The Mode in Costume

THE MODE IN COSTUME

By

R. Turner Wilcox

CHARLES SCRIBNER'S SONS

NEW YORK

5 7 9 11 13 15 17 19 C/P 20 18 16 14 12 10 8 6 4
7 9 11 13 15 17 19 C/C 20 18 16 14 12 10 8 6

PRINTED IN THE UNITED STATES OF AMERICA
LIBRARY OF CONGRESS CATALOG CARD NUMBER 58-12732
ISBN 0-684-13913-8 (pbk.)
ISBN 0 684-10663-9 (cloth)

To

RAY WILCOX

AND

RUTH WILCOX

Foreword

"He is only fantastical that is not in fashion."
Anatomy of Melancholy, Robert Burton, 1577–1640.

The wearing of clothes being a necessity, the individual owes it to himself to display in the front he presents to the world, the most pleasing exterior possible. Wearing apparel therefore, should be artistic in color and design, charming and flattering according to the fashion and the circumstance.

The idea which prompted the execution of this work was to place before the student a study of the mode in civil costume of all ages. I have endeavored to portray and explain, as simply as possible, for each period, the prevailing design of costume worn and, wherever available, to give the information regarding origin, actual dates, fabrics, colors and accessories.

To produce a handbook of the mode in all the important periods and for the reader's convenience, under one cover, I found a task of considerable proportions, requiring the utilization of wide information acquired over many years of study and work in this field.

I have confined my research to the original contemporary sources, such as medals, coins, sculpture, tapestries, pictures or decorations extant of the various periods. My aim has been to simplify, especially in ancient costume, the basic garments by avoiding the use of unnecessary foreign names. In many cases, I find that authors of works on this subject do not always agree on the meaning of terms which are, very often, of singular importance.

The calamity which befell France in 1940 has stopped the exportation of the designs of the French couturiers to the women of America, for a time at least. This furnishes an opportunity to the designers of the United States to display their abilities in this field. Some progress, undoubtedly, has been made, but the production seriously lacks the authority and prestige of the famous names of the French Couture.

Talent of no mean caliber is at work on the problem of creating that which for so many years was a matter of copying and adapting. To supplant the work of the French couturiers will take time and any success will be grudgingly admitted. It is hoped the problem of the production of "exclusive" fabrics will be more easily solved due to our American quality manufacturers.

While maintained contact with London should take care of the style features of masculine clothing, the United States Government limitations on the "Victory suit" and overcoat will force the designers in men's apparel to mark time for the duration of this war.

R. T. W.

May, 1942
Tenafly, New Jersey

Foreword—1948

MORE THAN four years of the German Occupation effectively shut Paris off from the rest of the world, four years in which American designers were compelled to stand on their own feet. Working under the limitations in design and fabric imposed by Washington's L85, our designers truly found themselves and produced lovely, wearable and functional clothes. Meanwhile, the Haute Couture hoping and working for the Day of Liberation, gallantly plied their creative talents for the good and continuance of the French fashion industry. And despite "blood, sweat and tears" and scarcity of materials, our valiant English cousins carried on, producing and shipping to America a few of their inimitable tailleurs, models of perfection as ever.

Now in 1948 in this world of closer neighbors, we realize that Paris still carries the torch of fashion, yet at the same time the brilliant designers of London, New York and California continue to create equally individual creations, each fashion center affording inspiration to the other.

This after-war world is a changed place. So is the world of fashion and it seems fitting in this history-making period that we record 1947 in "The Mode in Costume" by adding another chapter to the original work.

R. T. W.

Foreword—1958

SINCE WORLD WAR II the realm of fashion has become world-wide with worthy contributions coming from many lands. A decade has passed since Christian Dior revolutionized the mode in western woman's costume with his famous presentation of "The New Look." He framed milady in an aura of beauty and femininity and until his untimely death in 1957, was a brilliant style creator and leader of the French couture.

In 1951 in Florence, the leading Italian couturiers made their debut, the tailors and dressmakers putting on a fine show. Venice held an international display in 1956 in the eighteenth century Palazzo Grassi bringing to mind that it was in this Medieval City of the Doges that modish clothes first began to replace traditional costume. The gay casuals of the Italian designers are especially alluring while their beautiful ball gowns bear the stamp of their chic Latin flair for style and richness. Spain is represented by Cristobal Balenciaga, a truly great artist who exhibits his collections in Paris and his own country, and the well-known designer Pedro Rodriguez.

Brilliant Irish designers have entered the field with important clothes done in their inimitable hand-woven tweeds, linens and laces. The artistic influence of Austrian and German Tyrolean peasant dress has colored smart country clothes and from Munich in particular have come unusual designs especially suitable to American suburbia living. From the Far East, the fabulous and hand-woven sari has entered the western mode, as has the Oriental silhouette in sheath and kimono. And lastly but certainly not least there are our own top-ranking designers turning out that enviable "American Look." At the international show in Venice the Europeans were intrigued by the American country evening clothes, a form of dress new to them.

So, in taking note of the ever-changing picture, we are prompted to revise "The Mode in Costume" bringing it up to the moment for the designer, for the student and for all who wish a complete record of the mode.

R. T. W.

Table of Contents

CHAPTER EIGHT

CHAPTER NINE

CHAPTER TEN

CHAPTER FOURTEEN

CHAPTER FIFTEEN

CHAPTER SIXTEEN

CHAPTER TWENTY-ONE

CHAPTER TWENTY-TWO

CHAPTER TWENTY-THREE

The Mode in Costume

Chapter One

Egyptian

3000 TO 525 B.C.

THE GARMENTS of the Egyptians were few in number. Because of an even, warm climate, they were made of cotton and linen. The upper class wore a fine transparent muslin, similar to that of contemporary East Indian make, woven from flax grown in the rich mud flats of the Nile. The predominant color was white, but all colors, both brilliant and somber, were worn, color, however, being more ancient.

The first and principal garment of the men was the *schenti,* or loin cloth, which was a long scarf wrapped around the hips and held in place by a tied belt or girdle. When worn by high dignitaries, it was finished in front with a pleated apron. The pleats radiated from the low corner of the apron upward toward the belt, representing the rays of the sun, the emblem of Uraeus. From 1500 to 332 B.C. a long apron like a wrap-around skirt was worn and over that a transparent coat, the hems of which were often edged with fringe. The emblem of Uraeus, attached to the girdle, hung in front. Pleats were a distinct decorative feature of the costume of this later period.

Women wore a straight, narrow-sheath gown, which hung from under the breasts to the ankles and was held up by either a single shoulder strap, or one on each shoulder. In early Egypt only the priests wore sandals; the feet of the others were bare. Sandals had soles of leather, papyrus or sometimes wood and were held on by a couple of straps.

Both sexes shaved their heads for such reasons as religious ordinance, cleanliness and heat, but hair and beards were left to grow when in mourning. The rich wore wigs of false hair, wool or palm-leaf fiber, while the poorer classes wore skull caps of felt. Wigs were really a protection against the rays of the sun, the foundation being a porous fabric, to which human hair or sheep's wool was attached. Heavy bonnets of cotton, linen or wool, striped or embroidered, were worn for the same purpose. The ornaments were significant of rank or office, such as the lotus, meaning abundance; the asp, royal power; the sacred feather, emblem of the ruler. The headband with hanging ends in back was worn by men and women. Women often added flowers to their headdress, a favorite being the lotus.

Women used two colors of kohl for the eyes, green and black. They outlined the veins of the chest in blue, painted their lips with carmine, colored their cheeks with red and white and tipped their fingers with orange henna. They made general use of perfumes and ointments. The men wore no beard or mustache, but the pharaohs and high dignitaries wore the *postiche* or false beard, with which a woman, if queen, also adorned herself. In the examples which exist, the *postiche* was attached to a chin strap, gold no doubt, which was part of a frame or cap worn under the wig or bonnet.

The later period was one of great extravagance, dating from 1500 to 1150 B.C. Men and women wore earrings, pendants, necklaces, bracelets and anklets in pairs, also jewelled girdles. They were encrusted with cabochons of turquoise, carnelian, coral and lapis lazuli. Pearls and amber were used and beads fashioned of many stones, of various shapes. The deep flat collar of strung beads was especially favored. The exquisite jewelry of the Egyptians has never been surpassed in design or workmanship and the clasps of those pieces extant usually function as perfectly as when made. The signet ring and the jewelled girdle date from ancient Egypt.

In this later period, tunics were gorgeously embroidered. The Egyptians practised the art of embroidery, done with gold thread made of strips of the metal, beaten and rounded. The Greeks, however, are supposed to have been the first to make a gold thread fine enough to be used with needle. Sandals, too, became more elaborate, of soft leather dyed purple or crimson, embossed with gold and enriched with precious stones. There was also an Oriental style of sandal having long, turned-up toes. Others were of plaited palm, painted vermilion and ornamented with gold. It had become improper to go barefooted in the streets.

The umbrella was in use as a protection against the sun and the fan of feathers or papyrus for cooling the air. Both had long handles and were carried by bearers, that position being one of honor. Umbrellas and fans were permitted only to persons of rank.

Egyptian

schenti or
loin cloth

embroidered
sheath gown

white
sheath gown
RTW

triangular
apron

Egyptian
viceroy

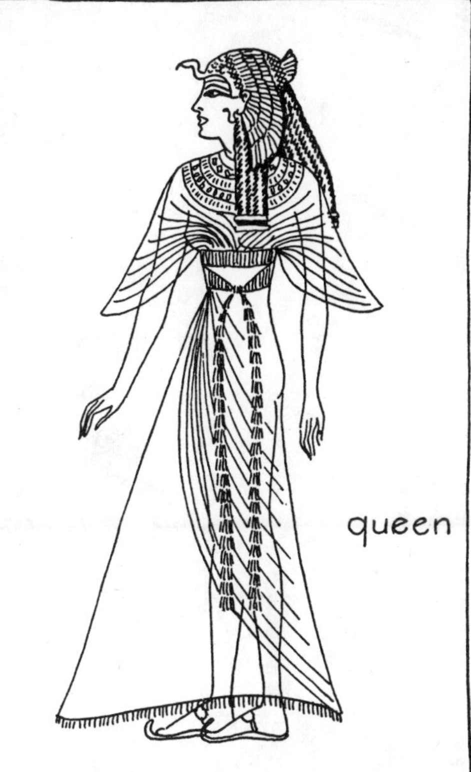
queen

priest
wearing
panther
skin

King in
long
apron
and coat
RTW

Egyptian
King
Tut-Ankh-Amen
Queen
Nefertiti
bead
necklace
hand mirror
fan
King Mycerinus
palm sandal
feather fan
RTW

Chapter Two

Babylonian and Assyrian

1500 B.C. TO 550 B.C.

BABYLONIAN civilization dated back nearly as far as that of the Egyptian, but never reached so high a state. In 1917 B.C. Elam, Assyria and Syria were united under the Babylonian Empire. Assyria conquered the empire in 1250 B.C., reaching its height in the mingled cultures in the eighth and seventh centuries B.C.

The costumes of the Babylonians and the Assyrians consisted of two garments, a straight tunic edged with fringe, either long or short, called the *candys,* and a fringed shawl of varying dimensions. Both men and women wore the same outfit, with the difference that the shawls of the women were more ample and draped loosely about the figure. The tunic appears often with a set-in sleeve.

Linen was used, but the principal fabric seems to have been wool elaborately embroidered with separate motifs founded upon the design of the rosette. Their embroideries came to be known as "Babylonian work." Garments were always trimmed with fringe and tassels. They were fond of brilliant colors in reds, greens, blues and purples. The purple candys embroidered with gold was reserved for the king. His hood was of wool decorated with embroideries and jewels, sometimes finished with a row of small feathers around the top. Jewelled tiaras were worn by high dignitaries.

The men wore their hair and beards long, done in carefully arranged tight corkscrew curls and are known to have powdered their hair with gold dust. Men and women wore jewelry of gold and silver in the form of earrings, necklaces and bracelets set with pearls and other precious stones. Their sandals had a sole of leather with heel straps or a heel cap, a ring for the large toe and laces tied around the ankle. The Greeks termed their footgear "miserable" as compared with the rest of the costume. Soldiers wore a buskin knee-high of leather laced from toe to knee. Umbrellas were used as a protection against the sun, but were permitted only to persons of rank, the same being true of fans. Both were carried by bearers.

Little is known of the feminine costume. Women led a most secluded life and are not represented in the bas-reliefs or sculpture, which have come down to us.

Babylonian
high
priest

and Assyrian
King

dignitary
RTW

attendant

Babylonian and Assyrian
hand bag
carried in
religious ceremonials
earrings
Babylonian King
Assyrian King
feather
fan
bracelets
sandals
umbrella
RTW

Chapter Three

Ancient Greek

1500 B.C. TO THE FIRST CENTURY B.C.

IN THE Mycenæan Period, contemporary with Egyptian civilization, Greek women wore corsets, also a sewn and fitted dress, the material of which is unknown. The colors were bright. The flaring skirt was fitted at the hips, ankle-length and had several rows of ruffles, sometimes pleated flounces. The short decorated tailored jacket in bolero style, reached to the waist, open in front, leaving the breasts bare.

In the Greek period from the seventh to the first century B.C., the feminine garment reached to the ankles, that of the men to the knees, and was called the *chiton*. It was a rectangular piece of woolen or linen fabric sewn partway up the sides and fastened on each shoulder by a fibula. The fibula was a sort of clasp or buckle resembling our safety pin and was introduced by the Dorians about 1100 B.C. The chiton was worn with or without a belt and there were two distinct styles. The Doric, of soft wool, was folded over at the top and held at the waist by a tied belt. The Ionic, of Oriental origin, was a rectangle of sheer linen or fine Indian cotton, later of silk, but was caught together over the arms by fibulæ or buttons forming loose sleeves when belted. Too, there was a chiton with a short sleeve.

Men of action fastened the chiton on the left shoulder, leaving the right arm free, and sometimes wore a second belt around the hips, creating a second bloused section between the two belts. Women often bloused their tunic in the same fashion. Men retained the long chiton for ceremonial occasions.

A garment worn by women over the chiton was the peplos or peplum. It was a rectangle of woolen fabric of variable size, unsewn and fastened on the shoulders. It was draped like the chiton. The bloused section called the kolpos or deploidion, was carefully arranged in artistic folds which were weighted with lead pellets.

The *chlamys,* a light summer mantle, was originally worn on horseback. Later, it became the cloak of young men, made in expensive material and worn over the chiton. It was a rectangle about one by two yards in dimension and of woolen material, with small weights at the four corners to prevent its blowing. A clasp fastened it on the shoulder or in front and it was used as a protection against cold and rain, also serving as a cover when sleeping.

The *himation,* or cloak, was worn by both sexes. It was composed of a piece of fabric about one and a half yards by three in size, draped about the figure, usually over but one shoulder. Young men and philosophers are pictured using it as their sole garment, in which case it appears securely fastened at the waist by a belt. Women too wore it, often without the chiton underneath.

A sign of mourning in Greek costume was the unbelted trailing garments of either sex, presumably of a brownish hue.

Pleats were a favorite decoration and were made by wetting the garment in thin starch, twisting it carefully, then laying it in the sun to dry. In the earliest period woolen fabric was employed, later linen appeared, and in the latest period there was pure silk, also flax and silk combined.

An important article of dress worn by women, even when sleeping, was the *bandelette,* a tape or ribbon which, while most decorative, acted as a support to the breasts. It was sometimes worn under, but usually outside the chiton.

Both sexes were greatly addicted to the use of perfumes, and oils and essences were freely applied to the body.

It is recorded that men wore beards until Alexander's time. They wore their hair cut short, often held in place by a band tied around the head. Women wore their hair long, sometimes frizzed or in corkscrew curls, or parted in the middle and drawn into a chignon at back of the neck. They fastened their hair with hairpins of bone or ivory, which were plain or mounted with gold. They also had a spiral type of hairpin of gold wire. They were naturally blond, but often made use of wigs, dyed their hair and wore rich sheer veils. The veils were occasionally floating or, again, wound in the hair. Too, they dressed their hair with perfume, flowers and colored ribbons, wore jewelled tiaras and crowns of gold or silver wire, also the caul or net. The Greek bride wore a long sheer white veil attached to the back of her headdress, which was ornamented with pearls. Another bridal headdress was a wreath of violets and myrtle.

Some of the Tanagra statuettes have large hats with wide brims, set on the head over the veil. From Phrygia in Asia Minor came the "Phrygian bonnet," revived now and then down the ages, notably in the French Revolution, as the cap on the figure of "Liberty."

The Phrygians are credited also with being the first people to make gold wire into strands thin enough to use with needle for embroidery, and are believed to have taught the art to the Egyptians. Greek women of the later period were noted for their skill in weaving and embroidery, the borders, necks and armscyes of their garments being richly decorated. The handwork was executed in wool or linen.

When Greek men travelled, they wore, with the chlamys, a hat of felt with a broad brim, as protection against heat and rain. It was secured by a chin strap, which permitted the hat to hang down in back, when not in use. This hat was called a petasos.

Felt was also used for cloaks and caps. Wool or hair matted together while moist was the means employed then, as today, in its manufacture.

Men and women wore sandals, having a sturdy leather sole, held on the foot by leather straps. The *cothurn,* which was the shoe of the actor, had a thick cork or wooden sole. Buskins, also worn, reached to the middle of the calf and were laced in front. They were usually lined and ornamented with skins of small animals, the heads and claws of which hung over the tops. It was the custom among the early Greeks to remove their footwear upon entering the house. At a later period, all classes wore sandals, boots and shoes. In the Periclean Age, men's sandals were ornamented with gold, while those of the women were adorned with colored embroidery and gold; in fact, sandals became a very costly part of the costume. The Greeks are known to have shaped the soles to conform to the right and left foot.

Earrings, necklaces, bracelets and rings of the classic period were artistic and of beautiful workmanship. Beads of various stones enamelled with gold were used and the exquisite stone cameos of that time have never been equalled.

Umbrellas were used by Greek women as shade protection and fans as a cooling device. The long-handled fans were carried by bearers, but women carried dainty ones in the hand. The hand mirror was usually of thin bronze slightly convex, one side polished and the reverse ornamented with an incised decoration. Silver was also used and they are known to have made glass mirrors coated with tin.

Ancient Greek

Ancient Greek

Mycenaean
1500 B.C.

long tunic
himation
and hat

Doric
woolen
chiton

Ionic
linen chiton
himation

RTW

Ancient Greek
umbrella
wig
mirror
fibulae
bracelet
caul
earrings
sandal
buskin
Venus
Phrygian bonnet
sandal
peacock feather fan
RTW

Chapter Four

Ancient Roman

THE FIRST CENTURY B.C. TO THE FIFTH A.D.

DURING the first three centuries of this period, the principal garment of the Romans was the *toga,* which was worn by both sexes. The feminine wrap later took the name of *palla.* Its use was the same as that of the Greek himation, but it differed in shape, the Greek wrap being a rectangle and the Roman mantle, when folded, a semicircle.

The toga was much larger than its Greek predecessor, being about two and one half by six yards long, making the draping of it heavier and more complicated. It was of wool and draped thus: an end was laid against the chest, then carried over the left shoulder, around the back and brought under the right arm to the front, again over the left shoulder to tie in the back, which arrangement left the right arm free. The draping of the toga became an art, with its straight-hanging folds, each one weighted with a pellet and, when the folds were in place, each had its name.

The ordinary citizen wore a plain white toga. Magistrates, priests and boys up to sixteen years old of the upper class wore the purple-bordered toga. The embroidered purple toga worn with the gold-embroidered tunic was the ceremonial dress of magistrates and generals and became the traditional costume of the emperors.

The origin of the word purple is the Latin "purpura," the name of a shellfish which yielded the famous Tyrian dye and was not violet but a deep crimson color.

Later, both sexes wore a tunic corresponding to the Greek chiton, underneath the toga or palla. Under that, men and women wore an undergarment reaching to the knees, similar to a shirt. It was made of wool for men and linen for women.

Over the undertunic, women wore the *stola,* a long, straight robe reaching to the feet. It hung straight or was bloused over a belt or girdle and had short set-in sleeves. The stola was usually fashioned of linen or soft, light wool, giving way later to silk and very sheer costly fabrics from the East.

Heliogabalus was the first Roman emperor (218 to 222 A.D.) to wear silk. In 533 A.D., looms were set up in the palace for the weaving of silk, but the raw material was imported from the East.

A wide purple band, called the *clavus,* insignia of rank, ornamented the center front from neck to hem, of the senator's tunic. The tunic of the knight bore narrow bands. The feminine tunic often had an embroidered band at the neck and the hem. Like the custom of the Greeks, the unbelted tunic of either sex signified mourning.

The art of embroidery was an art of great pride among Roman ladies. It was usually executed in wool, and for special costumes gold thread was added. Gold was lavishly used in the imperial periods.

Romans wore their shoes indoors and out, but did remove their sandals when dining. Their footgear was based upon Etruscan design. There were sandals, a short socklike foot covering, boots, and the buskin or *cothurnus.* These, in the later period, became elaborate and costly among people of wealth and rank. They were made of fine leathers, colorfully dyed and decorated with gold, silver and precious stones. Women generally wore the sandal or soft shoe. Men added to their height by means of a wedge placed inside the buskin at the heel.

Roman men were fastidious in the care of their hair and beards. Barber shops existed in their main streets, but shaving did not become the style until 454 A.D., when a group of barbers was imported from Sicily. From 68 A.D. to about 268, the nobles powdered their hair with gold dust on festive occasions. The hair of the women was usually parted in the middle and drawn into a chignon at the nape of the neck. It was waved and tightly curled.

Blond hair was much admired and desired and it is known that they wore wigs of that color made of hair bought from the northern Gauls. Too, they dyed their hair black or chestnut with soap imported from the Germanic tribes. Cauls of gold and silver net interspersed with pearls and other gems were worn by the women. They also wore veils, but for a general head covering draped themselves with a fold of the palla. Roman brides wore a flame-colored veil, while the Christian bride donned one of white or purple.

Beauty patches on the face were indulged in by the Roman women. The use of perfume by men and women probably surpassed that of any nation of all time. It was available in liquid, solid and powdered form and was applied not only to their persons, but to all articles and personal possessions with which they came in contact.

Umbrellas were used as a protection against the sun by the women and were later adopted by the men. The lady of early Roman period was cooled by a fan carried by an attendant, but later small fans were carried by fashionable women.

In the earlier period, jewelry consisted of wrought gold ornaments with engraved gems, which later developed into artistic and exquisite pieces. The Romans made use of many precious stones such as diamonds, rubies, sapphires, emeralds, pearls being favorites, set in rings, earrings, necklaces and bracelets. Their jewelry had not the refinement of that of the Greeks, being heavier and given more to display. The hand mirror of polished metal with incised ornamented back was usually disk-shaped.

Ancient Roman

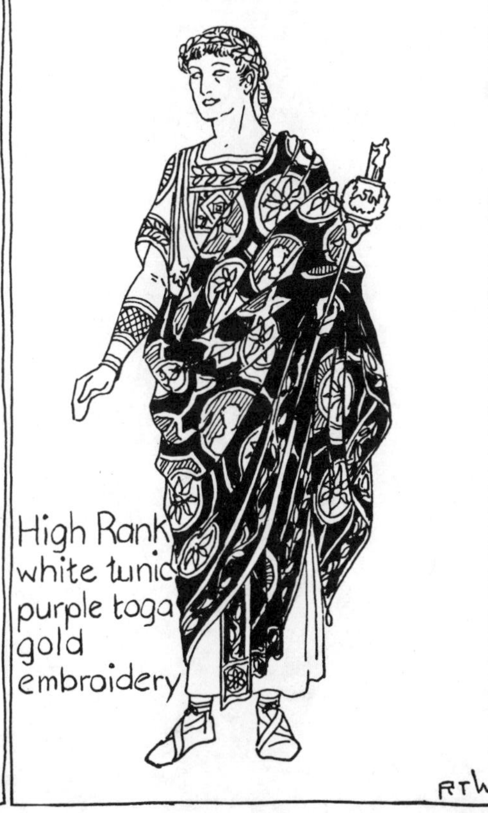

Ancient Roman
under tunic
stola
palla

under tunic
stola
palla

purple stola
gold
embroidery

young
woman
under tunic
stola
RTW

Ancient Roman
sandal
plumed helmet
hair pins
sandal
ring
soft leather shoe
wig and necklace
buskin
earring
fibula
corselets with kilts
RTW

Chapter Five

Ancient Persian

550 B.C. THROUGH THE CRUSADES

THE PERSIAN costume, while originally a continuation of the Babylonian and Assyrian mode, furnished many striking and different features. The *candys* of wool or linen was worn, also of silk imported from the East. But this candys was a shaped and sewn garment with flowing sleeves, which fell into set pleats at the back of the arm. The skirt was drawn up into the belt in center front or at the sides, forming carefully arranged pleats, somewhat like the Egyptian robe.

Under it was worn a shirt, drawers and stockings, which were also shaped and sewn. It is the first time that underclothes are noted and it is also the first encounter with tailored garments and a definitely set-in sleeve.

Only high dignitaries were permitted to wear the candys, which the king gave as gifts. His were of bluish purple, ornamented with white and silver, while people of inferior rank wore garments dyed red. This color was called "Sardian red" from a dye made from the blossoms of the sandix tree. Later, they had silk and woolen robes of all colors, but the predominant Persian colors were red, yellow and dark blue. Royal purple, dark blue and white appear to be the royal colors. Brown was the color of mourning.

Sashes were important, the king's being of cloth of gold. The king's wives wore golden girdles with a bag attached holding their "girdle money." The wives of some of the kings were allotted the revenue of entire cities for "pin money," as we term it today.

One decoration shows a king with a purple stole or shawl embroidered with gold thread and ornamented with precious stones. Later, the candys appears to have been replaced by a coat worn over trousers, surely the forerunner of today's standard civil costume for men.

Garments were elaborated with beautiful and colorful embroidery. Appliqué work was originated by the ancient Persians, serving in place of the all-over needlework. It was carried into Europe as a result of the Crusades and became very popular there.

A soft shoe was worn, always of yellow leather, shaped and covering the foot to the ankle, where it fastened by means of straps and buttons. In a later period, the shoe was heavily embroidered with pearls and other jewels. Gloves were known, and the gorgeous parasol and fan with long handles, carried by attendants, were only for royalty.

Their jewels were handsome, of heavy gold with colored enamels, set with pearls and rare gems. Stones were polished in cabochon form. There were earrings, bracelets and necklaces, especially the signet ring, symbol of authority. They had exquisitely wrought boxes and bottles of alabaster to hold their elaborately prepared perfumes and cosmetics. Girls, at the marriageable age of fifteen years, were given earrings. Also at that age, boys and girls were obliged to wear the sacred girdle or cord.

The men wore their hair and beards long, both meticulously fashioned in tight curls, and they dusted their hair with gold powder. Royalty wore headgear in the form of a tiara, miter or toque of white felt or striped in blue and white. Both the miter and tiara are of Persian origin, the miter being originally a turban or conical hat. Another head covering was the chincloth, seemingly of white linen, wrapped about the head and neck, extending up over the chin.

Few records of sculpture exist of feminine dress, women having led an entirely secluded life. In a bas-relief of the fifth century B.C., a queen wears the tunic and full trousers, known to us at a later period, which would lead us to believe that such had always been the costume of the women.

Ancient Persian
royal
body
guard

king in
purple
candys
blue and
white
striped
tiara

embroidered
coat and felt
mitre
RTW

embroidered
candys

Ancient Persian
umbrella
Nobleman
feather fan
white felt toque
warrior
soft shoes of yellow leather
white felt toque
RTW

Chapter Six

The Northern Europeans

The First Centuries A.D.

Of the Northern Europeans there exists little documentation except that furnished us by some coins, a few figurines and bas-reliefs. Only their arms and jewelry have survived the climatic conditions of their tombs.

The "Northern Barbarians," as they were called, wore a garment like that of the ancient Persians, a kind of drawers or breeches, shaped and sewn, rather like tights, which was later adopted by the Roman soldiers. Originally, it was made of skins, held around the waist by a belt and held close to the leg above the knee by cross-gartering of thongs or bands. Such a garment, no doubt, was the result of necessity for protection against severe climate. They are known to have worn a shoulder covering, a rather small square of leather or wool, folded diagonally like a shawl.

The women wore a long or short tunic with petticoat or kirtle of coarse woolen cloth. Their wrap was a square blanket fastened on one shoulder or in front with a clasp or buckle. A belt just below the breasts held the tunic in soft folds.

By the time the Romans penetrated into the northern parts of Europe, they found people there wearing trousers, a short belted tunic with sleeves, a cloak or mantle and perhaps, in winter, a cap of fur. They were proficient in weaving and dyeing. They wore squares of heavy woolen cloth in blue or black, rough on one side. Tunics and trousers were bright-colored, striped and checkered, red being the predominant color.

Long hair was a source of great pride to the Northern women and was worn flowing or hanging in long braids. The hair of the men reached to the shoulders. The women are known to have worn wigs, as the remains of brightly colored wool and silk wigs have been found in the catacombs. Red hair was a favorite of the Gauls and they resorted to dyeing to attain that color.

Many pieces of their jewelry have been found, most artistic and decorative in design, in fibulæ, buckles, armlets, necklaces or torques, hairpins, fashioned of bronze, occasionally a gold piece. The collar, or torque, was unique to the Northern tribes. It was heavy, of bronze or bronze and gold, and usually represented the wealth of the wearer. These collars were often taken as spoils by the conquering Romans and, in turn, handed out as rewards to the soldiers. Use was made of ivory for pins, and beads were made of brass, jet and amber from their own coasts, while they bought glass from Southern merchants.

After being conquered by the Romans, both sexes wore the tunic, short for men, long for women, in white, red, green or violet, decorated with bands of color. We learn from the Romans that the women wore white tunics ornamented with a purple design and that they were woven and dyed by the wearers. The wrap which followed Roman lines was sometimes trimmed with contrasting colored strips of cloth.

Important in the costume of these Northern tribes was the wearing of a real undergarment by the women, a sort of shirt of thin material, usually white. The Romans, who themselves were given to much bathing, were impressed by the Northerners' cult of cleanliness.

Footgear was simple, of moccasin type and sandals with straps by which to fasten them, also boots of undressed leather with wooden soles.

These boots reached almost to the knees and were decorated with pleasing designs.

Men had bonnets of leather or wool, while the women wore kerchiefs, utilizing mostly, however, a fold of the palla as a headcovering.

Still later, Byzantine influence became evident in the use of luxurious fabrics. Men wore, over their long breeches, a short tunic with long sleeves, belted at the waist, and a mantle fastened on one shoulder. They wore gloves too, in mitten style, without fingers.

The women wore two tunics, the under one of woven thread with long sleeves, which is the first noted body linen, or, as later called, lingerie. The outer tunic was long and straight, of rich fabric, cut with flowing sleeves and a train and often embroidered with gold and precious stones. Then, a mantle fastened on one shoulder or in front, and a scarf covering the head and shoulders. The head covering was the result of their adoption of the Christian religion, since women were compelled to cover their heads upon entering the church, as a sign of humility.

Jewelry had become works of art, usually intricate, in gold and silver encrusted with pearls and precious stones. There were clasps, buckles, necklaces, bracelets and rings. Girdles were embroidered with gold and decorated with gems.

Northern Europeans of the first Centuries A.D.
German-
linen and
woolen fabrics-
bronze jewelry
Gaul-
fur cap-plaid
and striped
woolen-leather
breeches and
moccasins
Frank-
fur jumper-
woolen tunic-
leather breeches,
moccasins and
cross-gartering
Briton-
plaid woolen
tunic-woolen
mantle-gold
jewelry
RTW

Chapter Seven

Byzantine

Fourth Century to the Middle Ages

Byzantium made two important contributions to the mode. In the third century A.D., Syrian weavers developed the weaving of patterned fabrics by the use of shuttles. Then, under Emperor Justinian, who reigned from 527 to 565, the process of raising the silkworm from the cocoon was established in the Occident. Under his patronage, eggs of the silkworm and seeds of the mulberry bush concealed in their hollow bamboo staffs, were brought from China by two Persian monks.

Byzantine costume revealed both Greco-Roman and Oriental influence, combining Roman drapery with the gorgeousness of the East, in heavy silks, damasks, brocades and cloth of gold. Due to the Christian religion, the body was now entirely concealed. Both sexes wore a long, straight tunic with long sleeves. It was made of silk or linen and confined at the waist by a girdle. Girdles were handsome and costly, of leather or small plaques of gold linked together and encrusted with colored stones.

Men of quality draped themselves in a rich mantle or dalmatique, reminiscent of the Roman toga, semicircular in shape. On the left front edge was placed the clavus, insignia of high dignitaries. It was a large decoration, rectangular in shape, fashioned of jewels and gold embroidery. Women wore over their tunic a stola or palla, using a fold of the palla as head covering. Men and women fastened their mantles on the right shoulder with a gorgeous jewelled fibula or clasp.

The materials used in the masculine costume were usually of solid color with embroidered contrasting bands of color, while the feminine costume employed patterned fabrics. But the garments of both sexes were heavy with the weight of elaborate embroidery encrusted with precious stones.

Eventually, beneath the tunic, was worn an undergarment, short and made of linen or thin silk, really a shirt. The long tunic evolved into the *gunna,* or gown. Of a later period, was a short feminine garment, termed *juppe,* worn over the long tunic or robe. The sleeves were usually long and in dolman style.

Women enveloped their hair in a coif of silk or a network of pearls, a style later adopted by Medieval Europe. Pearls were plentiful and much used in company with diamonds and other gems, but later, bits of glass and even tiny mirrors were added to their embroideries. Their goldsmiths wrought beautiful jewelry, surpassing that of Italy. There were rings, bracelets, brooches, buckles and earrings of elaborate design. A favorite motif in earrings was birds in pairs. Oriental perfumes and incense were lavishly used.

Sandals were still worn, but the foot covering of the rich was a soft boot reaching to the ankle. It was of dyed leather with a rather long pointed toe. These shoes were bright in color and embroidered with gold thread and pearls.

The Byzantine mode became more sumptuous with the centuries and its influence is evident through the Medieval and Renaissance periods of Europe. It was the foundation of Russia's costume and survives today in the vestments of her church.

Byzantine

princess in white tunic-green mantle lined with purple-cerise boots-gold and jewelled embroidery

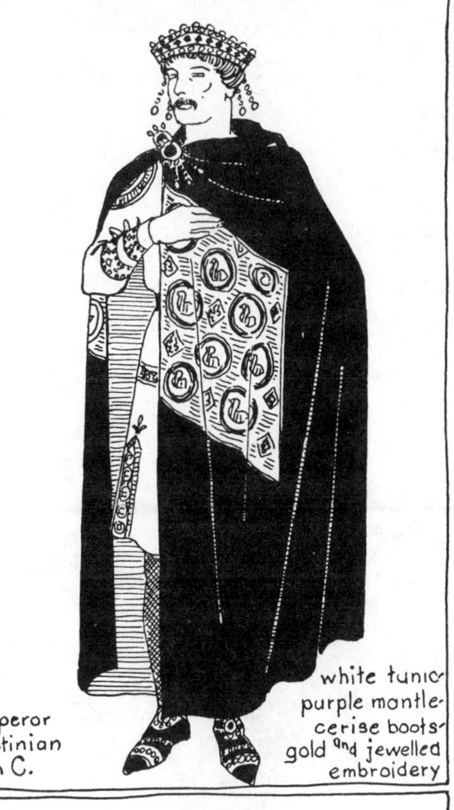

Emperor Justinian 6th C.

white tunic-purple mantle-cerise boots-gold and jewelled embroidery

emperor in white tunic-purple mantle lined with green-cerise boots-gold and jewelled embroidery

Empress Eudocie 5th C.

Byzantine
Queen
sandals
fibula
Emperor
11 th C.
Emperor
9th C.
short tunic
or "juppe"
12 th C.
soft leather
boots with
jewels
patterns of mantles
RTW

Chapter Eight

Italian Medieval or Gothic

HISTORIANS place the Middle Ages as the period between the fall of Rome, A.D. 476, and the fall of Constantinople in 1453. Others designate the period between the tenth and eleventh and the fifteenth centuries, as the flowering of the Gothic Period.

With the end of the Dark Ages, men and women were still wearing the Greco-Roman costume showing its Byzantine influence, but which, due to the teachings of Christianity, tended more and more to conceal the figure. In fact, the ecclesiastical mode definitely affected both style and color of clothes.

At first was worn the *bliaud,* a tunic with long sleeves, reaching to the knees on the men and to the feet on the women. Over that the *pallium,* or cloak, fastened in front by a large brooch or buckle. The men wore long, fitted and sewn stockings, a contribution of the Northern Barbarians. These stockings or tights were held up by a belt around the waist and were cross-gartered from the knees down. Later, the man's bliaud lengthened to the ankles.

By the eleventh century, the bliaud and mantle were worn by both sexes. The *chainse,* or undertunic, was made of wool, linen, hemp or silk, fastened at neck and wrist by buttons or tied with tassels. Later, it became really a piece of lingerie and was made of sheer washable fabric, with an embroidered edge showing at neck and wrists. Over that was worn the bliaud or long tunic, alike for men and women, reaching to the floor. The gown either hung straight or was belted with a plain or jewelled girdle and had long sleeves.

The fabrics had become rich and heavy, handsomely embroidered, fur-trimmed and fur-lined for cold weather. Ermine was the preferred pelt, but a fur called *miniver,* or *menu vair,* was also used extensively by fashionable people. It was gray and white, in small skins, and was a species of Russian and Siberian squirrel, also called *petit-gris.*

With the thirteenth century, the full overtunic of the men had shortened to the knees and by the latter part of that century, young men were wearing their tunics "shockingly" short. The tunic either hung straight or was belted, with a skirt of only a few inches below the waist. Hip-length stockings or tights were worn, made of bias material, usually red with gold and jewelled garters, accompanied by soft leather shoes.

Fabrics were dyed scarlet, green, blue and purple, of which there were fine linens, handsome brocades, embroideries and velvets. Sicilian brocades of the twelfth and thirteenth centuries were the finest in the world. All kinds of fur continued to be used, ermine being the favorite. Dull black cloth was worn for mourning, with tunic and mantle banded with white. The woman wore a white gauze cap, over which she draped her mantle.

Both sexes wore sumptuous loose full mantles. A particular masculine style was a long full cape with no opening except that for the head. The feminine tunic invariably had a train and many attempts were made to regulate the length of it.

The masculine head covering was a hood and shoulder cape in one. The hood, or *chaperon,* always had a point and this point, or *liripipe,* grew to all lengths over the years, to where it was worn wrapped about the neck or arm, or left to hang in back. Many arrangements of draping it about the head evolved. Later, the liripipe was draped over a padded roll, turban in shape, called the roundlet. In the second half of the fourteenth century, the liripipe, as well as other garments, was ornamented with "petal-scalloped" or castellated edge. The long hood was permitted only to the noble, the commoner was compelled to content himself with a very short one.

Men also wore skullcaps, peaked bonnets and bonnets with rolled brims and a long feather. This is the first appearance of the feather in modish dress. Felt bonnets were often worn over the hood. Men wore their hair moderately long with a deep fringe over the forehead.

A later style of feminine robe, which appeared in the early fourteenth century, is important, as being the cause of the second advent of the corset, its first appearance being noted in prehistoric Greece. It is also noteworthy, as being a real frock instead of a tunic. This was a gown with snug-fitting bodice, from which flowed a full trailing skirt. It created a vogue for a slim figure and both lacing and dieting were resorted to, to acquire the necessary silhouette.

The principal head covering for women in the Middle Ages was a piece of fabric, either cotton or linen, square, oblong or circular in shape, hanging to the shoulders or below. It was a continuation of the palla and was known as the *couvrechef,* "headrail" or "wimple." Crowns were placed over it. Crowns, by the way, were but signs of wealth and position in those days, and did not become insignia of rank until the sixteenth century. In the twelfth century, the hair was often worn flowing. Blond hair being the desired color, women sat for hours in roofless belvedere towers atop their houses, bleaching their hair in the sun. False hair and cosmetics were also used.

Then came the chinband in the next century, a fold of white linen which passed under the chin, fastened by pinning to a band around the forehead. Sometimes, the chinband went completely round the head. In another style, the headband was stiffened, forming a low crownlike or toque type of headdress. Sometimes, the toque had no top.

In the fourteenth century, the hair was dressed close to the head, usually parted in the middle in Madonna style, sometimes with a coronet braid. Small caps, nets and cauls of exquisite filigree work were much used, covered with sheer veils of silk or linen, shot with gold, which hung to the shoulders. The hennin and its many variations appeared in the latter part of the fourteenth century, to last a hundred years or more, and was the invention of Medieval Italy.

The hennin was a long-pointed conical headdress. The *escoffion,* a very ugly style, said to have originated in England, had two horns. Veils of different lengths, sometimes long enough to reach the floor, hung from these strange bonnets. The hennin was held on the head by means of the frontlet, to which the bonnet was fastened. The frontlet or ring which showed on the forehead was part of a cap of wire netting worn under the bonnet. The frontlet was covered with silk or black velvet and with gold, when worn by nobles. Veils alone were often worn. Elaborate stuffed rolls, turbanlike in shape, of Byzantine origin, were worn by Venetian ladies.

In the early thirteenth century, the Crusaders, returning from the East, brought beautifully embroidered costume accessories, which gave rise to a great vogue for such decoration. Pouches, bags, shoes, girdles and gloves were richly embroidered by ladies, who were proud of their accomplishment. In the same period, the Persian art of appliqué was copied. In the fourteenth century, pearls and spangles were added to the colorful embroidery.

In the fourteenth century appeared parti-colored clothes for men, which idea women later copied. The garment was divided into halves or quarters and each section was of a different contrasting color, even each shoe and stocking varying in color. Later, they took to dividing the costume diagonally and, by the end of the fourteenth century, men and women were wearing the coat of arms of both sides of their families appliquéd or embroidered on their costumes.

Shoes of both sexes were soft and pliable, having pointed toes and covering the foot to the ankle. They were works of art, executed in scarlet or violet velvet, even cloth of gold, ornamented with colored embroidery, strips of gold and sometimes encrusted with gems. Later, they were also fashioned of very soft leathers. The toes of men's shoes grew to such lengths, being stuffed too, that they finally reached a point where they were held up by fine chains attached to the knees. These shoes were called *poulaines.* Also called poulaines were the clogs, or pattens, made of wood and worn to protect the soft shoes. They had very thick soles of wood or cork and a heel about an inch high. Pattens appeared about 1377, lasting into the eighteenth century. The *chopine,* adopted principally in Venice, came from Turkey. It was of wood, a stiltlike affair, painted and gilded.

Among the accessories were embroidered gloves of leather, occasionally ornamented with jewels and often with a single gem on the back. They were worn first by the men and later adopted by the women. The scented glove of Eastern origin appeared in Venice in the eleventh century and the vogue lasted for several hundred years. The handkerchief, a very costly accessory of display, was in the possession of the fashionable wealthy only, and usually that person owned but one.

Fans, of the hand-screen design, were imported from the Orient in the twelfth century and became generally used. Ostrich, parrot or peacock feathers were fastened to handles of ivory or gold set with precious stones.

It was a period of heavy massive chains and jewelled belts. From the belt or girdle hung a purse or pouch, from which wealthy people of both sexes scattered coins or alms to the poor. Jewelled daggers were also suspended from the belt.

The making of silk in Italy dates from 1148 at Palermo. Other beautiful silks came from the Orient and cotton from Egypt. Typical of the period were costly materials in diapered pattern with repeated motif, principally of conventionalized flower design.

By way of the ports of Venice and Genoa, Oriental luxuries reached the courts of Europe, Italy being thus the first to feel the effects of the more refined culture of the East. Venice reached its height of prosperity about 1400, with the Venetian mode influencing all Europe. However, it is recorded that in the fourteenth century Venice imported yearly a fashion doll from Paris.

The making of glass mirrors on a commercial scale was first developed in Venice in the fourteenth century, and from then on to the middle of the seventeenth century, when large mirrors were made, fashionable men and women carried small pocket mirrors in little cases of silk or ivory.

In the Middle Ages, the limit of one's extravagance in dress was specifically determined by one's position in society. Rich clothes were worn only by nobility. About 1476, the cost of robes, buttons, belts, jewels and furs, also the length of trains, were regulated by sumptuary laws, which held until the early part of the sixteenth century.

Italian Medieval or Gothic

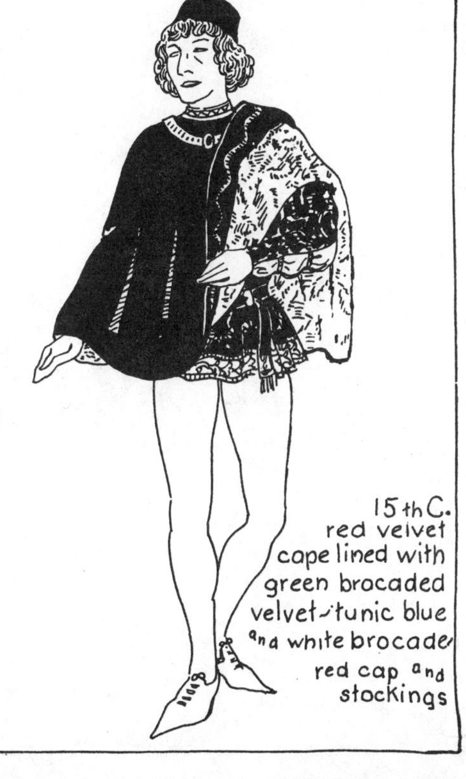

Italian Medieval or Gothic

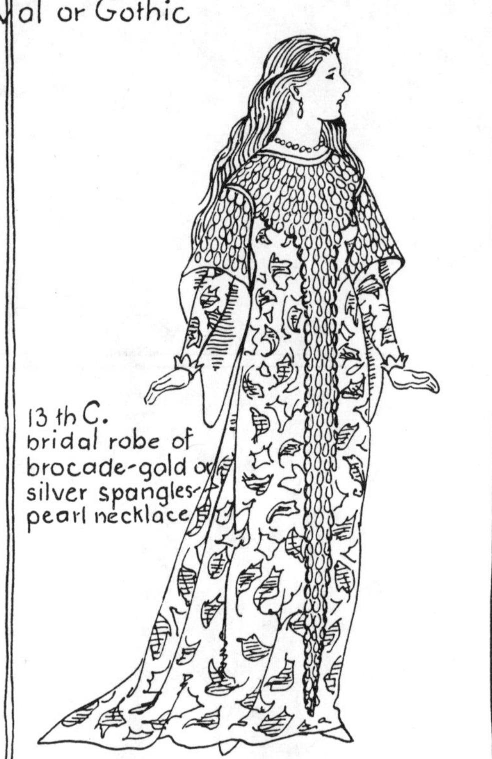

Italian-Medieval or Gothic
turban
with moiré
leaves-11th C.
wimple
chinband
of linen
folds-12th C.
net of gold cord
and pearls
over silk
bag-
12th C.
13th C.
chinband and
toque of white
linen folds
15th C.
two-horned
hennin
man's hood or chaperon
14th C.
14th C.
wooden patten
14th C.
man's
hat
with feather
lady's
chopine
15th C.
man's velvet hat
15th C.
man's boot
RTW

Chapter Nine

French Medieval or Gothic

THE FRENCH medieval scene opens with men and women still wearing clothes of Roman origin, consisting of two tunics and a mantle for both sexes. The undergarment, or chainse, reached to the ankles, had long, straight sleeves and was usually belted. Over it men and women wore the bliaud or bliaut which exposed the sleeves and neck of the undergarment. Then a mantle fastened in front or on the right shoulder, leaving the right arm free. Later, the women held the ends of the mantle in the hands and the wraps of both sexes were often entirely pleated. The bliaud, origin of blouse, was sometimes ornamented with a handsome jewelled girdle.

In the thirteenth century, the chainse finally developed into the chemise or body garment, made of soft wool or linen, really the beginning of lingerie, but in saffron color. For a long period to come, it showed at the neck and wrists and was no doubt made principally of batiste, a closely woven sheer fabric which appeared in the thirteenth century. Batiste was named after its inventor, Batiste Chambray, but unlike the cotton batiste of today, was of very fine linen thread.

Later, an extra garment, the surcoat, appeared. It was derived from the armor covering worn by the crusading knight to eliminate the glare of the sun on his armor, when in the East. The original covering hung straight, front and back, reaching to the knees and was caught at the sides. There was a hole for the head to pass through. His lady's surcoat was also short and sleeveless, with wide armholes and was worn over the bliaud. It was fastened by means of buttons on the shoulders. In cold weather, men and women wore a short jacket or doublet of fur or fur-lined between the chainse or body garment and the outer tunic, and over that the mantle.

Men wore beards and their hair shoulder-length until the tenth century, when beards disappeared and the hair was bobbed with a long bang over the forehead, but shaved quite high in the back. In the following centuries of the period, it appears to have been worn moderately long, with the bob the prevailing style.

Women parted their hair in the middle and dressed it in two hanging braids, to which they often added false hair for length. The head covering consisted of a square of sheer colored linen or cotton and was known as the *couvrechef* in French, the wimple in English. Veils were required to be worn in church, women being forbidden to enter bareheaded. Crowns were worn by all members of the upper class, and not until the sixteenth century were designs settled to designate the rank of the wearer. Women wore the crown over the wimple.

In the thirteenth century, the surcoat took the place of the bliaud for both sexes. That of the man reached a point below his knees, hung straight or was belted, had short sleeves or none. In the fourteenth century, it shortened to the knees, while the sleeves lengthened considerably, sometimes almost reaching to the floor. These sleeves hung over the hands, or had openings halfway up from which the arms protruded. The long sleeves were often in knots at the ends. With the longer surcoat, a man wore long, sewn and fitted stockings, which were usually red and fastened under the surcoat by lacings with points.

The lady's surcoat of the thirteenth century was a long full robe touching the floor, belted at the waist. The lady copied the very long sleeves of her lord and often they were really false sleeves attached to the shoulders of her dress. The fantastic sleeves of both sexes lasted well into the sixteenth century. "Petal scalloped" or castellated edges on all garments became very popular.

In the fourteenth century, the feminine surcoat opened at the sides, revealing a fitted dress underneath, known as the *cotehardie.* The cotehardie was either laced or buttoned in center front from neck to below the waist and had long tight sleeves with a row of buttons from elbow to the little finger. With it was usually worn a low-placed jewelled girdle, which showed in the side openings of the overdress.

Men also wore the cotehardie, of which the masculine version was a tight-fitting tunic buttoned down center front, having also the same long sleeves with buttons. Like the woman's dress, it too had a low-placed girdle.

The surcoat disappeared in the fifteenth century, women then wearing a real dress called *la robe,* in which the fitted bodice with tight sleeves was joined by a belt to a full skirt.

The man's surcoat was replaced by a jacket, under which he wore the *justaucorps,* or *pourpoint,* a sort of body coat, quilted and closed by lacings either back or front. The pourpoint originated as a garment worn under armor and was made with or without sleeves. It was also worn as the jacket proper and its vogue lasted from the thirteenth to the seventeenth centuries.

Shoes of the eleventh, twelfth, thirteenth and fourteenth centuries were of velvet and soft leather fastened by a jewelled button or buckle, often ornamented with embroidery, strips of gold and gems. As in Italy, pattens were worn to protect the soft sole. The stiltlike chopine of Turkish origin adopted by Venetian women was also worn by French ladies.

In the middle of the fourteenth century, shoes *à la poulaine* became the style, lasting until 1480. Their long, pointed toes grew to such lengths that it became necessary to hold up the stuffed points by gold chains attached to the ankles or knees. Noblemen were permitted toe lengths of two feet, gentlemen one foot, while the common man could have but six inches beyond his toes. They originated in Cracow, Poland, and became fashionable at all European courts. The French called them *poulaines* after Poland and the English *crackowes* after Cracow.

Due to the influence of the Christian religion, all during the thirteenth century, women's hair was more or less concealed by the wimple and neckcloth or gorget, which covered head and neck. Variations of these medieval headdresses survive today in many religious orders.

Then followed a small crownlike toque worn over a headband and chinband, all of white linen. The hair was dressed Madonna style, parted in the middle and drawn into a chignon. Following that period, the hair was parted down the center back, plaited and the two braids dressed over the ears in wheel fashion, or wound in loops at the sides of the face, covering the ears. The neckcloth or gorget was fastened to the hair over the ears with pins and the headcloth draped over it.

A most decorative style, the reticulated headdress or golden net caul, reminiscent of the Byzantine fashion, appeared in the fourteenth century, lasting until the middle of the fifteenth century. In that style, a low metal band or jewelled crown held the cauls of gold braid or wire set with gems with which the hair was covered. Cauls were also fashioned of gold braid, the checkered openings filled in with crimson silk. In this period of the golden net caul and hennin, both of which entirely concealed the hair, the short hairs at the nape of the neck were shaved off. Eyebrows were plucked to give a fine line.

In the fifteenth century, turbans were worn, which, too, concealed the hair. They were large stuffed rolls over which the wimple was sometimes draped. These stuffed rolls were also used to form some shapes of the hennin, principally the heart-shaped style. The hennin was brought to France by Isabella of Bavaria in the latter part of the fourteenth century and its vogue lasted a hundred years. There were many styles of the hennin, invariably draped with a veil, floating or with wired edge. They became so extravagant in size that the authorities found it necessary to regulate the height according to the social position of the wearer.

Women wore a huge cloaklike cape, which in winter was lined with fur. Of men's cloaks there were several styles, principally a voluminous cape, with collar and fastened on one shoulder. The *houppelande,* which originated in the Low Countries, was a long, full robe with long, full, flowing sleeves, held in folds at the waist by a leather or jewelled belt.

Men wore hoods, toques, chaperons and felt hats in sugar-loaf shape and with brims. Feathers as hat ornamentation first appeared in the Middle Ages, peacock plumage being favored. The cowl, or capuchon, was attached to the cloak, but the chaperon was originally the hood attached to the shoulder cape. Its point, which began to lengthen in the latter part of the thirteenth century, grew until, in the fourteenth century, it was wound round the head, and by the fifteenth century the pipelike tail, or liripipe, sometimes reached the floor. Eventually, the liripipe became merely a trimming added to a real hat or turban. The turban, or stuffed roll, was called *roundlet* and, when trimmed with the liripipe, was known as the *chaperon turban*. Dashing young men often slung the chaperon turban over their shoulders, instead of wearing it on their heads.

Parti-colored clothes became the style, with the entire costume being divided into sections of contrasting colors. Ladies and gentlemen of the fourteenth and fifteenth centuries wore their coats of arms emblazoned upon their costumes, stamped into the fabric in gold and silver leaf and enamels. Such costumes bore the name of *cottes historiées*.

Small silver bells, that odd form of ornamentation, were in vogue in the fourteenth and early fifteenth centuries. They were suspended from leather belts, jewelled girdles, around the neck, and were worn by men and women.

Both men and women wore heavy massive chains and jewelled belts. For a time, around 1300, women replaced gloves with mittens. The fashion of wearing gloves spread and several small French towns specialized in the making of them. They were made of doeskin, sheepskin and hareskin. Perfumed gloves were most fashionable, especially violet-scented ones, which appeared around 1400. Walking sticks were carried by men in the fifteenth century.

The principal fabric was cloth of Scotch wool, woven in Flanders and England, but there were also gorgeous silks from the Orient and Italy. Louis XI, in 1466, first established silk weaving at Lyons. Velvet, the greatest favorite, appeared in the thirteenth century and was woven in Paris. The tapestries of the Saracens were imitated and, as in Italy, the vogue for diapered patterns prevailed. Ermine was the costliest fur, but marten and miniver were much used. The idea of ornamenting white ermine with the small black tails originated in the twelfth century.

French queens of the Middle Ages wore white for mourning, but the Spaniards had been using black since 1100. In that feudal era, once a year at a stated time, the seigneur of a castle made gifts to the noblemen attached to his estate, of cloth or costume. The gift was called *livrée,* which is the origin of our word livery, or uniform of a servitor. The law governed the amount of one's possessions in wearing apparel, also the size of a cloak and the width of trimming. Nobles were permitted to own hoods with long liripipes, while the commoner was compelled to content himself with just a hood.

We read that in the thirteenth century, Paris was already giving proof of its great flair for the creation of artistic clothes and that in the fourteenth century Venice imported annually a French fashion doll. The small waxen mannequin attired in the very latest style was exhibited to the Venetian ladies. This method of "fashion-journalism" lasted to our own Colonial Period, when we read of "fashion dolls," or "fashion babies," coming to New York or Philadelphia by way of London. The thirteenth century is considered the most brilliant period of the Moyen Âge. The French Medieval Period is supposed to have reached its end with the reign of Louis XI, 1461 to 1483. An establishment for the making of silk under royal patronage was decreed by Louis in November, 1466.

Many luxuries reached the Western World through contact with the Orient during the Crusades, such as the cotton plant, with its name of Arabic origin and the Arabian invention of cotton paper, replacing parchment. Satin and velvet, with their names of Byzantine origin, and the knowledge of embroidery and carpet weaving came from the East. Toilet articles, such as rouge and glass mirrors instead of polished plates, were first used in the Orient. The revival of the custom of wearing beards by the end of the Middle Ages was a direct influence of Arabian contact.

French Medieval or Gothic

King-crimson mantle-gold cloth bliaud-white chainse gold embroidery 9th C.

surcoat over chainse-skullcap-13 th C.

Houppelande with petal scalloping-roundlet with chaperon-15th C.

Brocaded cloth jacket-fur trimmed-jewelled necklace-roundlet with chaperon-15 th C.

French Medieval or Gothic

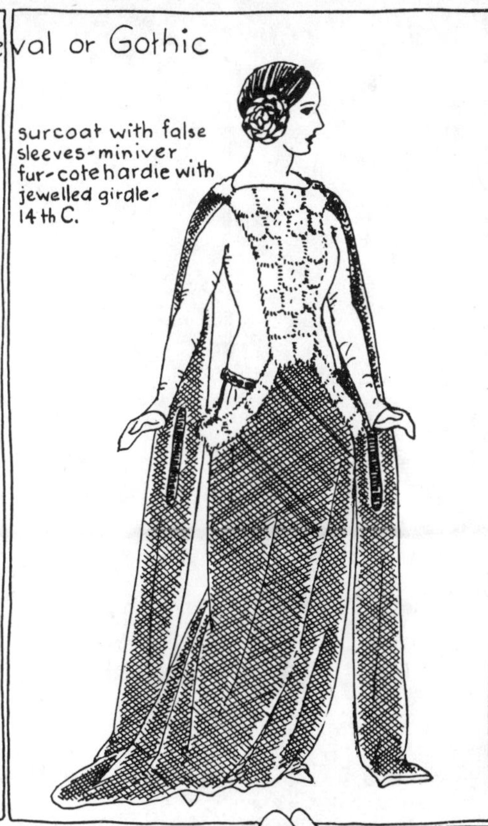

French Medieval or Gothic
white linen toque and chinband 12th and 13th C.
parti-colored hennin-15th C.
man's chaperon-turban 14th C.
shoe 13th C.
man's sugar-loaf hat with feather, jewels and cord - 15th C.
wooden patten 15th C.
hennin with white under-cap - black velvet fold - 15th C.
man's white felt hat - peacock feathers - red bandeau crossed with gold braid 15th C.
small bonnet with wired veil - 15th C.
reticulated headdress - wimple over golden net cauls - 15th C.
reticulated headdress - gold braid over crimson silk - stuffed roll with jewels - 14th C.
shoe and wooden patten 15th C.
RTW

Chapter Ten

English Medieval or Gothic

In the early part of this period, the Britons, both men and women, were still wearing three important garments, the stola or cotte, the bliaud or overtunic, and the palla or mantle, all reminiscent of Greco-Roman style. But they also wore, next to the body, a piece of lingerie, a garment of thin white material, either wool or linen, called a *shert,* or camise. The bliaud, bliaut or bliaus, is the origin of the blouse and the camise of the chemise.

The feminine bliaud or overtunic, a sleeveless garment worn indoors, was often long, but sometimes reached only to the knees, below which hung the long underdress, or cotte. The masculine tunic stopped halfway below the knees, showing his chausses or long thick stockings with feet, which were cross-gartered with leather thongs.

Men and women wore loose cord or leather belts. The men wore low leather shoes fastened at the ankles, the women soft shoes of either leather or fabric. Women were accomplished in weaving and embroidering and the tunics of both sexes were ornamented with bands of needlework at the neck and hem. Men wore simple hoods or skullcaps, while the women concealed their hair under a scarf or "headrail" of linen or cotton. It was circular, square or oblong and was wrapped about the neck like the Persian or Roman chincloth. A crown, if worn, was placed on top the headrail.

With the coming of the Normans, costume, while remaining about the same in style, became richer in fabric, to which were added costly silks, furs and jewels. The first princess style of dress appeared in the time of William II in 1100. An opening in the center back, reaching from the waist to between the shoulder blades was laced, not tightly, but just enough to eliminate the wrinkles around the diaphragm. A cord girdle was added, on which hung purse, keys and mirror.

The coiffure then changed, the hair being worn parted in the middle with long braids, to which false hair was often added for length and finished with ribbons wound about. The headrail developed into the wimple of fine white or colored fabric, held on the head by a snood or metal circlet. Later appeared the chinband and small toque of stiffened white linen. Sometimes it was crownless, with the wimple drawn through and draped in folds.

There was a long-lasting vogue for diapered fabrics, patterned with designs in lozenges, crescents and stars. The clothing of nobility was made only of costly cloths, silks and finest linens, richly embroidered. So much gold tissue was worn that it became necessary to lay thin paper between the folds to prevent tarnishing and that is the origin of our "tissue paper."

Gloves with jewels on the backs were worn by the men. Their long loose drawers gave way to more fitted hose in gay colors, cross-gartered with gold bands. It is interesting to note the leather belt with buckle worn by men and women, with the long tongue left hanging in front. The length of the yard measure was established in the reign of Henry II, 1154 to 1189, by the length of the King's arm. In that period, men's tunics were fastened at the neck by means of small gold studs.

In the twelfth century, a new garment appeared for women called the *pelisse*. It was a loose coat reaching to the knees, had flowing sleeves and fastened at the waist. In fabrics, there were wools woven in Flanders, brocades from Venice and, as on the Continent, ermine was the favored fur.

Between 1199 and 1216, the *surcoat* was adopted in England by men and women, copied after the panel of fabric worn over the knight's armor. Surcoat was the original name for the garment, the cotte or coat being the dress underneath. The surcoat was held in place by a cord girdle or belt. The cotte eventually became the petticoat, while the surcoat developed into the dress.

Gloves were made of wool and leather, and ladies carried theirs tucked into their belts. The shoes of both sexes in this period were of fabric or leather, often embroidered. Toward 1200, women dressed their hair up and adopted the chinband, to which the wimple was pinned, all of sheer linen.

In the early part of the thirteenth century, the *cotehardie* took the place of the surcoat. For men, it was a tight-fitting jacket buttoned down center front. It had long, tight sleeves which buttoned from elbow to the little finger and was finished with a jewelled belt placed low on the hips. The now long, fitted stockings or tights were fastened under the jacket with laces and points.

In the fourteenth century, parti-colored clothes appeared and lasted a half century. At the same time, the toes of the soft, plain or embroidered shoes grew to very long points, which were stuffed and stiffened. Pattens were worn outdoors to protect the soft soles.

In the latter part of the thirteenth century, appeared the *liripipe,* or hood with tail. In the fourteenth century, men wore the draped turban of the Continent with its very long tail, which was either wrapped around the neck or left hanging in the back. By the end of that century, the liripipe became part of the folds of the turban, looking very much like a cock's comb, thence the term "coxcomb," designating a dandy. That ornament dwindled in size, becoming finally, an insignia, the remains of which we have today in the cockade on the coachman's hat. Skullcaps, tall-crowned felt bonnets with narrow rolled brims, were in style too, often the bonnet worn over the hood. The roundlet, the evolution of the chaperon turban, was adopted by Englishmen in the fifteenth century. They also copied the Continental fashion of wearing it slung over one shoulder, holding the liripipe in one hand.

The masculine haircut was usually moderately short, but, in contrast to that style, some men wore their hair cropped short like a priest's and the back of the neck shaved.

There were several styles of cloaks, long and loose, square or circular, with or without hood, wide at the neck or buttoned with two or three buttons. Some had collars and lapels of fur. There were also men's hats with fur brims. Nearly always the masculine costume was finished with a black leather belt, from which hung a triangular pouch and dagger.

At that time there was little change in women's costume, which consisted usually of three garments: the cotte, or robe of cloth with long, tight sleeves and high at the neck; a tunic over that, having shorter and wider sleeves and fuller skirt, of which one or the other had a train; worn over the two was the surcoat, and around the throat a gorget of sheer white material, to which the wimple was pinned.

The hair was done in braids, which were looped up on either side of the face. Later, the wimple was replaced by cauls of various shapes, nets of gold thread or braid interspersed with jewels. This style is known as the golden net caul or the reticulated headdress. Any hair that showed on the back of the neck below the caul was plucked; even eyebrows were plucked in those days and rouge was in fashion.

In the fourteenth century, the *houppelande* came from the Low Countries and was adopted by men and women. It was long and voluminous, belted at the waist, often fur-trimmed and occasionally fur-lined. Young men wore a short version of it, but the various styles of the houppelande were in rich fabrics, sometimes elaborately embroidered. In the same period, edges of garments were petal-scalloped and castellated. Later, the houppelande was belted into evenly arranged pleats.

The heavy gold chain of the period has survived as a badge of office, worn today by mayors, judges and various orders. Large thumb rings were worn, and masculine and feminine costumes were ornamented with heraldic designs stamped on the cloth and velvet in gold, silver and colored enamels.

In the fourteenth century, the underdress with low-placed girdle, the cotehardie, became the mode, also the various styles of the hennin. The tall hennin was called the "steeple headdress" and the two-horned one the *escoffion,* which is said to have originated in England. As on the Continent, the hennin was fastened to a tiny skullcap worn underneath with the frontlet showing on the forehead. The frontlet was of black velvet and was permitted only to persons having ten pounds a year or more. Then came colored wimples after centuries of only saffron or white having been used.

Along with the more elaborate hennins came the higher-waisted gown with fitted bodice, while men adopted short tunics with full sleeves and the broad shoulders of Venetian influence. The long-pointed masculine shoes, called in England "crackowes" after the town of their origin, Cracow, Poland, lengthened to such a degree that, in 1463, an ordinance was passed permitting persons of rank to have points but two inches beyond their toes.

Small silver bells were a fashionable adornment in the late fourteenth and early fifteenth centuries. The jester's costume of parti-colored clothes, hood with short cape, castellated edges, tinkling with bells, has come down to us intact, as the dress of that period.

English Medieval or Gothic

English Medieval or Gothic

English Medieval or Gothic
chinband wimple and toque - 13th C.
man's shoe - 14th C.
headrail drawn through crownless toque - white linen - 13th C.
dress laced in back - 11th C.
pelisse - 12th C.
sugar-loaf hat worn over hood - 14th C.
jewelled circlet - headrail - 14th C.
a haircut of the 15th C.
wired veil - jewelled cap - 15th C.
man's money pouch worn on belt - 14th C.
cylindrical cauls of reticulated headdress - 14th C.
crackowe and patten - 14th C.
woman's bag worn on girdle - 14th C.
chaperon turban - 15th C.
jewelled reticulated headdress - 15th C.
RTW

Chapter Eleven

Flemish and German

Medieval or Gothic

The Flemings were skillful weavers, their craft dating from 900. Tapestry weaving in Europe originated in their city of Arras in the fourteenth century. They produced beautiful patterned leathers which rivalled those of Spain. They wove woolen cloth from English and Scotch wool, which was worn by all the other countries and sent to the East in exchange for the luxuries from those regions.

In the thirteenth century, the long tunic and mantle were still worn in the Low Countries. The tunic reached to the ankles on the men and was full-length on the women. Men wore their hair long, curled at the ends, while that of the women was long and flowing.

By 1300, the same development in the tunic as that in the neighboring countries had arrived. The women's tunic gradually changed into a robe, which was important as a German style, because it was worn over a corset. It was a fitted dress with flowing sleeves and unadorned neck and was worn over a complete undergarment, the chainse or chemise.

About the middle of the fourteenth century, the cotehardie appeared. For men, it was a short, fitted tunic, reaching halfway down between thigh and knee. It buttoned down center front and had long, tight sleeves with buttons from elbow to the little finger. The women's cotehardie resembled that of the man, except that the skirt lay in folds on the ground. Over it was worn the surcoat with large armscye, exposing to view the jewelled girdle at the hips.

The man's tunic changed into the *pourpoint,* a quilted jacket, short of skirt, the body laced either front or back and worn with long, fitted stockings or tights. When the pourpoint was sleeveless, it was worn under the jacket. The later carefully pleated tunic worn by all fashionable Europe originated in Flanders.

Because of the colder climate, fabrics were practical and heavy, richly patterned, but not distinguished. There were silks, brocades, velvets and cloth of gold, also their own beautiful woolens. The Flemings had developed the weaving of linen and cotton to a high degree, producing sheer veiling, muslin and delicate gauze, which were used for headdresses.

The hair was now dressed close to the head, a favorite style being long braids coiled on each side of the face, then, draped over that arrangement, the wimple, which in Germany and Flanders was most intricate and of many styles. Cauls and circlets of gold were worn too and crowns were placed on top of the wimple. The gorget enjoyed its vogue, worn pinned to the wimple.

Men wore hoods, the draped or chaperon turban and hats with brims. Men and women wore the soft, fitted shoe of leather or fabric like those of the other countries and used pattens in the streets. Both sexes were fond of many finger rings, worn also on the thumbs. The women did not use cosmetics. Fashionable people of the Low Countries, in the late fourteenth and early fifteenth centuries, adopted the fad of utilizing small silver bells as ornamentation on their clothes.

This people liked brilliant colors. They wore the parti-colored costumes of the period and surpassed all the other countries in their use of petal-scalloped or castellated edges of garments. A peculiar style of the fifteenth century was the silhouette with a straight back and what we might describe as a bustle worn in front over the stomach.

People of the Low Countries did not wear their clothes with the same style as their neighbors, their figures being heavier and shorter of waist. They did not have that innate feeling for the mode, so that their costumes became over elaborate and bulky.

Despite that fact, certain German styles did influence the northern countries. They furnished an important garment to the rest of Europe in the houppelande, a mode which lasted until the sixteenth century. Their adoption of that fantastic style of slashings and puffings in the last quarter of the fifteenth century, spread to the other courts of Europe, reaching its peak between 1520 and 1535.

The starching of sheer fabrics used for caps, wimples and collars originated in Flanders. In the fondness of the inhabitants of the Low Countries for excessive ornament, not only in dress but also in architecture, can be seen the foundation of the baroque or rococo period of the seventeenth and early eighteenth centuries.

Record has it that steel needles were made in Nuremberg in 1370.

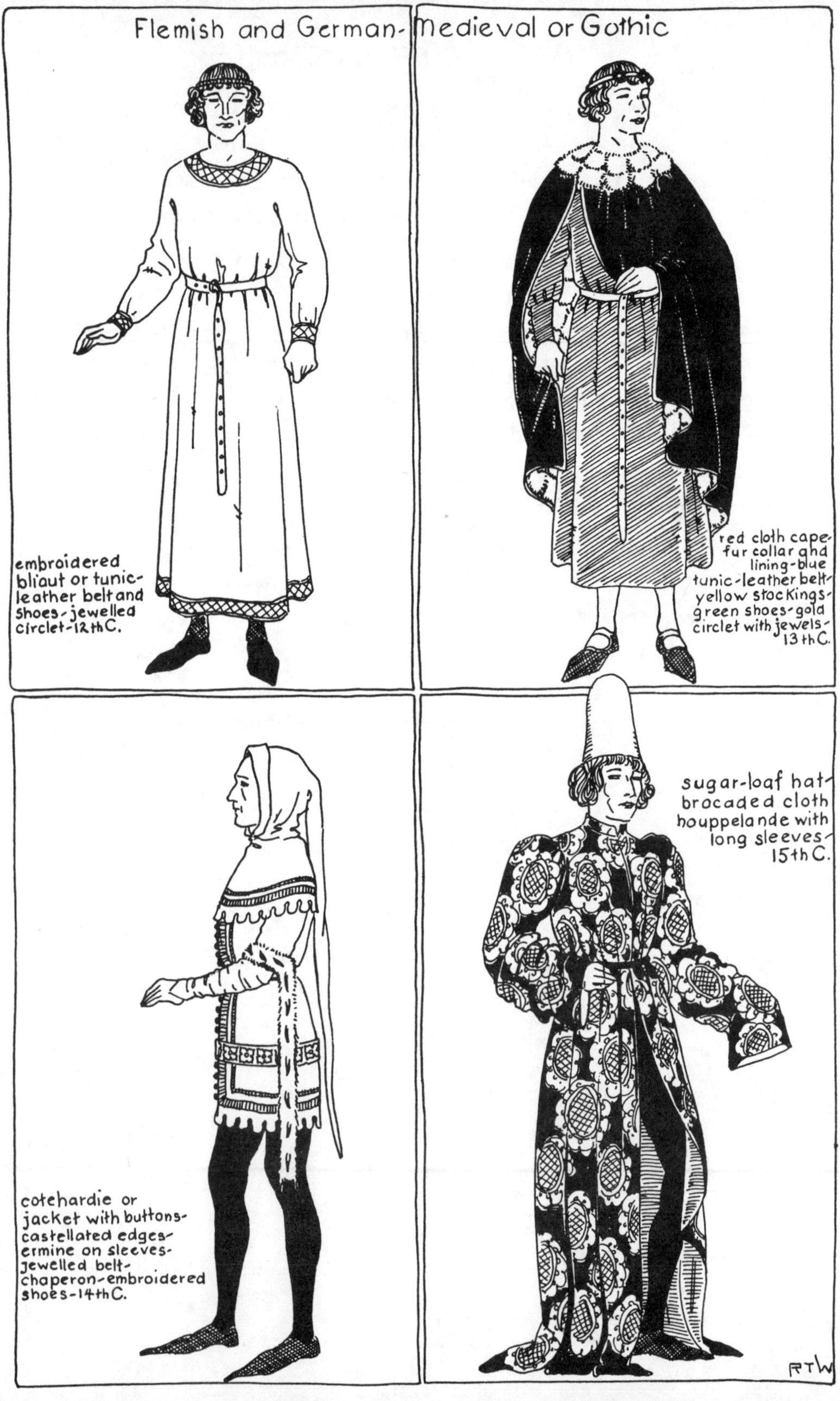

Flemish and German-Medieval or Gothic
embroidered bliaut or tunic-leather belt and shoes-jewelled circlet-12th C.
red cloth cape-fur collar and lining-blue tunic-leather belt-yellow stockings-green shoes-gold circlet with jewels-13th C.
cotehardie or jacket with buttons-castellated edges-ermine on sleeves-jewelled belt-chaperon-embroidered shoes-14th C.
sugar-loaf hat-brocaded cloth houppelande with long sleeves-15th C.
RTW

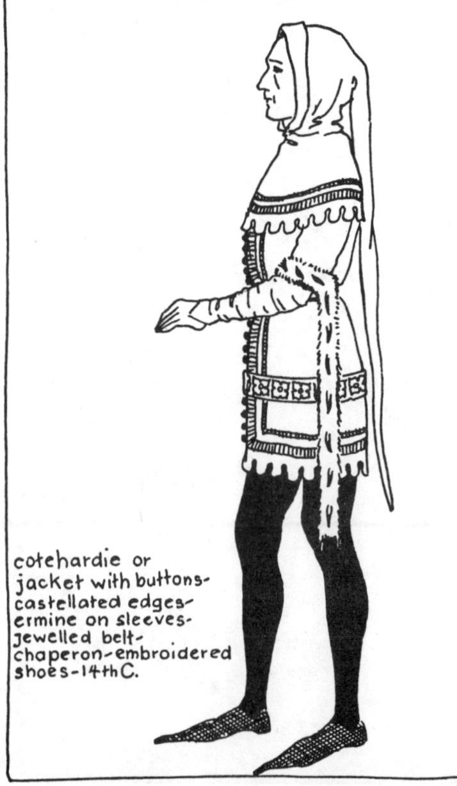

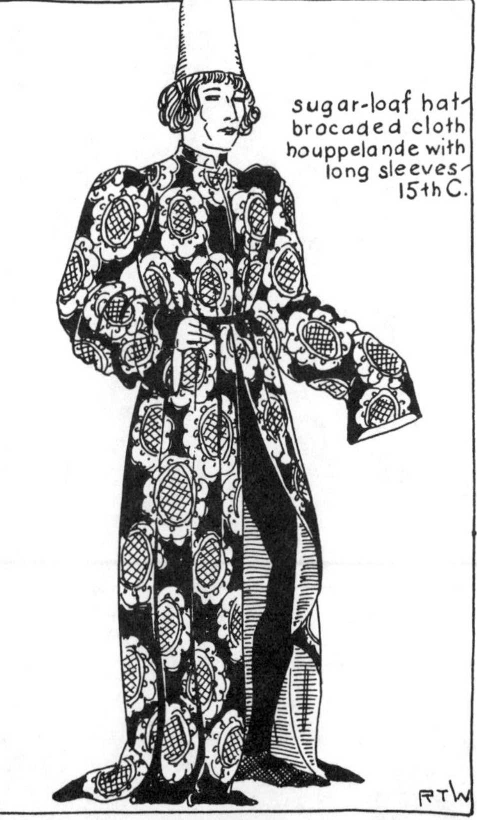

Flemish and German-Medieval or Gothic

Flemish and German-Medieval or Gothic
gold crown-white linen cap and chinband-12th C.
shoe of gold strips and pearls-11th C.
jewelled circlet-net of crocheted wool or Knotted cords of silk, gold or silver-13th C.
woman's belt with purse and keys-14th C.
turban of red and white linen-jewel and heron plumes-bell trimming on dress-15th C.
13th C. toque and chinband of embroidered linen
leather boot 11th C.
turban of white linen-jewel and gold braid-15th C.
roundlet with chaperon-15th C.
reticulated headdress-gold braid and pearls-15th C.
hennin and gorget-15th C.
tunic and baldric with bells-15th C.
shoe with straps-14th C.
man's felt hat with feather-15th C.
RTW

Chapter Twelve

Italian Renaissance

THE RENAISSANCE in Europe originated in Italy, brought about by the decline of Greco-Roman influence and the undertaking of the Crusades. It began in the thirteenth and fourteenth centuries, was fully under way at the beginning of the fifteenth, its height being about the middle of the century and its climax about 1500. At its height, there had existed no parallel except that of the Roman Empire in its greatest glory.

It affected men's costume more than women's. The feminine mode of the early part of the period was of a religious or so-called "conventional" style. Because printing began to be used in Europe about the middle of the fifteenth century, we have much authentic material.

The masculine costume consisted of a shirt, tunic or doublet and hose. Over the doublet was sometimes worn a garment called *pourpoint,* jerkin or jacket and sometimes a robe, called a gown. The shirt or body linen was made quite full, gathered at neck and wrists, the gatherings edged with fine embroidery in gold or red and black silk. This decoration, of ancient Persian origin, came from Spain and was known in Europe as Spanish blackwork.

The neck was either round or V-shaped, square neck predominating from 1500 to 1525. Then came the small turned-down collar, followed by the ruche of Spanish origin, which developed into the ruff in the second half of the sixteenth century. The doublet was a short tunic, jacket-like with sleeves, originally tight, but later tight over the forearm and puffed above.

Slashings appeared in the last quarter of the fifteenth century, lasting until the middle of the seventeenth century. That style originated among the Swiss soldiers, was adopted to an extreme degree in Germany and definitely marked the costume of France and England. The sleeves of the doublet in this period were often slashed and paned, revealing the shirt of rich material. Panes were strips of fabric used vertically over puffings, and these strips were, in turn, ornamented with slashes edged with stitching or gimp.

Wings, or puffs at the shoulders, masking the junction of sleeve and shoulder or the armscye, appeared in the second half of the sixteenth century.

The jerkin or jacket was now a rather short, full tunic, which either hung loose, or was belted into carefully arranged pleats. It had square or round neck, often long full sleeves. Sleeves were frequently detachable from doublet or jerkin, as were fronts or vest pieces, called stomachers.

The man's gown, which opened in front, varied in length, usually had long full sleeves and was made with or without collar. It was lined with rich fabric or fur. Voluminous cloaks were the fashion, both short and long, capelike or circular in cut. They were draped about the figure or simply hung from the shoulders and usually had broad collars.

The men wore fitted and sewn tights, which reached from waist to toe and were made of cloth or silk. Parti-colored hose were worn to the end of the fifteenth century. The short puffed trunks attached to the long stockings or tights were called trunk hose and were in fashion from 1575 to 1595. Trunk hose and codpiece were secured to the doublet by points or lacings. The codpiece was a decorated bag which held the sex piece and continued in fashion until 1580. It was of fabric, usually silk and often elaborately embroidered. From 1560 on, trunk hose were usually slashed or paned, revealing a full, padded silk lining.

Knee breeches followed in the 'seventies, tied below the knee with fringed or tasselled ribbon garters. Such breeches were known as "Venetians."

Footgear with long, pointed toes was replaced by a soft heelless shoe with broad toe. During the period of slashings, these broad toes were also slashed. Boots of varying height were worn until 1510.

Men's hair ranged in length from moderately short to shoulder length with a fringe over the forehead, occasionally in ringlets. Toward the end of the sixteenth century, mustache and beard reappeared.

The masculine head covering was principally a small toque and the béret-crowned hat with plume or jewel. The béret, in its various styles, which was to last a long time and be worn all over Europe, originated in Italy. It was made of felt, cloth, velvet and silk and was first a circular piece of fabric, drawn up on a string or band to fit the head. The tiny bow on the inside leather band of the man's hat of today, is a survival of that string. The béret was ornamented with a jewelled or embroidered band, sometimes a jewelled necklace being used. Brims of hats were sometimes laced with points as trimming.

Points were little metal tags or aglets attached to strings, ribbon, yarn or leather used as lacings and were a definite feature of the period. All parts of the costume were fastened in this manner. For ordinary wear, they were of metal, later they were made of gold and silver and set with precious stones. Points appear to have served for three centuries.

The gown of the lady of Renaissance Italy was artistic in design and rich in fabric. She made use of handsome brocades, embroidered velvets, satins, damasks and pearl-sewn cloth of gold. The Renaissance is sometimes called the "Pearl Age." From the East came gems and rare stones, cloth of gold and silver tissue; from Russia and the North furs such as sable, ermine, vair, marten, lynx, fox and lambskin; from Rheims rich brocades, while Venice made gorgeous silks and velvets.

The bodice of the gown was snug and short-waisted, which brought about the wearing of a heavy-fitted linen corset. The petticoat or "la robe" was of costly green or crimson satin or velvet. The early sleeves were long and tight, later puffed and slashed to reveal the sheer full lingerie undergarment. Necks were round, V-shaped, more often square. The ruff was adopted in the second half of the sixteenth century. Mantles or cloaks were fastened by brooches or cords and tassels.

Sewn stockings were held up by a garter above the knee, while shoes were of the same style as that of the men. The beginning of the heel can be seen in the thick wedge sole attached to the soft shoe, which appeared in the sixteenth century. When a belt or girdle was worn, it was jewelled and held a money pouch, a rosary, sometimes a feather fan and even a dagger.

The hair was worn off the forehead, parted in the middle and drawn into a chignon at the nape of the neck, although early in the period it was dressed in a hanging braid wound with ribbon. In another style, the parted front hair was cut short to below the cheek, curled and left to hang like a bob. The thin gauze or voile veil floating from the back of the head was a favorite fashion, too; ribbons, cauls and caps were worn. Brides wore their hair flowing, parted in the middle and crowned with a wreath of flowers.

False hair, especially blond color, was much worn, also wigs made of white and yellow silk. A favorite was a single jewel which hung in the middle of the forehead attached to a fine chain. That headdress is known to us as the ferronière.

Earrings appeared and became a popular adornment. Jewelry was ornate in design. There were heavy gold chains, strings of pearls and belts of gold and silver filigree. Buttons and clasps were fashioned of gold, silver, enamel, amber, crystal and pearls. Jewelled feathers were worn on men's hats, both sexes wore diamonds and rubies and gold and pearl embroidery.

From antiquity to the sixteenth century, all garments carried some touch of embroidery, Italy now holding the foremost position in this form of decoration. Gloves, hats, shoes, even furs carried decorative handwork, and men's clothes were embroidered in gold and silver or edged in fine red and black stitching. With the advent of the steel needle from the Orient, introduced into Europe by the Moors, embroidery became finer and more elaborate. All fabrics were decorated in colored silks, gold, silver, pearls and other gems.

During this period, the invention of lace took place, and while sparingly used before the seventeenth century, eventually ornamented every article of clothing for both men and women. Before the middle of the sixteenth century, the word lace designated tapes, cords and narrow braids, which were used as trimming and also served to lace together various parts of the costume. Laces were made of two to fifteen strands twisted together. The first lace with pattern was made of these twisted threads, usually white linen. Lace of fine and delicate pattern seems to have been an evolution of embroidery, the design cut out and edged with the buttonhole stitch. It appeared in Italy and Flanders about the middle of the sixteenth century.

It is noted that from the middle of the sixteenth century, both men and women used sunshades which were called umbrellas, even to carrying them on horseback. "Dandies" carried small thin canes, like the "swagger sticks" of today.

Fans, of Oriental origin, returned to vogue. Feather fans and small flag-shaped ones were fashionable in Venice. The flag fans were small squares of plaited straw, linen, parchment or silk, painted or embroidered in colors and attached to a slim ivory stick. Small flat muffs of brocade, silk or velvet were carried by Venetian ladies around the end of the fifteenth century. The possession and use of handkerchiefs became more general, both men and women carrying this accessory of embroidered silk or cambric. Most exquisite ones were adorned with drawn work, leaving very little of the original fabric.

Women made use of cosmetics, perfumes and lavender water and whitened their bare chests. The making of perfume in Europe originated in Renaissance Italy, founded upon the knowledge brought back from the Orient by the Crusaders. René, an Italian perfumer, opened the first perfume shop in Paris about 1500.

Italian Renaissance

satin gown with velvet collar and lining-doublet with lacings over white shirt-jewelled necklace-slashed sleeves-velvet cap-parti-colored tights-embroidered gloves-gold chain-late 15th C.

cloak of silk brocade with velvet-silk tunic-slashed velvet hat-silk tights-velvet shoes-16th C.

slashed satin pourpoint and trunk hose-fur collared mantle-velvet hat-black leather shoes-sword-gold chain and buttons-16th C.

cloth mantle with buttons-brocaded tunic and Venetians-sword-silk hat-late 16th C.

RTW

Italian Renaissance

Italian Renaissance
crown with pearls-late 15th C.
late 15th C.
Pearls and silk voile-late 16th C.
man's hat of braid-15th C.
flag fan of plaited straw-16th C.
man's felt hat-15th C.
lady of Lombardy-braids in rolls-silk voile scarf-16th C.
young woman of Piedmont-braided coiffure-16th C.
late 16th C. fringed muff of brocade
"trembling cap"-net over silk voile-edged with pearls-late 16th C.
wedge sole-beginning of heel-16th C.
Points-paned trunk hose-codpiece-middle 16th C.
fabric boot fastened on inside of leg-pearls-late 15th C.
silk fan-ivory handle-16th C.
RTW

Chapter Thirteen

German Puffs and Slashes

The First Half of the Sixteenth Century

Slashings originated in the costumes of the Swiss soldiers after 1477, when they won their battle against the Duke of Burgundy and mended their ragged uniforms with strips of tents, banners and furnishings left behind in the flight of the Burgundians. It became a fashion and was indulged in to the extreme by the Germans, especially the soldiers, mercenaries called Lansquenets. From them, the style passed to the rest of Europe, reaching its height from 1520 to 1535.

All articles of clothing, even gloves, shoes and stockings were slashed and paned, revealing puffings of contrasting fabric and color. The high waistline prevailed in both masculine and feminine dress. Narrow shoulders, a small tight waist and full hips were the characteristic features of the feminine silhouette, while the masculine effect was broad to squareness.

An exaggerated fullness over the abdomen, below the tight waist, was affected by the women. The underskirt was of heavy contrasting fabric and color, either edged with a wide band of embroidery or bands of velvet. Under that, several linen petticoats were worn. The body garment consisted of a shirt.

Under the large hats, men often wore a cap, while women wore either caul or cap. Hats were ornamented with jewels, embroidery and that great favorite, the ostrich plume. Brims were slashed. Instead of a cap, the man often resorted to a chinstrap or string to hold his hat in place. The string also enabled him to drop his hat to the back of his neck and there the hat was often carried.

Women drew their hair tightly off their faces and invariably concealed it beneath a caul or cap, while men featured theirs in waves and ringlets.

The fronts of shoes were square, of a much broader width than the foot. Daggers, swords and rapiers in ornate cases were suspended from belts. A woman, too, carried a small dagger in company with a decorative bag attached to the end of the girdle. Both sexes wore many rings on various fingers and heavy gold necklaces around their necks. The women used no cosmetics and were not addicted to the use of perfume.

Rich and heavy fabrics, in wool and brocades from the Orient, were used to make the evenly arranged organ-pipe folds of tunic and robe. The supremacy of the English woolen weavers caused the Germans to turn to the weaving of linens and cottons. They produced sheer gauzes, veilings and muslins of exceptionally fine textures.

German Puffs and Slashes

tunic with velvet bands-jewelled clasp-doublet over white linen shirt-paned breeches-ribbon garters with beads-parti-colored stockings-béret hat with plumes-dagger and rapier-1538

scarlet with white puffings-gold décolletage and belt-full white yoke-jewelled girdle with dagger and bag-scarlet béret hat-white plumes-gold caul and necklaces-1st half 16th C.

young woman in pale blue-bodice with white puffings and red embroidery-red band at neck-blue cape lined with violet-violet apron-black velvet bands-hair in pigtail wound with silk-red béret hat with green and white plumes-gold and pearl necklaces-1st half 16th C.

soldier-doublet with paned and slashed sleeves-waistcoat with scallops-paned and slashed breeches-slashed codpiece-ribbon garters-parti-colored stockings-hat with plumes-brim in two pieces-sword-early 16th C.

German Puffs and Slashes
1st half of the 16th Century
hat with
rolled velvet
edge-ostrich
tips
bêret with
slashed brim-
ostrich plumes
coif of gold striped
tissue over crest
shaped cap
flat bêret attached
to seed-pearl sewn
caul-ostrich plume
with pearls on spine
felt hat with
castellated edge
and slashes-attached
to cap-chin strap
velvet hat with
shallow crown-
brim in two halves-
attached to cap
bêret hat with
gold embroidery-attached
to seed-pearl sewn caul
lady's bag of pleated silk
and jewelled frame
velvet bêret with
tiny gold loops
under brim
bêret with
castellated edge-
net caul-ostrich
plumes-chinstrap
shoe with slashed heel
hat with castellated
edge-satin threaded
through slashes
shoe with
strap and buckle
RTW

Chapter Fourteen

French Renaissance The Valois

Charles VIII—1483–1498 Louis XII—1498–1515

In these two reigns, the Renaissance in France was taking root to reach full bloom in the reign of François I. By this time, it had already existed for one hundred years in Italy. The French mode of the sixteenth century was inspired by the Venetian mode of the fifteenth century, but was not as restrained and elegant. There were, however, the same heavy silks and satins, velvets and jewelled embroidery, metal braids, ribbons and costly furs.

Men wore the long tights reaching to the waist, the pourpoint or doublet which now had a low neck, usually square, worn over a full sheer lingerie shirt. The tights were often parti-colored, in silk or cloth of gold appliquéd in velvet or passementerie.

There were two styles of cloaks, both were full and had large openings for the arms to pass through. The long one, reaching to the ground, had long hanging false sleeves and the body was sometimes confined by a girdle around the waist. The shorter one, too, hung loose, reaching to a point below the knees. Both had lapels or wide collars and were often fur-trimmed and fur-lined. Hats were rather flat in béret style, soft-shirred crowns with brims of varied shape, turned up and frequently ornamented with a jewel and a plume.

The predominant style in women's dress appears to have been a snugly fitted bodice, under which was worn a fitted corset of heavy linen. There were two variations of this mode, Italian and French, the difference being in the sleeves. Those of the Italian gown were long and fairly slim, broken by small puffs, while the French sleeves flared into wide, turned-back cuffs. The neck of the bodice was usually square. The full skirt flared out from the waist on a straight line, opening over a petticoat of contrasting, heavy, rich fabric to which embroidery and jewels were added. Other ornamentation consisted of wide bands of fur, velvet and embroidery. Under this there was a foundation petticoat of taffeta-covered canvas. The wide-flowing sleeves showed their linings of fur or velvet. Later, sleeves of many puffs came in, wide at the top and tight at the wrists. Elaborate necklaces, strings of pearls and the jewelled pendant or cross attached to a fine, black silk cord were of the period. Jewelled girdles with a long end hanging in center front were worn, from which hung rosary or mirror.

The shoes of both sexes were soft, in leather, silk or velvet, with a round toe which finally became square. A buckled or buttoned strap served as fastening. Metal or gold points attached to laces were used to secure the different parts of the costume.

Men wore their hair in a bob to a line just below the cheek. Women dressed theirs in the Italian or Madonna fashion, parted in the middle and drawn back into a chignon at the nape of the neck. Over it was worn a hood with hanging folds at the sides and the back. The curtain or loose back piece of the hood was called the "fall," and the narrow side pieces "lappets." The favorite hood was of black velvet, embroidered and lined with red or white. The cap, or "coif," worn under the hood, was either sheer white or gold tissue, usually edged with a narrow frill. Many variations of the hood developed with the eventual pinning up of the fall and the lappets. The hair was concealed in silken cases.

Ladies of rank wore enveloping mantles of rich fabric, caught together at the neck by buckles, brooches or cords with tassels.

French Renaissance

crimson velvet gown-gray fur-false sleeves-gold satin pourpoint-gold necklace-black velvet hat-white silk tights-white shoes-end of 15th C.

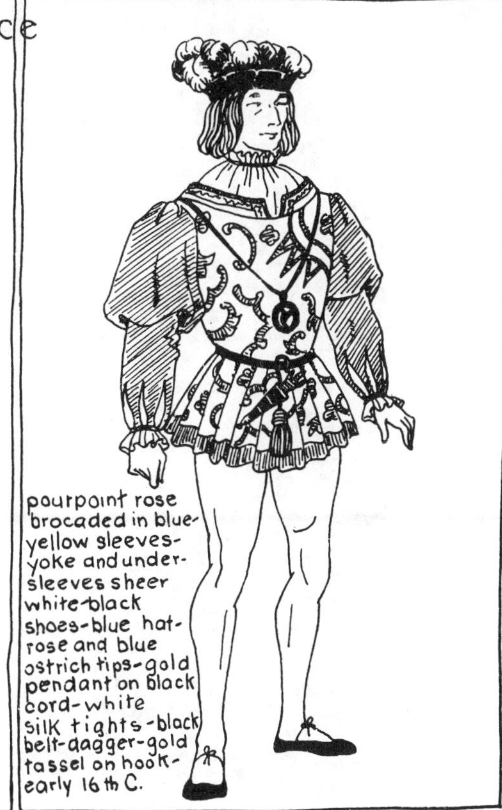

pourpoint rose brocaded in blue-yellow sleeves-yoke and under-sleeves sheer white-black shoes-blue hat-rose and blue ostrich tips-gold pendant on black cord-white silk tights-black belt-dagger-gold tassel on hook-early 16th C.

brown cloth jacket over red velvet pourpoint-black fur-black hat-purple tights-black shoes-gold belt-swagger stick-shirred sheer white at neck edged with jewels-gold pendant on black cord-early 16th C.

RTW

brocaded gold cloak-fur-lined and edged-white shirt and sleeves embroidered in gold-gold, red and black embroidery at neck-red tights with blue and gold bands-black shoes and hat-gold chain-early 16th C.

French Renaissance

French Renaissance

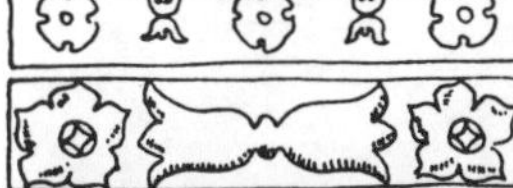

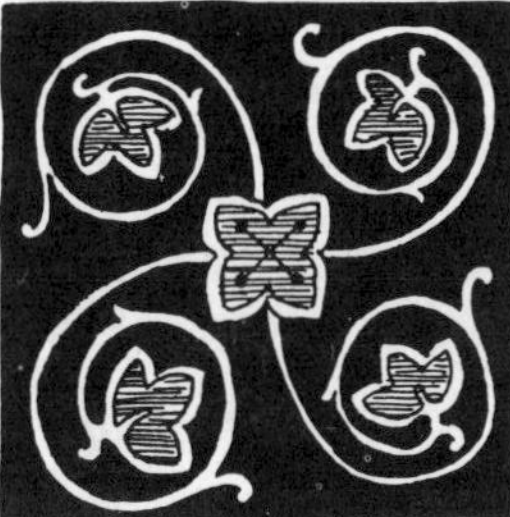

felt béret with brim-late 15th and early 16th C.

girdle of strands of yarn with pearl knots-16th C.

caul with jewelled band-velvet lappets-jewel on head, 16th C.

jewelled girdle-16th C.

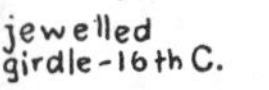

hood of tapestry and silk-large jewel-velvet lappets-sheer wired peak-late 15th and early 16th C.

cap with bound strands of yarn-velvet lappets-embroidered edge-16th C.

felt hat-jewels and crenellated edge-early 16th C.

rose velvet band with jewels-hair bound with ribbon-early 16th C.

lady's "hand bag" or small satchel-velvet with embroidery and pearls-early 16th C.

hat of brocade and felt-late 15th C.

felt hat with wired ostrich plume-jewelled ornament-late 15th C.

RTW

Chapter Fifteen

French Renaissance
The Valois

François I—1515–1547
Henri II—1547–1559

With the reign of François I, the French Court became definitely established and by its brilliancy revealed its Venetian origin and influence. The mode for both men and women was decidedly broad and square with much slashing in all parts of the costume. Colors were in a lighter vein than those of Italy, sky blue and white, lilac tones, rose, gold and silver being much favored.

The embroidered low-neck chemise or shirt of the man was shirred into a higher neckline, finishing in a narrow frill, the beginning of the ruche in France. The full sleeves were gathered at the wrist. The pourpoint, or doublet, had a low square neck, a fitted body and very full puffed and slashed sleeves, which were tight at the wrists. Early in the century, the pourpoint was skirtless, but later developed a short skirt often with scalloped or crenellated edge. The jerkin or jacket, really a tunic wrap, in this period was voluminous but short, with huge flowing sleeves that sometimes had wide turned-back cuffs. Occasionally it had hanging false sleeves or, again, puffed sleeves to the elbow with deep, tight cuff.

Trunk hose, stuffed or bombasted with horsehair, bran or other padding, became very short. They were paned and slashed, of different fabric from the stockings, but trunks and stockings were often made in one. Trunks or breeches were called upper stocks, while stockings were known as nether stocks. When trunks were fashioned of pieces or strips placed vertically, the English term for the strips was panes, thus paned breeches. Stockings were parti-colored, one plain and the other striped with garters and ribbon bows worn just below the knees. The codpiece attached to the trunks was still prominent and elaborately embroidered. In fact, the entire costume was decorated, slashed with puffings of different materials of contrasting colors showing through the openings. The puffings were also embroidered and the edges of the slashings finished with braid or gimp of silk, gold or silver.

Jewelled swords were worn at the side. Hats were the same for both men and women, the béret crown with narrow brim and trimmed with a white feather, which might have been ostrich, peacock or wool imitation of feathers. The same shapes in straw were worn in the summer.

The masculine undergarment was of finest linen, white with delicate black embroidery, known as Spanish blackwork. The outer garments were in colors of white, rose, sky blue and soft yellow, while at court functions, white and cloth of gold were worn. Men wore beards and mustaches, with their hair bobbed short.

The hoop came to France in 1530 with Eleanor of Castille, the second wife of François I. It was a petticoat of heavy canvas, with the lower part a wicker hoop covered with heavy taffeta. It flared out from the waist to the ground, creating a conical shape. The cotte or robe opened over an elaborately embroidered petticoat of rich fabric, under which was worn the hoop, women wearing for the first time three skirts.

Also an innovation, was the corset, or bodice, called the *basquine,* separate from the skirt and of different material and color. It was very tight, usually with low, square neck, which now curved upward across the front. Under it was worn the fitted corset of heavy linen, while steel rods were added to the bodice itself. Sleeves, which were often separate from the costume, were puffed and slashed and elaborately ornamented.

A distinctive feature of both men's and women's costume was the full sheer guimpe, or chemise, which appeared above the square neck of tunic or bodice. The jewelled girdle with long end in front, as worn by Catherine de' Medici, was really a rosary with a mirror at the end.

Women gathered their hair into a chignon at the back of the head. They parted it in the middle, over which were worn lovely caps of sheer gauze or linen, cauls of gold threads and jewels and nets of pearls. In the style known as "la ferronière," so called after "la Belle Ferronière," mistress of Francois I, a jewel hung in the center of the forehead, suspended from a fine chain around the head. In this period, the ornate jewelled gold necklace was popular.

Men and women wore squared-toed shoes of soft Spanish leather, silk or velvet. The toes were slashed and the feminine shoe ornamented with embroidery and jewels. Ladies wore stockings in crimson or scarlet with an embroidered or cut edge which rose three inches above the knee. Garters above and below the knee held them in place.

The Venetian mask of black velvet lined with white satin was the fashion for both sexes. Women wore them outdoors to protect their complexions and make-up and to the theatre to conceal their identity. There was a small mask which covered the upper half of the face. A larger one covered the entire visage, held in position by means of a button attached to the inside, which was inserted between the teeth.

Fabrics were indeed gorgeous with embroideries and jewels, patterned cloths, brocaded silks and velvets. Trimmings consisted of wide bands of contrasting colored cloth, embroidery or fur, such as sable, marten and ermine. Scarfs of fur were finished with head and claws encrusted with jewels and were worn throughout the entire sixteenth century. Other ornamentation was of gold and silver in thread lace and rosettes. There were also plain heavy silks, satins and velvets, velvet being the favorite.

The beginning of the supremacy of France in perfumes dates from this reign, François I encouraging the celebrated Italian perfumers to establish themselves in France.

With the reign of Henri II, the Protestant influence and severe restrictions in the use of silks and velvets, came a sobering of the mode. More somber colors and a great deal of black was worn. The broad silhouette disappeared, the Spanish style of bombast or padding taking its place. The distinctive features were the high collar, long wasp waist and padded hips. The first silk knit stockings, a Spanish invention, were worn by Henri II.

The man's pourpoint, or doublet, still embroidered and braid-trimmed, became high-necked with the narrow ruche of the chemise showing above the collar. Sleeves lost their extreme fullness, but were still tight at the wrists. The short skirt of the doublet opened in front, revealing the codpiece. Trunk hose became shorter and fuller, were still padded, while stockings knitted of silk or wool were better fitting. The soft shoe, still slashed, conformed more to the shape of the foot. Sword and pouch or money bag were worn in the belt. Pockets, inserted in the trunks, appeared in the latter part of this period.

The style of hat remained the same, with the brim a bit narrower. The hair was worn short with mustache and clipped beard. The long gown or robe continued to be worn, but the short circular cape of cloth or velvet was newer.

Catherine de' Medici, wife of Henri II, is credited with bringing to France the steel corset in the form of the stomacher. The stomacher, which was the outer bodice, was fashioned of splints of ivory, steel, mother-of-pearl or silver covered with fabric and heavily embroidered with gold, silver and jewels. Under it was worn a garment of heavy linen, reaching from chest and underarms to the waist, tightly laced in back.

The basic design of the robe had changed little, except that the neck rose high, as did the men's, finishing with the narrow ruche or frill, also at the wrists. This narrow ruche of Spanish origin and the beginning of the ruff was also introduced into France by Catherine. Narrow thread lace now began to edge these frills.

When hats were worn, they were of the same béret style as the men's. The small and very becoming cap of the period was of sheer gauze with wired edge, its characteristic feature being the dip over the forehead. It is known as the "Marie Stuart cap," but Catherine seems to have established it as the "widow's cap." The hair was parted in the middle, drawn over puffs, pads or wires at the temples and rolled into a chignon at the back. A contemporary painting of Mary Stuart in her mourning headdress of white, portrays her with a cap to which is attached a gorget, or *barbe,* biblike in shape, of pleated sheer white linen.

Crimson satin was a passion of Catherine's, but after the death of the King, she never relinquished wearing black for mourning.

The vogue for paint, powder and perfume grew and Catherine, like François I, encouraged the settling in France of celebrated Italian perfumers. Perfumed gloves of fine leather were introduced to the court by Count Frangipani and manufactured at Blois after the Italian model. They were named "gants à la frangipane." Knitted silk gloves were also worn.

The shoes of Mary Stuart and Catherine de' Medici are the first shoes made with high heels in the modern fashion, that is, the heel in pedestal form, separate from the sole.

Men and women wore a great deal of jewelry, even the men adorning themselves with earrings. Pearls and other jewels were freely sewn over both masculine and feminine costumes and women added jewels to their coiffures. Both sexes wore gloves, carried needle-worked handkerchiefs and, throughout the Renaissance Period, made free use of cosmetics to enhance their appearance. The art of "face-painting," if we could call the use of white lead and vermilion such, was introduced into France by Catherine. Drawn and cut-work ornamentation appeared about the middle of the sixteenth century. It was executed in white thread upon white linen. The fact that linen became sheerer and the handwork closer and finer, explains the origin and evolution of lacemaking.

French Renaissance

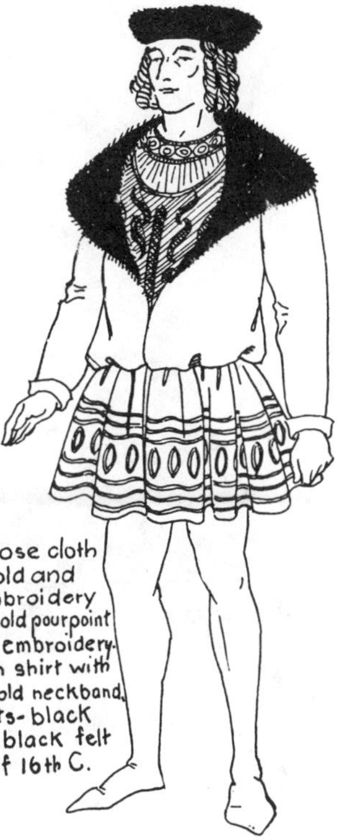

page in rose cloth jacket-gold and purple embroidery on skirt-gold pourpoint with blue embroidery. white linen shirt with blue and gold neckband, white tights- black fur collar-black felt hat-1st half 16th C.

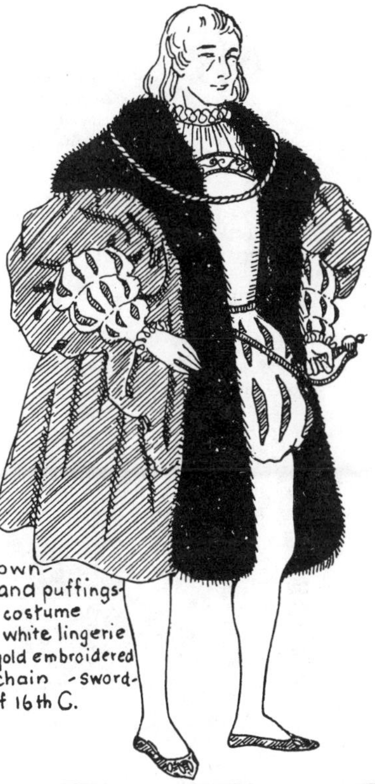

blue gown- shoes and puffings- rest of costume white-white lingerie shirt-gold embroidered band-chain -sword- 1st half 16th C.

black cape- pale blue pourpoint with yellow band- blue neckband- all braid gold-white shirt showing under slashes- wine trunk hose over white- white stockings- yellow shoes- gray-green hat with jewels and white plume-sword- 1st half 16th C.

black velvet jacket with ermine- silver galloon- and loops- slashed pourpoint- black leather belt-slashed codpiece-white paned trunk hose- white shoes and stockings-black hat-white plume- sword-1st half 16th C.

RTW

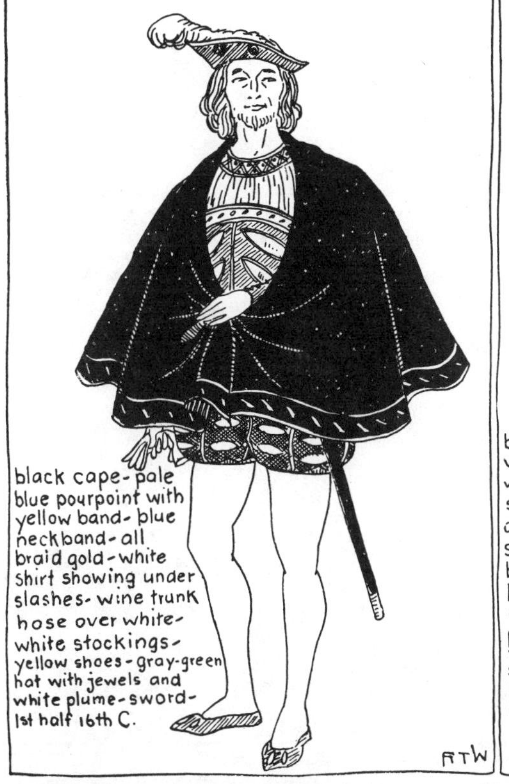

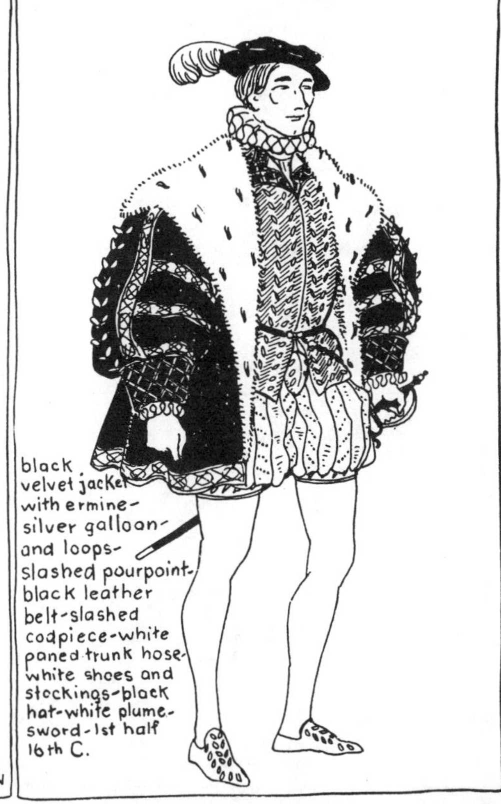

French Renaissance

French Renaissance

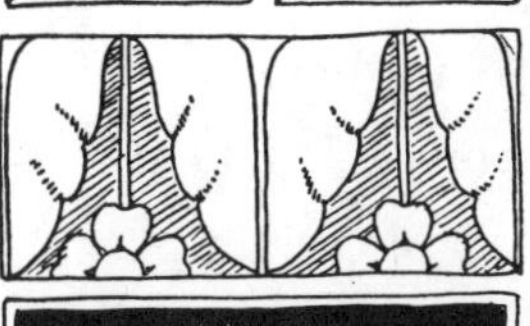

la ferronière-
gold chain with
jewel-early 16th C.

black felt hat-cap
gold braid over rose-
pearls-white feathers-
middle 16th C.

gray leather shoe-
inverted pleat and
jewel-1st half 16th C.

braids and pearls-
middle 16th C.

net of gold ribbon
over red velvet-
jewels and tassel-
1524

black velvet trimmed
with gold-1st half 16th C.

black velvet trimmed
with gold-white
feather-1st half 16th C.

white linen cap with
pearls-metal frame-black
velvet fall-early 16th C.

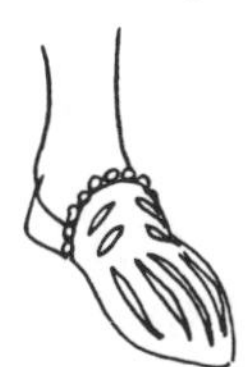

slashed leather
shoe with pearls-
middle 16th C.

black velvet-pearls-
white ostrich tip-
middle 16th C.

white mourning-cap
with wimple and gorget-
band with pearls-1560

slashed white fabric
shoe-1st half 16th C.

RTW

Chapter Sixteen

French Renaissance
The Valois

Charles IX—1560–1574
Henri III—1574–1589

Under Charles IX, men's costumes changed slightly, the Spanish influence still dominating the mode in the padded or bombast style. The long-bodied, small-waisted pourpoint or doublet became really a corset. It had stiffening, a busk in center front and the skirt of the garment was short. Sleeves were still tight at the wrists and padded, but not full. The embroidered linen shirt was still worn with a turned-down collar showing above the neck of the doublet. Buttons fastened the doublet down center front. The newly invented watches were carried in the pockets inserted in the trunk hose. Pockets were also inserted in the doublet sleeves.

Also worn were Venetians, which were breeches, full at the upper section of the leg, tying or buttoning below the knee. The codpiece embroidered with gold thread and jewels was still seen, but in the 'seventies, began to disappear, to be entirely gone by the 'nineties.

Gowns, cloaks and jerkins developed wings or shoulder puffs. An unusual jerkin worn by soldiers was the *mandilion,* short and wide with hanging sleeves, a garment which later became part of livery. The short Spanish cape continued in fashion. An interesting note in men's costume is that after 1565, the long robe and the flat béret cap continued to be worn only by elderly men and city people, eventually becoming the uniform of professional classes.

The soft crown of the béret grew high over a wire foundation and a narrow rolled brim appeared. The hat was fashioned of velvet or silk with a small standing plume, the crown encircled by a cord or perhaps a jewelled band. This toque was adopted by both men and women. The hair was worn short, beards were cropped and pointed and mustaches were the style. Pearl earrings were worn by both sexes.

Women now wore the Spanish hoop, called verdingale or farthingale, a petticoat of graduated hoops, or the French cartwheel which was a padded bolster tied around the hips. The corset-shaped bodice was high-necked with a ruff. Puffs and wings ornamented the shoulders and false or hanging sleeves were worn.

The hair continued to be dressed simply, off the face, parted in the middle and slightly rolled or puffed at the temples. Powdered hair was in vogue during most of the second half of the sixteenth century. The desired hue was black with a lighter shade showing through, blonds tinting theirs to gain the effect.

Caps ornamented with pearls and other gems were worn, also a hat of the same style as that of the men, narrow brim with béret crown, trimmed with a feather and jewels.

Masks of black velvet continued to be worn out of doors and to the theatre. They were to last well through the eighteenth century, passing from people of quality to the bourgeoisie. Later on, masks were worn as a protection against the winter cold. Green silk ones, covering the entire visage, were used on horseback to shield the complexion from the sun. Such a mask was held in position by a button clenched between the teeth. The wearing of them persisted to the time of our American Colonies.

When riding horseback, women wore, under the gown, a kind of doublet with upper hose, called *caleçons,* rather resembling the union suit of today.

Small muffs came into fashion in this reign, with colored furs being reserved to ladies, black only permitted to the bourgeoisie. The wearing of velvet was forbidden to the lower classes.

The period of Henri III was marked by an extreme decadence and degeneracy in the character of the fashionable men at court. In fact, Henri III has come down to us as the synonym for effeminacy and profligate living. Men used cosmetics and perfumes, and slept with masks and gloves to soften the skin. They plucked their eyebrows and mustaches to make a fine line. Both men and women used violet-scented powder in the hair and wore much jewelry, including earrings.

The doublet developed an ugly shape in front, called the peasecod-belly, a busk down the center front and a stuffed-out hump protruding over the belt. Men are supposed to have worn a corset. The skirt of the doublet was quite short, the neck high and finished with a ruff, sleeves still puffed, slashed and tight at the wrists. Sleeves were finished with narrow ruches or lingerie cuffs, but the neck ruff, following the Spanish fashion, had grown much larger. It was now starched, its edge wired, and was tied in front with the strings left hanging.

Trunk hose became so short that sometimes they were only a short puff below the waist, but the space from there to the knee was covered with a garment called *canions.* Canions were breeches conforming to the shape of the leg, usually made in many rows of slashed puffs. With them were worn stockings reaching halfway up the leg, gartered conspicuously at the knee with ribbons having fringed ends.

The béret crown rose still higher, supported on wire, but another style was also worn by Frenchmen during the 'eighties. It was a sort of bonnet with very narrow rolled brim, shirred crown, the whole worn on the back of the head. In center front was perched an ornament of small feathers and jewels.

The hair was short and brushed up at the temples like the feminine coiffure. Mustaches and cropped, pointed beards continued in fashion.

Henri III is supposed to have disliked beards. Men wore pearl earrings and carried their pocket mirrors in their breeches pockets.

Capes and cloaks were of all styles and lengths. The short Spanish cape sometimes had a cowl in back, while the French cape of three quarters and knee length had a collar or shoulder cape. Capes were worn in any manner possible, over both shoulders or just hanging from one shoulder, then again draped diagonally across the back and held in front.

Shoes were still slashed, but in a smaller design. They conformed to the shape of the foot, covering it to the ankle. Pantoffles, or pattens, which had a cork sole and a piece over the instep, were worn over these shoes outdoors. A style of shoe, no doubt inspired by the chopine, had a second sole or platform placed under the sole and heel of the shoe. A portrait of Henri III pictures him wearing such a pair of shoes with red heels. Cork soles appeared in this period, often being placed between the sole and upper leather. Boots of Spanish leather, preferably white, rose above the knee and were fitted to the leg. They were held up by narrow straps and sometimes fastened down the leg by means of buckles or buttons. The tops were often turned down in Spanish fashion and the edges cut in tabs or scallops. A low, flat heel began to appear.

Along with gloves of leather, there is mention of knitted gloves of silk.

The Spanish style persisted for women with the corseted bodice, busk and long point in front and the large ruff, starched and with wired edge. Under the bodice was worn a veritable instrument of torture, the *corps piqué,* or "stitched body," which, according to description, seems to have been a corset fashioned of wooden splints covered with heavy linen.

The hoop skirt went to the extreme in shape. The Spanish skirt with its petticoat of graduated hoops was conical in silhouette, while the French was drum-shaped because of the padded bolster set on the hips.

A feature of this period was the *conch,* a shell-like wrap with large wired wings, rising above the shoulders in back, framing the face. It was fashioned of sheer material and hung to the floor. The style of waving the hair in small, tight curls came in and the center part gave way to a pompadour dressed over pads or wire frames, ending in a flat bun in the back.

Hats followed the masculine style, along with jewelled caps, which were still the mode. Shoes were like those of the men.

Collars and cuffs were now being edged with lace and Catherine de' Medici is noted as having had handkerchiefs of silk or linen edged with gold lace. Henri III introduced lace-making to France by bringing to his court Venetian pattern makers of lace and linen needlework. The cartwheel ruff was changing into a fan-shaped lace-edged collar, open in front, where it rose from a low décolletage which exposed the bosom, sometimes the entire bosom. The velvet mask continued in use by both sexes.

During the second half of the sixteenth century, all modish European women wore the same cloak, with slight variations. It was a simple flaring coat with collar and short puffed sleeves, reaching to the hem of the skirt. It fastened only at the neck, flaring open in front, and was made of elaborately embroidered or brocaded fabric, the edges often finished with wide braid.

The vogue for small muffs continued. Fans of plumes attached to decorated sticks or handles came into fashion. To Catherine is accredited the introduction into France of the folding fan. It was of Spanish origin and came by way of Italy. Both men and women used this fan of heavily scented leather. In this period of needlework, men vied with women in the art of embroidering their gloves and shoes.

French Renaissance

jacket with "wings", velvet bands, buttons and loops-slashed pourpoint-paned trunk hose-codpiece-béret with brim-sword-1560's

all black-cape with heavy gold braid-white collar with lace edge-white wrist frills-trunk hose-canions-rapier-béret-2nd third 16th C.

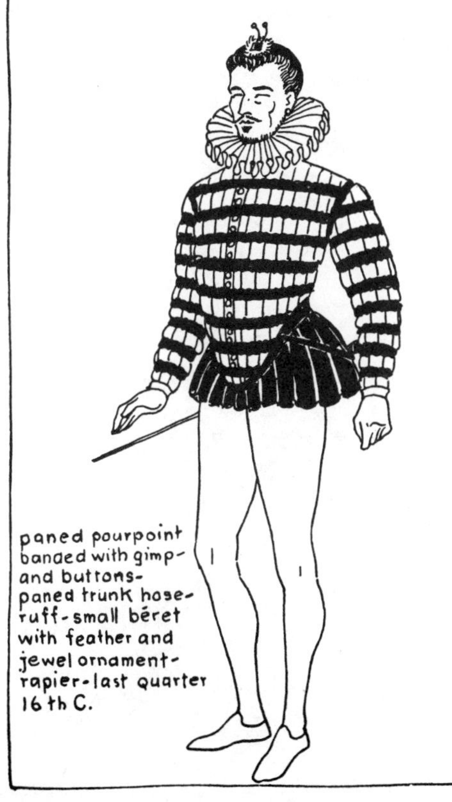

paned pourpoint banded with gimp-and buttons-paned trunk hose-ruff-small béret with feather and jewel ornament-rapier-last quarter 16th C.

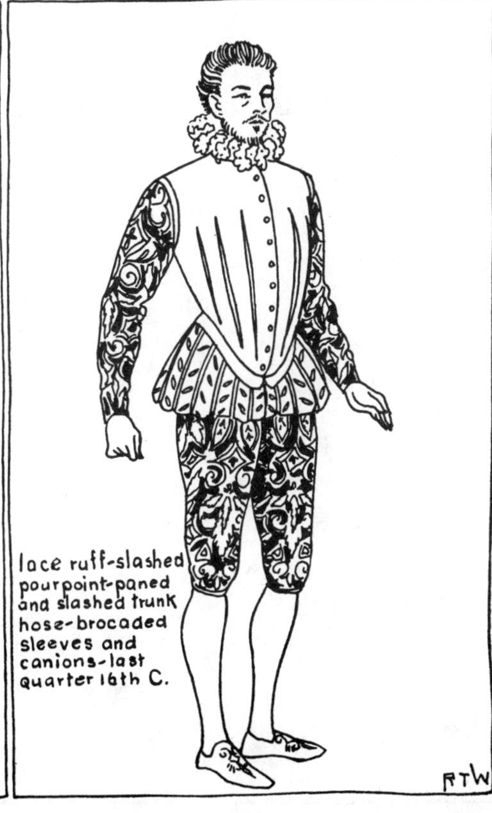

lace ruff-slashed pourpoint-paned and slashed trunk hose-brocaded sleeves and canions-last quarter 16th C.

French Renaissance

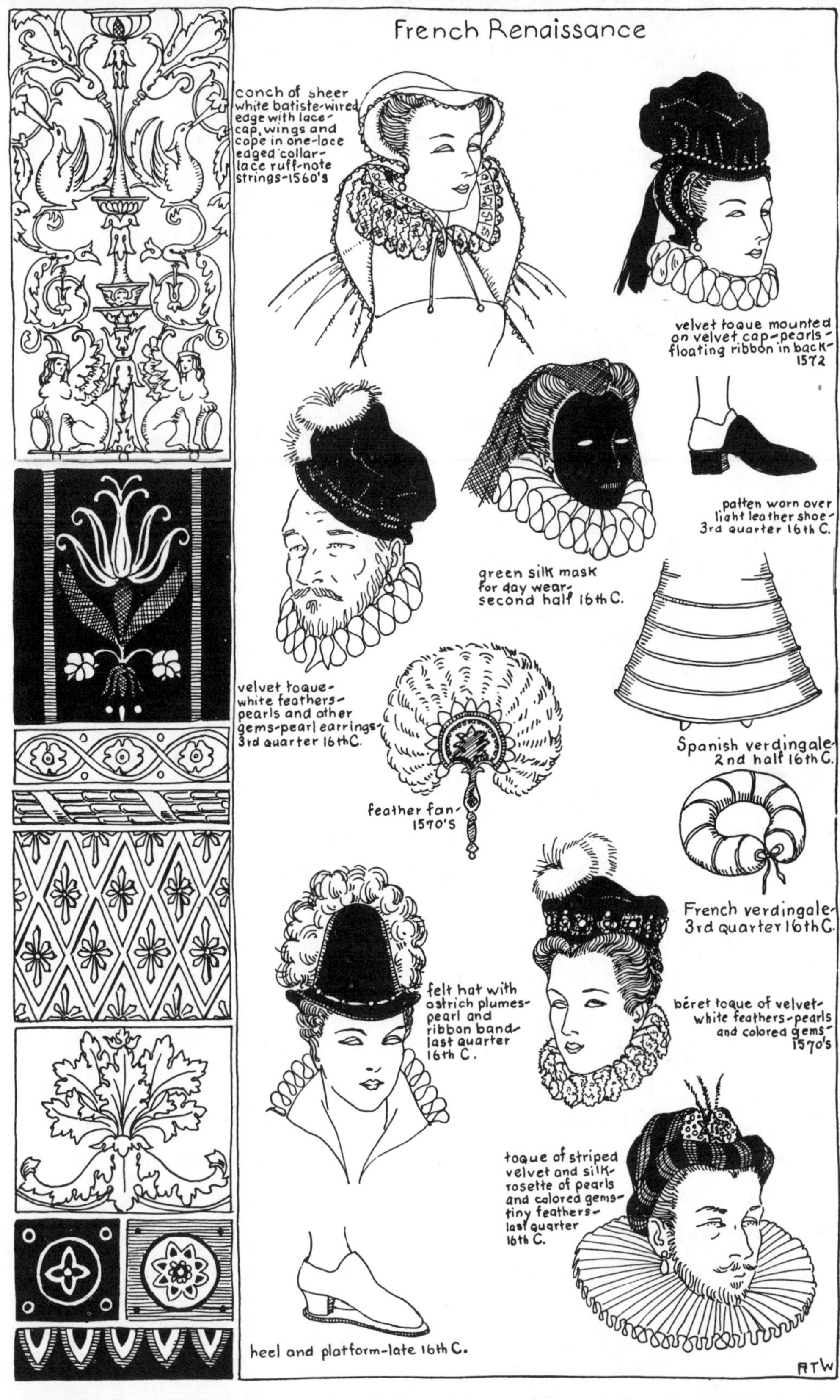
French Renaissance
conch of sheer white batiste-wired edge with lace-cap, wings and cape in one-lace edged collar-lace ruff-note strings-1560's
velvet toque mounted on velvet cap-pearls-floating ribbon in back-1572
green silk mask for day wear-second half 16th C.
patten worn over light leather shoe-3rd quarter 16th C.
velvet toque-white feathers-pearls and other gems-pearl earrings-3rd quarter 16th C.
Spanish verdingale-2nd half 16th C.
feather fan-1570's
French verdingale-3rd quarter 16th C.
felt hat with ostrich plumes-pearl and ribbon band-last quarter 16th C.
béret toque of velvet-white feathers-pearls and colored gems-1570's
toque of striped velvet and silk-rosette of pearls and colored gems-tiny feathers-last quarter 16th C.
heel and platform-late 16th C.
RTW

Chapter Seventeen

The Hispano-Moresque Period of Spain

THE SARACENS, by the middle of the eighth century, had conquered the entire Near East and settled in North Africa, Southern Italy and Spain. They ruled Spain for the next eight centuries. The Saracens, or Moors, were a people who had absorbed the culture of the other civilized countries, and thereby kept alive during the Dark Ages the development of art and science. They were the teachers of Medieval Europe and their period in Spain is known as the Saracenic or Hispano-Moresque. The influence and richness of their design are revealed in the arms, armor, jewelry and fabrics of the Gothic or Medieval and Renaissance Periods. Steel needles were introduced into Europe by the Moors.

In the earlier examples, their costumes were simple and voluminous, of plain wool, designed to protect them from the heat by covering the body almost entirely. As with other nations, the basic costume seems to have consisted of two garments or tunics, a long, straight, sleeveless one, ankle-length, called the *gandoura,* and over that another, more ample, with long, flowing sleeves. The outer tunic was drawn up and bloused over a girdle, shortening its length, thereby revealing the under one. Attached to the masculine outer tunic was a hood. The whole garment is known by the name of *burnous* and is still worn by the Arabs. Over their hoods, the men wore twisted turbans. Both sexes wore trousers.

That costume remains practically the same today among the Arabian peoples of the desert. Later, the Saracenic mode combined Arabian of the desert with Persian. During the Middle Ages, the costume was fashioned of gorgeous fabrics in cloths, silks, damasks, metal brocades, gauzes and sheer muslins in lovely colors.

The coat of Persian origin became, ultimately, almost regulation for men. It was of varying length, with long, straight, narrow sleeves. Sometimes the sleeves reached to the knees in length. A crushed, wide, soft sash usually accompanied it and trousers were worn underneath. The coat, of varied length and cut, worn over trousers, was also a feminine mode. Trousers were in three styles—long, straight ones slightly shaped to the leg, petticoat trousers, long and flaring, and very full ones, gathered at the ankles. The long, straight, feminine ones were of silk embroidered from knee to the ankle.

Women wore a short, full, pleated skirt or a scant one, just covering the knees, with the trousers or pantaloons showing below. Sometimes they wore a long robe or tunic like a candys, with a wide sash tied at the hips. When in public, baggy pantaloons covered feet and legs to the waist and an enveloping mantle concealed the body and head. It also covered the face, either having slits for the eyes or being worn just below the eyes.

Men and women wore sandals and slippers of soft leathers, colorfully dyed. A portrait of a Persian lady of the late sixteenth century pictures her wearing a short skirt about twelve inches from the floor, revealing embroidered trousers, below which appear well-fitted soft-leather boots with heels and pointed toes.

The women colored their fingers and toenails with henna, used rouge and darkened their eyes with kohl and indigo and were fond of perfumes. Both sexes adorned themselves with ornate jewelry.

Spanish blackwork, that fine black embroidery stitching combined with gold and silver thread which enjoyed such a long and tremendous vogue during the sixteenth century, came from the Moors and was, no doubt, of Persian origin. It edged the neck and wrists of the white linen or batiste shirts of the fashionable man of all the European courts.

The Christian Spaniards of the Middle Ages wore the costume of Medieval Europe, similar to that of Italy, but revealing the influence of their Oriental rulers in its color and decorative motif, employing much red, black and white.

Moorish or Saracenic Spain

Turkish Moorish-dark green turban green tunic over yellow-violet scarf, yellow fringe-yellow leather shoes embroidered-leather shoulder strap with jewels

Arabian Moorish-blue shawl over red pill-box cap-yellow brocade pleated skirt-red pantaloons

Persian Moorish-coat of painted, brocaded or embroidered silk-loops and buttons at sides-voile under garment, turban and gorget-jewelled headband-moiré trousers embroidered to knee-dyed leather boots

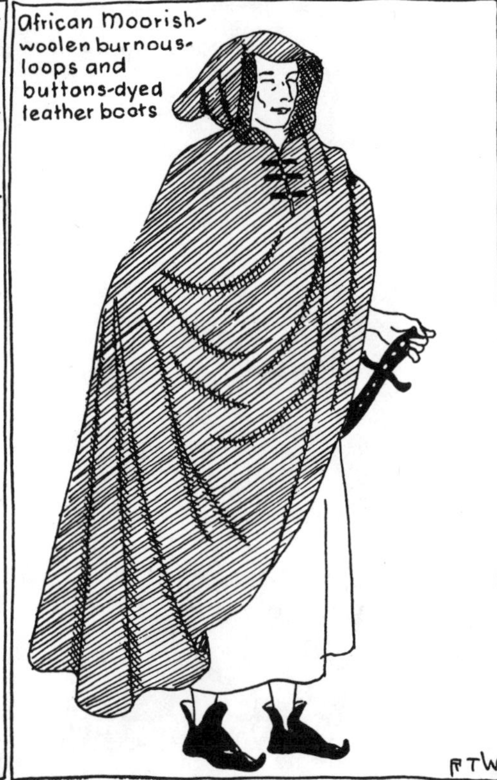

African Moorish-woolen burnous-loops and buttons-dyed leather boots

Moorish or Saracenic Spain

Knight in red surcoat-gold buttons-white cotehardie-undersleeves striped red and black-yellow bands-white tabs at neck-white stockings-jewelled yellow leather shoes-13th C.

white surcoat over red cotehardie-black velvet undersleeves and shoes-yellow bands-gold buttons-jewelled headband and necklace-13th C.

matron-brocaded gown of gold cloth, silk or damask-white headcloth and gorget-black mantle-soft shoes and chopines-16th C.

a toga-like mantle of dark green cloth-red cap-brown leather boots and shoulder strap-15th C.

RTW

Moorish or Saracenic Spain
Arabic inscription from the Alhambra-"There is no conqueror but God".
Persian Moorish-young woman-gold brocade-voile scarf with fringe-jewelled gold disques
Arabian Moorish-front and back of shawl with pleats
Persian Moorish-young woman-gold brocade-white feathers-jewelled ornament
African Moorish-white cotton turban
African Moorish-young woman-draped band with silk tabs resembling feathers
Persian Moorish-married woman-white linen or cotton gorget-draped velvet turban and bonnet
RTW

Chapter Eighteen

Spain of the Sixteenth Century

By the eighth century, Spain was almost entirely conquered by the Saracens, who ruled the land for the following eight centuries, stamping their Moorish civilization upon the Christian native. Eventually, bit by bit, the Spaniards regained their country, but the centuries of intercourse with the Moors, who possessed a much higher culture than any of their contemporaries in Europe, produced a remarkable character, which was individual in living, art and dress.

Their style was elegant and distinctive and it influenced, not a little, the mode of the other countries. They gave to Europe the ruche, the ruff, the short cape, the corset, the hoop, the bombast style of the padded doublet and trunk hose, followed by the unpadded trunks or breeches. Silk knit stockings were a Spanish invention and for a long time surpassed those of other countries.

They contributed also that great note of smartness in any period, the wearing of black in rich fabric. Black was the color for the general occasion, color being reserved for festive events. Black for mourning had been worn by the Spanish from the twelfth century, which custom was unusual, as the wives of most European kings wore white in like circumstance.

Despite the hoop, slimness of body for both men and women was the desired form and we read of the French resorting to diet to accomplish the "Spanish figure."

In the first half of the sixteenth century, men wore the elaborately embroidered doublet with short skirt and puffed sleeves over an embroidered lingerie shirt. The narrow ruffles or ruches which finished neck and sleeves showed at neck and wrist. After the middle of the century, the tiny neck ruffle became a fully developed ruff; then, in the 'eighties, a huge cartwheel, starched and wired. Later, narrow lace edging appeared. The width of the fashionable ruff was about a quarter of a yard and the frills contained eighteen or nineteen yards of fine linen lawn or Holland cambric, a luxury for the wealthy only. A frame of fine wire covered with silk thread was worn under it, the edge of the ruff being wired also. Ruffs were starched in various colors, blue, green, with yellow being a favorite and worn all over Europe.

The general style of sleeve had moderate fullness, tight at the wrist with puffs or wings masking the armscye. Later in the century, bishop and leg-of-mutton shapes were paned and slashed, as were trunks and hose.

Trunk hose were bombasted or padded to great bulk with rags, bran, wool, almost anything that could be used for stuffing. Canions appeared, covering the leg from the trunks to the knee. Venetians were knickerbockers tied or buttoned below the knee. French breeches reached to the knee, conforming to the shape of the leg, but were divided into horizontal rows of puffs. The short, full unpadded breeches were known in England as "Spanish slops," and the full unpadded breeches reaching to the knees, as "full slops." Knitted stockings appeared during this period.

The typical hat of the period, worn by both men and women, was of velvet or satin with béret crown, which grew very tall toward the end of the century. It was trimmed with jewels and a tuft of feathers, usually small ostrich tips with aigrettes. The hair was worn fairly short by the men, accompanied by mustache and clipped beard.

The shoes of both sexes were shaped to the foot, reaching to the ankle with fronts pierced in various designs. Pantoffles and chopines covered them for street wear. Men also wore a high, fitted boot and, before the end of the century, a low heel came into vogue.

Until after the first half of the sixteenth century, men wore a cloak just covering the trunks. It was a gorgeous garment of velvet or brocaded fabric with full sleeves in many puffs. The winter cloak had wide collar and revers faced with fur, which also lined the wrap. Later, the short cape became universally worn, of cloth with taffeta lining in summer and of velvet or cloth, fur-lined, in winter. The cape often had hanging sleeves. The high collar of doublet or cape when worn open, with fronts folded back in revers, now showed the nick or notch which survives today.

The dagger or rapier was carried, attached to the belt, gloves were part of the costume and dandies sported a rose behind the ear.

Women wore the corseted bodice, deeply pointed in front, and the bell-shaped hoop of Spanish origin. Sleeves were full and flowing, over undersleeves of lingerie material with lace insertions and edgings. The gown was usually of black velvet or satin, ornamented with bands of embroidery or galloon. Lace-edged ruchings finished neck and wrists.

Also part of the costume were large jewelled brooches, ropes of pearls and knotted loops of ribbon with jewelled points. Both men and women wore heavy gold necklaces set with large gems. A favorite feminine ornament was the ornate brooch with pendant, also pearl earrings. Women wore cauls of gold wire or pearl strings set with jewels, over which the velvet hat with béret crown was placed. The hair was drawn off the forehead in pompadour fashion, waved or tightly curled, and dressed over a wire frame.

Gloves were carried, and invariably the sheer handkerchief edged with most exquisite lace. The embroidered and perfumed Spanish leather gloves were greatly desired by the fashionables of Europe. They surpassed those of Italian and French make in retaining the odor of the scent and were in demand for several centuries.

There were fans of feathers attached to ivory handles, folding fans of vellum and the fan of scented leather. The folding fan of heavily scented leather, of Oriental origin, was first used in Spain, passing to Italy and appearing in France in the reign of Henri III, 1574–1589. Sunshades were in use by both men and women from the middle of the sixteenth century.

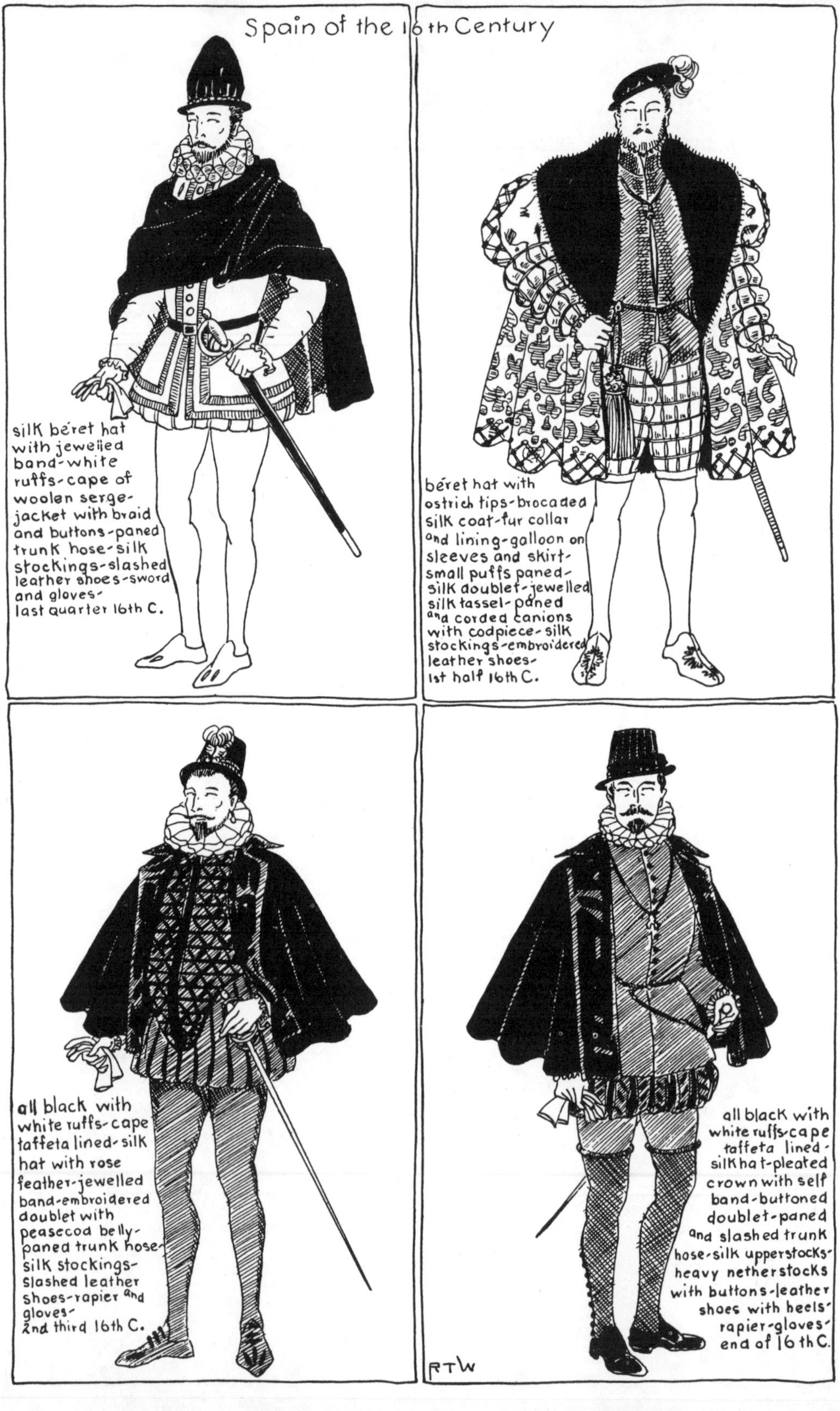
Spain of the 16th Century
silk béret hat
with jewelled
band-white
ruffs-cape of
woolen serge-
jacket with braid
and buttons-paned
trunk hose-silk
stockings-slashed
leather shoes-sword
and gloves-
last quarter 16th C.
béret hat with
ostrich tips-brocaded
silk coat-fur collar
and lining-galloon on
sleeves and skirt-
small puffs paned-
silk doublet-jewelled
silk tassel-paned
and corded canions
with codpiece-silk
stockings-embroidered
leather shoes-
1st half 16th C.
all black with
white ruffs-cape
taffeta lined-silk
hat with rose
feather-jewelled
band-embroidered
doublet with
peasecod belly-
paned trunk hose-
silk stockings-
slashed leather
shoes-rapier and
gloves-
2nd third 16th C.
all black with
white ruffs-cape
taffeta lined-
silk hat-pleated
crown with self
band-buttoned
doublet-paned
and slashed trunk
hose-silk upperstocks-
heavy netherstocks
with buttons-leather
shoes with heels-
rapier-gloves-
end of 16th C.
RTW

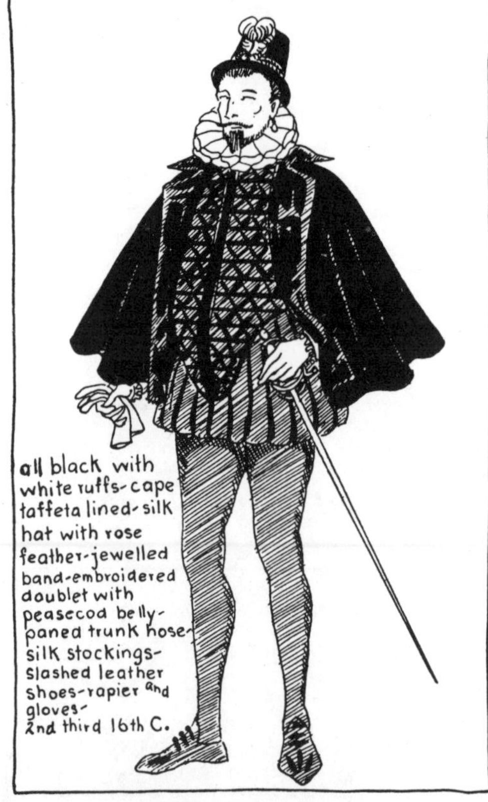

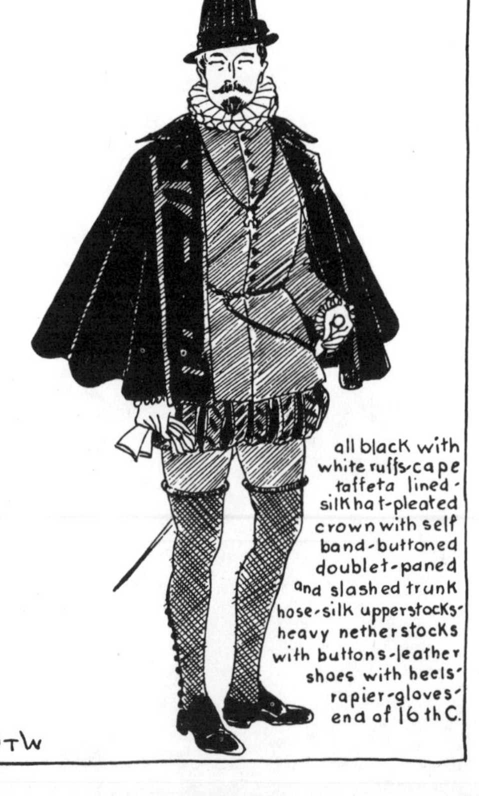

Spain of the 16th Century

Spain of the 16th Century
ribbon loop with
ivory points-
last half 16th C.
velvet béret over
jewelled caul-
pearls, ostrich tips
and aigrettes-
2nd half 16th C.
cap of pearls with
aigrettes-ruff of lace
edged embroidered
lawn-wired supporting
frame-late 16th C.
pearl bands and
jewel-early
16th C.
velvet béret
with pearls and
ostrich tips-
1560
flat velvet béret-
early 16th C.
"Spanish blackwork"
fine stitching in black-
sometimes red and
gold added
folding fan
of vellum or
paper-ivory sticks-
second half 16th C.
velvet hat-pearls
and jewels-ostrich
tips-1585
scented leather
fan in permanent
folds-ivory handle-
middle 16th C.
man's embroidered
money pouch
suspended from belt-
middle 16th C.
man's cloak with
hanging sleeves-
brocaded silk and
embroidery-edged and lined
with ermine-pearls on collar
and front edges-1560
RTW

Chapter Nineteen

Spain of the Velasquez Portraits

VELASQUEZ, who painted during the reign of Philip IV, 1621–1665, has left such magnificent portraits of this period, that his name has become definitely associated with the Spanish mode of his time.

The predominant color for both men and women was black in rich fabrics such as velvet and satin, ornamented with much gold and silver, often lightened by the use of white taffeta or lingerie fabric in the sleeves and about the neck. Cerise and vermilion were favorite colors too, with occasionally a costume of white. All-over embroidery of jewels, especially pearls, were lavishly used on the feminine costume, also ribbons, gimp and galloon.

To Philip is accredited the invention of the small, neat collar of thin lingerie fabric mounted over pasteboard. It flared out of the standing collar of the doublet, a sheer round, flat shape with pointed corners, open in front. This small flaring collar was known in English as the "neck whisk" and the lay-down style as the "falling band." Compared with the ruff, it was a tremendous change and improvement in comfort.

Men wore the heavy gold chain necklace and their shoe ties became large bows and rosettes, called shoe roses.

The bell-shaped hoop skirt was still being worn in the 1630's, with the long, pointed corseted bodice. The ruff too, was still the mode, and Velasquez painted a portrait of the Queen Marie-Anne, wearing a ruff of fur instead of lingerie material.

Later, the bell-shaped skirt changed to a hoop skirt of entirely different silhouette, flat front and back, but very wide at the sides. It spread abruptly out from the waist over hips, dropping as abruptly to the floor, creating a decidedly square outline, the width at the floor being as wide as the height of the figure. A circular peplum usually spread out from the waist.

The low, round neckline, horizontal from shoulder to shoulder, bateau-shaped, finished with a flaring bertha, a most artistic effect. In the center front of the bosom was usually placed a large ribbon rosette with an elaborate jewelled brooch.

The women wore many rings. A portrait of the Infanta Maria Thérésa shows her wearing the two watches hanging from fobs or cords attached at the waistline. That style became popular later in the other countries, with the difference that the watches were worn, one on each hip.

The hair was dressed flat on top of the head, hanging to the shoulders in extreme fluffiness, continuing the broad width of the silhouette, when seen from back or front. Added to the coiffure, hanging plumes, rosettes and many bowknots helped to give breadth to the contour. Rosettes of ribbon adorned the wrists, and a costly, large, sheer lace-edged handkerchief in the hand completed the picture.

A contemporary writing tells us that when the women married they were permitted to wear high heels and use cosmetics. The Moorish fashion of being veiled in public was observed.

A later distinctive Spanish style, which did not appear until 1790, was the gown and mantilla of black lace. The black silk was imported from Chantilly, France, and called by that name. The high comb, shawl and fan of our day appeared in the nineteenth century.

Spain of the Velasquez Portraits

all black-sheer white "neck whisk" and cuffs-striped silk doublet-velvet "full Spanish slops"-pendant on moire ribbon-shoulder wings-cloth cape-shoe roses- 1623

gold and pearl sewn black velvet with gold braid-shoulder wings and hanging sleeves-brown fox ruff-large brooch-necklace-jewelled buttons-lace edged handkerchief-1630

velvet with metal cloth and galloon-shirred sheer fabric yoke-jewelled rosette-brooch and chain-headdress in curls-bowknots-flowers-feathers-embroidered handkerchief-1658

embroidered jerkin with hanging sleeves-over doublet metal tissue-embroidered lingerie "falling band" and cuffs-"Venetians" tied with fringed ribbons-silk stockings-shoe roses-beaver hat with plumes-rapier on sash-middle 17th C.

Chapter Twenty

Renaissance England
The Tudors

Henry VII—1485–1509
Henry VIII—1509–1547

While signs of the Renaissance were evident in the reign of Richard III, the true Renaissance is considered to date from 1485 to 1603, that is during the reigns of the five Tudors.

In the first years of the reign of Henry VII, the medieval mode was still in existence, with the long, fitted stockings and short tunics for men. The women were still wearing the towering hennin or the wired sheer linen arrangement over a cap. The gown was long and full with a slightly fitted bodice, belted high. Ofttimes, the one-piece princess gown was laced in back to give the fitted look.

With the Renaissance years, the masculine tunic, which was short, opened over a waistcoat or stomacher of gorgeous brocaded material. The waistcoat was sometimes laced across in front, or sometimes laced together in back. Above it, at the neck, showed the sheer linen shirt gathered into a narrow frill.

Over the waistcoat was worn the gown or long coat, with loose, full sleeves, slashed to show the tunic sleeve, which in turn was slashed again, revealing the white linen shirt. The long gown was usually belted. When the gown or coat was cut short, it was called a petti-coat. Jerkin was the term for the short fitted jacket.

The long, fitted sewn stockings of every color and design were worn along with the conspicuous pouch or codpiece, embroidered and tied with colored ribbons.

For men, the bob with bangs was the style in hairdressing, with the black velvet hat of béret crown, ornamented with feather and jewel. Shoes had become more practical in design, the same for both men and women, made of cloth, leather and velvet, often embroidered and with ankle straps. Black velvet bands and facings trimmed the costumes of both sexes. Gloves were beautifully embroidered, and in the girdle or sash were carried purse and dagger.

The bell-shaped canvas underskirt, forerunner of the hoop, came to England in this reign. The skirt proper was long and full. The bodice was still slightly fitted with low, square neck, filled in with shirred white linen. Sleeves were of all styles, but principally long, wide and flowing, revealing a contrasting lining and a tight undersleeve. These gowns were often lined with fine fur and draped up in back, held by a button or brooch at the waist, to show the fur. Sometimes the skirt opened in front over a brocaded underskirt, or again the bodice opened V-shaped over a stomacher of handsomely decorated fabric.

A peculiar style of headdress, of English origin, was worn until 1550. Because of its outline, it was called *gable* hood, *kennel* or *pedimental* headdress, and covered the hair entirely. Over a close-fitting cap of linen, gold tissue or velvet, which showed at the forehead, was placed a broad fold of black silk or velvet. This fold, or lappet, was wired into a gable point in center front and fell to the shoulders. The lappet was richly embroidered with jewels and often edged with gold. Over the top of the head and hanging in back, was the *fall,* usually of black silk or velvet. The hair was concealed in silk cases. In a later style, the fall or back piece was often tied back by strings with metal points which were attached at the sides of the headdress. Puffed silk turbans, embroidered with gold and jewels, were also the fashion. The *barbe* was also worn, a biblike pleated piece of white linen passing under the chin and attached to the cap at the side like a gorget.

Fabrics for the costumes of both sexes were covered with a pattern semi-Spanish in design. Gorgeous figured silks and brocades came from the Orient, velvets and gold cloth brocaded in velvet from Venice, silks and satins from Bruges, the finest linen from Ypres and cambric from Cambrai. There were domestic linens, also hand-blocked linens of great beauty.

Necklaces of gold, jewels and beads were worn and the purse continued to be carried in the girdle. A fine, black-silk cord was in vogue for beads, jewelled pendants and the cross.

In the time of Henry VIII, there were two distinct fashions for men, the very square style with padded shoulders, as portrayed in Holbein's paintings, and another, fairly slim. Both, however, were influenced by the German-Swiss fashion of slashings and puffings either in a moderate or extravagant manner. The slashed and puffed sleeves of the masculine and feminine costume grew very large, full and elaborate and an outfit often had several pairs of detachable sleeves. They were attached by means of lacings, with points.

The slimmer costume of the man had a short waistcoat, cut straight across the chest, short at the waist with shirt showing above and below. The space left between waistcoat and breeches was filled in with shirt, the two edges being laced with strips of leather or ribbon having metal points.

The style usually connected with Henry VIII had the long, fitted sewn stockings, slashed and puffed, slashed, square-toed shoes and the elaborately embroidered and slashed tunic of length between thigh and knee, held at the waist by a belt from which hung the dagger. Silk knit stockings from Spain are known to have been presented to Henry VIII. In the opening of the shirt appeared the embroidered and jewelled codpiece of the period.

The collar of the white shirt was either a narrow ruffle or a narrow straight piece, embroidered in black silk. The latter had strings which were either tied or left hanging. Ruffles showed at the wrists, and if the tunic, jacket or jerkin was open in front, the shirt front ornamented with "Spanish blackwork" was revealed. This black silk embroidery, often combined with gold and red stitching on white linen, was of ancient Persian origin and its vogue lasted for more than a hundred years.

The handkerchiefs of Henry VIII were of Holland lawn, edged with gold fringe from Venice and embroidered in red and white silk.

Men and women wore several rings on the thumb, first and last fingers of both hands and heavy jewelled necklaces around their necks. They carried the perfumed and embroidered gloves of the time.

About 1521, short hair came in with the cropped beard and mustache; in fact, this French style was rigorously enforced at the court of Henry VIII. The béret hat continued in vogue.

In women's costume, the skirt now worn over a larger hoop, opened over a handsome kirtle or underskirt of embroidered satin or brocaded velvet of a contrasting color from the rest of the gown or cotte. The bodice still had the low square neck, but the sleeves had very wide cuffs, sometimes turned back, which were of black or colored velvet, of fur or gold net.

The gable or diamond-shaped headdress which now permitted the hair over the forehead to show, had become much more elaborate, with the fall and lappets caught up on top and stiffened into shape. Then came the smaller hood, known as the French hood, which left the front hair uncovered. The back hair was always concealed in a bag of black velvet, called the *cale*. The bonnetlike fold of velvet or satin was placed over a small cap or coif of white linen or gold net, edged with embroidery, gimp or jewels. Women also wore the béret-crowned hat, with narrow brim like that of the man, but placed over the cap.

The ruffles of the chemise appeared at the wrists. Sometimes the bodice opened over a rich stomacher, which was occasionally crossed with lacings.

There were long capes, open in front, and voluminous cloaks with the large puffed sleeves, very much like the men's. Only the royal were permitted to wear genet, a species of civet; only those above the rank of viscount could wear sable and to wear martin or velvet one had to be worth over two hundred marks a year.

The first mention of a nightgown is of that worn by Anne Boleyn, which was of black satin trimmed with black velvet. Perfume was excessively used, even such accessories as gloves, fans and shoes being saturated with it. The perfumed leather fan mounted on a carved ivory stick remained the favorite.

Queen Catherine used pins imported from France. That useful article came from France till about 1626, when the manufacture of pins was introduced into England. The pin was a fairly costly gadget in those days, whence the origin of the term "pin money."

Renaissance England

Renaissance England

Renaissance England
man's shirt collar-
Spanish blackwork
and tie strings-
2nd quarter 16th C.
gable hood-
black velvet
lappets and
fall-white
cap-pearls
and jewels-
around 1500
felt cap with
jewelled ornament-
late 15th C.
gable hood with
pinned up lappets-
black velvet fall-
pearl trimmed-1530-
back view to right
gable hood with
pinned up lappets and
fall-pearl sewn-
1528
back view gable hood-
lappets with square crown-
front view to left
black velvet béret-white
plume-topaz ornaments-
pearls on chains-tied
shirt collar-Spanish
blackwork-1537
slashed glove-
1549
sheer white cap-
wired edge-seed
pearls and colored
gems-over
embroidered coif-
jewelled rosette
with bead fringe-
1539
velvet béret
with white plume
over jewelled and
embroidered cap-
2nd quarter 16th C.
velvet béret-
jewel and tiny
gold loops-1536
wrist frill-
Spanish blackwork
white cap with
gold framework-
fluted ribbon next to
hair-black velvet fall-
2nd quarter 16th C.
RTW

Chapter Twenty-one

Renaissance England
The Tudors

EDWARD VI—1547–1553
MARY—1553–1558
ELIZABETH—1558–1603

DURING THE SIX YEARS' reign of Edward VI, costume lost much of its ornamentation and slashing. The square outline of the masculine costume waned and shoes were designed more to the shape of the foot. The cloaks of men and women had hanging sleeves. Record has it that Edward VI was presented with a pair of silk stockings from Spain by one of his lords. The flat velvet béret with narrow brim continued to be worn, with the end of its vogue in sight for the fashionable world. It has remained the headgear of the Beefeaters of the Tower of London to the present day. Men and women wore velvet nightcaps.

The marriage of Philip II of Spain to Mary brought about the Spanish influence in dress. Men adopted the narrow-brimmed bag hat with shirred high crown, all of black velvet, the small ruff, the short mustache and the clipped beard. The short cape came in with its standing collar and the notch (its first appearance) at the junction of collar and front. Gowns or cloaks, too, had standing collars, hanging leg-of-mutton sleeves and a skirt length which covered trunks and doublet skirts underneath. The vogue of the boot was in the making. Boots reached to the knee or stopped halfway up with turned-back cuffs.

Women's gowns had changed little, were simpler, with higher necks. Embroidered flaring collars were of linen or silk, usually white, sometimes with a wired edge. The hair was dressed simply, parted in the middle and knotted in the back, tending to be puffed at the temples. Hoods grew smaller, short at the sides and in back. The jewelled girdle with rosary or mirror at the end was worn, and small bouquets of flowers were carried in the hand or tucked into the neck of the bodice. The skirt flared open in front to show an embroidered or brocaded velvet petticoat of contrasting color. In jewelry, there were heavy gold chains, large jewelled pendants, rings and buttons. Gold and jewelled buttons by the dozens were worn by men and women.

In Elizabeth's time, the Spanish influence of the previous reign evolved into a definite style. Men wore Venetian breeches, full at the top, narrowing to the knee, paned, slashed or puffed, French breeches were tight, but done in horizontal puffs, and the short, full-padded trunk hose.

Trunk hose were the very short puffs which covered the thighs and were often made in one with the stockings. There is much confusion over the name "trunk hose." While the garment itself was of Spanish origin, there was a definite German influence in the mode at that time, and the name appears to be from the German, hose, or *hosen,* signifying drawers, breeches or trousers, thus "trunk hose." The later unpadded trunk hose were termed "Spanish slops," and the very full breeches bagging at the knees "full slops."

Pockets were inserted in the lining. Canions, those leg coverings which filled in the space between stockings and trunk hose, were also worn. Stockings which met the breeches at the knees were called netherstocks, and the breeches upperstocks. Stockings were of yarn, silk or wool, clocked at the ankles in various patterns, and in gold and silver thread. Clocks are the remains of the fitted seams, concealed by embroidery. Ribbon garters, tied just below the knees, held the stockings in place.

There was the fitted doublet with short skirt, and the "peasecod bellied" doublet of Spanish origin with its padded long-pointed projecting front. Both were slashed and embroidered. The Englishman appears to have adopted a less extreme version of the doublet with wooden busk and overhanging point than his Continental neighbor. At the neck there was a linen collar edged with lace, perhaps two small collars or a ruff. The small, detachable collar, which came from Spain and was worn by both sexes, came to be known as the partlet, or partlet strip. The doublet armscye was ornamented with wings, and the sleeves were tied into it by means of points.

The hair was short, accompanied by a trim mustache and beard, sometimes a beard with two points. Hats were of various shapes, narrow brims with high or low crowns, trimmed with bands of silk, wool, shirred lace, gold and jewelled chains and plumes. From this period dates the popularity of beaver felt for hats and the tendency toward the broad-brimmed Jacobean headpiece is apparent. Shoes became extravagant parts of the costumes, ornamented with embroidery, lace and jewels. They were shaped to the foot, tied with shoe roses and often had red heels. Boots reached to the ankles or to the knees, held up by leather straps.

Both men and women began to use lace, which is supposed to have been introduced into England by Catherine of Aragon. There were imported Italian lace and bone-bobbin lace made at Honiton. Large earrings were in fashion, worn principally by the men.

Gowns or cloaks and capes were worn, with a long, plain cape for travelling. The short Spanish cape for men was the most fashionable, often made of perfumed leather. Gloves, too, were made of perfumed leather, embroidered and fringed for both men and women. Although worn in Italy and France for several centuries and at the court of Henry VIII, the perfumed glove did not become the vogue in England until this period. The scented fan was taken up and perfumes were freely used.

In Elizabeth's reign the hoop or wheel farthingale and the ruff grew to exaggerated proportions, with the steel and buckram corset a definite feature of the mode. The corset consisted of two garments, an under one of buckram, which was laced tightly over the body, then a case of sheet steel, which opened on hinges at one side and was fastened by hooks on the other. It was perforated with a decorative design and encased in velvet. It sometimes formed the bodice proper, or was covered with the stomacher of the gown.

The Spanish ruff began as a cambric collar, became larger, more pleated and then wired. A wired support was called the *underproper,* or *supportasse.*

Handkerchiefs, which were still a luxury, and carried conspicuously by men and women, were of cambric or silk. They were trimmed with lace, some were stitched with blue, while others were fashioned of cut-work embroidery.

Calico, which came from Calcutta, India, was new in this period.

There were two styles of gowns, the exaggerated silhouette with long, pointed bodice and wheel farthingale, the other with moderate hoop and moderately fitted bodice. The skirt of the latter opened in front over a petticoat of contrasting color, richly embroidered and trimmed with gimp and fringe. Several linen petticoats were worn. Both styles had a low, straight décolletage with either a fan-shaped collar or a ruff. Sleeves were full, tight at the wrists and finished with lingerie cuffs or ruffles. False hanging sleeves and separate sleeves were the fashion, which were laced to the armscye with points.

The wired wings of the shell-like shaped wrap, which rose in back above the shoulders, were worn, with the long ends hanging to the floor. The very low décolletage, which bared the bosom, introduced by Catherine de' Medici, was also affected. In England, it was worn by maiden ladies, the queen wearing it in her later years. Quantities of pearls and precious stones were added to the costume.

Feminine hats, like those of the men, had brims and a feather, the crown encircled by a band or necklace. Lawn caps were of all shapes and close to the head. Velvet nightcaps continued to be worn. A particular style of bonnet is that known to us as the "Mary Stuart cap," of cambric and lace, wired into shape, its feature being the dip over the forehead.

False hair and wigs dressed with jewels, glass ornaments or feathers, were in vogue. Red and blond were the favorite colors, and in this period hair was often dyed red in compliment to the Queen's red hair, since Elizabeth set the fashion at her court. Powder and rouge were used. Little balls of scent, encased in gold or silver, sometimes enamelled and set with jewels, hung from girdle or rosary, also the fan and looking glass. The little ball was called a dry-scent box, or pomander. All accessories of costume, such as gloves, handkerchiefs, ruffs, fans and bags were scented. Beautiful feather fans were carried and the black velvet mask was worn in the street and to the theatre.

Elizabeth, like Catherine de' Medici and Mary Stuart, wore a slipper with a high heel. It is in this period that the low-cut shoe or slipper first appears, and "pumps" are mentioned for the first time. Shoes had cork soles, the uppers of leather or velvet, stamped with designs or embroidered in gold or silver. It is also stated that Elizabeth was the first Englishwoman to wear silk stockings. Perhaps silk stockings and the new heel were *la raison d'être* of the ankle-length gown seen in several of the Queen's portraits. From this time on, women began to wear the costly hand-knitted silk stockings, decorated with clocks in gold, silver and color. Red stockings were fashionable, worn with red or blue slippers.

The first knitting machine for stockings was invented by an Englishman, William Lee, in 1589. Ignored by Elizabeth and offered patronage by Henri IV, he established himself at Rouen with success. His workmen returned to England with the invention after his death and the assassination of Henri IV.

As on the Continent, chopines, pattens or clogs and pantoffles were worn over the shoes of both men and women, when outdoors. The Venetian chopine was less popular than the patten. Pattens and pantoffles were also used in the American Colonies. Chopines had stilts from four to as high as seven inches, pattens had wooden or cork soles, while pantoffles, with their cork soles, had only front uppers.

In this period, no person, unless of royalty, was permitted to wear crimson, except in underclothes, and the use of velvet, for sleeves only, was allowed the middle classes. In all, it was an era of great richness, extravagance and overdressing.

Elizabeth, in her many regulations pertaining to overdressing, issued a decree forbidding the wearing of "cut or pansied hose, or bryches, and of pansied doublets," which leads one to consider that the origin of the descriptive word "pansy" might perhaps be a result of this law and thus of early origin.

Renaissance England
doublet with buttons
galloon and embroidery-
paned trunk-hose
with cutwork-silk
stockings-ribbon
garters-shoe-roses-
braided leather belts-
rapier-bag hat-
jewelled band-ostrich-
jewelled necklace
with pendant-1567
padded
satin doublet
with peasecod
front and buttons-
jerkin with paned
wings and skirt-
points untied-
knotted cord
round neck-
Venetians with
paned frills-slashed
shoes-sword
1572
bag hat with ostrich
and jewelled band-
neck ribbon with
pendant-mandillion
of velvet, taffeta and
gold braid-embroid-
ered doublet with
wings-enbroidered
paned trunk hose-
wrinkled taffeta
canions-ribbon cross-
garters-pantoffles
over light colored
shoes-1575
black taffeta
doublet, trunk hose
and canions-cord-
ings-neck whisk
and cuffs with
point lace-
beaded belt-
jewel on cord-
beaver hat with
crêpe band-
pantoffles over
shoes-1597
RTW

Renaissance England

velvet gown-brocaded undergown-sleeve straps with jewelled buttons-jewelled girdle-jewelled mirror on silk cord-black velvet hood with white lawn and pearls-collars embroidered-pearl sewn gloves-1554

velvet gown-embroidered and jewelled petticoat-pearl sewn galloon-cap, ruff, yoke of white lawn-white plaid gauze mantle with wired edge-point lace-pendant on ribbon-jewelled girdle with mirror-satin slippers-1560's

rose satin cloak-fox collar-gold buttons-leather belt-quilted yellow gown-red sleeves-white lawn yoke and ruff-black felt hat-crown in folds-blue ostrich-1590

queen's gown-velvet with jewels, pearls, gold braid loops-oriental satin petticoat, stomacher and slippers-mantle and ruff white gauze, point lace and pearls-wired wings-wig with jewels-jewelled feather fan-pearl sewn gloves-knotted pearl necklace-end of 16th C.

RTW

Renaissance England
wired edged cap over wig-pearls-lawn and lace ruff-1570's
game bag for hawking-leather, cords and tassels-1575
beaver hat-wing-gold mount and pearl-1602
black velvet-crown in folds-yellow ostrich, cords and caul-1590
fan of ostrich plumes-jewelled handle-late 16th C.
man's pouch hung from belt-velvet with gold-1560's
black velvet with jewel-end of 16th C.
woman's satin bag hung from girdle-metal frame-1590
man's shoe-black velvet-white shoe-rose-late 16th C.
beaver hat with ostrich-small gold loops-1583
embroidered canions-ribbon cross-garter-fringe-gold buttons-1583
back view-side view ribbon cross-garters-1577
lady's satin slipper-shoe-rose-around 1600
RTW

Chapter Twenty-two

Henry Fourth and Marie de' Medici

1589–1610–1617

From this period on, one is able to note the evolution of men's costume as we know it today; the tunic, pourpoint or doublet into the vest or waistcoat, the justaucorps or jerkin into the jacket and the gown, cloak or cape into the topcoat; and in women's costume, the tunic into the cotte, or dress, and the kirtle into the petticoat.

Henri IV was more interested in furthering the growing French industries than in spending any time or thought on his personal wardrobe. Beautiful brocades, velvets and silks were made at Lyons, while Tours produced the heavy taffetas.

In his reign, the stuffed beak of the doublet disappeared, the doublet having a normal waistline and short skirt. The sleeves of the doublet were of contrasting fabric and color, often separate and laced on with points, but occasionally the doublet might be sleeveless. The shoulders were invariably finished with wings.

The Spanish cape and paned trunk hose were worn, also "Spanish slops" and "full slops." The full breeches reaching to the knees were tied with ribbon garters, which had lace ends, for lace was now in vogue for both men and women. Pockets were inserted in the lining of the breeches.

The courtier wore elbow-length gauntlet gloves of velvet or satin, silk or gold fringed, with backs embroidered or sewn with jewels. Riding gloves were of doeskin. Men's shoes now took on high heels and the front fastening of the low-cut shoe was covered with a huge shoe rose. High-dress boots of Russian leather were introduced, made by craftsmen who had been sent to Hungary to learn the art of dressing leather. These boots appeared in the salon and at balls. Turkish and Spanish morocco leathers were also used for boots. Leggings were in use, worn to protect the fragile and costly silk stocking. For country wear, they were of velvet with gold and silver embroidery; and of leather, for horseback riding.

The baldric, or shoulder sash of satin, was the fashion for both men and women, white being for the King only. The sword hung from a narrow leather belt. Henri IV is recorded as the first owner of an especially designed walking stick.

The costumes of both sexes were in all colors, but in subtle and beautiful shades, and for the first time we note that colors were given descriptive and fantastic names. The most distinguished masculine costume was of velvet.

Worn in the early part of the reign was a hat of felt with narrow brim and tall crown, ornamented with a band, jewel and plumes. Around 1600, from America came beaver pelts for the costly beaver hat with wide and rolling brim and crown of moderate height. Hats of castor, the European species of beaver, had been imported from Flanders before this period.

Henri IV permitted all styles of hair and beard. The hair was moderately short, with trim mustache and cropped beard. Lovelocks appeared, a long, plaited length of hair on one side, with a ribbon tied at the end.

The hoop, verdingale or farthingale grew to enormous proportions in this reign, spreading out straight from the waist, creating a cylindrical drumlike shape or, again, wide at the sides and flat front and back The hoop, or foundation-skirt was of canvas or heavy linen, with hoops of wood or steel. Over it and tied round the hips was placed the round bolster. Three elaborately trimmed and embroidered petticoats of contrasting colors were worn under the skirt proper.

Women wore the corset or stomacher to acquire the figure of the period. First, laced very tightly, was a bodice of heavy linen, over which was placed a steel case or garment, hinged on one side and fastened on the other by clasps. This "armor" was perforated in a most intricate design and encased in velvet. It sometimes formed the outside bodice or stomacher of the gown, in which case it was covered with elaborate embroidery.

To silk and jewel-encrusted embroideries were added lace and ribbons.

Lingerie ruffs, ruffles, bands and cuffs finished the neck and wrists of the bodice. The lace-edged ruff of the earlier part of the period opened into a standing fan-shaped frill, high in the back with low décolletage. This collar is known as the Medici collar and was accompanied by cuffs to match. The mantle of sheer material, with wired wings which rose above the shoulders continued to be worn and the false hanging sleeves were still in evidence.

Gowns for state occasions were intricately embroidered with gold, silver, pearls and other gems. Watches became the fashion, long ropes of pearls were worn, also pendant earrings and rings.

The riding habit of Marguerite de Valois, first wife of Henri IV, was of black velvet faced with cloth of gold, with which she wore a plumed hat having a diamond aigrette.

Marie de' Medici, second wife of the King, wore slippers of Spanish Moroccan leather, with high heels connected with the sole by a platform. With them she wore knitted silk stockings imported from Spain and Italy. They were red, orange or purple and embroidered with French lilies or the Medici crest.

Women dressed their hair high off the forehead, waved and rolled over a pad, usually in a heart-shaped silhouette. False hair was used, and for a while wigs were worn in blond and brown. Powder for wigs was used in the form of starch mixed with pomade and perfumed with violet or iris, violet for brunettes and iris for blonds. The hair was often sprinkled with jewels. The fashion of wearing a jewel on a fine gold chain in the middle of the forehead was originated by one of the mistresses of Francois I, la Belle Ferronnière. The "Mary Stuart cap" was worn in its many versions.

Paint, powder and beauty patches adorned the feminine face. Beauty patches of black taffeta were the fashion, and in public the mask of black taffeta was worn, the velvet mask being permitted to women of quality only. Masks in those days served as a protection against the hot sun and were worn both when walking and when horseback riding. Embroidered and lace-edged handkerchiefs were carried.

From Italy came beautiful fabrics and laces, especially Venetian point, also the parasol, which did not become popular. From Spain and the Orient were imported perfumes, sachets and rare scents. During this reign there were periodic restrictions against the excessive importation of luxuries, which took money out of France.

The perfumed gloves known as "Frangipani gloves" continued in vogue. Like those of the men, satin and velvet gloves fringed with gold, silver or silk were worn by women at court and doeskin ones of elbow length for the hunt. Colored furs were permitted to the nobility only, while black was decreed to the bourgeoisie. Muffs were carried in the winter and fans in the summer. The latter were made of ornamented silk, sheepskin and goatskin, but the most fashionable and costly were of ostrich plumes mounted on gold, silver or carved ivory handles.

To assure the prosperity of the silkworm culture, Henri IV ordered extensive planting of mulberry bushes.

After the death of Henri IV, it is noted for the first time in history that the mode in costume was indulged in by the middle class.

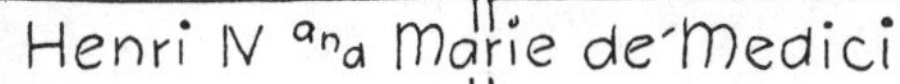
Henri IV and Marie de Medici

paned doublet-
buttons-wings-
skirt tabs-moire
baldric with cross-
paned trunk-hose-
codpiece-beaver
hat with jewel,
feather and cord-
shoe-roses-
1602

satin gown with
galloon and pearls-
jewelled buttons
on skirt-ruff of
cambric and
point lace-jewel
in hair-1595

taffeta with wheel
verdingale-wired fan
shaped pleated collar-
point lace-corded
puffed sleeves-contrasting
colored corded petticoat-
pearl necklaces-
jewelled hair
ornament with
aigrette-late
16th C

doublet with
wings and remains
of hanging sleeves-
buttons-skirt tabs-
falling ruff-"slops"-
Russian leather boots
with spur leathers-
baldric sash-sword-
beaver hat with
plumes-1st quarter
17th C.
RTW

Henri IV and Marie de' Medici
soldier's hat
worn until 1600-
embroidery and
ostrich plumes
tucked
cambric
cuff-lace
edged
handkerchief-
pearls
felt hat with
plumes
leather boot
which
buttoned to
trunks-spur
and spur
leathers
beaver hat
with jewels
and plumes
heart shaped coiffure
with topknot and
jewel
turned down
collar attached
to shirt
black velvet cap
with pearls-white
cambric ruff
embroidered
and fringed
doeskin glove
felt hat with
appliqué motifs-
cord-jewel-
ostrich tips
man's leather
shoe-cork sole
and heel-
jewelled shoe-rose
beaver hat-
crushed ribbon
band-ostrich
tips
FTW

Chapter Twenty-three

Louis Thirteenth

1610–1643

This is an important period in costume because, during it, France definitely established herself as arbiter of the mode. The first part of the reign was still given to elaboration and overindulgence in rich fabrics and embroideries, but with Richelieu's ban in 1625 against the importation of gold and silver cloth, galloons, passementeries and velvet brocades from Italy and Spain, costume took on a rich simplicity. Then followed, in 1633 and 1634, an edict against the wearing of gold or silver galloons, lace passementerie or embroidery.

Garments were fashioned of French fabrics, such as the plain but heavy satins and velvets and simpler patterned materials in more neutral tones. The new thread laces and embroideries began gradually to usurp the position held by rich embroideries. About this time, ribbon as we know it, a narrow band of silk with two selvedges, became fashionable. Lace, as a trimming, became very important, especially for the edge of the wide flat collar or falling band, known as the Louis XIII collar.

In the early part of the reign, men still wore the doublet with corseted body and the deep-busked point in front, shoulder wings and short skirt. A lace-edged ruff finished the neck and sleeves. The sleeves were usually slashed. In breeches, Spanish slops or full slops were worn, with ribbon garters tied at the knees and edged with points, lace or fringe. Trunk hose, except as livery for pages, had gone out of fashion. Pockets, which were vertical linings, braid-bound, were placed near the waist to either side of the front of the breeches.

With the seventeenth century came the development of the "Cavalier fashion," elegant in color and cut. The corseted shape was discarded and the doublet became a waistcoat with sleeves, while the ruff changed to a whisk, a falling ruff, a turned-down collar or falling band of fine lawn or cambric edged with lace. The sleeves and upper part of the doublet were often slashed, revealing the shirt, also of fine lawn or cambric. Occasionally, the doublet was buttoned from the neck to a few inches below, opening over the shirt. The doublet was often buttoned down center back. The shirt became of great importance, very full in body and sleeve, and of lingerie fabric. The shirt showed through a long slit in the back of the doublet and in the open front seam of the sleeve.

Neckpieces were tied in front with "band strings," which were cords or strings with tassels of yarn, silk or ribbon attached to the ends. A distinct style feature in neckwear was the falling band of sheer white fabric without the lace edge, made familiar in the portrait of Richelieu by Philippe de Champaigne. Bands diminished in size from about 1640.

The cravat, which was to enjoy such a long vogue from the next reign on, originated in this period. It appeared in 1636, a length of folded white linen, lawn or mull, tied loosely around the neck, its ends finished with lace. It was founded upon the custom of the Cravates, or Croats, serving in the French army, who wore a like fashion, a cloth muffled about the neck as a protection for the throat. A bow was added later. Dating from this period, the neck of the "well-dressed man" has never gone without a scarf or cravat in some form.

The baldric, or satin sash, tied from left hip to right shoulder, continued to be worn.

Ribbons and points now became ornaments instead of fastenings, large metal hooks and eyes supplanting them. However, points were functional and ornamental in the front closing of breeches. Brandenburgs, an innovation in both fastening and ornament, appeared in this period. They were horizontal strips of braid or loops with buttons or frogs, and originated on the jackets of the German Brandenburgers.

Breeches were moderately full, descending to below the knee, where they were tied with ribbons, or finished with a ruche of ribbon loops called *cannons*.

Short leather boots, of Spanish origin, with falling tops, became the fashion about 1625. They were of soft leather in very light colors, such as buff, beige, yellow, pale blue, a favorite being white. The fashionable stocking was of knitted red Milanese silk, and in winter several pairs were worn, one over the other. Worn between the boot and the silk stocking were boot hose of heavy linen finished with a deep, lace-edged or embroidered cuff. The cuff was turned down over the top of the boot, permitting the variegated colored loops or cannons of the breeches to show. Spurs were worn and the accompanying spur leathers grew in size and shape. Boots and spurs were not confined to the out-of-doors but were worn indoors and even at balls. Shoes with high red heels and red soles were in vogue and pantoffles continued in fashion. Shoes became long and narrow, with square toes, and took on very large and costly ribbon shoe roses centered with jewels.

Slightly longer capes, with a broad, square collar or none at all, were draped about the figure in every conceivable manner and were called manteaux instead of capes. Two cords, sewn inside the collar and tied around one shoulder, made it possible to hold the garment in place. The cassock, a loose greatcoat, had big sleeves, usually three-quarter length, with turned-back cuffs. Capes and coats had rich linings which were displayed by turning back the wrap.

The large felt or beaver hat, with sweeping or cocked brim, which style originated in Flanders, had one or more ostrich feathers with long flues, "weeping plumes," they were called. It was worn over waved and curled hair, parted in the middle and flowing to the shoulders. This style brought about the wearing of wigs, which were definitely accepted about 1600. The *cadenette,* or lovelock, a long curl or strand over one shoulder, was worn by the cavalier. It was often tied with a ribbon or a string with a rosette at one end. Hats were worn indoors until 1685. A large pearl earring often adorned the masculine left ear.

The beard, which had been banned by Henri III and again permitted by Henri IV, was worn by magistrates and ecclesiastics to Richelieu's time, who then authorized the wearing of a small chin beard only.

A long ebony stick with ivory top, often tied with ribbons, was carried by the King. The wearing of galloons, plumes, boots or spurs was not permitted the bourgeoisie.

The modish woman of the period wore a chemise, a corset, then several petticoats over the verdingale, or hoop. The hoop had grown smaller but continued to be worn until 1630. Over that was the gown, consisting of skirt and bodice or stomacher, with sleeves of light-colored satin or other fabric. And, over that, a robe or sort of redingote of darker or contrasting colored material, opened the full length in front. The robe usually had slashed sleeves showing the undersleeves. This robe was invariably worn until 1645. The outer robe was called *la modeste,* and when there were two skirts the outer one was called *la friponne* ("hussy," in English), the under one *la secret.*

An important style of the Louis XIII period was the looped-up outer skirt, adopted principally by the bourgeoisie. The overskirt was drawn up at the sides or sometimes drawn to the front and pinned in place.

The bodice of both robe and gown were in separate parts. The décolletage was low, straight across, round or pointed, with the moderate ruff or fan-shaped collar. From then on the gown changed, the hoop disappeared, the corset became less confining, with the bosom left free. The bodice was high-waisted, with a short peplum opening over a round-pointed stomacher and sometimes the bodice was laced in back. Wide lingerie collars and cuffs always finished the gown, and occasionally lace-trimmed aprons were added. The lace-edged collar or falling band was made popular by Anne of Austria, wife of Louis XIII.

The headdress, also introduced by Anne of Austria, had a fringe across the forehead, with the side hair cut short and hanging in ringlets over the ears, the remainder drawn to a knot at the back of the head. Out of doors, fashion decreed that the head be bare, only the bourgeoisie wearing hats. Veils and kerchieflike hoods of lace or dark-colored fabric were worn, sometimes tied under the chin. Hats, resembling those of the men, wide-brimmed and ornamented with plumes, were worn when hunting. An odd, cagelike hood of wired chiffon enveloped the head and shoulders, when in mourning. See Page 166.

Shoes were of satin or Moroccan leather, with high heels and usually worn with rose-colored stockings. Slippers developed flaps in front like the masculine shoe and were tied above the instep. New were pattens of crimson velvet with very thick soles, presumably of cork.

Capes were worn in winter, but the gowns were heavily lined with weight enough to require no wraps. Long kid gloves and fur muffs were in fashion. The vogue of the perfumed leather gauntlet continued. In this reign Marquis Frangipani, a descendant of Count Frangipani of "perfumed-glove fame," discovered that, by treating solid scents with alcohol, a perfume could be produced in liquid form. Beauty patches and masks of taffeta continued in the mode, with velvet still reserved to ladies of quality. Cosmetics were freely applied to the face, producing an artificial effect. The fan became very popular, in use by both men and women, the folding style being the favorite, hand-painted on vellum or silk. Jewelry was sparingly worn, while from the belt were suspended the small mirror and the perfume box.

The umbrella, of Italian name, fashionable in Italy at this time, does not appear to have been taken up in France until the next reign. It was carried by the individual whom it shaded, was of leather, folded, and when carried by horsemen was attached to the hip.

Louis XIII

slashed doublet-falling ruff-wings-buttons-paned sleeves and breeches-plaited leather belt and straps-fringed gauntlets with braid-beaver hat with plumes-1620's

cavalier wearing wig-falling band tied with bandstrings-slashed sleeves-frogs, buttons braid loops-breeches tied with tasseled strings-cannons at knees-linen and lace boot hose-spur leathers with ribbon rosettes-embroidered gauntlets-1630's

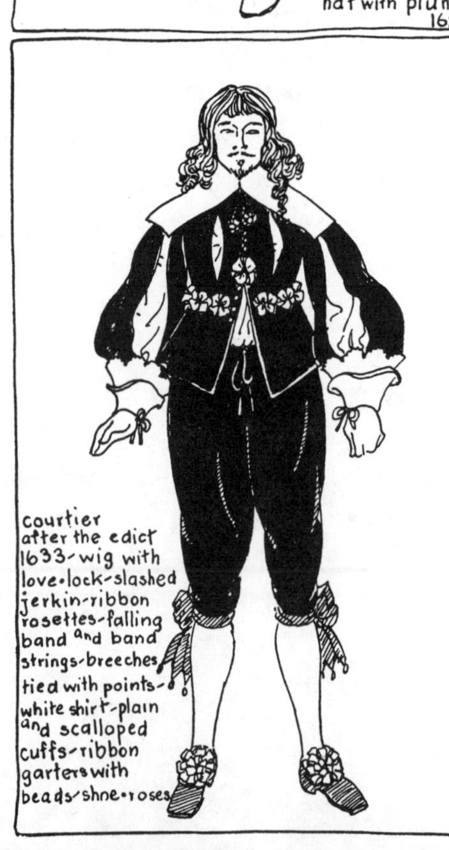

courtier after the edict 1633-wig with love•lock-slashed jerkin-ribbon rosettes-falling band and band strings-breeches tied with points-white shirt-plain and scalloped cuffs-ribbon garters with beads-shoe-roses

slashed jerkin-falling band-wings-paned sleeves-bowknots with points-gimp and buttons-leather baldric-breeches tied with points-slashed spur leathers-fringed braided gauntlets-beaver hat with plume-love•lock-1630

RTW

Louis XIII

three different fabrics-
tucked and embroidered
lingerie collar and double
cuffs-tied oversleeves-
paned undersleeves-
ribbon belt-button
trimming-rosette
on bosom-ostrich
tip in hair-velvet
mask-pearl
necklaces-
1620's

taffeta and brocade-
tucked and lace edged
lingerie collar, yoke
and cuffs-pinned up
overskirt-kerchief
hood-fur and
fabric muff-
necklace, rosary
and watch-
1620's

taffeta over satin-
slashed sleeves-
lingerie collar, yoke and
cuffs-shirred ribbon
on bodice and sleeves-
gimp on stomacher
and underskirt-
ribbon rosette on
bosom-knitted
cap-mirror-
vanity case-
1630's

cloth with lingerie
collar, yoke and
cuffs-slashed
sleeves-rosette
at bosom and
belt-cord with
bag-kerchief
hood-after
1633
RTW

Louis XIII
painted vellum fan
slashed felt hat with plumes
beaver hat with ostrich plumes-falling band-wig-love-lock with rosette
wig with love-lock and rosette-falling band with band strings
man's shoe and pantoffle-shoe-rose
first form of the cravat
hunting hat-beaver with ostrich plumes
felt hat-love-lock-falling band
hair dressed with ribbon bows
woman's striped silk slipper-red heel-red velvet pantoffle
red calotte or skullcap-falling band-band strings
braid and ringlets
head covering for street wear
cassock
embroidered linen boot hose-patten
pattern of circular cape-strings tied around shoulder
leather boot-extra sole-red heel
RTW

Chapter Twenty-four

England Under James First and Charles First

1603–1625

1625–1649

THE MODE of this period was founded upon French influence, brought about, no doubt, by the relationship of the English and French ruling class. Some of the wild extravagance of the preceding reign was now discarded.

The stiff doublet had a more normal waistline in position and girth, with a short skirt and shoulder puffs or wings. Sleeves were of self material or contrasting fabric and color, sometimes paned, finished with a turned-back cuff. The small ruff was still worn, but newer was a large collar of sheer linen or lawn-edged with exquisite lace, as were the cuffs. The rich embroideries were replaced by the new thread laces and white embroidery. The collar, or "band," was usually tied in front with strings or ribbons finished with small tassels, called "band strings." The pleats, or "pinches," of the ruff were often formed by pinning. Yellow starch from France stiffened the ruff or collar, but other colors were also used, such as red, blue, purple and green.

Breeches were very full, unpadded and bagging at the knees or sometimes moderately full at the top and tight over the knees, where they either buttoned or tied with ribbon garters, ending in a bunch of ribbon loops. Shoes with costly jewelled ribbon shoe roses were worn, but high, soft leather boots in pale colors and white were popular too. The knitted stockings were of silk, worsted and thread, yellow being a favorite color.

Mustache and hair were not as trim as in the preceding period, the hair being of moderate length. Beaver hats had been imported from Flanders for more than two centuries, but it remained for the beautiful pelts from America to create the tremendous vogue for the costly beaver hat. The style of this period had a tall, tapering crown with rolling brim of moderate width, ornamented with a band and plumes. The band was either cord, ribbon or a jewelled necklace. Men wore their hats indoors and out, at church and at table, and the custom held throughout the seventeenth century.

The full cape reached almost to the knees and embroidered gloves were worn. The sword hung from the belt and a new and important accessory was a small tobacco box with an inserted looking glass. Another new accessory was the gold-and-ivory-headed cane. Both sexes were lavish in their use of jewelry, wearing earrings and favoring diamonds and pearls.

The verdingale, vardingale, farthingale or Catherine-wheel made of whalebone, was still being worn along with the long and tapering waist. Sometimes, two Catherine-wheels were worn over the elaborately embroidered underskirt. The full drum-shaped hoop skirt cleared the floor, often ankle-length, revealing satin shoes with high heels and fastened with large shoe roses. Sleeves fitted the arm, ending in lace-edged cuffs and often there were long-hanging dummy oversleeves. Ruffs were still in evidence, but, when the neck of the gown was low in front, it usually had the wired, fan-shaped collar edged with lace. Sometimes the décolletage was cut below the bosom in England, a sign of maidenhood. Then came the round or "Dutch waist."

For both sexes there was a vogue for white in silk, cloth and velvet, and the first mention of an all-white wedding gown occurs at this time at the marriage of Princess Elizabeth to Prince Palatine.

The hair was dressed up off the forehead over a wire frame and sprinkled with jewels. In a variation of this style, the front hair framed the face in a small roll, held in place by a concealed band. Then the frizzled length was dressed over the high frame. In addition, false hair and hair dye were employed along with paint and powder, also patches of all shapes. "Patching the face" was the English expression for that practice. Masks were worn in public, and gloves, fans and small muffs were of this period.

Hats, when worn, resembled the masculine type, a rather stiff shape but very smart, with narrow brim and high crown, ornamented with ostrich plumes. The style is known to us as "postilion." Turbans trimmed with pearls and feathers are to be seen in contemporary portraits, also wide-brimmed hats of soft fabric with either lace or embroidered edge, which set on the back of the head, framing the high headdress in halo form.

The reign of Charles I is contemporary with the second half of the regime of Louis XIII, and, being under French influence in dress, costume became rich, simple and artistic. It was during that time that Van Dyck painted his beautiful and aristocratic portraits.

The man's costume of this period has come down to us under the name "Cavalier." Along with more serious political reasons, the Cavaliers scorned the Roundheads as being too soberly dressed and living too solemnly. The Roundheads disliked the long-ribbon-tied curls of their aristocratic friends and cropped their own hair close, to show their disapproval.

The tight and bombasted look disappeared, the waistline became normal. The doublet became a jacket, buttoned from the neck to over the chest, open from there down to expose a full sheer lingerie shirt. The long slit, down center back, and the open front seams of the jacket sleeves also permitted the showing of the shirt. With this style, half shirts or stomachers came into fashion. Points in bowknots, as an ornamentation, were placed around the waistline of the jacket. Over the jacket was worn the baldric, a satin sash or leather belt with jewelled buckles, reaching diagonally from right shoulder to left hip.

The falling band of sheer lingerie material, with its fine lace and embroidery, is a definite feature of the period and is known to us as the Van Dyck collar. The untrimmed band of the same shape was called a "playne band." These bands were kept in especially made decorated boxes which were called bandboxes.

Breeches were full to the knees where they were tied with colored ribbons and points. Or they were fairly tight to the leg, finished at the knee with loops or points. A new idea in trimming was the bunch of ribbon loops placed on different parts of the costume.

Shoes had square toes, medium heels and large ribbon ties or shoe roses. Boots had become popular for walking and were of soft leathers in light colors, with tops and cuffs in various styles. Boots had heels of moderate height and occasionally the added platform sole. Heel and sole were often red. Spurs and large spur leathers were worn or, again, just spur leathers for ornamentation. Over the falling tops of the boots hung the embroidered and lace-edged tops of the boot hose, linen stockings which were worn between the boot and the silk stocking. When boot hose were not worn, separate flounces or ruffles were attached at the knees, and sometimes boot cuffs were lined with elaborate frills.

Canes with heads of gold, silver or bone and further decoration of bunches of colored ribbons were carried. The hair fell to the shoulders, often in ringlets, and there were lovelocks tied with bows of colored ribbon. The lovelock introduced by Charles I was worn on the left side, a curl longer than the other ringlets. The trim mustache and the small "Van Dyck" beard were in vogue at the same time. Pearl earrings were worn by the smart masculine world. Jewelled buttons became very fashionable, being sewn even to handkerchiefs and called "handkerchief buttons."

Hats were in Cavalier fashion, of beaver and felt, wide brim with crown of normal height, or narrow brim with tall crown encircled by a jewelled band and with or without plumes. A ruling of Charles I finally prohibited the use of any fur but beaver to be fashioned into hats. This was probably intended as an aid to the North American colonists, to whom beaver was an important export.

Cloaks were short and capelike, draped in every possible manner, revealing rich satin linings. Ivory, light blue and pale green were the fashionable colors, but men were inclined more and more toward the wearing of black. Muffetees appeared in this reign, a pair of small fur muffs, one for each hand. They were also made of various colored worsted fabrics.

In women's costume, the ruff and farthingale disappeared along with the stiff-corseted silhouette. In that evolution came first, with the higher waistline, a loose overdress open in front over another dress which still retained its stomacher. Both garments were made separate in bodice and skirt, the whole tied with a narrow sash or belt.

Next, the stiffly boned stomacher and the overdress disappeared. The skirt was long and full, the bodice often low-necked and short-waisted with short peplum, the edge of which was straight, scalloped or crenelated. The bodice was more often laced in back. The original word was boddie, thus, later on, stays which were laced in back and fastened in front, were a pair of boddies and, finally, a bodice. Occasionally an overskirt was caught up at the sides or in front.

The neck was finished with the falling band, a wide collar which reached from neck to shoulder in width. It had square or round corners, was edged with lace or embroidery and was sometimes composed of two or three layers. Sleeves were full, reaching to elbow or wrist, finished with the sheer lingerie cuff matching the collar. When of elbow length, long kid gloves were worn, which, too, were often edged with lace. Also worn, and matching these lingerie accessories, were aprons of exquisite workmanship which in England were called *pinners*.

Women wore a capelike wrap resembling that of the men for winter, and there was the loose, short Dutch jacket, edged and lined with fur. Added to the latter, for warmth, were the long gloves and muffs. As with the masculine costume, bunches of ribbon loops or points ornamented the costume.

The coiffure was that made familiar by the portraits painted by Van Dyck of Queen Henrietta Maria, wife of Charles I. It had a fringe over the forehead and loose, short, hanging curls on either side of the face, with a bun on the back of the head. False hair continued in fashion and wigs came into vogue.

For horseback riding, women wore the soft leather top boot, safeguards or outer petticoats of red, gray or black homespun and large beaver hats. In public, they wore hoods or kerchiefs tied under the chin, or occasionally just hung a short veil over the head. The mask was also worn. Their shoes were of the same pattern as those of the men, but with very high heels and with huge shoe roses which were costly to have made. The perfume box and the small mirror hung from the girdle.

The manufacture of pins was introduced into England about 1626, pins until this time being imported from France.

English - James I - Charles I

brocaded
silk-doublet with
wings and tabs-lace
edged ruff and cuffs-
full slops-ribbon
garters-slashed shoes-
shoe-roses-satin cape-
brocade lining-sword-
jewelled belt and
strap-1st decade
17th C.

flowered silk doublet-
lace neck-whisk
over scalloped gorget-
wings-tabs-points
tied in bowknots
around waist-lace
cuffs-one boot
turned down show-
ing stocking-
sword on strap-
1614

black taffeta with
gimp-velvet wings-
lace edged ruff and
cuffs-ribbon bows
with points-Spanish
slops-wrinkled
canions-ribbon
garters-satin shoes
with taffeta ties-
pendant on
moiré ribbon-
1624

velvet jacket-
slashed
sleeves-
brandenburgs and
frogs-falling
embroidered band
and cuffs-band
strings-cloth
breeches tied in
front with points-
loops at knees-
embroidered linen
boot hose-boots
with platform soles
and spur leathers-
1630's

RTW

English-James I-Charles I

English-James I-Charles I
beaver hat-ostrich and aigrette-1st decade 17th C.
laced stomacher-1644
man's slipper-ribbon rosette with jewel-1612
lawn and lace cap-wired ruff-1614
spiral love-lock-lace whisk-ropes of pearls-2nd decade 17th C.
falling band-hair short on right side-love-lock on left-1630's
beaver cavalier hat-pearl earring-hair short on right side-love-lock on left-1630's
felt hat-rolled bands-jewelled brooch-ostrich and aigrette-1st decade 17th C.
man's shoe-black velvet-silver and green ribbon-red sole and heel-1641
tightly curled hair-cap with rolled edge-thread lace collar-1621
falling band-love-lock-1630's
wife of the Lordmayor of London-1646
cravat-1630's
fringe-ringlets and pearls-1630's
formal coiffure-hair curled and banded around face-jewels-ostrich-aigrette-1st decade 17th C
feather fan-1st decade 17th C.
white leather boot-red heel-spur leathers-platform sole-1630's
man's white leather shoe-red heel-shoe-rose-punched design-1633
woman's jacket-velvet and ermine-2nd third-17th C.
folding fan-2nd decade 17th C.
R.J.W.

Chapter Twenty-five

England Under Cromwell

PURITAN—1649–1660

THE REAL mode of this period was the Cavalier fashion, but the Puritans were the ruling power in England at this time. They did not create a style, but simply denuded the Stuart mode of all its fripperies. It should be remembered that the severely plain costume was not worn by all Puritans, as many of the sect wore the prevailing mode with its many colors and ornamentation, while only fanatics seem to have taken on the very sober garb. However, "sadd colours" were the fashion, meaning the grayed tones of any color.

The man's jacket was shorn of all trimming, breeches were moderately full and tight at the knee or sometimes cut straight at the knee, ending with a very simple frill or pleated ruffle. He wore no lace-edged collar or cuffs and his collar was tied with plain strings. The plain collar or band eventually became the two plain tabs of lawn or cambric worn by the professional class. The two tabs were attached to a neckband which fastened in back.

He wore the square-toed shoes or high boots of soft leather, with the broad spur leathers but no lace in the tops. Buckles replaced the spur leathers on the shoes in the next period. The broad-brimmed, high-crowned hat was worn by men and women, usually ornamented with a ribbon or band and buckle. While the Cavalier wore his curled locks flowing to the shoulders, the Puritan, or "Roundhead," as he was called, cut his hair fairly short and, if he wore a mustache, kept it very trim. The heavy oaken stick made familiar in portrayals of the Puritan, was first carried in the 1680's.

The most usual colors were black, dark brown and dull gray, but the jacket sometimes had sleeves of dull red and yellow striped material.

Women discarded the short peplum cut in tabs, leaving only a little tail to the bodice in back. The sheer linen cap which covered the hair, the wide collar and cuffs and the apron had no lace edging.

Comparatively simpler but dressier than the costume of the fanatic was the one with full skirt caught up, showing a petticoat, sometimes quilted of contrasting color, and a low-necked bodice, veiled by the collar or falling band. The cap, collar and cuffs might then be finished with very simple embroidery.

The large felt or beaver hat was worn over the lingerie cap in summer and in the winter over a black hood tied under the chin. Women also wore the voluminous cloaks and carried large muffs. Shoes, like those of the men, were square-toed and had neat shoe roses. Ribbons, in sober colors, were sparingly used, and the materials employed, such as lutestring, heavy silk, cloth and velvet, were in rich subdued tones.

England Under Cromwell-1649-1660

Chapter Twenty-six

Louis Fourteenth

First Period—1644–1661

The first period in this reign is one of transition in the mode. By this time, with the exception of Spain, all Europe followed France in culture and the mode.

The edicts against the importation of lace, gold and silver trimmings were ignored after Richelieu's death. Mazarin, in 1644, permitted only the employment of silks, to the exclusion of extravagant embroideries, metal and brocaded tissues, thus bringing about a new trimming, that of ribbon. The use of ribbon as ornamentation was carried to such extremes that by the end of this period loops (or *galants,* the French term) of variegated colors were placed all over the costume.

The last sumptuary decrees of Mazarin in 1656 and 1660 were very severe, forbidding the use of lace, passementeries and embroideries in the effort to prevent the outgoing of so much gold. The importation of Venetian and Flemish laces was banned.

After Mazarin's death, Louis XIV, acting upon the advice of his minister Colbert, brought Venetian lacemakers to France. Lacemaking centers were established at Alençon, Quesney, Arras, Reims, Sedan, Château-Thierry, Loudun and elsewhere. Colbert presented to the King the first pieces of lace made; he found them beautiful and encouraged the wearing of lace by the court. Gold and silver trimmings were reserved for the exclusive use of the King and his court.

The masculine jacket shortened to above the waistline, below which the full lingerie shirt bloused all around. The very full shirt sleeves were exposed below the three-quarter-length jacket sleeves.

The wide collar, because of the lengthening full wig, grew smaller and smaller. Neckcloths and cravats had appeared in the 'thirties and the falling band with its rounded corners now fell into two wide pleats over the chest. The jabot appeared, a falling lace ruffle, which filled in the opening of the jacket in front. White lawn, linen, mull and lace were employed for neckwear.

With the man's short jacket, a camisole was worn underneath as protection against the cold. The need for more adequate body covering brought about the wearing of a coat, adopting the style of the soldier's cassock. It reached to the knees, buttoned in front, and usually had short sleeves with turned-back cuffs and no collar. It was worn over the short jacket and is the origin of the classic coat and vest. A short full cape reaching almost to the knees was also in vogue. Large loose cloaks were worn only in bad weather or for travelling.

The tubular-shaped breeches continued to be worn, finished with a frill of ribbon loops. Rhinegrave or petticoat breeches made their appearance in this period. They were brought from Holland by Count Salm, whose title was Count of the Rhine or Rheingraf. Petticoat breeches were in two styles, either in one piece like a kilt, or in divided-skirt fashion and elaborately ornamented with ruches, ruffles, lace and ribbon loops. Often, separate lingerie and lace ruffles, called cannons, were worn just below the knees. A small apron of ribbon loops covered the front closing of the breeches.

Glove-fitting silk stockings with embroidered clocks were worn with shoes reaching to the ankles. The shoes had red heels and stiff wide bows, called butterfly bows or windmill wings. At the end of this period appeared the small jewelled buckle for shoe and garter. Shoes and boots had moderately high heels and square toes. Soft leather boots, called buskins, had wide cuffs, over which fell the lace-edged linen flounces of the boot hose. Sometimes the leather cuffs were lined simply with separate frills.

Buttons became popular—in fact, became a great extravagance—with dozens of jewelled buttons added to a costume.

The sword baldric of fabric or leather was occasionally seen. The hat had a sloping crown and a brim of moderate width and was usually bedecked with ostrich plumes. The hair continued to be worn in flowing curls, shoulder length, with the *perruque,* or wig, gaining in favor. The head was then regularly shaved, the wig taking the place of the man's own hair. At first, the wig was made to look like natural hair, but eventually, an artificial effect was intentionally cultivated. Masses of ringlets fell over the shoulders and down the back. By 1660, wigmaking in France reached such a stage of perfection that the French *perruque* was in demand all over Europe.

In this first period of the reign, the feminine costume remained about the same, but its coming changes were apparent. The bodice was tight and growing tighter, again shaping into the deep point in front and often laced in back. It was worn over a slim corset, which rose high under the armpits and over the breasts. The low neck was ornamented with the deep falling collar of sheer fabric introduced into France by Anne of Austria. The collar and the deep cuffs of the three-quarter-length sleeves were edged with fine lace or embroidery. Another style was the *fichu* of lace which finished the horizontal neckline, baring the shoulders. When the bodice opened over a stomacher of contrasting material, ornamental lacings of narrow ribbon or chenille were sometimes used.

Under the full skirt reaching to the floor was worn the spreading bell-shaped hoop of moderate dimension. Often the skirt opened in front over another of contrasting color bordered with gold and silk embroidery. A favorite style was the overskirt looped up toward the back.

The hair was dressed in the style introduced by Henrietta Maria into England, later called in France "coiffure à la Ninon." The sides were cut short, hanging to the shoulders in ringlets, often wired, short curls running over the forehead and the top drawn to a knot on the back of the head. The wired curls were known as "heartbreakers." Lace scarfs, kerchiefs and hoods served as head covering.

For hunting and horseback, the masculine attire was copied, the hat and often the wig, along with the coat, vest, cravat and sash, even to the light dress sword. Too, like that of the men, bunches of ribbon loops ornamented the costume. Cosmetics and beauty patches were as popular as ever, the mask continued to be worn, riding or walking. Brightly colored boutonnières of silk floss furnished an accent to the costume and were worn on the left shoulder.

In 1660, the King married the Spanish Infanta and there followed a vogue for black lace. This early black lace, resembling Chantilly lace of today, was made at Bayeux, hence the name, Bayeux lace.

Louis XIV - First Period

Louis XIV - First Period

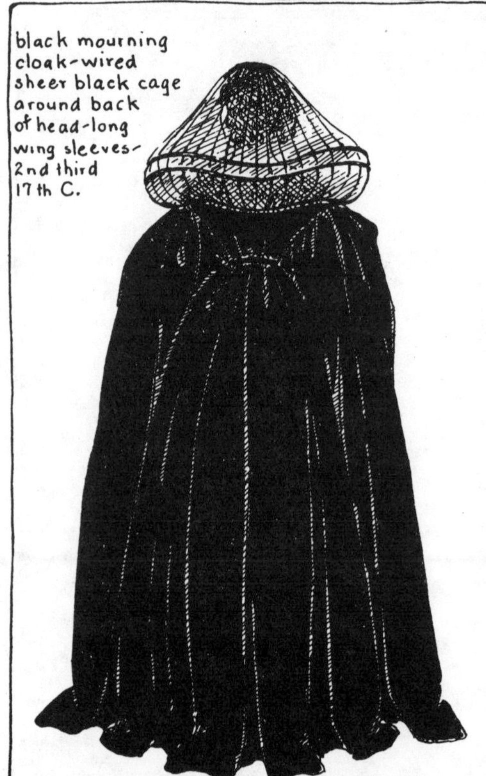

Chapter Twenty-seven

Louis Fourteenth

SECOND PERIOD—1661–1670

IN THIS period, Louis reached the height of his reign and France was now, definitely, the arbiter of the mode.

In the masculine jacket, which had become very short, elbow-length, is seen the last stage of the doublet. Below it the full lingerie shirt bloused all around. The short jacket sleeves had either plain edge or turned-back cuffs, often buttoned in place. The full shirt sleeves, tight at the wrists and finished with ribbon loops, ended with ruffles of lawn or lace.

The *rabat,* or lace falling band, with its round corners, became broad and long, and the *jabot,* or frill on the shirt front, frequently appeared with it. By the end of this decade, the ends of the cravat became full lace tabs, tied under the chin with "cravat strings," which were of ribbon or lace.

Rhinegrave or petticoat breeches were the definite feature of this period. They were in various syles, the full gathered skirt, the divided skirt and a shorter skirt which exposed to view the very full knee breeches. They were lavishly ornamented with galloon, lace and ribbon loops, and pockets were inserted in front of the skirt. Ribbon loops now encircled the waist and deep cannons of lingerie material and lace hung from just below the knees. Rhinegrave breeches lasted through the 'seventies, finally surviving in the livery of footmen.

Boots went out of fashion, even in the army, worn only by officers and the cavalry. From 1660 to 1690 buskins were worn. The buskin was a half boot of leather or fabric reaching to the calf of the leg, fitting snugly, fastened in front and having a turned-down cuff. The man's leather shoe of the period had square toes and a broad heel. The upstanding fronts formed little cuffs over the instep and cuffs, heel and sole were often red, the shoe itself being brown or gray. The stiff wide bows lasted until 1680. A bunch of ribbon loops was often placed on the outer sides of the shoes. More important was the jewelled buckle, which appeared about 1660 and, gradually growing larger, entirely replaced the tie fastening in the 'eighties.

Sashes were worn, fringed, lace-edged and tasseled, as was the sword baldric. During the 'sixties, loops and bowknots of ribbon were placed over the entire costume. Handkerchiefs hung from coat pockets, exquisite snuffboxes and elegant combs were carried to be used in public. Handsome, slim walking sticks, ornamented with ribbon bowknots, were in fashion, with gold, silver or carved ivory heads. The muff was a masculine as well as a feminine accessory in those days and hung suspended from a ribbon around the neck. It was small and round, either of cloth, velvet brocade or fur, and lined with either fur or silk, trimmed with lace, ribbon and embroidery. Its greatest popularity in this century dated from 1660 to 1680.

Wigs grew in favor, but the King, having a fine head of hair, did not adopt the fashion until 1673, when he was thirty-five. The full curled wig was worn with the low-crowned hat having a brim of moderate width and adorned with ostrich plumes. The hat was more often carried than worn on the head, so as not to disarrange the dressing of the wig. The mustache became a very thin line.

Woman's costume also took on extravagant ornamentation in gold and silver passementeries, laces and ribbons. *Galants,* or favors, as the bunches of ribbon loops were called, were of variegated colors. Striped and watered silks and gauzes, hand-painted with flowers in large designs, were popular. The motif in design on fabrics consisted principally of flowers and fruits in realistic form. An interesting note is that, for the first time in weaving, the play of lights and shadows was accomplished. In this flamboyant age of Louis XIV, the flower motif was larger than natural size, just slightly undersize in the reign of Louis XV, becoming diminutive under Louis XVI.

Skirts were long and full with the overskirt, or *manteau,* looped back, held by ribbon bows. The looped-up folds were often bunched in back. Over an underskirt of taffeta, the looped-up outer skirt of brocaded silk ended in a train, the length of which was determined by the lady's social position. The train was carried over the left arm, except in the presence of royalty, when it trailed on the floor.

The long slim-pointed bodice over the tight high corset persisted. Lace was now used principally on the sleeves, which were usually in several puffs and three-quarter or elbow length. The bodice often laced in back, but when fastened in front it had jewelled clasps, buttons or many bowknots. Bowknots of graduated size on the stomacher were called *échelon*. The décolletage was usually bateau-shaped, finished with a scarf or fichu of lawn or lace. The large collar of lace or point coupé, which had been originally introduced into France by Anne of Austria, became passé after her death and by the 'seventies had disappeared.

Transparents, made famous by Madame de Sévigné's description in one of her letters, were gowns of sheer muslin or lawn, painted with bunches of colored flowers and worn over another gown of moiré satin of a bright color. Transparents were also of gold or lace tissue, worn over figured brocades.

Slippers with very pointed toes and very high heels, known as "Louis heels," were of satin, brocade, embroidered fabrics and kid, fastened with jewelled buckles, ribbon and rosettes. Elbow-length gloves were of glacé kid or silk in white or pale colors. The all-lace fan made its appearance in the second half of this century. Women, too, carried the tall, slim cane with head of gold, silver or ivory. Parasols of Chinese shape, edged with fringe, were held over ladies by pages. The necklace of small pearls, which encircled the neck, was worn invariably with the low décolletage. A necklace with a pendant was worn by Louise de la Vallière, first mistress of Louis XIV, the style of which became known as *lavallière*. Rings, earrings, brooches and necklaces of gold were much worn, heavily encrusted with diamonds and colored gems.

There was also a tremendous vogue for artificial or "costume jewelry," as we call it today, fashioned of brilliantly colored stones. This artificial jewelry, which became very fashionable, was made on the Rue de Temple, and from that derived its name of "temple" jewelry. There was also a great fad for extravagant jewelled buttons, dozens of which were used on a costume.

Louis XIV-Second Period

Louis XIV-Second Period

Louis XIV-Second Period-1660's
falling band-bandstring with pom-pom of crocheted petals-natural hair
black silk hood lined with rose silk
lady's shoe-white kid with silk embroidery
felt hat-white plumes-lace falling band-natural hair-1665
ringlets dressed over wire frames-ribbon bowknots-tiny cap
corset laced back and front
fringed silk sash
lawn and lace cravat tied with ribbon-natural hair-1665
fringed embroidered sword baldric
men's shoes-leather with red tongue and heel-buckle fastening
lace wind mill wings-ribbon loops-red heel-up to 1680
RTW

Chapter Twenty-eight

Louis Fourteenth

Third Period—1670–1715

The beginning of this period was one of great pomp and luxury, which finally settled down to a more conservative style as it neared its end.

A great and lasting change came over men's attire, the doublet becoming a vest and the justaucorps, or jerkin, changing into coat or *habit,* as it was called in French. At first, the length of the waistcoat was just below the waistline, with the coat reaching halfway between thigh and knee. About 1670, the coat lengthened to the knee, with the vest reaching there about 1680. After 1675, the waistline became definitely shaped, even to a flaring skirt, which was later stiffened to stand out from the figure. To the back of either hip the skirt was slit and decorated with a row of buttons. Another style was the insertion of fan-shaped pleats at the side-back, headed by a button, which is the origin of the back buttons on today's tail coat.

From about 1680, buttons and buttonholes were lavishly used on the vest, cuffs and pockets. They were covered with yellow and white silk, simulating gold and silver. When buttons and buttonholes were applied in conjunction with braid, they were termed *brandenburgs* by the French after contact in 1674 with the Brandenburg troops whose cassocks were ornamented with like braided loops and buttons.

Embroidery in gold and silk, which was often elaborate, confined itself to the wide cuffs on the coat sleeves and the fronts of the waistcoat. Shoulders and sleeves were ornamented with huge bunches of ribbon loops. French cloth now rivalled that of England and Holland, and after 1677, following the edict of Louis XIV, the justaucorps was made of cloth instead of silk and trimming eliminated, leaving only the ribbon loops on the shoulders. Pockets were placed low in front, and coat and vest were collarless, no doubt due to the full wig. Until 1690, the waistcoat was buttoned with the coat either open or closed. Often the waistcoat had a sleeve which turned back over the cuff of the coat. Gold braid finished seams and edges and was often part of the embroidery design.

Petticoat breeches lasted until about 1678, replaced then by the full knickerbockers, blousing over the knees, where they were finished with ribbon loops or cannons. Plain, close-fitting breeches, knee-length and concealed by the coat, came in the 'nineties, fastened either with buttons or with one, two or three buckles at the side of the knee. These breeches, when not made of the coat fabric, were black, which became standard.

Shirts were full in body and sleeve, gathered at the wrists. The growing size of the wig, with its curls reaching to the shoulders, caused the wide falling band to give way to the cravat of lawn or lace, tied at the neck with the cravat-string of ribbon. The jabot of lace and lawn concealed the front opening of the shirt. The *steinkirk* came in in the 'nineties, a scarf of lace or lawn, loosely tied, with the ends casually twisted into the vest or shirt front or drawn through a buttonhole or ring. Black silk steinkirks were also worn. The name came from the Battle of Steinkerque in 1692, when the victorious French charged the opposing cavalry with their dress in disorder and their cravats untied and flying.

House gowns of Oriental design were worn by men for negligee. They were loose, with flowing sleeves, and were first made of India cottons in bright figured designs, but later developed in velvets, brocades, damasks, striped and figured silks in gay colors with linings of contrasting colored silks.

Mention must be made of the muffs of beautiful furs, carried by men in the winter, attached to a ribbon belt around the waist. The muff was a French fashion and had been carried since the sixteenth century. It now became most luxurious, made of gold and silver tissue, ribbons, feathers and fur, to which embroidery was often added. Fashionable for both men and women was the small plush muff, *couleur de feu,* presumably Chinese red.

Wigs grew in size, becoming more artificial in appearance, being now made of horsehair, which proved more satisfactory in retaining its curl. Louis, who as a young man had a fine head of hair, did not take to wig wearing until 1673, when he was thirty-five years old. In the 'nineties, the "full-bottomed" wigs were parted in the middle, standing high over the brow in double peaks, with curls falling on the shoulders and down the back. The wig was now sometimes powdered, and the hat carried instead of being worn, to avoid disturbing the coiffure. Indoors, for negligee, a nightcap was often worn instead of the wig. By 1685, the thin mustache disappeared and the face was clean-shaven.

From about 1670, the wide-cocked brim was the style in hats with moderate crown and, around 1690, the three-cornered hat became definitely the mode. It was bound or edged with metal braid or lace and trimmed with ribbon and plumes. Later, the tricorne was ornamented with uncurled ostrich plumes or ostrich fringe. The masculine hat was worn indoors until 1685.

Baldrics of leather or embroidered silk or velvet were worn, from which the dress sword hung, the fashion lasting until after 1695. The small dress sword which appeared in the opening of the coat skirt was attached to a braid loop beneath the vest. The sword was often ornamented with a broad ribbon "sword knot" having fringed ends. Even the cane had its ribbon bowknots or tasselled cords. Handkerchiefs were tasselled or edged with lace and were carried hanging from pockets. Paint, patches, handsome snuffboxes, tobacco boxes and combs were all part of the costume.

From the 'seventies, black became the color for men's shoes, brown for hunting. Shoes were square-toed, with red heels and soles, which only nobility and gentlemen at court wore. The tongue over the instep hung down, revealing its red lining. A famous pair of the King's shoes had the heels painted by Van der Meulen, portraying scenes of the victorious Rhenish battles. Until the 'eighties, shoes were fastened with ribbon or lace bows, sometimes very wide, but were then superseded by small oval buckles which grew larger and became square. Eventually, buckles were fashioned with pearls and diamonds, plain bronze being worn for mourning.

Soft fitted boots or buskins without cuffs, from 1675 to about 1690, were fastened at the small of the leg by buckles or buttons. High leather leggings, or *spatterdashes,* came in about 1700. The joining of legging and shoe was covered by spur leathers.

In the 'eighties, cannons and ribbon garters disappeared, giving way to narrow bands with buckles. Stockings were drawn up over the breeches with the garter on the outside, or perhaps hidden in the stocking roll. Stockings were invariably clocked and of different color from the shoe.

Women's costume, at the height of this last period, reached a state of overdecoration, but the King's marriage to Madame de Maintenon, plus critical times for France, had a sobering effect in the latter part of the reign.

Until 1675, only tailors fashioned women's garments, but now there were established couturiers or dressmakers, mantua or cloak makers, modistes or milliners, shoemakers, furriers, glovers, fan makers, jewellers, beauty specialists and coiffeurs or hairdressers, all high-class and very costly. The stage became an influence in launching new fashions. An extravagant use of powder, rouge and patches was the vogue. There were rules of etiquette for the wearing of the mask and definite rules for the length of trains and the wearing of certain fabrics, governed by one's station. The use of perfume declined in this reign, sweet odors being objectionable to the King.

A silkworm which produced pure white silk was cultured in France. Painted and printed linens and cottons became the rage, to last for the next two reigns. Lace ornamented not only clothes but was applied to bedcovers, carriages, horse blankets, even shrouds. There was point de Paris, d'Alençon, de Malines, de Valenciennes, de Bruxelles, also gold and silver lace made at Paris and Lyon.

The waistline of the long, slim, tightly corseted bodice had become very small, with the bust held high. The low neck was finished with a fichu, frills or a falling band. Bows and lace ruffles ended the elbow-length sleeves. There were deep capelike collars of lawn or lace which lay about the shoulders, either cut high to the neck or in bateau line. This style is familiar to us in American colonial dresses. Little capes, first made of fur and known as "palatines," or "pèlerines," were introduced into France by the Palatine Princess Charlotte Elizabeth of Bavaria, who married the King's brother, Duc d'Orléans, in 1671. Women adopted steinkirks in the 'nineties.

In the 'eighties, over a full skirt which hung to the floor, an overskirt with long train was drawn up and bunched toward the back over a bustle. Then the old verdingale, or farthingale, returned by way of England, under the new name of pannier, or hoop. This new hoop was made of cane or reed, rather like a bird cage, thus the French name of *panier,* or basket. But this style did not fully establish itself for years to come.

Gowns were trimmed with heavy embroideries, lace, braid, fringe and tassels. Ribbon bowknots in échelle form adorned the front of the bodice. Cut-out motifs of lace or gold embroidery, called *prentintailles,* were appliquéd or gummed to the skirts, making elaborate ornamentation. The heavy ruffles were called *fabalas,* which, anglicized, became "furbelows." Gowns often had separate sets of false sleeves.

The long trains were carried by pages. The small Negro boy servant or slave, dressed and turbaned in brilliant colors, appeared for the first time in this period. He held the long-handled parasol over the lady.

At home, for negligee, a loose, beltless coatlike robe called a *manteau,* or mantua, came into fashion. It was not unlike the kimono version of modern times and was of a dark color or black. To Madame de Maintenon is accredited its name, the "innocent." The gown worn at home was usually black, accompanied by the lace-trimmed white apron. Aprons were often of silk, edged with gold lace and were called *laisse-tout-faire.* Near the end of the century, there was a fad for *transparents* of black lace worn over colorful brocades. The name transparents was also applied to the sheer fabrics employed in the tall ruffled caps then in vogue.

The wrap of the period was a short, scarflike cape edged with ruffles or lace, called a *mante.* This wrap and the mantua were probably made of a silk imported from Italy in the eighteenth and nineteenth centuries and called mantua silk. No doubt, from that fact, came the name "mantuamaker." Mantes, or broad scarfs of gold and silver tissue, were worn only by women of high rank at court. The scarf of fur loosely tied around the neck was also called a *palatine,* though of different shape from the little cape. Muffs were carried in winter and were often large enough to hold the little pet dogs which were then the fashion.

A coiffure which appeared in 1671 and lasted but a few years was the *hurluberlu,* a madcap, or "windblown bob," the hair cut short and in ringlets. From about 1675, the hair was dressed high off the forehead in clusters of curls, arranged over a silk-covered wire frame, called a *commode.* Occasionally, the hair was powdered. In 1680, the Duchesse de Fontanges, having her hat blown off at a royal hunting party, tied her curls in place with her garter, arranging a bow with ends in front. From that incident, fastened to a cap, grew tier upon tier of upstanding, wired, pleated ruffles of lawn, lace and ribbons. The hair dressed in that fashion was called *coiffure à la Fontanges,* and the cap with its narrow rising front was known as *le bonnet à la Fontanges,* in English, the *fontange.* The cap often had two floating lappets of ribbon or lace in back, and over the whole arrangement was often worn the black silk hood or kerchief. In 1691, the headdress was reduced to two tiers of pleats and became known as the *commode*. About 1710, under ridicule, the cap lost its fantastic front tower and became just a little linen or lace cap. Patches, placed near the mouth and eyes and on the forehead, accompanied this headdress.

The riding habit was founded upon the masculine costume of coat and waistcoat. The skirt was draped for side saddle. At the neck was the lace cravat with huge ribbon bow. The three-cornered hat with plumes and heavy leather gloves were worn with the outfit. The equestrienne held the reins in her left hand, and on sunny days a parasol was carried in her right.

The tall cane continued in fashion; in fact, cane and parasol are shown being carried at the same time. Masks were still worn, hanging from the belt when not in use. Fans of rare beauty were created, miniature paintings mounted on sticks of gold, carved ivory, mother-of-pearl and carved and painted wood. A new accessory was the snuffbox, carried by "ladies of quality" who made use of snuff, a habit which was very displeasing to Madame de Maintenon.

Fine shoes, of exquisite fabrics and beautifully embroidered, were worn with the high "Louis heels." There were also high-heeled slippers with just the front covering, called *pantoffles*. Fastenings were ribbons and jewelled buckles.

The feminine vogue of wearing a small bouquet, or boutonnière, of fresh flowers brought about the invention of the "bosom bottle," to keep the blooms from wilting. It was a small glass or tin bottle about four inches long, covered with green ribbon and holding water, which was tucked into the bosom or the hair. Boutonnières of flowers fashioned of silk floss preceded the fashion of fresh flowers.

The process of manufacturing artificial pearls was perfected by Jaquin of Paris about 1680. Accepted everywhere, the imitation pearl vied with real gem as adornment. The single string around the throat without pendant became classic.

The clothes of children still resembled those of their elders.

Venetian mirrors were now excelled in quality by those of French manufacture. The method of making plate glass was invented in 1691 in Nehou, France, by Louis Lucas, a Frenchman.

Louis XIV - Third Period

cloth coat-braid and buttons-petticoat breeches-ribbon loops-lingerie cravat and shirt-fringed gauntlets-felt hat with ostrich-powdered wig-leather shoes-red tongues, heels-buckles-cane with bowknot-sword-1670's

orange cloth cape-gold and silver embroidery-gray cloth coat-orange embroidery-orange satin vest-orange plush muff attached to ribbon belt-lawn and lace cravat-fringed gauntlets-hat gray beaver-ostrich and ribbon-wig-stockings drawn over breeches-black shoes-red heels-gold buckles-1678

cloth coat with turned back fronts-striped waistcoat with sleeves-lace frills-steinkirk-fur muff on ribbon-beaver hat, uncurled ostrich-stockings gartered over breeches-black leather shoes-red heels-buckles-sword with fringed ribbon-snuff box-1694

cloth coat with braid and buttons-side pleats-lace frills-tricorne hat with braid-wig-cane-1706

Louis XIV - Third Period

heavy satin with fringe and pretintailles-lace on bodice and sleeves-velvet paniers and "manteau"-lace vestee-fur "palatine" and muff-fontange of lace and ribbon with lappets-beauty patches-late 17 th C.

silk and lace with "manteau" of contrasting color-lingerie sleeves-lace edged silk apron-handkerchief in pocket-ribbon échelle-fontange of lace and ribbon-late 17 th C.

brocade with ribbon and tassels-silk "manteau"-velvet mante with lace-lace fontange with lappets-fan-beauty patches-late 17 th C.

hunting habit-brocaded green velvet coat-lingerie shirt and cravat-brocaded deep rose cloth skirt-brown beaver hat-rose ostrich-handkerchief in pocket-game bag-gun-negro servant-1690's

Louis XIV - Third Period

Chapter Twenty-nine

The English Restoration

CHARLES II—1660–1685
JAMES II—1685–1689

THESE two reigns mark the return of the Stuarts to England. Charles brought back with him the costume worn at the Court of Louis XIV, where he had spent his exile. It was bedecked with ribbons, the very short jacket with short sleeves exposing the full, sheer lace-trimmed shirt with correspondingly full sleeves tied with ribbons.

This was accompanied by full breeches ending in deep lace ruffles or cannons, as they were called, or the petticoat or "rhinegrave breeches." There were two styles of petticoat breeches, one which resembled a kilt, the other like a divided skirt. At the neck appeared the lace or lawn falling band, the cravat or the oblong tabs. The costume was ornamented with glittering buttons, loops or buttonholes, braid, gimp or galloon.

There were the long bushy *peryke,* later called "periwig" (a misconstruction of the French word, perruque), the small mustache, tiny lip beard, silk stockings, squared-toed shoes with high red heels and wide ribbon ties, a cane and the wide-brimmed beaver hat with sweeping plumes. Curls were tied with ribbons.

With the graying of the king's own black hair, he adopted a black wig, which created a fad for that hue. Later, fair and light-brown periwigs became popular. For travelling, short bushy wigs replaced those in long ringlets.

With the return of Charles II, the boot again flared out in a wide falling cuff, finished with the ruffle and lace of the boot hose. Cannons, or bunches of ribbon loops, were affixed at the knee from 1660 to 1670. After the 'eighties, breeches were finished with a buckled garter band or the stockings were rolled over the breeches. Black seems to have been the popular color in leather boots after the 'seventies. Buckles appeared for the first time in this age on shoes and garters. Small jewelled buckles were worn, with the butterfly or "windmill wings" gradually growing in size, until, in the 'eighties, they were the only fastening or ornament on shoes.

About 1665 appeared the *jack boot,* a rigid leather boot for hard wear, which had a wide leather cuff, worn either up or down. There were also wide spur leathers, spatterdashes and buttoned or buckled leather leggings. The buskin, a soft fitted boot of leather or fabric, appeared in this period. It sometimes fastened in front with clasps.

Contemporary with the change in men's costume during the early part of the reign of Louis XIV, in fact definitely in October, 1666, came a change in the Englishman's apparel. Giving his court a month's notice, Charles II dressed all his courtiers in a new vest and coat "after ye Persian mode." According to Pepys's description, it was all black and white, the vest reaching the calf of the leg and over the vest, a coat six inches shorter.

The breeches, which were concealed by the vest, were of "Spanish cut," finished with cannons of black ribbon loops. The buskins worn with the outfit were either of cloth or leather, the same color as that of the vest or coat. The lining of the coat and vest was white, which scheme made Charles decide that they all looked too much like magpies, whereupon he ordered a new costume, entirely of black velvet. This somber hue did not survive at that time, but the idea of coat and vest replacing the tunic or doublet, was to last to our day.

From the portrait of Henry Bennet, Earl of Arlington, who was painted in the new coat and vest, the coat appears to be of black velvet, with white taffeta lining and undersleeves. The undersleeves are tied with black velvet ribbons. The vest seems to be of silk brocade in an Oriental design with narrow belt. The sword baldric, coat cuffs and the band on the vest appear to be of contrasting colored silk, ornamented with Italian cutwork. A white lawn and lace falling band tops the costume.

The new coat becoming quite generally worn, the cloak then became of secondary importance.

It was in this period that men adopted robes and turbans for negligee. Though originally worn at home, the use finally spread to the countinghouse or "office." The Oriental turban gave respite from the heat of the wig and the East Indian banyan, or banian, became the lounging robe. The Oriental influence came about through trade intercourse with Persia, India and Arabia. These loose gowns were first made of Indian cottons, but later appeared in silks, damasks and brocades, with contrasting linings and varied in style from the robe with wide sleeves to the flowing coat with turned-down collar and fitted sleeves. The robes were always of brilliantly colored figured or striped fabrics.

The pair of small muffs, or *muffetees,* was still worn in the winter by the men, in the beginning of this reign, but, by 1663, the single larger muff had become the fashion. It hung from a ribbon around the neck or from a button of the coat, and was usually of fabric with fur lining. The sword was suspended from a wide baldric of decorated leather or embroidered velvet.

The feminine gown of the period was quite simple and charming, usually of plain satin or velvet, although brocade, gold and silver tissue are also mentioned. The corset was laced tighter, creating a slimmer figure than that of the previous reign. The waistline was moderately pointed in front, round in back and the neckline either round or bateau-shaped. The center front of the bodice and the short full sleeve were left open at intervals and tied with ribbon bowknots, revealing the chemisette of sheer lawn, linen or muslin worn underneath. The chemisette showed in a tiny edge at the neck, and neck and sleeves were often finished with lace ruffles.

The full skirt was caught up over a petticoat which was of contrasting fabric and color and usually had a train. Petticoats were often elaborately embroidered with gold and silver and sometimes edged with ermine. Skirts of ankle-length were also fashionable.

Muffs, like those of the men, were carried in the winter, and the short cape or palatine, of German origin, called tippet in England, was worn. It later became known as a *pèlerine*. When travelling, women wore cloaks with enveloping hoods. For horseback and hunting, their hats, decked with plumes, resembled the masculine style. The hair was dressed in ringlets at the sides over wire frames, a fringe of curls on the forehead and a knot at the back. The side bunches of curls were often tied with ribbons.

"Pinners," or aprons of intricate workmanship, were the vogue. A negligee garment for women was the nightgown, worn in the boudoir but not in bed. It hung full from the neck, where it fastened and had full sleeves, gathered at the wrists. It was usually of striped satin or damask, padded and lined with taffeta to match.

A special "habit" for horseback was designed in this period, which had a long-skirted, buttoned-up coat worn over a sidesaddle skirt. See Page 166. With it were worn a doublet, the peruke and a tall crowned hat. In bad weather, a "safeguard," or "riding petticoat," of heavy linen protected the habit. Masks were worn in winter to protect the face from the cold, even on horseback. Masks were much used in our colonies for the same reason.

In accessories, added to the mask, there were the fan, patches, powder, rouge, the muff and long gloves of soft chamois or doeskin delicately scented. A new note for women was the garter of ribbon and lace fastened with a beautiful jewelled buckle. The English Court took up Bayeux lace, a black lace introduced at the French Court upon the marriage of the Spanish Infanta to Louis XIV. A novelty was the bouquet or nosegay of flowers worn on the left shoulder.

In the reign of James II, the coat and vest of the preceding regime became the accepted costume of men, taking on more of the French cut with shaped waist and flaring skirt. The coat was worn half-buttoned and the skirt was slit up center-back and at the sides. A wide turned-back cuff finished the sleeve, with the puffs and frills of the full lingerie shirt showing below. The coat front, cuffs, slits and low-placed pockets were trimmed with buttons and braid loops and galloon or all three. The cravat of fine lawn and lace finished the neck.

Breeches were moderately full, bagging at the knees, and shoes were now fastened with buckles on straps instead of strings. The cotton stockings made in England appeared in the 'eighties and, though the silk stocking remained the smart thing, knitted stockings of cotton or wool were generally worn.

Hats had brims of medium width and low crowns, with the newer trimming of ribbon loops. Although always removed in the presence of royalty, hats were worn indoors until 1685. There does not seem to be any definite record of when it became bad manners for a man to keep his hat on the head in house or at church. Broad sashes and the baldric were worn outside the coat.

The changes in the feminine gown were slight. The neck of the bodice was higher, and the wide, flat collar, whisk or falling band continued in fashion. The stomacher or front of the bodice was ornamented with ribbon bowknots in graduated size, a style called *échelle,* or ladder. Another decoration of the stomacher was the cross-lacing of narrow ribbon. Sleeves had wide turned-back cuffs, with the white lingerie puffs of the chemisette showing below. The popularity of sheer aprons, or pinners, continued.

The hair was now waved and parted in the middle, the hanging ringlets were retained, placed lower, also coming over the shoulders from the back. Black hoods, with or without capes, were fashionable, also the large hat finished simply with a ribbon band. While sunshades and umbrellas, coming by way of Spain, appeared in France about the middle of this century, they did not reach England until the end of the seventeenth century.

The first of the great "dandies" who exercised an influence over fashion lived in these two periods. His name was Robert Feilding. "Beau Feilding" was known at the Court of Charles II as "Handsome Feilding." He died in 1712.

The second dandy, of later date, was Richard Nash, called "Beau Nash," a leader of English society and fashion. The King appointed him master of ceremonies at Bath, where he ruled in matters of deportment and dress. He was born in 1674 and died in 1761.

The English Restoration

short doublet open front and back-slashed sleeves-lace edged pleated falling band-lawn shirt-petticoat breeches-ribbon loops-leather boots-lace edged boot hose-beaver hat with ostrich-cloth cloak-before 1666

coat and petticoat breeches-cloth with velvet loops-taffeta lining and cuffs-low pockets-handkerchief with jewelled button-white lawn shirt-pleated lace falling band-black wig-beaver hat-leather shoes-red heels after 1666

velvet with taffeta lining-satin vest-velvet baldric-lawn cravat and shirt-lace ruffles-satin bows-wig-felt hat-cane and a sword-1670

cloth with silk vest-cloth cloak-fur lined cloth muff with velvet loops-leather shoes-red heels-wig-felt hat with ribbon loops-1688

RTW

The English Restoration

The English Restoration
lady's shoe-white kid-black velvet-punched design-attached clog
black wig-bowknots-beaver hat-ostrich-lawn and lace cravat
beaver hat-ostrich plumes-ribbon loops-hair late in the period
wig and falling band
man's shoe-red heel and buckle-1682
corset to lace in back-false lacing in front
wig-falling band and bandstrings
pearls-knot in back-wired ringlets
man's shoe-"wind mill wing" ties-red heel
fitted buskin-boot hose frill
jack boot
slit in coat back-manner of wearing sword
coat-vest and breeches "after ye Persian mode" October 1666-for description see text
sword baldric
two styles of petticoat breeches
FTW

Chapter Thirty

Louis Fifteenth

1715–1774

In the eighteenth century, from 1750 to 1770, French costume is considered to have reached its perfection. There are definitely two periods: that from 1724 to 1750, known as "Rococo," with its basic motif, the shell combined with flowers, feathers, ribbon bowknots and all manner of curves and curls, often all in one design; the second, from 1750 to 1770, was less fantastic, more dignified. The manners and fashions of the French Court influenced social life throughout the civilized world.

The *habit à la française,* while adhering to the three fundamentals of coat, vest and breeches settled in the reign of Louis XIV, became perfected in design during the Regency, from then becoming the formal attire of the gentleman of Europe, lasting a century. The coat retained its name, *habit à la française,* to the end of the eighteenth century, with very little change in cut. Up the center back to the waist has always appeared the slash, originally necessary on horseback.

The sleeves, usually slit part way up in back, were straight with wide cuffs. The skirt of the coat, reaching to the knees, was reinforced with linen, buckram or whalebone and cut to flare when buttoned at the waist. The hilt of the sword protruded from these pleats, attached to a baldric or belt worn under the coat or vest. The full, rich-looking undersleeves were often part of the vest, in which case the back, sometimes laced, the fronts and the lower section of the sleeves were all of one material. The vest was buttoned or simulated thus, by three or four buttons at the waist. Under the vest was worn the lingerie *chemise,* with cravat or jabot attached.

In the 'fifties, the fronts of the coat began to slope away from the waist and the side pleats with buttons moved toward the back. The skirt of the vest gradually shortened, by the middle of the century, reaching just over the hips and cut away in front at the waist. The neck was cut away in front, leaving an opening filled in with cravat or jabot. The small, flat, turned-back collar developed along with pointed lapels, and the sleeve became tight with a small cuff. From the 'fifties, the large pocket flaps disappeared.

The tight breeches were either buttoned or buckled above the knee, with the silk stockings rolled over the breeches. The garters were concealed in the roll. Breeches were furnished with pockets, sometimes as many as eight, made of white kid. Later, the breeches, still fastened with buttons or buckles, came below the knees. Although *gallowses* appeared at the beginning of the century, breeches were still held by their cut and fit over the hips.

Fabrics employed for the *habit* were silks, velvets or woolens. Vests were brocaded or embroidered, as embroidery had returned to favor for both men's and women's garments. Designs were more delicate, executed in silk, gold and silver thread, which was finer than that of the preceding century. The most popular ornamentation consisted of loops and buttons in metal, jewels or silk.

Greatcoats, or overcoats, were full with a flat collar and wide cuffs. The redingote, or riding coat, came from England in 1725 and was worn throughout the century. It often had two or three small shoulder capes.

The heels of men's shoes were lower, but still red for the noble and the gentleman at court, worn with blue or red silk stockings, clocked in gold or silver. Leggings or spatterdashes, buttoned or buckled at the side, became fashionable for riding. In the 'seventies appeared the large square buckles.

Also in the 'seventies, men took to wearing the boutonnière of artificial flowers.

At the beginning of the century, the full-bottomed wig was drawn to the back and tied at the nape of the neck with a black silk ribbon, which style was known as the "tie." The wig was now dressed up off the forehead, with a soft roll or bunches of curls at either side of the face. The bunches of curls were called "pigeon's wings." Pigeon's wings were replaced by set rolls over the ears about 1755, when the *cadogan, catogan* or "club style" began to appear.

In the cadogan wig, the back hair was looped under and tied with a concealed string or the *solitaire* of black taffeta, satin or velvet. The solitaire, which no doubt is the origin of the black tie, was the black ribbon tied to the wig in a bow at the back, with the ends—brought around over the white cravat and tied in a bow under the chin. Sometimes the solitaire was held in front by a diamond pin or a barette. The "Macaronies," or "exquisites," of England were the first to adopt the cadogan wig. The name of the wig is attributed to the first Earl of Cadogan, of earlier period.

Another popular style was the bagwig, in which the black silk bag, with draw string at the back of the neck, encased the ends of the wig. This idea is supposed to have originated with the French servant, who thus kept his hair covered when at work. The solitaire was attached under the bag and the ends carried around the neck and fastened in front.

Among the many styles, there was the *ramillie* wig, of English origin, named in honor of the victorious battle of Ramillies in 1706, of Duke of Marlborough fame. The wig had one or two hanging braids tied top and bottom with black ribbon. Later, the end of the braid was often looped under and tied. Another was the knotted or full-bottomed wig, with several of its hanging curls tied in knots. The pigtail wig had its tail bound spirally by black ribbon and tied top and bottom.

White wigs were most popular in the first quarter of the century, changing to gray in the next quarter. From 1760, many wore their own hair dressed and powdered in wig fashion, but the use of powder declined. Under the wig, the head was shaved or close-cropped.

The hat of the period was the *tricorne,* three-cornered or cocked hat, edged with braid and trimmed with ostrich fringe or a ribbon band. It was fairly small, often being carried under the arm to avoid disturbing the wig.

The vogue of the cane continued, in various woods, including bamboo and ivory.

In women's costume, the gown designed by and named after the painter Watteau is the principal style of the Regency. The original Watteau gown was a loose sack or dress worn over a tight bodice and very full underskirt. The loose folds, falling from the shoulders in back, became part of the skirt. The front of the gown varied in design, either hanging loose or fitting at the waist, worn closed or open, and if open revealing a bodice and underskirt. The elbow-length sleeves had vertical pleats and soft wide cuffs, but from the 'forties the pagoda sleeve took hold, tight from shoulder to elbow, where it spread into flaring ruffles, headed by ribbon bows. The neck in front was low and the stomacher was ornamented with ribbon loops in graduated size or lacings of narrow ribbon finished with gauze or lace known as the *modestie*—in English the "modesty bit."

In the 'thirties, the Watteau gown became the *robe à la française,* and, by 1770, this loose gown was the formal dress for court functions, developing six box pleats, stitched flat to the back and ending in a train. Under the upper part of the gown, attached to the bodice, was a fitted lining which was laced in back.

The *robe volant,* or flying gown, was a variation of the gown with the Watteau pleats. The soft pleats flowed from shoulder to hem, both back and front. The dress was usually ankle-length, worn over a wide hoop which created an undulating movement as the wearer walked. The style lasted to the end of the reign.

Panniers returned in 1718 by way of England, where they had already been in fashion for six or seven years under the name of hoop skirt, but did not really take hold in France until 1730. The hoops were of reed or whalebone, held together by ribbons, basket-like, thus the French name *panier* meaning basket. The frame work was covered with taffeta or brocade, and was called accordingly a taffeta or brocade hoop. The hoop was first funnel-shaped, but from the 'thirties to the 'forties grew very broad at the sides and flat front and back. The circumference is said to have reached, later, eighteen feet. A Mademoiselle Margot, a coutourière, invented an inexpensive pannier, which made the fashion accessible to women of all classes.

About 1750, the hoop was divided into two sections with pocket openings in the sides, from which, on the inside, hung pockets in the form of bags. The wearer reached the pockets through openings in both the outer and under skirts.

In a popular style, called "pocket panniers," the panniers were formed by pulling the drapery through the pocket holes. This dress, which was usually ankle-length, also had the box pleats attached to the shoulders in back. This fashion, by the next reign, had spread to the bourgeoisie, finally becoming the habitual costume of servants. See Page 216.

The extremely broad panniers on which the elbows could be rested were named "elbow panniers," and the very small ones, worn for morning or negligee, *considérations*.

The feminine riding habit continued along masculine lines in coat and waistcoat with cravat. Its full skirt was worn over panniers, and the three-cornered hat topped the costume. By the 'forties, women were changing their costume three or four times a day. There were special toilettes for morning or negligee, walking, theatre, supper, and formal for night.

The "pair of bodies," bodice or corset was long and slim, laced in back, made of heavy linen or brocade, reinforced by whalebone, still a confining garment but of lighter weight than its predecessor. It had eyelets on tabs below the waist, to which the underskirt was held by lacing.

Fabrics changed from heaviness to daintiness in crisp taffetas, flowered, striped or plain, lustrous satins and damasks, lutestring, or lustring, flowered lawns and dimities, in pastel shades and all trimmed with lace, ribbons and artificial flowers. A fine soft lace in natural silk, known as *blonde lace,* appeared in 1757 and became very fashionable. Flower and fruit motifs on fabrics were just under natural size.

Aprons continued in fashion, now short and of silk, satin or gauze, edged with fringe or bobbin lace either in gold or silver.

Petticoats of silk or satin with wadding between the outer fabric and a lining, were quilted in attractive designs. These underskirts were especially popular in England and the American Colonies.

There were all styles of scarflike wraps and mantillas, edged with ruffles and ruches; in fact, the vogue of the shawl is supposed to have had its beginning in the 'seventies of this reign. These wraps were short for summer and long for winter, some had armholes and some had loose hoods attached. The long winter *mante,* or mantle, was fur-lined throughout and buttoned down the length of the front. The summer mantilla was draped over the head, loosely tied in front or crossed over the bosom and tied in back.

From 1730, collarettes of ribbon and lace were worn around the throat. Gloves were of light-colored kid or silk, and silk and lace mittens were of the period.

The hair was dressed simply, close to the head, off the forehead and up in back, until past the middle of the century. From about 1750, the front hair, cut short, was dressed off the forehead with the ends set in curls, going over the head from ear to ear. A dressing of pomatum and flour held the ringlets in place, and a tiny black taffeta cushion stuffed with straw or cotton supported the curls. False hair, flowers and aigrettes were also attached to the cushion. Powder was used on the hair for full dress. From 1760, the coiffure gradually increased in height. An interesting note is that, by 1769, there were twelve hundred hairdressers in Paris.

For everyday wear until the 'fifties, small dainty caps of lawn and lace were worn, but, from 1760, they grew in all dimensions with the coiffure, frills and ruchings framing the face and lappets hanging in back. About the 'seventies, hats became fashionable. They were of straw, felt and fabric, in all styles, worn at all angles, trimmed with lace, ribbons, feathers, artificial flowers and fruits and jewelled buckles. A great favorite was the leghorn hat encircled with a wreath of flowers.

Make-up, though still applied too freely, was done with more artistic technique than in the preceding reign. Paint and powder were a court requirement and patches of all shapes and sizes were worn. Madame de Pompadour and Madame du Barry both made extravagant use of perfume, a fashion which the whole court followed. All personal articles and clothes were scented. There were exquisite perfume cases and rings with tiny compartments for holding scent. Parasols did away with the necessity of wearing the mask. The parasol became smaller and could now be carried by the lady herself. Parasols or sunshades did not close. The invention of a folding frame was employed only for the *parapluie,* or rain umbrella.

Slippers of satin and brocade, with the high Louis XV heel, slim and curving, were worn; they were also made of kid in all colors, embroidered in gold and silver, and ornamented with buckles in gold and cut steel. Silk stockings had gold or silver clocks, and white cotton stockings, which were popular, had colored clocks.

Less jewelry was worn but there were such gadgets as patch boxes, vanity boxes and rouge pots. Watches were beautiful works of art. Women carried the lorgnette, and men the single glass, or *perspective.* Tall, gold-headed canes for feminine use were made of scented wood, tortoise shell and ivory, and were held halfway down the stick. Very small handkerchiefs embroidered in colored silks and edged with costly lace were used as ornaments, while the most beautiful fans were created in the eighteenth century.

The folding fan had sticks of ivory, tortoise shell, mother-of-pearl, gold or silver. Satin, kid or vellum leaf, stretched over the sticks, was decorated with miniature scenes, painted by the great artists of the day. Women, like the men, wore the small bouquets of artificial flowers. Small bags and purses were carried throughout the century, made of the costliest fabrics, beautifully embroidered in silk, steel, gilt or colored beads. Of that period is the beaded bag of heavy silk thread done with crochet hook or knitting needle. Muffs grew larger for both sexes, fashioned of rich furs and finished with frills of lace and ribbon.

A novelty in jewelry of the eighteenth century was paste, or *strass,* invented by a German jeweller named Strasser. Buckles, buttons, court and military orders glittered with the clear, brilliant sparkling stones. Paste seems to have been considered more as a substitute than an imitation, and was worn by the aristocracy. The French employment of paste surpassed that of the other countries in delicacy of design, and the periods of Louis XV and Louis XVI have been noted as the "golden age of paste."

Louis-XV

cloth coat-silk vest and breeches-buttons and buttonholes-white lawn shirt, cravat and jabot-powdered bag-wig with pigeon's wings- cocked hat-gold braid-black leather shoes with buckles-sword-cane-1st half 18th C.

habit of silk-coat-vest-breeches-buttons and buttonholes-white lawn shirt, cravat and jabot-cocked hat with braid-powdered bag-wig-pigeon's wings-leather shoes with buckles-1st half 18th C.

heavy cloth redingote-buttons and buttonholes-leather belt-habit cuffs showing-Ramillies hat with braid-powdered bag-wig-pigeon's wings-buckled leather shoes-sword-muffler-1740

habit with shortened vest-lawn shirt, cravat, jabot-handkerchief in coat pocket-watch fobs-clocked stockings-leather shoes-large buckles-sword-powdered cadogan wig-hat under arm-3rd quarter 18th C.

Louis-XV

"flying gown" of pink taffeta-underskirt same edged with gimp-lingerie neck and sleeve ruffles-lingerie cap with lappets-powdered hair-embroidered yellow slippers-green stockings-1st quarter 18th C.

changeable pink and green striped satin-gray satin stomacher-tiny peplum-lingerie ruffles and cap-twisted lace scarf-black silk mantilla with self ruche-gray kid gloves-1st quarter 18th C.

"Watteau pleats" and train-taffeta gown and underskirt-bowknot-lace frills-lace edged lingerie cap with lappets-2nd quarter 18th C.

"flying gown" of satin-underskirt same-tightly laced underbodice-velvet bows-pagoda sleeves-lingerie cap and frills-powdered hair-1730

Louis XV

taffeta with self ruchings-double panniers-satin bows-jewelled buttons-pagoda sleeves with lace ruffles-collarette of bowknots and pearls-satin slippers-powdered hair with velvet and satin ribbon and pearls-earrings-1762

"robe à la française" with pleats in back-old blue taffeta-scalloped edged ruffles-rose ribbon bows, stomacher and collarette-pagoda sleeves-lace ruffles-pink roses, green foliage-rose in powdered hair-fresh flowers on shoulder-embroidered gold slippers-pearl bracelets-1760's

satin gown with lace frills-powdered hair with velvet ribbon-middle 18th C.

"robe à la française"-satin witb contrasting colored underskirt-pleats stitched to fitted bodice-pagoda sleeves-lingerie frills-self ruching on skirt-powdered hair-cap with bowknot-3rd quarter 18th C.

Louis XV

silk hood with shoulder cape-mantilla of flowered silk presumably held to the figure by a cord or ribbon belt-1730's

riding habit with double panniers-coat and waistcoat resembling masculine cut-lingerie blouse-powdered hair with bowknot-tricorne-boots-1st half 18th C.

fur-lined mantle of cloth-silk hood with shoulder cape-1755

taffeta cloak with wide self ruching at waist-elbow sleeves with deep cuffs-silk hood with ribbon lappets-lorgnette-1720's

RTW

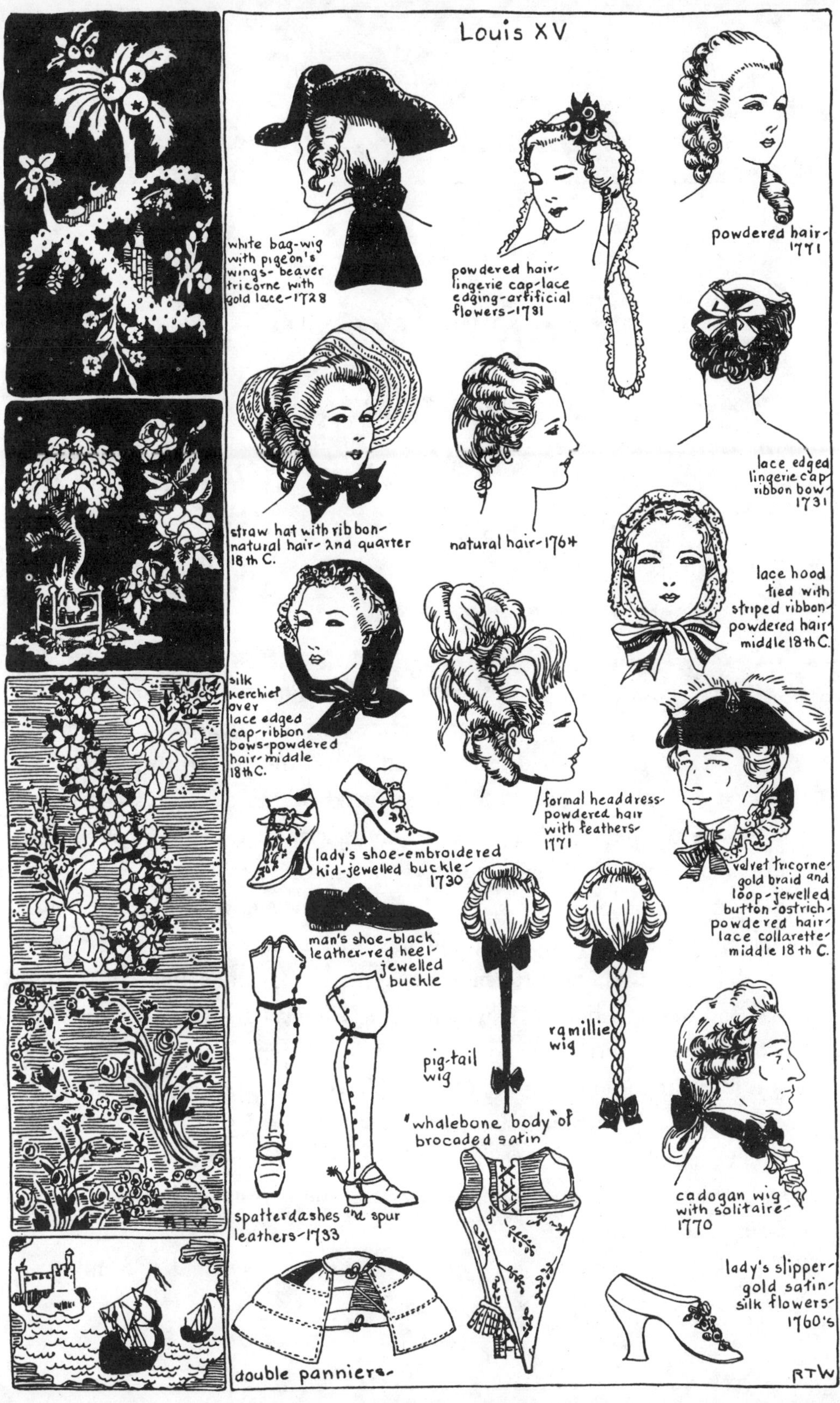
Louis XV
white bag-wig with pigeon's wings-beaver tricorne with gold lace-1728
powdered hair-lingerie cap-lace edging-artificial flowers-1731
powdered hair-1771
straw hat with ribbon-natural hair-2nd quarter 18th C.
natural hair-1764
lace edged lingerie cap ribbon bow-1731
lace hood tied with striped ribbon-powdered hair middle 18th C.
silk kerchief over lace edged cap-ribbon bows-powdered hair-middle 18th C.
formal headdress-powdered hair with feathers-1771
lady's shoe-embroidered kid-jewelled buckle-1730
velvet tricorne-gold braid and loop-jewelled button-ostrich-powdered hair-lace collarette-middle 18th C.
man's shoe-black leather-red heel-jewelled buckle
ramillie wig
pig-tail wig
"whalebone body" of brocaded satin
cadogan wig with solitaire-1770
spatterdashes and spur leathers-1733
lady's slipper-gold satin-silk flowers-1760's
double panniers-
RTW

Chapter Thirty-one

Louis Sixteenth—Marie Antoinette

To the French Revolution—1774–1789

The beginning of this reign was a period of great extravagance, artificialty and daintiness. The mode had spread to all classes and was worn by all who could afford to spend. By 1780, came a complete change toward simplicity, with a dominant English influence in both men's and women's costume. The English have held, up to the present day, the leadership they now acquired for the first time, as arbiters in designing men's apparel.

There was slight difference between the masculine mode of Louis XV and that of Louis XVI. The *habit à la française* still existed but was worn only at court. The coat opened wide in front over the vest. Color was more important, with a distinct preference for apple green and light yellow. Waistcoats were usually white, with colored silk embroideries in bouquets and garlands of flowers. There was a tremendous vogue for spotted and ribbed silks. Dress suits were often white with handsomely embroidered waistcoats.

The *frac,* or frock coat, origin of the cutaway, had a turndown collar, no visible pockets, the coat itself usually plain green or striped yellow. Near the end of the reign, striped fabrics dominated in frock coats. About 1780 appeared the English frock coat, usually buttoned in front, the waistcoat showing below and the frilled jabot of soft batiste at the neck. It, too, had the collar of contrasting fabric. Woolen fabrics were usurping the place of silk in the masculine coat.

Also of English derivation was the *redingote à la lévite,* a double-breasted long coat with turndown collar and two or three shoulder capes. The English also called the garment the carrick.

From under the vest, on either side of the breeches, hung tassels or fobs attached to key, locket or a pair of watches, the second watch often being false. The wearing of two fobs or charms originated with the idea of concealing the closing of the breeches to either side of the center front. However, watches were often made in pairs, probably so that, one failing, the other would still give service. Buttons were enameled, painted or of cut steel.

Breeches were very tight, fitting the thighs and ending below the knees, where they fastened with buckles, buttons and occasionally bunches of ribbon. The stocking was often rolled over the breeches, with the garter concealed therein. Both silk and cotton stockings were usually white, and silk stockings for dress wear were clocked with gold or silver.

Men's shoes retained their square toes and, for dress, red heels. Large square buckles were still worn, but their vogue began to decline in the 'seventies, giving way to string ties. Escarpins, or pumps, low-cut slippers with a thin flexible sole, were fashionable, also walking boots of soft black leather. *Guêtres,* or gaiters, known in England as leggings, or spatterdashes, were worn as protection in bad weather. They were of leather and buttoned at the sides.

Black was worn more and more as an economy by gentle people of small means, because it saved the expense of a mourning costume. Upon the death of a royal person, custom required every one to observe such an event occurring among crowned heads. The period of mourning, lasting a year, was reduced to a period of three months just before the Revolution.

The wigs of the preceding period and hair arranged in a postiche were worn for the greater part of this reign, but by 1779 wigs had begun to disappear, to be retained only by men in certain professions. The principal styles were the bagwig and the cadogan. The wig or hair was dressed high off the forehead, often with a single large roll over the top from ear to ear or with two smaller rolls over each ear. The Brutus, or "hedgehog," cut was popular in the 'eighties, its name describing very well the style.

The tricorne, or cocked hat, of Louis XV continued to be worn. From the 'eighties, a very small version was especially favored by the Macaronies of England, where it was known as the Nivernois hat, so named after the French diplomatist and writer.

The Macaronies were a group of idle young Englishmen, who, upon returning from a tour of Italy, formed the Macaroni Club in London, and thereafter everything extreme in dress was attributed to them.

The most popular hat of the period was a variation of the Swiss military hat. It was really a bicorne, having a front and back flap, with the highest point or corner in center front, caused by a pinching of the front flap, thereby resembling a tricorne. The French called their version the *Androsmane,* and the English named theirs the *Khevenhüller,* or *Kevenhuller,* after the famous Austrian field-marshal of that name. It set comfortably down on the head.

A forerunner of the top hat made its appearance in the 'eighties, a high crown with rolling brim. Other styles were the Holland, or Pennsylvania hat with flat crown and rolling brim, the Quaker hat with low crown and rolling brim and the jockey hat. The jockey hat also had a low crown, but its brim of moderate width was bent down in front to shade the eyes. This hat came from England, where it was first worn by grooms, then adopted by their masters. It was ornamented with a band and a cockade at the side or a buckle in the front.

The lingerie shirt was of fine material, with jabot and wrist ruffles of plain or embroidered lawn and lace. With the decline of the vogue of the wig in the 'seventies, the neckcloth appeared, lasting well into the nineteenth century. It was wrapped around the neck and tied in front in a soft bow.

Malacca canes were of all heights, with various styles of heads and tasselled cords and muffs were still used by the masculine sex in winter. Lace-trimmed handkerchiefs and exquisite snuffboxes were other accessories.

In feminine costume, all Europe now followed the French fashions, of which Marie Antoinette and her modiste, Mlle. Rose Bertin, were the dictators. Large dolls dressed in the latest creations, called "fashion dolls" or "fashion babies," were sent periodically from Paris to the capitals of the other countries, to be exhibited to the eagerly waiting fashionable world. There were many changes of style in this period, but from 1784 to 1789 the changes were constant.

Still worn was the whalebone corset, with eyelets in the tabs around the waist, to which the underskirt was laced. The garment was softer and more normal in shape, curving in decidedly to accentuate the small waist and curving out above to accent the line of the bosom. It gave a long, slim look to the body and was laced in back. Very wide side panniers were fashioned of metal bands connected by tapes, by means of which the hoops could be drawn up under the arms. In the 'eighties, panniers, though still retained for formal court wear, were supplanted by the *tournure,* or bustle.

The most extravagant use of ornamentation, pearls and jewels by the court marked the years 1776 to 1778, even slippers being encrusted with diamonds.

Gowns were made of plain, striped and painted satins, plain and striped taffetas, soft lustrous velvets and brocades. The motifs used on figured fabrics were small and dainty, festoons of flowers, bowknots, flower baskets and the like. Trimmings consisted of lace, tulle, ribbon and fur. Over the shoulders were draped scarfs of lace, tulle and ribbon. Hoop and pannier gowns were lavishly ornamented, knots of ribbon, puffs, loops, garlands of flowers, fluted flounces or quilting, all on one dress. Straw-colored satin was a great favorite; other colors were apple green, lemon yellow, canary yellow and pink.

The black silk laces of Chantilly were introduced in the last quarter of this century and were popular for scarfs and headdresses. Blonde lace, that soft fine lace of natural silk, was a great favorite of the Queen's. All parts of the costume were given curious names, an amusing example being *puce,* or flea color. The bowknot of ribbon which hid the fastening of the décolletage on the bosom was called "perfect contentment."

The sacque, or *robe à la française,* of the preceding reign, with its very broad panniers and stitched back pleats, became full dress for court, theatre and balls. It was most elaborate, ornamented with garlands of artificial flowers, furbelows, pearls and other gems.

The pocket panniers of the last period were taken up by the bourgeoisie, eventually becoming the costume of servants. The principal styles of gowns of this period were the *polonaise,* the *circassienne,* the *anglaise,* the *lévite,* the *caraco,* the English and the Queen's gown.

The *polonaise* lasted from 1776 to 1787, and its special feature consisted of three panniers, one back and two side sections, which rounded away in front. The panniers of the polonaise were drawn up on cords and could also be let down to form a flying gown. The cords were run through slots and were finished with tassels or rosettes, although later the panniers were sewn in position, with the cords simply ornamental.

The *circassienne* was a variation of the polonaise. It too had three panniers run on cords, but very short and of even length. The gown had double sleeves, that is, the outer bodice had short cap sleeves worn over the longer sleeves of the underbodice.

The *caraco* was a gown with long basque, finished with a peplum ruffle, and often a train, called a *figaro,* was attached under the peplum.

The *lévite* gown was really a type of redingote with train. Its creation was inspired by the Englishman's redingote of the same period. There was a definite redingote gown, which had a jacket, double breasted and with wide lapels. This costume was considered "very mannish."

The masculine wig and cravat, the redingote with its capes, were adopted for horseback, while from under the waistcoat hung the two watches or charms, such as the men wore. Shoes with low heels and a "switch stick" completed the attire of the "Amazons."

The Queen's playing at farming brought about a vogue for cotton prints, sheer aprons and fichus, large simple leghorn hats combined with feathers and jewels.

A very popular style, from 1781, was the *chemise à la reine,* worn by Marie Antoinette. Comparatively speaking, it was a simple frock made of sheer cotton or light silk. The neck was low in front, finished with a full standing ruffle. The skirt was edged with a deep-fluted flounce and a soft, wide sash was tied around the waist. It is noteworthy, as being the introduction of the lingerie frock into Europe. It was nevertheless a luxury, as cottons and prints were still imported from India.

In 1783, fashion suddenly changed from utter extravagance to extreme simplicity, and, by 1786, panniers, trains and trimming had all disappeared. There were several reasons for the change, the loss of immense fortunes, the writings of Jean-Jacques Rousseau, the country clothes of the Queen at the Petit-Trianon and the influence of English simplicity in dress.

About the middle of the century, at Jouy, France, had been established a shop for the hand-block printing of linen, cambric and cotton, which now came into its own with the vogue for *indiennes,* as they were called. *Tulle* made its first appearance in this period, named after the town of its fabrication, Tulle, France.

The *robe à l'anglaise* was simple, rich-looking and artistic, a great delight to the portrait painters of the period. It was usually of satin in plain colors, with tight bodice and long full skirt, a soft full fichu finishing the neck. The sleeves varied from the long, slim shape to the soft, full elbow-length puff.

The fichu was a feature of the period, worn with the different styles of gowns. It was bunched above the small, tight waist, giving a pouter-pigeon look to the figure.

Sheer cottons, fine linens and cambrics were embroidered with white cotton, the finest embroidery being done in Saxony. Such fabrics were employed for scarfs, collars and cuffs. The apron was now all white, of soft cotton ornamented with needlework and drawn work.

In the beginning of the period, the hair rose high off the forehead, dressed over pads at the sides and back of the neck. For full dress, strings of pearls and flowers were added. Later, the hair was kneaded with pomatum and flour, twisted into rolls and curls and dressed over a cushion or pad of wool. False hair was added to build up the coiffure, from then growing to unbelievable heights, with every conceivable decoration placed on top. To rows of curls were added ribbons, flowers, laces, feathers, blown glass or straw, models of ships, coaches and windmills. The back hair was dressed in loose curls, in chignon or cadogan fashion.

There were many styles of headdress, but two unusual ones in the 'eighties were the coiffure *à la l'enfant* and *à la hérisson*. *L'enfant,* or "baby headdress," was cut short like a bob, due to the Queen's illness necessitating the cutting of the hair. The *coiffure à la hérisson,* or hedgehog fashion, appeared in 1778, resembling that of the men, cut fairly short in front, frizzed to the ends and brushed up high off the face, with long loose curls or the cadogan in back.

Toward the end of the period, powder, always used for full dress, was but lightly employed for ordinary wear. After her hair was dressed, the lady covered her face with a paper bag and powder was thickly applied. Pertaining to the elaborate headdress, contemporary advice was that the head should be "opened up" at least once a week.

The face was literally painted red and white, accented with various shapes of black taffeta patches. The use of heavily scented perfume declined, the Queen preferring delicate rose and violet odors.

As the size of the coiffure increased, so did the lingerie caps, or *bonnets,* as they were now called, the name bonnet having been applied to men's toques heretofore. The *dormeuse,* or sleeping bonnet, so named because it was also worn at night, hugged the head tightly, covering the cheeks, and was threaded with a ribbon tied into a bow on top of the head. The dormeuse of daytime wear was worn higher on the head, revealing the ears and back of the head.

Then came the *demi-bonnets* and bonnet-hats imported from England. They were very large, with soft full crowns, wide brims which almost hid the face, and they were usually trimmed with ribbon bands and loops. The large cap was known in England as the *mob-cap,* or Ranelagh mob, because much worn in the Ranelagh Gardens, a place of entertainment founded by Lord Ranelagh upon his estate and frequented by the fashionables. The English name for the small cap was *close Joan.*

The bonnets called *thérèse* and *caliche* or calash were, according to a French description, cages. They covered the huge coiffures and were therefore very large. The thérèse was of gauze or tulle, sometimes of black taffeta edged with tulle and made over wires or whalebone. The calash had reed or whalebone hoops which could be raised or lowered by a ribbon like the hood of a carriage.

About 1783, with the lowered style of hairdressing, bonnets became smaller and hats appeared. Hats were of felt or beaver, in all sizes and shapes, worn at all angles, trimmed with plumes, ribbons, fruits and flowers. Very wide brims originated in England, as did the most elegant hat of all time, known today as the Marlborough or Gainsborough hat, perpetuating in the mode not only the name of the British painter, Gainsborough, but also that of his sitter, the Duchess of Marlborough.

Straw hats, with very wide brims and a simple ribbon band around the low crown, became popular during the Queen's "milkmaid period." That style, considered a "rustic fashion," also came from England, where people were very fond of country life. Straw was new for fashionable hats, and enjoyed quite a vogue, great quantities being imported from Italy, leghorn, horsehair and chip being the most fashionable.

The pelisse, a fur-trimmed wrap, capelike with armholes and broad collar, continued to be worn. In the winter, large fur muffs protected the arms and hands against the cold. Muffs were occasionally tiny, of silk and satin with ribbon bows and embroidery. They were carried in the summer and to balls. Long gloves of soft light-colored kid were worn during the whole century.

Slippers of satin, brocade and kid were the fashion, with moderately high heels, sometimes covered with white kid. The back seam was occasionally encrusted with gems. Women of quality wore fabric slippers of reddish brown or pigeon gray. Leather slippers were worn only by the demimonde and the lower class. Stockings were white in both silk and cotton.

Jewels were many and exquisite in necklaces, lockets, beautiful crosses, ivory writing tablets, with tassels, needlecases, handsome watches and eyeglasses mounted in gold and enamel. The use of paste or strass in jewelry reached its height in this period. Cut steel was employed for buttons and buckles. Necklaces were finally supplanted by a simple velvet ribbon tied around the neck. Later, a pendant or miniature was suspended from the ribbon. Exquisite and costly fans remained in vogue. The boutonnière of fresh or artificial flowers was worn by both sexes.

Dress for children had begun to change from the tightly fitted clothes of their elders. A portrait of Marie Antoinette with her two children, painted in 1785 by Wertmüller, portrays the Dauphin in long trousers and a short buttoned jacket with a frill at the open neck. The little girl wears a simple frock of English style, also with a frill at the low round neck and a sash about the waist.

Louis XVI - Marie Antoinette

Louis XVI - Marie Antoinette

pocket panniers-
heavy silk with
lingerie fichu
and pleated ruffles-
powdered hair-
lingerie cap-
1775

polonaise gown-
striped and plain
silk-cords, tassels
and ruches-hat
with turned-up
back-ribbon, ostrich
and aigrettes-neck
ribbon-satin
slippers with
buckles-
1776

circassienne gown-
silk in two colors-
Medici collar-
boutonnière-
tassels-hat with
flowers, ribbon,
ostrich, pleated
frill-powdered
hair-fan-satin
shoes-buckles-
handkerchief-
1780

RTW

caraco gown of
hunter's green
silk-white lawn
frills, fichu and
apron-black hat
with dotted rose
ribbon-white
ostrich-blond hair
in cadogan-
fan-
1785

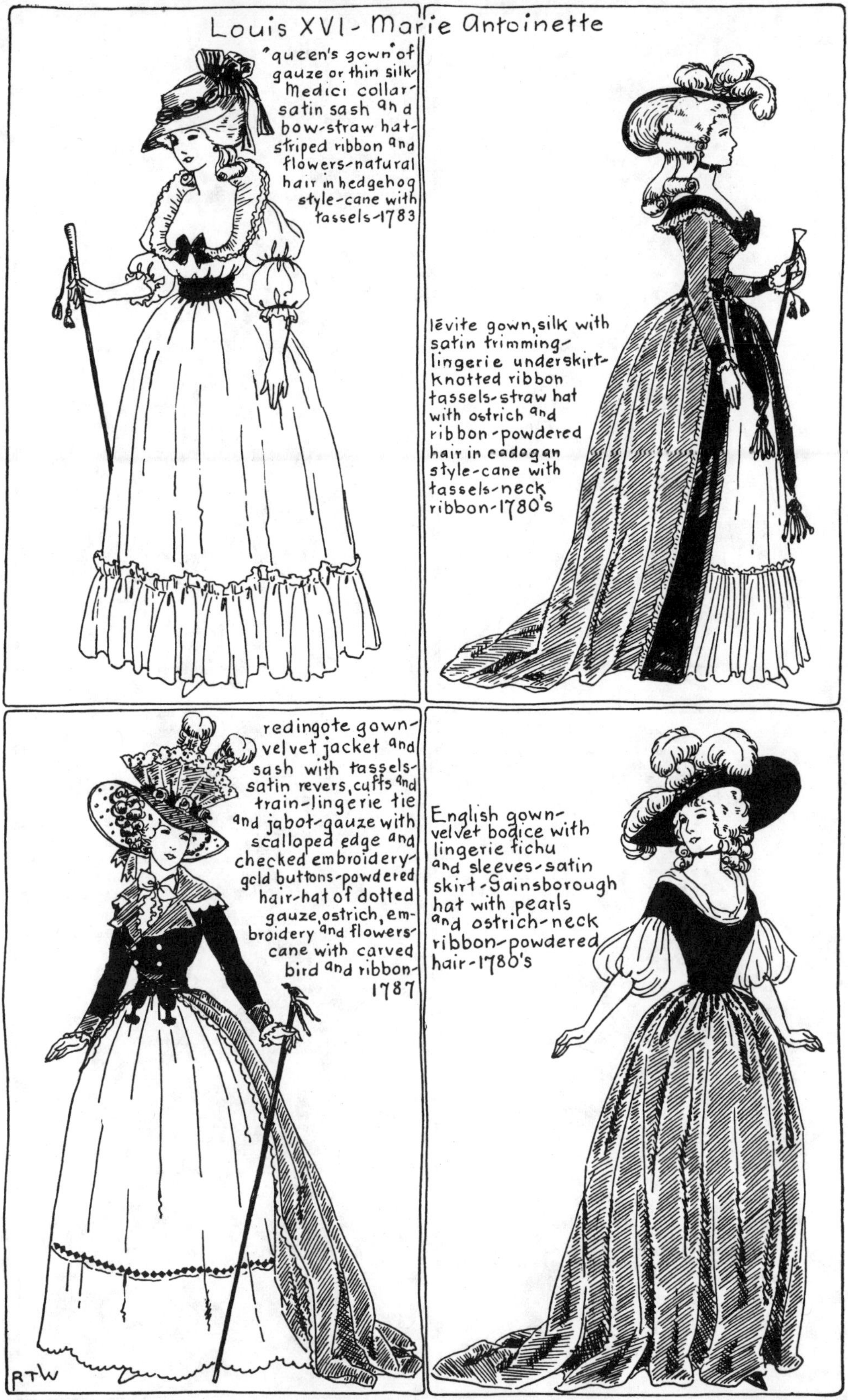
Louis XVI - Marie Antoinette
"queen's gown" of gauze or thin silk-Medici collar-satin sash and bow-straw hat-striped ribbon and flowers-natural hair in hedgehog style-cane with tassels-1783
lévite gown, silk with satin trimming-lingerie underskirt-knotted ribbon tassels-straw hat with ostrich and ribbon-powdered hair in cadogan style-cane with tassels-neck ribbon-1780's
redingote gown-velvet jacket and sash with tassels-satin revers, cuffs and train-lingerie tie and jabot-gauze with scalloped edge and checked embroidery-gold buttons-powdered hair-hat of dotted gauze, ostrich, embroidery and flowers-cane with carved bird and ribbon-1787
English gown-velvet bodice with lingerie fichu and sleeves-satin skirt-Gainsborough hat with pearls and ostrich-neck ribbon-powdered hair-1780's
RTW

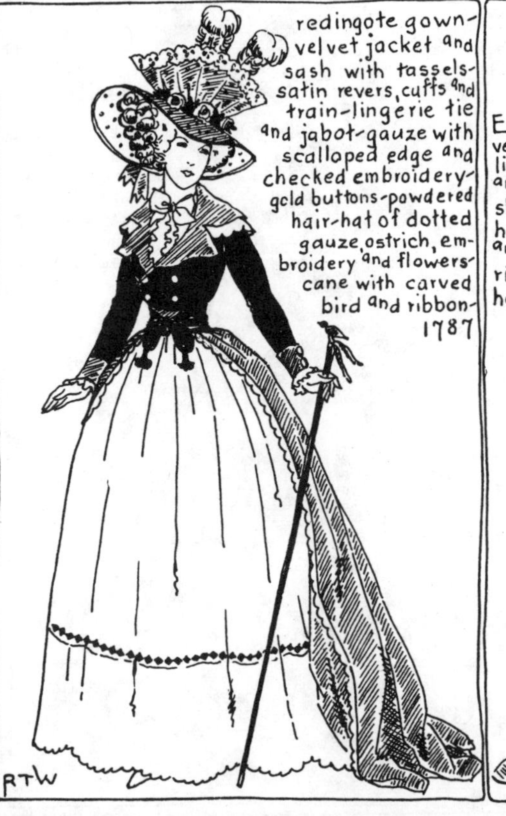

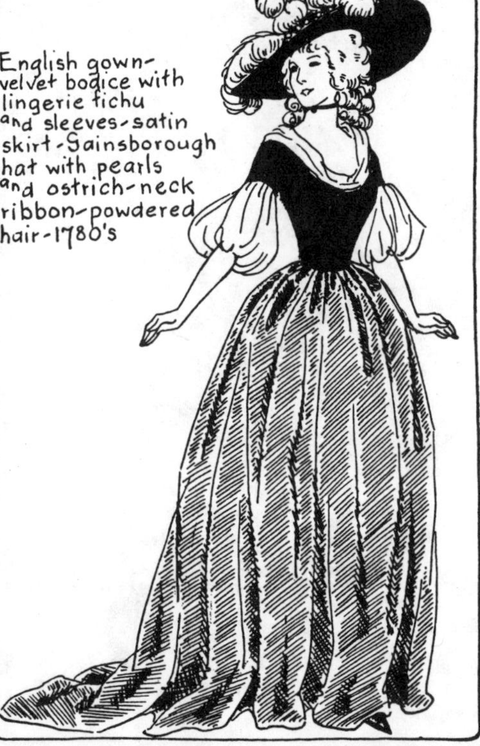

Louis XVI - Marie Antoinette

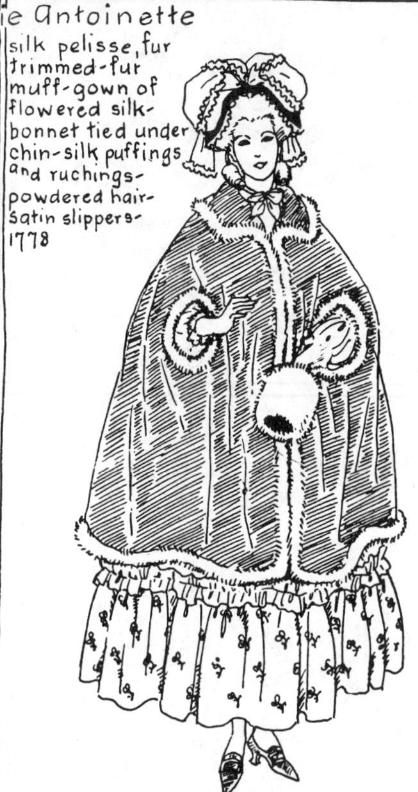

Louis XVI-Marie Antoinette
dormeuse bonnet-sheer muslin-satin ribbon-1770's
man's coiffure-natural hair-1780's
dormeuse bonnet-sheer muslin-taffeta ribbon-1770's
hedgehog and pigtail-1780's
powdered hair-thérèse of sheer black-satin band-colored bow-1784
back view of calash
hedgehog-1788
calash of black silk shirred on wire hoops-1780's
Quaker beaver hat-ribbon and buckle-1780's
beaver hat-natural hair in cadogan-late 1780's
Pennsylvania hat-beaver with ribbon-powdered hair in cadogan-1780's
lady's riding boot-1780's
formal headdress-powdered-cadogan-pearls, flowers and feathers-1780's
silk kerchief-powdered hair-ribbon-back in cadogan-1780's
folding metal panniers with tapes
RTW

Chapter Thirty-two

The French Revolution

1789–1795

In the years before the Revolution, the mode had begun to change. A desire for simpler design in dress, less splendor and less class distinction was indicated. The English, with their love of country life, had already eliminated formality from their everyday clothes, and thus it came about that they became a distinct influence in the modish world.

With the crash of the upheaval, hoops, paint, powder, beauty patches, artificial flowers and fruit and magnificence in costume disappeared. A very few dared display elegance in public. Social life ceased with the ending of court, and fashion journals were no more. Information of the mode in Paris must be had from contemporary English and German sources. Evidence of social distinction by means of dress was abolished by the National Assembly. The privilege of wearing brocades, feathers, red heels and embroideries, now extended to the citizens, was scorned, surviving only in servants' costume.

The standard simplicity of masculine costume worn today dates from the French Revolution. The principal change was the substitution of trousers for breeches or culottes. The wearing of trousers created a new trade, the manufacturing of suspenders, and caused stockings to shorten into socks.

The trousers opened in front by means of a panel buttoned to the vest by three buttons and were called *pantalons à pont,* bridge trousers, the panel operating like drawbridge. These trousers, hitherto worn only by British sailors, were accompanied by either a vest or jacket, named a *carmagnole*. The carmagnole was originally worn by Piedmont workers who came from "Carmagnola," and the deputies of Marseilles took the garment to Paris, where it was adopted by the Revolutionaries.

Those who wore trousers were called *sans-culottes,* meaning "without breeches," differentiating them from the aristocrat, but eventually the term came to signify the patriot. The red bonnet or cap, symbol of liberty with its cockade, completed the costume of the patriot or democrat.

The red liberty bonnet or cap varied in shape, being of Phrygian origin, or with hanging pointed crown, or just a skullcap with the pointed crown, but always ornamented with the tricolor cockade. The large felt hat with brim held up in front by the cockade was also seen. The red was always placed between the blue and the white.

The patriot of 1789-1790 wore the frock coat, with high turndown collar and lapels, cut away in front with tail in back. His breeches were tight, descending below the knees, sometimes finished with ribbon loops.

Heels, buckles and rosettes disappeared with the Revolution, leaving a soft, heelless slipper fastened with plain strings, worn with white or striped silk stockings. The indecision as to the length of the trousers was settled by wearing boots. They were of soft, highly polished black leather, with light-brown leather turndown cuffs and bootstraps hanging at the sides. This was the English jockey boot, commonly known as the top boot. The white or striped stockings showed between boot top and stocking. Well-fitting gaiters were also the fashion.

Wigs continued to be worn but powder was sparingly applied, a fashion note of 1790 being the use of mouse-colored powder. The back hair was generally worn in a very short pigtail wound with narrow ribbon. In the army, the short pigtail or cue was often false, fashioned of chamois or black leather, with a tuff of hair at the end.

The tricorne, or three-cornered hat, disappeared, supplanted by the bicorne and a round shape with brim of even width, tall tapering crown encircled by a silk cord and the red, white and blue cockade at one side.

The anti-revolutionist wore a black turndown collar, as a sign of mourning, on a light-colored coat. He changed, in 1791, to a coat of green with rose collar. About 1792, elegants or muscadins, in protest against the negligee appearance of the sans-culottes, returned to the frock coat with lapels, its collar of brilliant contrasting color and the frilled shirt front. The fronts of the coat, ornamented with two rows of steel buttons, did not close. The frock-redingote fastened by means of tabs or frogs.

A *muscadine* is a pastille scented with musk, and the name was applied to effeminate men who overdressed and used quantities of this scent. The muscadine carried a short or long stick weighted with lead.

A costume called the "true patriot" became official in 1794. It consisted of the pantalons à pont, the carmagnole, a brown redingote with collar and lapels faced with red, sabots and a bonnet or low bicorne. However, it did not meet with success, and the Convention commissioned the painter David to create a national costume. David's design consisted of tight trousers with boots, a tunic and short coat, in an attempt to fill the requirements of an outfit suitable to the new social order and work.

As with that of the men, women's costume took on a simplicity, while retaining the basic lines of the style of the last years of the Louis XVI period. The only noticeable change was in the raised waistline. This fashion, which is wrongly referred to as English, was created by Rose Bertin in London, whither she and her assistants had fled.

The bodice was tightly laced from waist to breasts, emphasizing the bosom. Still more emphasis was given by a full fichu of sheer white fabric, usually tulle or gauze, tucked into the neck of the bodice. Full folds of satin were often added, causing the whole to reach the chin in pouter-pigeon effect. Sleeves were long and tight, skirts were full, shirred at the waist and worn over many petticoats.

A ban against silks and velvets caused the increase of simple figured cottons and linens. The soft full lingerie gown, called the *chemise à l'anglaise* with its crushed satin sash, was worn both summer and winter. Satin, sparingly used, was brownish green or dull blue, while mat-surfaced silks such as *crêpon de chine* were in plain color or simple stripes of one color.

There were high-crowned hats trimmed with flowers and ribbons, and bonnet-shaped hats with ribbon loops and streamers which tied under the chin. Ostrich plumes reappeared by the end of the period. Added to these were toques and caps of various shapes with puffed crowns, ribbon-trimmed. The peasant or milkmaid cap, called today the "Charlotte Corday cap" and termed by the English the mobcap, had a full crown, shirred frills, ornamented with the tricolor cockade. The national colors were used throughout the whole costume.

The prevailing coiffure was dressed low on top, sometimes parted in the middle, with soft puffs placed low at the sides, the back hair hanging in cadogan or ringlets.

Along with other aristocratic frivolities, heels of slippers disappeared. Instead was worn a soft, flat slipper of fabric or kid, cut low, sandallike in appearance, occasionally laced across the instep and round the ankle with ribbon. A tiny bow or edging finished the slipper.

By the end of this period, the feminine English redingote of the previous period had taken on a full shirred skirt in place of the broad silk train, and was made of cloth. While occasionally seen, the enveloping buttoned coat with its turndown collar and lapels did not really become the fashion until after 1800.

The embroidered handkerchief and the fan continued to be carried, but, in place of the exquisite and costly works of art of the preceding period, fans were smaller, made of tulle and gauze, spangled and scented.

Because of royal patronage, the lace factories were demolished, especially those of Chantilly, while some of the lacemakers were put to death and their patterns destroyed.

With the ending of this period, we find the democratic mode turning toward Ancient Greece and Rome for its inspiration.

It is recorded that shops carrying ready-made clothes, which filled the needs of the citizen and his wife, have existed in Paris since 1791.

The French Revolution

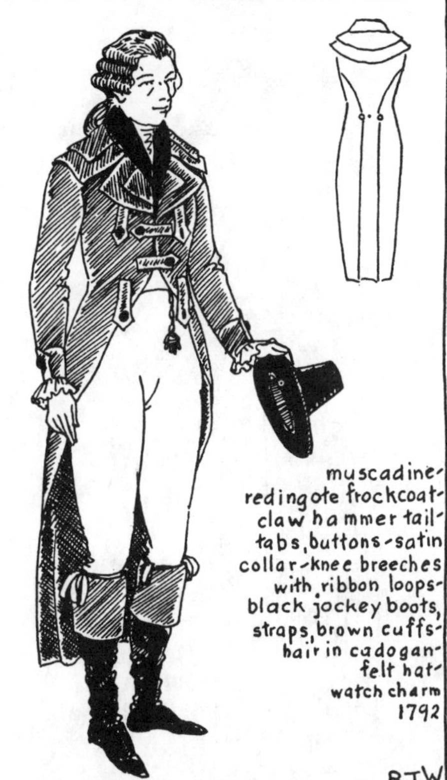

The French Revolution

The French Revolution
felt bicorne-
tricolor cockade-
hair in pigtail
the Phrygian
bonnet-red
wool with
tricolor
cockade-
earrings
soldier's bonnet-
red cuff, piping
and tassel-blue
crown-cockade
on left
side
bonnet of the
populace-
tricolor band
and rosette
bonnet of gauze
and taffeta-
tricolor
cockade-hair
in cadogan-
earrings
straw hat-
taffeta in
several colors-
flowers-hair
in cadogan
bonnet of tulle
and taffeta
felt hat with
satin ribbon
gauze bonnet-
ribbon loops
and ruching-
ostrich plume
straw bonnet
with
ribbon band
hair dressed
with flowered
ribbon
lady's hair
in cadogan
RTW

Chapter Thirty-three

Directoire

1795–1799

WITH the Directoire came the trend toward the classic style of Ancient Greece and Rome. Gradually the luxuries of living returned to daily life, even fashion journals making their reappearance.

The muscadines of the preceding period were to be seen in a group of young dandies, who went to extremes in their dress and were known as the *incroyables,* or *impossibles.* Their coats, which sloped away in front from the waist, when buttoned, had a high turndown collar, very wide lapels and were usually worn open. Sometimes the coat had bulky pleats across the back, giving the ugly effect of a hump; in fact, the incroyable strove for a careless, wrinkled appearance.

With this coat was worn a waistcoat of contrasting colored satin and a very full, sheer white cambric cravat. The cravat, or neckcloth, was loosely wound round the neck several times, often over padded cushions, so that it rose up over the chin, its ends tied in front.

The culottes, or breeches, ended below the knees, where they fastened with buttons and finished with ribbon loops. A strange idea was a button at the knee which came through a buttonhole in the breeches, presumably holding the stocking underneath. If the coat were of solid color, the waistcoat was striped, but, as often, the coat was of striped fabric and the waistcoat plain. Blue and white and green and white were favorite striped combinations.

When the refugee aristocrat returned to France, he wore, with his blond wig, the black collar as a sign of mourning on his light-colored coat. His green cravat or neckcloth was symbolic of royalty. The blond wig of the anti-revolutionist of the preceding period had now become the fashionable coiffure for both sexes.

The revolutionist finally gave up the sans-culottes, adopting the dress of the rest of the world, but wore a red collar on his coat, which gave rise to many bloody street quarrels between the "blacks" and the "reds."

The incroyable cut his hair raggedly in "dog's ears." His hat was extreme in size, either bicorne or with tall crown and hoop earrings hanging from his ears. Later, he changed to simple ringlets, lightly powdered, or the shaggy "Brutus" cut.

A more elegant costume was in vogue in this same period, consisting of frock coat and "hussar" breeches of dull blue cloth with black satin waistcoat, sometimes the breeches of satin. Hussar breeches were different only in that they were very tight. Favorite colors for breeches were canary yellow and bottle green, with the coat usually brown. The lapels of the coat were generally small and there was a small standing collar of black or violet velvet. The cravat, of fine white muslin or silk, in green, black or scarlet, was worn in the fashion of the incroyable. The hair was cut short in "Brutus" style.

There were boots of various heights and pumps, or *escarpins,* all of soft leather with pointed toes, worn with silk stockings, either plain white or striped on white.

The two watches were worn with the charms or fob seals hanging below the vest. The single eyeglass was fashionable, attached either to a long slim stick or a short one. Canes and short sticks of knotty and twisted wood, weighted with lead, were part of the ensemble.

The Directoire Period in the feminine mode is interesting in the fact of its being the first time that the creators of fashion turned back to another period for inspiration, this time to Greece and Rome of antiquity. Lacking the knowledge that we now possess of the ancient colors employed, it was thought, because of the aged and bleached-out ruins unearthed, that everything had been originally white. So white in interiors, fabrics, even complexions became the predominant color of the Directoire, the Consulate and the Empire Periods to follow.

Sheath or chemise gowns were the fashion, slightly fulled over the breasts with a sash tied directly under. The skirt hung soft and full, usually with a train which was carried over the arm or pulled through the girdle, often leaving the leg exposed to the knee. There were tunics, knee-length with a skirt below, and long slim gowns, slit up at the side, revealing a bare limb or flesh-colored tights. Sleeves were either long and tight or very short with long gloves covering the bare arm. For conservative ladies, there was the Roman style of gown with underslip.

Sheer white materials, in mull, linen, lawn and silk, were employed for these gowns, regardless of the season in which they were worn and this was instrumental in bringing on an epidemic of tuberculosis.

These "Athenians" and "Romans" wore very long narrow scarfs, and in winter carried very large muffs of fur or silk. Scarfs were of cashmere, cloth, serge, knitted silk and very often of gray rabbit wool, in such colors as flame, orange, apricot and black and white. Bonnet and scarf generally matched in color.

The white cashmere shawl was making its first appearance. The English and French armies, in the Egyptian campaign, took note of the Oriental shawl, thus bringing about the great vogue for the lovely Egyptian, Persian, Turkish and Indian shawls.

Although the Spencer jacket appeared in 1799, it did not become a fashion until the Consulate and Empire Periods, the same being true of the feminine redingote of English origin.

Since the lines of the figure were entirely revealed, no pockets were possible, necessitating the use of a small bag or reticule, which name was humorously changed to "ridicule." A larger receptacle for toilet articles was the *sabretache*. It hung from the belt or balantine and was rather like a cavalry bag, elaborately embroidered, fringed and tasselled.

The *merveilleuse* was the feminine counterpart of the incroyable. The neck of the short tight bodice of her diaphanous gown was very low. The sheer lingerie muffler, resembling the masculine neckcloth, was often added and worn in the same fashion. The merveilleuse went bareheaded or wore an extreme style of hat. It frequently was a bonnet with a very large brim rising high off the forehead, an exaggerated version of the English jockey hat.

Wigs came in again after 1794, with blond the favorite color. Madame Tallien wore a black wig, but is known to have had thirty wigs of various colors. She was a great beauty of royal Spanish birth, wife of Jean-Lambert Tallien, later Princess Chimay, and is credited with introducing the Greek gown to the mode under the Directoire.

The classic coiffure with the psyche knot and net was adopted, in which the hair was plaited or curled and waved like the ancients' and made glossy with "antique oil." The wide, jewelled band was also seen. In the hairdressing establishments were exhibited busts of goddesses and empresses of antiquity.

Then followed various bobs, particularly the Titus style, in which the hair was cut short and brushed in all directions from the crown of the head, with uneven ends hanging over the forehead and ears. There was also the feminine "dog's ears," long, straggling ends hanging at the sides of the face.

Much jewelry was worn, bracelets, necklaces, rings, cameos and, in the hair, bands or strings of pearls. Jewelled "corset belts" about two inches wide were placed just under the breasts.

The styles in headgear were many, in caps, turbans and bonnets of all sizes, fashioned principally of crêpe and tulle, trimmed with ribbons, feathers, aigrettes and flowers. It is interesting to note that the word bonnet, from this time, designates a woman's hat tied under the chin. In the Middle Ages, the name was used in connection with men's head covering; then, to the latter part of the eighteenth century, was applied generally to all feminine headgear.

Shoes followed the classic design in sandals or cothurns and buskins laced with narrow red bands, inset with gold and precious stones. More generally worn was the very soft, pointed, heelless slipper of kid in red or the favored color of apple green. Stockings, when worn, were of white silk with inserted pointed clocks of pink or lilac satin. The "Grecian lady," with her bare feet encased in sandals or buskins, wore jewelled rings on her toes and bracelets around her ankles.

Artificial flowers became an important accessory in feminine costume, and a gruesome fad of a moment was a neck ribbon of red velvet, recalling the victims of the guillotine.

It is to be noted that from this period, with the elimination of tradition or social background, especially in women's costume, there has been constant change and, in her desire for distinction in dress, woman discards the mode as soon as it reaches the masses.

Directoire

incroyable-cloth
costume-velvet collar
and cuffs-striped satin
waistcoat-muslin
cravat-button and
buttonhole on knee-
ribbon loops-leather
boots-silk stockings-
beaver hat-hair in
"dog's ears"-hoop
earrings-heavy
stick-1796

incroyable-cloth
costume-embroidered
satin revers-velvet
collar and cuffs-braid
and buttons-figured
silk waistcoat and
cravat-ribbon loops on
breeches-leather
pumps-silk stockings-
felt bicorne-cockade-
hair in "dog's ears"-
short heavy stick

incroyable-
cloth costume-
velvet collar and
cuffs-figured silk
cravat-crescent
brooch-ribbon
loops on breeches-
silk stockings-
leather pumps-
felt bicorne with
cockade-heavy
stick

a conservative
costume-cloth
with velvet
collar-muslin
cravat-light
silk waistcoat-
leather boots-
hair Brutus style-
beaver hat-short
light stick
RTW

Directoire

a "merveilleuse" in
white lingerie gown - silk
bodice - cashmere
scarf with fringe -
muslin cravat -
velvet bonnet - hair
cut in "dog's ears" -
clocked silk
stockings - red
kid slipper with
jewel - long
gloves - 1796

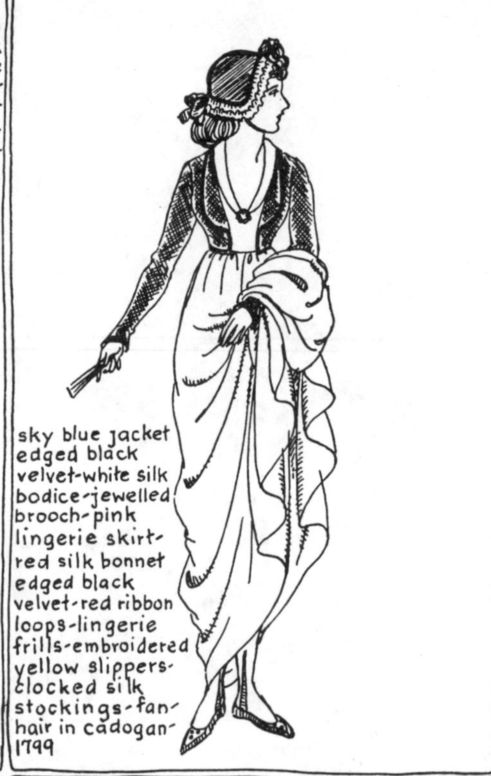
sky blue jacket
edged black
velvet - white silk
bodice - jewelled
brooch - pink
lingerie skirt -
red silk bonnet
edged black
velvet - red ribbon
loops - lingerie
frills - embroidered
yellow slippers -
clocked silk
stockings - fan -
hair in cadogan -
1799

Roman style in
embroidered linen -
balantine of heavy
cord, tassels, fringe
and embroidery -
earrings, chain
necklace and
brooch - sandals -
hair in Titus
cut
RTW

riding habit of
cloth - velvet
collar - striped
silk waistcoat -
muslin cravat -
felt bonnet with
cord and tassels -
hair in Titus cut -
clocked silk
stockings - kid
slippers - riding
crop

Directoire
poke bonnet worn by a "merveilleuse"- moiré silk-ribbon loops-lace frill-earrings
velvet béret-beads around band-ribbon flowers, aigrette, plume-hair in cadogan-sheer muslin neckcloth
man's beaver hat-cadogan wig with "dog's ears"-single eyeglass 1797
classic headdress-band with figures in relief-jewelled comb
Titus hair cut-straw bonnet-ribbons and violets-1797
hair in "dog's ears"-bicorne of felt-ribbon and cockade-green silk neckcloth-single eyeglass
swagger stick-about two feet long
reticule striped silk-ribbon and embroidery
classic buskin of red kid-rings on toes-1796
gauze turban with chin strap-aigrette-hair in Titus cut-earrings-1797
reticule of embroidered silk-tassels
red slipper with red ribbons-1796
white silk stocking-pink or lilac satin clock-apple green slipper-jewel-1798
hair in Brutus cut-scarlet silk neckcloth-jewel
RTW

Chapter Thirty-four

The French Consulate and First Empire

1799–1815

THE MODE was no longer dictated by Versailles but was launched at summer gardens and at public winter balls.

With the nineteenth century, pantaloons or trousers became definitely a feature of the masculine mode. In the opening years, under the Consulate, breeches still ended below the knees, the full-length trousers not making a more general appearance until the Empire. Breeches and trousers were tight-fitting, of elastic fabrics such as stockinet, buckskin or finely striped cotton, but the most popular material of the period for formal and informal wear, for young and old, in summer and in winter, was buff or yellow nankeen, imported from Nanking, China. Between 1810 and 1815, trousers and gaiters, made in one, appeared.

The coat of the incroyable of the Directoire left its mark in the bulky effect around the neck, also retaining its casual look of wrinkles around the armscye and through the body. Habits or suits were of cloth in dark blue, green and brown, with tobacco brown and pea green favorite colors. Waistcoats were usually of colored piqué or percale, with a border of contrasting color and a row of ball buttons down the front. Quilted piqué waistcoats appeared about 1811. The starched points of the shirt collar showed above the cravat or neckcloth. Two cravats were often worn, to give the desired thick look around the neck, a black satin over one of white linen.

Full dress consisted of velvet coat in color, black satin breeches, an elaborately embroidered silk waistcoat and a shirt having frilled wrist ruffles, a jabot and neckcloth. The powdered tie wig, bicorne and sword accompanied this habit, which was worn for evening and all ceremonial occasions.

For winter wear, there were two styles of greatcoats, both double-breasted: the redingote, a fitted coat and the carrick with its several capes. Both had a rather wide square collar which in winter was often of astrakhan. The single-breasted did not appear until the end of the Empire Period.

Only hats with narrow brims and tall crowns were worn, but brims and crowns varied in shape. They were fashioned of felt, made from beaver, shaved or long-haired angora, in the summer, of straw; and the colors were gray, beige and black. A silk cord or galloon encircled the crown, fastened by a steel buckle. The polished tall hat invented in Florence, Italy, in 1760, appeared in 1803, but was not adopted until 1823. The process of polishing was not perfected until the 'thirties.

The string or ribbon, laced through the béret of the Renaissance to hold the hat to the head, reappeared in the tall hat for hunting. An inner band was drawn tight by a narrow ribbon, the leather sweatband with the tiny bow in the modern hat being the remains of that idea.

Boots were worn with breeches and under trousers. They were elegant, well-fitted, usually of British make, of soft black leather, the white stocking often showing between boot and breeches. Short gaiters appeared about 1804. Low-cut escarpins, or pumps having very flat heels or none at all, were worn with striped or plain white silk or wool stockings. Trousers brought in the short stocking or sock for men.

The English jockey boot continued in favor, with cuffs of buff or chamois leather, or gray or beige cloth. The hussar, or Souvaroff boot, named after the Russian general, appeared around 1800. It was cut lower in back than in front, the front often ornamented with a swinging tassel. It varied in height, and was known in England as the Hessian boot. Another boot of military style was popular, high over the knee in front and cut out below the knee in back. Though known as the Wellington boot, it is seen worn by Napoléon in many of his portraits.

The Brutus haircut was the vogue, wigs and powder having disappeared in the masculine world. Slim, small bamboo sticks or riding whips were carried.

In the feminine costume, the mode of the Directoire Period continued in the semi-transparent lingerie chemise gown, belted under the breasts and worn over a sheer slip, sometimes of thin taffeta. The continued wearing of sheer cottons in winter brought on an epidemic of influenza in Paris in 1803, which was called "muslin disease."

A variation of the classic style was the wearing of a tunic of colored silk, satin or velvet over the white sheath gown. In materials, there were fine muslin, batiste, lawn, mull, also tulle, gauze, taffeta and moiré, and in cloth, rep and cashmere. Embroidery in delicate classic designs was popular, even muslin dresses being ornamented with gold or silver thread or tinsel and spangles in gold, silver, copper or steel.

Long sleeves, divided into several puffs by narrow bands or ribbons, were called "mameluke sleeves." "Betsies," small neck ruffs, came from England. They were introduced in Paris by the famous tailor Leroy, who named them *cherusses*.

Due to the sheer frocks, petticoats edged with lace frills became an important feature, often showing 'neath the hem of the dress. Sheer gowns also brought in the singular fashion of pantalets of flesh-colored satin instead of a petticoat. About 1805, muslin pantaloons edged with lace frills were shown in fashion publications, and there is a note of their being worn in 1807, but they do not seem to have become popular in France. The wearing of pantalets, or drawers, did not become an established custom until the 'thirties; until this time, woman's body linen never consisted of other than a chemise or smock, under-petticoats and stockings.

A bandeau which held the breasts firm was now worn over the slip or chemise and, about 1811, stays returned in the form of a corset waist fitted to the normal figure and but slightly boned.

Definitely of this period was the spencer, which originated in England. It was a very short jacket, or bolero, open in front and with long, tight sleeves. It was usually in velvet of a dark color, which contrasted with the gown, had a standing collar, the whole often edged with fringe or a narrow band of fur or swansdown. A variation of the spencer was the *canezou,* or little "hussar" vest, its difference being that it was pulled on over the head, did not open in front and was tight at the lower edge.

Women also wore the redingote, a long coat with several short capes, the coat built on the same lines as the gown, fastened down center-front and belted under the breasts. It had a standing collar, and in winter was often edged with bands of fur such as astrakhan, martin or sable. Around 1808 appeared the same coat of fur, silk-lined, or of cloth, fur-lined, called by the Russian name *witzschoura,* fur coats having come originally from Russia. The same style of coat was made of percale for summer wear.

Such colors as Egyptian earth, pea green and tobacco brown were used for the long coat and the tiny jacket, with the dress invariably white.

An outstanding style of the Empire Period was the court dress established by Josephine. She wore two costumes, one the "little costume," the other the "grand costume." The "little gown" was of embroidered blue satin with short puffed sleeves and the train falling from the belt. The "grand gown" was of brocaded silver with long, tight sleeves, the gorgeous train falling from the left shoulder. The neckline of both was square in front, with a standing lace collar, rather like the Medici collar, but ending at the corners of the décolletage. Both gowns were embroidered in silk, pearls and spangles, the most elaborate ornamentation being confined to the grand costume.

An accessory of importance which took hold in this period and continued to be worn for a century was the shawl, of fine cashmere with embroidered border, an article of great luxury. Shawls, though not unknown in Europe, had never before become a vogue. This fashion dates from the return of Napoléon's armies from Egypt. Shawls were large and small, hand-woven and embroidered, of silk, wool, chiffon, lace or cotton. Although originally made on hand looms in the Orient, beautiful ones were now made in France. From Paisley, Scotland, came shawls woven on power looms, following the intricate East Indian patterns, in which "Paisleys" achieved a high artistic value. While the design layout required four months, the actual weaving on the British power looms was accomplished in a week.

Josephine is said to have owned three to four hundred of them, costing fifteen to twenty thousand francs each. Ladies took lessons in the art of posing in and draping the shawl.

In the beginning of this period, wigs were still worn, and the simple classic coiffure was fashionable, but the Titus cut seems to have been the favored style. Another coiffure was *à la Chinoise,* with the hair drawn tightly back. From 1809, the headdress rose in height and all through the period the ears were uncovered.

The Egyptian campaign was responsible for luxurious turbans of brocade, satin, striped sheer gauze and velvet trimmed with aigrettes and feathers. Bonnets were of all shapes and sizes, the pokebonnet, or cabriolet hood, predominating, made of plush, velvet or satin for winter, of gauze or straw for summer. Headgear was ornamented with plumes, ribbons and flowers and invariably tied under the chin. With the return of lace to favor, due to Napoléon's interest in the industries, lovely lace veils hung over the front edges of bonnets. Fur bonnets were worn with the long fur coats.

The feminine riding habit resembled that of the Directoire Period, the short-waisted, double-breasted jacket with lapels over a waistcoat and lingerie shirt with full cravat, but the masculine top hat was now adopted.

Lace was used to edge caps, aprons, gowns and handkerchiefs.

In the early part of the period, crocheted bags, enriched with embroidery, colored beads, tassels and fringe were in fashion, but later waned in popularity. The handkerchief was carried in the hand and a small purse for money was concealed in the bosom of the dress.

Very small fans, about five or six inches long, came back into the mode. They were made of fine silk and decorated with designs using spangles of gold, silver, copper and steel. The costly, exquisitely painted fan and the jewelled fan reappeared.

The slippers of the period were cut very low and were heelless; they were made of kid or fabric, laced across the instep and tied around the ankle.

In jewelry, there were rings, long earrings, jewelled hairpins and hatpins, lockets and watches worn on chains. Cameos were very popular and beaded and gold chains were twisted six or seven times around the neck.

Artificial flowers were worn in the hair, on bonnets and as corsages, the workmanship having reached a high artistic standard.

Bathing and lingerie became very important. Men and women began their day with a bath, perhaps perfumed, and now changed their undergarments once a day. Both Napoléon and Josephine used perfume and toilet water lavishly. Rouge was discarded by the feminine sex and left to the men, women adopting a white or pale complexion.

In 1801, Joseph Marie Jacquard, son of a weaver, revolutionized the textile industry by inventing a mechanical loom to weave patterns or brocaded fabrics. The French government bought his loom in 1806, granting him a royalty and a yearly pension.

A Frenchman named Camus, Jr., in 1808, patented the first known invention for the production of hooks and eyes by power.

Consulate • First Empire

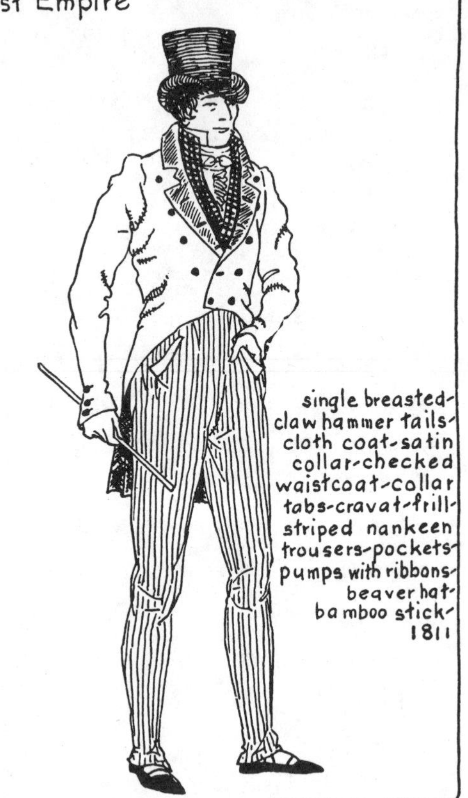

Consulate·First Empire

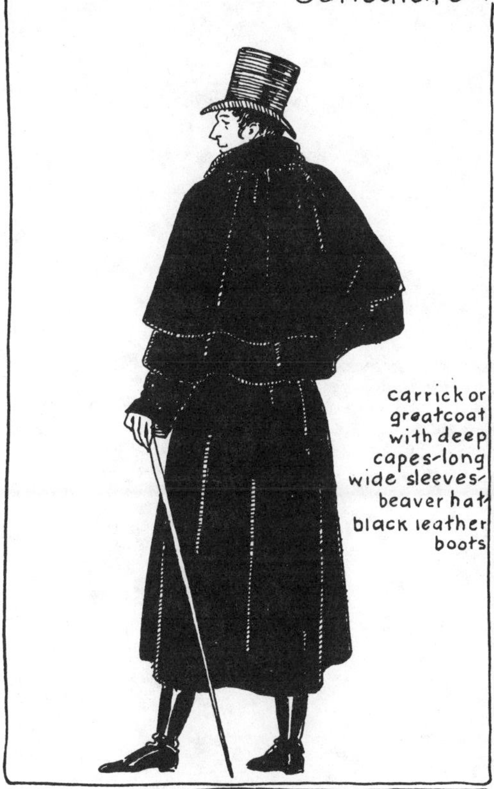

carrick or greatcoat with deep capes-long wide sleeves-beaver hat-black leather boots

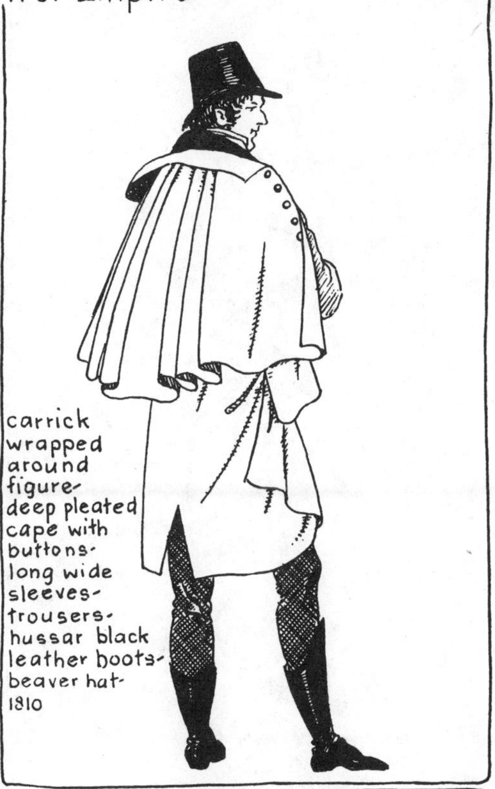

carrick wrapped around figure-deep pleated cape with buttons-long wide sleeves-trousers-hussar black leather boots-beaver hat-1810

double breasted redingote-satin collar-pockets with flaps-buttoned bands on sleeves-neckcloth-collar points-beaver hat-leather boots-1814

carrick or greatcoat-over formal habit-tabs and buttons-slashed pockets-neckcloth-collar points-black satin breeches-white silk stockings-black pumps-beaver hat-1814
RTW

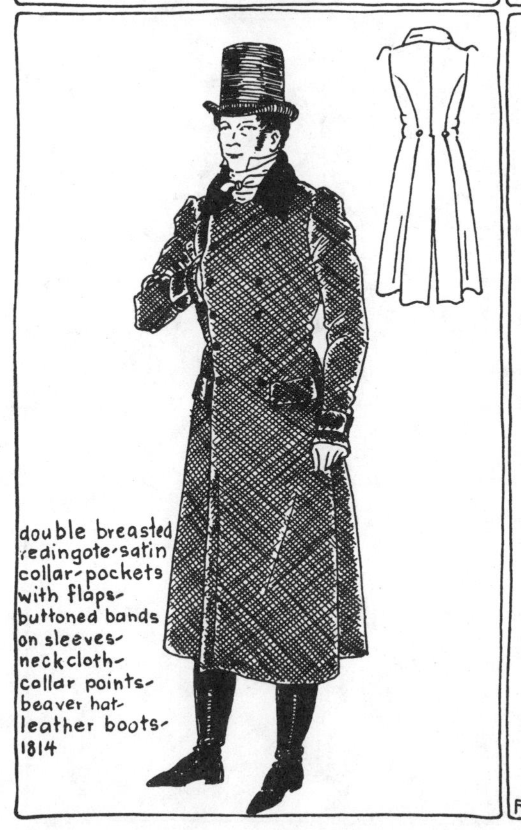

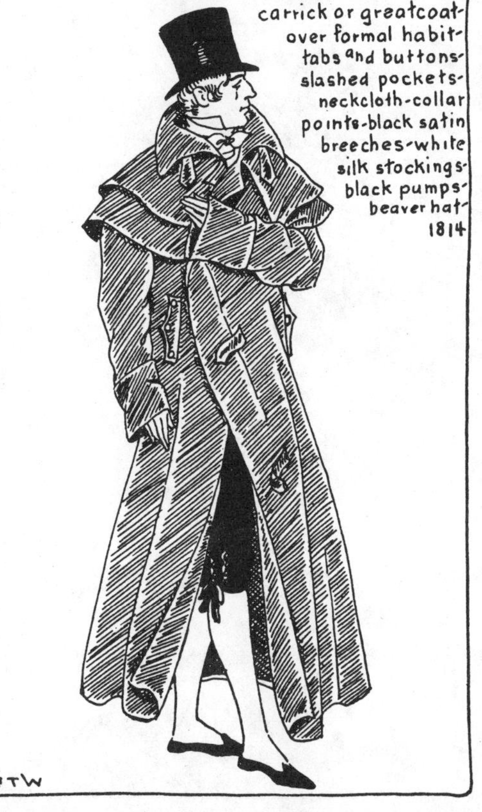

Consulate·First Empire

white muslin gown-elbow sleeves-open center front over slip-pearl buttons-Paisley shawl amber tones-yellow straw bonnet-cobalt blue ribbon-yellow flowers-Titus hair-yellow slippers-white stockings-1800

white muslin-tobacco brown velvet tunic-trimming, pearl beads on yellow discs-white silk stockings-white slippers-Titus hair-1802

embroidered white muslin-deep bertha edged with lace-short puffed sleeves-"cherusse" or "Betsie" of pleated muslin-green velvet sash-green slippers-white silk stockings-Titus hair-long gloves-fan-1803

white percale dress with pleats-mameluke sleeves-triple shoulder ruffles-straw hat with white cotton embroidery-velvet ribbon-foliage-colored slippers-white silk stockings-1811

Consulate · First Empire

velvet spencer-
white muslin
gown-cord
with tassels-
embroidered bag
with tassels-
tucked silk
bonnet with
lace frills-
ribbon bowknot-
Titus hair-
1800

cloth redingote-
satin collar and
and lapels-tabs
and buttons-
bonnet with
bead trimming-
frilled lace
neck ruche-
handkerchief-
Titus hair-
1806

velvet canezou-
self ruffles-silk
gown-embroidered
band and pleated
frill-lace "Betsie"
around neck-
velvet bonnet-
pleated taffeta
pompons-
handkerchief
in hand-
1810

dark green cloth
coat-yellow
collar-black
felt bonnet-
velvet and white
ruches-black
satin ribbon-
black ostrich-
handkerchief-
Titus hair-
black slippers-
white stockings-
1814

RTW

Consulate • First Empire
collar points and neckcloth
lace cherusse or "Betsy" - 1814
embroidered veil over straw and lace bonnet - 1804
embroidered veil tied round hair and over frame - muslin cherusse or Betsy - 1811
single eyeglass
white gauze bonnet - tea roses - green foliage - 1811
green velvet - white satin - white coque feathers - 1814
coiled braids and flowers - 1814
pleated turban - gray gauze - gold braid and spangles - 1803
profile of rose silk bonnet tied under chin - self cording - lace veil - 1806
corset - 1811
military - Napoléon and Wellington
trousers with strap over boot - 1813
muslin bandeau - 1810
hussar or Hessian boot - 1800
man's blue gaiter over trousers and pumps
FTW

Chapter Thirty-five

The French Restoration

Louis XVIII—1815–1824
Charles X—1824–1830

Men's costume varied little, except in the style of the waistcoat, which was single or double breasted, of bright color in silk, velvet or striped piqué. For some years, an evening fashion was the wearing of two waistcoats, one of white piqué over one of black velvet, with the velvet lapel rolled over the white. The lapels were cut in shawl collar shape. The waistcoat points sometimes showed below the coat and gold buttons were popular.

Coinciding with the smaller-growing waist of the women and the general wearing of stays, men's coats and waistcoats also became tightly fitted at the waist. This style necessitated some sort of lacing, which was secured by a basque belt worn next to the body. Padding was employed at the chest and the hips to give the exaggerated fitted look. Instead of being cut in one with the body as formerly, coattails were now cut separately and fitted to the body of the coat.

Knee-length redingotes appeared, single or double breasted with flaring skirt and a shawl collar buttoned up high. Redingotes of alpaca became the fashion about 1824, becoming very popular. Greatcoats, often worn thrown about the shoulders and held in front, were generally double-breasted.

Trousers continued tight, often ankle-length, but the popular style seems to have been that with the strap under the boot. They were made of nankeen, drill, white piqué or of fine white corduroy.

Coat colors were blue, claret, buff, with velvet collars and buttons of pearl, steel or gilt. Topcoat colors were gray, buff, with blue and bronze green most popular.

Habits or suits were topped off by handsome cravats or neckcloths of fine white linen, black satin or figured silk. Heavy silk mufflers were also in fashion pinned at the neck with a single jewel. A watch fob hung from under the vest.

A book published in the 1820's by H. Le Blanc, supposedly none other than Honoré de Balzac, described thirty-two styles of tying a cravat. The manual was republished in English in London and again in Philadelphia in 1828.

The hair was moderately short, and, if straight, curled by tongs into ringlets, with a thin line of whiskers on the cheeks. The mustache and a very small Vandyck reappeared.

Hats of beaver felt, in fawn, gray or white, were high with varying-shaped crowns, the most popular being that widest at the top. The silk hat, or polished beaver, invented in Florence, Italy, in 1760, began to be taken up about 1823 but was not generally worn until the 'thirties. Later, plush was employed in its fabrication. A Frenchman named Gibus, in 1823, invented the collapsible top hat.

Boots were short, only about fifteen inches high, the vogue being for the hussar, or Hessian, and the military guard boot, called the Wellington in England. Spatterdashes and gaiters regained popularity. In the late 'twenties appeared the first high shoe, worn by both men and women. It rose about three inches above the ankle, had a leather vamp and a cloth top, usually nankeen, laced on the inner side. The toe was long, narrow and square and, for street wear, the masculine version often had a low, flat heel.

With the Restoration, a complete change in style occurred in women's dress. From 1819, the corset, with a steel busk front fastening, became a definite part of the costume, the waist becoming very small in the 'twenties and placed normally. The slim, straight skirt changed to a bell shape, clearing the ground and revealing the tiny heelless slippers, laced with ribbons. The lower edge of the skirt was stiffened with buckram and ornamented with rows of trimming, which consisted of ruffles, puffs, scalloped flounces, lace, ribbon, bowknots, flowers and, later, rows of braid.

The shoulders were broadened by the cut of the garment, epaulettes and berthas, while sleeves were stuffed and wired. Sleeves were long and short, of various shapes, the leg-of-mutton shape appearing in 1820. Large full transparent sleeves of gauze were a feature, also the "pagoda sleeve," a long sleeve in a series of puffs, large at the top and diminishing in size to the wrist.

Chemise and petticoats were lavishly ornamented with lace and embroidery. Ribbon sashes were favored on dresses.

Colors were light, the favorite being white, and the materials used were principally sheer muslins, unbleached batiste and cambric. There were striped gowns and fine pink or blue checked ones. Gauzes, silks and tulles were employed in evening gowns. Woolen cloth for dresses appeared in 1828, and was indeed a novelty after so many years of the use of cotton. Every new color, fabric or article of dress was given a fanciful name, such as "water of the Nile," "frightened mouse," "amorous toad" and many others. Upon the occasion of a gift of a giraffe from Egypt to Charles X, various accessories of dress of both sexes were called *à la giraffe*. English, Russian and Polish ornaments came into fashion with the presence of the Allied troops in France.

The modern wedding gown of white seems to have originated in this period, a result of the prevailing mode for that color. Another new idea was a bodice of contrasting colored material from that of the skirt, a dark one with a light skirt or the other way around.

The canezou spencer was now made of embroidered cotton or lace; in fact, it became a transparent overbodice. See Page 280.

The redingote, or full-length coat, was made of cloth or velvet, and when fur-trimmed was known as a pelisse.

The tippet of fur and the boa of ostrich originated in this period. Huge muffs of fox and chinchilla were carried. Scarfs were of tulle, lace and silk, and shawls were of crêpe, silk and fine cashmere, in brilliant colors, red being much used. They were also in plaids and stripes, the East Indian scarf being known as the *bayadère*. Cashmere shawls were the "rage" and very costly. Shawls of French cashmere and the British Paisley were beautiful and desirable substitutes, inspired by the East Indian originals.

Long gloves, which were most expensive, were worn with the short sleeves and were often chamois-colored.

Bonnets and hats varied in shape and fabric, fashioned of straw, leghorn, silk plush, velvet and felt lined with taffeta. Long ribbon streamers floated from bonnet or hat and the ends of ribbon were cut into many points. Caps were military in style, such as Polish, Austrian or simple morning ones of white muslin or black velvet edged with tulle. There were turbans and bérets in tam-o'-shanter style, turbans later being worn only by older women. All this headgear was ornamented with feathers, ribbons, flowers, cockades, puffs and ruches, several different articles of trimming being applied to one hat. A flattering note was the lace cap worn under the bonnet.

The hair was dressed up off the ears and high in back, with curled puffs at each temple. Sections of the hair were tightly braided and the coiffure *à la Chinoise* remained in fashion. The latter was tightly drawn up into a knot with a high tortoise-shell comb to hold it in place. The ferronière was revived, a very fine chain around the head, with a jewel, either a pearl or ruby, hanging in the middle of the forehead. The band was also fashioned of tiny artificial flowers, strings of beads or a narrow velvet ribbon. For evening wear, large flaring fans of lace, sheer lawn, gauze, or silk were worn in the hair, to which flowers or a jewelled ornament was added.

Little jewelry was worn in the early part of the period, but later on its use became general. Cameos were popular and the favorite stones were pearls and garnets, set in bracelets, rings, long earrings, necklaces, brooches and the large ornate belt buckle. Nearly all these articles were often worn at the same time. When in mourning, hand-wrought silver jewelry was substituted for gold.

The soft slipper, with narrow ribbons tied around the ankle, had long, rounded pointed toes at first, changing to long, slim square toes later. Women also wore the soft high shoe, which appeared late in the 1820's, described earlier in this chapter.

Toward the end of the period, horseback riding became general, brought about by the returning émigrés from England. The feminine habit was of cloth, with satin collar and full skirt and a tightly fitted jacket with leg-of-mutton sleeves. A military cap or the masculine top hat of silk or beaver was worn, from which hung a floating green veil. Under the full skirt, fitted tricot drawers were worn, which were tight over the instep and held in place by a strap passing under the shoe.

Parasols gained in popularity, often the tilting parasol used when walking. The handkerchief was carried in the hand and in the evening the tiny bouquet and a small fan were added accessories. Fans, as formerly, were decorated by famous artists of the day.

French Restoration
formal cloth habit-
white satin piping
and lining-lingerie
neckcloth and frills-
cut steel buttons-
black felt bicorne-
black ostrich fringe-
sword hung from
belt-white silk
stockings-black
leather pumps-
self buckles-
1818
cloth habit,
velvet collar-
waistcoat of
checked silk,
shawl collar-
muffler with
pin-neckcloth-
monocle on ribbon-
handkerchief in
trousers pocket-
white stockings-
black pumps with
elastic bands-
beaver hat-
1820
cloth habit-
velvet collar-
vest with shawl
collar-gold braid
frogs-muffler
with pin-trousers
with straps-black
leather boots-
spurs-silk top
hat-cane-
1829
formal habit-blue or
black-self buttons-
gold embroidery-white
satin vest, breeches and
lining-lingerie shirt,
neckcloth, frills-white
silk stockings-black
pumps-self buckles-
sword on belt passing
under closure-black
felt bicorne-white
ostrich-1829
RTW

French Restoration

pelisse-ash
gray cloth-mink
collar and cuffs-
gray frogs-blue
neckcloth-violet
trousers with
straps-striped
waistcoat wine
and black-yellow
gloves-black
beaver hat-black
boots-cane-
1823

French Restoration

embroidered colored silk bodice-white muslin skirt with cotton embroidery-sleeves, interlaced silk strips-lingerie neck frill-straw hat-ostrich plumes-embroidered cashmere shawl-white silk stockings-colored slippers-1822

pink taffeta-pleated surplice-sleeve tabs edged white lace-taffeta petals, tabs, buttons on skirt-white gloves, stockings, slippers-pink roses in hair-fan-earrings-gloves handkerchief-1825

yellow cotton printed in black-white lingerie ruche, bertha and sleeves-cut-out work on bertha-embroidered white cravat-ruffle and tabs edged narrow black velvet ribbon-black straw hat-yellow flowers-yellow flowered ribbon-white frills-white silk stockings-black slippers-1828

pink cotton, green embroidery-white muslin bodice and frills-pink and green tie-white straw hat-pink flowers and ribbon-pink and green bag-white silk stockings-black slippers-1829

French Restoration

pelisse of peacock blue velvet-chinchilla fur-gray silk belt-embroidered white cotton dress-black and white velvet bonnet over lace cap-black plume-lingerie neck frill-white stockings-blue fabric slippers-ribbon bows-1818

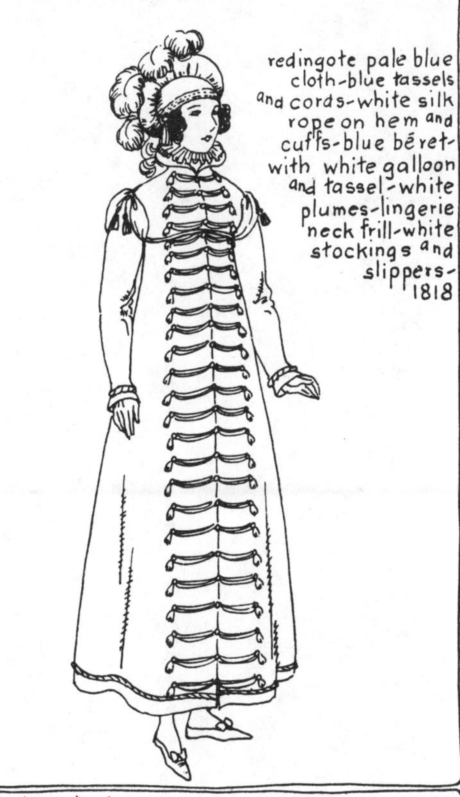

redingote pale blue cloth-blue tassels and cords-white silk rope on hem and cuffs-blue béret-with white galloon and tassel-white plumes-lingerie neck frill-white stockings and slippers-1818

cloth riding habit-white pantaloons-three rows of buttons-satin collar and cravat-lingerie frill-beaver hat-green veil-black boots-1828

woolen cloak embroidered in cashmere shawl motifs-velvet collar-jewelled fastening-taffeta dress-lingerie frill-belt with buckle-felt hat-striped ribbon-silk ruched edge-cloth top shoes-leather toecap-side lacing-1829

French Restoration
small black lace fan-1829
velvet hat-ribbon, rose and wheat-lace cap-neck frills-fur tippet-1823
beaver hat-plaid silk scarf-1823
silk parasol-ivory and ebony handle-1827
turban pleated gauze and galloon-ferronière-1829
turban of pearls and rose silk-1820
evening headdress-jewelled buckle-embroidered sheer white lawn-1828
turban of peacock blue velvet-striped white silk-aigrettes-1826
evening headdress-floral wreath-see below-1828
cloth top shoe-leather vamp-laced on inner side-men and women-late 1820's
surplice spencer with tassels-1820
bayadere scarf-1820's
evening headdress floral wreath-1828
RTW

Chapter Thirty-six

English Fashions

1790–1830

THE FRENCH REVOLUTION had a far-reaching effect upon society and, with the elimination of class distinction in dress, men's costume gradually settled into a more conventional style. French refugee couturiers in London continued to create fashions for women, but in the masculine mode, English tailors, seizing the ascendency in taste and design, continued their hold to the present day.

The *habit à la Française* of the Court of Louis XV, of velvet and satin with rich embroidery and sword, remained the masculine formal dress of Europe into the nineteenth century, but the English riding coat, which first appeared in 1725, developed, from 1780, into the frock coat or cutaway, which is today the morning or evening coat of formal dress.

The fine boots, hats and shoe polish of British make were in use by the "well-dressed man" over the Continent.

With the wearing of somber hues, the cut of a garment was concentrated upon, as never before. A marked change in men's clothes was in fabric, dark tones of brown, blue and green cloth and leather being used instead of light-colored silks and velvets. There was an ease or air of studied carelessness about the whole costume.

The trousers of the sans-culotte became the fashion, knee breeches, or "smallclothes," gradually lengthening, until the original short ones for informal wear, were seen only on elderly gentlemen. After the Battle of Waterloo in 1815, when George IV, as Regent, decreed the wearing of trousers, knee breeches disappeared, to be seen thereafter only upon ceremonial occasions. Trousers with the strap under the boot appeared, also those of ankle length. They were made of cloth, nankeen, drill, piqué, corduroy and stockinet in light colors, especially white and chamois yellow.

Evening breeches were very close-fitting, reaching just below the knee or above the ankle, where an opening at the side was buttoned part way up. This latter style was invented by Beau Brummel. It is said that the smartness of his black pantaloons made trousers popular. A great departure was his evening coat of dark blue, worn with a white waistcoat.

The frock coat was double-breasted with lapels, and a high turned-down collar and claw-hammer tails. In the 1820's, a closer fit was secured by cutting the tails separately and sewing them to the body of the coat. Padding was resorted to on the chest and hips to make the waist appear smaller. The black frock coat and evening coat appeared in 1828. Colors were gray, buff, green, blue and claret and a fine cord edged the coat.

The overcoats of the period were the carrick with its several capes and the long-skirted redingote.

The already muffling cravat grew in dimensions. In the first decade of the nineteenth century, two cravats were often worn, one of white lingerie material, the other of black silk. The white one was put on first, then covered by the black, thus giving the desired bulky look of the period. Eventually, the white cravat was replaced by the standing collar of white linen with pointed corners. The cravat then began to decrease in bulk, while the collar points rose higher, finally touching the cheeks. Black or white was favored for the neck dressing, tied into a bow in front.

Late in the 'twenties, mufflers fastened with a stud or tie pin, became fashionable.

Beau Brummel was famed for his skill in tying a cravat. His muslin scarf, which he changed three times daily, was only slightly starched. Gentlemen took lessons in the art of tying the cravat, which were given by experts.

Of the "Beau," it is said that he raised good dressing to cleanliness, conservatism and therefore to elegance. He introduced daily bathing and daily clean linen into English society, a luxurious supply of underlinen becoming one of the requisites of a well-dressed man.

As in France, the cocked hat gave way to the tall round hat of felt or beaver. Beaver hats, from 1818 to 1830, were in light colors, usually fawn, gray or white. The "silk hat," invented in 1760 in Florence, Italy, was seen in the early 1820's, but did not reach perfection until the 'thirties, when it was generally adopted. It was first made of polished beaver, called silk beaver, but later was fashioned of plush.

Wigs were demoded by 1800. The hair was worn short in the ragged Brutus style, brushed down over the forehead. From about 1809, short loose curled locks and side whiskers prevailed, with curling resorted to, if the hair was straight. The short cut, with slight variations, has lasted from that time. Powder was occasionally seen in dull pink, violet, gray or blue, but, by 1820, powder and the wig had completely disappeared, retained only by the English judiciary as part of the professional uniform.

Elegant footgear in high and low boots of black leather were part of the costume, with silk or wool stockings, white or striped. Pumps were popular, low-cut slippers with a flexible sole, always worn with the dress habit. Shoe roses were no more, shoes now being fastened with plain strings or latchets.

In the first decade of the century, the Hessian boot with swinging tassel and the English jockey boot with turndown leather cuff were seen. The turndown cuff was usually yellow, but, about 1818, cuffs of gray or beige cloth appeared. The Hessian and Wellington boots (see Page 246) were the fashion from 1820 to 1830. Boots grew quite short and were worn under trousers. Gaiters and spatterdashes appeared intermittently throughout the period.

Due to the increased popularity of horseback riding, the riding habit was often seen indoors, even in the drawing room. Morning or "office" coats, made of flowered chintz, appeared in the late 'twenties, the style lasting into the 'forties.

Muffs, which men had carried since the sixteenth century, were still modish; in fact, the muff was also a mark of dignity, and was in use even by judges of the court. From 1790 to 1820, the muff was very large, reaching to the elbows, attaining its largest size around 1810. It was first made of fabric filled with feathers, later, of single large fur pelts. This masculine fashion was also popular in our American Colonies.

Before 1800, sword sticks and heavy club sticks were carried, the short bamboo stick and riding whip becoming more popular later.

In this period, men's handkerchiefs settled into an accepted size of about eighteen inches square, of white linen with perhaps a hemstitched border and a monogram in one corner.

A watch with a dangling fob seal was often carried in each of the two front pockets of the trousers, but a single timepiece occupied the right-hand pocket.

Perfection and a low cost in gilding brass buttons was reached about 1818, making gilt buttons accessible to those dressy young men who could not afford hand-wrought gold.

In accessories, men carried the indispensable snuffbox and the small bag purse. Purses were of leather set in gilt mounts or of knitted silk worked with steel beads and tasselled ends.

The single lens, or monocle, came into fashion in the early years of the eighteenth century. It was carried in England and on the Continent. The use of the monocle has been and continues to be more favored in England than elsewhere. Pince-nez, worn on a heavy black cord, appeared in the 1820's.

Both the English and the French claim credit for the feminine classic mode, but the truth is that all Europe, influenced by the writings of Rousseau and Voltaire, was considering a reform in dress. The English, with their well-known love of country life, were the first to adopt simpler clothes.

Dresses were made of cottons, such as lawn, percale, batiste and calico, with ribbon sashes. The chemise gown, fuller than the French model, had a belt just under the breasts and had usually high neck and long sleeves. It also had the long train and there were knee-length tunics of colored cloth, silk or velvet, worn over the invariably cotton sheath gown.

Corsets were discarded, but the Englishwoman, being more conservative, wore more underclothing under the sheath gown than did her French neighbor, usually several petticoats of fine muslin edged with embroidery and lace.

The low-necked gown brought in a small neck ruff of several rows of fluted or ruffled Brabant lace. (See Page 246.) This fashion originated in England and was called a "Betsie" after Queen Elizabeth, which style was taken up in Paris by the tailor Leroy and renamed *cherusse*. By 1807, the collarettes were of six or seven falls of lace.

About 1808, the train disappeared, the feet were revealed and, by 1809, the skirt was ankle-length. During the winter of 1809, stays returned in the English mode.

The very short waist remained through the next decade, but skirts became fuller, bands of trimming ornamenting the lower edge. Sleeves developed puffs, and both neck and wrists were finished with frills. There were satin and velvet evening gowns, swansdown being used as a border, and color was making its appearance. Morning dresses of chintz were worn, and bombazine, a mixture of silk and cotton, was considered very smart, both in England and the American Colonies. Transparent fabrics were worn over colored satins.

Between 1820 and 1830, the waistline gradually dropped back to normal, shoulder lines lowered and sleeves grew very full, especially at the top. By 1830, the fullness was puffed out with the aid of tiny feather cushions or wicker frames. The skirts of both day and evening gowns cleared the ground or were ankle-length. Delicate colors were the vogue, white still retaining favor, but Indian red became very popular. Late in the 'twenties, chintzes and printed muslins were reserved for morning dresses and the very young. From 1820, ribbon became a featured trimming on both dress and hat.

From 1796, a demand for English flannels for scarfs developed with the wearing of muslin dresses in all seasons. Cloaks were not popular, because they concealed the figure, and thus came about the great vogue of the shawl, which was to last a century or more.

The shawl of English cashmere first appeared in London about 1786 and immediately took hold. It was a piece of fabric six yards long and two wide, making it quite understandable why the ladies of that day took instructions in the draping of such a garment. While the original hailed from India, beautiful imitations woven on power looms were made at Paisley, Scotland. At the height of the fashion, shawls were of all sizes and fabrics, fine wool, silk, lace, chiffon or cotton, often hand-woven and embroidered. At the end of the first quarter of the century, shawls of bright red cashmere were fashionable, also plaids and stripes

In the first two decades of the nineteenth century, the mantelet, a capelike garment, was worn. It was fastened at the neck, was cut away in front and hung to the knees at different points. It was usually of silk, lined or not, and often edged with a lace ruffle.

The spencer, a very short-waisted jacket, was worn with the Empire dress. It was invented by Lord Spencer, who claimed that fashion was so absurd that he himself could concoct a ridiculous, impractical style and it would become the "rage." He cut the tails off his own coat and went for a stroll. In two weeks, all London was wearing the "spencer," and soon fashionable men, women and children of the Continent and the colonies were wearing the same little jacket. The masculine spencer has come down to date in the mess jacket of the officers of the British Army. It certainly filled a serious need in women's costume. Spencer jackets were in black, purple, mulberry or bottle green, of satin or velvet, lined and sometimes padded. Occasionally, a narrow peplum was added and very elegant jackets were bordered with swansdown. The short spencer type of overjacket, of sheer muslin or lace, was called a canezou spencer or a cannezout. See Page 280.

Muffs of silk and lace were carried in the summer, but added warmth was furnished in the winter by the large muffs in vogue from 1790 to 1830. They covered the arms to the elbows and were made of various fabrics, gathered cloth and strips of fur or large single skins.

About 1812, the long cloth or velvet coat, called the *redingote* by the French, became the fashion. It was high-waisted, was at first knee-length, later reaching to nine or ten inches above the hem of the dress. By the end of the decade, the coat was full-length and edged with wide bands of fur. The pelisse, or fur coat of Russian origin, was first worn in Vienna in 1808. *Pelisse,* a word whose root means pelt, signified a fur-lined or fur-trimmed cloth coat, and was so used in France, but it seems that the English applied the name to any long outer coat.

An entirely new garment for women came into existence in this period, namely drawers, later called pantalets. Until 1800, only two or three known references to them exist, but the sheath gown made some leg covering necessary. Even so, drawers, as then conceived, were a decorative part of the costume. From about 1805, English and French fashion journals occasionally displayed evening gowns of shoe-top length, with fancy frilled satin pantalets showing below. Frequent references to them occur until about 1820, and from then they were worn only by little girls. Such drawers were of merino for winter and of lace-edged white dimity or colored calico for summer. Pantalets were often false, being ruffles held at the knees with tapes. Drawers were not generally worn by the feminine sex until the 1830's.

The classic style of headdress prevailed in the latter part of the eighteenth century, dressed close to the head with plaits, curls, the psyche knot finished with antique oil. The Queen and the court ceased powdering in 1793, but wigs were still worn and not always in the wearer's natural color. Later, the hair was formed in short ringlets, very few, however, adopting the shaggy Titus cut worn in Paris. In the 'twenties, it was parted in the center, with bunches of curls at the sides over the ears and a topknot on the crown of the head. The evening coiffure was bedecked with striped tinsel ribbon, flowers and high tortoise-shell combs. Upon the death of George IV, black-and-white crêpe flowers were worn in the hair for full dress.

The standing ostrich plumes in the coiffure of English court dress is a survival of the feathers worn in the Paris of Marie Antoinette.

In the first decade of the nineteenth century, draped turbans with feathers were inspired by the Egyptian campaigns. In the next ten years appeared bonnets of all shapes and dimensions, of straw, tulle, silk and light felt trimmed with ribbons, ruches, flowers and feathers. Lace caps edged with frills were often worn under hat or bonnet. Hats grew very large in the 'twenties, were faced with silk or velvet and ornamented with plumes, flowers and wide ribbon, looped, fringed and pinked. The plumed hat was worn at the opera and at dinner parties.

The use of jewelry in these unsettled times waned, although on formal occasions pearls and garnets were seen. Women also wore the monocle on a black ribbon. Handbags were of silk on gilt frames or of silk knitted with beads, and were called reticules. They were embroidered, appliquéd and painted.

Late in the eighteenth century and early in the nineteenth century, machines were invented in England making the mechanical manufacture of net and lace in large pieces possible for shawls and bridal veils. Lace or net veils were attached to the brims of bonnets or hats, either a short frill to the eyes or one hanging to the knees.

Early in the nineteenth century, shoes were soft heelless slippers tied with ribbon across the instep. These fabric shoes grew higher in the 'twenties, sometimes had leather toecaps and were laced in the back or at the inner side. (See Page 256.) Various fabrics were employed but satin and morocco were the principal ones. Slippers were often made at home by English and American women.

Long gloves were of kid in delicate colors and there were also long knitted ones and mittens.

The umbrella, or parasol, which had been in use in France from the middle of the eighteenth century, became popular in England from the beginning of this period. The year 1787 is the first date of their manufacture in that country, and many styles are to be noted in the fashion illustrations thereafter. The small tilting parasol was often carried when walking.

The first patent for making rubberized cloth was taken out in 1801 in London by Rudolph Ackerman, but another note says that E. Mackintosh, of England, patented the first practical process for waterproofing in 1823. In 1820, we find that T. Hancock, of Middlesex, England, invented the first elastic fabric with rubber in it. Elastic cloth or *webbing,* as it was called, replaced ribbon garters and the ribbons which secured the low slippers.

In Birmingham, England, in 1807, B. Sanders invented the metal button formed of two disks locked together by turning the edges, and the shell button with metal shank; and in the United States, in 1827, Samuel Williston of East Hampton, Massachusetts, patented the invention of a machine to produce cloth-covered buttons.

In 1831, also in the United States, the first successful machine for making solid-headed pins was invented by John Ireland Howe, of New York.

English-1790 to 1830

cloth frock coat-white linen cravat-buckskin trousers-fob seals covering the two front pockets-Hessian boots with tassels-beaver hat-1797

formal habit-chocolate brown cloth frockcoat-self buttons-beige drill breeches buttoned and tied-white waistcoat, shirt and cravat-black bicorne-white silk stockings-black pumps-watch fob seal-1810

Court habit-violet satin frockcoat-white satin lining, waistcoat and breeches-gold and green embroidery-jewelled buttons-lingerie shirt, jabot, cravat and collar points-lace wrist frills-white silk stockings-black pumps, gold buckles-black felt hat-white frill and lining-sword on violet ribbon-1810

green cloth frockcoat-flowered embroidered white waistcoat-light brown muffler-white collar tabs-white stockinet breeches-white stockings-black pumps with small spurs-brown beaver hat-riding whip-1830

English - 1790 to 1830

English-1790 to 1830

English-1790 to 1830

embroidered white lingerie gown-lace edged petticoat-blue velvet spencer-lapels edged red-lingerie Betsie-black velvet hat-dotted yellow lawn-yellow and black ribbon-powdered hair-white slippers-brown fur muff-brown kid gloves-
1795

swansdown edged velvet stole-brown and black fur muff-striped cotton gown-striped silk bonnet, ribbon and slippers-powdered hair in cadogan and curls-
1796

cloth redingote-velvet bands and tassels-pleated dotted lingerie dress with self frill-lingerie neck and wrist frills-cloth béret-velvet band with ruche-ostrich plume-fabric slippers-
1812

wine colored velvet pelisse with ermine-ermine "shako" with orange beads and tassels-ermine muff-white silk dress and slippers-
1817

English - 1790 to 1830
silk tilting parasol - about 18 inches diameter - 1795
silk tilting parasol - 1796
formal headdress - powdered wig - curls and cadogan - yellow roses - green foliage - white band - 1795
embroidered silk bag with beads - 1814
silk turban in two colors - wheat - 1796
flat straw hat - pleated silk band and facing - daisies - 1809
silk with galloon and gauze ruffle - 1810
lace bonnet - cordings and ruchings - flowers - 1816
embroidered silk bag - 1820's
plaid scarf - striped waistcoat - 1820's
pale blue silk with fringe - 1813
evening coiffure with roses 1820's
silk parasol - ivory and ebony handle - 1813
straw bonnet - striped ribbon - 1820's
Beau Brummel's evening trousers 1820-1840
lady's slipper - striped silk - 1814
lady's slipper - 1813
lady's overshoe - presumably felt - 1813
silk mantelet - shirred ribbon edge - lace frill - 1810
pantalets with chemise dress - pink satin - lace frills - 1811
chintz morning coat - 1820-1840
ankle trousers - 1820 to 1840
RTW

Chapter Thirty-seven

Louis-Philippe

1830–1848

DEFINITELY ESTABLISHED by now were trousers, the frock coat, top hat and the greatcoat, change or variation being furnished only by details. English influence held in the masculine mode.

The fitted waist or corseted look continued, smallness being acquired by the wearing of a basque belt or corset. Comparatively speaking, colors were somber, albeit greens, blues and violets were worn, but in grayed tones. Waistcoats were in bright colors, even to the use of crimson velvet with gold embroidery, and sometimes fastened with jewelled buckles. Blue and black became the accepted colors for evening wear, with embroidered waistcoats of velvet, satin, brocade, piqué or cashmere.

The shirt for informal dress was generally finished with a pleated frill at the opening, the goffered shirt it was called, because the pleats were set with the aid of a goffering iron. The evening shirt was of embroidered linen, finely pleated and fastened with a diamond stud. A bow-tied white neckcloth or cravat dressed the neck.

For informal wear, cravats, neckcloths and mufflers varied in fabric and color, black satin usually worn while white was *de rigueur* for dress. Mufflers filled in the space above the waistcoat to the chin and were tied in back. Long scarfs began to be worn in the 'forties, passing twice around the neck, loosely tied in front and held in place by a stickpin, the ends left hanging.

In the short redingote, with its flaring skirt, can be seen the "Prince Albert" of the next period. The collar was generally of velvet, changing to silk about 1845. In the 'forties, overcoats had flaring collars and were often trimmed with braid and frogs or brandenburgs. Coats and capes were lined with colored silks, usually white for dress.

In the 'thirties, or about 1837, appeared a short topcoat, entirely new in shape, the box coat. It was made of fawn-colored cloth, single or double breasted, and had a shawl collar of either velvet or satin.

Early in this period, the breeches of the formal habit were tight and ended above the ankles, below which showed silk socks in white or brown and the heelless pumps. For day wear, yellow, fawn or gray striped trousers were popular, with a dark coat, finished with canary-yellow gloves.

The black boot, especially the Wellington, soft, high and fitted, continued to be the fashion. It was covered by the long trouser with a strap under the shank of the boot, this style lasting to 1848.

Top hats of beaver or silk, in gray, fawn and white, remained in style, although the black silk hat appears to have been the favorite. The hair was brushed over the forehead in short ringlets, accompanied by short side whiskers. The "imperial" and the mustache were also worn.

At home, for negligee, men wore "lounging clothes" or smoking suits, with a velvet cap. The *robe d'intérieur* was of brilliantly figured silk or velvet.

In the feminine world, the leg-of-mutton sleeve, by 1830, had reached its largest size, stiffened with horsehair and whalebone. From then, the stiffening gradually diminished; by 1835, the large full sleeve falling softly over the tight cuff. Sleeves then grew smaller, the fullness disappeared, evolving into the fitted top or cap in the 'forties, eventually flaring at the forearm over a puff of contrasting fabric. The plain tight sleeve was also in fashion. To about 1835, the sleeves of evening gowns, while short, were full and stiffened, and called the béret or pancake sleeve.

Berthas, fichus and frills always accentuated the dropped shoulder line and the high necks of day dresses were always finished with a lingerie collar or frill.

Skirts became longer, ankle-length or just clearing the ground, with ornamentation sparingly used. Worn over five or six petticoats, the coming of the crinoline is apparent in the silhouette of extreme fullness.

Crinoline made its appearance in the early 'forties and was a band or braid of horsehair, *crin* being the French word for horsehair. The *crinoline* was a petticoat, corded and lined with horsehair and finished with braid straw at the hem. A flannel petticoat, in winter, was put on first, then the crinoline, then another corded calico skirt, over that a wheel of plaited horsehair and finally the starched white muslin petticoat.

The tightly laced waist of the fitted bodice remained in normal position but gradually dipped to a point in front.

The feminine greatcoat of the period was dresslike in design, full-length with small fitted waist, leg-of-mutton sleeves and a broad collar, lined for winter and of sheer material for summer. There were also mantles, shawls, scarfs, fur tippets and boas.

Shawls were of fine cashmere; lace-edged ones came from Spain, and from China those of silk crêpe, fringed and embroidered. The canezou spencer was a separate short transparent jacket with sleeves, its two scarf-like ends held in place by the dress belt. It was usually of sheer muslin, with embroidery, and was worn over the bodice. The false canezou was a deep ruffle, or bretelle, falling over the short puffed sleeve.

After the conquest of Algeria, there appeared the burnous (see Pages 289–292), a wrap for both sexes, but the feminine side did not take up the style until the next period.

For evening wear, much pink and white gauze and white organdie were worn, other favored colors being yellow, blue, lilac and violet de Parme. By the 'forties, heavy fabrics were in fashion, such as brocade, poplin, damask, moiré and velvet. Black tulle and net were extensively used, often embroidered in color and spangles. Black Chantilly lace was revived and, between 1830 and 1840, was especially seen in scarfs, shawls, flounces and frills, covering almost the entire foundation gown of satin or taffeta. Challis was a new material and stripes, checks and plaids were revived late in the period. Striped ribbons were very popular.

The bonnet, which appeared in the 'twenties, continued in high favor, to be worn for fifty years. It was made of all fabrics, often draped with a lace veil either white or black, and there were such shapes as the coal-scuttle bonnet, the poke bonnet and the calash.

Important, too, were caps of sheer lingerie fabric, lace-edged and trimmed with ribbons, worn principally at home. The bonnet was often worn over the cap, the exposed ruche framing the face. An evolution of the cap was a wire band with an outstanding lace frill, flowers and ribbon, this arrangement also framing the face. The English named the latter an *arcade*.

The coiffure of the period was sleek in silhouette, despite its braids and prim curls. In the 'thirties, the hair was elaborately dressed and, in the evening, ornamented with flowers, ribbons, feathers and the ferronière around the forehead. Late in the 'thirties, the "English ringlets" at the sides of the face began to descend, reaching the shoulders by 1840. In the 'forties, for evening dress, Oriental scarfs were tied around the head in turban fashion.

Silk mittens, especially black ones, became more and more popular, and the fine lace handkerchief was again brought into view as an important accessory.

The vogue for jewelry grew, specially in gold and elaborate settings in brooches, rings, long earrings and bracelets. Favorite gems were the diamond, pearl, ruby, emerald and topaz. Fine gold-chain fringe, onyx jet and cameos were characteristic of the time, as were "sets," which consisted of a brooch, a pair of bracelets and earrings. Very small, carefully arranged bouquets of fresh flowers were often carried in jewelled holders, attached by a chain to a finger ring.

A low broad heel appeared in the late 'thirties, but the low slipper with crossed elastic bands and the ankle shoe, both of fabric, were still worn. White slippers and light-colored silk boots were popular, while black satin slippers, with a fine white silk stocking, seem to have been the thing for evening. A novelty was the black net stocking worn over one of flesh color.

From 1836, when Charles Goodyear made his important discovery of a method of treating the surface of gum, the use of elastic in dress became more practicable.

Horseback riding was very popular for both sexes. A particular feminine riding habit is noted, of "London" smoke-colored cloth, with white cambric jacket, really a blouse, with full sleeves, a full skirt over petticoats, riding trousers, boots with silver spurs and yellow gauntlets. These particular riding trousers of white muslin were finished with a two-inch frill over the boot. In the cambric bodice can be seen the origin of the shirtwaist. As noted, it was of cambric, finely tucked and lace-trimmed.

Only young girls wore pantalets in France, but in England and America, both women and children adopted the fashion.

The small hinged or tilting parasol was used when riding in a carriage.

A machine for making flowered net, resembling the handmade lace, was invented in 1837, by Joseph Marie Jacquard, the inventor of the history-making mechanical loom for weaving patterned fabrics.

Louis-Philippe 1830-1848

Louis-Philippe 1830-1848

Louis-Philippe 1830-1848

rose taffeta skirt and sleeves-fluted white organdie ruffles-double organdie hem-embroidered neck and belt-straw hat-drooping plume-striped ribbon-shirred frills at cheeks-black satin slippers-white silk stockings-embroidered handkerchief-fan-1832

black taffeta and black lace net-braid ornaments on cord-tassels-black taffeta rose on bosom-white lace bonnet-pink roses and ribbon-fur boa-white silk stockings-black satin slippers-necklace-buckles on cuffs-1834

velvet gown-lace bertha and collar-three jewelled buttons-bonnet of shirred and corded silk-lace veil-1842

"London smoke" gray cloth riding habit-velvet collar-black satin stock-white ruche and shirt-black silk hat-gray veil-white muslin strap trousers-black boots-1844

RTW

Louis-Philippe 1830-1848

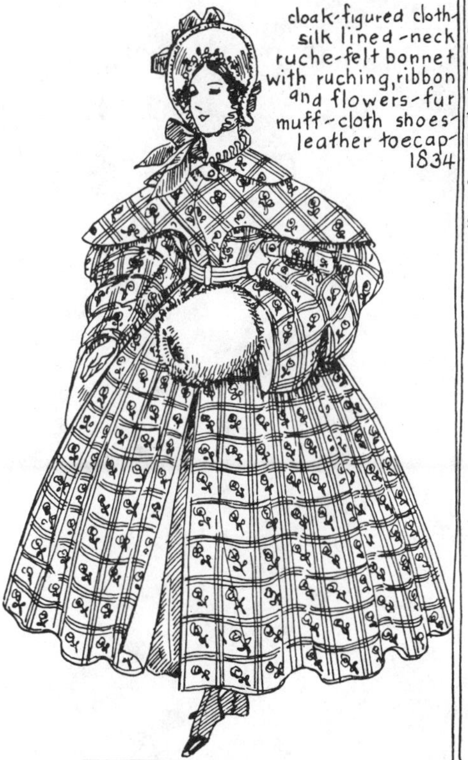

cloak-figured cloth-silk lined-neck ruche-felt bonnet with ruching, ribbon and flowers-fur muff-cloth shoes-leather toecap-1834

pelisse-brown cashmere-lined mauve silk and wadding-white fur-gray felt bonnet-paradise gray and magenta-gray ribbon-black silk shoes-1833

taffeta cape-self rope trimming-gown with lingerie collar and cuffs-embroidered handkerchief-fabric bonnet-ostrich plumes-1841

ermine stole and muff-white bowknot on muff-black silk gown-green velvet shirred and corded bonnet-green ribbons-green and gray ostrich-1844

RTW

Louis-Philippe 1830-1848
evening coiffure-wired black velvet ribbon bands-earrings-flowers-1838
evening coiffure-looped braids-wired black velvet ribbon-flowers-1838
striped cravat-collar tabs-flowered waistcoat-1831
black net over flesh color-black satin slipper-crossed elastic-1830's
black velvet cap worn with lounging robe or smoking suit-1839
corset-back lacing-1837
evening coiffure-braids-pearls-roses-lily of the valley-earrings-1830
negligée headdress-shirred lace on ribbon band-lace rosettes-1839
lady's boot-fur top-tied with ribbons-1830
waves and curls-collar tabs-satin stock-pearl stud-1848
curls and braid-1844
man's shoe-cloth top-leather toecap-laced on inner side-1832
white lace and taffeta-appliqueed green leaves-1838
black organdie-self ruched edge-yellow tie-red roses-green foliage-1835
white organdie canezou-1832
black silk mitten
RTW

Chapter Thirty-eight

French

Second Republic, 1848–1852
Second Empire, 1852–1870

The masculine mode had now settled into its severely tailored state of somber colors, plain, striped, or checked, colored waistcoats and black for formal wear, with but slight variations in accessories. It should be borne in mind that the basic style element in male attire had its origin in London; nevertheless, certain Latin preferences have always been apparent in the clothes of Frenchmen.

After 1850, the jacket or sack coat became definitely the costume for informal occasions, with the frock and tail coat reserved for dress. The sack coat was the outcome of the lounging or smoking habit, and since has signified any jacket with body and skirt cut in one or without waist seam. The double-breasted frock coat was named the "Prince Albert," after the consort of Queen Victoria of England.

The fold of white piqué edged the neck of the cloth vest or waistcoat.

The tight trousers, with straps under the boots, disappeared in the 'fifties; from then, the leg gradually widened. Stripes, checks and plaids were used and fancy braid appeared at the sides.

About the same time, the boot worn under the trousers gave way to the laced-up shoe which was followed in the 'sixties by the side-buttoned shoe. Pumps were revived at the Court of Napoleon III. Patent leather for shoes became very popular. It was japanned or lacquered leather which came into existence in the first quarter of the nineteenth century and was used for harness. A harness maker, Seth Boyden of Newark, New Jersey, in America, seeing harness blinders which came from Paris, experimented on his own and is known to have made the first patent leather in this country in 1822.

There were many styles in topcoats: among them, the short box coat of fawn-colored cloth with shawl collar; a short capelike coat; the MacFarlan, with its separate sleeve capes (see Page 304); the burnous, a variation of the Arab's cloak; and the *paletot*. The paletot, pall coat in English, worn past the middle of the century, was a heavy overcoat, three-quarter length, with the waist slightly repressed. An important coat which appeared in the 'fifties was the raglan topcoat, named after Lord Henry Raglan, hero of the Crimean War. The wide armhole was, no doubt, the result of his having lost an arm. Linings of winter coats were often of brilliant colored silks, padded and quilted. Overcoats were also fur-trimmed and fur-lined and fastened with heavy braided loops.

The steam locomotive brought about travelling to the seaside and inland watering places, with "casual clothes" for such visits. Sport clothes, although not so called, first appeared in the 'fifties and were made of alpaca, nankeen and foulard in white and light colors.

With these sport clothes were worn the long loosely tied scarf and the wide laydown soft collar of the shirt. Neck dressing became more trim, with soft collar rising above the cravat. In the 'fifties, the cravat was stiffened by an inner lining. It was often fastened in back by means of a strap and buckle with a sewn-on, made-up bow in front. A flat scarf, the forerunner of the later puff or Ascot tie, made its debut in the early 'fifties, the two ends crossed in front and held by a stickpin. In the 'sixties, starched detachable cuffs and collars replaced the soft attached shirt collars.

Wide woolen scarfs or folded shawls of dark colors and plaids were often worn around the shoulders when travelling.

In hats, the vogue of the gray, fawn and white beavers continued, with the black silk top hat becoming more and more the headgear for dress. Hats worn with sport clothes were of felt or straw, low-crowned with wide rolling brim, a ribbon tied round the crown, the ends often hanging to the neck in back. The melon-shaped hat appeared. The hard felt hat, known in France as the melon, in England as the bowler and to us as the derby, was designed in 1850 by William Bowler, the hatter.

Men still curled their hair, but wore it trimmed up higher on the back of the neck. The mustache, side whiskers, or "cutlets," the French name, and "Dundreary" in English, and the "imperial," the tuff of hair on the chin and lower lip, were worn even by very young men.

The use of the walking stick had become general. The monocle, in either round or square frame, was worn round the neck on a fine chain, cord or ribbon, also the pince-nez in like frame and fashion.

In feminine costume, the tight steel corset persisted and the full skirt widened, until it measured ten yards around by 1860, in this period of flounces.

Underclothing, in the early 'fifties, consisted of long lace-trimmed white muslin drawers, a flannel petticoat in winter, the crinoline or petticoat of calico, quilted and reinforced with whalebone, and several starched, checked, striped or white muslin petticoats with flounces. The outer petticoat was invariably tucked and embroidered.

These many petticoats were replaced by a cagelike frame of steel hoops, still called a crinoline. An improvement in crinolines was the *cage américaine,* in which the crinoline could be raised, making it possible to wear the garment in the street with short dresses. The decline of the crinoline began in 1860.

The bell-shaped skirt took on the shape of a cone, with steel hoops only from the knees down. The skirt still flared into a wide circumference on the ground, but was smooth and flat over the hips. In the early 'sixties, both trains and ankle-length skirts appeared. The short skirt brought into vogue petticoats of colored taffeta.

In 1869, the bustle replaced the crinoline. The bustle was really a crinoline, but with the rows of whalebone running only from the sides round the back. The wide flare at the bottom of the skirt disappeared, but the bunched-up polonaise or tunic in back created the bustle silhouette. Women returned to the stiffly starched muslin petticoats.

The fitted, boned bodice was finished high at the neck with a frill or small collar, while the décolletage was low for evening wear, its off-the-shoulder line finished with fichu or bertha. The *péplum Impératrice* of the late 'sixties was a basque bodice with draped-up tunic or panniers. From 1850, for about ten years, the pagoda sleeve prevailed with its full white lace-trimmed and tucked undersleeve, puffed out by light steel hoops. Then came the long tight sleeve.

The princess dress, called the "Gabriel," appeared in the 'sixties. It was in one piece from neck to hem, ornamented with buttons or bow-knots the length of the center front. Women also had clothes for the country and the seashore in pilot coats, boating jackets and rowing blouses worn with the short skirt.

Shawls, mantles, capes and flaring coats, hip-length and three-quarter, accompanied the full flaring skirt. A short coat which was fashionable in the 'sixties gave rise to the name of "turkey back silhouette." It hung fairly straight in the front, flaring out abruptly in the back from the neck.

In shawls there were black silk ones, the Indian cashmeres and those of fine wool, the striped Tunisian and those of crêpe de chine with embroidery and deep fringe. Mantles were made of woolen cloth, velvet, lace and changeable taffeta, finished with ruffles of all widths, fringes, cords and tassels.

Fashions in cloaks changed constantly with the Swedish cape, the Moldavian mantle, the Algerian burnous, the Talma and others. Then there were the Greek, Turkish and Zouave jackets. All these were made of rep, heavy silks and damasks.

The feminine jacket and skirt costume appeared for the first time in this period and, comparatively speaking, was a tailored mannish costume with its jacket shorn of lace and frills. The separate shirt or blouse often had a masculine collar, with a narrow bow tie and the tightly buttoned waistcoat also was adopted.

Ornamentation on gowns and wraps was lavish in embroidery, galloon, silk or woolen lace, braid, frogs, tassels, fringe and passementerie. Gowns for formal wear were of such fabrics as gold and silver brocades, handsome patterned materials, heavy satins, silks and moirés. Taffeta became the most popular of all fabrics. Ribbon continued in high favor, plaids and tartans especially so. Day dresses were made of fine wool, alpaca, mohair, English velveteen and foulards. Ball gowns were of gauze, tulle and tarlatan, and lace and summer dresses were of linen, cambric, muslin and batiste. Fashionable laces were Brussels net, Mechlin, point laces, with the black Spanish and Chantilly laces most popular.

Colors typical of the period were tender browns, olive, amber and vanilla. A color scheme introduced by Empress Eugénie was the combination of various shades of brown silk, combined with black velvet. Stripes of all widths were popular, and dyed astrakhan was much used.

Every lady had her dressing gown of thin silk or lingerie material for summer and for winter, of satin or brocade, often lined with quilted silk and trimmed with lace, velvet, ribbon or galloon. Relief from tight lacing was afforded in the boudoir when the stays were taken off and the dressing gown worn.

By 1860, bonnets and caps were replaced by the hat, fastened to the hair by hatpins. The little round hat with low crown was known in England as the "pork pie." The crown was encircled with flowers and a ribbon. The two long streamers hanging in back were named *suivez-moi jeune homme,* or "follow me, young man," in English. An important hat known in France as the "Empress hat" was revived in 1931 as the "Empress Eugénie." Other styles were the Windsor cap, with its peak, and the tiny shepherdess hat, which tilted down over the eyes. Paradise and aigrettes were added to millinery ornamentation.

The "nose veil," a short veil reaching only to the nose, came in in 1860, and the "face veil," longer and covering the face, in 1863.

The hair was parted in Madonna style, drawn into a cadogan or large bun at the back of the neck and often held in place by a coarse net. Nets were very popular and were made of silk or velvet ribbon, followed by nets of chenille and, in the 'sixties, by nets of human hair. From 1860 to 1865, the chignon was placed higher and grew very large, finally reaching the crown of the head, with cascading curls. Evening coiffures were ornamented with lace, flowers, ribbon, gold and silver nets and jewelled combs. The hair was waved by means of hot irons or tongs, and many women resorted to coloring and bleaching to effect the desired blond type.

Caps finally retired to the boudoir and eventually were worn only by elderly women.

High shoes, of very soft black leather, appeared in the 'sixties, in black or gray, of black patent leather, satin or kid or a combination of satin and leather. They had very high heels and very thin soles and were either buttoned at the side or laced up center front. The trim Hessian boot worn with the short skirt often flaunted a tassel at the top. Carriage shoes were made of brocade. Day shoes were usually black and the stocking generally white.

Colored stockings came in with colored silk petticoats in the 'sixties, although the first to appear were gray with red clocks. For evening wear, stockings matched the gown. Later, bright-colored stripes running round the leg and even red stockings were worn.

Accessories carried in the hand were the handkerchief, the fan, gloves and a parasol, while, in the evening, the conventionally arranged small bouquet of fresh flowers was an added note to the costume. Gloves were always worn and were of various lengths, of beautiful kid in white and delicate colors. Silk and lace parasols were trimmed with ruffles and fringe, and the small tilting carriage parasol continued very much in fashion.

There was a tremendous vogue for artificial flowers, which were sewn on evening gowns. Very elegant ladies employed fresh flowers, however.

The gold locket and shell cameo were favorite ornaments, worn on a black velvet ribbon round the neck, also the cross. Black velvet ribbon was tied round the wrists. There were jewelled hatpins, long and short earrings, rings, bracelets, brooches, necklaces, bandeaux and tiaras. A combination in design, characteristic of the period, was several colors of gold employed in one piece with small pearls and black enamel. Tiny scent boxes of gold and silver were carried, containing a small sponge saturated with perfume. Beads, pearls, coral, amber, marcasite and the newcomer crystal were more often worn in the daytime.

The frame of the feminine lorgnette, like that of the masculine monocle, had also taken on a square shape.

An event of great importance was the introduction into Europe, in the 'fifties, of the American sewing machine.

The Empress Eugénie was dressed by the famous couturier, Worth, whose clientele comprised most of the European royalty. Monsieur Charles Frederick Worth, an English lad of Lincolnshire, England, came to Paris before twenty years of age and, in 1858, founded the House of Worth. He was the first to exhibit his new creations on living mannequins.

French 1848-1870

striped cloth suit-satin cravat-collar tabs-beaver hat-black boots-1849

evening dress-black cloth-self buttons-white silk waistcoat-pearl studs-white linen shirt and cravat-tucked front with pearl studs-black silk hat-black patent leather shoes-chamois gloves-monocle on fine chain-1858

striped sack coat with plaid trousers-hard felt melon hat-black patent leather shoes-1862

sack coat-satin facing on lapels-cloth waist-coat with collar-stiff turned-down collar over cravat-scarf pin-striped trousers with braid stripe-black silk hat-black patent leather shoes-1870

French 1848-1870

cloth burnous-hood with tassel-silk cravat-trousers with braid-silk hat-black leather shoes-1851

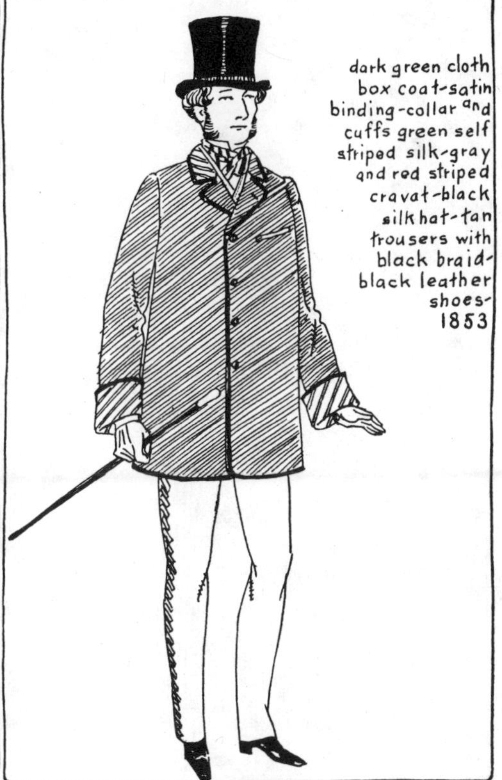

dark green cloth box coat-satin binding-collar and cuffs green self striped silk-gray and red striped cravat-black silk hat-tan trousers with black braid-black leather shoes-1853

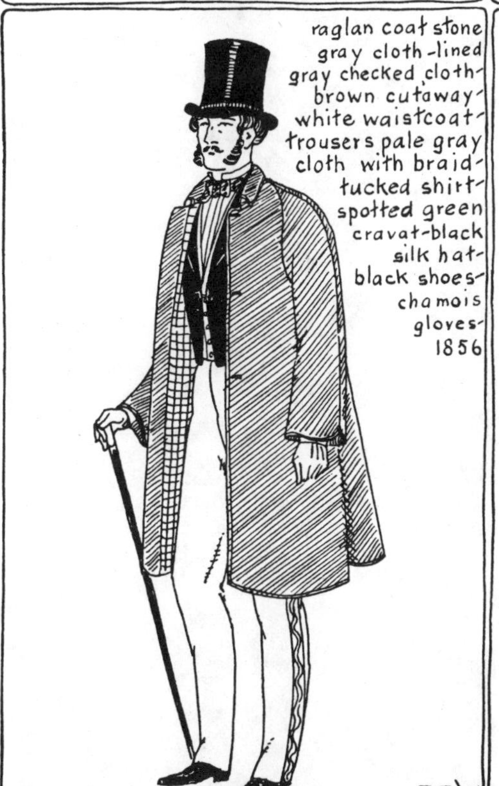

raglan coat stone gray cloth-lined gray checked cloth-brown cutaway-white waistcoat-trousers pale gray cloth with braid-tucked shirt-spotted green cravat-black silk hat-black shoes-chamois gloves-1856

black cloth overcoat-self buttons-brown trousers striped black-brown silk "flat scarf" with jewelled pin-black silk hat-black shoes-1858

French 1848-1870
hunting suit-striped coat-striped waistcoat-striped trousers-leather belt and pouch-silk cravat-plush melon hat-shoes striped cloth and leather-1849
white linen coat-royal blue moire waistcoat-tan moire lapels-biscuit colored trousers-checked shirt-polka dot silk cravat-natural straw hat-black pumps-black silk hose-chamois gloves-1855
tan cloth coat-white waistcoat-white trousers-tan and white checked shirt-blue and black checked scarf-natural straw hat-black pumps-red and white striped socks-1857
figured light blue foulard suit-double breasted white waistcoat with pink design-green silk cravat-brown felt hat-black pumps-light blue socks-1857
RTW

French 1848-1870

bridal gown-white satin-self buttons-embroidered white satin flounces-pleated chiffon-short white kid gloves-veil and orange blossoms-1858

"mannish" taffeta costume-plain and plaid-braid, cord and tassels-waistcoat-tucked lingerie blouse-bow tie-Empress hat-ostrich and bowknot-leather shoes-1860

"turkey back" silhouette-faille silk-self ruching-braid trimmed-shirred hood-cords and tassels-striped silk skirt-straw bonnet-lace ruffle-ostrich tips-1867

princess gown-gray silk with gray cords and buttons-sheer white collar-yellow gloves-blue ribbon and grapes in hair-1867

French 1848-1870

black riding habit-white lace collar and undersleeves-white muslin petticoat with lace insertion and tucks-black hat-velvet crown-straw brim-ostrich tips-yellow gloves-mauve veil-1857

burnous of white cloth striped green-green velvet band-green silk tassel-green velvet bonnet with white frill-green silk gown-1850's

black plush pelisse-beaver fur-green silk gown with lingerie collar and puffs-green bonnet of silk and velvet with ostrich tips-1862

black lace mantelet attached to "old blue" silk yoke-blue silk gown-blue straw bonnet-ribbon-white roses-green foliage-1866

French 1848-1870
brown felt hat-beige ostrich-black lace-royal blue ribbons-1857
"pork pie" straw hat-ribbon loops-"flirtation" ribbons-1865
men's cravats
1854
1858
1856
evening head dress-satin ribbon-black lace-roses-1859
evening cravat-embroidered ends-embroidered and tucked shirt-1854
shepherdess hat-felt-rolled velvet ribbon-black and white lace-aigrettes-1869
man's cravat-1853
evening coiffure-pink roses-sky blue ribbon-1867
black straw bonnet-rolled peacock blue velvet ribbon-blue tassels-net over hair-1861
Windsor cap of straw-ostrich tip-velvet ribbon-1864
crinoline of steel hoops-opening in front-1857
lady's patent leather boot-tassel-1864
man's long end scarf-soft shirt collar-1854
man's flat scarf-starched shirt collar-scarf pin-1857
false lingerie undersleeve-1853
RTW

Chapter Thirty-nine

Victorian England

1837–1901

In the masculine costume of the early part of this period, color, while more subdued than in preceding times, was still being worn, especially in day clothes. Colors were in various shades of brown, dark green, blue and violet. For evening wear, blue or black with white became the accepted mode. After 1850, the claw-hammer, or swallowtail coat and the frock coat were reserved for formal occasions. Coats were fitted at the waist with short flaring skirts. The double-breasted frock coat with silk-faced lapels and closed skirt front has always been known as the "Prince Albert," since it was worn by the Prince Consort of Queen Victoria. The pockets were placed in the back of the skirt and sometimes the coat had a velvet collar.

The morning coat, with rounded-off skirt fronts, appeared in the 'fifties, and about the same time appeared the short lounge jacket or sack coat, which became the coat for informal wear. It was called the *sakko,* a German contraction of sack coat, due, no doubt, to the nationality of the Prince Consort. The sack is any coat without a waist seam, that is body and skirt cut in one. Though originally considered eccentric, by 1870, the sack coat became generally worn.

Heavy tweed suits came into vogue for sportswear.

The dinner coat first appeared in England in the 'eighties and was called the "Cowes" or dress sack coat. It was described as a dress coat without tails, and was used for dinners and dances in country homes. It was not intended to take the place of the swallowtail, but to be worn on less formal occasions. In the United States, the coat was named the "Tuxedo," being first worn at Tuxedo Park. In France, it is known as the "smoking," its design having originated in the smoking or lounging suits of the 'forties. Berry Wall, a prominent society man and dress authority, was refused admission to a dance at the Grand Union Hotel in Saratoga, New York, because he wore "the latest English fad in dress coats." It later became more popular here than on the Continent, American men appreciating its informality.

Braid trimming on men's clothes came in about 1850, used as binding on coats and stitched down the side seams of trousers, surviving today on the trousers of the tail coat and the dinner coat.

Both trousers and black satin knee breeches remained the style for evening, breeches being the full dress for many British officials. Until the 'fifties, trousers were very tight, worn over the high boot with a strap passing underneath, from then gradually widening in the leg, the straps lasting into the 'sixties. Trousers were of striped, checked and plaid fabrics in various colors, the coat usually in solid color. The front closing flap gave way to buttons down the center front about 1845, with side pockets becoming general about the same time.

There were early attempts to introduce creases in trousers, but the style was not accepted. The Prince of Wales, later Edward VII, upon his visit to America in 1860 wore his trousers creased on the sides of the leg as well as at front and back. Creases down the front and back of the leg became general by the 'nineties, having first been introduced by army officers.

Cuffs on trousers, which began to appear with the turn of the century, were the result of Englishmen turning up their trousers on rainy days in the muddy paddock. An English nobleman, on his way to a wedding in New York, turned up his trousers for the same reason. He arrived late, neglected to turn down the cuffs and the fashion was on.

Waistcoats, until the 'eighties, were of colorful handsome fabrics and until the 'sixties, often embroidered. The white evening waistcoat was of brocade, satin, velvet, cashmere or piqué. Although the white waistcoat was first worn by Beau Brummel with his dark blue evening habit, the white waistcoat for day wear is noted as being made popular by Count Gabriel d'Orsay, a celebrated dandy who married Lady Blessington. He became successor to the "Beau" as fashion arbiter. He not only was a brilliant conversationalist but a painter and sculptor of talent and author of a book on etiquette. The white piqué fold which edged the neck of the dark vest from the 'fifties to the end of the century was the survival of the white waistcoat.

In the 'thirties and the 'forties, neckcloths and cravats were tied in front and mufflers, which filled in the space above the waistcoat to the chin, were tied in back. Until the 'sixties, the white evening bow tie often had embroidered ends (see Page 293). The jewelled stickpin appeared. The collar points which showed above began to turn down over the cravat in the 'forties, becoming a real turndown collar in the 'fifties. Also in the 'fifties appeared the stiff starched standing collar, with its narrow bow tie, to be followed, in the 'sixties, by detachable starched linen cuffs and collar. The round high collar came in in the 'seventies. Collars and cuffs of paper, to be worn once and then discarded, appeared for a short time.

The small cravat, tied in a bow in front, was worn from the 'fifties. It was stiffened by an inner lining and often the bow was sewn on, the scarf fastened in back by means of a strap and buckle, the original ready-made scarf. The scarf with long ends was first worn in the 'forties. It passed round the neck twice, was loosely tied in front and held in place by a scarfpin.

The flat scarf with wide crossed ends appeared in the 'fifties, and was the origin of the Ascot puff of the 'seventies. The Ascot, first worn at the

Ascot Heath races, was responsible for the great vogue of the ready-made cravat and was made of heavy colorful silks and novelty weaves. Variations of the style were the de Joinville, named after Prince de Joinville, and the four-in-hand or Teck, named after the Prince of Teck. The four-in-hand gained in popularity, replacing the made-up scarf by the end of the century. The bow tie continued in fashion to the end of the period.

Shirts of light colors, line checks and stripes, were worn with casual clothes past the middle of the century, but the fine white shirt for day and formal wear appears to have been the mark of the gentleman to the end of the century. An innovation, in the 'thirties, was the separate shirt front, or "dickey," which was replaced in the 'forties by the shirt with an inserted, tucked, pleated or embroidered bosom, of finer linen than that of the body of the garment.

Travel over the country, made easy by the railroads, carried people to "country, seaside or watering place," so that, by the 'fifties, country clothes came into existence. Men's casual clothes were in light colors, of fabrics such as nankeen, alpaca and foulard. Heavy tweed suits appeared for sportswear. The coat of the Duke of Norfolk's hunting suit, known as the Norfolk jacket, appeared in the 'eighties with knickerbockers, a first revival of knee breeches for day wear. Velveteen or corduroy breeches were for winter use and those of dark waterproof English cloth were preferred for autumn wear.

A fashion note of November, 1886, describes a "shooting jacket of strong plain or striped sail-cloth, gaiters of gray linen and a linen hat with cork lining."

There were many styles of topcoats. The short box coat dates back to the late 'thirties (see Page 277). It was single or double-breasted and has always been of fawn-colored cloth. An amusing fashion in the 'nineties was the use of the box coat over the evening habit, the tails hanging below to five or six inches. The burnous appeared in the late 'forties (see Page 289). The raglan, which is shown on Page 289, is of the 'fifties. It was named after the hero of the Crimean War, Lord Raglan, the loose armscye no doubt the result of his having lost an arm. There was a short sleeveless coat with cape, a flaring coat with straight sleeves and the MacFarlan, with its separate sleeve capes. In the 'eighties appeared the sleeveless Inverness cape coat of Scotch origin, the ulster of Irish origin, also the short double-breasted reefer adopted from the coat of the British Navy. The pall coat, or paletot, of the 'sixties was a heavy overcoat with a slight repression at the waist, a three-quarter-length garment. The Chesterfield, named after the Earl of Chesterfield, that classic dress overcoat of the twentieth century, also appeared in this period. Overcoats often had velvet collars, were fur-trimmed and fur-lined and were fastened by heavy braided loops.

There was also a vogue for shawls in masculine costume, that accessory being worn from 1840 to 1860. They were folded across the shoulders and were in wool in plaids and dark colors.

Until the 'sixties, the hair was worn moderately long and curled, usually parted at one side with side whiskers or beard all around the face. Whiskers separated by a shaven chin were called "Dundreary whiskers." Past the middle of the century, the mustache and the "imperial" appeared. Beards and whiskers disappeared in the 'eighties, but the mustache retained its popularity. At the same time, the hair was flattened on the top of the head and parted in the middle, sometimes from front to down the back. The preference appears to have been for straight hair in the 'nineties. The hair was dressed with Macassar oil all through this period, whence the vogue of the antimacassar, a tidy or doily which protected the back of the chair.

In tall hats, the fashion of fawn, gray or white beaver lasted until the 'nineties, with the black silk hat the headgear for formal dress. The invention of a machine for the manufacture of felt, in 1846, brought many new styles into vogue. In 1850, a round hard hat with straight brim and low round crown made its debut. It was designed by an English hatter, William Bowler, and was the original model of the bowler or derby. Another English name was the "billycock," a contraction of the name William Coke, the first Englishman to sponsor the style. Derby, the American name, had its origin in the fact that the Earl of Derby popularized the style by wearing the hat to the English races. His hat was gray with a black band. It was quite generally adopted in the 'seventies. A soft felt hat with wide brim and low flat crown appeared in the 'fifties, also the same model in straw and hats of woolen plaid for country wear. Caps had always been worn, but, with increase in travelling and sports, they now took a definite place in the wardrobe of the well-dressed man.

It seems well established that soft felt hats for men originated in Germany or Austria in the mountains of the Tyrol. After considerable British styling, these hats emerged as the Homburg or the fedora. The Homburg was named after Homburg, Germany, the place of its first manufacture. This hat was made fashionably important by being worn by the Prince of Wales (Edward VII), at Bad Homburg. The fedora took its name from the heroine of the drama by Sardou and was worn by both sexes in the 'eighties and the 'nineties.

The machine for sewing straw was perfected in 1870 and, by the 'eighties, the "boater" or hard straw hat was being worn when punting on the Thames. The Panama hat had been made for nearly three centuries in Ecuador and has always been in use by the Britisher in tropical countries. It was marketed at Panama, thus acquiring its name. The hat is known to have been worn in America in the eighteenth century.

Short Wellington boots worn under the trousers with straps lasted to the 'sixties. The laced-up shoe appeared in the 'fifties, followed by the side-buttoned shoe in 'sixties and the gaiter shoe in the 'seventies. The gaiter shoe had inserts of elastic at the sides or over the insteps and was known in America as the "congress shoe." In the second half of the century, black patent leather became fashionable for shoes. With the successful manufacturing of shoes, styles began to change often and special shoes were made for special occasions, such as dress shoes, evening shoes and sport shoes. Cloth spats and the gaiter halfway up the leg were fashionable throughout the period. Toward the end of the period came the cloth-top buttoned shoe.

A startling novelty in the early 'eighties were sleeping pajamas of Oriental origin, supplanting for many the long nightshirt with slashed sides.

Handsome gold-headed canes were carried, but were shorter than those of previous periods, being now cut to measure to reach from the man's hand of his slightly bent arm to the ground. Rings, scarfpins, heavy gold watches with heavy gold chains came into fashion about the middle of the century. Watches were carried in the vest pocket in the 'forties, when the shorter vest acquired the small watch pocket.

Buttons on suits and coats matched the cloth in color, often cloth-covered. Horn buttons were used and, by the middle of the century, buttons of dyed vegetable ivory were most popular, continuing in use today.

Cloth-covered buttons were first manufactured in the United States in 1826 and pearl buttons about 1885.

In women's clothes, the period known as "mid-Victorian" is the mode of the crinoline with its many flounces and ruffles, Queen Victoria living virtually in retirement after the death of the Prince Consort in 1861. The Queen attended the Paris Exhibition in state in 1855, thereby bringing about an acceptance of French ideas and feminine fashions into England.

The general style of the costume was that of the contemporary French, but it lacked the Gallic flair for lightness in clothes and, while it was definitely a period of ornamentation of all kinds, it was truly overdone in the English mode.

Boys' clothes became much simpler, with a leaning toward the peasant style of smock and trousers. An interesting fact is that, while the costume of the little girl followed closely, in design and trimming, that of her grownups, the design of the small boy's clothes appears to have been based upon the various European national costumes.

In 1851, Mrs. Amelia J. Bloomer of Seneca Falls, New York, attempted a reform in women's dress by appearing in full Oriental trousers with a very short skirt or tunic, not unlike Paul Poiret's minaret costume of more than half a century later. The event is noted here, because of her visit to London, where she met with some success, and because of the reappearance in the 'eighties of "bloomers" worn by women when bicycling.

Victorian England

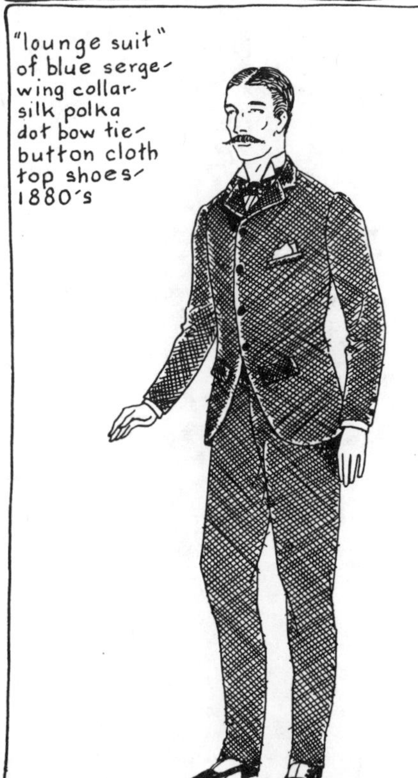

Victorian England

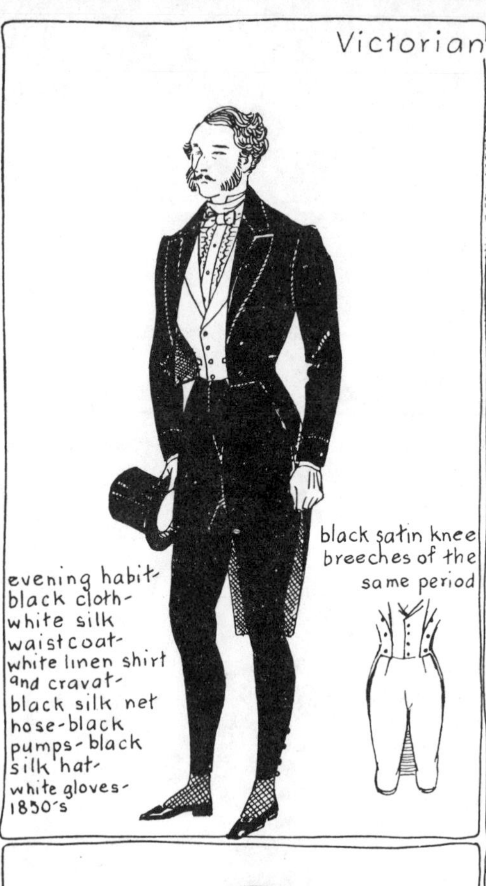

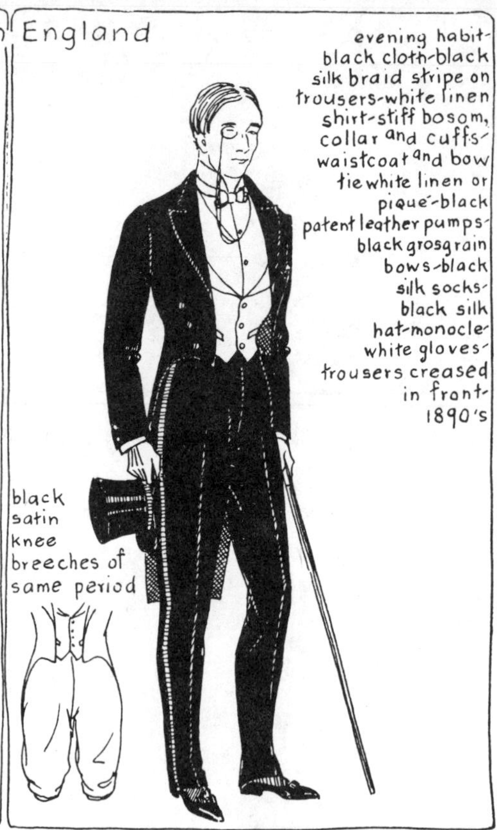

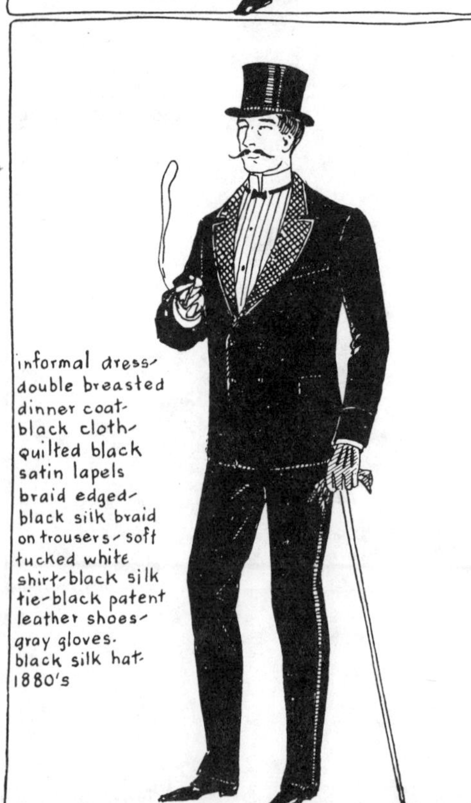

Victorian England

cloth redingote-velvet collar-cloth waistcoat-plaid trousers with straps-black silk scarf-collar tabs-beaver hat-black boots-1840's

sack coat with self vest-contrasting striped trousers-silk scarf-soft felt felt hat-buttoned cloth top shoes-1870's

"seaside" costume-flannel coat-flannel trousers-woolen sweater-straw boater with striped band-shoes of sailcloth and leather-1880's

Norfolk jacket and knickerbockers-heavy woolen cloth brown plaid on tan ground-yellow and brown knitted socks with cuffs-white linen spats-brown shoes-1890's

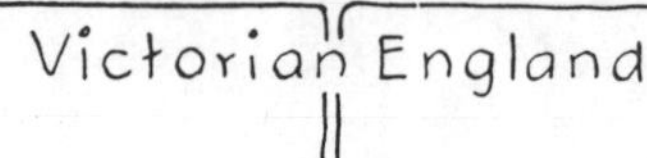
Victorian England

MacFarlan coat-
plaid trousers
over black
boots-silk
cravat-
standing
soft collar-
black silk
hat-
1850's

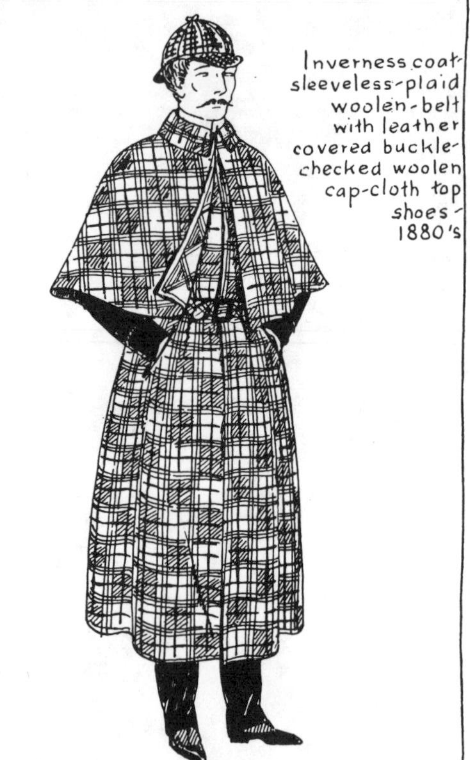
Inverness coat-
sleeveless-plaid
woolen-belt
with leather
covered buckle-
checked woolen
cap-cloth top
shoes-
1880's

dress overcoat-
heavy tan
broadcloth-black
velvet collar-
machine stitching-
horn buttons-
wing collar-
four-in-hand
scarf-black
shoes-tan
spats-black
silk hat-
1890's

Chesterfield overcoat-
black cloth with
velvet collar-
fly front-Ascot
scarf striped
red on black-
gray and black
striped trousers-
gray spats-
black shoes-
black silk
hat-
1890's
RTW

Victorian England

Victorian England
striped silk cravat-standing collar-1830's
light beaver hat-black silk cravat-pleated shirt-1830's
long black silk scarf-turn-down collar-1830's
black silk hat-black silk cravat-pleated shirt-1840's
natural straw-black ribbon-turn-down collar-bow tie-1850's
black silk hat-loosely tied scarf-standing collar-pearl pin-1850's
white felt Homburg-ribbon edge-Teck scarf-1890's
1840
gray felt top hat-loosely tied scarf-1870's
1850
black silk hat-long silk scarf-monocle-1860's
1860
1885
gray bowler-black ribbon-1879
1850
flat scarf
1890's
de Joinville scarf
straw "boater"-striped band-bow tie-monocle-1890's
plaid cap-silk muffler-pearl scarf pin-1890's
Ascot or "puff" scarf-pearl pin-1899
RTW

Chapter Forty

French

1870–1880

In this decade, the feminine interest was centered in the back of the costume. The pannier, or overskirt, of the late 'sixties was now bunched up in back, necessitating the tournure, or bustle. The style is known in England as "tied-back time." The skirt proper was long, usually ending in a train, even for street wear. The short-waisted bodice was lined with silk or muslin and shaped with inserted whalebones, fastening in front. Toward the end of the decade, the tunic, or peplum, descended over the hips, the bunched-up drapery in back dropped down, leaving the upper part of the costume quite sleek and in basque style. Sleeves for day wear were long, generally flaring at the lower edge. Evening-gown sleeves were tiny caps and the décolletage was square.

The design was most elaborate, several fabrics and trimmings employed in one garment. For winter, materials used were cashmere, satin, taffeta, moiré, velvet, faille, and, in the summer, surah, mohair, foulard, and lace, jet, tulle for evening with much bead and jet ornamentation. Pale blue was a favorite color, but bright colors were predominant, among them verdigris, royal blue, purple and garnet. Very much of the period were checks and stripes. Ribbons, braids, tassels and knotted fringe continued fashionable. A new style note was the pleated flounce. Black lace motifs were applied to velvet, silk and net. It still was a period of ribbon.

Coats, mantles and dolman wraps were of heavy silk trimmed with jet and passementeries edged with lace or fringe. For winter, there were sealskin coats in three-quarter or full length. Sealskin was dyed brown, not black as in the twentieth century, changing to a golden brown near the skin. The secret of the process disappeared with the death of the London furrier who discovered it. Silk plush was also smart, either sealskin or plush, edged with a band of beaver, and finished with collar and cuffs of the fur. Sable, mink, martin and chinchilla too, were fashionable.

In this period lingerie took on importance with drawers, petticoats and the chemise of fine cottons, ornamented with filmy lace and delicate embroidery. Wrappers and dressing gowns for wear at home were of transparent muslin and sheer nainsook, lace-trimmed.

High-heeled shoes were of fine kid or fabric, laced or buttoned and, toward the 'eighties, a narrow pointed toe came into fashion. Women also wore a congress boot, a shoe with elastic inserts at the sides, which proved unsatisfactory, the elasticity quickly disappearing. Rich fabrics were still used for evening slippers. Stockings, which were never seen, matched the evening gown and, for day wear, the silk petticoat. Purple and red, in petticoats and stockings, were great favorites.

In the first half of the decade, the hair, like the costume, was drawn up toward the back away from the face, exposing the ears, with the ends cascading down the back in cadogan fashion, in ringlets or looped braids. The thickness of the braids was exaggerated by being dressed loosely and over a cushion. A fringe or bangs often softened the brow, and long earrings were worn. By the end of the decade, the hair was dressed up the back in simpler fashion.

Bonnets were still elaborate but very small and worn high on the head, ribbons occasionally tied under the chin. Toward the end of the period, the hat replaced the bonnet, but ribbons, flowers and ostrich plumes continued as ornamentation. The short tightly tied face veil appeared.

Much attention was given to parasols, or sunshades, and to fans, which were of lace and chiffon, embroidered and spangled. Gloves were of kid in light colors, short and long, the latter buttoning to the elbow.

There was a marked trend toward a more active life, with young women taking to sports or "games," such as fencing, boating, tennis and bicycling.

French 1870-1880

gray cashmere over pleated royal blue silk skirt-narrow royal blue velvet ribbon-blue buttons-white ruching at neck and sleeves-1871

plum purple velvet jacket and skirt-lilac velvet drapery-mink fur bands-buttons-self ruche on skirt-lilac silk bonnet-béret crown-purple ribbon-white roses-green foliage-black shoes-beige gloves-1873

heavy tan faille silk gown and bowknots-pointed train-white taffeta drapery with pearl embroidery-white ostrich tips and aigrettes in hair-white slippers-1875

black satin-accordion pleated ruffles-jet beaded cording-velvet loops-wisteria blossoms-white chiffon vestee and sleeve caps edged with rhinestones-velvet neckband-jet jewelry-1879

French 1870-1880
natural straw-
black velvet
band and
ruching-
1871
natural straw-
mixed flowers-
old blue
ribbon-
1876
gray felt-French
blue velvet
ribbon-gray
ostrich-back
bandeau-
1872
bottle green
velvet-shaded
gray and brown
plume-pink
roses-green
foliage-green
bow-1875
brown velvet-
brown satin
loops-beige
plumes-
1875
pleated
pink
ribbon-
yellow velvet
bow-pink and
yellow flowers-
green foliage-
1876
buttoned fabric
top-patent leather
heel and toe
laced shoe-
kid or fabric
corset and
whalebone
petticoat
purple satin hat
and ribbon-shaded
purple and pink plume-
1878
whalebone and
silk
satin shoe-
elastic sides-
rosette
satin slipper
whalebone and wire
laced shoe-
kid with rosette
whalebone
and tape
whalebone and shirred silk
RTW

Chapter Forty-one

French

1880–1890

HE TOURNURE, or bustle, really a slim crinoline of the early 'seventies, grew less important in the latter part of that decade, to become again a definite feature of the mode of the 'eighties and to disappear by the 'nineties.

The costume was still complicated in design and composed of several fabrics and trimmings. Although short dresses appeared for dancing, street and country wear, the long train gown held its own. The straight foundation skirt continued to be superimposed by a shorter overskirt or draperies caught up in back. The pleated flounce of the underskirt developed into a real pleated skirt in this period.

The fitted, boned basque bodice, always made separate from the skirt and worn over the tightly laced stays or corsets, still reigned. The basque gradually shortened but the bodice retained its long waist, by the middle of the decade, dipping into a point in front. The silhouette was shaping into the "hour-glass figure" of the 'nineties. Forms of fine braided wire were used to enhance the curves of undersized breasts. Stockinet, or jersey, a cloth manufactured in the Isle of Jersey, was the fabric usually employed for the basque bodice.

The bodice often had an inserted front, a full shirred or pleated vestee of soft silk, chiffon or lace. The folds of this bloused front often fell five or six inches below the waistline or, again, hung peplum-like below a short "jacket bodice" and were called a "jabot."

The high neck prevailed in day gowns and, by the middle of the decade, high standing stiff collars and starched linen collars and cuffs became the fashion. The décolletage of the evening gown was moderately low, and sleeves were usually of elbow or cap length. The slim day sleeve was generally long or "bracelet length."

History making in the mode was the tailored suit of cloth, comprising coat, skirt and bodice brought out by Doucet of Paris. That event occurred near the end of this period and has survived over half a century. Doucet, originally founded as a house of lingerie in 1824, became a *maison de couture* late in the 'seventies. This couturier also originated the coat with "fur sides outside," conceiving the idea of using fur as a fabric.

Winter materials were heavy in velvet, satin, poplin, damask, serge and brocade. Summer fabrics consisted of light silks, foulard, muslin, tulle and such laces as Chantilly, Mechlin, English, Valenciennes and blonde. Appliquéd motifs of black, écru or cream-colored lace and passementerie were employed with velvet, ribbon and jet.

Lingerie and petticoats were of silk in delicate colors lavishly ornamented with embroidery and lace. In winter, an underpetticoat of woolen or flannel was always worn and edged with colored crochet woolen lace. The top petticoat was usually reinforced with stiff muslin below the waist in back, to accent the silhouette of the tournure or bustle.

Wraps were indeed varied in shape with long loose coats, long and short mantles, dolman wraps, long circular capes lined throughout with squirrel. Sleeves were flaring, cape-like or cut in one with the body, pointing the way to the all-out revival of the cape in the next decade. Tightly fitted jackets or long coats were known as paletots. Winter wraps, usually full length, were of velvet, sealskin, plush and cut velvet and often trimmed with bands of beaver. For summer, there were mantelets of cashmere, faille silk or heavy lace edged with lace frills and trimmed with passementerie. Very small round muffs of fur or fabric were carried and the feather boa reappeared.

Bonnets tied under the chin and called "carriage bonnets" resembled the fontange headdress of the latter part of the seventeenth century, even to the curled fringe of hair over the forehead. The ribbons were attached farther back on the bonnet, coming down behind the ears. Hats were being worn more and more, a favorite shape being the recurring postillion hat, now named the Rembrandt hat. It was ornamented with ostrich plumes and the brim was usually turned up at one side. To all the usual millinery trimmings in vogue, a new one was now added, that of stuffed birds.

The hair was drawn back off the ears, sometimes low in a chignon, cascading curls or dressed high in a bun. The front hair was often cut short and curled into a mass on the forehead. Flowers, velvet bows, small ostrich tips and aigrettes adorned the evening coiffure.

Long white kid gloves were *de rigueur* for evening, with delicate colors worn in the daytime. Sunshades were of chiffon and silk finished with lace and ruffles, a large ribbon bow tied on the handle. The use of jewels, especially diamonds, was extravagant. Onyx and black cut jet were very fashionable, dull jet being reserved for the mourning costume.

Mourning was strictly observed in dress, the entire costume of gown, coat and hat trimmed with heavy, dull black crêpe.

The fashionable woman's footwear consisted of heavy English shoes for morning, button or laced shoes of kid or a combination of kid and cloth for afternoon, while "opera slippers," of plain satin or kid to match the gown, were worn for evening. Stockings were mostly cotton thread instead of silk, hidden by trailing skirts. The vogue of the colored stocking continued, bright red stockings being noted in contemporary fashion plates of young women.

Large embroidered silk and feather fans were carried. Two styles of folding scented fans, of violet wood, are described as a Parisian novelty in a fashion journal of October, 1886. One was entirely of wood spotted with silver dots, the other, a wooden frame covered with Swedish leather and embroidered with birds, flowers and other motifs.

Small fabric bags with metal and jewelled mounts were in fashion and the knitted-silk beaded bag returned to favor.

The vogue for aprons was revived in the "tea apron" of sheer white lingerie fabric trimmed with lace, colored embroidery and colored satin and velvet ribbon.

That famous English dressmaker Redfern founded his Paris house in 1881, maintaining also a branch in London, and later, one in New York.

French 1880-1890

French 1880-1890

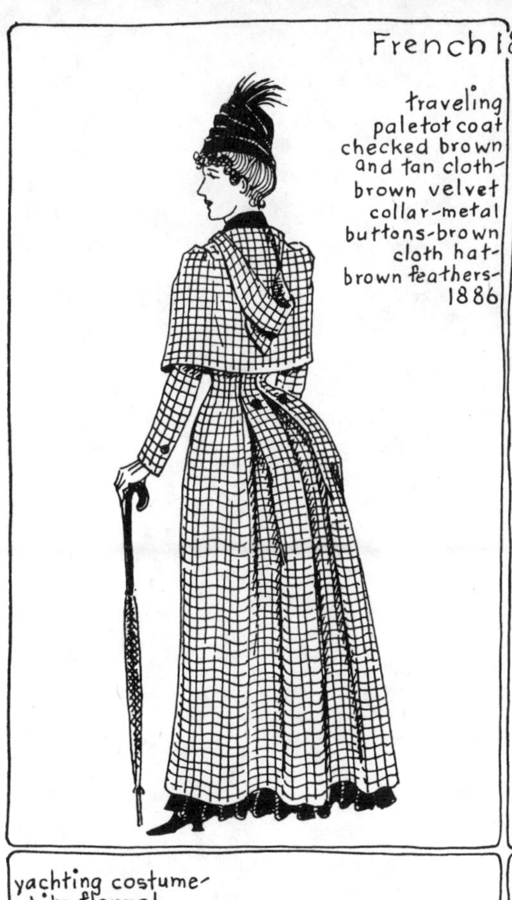

traveling paletot coat checked brown and tan cloth-brown velvet collar-metal buttons-brown cloth hat-brown feathers-1886

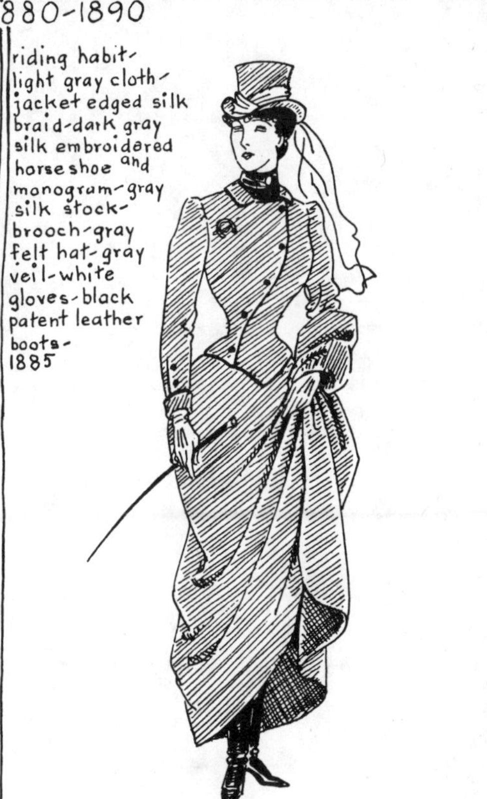

riding habit-light gray cloth-jacket edged silk braid-dark gray silk embroidered horseshoe and monogram-gray silk stock-brooch-gray felt hat-gray veil-white gloves-black patent leather boots-1885

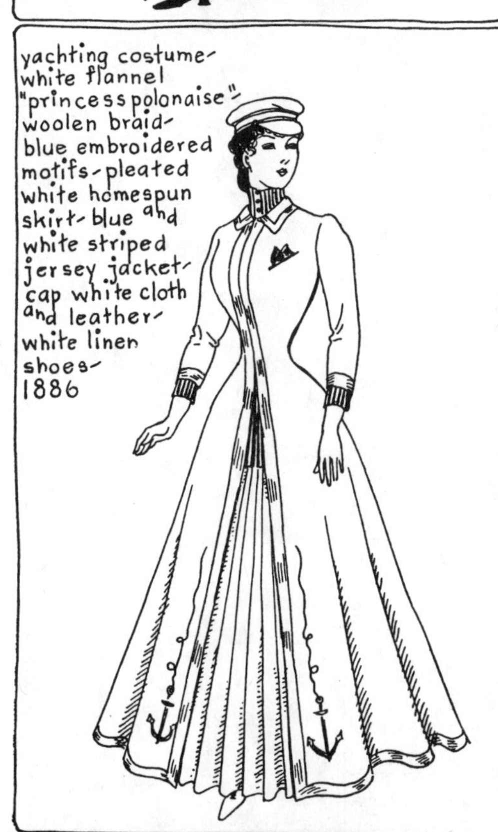

yachting costume-white flannel "princess polonaise"-woolen braid-blue embroidered motifs-pleated white homespun skirt-blue and white striped jersey jacket-cap white cloth and leather-white linen shoes-1886

hunting dress-light and dark brown checked cloth-velvet collar, cuffs and pockets-leather waistcoat-leather gaiters-brown tweed hat-1887

French 1880-1890
lace fichu-pleated crêpe-yellow and black velvet ribbon
black silk bonnet-jet leaves-white lace-yellow ribbon-black lace veil-jabot lace and lawn-pearls
black lace bonnet-black satin ribbon-pink roses-green foliage
brown velvet bonnet-pearls-brown ribbon-three birds
straw sailor-gros grain band
evening gloves painted in color
jet and gold comb
parasol-striped red and blue silk-red ribbon
Rembrandt hat-felt-ribbon and ostrich
velvet bows
bag of velvet and nickel
fan-ebony frame-shaded red feathers
evening petticoat-pale blue surah-scalloped flounces-lace flounce-pleated under frill
silk "jacket bodice" edged chenille-jet bead embroidery-white gauze "jabot" and sleeve frills
braided wire bustles
kid evening slipper
satin house slipper
lawn apron-lace-velvet ribbon and belt-cord and pompoms
RTW

Chapter Forty-two

French

1890–1900

WITH 1890, the bustle disappeared, along with tied-up skirt drapery, though occasional folds and shirred peplums were still seen on the hips. The general design in costume became less complicated, albeit that two or three fabrics were combined in one garment. As a rule, skirts fitted snugly over the hips, flaring to the floor in bell shape and ending in a train, which was worn all hours of the day, even when walking. In the streets, skirts were held up to one side, the proper handling of which became an art and a gesture, very characteristic of the period.

The skirt was cut in many gores and not only lined from waist to hem with silk, cambric or sateen but also interlined with stiffening, the whole hanging from a narrow belt. In fact, in this period, even washable fabrics were silk-lined, stiff taffeta being the most desirable because of its rustling sound or "frou-frou." Added to which were the beruffled taffeta petticoats of all colors, snug-fitting to the knee and flaring below. The sleek "hourglass" silhouette caused the elimination of petticoats down to but one, and that well fitted over the hips.

The leg-of-mutton sleeve, stiffened with tarltan, buckram and lining, reappeared and grew to enormous proportions. The puff reached to the elbow with the forearm section tightly fitted, followed in 1899 by the long slim tight sleeve. Evening gowns were sleeveless or had short puffs. The breadth of the shoulders was further enhanced by short capes, deep lace ruffles from neck to shoulder and wide circular bretelles. The deep-pointed bodice was reinforced with whalebone and lining.

The soft, full overhanging blouse, either separate or part of the gown and always finished with a belt, is definitely of the 'nineties. It was fashioned of any soft, sheer fabric and ornamented with embroidery, beads, braid, lace and insertion.

The collar of the day dress was high, sometimes edged with ruching, sometimes finished with a large tulle or lace bow placed either front or back. Small neck ruffs of tulle or ribbon loops were often worn with the low round décolletage.

The tailored suit, with jacket, skirt and "shirtwaist," took firm hold and has survived half a century. The appearance of coat, skirt, waistcoat and lingerie shirt for sportswear in the feminine world dates back to the middle seventeenth century of Louis XIV and Charles II, when women took over the masculine design for their riding habit. The short jacket, with skirt of walking length, first appeared in the 1850's. In its strictly English, mannish design and fabric, the suit dates from the 'eighties, but its whole-hearted acceptance took place in the 'nineties. The blouse of lingerie fabric had been making intermittent appearances since the 1830's, but now followed the masculine model in having shirt length instead of being fitted and sewn to a belt.

The princess silhouette of glove-like fit, gored from neck to hem, appeared in the 'nineties in tailleur, tea gown and ball gown, and, in 1899, the striking black-spangled evening gown, followed later by colored spangles. Of the period was the fitted bolero jacket worn over the princess gown or the full blouse.

The influence of the Maison Callot increased the vogue for costly lace, a novelty being bands of black lace insertion. Necks, wrists and fronts of blouses were finished with lace frills and voluminous jabots were in fashion. There were evening gowns made entirely of lace over taffeta. The chemise and drawers of fine linen, batiste, pale silks and satinet were lavishly lace-trimmed and beribboned. The lace-edged, beflounced petticoat in silk, linen or nainsook created a pretty effect, typical of the period, held to one side when walking.

Flounces were concentrated upon and accordion pleating was much favored, sometimes the whole gown being thus pleated. Materials were tucked, quilted, smocked, and laces were threaded with silk or velvet ribbon. Embroidery in silk or wool extended to tailored dresses and suits. Added ornamentation consisted of embroideries in silk and gold tinsel, pearl and crystal beads and gold lace insertion. The textiles of the decade were foulard, moiré, figured satin, damask, poplin, serge, muslin and tulle. Cloth was trimmed with rows of machine stitching.

As to wraps, for which fawn and gray were the favorite colors, there were Eton jackets and finger-tip length capes. Capes were two or three tiered, severely tailored or elaborately trimmed. Winter wraps were of velvet or cloth bordered with fur, while summer mantles were of silk and finished with embroidery, lace and pleated ruffles. Characteristic of the period is the full-length redingote of mastic-colored cloth with wide lapels and flaring collar.

The specialization of costume for the specific occasion began to take shape in the 'nineties, sports clothes following the English style. Yachting, "lawn tennis," bicycling and golf became popular, necessitating more practical clothes. The smart woman wore the "shirtwaist" and separate skirt with golf cape or Norfolk jacket for golf, and when bicycling, a short skirt or full bloomers with a fitted jacket. The tailored separate skirt of walking length was called the "rainy day skirt."

Such sports clothes were made of homespuns, coarse masculine tweeds and double-faced Oxford cloths. Colors were somber in dark blue, brown, Oxford gray and plaids. The tailored shirtwaist which accompanied such a suit was mannish with stiffly starched collar and cuffs, the collar either standing or turned-down. A small felt fedora, cloth tam-o'-

shanter or sailor completed the costume. By this time, the long riding skirt had been replaced by a shorter one, below which showed the mannish English leather boots.

The corset of firm heavy satin, in black or color, while lower than that of preceding years and only just covering the hips, was straight in front and decidedly fitted in at the waist, producing the "wasp-waist" effect. The entire garment was heavily boned with steel and whalebone. An eighteen-inch waist was the desired and admired size of that day. "Kangaroo walk" was the name given by humorists to the movement resulting from the figure encased in the straight front corset. The chemise was worn next to the body, the corset over and the drawers over the corset.

Small hats in toque form and hats with brims of moderate size were perched high on the head, invariably worn with the lace veil tied in back. Ornamentation comprised paradise plumes, aigrettes, ostrich plumes, wings, ribbon, jet, artificial violets and roses.

The former sleek effect in hairdressing was discarded in favor of a fluffy effect in which tiny curls softened the neckline and framed the face. The hair was simply dressed, drawn up into a knot on the top of the head and done in the new Marcel wave invented by the Parisian coiffeur. Small black and white ostrich tips with short aigrettes were added for evening wear.

A touch of rouge and a dash of rice powder sufficed in cosmetics, although, before the end of the period, cold cream was being used and "costly" perfumes were introduced.

The fashionable furs were chinchilla, Russian sable, seal and Persian lamb, of which scarfs, capes, jackets and small round muffs were made. Bands of fur trimmed the velvet or cloth costume, while revers and flaring collars were faced with it.

The fashionable shoe wardrobe contained walking boots and plain Oxford shoes, which were heavy in the English manner, and high button boots of kid to be worn under the trailing gown. Dressy slippers were of black or brown kid, black patent leather, also bronze slippers with stockings to match. Stockings were black in cotton thread or silk. That style note of the gay 'nineties, the open-worked black silk stocking, made its appearance.

Accessories were fans, suéde gloves, parasols and umbrellas. Small gold watches worn on long fine chains were tucked into the belt or concealed at the waist. Purses were small and of fabric or leather, the favorite style being the "pocketbook," a flat folding book-shaped purse with compartments.

The bathing suit was of serge, alpaca or flannel in dark blue or black and usually trimmed with white braid. The fitted bodice, high neck and elbow-length leg-of-mutton sleeves were of the prevailing mode. Bloomers were worn under the knee-length skirt with black stockings and low canvas shoes.

Fresh violets were very popular, worn in the evening and on coats, suits, dresses and muffs. The vogue of violets lasted through the first decade of the twentieth century. Here, in America, an admirer presented his lady-love with dozens of the showy, long-stemmed rose of bluish red called the American Beauty rose. Orchids in those days were sent only to actresses and were considered flowers of the *nouveaux riches.*

French 1890-1900

French 1890-1900

gown with separate double cape-old blue velvet and black velvet-mink bands and muff-black felt hat-black and blue ostrich plumes-1893

princess gown with jacket-old rose cloth-white soutache embroidery on white-gored skirt-batiste and lace jabot-lace frills-black felt hat-black ostrich-rose silk rosettes-white satin loops-white face veil-mink and lace muff with lace bowknot-1895

changeable brown checked taffeta-ivory lace bolero-brown velvet ribbon-pearl buckles-accordion pleated white blouse-white neck bow and frills-turban of red roses-green foliage-white lace-black silk umbrella-1897

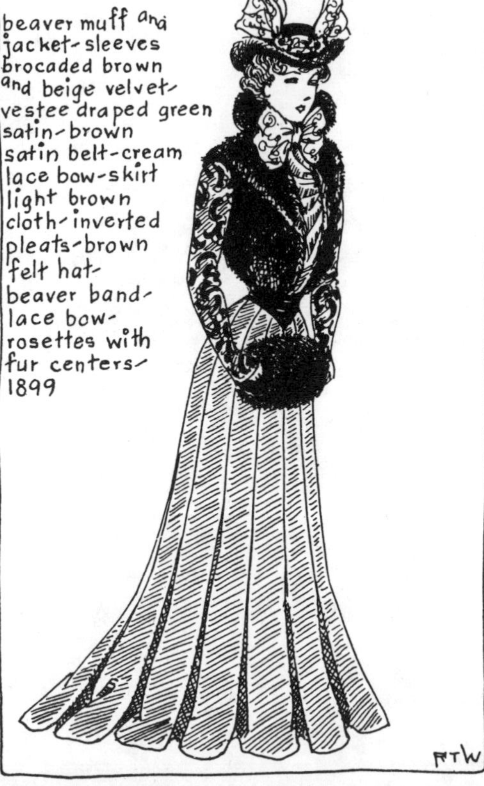

beaver muff and jacket-sleeves brocaded brown and beige velvet-vestee draped green satin-brown satin belt-cream lace bow-skirt light brown cloth-inverted pleats-brown felt hat-beaver band-lace bow-rosettes with fur centers-1899

FTW

French 1890-1900

redingote-mastic colored broadcloth-bone buttons-muff and toque black Persian lamb-black wings-blue brocaded ribbon-white gloves-black shoes-1894

summer cape-black taffeta-accordion pleated frills-white lawn collar and jabot with lace-taffeta rosettes-straw hat-pleated taffeta fans-light cloth dress-white kid gloves-black shoes-black silk umbrella-1895

black broadcloth cape-satin bound edges-tabs with large buttons-straw hat-violets-satin ribbon-spotted veil-1895

evening cape-black velvet lined and trimmed with mink-black embroidery on gold cloth-black silk tassels-white satin gown-lace and roses-white ostrich fan and headdress-aigrettes-1897

French 1890-1900

Chapter Forty-three

Masculine Costume

1900–1942

BY THE twentieth century, masculine costume had become thoroughly standardized, with a distinct code of rules as to the wearing of it. The cut of the garment, length of coat, breadth and shape of the shoulders, shape of the lapel, width of trousers and number of buttons vary, but the changes are barely perceptible from season to season. Directly after the First World War, there became evident some slight influence of Italian tailors presenting a military expression, and occasionally also a Hollywood note is brought to our attention, but it can be definitely stated that thus far in the twentieth century, as in the nineteenth century, London is the style source for men's fashions in clothing.

In the first decade appeared the concave shoulder, very broad with considerable padding in the shoulder head, creating a dip in the shoulder line. This extreme style was responsible around 1910 for the introduction of a natural shoulder without padding, which is still worn by conservative men. A straight-sided, straight-back short jacket originated in the 'twenties in a college town, a revolt against the nipped-in waist and spiderlike silhouette of the ready-made.

An attempt was made in the middle 'twenties to accentuate the chest and straight-line shoulder, by means of a high waistline which necessitated high-rise trousers. The high waistline was further accentuated by the use of a double-breasted vest with horizontal bottom. (See Page 343). The idea originated in London but was of short duration. In the 'thirties, London designers set up a straight military shoulder and found it advisable to break the line on the chest with folds. This is the drape idea. Through the use of dynamic principles of design, in the last ten years, it has been possible for the tailor to make a short man appear taller and a corpulent man slimmer.

The slim trousers of the late nineteenth century took on fullness in the first decade of the new century; in fact, a very exaggerated form appeared in the "peg-top" trousers. This style did not last. The slim silhouette persisted until the early years of the 1920's, when "Oxford bags" came into vogue. They were sometimes as much as twenty-four inches in width at the bottoms. The very wide trousers lasted through the 'twenties, then were cut narrower with a taper toward the foot. Pleats at the waist appeared in the early 'thirties.

The sports costume in the first half of the period consisted of the Norfolk jacket, knickerbockers and heavy woolen hose with deep turned-down cuff. The cap with wide visor and ample crown accompanied the outfit. In the latter part of the 'twenties, knickers became voluminous in width and length and were known as "plus fours." That term originated in the British Army, when breeches were measured as reaching to the knees, plus four inches. White linen knickers were much in evidence in the summer. The sports coat with pleated back and half belt stitched on or in, appeared in the middle of the 'twenties.

A revival was the dress sack or formal lounge, sometimes braid bound, which came in, in the 'twenties. It is worn with formal striped gray and black trousers and has either a peaked or notched lapel.

Early in the 'thirties, the white mess jacket, copied after that worn by the British officer on tropical duty, appeared. It was worn during the summer with black tie and the cummerbund of East Indian origin, which often took the place of the waistcoat. Then came the white dinner coat either single or double breasted, also worn with black tie. Black mohair breeches trimmed with braid accompany the white dress coat. The white shirt with soft turned-down or fall collar and soft bosom of piqué or linen is usually worn with the summer dinner coat, either black or white. The introduction of summer evening clothes was due to the popularity enjoyed by many semitropical summer resorts in the Bahamas, along the Mediterranean and the coast of Florida.

After the First World War, the summer suit for day wear in the States came to the fore and is worn not only to business in the South but in the North as well. Materials consist of heavy linen, seersucker, tussah, shantung, tropical worsteds and a fabric of cotton and mohair which is popular. Smart suitings of good texture woven with synthetic yarns as the base are also employed. Wool gabardine was developed for wear in the summer months in tans, grays and blues. The fabric derives from the famous East Indian gabardine with a red back known as suncloth.

The English walking coat was a style which met with acceptance by the middle class in that country. It enabled one to dress differently from the clerk and yet was not formal attire. (See Page 338.)

Black or midnight blue continues *en règle* for evening clothes, but the classic dark-blue business suit of the early part of the period has been supplanted by the wearer's own choice of fabric and color. Woolen textiles for suits consist of tweeds, shetlands, serges, flannels, gabardines and worsteds, in beautiful grayed color mixtures. After years and years of black, gray, brown and dark blue, we now have suits of French blue, blue-green, pinkish beiges, while in sports clothes much liberty in color is permitted. In patterns, there are diagonals, pin stripes and checks, herringbones, glen or "glenurquhart" plaids, the pin dot or sharkskin pattern.

The hand-stitched or "hand-pricked edge," instead of machine-stitching of collar and lapel of the informal suit, was a new feature which appeared in the 'thirties.

The crudely woven but artistic Harris tweed of heather colors, originally made in the Isle of Harris in the Hebrides, enjoyed a great demand in the early half of the period. Great advances have been made in the last twenty years in the styling of fabrics. German manufacturers, in the 'twenties, made an unsuccessful attempt to gain a portion of the American woolen cloth trade and undersold the British weavers to such an extent that, for a time, there was an influx of cloth fair in quality but poor in design.

The great advance in the weaving and dyeing of synthetic fibers or yarns has largely supplanted the use of silk as lining in men's clothing.

Definitely of the twentieth century is the polo coat of natural-color camel's hair. It appeared in the first decade, is still good and was evolved from the cricket "wait coat" thrown over the shoulders between periods of play.

The successful attempts of cloth processors to produce a water-repellent cloth are attested by first, the raincoat and then the trenchcoat of the First World War. These coats, both in England and the United States, are well designed, smartly tailored and some of the British makes are world renowned.

The following overcoats of the preceding century, with style variation, are still with us, namely, the raglan, the Ulster, the Inverness and the Chesterfield. The paletot, or paddock, of the early years of the century was a fitted overcoat with waist seam and skirt pleats in back, headed with the two buttons. It was the evolution of the original English riding coat, or redingote. The Chesterfield seems to have established itself as the classic dress overcoat. In the list of overcoatings are vicunas, thibets, friezes, chinchillas, undressed worsteds, Meltons and Montagnacs.

The huge racoon coat for winter wear was the result of riding in the open car and was considered proper equipment for attending football games. In the late 'twenties its popularity was challenged by another coat of deep-pile camel's hair.

The dress shirt continues to be made of fine white cotton or linen with stiff or pleated bosom of linen or piqué, while the informal white shirt is usually of cotton broadcloth, poplin or a basket weave. Other fabrics are figured silks, plain, plaid, striped cottons and flannels in all colors. An innovation in the 'thirties was the dark-colored shirt in navy, wine red or brown, with light-toned coat and trousers.

The backless evening waistcoat of white piqué, cooler for night club wear and dancing, has been popular for several years.

A detached soft collar, wrinkle-proof and requiring no starch, was introduced by some shirtmakers in the 'twenties. Later on, the soft collar was still further improved by the use of a rayon fabric in the lining, collar and shirt being now attached. Of the 'twenties and the 'thirties is the pin collar, in which the turned-down collar points are held by a long gold pin passing under the scarf knot.

The polo shirt, with long collar points which lay over coat or sweater, is popular and much in evidence in the summer. To conceal the bare neck, a brilliantly colored bandeau scarf is loosely tied around the neck, filling in the V.

The predominant note in neckwear for the period is the four-in-hand, with the occasional appearance of the bow tie. All fabrics, weaves, patterns and colors hold with club and regimental stripes, the favored of the whole period.

In the early years of the twentieth century and contemporary with the "shirtwaist girl," men, in the summer, discarded their vest and carried their coat over the arm. This fad created the vogue of the leather belt, which has been worn since. Buckles are of leather, gold, silver or other metal. Gallowses or suspenders continue to be worn with evening clothes and are still preferred by many in place of the belt.

The derby and the black or blue fedora or Homburg vie with each other for day town wear and with the dinner jacket. The collapsible opera hat of black grosgrain silk accompanies full dress and the silk top hat is worn with the cutaway or formal day clothes. The gray top hat is still seen in England at the races.

The hard straw hat, sailor or boater is still with us for wear in town, although a lighter style of the Homburg type in coarsely woven straw, jute, hemp or other exotic material is usurping its place. The newer hat is bound with a wide, pleated, brightly colored silk puggree, originally tied about the East Indian helmet. Panama hats in the hands of stylists have taken on a more acceptable shape.

The open-air activities of men in the late 'twenties brought into existence for use on the golf course, at the races and for country wear generally, a light-weight, paper-thin felt hat which could be rolled up and packed into a suitcase. The cap, though still used for sports in England, gave way to the soft felt in the United States.

The derby and hard straw hat of the first decade retained the black silk cord of English origin to about 1915. It was wound round the ribbon band, one end formerly used in anchoring the hat to the buttonhole in the coat lapel. English hats often had eyelets in pairs at the side of the crown for ventilation.

A noteworthy style of dressing the hair occurred in the first decade, when men wore their hair straight, parted in the middle, the side pieces reaching to the ears in length.

The turtle-neck sweater of solid color, which first appeared in the 'eighties with the fad for bicycling, football, lawn tennis and yachting, lasted through the first decade of the twentieth century. Then the gay, colorful sweater of Fair Isle, England, completely changed the trend in this garment. The V-neck appeared, also the coat sweater in varied color designs. In the wake of the V-neck came the soft shirt and the colorful scarf.

Negligee or house robes became general, and here masculine taste was permitted to indulge not only in plain silks, flannels or velveteens, but in the most colorful of figured silks. Beach robes are of bright-colored cottons and flannels in bold patterns, stripes or solid color. The blazer, a separate unlined sports jacket, originally of navy blue flannel bound with white braid, also took on very gay stripes.

From the 'nineties, men's underwear experienced a radical change. Until then, the long union suit of lisle or cotton was worn for summer, changing to one of wool for winter. The great vogue for sports brought in an entirely new fashion. Founded upon the athlete's running pants and skeleton shirt, undergarments changed to sleeveless lisle shirts and shorts of fine cottons, first white and later to highly colored stripes, plaids and prints. Union suits of lisle or silk, form-fitting, often knee length, continue to be worn, principally by horsemen.

Hose or socks are of silk, lisle and wool, of varied colors and clocked. Plain brown, blue and black in ribbed weave are the most popular.

Pajamas are made of many different fabrics, either cotton or silk, plain colored or striped. The tunic either buttons jacket-like or slips on over the head. There is also a knee-length coat with long lapel, buttoned and belted and worn without trousers.

In the early years of 1900, high shoes, either laced or buttoned, were worn in the fall and winter and low shoes, also either laced or buttoned, in the summer. They were to be had in tan, brown, gun-metal calf or patent leather. By 1930, high shoes had disappeared from the wardrobe of the well-dressed man. Blucher, signifying the style of lacing, originally designated the half boot named after the Prussian General Blücher.

The fringed leather piece which drops over the lacing of the sports Oxford was originally intended as protection to the laces when tramping over the Scottish moors.

Sports shoes were fashioned of white buckskin or a combination of white buckskin and black or brown leather saddles, but, with the late 'twenties, came various styles in pigskin, followed by sandals of interlaced strips of colored leather. A popular sports style is the moccasin type of low shoe, slipperlike, made with a firm leather sole. The very thick crêpe rubber has become a staple. The black-waxed calf Oxford is worn with formal day clothes and the black patent-leather Oxford with tails or the dinner coat.

Spats have been worn throughout the period with the low shoe or Oxford, always of gray or beige and usually of broadcloth, though occasionally of linen for summer.

Colored handkerchiefs, striped or plaid or in deep rich colors, and of fine cottons and linens, are used only with informal clothes. The fine white linen or batiste handkerchief with exquisite hand-turned or hemstitched edge and monogram continues in demand.

The walking stick, much used in England and on the Continent is but occasionally seen in the States. Gold or silver headed sticks of rare and exotic woods gradually gave way to those of heavy Malacca with a crooked handle. Gloves are of white buck or kid for dress and chamois, mocha or pigskin for informal wear. The wrist watch, a small watch attached to an adjustable bracelet of leather, silver or gold became more popular after its use in the First World War. It was worn as early as 1910 by the British officer. The heavy gold watch in use for centuries has been replaced by one, wafer-thin, of gold or platinum with a very fine chain. Another gadget of the twentieth century is the tie clip of gold holding the scarf to the shirt when the vest is dispensed with.

The fashion in boutonnières is a dark red carnation, either fresh or artificial, worn on the lapel of the dinner coat and a white carnation with "tails."

Englishmen continue to demand custom-made clothes, or, as they term it, "bespoke tailoring." English ready-to-wear clothing has never achieved the excellence of design and tailoring that has, since the middle of the 1890's characterized the product of the best American manufacturers. The only ready-to-wear used extensively by the well-dressed Britisher is confined almost exclusively to certain overcoats and raincoats or utility sports topcoats of outstanding design.

In the first quarter of the present century, American designers of the ready-made endeavored to evolve a real American style, but, with the exception of a few so-called university styles, the manufacturers are willing to follow the custom tailors, deriving their ideas and design from London.

In the first decade of the twentieth century, the small boy, who had been wearing straight knee-length breeches, changed to knickerbockers with the accompanying Norfolk jacket. His overcoat followed the style of his elders. Again, copying his seniors, he changed to slacks in the 'thirties. The vogue for sports clothes has fitted in beautifully with the youngster's way of life.

In this year of 1942, the designers of England and the States have brought out clothes which will conserve materials for the armed forces.

The fabric is composed of synthetic yarn, using sixty-five per cent or less of wool. The suit is shorn of cuffs, pleats, buttons on sleeves, and patch pockets. The jacket is shorter, trousers are narrower and the vest is eliminated from the double-breasted. The British model is called "the Utility Suit," while we have named ours "the Victory Suit."

Formal evening wear: Tail coat, black or midnight blue, unfinished worsted; trousers same, braided side seams, uncuffed bottoms; waistcoat, white washable piqué, single-breasted; white shirt, stiff bosom plain or piqué; bow tie, to match bosom; wing collar; pearl studs; white buck or kid gloves; shoes, patent leather Oxfords or pumps; hose, black or dark blue silk with or without clocks, also lisle; silk top hat or opera hat; overcoat, black or dark-blue Chesterfield, single or double-breasted.

Informal evening: Dinner jacket, black or midnight blue, unfinished worsted; trousers same, braided side seams, uncuffed bottoms; waistcoat, white washable piqué or black silk, single or double-breasted, or black cummerbund; white shirt, stiff bosom, piqué or wide box pleat; wing or fold collar; silk bow tie, black or midnight blue; gloves, white mocha, buck or chamois; shoes, patent leather, low shoes or pumps; studs, pearl, mother-of-pearl, enamel or colored stones or plain gold; hose, blue or black silk, plain or clocked; overcoat, single or double-breasted Chesterfield, belted guard coat or box coat in black, Oxford or midnight blue.

Formal day: Cutaway, black or Oxford cheviot or unfinished worsted; waistcoat, same or light-toned washable fabric, as linen, single or double-breasted; trousers, black and gray, striped worsted, uncuffed bottoms; silk top hat; white shirt, stiff bosom, plain or pleated linen or piqué; wing or fold collar; cravat, Ascot or four-in-hand, gray or conservative stripings; gloves, white or gray buck, mocha, fawn calf or white chamois; pearl or jewel scarf-pin; hose, plain or ribbed, silk or lisle, black or dark blue; shoes, black or gun-metal calf Oxfords; overcoat, blue, black or Oxford Chesterfield.

1900-1942

single breasted sack suit-gray striped worsted-modified peg-top trousers-black leather shoes-brown capeskin gloves-gray fedora hat-wing collar-polka dot bow tie-1905

single breasted sack suit-herringbone shetland-striped silk four-in-hand scarf-white collar attached shirt-snap brim felt fedora-tan Oxford shoes-1941

double breasted sack suit-plaid over diagonal-high turned-down collar-very narrow four-in-hand scarf-black shoes-1906

double breasted sack suit-blue sharkskin fabric-white collar and shirt-striped four-in-hand scarf-black Oxfords-1941

RTW

1900-1942

formal day dress-
Prince Albert frockcoat-
satin faced lapels-
silk buttons-pearl
gray silk Ascot
scarf-high white
collar-trousers
striped gray and
black-black
patent leather
shoes-white
spats-black
silk top hat-
black
stick-
1906

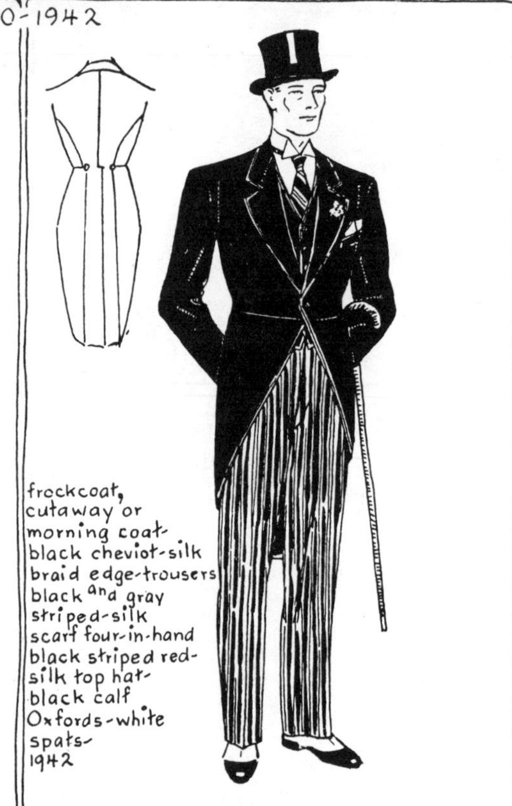
frockcoat,
cutaway or
morning coat-
black cheviot-silk
braid edge-trousers
black and gray
striped-silk
scarf four-in-hand
black striped red-
silk top hat-
black calf
Oxfords-white
spats-
1942

English walking
suit-tan worsted-
white piqué
waistcoat-white
figured brown
four-in-hand scarf-
mocha
gloves-brown
derby-black
calf shoes-
tan spats-
1906
RTW

informal evening
single breasted-
dinner coat-black
or midnight blue
unfinished worsted-
black silk braid
on trousers-white
piqué bosom, fold
collar and waistcoat-
black silk bat
wing cravat-patent
leather Oxford ties-
1938

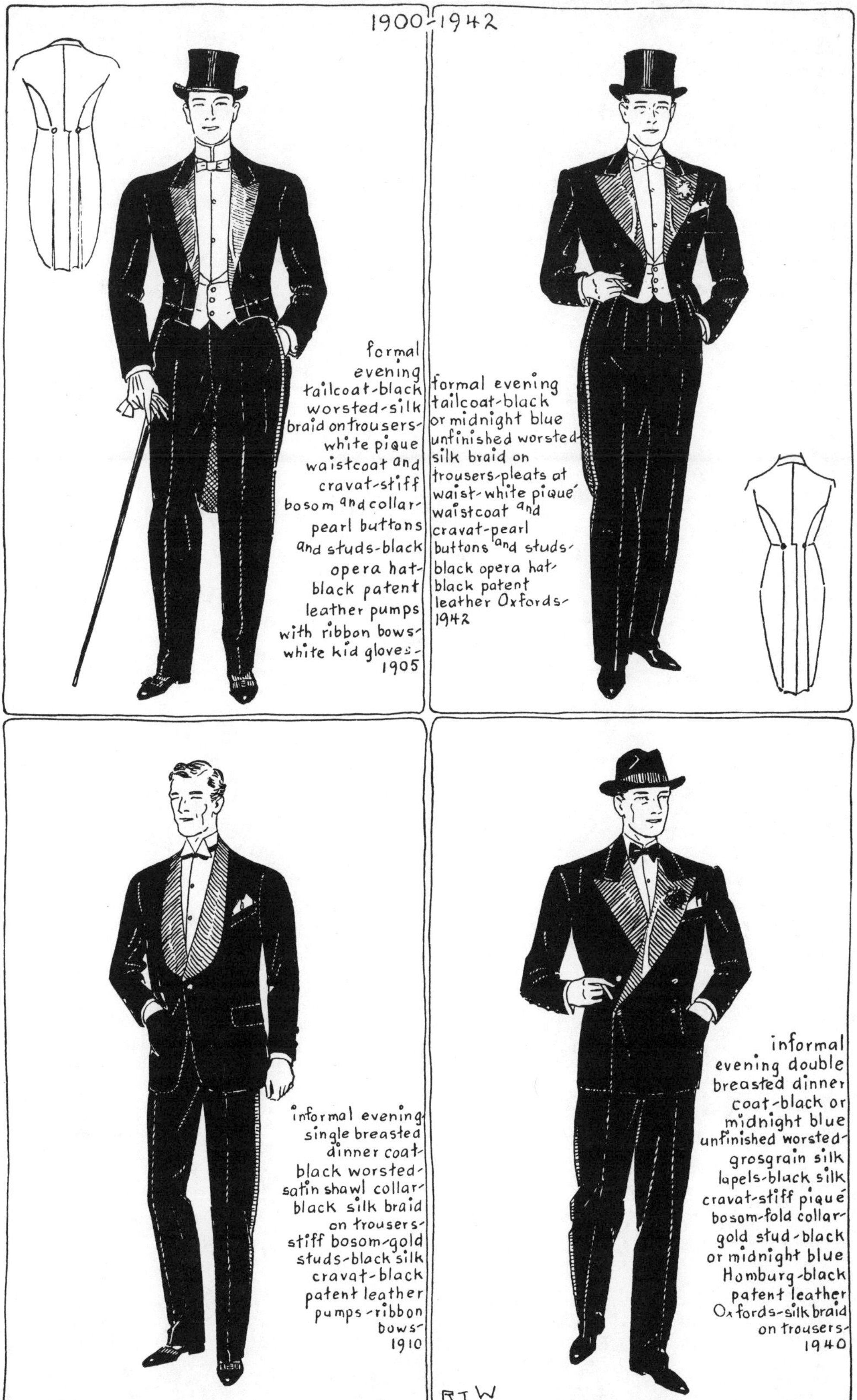

1900-1942

formal evening tailcoat-black worsted-silk braid on trousers-white pique waistcoat and cravat-stiff bosom and collar-pearl buttons and studs-black opera hat-black patent leather pumps with ribbon bows-white kid gloves-1905

formal evening tailcoat-black or midnight blue unfinished worsted-silk braid on trousers-pleats at waist-white piqué waistcoat and cravat-pearl buttons and studs-black opera hat-black patent leather Oxfords-1942

informal evening single breasted dinner coat-black worsted-satin shawl collar-black silk braid on trousers-stiff bosom-gold studs-black silk cravat-black patent leather pumps-ribbon bows-1910

informal evening double breasted dinner coat-black or midnight blue unfinished worsted-grosgrain silk lapels-black silk cravat-stiff piqué bosom-fold collar-gold stud-black or midnight blue Homburg-black patent leather Oxfords-silk braid on trousers-1940

RTW

golf suit with "plus fours"-vest self material-gray toned shetland-knitted plaid woolen golf hose-fringed brogues heavy tan leather-striped silk four-in-hand scarf-hat beige feather weight felt-1927

casual clothes golf and country wear-shirt wine red cotton basket weave-varied colored silk muffler-beige flannel slacks-pleats at waist-tan leather mocassins-1941

country clothes Norfolk jacket-blue serge jacket and vest-gray whipcord breeches-white washable stock-heavy knitted golf hose-heavy tan blucher shoes-checked woolen cap-1901

golf suit-sports coat checked worsted-slacks light colored flannel-hat light brown coarse woven straw-draped striped silk puggree band-shoes turned calf-dark silk handkerchief in pocket-1940

1900-1942

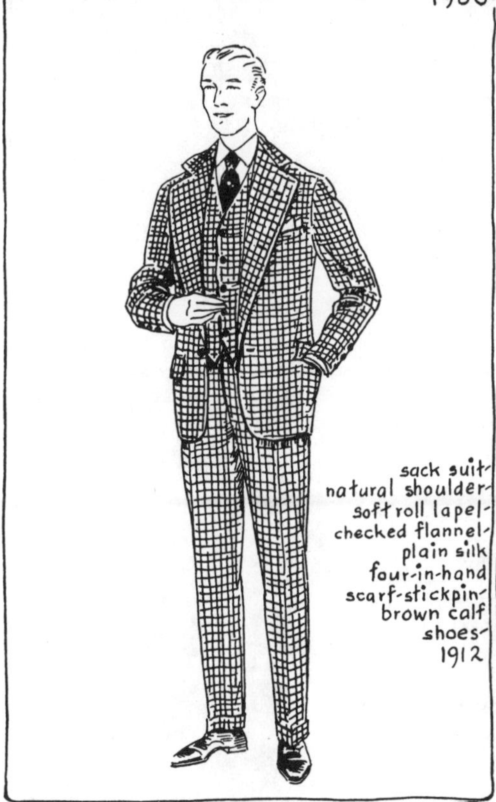

sack suit-
natural shoulder-
soft roll lapel-
checked flannel-
plain silk
four-in-hand
scarf-stickpin-
brown calf
shoes-
1912

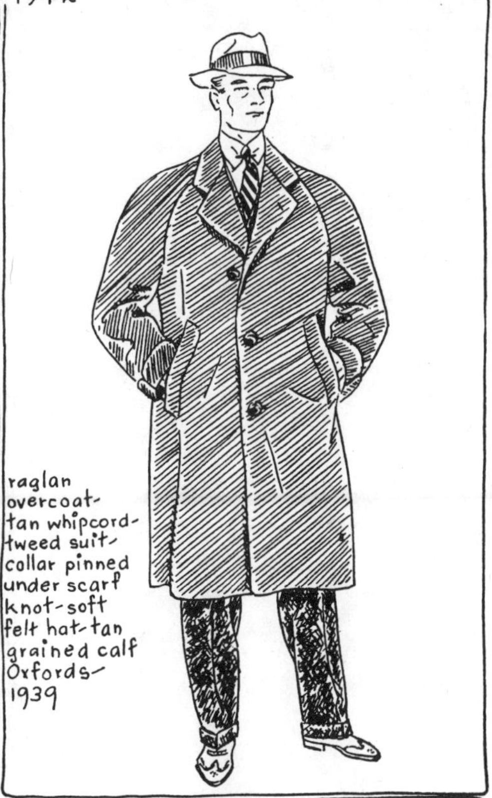

raglan
overcoat-
tan whipcord-
tweed suit-
collar pinned
under scarf
knot-soft
felt hat-tan
grained calf
Oxfords-
1939

overcoat-
dark blue
chinchilla-
gray suit-
gray spats-
black calf Oxfords-
black derby-
chamois gloves-
1924
RTW

polo coat
natural color
camel's hair-
long belt-
leather
buckle-
horn
buttons-
tweed suit-
soft brown felt
hat-brown
calf shoes-
1936

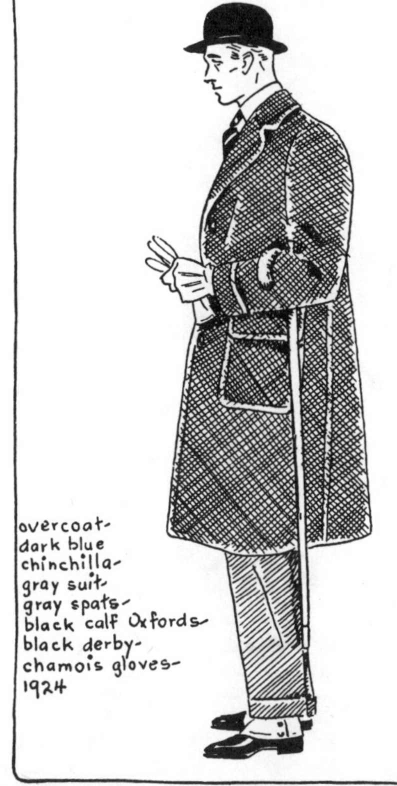

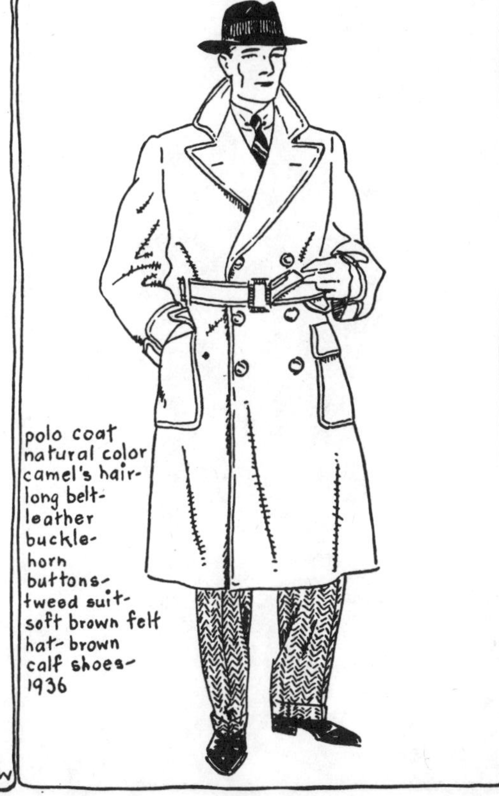

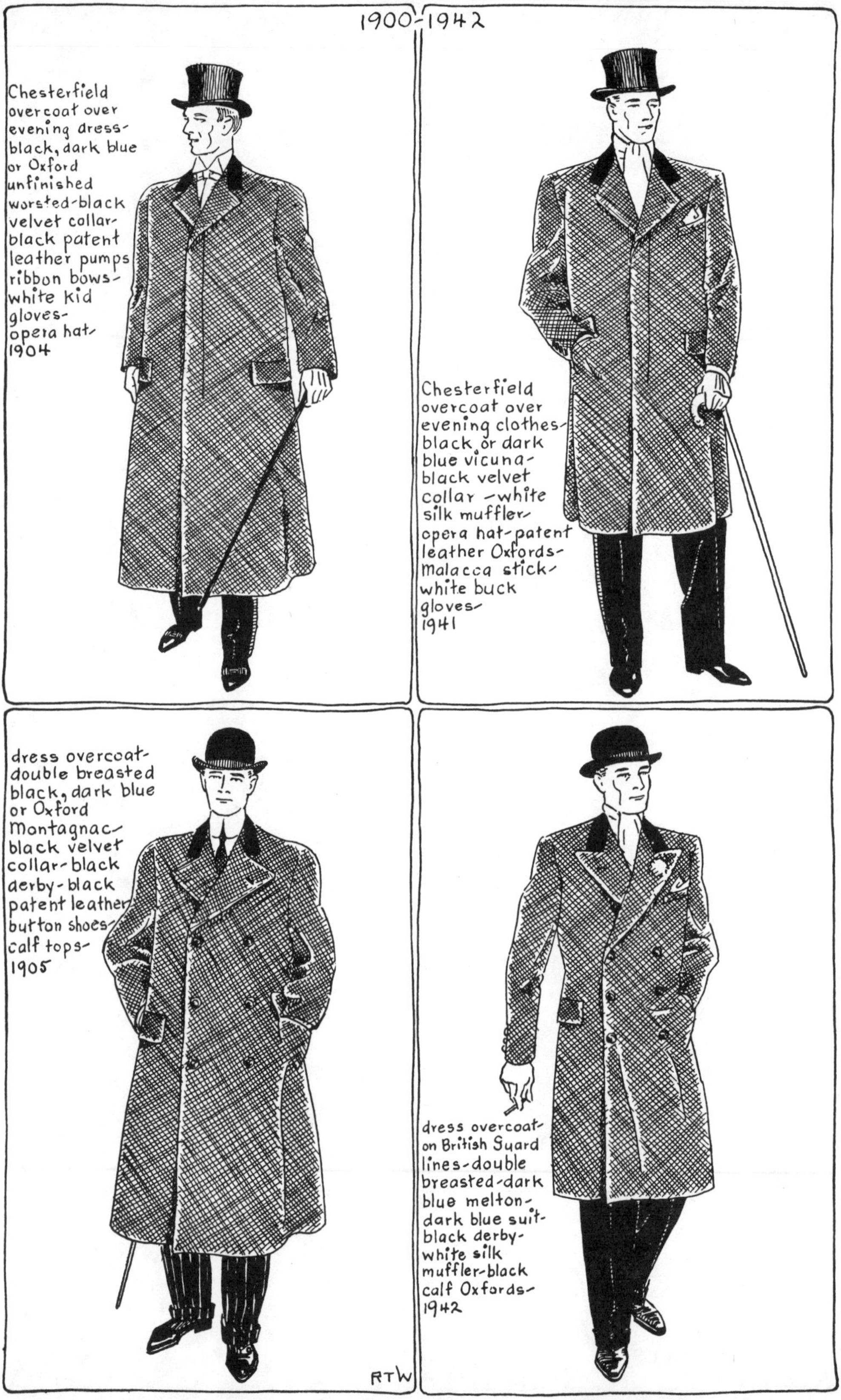

1900-1942
Chesterfield overcoat over evening dress-black, dark blue or Oxford unfinished worsted-black velvet collar-black patent leather pumps ribbon bows-white kid gloves-opera hat-1904
Chesterfield overcoat over evening clothes-black or dark blue vicuna-black velvet collar -white silk muffler-opera hat-patent leather Oxfords-malacca stick-white buck gloves-1941
dress overcoat-double breasted black, dark blue or Oxford Montagnac-black velvet collar-black derby-black patent leather button shoes-calf tops-1905
dress overcoat-on British Guard lines-double breasted-dark blue melton-dark blue suit-black derby-white silk muffler-black calf Oxfords-1942
RTW

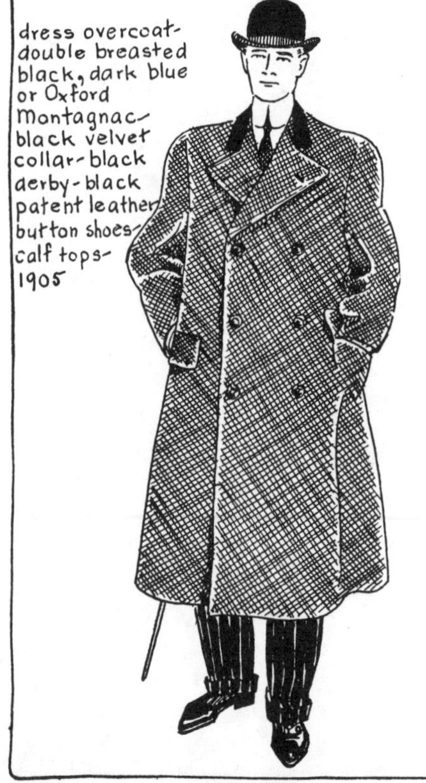

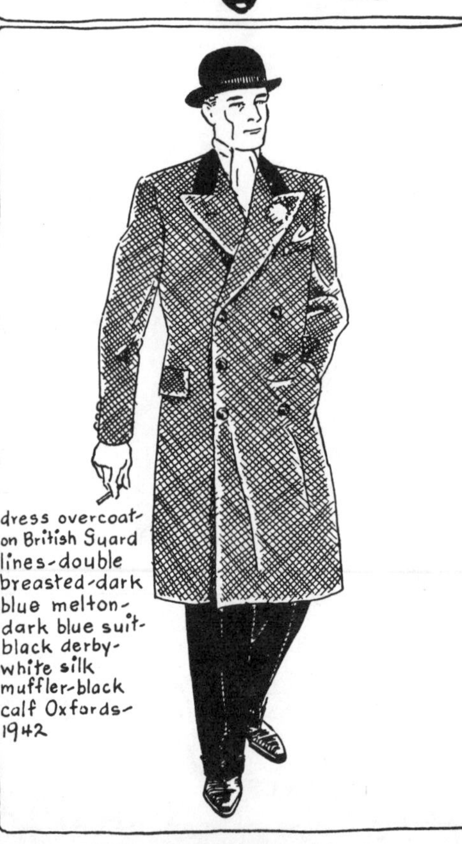

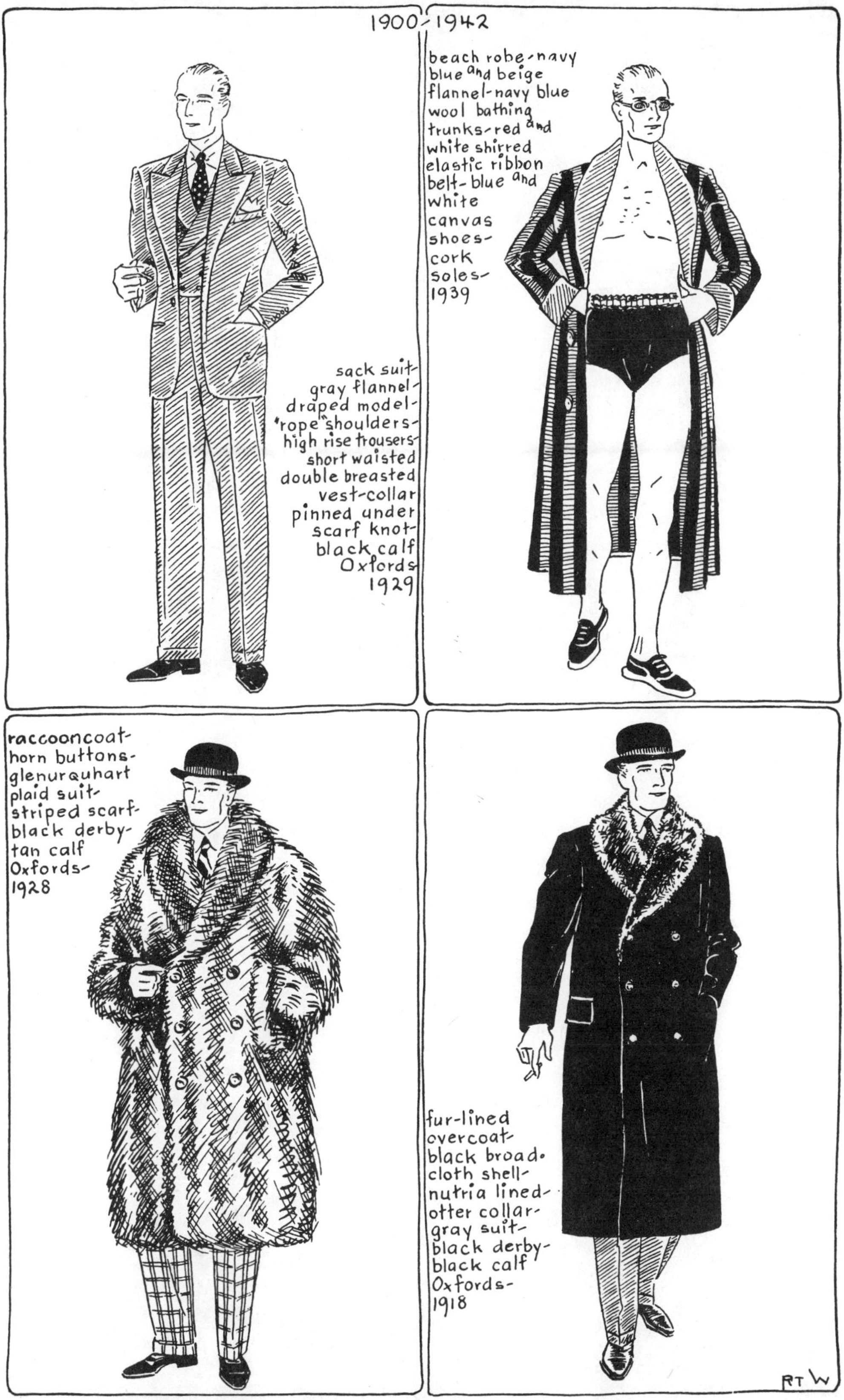
1900-1942
sack suit-
gray flannel-
draped model-
"rope" shoulders-
high rise trousers-
short waisted
double breasted
vest-collar
pinned under
scarf knot-
black calf
Oxfords-
1929
beach robe-navy
blue and beige
flannel-navy blue
wool bathing
trunks-red and
white shirred
elastic ribbon
belt-blue and
white
canvas
shoes-
cork
soles-
1939
raccooncoat-
horn buttons-
glenurquhart
plaid suit-
striped scarf-
black derby-
tan calf
Oxfords-
1928
fur-lined
overcoat-
black broad-
cloth shell-
nutria lined-
otter collar-
gray suit-
black derby-
black calf
Oxfords-
1918
RTW

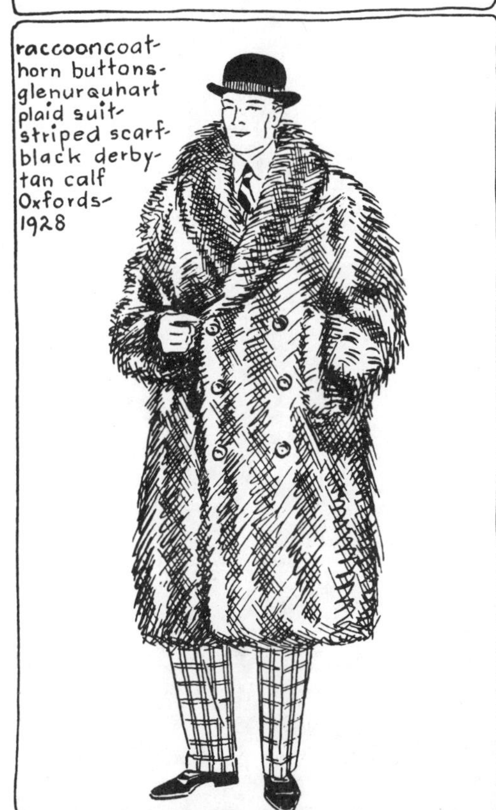

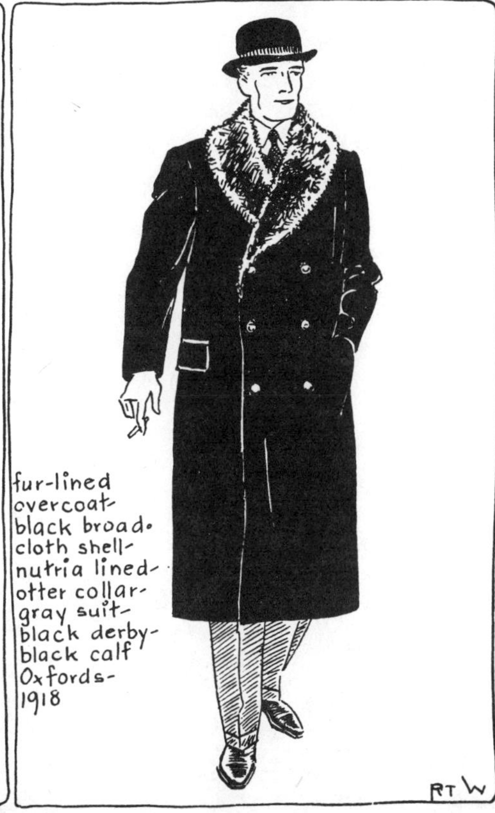

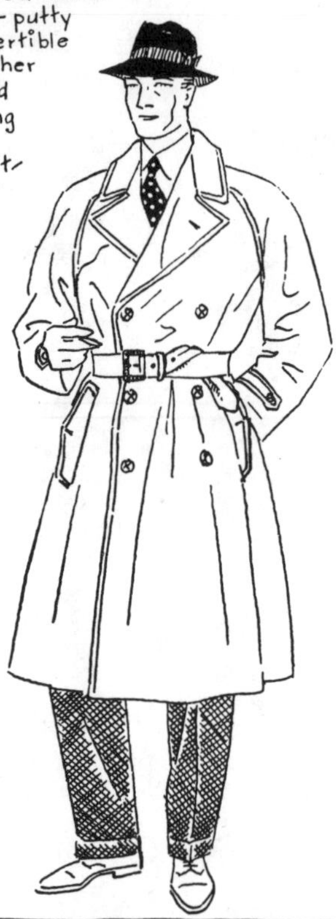

trench coat-waterproofed cotton gabardine-putty color-convertible collar-leather buttons and buckle-long belt-gray flannel suit-brown felt hat-tan Oxfords-1924

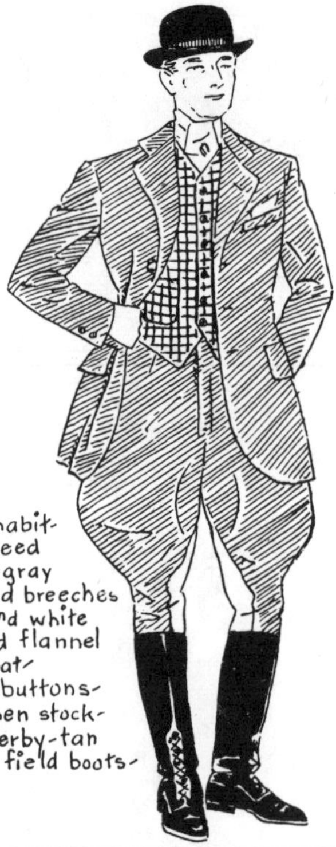

riding habit-gray tweed jacket-gray whipcord breeches black and white checked flannel waistcoat-leather buttons-white linen stock-black derby-tan leather field boots-1930

summer suit-oyster white linen-vegetable ivory buttons-navy blue basketweave cotton shirt-collar attached-scarf white silk blue dots-navy blue handkerchief-sport shoes white buckskin black calf trimmings-1938

summer single breasted dinner coat-white synthetic fabric-soft white pique shirt-collar attached-black silk tie-black grosgrain cummerbund-black mohair trousers with silk braid stripe-1936

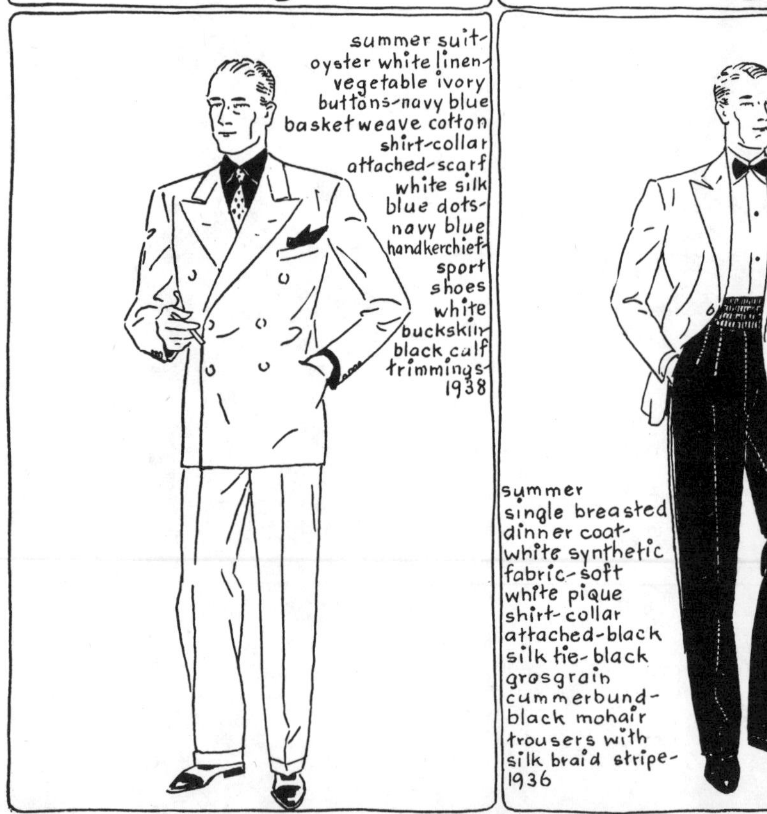

Chapter Forty-four

French

1900–1910

In this decade, a great change took place in the shape of the corset. In the early years, it retained its very small waist but grew longer in the hips and had a straight front. In 1907, the curve of the hips was reduced, a less tight lacing widening the waist. Curves almost entirely disappeared in the following year, the corset became straight and long over the hips and lower under the bosom. With the added length of hip, attached garters appeared, replacing the round garter worn above or below the knee.

In the first part of the decade, skirts fitted in molded form over the hips, flared out in bell fashion to lie on the ground with a train at the back. To the flounces of evening and summer gowns of lighter materials were added pleatings and ruffles of chiffon and lace. Petticoats were much beflounced and ruffles of silk, called "dust ruffles," were added to the under side of cloth skirts.

Trains persisted on the skirts of tailored suits until the middle of the period, when the skirt, straight of silhouette appeared, a decidedly new note. It cleared the ground, had a raised waistline and was made with groups of side pleats or wide inverted box pleats. Linings were dispensed with in the new straight skirt.

Short fitted jackets and boleros were worn with the flaring skirt, but with the straight skirt, jackets became longer, semifitted and usually had the mannish collar and lapels. The tailored suit became the accepted street costume, of navy serge or black broadcloth. For resort wear in the summer, tailored white suits of mannish fabrics were made, after the English style with Norfolk jacket. Shirtwaists were severely tailored and blouses were soft, sheer and filmy. Stiff starched collars with a small bow tie or the four-in-hand were worn with the shirtwaist. In general, collars of day dresses and blouses were boned and often reached up to just behind the ear.

The sleeve of the tailleur was fairly straight, but that of the gown widened into fullness over the forearms, by 1903 falling over a tight cuff. It was known as the pouch or bishop sleeve. Another style was the full drooping elbow-length sleeve finished with a deep ruffle of lace or self material. The dropped shoulder line of 1905, in which the collar, yoke and shoulders were in one flowing line, was very pleasing. The next move, in 1910, was the kimono sleeve or kimono-sleeve construction, of Japanese origin.

In the second half of this decade, the waistline rose higher, the silhouette straightened and narrowed, culminating, by 1910, in the style inspired by that of the First Empire. Evening gowns became tubelike and trainless. When trains were worn, as for full dress, they were only narrow slithering tails. The tube-shaped skirt of the suit, but a yard in width, necessitated a slit at the side to the knee. Another style had a wide band placed just below the knees, suggesting the much-used expression "hobble skirt."

Separate coats were in dressmaker style, semifitted, either seven-eighths or full length, with straight sleeves and made of black satin, broadcloth or navy serge in winter or of black taffeta or natural pongee for summer wear. The dolman sleeve was revived for coats near the end of the period. There were long coats of rich furs, such as chinchilla, ermine, mink and sable. A newcomer in fur coats was ponyskin, in rich black. Stoles, boas, long neckpieces and very large muffs were in vogue. Evening wraps in dolman style were of heavy brocades and velvets ornamented with fur bands, lace and passementerie.

The fabrics of the period were velvet, satin, foulard, poplin, mousseline-de-soie, surah, damask, crêpe de Chine trimmed with silk or bead embroidery and appliquéd lace motifs. In cloths, there were serge, cashmere and mohair, but broadcloth was the most popular. Rows and rows of shirring were used and lace insertion and beading threaded with ribbon continued in fashion. Among the many laces, a particular pattern was that of Irish crochet, of which jackets and coats were made, even entire dresses.

The coiffure of the period was the pompadour, drawn up high over a pad or roll of false hair (a rat, it was called). The chignon at the neck was worn also. There were ornamental combs of amber or tortoise shell decorated with gold filigree work and jewels. These combs were worn in pairs and a third was the back comb, all three holding the hair in place.

Hats, fairly large, were perched on the top of the head, a bandeau underneath to set them up still higher. The large black velvet hat trimmed with ostrich plumes was a revival of the "Gainsborough." A black straw sailor, with very wide straight brim, was known as the "Merry Widow," after the popular operetta by Franz Lehar, the Viennese composer. From 1907, both crown and brim grew in size, the hat settling down on the head and attaining huge proportions by 1909. The brims that had flared off the face, now drooped over the face. Heron and bird-of-paradise plumes, and willow plumes which were ostrich feathers with added tied flues, were the favorite ornamentation. Such dressy hats were worn with street clothes at any hour of the day, accompanied by the flattering face veil of lace or spotted net tied in back.

High button or laced shoes of kid were worn in the winter and Oxford shoes or slippers in the summer. Pumps of patent leather or calf, with flat bows of grosgrain ribbon, resembling the man's evening pump, appeared in the middle of the decade. Day shoes were either black or brown, matched by lisle or silk stockings, with the black silk stocking becoming general. A popular combination was the black stocking worn with a tan Oxford. Dressy slippers were of bronze kid, and evening slippers were of satin or brocade, with stockings to match the gown. Silk stockings, with cut-out lace inserts over the instep, were very smart.

Long suède or kid gloves, in white, black or brown, were always worn with short sleeves and gloves of silk in the same colors in the summer. Parasols, too, were carried in the summer, fashioned of silk, lace or chiffon, edged with ruffles or trimmed with velvet ribbon.

In this period, white batiste and the finest linen, embroidered, beribboned and lace-trimmed, gradually usurped the place of fine muslin and nainsook for lingerie. "Umbrella drawers," with a full skirted leg did away with "open drawers." Undergarments consisted of a chemise, over which the corset was worn. Then, a "corset cover," to which were added rows of narrow ruffles, if the bosom were too flat. The pantaloons were trimmed with lace and ribbon and the petticoat was of nainsook, fine linen or changeable taffeta, embroidered, frilled or lace-edged.

Small leather bags and "pocketbooks" were in use until the Empire mode brought in the large handbag of "saddle-bag style," the sabretache, of a century back, that same bag that accompanied the Directoire costume. It was of tapestry or brocade, with long gilt or silk cord rope which hung from the arm or shoulder.

The "dog collar," composed of several rows of small pearls held together by bars of diamonds or brilliants, was a definite style feature in this period of high collars. Earrings with screw fastenings appeared.

The automobile was responsible for the long coat, or "duster," of natural pongee or linen and the chiffon veil two to three yards long, worn over the large hat and tied under the chin. Then followed many styles of "automobile bonnets," designed especially for riding in the open cars. Unpaved, dusty roads made these enveloping garments and goggles or colored spectacles for the eyes very necessary.

Riding breeches were becoming popular for horseback, the habit retaining its draped side-saddle skirt for dress.

The bathing suit was still dresslike in design, but dispensed with its high collar and long sleeves and the skirt reached only to the knees. Bloomers and black stockings continued part of the ensemble. Silk suits, of colors other than black or navy blue, were making their appearance.

The indulgence in cigarette smoking among women was on the increase.

French 1900-1910

tailored suit-blue serge and black satin-bolero jacket-tailored shirtwaist-black silk bow tie-natural straw sailor-black ribbon band-1902

tailored suit-tan broadcloth-black velvet collar and cuffs-lace blouse-tan felt hat faced with black velvet-bright green bird-1905

bolero and skirt-dark red cloth-inverted box pleats-high waistline-black braid on jacket-tailored shirtwaist-green straw hat-flowers-black aigrettes-1906

midnight blue charmeuse-dolman wrap-knife pleated skirt-satin cording-lace collar and jabot-long suéde gloves-black velvet hat-willow plumes shaded rose and blue-leather hand bag-1908

RTW

French-1900-1910
rose silk with Irish crochet lace-black velvet bows and belt-bertha-bishop sleeves-fitted hip yoke edged self cording-inverted box pleats-lace hat-black velvet band and bow-1903
emerald green satin-cream lace-yoke of tucks and lace insertion-lace bow with long ends-rose colored velvet hat-green ostrich plumes-long white kid gloves-hair in marcel wave-1904
princess gown-white batiste-Valenciennes lace-embroidery-fine tucks-black straw hat-black aigrettes-white parasol-chiffon and lace-white kid slippers-1909
French blue silk-and black velvet-kimono sleeves-cream lace yoke and collar-silk embroidery on skirt-black straw hat-pink roses-blue silk parasol-chamois gloves-blue slippers-1910
RTW

French 1900-1910

evening gown-
yellow satin-
deep lace bertha-
black velvet
ribbon-fitted
shirring over
hips-crushed
self belt-pearl
"dog collar"-
1904

evening gown-
coral velvet-
turquoise blue
chiffon fichu-
bead embroidery-
black velvet belt
and bow-jewelled
buckle-fox fur-
self colored
embroidery-pink
rose and black
velvet ribbon
in hair-
1908

evening wrap-
mauve velvet-
black velvet
collar-gold
passementerie,
cord and tassels-
paradise in hair-
black velvet
gown-
1909

black silk coat-
black silk braid
on collar and lapels-
lace blouse with
jabot-cloth skirt-
pleated chiffon
hat-pink rose-
black silk
umbrella-
1902

RTW

French 1900-1910
satin corset-insertion threaded with ribbon-1901
brocaded satin corset-lace top-shirred ribbon garters-1905
satin corset-lace top-bowknot-1910
black calf or patent leather pump-grosgrain bow
patent leather-white kid top-black buttons
satin opera slipper-rhinestone buckle
chemise-white nainsook or crêpe de chine-tucks-lace-colored ribbon
soft brown kid or patent leather
umbrella drawers-nainsook-lace-beading-ribbon
corset cover-nainsook-beading and ribbon
black or brown kid Oxford
combination corset cover and petticoat-nainsook-lace-tucks-ribbon threaded through insertion
colored changeable taffeta petticoat
petticoat-white nainsook or crêpe de chine-tucks-lace-colored ribbon
RTW

Chapter Forty-five

French

1910–1920

Two important events took place in this period; first, the return to the natural figure; and second, as a result of the First World War, the adoption of the simple tailored, unadorned frock for day or informal wear. Another influence of the war was the all-black costume relieved only by jewelry.

This decade found the straight silhouette with raised waistline definitely established in the mode, with Paul Poiret the first couturier daring enough to place the belt just under the breasts in true Empire style. He was also responsible for the open-neck kimono waist, which did away with high collar and set-in sleeves for many years to come. Another striking departure was his use of brilliant color in emerald green, cerise, vermilion, royal blue and purple. Startling at first was his combination of cerise and purple.

The long tunic hanging over a narrow underskirt appeared in 1911. Sometimes a wide band or sash finished the edge of the tunic or was tied around the underskirt at a place below the knees. This narrow skirt of suits, dresses and evening gowns was called the tube, or hobble skirt.

It was one and a quarter yards in width, though often but a yard around. As walking thus became almost impossible, a slit at the side or front remedied the situation.

The tunic shortened and became fuller, turning into panniers or draped fullness at the hips in 1912. Next, the fullness dropped halfway down the skirt length, sloping in to the ankles. This was the peg-top silhouette.

An attempt was made to introduce a divided or trouser skirt into the mode under the name of "harem skirt." Though worn by mannequins in public, it did not meet with success.

In 1912, Poiret designed the Persian costumes for "Le Minaret," creating a belted tunic, knee-length, with wired flaring edge over a slim silhouette. The minaret tunic shared honors with the peg-top silhouette until the First World War.

Then appeared the short full skirt, "eight inches" from the ground. The skirts of evening gowns were given added flare by two or three flounces with whalebone edge. This fashion, for which Lanvin became famous, is known as the *infanta style,* or the *robe de style,* and the skirt length, changing from period to period, is still good in evening dresses.

1914 saw the birth of the chemise frock of medieval origin, but it was not taken up until 1916, and did not become general until the following year. At first, it was a straight slip, over which was worn a straight tunic or overblouse with long tight sleeves. Then the tunic lengthened, took on a belt placed low at the hips and the underslip disappeared.

In 1917, came the "tonneau silhouette," which met with little success. The skirt widened at a place halfway between waist and hem in barrel shape.

In 1918 and 1919, the skirt of the chemise gown shortened to just below the knee. Its shortest length was still to come in 1925, when it frankly reached the knee. The day frock was a scant affair, with fairly low round neck and sleeveless. The evening model, as short and sleeveless, had no back and often, a long narrow trailing panel which acted as train.

Vionnet, in 1919, created a sensation with her tubular frock of crêpe de Chine which slipped on over the head. She made unlined gowns of fabrics cut on the bias. Noteworthy, too, was her handkerchief tunic, with its corners hanging to the hem of the underskirt.

Navy blue and black were the colors for day dresses in such fabrics as foulard, satin, charmeuse and serge. Materials became soft in finish like duvetyn, suède cloth, chiffon broadcloth, soft twill gabardine, and there were crêpes of every description, crêpe de Chine, georgette crêpe, crêpe marocain and Canton crêpe.

Chanel, in 1918, introduced jersey cloth to the mode which jumped to the fore for the chemise frock and the dressmaker suit. The evening version of the chemise frock was of silk crêpe or georgette embroidered with beads, crêpe lamé, metal brocade or gold or silver cloth. Gold and silver fringe edged the tunics. Picot-edged and grosgrain ribbon became great favorites. Ostrich fringe was a novelty for gown and hat.

As far back as 1915, Chanel displayed models at Deauville made of artificial silk. Artificial or glazed satin was used for sports skirts.

Soft woolens in novelty weaves were used for sports clothes. The tailleur of dressmaker style usurped the position of the strictly tailored suit. Late in the period, the white piqué waistcoat worn with the blue or black suit was a smart accessory.

Dress coats had dolman sleeves and wrap-around fronts with but one fastening. Evening cloaks were a combination of cape and coat design, with large, standing, fold-over collars. The raglan was favored for the separate sports coat, made of such cloths as chinchilla and camel's hair. Along with the same sports coat for men, appeared the raccoon coat, which enjoyed a great popularity.

Fur coats and capes followed the lines of cloth dress coats and were trimmed with contrasting furs. Muffs were very large, soft and flat. Bands of fur not only ornamented suits but even chiffon gowns. The scarf of large skins and the long stole were worn also in the summer over light dresses. The most lowly skins were now dressed into pliable pelts, such as muskrat, skunk, rabbit and lamb. Other furs were chinchilla, ermine, sable and mink principally for evening, and caracul, Persian lamb, broadtail, ponyskin and kolinsky.

The Spanish shawl returned to the mode, with the revival of fringe, tassels and the dolman type of wrap.

The sweater acquired new styling in lovely colors, not only of wool but of spun silk and artificial silk worked with metal threads. The cardigan with knitted sash was smart. Another sports jacket was of black velveteen worn with colored or white wool or silk skirt.

Brims of hats were large, flaring, drooping or turned-up and, as the crown settled down to the eyes, it too grew very large. The automobile, especially the open car, had much to do with the change of style in millinery. It necessitated the crown fitting the head, and long chiffon veils, tied over hat and under chin, held the headgear secure. Then hats became small, hugging the head. A revival of the sailor occurred in the second half of the decade; another revival was the tricorne. A forerunner of the cloche of the next decade was the pillbox shape.

Trimmings were confined to feathers or wired wings of silk or velvet. Hats were weighted down under great quantities of plumes. So devastating to bird life was this fad for fine plumage that, through the efforts of the Audubon Society of America, protective measures were passed, bringing about the passing of the craze.

Face veils of lace or net, spotted with chenille dots or velvet disks, were worn, also large veils of silk lace or net draped over the hat. The "harem veil," leaving the eyes exposed and fastened to the brim in back, was a summer fashion. (See Page 364.)

The hair was dressed off the face and over the ears, wrapped or swirled close to the head, paving the way for the universal bob of the next decade. Occasional bobbed heads were seen toward the end of this period, but the style did not become the mode until the 'twenties. The "beauty shop" now made it possible for all women, regardless of wealth, to enjoy the services of a hairdresser. All women could have curly locks by means of electrical machines which produced a "permanent wave." Auburn, the favorite color of hair of the twentieth century, was responsible for the fad of dyeing locks a reddish hue with henna. Cosmetics of natural tone and artfully applied were less frowned upon than formerly. Lipstick was added to rouge and powder.

The new mode required very little corseting, that garment becoming a soft girdle of tricot or knitted elastic, waistline-high and just covering the hips. The breasts were held firm and flat by a soft bandeau, camisole or brassière. An entirely new carriage or posture was adopted. The hips and abdomen were thrown forward, helping to produce the much-desired flattening silhouette of the bosom. The pose of arms akimbo or hands on the hips, which had always been avoided by the "lady," was now à la mode. This new figure was called the "boyish form" and the "debutante slouch."

Simple lingerie, with just a touch of lace or embroidery of white batiste or fine handkerchief linen, was worn until 1918, when crêpe de Chine and silk jersey came in for undergarments. Silk met with huge success and delicate shades of pink, blue and mauve became popular. The petticoat disappeared entirely and sheer silk slips were worn under only such evening frocks as required them. Often, just a bandeau and a pair of silk knickers sufficed under the chemise frock. Many women took to wearing silk pajamas instead of the nightgown.

Footgear for day wear consisted of shoes with high-laced or buttoned tops of gabardine, kid or suède, the buttoned Oxford, the plain pump, the slipper with cut steel or rhinestone buckle, all with the slim French heel and long, pointed toe. With the short chemise frock came a great change in footwear. The long, pointed shoe, conservative in style and color, was supplanted by the so-called French last, with short vamp and round toe, the slender curving Louis XV heel or the lower, "baby Louis" heel. Shoes were cut in intricate strap-fastening designs, ornamented with buckles, even to jewelled heels. Day shoes were beige, sand, taupe, gray or black, while evening shoes matched the gown in color, made of satin, gold or silver brocade. Sports Oxfords were of white buck, with black or brown leather trimming for summer and of brown leather for winter.

The black or tan silk stocking of the earlier part of the decade gave way to gray, taupe, Cordovan and sand tones matching shoes of like colors. Gray stockings were general. Beige stockings matched beige spats worn with black pumps. Nude or blond hosiery was first worn in Paris in the second half of the decade. It was introduced by a small French shop where stockings were dyed to order. Black was rare by the end of the period. White was the color for summer sports wear. The instep of the evening stocking was often decorated with embroidery or a lace insert.

There were bags of very fine beads in exquisite design and color, bags of gold and silver mesh, also those of tapestry, while the leather handbags became the accessory for street and sports. From this time, the fittings of the bag were given as much thought as the bag itself. Still with us are the several inside pockets containing small change purse, small mirror and comb, and these articles are to be found in the lowliest bag. Jewelled cigarette holders and cases were among the contents of the bag, the habit of smoking having become general in the feminine world.

Bead necklaces of all kinds and all lengths came into fashion. The short pearl necklace, with the accompanying button pearl earrings, became especially popular. Large ornamental hairpins, usually worn in pairs, were of amber or tortoise shell, often studded with brilliants. The simple untrimmed frock was the beginning of the craze for costume jewelry which exists today. Pieces effective in design and color were used with certain gowns, the intrinsic value being unimportant.

War work proved the great convenience of the wrist watch, which became very popular. While the practical model was worn on a leather-strap bracelet, the dressier timepiece was attached to a matching jewelled bracelet or a black grosgrain ribbon. The watch became unbelievably small, and an exquisite ornament in gold or platinum set with tiny jewels.

The bathing suit followed the dress design with high or low neck and shoulder cap sleeves. Skirt and knickers grew shorter, about five or six inches above the knee. American women wore long stockings with sandals. French women did not wear stockings either with the one-piece knitted maillot or swimming suit or with the conventional suit with short skirt. Various new fabrics were employed in its making, such as silk jersey and awning-striped materials.

The "pencil umbrella," a long, slim affair of black silk, was carried in this period. Raincoats of waterproofed gabardine were usually tan in color.

With the "robe de style" came a vogue for the small old-fashioned bouquet of fresh flowers set in a frill of lace. The craze for violets had passed but roses were as popular as ever. Orchids or gardenias worn singly or in a corsage of two or three were very "swank."

French 1910-1920

French 1910-1920

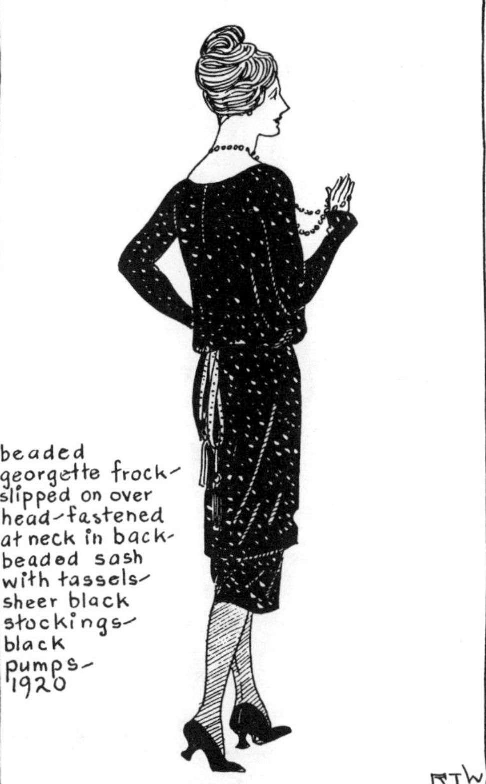

French 1910-1920

French 1910-1920

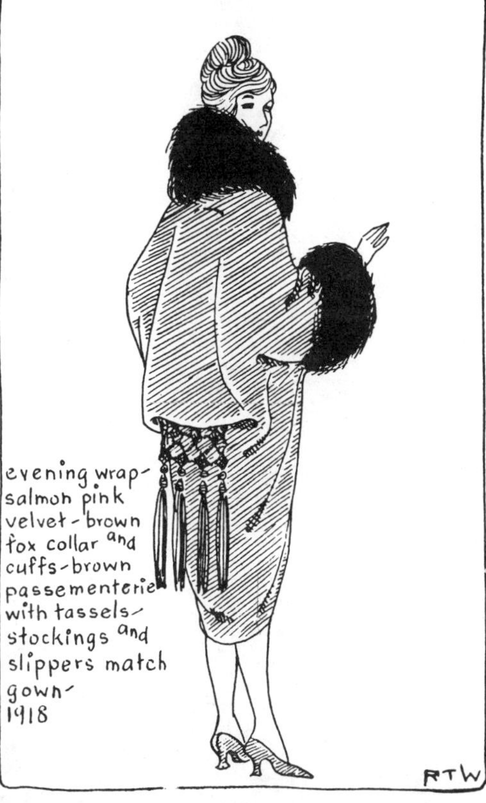

1910-1920
golf costume-
tweed skirt-
knitted cardigan-
tailored white
washable shirt-
felt hat-white
buck shoes
with leather
fringe-
1913
tennis costume-
lingerie blouse-
silk scarf-
awning
striped cotton
skirt-panama
hat with
striped ribbon-
white buck
shoes-brown
trimming-
white
stockings-
1915
summer sports
costume-white
satin glacé skirt-
knitted tan
woolen cardigan-
knitted and
fringed sash or
scarf-black
straw sailor
with harem veil-
striped ribbon
band-white buck
shoes-black
leather trim-black
silk stockings-
1918
"country suit" of
tweed-leather
buttons-black
silk sailor-
white Ascot
scarf-tan
leather gauntlets-
fringed woolen
scarf-woolen
stockings-
beige suède
shoes-
1919
RTW

French 1910-1920
pink satin corset worn over chemise-1914
beaded bag-1918
corset-silk brocade-elastic waistband-1918
green gold mesh bag-1919
"slipover" corset-silk tricot mesh-worn over knickers-brassière on georgette bodice-1914
square toe-short vamp-brocade and velvet-1919
patent leather and kid-1912
gray spat over black pump-1917
embroidered nainsook combination-1911
laced shoe-white kid-black patent leather-1916
satin slipper-velvet frill-rhinestone buckle-1917
button shoe-gray or beige suede-black patent leather heel and toe-1915
combination with knickers-crêpe de Chine-1918
Oxford-black or brown kid-1918
cothurn-brocaded silk-1916
envelope combination-crêpe de Chine-1918
fan-green ostrich-amber stick-silk tassel-1916
brassière-pink satin-embroidery-Cluny lace-1919
black satin slipper-jewelled buckle-black silk stocking-lace insert-1918
black velvet bag-bead embroidery-silk tassels-1916
RTW

Chapter Forty-six

French

1920–1930

THE LONGER SKIRT arrived by 1921, having been eased in by the uneven hemline with panels and drapery hanging below the short skirt. Then the hemline started back upward, growing shorter and shorter until 1925, when it reached the knee. Never before, in the history of the mode, was so short a skirt worn by the fashionable woman. That lasted several years, when the hemline again began its descent, by 1930 touching the floor in evening gowns, with day dresses ten to twelve inches off the floor.

Since this time there have been two distinct hemlines, a long one for evening wear and a short for day dresses.

The uncorseted figure was definitely established, with its low-waisted girdle of satin or knitted elastic practically boneless. For the first time in the history of the corset, that garment was worn next to the body. The "foundation garment" of brassière and "panties" in one, well fitted and fashioned of firmly woven or knitted fabric, was as generally worn as girdle, brassière and knickers. The petticoat or slip was eliminated under the day or evening gown unless the transparency of that garment necessitated an underpiece. The few undergarments worn were simple, usually unadorned, and of crêpe de Chine or silk jersey. Lace when used was blond or deep écru in color.

The straight silhouette prevailed throughout the period. The belt line placed low on the hips lasted until the last few years of the decade, when it began to creep slowly up, reaching normalcy in 1930.

In evening gowns, a continuation of the *robe de style* was the long straight basque, with very full skirt of ankle length. The décolletage was round, square or straight across, to the waist in back and with narrow shoulder straps. The low waistline was marked by embroidered motifs, cockades, sashes and belts of all fabrics and widths, finished with sash ends or drapery. Too, floating panels and gathered sections of chiffon hung from the hips.

Evening gowns revealed an Indo-Chinese influence in ornamentation and color, also in the gold and silver turbans often worn with them. The all-white costume for evening became fashionable. There were dull crêpes in all varieties of weaves. Lace dyed in dark colors was employed for entire dresses. Bead embroidery continued in fashion for both day and evening. Transparent velvet became the vogue, a lustrous sheer velvet of artificial silk with beautiful draping quality.

While synthetic fabrics had been in use for some time, it was not until the late years of the decade that the French couturiers frankly employed artificial silks and velvets for their creations. The rich colors and lovely folds of these materials account for their success.

The navy-blue dress and the "little black dress" in either jersey, crêpe or crêpe georgette became standard for day wear in town. Over it was worn a black coat of the same length, fur-trimmed in winter. Necks were high, round or in *bâteau line,* straight across from shoulder to shoulder. There was also the "cowl neck," with loosely draped front.

With the exception of the hunting suit, sports clothes lost their severely tailored cut. The former was of rough tweed with belted jacket and a simple skirt which unbuttoned down the center front, revealing tweed knee breeches. Heavy knitted woolen stockings, brogues and a simple hat completed the outfit. The tailored suit and coat have always been of English origin, but it remained for Paris to create, for sports wear, the three-piece *ensemble* of dressmaker type, consisting of dress and coat or overblouse, skirt and coat.

The overblouse was the result of the low waistline, necessitating wearing the blouse outside the skirt, even the lingerie blouse. The blouse was usually of crêpe de Chine, but the knitted silk or woolen sweater or jumper, heretofore worn only for active sports, enjoyed great popularity. With this style originated the fashion of wearing a single short string of pearls with the sweater. Colorful woolens in soft lovely weaves and patterns, suède cloth, knitted and angora fabrics were used, the most popular material being wool jersey, especially in beige and brown. Awning stripes for skirts were smart.

The *ensemble* finally eclipsed all other styles for daytime wear. A wardrobe composed of evening clothes, the indispensable "little black dress" with accompanying long coat and the three-piece ensemble, proved adequate to fill the requirements of the well-dressed woman.

In the second half of the period appeared the low-necked, sleeveless sports dress, with gaily colored handkerchief or scarf tied loosely about the shoulders. A cloche, or tied headband, and short gloves were worn with it.

Coats were in wrap-around style, one side fastened underneath on one hip, the other either fastened or simply held in place with the hand. Scarfs of self material were part of or attached to the coat or jacket, one end thrown over the shoulder.

Bobbed hair of the beginning of the decade evolved into the "shingle" by 1922, lasting several years. A shaggy cut like the Titus headdress of the Directoire, but called the "wind-blown bob," was a popular style. Tinting gray hair with bluing originated in this period. Before the end of the 'twenties, the hair was worn a little longer, making an arranged coiffure possible, but always retaining the small head shape.

Bobbed hair revived the use of the wig or transformation, a skillfully made caplike coiffure which entirely concealed the wearer's own hair. In the early 'twenties, there was a short-lived fad for transformations of orange, red, green and purple for evening. While the transformation is not generally worn, it is still in use by many women with unsatisfactory hair. The wig of today has reached such perfection that it seldom reveals its artificiality.

With the short hair appeared a new metal hairpin, fashioned, like the cotter pin, of machinery, and called a "bobby pin."

Hats grew smaller and shed their trimmings, evolving into the cloche or mushroom shape about 1923 and surviving through 1930. It was a simple round crowned hat with tiny brim, usually of beige or black felt, winter or summer, enveloping the head to the neck in back and to the eyes in front. Reboux produced this hat, which became classic, often with no decoration but the ornamental shaping of the felt. Sometimes the simple hat was relieved by a grosgrain ribbon band or a single jewelled brooch or buckle. The béret, especially the Basque béret for sports, took firm hold and in its many variations continues in style. Veils of all kinds disappeared.

In furs there were long enveloping capes and coats with wide standing collars in moleskins, squirrel, gray and dyed kolinsky, beaver, Hudson seal, broadtail, caracul, mink, sable and ermine. New were babylamb, honey beige-sheared goat, honey beige or summer ermine. Furs were used on suits and dresses in very wide bands and a novelty was monkey fur. Fox skins of one to four skins in length were worn, a costly one being silver fox.

The high shoe disappeared, replaced by the pump and slipper. The low shoe became the "all-year-round" foot covering, protected in bad weather by galoshes or *arctics,* overshoes of rubber. Shoes had rounded toes, French heels, spike heels, straps crossed in every conceivable manner, upstanding tongues or frills with large buckles of metal, cut steel, marquisite or rhinestones. Street slippers were of patent leather, kid or suède. A newcomer for day wear was the dark-blue kid pump or slipper. Turned calf, resembling suède but much more durable, also appeared.

Oxfords or brogues in white buckskin for summer sports wear had brown or black leather trimmings, the winter model in brown leather. Gillies, sports shoes in brown leather or white buck with laces tied around the ankles, were also smart.

The white buckskin with high heel and brown leather trimming became standard for summer wear in the country, accompanying frocks or suits. Heels were either moderately high Cuban or the very high spike heel.

Evening slippers were of satin, brocade shot with gold or silver, while those of plain gold or silver took the place of the former bronze slipper as the "go-with-everything."

The light-colored stockings led the way to the flesh-colored, nude or blond stockings which fashion decreed. Woolen or lisle stockings were worn with sports shoes.

The buttoned glove was replaced by the "slip-on" glove of chamois, suède or doeskin, wrist-length or reaching halfway up the forearm. White, black or beige were the preferred colors with beige or brown for sports. With the growing casual feeling in clothes came the elimination of gloves for evening. The long glove disappeared, not being seen even upon formal occasions. It became the fad to wear one's gloves a size larger than formerly, giving the desired loose wrinkled effect.

Pajamas of crêpe de Chine, in brilliant colors, became the fashion for boudoir and lounging on the beach.

The use of cosmetics became general, powder, rouge, lipstick, eye shadow and eyebrow pencil over a make-up base being employed by young and old, the lady of leisure and the business woman. The vanity case was carried as generally as the purse, and could be had in beautiful design, regardless of its price. Repairs to the make-up, such as powdering the nose or adding lipstick, were calmly made in public with the aid of a small mirror. The vogue for "sunbathing" brought in the sun-tanned or very brown complexion.

Parasols disappeared and the umbrella grew smaller, gave up its long handle and took to colored silks instead of the former black. When closed, it was a stubby affair of about twenty inches in length. Raincoats also changed to gaily colored waterproofed silks.

Much attention was given to handbags, which became fairly large. After the war, travelling increased, especially to and over Europe, with the passport a requirement. That, with vanity case, the cigarette case and holder and the usual articles to be found in a woman's bag, made the larger container a necessity. The flat envelope design predominated, staying with us to date. Evening bags of both envelope and pouch shape were in costly fabrics with jewelled clasps and mounts. Every possible leather was employed for the more practical bag, beautifully lined and fitted with "gadgets."

It was in this period of simple unadorned dress necks, that costume jewelry settled down for a long stay. Pieces were designed for certain gowns, furnishing an effect or a color note, the intrinsic value of the bauble being of no matter, so that silver and gold plated metal with semi-precious stones sufficed. The slave bracelet of links appeared and long earrings were important for day and evening. The clip, a jewelled ornament which fastened to the garment by a clip, was newer and smarter than the brooch.

The lovely feather fan of the previous decade continued as a decorative evening accessory. A revival of artificial flowers in this period brought the nosegay and corsage into fashion. The nosegay, or boutonnière, was worn with the tailor-made as well as with the gown.

Because of the fashionable slim figure, exercise was scientifically taken up, necessitating a "play suit," which was of washable cotton, resembling the rompers of the youngster.

Many horsewomen adopted *jodhpurs* for active riding, long breeches tight from the knees to the ankle, with low boots worn underneath.

Bathing suits, in the first years of the period, were still accompanied by long stockings. They disappeared by the middle of the decade, the dressmaker type of suit being replaced by the French style of knitted woolen one-piece swimming suit or a combination of knitted maillot or jumper with flannel or knitted shorts of contrasting color.

The use of colored spectacles as a protection for the eyes, which originated with the automobile, was becoming popular for both winter and summer sports.

Winter sports grew in popularity and the fluffy angora type of knitted sweater, tam-o'-shanter and socks worn with knickerbockers early in the period were replaced by the simple tailored dark-colored mannish costume. It consisted of long trousers and jacket of jersey, gabardine, whipcord or flannel with the tailored flannel shirt or knitted sweater.

French 1920-1930

Madelaine et Madelaine-Directoire suit-bottle green cloth-braided skirt-black satin cravat-lingerie blouse-black velvet bicorne-sand colored pumps and stockings-envelope bag-1920

tailored suit-black broadcloth-silk braid-lingerie blouse-black velvet bicorne-black patent leather shoes-silver buckles-sheer black stockings-black suéde bag-1921

Molyneux-ensemble-brown wool with beaver-tunic blouse with bias jabot-cloth belt and buckcle-beige felt hat-beige suéde slippers-blond stockings-tan leather bag-1928

Gervais-ensemble-red woolen coat-lining and dress red and white printed crêpe-accordion pleating-red suéde belt-red felt hat-black suéde pumps-blond stockings-1930

French 1920-1930

navy wool jersey-self sash in back-self covered buttons-dark blue leather pumps-blond stockings-shingle bob-1925

Patou-lime-green wool sweater-skirt crêpella accordion pleated-scarf georgette with black and white bands-black belt-beige felt hat-green and white grosgrain band-stitched crossed tucks on crown-pearl necklace-brown leather gillies-blond stockings-1927

printed voile-red, yellow and green on black ground-cowl neck-skirt and drapery one piece, length of fabric-black velvet sash-beige straw hat-red and yellow grosgrain-beige leather envelope bag-black suéde pumps-blond stockings-1928

Suzanne Talbot-sleeveless sports frock-white and yellow silk-belt with buckle-béret shirred yellow silk-white doeskin slip-on gloves-grège silk stockings and shoes-brown leather trim-brown suéde bag-1929

French 1920-1930

Lanvin-robe de style-heavy white satin-bands of crystal beads-cockade of bead roses with silver leaves-crystal and bead caul on chignon-1923

Premet-cinnamon colored satin with delicate silver brocade-elaborate ornament-brown satin slippers-jewelled buckles-blond stockings-1923

Chéruit-black moiré with circular design-green taffeta scarf-drapery with green taffeta lining-silver slippers-pearl straps-blond stockings-shingle bob-1926

Augustabernard-black satin-draped scarf knotted to shoulder strap-faced with rose satin-jewelled buckles-black velvet pumps-blond stockings-short slip-on white doeskin gloves-1930

FTW

French 1920-1930

madelaine et madelaine- cape of monkey fur mounted on black chiffon- muff of monkey fur-draped black velvet turban- taupe suede shoes- gun metal buckles- taupe stockings- 1920

day coat- tan kasha cloth- embroidery in bright peasant colors-hat tan cloth-black cloth facing-peasant embroidery-black patent leather shoes-sand colored stockings- 1921

Vionnet- day and sports coat- golden-beige sheared goatskin- cuffs, collar and band of unsheared goat- beige felt hat- black grosgrain band-beige suéde pumps- blond stockings- black leather bag- 1927

Chanel- evening wrap- white velvet- white fox- fine stitched tucks-white velvet bag- jewelled mount- white gown- white slippers- 1930

French 1920-1930

French 1920-1930
uncurled ostrich fan-ivory sticks
Reboux-red felt hat-red velvet bow and band-1927
Basque béret for sports
elastic girdle-back lacing-no bones-flounce net with crystals-1920
one piece black wool jersey swimming suit-white bands-1930
combination brassiere, vest and bloomers-silk jersey-1930
combination brassiere, girdle and drawers-pink silk jersey-ecru lace-1930
black and white knitted swimming suit-1929
beach pyjamas-white silk jersey-royal blue bands-1924
brassière and panties-pink silk jersey-colored applique-1927
bathing suit-silk jersey-top sulphur-middle orange-skirt and sash black-sheer black stockings-1921
brown and beige silk umbrella-amber and wood handle-1922
Perugia-cothurn of lamé or satin-1922
Perugia-black leather with red edge-1922
Perugia-evening slipper-velvet and lamé-1922
RTW

Chapter Forty-seven

French

1930–1942

By this period, clothes had become so thoroughly specialized that the wardrobe of a well-dressed woman contained costumes suitable for all occasions. There were clothes for town, for the country, for tea or cocktail parties, the hostess gown for informal evenings, formal evening dress, for the various sports and if, at sports, she was only a spectator, then there was the "spectator sports" costume.

The waistline settled back into its normal position, but the figure retained its natural lines till the winter of 1937 and 1938, when the Paris couturiers presented the fashionable woman with a new corset or girdle. It was made of the same fabrics, but came up higher under the bosom and confined the figure by means of extra bones, producing the required smaller waist of the new mode.

The change is supposed to have been influenced by the appearance and success, both here and abroad, of the photoplays of Mae West, especially her first picture "Diamond Lil," in which she portrayed a siren of the 'nineties with all her voluptuous curves.

The "all-in-one," or foundation garment, now as generally worn as the girdle and brassière, also took on more form by means of careful fitting and added bones. Instead of the flat silhouette, the shape of the breasts was enhanced by cuplike-shaped brassières, called "uplift style." Carriage and posture changed from a slouch of standing on one leg to a firm position on both feet, with chest out and shoulders thrown back. The corset, girdle and foundation garment were made of satin and elastic or knitted elastic. An improvement in knitted elastic fabric was the "two-way stretch" weave which did not ride up on the figure. It was also firmer, more elastic and eliminated the need of bones.

Hemlines of day clothes were from six to eight inches off the ground till 1939, when they again rose, reaching fifteen inches by the spring of 1940. Evening gowns still touched the floor or were ankle-length.

There were several evening silhouettes in the 'thirties, the long basque bodice with bouffant skirt, the gown with classic drapery and the slim, sleek gown with or without train. The bouffant gown was fashioned of such fabrics as taffeta, slipper satin, heavy velvet or organza with horsehair. The classic and the slim models took materials which fell in clinging folds, such as sheer velvet, jersey and crêpes.

New, in the beginning of the period, was the summer gown of cotton, appearing first in white piqué, then in organdie and that billowy synthetic fabric organza, in lovely designs and color. Crêpes and printed georgettes were also popular for summer. Other warm-weather fabrics were cotton denim and knitted ordinary cotton string. The former was used for play clothes and the latter for sweaters, turbans and gloves.

Lace, especially in black and jet came back as trimmings in the second half of the decade, and faille silk returned to the mode, especially for the dressmaker suit. The most unusual color of the period was Schiaparelli's "shocking pink," a fuchsia pink.

Lingerie consisted of panties worn over a girdle, a silk petticoat and shaped brassière, or a form-fitting silk slip, which eliminated petticoat and brassière.

Another change in the silhouette occurred in 1933 with the broad and exaggerated square shoulders of tailored clothes. Sleeves varied from the leg-of-mutton to the long, tight style and in all lengths. They were shirred or pleated into the armscye and padded into the square effect. In the second half of the period, the simulated bustle in tied-back drapery tried to assert itself, but the style was temporary.

A fashion of several years was the evening gown, high of neck in front and entirely minus back. There was also the "halter dress," of beach origin, with a bib for a bodice in front, drawn up, gathered and held at the neck by a cord or ribbon. The halter neck was adopted in summer day frocks too.

Dinner suits appeared, copying the man's summer informal evening outfit with white jacket, long black skirt and blouse. The masculine cummerbund was also imitated. Winter evening gowns of sheer wool crêpe or wool jersey became a fashion. Late in the period, the evening sweater came into the mode, of wool embroidered in silver and gold, silk and beads.

The remainder of the period was one of jackets accompanying evening gowns. Jackets either matched or contrasted with the dress and were of velvet, cloth or crêpe, embroidered with gilt or sequins. The "covered-up look" became the required effect for theatre or restaurant dining; in fact, the dinner dress came to stay.

A startling new idea in summer evening gowns appeared in 1939. It was the bare midriff which originated on the beach. The long skirt and the very short bodice were separated by an expanse of bare torso, which effect was often heightened by long tight sleeves. Sometimes, the bare midriff was simulated by a joining of flesh-colored chiffon between skirt and bodice.

The "little black dress" of crêpe, georgette or silk jersey retained its hold. A less formal, simpler frock was the "run-about dress" of wool jersey or flannel for winter, of colored silk or cotton for summer. The shirtwaist dress appeared with skirt and blouse joined together. The blouse was of shirtwaist design, and the skirt either plain or pleated, in silk, wool or cotton according to season.

With the return to the normal waistline, sweaters and blouses were worn under the skirt instead of outside.

The jackets of suits were short in reefer or semifitted style. In the second half of the period, the contrasting jacket and skirt appeared, a light jacket with dark skirt or the other way round. The country suit of color and novelty weave replaced the black or navy blue suit for town wear. Oxford gray became smart. Jacket and coat edges were finished with saddle stitching.

The long straight coat of the early years acquired a fitted body. The redingote appeared and the untrimmed dress coat, with which a fur scarf or short fur cape was worn. There were long coats over which fur boleros were worn. Sports coats were in several styles, the reefer, the redingote and that great stand-by, the loose coat of camel's hair. Much leeway in color became the vogue, with pastel shades to the fore for country wear.

Evening coats, in general, followed Victorian lines, long and fitted at the waist in redingote style, of woolen cloth or velvet and often untrimmed and collarless. The short jacket of silver fox, bulky and square, was worn both with evening and day clothes.

Hats varied constantly but seemed to agree on the shallow crown or no crown at all. There were sailors and huge cartwheels, the Eugénie hat with its drooping plume, the Watteau hat, the pillbox, the tiny pancake hat, or "doll hat." The calotte, with ribbon bow or flowers known as the pompadour hat, and designed by Talbot for the Duchess of Windsor, became very popular. The shape of the béret varied and we had Victorian bonnets, little flower hats and turbans. Large brims flared up off the face. Felt hats of Tyrolese shape were worn with sports clothes. Veils enjoyed a distinct vogue, especially the short one of horsehair and in wide mesh.

Cauls, filets or nets, now erroneously called snoods and made of chenille, appeared in the middle of the decade; in fact, it was by means of the net that the tiny hat was held to the head. The original snood was a ribbon tied round the head, and in this period small hats were attached to snoods. For casual dress or sports, there were the hand-tied turban and the peasant handkerchief tied under the chin.

Wimples, tiny medieval caps, gold nets and small lace mantillas were worn in the evening. Artificial flowers, ribbons and feathers were again worn in the hair, also jewelled ornaments or clips.

Every style of coiffure or hair-do was modish, providing it did not conceal the contour of the head. The hair was kept shoulder-length, making it possible to adopt any headdress. In general, the hair close to the head was not curled; only the ends were curled, usually by a permanent wave. The hair dressed high in the back, in the style of the 'nineties, returned to favor in 1937, with the pompadour following the next year. Coiffures had straight bangs or curled fringes over the forehead, puffs, rolls and cadogan loops, even lacquered curls dusted with gold flakes in the evening.

The short slip-on or pull-on glove, loose-fitting and with hand stitching, remained in fashion, made of all fabrics and combinations of fabrics. The staple glove was of beige doeskin or suède for street, pigskin for sports and cotton suède for summer. Gloves contrasted with the costume, light with dark and *vice versa*.

All furs, both costly and lowly, were smart in this period, according to the occasion. The most popular furs for the long coat were sable, mink, chinchilla, baum marten, broadtail, Persian lamb and caracul, with silver fox for the short coat and scarf. Fashionable also, were furs of lesser value, such as beaver, nutria and plucked muskrat. For sports, there were leopard and the various dressed goat and lamb skins in light colors; for evening, tailless ermine, coffee-dyed ermine, summer ermine and white broadtail. Small muffs and those of moderate size were carried.

In this period, many of the Victorian colors returned to the mode, such as garnet red, cabbage red, eggplant purple, chartreuse, lime yellow, gray pinks and raw vivid pinks.

Low shoes or slippers became elaborate and fantastic. The slim spike heel replaced the Louis heel. There were sandals fashioned only of narrow strips with high heels, sandals without backs or toes and slippers with open toes or a hole where the toecau should have been. They were of many fabrics and leathers. The shoe with the wedge sole, a revival of the Italian Renaissance, appeared in the middle of the decade. That was followed by the platform sole, a sole of great thickness, with high heel. Pumps, Oxfords and brogues were utility shoes in leather, kid, suède, alligator, lizard, toadskin, snakeskin, calf and turned calf. Bronze kid reappeared for afternoon wear in 1940. The blond stocking retained its hold, while, coinciding with the rage for the sun-tanned complexion, young women went stockingless in the summer.

Costume jewelry remained very important as a costume accent in gold and silver with semiprecious stones. Following the vogue for jewelled clips, tiny watches were clip-fastened and earrings were made with clips instead of screws.

The mechanical slide fastener was perfected and manufactured in all colors and was used to fasten girdles, foundation garments, dresses, coats, handbags; in fact, wherever a trim concealed closing was required.

The large handbag remained in vogue, of fabric or leather, of varied shape, with the smaller jewelled bag of precious fabric for evening use.

Play clothes consisted of the cotton dress, with skirt covering the thighs, or a knee-length skirt buttoned down center front, or the dirndl skirt of peasant origin, with shorts underneath. Shorts and slacks became very popular for sports. "Girdle panties" of elastic tricot confined the figure under the slacks. Generally worn was the one-piece swimming suit of knitted or elastic fabric in pleasing patterns and colors.

The tailored mannish costume of pants and jacket became standard for winter sports, especially for skiing. Navy blue, even black, were the favorite colors in gabardine, whipcord, jersey or flannel. A tailored knee-length skirt for skiing, worn with high knitted socks, appeared late in the period. The tailored knee-length dress with flaring circular skirt was the favored style for rink ice skating.

Cosmetics, powder, rouge, lipstick, eye shadow and eyebrow pencil were employed by all well-dressed women. Finger-nails were lacquered in all shades of red, varying from a delicate pink to that of mahogany red, the use of a certain color governed by preference. Gray hair, no longer dyed by the smart woman, was given a blue or mauve tint by a rinse in a tinted bath.

French 1930-1942

Schiaparelli-
black ribbed
wool-blouse
white crochet
string-S-clips-
pull-on gloves-
Eugénie hat-
blond
stockings-
black antelope
bag and pumps-
1931

Molyneux-
navy blue cloth
dress-jacket
fuchsia pink
cloth-white
flower at neck-
Tyrolese hat
black felt-
grosgrain band-
gloves and
pumps blue
antelope-
blond
stockings-
1937

Balenciaga-
jacket, café au
lait satin-
twisted black
buttons-black
crêpe dress-
circular pleating-
Suzy hat-fancy
straw-veil-
black antelope
gloves and pumps-
beige crocodile
bag-blond
stockings-
1939

Lelong-
black cloth
jacket-Persian
lamb-plaid
skirt of sewn
squares-Suzy
hat-cerise
beaver crown-
white felt brim-
black ribbon-
beige and black
feather-blond
stockings-black
patent leather
pumps-
1939

RTW

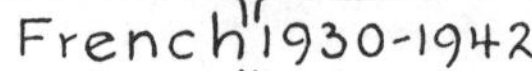
French 1930-1942

Lucien Lelong-
black silk
crêpe-bias
seams-self
bowknots-black
velvet Eugénie
hat-blond
stockings-
black antelope
pumps-
1931

Marcel Rochas-
flowered
taffeta with
velvet
trimming-
black felt
hat-
blond
stockings-
black
suede
pumps-
1935

Worth-
black satin-
shirred into
raglan shoulder-
pleats on hip-
self buttons-
velvet hat-
satin crown-
black
antelope
bag and
pumps-
blond
stockings-
1935

Alix-
brocaded
navy blue
silk-stand-
out panniers-
self buttons
and tie belt-
pleats in
front of skirt-
blond stockings-
blue kid
pumps-
1939
RTW

French 1930-1942

Paquin-
coat of
pomegranate
red wool-
brown sealskin
bolero and
muff-
Maria Guy hat-
black taupé-
brown suède
slippers-blond
stockings-
1931

Vionnet-
coat of
soft red
woolen cloth-
Persian lamb-
velvet béret-
blond
stockings-
black patent
leather
pumps-
1932

Molyneux-
green wool
coat-green
straw hat-
ribbon bow-
chamois
pull-on gloves-
blond stockings-
copper colored
suède open-toed
sandals-
1936

Creed-
redingote
butter yellow
cotton whipcord-
black felt
sailor-black
silk muffler
and handkerchief-
black leather
shoes-blond
stockings-
1937

French 1930-1942

French 1930-1942

Patou-
evening wrap-
two shades of
red-trimmed
with sable-
1931

silver fox
jacket
over black
crêpe gown-
late
'thirties-

Mainbocher-
evening greatcoat
red woolen
cloth trimmed
with blue fox-
red velvet
hat with
ostrich feather-
1938

Creed-
evening coat-
brown velvet
with black
passementerie-
1939

RTW

French 1930-1942

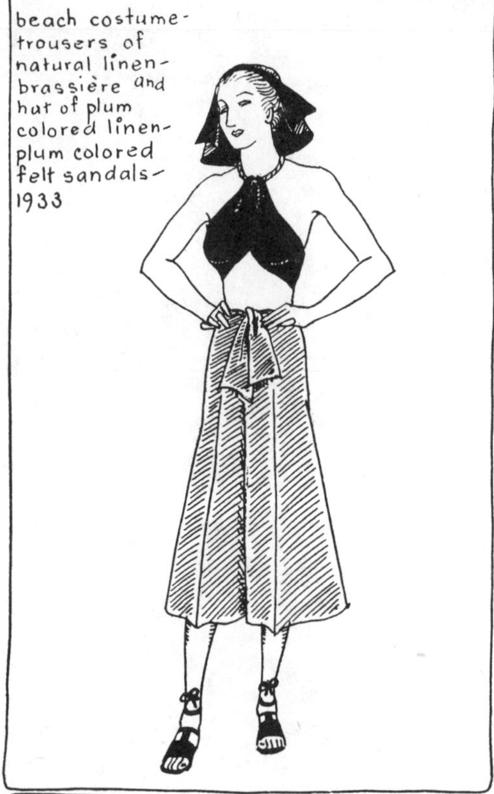

beach costume-
trousers of
natural linen-
brassière and
hat of plum
colored linen-
plum colored
felt sandals-
1933

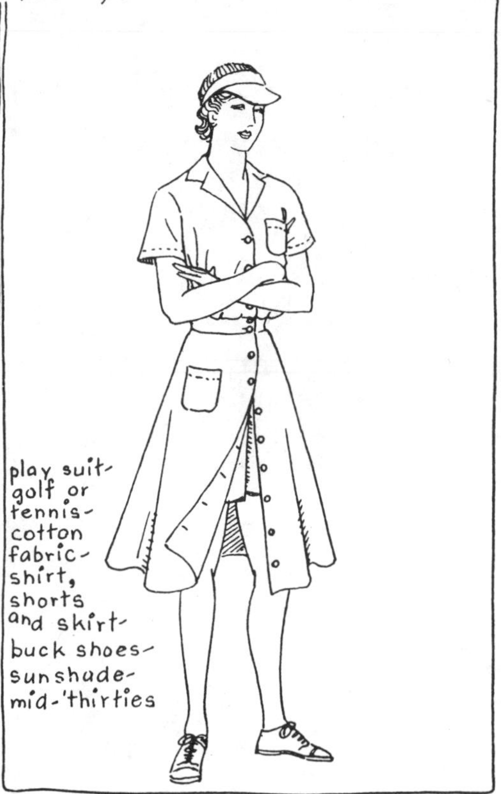

play suit-
golf or
tennis-
cotton
fabric-
shirt,
shorts
and skirt-
buck shoes-
sunshade-
mid-'thirties

shirtwaist frock-
silk or
cotton-
tied silk or
knitted fabric
turban-
leather sandals-
mid-'thirties
RTW

winter play
costume-
yellow woolen
coat-beaver
collar-red suede
waistcoat-
beige slacks-
beige shirt-
beige leather
shoes-red
knitted calotte and
socks-
mid-'thirties

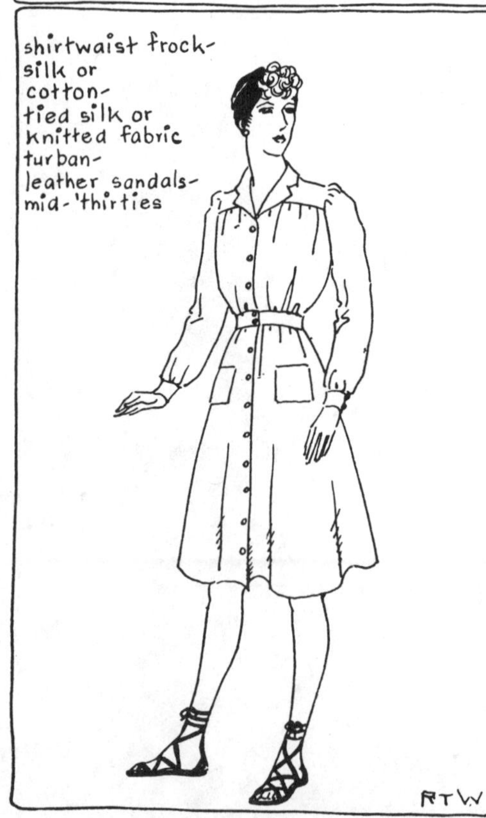

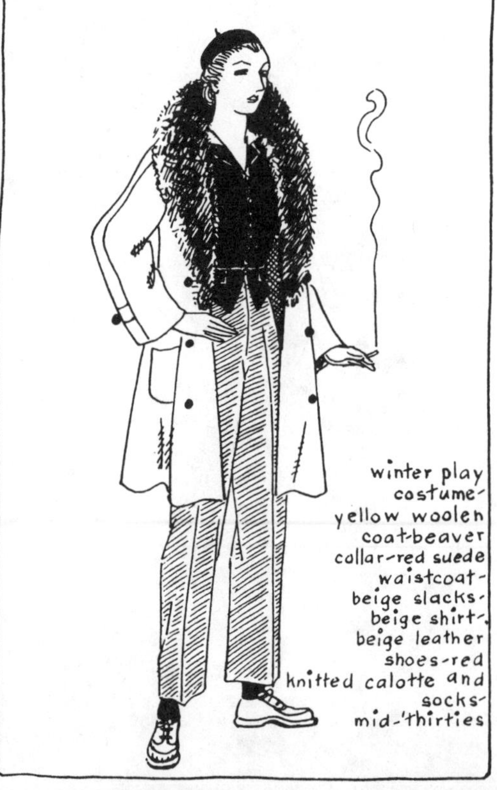

French 1930-1942
Schiaparelli-knitted cap-1932
Maria Guy-green velvet-gold metal stripe-1934
"off-the-face" felt hat-velvet ribbon-1936
Suzy-black beaver-black satin-1939
Schiaparelli-black felt-black chenille net-1936
J. Suzanne Talbot-black velvet-pink roses-1940
Suzy-pink flowers green foliage-1940
Reboux-sailor of East Indian scarf-black velvet brim-1940
velvet calotte-late 'thirties
peasant handkerchief style-late 'thirties
pan cake béret
colored silk umbrella
knitted swimming suit-1940
satin and elastic girdle-lace brassiere-1934
seamless elastic foundation garment-1934
pink satin corset-slide fastener-1939
empire sandal-petunia satin-1936
beige calf-crêpe rubber sole-1940
summer sandals-red felt-braided straw soles-1940
platform sandals-red velvet-1940
gold sandals straps edged black-1935
RTW

Chapter Forty-eight

1947 and The New Look

THIS MOMENT appears of the greatest importance in the feminine mode. A new couturier, Christian Dior, said to be a former successful Paris art dealer, has turned his creative talents to women's clothes and therein has launched a breath-taking silhouette. Breath-taking to the lay public, because entirely opposite to the pencil-slim form of the past decades. It was not without warning, however, because those who know could sense some suspicious signs of the coming change in the late 'thirties. Even then the trend was toward a rounder figure, a smaller waist, snug bodices and, occasionally, full flaring skirts.

As ever, woman takes on a new allure which is laid at her feet by that goddess of changeable whims, Fashion. In these very whims lies the fascination of the mode, because fashion cannot and never does remain static for long. There is nothing new in fashion—it is only the modern interpretation of a given style that makes it so.

Milady has taken on a bosom, hips, stomach and derrière, all this happening despite a terrific wailing of the many opponents of the "New Look." We find ourselves giving up the broad, square, masculine look, a surprising distortion of round, feminine shoulders. We are slipping into a new form, requiring an hourglass corset, the guêpière or waist-clincher, with costumes boned, lined and padded; bustles, peplums, basques, tippets—in fact, all the blandishments of other days.

Call it what you will, guêpière (wasp), waist-cincher or waist-liner, the corset is back as the foundation of the mode. True, it is unlike the torturing garment of other days, being fashioned of lighter fabric and judiciously boned to control the figure. But the firm intent is to produce a small, tight waist, trim above and rounding below. Even the bathing maillot calls for some kind of girdle to give a defined waistline.

The vogue for bare shoulders, which has invaded day, country and play clothes, is responsible for a new engineering feat in brassières, a strapless wired "bra." This wired piece of structure does away with the binding shoulder strap for active sports, at the same time offering firm hold and support. A single wire arched over each breast and bent into a small loop between is the secret. Waist-length brassières with boned seams give a trim look to the tight bodice.

Aside from the stimulus it affords industry, the new style is a boon to many women who have been unable to display a slim silhouette. Of course the smaller waist offers a problem, but they can at least feel happy in possessing bosom and hips instead of the pads which the lithe young creatures must needs adopt.

The short, straight style in suit and dress was practical and fabric-saving during the war, but hemlines have been lengthening by half inches since. Then came the drop to fourteen and twelve, with a prophecy of ten for day wear. In England and in many sections of the United States, many women openly rebelled, but in spite of protests the long skirt is appearing in the metropolis and on Main Street.

The Dior or infanta silhouette is not fashion's ultimate dictum but by far the most important. Other contours are labelled the triangle which flares from neck to hem, back fullness with bustle drapery and the cocoon or wrap-around effect. One can choose between a narrow skirt and a full flaring model in suits.

A sensational circular skirt of Dior's is made with many seams, each panel reinforced with muslin and the hemline faced upward with calico for eight or ten inches. All of which makes the skirt stand away from the figure. And that quite naturally brings us to the subject of petticoats.

For nearly a half century but one petticoat has been worn, a sheath-like garment of silk and occasionally lace-trimmed. Now, all of a sudden, there are definite signs of "petticoat fever," with women wearing two and three at a time in taffetas of all colors, heavily flounced, and many crinoline-stiffened with horsehair or featherboning. White cotton ones are back, frilled with embroideries, and dainty organdy skirts have eyelet edging run with ribbons.

Beautiful lace again adorns slips and panties. Lingerie colors are peach, white, pale blue with black, a growing favorite, the latter further enhanced with black lace. Formerly only the demimondaine availed herself of such glamour.

Lace is once more in fashion; laces of all kinds and qualities. Lace for several decades has led a distinctively dimmed existence in the mode, but the devastation caused by the war in Europe made it imperative to restore and revive the industry to save the very lives of the lacemakers.

The long-sleeved nightgown of fine silk and lace-trimmed of the gay nineties is again worn for winter and not just by the lady of a certain age. This garment was re-introduced by gay, sensible young people. To them goes credit for a revolutionary feminine sleeping tunic, a knee-length affair resembling a man's nightshirt.

Dressing for the cocktail hour is a happy postwar custom, with the "five-o'clock-and-on" frock of ballet length fitting well into the picture. This short evening or dinner dress was an origination brought out in the early 'forties by the American couturière Valentina. The "ballerina," as the style is known, fills a woman's need for the dressy look when her escort is in business clothes. The tailored costume of jacket and skirt of handsome brocade is also meeting with decided approval.

One must note the much-publicized sensational décolletage of a Dior gown which he called "Cabaret." A wide V neckline opens to the waist and partially exposes the breasts. The bosom-baring décolletage is a revival of many appearances in the mode. The Cretan ladies displayed their breasts openly; the deep V neck appeared in the late fourteenth century worn with the hennin, and Agnès Sorel, "la Dame de Beauté" and favorite of the French Charles VII in the fifteenth century, had her portrait painted so.

A century later we find Marie de Médicis wearing the low neck at the French court, where it was designated as the "Italian Style," and 'tis said that it became really popular. In England it was worn, oddly enough, by maiden ladies, and Queen Elizabeth indulged in the low-cut front. We read that the French ambassador was deeply disconcerted during an audience with the English monarch, who was wearing her open-front gown.

After a period of "sans chapeau"—a casual fashion seen even on city streets—the smart feminine head is once again coifed, in a real hat. Dinner and evening gowns, too, are accompanied by chic little hats. There are berets, turbans, pillboxes, some large hats; but again we turn to Dior to mention his profile hats, made after his designs by Maud Roser. His is a new half-hat, half-hairdo idea, a modern version of the very jaunty soft hat which the dandy of the Renaissance wore over one ear. Some of those gentlemen attached the hat to a caul and thus kept the piece perched at the side of their heads but today's smart woman pins hers to a one sided up-hairdo.

The small soignée head with the hair dressed up in back is the fitting style atop the new figure. Many young women affect a medieval bob, an artistic headdress of beautifully brushed, swirled locks. Technicolor photography, which tinges all colors with a suspicion of red, has introduced a new shade in blonds. The color is lighter and pinker than Titian, rather like a pale tone of copper foil, a metallic but beautiful tint.

The greatcoat is with us, of heavy but soft cloth and with flaring skirt, also the coachman's cloak with its little capes. Attached to many a coat is an enveloping hood, the result of the hatless fashion.

Furs, which are still scarce in Paris, have adopted the rounded silhouette with softened shoulders. They are fashioned in jacket, three-quarter and full length with full sleeves. Sumptuous indeed are the new long capes of luxurious silver fox. Precious furs, of which there is a profusion in the United States, are given simple, casual treatment in design.

Successful ranch-raising of animals for their fur has augmented the supply of pelts in the world's fur markets, while successful experiments with mutation have produced new colors in valuable skins especially in mink and silver fox. From the ranch come deep-blue tones, black mink sprinkled with white, and, rarest and costliest of all, white mink.

Very popular for the modern way of life is the separate skirt, especially the dirndl of Tyrolean origin, worn with the tuck-in blouse. This style makes for many changes and offers a wide choice of color combinations and fabrics, in either long or short, for day or evening. It is also responsible for the very youthful and very American "mother and daughter" ensembles.

The world of fashion is enjoying the return of the many fabrics which had disappeared because of war priorities. Most worthy of note is the reinstatement in the mode, after an absence of some decades, of black broadcloth, a fabric of great elegance. There are sheer woolens, suède-surfaced woolens and wool jerseys, all of which tailor well and drape beautifully; also rare fleeces, tweeds and practically all the known cloths, silks and velvets. From our good neighbors to the south come Mexican and Guatemalan cottons, hand-woven and hand-loomed in brilliant color and interesting texture.

Suèded leather is not new for hunting clothes, the Spanish having made use of the soft, beautifully toned leather centuries back. But today, in this era of informal living, suède enters into every phase of costume, being carried into feminine evening dress. The chamoised leather, dyed in many subdued colors, lends itself to a simple unadorned mode.

Feminine footwear is inspired by the shoes of the peoples of all ages: the primitive fur boot, the alpargata, the moccasin, the sandal, the mule, the peaked toe, fashioned of all possible materials into models suitable to any and every occasion. In general, heels are of either extreme—that is, low and broad or high and spiked. The designers are creating footwear as simple or as extravagant as one might desire. Bronze slippers are staging a return. Suède, fancy and colored leathers, velvet and satin remain staple, and dress and weather shoes show signs of rising to ankle height. "Open-toed" shoes for day wear have been blacked out by the classic pump.

Time was when a pair of lady's rubbers covered any pair of shoes but the varied styles in any wardrobe have made overshoes a problem. The designers have got busy on that dilemma, and from California comes a protective boot to accommodate heels of all kinds. It borrows the clog idea of Colonial days, a flat sole of synthetic rubber cushioned with cork from which a bag rises to encase the foot. Strapped round the ankle, it is a modern contraption, with the uppers of transparent, sheer but sturdy fabric. The picture given on our accessory page will illustrate the result better than a description.

With the quantities of exquisite sheer nylon stockings again available, the bare-legged fashion has left us. The general color is darker and in many hues of muted tones of green, plum, brown and black, but so gossamer sheer are the stockings that such colors appear but as shadows over the flesh. There are lisles and wools for sportswear in knee-high or ankle socks, the latter called anklets. For spectator sports there is a very sheer lace mesh nylon, a flattering and almost indestructible stocking.

The beautiful white mousquetaire glove is back for evening wear in eight, twelve, sixteen, or twenty-button lengths, and the classic pull-on in black or brown doeskin is the preferred afternoon or cocktail glove. For street and casual wear we find slip-ons, one- or two-button shorties and wrist-strap gloves, the same styles for sportswear but of heavier leather such as pigskin, buckskin, goatskin and the like. White pigskin in the longer lengths, however, is a recent and truly chic addition to glove leathers for afternoon and evening dress.

One could devote many paragraphs to scarfs and mufflers, which are to be had in all possible lovely fabrics, printed, hand-blocked and hand-painted. The influence of the artist is evident today in all walks of life, because, regardless of the quality or price of the article, the applied design is artistic in motif and color—a statement which holds good for practically all of our modern materials.

We have passed through a period of bags in sabretache style with the long shoulder strap, a very convenient war fashion. The wrist strap seems newer and is attached to many different shapes which range from pouch to box forms. A novelty in this day is a chatelaine bag swinging from the belt. All styles are tailored and done in leathers and fabrics, a fairly new one being black broadcloth. Handbags usually bear some gilt or gold decoration in clasps, chains or monograms. The war left its mark in a trail of gilt insignia and other martial motifs.

Evening bags, smaller in size than the day pieces, are of satin, brocade, tapestry, embroidery or beading, making a featured note of the ensemble. It is possible for a woman of means to indulge her fancy in its wildest flight, so beautiful, extravagant, precious and costly are some of these receptacles.

There have been several attempts to bring back the long-handled umbrella, but the short, stubby model still holds its own. Designers have given much attention to clothes for inclement weather, creating raincoats which are not only utilitarian but smart enough in appearance to wear on the sunniest day.

Touching upon the masculine mode, signs of a new trend are to be observed. Not to be outdone by Madame, the well-dressed man appears to be taking note of the feminine shoulder treatment by giving up the exaggerated square physique. High-class ready-mades are being prepared with narrower and rounder shoulders.

The popularity of the single-breasted fly-front topcoat for day wear is on the wane. Double-breasted overcoats are being made of handsome soft fabrics and accordingly are being tagged with very high prices. For instance, a coat of the South American vicuña, a small animal of the camel family with the finest and rarest wool in the world, can be had for approximately five hundred dollars. Guanaco, also of the camel species and of the same country, provides hair for a costly fabric similar to vicuña but slightly coarser in texture.

The topcoat of camel's hair or tweed and the raglan of light brown whipcord are staples for general use. Also to be noted for knock-about service are casual loafer coat of suèded cloth, the army coat of water-repellent cotton gabardine, sheepskin lined and collared, and the wind-breaker of ponyskin.

The influence of battle dress is evident in civilian life, especially in sports clothes. The short battle jacket is of particular interest, a London tailor having designed an informal evening suit on the same lines in midnight-blue cloth for wear with the black tie. Its acceptance is a matter of conjecture—men do not as a rule like change (a woman's statement); and there is an objection to the outfit resembling too closely that of the uniformed attendant. The double-breasted Tuxedo or dinner jacket has definitely come to the fore in popularity.

The war, with attending curtailment of civilian manufacturing, followed by the army of returning veterans clamoring for clothes, created a dearth of all necessities. It has taken two years to reach anything near normalcy.

White cotton for shirts and underwear was simply unobtainable and so men wore what could be had. From California came the idea of shirts, shorts and robes done in bright-colored materials for sportswear. Necessity and the scarcity of woolen cloth put men into ensembles of light colors and combinations of colors. This latter scheme evolved a jacket in two colors, of a plain and a fancy weave, the front in one color or pattern and the sleeves and back in another. The latest tendency appears to be toward no pattern and cloth light in color for sports jackets.

Trousers continue to be made with pleats at the waist, affording some fulness in front. A new patented design in slacks, called "Daks," is a recent English contribution of importance in breeches that requires no belt.

There is a rise in the cut of some day shoes, a noticeably smart style founded upon the polo player's and army officer's boot and so named the "chukka" or "flight boot." The comfortable, casual Norwegian slipper, called the "loafer shoe," has become a staple. It is gradually working its way into the class for general wear, since shoe designers have given their attention to a dress version of the laceless slip-on.

The hats of the average man's wardrobe afford him a wide choice of what to wear, but pre-war rules still hold with the same insistence on when and where to wear a certain hat.

The well-dressed man likes a scarf of rich color but he also delights in a cravat gayly patterned perhaps with contrasting colors. According to his ensemble, it will be of silk, wool, cotton or synthetic fabric, in club or regimental stripes, weaves of small design or just plain. At the moment an incredible craze is current for garish colored neckties of truly startling motifs, very often hand-painted and for that reason costing a goodly sum. Such neckpieces are appearing not only with loafing clothes but with the town habit.

The notes given in Chapter Forty-three on men's robes, underwear, sweaters, hose and sleeping garments continue to appertain in this post-war period.

1947 "The New Look"

1947

black wool suit-
turtle neck jersey
shirt-crushed fedora
of cinnamon velour-
Dior

beige cloth suit-
skirt pleated over hips-
plaid wool blouse,
béret and muffler-
Molyneux

black cloth jacket edged
with black serpentine
braid-green cloth
circular skirt with
gathers in back-
black velvet
béret-
Jacques Fath

gray herringbone woolen
suit-self-banded at
hip and hem-
embroidered
black velvet
pillbox-
Mainbocher
RTW

1947
evening gown of
black chiffon and dark
red taffeta-black
leather belt with
gun metal buckle-
Dior

evening ensemble of
cocoanut colored
satin and velvet-
velvet basque-gold
and silver embroidery-
sable fur-
Jacques Fath

white satin
and heavy white
cotton Venetian lace-
Maggy Rouff

black woolen
dinner suit-dress
worn with short
basque jacket-
black ostrich
trim and muff-
black béret-
Dior
RTW

1947

boulevardier greatcoat
of heavy woolen
cloth-
Balenciaga

Cossack coat of
bright blue cloth-
Persian lamb-
squirrel lining-
Dior

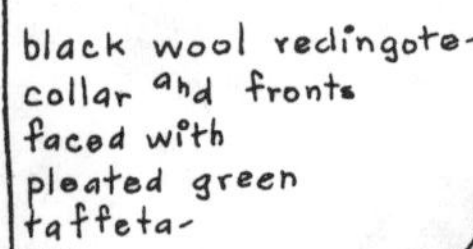
black wool redingote-
collar and fronts
faced with
pleated green
taffeta-
Dior

coachman's coat
of heavy woolen
cloth-
Grès
RTW

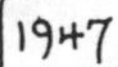

circular capes of gray flannel-
Grès

triangle silhouette-
greatcoat of thick beige woolen cloth with stitching-
Paquin

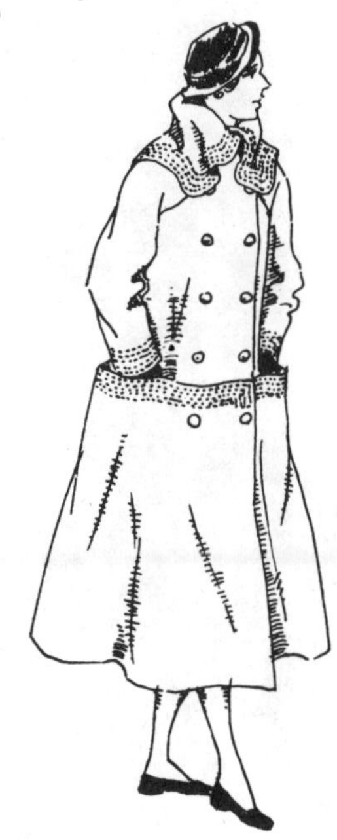

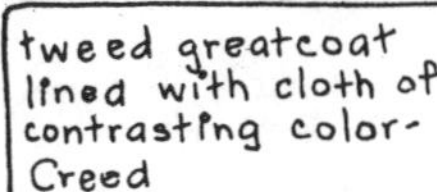

short hooded cape of gray and gold plaid cloth-
Grès

RTW

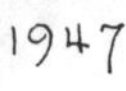
1947

Alaska sealskin
coat created
for Fredrica
by Dior

cape of
silver fox-
Fromm

coat of
champagne colored
nutria-coif of
Venetian lace-
Maximilian

coat of
dark ranch mink-
Esther Dorothy

RTW

1947
raincoat of
rain repellent
cloth with
detachable hood-
rubber boots

green suède leather
skeet jacket-
chamois patch
at shoulder-
bellows pockets-
tweed skirt-
calf gillie shoes

ski ensemble-
gray gabardine
jacket-dark blue
lining, hood,
mittens and
trousers

American
"mother and daughter"
design-of black
taffeta or velveteen
over white organdie
blouse
RTW

1947

for beach or sailing-
blue denim and
red and white striped
cotton-short slacks
or "pedal pushers"-
coolie jacket-
red and white
clogs

all-in-one beach suit-
beige wool jersey-
striped green belt-
wooden clogs with
green cotton straps

ranch or western riding
togs-whipcord frontier
pants and jacket-
wool shirt-colored
embroidery-leather
boots with heels
and colored leather
motifs-leather
and silver belt-
felt hat with
leather bride

for dinner at home-
black velvet slacks-
colorful silk
blouse-
ballet slippers

RTW

1947
white sharkskin bathing suit-tucked body-clogs of painted wood and cotton-Brigance
black nylon elastic swim suit-zippered back-Mabs

beach dress of striped linen worn over pantaloons-Molyneux

brown jersey one-piece beach suit with full bloomers-jersey skirt striped green, brown and black-striped cotton clogs-Jacques Fath

sun-dress in culotte fashion-printed batiste-colorful cotton wedge clogs-De De Johnson
RTW

1947
modern farthingale of taffeta with ruffles
colored taffeta petticoat white cotton ruffle-lace edge-bands of horsehair braid
woman's sleeping tunic of silk or batiste-lace-edged
black chiffon gown with corselet of black lace
lace-trimmed silk slip
laced and hooked guêpière-black satin-lace-edged
long-sleeved gown of silk or batiste-lace-edged
woman's sleeping tunic of silk or batiste
lace and satin pantie girdle
removable wire
gartered brassière of nylon-elastic-black or white
boned "waist-liner" of nylon marquisette-laced in front
strapless brassière with removable arched wire
RTW

1947
soft felt brimmed béret-Dior design made by Sygur
suède shoe with satin bowknot-Adrian
coiffure by Antoine
black suède pouch on leopard skin belt
pouch bag-black suède or fabric-Pichel
black felt or velvet toque-black brush-Dior
suède or satin pump-moiré tie-La Valle
evening sandal-black velvet edged gold braid-yellow thongs tied in back
wide girdle of pink antelope-Balenciaga
casual shoe-cocoa suède-Cobblers
gray sèude and black patent leather-Drettas
black suède bag-gilt decoration-Rosenfeld
silk umbrella-cobra handle, case and shoulder strap
silk umbrella leather covered handle
California rain boot-transparent plastic-cork and rubber sole
sports glove-yellow crochet string with pigskin palm
return of the formal white glacé or suède glove
tailored cloth hat with fantasy feather-Schiaparelli
small suitcase-canvas and pigskin with silk umbrella Schiaparelli
black faille bag-silk umbrella in zippered compartment
RTW

1947

Country Clothes

sports jacket, green plaid-
green foulard scarf,
white polka dots-
beige flannel slacks-
brown reverse calf
shoes-crêpe
rubber soles

leisure jacket, rust gabardine-
colorful plaid wool sleeves and
collar-white shirt-
gray knitted pull-on
sweater-gray
gabardine slacks-
jippi-jappa hat-
brown and white
Norwegian
slippers

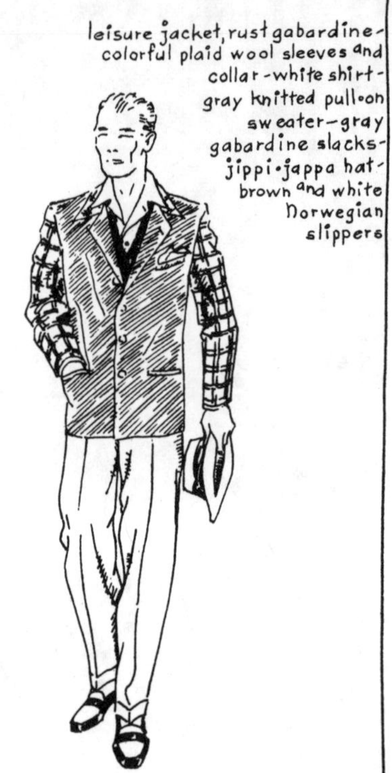

leisure jacket, camel's hair, natural
color- **dark** shirt-knitted scarf-
gold colored cotton slacks-
hemp hat with striped
puggree band-
brown and white
casual shoes

leisure jacket, brown suède
leather-beige corduroy slacks-
yellow flannel shirt-
maroon scarf-
brown and tan
casual shoes

RTW

1947-

Sports Clothes

hunting costume-
maroon and black plaid wool-
maroon wool shirt-
scarlet wool cap-
moccasin boot of
grained leather-
white wool hose with
maroon stripe

active sports costume-
"bush jacket" of tan cotton twill-
bellows and pleated pockets-
tan twill shorts-white lisle
pullover shirt-
white knitted wool
hose-brown turned
calf shoes-
sun helmet, tan
cotton over
fiber

RTW

1947 Beach Clothes

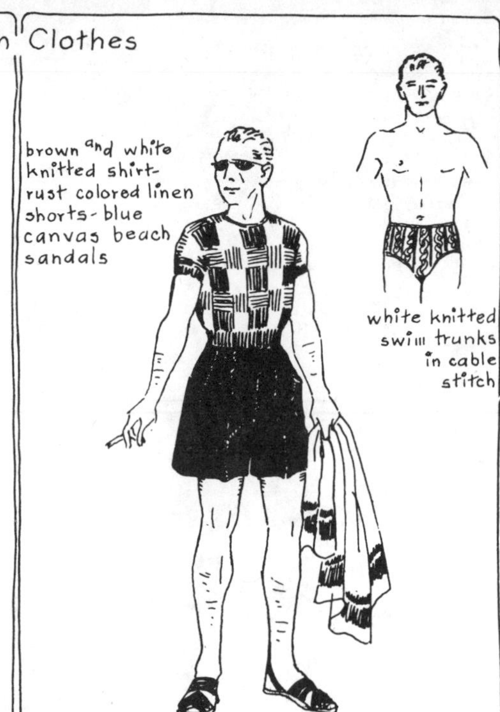

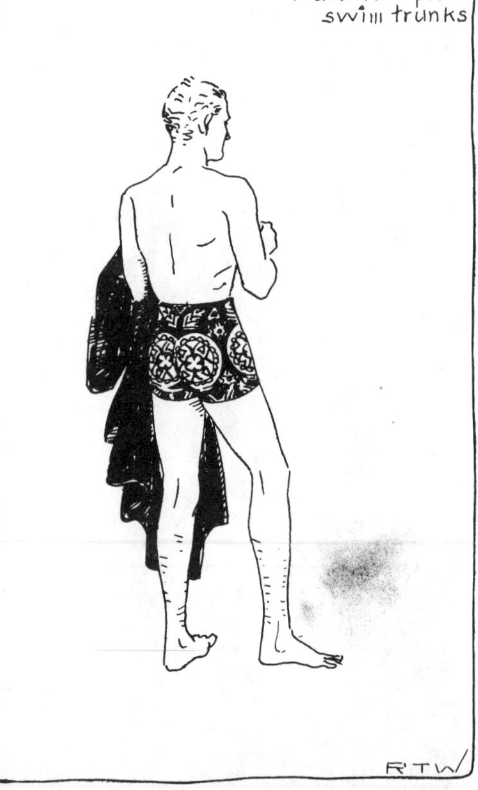

1947
thong laced to one side-reversed calf
the classic Homburg-dark blue and other colors
knitted ski sweater-navy or red on white
chukka boot of brown or black calf
cocoanut hat-polka dot puggree band
cotton shirt of two fabrics-white and colored check
scarf designs
English evening suit founded on battle dress-midnight blue with silk shawl collar
dress version of the Norwegian slipper-calf or suède
jippi•jappa hat with wide puggree band
cap for active sports-of straw or canvas
moccasin with platform sole-white buck-tan reverse calf.
tri•colored straw with puggree band
horsehide jacket for roughing it-wool lined
RTW

Chapter Forty-nine

1948-1958

Going back over the period, the shirtwaist dress appears to have been and continues to be outstanding with the sheath a close second. Whether in silk, wool or cotton, the shirt dress and certainly the shirt itself have attained fashionable importance comparable to the days of the Gibson girl. Both dressmaker and tailored models have become basic whether worn with the slim, cloth skirt for office or sports or with the full skirt for dining and dancing.

A complete shirt wardrobe includes one each of lawn, voile or organdie, a white satin and a splashy silk print. The satin model embodies true elegance, also the chiffon shirt made of two layers, wearable with dinner skirt or with dressy slacks for home entertaining. Handsome jeweled links fasten the French cuffs of long sleeves and ropes of beads ornament the neck. The revival of the over-blouse coincides with the present vogue of the chemise frock. Very popular indeed has been the mannish pink cotton shirt brought out in 1949 by Brooks Brothers of New York as a concession to the ladies who until then had been raiding the small sizes in that particular men's shop.

Since 1950, the sheath, shift, chemise or "sack" has been stealthily gaining a foothold in the mode. In 1954 appeared a knit chemise which *Vogue* Magazine, its creator, called the "T-shirt dress" and which was nothing more than the popular sport shirt of stockinette knitted to dress length. Finally in 1954 the Paris designers displayed versions of the chemise frock, thus making it a most controversial fashion and who knows, perhaps the standard, uniform style today's globe-trotting calls for. At this writing (February 1958) Yves Saint-Laurent, a young designer, protégé and successor to M. Dior has made his debut. He is being acclaimed for his "Trapeze Line" which adds a new dimension to the chemise, a narrow-shouldered, high-waisted but shaped bodice with a flaring and waistless line "swinging" from bodice to knees.

It was in 1948 that Balenciaga showed an Empire-waisted dress. Repeated attempts have been made to revive the style but, thus far, its acceptance has been lukewarm. For the moment the ayes in favor of the hip-line girdle vie with those leaning toward the belt under the bosom. In the early 1950's Paris featured the bloused top or "blouson", long-haired furs and the large hat. Deep-collared coats paved the way for the Paris cape craze in the fall of 1956 and Dior named his barrel-shaped silhouette the "Magnet Line" after the horseshoe-shaped magnet. This shape was further developed, becoming an egg-shaped outline called "cocoon." A new interlining shapes garments today in both men's and women's wear. Not woven but of pressed fibers, it is crease-resistant and washable and usable with all fabrics.

Cecil Beaton made fashion history in 1956 by creating the beautiful costumes for the musical play "My Fair Lady" presented in New York. He, too, stressed the Empire mode of the first two decades of our century recalling the nostalgic past of Paul Poiret, Balieff's ballet and the artist, Leon Bakst. Slim, high-waisted, full-length gowns of elegant silks, chiffons and laces in long-line draperies with bead embroideries, it was a fashion for well-mannered ladies.

In suits, a departure from the traditional neck-hugging collar of the tailleur came about in 1952 when Balenciaga placed the collar of jacket and coat at a cut-away neckline. A current fashion is the youthful, short-jacketed suit of tweed or wool jersey created by Chanel in the 1920's. Back into the haute couture in 1954 after an absence of fifteen years came Gabrielle Chanel bringing her famed "Chanel Look" with her in a simple, little tailleur set off by a brilliant silk print used for blouse and lining. An event of tremendous importance and an instant success! In this period the "tricot" or sweater was elevated to fashionable formal dress.

The knitted cardigan became high fashion in the hands of Mainbocher who created a lovely butterfly from a utilitarian piece of knitting. It began in 1949 when he remade some cardigans into smart little jackets for some of society's best-dressed women. In 1950, the revamped sweater appeared in Palm Beach, went on to Long Island, worn day and night in the country and in the city. What had been a simple, light, shoulder protection now turned out chiffon-lined and enhanced with glittering paillettes and beads, braid and ribbon embroidery, jeweled buttons and what not! And those who own real gems pin on their fabulous brooches as well. Another type of cardigan in the mode is the bulky knit in jacket or full coat length becoming, according to the color, a good travel piece and smart for town or country.

Daytime styles of 1957 followed an uncluttered, relaxed simplicity with hems of variable lengths, evening dress going all out for the exotic, Oriental splendor in mandarin sheaths, hooded saris and kimono coats. After sundown the skirt ranged from short, puffed harem hems to the newest fishtail trains, while the showing of an occasional knee-length by Dior, Balenciaga and Patou put the fashion world in a tizzy. Silk crêpe in black and pastel colors is again with us in the fabric department, sharing honors with silk and wool jersey, loosely woven wools, beautiful brocades, striking prints and shantung. Chiffon is in its heyday with miles of double layers fashioned into simple, untrimmed dresses, blouses and floating, filmy evening gowns. Lace has staged a comeback and picture bowknots are rampant.

Black and white are first on the color chart, then a gamut of beiges, browns and red. However, come summer the palette runs wild in Matisse-like hues and color combinations in all shades of yellow, lime, orange, coral and turquoise. A return to the Poiret Era, indeed.

The staple coat remains that founded upon the man's polo coat, the feminine model of the 1950's either three-quarter or full-length, still made of camel's hair cloth, costlier in cashmere and fabulous in vicuña. Although the traditional color is blond or honey, today's polo coat cloths are also dyed red, black, wine red, French blue and gray. And what with world travel it has become the one coat every woman must own. It is an all-year-round, all-occasion cloak and when lined with lustrous, delicately tinted or white satin is fitting for formal evening wear as well.

In the domain of furs a mink coat whether long or short continues to be one of the most coveted of wraps, and due to the progress of scientifically cultivated mutation in various shades, a woman can choose the perfect foil for her own coloring. The breeding of chinchilla in America which got under way in the 1920's now makes capelets and even long coats of the fur available "at a price." Fine furs made up on dressmaker lines are frequently finished with braid, suède and occasionally with a crushed satin cummerbund.

The colorful dyeing of pelts was a new idea in the early 1950's with coney, mouton and moleskin turning up in all the rainbow hues of the spectrum. Today, following the lead set by broadtail, Persian lamb and Alaska seal, the most precious furs have gone casual in middy jacket and smock fashion. Though ingénue and sports-like, black is the predominating color with sable, mink, ermine and even chinchilla being dyed black. New in 1957 is "Kitovi", a plum-dyed Alaskan seal which tones to navy blue or brown when worn with those colors.

The past few years have noted the growing popularity of long-haired furs culminating this season in a lavish use of such pelts. To the fore have come fox, lynx, civet cat, opossum and raccoon. Fur muffs and hats are back in the mode so that, to be really chic, one should be as fur-wrapped and fur-capped as any Russian Cossack ever was.

A skin of new fashion importance is river otter which made its appearance around 1950 as an all-weather coat. The sleek, shiny Brazilian pelts are employed for the body of the coat while collar and cuffs might be the long-haired Canadian otter or mink. The same use is made of Labrador hair seal which is either dyed a rich brown or bleached to a pale beige.

Also around 1950 appeared the "frankly fake furs" which, while making no pretence, became fashion news. Designed at first with the college girl in mind the manufacturer has improved his product to the point where designers are successfully using the woven synthetic fur cloths in sophisticated styles such as cocktail jackets, at the same time turning out handsome greatcoats for day and evening. Among the imitations are Persian lamb, broadtail, moleskin, beaver, sealskin, krimmer and other short-haired skins. Of course, the cloth lacks the warmth of the impermeable pelt but even that can be overcome by an insulated lining thus making real glamour available at comparatively low cost.

Most remarkable is the story of man-made fibers. After thousands of years of weaving the natural yarns, wool, linen, cotton and silk into cloth for man's dress, the invention of rayon in the last century and the eventual perfection of synthetic filaments, the industry producing the new textiles has come far indeed. Chanel was the first of the French couture to make use of rayon cloth in models which were displayed by her mannequins at Deauville in 1915. By the 1940's synthetic yarn in the United States exceeded in quantity that of the world with Japan following in second place.

Since World War II an ever-increasing flow of yarns has come from the laboratories to be woven into fabric for male and female dress. In America we have Acetate, Nylon, Orlon, Dacron, Cynel and Vicara which are names relatively of the moment. These test-tube yarns have remarkable properties in lowered cost, can be washed and dry cleaned, have insulation qualities against heat and cold and are light in weight. Furthermore, miracles in fashion are evolved by blending the artificial fibers with the natural thereby utilizing the advantages of both in crease and moth resistance plus greater durability.

Perhaps even more amazing is the stretchable yarn which is fashioned into all manner of form-fitting undergarments, thus eliminating the need of varied size and shape in a given item. Added to all this, stretchables give the luxurious feel of fitting. But, wonderful as are the new fabrics, wool, linen, silk and cotton continue to hold their own except in women's stockings. It is here that nylon because possessed of unusual tensile strength no matter how sheer, has surpassed and supplanted natural silk.

A pencil seam is the feature of the shadowy hose but for wear with the naked looking sandals there are seamless nylons and those woven with toes to carry out the bare look. In 1954 the French couturier, Jacques Fath, designed nylon stockings with exquisite lace tops. Other glamorous ideas are nylons sprinkled with tiny sparkling jewels and others spun with gold thread. For hot weather comfort, knee-high sheers come woven with garter tops.

A forty-inch nylon stocking appeared in 1955 to be fastened to the panty girdle. This was followed by black tights reaching to the waist and intended as casual dress for evenings at home. By 1956 this garment of stretch nylon had grown into a footed leotard reaching from neck to toe, available in red, green and blue and worn with Bermuda shorts, the kilt, country tweeds and ski and skating togs. Which brings to mind the colorful hose of the medieval dandy except that he, poor fellow, wore cloth tights shaped by hand-sewn seams.

The shoe story is that of the pump but new, in the long, slim last, sharply pointed as to toe, with an exceedingly high spike or needle heel, or a baby French heel. The elegant French woman has been wearing the pointed toe for some years.

Perhaps the biggest style note is "hats." The fashionable woman is actually wearing a hat, a real hat! Hats vary in shape and over-all size. Many are tall and have feathery ornaments rising to surprising height. Feathers, flowers, ribbons, velvets, tulle, jewels, buckles, felts and straws are once more on the shelves of the milliner. The modiste is again designing hats for each season of the year and for every occasion, but for real practical purposes the stay-on cloche, the turban and the sailor have returned. At the same time, all signs portend that the tiny hat will continue its firm hold on the smart head and our guess is that come mild weather many women will refuse to forgo the fun of going hatless. And many will cling to headkerchiefs and hoods, especially the sportscar addicts.

Gloves are definitely in the news what with the vogue for short-sleeved coats, suits and dresses. From "shortie" to shoulder length, gloves will be worn more than in many seasons past. Leathers, cottons and nylons come in pastel shades but gray, beige and white predominate, especially with the dark costume, and black as an accent with the light scheme. The shortened sleeve calls for gloves reaching halfway up the forearm except for evening décolleté when the shoulder-high glove is worn. Much thought has been given to country gloves which are available in leather, cotton and crochet string and combinations of leather and fabric. The favored leather for driving and sportswear is pigskin. Whether of leather or fabric, "lavable" or washable gloves are in most demand.

A new idea in jewelry was the tiny patch of diamonds, real ones, first worn in 1951 applied to cheek or neck by means of a special stickum. The chignon and French twist, whether one's own or added, is bringing back jeweled combs and jeweled hairpins for evening. Wide picture necklines have influenced the flair for costume jewelry, a particular note being the chandelier earrings. Fabulous brooches, clips, tiaras and long necklaces are modish. And beads! beads! beads! long ropes either matching or of different colors all worn at the same time cascading from throat to waist.

Lingerie ranges from the most fairy-like loveliness to the most practical and common sense designs. A wide choice of fabrics goes into their making, cottons, silks and synthetics in airy, gossamer tissues or heavier weight fabrics. Of almost unbelievable charm are the nightgowns with matching négligés made of yards and yards of lace-trimmed, permanently pleated nylon chiffon, this luxury a newcomer in 1947. Quaint and picturesque is the Victorian full-length gown, high of neck with long full sleeves. A hip-length version has been adopted by the young woman and is worn over the very shortest of bloomers.

The petticoat vogue continues, slim for the sheath, full and hooped as the underprop for formal, bouffant skirts, sometimes as many as six bolstering the full-skirted ball gown. The silk-lined sheath and the silk-lined suit skirt are responsible for the return of the chemise which in its modern form of combination camisole and panty eliminates the petticoat. In today's vernacular, a slim underskirt is a "half slip" while a "full slip" is a petticoat with top. In general, lingerie colors run to pale peach, pale blue, delicate green, mauve, black or white, even French gray, but smartest are the beige and brown tones with ecru lace. This beige and brown fashion has led to a craze for lingerie fabrics printed in leopard pattern.

In corsetry there is the corselette or all-in-one, the step-in girdle, the girdle with zipper, the waist cincher and the garter belt. Under the same heading are brassières or "bras" and "falsies" or "mystifiers", this latter a trade name. Some all-in-ones are actually combination girdle, panties and bra, while others also combine a slip. Today's corset is comfortable to wear because of the stretchable, glove-fitting textiles, few bones and the garment being worn next to the skin. Fashioned from dainty and seemingly fragile fabric, Lastex (nylon elastic), satin, power net and lace, the garment belies its looks. The modern foundation is a far cry from that of earlier decades. In fact, so far removed from the traditional "stays" is our garment that the manufacturer would gladly welcome a new name, one less grim than the word corset.

For golf and tennis the tailored shirtwaist dress of yore has been pretty well replaced by Bermuda shorts which are knee-length, the newer above knee-length termed Jamaica shorts and the kilt. The change got under way about 1950 when the younger players adopted more abbreviated play dress. Topped by a tailored shirt, shorts or kilt secured by a golf belt are now considered appropriate on the fairways from conservative Palm Beach to California. Golf shorts may be of tweed or cotton according to season but the tennis theme is invariably white and definitely without frills.

Feminine breeches of dressier type such as satin or velvet are usually black and in jodhpur or Spanish toreador cut, worn when giving a cocktail party or the little dinner at home. With a cashmere sweater or a tailored silk shirt the ensemble is at once both casual and chic.

With youthful marriages so prevalent at present and with definite plans for larger familes, maternity dress now comes under the heading of the mode. Time was when the young matron went into seclusion for a certain period but not so today! A whole new field of designing has grown up to glamorize the "lady-in-waiting", making it possible for young women to step out until the very last minute in appropriate and lovely clothes. In 1940 Elsa Schiaparelli created a stunning evening gown, a white silk choir-boy smock lace-edged and worn over a slim black skirt, and one wonders if she realized what a wonderful costume it was to make for the mother-to-be. The skirt permits constant reshaping and the hem hangs straight because of the cut-out over the abdomen covered by the smock or overblouse.

The most abbreviated of all bathing attire appeared in 1947 and 1948. It consisted of two bits of fabric, the very slimmest of bra and a kind of G-string, the "bikini" of the French Rivièra, producing an effect more naked than the nude figure. Needless to say, the American version required a few more inches to be wearable. Eventually bathing dress took a trend toward a more covered-up look, some later models having long or push-up sleeves though designed with low back. Those with a strapless décolletage are made with a built-in bra and some with an all-in-one foundation for proper fit. Often the suit is equipped with a wrap-around skirt so that the wearer may dine at the beach club or restaurant without having to dress. Swim suit fabrics comprise cotton, jersey, Lastex and a fine woolen cloth in glen-plaids and herringbones like that used in men's day suits. Most popular, however, is Lastex, especially for the maillot model.

Fashion is as much a part of and as changeable in swim suits as the rest of the feminine wardrobe. Instead of one such garment, most women now have three or four numbers for beach, sun bathing and even cocktail hour at club or private pool. And what with the popularity of vacation cruises, the swim suit is almost a year-round necessity and a costlier item than formerly.

Though the shingle haircut marks the beginning of this period many smart women were observed pinning on a chignon, especially for evening. The pony tail secured by an elastic band was the result among young women of growing a length of hair and being reluctant to cut it off again. We next see the poodle clip, no doubt inspired by Mary Martin's hairdo of tight curls which she shampooed daily on the stage in "South Pacific." A startling new shape appeared in 1951 when Michel created his "Pompon" cut, an outline different from the usual curls. The fairly straight locks were puffed out in rolls over a manipulated undercutting. So new it was that it lay dormant a while to bloom forth as the bouffant hairdo of 1956.

Meanwhile the hairdo of the Italian movie stars took hold, a mass of loose ringlets coiffed high in a sculptured effect over the forehead. This prompted the return of the pompadour or "portrait style" of high wide waves, giving a patrician look to most wearers. The new coiffures are as much the result of skill in handling the shears and comb as in the setting of the shape. Of the moment is the soft bouffant cut, a perfect foil for the larger hat.

In these days women dye their hair and do not keep it secret either! It is done professionally or at home by thousands of women. There are many safe coloring kits on the market under the headings of rinse, tint, bleach or dye which can be combed in, brushed in or washed in as in a shampoo. Some are permanent, some wash out in the next shampoo, so one need not fear the horror of regret over a wrong choice of color. Many women simply touch up their hair while others delight in painting on a silver or white streak for the fun of it.

As to the use of cosmetics, they are on the dressing table and in the handbag of every well-dressed woman. Never have beauty aids been so universally a part of good grooming. At the French court of the eighteenth century paint and powder were compulsory and glaringly applied but ladies did not wear paint and powder in public. Today, however, the use of make-up is a natural, necessary and flattering finish to the ensemble from the moment of rising to retiring. Most women take advantage of the glamour-giving concoctions and what's more, modern men expect their women to do so.

The fashion of the suntan complexion has faded, giving way to a delicate, subtle palette and a very feminine look. Except in the case of the perfect youthful complexion, make-up in general consists of a fluid foundation base, rouge applied sparingly, lipstick, eye shadow and a touch of eye liner. If the eyebrows require a bit of accent, that is done too. Mahogany and scarlet fingernails have had their day, for which men are grateful; instead nail enamels are more powdery in tone to harmonize with the lighter facial coloring.

While the ups and downs of skirt hems serve to stir up no small tempest in a woman's world, still more provocative is some American news of "throw away" paper clothes developed by a manufacturer of paper tissues. These paper clothes with flame resistance and wet strength properties are already available as dungarees to workers in atomic energy. The paper cloth for feminine wear has been exhibited in a dirndl skirt which was worn by a model on television. The fabric was decorated with a beautiful fern motif hand-screened in gold and black. Just think of the endless possibilities in store for the woman with "nothing to wear"!

Masculine dress has adopted definite fashion changes, the "drape" giving way to a slimming down of the silhouette with narrower shoulders, tapered sleeves, a hat narrowed in brim with rising, tapered crown, all these features creating figure height. An Edwardian trend is responsible for the return of some old-time fashions such as plaids, knickerbockers, peaked caps, scarf pins and cuff links, a trend which ties up with our American "Ivy League" look.

From the very first years of this century a cult has grown up among certain gentlemen based upon the conservative elegance made traditional by Bond Street, London, and Madison Avenue, New York. It has come to be known as the Ivy League manner of dressing and was first observed among some Yale, Harvard and Princeton men. After many decades of sons following fathers' footstps, the class now includes groups of smaller schools along the Atlantic coast from New England to the University of Virginia. No "collegiate airs" these but a strict observance of what the well-dressed man should and does wear.

All through the straight and broad-shouldered era the suit bearing the Ivy League look displayed slender trousers, natural shoulders, narrow lapels on a straight unshaped coat and above all, unpadded. And no real Ivy Leaguer ever wore a hand-painted scarf or an eccentric handkerchief.

Two world wars with attendant shortages and privations have all but eliminated formality in day and evening dress. Tails with white tie and white waistcoat have practically been replaced by the dinner coat or "black tie." The formal cutaway or morning coat with striped trousers and top hat is rarely seen, as true on the Continent as in America. In fact, a surprising number of young men of the class that formerly owned such dress habits now rent them when occasion demands.

Masculine clothes have settled into a pattern much influenced by our modern flare for casual smartness which spectator sportswear has made so popular. Dressing "black tie" is like putting on one's most comfortable business suit, men having demanded lighter weight garments which comprise tropical worsteds, wool blended with synthetic fibers and winter-weight silks for the year round. The stiff collar and board-like bosom have been replaced by a soft, pleated front and attached soft collar while the cummerbund in sash or vest style has supplanted the heavier waistcoat. Men have finally and sensibly copied their women who really undress for evening parties.

The informal dinner jacket of tartan seems to attract even those who have little claim to Scotch descent, wearing it at home parties in the city and to club dances in the suburbs. This interest in Scottish national dress has prompted one of England's leading tailors to promote the sale through a New York merchant where the fittings of a formal habit with all the proper accessories may be ordered direct from Scotland.

An ingenious solution to curtailed luggage has just originated in a business suit of midnight blue worsted with the traditional two-button jacket. It is made to double for dinner jacket by separate black satin lapels which are slipped over the cloth lapels and hooked very simply into place. Three lightweight extras, a dress shirt, black bow tie and the silk lapels give the wearer the comfortable feeling of being prepared for day or evening.

The gray flannel suit given much publicity by the advertising fraternity holds the center of the stage, especially in a dark tone called charcoal or carbon gray. Evening dress as well has switched to charcoal and charcoal blue, the latter a real blue black. After a surfeit of color and by way of the gray suit we have arrived at a "black period" in men's wear, a London-inspired revival which made its appearance in 1952, not only, as one would suppose, for city wear but for sportswear too. City black is offset in combination with dark green, brown or gray, dulled white chalk stripes and a woven black and brown stripe called "tawny black." In smart sports clothes the use of black is extremely sophisticated when complemented by colorful accessories.

Combining synthetic fabrics such as Dacron with cotton has made possible a man's suit that will take a real washing, even in a washing machine, and then drip-dry in a matter of hours or overnight. Added to this virtue, no pressing is required, making the suit a boon for travel by air and wear in hot cities. The suit is well tailored and is available in fabrics of varied pattern and dark as well as light colors.

The suit vest became a casualty of World War II, wool yardage being curtailed in civilian dress. Included in the ban were patch pockets, pocket flaps and trouser turn-ups. The latter have returned but not the vest in American ready-made clothing unless specifically ordered. Signs point to the return of the double-breasted jacket, no doubt because of the absence of the vest. The vest is a traditional piece of a man's ensemble furnishing in addition to style and warmth the necessary pockets, a need often filled by a separate waistcoat of contrasting fabric. It might be of wool, corduroy, suède leather, printed challis, figured or ribbed heavy silk and plaids of every description, especially the tartan and tattersalls.

Though the raglan remains ever popular, the Chesterfield, formerly of

Oxford gray, dark blue or black cloth has come back in a variety of fabrics from Harris tweeds, coverts, shetlands to cashmere, frequently topped with the dressy black velvet collar. The black collar is tied up with history, originating some one hundred and fifty years ago following the French Revolution when émigrés returning to France wore it on their redingotes in mourning for Louis XVI. Another elegant fashion of tradition appearing around town with dress evening clothes is the black cloth cape lined with satin, either black or white or even bright red.

The success of the "short warm" or "car coat" is significant of the vast growth of suburban living. It is often a reversible coat in two different fabrics for shell and lining. Men, women and children wear the duffer, duffle or tow coat (the latter name from use on the ski lift) which came into use in the post-years of World War II when surplus English Navy coats were made available to civilians through government stores without the ban of rationing. Usually of Loden cloth from the Tyrol, with wooden toggles and hemp loops, the coat has become the perfect all-weather, knock-about wrap and so well liked that a Continental fashion reporter objected to seeing it worn over dress clothes in the lobby of the opera in some European capitals.

The convertible car appears to have brought about a return engagement of the raccoon coat. It might be that some college men of the roaring 'twenties had carefully packed away their coonskin coats and that may account for some of those seen on young bloods at last year's football games. In any case, father's son and father's daughter made the raccoon coat, whether heirloom or newly bought, an American fashion of 1957.

As to the raincoat, it plays a very important role in the wardrobe, very often serving as the topcoat especially when traveling, the contemporary model being a far cry from the yellow gum raincoat of other days. Today's waterproofed garment is a top fashion item in gabardine, usually gray or beige and more recently black, and there is also a fine textile of silky cotton and dacron, crease and spot resistant.

After an era of hatless college youths the hat industry is working desperately on a campaign to influence the clothes-conscious man to wear a hat. The manufacturers hope by radically restyling the hat that every man will be forced to buy one but so far, the well-dressed man has avoided the new narrow brim which is unflattering even to the handsomest face. From London hails a new version of the derby, a more casual design developed in a softer felt which should add to its wearing comfort, while the peaked cap is back for sportswear.

Shorts and slacks share honors for casual wear, golf, on the beach or whatever according to the season. Slacks are cut in slimmer, tapering style. Bermuda shorts, those impeccably tailored breeches the Englishman wears in the tropics, made news in the 1950's. Perfect in the tropics and appropriate enough in Palm Beach, they were startling, even if cool, on the streets of New York City in the summer of 1953. And quite a few brave young men attended country club dances in shorts with dinner jacket. If it takes more than one swallow to make a summer, perhaps more than one sizzling New York summer will make shorts a hot weather fashion in the temperate zone.

The white nylon shirt came upon the scene in the 1940's during the scarcity of white cotton and it proved a sensation! The qualities of washability and quick drying, requiring no pressing or very little, made it seem a practical wonder. Each season since, newer and finer shirt cloths have come off the looms in cotton as well as the synthetic yarns. There are the innumerable staple cottons such as broadcloth, poplin, denim for service wear, while sheers such as batiste, piqué voile and others are for summer use. Too, there are cotton tweeds and finely ribbed corduroy for sports shirts, jackets, slacks and shorts.

Although there exists a preference for the colored shirt, white remains the classic in the well-dressed man's wardrobe. It was in the banking profession that white held out longest, worn with the dark blue suit, nicknamed "banker's blue." Only recently has a bit of color crept into that citadel. The modern shirt with attached soft collar and cuffs is much more comfortable than was its antecedent. The turned-down collar has spreading points, some long, some short, and there is the conservative and popular button-down collar. In leisure shirts whether for indoors, outdoors or active sports, fabrics have changed to neater prints, checks and plaids in toned-down colors. Cloths range from linen and cotton to silk and wool and the many handsome synthetic stuffs. The knit cotton shirt is ever popular, as well it might be, due to a wide variety of style, color and above all, easy washing.

Neckwear necessarily confines itself to the bow tie and the four-in-hand, trim in size, small in pattern and subtle in color because shirts themselves have taken on pattern and color. Small prints and dots, regimental and horizontal stripes are in the picture, and very smart is the single, miniature motif placed strategically on the scarf.

The négligé robe of the period retains its traditional style, a long or three-quarter length straight gown with shawl or notched collar and a sash of self material. Here is a man's chance to express his personality in cloth, color and elegance as he may desire. From the British Crown Colony of Hong Kong comes a new model, a short kimono design of cloth or silk with a sash belt.

Skeleton shirts and trunks of cotton cloth, cotton knit and synthetic fabric comprise masculine underwear today. Summer materials are often as fine as that used in feminine lingerie and why not! For several decades many young men have worn no undershirt, ever since Clark Gable in a successful movie of the 'thirties took off his shirt revealing that he "went bare." Winter shirts, shorts and long drawers are now fashioned mostly to slip on without the bother of buttons and buttonholes, this made possible by the elastically knitted neck and waistband. Gone is that laundry bogey of broken buttons and torn buttonholes.

Sport socks favor small patterns and solid colors with the exception of the very gay Argyle plaids in golf hose. For town there is the English ribbed weave known as 3x6 which the well-dressed man wears in dark blue, brown, black and heather mixtures. The manufacturers have brought out many new weaves in which they combine natural yarns with synthetics, especially in heel and toe reinforcement, making for durability and non-shrinkage. Socks of stretchable nylon with hug-fitting tops were first introduced in 1955 and met with real success due to better fit and wearing quality. As in other stretch items only four sizes are necessary to fit all leg types.

The new look in shoes is a longer, slimmer Continental last tapering either to a round or square tip. Slip-on types founded upon the moccasin and the buckle and strap shoes are high fashion. Styled in both casual and dressy leathers ranging from sports to dress, this footwear, while sturdily built, retains the slipper comfort of the original model.

The sleepcoat which is now popular, a well-designed garment of cotton or silk pongee, appeared in the early 1900's but the innovation required some decades to become launched in men's wear. Sleepwear, now indistinguishable from beachwear, is packaged in separates so that a man, if he wishes, need purchase only one part, be it trousers, shorts or top. A novelty reminiscent of the Edwardian Age is the knit nightshirt which slips on over the head, really a knee-length tunic with long or short sleeves. The knitted "snoozer" in separate polo shirt and pantaloons is for winter wear. Of balbriggan in stripes or solid color and finished with ribbed cuffs and anklets, the suit is also intended as a lounging ensemble.

The haircut of the period, particularly among young men, is the crew cut in which the hair is cropped close to the head except on top where an inch or less stands up bristly. Though known as the G.I. and the Prussian bob of World War II, it really is a collegiate fashion which originated among the varsity crews to differentiate them from other undergraduates and was called the varsity cut. When the top is slightly longer and casually tousled, it becomes a feather crew. "Ivy League cut" seems to be its latest name.

The very opposite in style is the well-established English or Continental cut which originated in London and has belatedly reached New York. In what the uninitiated would suppose to be "in need of a haircut", the locks are long enough in back to reach to the collar, a help to the older man with thinning hair. For the balding pate there are wonderful, natural appearing headpieces to be had. It is from the unbleached, undyed European peasant hair that these are made. And it is not unusual for the young man with a good head of hair to undergo a permanent to acquire a wave or two in a pompadour hairdo. Such wiles the stronger sex has indulged in all through the ages.

And that brings us to men's toiletries of which there exist at least a half dozen leading manufacturers in Europe and New York. An aftermath of the last war, it is thought that the life of living in tin huts, the mud and filth, the return in the crowded troop liners where cologne could be purchased at the PX aroused a longing for refreshing, perfumed odors. And so, the men who were already accustomed to talcum powder, shaving cream and scented soap took easily to deodorants, toilet water and after-shaving lotions, as the manufacturers' sales testify.

the large hat and Empire
waistline-hat and dress
of almond green faille-
black wings-black
cloth coat-
push-up
sleeves-
black fur-
Balenciaga-
1948

the slim and
chinoise
coat dress-
soft gray
wool with
black braid
and buttons-
Trigère-
1948

shirtwaist
dress of
pleated chiffon-
scarf ends
of self fabric
leather belt-
Dior-
1950

dinner shirtwaist
dress of two layers
of white organdie-
black belt
and black
poppy-
Traina-
Norell-
1949
RTW

wide open neck
and oval hips-
black taffeta
dinner dress-
with self belt-
taffeta hat draped
with chiffon-
Dior-
1951

dress of beige
cashmere bloused
over self belt and
buckle-white
felt tambourine
hat-black fox
muff-
Balenciaga-
1952

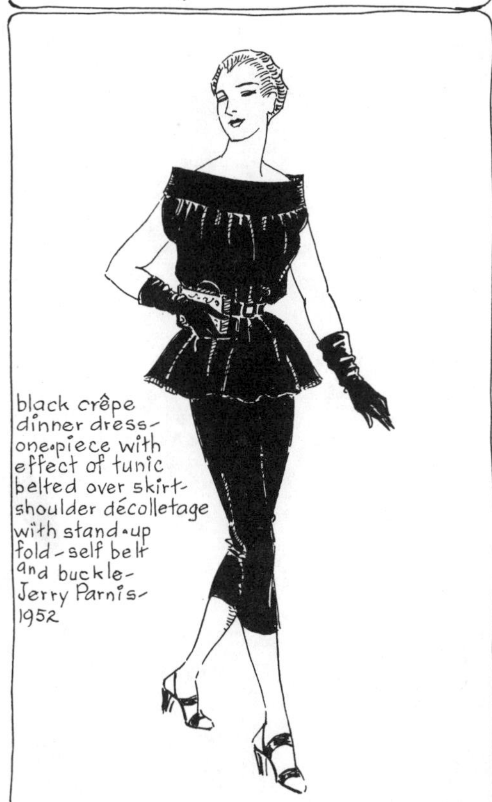
black crêpe
dinner dress-
one-piece with
effect of tunic
belted over skirt-
shoulder décolletage
with stand-up
fold-self belt
and buckle-
Jerry Parnis-
1952

dinner ensemble
of separates-
black velvet skirt
with gold
embroidery-black
silk jersey sweater-
fringed black silk
jersey shawl-
Italian
1952

day dress of
gray wool - sleeves
buttoned at
elbow - muff
and toque
of zebra-
Dior-
1953

"after•five" ensemble-
black broadtail skirt-
sleeveless beige cashmere
sweater with black
passementerie-tailored
beige cashmere jacket-
Mainbocher-
1954

white taffeta with
black polka dots-
flamenco flounce
set low in front-
black faille toque-
Givenchy-
1954

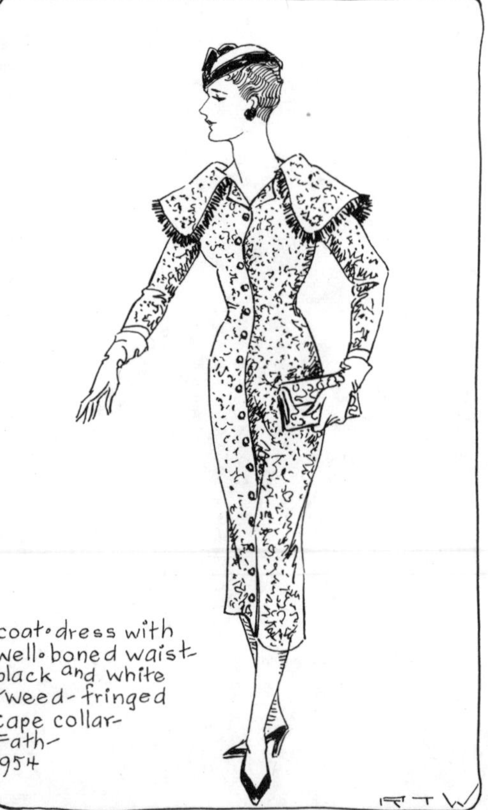
coat•dress with
well•boned waist-
black and white
tweed-fringed
cape collar-
Fath-
1954
RTW

dinner dress of black silk jersey lined throughout - high, flat bosom - long waisted bodice - tiny suède tricorne with jewel - Dior - 1954

popular, inexpensive machine-knit cotton "stocking dress" - stripes or solid color - leather belt - straw Breton sailor hat - tapestry "tote" bag - 1954

long-waisted day dress with a wide self collar - gray brushed wool flannel - Balenciaga - 1955

black crêpe dinner dress - gathered up in front to a ribbon bowknot and jewel - Griffe - 1956

the 1957 sacque or chemise
the
Hong Kong
sheath-
printed copper
colored silk-
self-colored
underskirt-
large folded
hat-necklace
of ropes of beads-
Dior
Empire sheath
of white satin-
folded over and
closed in front-
self bow knot-
front seam slit
at hemline-
Givenchy
black crêpe
sacque gown-
fitted front
and loose back-
string belt
tied in front-
Balenciaga
back-buttoned
molded chemise-
pea soup green
wool jersey-
cut on the bias-
Grès
RTW

introduction to "chemiserie"-
gown of black lace over black silk-
Spanish flounce-
Traina • Norell-
1950

Empire • waisted gown with train-
gray moiré faille-
jet flower corsage-
Molyneux-
1948

"after five" ensemble-
gray silk shantung-
lace and chiffon bodice-
black moiré bands sewn with black braid and large pearls-
Mainbocher-
1949

the "Black Tulip"-
black satin with flamenco flounce of black faille shaped with buckram and whalebone-
Charles James-
1949
RTW

gown of pleated mauve pink chiffon jersey-hem-length scarf of white jersey tied over breasts and shoulder-Grès-1952

gown of brown chiffon-shirred bodice-brown velvet ribbon sash-Fath-1953

Edwardian princess gown of black slipper satin with boned bodice-Galanos-1953

blouse of pleated fine white linen-skirt and cummerbund of pewter gray linen with white embroidery-Sybil Connolly-1954

straight tunic over
a skirt knotted in
back-marbleized
taffeta-
Balenciaga-
1955

black polka dot
organdie over bright,
deep blue taffeta-
stiffened peplum-
pale blue ribbon
sash and
a pink rose-
Dior-
1955

lilac pink faille
with puffed
overskirt-bodice
fold tied in front-
petticoat of
white tulle stitched
with sequins-
Balenciaga-
1955

cream-colored faille
with a frieze of
appliquéd crimson
velvet-three-cornered
shawl of crimson
velvet-
Lanvin-Costillo-
1955
RTW

white faille evening
gown stiffened
with buckram
and silk-fold
of self fabric
tied at
Empire
waistline-
Dior-
1956

corolla
gown of rose-red
taffeta-skirt
fashioned in
simulated
rose petals-
Capucci-
1956

sheath of pink
and white brocade-
buttoned jacket-
top bloused low
in back-
shoulder straps
tied in bow
knots-
Fabiani-
1956
RTW

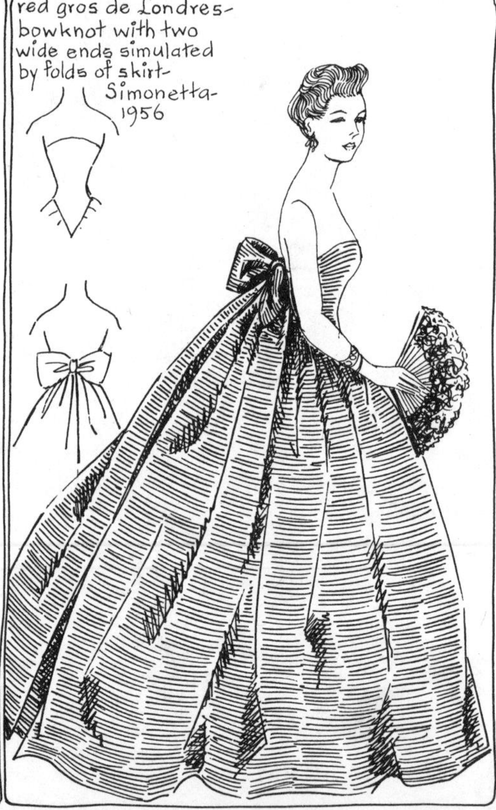
red gros de Londres-
bowknot with two
wide ends simulated
by folds of skirt-
Simonetta-
1956

deep-collared suit
of black broadcloth
or black faille-
slash pockets
in jacket-
Traina-Norell-
1949

suit of dark blue
wool with vest
of self fabric-
white piqué facing
at neck-curved
slashed pockets-
wing cuffs-
skirt of two
overlapping
aprons-
Dior-
1950

double-breasted
spring suit of
dark blue wool-
low-necked
jacket-fitted
front and straight
back-flap
pockets-
Balenciaga-
1952

brown wool suit-
leg-of-mutton sleeves-
black astrakan
choker and muff-
astrakan pillbox
with ribbon ties-
Fath-
1953
RTW

belted and bloused shirt-jacket over a sheath-ensemble of gray wool- self belt and buckle-pushed-up sleeves- Talmack- 1954

revival of the "Chanel Look"- navy blue wool jersey-jacket white-lined- white muslin blouse - blue bow tie- Chanel- 1954

cape-suit of black and white tweed-black wool sweater joined to high-waisted skirt- Traina-Norell- 1956

ankle-length day suit- nubby gray tweed- leather belt-white chiffon blouse- white melusine sailor- Dior- 1956

greatcoat of black
wool with enormous
revers-black leather
belt-squared
velvet cap
with pompon-
Dior-
1949

three-piece ensemble-
black wool topcoat-
belt-tied coat
of camel's hair-
sleeveless
striped red
sheath-
Bonnie Cashin-
1950

black wool coat
with kimono sleeve
and narrow
neckband-
black suède
pagoda hat-
black fox
muff-
Balenciaga-
1951

broadcloth greatcoat-
beaver or seal
collar-push-up
sleeves-fancy
buttons-leather
belt-felt
tricorne-
Griffe-
1951
RTW

greatcoat of fleece
cloth in nude color-
shirred to back
yoke-push-up
sleeves-deep
slashed
pockets-
Maguy-
1951

Empire waist in
front-straight
back-red
raspberry wool-
self fabric belt
with metal
buckle-
Schiaparelli-
1952

coat with
cape-collar-
speckled gray
wool tweed-
leopard cap
and bag-
Nettie Rosenstein-
1955

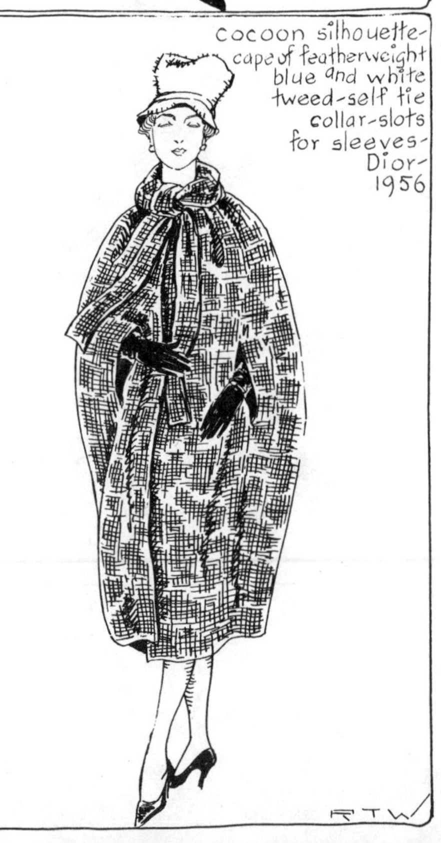
cocoon silhouette-
cape of featherweight
blue and white
tweed-self tie
collar-slots
for sleeves-
Dior-
1956
RTW

matara brown sealskin-full coat with cape-detachable Gothic hood with fur brides-Fredrica-1948

broadtail worn as sheath belted and buttoned in back-as coat when buttoned in front-Esther Dorothy-1953

coat of mutation mink with fullness hanging in straight, deep folds-Revillon-1952

town and travel coat of supple South American river otter-collar and cuffs of unplucked Canadian otter-Bergdorf Goodman-1953

brown Persian lamb
belted high in
front- full
flowing back-
Ritter-
mink béret
by Irene-
1953

chinchilla
evening coat
with full
sleeves-
Russeks-
1954

an opulent coat
of costly vicuña
and sable-reversible-
copper rose
cloth- for day
or evening wear-
Originala-
1954

lynx greatcoat
for
country wear-
Revillon-
1955
RTW

small furs and sweaters-
evening bolero mutation mink "Blue Frost"- Ritter- 1948
evening sweater- sewn with fake jewels, paillettes and gold braid- 1950
astrakhan sweater- bateau neck line- knitted waistband and cuffs- Griffe- 1949
red-dyed moleskin cardigan- Esther Dorothy- 1949
sport jacket- tan leather- sleeves of black rib knit wool- accordion pleated scarf- Givenchy- 1952
ermine sweater lined gold lamé- braid with paillettes- Maximilian- 1952
Persian lamb cape with fringe- Marano- 1952
Persian lamb middy coat- 1952
sweater of black mohair bouclé- white jersey vest- Grès- 1953
pull-over sweater- mink with rib knit wool bands- Revillon- 1953
sweater ensemble- gold colored cashmere cardigan- cut-out polka dots revealing under-sweater, half black and half white- Bernhard Altmann- 1956
jacket of African cheetah trimmed with black braid- Esther Dorothy- 1955
white cotton lace cardigan- Haymaker- 1956
RTW

playclothes-
the "bikini"- yellow and orange striped linen- 1948
sheath and kilt of yellow and bright blue cotton- Carolyn Schnurer- 1948
denim overalls for "roughing it"- leather belt- white woolen hose- Norwegian style moccasins- 1952
beige linen shirt and shorts- tucked bosom- Anne Fogarty- 1951
two-piece playsuit- black cotton broadcloth- Simonetta-1952
three-piece ensemble- gray flannel cardigan and shorts- knit yellow woolen sweater and hose- Jantzen- 1956
bathing suit and wrap-around skirt of print cotton- brown on black- Greta Plattry- 1956
hooded beach sweater- black wool jersey- Claire McCardell- 1954
RTW

coat and nightgown of sheer batiste with eyelet embroidery-ribbon ties-1948
small waist-rounded hips-rayon satin elastic-zipped in back-1948
chemise of honey-colored nylon tricot and net-1950
strapless brassière cut low in front-embroidered nylon-1952
wrap-around strapless slip-white nylon crêpe and ecru lace-1949
Dior's corselet to lift bosom and mold a long body line-nylon power net and lace over satin-1954
halter brassière hooked to girdle in back-half-slip of pleated nylon net-1950
crinoline for evening or wedding gown-plastic frame-ribbon stays-1952
pajamas-white cotton and Valenciennes lace over red cotton briefs-1954
all-in-one-elasticized nylon net with lace brassière-1954
negligé ensemble-coat of ivory damask-breeches and sash of olive green satin-1956
crinoline-removable hoop-silk tricot over taffeta-ribbon and bowknot-1956
RTW

the pony tail-1948
Empire coiffure-1948
poodle clip-1950
false chignon-1950
bouffant style-1951
Italian cut-1953
short hair in French twist-1956
short hair-wide waves-Paris-1957
turban of beige jersey-Paulette-1948
felt pillbox with wings-in beige-Lilly Daché 1948
violet chiffon cornucopia with jewel-Dior-1956
calotte and shoulder cape of jersey-Paulette-1950
Chinese pagoda of plush felt-Dior-1950
"fur bonnet" brushed yellow beaver felt-Emme-1955
red velvet pillbox-Dior-1951
black velvet with ostrich-Dior-1951
toque with curled-up back-gold velvet-Balenciaga-1951
black satin bowknot-sequin embroidery-Galanos-1956
black satin evening hat-black ostrich panache-Tatiana-1956
dinner hat-black velvet and brown satin Adolfo-1956
brown striped velvet turban-black wing-Sally Victor-1956
"Ascot hat"-black organdie, ostrich and jewel Lilly Daché-1956
chetnik of royal blue fleecy fabric-Adolfo-1956
dinner hat-draped black panne velvet-Sally Victor-1956
chechia of ermine-John Frederics-1956
travel hat of beige felt-1956
RTW

black suède-red calf straps-Slater-1948
beach boot-Italian straw-Perugia-c.1950
black suède buttoned at side-Bally-1948
straw slipper-knotted toe-Givenchy-1950
peak toe-turquoise patent leather-black braid-Capezio-1951
black patent leather-lucite straps-1952
evening "tote" bag-white fur-gold handles-1953
black alligator handbag-Koret-1953
flower embroidered fabric glove-Dior for Shalimar-1953
black Paisley shawl from Italy-1953
"carpet bag" carryall-tapestry and leather-Mark Cross-1950
earring-white daisies on fine gold wires-Sutain-1952
suède and leather-Delman-1953
the favored eyeglass shape of the period-plain or jeweled-choice of colors
nylons with black lace-jeweled garter ribbon-Fath-1954
"giant carryall"-Paisley covered-black leather trim-Coronet-1954
mule of black suède and Vinylite-metal heel-Saks F.A.-1954
dinner party frivolity-red satin monkey hat with feathers-Balenciaga-1955
one pump with three heels-black alligator, red leather or rhinestones-Perugia-1956
chain with crystals encircling a metal spike-Delman-1956
RTW

1948-1957

"white tie"-
formal evening
tailcoat-midnight
blue worsted-
braid at sides of
trousers-satin
lapels-white
piqué shirt, cravat
and waistcoat-
starched bosom-
waistcoat single
or double breasted-
wing collar-
white pearl studs
and links-hose
black or dark blue
nylon, lisle or wool-
black patent
leather shoes or
pumps-high silk
or collapsible
opera hat-
1953

"black tie"-
semi-formal-
single breasted
dinner jacket
of charcoal blue,
gray or white fabric
according to season-
tartan or black silk
cummerbund-shirt
plain or pleated-fold
or wing collar-black or blue
trousers with braid
on seams-footwear
same as formal-
midnight blue, black or
dark gray Homburg
or derby-
1950

British lounge coat
often worn instead of
cutaway or morning
coat-black cheviot
with bluff edge or
braid-bound edge-
vest to match-heavy
silk four-in-hand
scarf-trousers
striped black and
gray-Homburg
or derby-
1950's

cutaway-see page 338

"black tie"-
semi-formal-double
breasted dinner
jacket-midnight
blue cloth-trousers
to match-see
above for
other
details-
1952

RTW

1948–1957 Town and Business Suits

Glen Urquhart plaid worsted–three button jacket–flap pockets

charcoal gray worsted or flannel–three button jacket–welt pockets

herringbone tweed–double breasted jacket–welt pockets–snap brim fedora

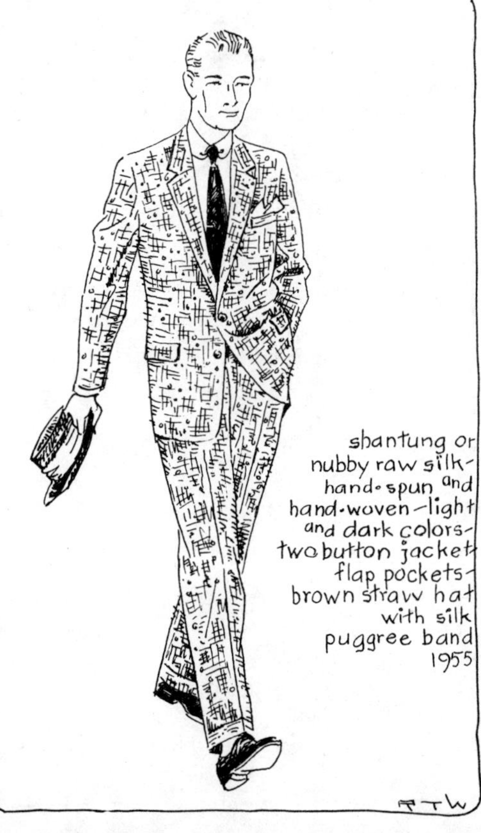

shantung or nubby raw silk–hand-spun and hand-woven–light and dark colors–two button jacket–flap pockets–brown straw hat with silk puggree band 1955

1948-1957
the classic polo coat of natural color camel's hair cloth-1949
raglan shoulder topcoat of tweed-sports felt hat in Tyrolese style-cord and feather-1951
town coat of light tan cashmere-saddle bag pockets-1956
a less formal Chesterfield-velvet collar on tweed, shetland, covert or cashmere-extra change pocket-fly front-1954
RTW

1948-1957
duffer, duffle, suburban or ski tow coat-wooden toggle closure-waterproofed cotton, wool or tweed-alpaca lined-concealed hood-worn from 1950
stormcoat-water-repellent wool gabardine-alpaca lined-mouton or raccoon collar-1950
pure silk sport jacket-hand-loomed nubby raw silk-two button-patch pockets
cotton sport jacket-coarse white and black weave-dropped shoulder-cuff buttons concealed-French-1956
topcoat of herring bone tweed-zippered-in plaid lining
British raincoat-water-resistant mercerized cotton-tartan plaid lining
British topcoat of covert cloth-saddle stitching-extra change pocket-blue and white polka dot ascot type muffler-1950
sport jacket of cashmere-wool blend check-three button-patch pockets
RTW

1948-1957

hot weather dress-Bermuda shorts of gray flannel-plaid India madras jacket-solid color sport shirt-gray and red argyle hose-1953

ski costume-black and red wool gabardine-jacket reversible with reversed colors-zipper fastened pockets-other ski fabrics, whipcord, nylon, waterproofed cotton cloth-1953

British shooting dress-rough tweed jacket and knickerbockers checked woolen cap-woolen hose-tan linen gaiters-1950

British horseman-checked tweed jacket and cap-whipcord breeches-sport shirt with bow tie-pull-over knit sweater-1950

RTW

1948-1957
striped knitted cotton-Italian boatman style-contrasting collar-1956
raglan style ski sweater-Italian-1956
flat top tan felt-dark green grosgrain ribbon-1950
backless waistcoat of foulard in muted tones-1953
casual derby-soft, rough felt-mohair braid band-British-1956
country hat herringbone tweed-self band-1953
kimono coat and swim trunks-white print on black-1955
evening shirt-voile body-broadcloth scalloping-pearl buttons-1955
waistcoat-rep tie silk-pearl buttons 1951
brown and tan woven straw-rope soles-1956
sennit or hard straw hat-black or striped grosgrain ribbon-1956
Hong Kong-made lounger-colored silk pongee-1956
sport shirt in lightweight wool with contrasting stripes-British-1953
cap of tartan worsted-1950
sport shirt-Paisley print challis-1953
sport-helmet-hat-waterproofed, pliable, green felt-British-1954
alligator tassel slip-ons-1954
town shoe of polished calf-leather-lined-1957
RTW

BIBLIOGRAPHY

ITALIAN —*Habiti Antichi et Moderni*—Cesare Vecellio—2 vols.

FRENCH —*Costumes français depuis Clovis*—Drawings by L. Massard.

Histoire du costume en France—J. Quicherat.

Le costume historique—A. Racinet.

Les arts—Moyen âge et la Renaissance—Paul Lacroix.

Vie militaire et religieuse—Moyen âge et la Renaissance—Paul Lacroix.

XVIIe siècle—Institutions, usages et costumes—Paul Lecroix.

Directoire, consulate et empire—Paul Lacroix.

The Eighteenth Century—Its Institutions, Customs, and Costumes—Paul Lacroix.

Un siècle de modes féminines, 1794–1894—Charpentier et Fasquelle.

Fashions in Paris—1797–1897—Octave Uzanne.

Mesdames nos aïeules: dix siècles à élégances—Robida.

Le costume civil en France du XIIIe au XIXe siècle—Camille Piton.

Histoire de la peinture classique—Jean De Foville.

Histoire du costume—Jacques Ruppert.

Histoire du costume—Librairie Hachette.

Le costume—Miguel Zamacoïs.

Les soieries d'art—Raymond Cox.

Cent ans de modes françaises—1800–1900—Mme. Cornil.

La mode féminine, 1900–1920—Éditions Nilsson.

GERMAN —*Die Trachten der Völker*—Albert Kretchmer.

Münchner Bilderbogen—Zur Geschichter des Kostüms.

An Egyptian Princess—George Ebers.

Die Mode im XVI. Jahrhundert—Max von Boehn.

Die Mode im XVII. Jahrhundert—Max von Boehn.

Die Mode im XVIII. Jahrhundert—Max von Boehn.

Die Moden des XIX. Jahrhunderts—Collection Geszler.

Modes and Manners of the XIX Century—Fischel-Von Boehn, 4 vols.

Le costume chez les peuples anciens et modernes—Fr. Hottenroth.

Kostümkunde—Hermann Weiss.

English —*Manners and Customs of the English*—Joseph Strutt, 3 vols.

Everyday Life in Anglo-Saxon, Viking and Norman Times—M. and C. H. B. Quennell.

Everyday Life in Roman Britain—M. and C. H. B. Quennell.

History of Everyday Things in England, 1066–1799—M. and C. H. B. Quennell.

Life and Work of the People of England—16th Century—Hartley and Elliot.

Life and Work of the People of England—17th Century—Hartley and Elliot.

London in the Time of the Tudors—Sir Walter Besant.

Chats on Costume—G. Woolliscroft Rhead, R.E.

The Grammar of Ornament—Owen Jones.

Historic Costume—Francis M. Kelley and Randolph Schwabe.

English Costume—Dion Clayton Calthrop.

Dress Design—Talbot Hughes.

English Costume from the 14th through the 19th Century—Brooke and Laver.

American—*Historic Dress in America*—Elizabeth McClellan.

Two Centuries of Costume in America—Alice Morse Earle, 2 vols.

Wimples and Crisping Pins—Theodore Child.

Accessories of Dress—Lester and Oerke.

The Psychology of Dress—Frank Alvah Parsons, B.S.

Economics of Fashion—Paul H. Nystrom, Ph.D.

The Ways of Fashion—M. D. C. Crawford.

Early American Costume—Edward Warwick and Henry Pitz.

A History of the Ancient World—George Willis Botsford, Ph.D.

Ancient Times—James Henry Breasted, Ph.D., LL.D.

The Fairchild Publications.

The Language of Fashion—Mary Brooks Picken.

Dressmakers of France—Mary Brooks Picken and Dora Loues Miller.

Apparel Arts.

Gentry.

Life.

Time.

The New York Times.

The New York Herald Tribune.

The Wall Street Journal.

Vogue.

Harper's Bazaar.

British-American—*The Encyclopædia Britannica.*

Swiss—*Ciba Review.*

Index

Newfoundland and Labrador
Pages 60–69

New Brunswick, Nova Scotia, and Prince Edward Is.
Pages 70–93

Montreal
Pages 102–123

Quebec City and the St. Lawrence River
Pages 124–141

Southern and Northern Quebec
Pages 142–153

Iqaluit

Toronto
Pages 162–187

Ottawa and Eastern Ontario
Pages 188–203

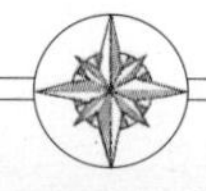

EYEWITNESS TRAVEL GUIDES

CANADA

EYEWITNESS TRAVEL GUIDES

CANADA

DK PUBLISHING

LONDON • NEW YORK • MUNICH
MELBOURNE • DELHI

Produced by Duncan Baird Publishers
London, England
MANAGING EDITOR Rebecca Miles
MANAGING ART EDITOR Vanessa Marsh
EDITORS Georgina Harris, Michelle de Larrabeiti, Zoë Ross
DESIGNERS Dawn Davies-Cook, Ian Midson
DESIGN ASSISTANCE Rosie Laing, Kelvin Mullins
VISUALIZER Gary Cross
PICTURE RESEARCH Victoria Peel
DTP DESIGNER Sarah Williams

Dorling Kindersley Limited
PROJECT EDITOR Paul Hines ART EDITOR Jane Ewart
US EDITOR Mary Sutherland EDITOR Hugh Thompson

CONTRIBUTORS
Paul Franklin, Sam Ion, Philip Lee, Cam Norton, Lorry Patton, Geoffrey Roy, Michael Snook, Donald Telfer, Paul Waters

PHOTOGRAPHERS
Alan Keohane, Peter Wilson, Francesca Yorke

ILLUSTRATORS
Joanna Cameron, Gary Cross, Chris Forsey, Paul Guest, Claire Littlejohn, Robbie Polley, Kevin Robinson, John Woodcock

Reproduced by Colourscan (Singapore)
Printed and bound by South China Printing Co. Ltd., China

First American Edition, 2000
02 03 04 05 10 9 8 7 6 5 4

Published in the United States by DK Publishing, Inc.,
375 Hudson Street, New York, New York 10014

Printed with revisions 2002

Published in Great Britain by Dorling Kindersley Limited.

A CATALOGING IN PUBLICATION RECORD IS AVAILABLE FROM THE LIBRARY OF CONGRESS.

ISSN 1542-1554
ISBN 0-7894-9561-9

See our complete product line at
www.dk.com

The information in this
Eyewitness Travel Guide is checked regularly.
Every effort has been made to ensure that this book is as up-to-date as possible at the time of going to press. Some details, however, such as telephone numbers, opening hours, prices, gallery hanging arrangements and travel information are liable to change. The publishers cannot accept responsibility for any consequences arising from the use of this book, nor for any material on third party websites, and cannot guarantee that any website address in this book will be a suitable source of travel information. We value the views and suggestions of our readers very highly. Please write to: Publisher, DK Eyewitness Travel Guides, Dorling Kindersley, 80 Strand, London WC2R 0RL, Great Britain.

◁ **The dazzling fall foliage of Quebec's maple forests**

CONTENTS

INTRODUCING CANADA

ATLANTIC CANADA

The historic reconstruction of Fortress Louisbourg, Nova Scotia

QUEBEC

Lake Moraine in Banff National Park in the Rockies

Château Frontenac in Quebec City

Ontario

Central Canada

British Columbia and the Rockies

Northern Canada

Travelers' Needs

Survival Guide

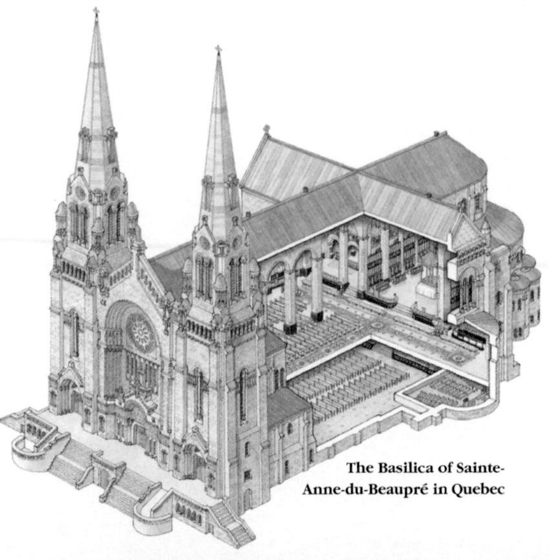
The Basilica of Sainte-Anne-du-Beaupré in Quebec

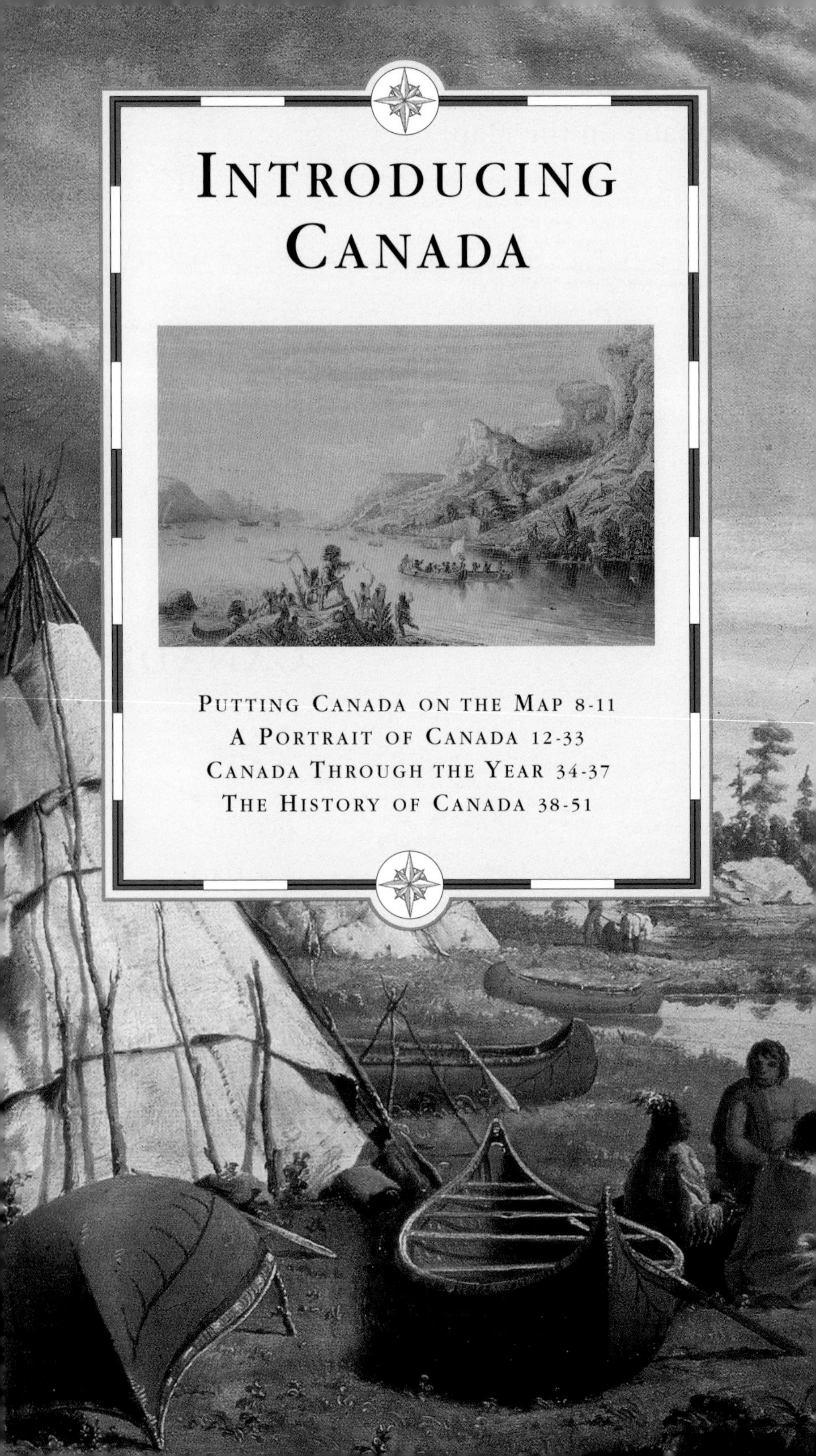

Introducing Canada

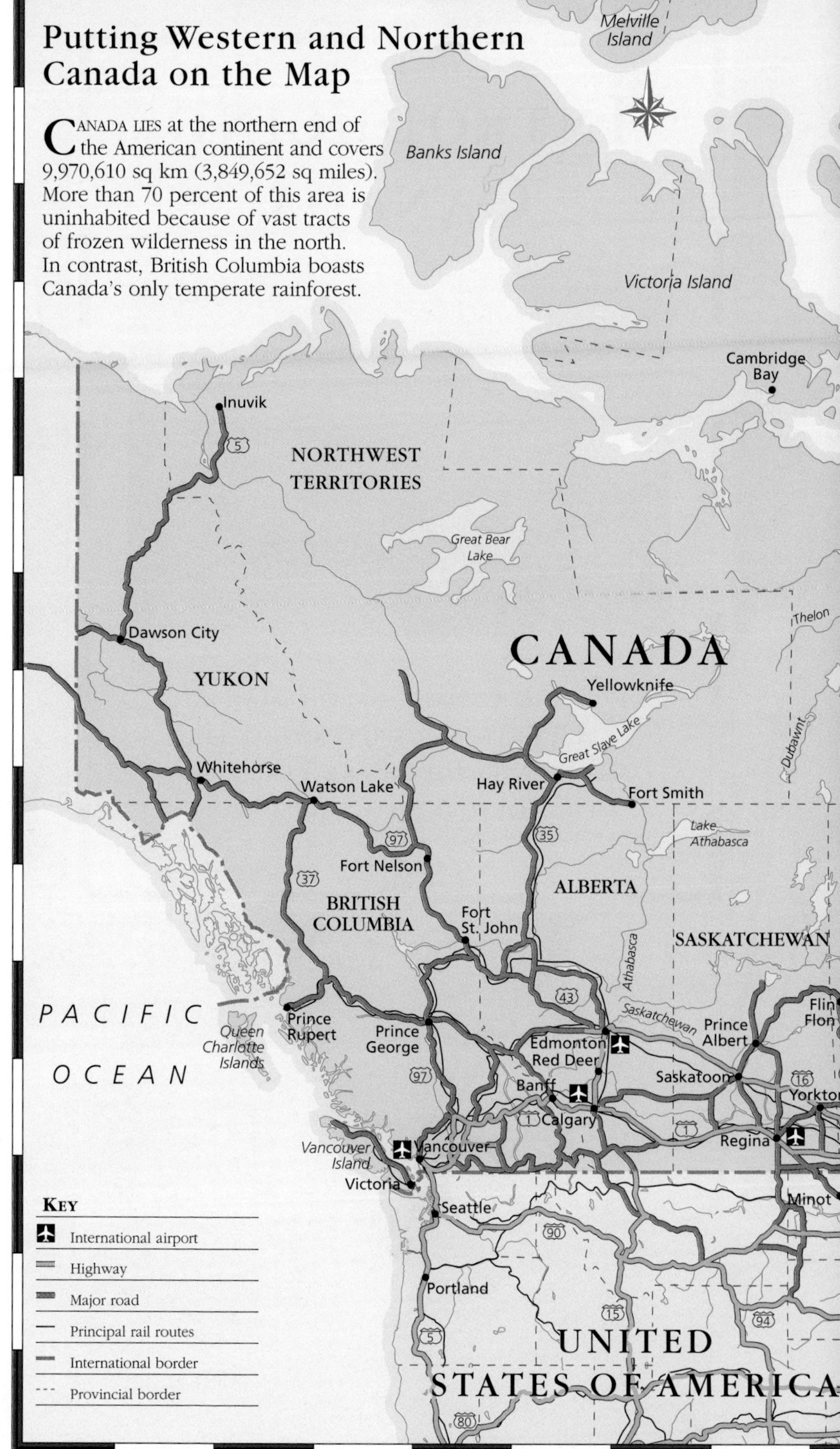
Putting Western and Northern Canada on the Map
CANADA LIES at the northern end of the American continent and covers 9,970,610 sq km (3,849,652 sq miles). More than 70 percent of this area is uninhabited because of vast tracts of frozen wilderness in the north. In contrast, British Columbia boasts Canada's only temperate rainforest.
Melville Island
Banks Island
Victoria Island
Cambridge Bay
Inuvik
5
NORTHWEST TERRITORIES
Great Bear Lake
Thelon
CANADA
Dawson City
YUKON
Yellowknife
Great Slave Lake
Dubawnt
Whitehorse
Watson Lake
Hay River
Fort Smith
35
Lake Athabasca
97
Fort Nelson
37
ALBERTA
BRITISH COLUMBIA
Fort St. John
Athabasca
SASKATCHEWAN
43
Flin Flon
PACIFIC
OCEAN
Prince Rupert
Queen Charlotte Islands
Prince George
Saskatchewan
Prince Albert
Edmonton
Red Deer
97
Saskatoon
16
Banff
Yorkton
1
Calgary
1
Regina
Vancouver Island
Vancouver
Victoria
Minot
Seattle
90
Portland
15
94
5
UNITED
STATES OF AMERICA
80
KEY
International airport
Highway
Major road
Principal rail routes
International border
Provincial border

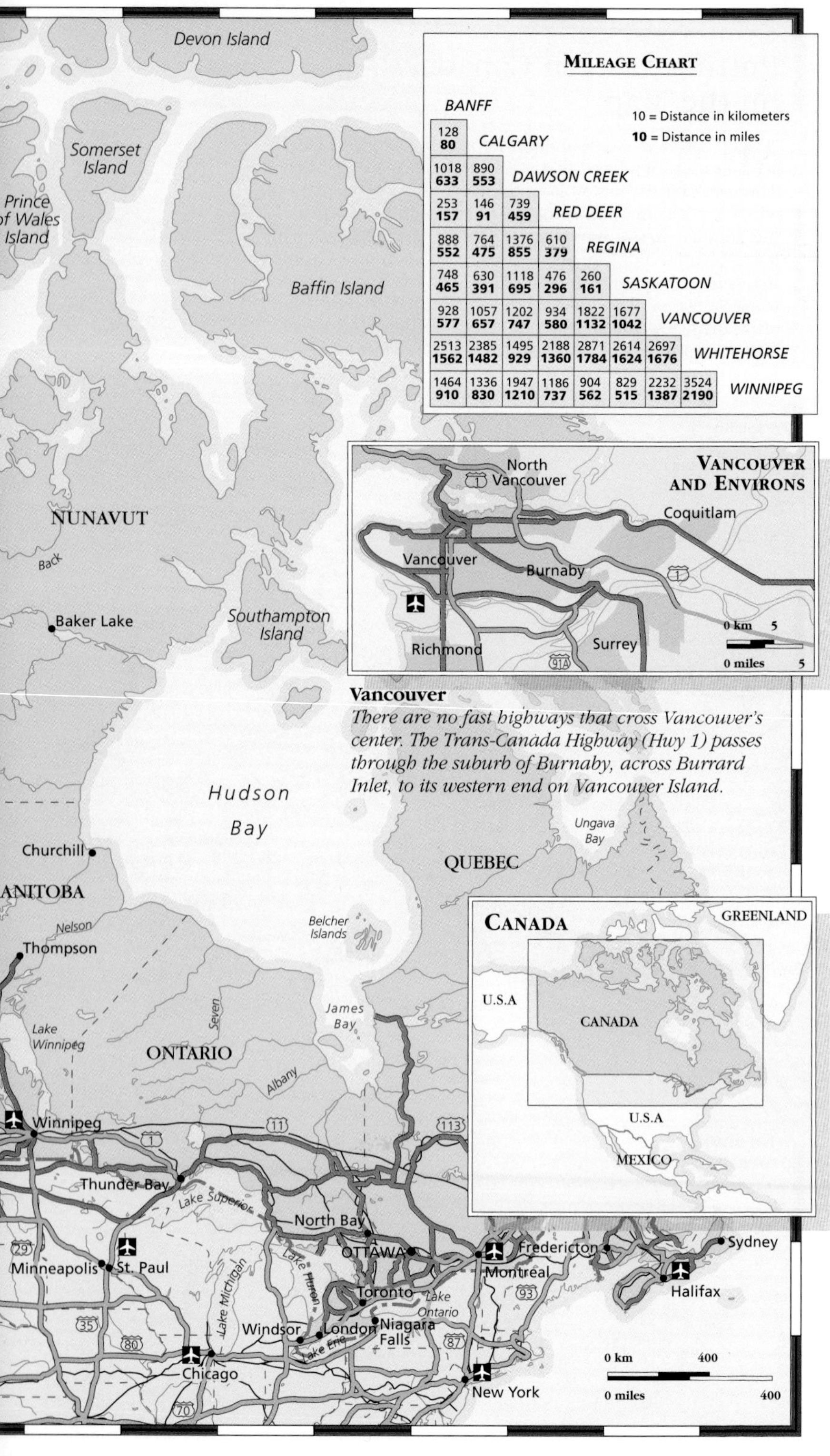

Mileage Chart

10 = Distance in kilometers
10 = Distance in miles

	BANFF	CALGARY	DAWSON CREEK	RED DEER	REGINA	SASKATOON	VANCOUVER	WHITEHORSE
CALGARY	128 **80**							
DAWSON CREEK	1018 **633**	890 **553**						
RED DEER	253 **157**	146 **91**	739 **459**					
REGINA	888 **552**	764 **475**	1376 **855**	610 **379**				
SASKATOON	748 **465**	630 **391**	1118 **695**	476 **296**	260 **161**			
VANCOUVER	928 **577**	1057 **657**	1202 **747**	934 **580**	1822 **1132**	1677 **1042**		
WHITEHORSE	2513 **1562**	2385 **1482**	1495 **929**	2188 **1360**	2871 **1784**	2614 **1624**	2697 **1676**	
WINNIPEG	1464 **910**	1336 **830**	1947 **1210**	1186 **737**	904 **562**	829 **515**	2232 **1387**	3524 **2190**

Vancouver
There are no fast highways that cross Vancouver's center. The Trans-Canada Highway (Hwy 1) passes through the suburb of Burnaby, across Burrard Inlet, to its western end on Vancouver Island.

Putting Eastern Canada on the Map

MOST OF CANADA'S 30 million people live close to the US border, in a band that stretches from the east coast across to British Columbia in the west. Over 60 percent of all Canadians are concentrated in the southeast corner of the country, in the provinces of Ontario and Quebec. This is the heartland of Canadian industry, including electronics, hydro-electricity, lumber, and paper. The maritime provinces of Nova Scotia, New Brunswick, and Prince Edward Island are Canada's smallest, but the beauty of their landscapes attracts thousands of tourists each year. Newfoundland and Labrador are also known for their rugged charm.

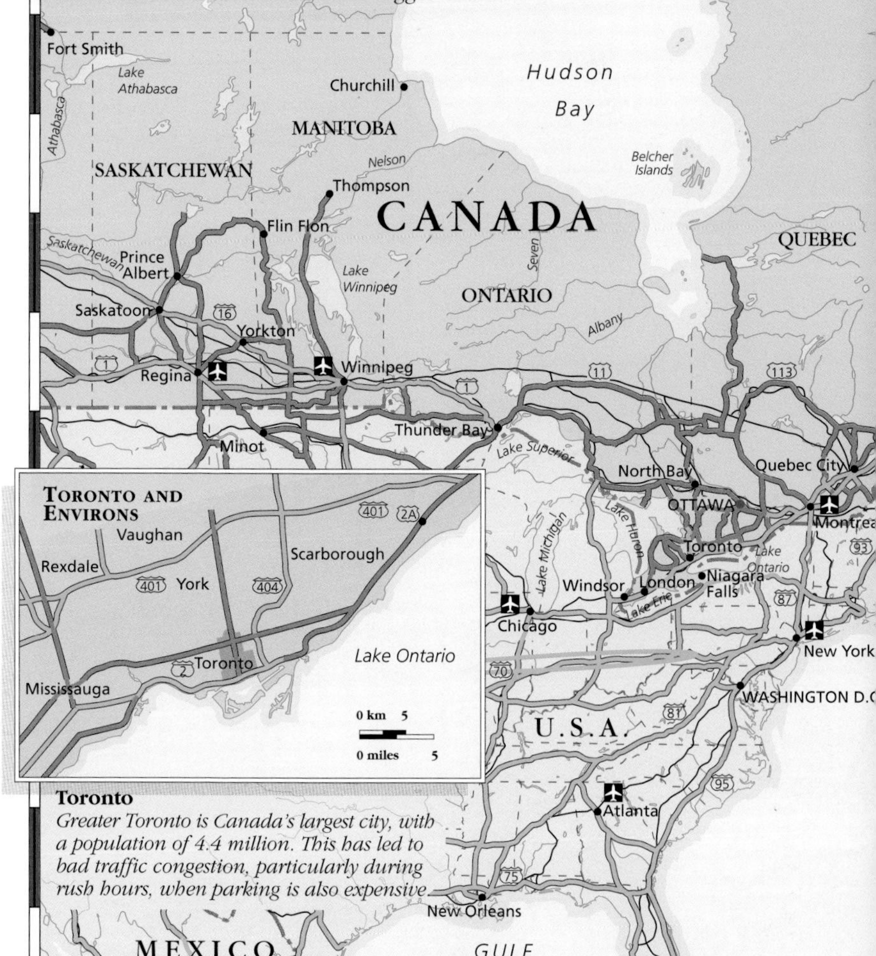

Toronto
Greater Toronto is Canada's largest city, with a population of 4.4 million. This has led to bad traffic congestion, particularly during rush hours, when parking is also expensive.

Mileage Chart

10 = Distance in kilometers
10 = Distance in miles

	Charlottetown	Fredericton	Halifax	Montreal	Niagara Falls	Ottawa	Quebec City	Sept-Iles	Thunder Bay
Fredericton	356 **221**								
Halifax	239 **148**	473 **294**							
Montreal	1149 **714**	834 **518**	1003 **623**						
Niagara Falls	1860 **1156**	1510 **938**	1925 **1196**	676 **420**					
Ottawa	1339 **832**	1016 **631**	1456 **905**	200 **124**	536 **333**				
Quebec City	954 **593**	598 **371**	1071 **665**	257 **160**	946 **588**	724 **450**			
Sept-Iles	1412 **877**	1267 **787**	1512 **939**	859 **534**	1569 **975**	1074 **667**	637 **396**		
Thunder Bay	2794 **1736**	2471 **1535**	2910 **1808**	1654 **1028**	1521 **945**	1503 **934**	1963 **1220**	2613 **1624**	
Toronto	1689 **1049**	1366 **849**	1806 **1122**	549 **341**	137 **85**	399 **248**	809 **503**	1449 **900**	1384 **860**

Iqaluit
Labrador Sea
LABRADOR
Labrador City
Happy Valley - Goose Bay
Sept-Iles
NEWFOUNDLAND
St. John's
Fredericton
Charlottetown
Sydney
Halifax
ATLANTIC OCEAN

Key

- International airport
- Highway
- Major road
- Principal rail routes
- International border
- Provincial border

0 km 500
0 miles 500

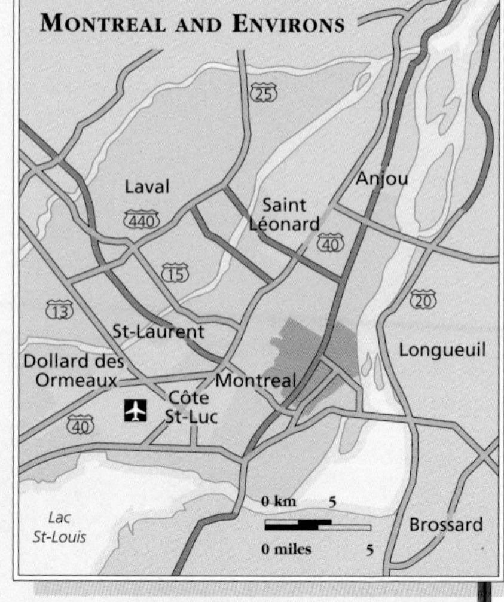

Montreal
Montreal is a well-established transportation hub. The city is surrounded by a network of highways: the Trans-Canada Highway, a hectic six-lane highway, crosses the city as number 20 or the Autoroute Métropolitain.

A PORTRAIT OF CANADA

BLESSED *with ancient forests, rugged mountains, and large cosmopolitan cities, Canada is unimaginably vast, stretching west from the Atlantic to the Pacific and north to the Arctic Ocean. Around 20,000 years ago Canada was inhabited by aboriginal peoples but by the 19th century it had been settled by Europeans. Today, the country is noted as a liberal, multicultural society.*

Inuit wooden mask

In part, Canada's heritage of tolerance is a result of its conflict-ridden past. Two centuries of compromise was necessary to fully establish the country. Following fighting between the British and French armies in the 1750s, the British won control of the country in 1759. The self-governing colonies of British North America spent three years hammering out the agreement that brought them together as the Dominion of Canada in 1867. Newfoundland did not become part of the nation until 1949. Powerful regional differences, particularly between French- and English-speaking Canada meant that the country has had difficulties evolving a national identity. When Pierre Berton, one of Canada's most prolific writers, was prompted to define a Canadian he evaded the question, replying: "Someone who knows how to make love in a canoe."

The second largest country in the world, Canada has a surface area of 9,970,610 sq km (3,849,652 sq miles). Over 40 percent of the land is north of the treeline at 60° latitude; this extraordinarily hostile and sparsely inhabited wilderness is bitterly cold in winter, averaging -30°C (-22°F), and plagued by millions of insects in summer. Not surprisingly, most

The snow-laden rooftops of Quebec City overlooking the St. Lawrence River at dusk

◁ **Bull elk grazing in Jasper National Park in the Rocky Mountains**

Canadians live in the more temperate regions farther to the south. Of the country's 30 million inhabitants, more than 80 percent live within 200 kilometers (124 miles) of the US border.

FLORA AND FAUNA

In the far north, the permafrost of the treeless tundra (or taiga) supports the growth of only the toughest flora, such as lichen, mosses, and a range of unusually hardy varieties of flowers and grasses. In spring and fall however, the tundra flora bursts into an impressive display of color. Animal life is abundant in this region, and includes the polar bear, arctic fox, wolf, seal, musk ox, and caribou.

Spring flower from the Bruce Peninsula

Farther south, the boreal or coniferous forest covers a wide band from Newfoundland in the east to the Yukon in the west. A variety of trees here, including spruce, balsam fir, and jack pine, provides a home for those animals most typically thought of as Canadian, primarily moose, beaver, lynx, and black bear. The beaver is Canada's national symbol. It was the European fashion for beaver hats that created and sustained the Canadian fur trade and opened up the interior to European settlers, paving the way for the growth of the modern nation.

In the east, deciduous forests containing the emblematic maple are populated by deer, skunk, and mink. Across central Canada, the grasslands, known as the Prairies, house elk, gophers, and the few thousand buffalo which are all that remain of the vast herds that once roamed here. British Columbia's temperate rain forests are rich in wildlife such as black tail deer, brown bear, and cougar. Rare orchids and ferns grow here, among towering cedars, firs, and spruce trees.

THE FIRST NATIONS

Although thought of as a new country, Canada's prehistory dates back about 20,000 years to the end of the first Ice Age. At that time there was a land bridge joining Siberia to Alaska; Siberian hunter-nomads crossed this bridge to become the first human inhabitants of North America, and over

The bald eagle, a common sight around the Charlotte Island archipelago in British Columbia

the succeeding centuries their descendants gradually moved south. Archaeological digs in the Old Crow River Basin in the Yukon have unearthed a collection of tools believed to date to this initial period of migration. These Siberian nomads were the ancestors of the continent's native peoples, who adapted to their new environment in a variety of ways.

Inuit children at Bathurst Inlet, Northern Peninsula, Newfoundland

By the 16th century, Spanish and Portuguese traders were the first Europeans to have close dealings with the aboriginal peoples of the Americas, whom they named "Indians" in the mistaken belief that they had reached India. The "Indian" appellation stuck, and the "Red" was added by British settlers in the 17th century when they met the Beothuks of Newfoundland, who daubed themselves in red ochre to repel insects. The native peoples of the far north were also given a name they did not want – "Eskimo," literally "eaters of raw meat." Given the history, it is hardly surprising that modern-day leaders of Canada's aboriginal peoples have rejected these names in favor of others: aboriginal, native Canadians, and First Nations are all acceptable, though the people of the north prefer Inuit (meaning "the people"). Included among Canada's native peoples are the Métis, mixed race descendants of aboriginal peoples and French-speaking European traders.

Society

The joint official languages of Canada are French and English, and the interplay between Canada's two largest linguistic and cultural groups is evident in the capital city of Ottawa, where every federal speech and bill has to be delivered in both languages. Canada's population is about 24 percent French Canadian, predominantly the descendants of French settlers who came to the colony of New France in the 17th and 18th centuries *(see p41)*. Their English-speaking compatriots are largely descended from 18th- and 19th-century British immigrants. Canada's reputation as a multicultural society began to be established in the 19th century when successive waves of immigration, along with various settlement plans, brought people from all over the world to Canada's cities and its rural areas. Today, perhaps the best way to experience modern Canada's vibrant cultural mix is to visit its three largest cities – Toronto, Montreal, and Vancouver.

View from Centre Island's parks and gardens on Lake Ontario toward Toronto's CN Tower

Changing of the Guard outside Ottawa's Parliament Building

Government and Politics

Canada is a parliamentary democracy with a federal political system. Each province or territory has its own democratically elected provincial legislature headed by a Premier, and also sends elected representatives to the federal parliament in Ottawa. The House of Commons is the main federal legislature. The Prime Minister is the head of the political structure, as well as an elected member of the House of Commons where he must be able to command a majority. Bills passed in the Commons are forwarded to an upper chamber, the Senate, for ratification. At present, the Prime Minister appoints senators, although there is increasing pressure to make the upper chamber elective too. The nominal head of state is the British monarch, currently Queen Elizabeth II, and her Canadian representative is the Governor-General.

The ceremonial unveiling of the new Nunavut flag in 1999

In recent years, the dominant political trend in Canadian politics has been regionalism. The provinces have sought to take back power from the center, which makes it difficult for any one political party to win majority support in all parts of the country at any one time. The most conspicuous aspect of this process has been the conflict over Quebec, where there is a strong separatist movement. Twice since 1981, the Quebecois have been asked to vote in referenda seeking their support to leave Canada and, although the electorate voted "No" on both occasions, it was a close result. Sadly, the issue of Quebec's relationship with the rest of Canada is still unresolved, and further political disputes seem inevitable.

Since the 1980s aboriginal politics has come to the fore with campaigns for constitutional, land, and mineral rights. The Assembly of First Nations have been at the forefront of the establishment of the Inuit homeland, Nunavut. Current issues include battles for self-government and schools to preserve native languages, as well as hunting and fishing rights.

Canada has played its part in the major events of the 20th century, including both world wars, and today holds a prominent position in international politics. The country is a member of NATO and one of the Group of Eight (G8) countries, which, with the US, UK, Italy, Japan, France, Germany, and Russia, decide on world trade agreements.

Art and Culture

The vast and beautiful landscape of the country is a defining feature of Canadian culture. Outdoor pursuits such as hiking, skiing, and canoeing are high on the list of popular activities. Canadians are also great sports fans, and ice hockey, baseball, basketball, and Canadian football attract huge

crowds of spectators, and foster deeply felt allegiances. In addition to their passion for sports, Canadians are also enthusiastic about the arts. This is the country that has produced internationally renowned classical pianist, Glenn Gould, and whose major cities possess well-respected orchestras. Canada has also produced more than its share of international rock stars, from Joni Mitchell and Gordon Lightfoot to contemporary artists such as Celine Dion, Bryan Adams, k.d. lang, Shania Twain, and Alanis Morissette. Canada's cosmopolitan culture also means that visitors are likely to find a wide choice of music in bars, cafés, and many other venues across the country. All kinds of drama from Shakespeare to new writing, can be seen at Canada's renowned Stratford Festival, which is held in Ontario every year.

Vancouver Canucks Ice hockey game

Both native and European artists have looked to the wilderness as a source of inspiration. The first artist to attempt to express a sense of national identity was Tom Thomson, with his distinctive landscapes. He influenced the country's most celebrated group of painters, the Group of Seven *(see pp160–61)*, who evolved a national style of painting uniquely capable of representing Canada's wilderness, a theme developed by their contemporaries and successors, notably Emily Carr.

Canada's world-class museums and galleries represent the country's pride in its art collections: Toronto businessman Ken Thompson, shows a range of Canadian art in his own gallery as well as lending his support to the outstanding Art Gallery of Ontario. The marvelous array of restored forts, towns, and native villages reflect Canadian respect for both their native and European heritage.

International rock star, Alanis Morissette

Among Canadian writers, there are distinguished practitioners in both English and French, and an impressive list of contemporary novelists includes such prize-winning authors as Margaret Atwood, Carol Shields, Michael Ondaatje, Jacques Poulin, and Germaine Guèvremont.

The Canadian film industry is thriving, and the country's varied landscapes have proved popular locations, particularly for US film and TV producers (until 1999, the popular TV series the *X-Files* was shot in Vancouver). Behind Canada's flourishing cultural life, lies a pride in its history and cosmopolitan heritage, and an affection for the land's daunting beauty.

Popular TV series, the *X-Files*, was shot in Vancouver

Landscape and Geology

CANADA IS THE LARGEST country in the world, covering an area almost as big as Europe. It was created from the world's oldest landmasses. The billion-year-old bowl-shaped Canadian Shield covers much of the country, dipping around Hudson Bay and rising to mountain ranges at its edges. The country is bordered by oceans on three sides, with a coastline 243,800 km (151,400 miles) long and an interior containing some two million lakes. Canada is well known for the impressive diversity of its interior landscapes: from the frozen, barren north that descends to the mountainous west with its forest and wheat plains, through the wooded, hilly east, and the flat, fertile lowlands of the southeast.

***The Great Lakes** region covers 3% of Canada's landmass, and comprises a fertile lowland bowl, vital to its agricultural economy.*

***The Interior Plains**, including the prairies, are the principal wheat-growing areas of the country, and range southeast 2,600 km (1,600 miles) from the Cordilleras to the US border. The plains are divided into three huge steppes.*

THE ROCKIES AND THE WESTERN CORDILLERA

This region is part of one of the world's longest mountain chains. In Canada, the Cordillera comprises the Pacific Coastal Mountains and forested basins. Graduated peaks and ridges reveal Ice Age erosion, as does the Columbia Icefield *(see p308)*. The Rockies developed from continental plate movement, which began about 120 million years ago *(see pp256–7)*.

GEOGRAPHICAL REGIONS

Characterized by its variety, Canadian landscape falls into six main areas. The north of the country offers a landscape of tundra, with the far north ice-covered for much of the year. In the west and south, the warmer, fertile lands of the Cordillera and interior plains support the rural population. To the east, the Great Lakes area is an agricultural center. The vast Canadian Shield cradles the plains and rises to form the northern Innuitian region and the Appalachians in the south.

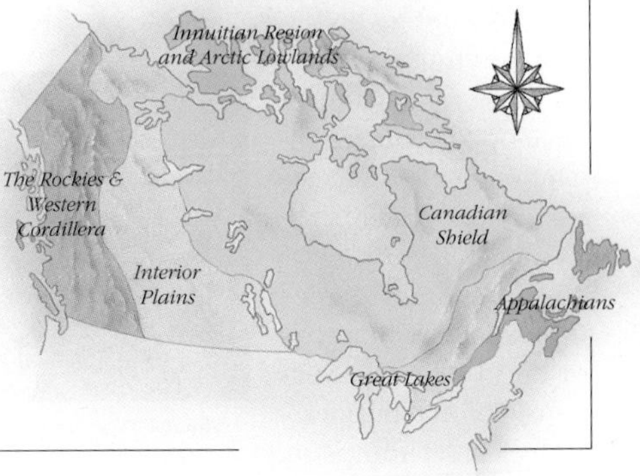

The Appalachians' *rolling landscape is two-thirds woodland and covers both arable lowland areas and the highest peaks in Quebec. These are found on the Gaspé Peninsula, the outer mountain ring of the Canadian Shield highland. Most of the Appalachian mountain chain lies in the US. They are nature's barrier between the eastern seaboard and the continental interior lowlands.*

The Canadian Shield, *formed of the 1,100-million-year-old bedrock of the North American continent, is the core of the country. It spreads out from Hudson Bay for 5 million sq km (1.9 million sq miles). The center is scrub and rock, and rises to steep mountains around the rim.*

The Innuitian *region stretches northward from the Arctic Lowlands' modest height of 100–700 m (330–2,000 ft) above sea level to the peaks of the Innuitian mountain range, at their highest on Ellesmere Island at 2,926 m (9,600 ft). Vigorous glaciation for millenia has developed deep fjords, sharp peaks, and frost patterns on the earth. This region is rich in oil, coal, and gas.*

Canada's Wildlife

By the time it emerged from the last Ice Age 10,000 years ago, Canada had developed a geography and climate that remains one of the most diverse on Earth. In the north, the Arctic weather produces a harsh, barren desert, in darkness for several months and frozen most of the year. By contrast, the country's most southerly province, Ontario, shares a latitude with northern California and offers fertile forests laced with rivers and lakes. In southern Canada, many varieties of wildlife flourish in the coniferous forest that covers the ancient rocks of the Canadian Shield. In the central plain are wheat-filled open prairies. From here, foothills lead to the Rocky Mountains, which gradually roll westward to coastal mountains and the balmy landscape of temperate rainforest along the Pacific coast.

***The muskox** is a gregarious herd animal and a remnant of the last Ice Age. Its thick topcoat of guard hair and undercoat of finer, fleecier hair keeps it warm even at –45°C (–50°F).*

The Boreal Forest

The boreal forest extends from eastern Canada, across most of Quebec and Ontario, and into the northern parts of the prairie provinces. It consists of a mix of spruce, pine, birch, and aspen, and occurs mostly on the giant rock outcrop of the Canadian Shield *(see pp18–9)*. Dotted with thousands of lakes, it is a rich habitat for some of Canada's best-known wildlife.

***The timber wolf**, or gray wolf, was hunted almost to extinction by 1950. It has now returned to the more isolated parts of its range in the boreal forest.*

***The loon** has a haunting call that rings out over northern lakes and is symbolic of the Canadian wilderness.*

The Prairies

Once referred to as a "sea of grass," the Canadian prairie is now predominantly agricultural in nature, specializing in growing wheat and other grains, and ranching prime beef cattle. While little original prairie wilderness remains, this is still a land of great open spaces that supports a surprising, often rare, wildlife population.

***The pronghorn** antelope is the last of its species to survive in North America. The fastest American mammal, it can reach speeds of over 75 km (47 miles) per hour.*

***The bison** now exists in only two remaining wild herds in Alberta and the Northwest Territories.*

Canada's Sports Fish

From the northern pike and lake trout in the north to the walleye and smallmouth bass in the south, Canada is blessed with a large number of sports fish species. Some fish that are much sought after as sport in Europe (the common carp, for example) are regarded as "trash," or undesirable, in Canada, and exist in large numbers in lakes and rivers across the Canadian Prairies. The arctic char, plentiful in the far north, is also prized for its taste.

Fishing *is one of Canada's most popular sports and is superbly supported by 37 national parks, each containing plentiful rivers and lakes.*

Salmon migrating *upriver provide an annual challenge for the keen sport fisherman. Canada has half the freshwater in the world, but deep sea angling can also prove rewarding.*

The Rocky Mountains

The Rocky Mountains begin in the foothills of western Alberta and rise into British Columbia. Along with the Columbia Mountains and the coastal mountains, they form a unique environment that ranges from heavily forested lower slopes, through alpine meadows, to snow-covered rocky peaks. This habitat is home to some of the most majestic wildlife in Canada.

The recurving horns *of a mature male bighorn sheep, found in more remote spots of the Rockies, weigh as much as all its bones put together.*

Canada's grizzly bear *stands up to 2.75 m (8.8 ft) high and weighs up to 350 kg (800 lbs). It feeds on roots, berries, and meat.*

The Canadian Arctic

North of the 60th parallel of latitude, the forest yields to arctic tundra and rock. The tundra is mostly bare, and frozen year-round a few inches below the surface, the icy ground being known as permafrost. During the brief summer the top layer thaws, and the Arctic bursts into bloom. Even though the Arctic is a freezing desert with little moisture, wildlife flourishes.

The great white polar bear *spends most of its life alone, out on the polar ice-pack, hunting for seals.*

The caribou *is a North American cousin of the reindeer. Caribou in the arctic migrate with the season in herds of 10,000, heading north on to the tundra in spring, south into the forest during winter.*

Multicultural Canada

Canada prides itself on its multiculturalism. The country has evolved a unique way of adjusting to the cultural needs of its increasingly diverse population. In contrast to the US's "melting pot," Canada has opted for what is often called the "Canadian mosaic," a model based on accepting diversity rather than assimilation. The origins of this tolerant and fruitful approach are embedded deep in Canadian history. Fearful of attack by the US in 1793, the British safeguarded the religious and civic institutions of their French-Canadian subjects in the hope that they would not ally with the Americans. This policy set the pattern of compromise that is now a hallmark of Canada. Citizens of British and French ancestry still make up the bulk of the population of 30 million, but there are around 60 significant minorities.

Young Inuit people in traditional dress huddled against the snow

Native Canadians

Today there are approximately one million Native Canadians, though national census figures usually break this group down into three sub-sections – aboriginals (750,000), métis (Indian and French mixed race 200,000), and Inuit (50,000). Of the million, about 60 percent are known as Status Indians, which means they are officially settled on reserve land. However, over 40 percent of Status Indians now live away from reserve land, and only 900 of Canada's 2,370 reserves are still inhabited. These lands are home to 608 First Nations groups, or bands, which exercise varying degrees of self-government through their own elected councils. Since the 1970s, progressive councils have played a key role in the reinvigoration of traditional native culture. Most non-Status Native Canadians are now integrated within the rest of Canada's population.

Rarely is the membership of a reserve descended from just one tribe. The largest band is the Six Nations of the Grand River, in Ontario, where the 19,000 inhabitants are made up of of 13 groups including the Mohawks, Delaware, and Seneca peoples.

In the far north, where white settlers have always been rare, the Inuit have a small majority. A recent result of their self-determination was the creation of Nunavut, a semi-autonomous Inuit homeland comprising 349,650 sq km (135,000 sq miles) of the eastern Arctic, created officially in April, 1999. Nunavut means "our land" in the Inuit language, and traditional skills of hunting and igloo-building are being reintroduced to this new region.

British and Irish Canadians

Canadians of British and Irish descent constitute about 60 percent of the country's population. The first English settlers arrived in the wake of the fleets that fished the waters off Newfoundland in the 16th century. Thereafter, there was a steady trickle of English, Scottish, Welsh, and Irish immigrants and several mass migrations, prompted either by adverse politics at home or fresh opportunities in Canada. Thousands of Scots arrived following the defeat of Bonnie Prince Charlie at Culloden in 1746, and the Irish poured across the Atlantic during and after the potato famine (1845–49). When the Prairie provinces opened up in the 1880s and at the end of both World Wars another large-scale migration took place.

These British and Irish settlers did much to shape Canada, establishing its social and cultural norms and founding its legal and political institutions. Canada's official Head of State is still the British monarch.

British poster of the 1920s promoting emigration to Canada

French Canadians

Canada's French-speakers make up about 25 percent of the total population, and are the country's second largest ethnic group. They are mainly based in just one of the 10 provinces, Quebec,

but other pockets thrive in other provinces. The French first reached the Canadian mainland in 1535 when Jacques Cartier sailed up the St. Lawrence River in search of a sea-route to Asia. Fur-traders, priests, and farmers followed in Cartier's footsteps and by the end of the 17th century, New France, as the colony was known, was well established. After the British captured New France in the Seven Years' War of 1756–63 *(see pp42–3)*, most French colonists stayed on as British subjects. The French-speakers maintained their own religious and civic institutions and a feeling of independence that has grown over time. Since the 1960s, the constitutional link between Quebec and the rest of the country has been the subject of political debate, with a strong minority of Quebecois pressing for full independence *(see p51)*.

German Canadians

Although there have been German-speakers in Canada since the 1660s, the first major migration came between 1850–1900, with other mass arrivals following both World Wars. On the whole, the English-speaking majority has absorbed the Germans, but distinctive pockets of German-speakers hold strong today in Lunenburg, Nova Scotia *(see p84)*, and Kitchener-Waterloo in Ontario *(see p216)*. The rural communities surrounding Kitchener-Waterloo are strongholds of the Amish, a German-speaking religious sect, whose members shun the trappings of modern life and travel around on horse-drawn buggies wearing traditional homemade clothes.

German food and drink, especially its beer-making techniques, have added to Canadian cuisine. Ethnic restaurants in German areas still run on traditional lines.

German beer stein

Street scene in Chinatown, Toronto

Italian Canadians

The widespread Italian presence in Canada can prove hard to see, as, for the most part, all 600,000 immigrants have merged almost seamlessly with the English speakers. There are, however, exceptions; in Toronto, a large and flourishing "Little Italy" neighborhood delights both visitors and the city's epicurean residents. The first major influx of Italian Canadians came in the wake of the civil wars that disrupted Italy in the second half of the 19th century; another wave arrived in the 1940s and 1950s after World War II. Immigration continues into the 21st century, with two percent of Canadians today speaking Italian as their first language.

Chinese Canadians

During the 1850s, Chinese laborers arrived in Canada to work in the gold fields of British Columbia. Thereafter, they played a key role in the construction of the railroads, settling new towns and cities as their work progressed eastward. During this period the Chinese suffered much brutal racism, including laws that enforced statutory discrimination.

A flood of Chinese immigration took place just before the return of Hong Kong to China by the British in 1997. Most settlers chose Toronto, Montreal, and Vancouver, but recently British Columbia has gained in popularity. With the Chinese focus on keeping large families together, most new arrivals today aim for an established community. About half of all Canada's new immigrants today come from Asia. Over two percent of the Canadian population claimed Chinese as their first language in the late 1990s.

Ukrainian Canadians

Although Ukrainians are a small fraction of the Canadian population, numbering less than three percent, they have had a strong cultural influence, especially in the Prairie Provinces where the cupolas of their churches rise above many midwestern villages. The first major wave of Ukrainian migrants arrived in the 1890s as refugees from Tsarist persecution. The Soviet regime and the aftermath of World War II caused a second influx in the 20th century.

Woman in native Ukrainian dress in Battleford, Saskatchewan

French Canada

"Free Quebec" demonstrator

MANY CANADIANS are quick to point out that Canada's origins are more French than British, that the first European Canadians were explorers from France, and therefore called *canadiens*. French Canadians have had a centuries-long history of conquest and battle to preserve their language and culture, strongest in Quebec and parts of Atlantic Canada. This has left large parts of the country with a French cultural base that lives on in language, religion, and the arts. More recently, the French-Canadian struggle for recognition in the 20th century has left unresolved the issue of Quebec's independence.

The heart of French Canada is Quebec, a province many times the size of France. Here, 85 percent of people count French as their mother tongue. French is not just the language of food, folklore, and love; it is also the language of business, government, and law.

LANGUAGE

FRENCH IS the joint official language of Canada, but it has mutated in much the same way that North American English has. *Canadiens*, especially those in the bigger cities, have adopted some anglicisms; modern English words relating to industries and trades introduced by English-speakers are favorites. Conversely, some words that have passed out of fashion in France survive here; Canada is one of the few places where a cart remains a *charette*, for example, instead of a *tombereau*, and the *fin-de-semaine* is the time to get away for some relaxation, rather than the now-universal *le weekend*. Young Quebecois in particular are also far more free in using the informal *tu*, than more formal *vous*, than their parents would perhaps consider polite.

Wide varieties exist in the quality and style of French spoken. The Paris-influenced intonation of Montreal's college-educated *haute bourgeoisie*, for example, is quite distinct from the rhythmic gutturals of the Acadian fishermen of the Maritimes. Residents of Quebec's Saguenay-Lac-Saint-Jean region speak a hard, clear French that must sound very like that of their Norman forbears.

Over the years Quebecois have evolved a dialect called *joual*, which is informal, slangy, and peppered with anglicisms. It is also very colorful and viewed with a mix of pride and disdain. The accent may be hard for foreigners to follow.

FOOD

CANADIENS HAVE always considered themselves the epicures of Canada, and with some justice, enjoying the delights of the table more passionately than their northern European counterparts. Traditional food is rich and hearty. Meat pies are a specialty: *cipaille* comprizes layers of game meat under a flaky crust, and the more common *tortière* has a filling made of ground beef spiced with cloves. Salmon pie, stews made with pigs' feet, and meatballs in a rich gravy are also typical. Desserts are rich; the Acadian *tarte au sucre* (sugar pie) is popular, as well as *pudding au chomeur* (literally "unemployed pudding"), an upside-down cake with a sweet, caramelized base of sugar baked into a rich batter.

Sugar pie, a traditional Acadian family dessert, served at celebrations

Musician Felix Leclerc, guardian of the folk music of Quebec

MUSIC

CHANSONIERS are the troubadours of French Canada. Rooted in the traditional music of the first settlers, their haunting songs and simple melodies, such as the ballads of Felix Leclerc, might be melancholy or upbeat, but they are almost always romantic. These folk songs, accompanied by guitar, usually reflect optimism and a deep love for the land. Quebec *chansonier* Gilles Vigneault's *Mon Pays* has become a nationalist anthem for those seeking independence. Of course, French music is not confined to the traditional; there are several successful rock, pop, and independent bands. Acadia's singers are often *chansonières*, including Edith Butler and Angèle Arseneault vividly evoking the sadness and joy of life by the sea.

Traditional Catholic church in Cheticamp, Cape Breton Island

Faith

The first French settlers were Roman Catholic, many very devout and zealous. The founders of Montreal, Paul Chomédy Sieur de Maisonneuve and Jeanne Mance, had hoped to create a new society based on Christian principles. Much of that devotion has evaporated in the modern age, especially in Quebec, which has one of the lowest church-attendance records in the country. Past fidelity has, however, left permanent monuments. Tiny French villages in Quebec and New Brunswick often have huge, stone churches with glittering tin roofs, gilding, and ornate interiors. Some parish churches in Montreal, like the magnificent Basilique Notre-Dame-de-Montréal *(see pp108–9)*, would pass for cathedrals in US cities.

Nationalism

There has been a nationalist strain to most *canadien* aspirations since the founding of Modern Canada. Quebecois entered the 1867 Canadian Confederation *(see p44)* only because French leaders persuaded them that the deal would preserve their faith and language. The 1960s and 1970s took the campaign into a new phase, with the aim being the independence of Quebec, as the politics of mere survival rose to the politics of assertiveness (with French President Charles de Gaulle adding his rallying cry *"Vive le Québec – libre!"* in 1966). Acadians in New Brunswick gained real political power to preserve their unique heritage, Franco-Ontarians fought for control over their own schools, and Manitobans used the courts to force their provincial government to translate all Manitoba statutes into French.

This resurgence of national pride was felt most strongly in Quebec, where the charismatic and popular politician René Lévesque and his Parti-Québecois won the provincial election in 1976 and made outright separatism respectable. The party now regularly wins local elections and has so far held two referenda on independence. Both times Quebecois said no by the narrowest of margins, but the threat still dominates Canada's political life.

Symbols

The Quebec flag has a white cross on a blue background with a white Bourbon lily in each quarter. Acadians have created their own flag by adding a gold star to the French tricolor, which symbolizes *Stella Maris* (Star of the Sea), named after the Virgin Mary. The patron saint of French Canada is St. Jean-Baptiste (St. John the Baptist); parades and parties mark his feast day on June 24. The celebrations take on a strongly nationalist style in Quebec, where the big day is called the *Fête National*. The provincial bird of Quebec is the snowy owl, and the flower remains the white lily, both of which flourish in the province.

Quebec flag with Bourbon lilies

Demonstrators during referendum vote for independence of Quebec

Native Canadians

Native mask from Vancouver

Europeans began to arrive *in numbers during the 17th century. In Newfoundland, the first part of Canada settled by whites, interracial relations were initially cordial but soured when new settlers encroached on ancient hunting grounds. In a pattern repeated across the continent, the native peoples, many dying from European diseases, were driven to inhospitable lands.*

Most archaeologists believe that the first inhabitants of North America crossed from Siberia to Alaska around 25,000 years ago. These hunter-nomads came in search of mammoth and bison, the ice-age animals that constituted their basic diet. The first wave of migrants was reinforced by a steady trickle of Siberian peoples over the next 15,000 years, and slowly the tribes worked their way east and south until they reached the Atlantic and South America. Over the centuries, the descendants of these hunter-nomads evolved a wide range of cultures, which were shaped by their particular environment. In the icy north or across the barren wastes of Newfoundland, life was austere; but the fertile soils of Ontario and the fish-rich shores of British Columbia nourished sophisticated societies based on fishing and farming.

The Iroquois

Spread along the St. Lawrence River and the shores of the Great Lakes, were the Iroquois-speaking tribes, among whom were the Mohawks, the Huron, and the Seneca. These tribes hunted and fished, but they also cultivated beans, pumpkins, squash, and corn, growing everything in abundance for a year-round food supply. This enabled them to live in large villages, often with several hundred inhabitants. Their traditional dwelling was the longhouse, built of cedar poles bent to form a protective arch and covered with bark. These settlements were all surrounded by high palisades made of sharpened wooden stakes, a necessary precaution as warfare between the tribes was endemic.

An Iroquois-built longhouse

Cornplanter, a 17th-century chief of the Seneca tribe

The Plains Peoples

War was also commonplace on the plains of southern Manitoba and Saskatchewan, where the majority Blackfoot tribe was totally reliant on the buffalo: they ate the meat, used the hide for clothes and tents, and filed the bones into tools. The first Blackfoot hunted the buffalo by means of cleverly conceived traps, herding the animals and stampeding them off steep cliffs *(see p294)*. Originally, the horse was unknown to the native peoples of the Americas – their largest beast of burden was the dog – but the Spanish conquistadores brought the horse with them when they colonized South America in the 1500s. Thereafter, horses were slowly traded north until they reached the Canadian plains. The arrival of the horse transformed Blackfoot life: it made the buffalo easy to hunt and, with a consistent food supply now assured, the tribe developed a militaristic culture, focusing particularly on the valor of their young men – the "braves."

Indians on horseback hunting buffalo with arrows

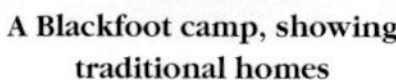

A Blackfoot camp, showing traditional homes

Peoples of the Pacific Coast

The native peoples of the Pacific Coast were divided into a large number of small tribes such as the Tlingit and the Salish. The ocean was an abundant source of food; with this necessity taken care of, they developed an elaborate ceremonial life featuring large and lively feasts, the potlachs, in which clans tried to outdo each other with the magnificence of their gifts. The peoples of this region were also superb woodcarvers, their most celebrated works of art being totem poles. Each pole featured a myth from the tribe's religion; magical birds and beasts mix with semi-human figures to tell a story in carved panels rising up the pole.

Sqylax tribal celebration in British Columbia

Totem pole in Stanley Park

Terminology

For many Canadians, the words "Eskimo" and "Red Indian" or just "Indian" are unacceptable. They are seen as terms of abuse, as they hark back to times when whites dominated the country and crushed its original population. The word "Eskimo" has been replaced by "Inuit," but modern substitutes for "Indian" are not as clear-cut. Some people choose "aboriginal" or "native," others prefer "indigenous," or speak of Canada's "First Nations." All are acceptable, and the simple rule, if in doubt, is to ask which word is preferred as this is a sensitive issue.

The Inuit and the Peoples of the Northern Forests

Stretching in a band from Alaska to Greenland, the far north was home to the Inuit, nomadic hunters who lived in skin tents in the summer and igloos in the winter. Arctic conditions and limited food supply meant that they foraged in small family groups and gathered together only in special circumstances – during the annual caribou migration, for instance. To the south of the Inuit, and also widespread across modern-day Canada, were the tribes of the northern forest, including the Naskapi, the Chipewyan, and the Wood Cree. These tribes were also nomadic hunters, dependent on fish and seal, or deer and moose. Successful hunters earned prestige, and the tribal priest (shaman) was expected to keep the spirit world benevolent, but there was little other social organization.

An Inuit hunter by his igloo home

Inuit in Caribou parka, checking his harpoon

Paul Okalik, Nunavut's first Premier, at his inauguration

Native Canadian Issues

Since the 1960s, Canada's native peoples have recovered some of their self-confidence. A key development was the creation of the Assembly of First Nations (AFN), an intertribal organization that has become an influential player on the national scene. In the 1980s, the AFN successfully argued for a greater degree of self-government on the reservations and tackled the federal government on land rights, sponsoring a series of court cases that highlighted the ways the native population had been stripped of its territories. The AFN was also involved in the establishment of Nunavut *(see p51)*, the new homeland for the Inuit created in 1999 from part of the former Northwest Territories. By comparison with their white compatriots, Canada's native population remains, nonetheless, poor and disadvantaged. The rectification of historic wrongs will take decades, even assuming that the political will remains strong enough to improve matters.

Art in Canada

INUIT AND OTHER First Nations groups have produced art in Canada since prehistoric times: the Inuit carved wood or antler sculptures, and other native groups were responsible for works from rock paintings to richly decorated pottery. Early European immigrants, both French and English, generally eschewed native traditions and followed European forms. Throughout the 19th and early 20th centuries, artists traveled, to Paris, London, and New York to study European art. It was in the 1900s that painters sought to develop a distinctly national style. However, one consistent subject of Canadian painting is the country itself: a preoccupation with its lush forests, stately landscapes, and expanse of freezing northern wilderness. Today, Canadian art reflects a wide range of art movements, with native art in particular fetching high prices among collectors.

***On the Saint Lawrence* (1897) oil painting by Maurice Cullen**

PAINTERS IN THE NEW WORLD

IN THE 1600s French settlers in Canada either imported religious paintings or commissioned stock subjects to adorn their new churches. Only Samuel de Champlain, the "Father of New France" *(see p41),* stands out for his sketches of the Huron tribe. After the English conquest in the 1760s, art moved from religion to matters of politics, the land, and the people. Army officers, such as Thomas Davies (1737–1812), painted fine detailed works, conveying their love of the landscape. Artists such as Robert Field (1769–1819), trained in Neo-Classicism, which was prevalent in Europe at the time, and became very popular, as did Quebec painters Antoine Plamondon (1817–95) and Théophile Hamel (1817–70). Cornelius Krieghoff (1815–72) settled in Quebec and was famous for his snow scenes of both settlers and natives. His contemporary, Paul Kane (1810–71), recorded the lives of the First Nations on an epic journey across Canada. He then completed over 100 sketches and paintings, of which *Mah Min*, or *The Feather*, (c.1856) is one of the most impressive *(see p36)*. During the 19th century, painters focused on the Canadian landscape. Homer Watson (1855–1936) and Ozias Leduc (1855–1964) were the first artists to learn their craft in Canada. Watson said, "I did not know enough to have Paris or Rome in mind. ... I felt Toronto had all I needed." His canvases portray Ontarian domestic scenes.

After Confederation in 1867, the Royal Canadian Academy of Arts and the National Gallery of Canada were founded in 1883. Artists could now train at home, but many still left to study in Paris. Curtis Williamson (1867–1944) and Edmund Morris (1871–1913) returned from France determined to revitalize their tired national art. They formed the Canadian Art Club in 1907, where new schools such as Impressionism were shown. James Wilson Morrice (1865–1924), Maurice Cullen (1866–1934), and Marc Aurèle de Foy Suzor-Coté (1869–1937) were key figures in this move toward modernity.

MODERN PAINTERS

THE INFLUENCE OF European art was criticized by perhaps the most influential set of Canadian artists, the Group of Seven *(see pp160–61)*. Before World War I, Toronto artists had objected to the lack of a national identity in art. By the 1920s the Group had defined Canadian painting in their boldly colored landscapes, such as A.Y. Jackson's *Terre Sauvage* (1913). Despite his early death, painter Tom Thomson was a founding influence. Three painters who came to prominence in the 1930s were influenced by the Group but followed highly individual muses, each of the artists were distinguished by a passion for their own province; David Milne (1882–1953), known for his still lifes, LeMoine Fitzgerald (1890–1956) for his domestic and backyard scenes, and Emily Carr (1871–1945) *(see p280)*

Lawren S. Harris, painter (1885–1970)

***Skidegate, Graham Island, BC,* (1928) a later work by Emily Carr**

for her striking depiction of the west coast Salish people and their totem poles. Carr was the first woman artist to achieve high regard. A writer as well as painter, her poem *Renfrew* (1929), describes her intense relationship with nature, which was reflected in her paintings: "... in the distance receding plane after plane... cold greens, gnarled stump of gray and brown."

The strong influence of the Group of Seven provoked a reaction among successive generations of painters. John Lyman (1866–1945) rejected the group's rugged nationalism. Inspired by Matisse, he moved away from using land as the dominant subject of painting. Lyman set up the Contemporary Arts Society in Montreal and promoted new art between 1939–48; even Surrealism reached the city.

Since World War II there has been an explosion of new forms based upon abstraction. In Montreal, Paul-Emile Borduas (1905–60) and two colleagues formed the Automatists, whose inspirations were Surrealism and Abstract Impressionism. By the 1950s Canadian painters achieved international acclaim. Postwar trends were also taken up in Toronto where The Painters Eleven produced abstract paintings. Today, artists work across the range of contemporary art movements, incorporating influences from around the world and from Canada's cultural mosaic. Experimental work by painters such as Jack Bush, Greg Carnoe, and Joyce Wieland continues strongly in the wake of ideas from the 1960s. Canada now boasts a plethora of public and private galleries, and exceptional collections of 20th-century art.

Aboriginal Art

The art of the Inuit *(see pp324–5)* and the Northwest First Nations is highly valued in Canada. Prehistoric Inuit finds reveal beautiful objects, from sculpted figurines to carved harpoon heads, which were largely created for religious use. With the coming of the Europeans the Inuit quickly adapted their artistic skills to make objects for sale such as sculptures made from ivory, bone, and stone. Today, Inuit artists such as Aqghadluk, Qaqaq Ashoona, and Tommy Ashevak are noted for their contribution to contemporary Canadian art, especially their sculpture and wallhangings. The sculpture of the Northwest coast First Nations people is known worldwide, particularly the cedar-wood carvings of Haida artist Bill Reid, the totem poles of Richard Krentz, and the Kwa Gulth Big House at Fort Rupert by Chief Tony Hunt.

Robert Murray's *Sculpture*

The celebrated Haida sculptor Bill Reid

Painters such as Norval Morisseau, Carl Ray, and Daphne Odjig cover a range of styles, from realism to abstract work. Native art celebrates the culture of its people, from their legendary survival skills, tales and myths, to their land and the fight for its preservation.

Sculpture

European sculpture arrived in Canada with the French who created sacred figures to adorn their churches. Sculptors such as Louis Quévillon (1749–1832) carved decorative altarpieces as well as fine marble statues in Montreal. European traditions continued to dominate through the 19th century, and it was not until the 20th century that Canada's new cities began to require civic monuments. The façade of the Quebec Parliament was designed by Louis-Phillipe Hébert (1850–1917).

Native subjects were incorporated into much 20th-century sculpture, as were European styles including Art Nouveau and Art Deco. Since the 1960s, sculptors such as Armand Vaillancourt (b.1932) and Robert Murray (b.1936) have sought to develop a Canadian style. Modern materials and the influence of conceptual art inform the work of such current artists as Michael Snow. Their work can be seen not just in museums but also in new commercial and civic buildings.

Literature and Music in Canada

As the Canadian poet the Reverend Edward Hartley Dewart wrote in 1864, "A national literature is an essential element in the formation of a national character." Much Canadian literature and music is concerned with defining a national consciousness but also reflects the cultural diversity of the country. Both English and French speakers have absorbed a variety of influences from the US, Britain, and France, as well as from the other nations whose immigrants make up the population. The Europeans' relationship with First Nations peoples has also affected the style and content of much Canadian fiction and poetry, as have the often harsh realities of living in a land of vast wilderness.

Stars of the popular 1934 film *Anne of Green Gables*

New Beginnings

Much of the earliest writing in Canada (between the mid-1500s and 1700s) was by explorers, fur traders, soldiers, and missionaries. French lawyer Marc Lescarbot's *Histoire de La Nouvelle France* (1609) is an early example of pioneer commentary and is a lively record of his adventures in Nova Scotia. After the English conquest of 1760, New France was subdued, but by the 19th century, French poets began producing patriotic poems such as *Le Vieux Soldat* (1855) by Octave Cremazie (1827–79), sparking a renaissance of poetry that continues today.

English writing was concerned with man's struggle with nature and life in the new world. *Roughing it in the Bush* (1852) by Mrs. Moodie is a tale of struggles in isolated northern Ontario. British Columbia was the last region to be settled, and a captivating memoir is *A Pioneer Gentlewoman in British Columbia: the recollections of Susan Allison* (1876). Allison came from England to teach in the town of Hope and was the first European woman to make the dangerous journey across the Hope Mountains on horseback. Much 19th-century Canadian fiction romanticizes the past, such as William Kirby's (1817–1906) *Golden Dog* (1877), with its idealized view of 18th-century Quebec. Epic novels of the time focused on native lives and cultures, notably *Wacousta* (1832) by John Richardson (1796–1852). Archibald Stansfield Belaney (1888–1938) took on a new identity as an Ojibway native named Grey Owl *(see p248)*, producing some of Canada's best-loved literature. *Pilgrims of the Wild* (1935) tells of his journey into Quebec to find sanctuary for the over-hunted beaver. *The Adventures of Sajo and her Beaver People* and *Tales of an Empty Cabin* (1935–6) are laments for the wild and lost traditions.

Classics of the early 1900s deal with domesticity. These include *Anne of Green Gables* (1908) by L.M. Montgomery (1874–1942). Humorous writing was led by Stephen Leacock *(see p216)*, and Thomas Chandler Haliburton (1796–1865), a judge who created Sam Slick, narrator of *The Clockmaker* (1876). Painter Emily Carr's *A House of all Sorts* (1944) describes her days as a landlady.

Poetry

Early English language poets Standish O'Grady (1793–1843) and Alexander McLachan (1818–76) wrote verse that reflected a colonial point of view. The genre looked critically at an iniquitous motherland (England), while praising the opportunities available in the New World. Creators of a "new" Canadian poetry in the 1870s and 80s used detailed descriptions of landscape to highlight man's efforts to conquer nature. Two notable authors were Charles Mair (1838–1927) and Isabella Velancey Crawford (1850–1887). By the 20th century the idea of the wilderness stayed at the center of Canadian poetry but was written

Internationally renowned poet and songwriter, Leonard Cohen

in a sparer style that mirrored the starkness of the Group of Seven's landscape paintings *(see pp160–1)*. Robert Service's (1874–1958) popular ballads deal with history, and he is noted for his gold rush poems such as *The Spell of the Yukon* (1907) and the later *Rhymes of a Roughneck* (1950). John McCrae (1872–1918) wrote one of the most famous World War I poems *In Flanders Fields* (1915).

Modern English and French poetry now has a worldwide audience, with writers such as Anne Wilkinson, Irving Layton, Earle Birney, E.J. Pratt, Leonard Cohen, and Patrick Anderson, whose *Poem on Canada* (1946) looks at the impact of nature on European mentalities. The simple power of French writer Anne Hébert's poems, such as *Le Tombeau des Rois* (The Kings' Tombs) (1953) focuses on the universal themes of childhood, memory, and death. A postwar boom in poetry and fiction was fostered by the Canada Council for the Arts.

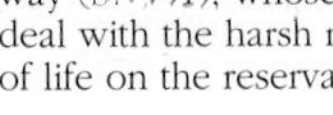

Canadian poet Robert Service in 1942

Native Canadian Writing

Despite a powerful oral tradition – where stories are both owned and passed down through families and clans – autobiography, children's books, plays, short stories, poetry, essays, and novels have been produced by Canadian native writers since the 19th century. One of the most popular autobiographies of this period was written by Ojibway native George Copway (1818–69). Titled *The Life, History, and Travels of Kah-ge-ga-ga-bowh* (1847), it had six editions in a year. The first book to be published by a native woman is thought to be *Cogewea, The Half-Blood* (1927), by Okanagan author Mourning Dove (1888–1936). Another Okanagan novelist, Jeanette Armstrong (b.1948), published *Slash* in 1985. The struggles of a Métis woman in modern Canada are described in the best-selling autobiography of Maria Campbell in *Halfbreed* (1973).

A mix of legend and political campaigning for native rights informs much aboriginal fiction, such as Pauline Johnson's *The White Wampum* (1895) and Beatrice Culleton's *In Search of April Raintree* (1983). The first Inuit work in English was *Harpoon of the Hunter* (1970), a story of coming of age in the northern Arctic by Markoosie (b.1942). One of Canada's top contemporary playwrights is Cree author Thompson Highway (b.1951), whose plays deal with the harsh reality of life on the reservations.

Modern Fiction

Since the 1940s, many Canadian writers have achieved international fame. Margaret Atwood (b.1939) for her poetry, novels, and criticism, while Carol Shields (b.1935) won the prestigious British Booker Prize for *The Stone Diaries* in 1996. Mordecai Richler (b.1931) and Robertson Davies (1913–95) are noted for their wry take on contemporary Canadian society. Many authors have reached a wider public through having their books adapted for the big screen. Gabrielle Roy's *Bonheur d'Occasion* (1945) became the 1982 movie *The Tin Flute*; a novel by W.P. Kinsella, *Shoeless Joe* (1982), became *Field of Dreams* starring Kevin Costner in 1989, and Michael Ondaatje's 1996 *The English Patient* won nine Oscars. There is a strong tradition of short-story writing, one master being Alice Munro (b.1931). Popular history is highly regarded; noted author Pierre Berton has written 40 books on the nation's history.

Legendary composer and Folk singer, Joni Mitchell

Michael Ondaatje, Oscar-winning author of *The English Patient*

Music in Canada

Some of the biggest names in the music industry are Canadian. A strong tradition of folk and soft rock has produced such artists as Leonard Cohen, Kate and Anna McGarrigle, Joni Mitchell, and Neil Young. A new generation of singer/songwriters that have continued the tradition of reflective, melodic hits include Alanis Morissette and k.d. lang; and the Cowboy Junkies and Shania Twain play new styles of country music. Superstars such as Celine Dion and Bryan Adams have made a huge impact in Europe and the US. In the classical sphere, orchestras such as the Montréal Orchestre Symphonique are world famous, as was the pianist Glenn Gould. Jazz is represented by the pianist Oscar Peterson, and every year Montreal hosts one of the world's most famous festivals.

Sports in Canada

Canadians are avid sports fans, and most of the country's cities and towns offer visitors a chance to see year-round sports entertainment. Although the official national game is lacrosse – a First Nations game in which the ball is caught and tossed in a leather cradle on a stick – Canadians' greatest enthusiasm is for ice hockey. Baseball, basketball, and Canadian football (similar to the US game) are also big crowd-pullers. Major cities regularly attract international stars to world-class racing, golf, and tennis tournaments. Even small towns provide the chance to watch minor professionals, amateurs, and student athletes. For visitors who prefer participating in sports, Canada offers a broad choice of activities from skiing to golf, fishing, and hiking.

National ice hockey heroes in action during a league game

Ice Hockey

The popularity of ice hockey in Canada knows no bounds. Every town has a rink, and every school, college, and university a team. The North American **National Hockey League** (NHL) was founded in 1917, and its principal prize, the Stanley Cup, was instituted in 1892 by Canadian Govenor General, Lord Stanley. Today, the league has 30 teams, six of which belong to Canadian cities; the Montreal Canadiens, Calgary Flames, Edmonton Oilers, Toronto Maple Leafs, Ottawa Senators, and the Vancouver Canucks. Although most of the players in both the US and Canada are Canadian, recent years have seen an influx of other nationalities such as Russian, American, and Swedish atheletes playing for the top teams. Renowned for its toughness, the game usually involves a skirmish or two among the players, which often means that this 60-minute game can last up to three hours. The season runs from October to April when the play-offs for the Stanley Cup begin.

Hockey stars such as Wayne Gretzky are national icons. He retired in 1999 after 20 years in the game, having captured 61 NHL scoring records.

Tickets to the major games can be hard to come by, and should be booked in advance. It is a good idea to contact the club's ticket lines, or book through **Ticketmaster**. Minor league and college games are easier to get into, and the University of Toronto and York, Concordia in Montreal, and the University of Alberta in Edmonton all have good teams. Tickets can be bought from the local arena, or direct from the administration center, and are usually a great bargain.

Baseball

Although baseball is seen as an American sport, the game has a large following in Canada. There are two teams that play in the US's two major leagues; the well-known **Toronto Blue Jays**, who won the World Series in 1992 and 1993, and the **Montreal Expos**, who became the first Canadian team to play in a US league in 1968. Baseball is played in the summer, and the season lasts from April to September (with play-offs through October) and can be a great family day out, with its beer, popcorn, and sunshine accompaniment.

The teams play their American league rivals in two outstanding stadiums; the Jays in Toronto's SkyDome, an architectural marvel with a roof that opens and closes depending on the weather *(see p169)*, and the Expos in Montreal's Olympic Stadium *(see pp120–21)*. Tickets have to be booked well in advance, and it is easier to obtain them for the Montreal Expos than it is for the Jays. Seeing one of the minor league teams such as the Edmonton Trappers is also fun.

Jose Canseco during his days with the Toronto Blue Jays

FOOTBALL

THE CANADIAN version of football (not soccer) is noted for being a more exciting version of American football. Although the best Canadian players tend to move to the US for higher salaries, the game still attracts substantial home audiences. The Canadian Football League has two divisions of four teams who each play over the July to November season.

The games tend to attract a lively family crowd and are fun, especially around the Grey Cup final. Played on the last Sunday of November, the game is preceded by a week of festivities and a big parade in the host city. Football is also played at most universities, where a Saturday afternoon game makes for an entertaining excursion. The annual college championship game is called the Vanier Cup and is played at Toronto's Skydome at the beginning of December. Tickets are relatively easy to come by and are reasonably priced.

BASKETBALL

WHAT ONCE was an American passion has now spread around the world to become one of the fastest growing international sports. The game was invented in the United States by a Canadian, Dr. James Naismith, and now enjoys huge popularity in his homeland. The **Toronto Raptors** and **Vancouver Grizzlies** both play in the National Basketball Association, the top professional league in the world, against the likes of the Chicago Bulls, Boston Celtics, Los Angeles Lakers, and New York Knicks. The season lasts from October until late spring, and it is well worth a visit to Vancouver's GM Place or Toronto's Air Canada Centre to watch a game. Most of Canada's universities have teams, and although crowds tend to be smaller than those drawn by the professionals, the competition is fierce and the atmosphere exhilarating, especially during the annual national championship tournament played in Halifax each March.

Toronto Raptors versus the L.A. Lakers basketball match

GOLF

CANADA HOSTS two major tournaments each year (both in September), which draw large crowds of spectators, as well as the world's greatest players. The biggest is the Canadian Open, usually played at Toronto's Glen Abbey on a course designed by Jack Nicklaus. The annual Greater Vancouver Open is a regular stop on the Professional Golfers' Association tour, although the field is not as strong as that of the Open.

Golf is an immensely popular participation sport, with over 1,700 beautiful courses across the country, from the Banff Springs course in the west to the many rolling fairways of Prince Edward Island in the east.

WINTER SPORTS

FAMOUS FOR the plentiful snow and sunshine of its cold winters, Canada is one of the top places both to watch and participate in winter sports. Canadian resorts are less crowded than their European counterparts, and are set among some of the most dramatic scenery in the world. Visitors can enjoy a range of options in resorts across the country, from Whistler in the Rockies to Mont Ste-Anne in Quebec. As well as downhill skiing, it is also possible to try snowboarding, snowmobiling, dogsledding, or even heli-skiing on pristine snow *(see p387)*.

DIRECTORY

National Hockey League
11th Floor, 50 Bay Street, Toronto.
(416) 981 2777.

Ticketmaster
(for hockey games)
(416) 870 8000.

Baseball
Toronto Blue Jays
Tickets: (416) 341 1234.
Montreal Expos
(514) 790 1245.

Football
Canadian Football League
110 Eglinton Avenue W. Toronto
(416) 322 9650.

Basketball
Toronto Raptors
Tickets: (416) 815 5600.
Vancouver Grizzlies
Tickets: (604) 899 4667.

Golf
Royal Canadian Golf Association
(905) 849 9700.

Snowboarder descending a slope at speed in powder snow

Canada Through the Year

Seasonal changes in Canada vary greatly across the country, but in general it is safe to say that the winters are long and cold and run from November to March, while spring and fall tend to be mild. British Columbia is the most temperate zone, with an average temperature of 5°C (40°F) in January. July and August are reliably warm and sunny in most places, even the far north, and most outdoor festivals tend to be held in the summer months. There are plenty of events held during winter, both indoors and out, some of which celebrate Canadians' ability to get the best out of the icy weather, especially activities such as dogsledding, snowmobiling, and ice-skating. A range of cultural events reflect the country's history, as well as its diverse peoples and culture.

Native powwow in Calgary

Spring

March and April bring the country some of its most unpredictable weather, moving from snow to sunshine in a day. In the north this is a time for welcoming the end of winter, while farther south spring is the start of an array of fun festivals.

Dogsledding at Yellowknife's Caribou Carnival in spring

March

The Caribou Carnival *(late March)* Yellowknife. A celebration of the arrival of spring, featuring dogsledding, snowmobiling, and delicious local foods.

April

Toonik Tyme *(mid-April)* Iqaluit. This week-long festival includes igloo building, traditional games, and community feasts.

Beaches Easter Parade *(April)* Toronto. This annual parade has become a popular spring institution. It follows a route along Queen St. E., between Victoria Park and Woodbine Avenue.

Shaw Festival *(April- October)* Niagara-on-the-Lake. Theater festival with classic plays by George Bernard Shaw and his contemporaries *(see p206)*.

Summer

Warm weather across most of the country means that there is an explosion of festivals, carnivals, and cultural events, from May through August.

May

Canadian Tulipfest *(mid-May)* Ottawa. Colorful display of millions of tulips is the centerpiece for a variety of events.

Stratford Festival *(May–November)* Stratford. World famous theater festival featuring a range of plays from Elizabethan to contemporary works *(see p209)*.

Shorebirds and Friends' Festival *(late May)* Wadena, Saskatchewan. Features guided bird-watching and tours of wildlife habitats.

Vancouver International Children's Festival *(last weekend in May)* Vancouver. Theater, circus, and music for children aged 3 and up.

June

Grand Prix du Canada *(early June)* Montreal. North America's only Formula One event.

Midnight Madness *(mid-June)* Inuvik. Celebration of the summer solstice, with parties under the midnight sun.

Mosaic – Festival of Cultures *(first weekend in June)* Regina. Cultural events from around the world.

Banff Festival of the Arts *(mid-June to mid-August)* Banff. Two months of opera, music, drama, and dance.

Vividly colored tulips at Ottawa spring festival, Canadian Tulipfest

Steer wrestling competition in the *Half Million Dollar Rodeo* at Calgary's Exhibition and Stampede

Jazz Fest International *(late June–July)* Victoria. Jazz and blues musicians play in venues all over town.
Red River Exhibition *(late June–July)* Winnipeg. A huge fair with a wide choice of entertainments.
Festival International de Jazz de Montréal *(late June–July)* Montreal. Famous jazz festival with a number of free outdoor concerts.
Nova Scotia International Tattoo *(late June–July)* Halifax. There are 2,000 participants in one of the world's largest indoor shows.

July

Folk on the Rocks *(second weekend)* Yellowknife. Inuit drummers, dancers, and throat singers perform here.
Klondike Days *(July)* Edmonton. Commemorates the city's frontier days. A highlight is the World Championship Sourdough Raft Race.
Calgary Exhibition and Stampede *(mid-July)* Calgary. Ten-day celebration of all things western, including parades and a major rodeo competition *(see p292)*.
Molson Indy *(mid-July)* Toronto. Indy car race held at Exhibition Place.
Quebec City Summer Festival *(second week)* Quebec City. Ten days of music and dance.
Just for Laughs Festival *(July 14–25)* Montreal. Twelve-day comedy festival with more than 600 comedians from around the world.
Canadian Open Tennis Championships *(July–Aug)* Montreal. Major international tennis tournament.
Caribana *(July–Aug)* Toronto. One of the largest cultural celebrations in North America. The main event is the parade.
Antigonish Highland Games *(mid-July)* Antigonish. Oldest traditional highland games in North America, with pipe bands and dancing.

Ford race car at the Molson Indy meeting held in Toronto

August

Royal St. John's Regatta *(Aug 4)* St. John's. Noted as North America's oldest sporting event, features rowing races and a carnival.
Wikwemikong Powwow *(first weekend)* Manitoulin Island. Ojibway native festival with a dancing and drum competition *(see p222)*.
Discovery Days Festival *(mid-Aug)* Dawson City. Commemorates gold rush days, with costumed parades and canoe races.
First People's Festival Victoria. *(mid-Aug)* Three days of exhibitions, dancing, and a traditional native gathering known as the potlatch.
Folklorama *(mid-Aug)* Winnipeg. Multicultural festival of food, performance, and the arts.
Victoria Park Arts and Crafts Fair *(mid-Aug)* Moncton. Atlantic Canada's largest outdoor sale of arts, antiques, and crafts.
Festival Acadien de Caraquet *(Aug 5–15)* Caraquet. Celebration of Acadian culture and history.
Halifax International Busker Festival *(second week)* Halifax. The best street entertainers from around the world.
Canadian National Exhibition *(Aug–Sep)* Toronto. Annual fair featuring spectacular air show, concerts, and a casino.
Folkfest *(mid-Aug)* Saskatoon. Saskatchewan's multicultural heritage celebrated in a variety of events.

Showjumping in the Masters equestrian event held in Calgary

Fall

Cool, but often sunny weather provides the best setting for the dramatic reds and golds of the fall foliage, which are mostly seen in the deciduous forests of the eastern provinces. In Ontario and Quebec, fall signals the end of the humid summer months and heralds crisp days that are perfect for outdoor pursuits.

September

The Masters *(first week)* Calgary. Equestrian event with top international riders.
Molson Indy *(early Sep)* Vancouver. This year's second Molson Indy sees car racing in downtown Vancouver.
Toronto International Film Festival *(Sep)* Toronto. Famous movie stars and directors attend this prestigious festival.
Flambée des Couleurs *(mid-Sep–Oct)* Eastern Townships. A series of celebrations of glorious fall leaf colors.
Niagara Grape and Wine Festival *(last week)* Niagara Falls. Vineyard tours, wine tastings, and concerts welcome the area's grape harvest.

October

Okanagan Wine Festival *(early-Oct)* Okanagan Valley. Tours and tastings throughout the valley *(see p315)*.
Oktoberfest *(mid-Oct)* Kitchener-Waterloo. Largest Bavarian festival outside Germany *(see p216)*.

Traditional Bavarian costumes and music at the Oktoberfest

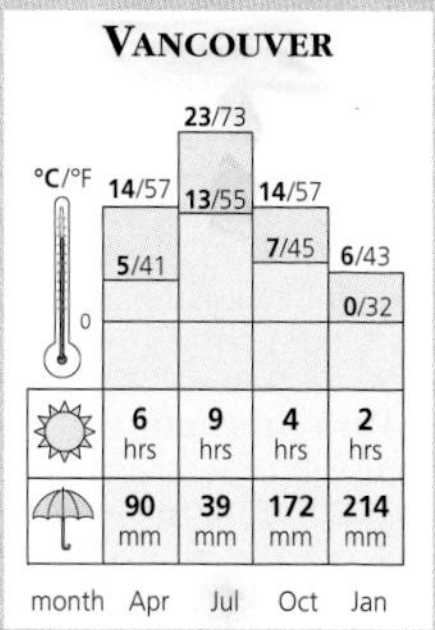

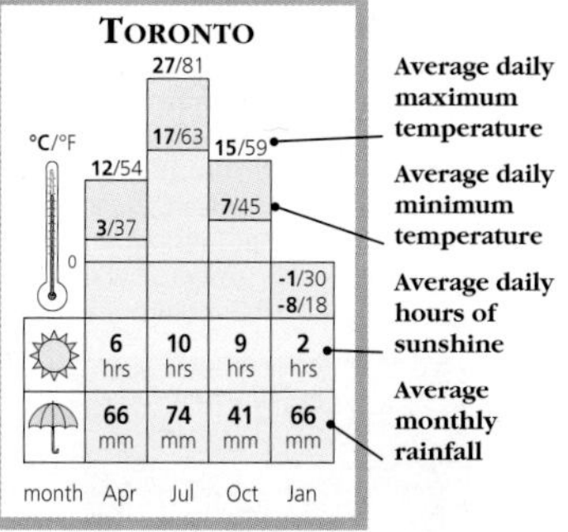

Climate
This vast country has a variable climate, despite being famous for having long, cold winters. Most Canadians live in the warmer south of the country, close to the US border. Southern Ontario and BC's south and central coast are the warmest areas, while central and northern Canada have the coldest winters.

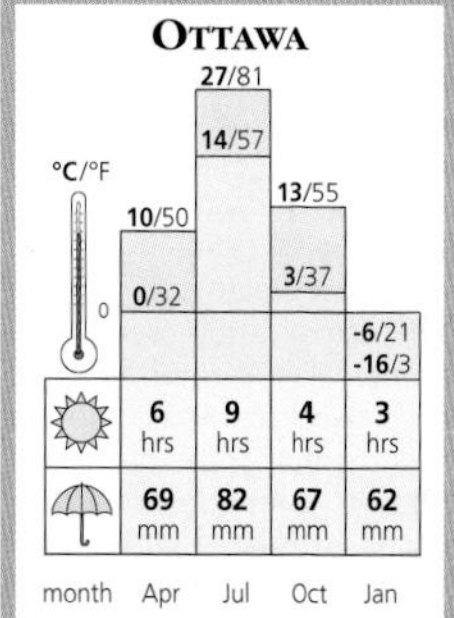

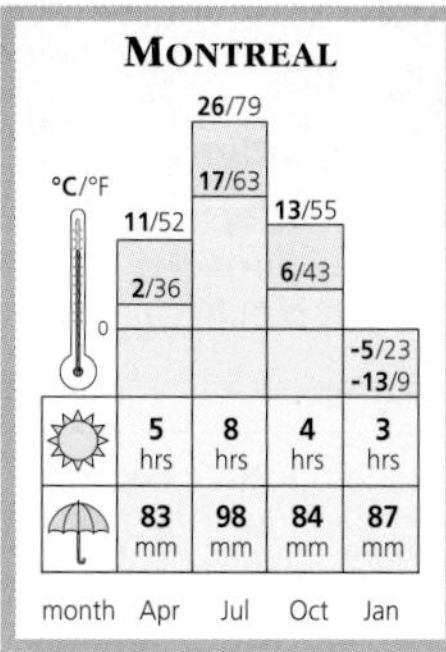

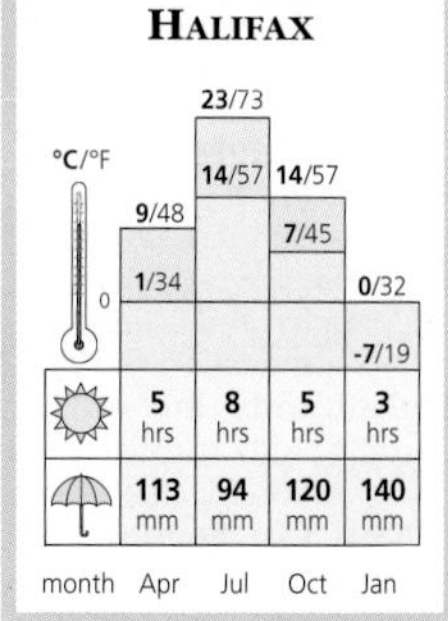

Celtic Colours *(mid-Oct)* Cape Breton Island. International Celtic music festival held across the island.

WINTER

APART FROM coastal British Columbia, Canadian winters are long and cold with lots of snow. Events focus on winter sports, with some of the best skiing in the world available at such resorts as Whistler in British Columbia. The Christmas holidays are a time of fun activities to cheer everyone up in the midst of long, dark days.

PUBLIC HOLIDAYS

New Years Day (Jan 1)
Good Friday (variable)
Easter Sunday (variable)
Easter Monday (variable) Vacation for government offices and schools only.
Victoria Day. (Monday before May 25)
Canada Day (July 1)
Labour Day (first Monday in September)
Thanksgiving (second Monday in October)
Remembrance Day (Nov 11)
Christmas Day (Dec 25)
Boxing Day (Dec 26)

An illuminated display of Christmas decorations

NOVEMBER

Royal Agricultural Winter Fair *(early–mid-Nov)* Toronto. The world's largest indoor agricultural fair features the Royal Horse Show and the Winter Garden Show.
Canadian Finals Rodeo *(mid-Nov)* Edmonton. Canada's cowboy champions are decided at this event.
Winter Festival of Lights *(mid-Nov–mid Jan)* Niagara Falls. Spectacular light displays and concerts.

DECEMBER

Canadian Open Sled Dog Race *(Dec)* Fort St. John and Fort Nelson. Snow sports and family fun-days as well as dogsled races.
Christmas Carolships Parade *(mid-Dec)* Vancouver. Boats are beautifully decorated with Christmas lights, and cruise Vancouver's waters.

JANUARY

Ice Magic *(mid-Jan)* Lake Louise. International ice sculpture competition.
Techni-Cal Challenge – Dog Sled Race *(mid-Jan)* Minden. Over 80 teams compete in international races.
Rossland Winter Carnival *(last weekend)* Rossland. Snowboarding contests, a torchlit parade, and lots of music and dancing at this weekend-long party.
Quebec Winter Carnival *(Jan-Feb)* Quebec. A famous canoe race across the St. Lawrence River is just one attraction at these huge winter celebrations.
Jasper in January *(last two weeks)* Jasper. Winter festivities include skiing parties, races, and food fairs.
Banff/Lake Louise Winter Festival *(last week)* Banff, Lake Louise. Variety of fun events, including skating parties and barn dances.

FEBRUARY

Yukon Quest International Sled Dog Race *(Feb)* Whitehorse. Famous 1,600 km (1,000 mile) race from Fairbanks, Alaska to Whitehorse.
Yukon Sourdough Rendevous *(Feb)* Whitehorse. A "mad trapper" competition and an array of children's events in this winter festival.
Frostbite Music Festival *(third weekend)* Whitehorse. Features a wide range of music from jazz to rock.
Calgary Winter Festival *(second week)* Calgary. Winter festival with lots of fun family activities, music, and feasting.
Festival du Voyageur *(mid-Feb)* Winnipeg. Celebration of fur trade history featuring an enormous street party.
Winterlude *(every weekend)* Ottawa. A wide array of activities including ice-skating on the Rideau Canal.

Two eagle ice sculptures at Ottawa's February festival, Winterlude

The History of Canada

Canada is known for its wild and beautiful terrain, yet with the help of the aboriginal peoples, European settlers adapted to their new land and built up a prosperous nation. Despite continuing divisions between its English- and French-speaking peoples, Canada has welcomed immigrants from around the globe and is respected as one of the most tolerant countries in the world today.

Long before the first Europeans crossed the Atlantic in AD 986, the landscape we now know as Canada was inhabited by various civilizations. Tribes of hunters came on foot, walking across a land bridge that once joined Asia with North America as part of the ancient land mass of Laurasia.

Detail of totem pole made by Haida peoples from the west

These first inhabitants, now referred to as the First Nations, endured centuries of hardship and adaptation, eventually developing the skills, technology, and culture required to survive the rigors of life in Canada.

Early Survival

Across most of the country, from the Yukon to the Atlantic, there were two main groups of hunter-gatherers, the Algonquins and the Athapaskans. They lived in small nomadic bands, which developed birch bark canoes and snowshoes to travel across this vast land. Food and clothing were procured through fishing and animal trapping, traditions that gave Canada the lucrative fish and fur trades.

To the north of these two groups were the Innu people, who mastered life in the Arctic, being able to survive in a region of dark, ice-bound winters and brief summers. To the south, the Iroquois settled in forest villages where they lived in longhouses and grew corn as their staple crop.

On the western plains, other tribes depended on the bison for their livelihood, while communities living along the Pacific Coast relied on fishing and trading. Their towering totem poles indicated a rich culture and spiritual belief system.

The common bond between all the First Nations, despite their disparate lifestyles, was that they saw themselves as part of nature and not as its masters. They believed the animals they hunted had kindred spirits, and misfortune befell those who offended such spirits by gratuitous killing.

The generosity of the natives toward Europeans may have hastened their own downfall. As Canadian historian Desmond Morton points out: "Without the full... assistance of natives showing the Europeans their methods of survival, their territory, and their resources, the early explorers and settlers would have perished in even greater numbers and possibly abandoned their quest, much as the Vikings had done 500 years before."

Timeline

9,000 BC Native peoples are living at least as far south as the Eramosa River near what is now Guelph, Ontario

Viking ship c.980 AD

AD 986 Bjarni Herjolfsson, a Viking sailing from Iceland to Greenland, is the first European to see the coastline of Labrador

1497 John Cabot's first voyage to North America

30,000 BC	20,000 BC	10,000 BC	AD1	500	1000	1500

30,000–10,000 BC Nomadic hunters arrive in North America across a land bridge from Asia

992 Leif "the Lucky" Ericsson visits Labrador and L'Anse aux Meadows, Newfoundland

1003 Thorfinn Karlsefni starts a colony in Labrador (Vinland) to trade with the natives, but it is abandoned two years later because of fighting with the hostile aboriginals

◁ ***Mah-Min*** **or** ***The Feather*****, painting of an Assiniboine chief by Paul Kane c.1856**

The First Europeans

The Norse sagas of Northern Europe tell how Vikings from Iceland first reached the coast of Labrador in AD 986 and made a series of unsuccessful attempts to establish a colony here. Leif "the Lucky" Ericsson sailed from Greenland in 988, naming the country he found in the west Vinland after the wild grapes found growing in abundance there. Around 1000 AD Thorfinn Karlsefni tried to establish a Vinland colony. Thorfinn's group wintered in Vinland but sailed home to Greenland in the spring, convinced that a colony was impossible as there were too few colonists and the *skraelings* (aboriginals) were hostile. Remarkably, remains of this early Viking settlement were discovered in Newfoundland in 1963 *(see p67)*.

The English Invasion

In 1497, the Italian navigator John Cabot (1450–98), on the commission of King Henry VII of England, set sail aboard the *Matthew*, bound for America. On June 24, he found a sheltered place on Cape Breton Island. Here he went ashore with a small party to claim the land for England. He then went on to chart the eastern coastline before sailing home, where he was greeted as a hero.

Italian navigator and explorer John Cabot

In May 1498, Cabot sailed again with five ships and 300 men hoping to find the Northwest Passage to China. Harsh weather drove Cabot to relinquish his efforts and head south to Nova Scotia. Cabot then found himself sailing through a sea littered with icebergs. The fleet perished off the coast of Greenland, and English interest in the new land faded.

The French Arrival

Originally from the port of St. Malo, explorer Jacques Cartier (1491–1557) made his first voyage to Canada in 1534. He reached Labrador, Newfoundland, and the Gulf of the St. Lawrence before landing on Anticosti Island where he

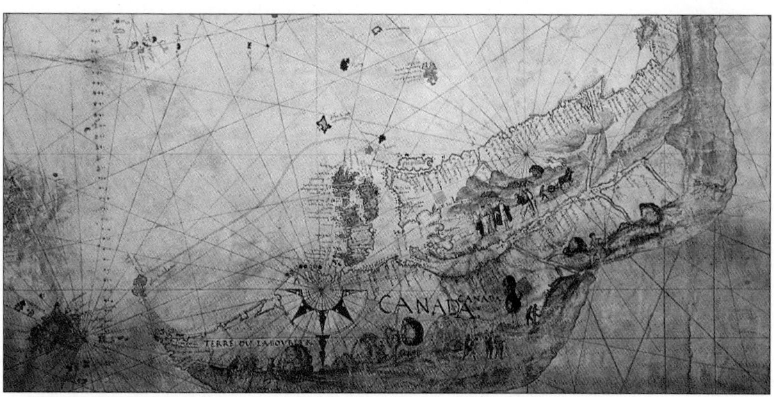

Map of the voyage of Jacques Cartier and his followers by Pierre Descaliers c.1534–1541

Timeline

1525

1535 Cartier sails up the St. Lawrence River to Stadacona (Quebec City) and Hochelaga (Montreal)

1541 At the mouth of the Cap Rouge River, Cartier founds Charlesbourg-Royal, the first French settlement in America – it is abandoned in 1543

1550

Jacques Cartier

1567 Samuel de Champlain "Father of New France" born

1575

1600

1605 Samuel de Champlain and the Sieur de Roberval found Port Royal, now Annapolis, Nova Scotia

1608 Champlain founds Quebec City, creating the first permanent European settlement in Canada

1610 Henry Hudson explores Hudson Bay

realized he was at the mouth of a great river. A year later, he returned and sailed up the St. Lawrence River to the site of what is now Quebec City, and then on to a native encampment at Hochelega, which he named Montreal. In 1543, Cartier's hopes for a successful colony died when, after a bitter and barren winter, he and his dispirited group returned to France. Seventy more years would pass before French colonists returned to Canada to stay.

Champlain, "Father of New France," fighting the Iroquois

The Father of New France

Samuel de Champlain (1567–1635) was a man of many parts – navigator, soldier, visionary – and first made the journey from France to Canada in 1603. While the ship that carried him across the Atlantic lay at Tadoussac, Champlain ascended the St. Lawrence River by canoe to the Lachine Rapids.

In 1605, Champlain's attempt to found a colony at Port Royal failed, but in 1608 the seeds of a first tiny French colony at Quebec City were planted, with the construction of three two-story houses, a courtyard, and a watch-tower, surrounded by a wooden wall.

The economic engine propelling Champlain was the fur trade. In its name he made alliances with the Algonquins and Hurons, fought their dreaded enemies, the Iroquois, traveled to the Huron country that is now central Ontario, and saw the Great Lakes. Champlain and the other Frenchmen who followed him not only established lasting settlements in the St. Lawrence Valley but also explored half a continent. They built a "New France" that, at its zenith, stretched south from Hudson Bay to New Orleans in Louisiana, and from Newfoundland almost as far west as the Rockies. In 1612 Champlain became French Canada's first head of government.

Champlain's efforts also helped to create the religious climate that enabled orders such as the Jesuits to establish missions. But his work also laid the seeds of conflict with the English that would last well into the next century and beyond.

The Hudson's Bay Company

Hudson's last voyage

In 1610, English voyager Henry Hudson landed at the bay that still bears his name. The bay's access to many key waterways and trading routes ensured the fortunes of the fur trade.

Founded in 1670, the Hudson's Bay Company won control of the lands that drained into the bay, gaining a fur-trading monopoly over the area. The company was challenged only by Scottish merchants who established the North West Company in Montreal in 1783. By 1821, these two companies amalgamated, and the Hudson's Bay Company remains Canada's largest fur trader to this day.

1625

1629 British adventurer David Kirke captures Quebec, but it is returned to France in 1632

Raccoon pelt

1648–49 The Iroquois disperse the Huron nation and Jesuit father Jean de Brébeuf is martyred during Iroquois raids on Huronia

1650

1670 The Hudson's Bay Company is founded by royal charter and underwritten by a group of English merchants

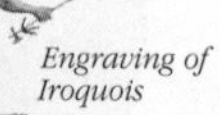
Engraving of Iroquois

1675

1676 population of New France swelled to 8,500 by settlers

1700

1702 French and British rivalries result in outbreak of Queen Anne's War

Anglo-French Hostilities

THROUGHOUT THE 18th century, hostilities between the French and English in Europe continued to spill over into the New World. By 1713, Britain ruled Nova Scotia, Newfoundland, and the Hudson Bay region and, after the Seven Years War in 1763, all of French Canada.

Anglo-French tensions were exacerbated by religion: the English were largely Protestant and almost all of the French Catholic. This resulted in the colony of Quebec being divided in 1791 into the mainly English-speaking Upper Canada (now Ontario), and majority French-speaking Lower Canada (now Quebec).

Taking advantage of the British conflict with Napoleon in Europe, the Americans invaded Canada in 1812. They were defeated by 1814, but the threat of another invasion colored Canadian history during much of the 19th century.

The Acadian Exodus
French-speaking Acadians were ruthlessly expelled from their homes by the British in the 1750s (see pp58–9).

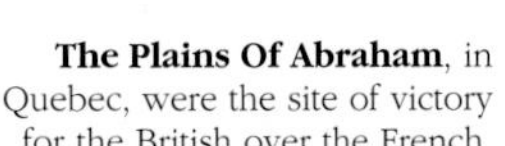

The Plains Of Abraham, in Quebec, were the site of victory for the British over the French.

General Isaac Brock
Brock's heroic exploits during the War of 1812, such as the capture of an American post at Detroit, buoyed the spirits of the Canadian people.

THE SEVEN YEARS WAR

The famous Battle of the Plains of Abraham in 1759 was the last between British and French forces to take place in Canada. The British launched a surprise assault from the cliffs of the St. Lawrence River at a site now known as Wolfe's Cove. Louis Joseph de Montcalm, the French commander, was defeated by General Wolfe and his army. Both generals were killed, and Quebec fell to the British. The war finally ended in 1763 with the Treaty of Paris, which ceded all French-Canadian territory to the British.

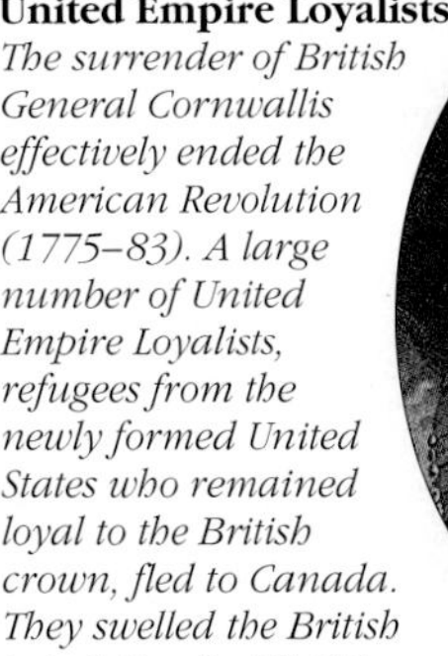

United Empire Loyalists
The surrender of British General Cornwallis effectively ended the American Revolution (1775–83). A large number of United Empire Loyalists, refugees from the newly formed United States who remained loyal to the British crown, fled to Canada. They swelled the British population by 50,000.

Louisbourg
The French fortress of Louisbourg on Cape Breton Island was built between 1720 and 1740, and was the head-quarters for the French fleet until it was destroyed by the British in 1758. Today, the restored fortress is a popular tourist attraction (see pp92–3).

General Wolfe
The distinguished British soldier, shown here fatally wounded at the Plains of Abraham, preceded his 1759 victory in Quebec with the taking of the French fortress, Louisbourg, in 1758.

General Wolfe's forces sailed up the St. Lawrence river overnight, allowing them to surprise the enemy at Quebec.

Wolfe's infantry scrambled up a steep, wooded cliff. They had to defeat an enemy post before the waiting boats of soldiers could join the battle.

French Rights
In 1774 the British government passed the Quebec Act, granting French-Canadians religious and linguistic freedom and giving official recognition to French Civil Law.

TIMELINE

1743 The La Vérendrye brothers discover the Rocky Mountains

1755 Expulsion of the Acadians from Nova Scotia

1758 Louisbourg, the French fortress on Cape Breton Island, falls to the British

Sir Alexander Mackenzie

1793 English explorer and fur trader Alexander Mackenzie crosses the Rockies and reaches the Pacific Ocean by land

1720 — 1740 — 1760 — 1780 — 1800

1713 British gain control of Nova Scotia, Newfoundland, and Hudson Bay

1759 Wolfe defeats de Montcalm in the Battle of the Plains of Abraham

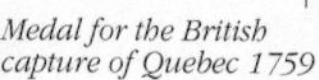

Medal for the British capture of Quebec 1759

1760 Montreal falls to the British

1774 The Quebec Act grants French colonists rights to their own language and religion

1812 The US at war with Britain until the Treaty of Ghent in 1814

A British Dominion

Representatives meet in London to discuss terms of union

Twenty-five years after the War of 1812 ended in stalemate, violence of a different sort flared in Canada. The English wanted supremacy in voting power and to limit the influence of the Catholic Church. By 1834 the French occupied one quarter of public positions, although they made up three-quarters of the population. Rebellions in Upper and Lower Canada during 1837–38 were prompted by both French and British reformers, who wanted accountable government with a broader electorate. The response of the British Government was to join together the two colonies into a united Province of Canada in 1840. The newly created assembly won increased independence when, in 1849, the majority Reform Party passed an Act compensating the 1837 rebels. Although the Governor-General, Lord Elgin, disapproved, he chose not to use his veto. The Province of Canada now had "responsible government," (the right to pass laws without the sanction of the British colonial representative.)

The rest of British North America, however, remained a series of self-governing colonies that, despite their economic successes, were anxious about American ambitions. Such fears were reinforced by a series of Fenian Raids on Canadian territory between 1866–70. (The Fenians were New York Irish immigrants hoping to take advantage of French Canada's anti-British feeling to help them to secure independence for Ireland.) The issue of confederation was raised and discussed at conferences held from 1864 onward. Only by uniting in the face of this common menace, said the politicians, could the British colonies hope to fend off these incursions.

Northwest rebel Louis Riel

The new country was born on July 1, 1867. Under the terms of the British North America Act the new provinces of Quebec (Canada East) and Ontario (Canada West) were created, and along with Nova Scotia and New Brunswick became the Dominion of Canada. The new government was based on the British parliamentary system, with a governor-general (the Crown's representative), a House of Commons, and a Senate. Parliament received power to legislate over matters of national interest; defense, criminal law, and trade, while the provinces ruled over local issues such as education.

The Métis Rebellion

Following confederation, the government purchased from the Hudson's Bay Company the area known as Rupert's Land, which extended south and west inland for thousands of kilometers from Hudson's Bay.

Timeline

- **1818** Canada's border with the United States is defined as the 49th Parallel from Lake of the Woods to the Rocky Mountains
- **1820**
- **1821** Merger of Hudson's Bay and North West Companies
- **1830**
- **1837** A general feeling that the government is not democratic leads to violent but unsuccessful rebellions in Upper and Lower Canada
- **1839** Lord Durham issues a report recommending the establishment of responsible government and the union of Upper and Lower Canada to speed the assimilation of French-speaking Canadians
- **1840**
- **1841** An Act of Union unites Upper and Lower Canada as the Province of Canada
- **1849** The boundary of the 49th Parallel is extended to the Pacific Ocean
- **1850**

The Métis people (descendants of mostly French fur-traders and natives) who lived here were alarmed by the expected influx of English-speaking settlers. In 1869, local leader Louis Riel took up their cause and led the first of two uprisings. The Red River Rebellion was an attempt to defend what the Métis saw as their ancestral rights to this land. A compromise was reached in 1870 and the new province of, Manitoba was created. However, many Métis moved westward to what was to become the province of Saskatchewan in 1905.

Riel was elected to the House of Commons in 1874 but, in 1875, he emigrated to the US. The government's intention to settle the west led the Métis of Saskatchewan to call Riel home in 1884 to lead the North-West Rebellion. It was short-lived. Defeated at Batoche in May, Riel was ultimately charged with treason and hanged in Regina on November 16, 1885.

Driving home the last spike of the Canadian Pacific Railroad, 1885

Birth of a Nation

The defeat of the Métis and the building of a transcontinental railroad were crucial factors in the settlement of the west. British Columbia, a Crown colony since 1858, chose to join the Dominion in 1871 on the promise of a rail link with the rest of the country. The first train to run from Montreal to Vancouver in 1886 paved the way for hundreds of thousands of settlers in the West in the late 1800s. Prince Edward Island, Canada's smallest province, joined the Dominion in 1873.

In 1898, the northern territory of Yukon was established to ensure Canadian jurisdiction over that area during the Klondike gold rush *(see pp46–7)*. In 1905, the provinces of Saskatchewan and Alberta were created out of Rupert's Land, with the residual area becoming the Northwest Territories. Each province gained its own premier and elected assembly. By 1911 new immigrants had doubled the populations of the new provinces.

For the time being, Newfoundland preferred to remain a British colony, but in 1949 it was brought into Canada as the country's tenth province.

The Métis People

The Métis people of central Canada were descended from native and largely French stock. Proud of their unique culture, this seminomadic group considered themselves separate from the rest of the Dominion. With their own social structure and lifestyle dependent almost entirely on buffalo hunting, they resisted integration. They responded to the unification of the country with two failed rebellions. The Métis won no land rights and were condemned to a life of poverty or enforced integration.

Métis hunt buffalo on the Prairie

Sir John MacDonald

1867 Dominion of Canada; Sir John A. Macdonald is Canada's first Prime Minister

1870 The Red River Rebellion is quashed by General Wolseley, and the the province of Manitoba is created

General Wolseley

1886 Gold found on the Forty-Mile River

1860 | **1870** | **1880**

1866 The Fenians raid Canadian territory to divert British troops from Ireland

1855 Queen Victoria designates Ottawa as capital of the Province of Canada

Canadian Pacific

1885 Riel leads the North-West Rebellion. The Métis are defeated at Batoche, and Riel is hanged in Regina. The last spike of the transcontinental railroad is put in place

The Klondike Gold Rush

THERE HAD BEEN rumors of gold in the Yukon since the 1830s, but the harsh land, together with the Chilkoot Indians' guarding of their territory, kept most prospectors away. Then, on August 16, 1896 the most frenzied and fabled gold rush in Canadian history started when George Washington Carmack and two Indian friends, Snookum Jim and Tagish Charlie, found a large gold nugget in the river they later named Bonanza Creek. For the next two years at least 100,000 prospectors set out for the new gold fields.

Only about 40,000 prospectors actually made it. Most took boats as far as Skagway or Dyea, on the Alaskan Panhandle, then struggled across the Coast Mountains by the White or Chilkoot passes to reach the headwaters of the Yukon River. From here boats took them 500 km (310 miles) to the gold fields. In all, the gold rush generated Can $50 million, although few miners managed to hold onto their fortunes.

Klondike Entrepreneur
Alex McDonald, a Nova Scotian with a canny business sense, bought up the claims of discouraged miners and hired others to work them for him. Known as "King of the Klondike," he made millions.

Skagway, Alaska
The jumping-off point for the Klondike was the tent city of Skagway. There were saloons and swindlers on every corner, and gunfire in the streets was commonplace. The most famous con man was Jefferson Randolph "Soapy" Smith, who died in a shoot-out in 1898.

The sternwheeler was a steamboat driven by a single paddle at the back.

The Yukon River rises in British Columbia's Coast Mountains, winding for 3,000 km (1,900 miles) to Alaska.

The Mounties Take Control
The safety of the Klondike Gold Rush was secured by Canada's red-coated Mounties. Thanks to them, the rush was remarkably peaceful. A small force of 19 Mounties led by Inspector Charles Constantine were sent to the Yukon in 1895, but by 1898 there were 285, operating out of Fort Herchmer at Dawson.

Klondike Fever
The outside world learnt of the riches in July 1897, when miners docked in Seattle and San Francisco hauling gold. In no time, Klondike fever was an epidemic.

Dawson City
As the gold rush developed in the summer of 1897, the small tent camp at the junction of the Klondike and Yukon rivers grew to a population of 5,000. A year on it had reached 40,000, making Dawson City one of the largest cities in Canada.

Steamboats and other craft brought thousands of prospectors up the long Yukon River to Dawson, where the boats jostled for space at the dock.

Capturing the Mood
Even literature had a place in the Klondike. The gold rush inspired novels such as Call of the Wild *(1903) by Jack London (shown here) and the 1907 verses* Songs of a Sourdough *by poet Robert Service.*

Crossing the Yukon River

The ferocious Yukon River rapids in Miles Canyon smashed so many boats to splinters that the Mounties decreed that every boat had to be guided by a competent pilot. Experienced sailors could earn up to Can$100 a trip taking boats through the canyon. Past the canyon, only one more stretch of rapids remained before the Yukon's waters grew calmer all the way to Dawson City.

Timeline

1896 George Carmack and two friends, Tagish Charlie and Snookum Jim, strike it rich on Bonanza Creek. Liberal Wilfred Laurier elected as the country's first French-Canadian prime minister

1897 Steamers from Alaska carry word of the strike to San Francisco and Seattle, setting off a frenzied gold rush

Klondike News 1898

1898 The Yukon is given territorial status, partly to assert British authority in the eyes of the Americans from neighboring Alaska

1899 Gold is discovered in Nome, Alaska, and Dawson begins to shrink as people leave to follow the new dream of riches farther west

1896 — 1898 — 1899

New optimism and arrivals

The impact of the Klondike gold rush was felt all over Canada. It led to an expansion of cities such as Vancouver and Edmonton, and the establishment of the Yukon territory. A period of optimism was ushered in by the new Liberal government, elected in 1896 under the first French-Canadian premier, Wilfred Laurier, who firmly believed that "the 20th century will belong to Canada."

The new central Canadian provinces provided a home for European immigrants eager to farm large tracts of prairie land. By 1913, this wave of immigration had peaked at 400,000. Finally Canada began to profit from a prosperous world economy and establish itself as an industrial and agricultural power.

1914 poster promoting immigration to Canada

Supporting the Allies

The first test of the fledgling nation came in 1899, when the Boer War broke out in South Africa; the second in 1914, when Europe entered World War I. Initially, Laurier was cautious in his approach to the South African crisis, but pressure from the English-speaking population led to the dispatch of 1,000 soldiers to Cape Town in 1899. Before the Boer War ended in 1902, some 6,000 men had made the journey to the South African battlefields. They returned with a stronger sense of national identity than many of their compatriots at home had expected. But, while the experience of war infused some with a new sense of national unity, it also laid bare divisions. There were fights between French- and English-speaking university students, as well as disputes among Ontario conservatives and French-speaking Quebec politicians.

Before matters could come to a head, another crisis loomed. Joining the Allies in Flanders, the Canadians found renewed glory during World War I. Canadian pilot, Billy Bishop, was the Allies' greatest air ace, and another Canadian, Roy Brown, was the pilot credited with downing the Red Baron. Canadian troops were the heroes of two major battles, Ypres (1915) and Vimy Ridge (1917). When peace was declared on November 11, 1918, there were 175,000 Canadian wounded, and 60,000 had died for their country.

Canadians advance at Paardeberg in the Boer War, 1900

Independent Status

Canada had played so significant a role during World War I that it gained recognition as an independent country, winning representation in the League of Nations. This independence was confirmed in 1931 with the passing of the Statute of Westminster,

Timeline

1899 The first Canadians are sent to fight in the Boer War

1903 Canada loses the Alaska boundary dispute when a British tribunal sides with the US

1911 Robert Borden and the Conservatives win federal election, defeating Liberal party leader, Wilfred Laurier on the issue of Reciprocity

1914 Britain declares war on Germany, automatically drawing Canada into the conflict in Europe. The War Measures Act orders German and Austro-Hungarian Canadians to carry identity cards

1917 Munitions ship explodes in Halifax harbor wiping out 5 sq km (2 sq miles) of the town, killing 2,000, and injuring 9,000

1918 Canadians break through the German trenches at Amiens beginning "Canada's Hundred Days"

1922 Canadians Charles Best, Frederick Banting, and John MacLeod win the Nobel Prize for the discovery of insulin

1900 | 1905 | 1910 | 1915 | 1920

Dr. Frederick Banting

which gave Canada political independence from Britain and created a commonwealth of sovereign nations under a single crown.

However, national optimism was curtailed by the Great Depression that originated with the Wall Street Crash in 1929. Drought laid waste the farms of Alberta, Saskatchewan, and Manitoba. One in four workers was unemployed, and the sight of men riding boxcars in a fruitless search for work became common.

Soup kitchen during the Great Depression

World War II

The need to supply the Allied armies during World War II boosted Canada out of the Depression. Canada's navy played a crucial role in winning the Battle of the Atlantic (1940–3) and thousands of Allied airmen were trained in Canada. Canadian regiments soon gained a reputation for bravery, for example, many died in the fiercly fought 1942 raid on Dieppe. Thousands battled up the boot of Italy, while others stormed ashore at Normandy. In the bitter fighting that followed, the Second and Third Canadian Divisions took more casualties holding the beachheads than any unit under British command. It was also the Canadians who liberated much of Holland.

The Canadian prime minister of the day was the Liberal, Mackenzie King (1935–48). He ordered a plebiscite to allow the sending of conscripts overseas, monitored the building of the Alaska Highway *(see pp260–61)* and, aided by his minister of munitions and supply, he directed a massive war effort.

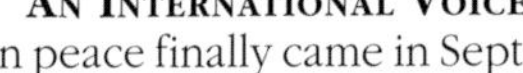

An International Voice

When peace finally came in September 1945, Canada had the third-largest navy in the world, the fourth-largest air force, and a standing army of 730,000 men. Although the price Canada had paid during World War II was high – 43,000 people died in action and the national debt quadrupled – the nation found itself in a strong position. A larger population was better able to cope with its losses and much of the debt had been spent on doubling the gross national product, creating durable industries that would power the postwar economy.

German prisoners captured by Canadian Infantry on D-Day, June 6, 1944

1926 The Balfour Report defines British dominions as autonomous and equal in status

Air Canada logo

1937 Trans-Canada Air Lines, now Air Canada, begins regular flights

1942 Around 22,000 Japanese Canadians are stripped of non-portable possessions and interned

1944 Canadian troops push farther inland than any other allied units on D-Day

1925 | 1930 | 1935 | 1940 | 1945

1929 The Great Depression begins

1931 The Statute of Westminster grants Canada full legislative authority

1941 Hong Kong falls to the Japanese, and Canadians are taken as POWs

1945 World War II ends. Canada joins the UN. Canada's first nuclear reactor goes on line in Chalk River, Ontario

Large Canadian grain carrier approaches the St. Lawrence Seaway in 1959 – its inaugural year

Since World War II, Canada's economy has continued to expand. This growth, combined with government social programs such as old-age security, unemployment insurance, and medicare, means Canadians have one of the world's highest standards of living and a quality of life which draws immigrants from around the world. Since 1945, those immigrants have been made up largely of southern Europeans, Asians, South Americans, and Caribbean islanders, all of whom have enriched the country's multicultural status.

Internationally, the nation's reputation and influence have grown. Canada has participated in the United Nations since its inception in 1945 and is the only nation to have taken part in almost all of the UN's major peacekeeping operations. Perhaps it is only fitting that it was a future Canadian prime minister, Lester Pearson, who fostered the peacekeeping process when he won the Nobel Peace Prize in 1957 for helping resolve the Suez Crisis. Canada is also a respected member of the British Commonwealth, la Francophonie, the Group of Eight industrialized nations, the OAS (Organization of American States), and NATO (North Atlantic Treaty Organization).

The French–English Divide

Given all these accomplishments, it seems ironic that the last quarter of a century has also seen Canadians deal with fundamental questions of national identity and unity. The driving force of this debate continues to be the historic English–French rivalry. The best-known players of these late 20th-century events are Prime Minister Pierre Trudeau (1968–84) and Quebec Premier René Lévesque (1968–87).

When Jean Lesage was elected as Quebec Premier in 1960, he instituted the "Quiet Revolution" – a series of reforms that increased provincial power. However, this was not enough to prevent the rise of revolutionary nationalists. In October 1970, British Trade Commissioner James Cross and Quebec Labor Minister Pierre Laporte were kidnapped by the French-Canadian terrorist organization, the

Quebec Premier René Levesque and Canadian Prime Minister Pierre Trudeau during the 1980 referendum

Timeline

1949 Newfoundland joins the Confederation. Canada joins NATO

1959 Prime Minister John Diefenbaker cancels the AVRO Arrow project, losing 14,000 jobs

The AVRO Arrow Delta High speed aircraft

1967 Expo '67 is held in Montreal and Canada celebrates its Centennial

1950 | 1955 | 1960 | 1965 | 1970

1950 The Canadian Army Special Force joins UN soldiers in the Korean War

Lester Pearson

1957 Lester Pearson wins the Nobel Peace Prize for helping resolve the Suez Crisis

1965 Canada's new flag is inaugurated after a bitter political debate

1972 Canada wins the first hockey challenge against the Soviets, touching off a huge nationwide celebration

1990 demonstration for Quebec independence in Montreal

Front du Libération de Québec (FLQ). Cross was rescued by police but Laporte was later found murdered. Trudeau invoked the War Measures Act, sent troops into Montreal, and banned the FLQ. His actions eventually led to nearly 500 arrests.

Trudeau devoted his political life to federalism, fighting separatism, and giving Canada its own constitution. In contrast, Lesage's successor, René Lévesque, campaigned for a 1980 referendum in Quebec on whether that province should become independent. A majority voted against, but the results were far from decisive, and separatism continued to dominate the country's political agenda. However, in 1982, the Constitution Act fulfilled Trudeau's dream, entrenching federal civil rights and liberties such as female equality.

A Move toward Conservatism

In 1984 the leader of the Progressive Conservatives, Brian Mulroney, won the general election with the largest majority in Canadian history. Dismissive of Trudeau's policies, Mulroney's emphasis was on closer links with Europe and, in particular, the US. In the years that followed, two major efforts were made to reform the constitutional system. The 1987 Meech Lake Accord aimed to recognize Quebec's claims to special status on the basis of its French culture, but Mulroney failed to implement the amendment since it did not obtain the consent of all provinces. When the Inuit began campaigning for more parliamentary representation it led to the Charlottetown Accord of 1991, which raised the issue of aboriginal self-government. The Accord was rejected in a national referendum held in 1992.

Today, many of these reforms are finally in place and hopefully aiding Canadian unity. Quebec's French heritage has official recognition, and the Inuit rule their own territory of Nunavut.

Independence for Nunavut

On April 1, 1999, Canada gained its newest territory, the Inuit homeland of Nunavut. The campaign for an Inuit state began in the 1960s when the Inuit desire for a political identity of their own was added to aboriginal land claims. Nunavut's first Premier is 34-year-old Paul Okalik, leader of the first-ever Inuit majority government over an 85 percent Inuit population. English is being replaced as the official language by the native Inuktitut, and traditional Inuit fishing and hunting skills are being reintroduced. By 2012, the federal government will invest over Can$1 billion in public services for Nunavut.

Signing ceremony in Iqaluit, April 1, 1999

1976 The Olympic games are held in Montreal under tight security. René Lévesque and the separatist *Parti Québecois* win a provincial election

1979 225,000 people of Mississauga, Ontario, are evacuated after a train derailment threatens to release clouds of chlorine gas

1984 Aboard the US shuttle *Challenger*, Marc Garneau becomes the first Canadian in space

1988 Calgary hosts the XV Winter Olympics

1989 The Canada–US Free Trade agreement goes into effect

1991 Canadian forces join the battle to drive Saddam Hussein's Iraqi troops from Kuwait

Canadian & Nunavut flags

1997 A 13-km (8-mile) bridge connecting Prince Edward Island to the mainland is opened

1999 The Inuit territory of Nunavut established

1975 | 1980 | 1985 | 1990 | 1995 | 2000

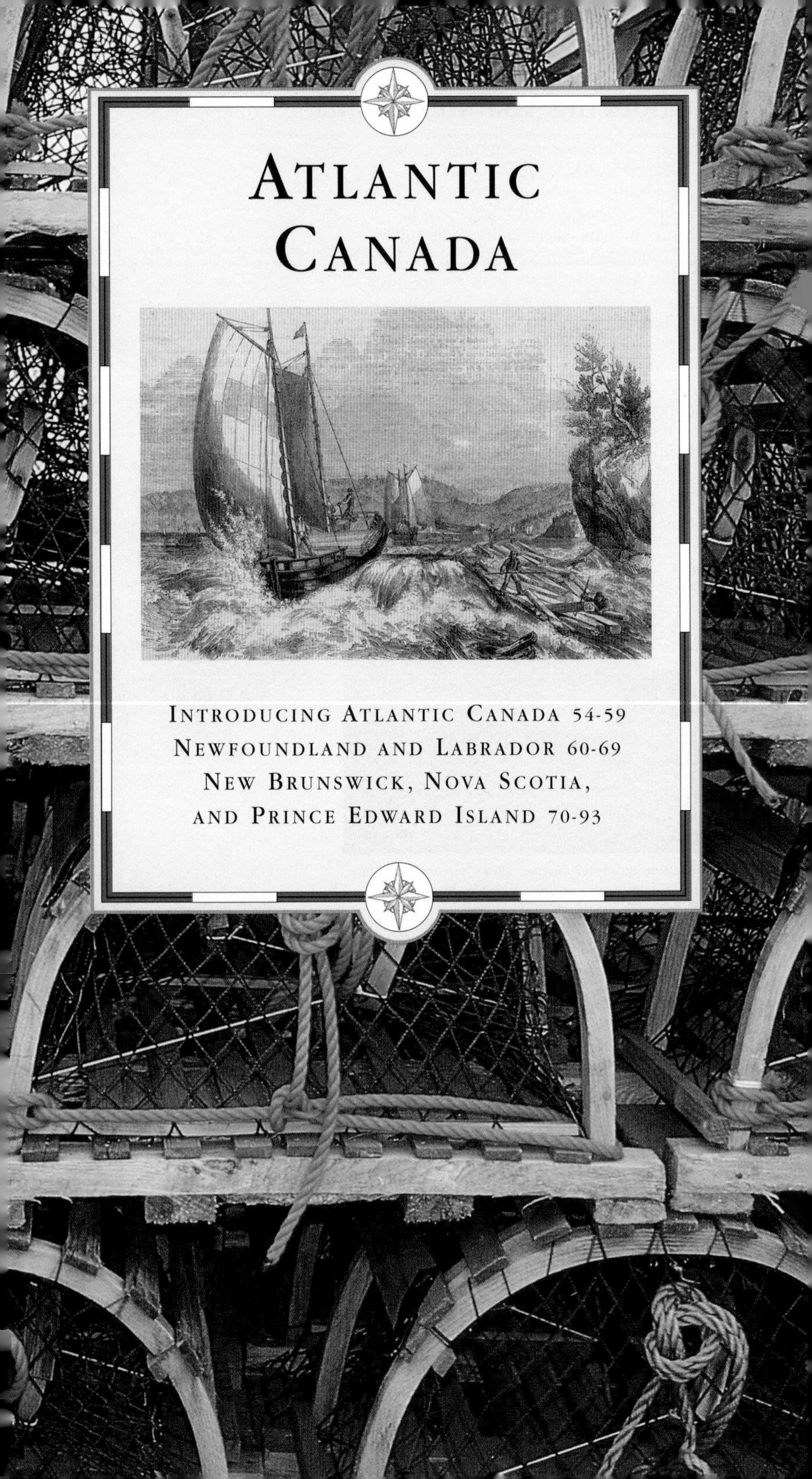

ATLANTIC CANADA

Introducing Atlantic Canada

ATLANTIC CANADA IS renowned for rocky coastlines, picturesque fishing villages, sun-warmed beaches, cozy country inns, and friendly people. Each province has a distinctive cultural flavor. In northeastern New Brunswick, French-speaking Acadian culture flourishes while the south coast offers the pristine, tide-carved beauty of the Bay of Fundy. Nova Scotia, famous for world-class attractions, such as the 18th-century Fortress Louisbourg and the stunning natural scenery of the Cabot Trail, is also home to historic towns like seafaring Lunenburg. Prince Edward Island is known for its emerald-green farmland, fine sandy beaches, and rich lobster catches. In Newfoundland, the mountains of Gros Morne National Park rise 800 m (2,625 ft) above sparkling blue fjords. Labrador offers an imposing and stunning coastal landscape, often with a backdrop of glittering icebergs.

Acadian homesteads still flourish after 400 years of a unique culture that dominates northeastern New Brunswick

The fresh maritime scenery of Two Islands beach, known as "The Brothers" for its twin offshore islands, in Parrsboro, Nova Scotia

GETTING AROUND

Air Canada and Air Nova offer regularly scheduled flights throughout the region. The Trans-Canada Highway (TCH) travels to all four provinces, but not through Newfoundland and Labrador. The new Confederation Bridge connects Prince Edward Island to Cape Tormentine, New Brunswick. Newfoundland must be accessed by air or by ferry from Sydney, Nova Scotia, to either Port aux Basques or Argentia. A ferry also travels between Nova Scotia and Bar Harbor, Maine. Bus services cross the provinces, but many areas are remote so availability should be checked.

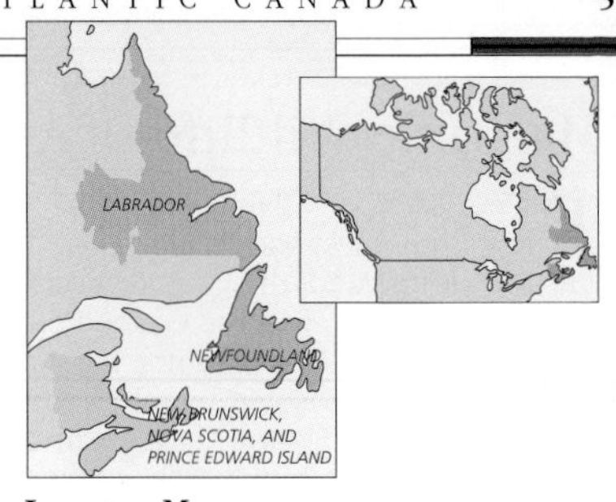

LOCATOR MAP

KEY

- Highway
- Major road
- Minor road
- River

SEE ALSO

- ***Where to stay*** pp344–346
- ***Where to eat*** pp364–366

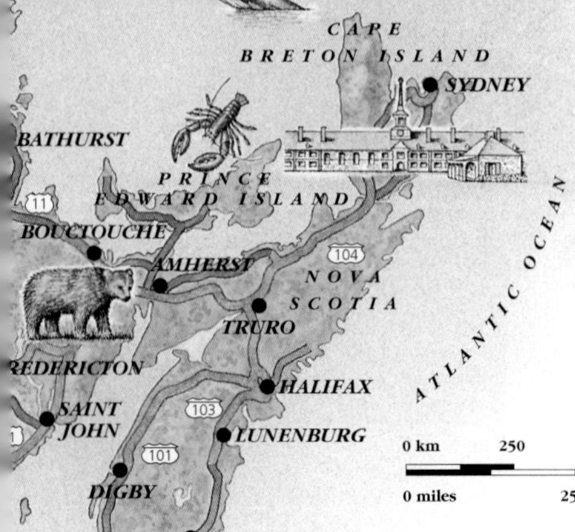

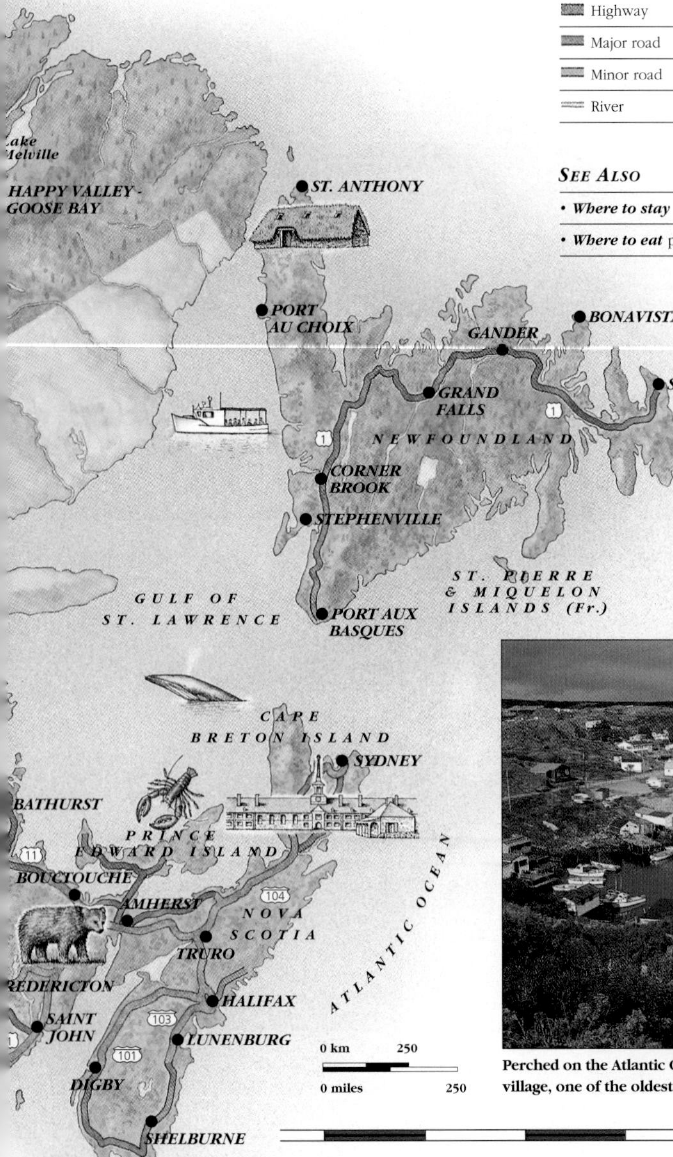

Perched on the Atlantic Coast, Quidi Vidi village, one of the oldest in Newfoundland

Maritime Wildlife of Atlantic Canada

THE PROVINCES OF Atlantic Canada – Nova Scotia, New Brunswick, and Prince Edward Island – along with Newfoundland, the Quebec north shore of the St. Lawrence River, and the Gaspé Peninsula, constitute a rich and diverse maritime habitat for wildlife. The climate is dominated by the ocean, being influenced by the moderating Gulf Stream that flows north from the Caribbean and by the southward flow of icy waters, often bearing icebergs, from the Canadian Arctic. The terrain of the eastern Canadian coastline varies from rocky headlands to soft, sandy beaches. Both sea and land mammals inhabit this coast, as do hundreds of species of seabird.

***The piping plover** is a small, endangered shore bird that lives and breeds along the Atlantic coast of Canada.*

SHORELINE HABITAT

The maritime shoreline encompasses rocky cliffs, sandy beaches, and salt-flat marshes. Moving a little inland, the landscape shifts to bog, forest, and meadow. It is an inviting habitat for many smaller mammals such as raccoons and beavers, and also provides a home for a diversity of bird life. Where the shoreline meets the water, fertile intertidal zones are a habitat for mollusks, algae, and invertebrae.

***The river otter** lives in "families," frequenting rivers, lakes, and ocean bays, in its search for fish.*

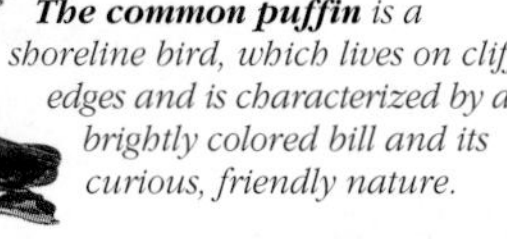

***The common puffin** is a shoreline bird, which lives on cliff edges and is characterized by a brightly colored bill and its curious, friendly nature.*

***The raccoon,** with its ringed tail and black-masked face, preys upon fish, crayfish, birds and their eggs.*

***The beaver,** symbol of Canada, lives in marshy woodland near the coast. It gnaws down trees, using them to build dams, its lodge, and for food.*

Ocean Habitat

The sea around Atlantic Canada is influenced by the cold Labrador Current flowing from the north, the Gulf Stream from the south, and the large outflow of fresh water at the mouth of the St. Lawrence River. The region is home to myriad ocean creatures, and the highest tides in the world at the nutrient-rich Bay of Fundy. Off Newfoundland lie the Grand Banks, once one of the Earth's richest fishing grounds. Over-fishing has endangered fish stocks, and quotas are now limited.

***Lobster**, a favorite seafood of the area, is caught in traps set near the shore. Rigid conservation rules have been put in force to protect its dwindling numbers.*

***The adult blue whale** is the world's largest mammal, reaching up to 30 m (100 ft) long. Today, whale-watching is a growing eco-tourism enterprise, particularly off the east coast, where this and other species congregate.*

***The Atlantic salmon**, unlike its Pacific cousins, returns to its home stream to spawn several times during its lifetime. Atlantic salmon are renowned sport fish* (see p21).

***Bottle-nosed dolphins**, characterized by their long beaks and "smiles," live off the east coast, in both New Brunswick and Nova Scotia.*

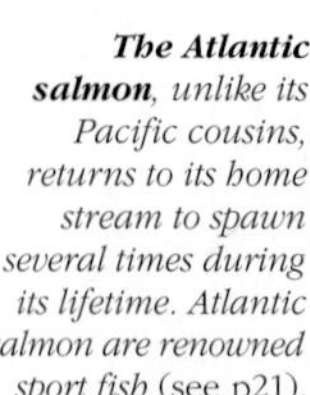

Seabirds of the Atlantic Coast

The maritime coast of eastern Canada is a perfect environment for seabirds. Rocky cliffs and headlands provide ideal rookeries. The rich coastal waters and intertidal zones ensure a generous larder for many species, including the cormorant and storm petrel. Some Atlantic Coast seabirds are at risk due to environmental changes, but puffins and razorbills, in particular, continue to thrive.

***The double-crested cormorant** or "sea crow," as it is sometimes known, is a diving fishing bird, capable of capturing food as deep as 10 m (30 ft) under water.*

***Leach's storm-petrel** is part of the Tubenose family of birds, whose acute sense of smell helps them navigate while out at sea.*

The Acadians

FEW STORIES SURROUNDING the settlement of the New World evoke as many feelings of tragedy and triumph as the tale of the Acadians. Colonizing Nova Scotia's fertile Annapolis Valley in the 1600s, 500 French settlers adopted the name Acadie, hoping to establish an ideal pastoral land. They prospered and, by 1750, numbered 14,000, becoming the dominant culture. The threat of this enclave proved too much for a province run by the British, and in 1755 the Acadians were expelled overseas, many to the US. When England and France made peace in 1763, the Acadians slowly returned. Today their French-speaking culture still thrives in coastal villages.

***Acadian women** play a part in summer festivals, displaying local woolcraft and linen textiles.*

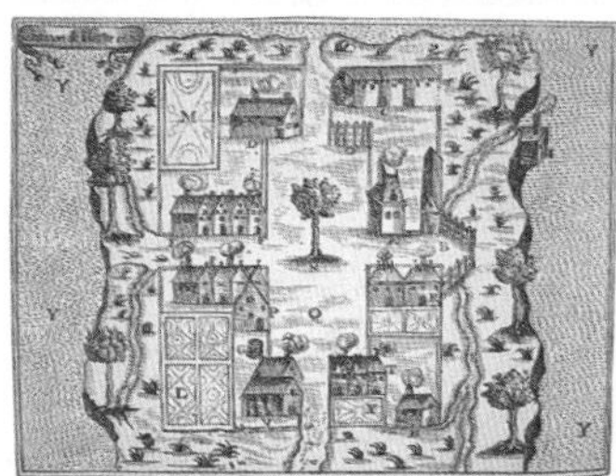

***Ile Sainte-Croix** was the earliest Acadian settlement, established by the French in New Brunswick in 1604. The neat, spacious layout of the village is typical.*

ACADIAN FARMING

As hardworking farmers, Acadians cleared the land of the Annapolis Valley, built villages, and developed an extensive system of dikes to reclaim the rich farmland from tidal waters. Summer crops were carefully harvested for the winter; potatoes and vegetables were put in cellars, and hay stored to feed cattle and goats. By the 19th century, Acadian farmers had expanded their crop range to include tobacco and flax.

An important crop, hay was raked into "*chafauds*," spiked haystacks that dried in the fields for use as winter animal feed.

***The Embarkation of the Acadians** took place in August 1755. British troops brutally rounded up the Acadians for enforced deportation. Over 6,000 Acadians were put on boats, some bound for the US, where they became the Cajuns of today. Others returned in later years, and today their descendants live in villages throughout Atlantic Canada.*

***The Acadian people** maintained a traditional farming and fishing lifestyle for centuries, re-created today at the Village Historique Acadien* (see p75).

***The Church of Saint Anne** in Sainte-Anne-du-Ruisseau represents Acadian style in its fresh simplicity and elegance. Catholicism was very important to the Acadians, who turned to their priests for succour during the 1755 diaspora.*

***Acadian musicians** have reflected their culture since the 17th century. Playing lively violin and guitar folk music, they are known for their upbeat tunes and ballads of unrequited love and social dispossession.*

Acadian life revolved around the farmsteads in each community. Men tilled the fields and fished while women helped with the annual harvest.

Henry Wadsworth Longfellow

One of the most popular poets of the 19th century, both in the US and Europe, the American Henry Longfellow (1807–82) is best known for his long, bittersweet narrative poems. Based on the trials and injustices of the Acadian civilization, *Evangeline*, published in 1847, traces the paths of a young Acadian couple. The poem, now regarded as a classic, stirringly records Evangeline's tragic loss in this land intended as an idyll when their love was destroyed through the upheavals and expulsion of the 18th century: "Loud from its rocky caverns, the deep-faced neighbouring ocean [sings], List to the mournful tradition sung by the pines of the Forest, ... List to a Tale of Love in Acadie, home of the happy."

Newfoundland and Labrador

With towering peaks, vast landscapes, and 17,000 kms (10,500 miles) of rugged coastline, Newfoundland and Labrador displays wild, open spaces and grand spectacles of nature. In this captivating land, massive icebergs drift lazily along the coast, whales swim in sparkling bays, and moose graze placidly in flat open marshes. Newfoundland's west coast offers some of the most dramatic landscapes east of the Rockies. The granite mountains of Gros Morne National Park shelter deep fjords, while the eastern part of the island has a more rounded terrain, featuring the bays and inlets of Terra Nova National Park. Part of the area's appeal is retracing the history of past cultures that have settled here, including Maritime Archaic Indians at Port au Choix, Vikings at L'Anse-Aux-Meadows, and Basque whalers at Red Bay in the Labrador Straits.

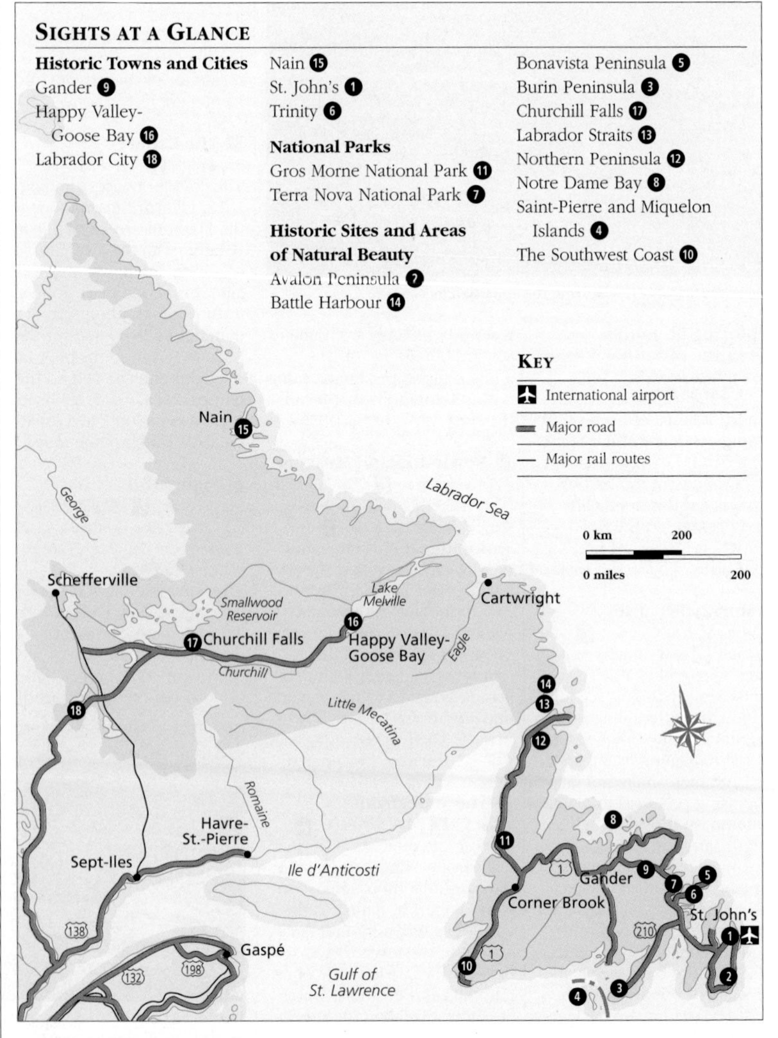

◁ **The weathered seaside fishing villages of Newfoundland have relied on the fishing trade for centuries**

St. John's ❶

Pendant in local museum

ITALIAN EXPLORER John Cabot *(see p40)* aroused great interest in Newfoundland (after his 1497 voyage on behalf of Henry VII of England) when he described "a sea so full of fish that a basket thrown overboard is hauled back brimming with cod." Cabot started a rush to the New World that made St. John's a center of the fishing industry, and North America's oldest and liveliest settlement. Today, St. John's still bustles with the commerce of the sea: fishing, oil exploration, and the ships of a hundred nations waiting to be serviced. The people of St. John's are known for their friendliness, a delightful counterpoint to the harsh, rugged beauty that surrounds this historic town.

Downtown St. John's, seen from the approach by sea

Exploring St. John's

The capital of Newfoundland is easily explored on foot. Most of the sights are within a short distance of each other moving east along Water Street. Approaching by sea offers the best view of the harbor, in particular the steep cliff-lined passage on the east side where pastel-colored old houses cling to the rocks.

Murray Premises

cnr Water St. & Beck's Cove. (709) 739 8899. *8am–10:30pm daily.*

At the west end of Water Street stands Murray Premises. Built in 1846, these rambling brick and timberframe buildings are the last remaining examples of the large mercantile and fish-processing premises that were common on the St. John's waterfront. Murray Premises once bustled with the work of shipping cod to world markets. The complex narrowly escaped destruction in a huge fire that engulfed much of the city in 1892, and the buildings mark the western boundary of the fire's devastation. Now a Provincial Historic Site, the restored buildings are home to several boutiques, offices, and a fine seafood restaurant, hung with photographs that recall the busy town of the 1900s.

Newfoundland Museum

285 Duckworth St. *(709) 729 2329.* *9am–5pm Tue, Wed, Fri; 9am–9pm Thu; 10am–6pm Sat & Sun.* *Mon.*

This museum illustrates the province's history over the past 9,000 years. The prehistory of Newfoundland is illustrated with artifacts excavated locally. Focusing on colonial times, restorations range from humble fishing cottages to the elegant drawing rooms of early townspeople. There is also a popular gallery of native Indian art.

The Waterfront

Water St. *(709) 576 8106.*

Tracing the edge of St. John's waterfront, Water Street is the oldest public thoroughfare in North America, dating to the late 1500s when trading first started in the town. Once a brawling wharfside lane of gin mills and brothels, Water Street and Duckworth Street now offer an array of colorful gift shops, art galleries, and some of Newfoundland's top restaurants. Also along the waterfront is Harbour Drive, a great place to stroll or relax. Nearby George Street is the hub of the city's nightlife.

East End

King's Bridge Rd. *(709) 576 8106.*

The East End is one of St. John's most architecturally rich neighborhoods, with narrow, cobblestone streets and elegant homes. Commissariat House, built in 1836, was once the home of 19th-century British officials. This simple but elegant historic dwelling is now a provincial museum. Nearby Government House, built during the 1820s, is the official residence of the province's Lieutenant Governor.

The Battery

Battery Rd. *(709) 576 8106.*

The colorful houses clinging to sheer cliffs at the entrance to the Harbour are known as the Battery. With the look and feel of a 19th-century fishing village, this is one of St. John's most photographed sites. The community is named for the military fortifications built here over centuries to defend the harbor. Local residents used the battery's guns in 1763 to fight off Dutch pirate ships.

Signal Hill

Signal Hill Rd. *(709) 772 5367.* *Interpretation Centre: Jun–Sep: 8:30am–8pm; Sep–May: 8:30am–4:30pm.*

This lofty rise of land presents spectacular views of the open Atlantic, the rocky harbor entrance, and the city of St. John's curled in historic splendor around the town harbor.

View of Signal Hill from St. John's picturesque fishing harbor

The Cabot Tower as it rises above Signal Hill over the harbor

Cabot Tower

Signal Hill Rd. *(709) 772 5367.* *Jun–Sep: 8:30am–8pm; Sep–May: 8:30am–4:30pm.*

The building of Cabot Tower at the top of Signal Hill began in 1897 to celebrate the 400th anniversary of Cabot's arrival. On summer weekends, soldiers in period dress perform 19th-century marching drills, with firing muskets and cannon. It was here that another Italian, Guglielmo Marconi, received the first transatlantic wireless signal in 1901.

Quidi Vidi Village

Quidi Vidi Village Rd. *(709) 729 2977.* *daily.*

On the other side of Signal Hill, the weathered buildings of ancient Quidi Vidi Village nestle around a small harbor. Visitors can browse through the eclectic collection of antiques for sale at Mallard Cottage, dating back to the 1750s. Above the village, the Quidi Vidi Battery was a fortified gun emplacement built in 1762 to defend the entrance of Quidi Vidi Harbour. Today, the site is a reconstruction of the small barracks that soldiers lived in. Guides in period military dress are on hand to relate tales of their lives and hardships.

Pippy Park

Nagles Place. *(709) 737 3655.* *daily.*

Visitors are sometimes startled to see moose roaming free in St. John's, but it happens often in this 1,400-ha (3,460-acre) nature park, 4 km (2 miles) from the town center. The park is also home to the ponds and gardens of the local Botanical Gardens. The only Fluvarium in North America is based here too, featuring nine underwater windows that look onto the natural activity of a rushing freshwater trout stream.

Visitors' Checklist

102,000. 6km (4 miles) N of the city. Memorial University. Argentia 130 km (80 miles) SE. St. John's City Hall, New Gower St. (709) 576 8106. St. John's Days Celebrations (Jun); Signal Hill Tattoo (Jul-Aug); Royal St. John's Regatta (Aug).

Cape Spear Lighthouse

(709) 772 5367. *mid-May–mid-Oct: daily.*

Ten km (6 miles) southeast of town, the Cape Spear National Historic Site marks the most easterly point in North America. Set atop seaside cliffs, as the ocean pounds rocks below, the majestic Cape Spear Lighthouse has long been a symbol of Newfoundland's independence. Two lighthouses sit here. The original, built in 1836 and the oldest in Newfoundland, stands beside a graceful, modern, automated lighthouse, added in 1955.

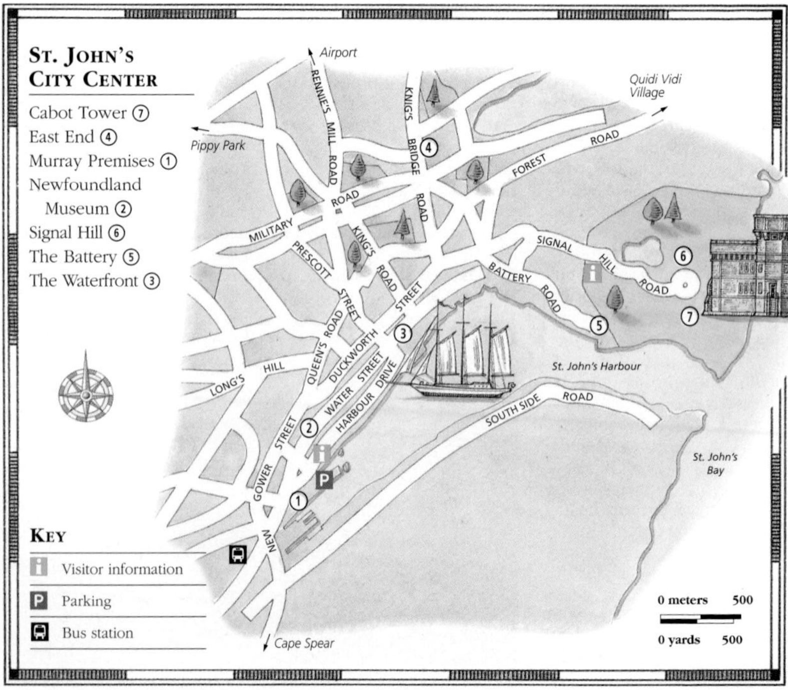

St. John's City Center

Cabot Tower ⑦
East End ④
Murray Premises ①
Newfoundland Museum ②
Signal Hill ⑥
The Battery ⑤
The Waterfront ③

Key

Visitor information
Parking
Bus station

0 meters 500
0 yards 500

Whale- and bird-watching boats tour the Avalon Peninsula frequently

Avalon Peninsula ❷

St. John's. Argentia. Dept. of Tourism, Confederation Building, St. John's (709) 729 2830.

THE PICTURESQUE community of Ferryland on the Avalon Peninsula is the site of a large-scale archeological excavation of Colony Avalon, a settlement founded by English explorer Lord Baltimore and 11 settlers in 1621. This was Baltimore's first New World venture, intended to be a self-sufficient colony engaged in fishing, agriculture, and trade, with firm principles of religious tolerance.

By the end of the following year there were 32 settlers. The population continued to grow, and for many years it was the only successful colony in the area. Although excavations to date have unearthed only five percent of the colony, it has proved to be one of the richest sources of artifacts from any early European settlement in North America. Over half a million pieces have been recovered, such as pottery, clay pipes, household implements, and structural parts of many buildings, including defensive works, a smithy, and a waterfront commercial complex. An interpretive center tells the story of the colony and a guided tour includes the chance to watch archeologists working on site and in the laboratory.

At the southern end of the peninsula, **Cape St. Mary's Ecological Reserve** is the only nesting seabird colony in the province that can be approached on foot. A short trail leads along spectacular seacliffs to a site where over 8,000 golden-headed gannets nest on a rock just a few yards over the cliff.

On the southwest side of the peninsula, overlooking the entrance to the historic French town of Placentia, visitors can stroll through **Castle Hill National Historic Site.** These French fortifications dating back to 1632 protected the town, and the site of the remains offers fine coastal views.

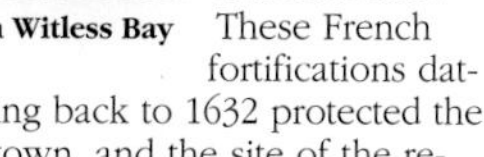

Boat-tour sign in Witless Bay

Cape St. Mary's Ecological Reserve
off Route 100. (709) 729 2429.
year round. **Interpretive Centre**
daily, May–Oct.

Castle Hill National Historic Site
Jerseyside, Placentia Bay. (709) 227 2401. Sep–mid-Jun: 8:30am–4:30pm; late Jun–Aug: 8:30am–8pm.

Burin Peninsula ❸

St. John's. Argentia. Columbia Drive, Marystown (709) 279 1211.

THE BURIN PENINSULA presents some of the most dramatic and impressive scenery in Newfoundland. Short, craggy peaks rise above a patchwork green carpet of heather, dotted by scores of glittering lakes. In the fishing town of Grand Bank, the **Southern Newfoundland Seaman's Museum** is a memorial to Newfoundland seamen who perished at sea. The nearby town of Fortune offers a ferry to the French-ruled islands of Saint-Pierre and Miquelon.

The Southern Newfoundland Seaman's Museum
Marine Drive. (709) 832 1484.
May–Oct: daily. limited.

Saint-Pierre and Miquelon ❹

6,400. 4274 Place de General DeGaulle (508) 41 23 84.

THESE TWO SMALL islands are not Canadian but French, and have been under Gallic rule since 1783. Saint-Pierre, the only town on the island of the same name, is a charming French seaside village, complete with gendarmes, bicycles, and fine French bakeries where people line up every morning for fresh baguettes. The **Saint-Pierre Museum** details the history of the islands, including their lively role as a bootlegger's haven during Prohibition in the 1930s when over 3 million cases of liquor passed

The Newfoundland Ferry collects visitors for Saint-Pierre and Miquelon

Cape Bonavista Lighthouse, built on the spot believed to be John Cabot's first landing place in the New World

through this tiny port annually. Many of the harborfront warehouses originally built for this trade are still standing.

A daily ferry leaves Saint-Pierre for the smaller village of Miquelon. Miquelon Island is made up of two smaller islands, Langlade and Grand Miquelon, joined by a narrow, 12-km (7-mile) long strand. The road across this sandy isthmus crosses grassy dunes where wild horses graze and surf pounds sandy beaches.

Saint-Pierre Museum
Rue du 11 Novembre. *011 508 41 35 70.* *2–5pm daily.*

Bonavista Peninsula 5

St. John's. *Argentia.* *Clarenville (709) 466 3100.*

Bonavista Peninsula juts out into the Atlantic ocean, a rugged coastal landscape of seacliffs, harbor inlets, and enchanting small villages such as Birchy Cove and Trouty.

The town of Bonavista is believed to be the point at which Italian explorer John Cabot *(see p40)* first stepped ashore in the New World. A monument to the explorer stands on a high, rocky promontory, near the Cape Bonavista Lighthouse, built in 1843.

Along the Bonavista waterfront, the huge 19th-century buildings of Ryan Premises, once a busy fish merchants' processing facility, are now restored as a National Historic Site. Ryan Premises include three large buildings where fish were dried, stored, and packed for shipping, and displays on the history of the fisheries in North America. The waterfront salt house offers local music.

Trinity 6

300. *Trinity Interpretation Centre, West St. (709) 464 2042.*

The charming village of Trinity, with its colorful 19th-century buildings overlooking the blue waters of Trinity Bay, is easily one of the most beautiful Newfoundland communities. Best explored on foot, Trinity has a range of craft shops and restaurants. The **Trinity Museum** contains over 2,000 artifacts, illustrating the town's past.

Also here is Hiscock House, a turn-of-the-century home, restored to the style of 1910, where merchant Emma Hiscock ran the village store, forge, and post office while raising her six children.

Trinity Museum
Church Rd. *(709) 464 2244.* *mid-Jun–mid-Sep: 10am–6pm daily.*

Terra Nova National Park 7

Trans-Canada Hwy. *from St. John's.* *Jun–mid-Oct: daily.* *limited.* *Glovertown (709) 533 2801.*

The gently rolling forested hills and deep fjords of northeastern Newfoundland are the setting for Terra Nova National Park. The park's Marine Interpretation Centre offers excellent displays on the local marine flora and fauna, including a fascinating underwater video monitor that broadcasts the busy life of the bay's seafloor. Whale-watching tours are also available.

A lookout over Terra Nova National Park

Notre Dame Bay 8

Gander. Port-aux-Basques. Notre Dame Junction, Rte 1 (709) 535 8547.

On the east side of Notre Dame Bay, traditional Newfoundland outports maintain a way of life that echoes their history. The **Twillingate Museum**, located in an elegant Edwardian rectory in Twillingate, has several rooms furnished with period antiques. Also on display are aboriginal artifacts collected from nearby sites, and marine memorabilia recounting the region's fascinating shipping history.

Boat tours take passengers out into the bay for a close-up look at the huge icebergs that float by in spring and summer, and to see the many whales that roam about offshore. Nearby Wild Cove and Durrell are romantic villages.

The elegant Edwardian rectory that houses the Twillingate Museum

Gander 9

1,300. 109 Trans-Canada Hwy (709) 256 7110.

Best known for its illustrious aviation history, Gander is a small town and a useful tourist center for fuel and food. In Grand Falls-Windsor, 50 km (31 miles) west of Gander, the Mary March Regional Museum, named after the last survivor of the now extinct Beothuk people, traces 5,000 years of human habitation in the Exploits Valley. Throughout Newfoundland, the Beothuks were decimated by disease and genocide between 1750 and 1829. Behind the museum, visitors can take a guided tour through the historic village.

A mamateek dwelling reveals a past way of life in Grand Falls Indian village

The Southwest Coast 10

Ferry dock terminal. Port-aux-Basques. Port-aux-Basques (709) 695 2262.

In southern Newfoundland a 45-km (28-mile) coastal drive along Route 470 from Channel Port-aux-Basques to Rose Blanche leads through a landscape of ancient, jagged, green mountains and along a rocky, surf-carved shoreline. Near Rose Blanche, a 500-m (545-yd) boardwalk trail winds through bright wildflower-strewn heath to the impressive Barachois Falls. There is a charming picnic spot at the foot of the 55 m (180 ft) falls. The Rose Blanche Lighthouse, built in 1873, stands in defiant splendor atop the harbor headland. The peninsula road offers marvelous scenery, especially near Petit Jardin.

Gros Morne National Park 11

(709) 458 2417. Corner Brook. St. Barbe. daily.

A United Nations World Heritage Site, Gros Morne is Newfoundland's scenic masterpiece. Here the Long Range Mountains rise 700 m (2,000 ft) above blue fjords that cut into the coastal range. Some of the world's oldest mountains, these are pre-Cambrian and several million years older than the Rockies.

The best way to see the park is on a boat tour along Western Brook Pond, a narrow fjord cradled between soaring cliffs where waterfalls vaporize as they tumble from great heights. Wildlife, including moose, caribou, and eagles, is frequently seen and heard.

The Long Range Mountains in Gros Morne National Park, seen from a walkway in the park

Northern Peninsula Tour ⓬

Road sign on Hwy 430

A LAND OF LEGENDS and mystery, the Northern Peninsula of Newfoundland offers adventurous travelers the chance to experience over 40 centuries of human history, from early aboriginal people through colonization to today's modern fishing life. The road north travels along a harsh and rocky coast. Along the way, important historic sites, such as L'Anse-aux-Meadows, tell the story of the earlier cultures who chose this wild land as their home.

TIPS FOR DRIVERS

Tour length: *690 km (430 miles) along Hwy 430.*
Starting point: *Deer Lake, at junction of Hwy 1.*
Stopping off points: *Gros Morne's Wiltondale Visitors' Centre and Tablelands; Port au Choix National Historic Site; Grenfell Museum in St. Anthony.*

Port au Choix ⑤
This historic site is dedicated to exhibitions of Maritime Archaic Indians and Dorset Eskimos who lived here in 2000 BC and AD 500.

Hawke's Bay ④
A whaling station early in the 20th century, Hawke's Bay boasts excellent salmon fishing waters.

The Arches ③
This lovely spot is named for three limestone arches that are probably 400 million years old.

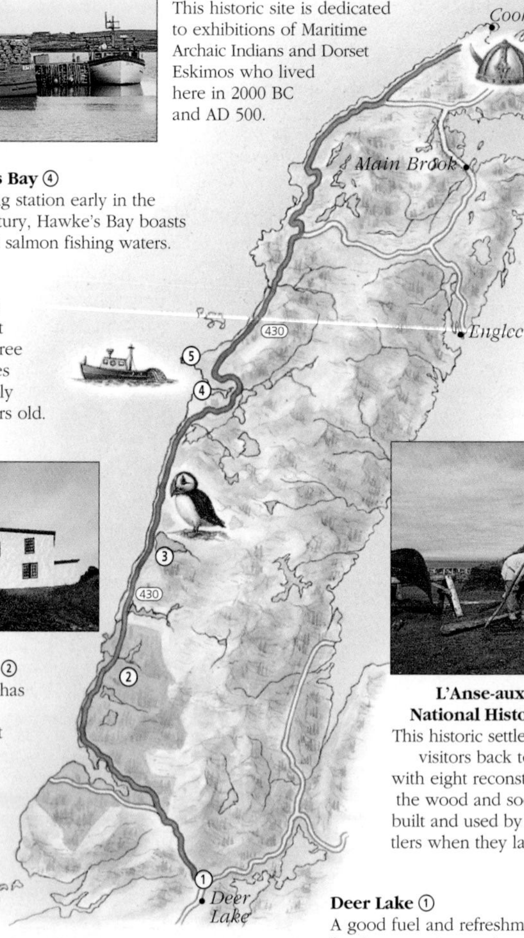

Gros Morne National Park ②
This fine place has a reputation as one of the most beautiful parks in the whole of Canada.

Cooks Harbour
L'Anse-aux-Meadows
St. Anthony
Main Brook
Englee
430
Deer Lake

L'Anse-aux-Meadows National Historic Site ⑥
This historic settlement takes visitors back to AD 1000, with eight reconstructions of the wood and sod buildings built and used by Viking settlers when they landed here.

Deer Lake ①
A good fuel and refreshment center for those starting on the tour, Deer Lake and its surrounding area is remarkable for its jagged landscape, glittering seas, wildlife, and tiny friendly fishing villages.

KEY

- Tour route
- Other roads
- Viewpoint

0 km 25
0 miles 25

Fishermen's huts in the village of Red Bay on the coast of Labrador

Labrador Straits ⓭

Blanc Sablon. *Labrador Straits Historical Development Association, Forteau (709) 927 5825.*

HAUNTINGLY beautiful coastal landscapes explain why the Labrador Straits is a popular place to visit in this province. A summer ferry service crosses the straits from Newfoundland to Blanc Sablon, Quebec, just a few kilometers from the Labrador border. From there, an 85-km (53-mile) road leads along the coast through a wild countryside of high, barren hills, thinly carpeted by heath and wind-twisted spruce.

The Labrador Straits was an important steamship route in the mid-19th century. To aid navigation in the often treacherous waters, the Point Amour Lighthouse was built in 1854 near L'Anse-Amour. Now a Provincial Historic Site, this 30-m (109-ft) tower is the second-tallest lighthouse in Canada. Visitors can ascend the tower for stunning views of the Labrador coast.

Along the road to the lighthouse is a monument that marks the site of the Maritime Archaic Burial Mound National Historic Site, North America's oldest burial mound, where a Maritime Archaic Indian child was laid to rest 7,500 years ago.

At the end of Rte. 510 lies **Red Bay National Historic Site**. Here visitors can take a short boat ride to an island where 16th-century Basque whalers operated the first factory in the New World. A tour around the island leads past the foundations of the shanties, shipworks, and cooper shops where as many as 1,500 men worked each season, rendering whale oil for lamps in Europe.

Red Bay National Historic Site
Route 510. *(709) 920 2051.*
mid-Jun–mid-Oct: daily.

Battle Harbour ⓮

Mary's Harbour, Newfoundland. (709) 921 6216.

ONCE CONSIDERED the unofficial capital of Labrador (from the 1870s to the 1930s), Battle Harbour, a small settlement on an island just off the southern coast of Labrador, was a thriving fishing community during the late 18th and 19th centuries. In 1966, the dwindling population was relocated to St. Mary's on the mainland, but all of the town's buildings, many of which date back 200 years, were left standing, and in the 1990s the town was restored. Today, visitors can tour the island and get a taste of the way life was in coastal Labrador a century ago.

Nain ⓯

1,000. *Town Council, Nain (709) 922 2842.*

TRAVELING NORTH, Nain is the final community of more than a few hundred people. The town can be reached by a coastal boat service that carries passengers and freight, but no cars. A large part of Nain's small population is Inuit, and Piulimatsivik (The Nain Museum) contains valuable artifacts from early Inuit culture. Nain is home to many of Labrador's most prominent Inuit artists. There are also exhibits highlighting the important role that the Moravian Missionaries, an evangelical Christian movement active in the late 18th century, played in bringing education and health care to this wilderness region.

Nearby Hopedale was the site of one of the many Moravian Missions built in Labrador. Today the main feature here is the **Hopedale Mission National Historic Site**. Visitors can tour the Mission, constructed in 1782, which is the oldest woodframe building in Atlantic Canada. Both the Mission and

Inuit children in Nain

Battle Harbour Island with icebergs on the horizon

A snowy street in Nain during the long winter

other structures were built in Germany, shipped across the Atlantic, and reassembled here.

Hopedale Mission National Historic Site

Agvituk Historical Society, Hopedale. *(709) 933 3777. daily.*

The Moravian Church in Happy Valley-Goose Bay

Happy Valley-Goose Bay 16

8,600. Labrador North Chamber of Commerce (709) 896 8787. obligatory, book ahead.

THE LARGEST town in the wilderness of Central Labrador, Happy Valley-Goose Bay was a strategically important stopover for transatlantic flights during World War II. A Canadian military base now tests fighter planes in the area.

Today, the town is home to the Labrador Heritage Museum, where exhibitions depict Labrador's fascinating history. The museum pays particular attention to the life of trappers, with displays that include samples of animal furs, trapper's tools, and a traditional tilt (wilderness shelter).

Churchill Falls 17

Churchill Falls Development Corporation (709) 925 3335. obligatory, book ahead.

THE TOWN of Churchill Falls is ideally placed for visitors to stock up on supplies, fill up with gas, and check tyres as there are no service stations between Happy Valley-Goose Bay and Labrador City. Churchill Falls is famous as the site of one of the largest hydro-electric power stations in the world. Built in the early 1970s, the plant is an extraordinary feat of engineering, diverting the Churchill River (it is Labrador's largest) and its incredible volume of water to power the underground turbines that produce 5,225 megawatts of power – enough to supply the needs of a small country. Guided tours are available of this impressive complex.

Labrador City 18

9,000. Labrador North Tourism Development Corporation (709) 944 7631.

IN THE MIDST of ancient tundra, Labrador City is a mining town that shows the modern, industrial face of Canada. The town is home to the largest open-pit iron mine in the world and the community has largely grown up around it since the late 1950s. The historic building that once held the town's first bank is now the Height of Land Heritage Centre, a museum of photographs, artifacts, and displays dedicated to preserving the history of the development of Labrador.

The vast open wilderness surrounding Labrador City, with its myriad pristine lakes and rivers, is renowned as a sportsman's paradise that attracts hunters and anglers from around the world. Every March, this region sponsors the Labrador 150 Dogsled Race, which has become one of the world's top dogsledding competitions. The western Labrador wilderness is also home to the 700,000 caribou of the George River herd. The herd moves freely through the area for most of the year, grazing the tundra in small bands. Professional outfitters take groups of visitors out to track the herd through the region. Many tourists make the trip to admire the animals.

The Labrador Coastal Ferry

The Labrador Coastal Ferry is the primary mode of transportation for many communities along the Coast. Departing from St. Anthony in northern Newfoundland, the ferry round-trip takes 12 days, visiting up to 48 communities, delivering goods, passengers, and supplies in each port. Half the passenger space is for tourists, half for locals. Along the way, the ferry calls at the historic port of Battle Harbour and travels into fjords. Icebergs are a common sight.

HAND BARRO

NEW BRUNSWICK, NOVA SCOTIA, AND PRINCE EDWARD ISLAND

THE BEAUTY AND lure of the sea is always close at hand here. Stunning coastal scenery, picturesque centuries-old villages, world-class historic sites, and a wealth of family attractions have turned these three Maritime Provinces into one of Canada's top vacation destinations. New Brunswick's ruggedly beautiful Bay of Fundy is matched by the gently rolling landscape of Acadian villages tucked into quiet coves and long sandy beaches. With its sparkling bays and ancient weathered fishing towns, Nova Scotia embodies the romance of the sea. Elegant country inns and historic sites bring the past to life. Canada's smallest province, Prince Edward Island, is known for its vibrant green farmlands, red bluffs, deep blue waters, and golf courses, and is enjoyed by cyclists, anglers, and hikers.

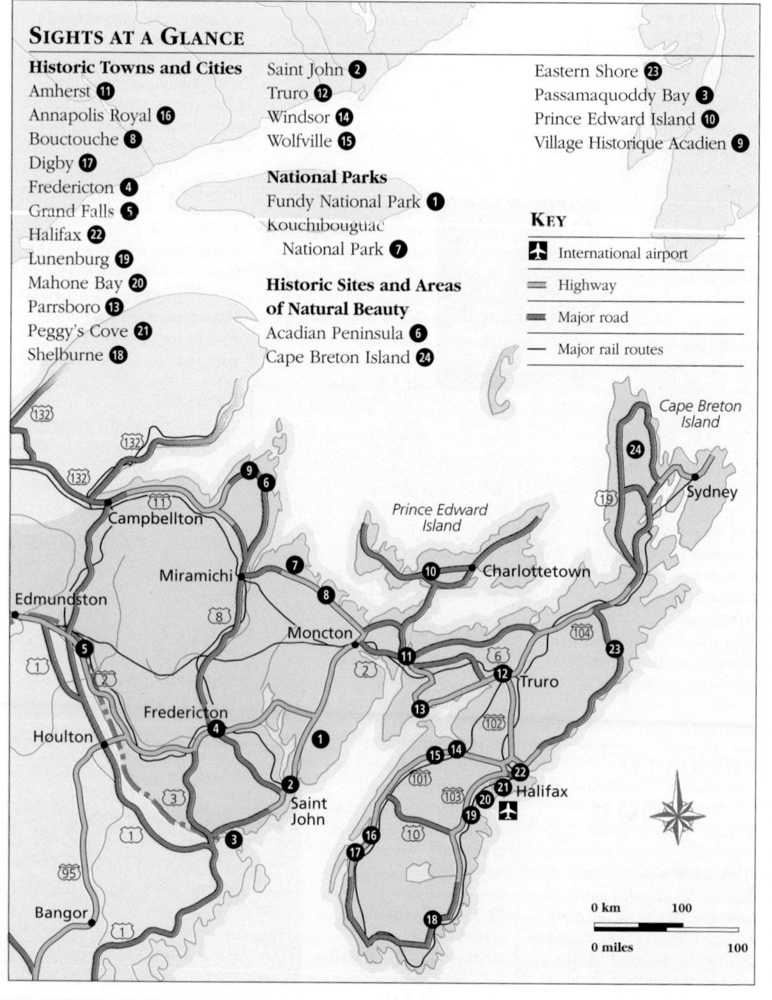

The Fisheries Museum of The Atlantic, Lunenburg, housed in a wooden fishing hut typical of the area

Humpback whales at play in the Bay of Fundy

Fundy National Park ❶

(506) 887 6000. Moncton. Sussex. Saint John. daily. Jun–Sep.

ALONG New Brunswick's eastern shore, the tremendous tides of the Bay of Fundy are a powerful feature of everyday life. Twice a day, over 100 billion tons of water swirl into and out of the bay, creating a tidal shift of up to 15 m (48 ft) and carving out a stunning wild and rocky shoreline.

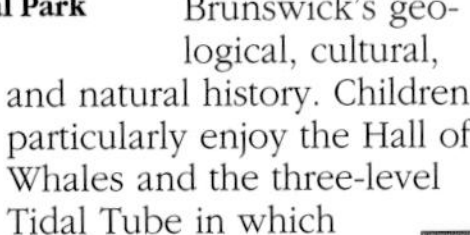
Moose in Fundy National Park

One of the best places to experience these world-famous tidal wonders is at Fundy National Park. Here at low tide, visitors can walk out over the Hopewell Rocks, looking for marine treasures. The Bay is a favorite with naturalists. Swirling tides make for nutrient-rich waters that attract the world's largest population of whales, including minke, humpback, finback, and even the rare right whale.

Saint John ❷

125,000. City Hall, King St. (506) 658 2990.

NEW BRUNSWICK'S largest city, Saint John, still retains the charm of a small town. In 1785, 14,000 loyalists escaping the turmoil of the American Revolution built Saint John in under a year. More recently, restoration has made Saint John's historic center a delightful place to explore. The Old City Market is a working public market, with colorful produce stacked high, fresh seafood vendors, cafés, and an excellent traditional fish restaurant.

In nearby Market Square, an airy atrium links buildings that were once the city's center of commerce. Here visitors will find upscale restaurants and stores. Market Square is also the home of the lively **New Brunswick Museum**. Three floors offer clever and entertaining exhibits on New Brunswick's geological, cultural, and natural history. Children particularly enjoy the Hall of Whales and the three-level Tidal Tube in which water rises and falls, re-creating the height of the tides roaring away just outside.

Nearby, the Loyalist House Museum is located in an impressive Georgian house built by Loyalist David Merritt in around 1810. Inside, the house has been renovated to reflect the lifestyle of a wealthy family of that time, with authentic period furnishings.

New Brunswick Museum
Market Square. (506) 643 2300. daily. Dec 25.

Passamaquoddy Bay ❸

St. Stephen. Black's Harbour & Letete. St. Stephen (506) 466 7390.

THERE IS A genteel historic charm to the villages surrounding the island-filled waters of Passamaquoddy Bay, and none is more charming or intriguing than the lovely holiday town of St. Andrews-by-the-Sea. Overlooking the town, the beautifully maintained Algonquin Resort, with its elegant grounds and 27-hole golf course, recalls early 20th-century days when St. Andrews was renowned as an exclusive getaway of the rich and powerful.

In town, Water Street is lined with intriguing boutiques, craft shops, and fine restaurants housed in century-old buildings. At the town dock, tour companies offer numerous sailing, whale-watching, and kayaking adventures. Nearby, the elegant Georgian home built for Loyalist Harris Hatch in 1824 is now the location of the **Ross Memorial Museum** which contains an extensive collection of antiques and art assembled early in the 20th century.

Two ferries leave from the St. George area nearby for Campobello and Grand Manan Islands, 20 km (12 miles) and 30 km (18 miles) south respectively of St.

Saint John town from the Saint John River

The charming Victorian vista of Fredericton seen from across the Saint John River

Andrews. The Roosevelt Campobello International Park is a 1,135-ha (2,800-acre) preserve on Campobello Island built around the elegant summer home of US President Franklin D. Roosevelt. The 34-room Roosevelt Cottage has been restored, and includes historic and personal artifacts belonging to Roosevelt and his family.

Renowned for its rugged coastal beauty, Grand Manan Island has high rocky cliffs, picturesque fishing villages, and brightly painted boats resting against weathered piers. It is popular with birdwatchers as it attracts large flocks of seabirds annually.

The Ross Memorial Museum
188 Montague St. (506) 529 5124. *late Jun–Sep: Mon–Sat; Sep & Oct: Tue–Sat.*

Fredericton 4

44,000. City Hall, Queen St. (506) 460 2041.

STRADDLING THE Saint John River, Fredericton is New Brunswick's provincial capital. Its Victorian homes and waterfront church make it one of the prettiest small cities in Atlantic Canada. Several historic buildings reflect the town's early role as a British military post. The **Beaverbrook Art Gallery** contains an impressive collection of 19th- and 20th-century paintings, including Salvador Dali's masterpiece *Santiago el Grande* (1957). **King's Landing Historical Settlement**, 37 km (22 miles) west of Fredericton is a living history museum that re-creates daily life in a rural New Brunswick village of the mid-1800s. Over a hundred costumed workers bring villagers' homes, church, and school to life.

Beaverbrook Art Gallery
703 Queen St. *(506) 458 8545.* *Jun–Oct: daily; late Oct–Jun: Tue–Sun.*

King's Landing Historical Settlement
Rte 2, W of Fredericton. *(506) 363 4999.* *Jun–mid-Oct: 10am–5pm daily.* *partial.*

Grand Falls 5

6,100. Malabeam Reception Centre (506) 475 7788.

FROM FREDERICTON to Edmundston, the Saint John River flows through a pastoral valley of rolling hills, woods, and farmland. The town of Grand Falls consists of one well-appointed main street, which is a useful refreshment stop. The town was named Grand Falls for the mighty cataract the Saint John's River creates as it tumbles through Grand Falls Gorge. Framed by parkland, the surge of water drops more than 25 m (40 ft). Over time it has carved a gorge 1.5 km (1 mile) long, with steep sides as high as 70 m (200 ft) in places.

Upriver and north through the valley, the town of Edmundston offers the **New Brunswick Botanical Gardens**. Paths lead through eight themed gardens and two arboretums that provide dazzling input for the senses. Bright colors, delicate scents, and even soft classical music delight visitors.

New Brunswick Botanical Gardens
Saint-Jacques, Edmundston. *(506) 739 6305.* *Jun–Oct: 9am–dusk daily.*

The deep waterfall valley of Grand Falls Gorge

Endless sandy beaches stretch to the horizon at Kouchibouguac National Park

The Acadian Peninsula 6

Bathurst. Bathurst. Dalhousie. Water St., Campbellton (506) 789 2367.

THE QUIET coastal villages, beaches, and gentle surf of the Acadian peninsula have made it a favorite vacation destination for years. Established here since the 1600s, the Acadians have long enjoyed a reputation for prosperous farming centered around pretty villages and a strong folk music tradition *(see pp58–9)*.

In Shippagan, the small fishing town at the tip of the mainland, the **Marine Centre and Aquarium** holds tanks with over 3,000 specimens of Atlantic sealife and displays on local fishing industries.

Nearby, the Lamèque and Miscou islands are connected by causeways to the mainland. On Miscou Island, a 1-km (0.5-mile) boardwalk leads through a peat bog with interpretive signs about this unique ecosystem. Nearby, the 35-m (85-ft) high Miscou Lighthouse is the oldest operating wooden lighthouse in Canada.

Home to many Acadian artists, Caraquet is the busy cultural center of the peninsula. On the waterfront, adventure centers offer guided kayak trips on the Baie des Chaleurs. For those wanting an introduction to the story of the Acadians, the **Acadian Wax Museum** features a self-guided audio tour past 23 tableaus from Acadian history. The scenes begin with the founding of the "Order of the Good Times" at Annapolis Royal in 1604 and focus on the expulsion of 1755.

Marine Centre and Aquarium
Rte 113, Shippagan. *(506) 336 3013. mid-May–mid-Oct: 10am–6pm daily.*

Acadian Wax Museum
Rte 11, Caraquet. *(506) 726 2682. Jun–Sep: daily.*

Kouchibouguac National Park 7

(506) 876 2443. Newcastle. Newcastle. Miramichi. daily.

THE NAME of this park comes from the native Mi'kmaq word for "River of Long Tides." The park's 238 sq km (92 sq miles) encompass a salt-spray world of wind-sculpted dunes, salt marshes packed with wild life, and 25 km (16 miles) of fine sand beaches, as well as excellent terrain for cyclists. One of the park's most popular activities is the Voyager Marine Adventure, a three-hour canoe paddle to offshore sandbanks where hundreds of gray seals relax in the warm sun.

Bouctouche 8

2,350. 14 Acadia St. (506) 743 8811.

A SEASIDE TOWN with a strong Acadian heritage, Bouctouche is home to **Le Pays de la Sagouine**. This theme village is named for La Sagouine, the wise washerwoman created by Acadian authoress Antonine Maillet (b. 1929), very much part of Canadian popular heritage. Ongoing theatrical shows here act out Maillet's tales.

Nearby, the Irving Eco-Centre studies and protects the beautiful 12-km (8-mile) network of dunes, saltmarshes, and beach that extend along the entrance to Bouctouche Harbour.

Le Pays de la Sagouine
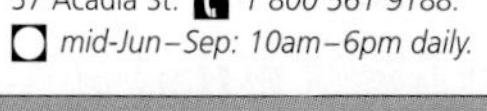
57 Acadia St. *1 800 561 9188. mid-Jun–Sep: 10am–6pm daily.*

The raised boardwalk at the Irving Eco-Centre, La Dune de Bouctouche

Village Historique Acadien ❾

After the tragic deportation of 1755–63 *(see p58–9)*, Acadians slowly returned to the Maritimes, clearing new farmlands and rebuilding their way of life. The Village Historique Acadien portrays a rural Acadian community between 1770 and 1890. The village's 45 restored historic buildings, including several working farms, cover 364 ha (900 acres). Throughout the village, period-costumed bilingual guides re-create the daily activities of the 19th century. Visitors can ride in a horse-drawn wagon, watch the work of the blacksmith, print shop, or gristmill, and also tour working farms and homes where women are busy spinning, weaving, and cooking.

Visitors' Checklist

Route 11, 10 km (6 miles) W of Caraquet. *(506) 726 2600.* *from Bathurst.* *Jun–Oct: 10am–6pm daily.* *late Oct–May.*

School and Chapel
Through centuries of turmoil, Catholicism was a vital mainstay of the Acadian people. Priests were also schoolteachers; education was highly prized by the community.

Men in horse-drawn cart
Traditional methods are used on the farms; tilled by local people arriving each day, the harvest is moved in carts to barns for winter.

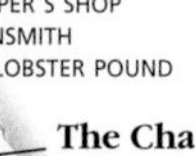

The Chapel was built by pioneer Acadians and dates from 1831.

Doucet Farm was first built in 1840 and has been fully restored to its original appearance.

Mazerolle Farm sells fresh bread and rolls, which are baked daily in a large oven in the farmhouse.

Robin shed

Poirier Tavern

Savoie House Education Centre

Godin House

Forge
In many ways the center of the community, the blacksmith was a feature of every Acadian village, repairing farm equipment and shoeing horses for the people of the area.

0 m 100
0 yards 100

The Visitors' Reception Centre offers an audiovisual presentation, and typical Acadian food in its restaurant.

Prince Edward Island ⑩

Beautiful and pastoral, Prince Edward Island is famous for its lush landscapes. Wherever you look, the island's rich colors, emerald green farmlands, red-clay roads, and sapphire sea, seem to combine and recombine in endless patterns to please the eye. The island is also a popular destination for golfers who come to tee off on some of Canada's best courses, as well as a haven for sun worshipers who revel in the sandy beaches that ring the island. Prince Edward Island seems made for exploring at a leisurely pace. Meandering coastal roads present an ever-changing panorama of sea, sand, and sky. Small historic towns are home to elegant country inns and art galleries. In the evenings, the island's famous lobster suppers await, caught fresh daily from the Atlantic Ocean.

Green Gables House
Set amid leafy green paths, this 19th-century home was the setting for the popular Anne of Green Gables *tales.*

Malpeque Bay
Cabot Beach Provincial Park covers part of the bay. Ten million of the world-famous Malpeque oysters are caught here each year.

Cedar Dunes Provincial Park features a restored 1875 lighthouse, sandy beaches, and a large coastal campground.

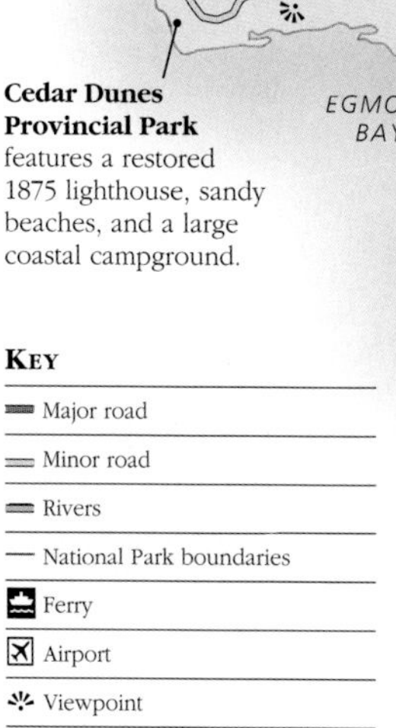

Key

- Major road
- Minor road
- Rivers
- National Park boundaries
- Ferry
- Airport
- Viewpoint

Star Sights

- ★ **PEI National Park**
- ★ **Charlottetown**

Main street, Summerside
This quiet city with its attractive tree-lined streets is known for its Lobster Carnival each July.

Confederation Bridge, opened in 1997 at a total cost of Can$900m, runs for 13 km (8 miles) to the mainland.

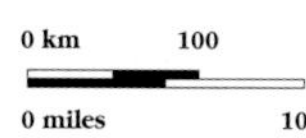

★ Prince Edward Island National Park
Characterized by 40 km (25 miles) of coastline leading onto red cliffs, pink and white sand beaches, and mild seas, this park offers unbeatable sport and vacationing facilities and has an educational Visitors' Centre for those interested in its marine wildlife.

VISITORS' CHECKLIST

Water St., Charlottetown. (902) 368 4444. Charlottetown. to Wood Islands, Borden-Carleton. to Wood Islands, Borden-Carleton, Souris.

East Point Lighthouse
The island's easternmost point is home to a 19th-century lighthouse with a restored radio room. Now unmanned and fully automatic, it is open to visitors.

★ Charlottetown
Elegant 19th-century row houses characterize the streets of this sleepy town, the smallest of Canada's provincial capitals; in 1867 the Confederation of Canada was decided here.

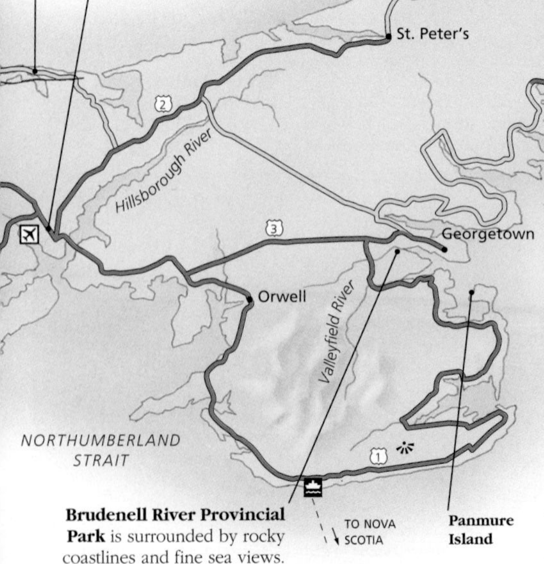

Red Point Beach
Characteristic red rocks lead down to wide beaches; the sand here mysteriously squeaks underfoot, much to the delight of vacationing children.

Brudenell River Provincial Park is surrounded by rocky coastlines and fine sea views.

Panmure Island

Exploring Prince Edward Island

The smallest province in Canada, Prince Edward Island's concentration of activity means every corner of the island is accessible. Charlottetown, known as the birthplace of Canada, is centrally located, and its tree-lined streets make a gentle start to exploring the outlying country. Red clay roads guide the visitor through farms and fishing villages to tiny provincial parks scattered throughout the island. Traveling the north coast takes in the splendid rolling green scenery of PEI National Park, with its famous beaches, while southward, warm swimming spots abound.

Fishing huts overlooking French River near Cavendish

Cavendish

This is such a busy little town that it can be hard to see the gentle, pastoral home of the *Anne of Green Gables* novels. The best place to get in touch with its charm is at the site of **Lucy Maud Montgomery's Cavendish Home**, where the author lived for many years, a simple and authentic site. The town is also the location of **Green Gables,** the novels' fictional 19th-century home.

Lucy Maud Montgomery's Cavendish Home
Route 6. *(902) 963 2231.*
Jun–Oct: 10am–5pm daily.

Green Gables
Route 6. *(902) 672 6350.*
May–Oct: 9am–8pm daily.

Cavendish
Routes 6 & 13. *(902) 963 7830.*

Prince Edward Island National Park

Green Gables is part of Prince Edward Island National Park, whose western entrance is in Cavendish. This is the park's busier side. The soft sand and gentle surf of Cavendish Beach make it one of the most popular beaches in the province. The park's coastal road leads to North Rustico Beach, which is a favorite with sightseers. At the park's western end, the Homestead Trail leads for 8 km (5 miles) through rustic green woodlands and meadows.

The park's quieter eastern side features a long stretch of pristine beach and dunes, and a coastal road that makes a scenic drive. The Reeds and Rushes Trail is a lovely short boardwalk track that leads to a freshwater marsh pond where local species of geese and duck nest and feed.

Prince Edward Island National Park
Charlottetown. *Wood Islands.*
(902) 672 6350. *daily.*

The South Coast

Enchanting vistas of farmland and seashore are found along the roads of the south shore, between Confederation Bridge and Charlottetown. This is also where visitors will find Victoria-by-the-Sea, a small village that is home to some of the island's most interesting craftshops.

En route to Charlottetown, visitors can make a short detour to **Fort Amherst-Port-la-Joye National Historic Site**. It was here, in 1720, that the French built the island's first permanent settlement. The British captured it in 1758, and built Fort Amherst to protect the entrance to Charlottetown Harbour. While the fort is long gone, the earthworks can still be seen in the park-like surroundings.

Fort Amherst-Port-la-Joye National Historic Site
Rocky Point. *(902) 566 7626.*
May–Oct: daily.

The red bluffs of Cavendish Beach, one of the most favored spots in Prince Edward Island National Park

View of 19th-century church at Orwell Corners Historic Village

Panmure Island

The natural beauty of the island's eastern area is easy to experience on Panmure Island, south of Georgetown. Level roads make it popular with cyclists. In summer, the octagonal wooden **Panmure Island Lighthouse** is open, and the view from the top takes in a long vista of the island's beaches, saltmarshes, and woodlands. The lighthouse still guides ships into port as it did when it was first built in 1853.

Panmure Island Lighthouse
Panmure Island. *(902) 838 3568.*
Jul–Aug: 9am–7pm daily.

Orwell Corners Historic Village

Just outside of the small hamlet of Orwell, Orwell Corners Historic Village re-creates the day-to-day life of a small 19th-century crossroads community. Orwell Corners was thriving until well into the 20th century, when changes in transportation and commerce lessened the importance of the settlement. Restored and opened in 1973, this small historic village radiates charm. Visitors can see several buildings including a blacksmith's, church, schoolhouse, and Clarke's store, the social center of the village. Upstairs is the workshop of Clarke's seamstresses, who made dresses for local ladies.

Just 1 km (0.5 mile) away is the **Sir Andrew Macphail Homestead**. This Victorian house and its surroundings were the much-loved home of Macphail, a local doctor, journalist, teacher, and soldier who counted among his friends prime ministers and acclaimed writers such as Kipling. The house features many exhibits dealing with Macphail's life. Outside, trails wind through deep woodlands.

Orwell Corners Historic Village
Orwell. *(902) 651 2013.*
May–Oct: daily.

Sir Andrew Macphail Homestead
off Rte 1, Orwell. *(902) 651 2789.*
Jun–Sep: 10am–5pm daily.

Charlottetown

The birthplace of Canada is a charming small city. Along Peake's Quay, sailboats lie snug against marina piers, and the waterside buildings are home to numerous intriguing shops and restaurants. The elegant **Confederation Centre of the Arts** hosts an array of shows including the popular musical of *Anne of Green Gables*. **Province House National Historic Site** is where the 1864 Charlottetown Conference was held *(see p46)*, which led to the formation of Canada as a nation. Several rooms have been meticulously restored to their 19th-century character.

Ardgowan National Historic Site was once the elegant home of William Pope, one of the Fathers of Confederation.

Confederation Centre of the Arts
145 Richmond St. *(902) 628 1864.*
daily.

Province House National Historic Site
165 Richmond St. *(902) 566 7626.*
daily; call ahead for hours.

Ardgowan National Historic Site
Mount Edward Rd. *(902) 566 7050.*
daily.

Charlottetown
Water St. (902) 368 4444.

Historic homes in Great George Street, Charlottetown

Lucy Maud Montgomery

The island's most famous author, Lucy Maud Montgomery, was born in Cavendish in 1874. Nearby Green Gables House became the setting of her internationally best-selling novel, *Anne of Green Gables* (1908), set in the late 19th century. The manuscript was accepted only on the sixth attempt. To date, millions of copies of *Anne* have been published, in 16 languages. In 1911, Lucy married and moved to Ontario, where she raised two sons. She continued to write, producing 17 more books, ten of which feature Anne, with all but one set on Prince Edward Island. She died in 1942 and was buried overlooking the farms and fields of her beloved native Cavendish, the Avonlea of which she wrote so often.

Author Lucy Maud Montgomery

Amherst ⓫

9,700. Rte 104, exit 1 (902) 667 8429.

A BUSY COMMERCIAL and agricultural town right in the center of Atlantic Canada, Amherst overlooks the world's largest marsh, the beautiful Tantramar. Along the edge of the marsh, hayfields grow on land reclaimed by Acadian dikes during the 18th century. **The Cumberland County Museum** in central Amherst is located in the family home of Senator R.B. Dickey, one of the Fathers of Confederation. The museum focuses on the region's industrial development, local, and natural history. Particularly interesting are examples of goods once made in the town's busy factories.

Cumberland County Museum
150 Church St. (902) 667 2561.
9am–5pm daily.

Truro ⓬

11,700. Victoria Square (902) 893 2922.

A PROSPEROUS TOWN at the hub of Nova Scotia's major transportation routes, Truro is also the site of a unique geographical phenomenon, the tidal bore. As the Great Fundy tides return landward, sweeping into the Minas Basin, they generate a wave or "bore" that is driven for several kilometers up the rivers that empty into the back of the basin. An information display next to the Salmon River explains each process and posts the tidal times. On the nearby Shubenacadie River, visitors can ride the bore in rafts. The waves generated can reach 2 m (7 ft) in height, particularly on the new and full moons, creating a churn of whitewater that the rafts race through as they follow it for miles upstream.

Façade of Haliburton House in Windsor, home of the famous humorist

Parrsboro ⓭

1,600. Main St. (902) 254 3266.

LOCATED ON the north shore of the Minas Basin, Parrsboro is famous as the home of the world's highest tides, which reach over 15 m (50 ft) in height. Rockhounds are drawn to the Minas Basin whose beaches are scattered with semiprecious gems and fossils. The excellent displays at **Fundy Geological Museum** in Parrsboro feature superb examples of the amethysts found locally. There are also dinosaur footprints and bones.

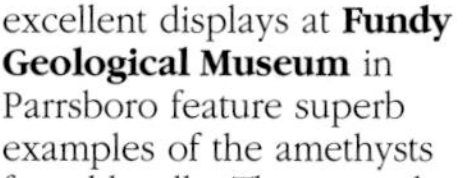

Prosauropod dinosaur skull from Fundy Museum

The Fundy Geological Museum
6 Two Islands Rd. (902) 254 3814.
Jun–mid-Oct: daily; late Oct–May: Tue–Sun.

Windsor ⓮

3,600. Hwy 101, exit 6 (902) 798 2690.

A QUIET TOWN whose elegant Victorian homes overlook the Avon River, Windsor was the home of Judge Thomas Chandler Haliburton, lawyer, historian, and the author of the Canadian "Sam Slick" stories, which achieved enormous popularity in the mid-1800s. Haliburton was one of the first widely recognized humorists in North America. His clever, fast-talking character Sam Slick was a Yankee clock peddler who coined idiomatic terms such as "the early bird gets the worm," and "raining cats and dogs." His elegant home is now the **Haliburton House Provincial Museum**. Surrounded by gardens that Haliburton tended and loved, the house is furnished in Victorian period antiques and contains many of his personal possessions, including his writing desk.

Haliburton House Provincial Museum
414 Clifton Ave. (902) 798 2915.
Jun–mid-Oct: daily. *limited.*

Two Island Beach in Parrsboro, famous for the two large rock outcrops known as the "Brothers Parrsboro"

Wolfville ⓯

3,500. Willow Park (902) 542 7000.

THE HOME of the acclaimed Acadia University, Wolfville and the surrounding countryside radiate a truly gracious charm. Here the green and fertile Annapolis Valley meets the shore of the Minas Basin, and keen visitors can follow country roads past lush farmlands, sun-warmed orchards, gentle tidal flats, and wildlife-filled salt marshes.

Much of the valley's rich farmland was created by dikes built by the Acadians in the 1700s. When the Acadians were deported in the Great Expulsion of 1755, the British offered the land to struggling New England villagers on the condition that the entire village would relocate. These hardworking settlers, known as Planters, proved so successful that the towns of the Annapolis Valley flourished.

Wolfville is a pretty town of tree-lined streets and inviting shops and restaurants. Nearby, the town's Visitor Information Center marks the beginning of a beautiful 5-km (3-mile) trail along the Acadian dikes to the graceful church at the **Grand Pré National Historic Site**. When the British marched into the Acadian village of Grand Pré in August 1755, it marked the beginning of the Great Uprooting, *Le Grand Dérangement*, which eventually forced thousands of peace-loving Acadians from Nova Scotia *(see pp58–9)*. In 1921 a beautiful stone church modeled after French country churches was built on the site of the old village of Grand Pré as a memorial to this tragedy. Today, visitors tour the church and stroll around the garden grounds where a statue of Evangeline, the heroine of Longfellow's epic poem about the Acadians, stands waiting for her lover, Gabriel. The site's information center features exhibits on the Acadians, their deportation and eventual resettlement in the Maritimes. Many families hid locally, but even deportees returned in the 18th century.

Longfellow's Evangeline

Grand Pré National Historic Site
Hwy 101, exit 10. *(902) 542 3631.* *daily.*

Annapolis Royal ⓰

630. Prince Albert Rd. (902) 532 5769.

AT THE EASTERN end of the Annapolis Valley lies the historic and picturesque town of Annapolis Royal. It was near here that Samuel de Champlain built the fur trading post of Port Royal in 1605 *(see p41)*. A purely commercial venture, this was the first European settlement in the New World north of Florida. **The Port Royal National Historic Site** is an exact replica of the original colony, based on French farms of the period, from plans drawn by Champlain.

Kejimkujik Park entrance sign

An hour's drive inland from Annapolis Royal lies **Kejimkujik National Park**, which covers 381 square km (148 sq miles) of inland wilderness laced with sparkling lakes and rivers. Throughout the park there are numerous paddling routes and 15 hiking trails, ranging from short walks to a 60-km (37-mile) perimeter wilderness and wildlife trail.

Port Royal National Historic Site
15 km W. of Annapolis Royal.
(902) 532 2898. *May–Oct: 9am–5pm.*

Kejimkujik National Park
Hwy 8. *(902) 682 2772.* *daily.* *mid-May–Oct.*

Digby ⓱

2,300. Shore Rd (902) 245 2201.

THE HARDWORKING fishing town of Digby is virtually synonymous with the plump, juicy scallops that are the prime quarry of the town's extensive fishing fleet. The area around Digby also offers splendid scenery and is the starting place for a scenic trip along Digby Neck to the rocky coastal landscape of beautiful Long and Brier Islands.

The waters off Long and Brier Islands brim with finback, minke, and humpback whales, and whale-watching tours are one of the region's favorite pastimes. Some visitors may even glimpse the rare right whale, as about 200 of the 350 left in the world spend their summers basking and breeding in the warm Bay of Fundy.

Children having fun in a canoeing lake at Kejimkujik National Park

Riverfront houses at Bridgewater near Lunenburg, Nova Scotia ▷

The Dory Shop Museum in Shelburne, center of local boat-building

Shelburne 18

2,250. Dock St. (902) 875 4547.

A QUIET HISTORIC town nestled on the shore of a deep harbor, Shelburne was founded hastily by 3,000 United Empire Loyalists fleeing persecution after the American Revolution in 1775. More loyalists followed over the next few years, and Shelburne's population swelled to 16,000, making it at the time the largest town in British North America. Many of these settlers were wealthy merchants who were unprepared for the rigors of living in a primitive land. Over time, many relocated to Halifax or returned to England, leaving behind the fine 18th-century homes they had built.

Today, a walk along Water Street leads past some of the town's most attractive historic homes to the **Dory Shop Museum**. This two-storey waterfront structure has been a commercial dory (flat-bottomed) boat building shop since its founding in 1880. During the days of the Grand Banks schooner fleet, Shelburne dories were famous for their strength and seaworthiness, and the town boasted seven shops that built thousands of boats each year. The museum's first floor features displays on the industry and the salt-cod fishery. Upstairs, skilled shipwrights demonstrate the techniques of dory building that have changed little in a century.

Dory Shop Museum
Dock St. (902) 875 3219.
Jun–Sep: daily. limited.

Lunenburg 19

2,800. Waterfront (902) 634 8100.

NO TOWN CAPTURES the seafaring romance of Nova Scotia as much as Lunenburg. In the mid-1700s the British, eager for another loyal settlement, laid out a town plan for Lunenburg. They then offered the land to Protestant settlers from Germany. Although these were mainly farmers, they soon turned to shipbuilding and fishing. In 1996 the town was declared a UNESCO World Heritage Site, one of the best-preserved planned settlements in the New World. Lunenburg is also the home port of *Bluenose II*, a replica of Canada's most famous schooner.

The Fisheries Museum of the Atlantic fills several historic buildings along the waterfront. The museum docks are home to many ships including the *Theresa E. Conner*, the last of the Grand Banks Schooners.

Fisheries Museum of the Atlantic
Bluenose Dr. (902) 634 4794.
mid-May–mid-Oct: daily; late Oct–May: Mon–Fri. limited.

One of Mahone Bay's three waterfront churches

Mahone Bay 20

1,100. Hwy 3 (902) 624 6151.

THE SMALL seaside town of Mahone Bay has been called the "prettiest town in Canada." Tucked into the shores of the bay that shares its name, the waterfront is lined with historic homes dating to the 1700s, and at

View of the Lunenberg Fisheries Museum of the Atlantic along the town's romantic waterfront

the back of the harbor three stately churches cast their reflection into the still waters.

The town has attracted some of Canada's finest artists and craftspeople, whose colorful shops line the main street. The small **Settlers Museum** offers exhibits and artifacts relating the town's settlement by foreign Protestants in 1754, and its prominence as a boat-building center. The museum's most popular exhibit is a collection of 18th- and 19th-century ceramics and antiques.

Settlers Museum
578 Main St. (902) 624 6263.
May–Sep: Tue–Sun.

Peggy's Cove ㉑

60. *Sou'wester Restaurant (902) 823 2561/1074.*

THE GRACEFUL Peggy's Cove Lighthouse stands atop wave-worn granite rocks and is one of the most photographed sights in Canada, a symbol of Nova Scotia's enduring bond with the sea. The village, with its colorful houses clinging to the rocks, and small harbor lined with weathered piers and fish sheds, has certainly earned its reputation as one of the province's most picturesque fishing villages. This is a delightful place to stroll through, but visitors may want to avoid midday in summer, when the number of tour buses can be a distraction. Early morning and late afternoon are the most peaceful times. Just outside the village is a memorial to the victims of the 1998 Swissair crash.

The village was also the home of well-known marine artist and sculptor, William E. deGarthe (1907–83). Just above the harbor, the deGarthe Gallery has a permanent exhibition of 65 of his best-known paintings and sculptures.

Right outside the gallery, the Memorial is a 30-m (90-ft) sculpture created by deGarthe as his monument to Nova Scotian Fishermen. Carved into an outcropping of native granite rock, the sculpture depicts 32 fishermen, and

The best-known symbol of Atlantic Canada, Peggy's Cove Lighthouse

their wives and children. The large angel in the sculpture is the original Peggy, sole survivor of a terrible 19th-century shipwreck, for whom the village was named.

Halifax ㉒

See pp86–7.

The Eastern Shore ㉓

Halifax. *Antigonish.* *Pictou.* *Canso (902) 366 2170.*

A TOUR ALONG the Eastern Shore is a trip through old-world Nova Scotia, through towns and villages where life has changed little since the turn of the 20th century. The tiny house and farm that comprise the Fisherman's Life Museum in Jeddore, Oyster Ponds (60 km/37 miles east of Halifax) was the home of an inshore fisherman, his wife, and 13 daughters around 1900. Today, the homestead is a living-history museum where guides in period costume (many of them wives of local fishermen) reenact the simple daily life of an inshore fishing family, still the heart of Nova Scotia culture. Visitors who arrive at midday may be invited to share lunch cooked over a woodburning stove. There are also daily demonstrations that include rug-hooking, quilting, and knitting, and visitors can tour the fishing stage where salted fish were stored.

Sherbrooke Village is the largest living-history museum in Nova Scotia. Between 1860 and 1890, this was a gold and lumber boomtown. As the gold ran out, Sherbrooke once again became a sleepy rural village. In the early 1970s, 25 of Sherbrooke's most historic buildings were restored. Within the village, scores of costumed guides bring 19th-century Nova Scotia to life. A ride on a horse-drawn wagon offers an overview of the town; the drivers share bits of local history as the horses trot along the village roads. At the Apothecary, visitors can watch the careful mixing of patent medicines, and those interested in the Ambrotype Studio can dress in period costumes, sitting very still while the vintage camera records their image on glass. Just outside town a massive waterwheel turns, powering the Lumber Mill.

Sherbrooke Village
off Hwy 7. *(902) 522 2400.*
Jun–Oct: daily.

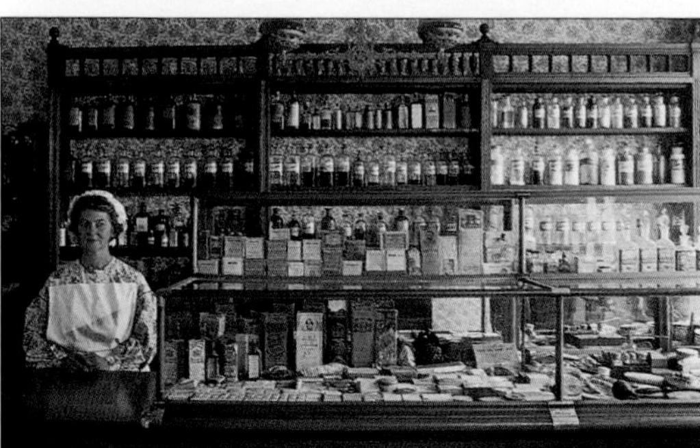

The Apothecary at the living history museum Sherbooke Village

Halifax ㉒

Town memorial to merchant seamen

WITH ITS GLEAMING waterfront, pretty parks, and unique blend of modern and historic architecture, Halifax is a romantic and fascinating small city. Its cultured flavor belies Halifax's 250-year history as a lusty, brawling, military town. Founded in 1749 by General George Cornwallis and 2,500 English settlers, Halifax was planned as Britain's military center north of Boston. The city has a long history of adventure, being the town where swashbuckling legalized pirates, or privateers, brought captured ships to be shared with the crown, at a time when men made huge fortunes from sea trading. Today, Halifax is best known as one of Canada's foremost centers of higher learning and has many colleges and five universities.

Exploring Halifax

This is an easy town to explore on foot, as many of the better museums, historic sites, shops, and restaurants are located within the fairly contained historic core.

Downtown, leading west from Brunswick Street, is hilly and green, ideal for a leisurely walk to appreciate the old-style architecture. Citadel Hill offers excellent views of the town as it stretches out over the water.

Historic Properties

1869 Upper Water St. *(902) 429 0530. daily. limited.*

The Historic Properties are a wharfside collection of elegant stone and timber-frame structures, which were originally built in the 19th century to hold the booty captured by privateers. Today, they house an intriguing collection of specialty and gift shops, pubs, and fine restaurants. This is the one of the city's favorite gathering spots on warm summer nights, with crowds of strollers enjoying the lights of the harbor and music drifting from nearby pubs, or placing bets at the Sheraton Casino.

Maritime Museum of the Atlantic

1675 Lower Water St. *(902) 424 7490. daily. summer. on request.*

This harborfront museum offers extensive displays on Nova Scotia's seafaring history, including small craft, a restored chandlery, and, at the dock outside, the elegantly refitted 1921 research vessel *Acadia*. The museum's most popular exhibit is the *Titanic* display, which offers artifacts recovered from the ship. There is also a grand staircase, a replica of the original, which was built for the 1997 movie, *Titanic*, partly filmed in Halifax. After the 1912 catastrophe, many of the bodies that were recovered were brought to Halifax, and 150 are buried in the town.

The waterfront of Halifax, seen from the town ferry

Harbourfront

(902) 490 5946.

The Harbourfront Walkway, features interesting gift shops, cafés, and restaurants in historic settings along the boardwalk. This delightful promenade leads to the Dartmouth Ferry, North America's oldest town ferry. A trip round the harbor is an inexpensive way to enjoy a panorama of Halifax.

Government House

1200 Barrington St.

The current home of Nova Scotia's lieutenant-general, this beautiful building is not open to the public but well worth exterior inspection for its historic and architectural interest. Its Georgian façade lends an urban grandeur. Completed in 1807, Government House cost over £30,000 (Can$72,000), a huge amount for a humble fishing village.

The bandstand of Halifax Public Gardens, framed in flowers

Pier 21

1055 Marginal Road *(902) 425 7770. 9:30am–5pm Wed–Fri, 10am–5pm Sat, noon–5pm Sun.*

Canada's entry point for more than a million immigrants and refugees, Pier 21 is now a National Historic Site. With powerful and emotional displays and fascinating images, Pier 21 provides a unique glimpse into Canadian history.

Halifax Public Gardens

Spring Garden Rd. *(902) 490 5946. daily. limited.*

Created in 1836, the Public Gardens are a beautiful 7-ha (17-acre) oasis of Victorian greenery and color in a

bustling city. A peaceful place to stroll, the gardens' paths wind past duck ponds, fountains, and a seemingly endless array of vivid flowerbeds. In the center of the gardens, an ornate bandstand is the site of Sunday concerts. On weekends, craftspeople gather outside the park's cast-iron fence to display their varied and colorful wares.

Halifax Citadel National Historic Site

Citadel Hill. (902) 426 5080. *May–Oct: daily.* *summer.*

Overlooking the city, this huge star-shaped fortress has a commanding view of the world's second-largest natural harbor. Built between 1828 and 1856, the citadel and its outlying fortifications provided a formidable defense. Visitors can stroll the parade grounds where the kilted regiment of the 78th Highlanders perform with twice-daily musket drills.

Halifax's famous town clock, built in 1803 as a gift from British royalty

Old Town Clock

Citadel Hill.

At the base of Citadel Hill stands the city's most recognized landmark, the Old Town Clock. The clock was a gift in 1803 from Edward, the British Duke of Kent and then military commander, who had a passion for punctuality. He designed the clock with four faces so that both soldiers and citizens would arrive at their appointed destinations on time.

Visitors' Checklist

115,000. 35 km (22 miles) N of the city. CN Station. 6040 Almon St. Halifax International Visitors' Centre, 1595 Barrington St. (902) 490 5946. Nova Scotia International Tattoo (Jul); Atlantic Jazz Festival (Jul).

Province House

1726 Hollis St. *(902) 424 4661.* *daily.*

Begun in 1811 and finished in 1819, Nova Scotia's Province House is the oldest seat of government in Canada. In 1864 the Fathers of Confederation held two days of meetings here on the formation of Canada *(see p44)*. Visitors can tour the rooms where these plans were laid.

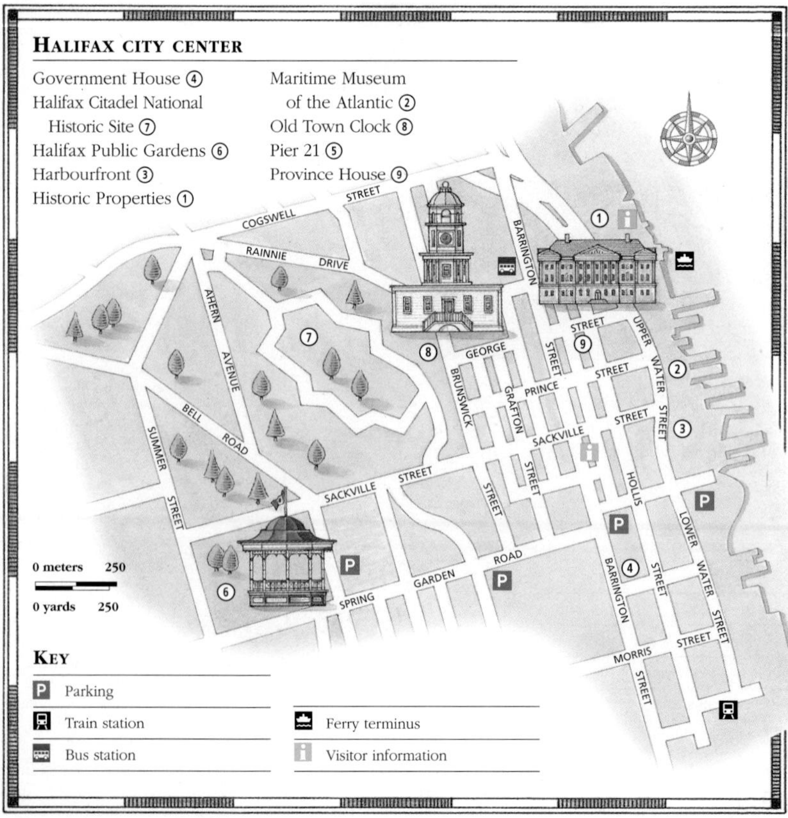

Halifax City Center

Government House ④
Halifax Citadel National Historic Site ⑦
Halifax Public Gardens ⑥
Harbourfront ③
Historic Properties ①
Maritime Museum of the Atlantic ②
Old Town Clock ⑧
Pier 21 ⑤
Province House ⑨

0 meters 250
0 yards 250

Key

- Parking
- Train station
- Bus station
- Ferry terminus
- Visitor information

Cape Breton Island 24

MAGNIFICENT NATURAL BEAUTY is the attraction on Cape Breton. Every year thousands of people travel the famous Cabot Trail through the craggy splendor of Cape Breton Highlands National Park *(see p90–1)*. But Cape Breton's beauty is not limited to these two renowned sights; it can be found along inviting country roads and in the less explored corners of this green, fertile island. Particularly stunning are the Mabou Highlands, which cradle the gentle waters of Lake Ainslee, Bras d'Or Lake where eagles soar over scenic shores, and romantic coastal villages such as windswept Gabarus. The reconstructed 18th-century French garrison and village, Fortress Louisbourg, is also highly popular.

Glenora Whisky

Cabot Trail Highway
This sublime 300-km (186-mile) drive around the island's northwest and its national park attracts more visitors each year.

St. Pierre Church at Cheticamp
Built in 1883, the silver spire of this church is typical of Catholic style. The church is in the center of the town of Cheticamp, which offers whale-watching opportunites and is the focus of the 3,000-strong local Acadian community.

Lake Ainslee
This tranquil lake, encircled by scenic roads, attracts many bird species, such as ospreys and loons, which feed on its shores.

KEY

- Major road
- Minor road
- Scenic route
- Rivers
- Visitor information
- Viewpoint
- Airport
- National Park boundary
- Ferry

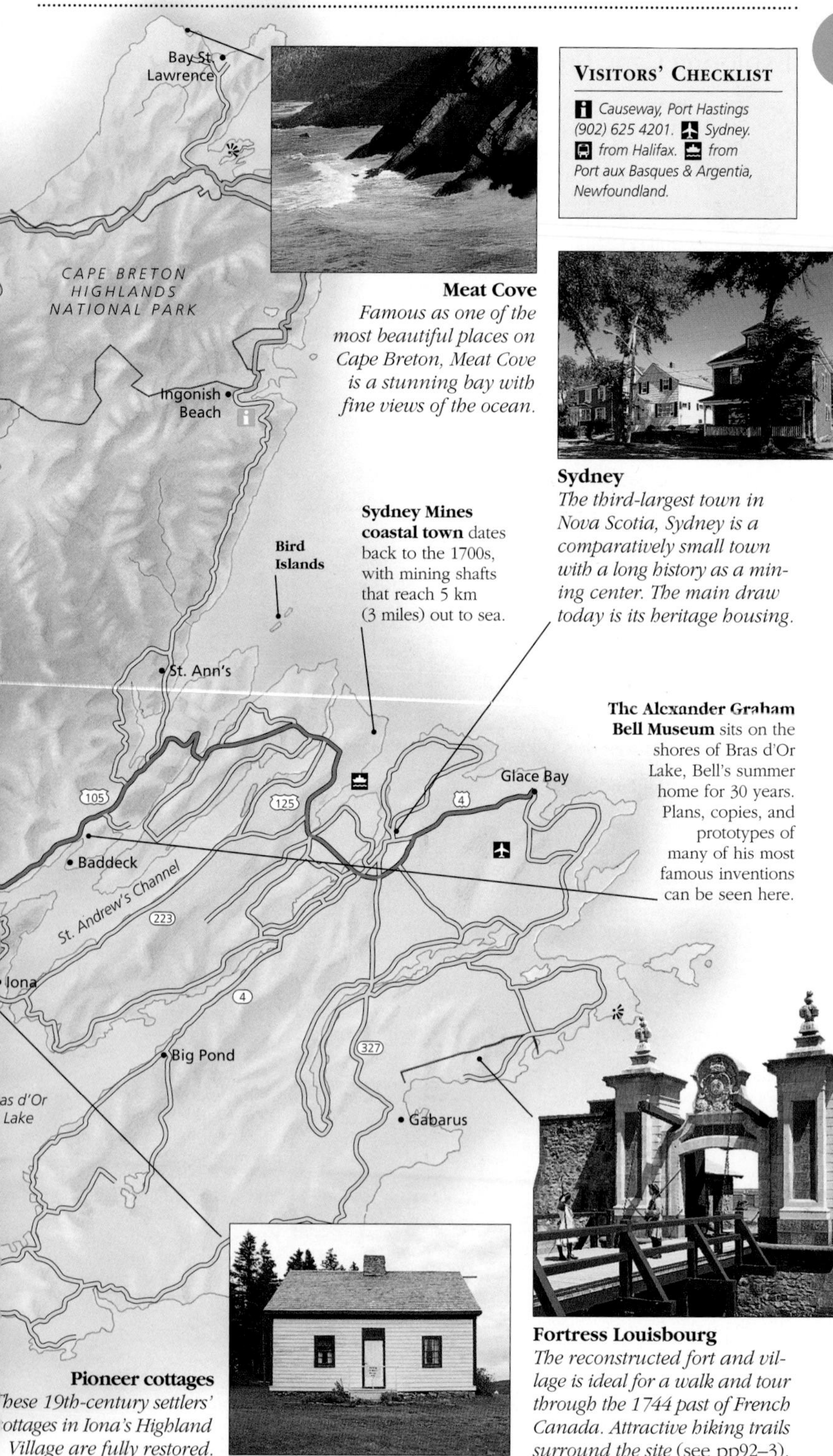

Meat Cove
Famous as one of the most beautiful places on Cape Breton, Meat Cove is a stunning bay with fine views of the ocean.

Sydney Mines coastal town dates back to the 1700s, with mining shafts that reach 5 km (3 miles) out to sea.

Sydney
The third-largest town in Nova Scotia, Sydney is a comparatively small town with a long history as a mining center. The main draw today is its heritage housing.

The Alexander Graham Bell Museum sits on the shores of Bras d'Or Lake, Bell's summer home for 30 years. Plans, copies, and prototypes of many of his most famous inventions can be seen here.

Pioneer cottages
These 19th-century settlers' cottages in Iona's Highland Village are fully restored.

Fortress Louisbourg
The reconstructed fort and village is ideal for a walk and tour through the 1744 past of French Canada. Attractive hiking trails surround the site (see pp92–3).

Visitors' Checklist

Causeway, Port Hastings (902) 625 4201. Sydney. from Halifax. from Port aux Basques & Argentia, Newfoundland.

Exploring Cape Breton Island

Cape Breton fresh lobster

THE LARGEST ISLAND in Nova Scotia, Cape Breton has a wild beauty and grandeur that makes for some of the most impressive scenery in Canada. From the rolling highlands, sprinkled with sparkling streams, to fine sandy beaches, the island's 300-km (200-mile) Cabot Trail provides one of the most memorable tours in Canada. Other inviting country roads lead to the stunning Mabou Hills, surrounding Lake Ainslee, and to romantic little towns including Baddeck and the Acadian settlement of Cheticamp near the green Margaree Valley.

Lobster fishing boats in the Main à Dieu harbor on Cape Breton Island

Cape Breton Highlands National Park

In the 1930s the Canadian Government set aside the 958 sq km (370 sq miles) of magnificent highlands in the northern tip of Cape Breton Island to form Cape Breton Highlands National Park. The park contains some of Canada's most famous scenery, with its mountains, green wilderness, and windswept coastal beauty. The best-known feature of the park is the spectacular 106-km (66-mile) section of the Cabot Trail highway, which traces much of the park's boundary in a loop from Cheticamp to Ingonish.

The Cabot Trail is the primary route through the park, and most attractions are found along it. Entering the park, the trail ascends along the flanks of the coastal mountains. Several viewpoints on this stretch present far-reaching views of the highlands rising from the sea. Continuing inland, the trail travels across the highland plateau. Just past French Lake, the short Bog Walk is a boardwalk trail through marshes, with educational panels that describe this unique bog-bound ecosystem, which is home to rare orchids. Visitors may even catch a glimpse of the park's many moose grazing here in a wetland marsh.

Crossing the French and Mackenzie Mountains, the trail descends dramatically to the charming old community of Pleasant Bay. It then re-enters the highlands, crossing North Mountain, which, at 475 m (1,560 ft), is the highest point in the park. The trail descends into the Aspy River Valley, where a side road leads to the base of the 30-m (100-ft) high Beulach Ban Falls.

Picturesque Ingonish Beach on Cape Breton Island

At Cape North, another side road leads to the scenic whale-watching destination of Bay St. Lawrence just outside the park and the stunningly pretty road to Meat Cove. Farther on, the Scenic Loop breaks away from the Cabot Trail and follows the coast, offering awesome views as it descends to White Point. This road rejoins the Cabot Trail to the east, where it reaches the resort town of Ingonish. The Highland Links Golf Course here is ranked among the top golf courses in Canada.

Cape Breton Highlands National Park
Ingonish Beach. *(902) 285 2691. daily. limited.*

Baddeck

Across the lake from the estate of Alexander Graham Bell, who loved the little town, Baddeck lies in rich farmland and is very much the island's premier resort destination. Set on the northwest side of Bras d'Or Lake, Baddeck is still the small, friendly town that charmed visitors in the 19th century. All amenities are within walking distance. The town's main street follows the waterfront and is lined with shops, cafés, and restaurants. Boat cruises around the lake are available from several places on Water Street by the shore.

The town's top attraction is the **Alexander Graham Bell National Historic Site**. The museum here contains the world's largest collection of photographs, artifacts, and documents about the life of this famous humanitarian and inventor. There are early telephones and several of his later inventions, including a copy of his HD-4 Hydrofoil.

Baddeck
Chebucto St. (902) 295 1911.

Alexander Graham Bell National Historic Site
559 Chebucto St. *(902) 295 2069. daily.*

A fly-fisher tries his hand in the salmon- and trout-filled waters of the Margaree River

Margaree River Valley

Small and emerald green, the Margaree River Valley is in a delightful world of its own. The river has attracted salmon and trout anglers in large numbers since the mid-19th century. Today the region is also a favorite with hikers, antique-hunters, and sightseers.

In the little town of North East Margaree, the tiny but elegant **Margaree Salmon Museum** will fascinate even non-anglers with its beautiful historic rods and reels.

Paved and gravel roads follow the Margaree River upstream to the scenic spot of Big Intervale, where the headwaters come tumbling out of the highlands. This area is ideal for a long hike, fishing, or cycling, and is dazzling when the hillsides are carpeted in the flaming colors of fall.

Margaree Valley
Margaree Fork (902) 248 2803.
Margaree Salmon Museum
60 E. Big Interval Rd. *(902) 248 2848.* *mid-Jun–mid-Oct: 9am–5pm daily.* *limited.*

Cheticamp

This vibrant town is the largest Acadian community in Nova Scotia. Its beautiful Saint Pierre Church is visible from miles out at sea. The Acadians of Cape Breton are skilled craftspeople, and the town's seven cooperatives produce pottery and hooked rugs. Cheticamp's best-known rug hooker was Elizabeth LeFort, whose large and intricate works depicting prominent moments in history have hung in the Vatican and in the White House. Several of her finest rugs are on display at the **Dr. Elizabeth LeFort Museum** at Les Trois Pignons.

Cheticamp is also a popular whale-watching destination; tours are available for seeing many varieties of whale.

Dr. Elizabeth LeFort Museum
15584 Main St. *(902) 224 2642.* *May–Oct: daily.*

Sydney

The only city on Cape Breton Island, Sydney is the third-largest town in Nova Scotia. Boasting the biggest steel plant in North America, the town is the region's industrial center. Despite this, Sydney has a small, attractive historic district around the Esplanade, with several restored buildings, such as Cossit House and Jost House, both dating from the 1870s. Downtown, boutiques, stores, and restaurants can be found along the town's main drag, Charlotte Street.

Sydney
Sydney (902) 539 9876.

Alexander Graham Bell

Alexander Graham Bell

Alexander Graham Bell was born in 1847 in Scotland. Bell's mother was deaf, and, as a child, he became fascinated by speech and communication. In 1870, Bell and his family moved to Ontario *(see p216)*. His work involved transmitting the voice electronically, and he began experimenting with variations of the technology used by the telegraph. In 1876 he transmitted the world's first telephone message, "Watson, come here, I want you." With the patenting of his invention, Bell secured his role as one of the men who changed the world. In 1877, Bell married Mabel Hubbard, one of his deaf students. In 1885, the couple visited Cape Breton, where Bell later built his beautiful estate, Beinn Bhreagh, by Bras d'Or Lake. There he lived and worked each summer until he died in 1922. In Baddeck, the Alexander Graham Bell Museum focuses on his life and varied work.

Fortress Louisbourg

Costumed interpreter

BUILT BETWEEN 1713 AND 1744, the magnificent Fortress Louisbourg was France's bastion of military strength in the New World. Today, it is the largest military reconstruction in North America. Visitors stepping through the fortress gate enter the year 1744, when war had just been declared between France and England. Inside, scores of historically costumed guides bring the excitement of an 18th-century French trading town to life. The streets and buildings are peopled with merchants, soldiers, fishmongers, and washerwomen, all going about the daily business of the 1700s. From the lowliest fisherman's cottage to the elegant home of the Chief Military Engineer, attention to detail throughout is superb. The costumed interpreters offer information about the fortress, its history, and the lives of people they portray.

Overview of the Fortress
The seat of government and the central command of French military power in the New World, the Fortress was home to a town of thousands.

0 meters 50

0 yards 50

The Quay and Frederic Gate
The Quay was the center of commercial activity in the town. It is still central to the fort, as many activities now take place at the Gate's imposing yellow arch.

★ The Engineer's Residence
Responsible for all public construction projects at the fortress, the engineer was one of the most important and powerful men in the community.

STAR FEATURES

- ★ King's Bastion
- ★ Engineer's Residence

Visitors' Checklist

Rte. 22 SW of Louisbourg. *(902) 733 2280.* *May, Jun, Sep & Oct: 9:30am–5pm daily; Jul & Aug: 9am–7pm daily.*

★ King's Bastion
The largest building in the Citadel, the King's Bastion Barracks was home to the 500 French soldiers who lived, ate, and slept here.

The Icehouse was used to store fresh food for the Governor's table.

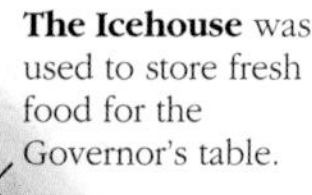

Officers' rooms

King's Bakery
Visitors can buy warm bread from this working bakery that produced the soldiers' daily rations.

The Forge
Traditional skills are in evidence here, with costumed workers demonstrating exactly the carefully learned craft of the 18th century.

The Guardhouse held the vital human line of defense; guards were stationed here while on duty.

The Dauphin Gate
Soldiers in historic uniforms at the gate challenge visitors, just as they would have in 1744. The gate's artistic details are based on archeological relics from the original gate recovered in the 1960s.

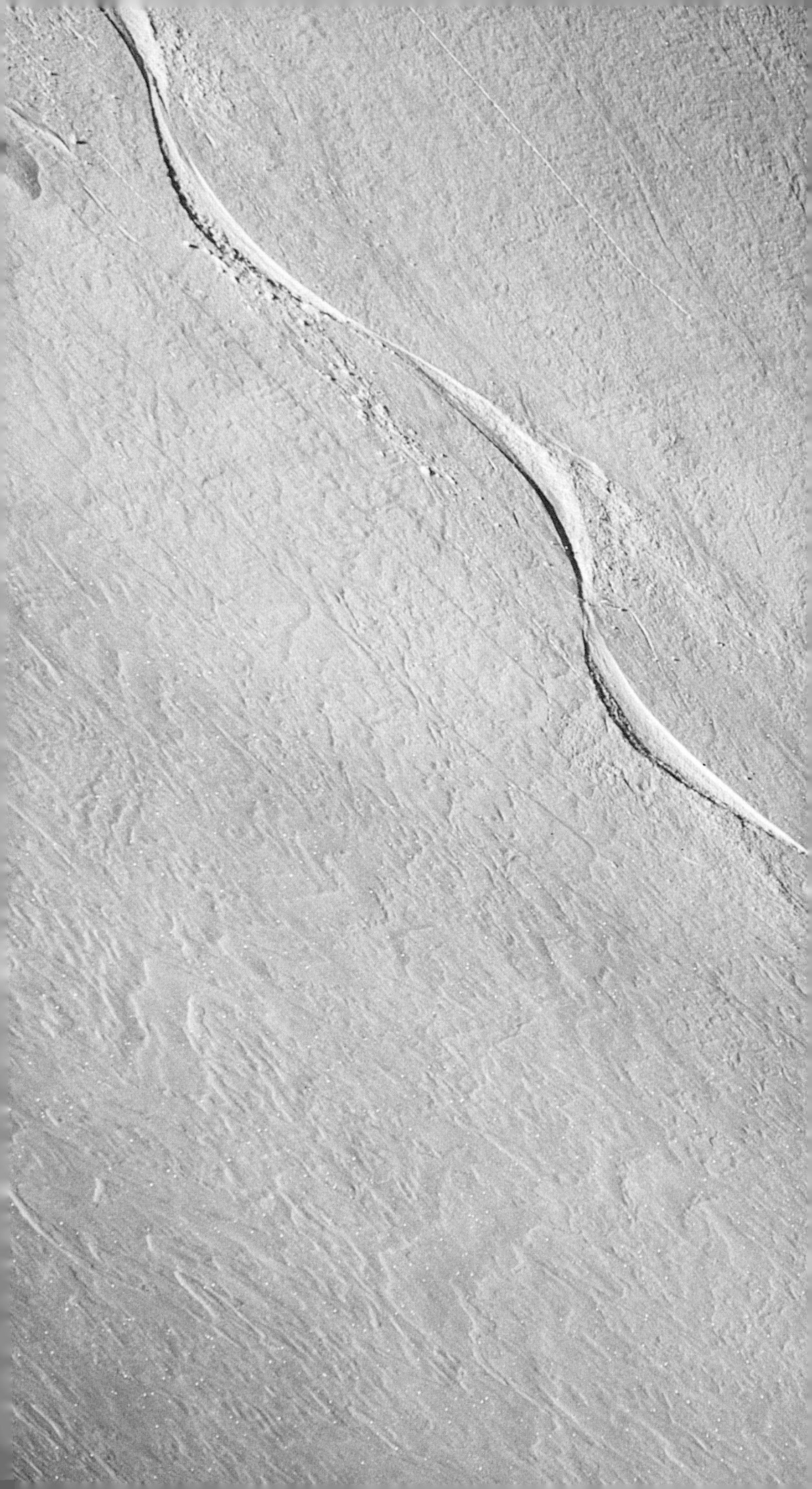

QUEBEC

Introducing Quebec

QUEBEC IS THE LARGEST of Canada's provinces and the biggest French-speaking territory in the world, with many of its seven million citizens holding firm to the language and culture inherited from their French ancestors. Landscapes range from pastoral valleys and villages along the American border, to vast expanses of tundra on the shores of Hudson Bay. At Quebec's heart is the St. Lawrence River. Its north shore begins with the scenic Charlevoix region edging a wilderness of lakes, forest, and tundra that stretches to the Hudson Strait, past one of the world's largest power projects at James Bay. To the south lies the mountainous Gaspé Peninsula. There are two major cities; multiethnic Montreal, and Quebec City, the provincial capital and North America's only walled city.

The picturesque lakeside resort of St- Jovite in the Laurentian Mountains set amid a backdrop of magnificent fall colors

Quebec's largest city, Montreal, has a vibrant downtown area that comes to life after dark

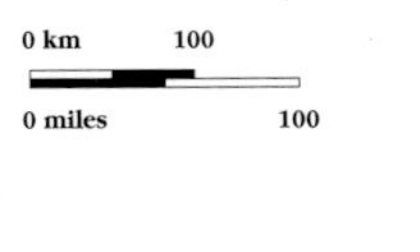

KEY

Highway

Major road

River

SEE ALSO

• ***Where to stay*** pp346–350

• ***Where to eat*** pp366–370

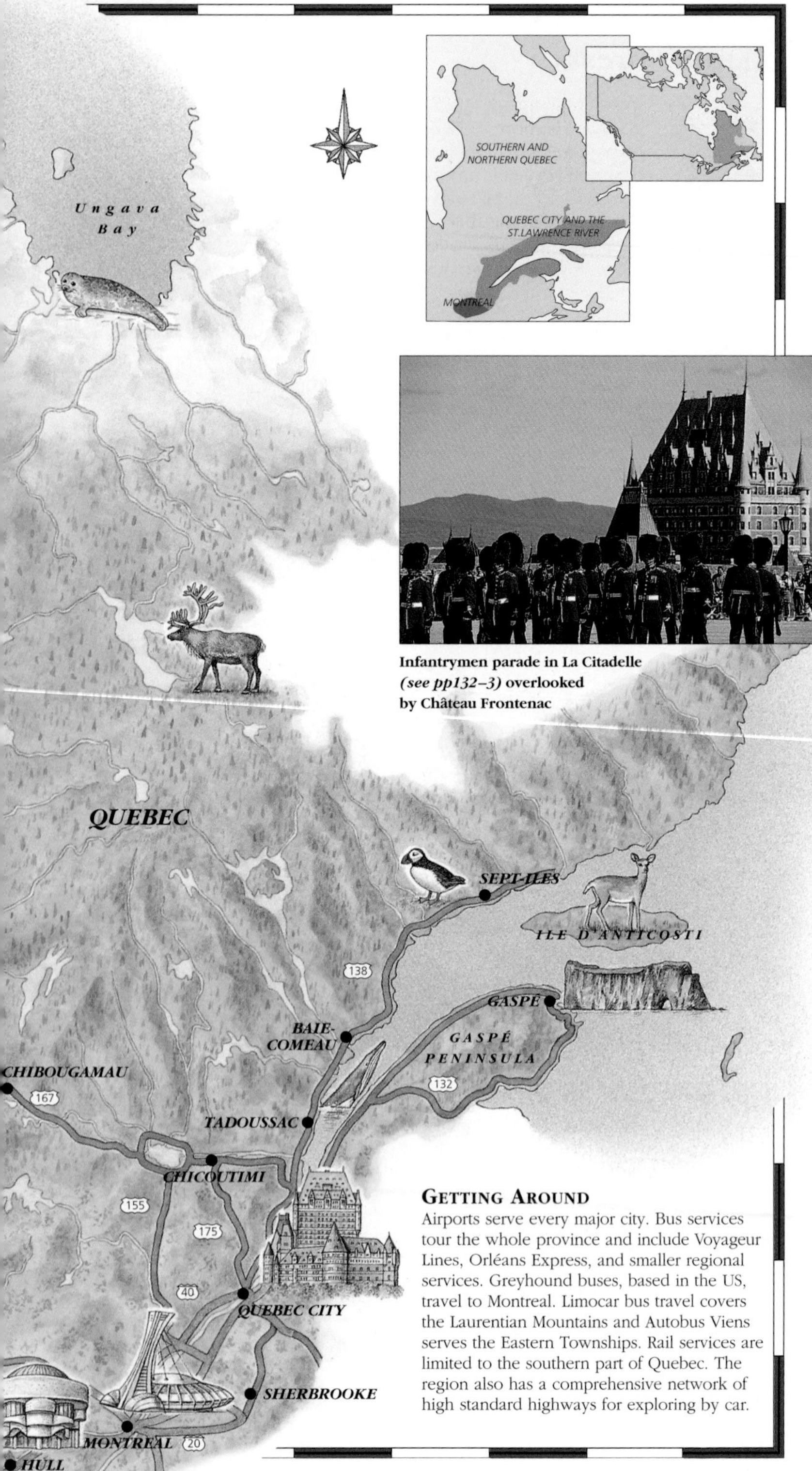

Infantrymen parade in La Citadelle ***(see pp132–3)*** **overlooked by Château Frontenac**

Getting Around

Airports serve every major city. Bus services tour the whole province and include Voyageur Lines, Orléans Express, and smaller regional services. Greyhound buses, based in the US, travel to Montreal. Limocar bus travel covers the Laurentian Mountains and Autobus Viens serves the Eastern Townships. Rail services are limited to the southern part of Quebec. The region also has a comprehensive network of high standard highways for exploring by car.

Maple Forests

The red maple leaf of Canada

LONG THE PRIDE of Quebec and Ontario, there is more to Canada's ancient maple forests than their annual display of beauty. Every fall, turning leaves splash crimson and orange across the south, but it is in springtime that the trees give up their most famous product: maple syrup. Extracting techniques which were developed by native peoples were passed to Europeans in the 17th century. Traditional methods changed little until the 1940s, when part of the process was mechanized. Many age-old methods remain, however, including the final hand-stirring of the syrup.

Maple trees, either red maple *(Acer rubrum)* or sugar maple *(Acer saccharum)*, grow to heights of well over 30 m (100 ft), with thick trunks a meter (3 ft) in diameter. While their main product is the syrup, the hard wood is used for furniture and, of course, the leaf itself is the national symbol of Canada, officially established on the flag in 1965.

Collecting sap from trees *by tapping maple trunks is the first step. Cuts are made low in the wood in spring as sap rises.*

Transporting the sap *in large barrels on a horse-drawn sleigh through the snowy forests is traditional. In the 1970s this was largely replaced by a network of plastic tubing that take the sap directly from tree trunks to the sugar shacks.*

Sugar shacks *are built in the forest in the center of the sugar bush, the cluster of maple trees that are producing sap. Men and women alike work long hours at slowly evaporating the sap, reducing it to syrup. Quebecois have their own rite of spring: when the first syrup is ready, it is poured onto the crisp snow outside the shacks to make a tasty frozen taffy.*

Maple Syrup Products

Maple products are used in a variety of foods, both sweet and savory

Although 80 percent of Canada's annual maple harvest eventually becomes maple syrup, there is more to the industry than simply a sweet sauce. Boiled for longer, the syrup hardens into a pale golden sugar that can be used to sweeten coffee or eaten like candy. Maple butter, which is whipped with sugar, is also popular. Savory products benefit too; ham and bacon can be cured in syrup, which is delicious. The sweet-toothed people of Quebec use the syrup to make sugar pie, a tart with a sweet, fudge filling.

Maple syrup

Syrup is graded according to quality; clear golden fluid, produced at the start of the season, is the most prized, and is generally bottled. Later, darker syrup is used in cooking, and the final, even darker, batch makes a base for synthetic flavors or syrups. Over Can$100 million is spent annually on maple products.

The Story of Maple Syrup

The first maple-sugar farmers were native Canadians. Long before European settlers arrived in the 16th century, tribes all over Northeast America sweetened savory dishes with syrup. An Iroquois legend tells the story of a chief in ancient times who, hurling an ax at a tree, found it stuck in the trunk at the end of the next day, dripping sweet fluid. That night the chief's wife boiled the day's hunt in the sap, and the syrup was born. Folk tales apart, it is certain that native people discovered the sap and techniques for refining it, few of which have changed, and passed their knowledge to Europeans freely.

Boiling maple sap *involves 40 liters (88 pts) of sap to create one liter (2.2 pts) of syrup. The gold color and maple flavor develop as distillation takes place. The paler first syrup of the season is the most valuable.*

Transforming sap into maple syrup *takes place very slowly. The sap bubbles over a wood fire (maple wood is prefered) until about 98 percent of its water content evaporates. Modern processes use mechanized evaporators to boil the sap and draw off the steam, but even hi-tech methods still require a final hand-stirred simmering.*

The St. Lawrence Seaway

EXTENDING FROM THE Gulf of St. Lawrence on the Atlantic coast to Duluth at the western end of Lake Superior in Minnesota, the St. Lawrence Seaway and Great Lakes System flows across North America for over 3,700 km (2,300 miles). The St. Lawrence Seaway itself stretches 553 km (344 miles) from Montreal to Lake Erie and covers 245,750 square km (95,000 sq miles) of navigable water. Open from March to December, it is the world's longest deep-draft inland waterway. Ships carry a huge quantity of domestic traffic, but over 60 per cent of the total freight travels to and from overseas ports, mainly from Europe, the Middle East, and Africa. Traffic varies: cargoes of grain travel in superships alongside pleasure boats.

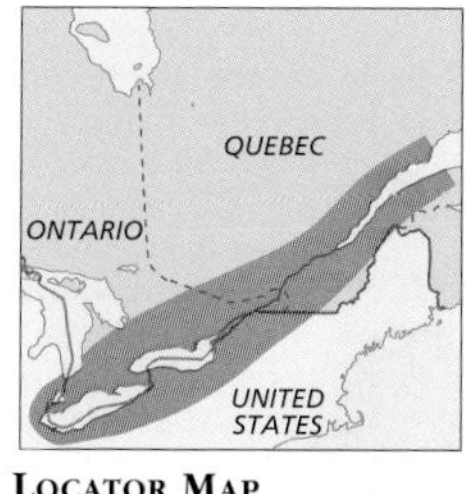

LOCATOR MAP

The St. Lawrence Seaway

THE HISTORY OF THE SEAWAY

The Seaway has ancient beginnings: in 1680, French monk Dollier de Casson started a campaign to build a mile-long canal linking Lac St. Louis and Montreal, which was finally opened in 1824 as the Lachine Canal. In 1833, the first Welland Canal (from Lake Ontario to Lake Erie) opened. The fourth Welland Canal was the first modern part of the Seaway to be built in 1932. 1951 brought US and Canadian cooperation to bear on a new seaway, which began in Canada in 1954. On April 25, 1959, the Seaway opened, linking the Great Lakes to the world.

The *D'Iberville*, first ship to cross the Seaway

Pleasure boats *cruise the Seaway near the Thousand Islands by Kingston, Ontario. Each summer, small craft take advantage of the excellent sailing and waterskiing available in this section of the Seaway.*

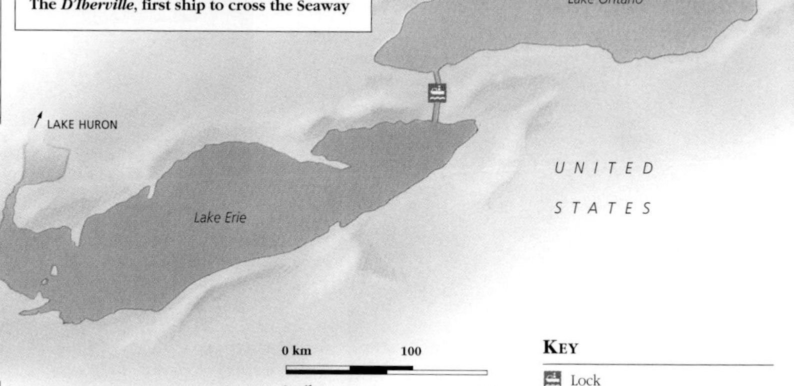

KEY

Lock

Montreal *is the historic beginning of the Seaway. It was here that the first link was built to the lakes during the 18th century, opening up pathways to the center of North America. The Seaway is open nine months each year, despite much freezing weather.*

Cargo ships *carry iron ore, grain, coal, and other bulk commodities through the waterway: more than 2 billion tons of cargo have been shipped since 1959. Canada's heavy industry could not continue without the Seaway.*

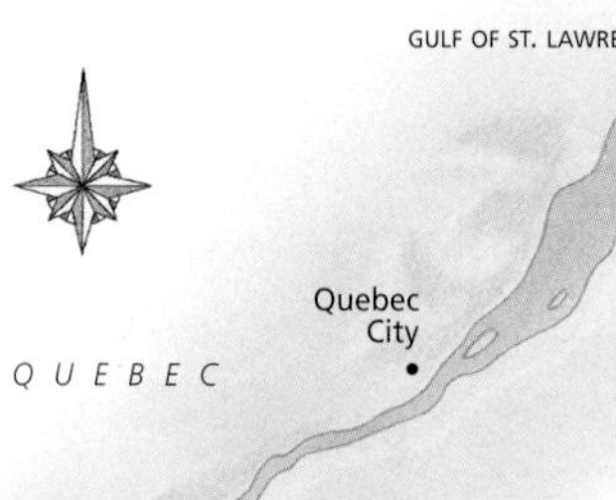

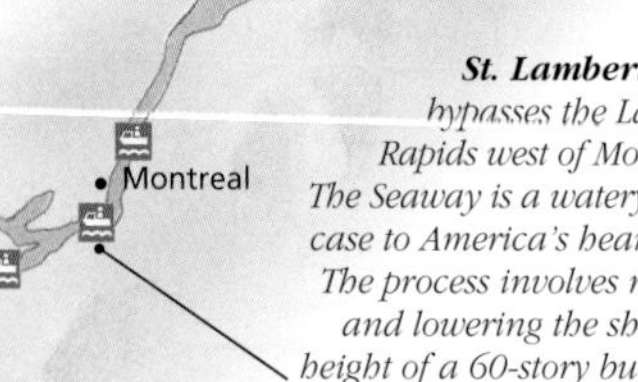

St. Lambert Lock *bypasses the Lachine Rapids west of Montreal. The Seaway is a watery staircase to America's heartland. The process involves raising and lowering the ships the height of a 60-story building.*

Construction of the Seaway

In 1895, the US and Canadian governments appointed a Deep Waterways Commission to study the feasibility of what was to become today's St. Lawrence Seaway; it reported in favor of the project two years later. After 50 years of intercountry wrangling, the jointly financed project was begun on August 10, 1954 – in the words of Canadian Prime Minister Louis St. Laurent "a bond rather than a barrier between Americans and Canadians." The massive undertaking was beset with problems not previously encountered, especially the discovery of ancient rock formations so hard that new machinery had to be created to dig through them. All work, including relocating villages and dredging the existing canals, had to be carried out with minimum disruption to the daily boat, rail, and car traffic of major cities. Nonetheless, the four-year construction was completed almost to the day.

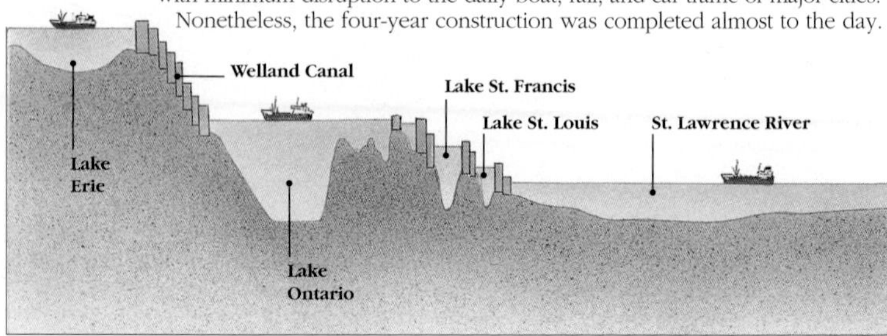

The Seaway in profile with locks and rising water levels

MONTREAL

MONTREAL IS *the second largest city in Canada, and the only French-speaking one in the Americas. The pious 17th-century French founders of this vibrant island metropolis might be a little surprised to have produced a place that revels so much in its reputation for joie de vivre, but at least their edifices remain; the spires of some of Canada's finest churches still rise above the skyline.*

Montreal's location at the convergence of the St. Lawrence and Ottawa rivers made it Canada's first great trading center. It was founded in 1642 by a group of French Catholics as a Christian community and port. Much of its economic power has now moved west to Toronto, and what makes Montreal interesting today is a cultural, rather than a geographical, confluence. About 70 percent of its 3 million residents are of French descent, another 15 percent have British origins, and the rest represent nearly every major ethnic group. Many speak three or more languages. The communities form a kind of mosaic, with the anglophones in the west, the francophones in the east, and other ethnic communities in pockets all over the island. There is nothing rigid about these divisions: Anglophones eat and drink in the restaurants and bistros of the historic French district, and francophones visit the traditionally English area. The most interesting neighborhoods sprawl along the southern slopes of Mont-Royal – the 234-m (767-ft) hill from which the city derives its name. Vieux-Montréal's network of narrow, cobblestone streets huddles near the waterfront, while the main shopping area is farther north along Rue Sainte-Catherine. It extends below the city's surface in the maze of tunnels that connect the Underground City, the complex of homes, stores, and leisure venues that spreads out beneath the bustling city. Other modern attractions include the Olympic Park stadium and the Musée d'Art Contemporain, built in the 1990s to complement Montreal's fine historic museums.

Visitors admiring the skyline of Montreal

◁ **Waiters posing outside a typically French traditonal bistro in downtown Montreal**

Exploring Montreal

MONTREAL SHARES A 50-kilometer (30-mile) long island in the St. Lawrence River with the 28 other municipalities that make up the Communauté Urbaine de Montréal (Montreal Urban Community). The city core lies between Mont-Royal and the river, and streets follow a fairly consistent grid pattern, with Boulevard Saint-Laurent, known as The Main, splitting the city into its western and eastern halves. Montreal is a large city but getting around is easy.

The skyscrapers of downtown Montreal at dusk

KEY

- Street-by-street: *see pp106–107*
- International airport
- Railroad station
- Bus terminus
- Ferry boarding point
- Visitor information
- Parking
- Métro station
- Highway
- Major road
- Pedestrian walkway

SIGHTS AT A GLANCE

Historic Buildings and Areas

Château Ramezay 3
Chinatown 7
Lachine 27
McGill University 13
Place des Arts 9
Plateau Mont-Royal 8
Sir George Etienne-Carter National Historic Site 4
Square Dorchester and Place du Canada 16
Rue Sherbrooke 19
Underground City 15
Vieux Port 1

Parks and Gardens

Jardin Botanique de Montréal 23
Olympic Park pp120–21 22
Parc Mont-Royal 21

Islands

Ile Notre-Dame 25
Ile Sainte-Hélène 24

Churches and Cathedrals

Basilique Notre-Dame-de-Montréal pp108–109 2
Cathédrale Marie-Reine-du-Monde 17
Christ Church Cathedral 11
Oratoire St-Joseph 20

Museums and Galleries

Centre d'Histoire de Montréal 6
Centre Canadien d'Architecture 18
Maison Saint-Gabriel 26
McCord Museum of Canadian History 12
Musée d'Art Contemporain pp112–13 10
Musée des Beaux-Arts pp114–15 14
Musée Marc-Aurèle Fortin 5

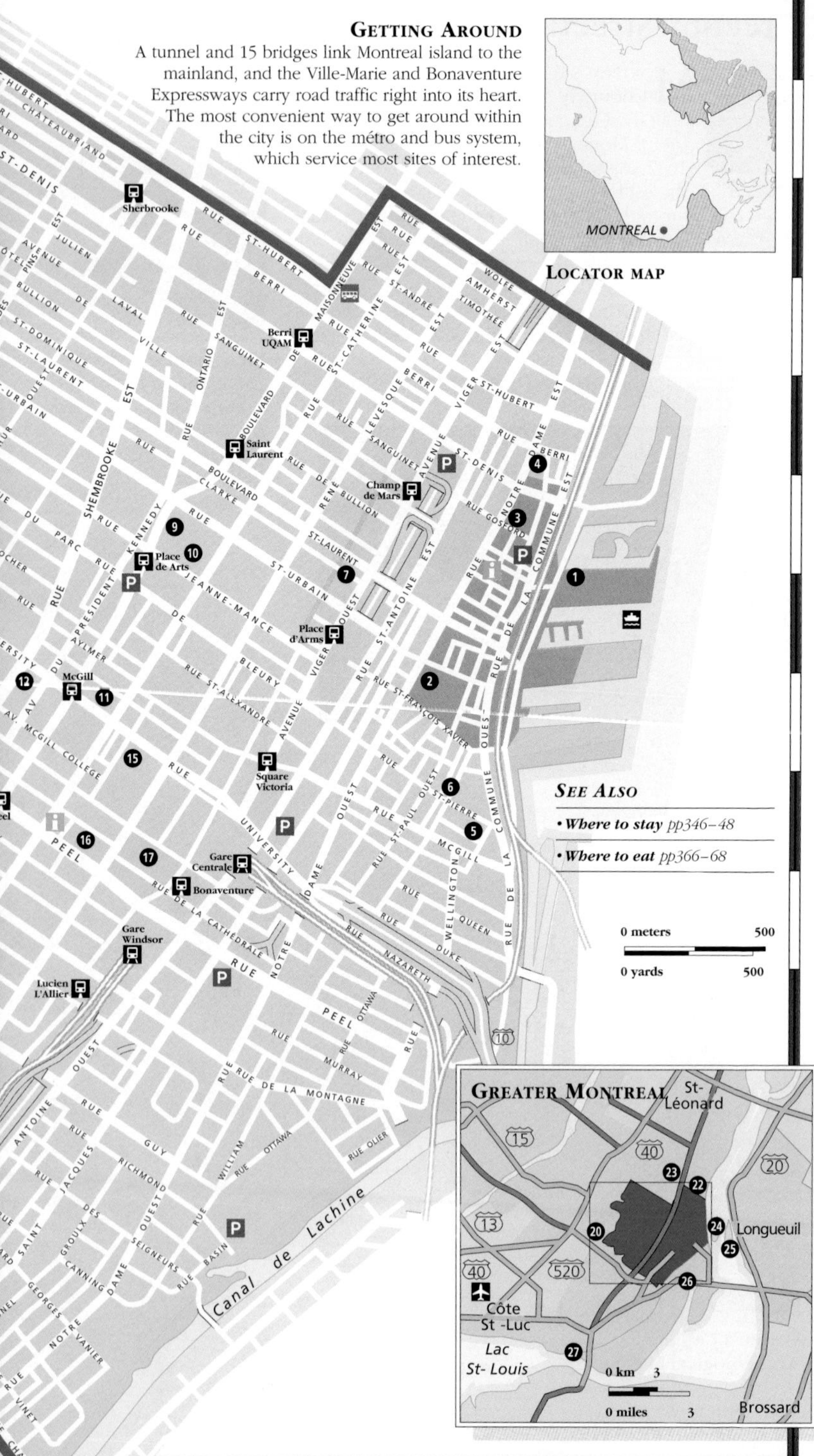

GETTING AROUND

A tunnel and 15 bridges link Montreal island to the mainland, and the Ville-Marie and Bonaventure Expressways carry road traffic right into its heart. The most convenient way to get around within the city is on the métro and bus system, which service most sites of interest.

SEE ALSO

- ***Where to stay*** *pp346–48*
- ***Where to eat*** *pp366–68*

Street-by-Street: Vieux-Montréal

Rue St-Paul street sign

MONTREAL'S FOUNDERS, led by Paul de Chomédy and Sieur de Maisonneuve, built the Catholic village that was to become Vieux-Montréal by the Lachine Rapids in 1642. Missionary efforts failed to flourish, but the settlement blossomed into a prosperous fur-trading town with fine homes and a stone stockade. As Montreal expanded in the 19th century, the old city, Vieux-Montréal, fell into decline. In the 1960s, however, the district underwent a renaissance. The remaining 18th-century buildings were renovated and transformed into the restaurants, bistros, and boutiques that are so fashionable today, especially those of rue Notre-Dame and rue St-Paul.

View from the river
This clutch of historic streets leading down to the great St. Lawrence River is a district of romance and charm in the midst of this modern city.

★ Basilique Notre-Dame
One of the most splendid churches in North America, the city's 1829 Catholic showpiece has a richly decorated and colorful interior ❷

Pointe-à-Callière Archeological Museum
An underground tour here leads visitors past excavated ruins and early water systems dating from the 17th century.

STAR SIGHTS

- ★ **Basilique Notre-Dame**
- ★ **Château Ramezay**

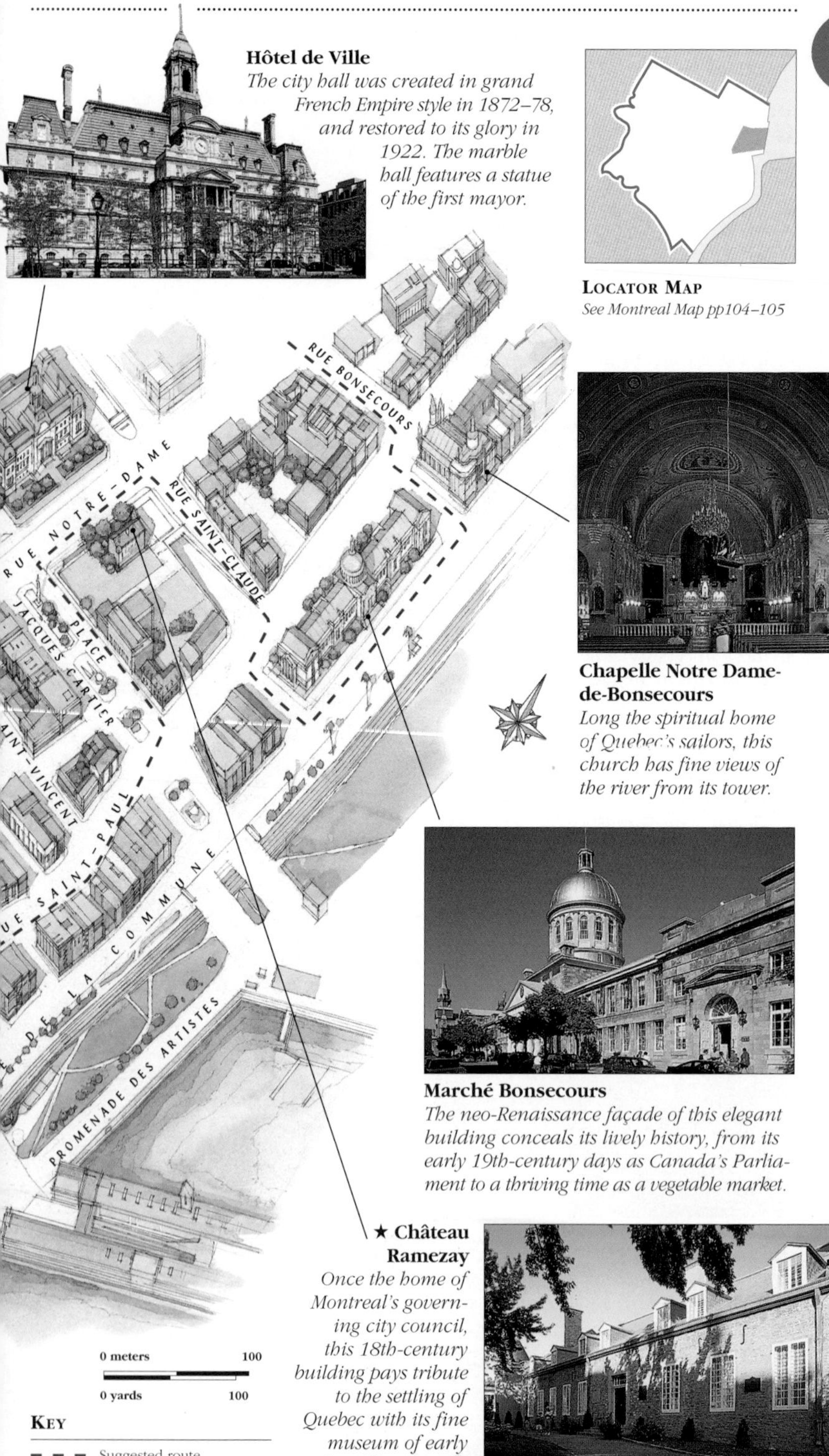

Hôtel de Ville
The city hall was created in grand French Empire style in 1872–78, and restored to its glory in 1922. The marble hall features a statue of the first mayor.

Locator Map
See Montreal Map pp104–105

Chapelle Notre Dame-de-Bonsecours
Long the spiritual home of Quebec's sailors, this church has fine views of the river from its tower.

Marché Bonsecours
The neo-Renaissance façade of this elegant building conceals its lively history, from its early 19th-century days as Canada's Parliament to a thriving time as a vegetable market.

★ Château Ramezay
Once the home of Montreal's governing city council, this 18th-century building pays tribute to the settling of Quebec with its fine museum of early tools and artifacts ❸

0 meters 100
0 yards 100

Key

– – – Suggested route

Vieux-Port ❶

333 Rue de la Commune. (514) 496 7678. Central Station. 55. Terminus Voyager. Square Victoria.

In its glory days of the 19th century, the Vieux-Port of Montreal was one of the most important inland harbors in North America, but it declined with the introduction of megaships and the airplane in the early 20th century. By the late 1980s, the Canadian government had begun to transform it into one of the most popular parks in Montreal. Its 12.5 km (8 miles) of waterside walkways and open grassy fields blend almost seamlessly into the lovely streets of Vieux-Montréal, giving the old city a wide window onto the river.

The port has a bustling, recreational atmosphere. On summer afternoons, visitors and Montrealers alike stroll, cycle, or in-line skate along the Promenade du Vieux Port.

Cyclists enjoying the waterfront promenade, Vieux-Port

Château Ramezay ❸

280 Rue Notre Dame E. (514) 861 3708. VIA Rail. 14, 55. Terminus Voyager. Champ-de-Mars. Jun–Sep: 10am–6pm daily; Oct–May: 10am–4:30pm Tue–Sun. Dec 25, Jan 1.

When Montreal's 11th governor, Claude de Ramezay, arrived in the city in 1702, he was homesick for Normandy and decided to build a residence for himself that was reminiscent of the châteaux back home, with stone walls, dormer windows, and copper roof. The squat round towers, added in the

Basilique Notre-Dame-de-Montréal ❷

In the center of Place d'Armes sits the Basilica, Montreal's oldest and grandest Catholic church. Originally built in the 17th century, a new building was commissioned in 1829. American architect James O'Donnell excelled himself with a vast vaulted cavern that combined elements of Neo-Classical and Neo-Gothic design, and provides 3,800 seats in the nave and two tiers of balconies. Splendidly redecorated in the 1870s, the intricate woodcarving and stained glass are the work of Canadian craftsman Victor Bourgeau.

The main altar is surrounded by delicate pine and walnut woodcarving.

The nave is illuminated by a rose window under an azure ceiling.

★ Reredos
The focus of the nave is backed by azure, beneath a golden starry sky.

★ Pulpit
This ornate construction was sculpted by Philippe Hébert. The prophets Ezekiel and Jeremiah stand at its base.

Star Sights

- **★ Reredos**
- **★ Pulpit**

19th century, reinforce the effect. Many of de Ramezay's governor successors lived here. Château Ramezay is one of the most impressive remnants of the French regime open to the public in Montreal.

The château has been restored to the style of Governor de Ramezay's day. Of particular interest is the Nantes Salon, with its 18th-century carved paneling by the French architect Germain Boffrand.

Uniforms, documents, and furniture on the main floor reflect the life of New France's ruling classes, while the cellars depict the doings of humbler colonists. The scarlet automobile, made for the city's first motorist, is an interesting sight.

Sir George-Etienne Cartier National Historic Site ❹

458 Rue Notre Dame. *(514) 283 2282. Central Station. Terminus Voyager. Champ-de-Mars. mid-May–Aug: daily; Sep–Dec & Apr–mid-May: Wed–Sun. Jan–Mar.*

GEORGE-ETIENNE Cartier (1814–73) was a Father of Confederation *(see p44)* and one of the most important French-Canadian politicians of his day. This national historic site comprises two adjoining graystone houses owned by the Cartiers on the eastern edge of the old town. One is dedicated to Cartier's career as a lawyer, politician, and railroad-builder. In this house, you can sit at a round table and listen in either French or English to a very good summary of the political founding of modern Canada.

Ormolu clock at the Etienne-Cartier

The second house focuses on the Cartiers' domestic life and the functioning of a Victorian upper middle-class family. Visitors can wander through formal rooms full of rich furniture and listen to snatches of taped conversation from "servants" talking about their lives.

The twin towers rise 69 m (226 ft) above the basilica and are visible across the old city.

The Vieux Séminaire dates from 1685 and still belongs to the Sulpician Fathers, the priests who also run the basilica. It is one of the oldest building in Montreal.

VISITORS' CHECKLIST

110 rue Notre Dame W, Place d'Armes. *(514) 842 2925. Place des Arts. Jun–Oct: 7am–8pm daily; Nov–May: 7am–6pm daily. Jun–Oct.*

Pipe Organ
The renowned maker Casavant built the organ above the north door in 1891. Recitals are still held frequently.

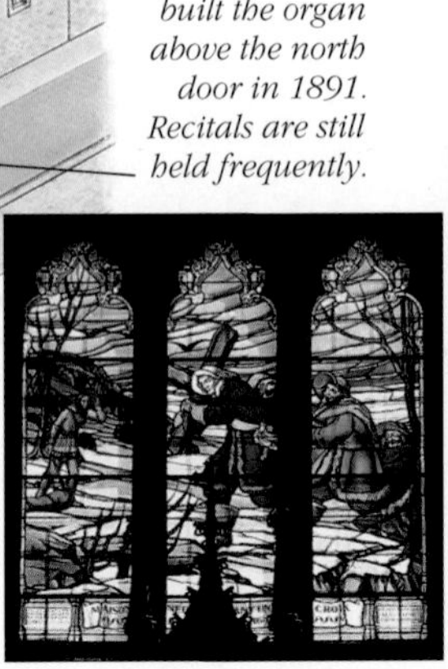

Stained-glass windows
The basilica's beautiful windows were imported from Limoges in 1930. Each tells a story of Montreal's past; this shows New World pioneer Maisonneuve climbing Mont Royal in 1643.

Musée Marc-Aurèle Fortin ❺

118 Rue Saint-Pierre. *(514) 845 6108.* *Central Station.* *Terminus Voyager.* M *Square Victoria.* *11am–5pm Tue–Sun.*

THIS MUSEUM, housed in an old stone warehouse belonging to an ancient order of nuns, has an extensive collection of Fortin's work, and it also mounts exhibitions of new painting by local artists.

Marc-Aurèle Fortin transformed landscape painting in Canada. He was born in 1888, when European styles dominated North American art. Fortin loved the light of his native province, and used many unusual techniques. To capture the "warm light of Quebec," for example, he painted some of his pictures over gray backgrounds. By the time he died in 1970, he left behind not only a staggering amount of work but a whole new way of looking at nature, especially the various rural areas of his native Quebec.

Gray stone façade of the Musée Marc-Aurèle Fortin

Centre d'Histoire de Montréal ❻

335 Place d'Youville. *(514) 872 3207.* *61.* M *Square Victoria.* *mid-May–Aug: daily; Sep–May: Tue–Sun.* *mid-Dec–mid-Jan.*

THIS MUSEUM is housed in a handsome, red-brick fire station, which has a gracefully gabled roof built in 1903. The exhibits trace the history of Montreal from the first Indian settlements to the modern age, with the focus on everyday life. A dummy 19th-century town crier, for example, warns residents of the penalties for letting their pigs and sheep run loose. Particularly interesting is the second floor, which depicts life in the 1930s and 1940s. Visitors can relax in a period living room and listen to snippets of Canadian radio broadcasts (ranging from a hockey game to the recitation of the rosary), or step into a phone booth and eavesdrop on a factory worker making a date with his shop-clerk girlfriend. A simulated ride in a city tram brings visitors back into modern times.

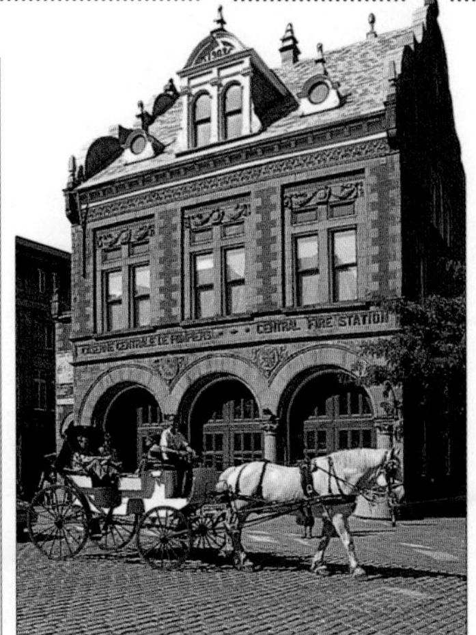

Centre d'Histoire de Montréal

Chinatown ❼

M *Champ-de-Mars; Place des Arts.*

THE NAME IS becoming a little anachronistic. Many of the restaurants and shops in this 18-block district just northeast of the Old City are now owned by Vietnamese and Thai immigrants, who arrived in Montreal in the wake of 20th-century upheavals in Southeast Asia. The Chinese, however, were here first. They began arriving in large numbers after 1880, along with many European immigants, and stuck together in this corner of the city in an attempt to avoid discrimination.

As they grew more prosperous, many of the descendants of the first immigrants moved to wealthier areas, leaving Chinatown to the old and to the newly arrived. Many thousands of them now return on weekends, and the narrow streets are busy with people shopping for silk, souvenirs, vegetables, records, and barbecued meat.

Restaurants specialize in a range of cuisines, serving Szechuan, Cantonese, Thai, Vietnamese, and Korean food, and the air is fragrant with the smell of hot barbecued pork and aromatic noodles.

For those seeking respite from the bustle, there is a lovely little garden dedicated to the charismatic Chinese leader Sun Yat-sen on Clarke Street. Other features of the area include two large, Chinese-style arches which span de la Gauchetière Street, and a pair of authentic pagodas on the roof of the modern Holiday Inn hotel.

A brightly colored market stall in vibrant Chinatown

Locals picknicking in the leisurely atmosphere of the Parc Lafontaine in Plateau Mont-Royal

Plateau Mont-Royal ❽

Tourisme Plateau Mont-Royal: (514) 524 8767. **M** *Sherbrooke; Mont-Royal.*

No neighborhood captures the essence of Montreal more fully than the Plateau. Its main thoroughfares are lined with bistros, bookstores, boutiques, and sidewalk cafés. Nightclubs veer from the eccentric to the classic, and eateries from snack bars and sandwich shops to some of the best dining locations in the city. Jazz bars, too, are popular in this area and range from the decorous to the distinctly shady.

The area's residents are a mix of students, working-class French-speakers, trendy young professionals, and ethnic families with roots in Europe and Latin America. They congregate either in Parc Lafontaine, a neighborly expanse of green with an outdoor theater, or in "Balconville," a distinctly Montrealer institution linked to the duplexes and triplexes that many residents live in. To save interior space, these stacks of single-floor flats are studded with balconies linked to the street by fanciful, wrought-iron stairways. Although treacherous in winter, in summer they are decked with flowers and barbecue grills, and become centers for parties, family gatherings, and picnics.

The large working-class families for whom these homes were built in the early part of the century lived very modestly, but they managed to amass enough money to build impressively large and beautiful parish churches, notably the Eglise Saint-Jean-Baptiste. The Catholic bourgeoisie lived just a little farther south, in gracious Second-Empire homes on Rue Saint-Denis or Carré Saint-Louis, one of the prettiest squares in the city.

Place des Arts ❾

183 Rue Ste-Catherine W. *(514) 842 2112.* **M** *Place des Arts.*

This complex of halls and theaters is Montreal's prime center for the performing arts. Both the Opéra de Montréal (Montreal Opera) and the Orchéstre Symphonique de Montréal (Montreal Symphony Orchestra) make their home in the Salle Wilfrid Pelletier. This is the largest of the center's five halls, and has 2,982 seats. The buildings of Place des Arts share a modern, spacious central plaza with the outstanding Musée d'art contemporain *(see pp112–13)*.

Place des Arts, Montreal's top entertainment venue

Musée d'Art Contemporain ⑩

Opened in 1964, the museum of Contemporary Art is the only institution in Canada dedicated exclusively to modern art. Located in downtown Montreal, more than 60 percent of the approximately 6,000 paintings, drawings, photographs, videos, and installations in the permanent collection are by Quebec artists. Works date from 1939, but the emphasis is on the contemporary. There are also works by innovative international talents, such as the controversial Bill Viola, Louise Bourgeois, and Andrès Serrano. The exhibits are in wide, well-lit galleries whose elegance helped to earn the Musée a Grand Prix from Montreal Council. The exhibition space is built around a rotunda, which runs up through the core of the building.

Les Dentelles de Montmirail
Young artist Natalie Roy's 1995 landscape (detail shown) is part of a large collection of new Quebec art.

First floor

★ **Niagara Sandstone Circle** *(1981)*
English sculptor Richard Long's work is literally ground breaking. Using materials from the natural environment, which itself is the theme of the work, his careful geometric placing acts as a spur to meditation.

Street Level

Key

- Permanent exhibition space
- Temporary exhibition space
- Pierre Granche sculpture
- Movie theater
- Video gallery
- Multimedia gallery
- Theater/Seminar hall
- Art workshops
- Nonexhibition space

Entrance Hall
The museum uses this airy modern space, hung in places with pieces from its collection, for special events and receptions. A pleasant first-floor restaurant overlooks the hall.

Star Exhibitors

★ **Pierre Granche**

★ **Richard Long**

Museum Guide

Only a small proportion of the exhibits in the museum are on permanent display. They occupy the upper floor space along with rotating and visiting items. There is also a sculpture garden, accessible from the main museum building, that has rotating exhibits and is a good spot to rest during a tour of the galleries.

VISITORS' CHECKLIST

185 Ste. Catherine St. W. *(514) 847 6226.* *Place-des-Arts.* *11am–6pm Tue, Thu–Sun; 11am–9pm Wed.* *Mon; Dec 25, Jan 1.* *by arrangement.* *www.macm.org*

★ **Comme si le temps ... de la rue** *(1991–2)*
Pierre Granche's permanent outdoor installation is based on Egyptian mythological figures whose shapes symbolize Montreal. Created to contrast with its urban milieu, the work exudes humor and poetry.

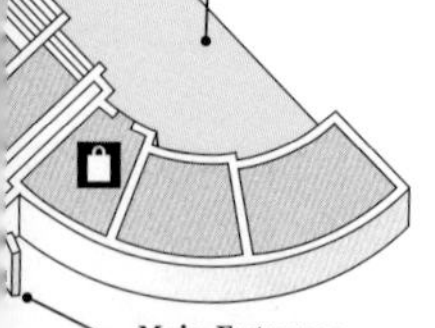

Main Entrance

Museum façade
Built in the 1990s, the MAC building shows 320 artworks, taken from their much larger rotating collection.

Christ Church Cathedral ⓫

1444 Union Ave. *(514) 843 6577.* *Central Station.* *15.* *McGill.* *8am–5:30pm daily.*

ARCHITECT Frank Wills completed Christ Church in 1859 as the seat of the Anglican bishop of Montreal. This graceful Gothic limestone building, with a triple portal and a tall slender spire, has exterior walls decorated with gargoyles. The church was too heavy for the land, and the stone spire was replaced in 1940 with a treated aluminum steeple. Many local workers find respite at noon concerts in the cathedral's cool, dim interior with its pointed arched nave and magnificent stained-glass windows, some from the William Morris studio in London.

Christ Church Cathedral, based on a 14th-century English design

McCord Museum of Canadian History ⓬

690 Rue Sherbrooke W. *(514) 398 7100.* *Central Station.* *24.* *McGill.* *10am–6pm Tue–Fri; 10am–5pm Sat & Sun.* *Mon.*

LAWYER DAVID Ross McCord (1844–1930) was an avid collector of virtually everything that had to do with life in Canada, including books, photographs, jewelry, furniture, clothing, documents, papers, paintings, toys, and porcelain. In 1919, he gave his considerable acquisitions to McGill University with a view to establishing a museum of Canadian social history. That collection, now more than 90,000 artifacts, is housed in a stately limestone building that was once a social center for McGill students. The museum has a good section of early history, as well as exceptional folk art. A particularly fine collection of Indian and Inuit items features clothing, weapons, jewelry, furs, and pottery.

Inuit slippers at the McCord Museum

A separate room is devoted to the social history of Montreal. The museum's most celebrated possession is the collection of 700,000 photographs, that painstakingly chronicle every detail of daily life in 19th-century Montreal.

McGill University ⓭

845 Rue Sherbrooke W. *(514) 398 4455.* *Central Station.* *24.* *McGill.* *9am–6pm Mon–Fri.* *book in advance.*

WHEN IT was founded in 1821, Canada's oldest university was set on land left for the purpose by fur trader and land speculator James McGill (1744–1813). The university's main entrance is guarded by the Classical Roddick Gates. Behind them an avenue leads to the domed Neoclassical Arts Building, which is the oldest structure on campus.

The rest of the 70 or so buildings range from the ornately Victorian to the starkly concrete. One of the loveliest is the **Redpath Museum of Natural History**, which holds one of the city's most eclectic and eccentric collections. A huge number of fossils, including a dinosaur skeleton, sit alongside African art, Roman coins, and a shrunken head.

Redpath Museum of Natural History
859 Rue Sherbrooke W. *(514) 398 4086.* *9am–5pm Mon–Thu; 1pm–5pm Sun.* *Fri & Sat.*

Musée des Beaux Arts ⓮

THE OLDEST AND LARGEST art collection in Quebec is housed in two dramatically different buildings that face each other across Rue Sherbrooke. On the north side is the Benaiah Gibb Pavilion with white marble pillars; on the south side is the huge concrete arch and tilting glass front of the Jean-Noël Desmarais Pavilion.

The galleries in the Desmarais Pavilion focus on European art from the Middle Ages to the 20th century, especially the Renaissance. Linking the two pavilions is the gallery of ancient cultures, with rich collections of artifacts, including Roman vases and Chinese incense boxes. The Benaiah Gibb Pavilion galleries focus on Canadiana, with Inuit art, furniture, and church silver from early settlers, and paintings from the 18th century to the 1960s.

Façade of Jean-Noël Desmarais Pavilion
Opened in 1991, the larger pavilion contains a collection that has grown from 1,860 to about 26,000 pieces.

★ Portrait of a Young Woman *(c.1665)*
This famous work originated in Rembrandt's native Holland. Painted in characteristically realist style, the sitter's pensive concentration is thrown into sharper relief by the deep black background.

Benaiah Gibb Pavilion

Named after a 19th-century benefactor, the Benaiah Gibb Pavilion is connected to the southern side by an underground tunnel that contains the gallery of ancient cultures. Dedicated to pre-1960 America, the Benaiah Gibb has Meso-American, Inuit, and Amerindian art, as well as early European-style furniture, domestic silver, and decorative art. Later galleries follow the history of Canadian painting, from church sacred art to early native studies by wandering artist Paul Kane and the impressionism of James Wilson Morrice. The Group of Seven and Paul-Emile Borduas are among those representing the 20th century.

18th-century silver teapot

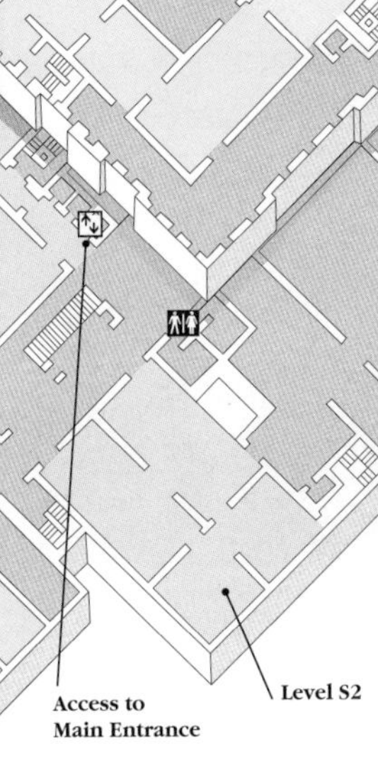

Star Exhibits

- ★ **Man of the House of Leiva by El Greco**
- ★ **Portrait of a Young Woman by Rembrandt**

VISITORS' CHECKLIST

1379–1380 Rue Sherbrooke W. *(514) 285 2000.* *Central Station.* *24.* *Guy Concordia.* *11am–6pm, Tue, Thu–Sun; 11am–9pm, Wed.* *Mon.* *for special exhibitions.* *www.mbam.qc.ca*

Level 4

★ Man of the House of Leiva *(1590)*
El Greco's haunting portrayals of the Spanish aristocracy are a Renaissance highlight.

GALLERY GUIDE
The exceptional painting collections are contained on both levels 3 and 4 of the Desmarais Pavilion. Levels 1 and 2 offer a fine café and shop. Level S2 continues the connecting tunnel display of ancient cultures. Access to the main entrance is available from the elevators situated on every exhibit level.

KEY

- Contemporary art
- Art of ancient cultures
- 19th-century European art
- 20th-century European art
- European Decorative arts
- Old Masters
- Temporary exhibitions
- Nonexhibition space

A street-level entrance to the labyrinthine Underground City

Underground City ⓯

Central Station. *Terminus Voyager.* *Place des Arts.*

WHEN MONTREAL OPENED its first métro (or subway) lines in 1966, it inadvertently created a whole new layer of urban life – the Underground City. It is theoretically possible to lead a rich life in Montreal without once stepping outside. The first métro stations had underground links to just the two main train stations, a few hotels, and the shopping mall under the Place Ville-Marie office tower. This has turned into a vast network of over 30 km (19 miles) of well-lit, boutique-lined passages that includes more than 1,600 shops, 200 restaurants, hotels, film theaters, and concert halls.

Square Dorchester and Place du Canada ⓰

1001 Rue Square Dorchester. *(514) 873 2015.* *Central Station.* *Terminus Voyager.*

THESE TWO open squares create a green oasis in central downtown Montreal. On the north side of Boulevard René-Lévesque, statues including Canada's first French-Canadian prime minister, Sir Wilfrid Laurier, share the shade of Square Dorchester's trees with a war memorial. On Place du Canada a statue of the country's first prime minister, Sir John A. Macdonald, looks out over the stately Boulevard René-Lévesque.

The buildings surrounding the park are eclectic. The mix includes a Gothic church, a shiny, black bank tower and the Sun Life Building (1933), a huge stone fortress that housed the British Crown Jewels during World War II.

Varied architecture, from historic to post-modern, in Square Dorchester

Montreal skyline at night ▷

LE REINE

Marie-Reine-du-Monde façade with statues of Montreal's patron saints

Cathédrale Marie-Reine-du-Monde ⑰

1085 Rue Cathédrale. (514) 866 1661. Central Station. Terminus Voyager. Bonaventure. 6:30am–7:30pm Mon–Fri, 7:30am–8:30pm Sat, 8:30am–7:30pm Sun.

When Montreal's first Catholic cathedral burned down in 1852, Bishop Ignace Bourget decided to demonstrate the importance of the Catholic Church in Canada by building a new one in a district dominated at the time by the English Protestant commercial elite. To show his flock's loyalty to the Pope, he modeled his new church on St. Peter's Basilica in Rome.

The cathedral, which was completed in 1894, has dimensions that are a quarter of those of St. Peter's. The statues on the roof represent the patron saints of all the parishes that constituted the Montreal diocese in 1890. The magnificent altar canopy, a replica of the one Bernini made for St. Peter's, was cast in copper and gold leaf. Another reminder of Bourget's loyalty to Rome can be found on the pillar in the northeast corner of the church. Here lies a marble plaque listing the names of all the Montrealers who served in the Papal armies during the Italian war of independence in the 1850s.

The altar canopy in the cathedral

Centre Canadien d'Architecture ⑱

1920 Rue Baille. (514) 939 7026. Central. Terminus Voyager. Guy Concordia. Jun–Sep: 11am–6pm Tue, Wed, Fri–Sun, 11am–9pm Thu; Oct–May: 11am–5pm Tue, Wed, Fri–Sun, 11am–8pm Thu. Mon. on request.

Visitors enter through an unobtrusive glass door in an almost windowless façade of gray limestone that fronts this large U-shaped building. Well-lit exhibition rooms house a series of rotating displays. While some can be fairly academic, others focus on the whimsical: doll's houses and miniature villages have been featured. The two arms of the modern building embrace the ornate, grand Shaughnessy Mansion, which faces Boulevard René-Lévesque Ouest. Now part of the Centre, the house was built in 1874 for the president of the Canadian Pacific Railway, Sir Thomas Shaughnessy, and has an art-nouveau conservatory with an intricately decorated ceiling.

The Centre is also a major scholarly institution. Its collection of architectural plans, drawings, models, and photographs is the most important of its kind anywhere. The library alone has over 165,000 volumes on the world's most significant buildings.

Rue Sherbrooke ⑲

Central Station. Terminus Voyager. Sherbrooke.

In the latter half of the 19th century, Montreal was one of the most important cities in the British Empire. Its traders and industrialists controlled about 70 percent of Canada's wealth, and many built themselves fine homes on the slopes of Mont Royal in an area that became known as the Golden, or Square, Mile. Rue Sherbrooke between Guy and University was their Main Street, and its shops, hotels, and churches were the most elegant in the country.

Some of that elegance survived the modernizing bulldozers of the 1960s. Holt Renfrew, Montreal's upscale department store, and the stately Ritz-Carlton Hotel still stand. So do two exquisite churches, the Presbyterian St. Andrew and St. Paul, and the Erskine American United at the corner of avenue du Musée, which boasts stained-glass windows by Tiffany. Boutiques, bookstores, and galleries fill many of the rows of graystone townhouses. Millionaires not quite wealthy enough to make it into the Square Mile built graceful row homes on rues de la Montagne, Crescent, and Bishop nearby. Many of these now house trendy shops and bistros.

Farther west is the Grande Seminaire, where Montreal's Roman Catholic archdiocese still trains its priests.

Historic home on Rue Sherbrooke, the "Golden Square Mile"

Montreal's largest shrine, Oratoire Saint-Joseph, showing the steps climbed annually by pilgrims

Oratoire Saint-Joseph ⓴

3800 Chemin Queen Mary. ☎ *(514) 733 8211.* 🚉 *Central Station.* 🚌 *Terminus Voyager.* 🚉 *Côte-des-Neiges.* ◯ *7am 9pm daily.* ♿

EVERY YEAR, thousands of pilgrims climb the 300 steps to the entrance of this enormous church on their knees. Their devotion would no doubt please Brother André (1845–1937), the truly remarkable man responsible for building this shrine to the husband of the Virgin Mary. It began when he built a hill-side chapel to St. Joseph in his spare time. Montreal's sick and disabled joined him at his prayers, and soon there were reports of miraculous cures. Brother André began to draw pilgrims, and the present oratory was built to receive them. He is buried here and was beatified in 1982.

The octagonal copper dome on the top of the church is one of the biggest in the world – 44.5 m (146 ft) high and 38 m (125 ft) in diameter. The interior is starkly modern; the elongated wooden statues of the apostles in the transepts are the work of Henri Charlier, who was also responsible for the main altar and the huge crucifix. The striking stained-glass windows were made by Marius Plamondon. The main building houses a museum depicting André's life and a crypt church, ablaze with hundreds of flickering candles lit by hopeful pilgrims, where daily masses are said.

Parc Mont-Royal ㉑

☎ *(514) 844 4928.* 🚉 *Central Station.* 🚌 *11.* 🚉 *Mont-Royal.* ◯ *6am–midnight daily.* ♿

THE STEEP GREEN bump that rises above the city center is only 234 m (767 ft) high, but Montrealers call it simply "the mountain" or "la mont-agne." Jacques Cartier gave the peak its name when he visited in 1535 and it, in turn, gave its name to the city. The hill became a park in 1876 when the city bought the land and hired Frederick Law Olmsted, the man re-sponsible for designing New York's Central Park, to landscape it. Olmsted tried to keep it natural, building a few lookouts linked by foot-paths. Succeeding generations have added a manmade pond (Beaver Lake), a 30-m high (98-ft) cross made of steel girders, and the Voie Camilien Houde, a thoroughfare that cuts through the park from east to west.

The mountain's 101 ha (250 acres) of meadows and hardwood forests still offer Montrealers a precious escape from urban life, as well as spectacular views of the city. The wide terrace in front of the Chalet du Mont-Royal pavilion looks out over the skyscrapers of the down-town core. The northern boundary of the park abuts two huge cemeteries, the Catholic Notre-Dame-Des-Neiges and the old and stately Protestant Mount Royal Cemetery, where many of Canada's finest rest.

A typical view of Montreal from the top of lofty Parc Mont-Royal

Olympic Park ㉒

Penguin at the Biodome

DESIGNED FOR the 1976 Olympic Games, Montreal's Olympic Park showpieces a number of stunning modern buildings. Paris architect Roger Taillibert created the Stadium, now known to many Montrealers as "The Big Owe," a reference not only to its round shape but the Can$695 million it cost to build. The stadium, seating 56,000, is used today for concerts by international stars, major league baseball and big exhibitions, and as a modern attraction in a historic city. Arching up the side of the stadium is the Montreal Tower, with its fine views. Nearby, the Biodome environmental museum replicates four world climates.

Aerial view of Olympic Park
An exceptional tourist attraction, the park can be toured fully during the day. Another popular way to visit is for a concert or ballgame.

The Biodome was first used as a velodrome for the 1976 Olympics – hence the unusual cycling hat design of its roof.

★ Biodome
Here are stunning re-creations of climate zones: a steamy rainforest, the freezing Polar World, the fertile forests of the Laurentian Mountains, and the fish-filled St. Lawrence ecosystem.

Sports Centre
Should any visitor become inspried by the international-standard sport on offer at the stadium, this fully equipped center offers unbeatable facilities, including a 15-m (50-ft) deep scuba diving pool.

★ Olympic Stadium
Finished in 1976, this magnificent hall does justice to the world stars and players who perform here.

Visitors' Checklist

4141 Ave Pierre-de-Coubertin. *(514) 252 8687. Viau Station. Jun–Sep: 10am–8pm daily; Oct–May: 10am–6pm daily. www.rio.gouv.qc.ca*

The stadium roof was originally intended to be retractable. However, due to structural problems, it was replaced in 1998 by a detached, permanently closed roof.

★ Montreal Tower
At 175 m (575 ft) this is the world's tallest inclined tower. It arches over the stadium and overhangs it in a graceful sweep. A cable car takes 76 visitors at a time up the side of the tower to its large viewing deck. The trip takes less than two minutes.

Viewing Deck
This glass platform provides some stunning views of the city. Signs point out sights of interest that can be as far as 80 km (50 miles) away.

A cable car shoots up the side of the tower at speed; tickets can be combined with a guided tour of the stadium or Biodome.

0 meters 50
0 yards 50

Plan of the Olympic Park Area

1 Sports Field
2 Sports Arena
3 Maurice-Richard Centre
4 Biodome
5 Olympic Stadium
6 Botanical Gardens

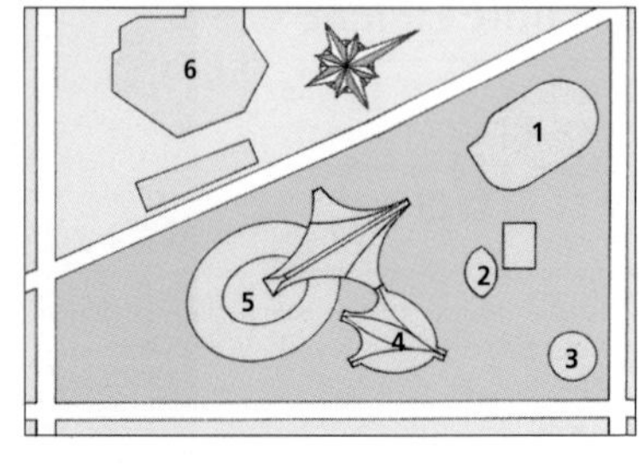

Star Sights

- ★ **Olympic Stadium**
- ★ **Montreal Tower**
- ★ **Biodome**

The Jardin Botanique is an oasis of calm away from the rush of the city

Jardin Botanique de Montréal ㉓

4101 Rue Sherbrooke E. (514) 872 1400. Pius-X. May–Oct: 9am–7pm daily; Nov–Apr: 9am–5pm daily.

MONTREAL'S botanical garden is among the largest in the world, a fine accomplishment for this northern city with a brutal climate. Its 73 ha (181 acres) enclose 30 outdoor gardens, 10 greenhouses, a popular display of poisonous plants, the largest collection of bonsai trees outside Asia, and a bug-shaped Insectarium full of creepy-crawlies, both dead and alive. Its most peaceful havens are the 2.5-ha (6-acre) Montreal–Shanghai Dream Lake Garden, a delightful replica of a 14th-century Ming garden, and the exquisite Japanese Garden and Pavilion where visitors can relax and appreciate the scenery.

Bonsai tree at the Jardin Botanique

Ile-Sainte-Hélène ㉔

20 Chemin Tour de Lille. (514) 844 5400. Ile-Ste-Hélène. Vieux-Port. 10am–5pm Wed–Tue. groups only.

THIS SMALL forested island in the middle of the St. Lawrence River has played a major role in Montreal's emergence as a modern city. Originally named after Samuel de Champlain's wife *(see pp41)*, Ile-Sainte-Hélène was the site of Expo '67, the world fair that brought millions of visitors to the city in the summer of 1967.

Several reminders of those days remain – most notably La Ronde, the fair's amusement park, and the dome that served as the United States Pavilion. This is now the Biosphere, an interpretive center that examines the Great Lakes and St. Lawrence River system. Between the dome and the roller coasters is the Fort de l'Ile-Sainte-Hélène, built in 1825 to protect Montreal from a potential American attack. Its red stone walls enclose a grassy parade square that is used today by members of the Olde 78th Fraser Highlanders and the Compagnie Franche de la Marine, re-creations of two 18th-century regimental military formations that fought each other over the future of New France until 1759. The fort also houses the **Musée David A. Stewart**, a small and excellent museum of social and military history.

Musée David A. Stewart
20 Chemin Tour de Lille. (514) 861 6701. 10am–5pm Wed–Mon. Tue; Dec 25, Jan 1.

Ile-Notre-Dame ㉕

110 Rue Notre-Dame. (514) 842 2925. Central Station. Terminus Voyager. Place d'Armes. late Jun–Aug: 7am–8pm daily; Sep–Jun: 7am–6pm daily. for a charge.

THIS 116-ha (286-acre) wedge of land encircled by the St. Lawrence Seaway did not exist until 1967, when it was created with rock excavated for the Montreal métro system. It shared Expo '67 with Ile-Sainte-Hélène, and today the two islands constitute the Parc-des-Iles. Ile-Notre-Dame's most popular attraction by far is the monumental Casino de Montréal, a province-owned gambling hall housed in the old French and Quebec pavilions. Every day, thousands line up at its tables and slot machines. The casino never closes. There are more refined entertainments – a rowing basin, excavated for the 1976 Olympics, superb floral gardens, and a carefully filtered body of water, which is the site of the city's only swimming beach.

Built for Expo '67, the Biosphere has displays on Canadian river systems

The province-owned Casino on Ile-Notre-Dame is open to the hopeful 24 hours a day

Ile-Notre-Dame's Circuit Gilles Villeneuve, named for the Canadian champion, plays host to Canada's Formula 1 Grand Prix every June.

Maison Saint-Gabriel ㉖

2146 Place de Dublin. *(514) 935 8136.* *Charlevoix.* *57.* *late Jun–Aug: daily; Sep–Jun: Tue–Sun.* *obligatory.*

THIS ISOLATED little fragment of New France at first appears lost among the apartment buildings of working-class Pointe-Saint-Charles. It was a farm when the formidable Marguerite Bourgeoys, Montreal's first schoolteacher and now a canonized saint, bought it in 1668 as a residence for the religious order she had founded in 1655.

The house, rebuilt in 1698 after a fire, is a fine example of 17th-century architecture, with thick stone walls and a steeply pitched roof built on an intricate frame of original heavy wooden timbers.

Marguerite Bourgeoys and her tireless sisters worked the farm and ran a school on the property for native and colonial children. They also housed and trained the *filles du roy* (the "king's daughters"), orphaned young girls sent abroad to be the women of his new colony. The house's chapel, kitchen, dormitory, and drawing rooms are full of artifacts dating from the 17th century. These include a writing desk the saint used herself and a magnificent vestment and cope, embroidered in silk, silver, and gold by a wealthy hermit who lived in a hut on the property.

Lachine ㉗

Blvd. St. Joseph. *(514) 873 2015.* *Lionel Groulx.* *191.*

LACHINE COMPRISES a suburb of southwest Montreal and includes a small island of the same name along the shore west of the Lachine Rapids, where the St. Lawrence River widens to form Lac-Saint-Louis. Lachine is now part of Montreal, but has a long history of its own, and the old town along Blvd. Saint-Joseph is charming. Many of its fine old homes have become restaurants and bistros with outdoor terraces that overlook Parc René-Lévesque and the lake. One of the oldest houses, built by merchants in 1670, is now the **Musée de Lachine**, a historical museum and art gallery. The **Fur Trade at Lachine National Historic Site** is a building dedicated to the fur trade, which for years was Montreal's main support.

The Lachine Canal, built in the 19th century to bypass the rapids, links the town directly to the Vieux-Port. The canal itself is now blocked to shipping, but the land along its banks has been turned into parkland with a bicycle trail.

Musée de Lachine
110 Chemin de LaSalle. *(514) 634 3471.* *Mar–Dec: 11:30am–4:30pm Wed–Sun.* *reserve.*

Fur Trade at Lachine National Historic Site
1255 Blvd. St. Joseph. *(514) 637 7433.* *Apr–Oct: daily.*

A view of the historical Musée de Lachine from the reclaimed canal

Quebec City and the St. Lawrence River

THE HEART AND soul of French Canada, Quebec City sits overlooking the St. Lawrence River on the cliffs of Cap Diamant. As provincial capital, the city is the seat of regional government, and nowadays is the heart of French-Canadian nationalism. Parisian in atmosphere, with every tiny street worth visiting, Quebec City is almost entirely French-speaking. The European ambiance, architecture, and the city's crucial historical importance all contributed to it being named as a United Nations World Heritage Site in 1985. One of the world's great waterways, the St. Lawrence River is home to rare marine wildlife. Right and minke whales swim as far upstream as Tadoussac and feed at the mouth of the Saguenay River. The Laurentian Mountains rise up above the St. Lawrence on the north shore, a year-round natural playground. Nearer Quebec City, the rich scenery of the Charlevoix region is among the most beautiful in the country, contrasting with the soaring cliffs and wilderness of the Gaspé Peninsula. Offshore, Ile d' Anticosti is a stunning nature preserve.

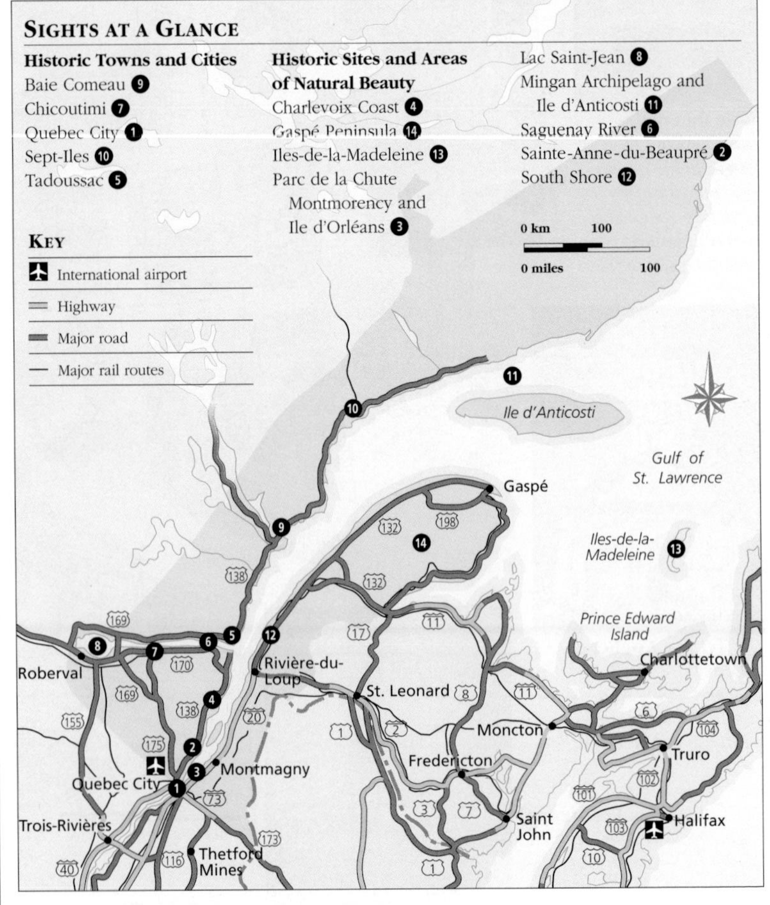

The historic architecture of Quebec City's Lower Town

Street-by-Street: Quebec City ❶

ONE OF THE OLDEST communities on the American continent, Quebec City was discovered as an Iroquois village by the French explorer Jacques Cartier and founded as a city in 1608 by explorer Samuel de Champlain *(see p41)*. The British gained dominance over the city and the rest of the province at the Plains of Abraham battle just outside the city walls in 1759. Today the town is renowned as the heart of French Canada. The oldest part of the city is Basse-Ville, or Lower Town, which was renovated in the 1970s. With its winding staircases and cafés, it is a charming destination.

★ Basilique Notre-Dame-de-Québec
This 1647 cathedral provides a rich setting for relics from early French rule in Quebec, and Old Master paintings.

Musée du Fort
Military history is brought to life here in sound-and-light shows reenacting six Quebec sieges and battles, and numerous war relics.

Holy Trinity Anglican Cathedral
An elegant 1804 stone Neo-Classical façade conceals an English oak interior.

Château Frontenac
Quebec City's best-known landmark has risen over the city since 1893, and has 600 luxurious guest rooms.

DES JARDINS
DE BUADE
SAINTE ANNE
DES JARDINS
DU FORT
SAINT LOUIS

0 meters 100
0 yards 100

KEY

– – – Suggested route

Musée de la Civilisation
Human history through the ages is explored in this airy modern building linked to historic houses in the rest of the town, including Maison Chevalier.

Visitors' Checklist

167,500. 16 km (10 miles) west of the city. 450 Rue de Gare-du-Palais. 320 Rue Abraham-Martin. 10 Rue des Praversiers. 835 Avenue Wilfrid-Laurier (418) 649 2608. Winter Carnival (Jan–Feb); Summer Festival (Jul). www.quebecregion.com

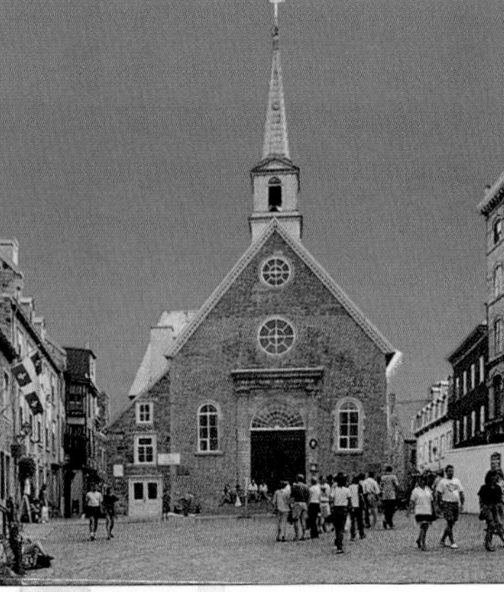

★ Place Royale
A virtual microcosm of Canadian history, Place Royale has experienced a renaissance, and the surrounding streets, with their 18th- and 19th-century architecture, have been sandblasted back to their original glory.

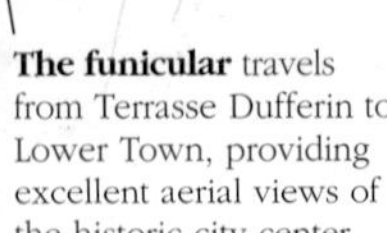

The funicular travels from Terrasse Dufferin to Lower Town, providing excellent aerial views of the historic city center.

Maison Chevalier
Linked with the Musée de la Civilisation, this home built for an 18th-century merchant showcases the decorative arts. Quebec furniture and the famous Quebec silverware feature in every room, as well as exhibits showing how well-to-do families lived in the 18th and 19th centuries.

Star Sights

- ★ Place Royale
- ★ Basilique Notre-Dame

Quebec City

Containing the only walled city north of the Rio Grande, Quebec City has narrow cobblestone streets and 18th-century buildings that lend a European air to this small provincial capital, just 93 square km (36 square miles). Most of the sights are packed into one accessible corner, above and below the Cap Diamant cliffs, with the Citadel rising up protectively at the top of the cliff. As Quebec's capital, the city is home to the provincial parliament, the Assemblée Nationale, which conducts its debates almost entirely in French in splendid chambers behind the ornate early 19th-century façade of the grandiose Hôtel du Parlement.

Château Frontenac dominates the skyline of Quebec City

Exploring Quebec City

Most of the main sights are easily reached on foot. The city can conveniently be divided into three parts. Basse-Ville, or Lower Town, is the oldest part, and rambles along the St. Lawrence River at the foot of Cap Diamant. Above lies the walled city, Haute-Ville, or Upper Town. This area is full of shops and restaurants, similar to the Basse-Ville, but both Catholic and Protestant cathedrals are here, as is the imposing Château Frontenac. Beyond the walls stretches Grande Allée, with the Hôtel du Parlement where the provincial parliament of Quebec sits.

Joan of Arc at Parc-des-Champs de Bataille

Terrasse Dufferin

Sweeping along the top of Cap Diamant from Château Frontenac to the edge of the Citadel, this boardwalk is well equiped with benches and kiosks, and offers unmatched views of the St. Lawrence River, the Laurentian Mountains, and Ile d'Orleans. During the freezing Quebec winter, the municipal authorities install an ice slide for toboggans on the terrace, known as Les Glissades de la Terrasse.

Parc des Champs-de-Bataille

835 Ave. Wilfrid Laurier. (418) 648 4071. daily.

Once a battlefield where the future of Canada was decided, the National Battlefields Park is now a delightful grassy recreation ground, with grand monuments and a dedicated fountain the only clues to the area's bloody and dramatic history. On September 13, 1759, British regulars under General James Wolfe defeated the French army on this clifftop field, the Plains of Abraham, just outside the walls of Quebec *(see pp42–3)*, establishing permanent British rule in Canada. In 1908, the 100-ha (250-acre) battlefield was turned into one of the largest urban parks in North America.

Assemblée Nationale

Ave. Honoré-Mercier & Grande Allée E. (418) 643 7239. late Jun–early Sep: daily; late Sep–Jun: Mon–Fri.

The Assemblée Nationale, Quebec's provincial parliament, meets just outside the walls of the Old City in this graceful Second-Empire building, completed in 1886 as a showcase of provincial history. Niches along the imposing façade and up the sides of the tall central tower display 22 bronze figures, each representing a person who played a vital role in Quebec's development. The first inhabitants of the territory are honored in a bronze rendition of a native Indian family by the main door. Inside, the blue chamber is the hub of Quebec's political activity.

Fortifications de Québec

(418) 648 7016. Apr–Oct: daily.

After a century of peace, the fortifications that had secured Quebec since their completion by the British in 1760 were transformed in the 1870s from a grim military necessity into this popular attraction. On the city's northern and eastern edges, low ramparts studded with cannon defend the clifftop, with the walls on the western side reaching 2.5 m (10 ft). Two elegant gates, the Saint-Jean and the Saint-Louis, pierce the western stretch. Visitors can walk along the top of the walls for 4 km (3 miles).

Quebec's 18th-century fortifications in the Parc d'Artillerie

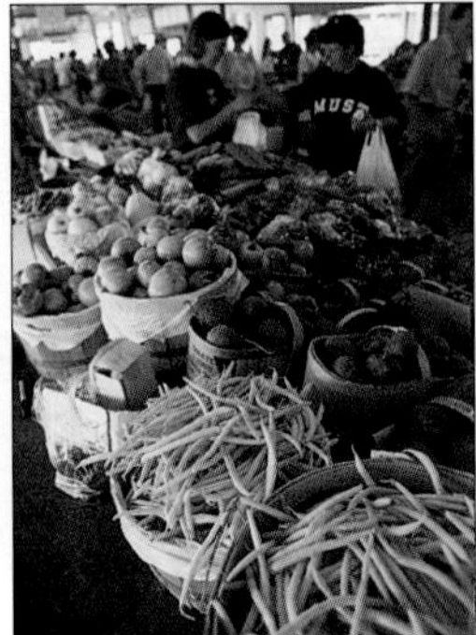

Abundant produce stalls draw crowds at the market in Vieux Port

Vieux Port

100 Quai Saint Andre. *(418) 648 3300.*

This delightful area has its focus around the old harbor northeast of the walled city. In contrast to the crammed heritage of much of the Lower Town, Vieux Port is an airy riverside walking site, full of new and restored modern attractions. Boat cruises which lead gently downriver to the Chute Montmorency waterfalls are available. Waterfront walks pass chic boutiques, apartment blocks, the city's concert stadium, and shops in trendy warehouse settings.

Musée de la Civilisation

85 Rue Dalhousie. *(418) 643 2158.* *late Jun–early Sep: daily; late Sep–early Jun: Tue–Sun.*

Top contemporary Canadian architect Moshe Safdie designed this modern limestone and glass building in Basse-Ville to house Quebec's new museum of history and culture. Although highly up-to-date in feel, the construction has won several prizes for blending in well with its historic surroundings. Three heritage buildings are part of the museum's structure including Maison d'Estebe, an 18th-century merchant's house. The museum also uses another nearby 18th-century house, Maison Chevalier, for displaying Quebec architecture and furniture in period setting.

Museum exhibits include a collection of Chinese imperial furniture and the remains of a 250-year-old French flat-bottomed boat. *Mémoires*, a permanent exhibit on the third floor, provides a real insight into 400 years of Quebec history with a collection of items from everyday life including tools, folk art, toys, carriages, and many religious articles.

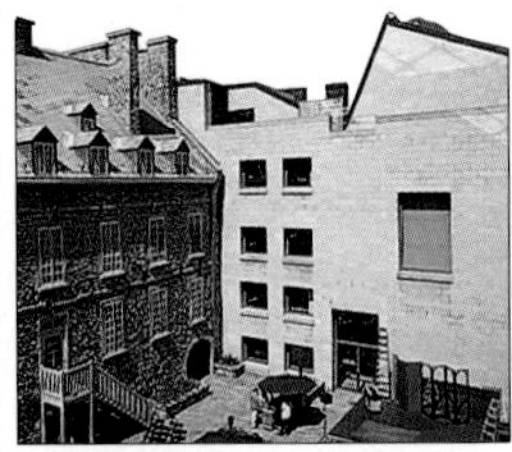

Antique and modern architecture of the Musée de la Civilisation

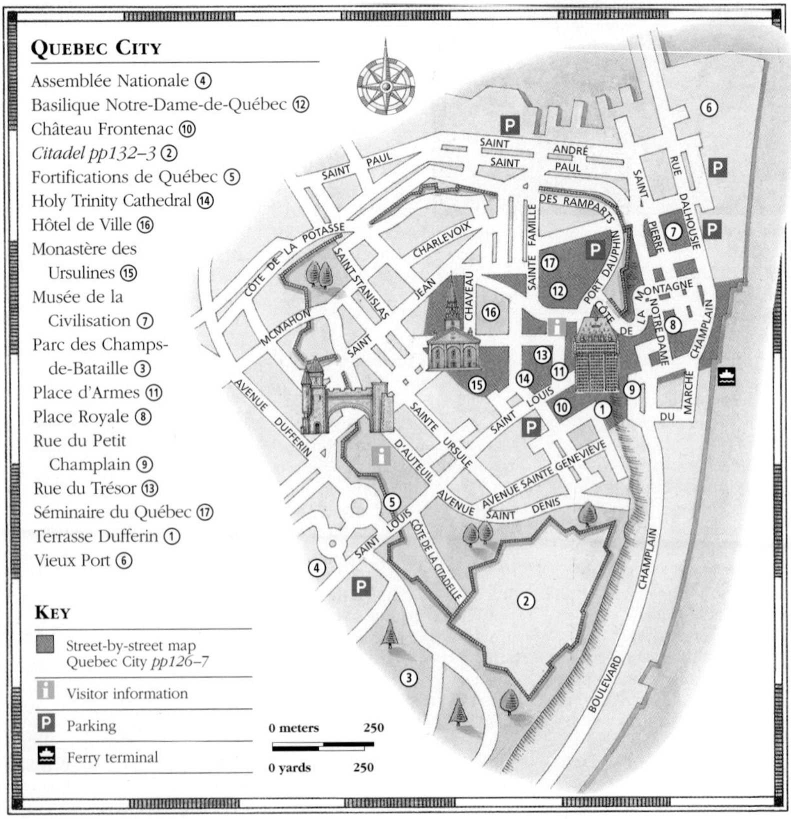
QUEBEC CITY
Assemblée Nationale ④
Basilique Notre-Dame-de-Québec ⑫
Château Frontenac ⑩
Citadel pp132–3 ②
Fortifications de Québec ⑤
Holy Trinity Cathedral ⑭
Hôtel de Ville ⑯
Monastère des Ursulines ⑮
Musée de la Civilisation ⑦
Parc des Champs-de-Bataille ③
Place d'Armes ⑪
Place Royale ⑧
Rue du Petit Champlain ⑨
Rue du Trésor ⑬
Séminaire du Québec ⑰
Terrasse Dufferin ①
Vieux Port ⑥
KEY
Street-by-street map Quebec City pp126–7
Visitor information
Parking
Ferry terminal
0 meters 250
0 yards 250
SAINT PAUL
SAINT ANDRÉ
SAINT PAUL
DES REMPARTS
RUE DALHOUSIE
SAINT-PIERRE
CÔTE DE LA POTASSE
CHARLEVOIX
SAINT STANISLAS
JEAN
CHAUVEAU
SAINTE FAMILLE
PORT DAUPHIN
CÔTE DE LA MONTAGNE
NOTRE DAME
CHAMPLAIN
MCMAHON
SAINT
AVENUE DUFFERIN
SAINTE URSULE
D'AUTEUIL
SAINT LOUIS
AVENUE SAINTE GENEVIEVE
AVENUE SAINT DENIS
CÔTE DE LA CITADELLE
MARCHÉ
DU
BOULEVARD CHAMPLAIN

Place Royale

Rue Saint Pierre.

Of all the squares in Canada, Place Royale has undoubtedly the most history. Samuel de Champlain, the founder of Quebec, planted his garden on this site, and the French colonial governor Frontenac turned it into a market in 1673. A bust of Louis XIV was installed in 1686, and the square was named Place Royale.

Today it remains much as it did in the 18th century, exuding an air of elegance and delicate grandeur. A cobblestone court in the center of Basse-Ville, Place Royale is surrounded by steep-roofed early 18th-century buildings with pastel-colored shutters that were once the homes of wealthy traders. The square declined in the 19th century but is now fully restored and a favorite for street performers.

A familiar landmark of the city, the 600-room Château Frontenac hotel

Place d'Armes

French colonial soldiers once used this attractive, grassy square just north of Château Frontenac as a parade ground, but its uses today are more congenial. Open horse-drawn carriages wait here to offer visitors a journey that reveals the square in all its charm. In the center, the Monument de la Foi commemorates the 300th anniversary of the 1615 arrival of Catholic Recollet missionaries. On the southwest corner next to the fine Anglican cathedral, lies the grand early 19th-century Palais de Justice. The Musée du Fort opposite contains a large scale model of Quebec City in the 19th century.

Rue du Petit Champlain bustling with shoppers

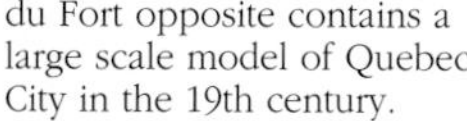

Rue du Petit Champlain

below Dufferin Terrace in Old City. (418) 692 2613. partial.

The rather aptly named Escalier Casse-Cou, or Breakneck Stairs, descends from Haute-Ville past several levels of gift shops to end on this narrow little walkway in the oldest part of the town. French artisans built homes along here as early as the 1680s, and Irish dockworkers moved to the area in the 19th century. Much of the historic architecture remained, but the area fell into decline early in the 20th century. Now fully refurbished, the workers' homes are transformed into shops and restaurants, and the short pedestrian walkway has become one of the liveliest spots in old Quebec City. While often crowded, some interesting boutiques can be found.

Château Frontenac

1 Rue des Carrières. (418) 692 3861.

The steep, green copper-roofed landmark that dominates the skyline of Old Quebec is a luxury hotel, built by the Canadian Pacific Railway on the heights overlooking the St. Lawrence River. In the 19th century, US architect Bruce Price designed the hotel as a French-style château on a huge scale, with dozens of turrets, towers, and a high copper roof studded with rows of dormer windows. Building continued for almost a century after the first section of the hotel was opened in 1893, with a final part completed in 1983. Made from brick and stone, the hotel now has over 600 rooms. The public salons are sumptuous and elegant; Salon Verchère and the Champlain are the most visited.

Basilique Notre-Dame-de-Québec

Place de l'Hôtel de Ville. (418) 694 0665. *7:30am–4.30pm daily.*

This magnificent cathedral is the principal seat of the Roman Catholic archbishop of Quebec, whose diocese once stretched from here to Mexico. Fire destroyed the first two churches on the site before 1640, and the first cathedral built here was torn down by the British in 1759. A fourth version burned down in 1922. The present cathedral replaced it in the style of the 1647 original. Some modern materials, including concrete, steel, and plaster, have been used to re-create the light feel; glowing stained-glass windows, richly gilded decoration, and the graceful baldachin over the main altar add to the effect.

Imposing façade of the Basilique-Notre-Dame-de-Québec

The Hôtel de Ville seen from the small park in its grounds

Rue du Trésor

off Place d'Armes.

This tiny alley just across rue de Buade from Holy Trinity cathedral is something of a Quebecois institution. Closed to cars, the little street is packed in summer with visitors eager to have their portraits drawn, painted, or caricatured by the dozens of street artists who gather here. Browsing for sketches and watercolors of Quebec scenes can be fun.

Holy Trinity Anglican Cathedral

31 Rue des Jardins. *(418) 692 2193.* *daily.*

After worshiping for nearly a century in the city's Catholic churches, in 1804 the Anglicans of Quebec finally had their own cathedral built at state expense. Their new mother church was the first Anglican cathedral outside Britain and is modeled on London's huge Neo-Classical St. Martin's in the Fields. To this day, gifts from England remain, including the prayer book and Bible donated by the British King George III. Cut from the King's Windsor Forest in England, the pews are of oak, and the eight-bell peal is the oldest in Canada. In the summer artists and artisans fill the verdant church grounds.

Reliquary from the Ursuline Convent

Monastère des Ursulines

Rue Donnacona. *(418) 694 0694.* *daily.*

In 1639, Mère Marie de l'Incarnation brought the Ursuline order of nuns to Quebec and oversaw the construction in 1641 of the nunnery here, which later burned down. Today, visitors can see the Saint-Augustin and Saint-Famille wings, which date from a period of rebuilding between 1685 and 1715. Surrounded by fruit orchards, the charming complex has gradually evolved over the past four centuries. One of the buildings is North America's oldest girls' school.

Nearly a hundred nuns still live and work here, so access is limited. The beautifully decorated chapel and French antiques, including Louis XIII furniture, antique scientific tools and instruments, paintings, and embroideries are displayed in the Musée des Ursulines within the monastery. The museum also tells the story of the nuns' educational and missionary achievements in the province. Mère Marie completed the first native Algonquin and Iroquois dictionaries, and these can be seen here, alongside native art and artifacts.

Hôtel de Ville

Côte de la Fabrique. *(418) 691 4606.* *Interpretive Centre: late Jun–Sep: daily; Oct–Jun: Tue–Sun.*

This imposing building stands at the western end of the rue de Buade, a popular gathering place for Quebec artists offering their wares. Built in 1833, and still the town hall to the city, it is the grounds that are the focus for the city's people. The small park here holds theater performances in the summertime and is a meeting place for festival-goers.

Séminaire de Québec

2 Côte de la Fabrique. *(418) 692 2843.* *summer.* *obligatory.*

In 1663, the first bishop of Quebec, Francois Laval, built a seminary next to his cathedral to train Catholic priests for his huge diocese. Over the centuries the school has been added to and now forms a graceful complex of historic 17th-, 18th-, and 19th-century buildings centered on a peaceful grassy courtyard.

Within the seminary, visitors can admire the excellent 18th-century paneling that covers the walls of the chapel. The Musée de l'Amérique Française is part of the complex and has a wonderfully eclectic collection, including a converted chapel decorated with fascinating wooden *trompe l'oeils.*

The 19th-century interior of the chapel at the Séminaire de Québec

La Citadelle

Regimental stained glass beaver badge

BOTH THE FRENCH and British armies contributed to the building of this magnificent fort. The French started construction in 1750, with work completed in 1831 by the British. The purpose of the fort was to defend Quebec against an American attack that never came. Today the fortifications are a pleasant walkway that provides a tour around the star-shaped fortress. The Citadel is home to the famous French Canadian regiment the Royal 22-ème (Van Doos). Because the Citadel is still a working military barracks, visitors can see the regiment perform their daily tasks as well as their parade drill.

The Fortifications
From the mid-19th century, the Citadel served as the eastern flank of Quebec City's defenses.

Old Military Prison

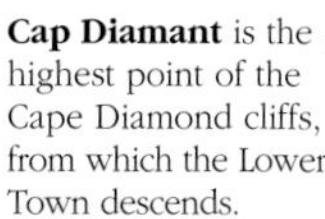

Cap Diamant is the highest point of the Cape Diamond cliffs, from which the Lower Town descends.

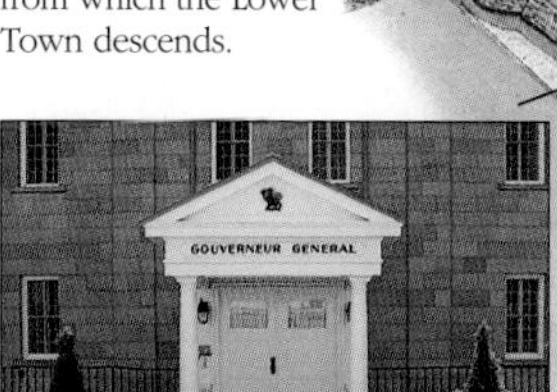

Governor-General's residence
This splendid mansion with its double central staircase and marble hall has been the official home of Canada's governors-general since the 19th century.

Cape Diamond Redoubt
The oldest building in the Citadel, the Redoubt dates back to 1693 when it was built under the leadership of the French Count Frontenac as a first citadel for Quebec. Now home to relics of war, the Redoubt offers fine views of the St. Lawrence River.

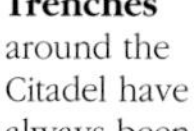

Trenches around the Citadel have always been key defensive structures.

The Vimy Cross was erected in memory of the Canadians who fell at the WWI battle of Vimy Ridge in 1917.

Chapel
A key part of the fortress, this private chapel used to be a British powder magazine and is now used for ceremonial purposes.

★ Changing of the Guard, Parade Square
Every day from June to Labour Day, the Changing of the Guard takes place. The ceremonial dress of the 22-ème, scarlet tunic and blue trousers, is of British design.

VISITORS' CHECKLIST

1 Cote de la Citadelle. *(418) 694 2815.* *daily.* *in museum.* *obligatory.* *www.lacitadelle.qc.ca*

The Barracks
As a fully operational military site, the barracks is home to Canada's most dashing regiment, the 22-ème, who fought with bravery in both world wars.

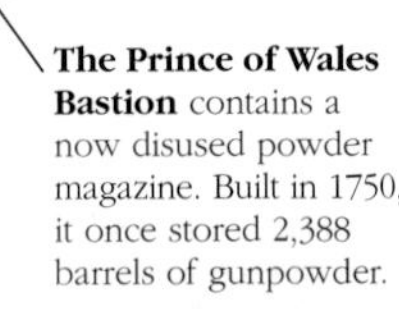

The Prince of Wales Bastion contains a now disused powder magazine. Built in 1750, it once stored 2,388 barrels of gunpowder.

0 meters 25

0 yards 25

★ Dalhousie Gate
One of the original structures remaining from the 19th century, Dalhousie Gate is surrounded by portholes and gun fittings. These helped the four-pointed fortress to cover its north, south, and west flanks with defensive fire.

STAR SIGHTS

- **★ Changing of the Guard**
- **★ Dalhousie Gate**

Sainte-Anne-de-Beaupré ❷

ONE OF CANADA'S most sacred places, the shrine to the mother of the Virgin Mary was originally built in the 17th century by a group of grateful sailors who landed here after narrowly surviving a shipwreck. Over 1.5 million sightseers and pilgrims now visit every year, including an annual pilgrimage on the Saint's Day in July. The focus of their homage is the ornate medieval-style basilica, which was built in the 1920s. Inside the entrance stand two columns of crutches, testimony to the faith of generations of Roman Catholics. Rows of thick columns divide the interior into five naves, and the dome-vaulted ceiling is decorated with gold mosaics portraying the life of Saint Anne. She is represented in a large gilt statue in the transept, cradling the Virgin Mary.

Statue of Saint Anne
The focus of the upper floor, the richly decorated statue sits in front of the relic of Saint Anne, presented to the shrine by Pope John XXIII in 1960.

Stained-glass windows show the progress of pilgrims through the shrine, with the rose window as centerpiece.

PLAN OF THE SHRINE

1 Basilica
2 Monastery
3 Seminary
4 Museum
5 Blessing Office

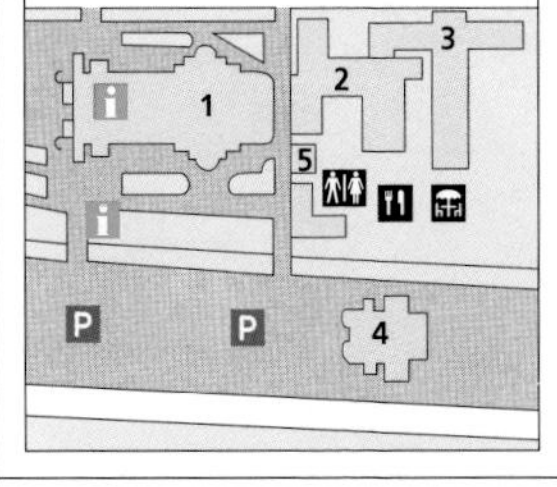

THE BASILICA
In 1876, Saint Anne was proclaimed patron saint of Quebec, and in 1887 the existing church was granted basilica status. The Redemptorist order of Catholic priests took charge of the shrine in 1878.

Entrance to Basilica's upper floor

Bright mosaic floor tiles echo ceiling patterns

★ The Basilica
There has been a church on this site since 1658. In 1922, the previous basilica burned down. Today's version was built in 1923 and consecrated in 1976.

STAR SIGHTS

★ The Basilica

★ Pietà

VISITORS' CHECKLIST

3,400. Quebec City. Quebec City. 10018 Av. Royale (418) 827 3781. Sainte-Anne (Jul 26). www.ssadb.qc.ca

★ **Pietà**

A faithful copy of Michelangelo's original in St. Peter's, Rome, this shows Christ at his death.

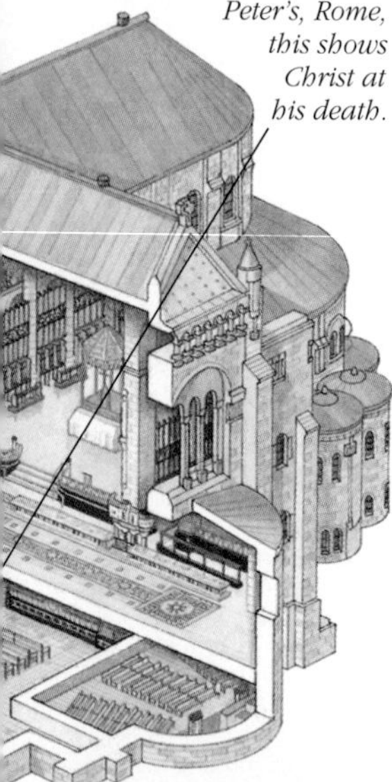

Basilica interior

Lit by sun streaming through the stained-glass windows, the cream and gold interior is decorated in every corner.

Montmorency Falls at Ile d'Orléans, Quebec's most dramatic waterfall

Parc de la Chute Montmorency and Ile d'Orléans ❸

Montmorency Falls (418) 663 3330. 8:30am–11pm daily. Ile d'Orléans Tourist Centre, 490 Cote du Pont, St. Pierre (418) 828 9411.

LOCATED 7 KM (4.5 miles) east of Quebec City, Montmorency Falls is Quebec's most celebrated waterfall. Higher than Niagara Falls, the cascade is created as the Montmorency River empties out into the St. Lawrence River – a total of 30 m (100 ft) higher than the 56-m (175-ft) plunge of Niagara Falls from the Niagara River to Lake Ontario. The park surrounding the Falls offers several ways to view the cascade; a suspension bridge, an aerial tram, and, for the fit and fearless, a series of trails that climb the surrounding cliffs.

A spidery modern bridge nearby crosses the river to the Ile d'Orléans. This richly fertile island is covered with flowers, strawberry fields, and flourishing farmland. Sprinkled with villages, it gives a fascinating look at the traditional Quebec routine of peaceful rural life.

Charlevoix Coast ❹

166 Blvd. de Comporte, La Malbaie (418) 665 4454.

THE CHARLEVOIX coast runs 200 km (130 miles) along the north shore of the St. Lawrence River, from Sainte-Anne-de-Beaupré in the west to the mouth of the Saguenay. A UNESCO World Biosphere Reserve because of its fine examples of boreal forest, the area is a slim band of flowery rural beauty on the southern edge of tundra that stretches northward. Gentle valleys protect old towns reaching to the river, with coastal villages sheltering beneath tall cliffs. Lying in a fertile valley is the exception-ally pretty Baie-Saint-Paul, its streets lined with historic houses and inns.

Just 35 km (21 miles) north of Baie-Saint-Paul lies the **Parc des Grands Jardins**, a vast expanse of lakes and black-spruce evergreen taiga forest with a herd of caribou. Small mountains offer walking and hiking. Farther downstream is the tiny and tranquil island Ile-aux-Coudres. The lush, green farmland here is sprinkled with historic farms and a windmill.

Parc des Grands Jardins

Rte. 381. (418) 439 1227. May–Oct: daily; Nov–Apr: Sat & Sun.

Moulin de L'Ile-aux-Coudres, in the Charlevoix region

The town of Tadoussac at the confluence of the St. Lawrence and Saguenay rivers

Tadoussac 5

850. 197 Rue des Pionniers (418) 235 4977.

Lined with boutiques, the old streets of this little town make a gentle start to exploring the local stretch of the St. Lawrence River. In 1600, French traders picked the village as the site of the first fur-trading post in Canada, noticing that for generations native Indians had held meetings here to trade and parley. In the 19th century, even while the fur trade was still a force, steamships began to transport well-heeled tourists to the village for a taste of its wilderness beauty.

Justifying two centuries of tourism, the scenery here is magnificent. Backed by rocky cliffs and towering sand dunes, Tadoussac's waterfront faces over the estuary at the confluence of the St. Lawrence and Saguenay rivers. In the town, the re-creation of the original 17th-century fur-trading post and the oldest wooden church in Canada, the Petite Chapelle built in 1747, are popular. However, the main attraction in Tadoussac lies offshore. Whale-watching tours offer trips into the estuary to see many species at close quarters. The thriving natural conditions in the estuary support a permanent colony of white beluga whales, which are joined in summer by minke, fin, and blue whales.

Saguenay River 6

Jonquière. Chicoutimi. 198 Rue Racine East (418) 543 9778.

The Saguenay River flows through the world's southernmost natural fjord. This was formed from a retreating glacier splitting a deep crack in the Earth's crust during the last Ice Age, 10,000 years ago. Inky waters, 300 m (985 ft) deep in places, run for 155 km (95 miles) beneath cliffs that average 450 m (1,500 ft) in height. Due to the exceptional depth, ocean liners can travel up to Chicoutimi on the river.

Running from Lac St. Jean to the St. Lawrence estuary, the Saguenay is best known for its lush borderlands and the wildlife that thrives in its lower reaches. Much of the pretty Bas Saguenay, the southern half of the river, is a federal marine park. Most visitors take a tour to view the colony of a thousand whales that have chosen the fjord as their home.

Beautiful views of the length of the fjord are available on the western shore at Cap Trinité, a cliff that rises 320 m (1,050 ft) over the channel, with a well-known 10-m (33-ft) statue of the Virgin Mary surveying the scenery from the lowest ledge.

Waterside view of a section of the deep Saguenay fjord

Chicoutimi 7

64,600. 198 Rue Racine East (418) 543 9778.

Snug in the crook of mountains on the western shore of the Saguenay, Chicoutimi is one of northern Quebec's most expansive towns, despite its modest population. The cultural and economic center of the Saguenay region, its waterfront district has now been restored. A stroll along the riverside offers good views of the surrounding mountains and the confluence of the Chicoutimi, Du-Moulin, and Saguenay rivers.

Once a center for the paper trade, Chicoutimi still features a large pulp mill, the **Pulperie de Chicoutimi**. Although no longer operational, the plant can be toured, and an adjacent museum shows visitors the intricacies of this long-standing Quebecois industry, which once supplied most of North America's paper needs.

Pulperie de Chicoutimi

300 Dubuc. (418) 698 3100.

late Jun–Sep: 9am–6pm daily. 

A Tour of Lac-Saint-Jean ❽

IN THE MIDST OF THE ROCKY, spruce-covered wilderness that characterizes central Quebec, Lac-Saint-Jean is an oasis of tranquillity. Dairy farms, charming villages such as Chambord, and warm sandy beaches border the lake itself, which covers 1,350 sq km (520 sq miles). The lake and its rolling green landscape fill a crater-sized basin left by advancing glaciers at the end of the last Ice Age. Tiny rivers flow to the lake and tumble dramatically down the basin's steep walls into the blue waters, to be reborn as the source of the Saguenay River.

Tips for Drivers

Starting point: *Chambord.*
Length: *180 km (112 miles).*
Getting around: *This is a long, though relaxed drive, and the road is well maintained. Inns and restaurants offer rest on the way in most towns and villages, including Mashteuiatsh. Small side roads make peaceful diversions.*

Parc de la Pointe-Taillon ⑥
Stretching into a peninsula that juts out into the lake, this park is excellent for cycling and hiking, but is best known for its fine, long beaches.

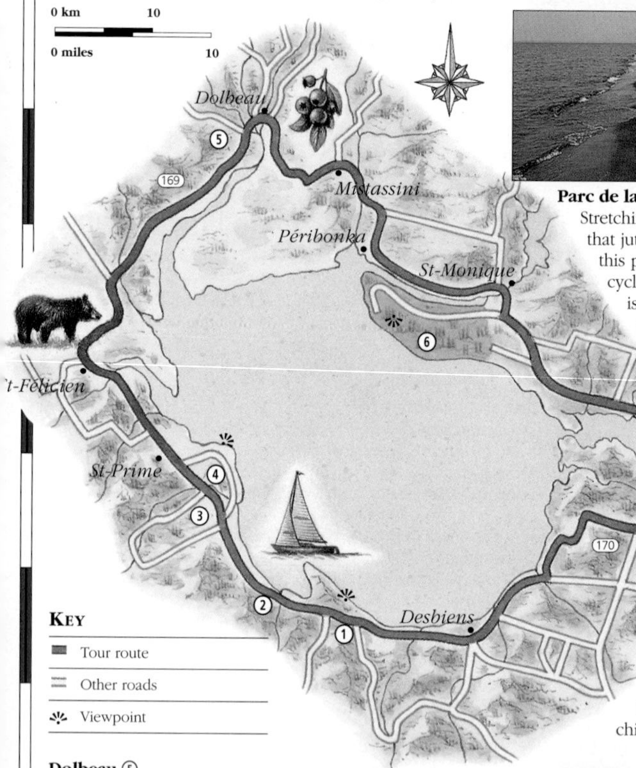

Chambord ①
Sailing and swimming are top activities here, especially for children and families.

Key

- Tour route
- Other roads
- Viewpoint

Dolbeau ⑤
Most visitors to Dolbeau arrive in July for the ten-day Western Festival, which features rodeos and cowboys in Stetsons.

Mashteuiatsh, Pointe Bleu ④
This Montagnais Indian village is open to visitors who can see at first hand age-old methods of carving, hunting, weaving, and cooking.

Roberval ③
This little village has a charming waterfront, from which spectators can see the finish of the swimming contest to cross the lake, which has taken place each July since 1946.

Val-Jalbert ②
This small town is dominated by the 70-m (200-ft) Ouiatchouan waterfall in the center, which once acted as power for a pulp mill here in the 1920s.

Manic Côte Nord, a hydroelectric power plant north of Baie-Comeau

Baie-Comeau 9

26,700. 337 La Salle (418) 294 2876.

THIS SMALL town owes its entire existence to the US newspaper, the *Chicago Tribune*, which in 1936 built a mill near the mouth of the Manicougan River to supply its newspaper presses with paper. Declared a historic district in 1985, Baie-Comeau's oldest area is the Quartier Amélie, with rows of fine homes and an impressive hotel dating from the 1930s.

Paper production remains a vital industry in this area, but Baie-Comeau is most important today as a gateway to the enormous Manic-Outardes hydroelectric power complex, situated along Hwy 389, from 22 km (14 miles) to 200 km (130 miles) north of town. The most spectacular example is Manic-5, 190 km (115 miles) from Baie-Comeau. Its gracefully arched Daniel Johnson Dam holds back a vast reservoir that fills a crater geophysicists believe might have been created by a meteorite several millennia ago.

Sept-Iles 10

26,000. 312 Ave. Brochu (418) 962 0808.

UNTIL THE 1950s, Sept-Iles led a quiet existence as a historic, sleepy fishing village. However, after World War II, the little settlement, set on the shores of a large, circular bay, drew the attention of large companies to use as a base for expanding the iron mining industry in northern Quebec. Now the largest town along the north shore of the Gulf of St. Lawrence, Sept-Iles has turned into Canada's second largest port as part of the St. Lawrence Seaway. A boardwalk along the waterfront offers visitors the chance to see the large ships in action, and to observe close-up the workings of a busy modern dock.

Although boasting the best of modern marine technology, the town also offers a reminder of its long-standing history. Vieux Poste near the center of the town is a fine reconstruction of a native trading post, where the original inhabitants of the area met to barter furs with French merchants. A small museum with aboriginal art and artifacts sells native crafts.

Despite its industrial importance, Sept-Iles is an area of considerable natural beauty.

Sept-Iles from the air, showing the bustling dock in action

Miles of sandy beaches rim the nearby coastline, and the salmon-rich Moisie River flows into the Gulf of St. Lawrence just 20 km (12 miles) east of the town. The seven rocky islands that gave the city its name make up the Sept-Iles Archipelago Park.

Ideal for campers and hikers with its beaches and nature trails, one of the seven islands, Ile Grand-Basque, is a popular local camping spot. Another small island, Ile du Corossol, has been turned into a bird sanctuary that teems with gulls, terns, and puffins, and can be toured with a guide. Cruises are available for guided trips between islands.

Mingan Archipelago and Ile d'Anticosti 11

Sept-Iles. Sept-Iles. 312 Ave. Brochu, Sept-Iles (418) 962 0808.

BARELY VISITED until recently, this unspoiled and unsettled area is fast gaining in popularity for its harsh landscape, rich wildlife, and untouched ecosystems. In 1984, the Mingan Archipelago islands became Canada's first insular national park. Puffins, terns, and several gull species find refuge in the Mingan Archipelago Wildlife Park, which comprises all 40 of the Mingan Islands that scatter along the north shore of the Gulf of St. Lawrence. Gray, harbor, and harp seals all cluster along the tiny coves and bays, and fin whales are occasional visitors. As well as the abundant wildlife, the islands are famous for their bizarre monoliths. Eroded over many centuries by the sea, these limestone carvings have surreal shapes. The best-known rocks look strikingly like flowerpots, with grasses sprouting from their peaks. Visitors can book a trip to admire this unique manifestation of nature by boat.

Until 1974, the Ile d'Anticosti, east of the archipelago, was private property – all 8,000 sq km (3,090 sq miles) of it. The past owner, French chocolate tycoon Henri Menier, bought

"Flowerpot" limestone monoliths at Mingan Archipelago National Park

the island in 1895 and stocked it with a herd of white-tailed deer for his friends to hunt. Now numbering 120,000, the deer herd is firmly ensconced but can still be hunted. Wildlife abounds; over 150 species of bird live happily in the relatively unspoiled forest and on the beaches. A lone village on the island, Port Menier, has 300 residents and acts as the local ferry terminus and lodging center.

Seal at Ile d'Anticosti

South Shore ⓬

Rivière-du-Loup. *Rivière-du-Loup.* *Rivière-du-Loup.*
Rivière-du-Loup (418) 867 3015.

COMMUNITIES here can trace their roots back to the old 18th-century settlers of New France. Dotted along the flat, fertile farmland of the south shore of the St. Lawrence River west of Gaspé and inland toward Montreal, the villages cover the area between the region's largest towns of Montmagny and Rimouski. Rivière-du-Loup, a seemingly unremarkable town in this stretch, provides for many people a taste of true Quebec. Featuring an ancient stone church that rears above the skyline, the old town rambles along hilly streets, and its old 18th-century cottages have an appealing French atmosphere. From the peak of the old town, views across the river valley are lovely. Other villages in this area feature unusual attractions. Farther along the main Route 32, Trois-Pistoles boasts a history that goes back to 1580, when Basque whalers arrived. The offshore Ile-aux-Basques was a whaling station in the 16th century, and today can be visited to tour the nature preserve in its place. Toward the region's commercial center, Rimouski, lies Parc Bic, a small preserve of 33 square km (13 square miles) dedicated to the two forest zones, deciduous and boreal, it encloses, and its varied coastal wildlife.

Iles-de-la-Madeleine ⓭

128 Chemin du Debarcadere, Cap-aux-Meules (418) 986 2245.

THE FEW FISHING families who make their homes on this remote archipelago in the middle of the huge gulf of St. Lawrence have taken to painting their cottages in a bright and beautiful assortment of mauves, yellows, and reds. The river gives striking views of the little communities on their low-lying, windswept islands, but the islands themselves have more to offer the visitor who makes the boat trip to see them. As well as the charming ancient villages, they are home to what are reputed to be some of the most relaxing beaches in Canada, celebrated for their fine sand and sheltered position.

Painted fisherman's cottage on L' Ile-du-Havre-Aubert, Iles-de-la-Madeleine

Gaspé Peninsula Tour ⓮

POPULARLY KNOWN as La Gaspésie, the Gaspé Peninsula stretches out north of New Brunswick to offer Quebec's wildest and most appealing scenery. As the peninsula spreads east, clumps of trees become dense pine forests, and the landscape becomes rough and rocky; cliffs along the northern coast reach 500 m (1,500 ft). The Chic-Choc mountains reach heights of 1,300 m (4,000 ft) and provide some of the province's best hiking. Shielded by the mountains, the southern coast harbors 18th-century fishing villages, inland fruit farms, exotic gardens, and wilderness national parks.

Parc de la Gaspésie ③
Here, over 800 sq km (300 sq miles) of rough, mossy terrain mark a change from boreal to subalpine forest.

Grand Métis ①
This small town is home to one of Canada's most beautiful gardens, an exotic haven of over 1,000 rare species.

Cap Chat ②
Named for a nearby cat-shaped rock, Cap Chat boasts the tallest windmill in the world at 110 m (160 ft).

Vallée de la Matapédia ⑨
Starting at the confluence of two excellent salmon-fishing rivers, the picturesque Matapédia Valley is crisscrossed by covered bridges dating from the 18th century. Concealing long-established fruit farms, the valley's elm and maple trees show stunning fall colors.

Carleton ⑧
Founded in 1756 by Acadians fleeing the Great Expulsion in Nova Scotia *(see pp58–9)*, Carleton today is a pleasant, relaxed resort town. Quality hotels and restaurants line the airy streets, and many visitors enjoy the mild coastal climate.

Sainte-Anne-des-Montes ④
The entrance to Gaspé's park and the wildlife reserves of the Chic-Chocs, this 19th-century village has fine restaurants, and good salmon fishing nearby.

Tips for Drivers

The main road on this tour is Hwy 132, which follows the coastline from Grand Métis along the peninsula in a round trip. While too long to complete in a day, the journey can be broken in many of the local villages. Trips into the interior on the secondary road 299 are ideal for seeing the rocky wilderness.

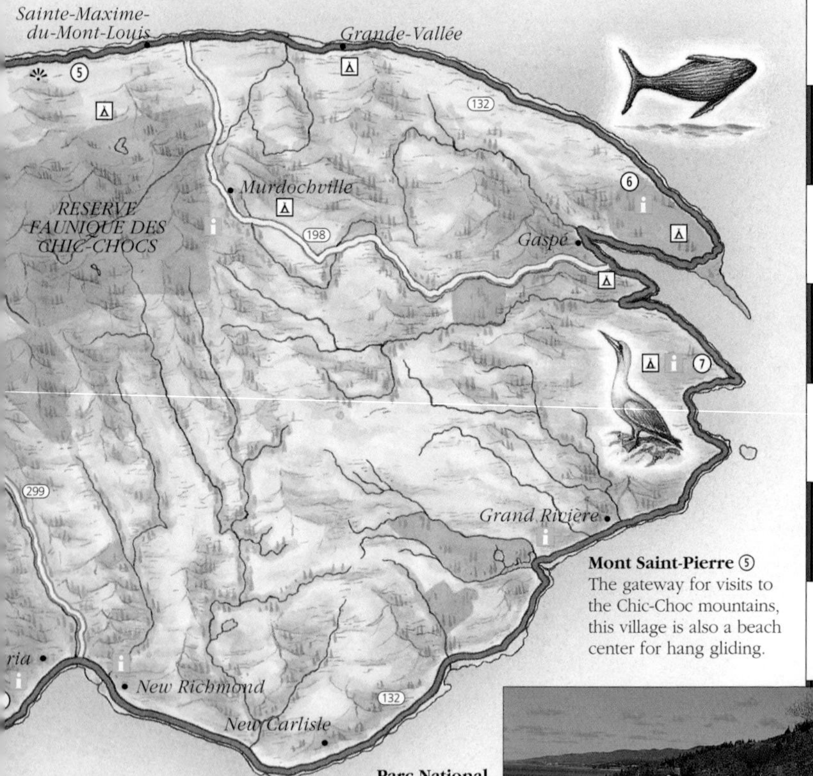

Sainte-Maxime-du-Mont-Louis
Grande-Vallée
⑤
132
⑥
Murdochville
RESERVE FAUNIQUE DES CHIC-CHOCS
198
Gaspé
⑦
299
Grand Rivière
ria
New Richmond
132
New Carlisle

Mont Saint-Pierre ⑤
The gateway for visits to the Chic-Choc mountains, this village is also a beach center for hang gliding.

Parc National Forillon ⑥
The park contains the tail end of the Appalachian Mountains, now cliffs worn into rugged formations by the sea.

Rocher Percé ⑦
Situated out to sea south of the small town of Percé, this famous pierced landmark is the result of tidal erosion. In the 1930s, Percé became a popular spot for Canadian artists and still contains many galleries.

Key

- Tour route
- Other roads
- Camp grounds
- Visitor information
- Viewpoint

SOUTHERN AND NORTHERN QUEBEC

THE VAST AREA of land that stretches across Quebec from the Ontario boundary to historic Quebec City is rewarding in its diversity. In the south, the rich hilly farmland of the Appalachians and scarlet forests of maple trees attract many visitors each year, while the stark beauty of Nunavik's icy northern coniferous forests bursts into a profusion of wildflowers in spring, alongside the largest hydroelectric projects in the world. The center of the region is Quebec's natural playground, the Laurentian Mountains, a pristine lake-filled landscape offering fine skiing on ancient mountains. Populated by native people until Europeans arrived in the 16th century, the area was fought over by the French and British until the British gained power in 1759. Today French-speakers dominate.

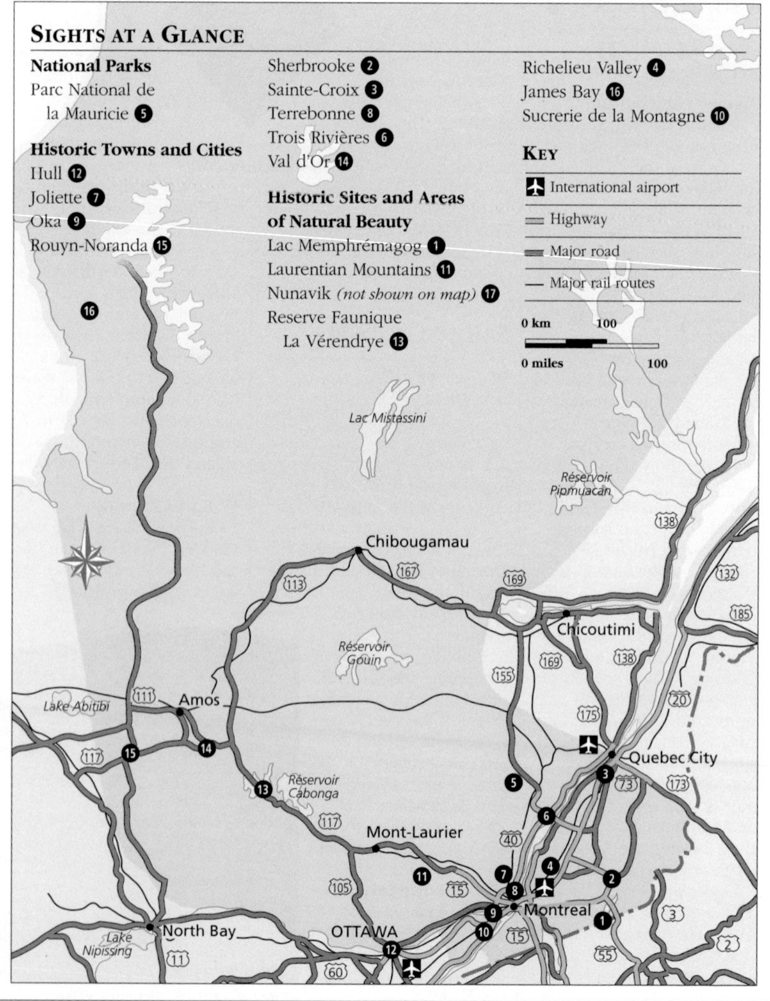

◁ **Colorful houses in St. Jovite, with the Laurentian Mountains rising behind**

Church by Lac Memphrémagog

Lac Memphrémagog ❶

Magog. Magog. 55 Cabana St., Magog 1 (800) 267 2744.

THIS AREA belongs to the Eastern Townships, or the "Garden of Quebec" that stretches from the Richelieu River valley to the Maine, New Hampshire and Vermont borders in the US. Set among rolling hills, farmland, woods, and lakes in a landscape similar to the Appalachians, the Townships are among Canada's top maple syrup producers *(see pp98–99)*.

Lac Memphrémagog itself is long, narrow, and surrounded by mountains. It even boasts its own monster, a creature named Memphré, first spotted in 1798. The lake's southern quarter dips into the state of Vermont, so it is no surprise that the British Loyalists fleeing the American Revolution were this region's first settlers. Their influence can be seen in the charming late 19th-century red-brick and wood-frame homes of lakeside villages such as enchanting Georgeville and Vale Perkins, and in the resort city of Magog that sits at the northern end of the scenic lake.

Benedictine monks from France bought one of the lake's most beautiful sites in 1912 and established the Abbaye Saint-Benoît-du-Lac. Today the monks produce cider and a celebrated blue cheese called l'Ermite. They are also renowned for Gregorian chant, and visitors can hear them sing mass in the abbey church.

Sherbrooke ❷

77,500. 3010 King St. W. 1 (800) 561 8331.

THE SELF-STYLED "Queen of the Eastern Townships," Sherbrooke is indeed this region's industrial, commercial, and cultural center. The city lies in a steep-sided valley, with the historic quarter delightfully situated among the rolling farmlands of the Saint-François and Magog Rivers. The first settlers were British Loyalists from the New England states. Although their heritage survives in the fine old homes and gardens of Sherbrooke's North Ward and in street names, today the city is overwhelmingly French speaking. The center of town is the starting point of the Riverside Trail, a lovely waterfront park with 20 km (12 miles) of cycling and walking trails along the banks of the Magog River.

Sainte-Croix ❸

2,600. 6375 rue Garneau (418) 926 2620.

A CHARMING, wooden manor house with bold sweeping front steps, pillars, and carved curlicues is the grandest old house in this pretty riverside town. It is the centerpiece of **Domaine Joly-De-Lotbinière**, a stunning estate built in 1851 by the local squire (seigneur). The house is surrounded by banks of geraniums and terraces of walnut trees stretching down to the river. Rare plant finds include 20 red oaks estimated to be more than 250 years old. The gardens are best known, however, for cultivating blue potatoes.

Domaine Joly-De-Lotbinière

Rte. de Pointe-Platon. *(418) 926 2462. Jun–Sep: daily; Oct–May: 10am–6pm Sat & Sun. partial.*

Richelieu Valley ❹

1080 Chemin des Patriotes Nord, Mont Saint-Hilaire (450) 536 0395.

THIS FERTILE VALLEY follows the 130-km (80-mile) Richelieu River north from Chambly to Saint-Denis. **Fort Chambly**, also known as Fort St. Louis, in the industrial town of Chambly along the valley on the Montreal Plain, is the best preserved of a series of ancient buildings that the French erected to defend this vital waterway from Dutch and British attack. Built from solid stone in 1709 to replace the wooden fortifications that the original settlers set up in 1655, the fort is very well preserved and is a popular attraction. A museum in Saint-Denis commemorates Quebecois patriots who fought in the failed 1837 rebellion against British rule.

A sign to Fort Chambly in the Richelieu Valley

Today the river flows past attractive villages surrounded by orchards and vineyards; Mont Saint-Hilaire affords fine views of Montreal, and is famed for its apple plantations. Its 19th-century church was declared a historic site in 1965 and features paintings by Canadian Ozias Leduc *(see p28)*.

Fort Chambly

2 Richelieu St., Chambly. *1 (800) 463 6769. Mar–mid-Jun: 10am–5pm Wed–Sun; mid-Jun–Sep: 10am–6pm daily. Nov–Feb.*

Mont Saint-Hilaire, Richelieu Valley

Canoeists on Lac Wapizagonke in Parc National de la Mauricie

Parc National de la Mauricie ❺

off Hwy 155 N. Shawinigan.
(819) 536 2638. *Shawinigan.* *Shawinigan.* *daily.* *partial.* *for a fee.*

CAMPERS, HIKERS, canoeists, and cross-country skiers love this 536-sq km (207-sq mile) stretch of forest, lakes, and pink Precambrian granite. The park includes part of the Laurentian Mountains *(see p147)*, which are part of the Canadian Shield, and were formed between 950 and 1,400 million years ago. La Mauricie's rugged beauty is also accessible to motorists, who can take the winding 63-km (40-mile) road between Saint-Mathieu and Saint-Jean-de-Piles.

Another great drive starts at Saint-Jean-de-Piles and has good views of the narrow Lac Wapizagonke Valley. With trout and pike in the lake, the area is an angler's delight. Moose and bear roam wild in the park.

Trois-Rivières ❻

51,800. *5775 Blvd. Jean XXIII (819) 536 3334.*

QUEBEC IS one of the major paper producers in North America, and Trois-Rivières, a pulp and paper town, is a main center of that industry in the province. This fact often hides the rich historical interest that Trois-Rivières has to offer. The first colonists arrived here in 1634 from France and, although not many of the colonial dwellings remain, the city's charming old section has a number of 18th- and 19th-century houses and shops, many of which have been recently converted into cafés and bars.

Ursuline nuns have been working in the city since 1697, and the core of the old city is the **Monastère des Ursulines**, a rambling complex with a central dome, a chapel, and a little garden that is now a public park. Rue des Ursulines features several little old houses with varying architectural styles, which can be viewed on a stroll around the area. Also here is an 18th-century manor house, the 1730 Manoir Boucher-de-Niverville, which contains the local chamber of commerce and rotates displays on the rich history of the area around the Eastern Townships.

The church of the Monastère des Ursulines in Trois-Rivières

Monastère des Ursulines
734 Ursulines. *(819) 375 7922.*
Mar & Apr: Wed–Sun; May–Oct: Tue–Sun; Nov–Feb: call ahead.

Joliette ❼

31,100. *500 rue Dollard (450) 759 5013.*

TWO CATHOLIC PRIESTS are responsible for turning the industrial town of Joliette on the Assomption River into a cultural center. In the 1920s, Father Wilfrid Corbeil founded the Musée d'Art de Joliette, whose permanent collection ranges from medieval religious art to modern works. In 1974, Father Fernand Lindsay started the Festival International de Lanaudière, a series of summer concerts by some of the world's best-known musicians.

The nearby town of Rawdon, 18 km (11 miles) west, has a deserved reputation as a place of great natural beauty. Trails wind away from the small town alongside the Ouareau River, leading to the picturesque, rushing Dorwin Falls.

Terrebonne 8

36,680. 3645 Queen Street (450) 834 2535.

JUST NORTHWEST of the outer fringe of Montreal's suburbs, this historic little town on the Mille-Iles River was founded in 1673, but a fire in 1922 engulfed many of its original buildings. However, some graceful 19th-century homes remain, on rue Saint-François-Xavier and rue Sainte-Marie, many of them converted into lively restaurants and bistros. The town's real gem is the **Ile-des-Moulins**, a pre-industrial complex of living history in the middle of the Mille-Iles River, with water-powered mills for grinding grain, carding wool, and sawing lumber. One of the biggest buildings on the site is the three-floor factory that was the first large-scale bakery in Canada. It was built by the Northwest Company in 1803 to make the saltless ship's biscuits that sustained the *voyageurs* who paddled west every year to collect furs for the company.

Terrebonne is also the center of Quebec's horse-riding culture. Popular with locals, rodeo and ranching events take place regularly.

Ile-des-Moulins

Autoroute 25, exit 22 E. *(450) 471 0619.* *Jun–Sep: 1–9 pm daily.*

Rue-St-Louis Church in Terrebonne

The Oka ferry as it travels across the Lake of Two Mountains

Oka 9

3,840. *183 rue des Anges (450) 479 8337.*

THE PRETTIEST WAY to approach this village north of Montreal is on the small ferry that chugs across the Lake of Two Mountains from Hudson. Framed by mountains and orchards, from the water the small Neo-Romanesque 1878 church is visible through the trees. Oka's best-known religious building is the **Abbaye Cistercienne**, founded by a group of monks who moved to Canada from France in 1881. The decor of the abbey church is somewhat stark, in the Cistercian tradition, but the Neo-Romanesque architecture is gracefully simple and the gardens peaceful. The abbey shop sells the soft Oka cheese that the monks have developed. Nearby, the Parc d'Oka covers about 20 sq kms (7 sq miles) of ponds and forests. It features the best beach and campground in the Montreal area, attracting sports lovers and visitors year-round.

Abbaye Cistercienne

1600 Chemin d'Oka.

(450) 479 8361.

8am–8pm Mon–Sat.

lunchtimes; Sun.

Quebecois Maple Syrup

Sucrerie de la Montagne 10

10 km South of Rigaud. *(450) 451 0831.* *year round but call ahead.* *obligatory.*

THIS TYPICALLY Canadian treat is set in a 50-ha (120-acre) maple forest on top of Rigaud Mountain near Rang Saint-Georges, Rigaud. It is entirely devoted to the many delights of Quebec's most famous commodity, the maple tree and its produce *(see pp98–99)*. The site features a reconstructed 19th-century sugar shack, where collected maple sap is distilled and boiled in large kettles to produce the internationally renowned syrup. Over 20 rustic buildings house a fine bakery, a general store, and comfortable cabins for overnight guests. The heart of the complex is a huge 500-seat restaurant that serves traditional banquets of ham, pea soup, baked beans, pork rinds (called *oreilles du Christ*, or Christ's ears), and pickles, and dozens of maple-based products, including syrup, sugar, candies, taffy, muffins, and bread. Folk music accompanies the nightly feast. The tour includes a thorough guided explanation of the maple syrup-making process, which is generally thought to have originated with the native people. They later imparted their secrets to European settlers, whose traditional methods are still in use today.

Laurentian Mountains Tour ⑪

Cycle sign

THIS WHOLE region, from the lively resort of Saint-Sauveur-des-Monts in the south to north of Sainte Jovite, is nature's own amusement park, full of beautiful lakes, rivers, hiking and cycling trails, and ski runs visited all through the year. The mountains are part of the ancient Laurentian Shield and are a billion years old. Dotted with pretty, old French-style towns, this is a superb area to relax in or indulge in some vigorous sports in the many national parks.

TIPS FOR DRIVERS

Although the 175-km round tour of the Laurentian Mountains can be made from Montreal in a day on Hwy 15, the region is best seen and enjoyed by taking advantage of the slower, but more scenic, Hwy 117. There may be traffic congestion at the peak times of July through August and from December to March.

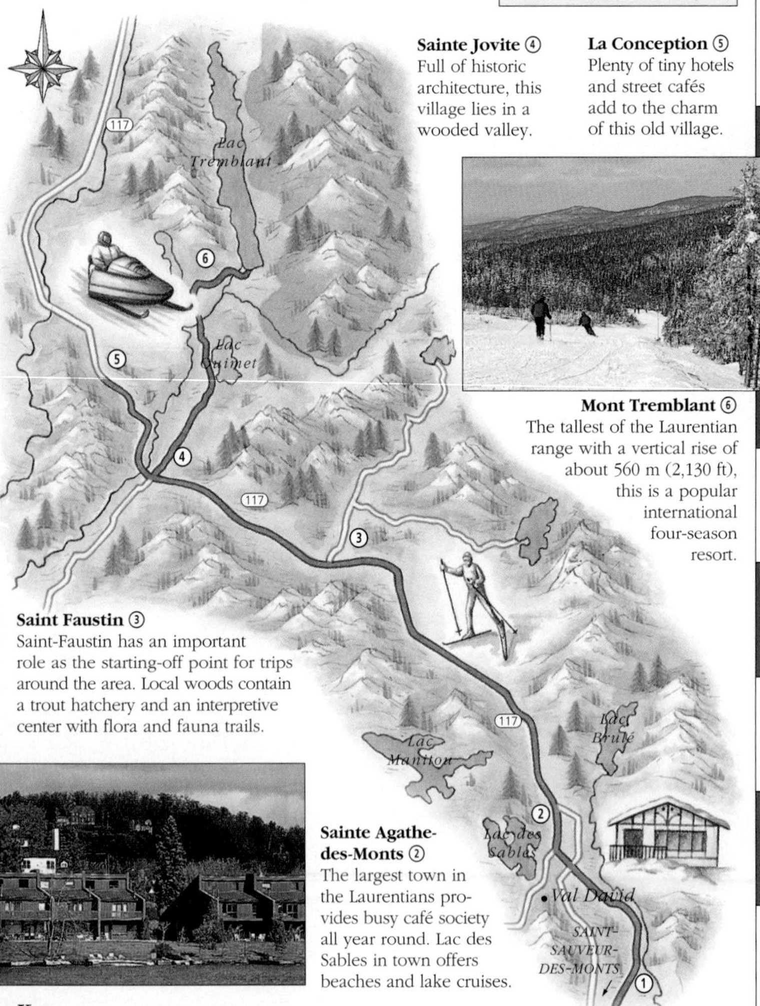

Sainte Jovite ④
Full of historic architecture, this village lies in a wooded valley.

La Conception ⑤
Plenty of tiny hotels and street cafés add to the charm of this old village.

Mont Tremblant ⑥
The tallest of the Laurentian range with a vertical rise of about 560 m (2,130 ft), this is a popular international four-season resort.

Saint Faustin ③
Saint-Faustin has an important role as the starting-off point for trips around the area. Local woods contain a trout hatchery and an interpretive center with flora and fauna trails.

Sainte Agathe-des-Monts ②
The largest town in the Laurentians provides busy café society all year round. Lac des Sables in town offers beaches and lake cruises.

Val Morin ①
This enchanting village is a charming introduction to the area, with traditional French homes and churches.

KEY

Tour route

Other roads

0 km 3

0 miles 3

The impressive beauty of Quebec's thundering Montmorency Falls ▷

Hull ⓬

Meditation center

HULL'S LINKS TO THE province of Ontario often appear stronger than its ties to its county position as the main city of Western Quebec. The town is based just across the river from Ottawa, and, as a result, many federal bureaucracies have their headquarters here. For years Hull has been a more relaxed and fun-loving counterpart to the capital, an attitude that reveals itself even in its officialdom – City Hall, for instance, boasts a meditation center. From Hull's establishment in 1800 until very recently, the city's liquor laws were far more lenient than Ottawa's, and this was where Ottawa politicians came to party. Hull contains one of Canada's best museums, the Museum of Civilization, which has a fascinating tour of Canada's history over the past 1,000 years.

VISITORS' CHECKLIST

60,700. Ottawa International 12 km (8 miles) south of the city. 200 Tremblay Rd, Ottawa. La Maison du Tourisme, 103 Rue Laurier (819) 778 2222. Fall Rhapsody (Sep/Oct).

Gatineau Park

Hwy 5. *(819) 827 2020. daily.*

This 360 sq km (140 sq miles) oasis of lakes and rolling hills between the Gatineau and Ottawa Rivers is a weekend playground for city residents. The park contains fragments of Gothic buildings, collected by the former Prime Minister, William Lyon MacKenzie-King, from demolition sites.

Casino de Hull

1 Casino Blvd. *(819) 772 2100.*

11am–3am daily.

Four million visitors a year are lured to this glittering Casino, which is equipped with 1,300 slot machines and 45 gaming tables. Owned by the Quebec Government, the Casino opened in 1996 and is set in a park full of flowers and fountains.

Gaming room in the Casino de Hull

Alexandra Bridge

Built in 1900, this handsome steel-framed bridge spans the Ottawa River and links Ontario to Quebec. From footpaths, drivers' lanes, and cycle routes, the bridge offers fine views of the river, the modern Museum of Civilization, and the Parliament Buildings in Ottawa.

Maison du Citoyen

25 Laurier St. *(819) 595 7100.*

8:30am–4:30pm Mon–Fri. public holidays.

The heart of this modern complex is a vast atrium, the Agora, meant to serve as an all-weather gathering place for Hull's citizens, as well as an airy meditation center for the city's workers. Opening from it are City Hall, a library, a theater, and an art gallery.

Promenade du Portage

Linked with the city bridges, this main route downtown is a good shopping center with large stores and lively cafés. After dark the area and nearby Place Aubry become the focus of the city's excellent nightlife.

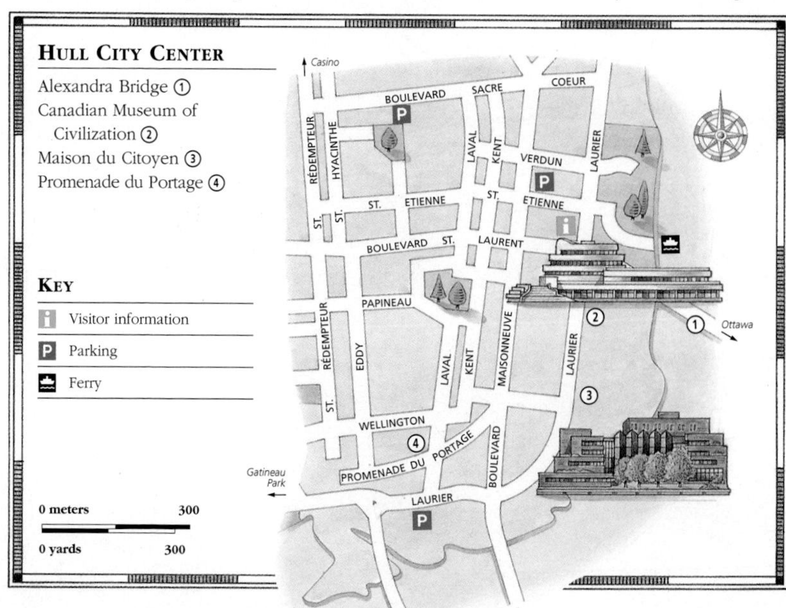

Canadian Museum of Civilization

THIS MUSEUM ON THE BANKS of the Ottawa River was built in the 1980s to be the storehouse of Canada's human history. The architect, Douglas Cardinal, wanted the undulating façades of both buildings to reflect the Canadian landscape. The more curved hall is the Canadian Shield Wing, home to the museum's offices. The Glacier Wing displays the exhibits. Its entry is stunning; the dramatic interior of the Grand Hall contains a forest of totem poles. Canada Hall traces the progress of the Canadian people from the Vikings through early settlers to the present day. The Children's Museum is delightfully diverting.

VISITORS' CHECKLIST

100 Laurier St. *(819) 776 7000.* *May–mid-Oct: 9am–6pm daily; mid-Oct–May: 9am–6pm Tue–Sun.*
www.civilization.ca

The museum façade echoes the rolling Quebec landscape

Canada Hall is a mazelike journey that traces the country's history from Norse settlers and colonial times to Acadian and Victorian villages.

Upper Level

David M. Stewart Salon

Street Level

Main Entrance

Lower Level

Library

The Children's Museum
This extremely popular space contains a "world tour" of interactive exhibits, a busy international market, and this brightly decorated Pakistani trolleybus.

★ The Grand Hall
Lit by windows three stories high, totem poles from the West Coast line the Grand Hall; each pole tells a native myth in wood carving.

STAR SIGHT

★ The Grand Hall

KEY TO FLOOR PLAN

- Children's Museum
- Grand Hall
- Canada Hall
- River Gallery
- Art Gallery
- Temporary exhibition halls
- Permanent exhibition galleries
- W.E. Taylor Research Gallery
- Marius Barbeau Salon
- IMAX/OMNIMAX™ movie theater
- Nonexhibition space

The wildlife preserve of La Vérendrye, seen from the air

Reserve Faunique La Vérendrye ⓭

(819) 736 7431. Maniwaki. summer. partial.

THIS WILDLIFE preserve is situated approximately 190 km (120 miles) to the northwest of Montreal on Hwy 117. It is celebrated for long, meandering waterways and streams and, with thousands of kilometers of canoe trails, is a legend among canoeists. Its rivers are usually gentle, and the 13,000 sq km (5,000 sq miles) of wilderness are home to large numbers of moose, bear, deer, and beaver. The land is practically untouched, but there are several campgrounds here for those who seek a truly peaceful break. In season, anglers can try for walleye, pike, lake trout, and bass. Hwy 117 traverses the park, providing access to many of its lakes and rivers, and is the starting point of hiking trails.

A moose at La Vérendrye

Val d'Or ⓮

25,000. 20 3rd Ave. E. (819) 824 9646.

VAL D'OR IS principally a mining town and is the major center in the northwestern part of Quebec. The town sights here are not architectural but vivid living history attractions of mines and historic villages from the area's heritage of lumber trade and mining. Miners have been digging gold, silver, and copper out of the ground around Val d'Or since the 1920s. A climb to the top of the 18-m (60-ft) Tour Rotary on the edge of town shows 10 still-active mineheads.

The Lamaque Goldmine, now abandoned, used to be one of the richest sources of gold in the area. In its heyday of the early 20th century, the mine had its very own small townsite with a hospital, a boarding house for all single workers, and neat streets lined with little log cabins for married men and their families. The mine managers had more elaborate homes nearby, and there was a sumptuous guesthouse for visiting executives. Much of this remains intact. The townsite and mine, **Village Minier de Bourlamaque** and **La Cité de l'Or**, were declared historic sites in 1979 and are a reconstruction of gold rush times of the 1850s. Visitors can tour the village, the old laboratories, and the minehead. For the brave there is a ride 90 m (300 ft) underground to see mining techniques through history.

Village Minier de Bourlamaque, La Cité de l'Or
123 Ave. Perrault. *(816) 825 7616. Jun–Sep: 9am–6pm daily. partial.*

Rouyn-Noranda ⓯

26,450. 191 Ave. du Lac (819) 797 3195.

AS WITH ALL developed areas in the north of Quebec, towns here are based on heavy industry. Rouyn and Noranda sprang up virtually overnight in the 1920s when prospectors found copper in the region. They merged into one city in 1986 but are quite different places. Noranda on the north shore of Lake Osisko is a carefully planned company town with its own churches and schools, built to house the employees of the now-defunct Noranda copper mine. The lawns and tree-lined streets have an almost English air. Nowadays its residents are likely to be employed in surrounding mines. The Horne Smelter, one of the biggest in the world, is based just outside the center of town and can be visited by arrangement.

Rouyn, on the south shore of the lake, is less structured and more commercial. It is also where Noranda residents used to go for recreation, and it is useful as a refreshment and fuel center for those traveling to the northern wilderness. The **Maison Dumulon**, a reconstruction of Rouyn's first post office and general store, celebrates its pioneer spirit with displays on the first settlers.

Maison Dumulon
191 Ave. du Lac. *(819) 797 7125. Jun–Sep: daily; Oct–Jun: Mon–Fri. Dec 25, Jan 1.*

Copper being smelted into huge nuggets for export, Noranda

Herds of caribou migrate south in summer across the Hudson Bay area into Nunavik

James Bay ⓰

Federation des Pourvoyeurs du Quebec, Jonquiere (418) 877 5191.

THE THINLY populated municipality of James Bay is roughly the size of Germany, which makes it much larger than most other municipalities in the region – about 350,000 square km (135,000 square miles). Its landscape, lakes, scrubby trees, and early pre-Cambrian rock is hardly urban, changing from forest to taiga to tundra and becoming gradually more inaccessible in the frozen northern parts. However, what the region lacks in infrastructure it makes up for amply in power capacity. Its six major rivers, which all flow into the Bay, can produce enough electricity to light up the whole of North America. So far, the Quebec government has spent over Can$20 billion in building a third of the number of dams for what is already one of the biggest hydroelectric projects in the world. Five power plants produce nearly 16,000 megawatts of electricity to power much of Quebec and parts of the northeastern US. Le Grand 2 (known as LG 2) is the biggest dam and underground generating station in the world.

The main town in the area is the small settlement of Radisson. A functional but useful tourist center, Radisson also offers good views of the surrounding country. Not all of the Bay's 215 dams and dikes can be seen, but the massive dams and series of reservoirs, especially LG 2, which is just east of town, are visible from above.

One of the vast power stations at James Bay

Nunavik ⓱

Association touristique du Nunavik (819) 964 2876.

IN THE FAR NORTH of Quebec, the municipality of Nunavik covers an area slightly larger than continental Spain. Its inhabitants number about 7,000, nearly all of them Inuit, who live in 14 communities along the shores of Hudson Bay, the Hudson Strait, and Ungava Bay. Nunavik is Quebec's last frontier, a wild and beautiful land that is virtually inaccessible except by airplane. Caribou herds, polar bears, and musk oxen roam the taiga coniferous forest and frozen Arctic tundra that covers this region. Seals and beluga whales can be found swimming in its icy waters.

Kuujjuaq, near Ungava Bay, is Nunavik's largest district, with a population of just over 1,400. This is a good jumping-off point for expeditions to the beautiful valley of Kangiqsujuaq near Wakeham Bay and the rugged mountains around Salluit.

Visitors come to Nunavik and Kuujjuaq to appreciate the many varieties of wildlife which roam freely in their natural setting. Summer is the best time for a trip; temperatures rise, but the ground remains frozen all year round. The region has no railroads (and hardly any roads) and should be explored only in the company of a seasoned and reliable guide. Many Inuit groups and communities offer guide services and the opportunity to experience life on the land with Inuit families. Visitors should be prepared for a very warm welcome and the chance to sample traditional Inuit foods and hospitality.

ONTARIO

Introducing Ontario

THE SHEER SIZE OF ONTARIO is daunting. It is Canada's second-largest province, covering over one million square miles and stretching all the way from the Great Lakes on the US border to the frozen shores of Hudson Bay. Northern Ontario is relatively inaccessible, but this wild and stunningly beautiful region of turbulent rivers, deep forests, and Arctic tundra can be reached by air, and by the occasional scenic road and railroad. Much of the north is also sparsely populated, in striking contrast to the fertile lands farther south, and bordering Lake Ontario, which have attracted many thousands of immigrants. Both Toronto, Canada's biggest city, and Niagara Falls, the country's leading tourist destination, are here.

The world's tallest free-standing structure, Toronto's CN Tower is illuminated at night

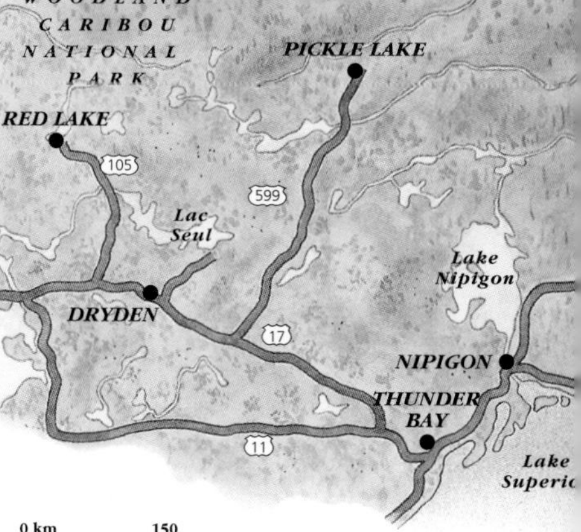

A tour boat approaches the spectacular Horseshoe Falls at Niagara

GETTING AROUND

Among several highways skirting the northern shore of Lake Ontario, the most important are Hwy 401, heading east from Toronto to Montreal, and the Queen Elizabeth Way (QEW), running south from Toronto to Niagara Falls. Niagara Falls, Toronto, and Ottawa, are connected by bus and VIA Rail. Traveling north from Toronto, Hwy 400 becomes part of the Trans-Canada Highway which travels west to Lake Superior. Trains and buses also cover many northerly routes.

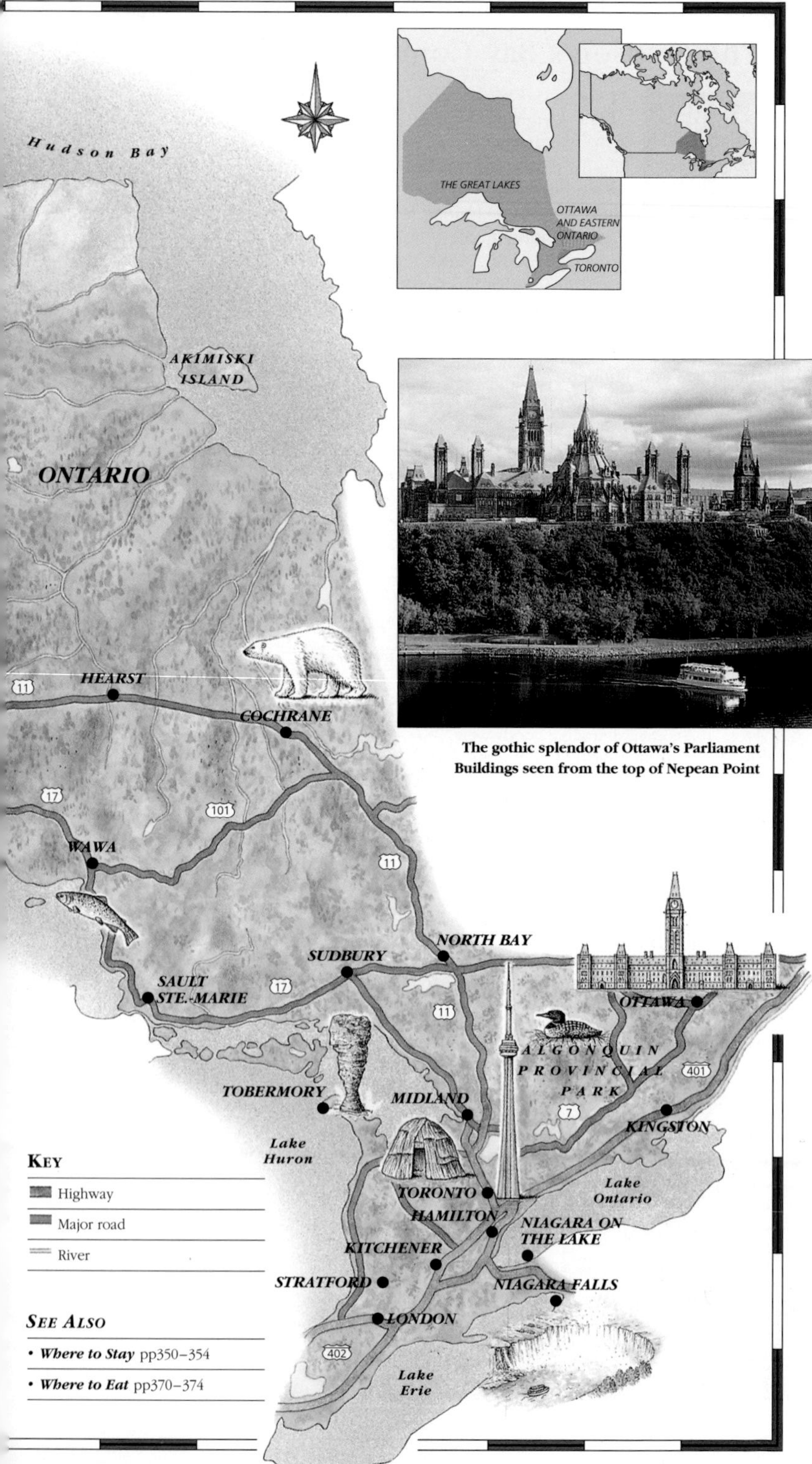

The gothic splendor of Ottawa's Parliament Buildings seen from the top of Nepean Point

KEY

- Highway
- Major road
- River

SEE ALSO

- ***Where to Stay*** pp350–354
- ***Where to Eat*** pp370–374

The Hudson's Bay Company

The Hudson's Bay Co. crest

The Hudson's Bay Company was incorporated by King Charles II of England on May 2, 1670. His decision was prompted by the successful voyage of the British ship *Nonsuch*, which returned from the recently discovered Hudson's Bay crammed with precious beaver furs. The king granted the new company wide powers, including a monopoly of trading rights to a huge block of territory bordering the Bay, then known as Rupert's Land. The Company was ordered to develop links with the native Americans of Rupert's Land, and trade took off swiftly. Here fashion played a part: the ladies and gentlemen of 18th-century Europe were gripped by a passion for the beaver hat, and the demand for beaver pelts became almost insatiable.

European fur couriers *rapidly built up a roaring trade with native fur trappers, which came to follow a seasonal pattern.*

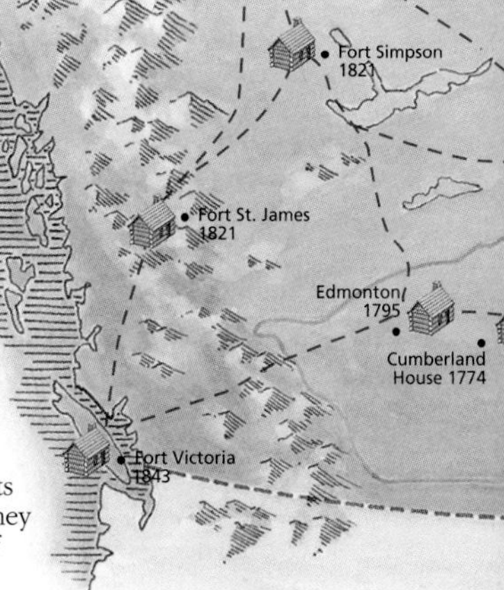

Lands and Trading Posts

From 1670 onward, trading goods were dispatched from England to the Company's main trading sites around Hudson Bay, modest stockaded settlements with safe stores for the merchandise. Larger outposts gradually became self-sufficient, catering to newer, smaller posts as the Company moved ever westward. By 1750, HBC camps were established at the mouths of all the major rivers flowing into Hudson Bay. James Bay's Fort Albany had a jail, a hospital, a smithy, a cooperage, a canoe-building jetty, and sheep and cattle barns, while gallant efforts were made to grow crops. Main trading posts serviced a network of smaller seasonal outposts. They continued their expansion west until the transfer of land rights to the new country of Canada in 1870.

Key

Trading post

-- Trading route

1670 boundary of Rupert's Land

The Sevenoaks Massacre *of June 1816 in Ontario occurred when HBC workers clashed with the rival North West Company, and 20 men were killed. The two companies agreed in 1820 to join territories and increased in power.*

English traders *assembled a variety of goods to trade with local tribes in return for the winter's supply of pelts. Transported by ship in spring, the merchandise ranged from trinkets to more substantial items including blankets, knives, and guns.*

The Changing Fortunes of HBC

Until the 1840s HBC reigned supreme in Canada, but civil disobedience led the British to relinquish claims to Washington State and Oregon in 1846, establishing the US border. Unable to continue enforcing its monopoly, HBC sold its land to Canada in 1870, retaining only areas around the trading posts. Since they were in key locations, this boosted HBC's expansion into real estate and retail in the 20th century. Today HBC is one of Canada's top companies and chain stores.

The Bay in Vancouver, one of HBC's modern department stores

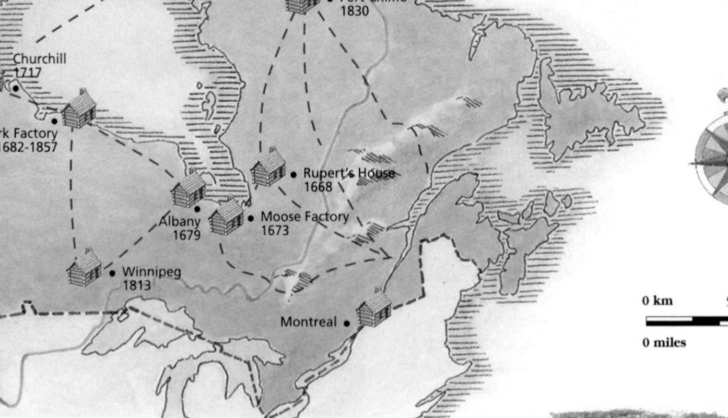

The beaver's coat *is at its thickest and most valuable in winter, when the natives ventured out into the ice and snow to trap the animal. In spring Indian trappers delivered bundles of soft pelts to the Company's trading posts, in exchange for goods.*

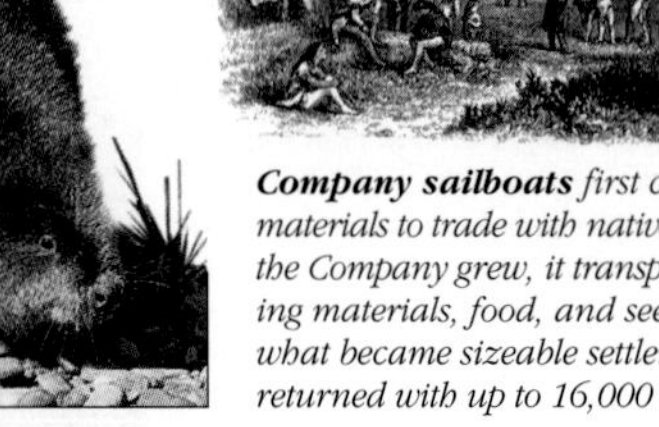

Company sailboats *first carried materials to trade with native peoples. As the Company grew, it transported building materials, food, and seeds to set up what became sizeable settlements. Ships returned with up to 16,000 beaver pelts.*

The Group of Seven

Tom Thomson, (1877–1917)

FORMED IN 1920, the Group of Seven revolutionized Canadian art. Mostly commercial artists working in an Ontario art firm, this small band of painters was inspired by a colleague, Tom Thomson. An avid outdoorsman, Thomson started making trips in 1912 into the wilderness of northern Ontario to produce dozens of brightly colored, impressionistic sketches. His friends realized that he was taking Canadian art in a new direction – these landscapes of their country were largely free of the rigid European focus that had characterized painting until then and a nationalist movement had begun. After World War I and the death of Thomson in 1917, these same friends started the Group and held their first exhibition in Toronto in 1920. Many of the paintings shown depicted Nova Scotian, Ontarian and Quebec wildernesses; a new art was born that forged a sense of national pride between the people and their land in this young country.

The Red Maple *is A.Y. Jackson's vibrant landmark of 1914, embodying the Group aim of creating a national consciousness.*

Edge of the Forest (1919) *by Frank Johnston is just one of the Group's works that illustrates their statement: "Art must grow and flower in the land before the country will be a real home for its people." Using the impressive surroundings of their homeland, the Group painters developed a spontaneous technique.*

Above Lake Superior *was produced by Lawren Harris in 1922. Known for his simple, heroic images, Harris captures the harsh, exhilarating climate of the Great Lakes region in winter, known as "the mystic north." Harris believed that spiritual fulfillment could best be obtained by studying landscape. The Group also held the ethos that truly meaningful expression was accomplished only when the the subject of the work was one the viewer shared with the artist, in this case local landscape.*

Falls, Montreal River *(1920) was painted by J. E. H. MacDonald, who chose Algoma as his work base. Each of the Group had a preferred individual region in which they found most inspiration, mostly in Ontario. Sketching trips regularly took place in summer, with painters showing each other favorite areas.*

Autumn, Algoma *(1920)*
This richly decorated canvas shows the extraordinary evening colors of the fall in Ontario. Algoma was J.E.H. MacDonald's chosen region, a Canadian Eden in northern Ontario that acted as his inspiration and where he regularly made sketching trips. MacDonald records uniquely Canadian subjects in this painting; the blazing foliage and looming pines serve to record and thus establish a Canadian identity. Influenced by the stark landscapes produced in Scandinavia from around 1900, MacDonald focuses on the chill drama in this scene to add a grandeur to his beloved landscape.

The Group of Seven

Based in a converted railway boxcar, the members hiked and boated to favorite places in Algonquin Park, Georgian Bay, Algoma, and Lake Superior to produce new art for their country. Following the 1920 exhibition, entitled The Group of Seven, their striking paintings immediately became popular and the Group went on to exhibit together almost every year. Native inspiration was vital to the Group's subject and technique. The apparently raw and coarse methods were a rejection of the heavy, realist oils produced in Europe at the time. Luminous colors and visible brushstrokes led one critic to remark that the Group had "thrown [their] paint pots in the face of the public." The Group held their final show in 1931 and disbanded the following year to make way for a wider group of painters from across Canada, the Canadian Group of Painters. Founders of a distinctive Canadian art movement based on a love of their country's natural beauty, the Group of Seven painters remain particularly celebrated in Canada and are still given prominence in top galleries across Ontario and the rest of the country today.

The photograph below, taken at Toronto's Arts & Letters Club in 1920, shows, from left to right: Varley, Jackson, Harris, Barker Fairley (a friend and writer), Johnston, Lismer and MacDonald. Carmichael was not present.

The Group of Seven in 1920

TORONTO

TORONTO HAS SHED *its prim, colonial image to become one of North America's most dynamic cities, a cosmopolitan mix of nearly 4 million inhabitants drawn from over one hundred ethnic groups. Reveling in its position as the richest city in the country's most prosperous region, Toronto is the financial and commercial center of Canada, with fine art museums, suave café-bars, and luxury stores.*

Toronto is an enterprising city. Located on the banks of Lake Ontario, it was originally a native Indian settlement dating from the 17th century, and, after 1720, a French fur-trading post. Fought over by the US and Britain in the War of 1812 *(see p41)*, Toronto has since been a peaceful city, growing dramatically after World War II with the arrival of over 500,000 immigrants, especially Italians, and, most recently, Chinese.

The first place to start a visit must be the CN Tower, the world's tallest free-standing structure and the city's most famous tourist attraction. From the top it is easy to pick out the sights of the city, and from the bottom a short stroll leads to the Skydome stadium or the banking district. To the north of downtown is the boisterous street-life of Chinatown and the superb paintings of the world-renowned Art Gallery of Ontario. Beyond sits the University of Toronto on whose perimeters lies the fine Royal Ontario Museum and also two delightful specialty collections, the historic Gardiner Museum of Ceramic Art and the contemporary Bata Shoe Museum. A quick subway ride takes the visitor north to both Casa Loma, an eccentric Edwardian mansion that richly merits a visit, and Spadina House, the elegant Victorian villa next door. Many more attractions are scattered around the peripheries of Toronto, including Toronto Zoo and the Ontario Science Centre. The McMichael Art Collection, in nearby Kleinburg, contains an outstanding collection of paintings by the Group of Seven in a modernist setting.

Toronto's café society doing what it does best in the downtown area

◁ **The spire of the CN Tower rearing above the city reflected in an office building**

Exploring Toronto

TORONTO IS A LARGE, sprawling metropolis that covers over 259 sq km (100 sq miles) on the north shore of Lake Ontario. The suburbs are divided into areas such as Etobicoke and Scarborough that, together with the inner city, form the GTA or Greater Toronto Area. The center consists of a series of interlocking neighborhoods such as the banking district between Front and Queen Streets (west of Yonge Street). Yonge Street is the main artery, bisecting the city from north to south.

SIGHTS AT A GLANCE

Historic Areas and Buildings
Casa Loma 21
Chinatown 12
First Post Office 8
Fort York 23
Little Italy 24
Ontario Parliament Buildings 16
Queen Street West 9
Royal Alexandra Theatre 7
Royal York Hotel 3
Spadina House 22
Toronto City Hall 11
University of Toronto 14
Yorkville 20

Parks and Gardens
Ontario Place 25
Queen's Park 16
Toronto Zoo 28

Islands and Beaches
Toronto Island 26
The Beaches and Scarborough Bluffs 27

Museums and Galleries
Art Gallery of Ontario pp174–5 10
The Bata Shoe Museum 19
Black Creek Pioneer Village 30
George R. Gardiner Museum of Ceramic Art 17
Hockey Hall of Fame 4
Hummingbird Centre for the Performing Arts 5
McMichael Art Collection 29
Ontario Science Centre 29
Royal Ontario Museum pp182–3 18
Toronto Dominion Gallery of Inuit Art 6

Modern Architecture
CN Tower p168 1
SkyDome 2

Shopping Areas
Kensington Market 13

GETTING AROUND

Toronto's public transportation system is excellent. One of the subway's three lines carries passengers east to west, while the other two run north to south. Buses and streetcars leave each subway station to service the surrounding area. Rush-hour traffic is heavy downtown.

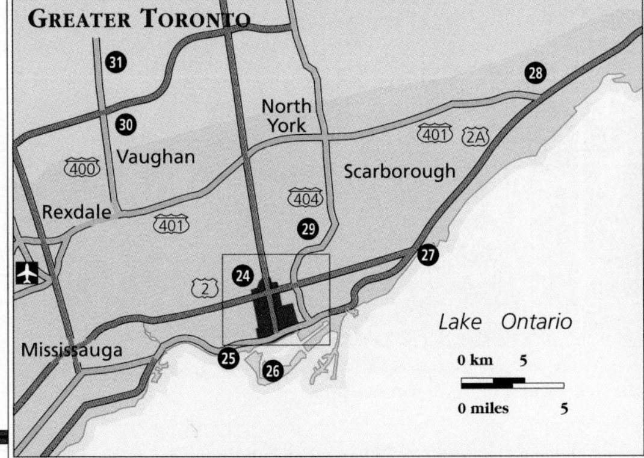

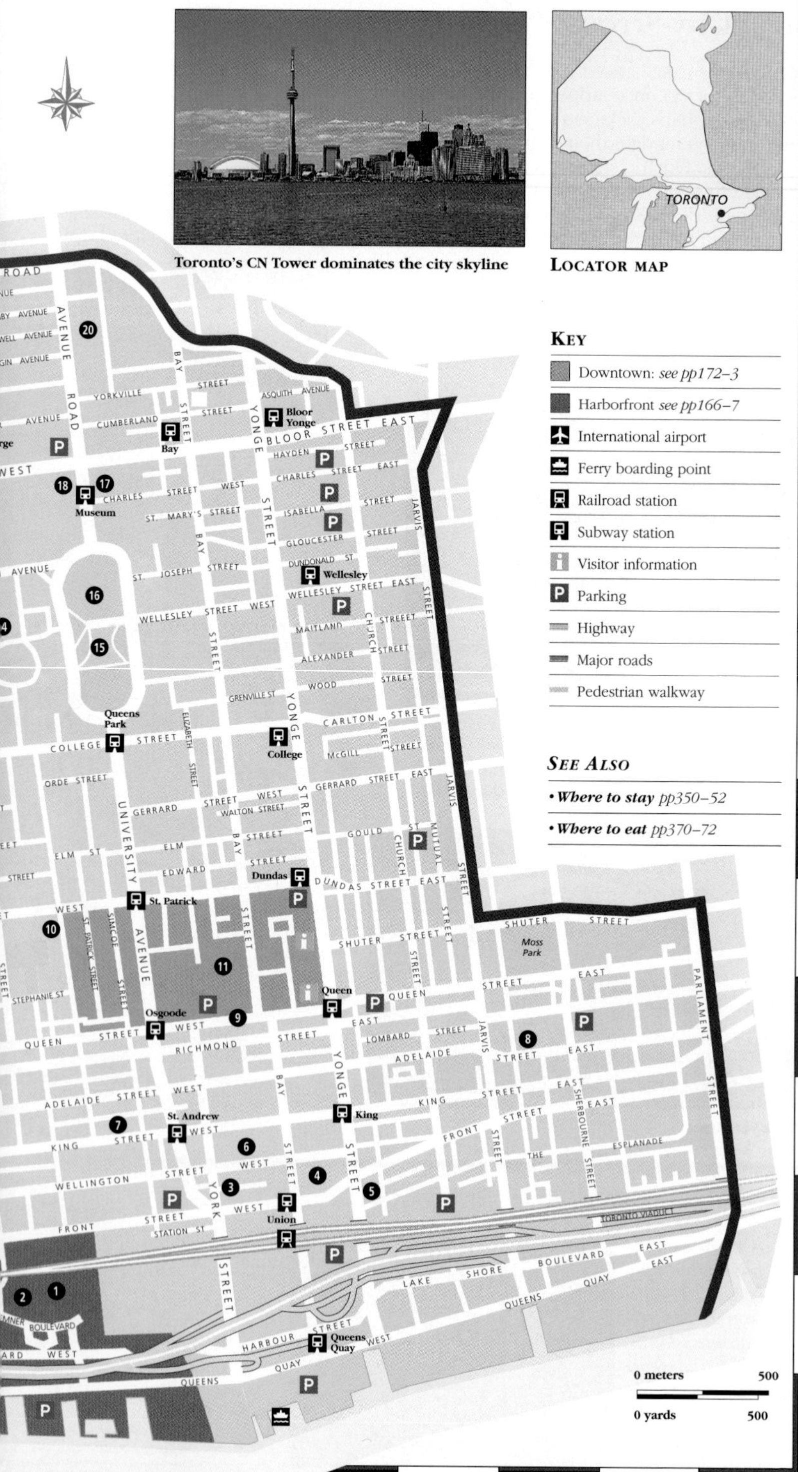

Toronto's CN Tower dominates the city skyline

LOCATOR MAP

KEY

- Downtown: *see pp172–3*
- Harborfront *see pp166–7*
- International airport
- Ferry boarding point
- Railroad station
- Subway station
- Visitor information
- Parking
- Highway
- Major roads
- Pedestrian walkway

SEE ALSO

- ***Where to stay*** *pp350–52*
- ***Where to eat*** *pp370–72*

Street-by-Street: Harborfront

TORONTO'S HARBORFRONT has had a varied history. Lake Ontario once lapped against Front Street, but the Victorians reclaimed 3 km (1.5 miles) of land to accommodate their railroad yards and warehouses. Ontario's exports and imports were funneled through this industrial strip until the 1960s, when trade declined. In the 1980s the harborfront had a new lease on life, when planners orchestrated the redevelopment of what has now become 10 sq km (4 sq miles) of reclaimed land. It now boasts grassy parks, walkways, smart apartments, many of the city's best hotels, and a cluster of tourist sights in and around the Harbourfront Centre.

★ View of the CN Tower
The highest free-standing tower in the world offers views of up to 160 km (100 miles) over Ontario, and a glass floor for those with iron nerves ❶

Convention Centre
Split into north and south arenas, the center is used for large-scale business shows as well as trade and consumer exhibitions for the public.

★ SkyDome
Using enough electricity to light the province of Prince Edward Island, a performance at the vast SkyDome stadium is an unforgettable experience ❷

Charter boats
Sailing out into Lake Ontario and around the three Toronto Islands provides fine views of the city. Small sailboats, motorboats, and tours are available.

0 m 150
0 yards 150

KEY

– – – Suggested route

Toronto Harborfront
The harborfront is a pleasing and relaxing addition to the city. Modern attractions consolidate Toronto's standing as the third-largest theater and dance center in the world.

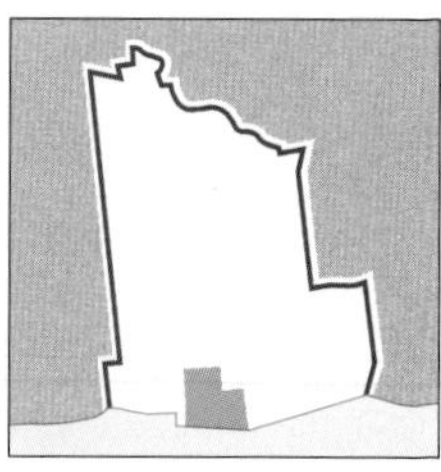

LOCATOR MAP
See pp164–5

Molson Place
Classical and modern performances run through the summer evenings in this open-air concert venue. Part of the Harbourfront Centre arts complex, nearby attractions include theater, dance, and film screenings.

The Gardiner Expressway slices through the city center, leading west to Niagara Falls *(see pp210–13)*.

Queen's Quay Terminal
The focus of activity on the harborfront, Queen's Quay is a lively area for visitors. Lined with cafés and restaurants, the walkway offers lakeside views as well as street performers and gift shops.

STAR SIGHTS

- ★ **SkyDome**
- ★ **CN Tower**

CN Tower ❶

No less than 553 m (1,815 ft) high, the CN Tower is the tallest free-standing structure in the world. In the 1970s, the Canadian Broadcasting Company (CBC) decided to build a new transmission mast in partnership with Canadian National (CN), the railroad conglomerate. The CN Tower was not originally designed as the world's tallest spire, but it so overwhelmed the city's visitors that it soon became one of Canada's prime tourist attractions. The tower houses the largest revolving restaurant in the world, which rotates fully every 72 minutes.

Visitors' Checklist

301 Front St. W. 416 868 6937. www.cntower.ca
10am–10pm daily.
Dec 25.

The Sky Pod is reached by its own elevator and is the highest accessible point on the tower at 447 m (1,465 ft).

The 360 Restaurant
Top-quality cuisine is available here as the restaurant revolves, allowing diners a spectacular view while they dine.

The CN Tower from the Lake
The tower offers fantastic views in every direction. On a clear day it is possible to see as far south as Niagara Falls (see pp210–13).

The exterior lookout level is protected by steel grilles and illustrates how high the tower is, especially in windy weather.

The interior lookout level offers visitors the chance to observe the city in comfort, away from the wind; signs identify main Toronto landmarks.

Glass Floor
The ground is over 300 m (1,000 ft) beneath this thick layer of reinforced glass, and even the courageous may feel a little daunted.

The outside elevators are glass-fronted and take visitors shooting up the outside of the Tower to the upper levels. Speeds take your breath away and make your ears pop; the elevators can reach the top in under a minute.

The inside staircase is the longest in the world, with 1,769 steps. Visitors would climb down only in an emergency. Even 70 major storms each year have no effect on the elevators.

View of the City from the Lookout Level
At 346 m (1,136 ft) above the city, the Lookout Level provides panoramas of Toronto from exterior and interior galleries.

SkyDome ❷

1 Blue Jay Way. 416 341 3663. *Union Station.* *Bay St. Terminal.* *Union.* *daily.*

OPENED IN 1989, the SkyDome was the first sports stadium in the world to have a fully rectractable roof. In good weather, the stadium is open to the elements, but in poor conditions the roof moves into position, protecting players and crowd alike. This remarkable feat of engineering is based on simple principles; four gigantic roof panels are mounted on rails and take just twenty minutes to cover the playing area. The design is certainly innovative and eminently practical, but the end result looks sort of like a giant hazelnut. However, the building's looks are partially redeemed by a matching pair of giant-sized cartoon-sculptures on the outside wall showing spectators at an imaginary game, the creation of a popular contemporary artist, Michael Snow.

The SkyDome is home to two major sports teams, the Toronto Argonauts from the Canadian Football League, and the Toronto Blue Jays of Major League Baseball. The Skydome is also used for special events and concerts. Guided tours allow a close look at the mechanics of the roof and include a 20-minute film outlining the story of its ground-breaking construction.

Lavish interior lobby of the Royal York

Royal York ❸

100 Front St. W. 416 368 2511. *Union Station.* *Bay St. Terminal.* *Union.* *121+.*

DATING FROM 1929, the Royal York was once Toronto's preeminent hotel, its plush luxury easily outshining its rivals. It was built opposite the city's main train station for the convenience of visiting dignitaries, but for thousands of immigrants the hotel was the first thing they saw of their new city, giving it a landmark resonance beyond its immediate commercial purpose. The Royal York was designed by the Montreal architects Ross and Macdonald in Beaux Arts contemporary style with a tumbling, irregular façade that resembles a large French château. Inside, the public areas are lavish and ornate with slender galleries providing extra grace and charm. Recently revamped, the Royal York remains a favorite with high-powered visitors, although other, newer hotels threaten to usurp its long-established position.

Doorman of the Royal York

Union Station, across the street from the Royal York, was also designed by Ross and Macdonald. The earlier building of the two, it shares a similar Beaux Arts style. The long and imposing stone exterior is punctuated by stone columns, and on the inside the cavernous main hall has a grand coffered ceiling supported by 22 sturdy marble pillars.

The retractable roof of the SkyDome rears above the playing field, site of many famous ballgames

The Hummingbird Centre, home to the National Ballet and Opera

Hockey Hall of Fame ❹

BCE Place, 30 Yonge St. *416 360 7735. Union Station. Bay Street Terminal. Union Station. 10am–5pm Mon–Fri, 9:30am–6pm Sat, 10:30am–5pm Sun.*

THE HOCKEY HALL of Fame is a lavish tribute to Canada's national sport, ice hockey *(see p32)*. Hockey, both ice and grass, originated in Canada; from its simple winter beginnings on frozen lakes and ponds, the game now ignites Canadian passions like no other. The Hall of Fame's ultra-modern exhibition area is inventive and resourceful, and features different sections devoted to particular aspects of the game. There are displays on everything from the jerseys of the great players, including Wayne Gretsky and Ray Ferraro, to a replica of the Montréal Canadiens' locker room, and antique hockey sticks and skates.

Another section traces the development of the goalie's mask from its beginnings to the elaborately painted versions of today. Interactive displays abound, and visitors can practice their shooting on a mini-ice rink. A small theater shows films of hockey's most celebrated games. A separate area at the front of the Hall displays a collection of trophies, including the Stanley Cup, hockey's premier award, donated by Lord Stanley in 1893.

The Stanley Cup at the Hockey Hall of Fame

Hummingbird Centre for the Performing Arts ❺

1 Front St. E. *416 393 7474. Union Station. Bay Street Terminal. Union Station.*

OWNED AND operated by City Hall, the Hummingbird Centre is one of Toronto's largest performing arts venues, with over 3,000 seats in the single large theater. It was known as the O'Keefe Centre until 1996 when the Hummingbird software company donated several million dollars to have the place refurbished. Now with a cavernous modern interior, it is home to both the Canadian Opera Company and the National Ballet of Canada. The Hummingbird also offers a wide-ranging program including light comedy shows, and childrens' entertainments, not to mention musicians famous worldwide. Recent productions have included Houston Ballet's *Dracula* and *The Nutcracker*. Top artists come from all over the world to the center – pop performers and classical musicians regularly star here. Despite this, the accoustics here have often been criticized, and many people try to avoid sitting in the front rows.

Toronto Dominion Gallery of Inuit Art ❻

Wellington St. *416 982 8473. Union Station. Union Station. Union Station. 8am–6pm Mon–Fri, 10am–4pm Sat & Sun.*

THE TORONTO Dominion Centre consists of five jet-black skyscrapers, a huge modern tribute to the money-making skills of the Toronto Dominion Bank. The southern tower displays a strong collection of Inuit Art on two levels of its foyer. The exhibits were assembled on behalf of the bank by a panel of art experts in the 1960s. They bought over 100 pieces in a variety of materials, including caribou antler and walrus ivory, but the kernel of the collection is the stone carving. Soapstone sculptures on display, mostly 30–60cm (1–2 ft) high, show mythological beasts and spirits as well as scenes from everyday life. Some of the finest were carved by Johnny Inukpuk (b.1911), whose *Mother Feeding Child* (1962) and *Tattooed Woman* (1958) have a raw, elemental force.

Royal Alexandra Theatre ❼

260 King St. W. *416 872 1212. Union Station. Bay Street Terminal. St. Andrew.*

IN THE 1960s, the Royal Alexandra Theatre was about to be flattened by modernizing bulldozers when a flamboyant Toronto retail

Façade of the Edwardian Royal Alexandra Theatre

Toronto's fashionable café society on Queen Street West

entrepreneur by the name of "Honest Ed" Mirvish, the king of the bargain store, came to the rescue. Mirvish saved a fine Edwardian theater, whose luxurious interior of red velvet, green marble, gold brocade, and flowing scrollwork once made it the most fashionable place in Toronto. Nowadays, the Royal Alex puts on blockbuster plays but specializes in big-hit Broadway musicals, which are often held over for months at a time. Evening performances are extremely popular; theater-goers stand in line to admire the interior as much as the show, and booking promptly is recommended. Early arrivals can enjoy the original Edwardian features in the bar before the show.

First Post Office 8

260 Adelaide St. E. *416 865 1833. Union Station. Bay Street Terminal. Yonge St. 9am–4pm Mon–Fri, 10am–4pm Sat & Sun. by arrangement.*

In the early Victorian era, the British Empire needed good communications for all its colonies. In 1829, the British House of Commons founded their colonial postal service and five years later established a post office in a far-flung outpost of the newly created town of Toronto. Remarkably, Toronto's First Post Office has survived, weathering various municipal attempts by the city to have it demolished. The only remaining example in the world of a post office dating from the British North American postal era still in operation, the First Post Office functions fully. Visitors make the trip to write a letter with a quill pen and have it sealed with hot wax by a clerk wearing period dress. Today's mail, however, is processed by the national service, Canada Post. After a devastating fire in 1978, the building was entirely restored and refurbished to its former carved and decorated appearance using old documents and historical city archive records.

Young visitors on Queen Street West

Queen Street West 9

Union Station. Bay Street Terminal. Queen.

Through the day and into the small hours of the morning, Queen Street West buzzes. Students and trendsetters reinvigorated this old warehouse area in the 1980s, but nowadays the street is more varied, with chic designer stores, downbeat bars, and stylish cafés mixed in with more mainstream offerings from the big chain stores. The chief merrymaking is concentrated between University and Spadina, a good place for budget restaurants and bars.

Worker at Toronto's First Post Office stamping mail by hand

Street-by-Street: Downtown

THROUGHOUT THE 19th century, Yonge Street was the commercial focus of Toronto, lined with scores of shops and suppliers. It also separated the city ethnically. In 1964, with the building of the new City Hall and Nathan Phillips Square just across from Old City Hall, Toronto's center of gravity shifted to Queen Street. South of Queen Street lay the banking district, where old Victorian buildings were replaced from the 1960s onward by gleaming concrete-and-glass tower blocks. The re-invigorated Harbourfront, with its yachts and cafés, provides light relief from the busy atmosphere. Yonge Street is now best known for the Eaton Centre emporium, one of the world's biggest malls.

Textile Museum
Based in a downtown office building, this collection features fabrics, embroidery, and clothing through the ages.

★ Art Gallery of Ontario
With exhibits ranging from the 14th to the 21st centuries, the AGO is also home to over 20 Henry Moore bronzes ⑩

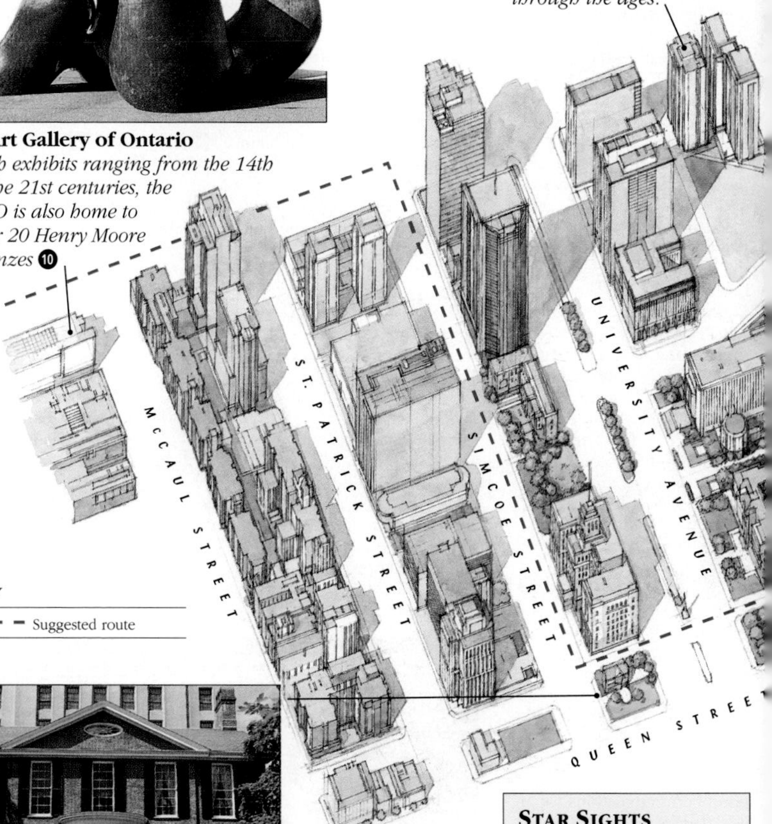

MCCAUL STREET

ST. PATRICK STREET

SIMCOE STREET

UNIVERSITY AVENUE

QUEEN STREET

KEY

– – – Suggested route

Campbell's House
This 19th-century home is a period piece from the days of the Victorian bourgeoisie.

STAR SIGHTS

- ★ Art Gallery of Ontario
- ★ Toronto City Hall

Eaton Centre
If Toronto has a specific core it would be outside the Eaton Centre shopping mall at the Yonge and Dundas intersection. The Eaton Centre boasts that it sells anything available in the world.

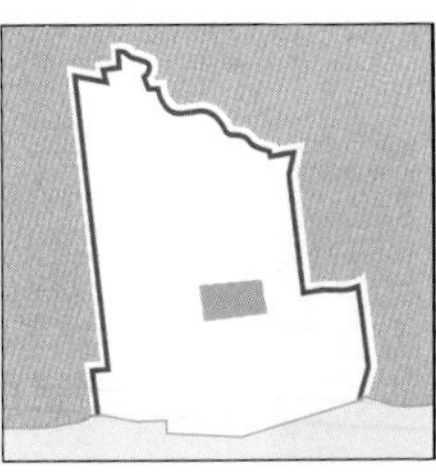

LOCATOR MAP
See Toronto Map pp164–5

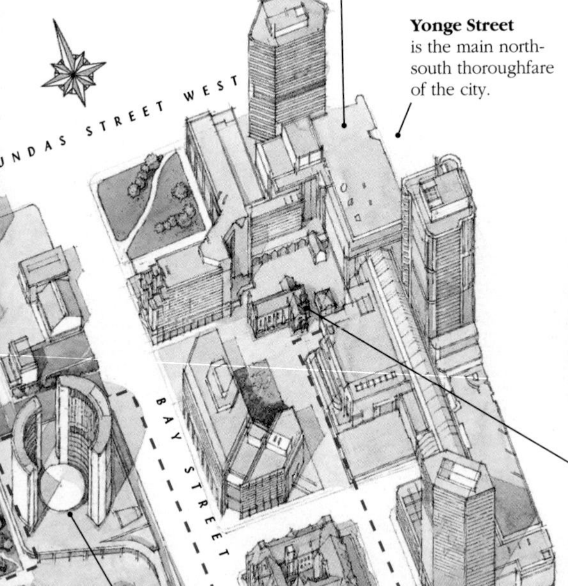

Yonge Street is the main north-south thoroughfare of the city.

Church of the Holy Trinity
This charming Catholic church was built in the 19th century and features an elegant interior.

Nathan Phillips Square is a center of the town's activity and is a popular rendezvous for young people.

★ Toronto City Hall
Built in 1964, this controversial development has slowly become popular with locals, who use the plaza as a skating rink in winter ⓫

Old City Hall
In sharp contrast to its ultra-modern replacement across the street, the elegant 19th-century Old City Hall now houses Toronto's Law Courts and the Justice Department.

Art Gallery of Ontario ⑩

***Hina and Fatu* (1892), Paul Gauguin**

FOUNDED IN 1900, the Art Gallery of Ontario holds one of Canada's most extensive collections of fine art and modern sculpture. Its first permanent home was The Grange, an English-style manor built in 1817 and left to the gallery in 1913. In 1973 The Grange was restored in 1830s style and opened to the public as a historic house which is now connected to the main gallery building. This modern structure houses European Art ranging from Rembrandt to Picasso, a superb collection of Canadian painting including Group of Seven work *(see pp 160–1)*, Inuit art, and an entire gallery of Henry Moore sculptures.

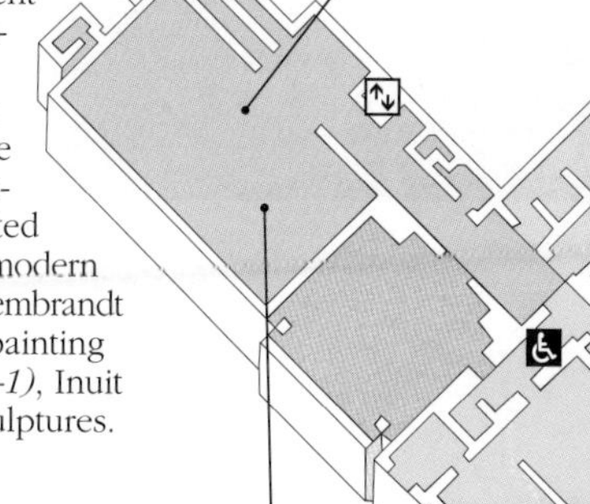

★ Henry Moore Sculpture
Opened in 1974, the Henry Moore Sculpture Centre houses the world's largest public collection of his works, including Draped Reclining Figure *(1952–3).*

Street Level

Floor Burger *(1962)*
Claes Oldenburg's giant hamburger is made of painted sailcloth and foam rubber and is an iconic work of the Pop Art movement.

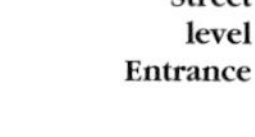

Street level Entrance

Gallery Façade
The gallery was reopened in 1993 after four years of architectural renovation that unified a range of styles, from Georgian to Modernist. Outside, the stern Henry Moore bronze, Large Two Forms *(1966–9), dominates the forecourt.*

STAR SIGHTS

- ★ **The West Wind by Tom Thomson**
- ★ **Henry Moore Sculpture Centre**
- ★ **Inuit Collection**

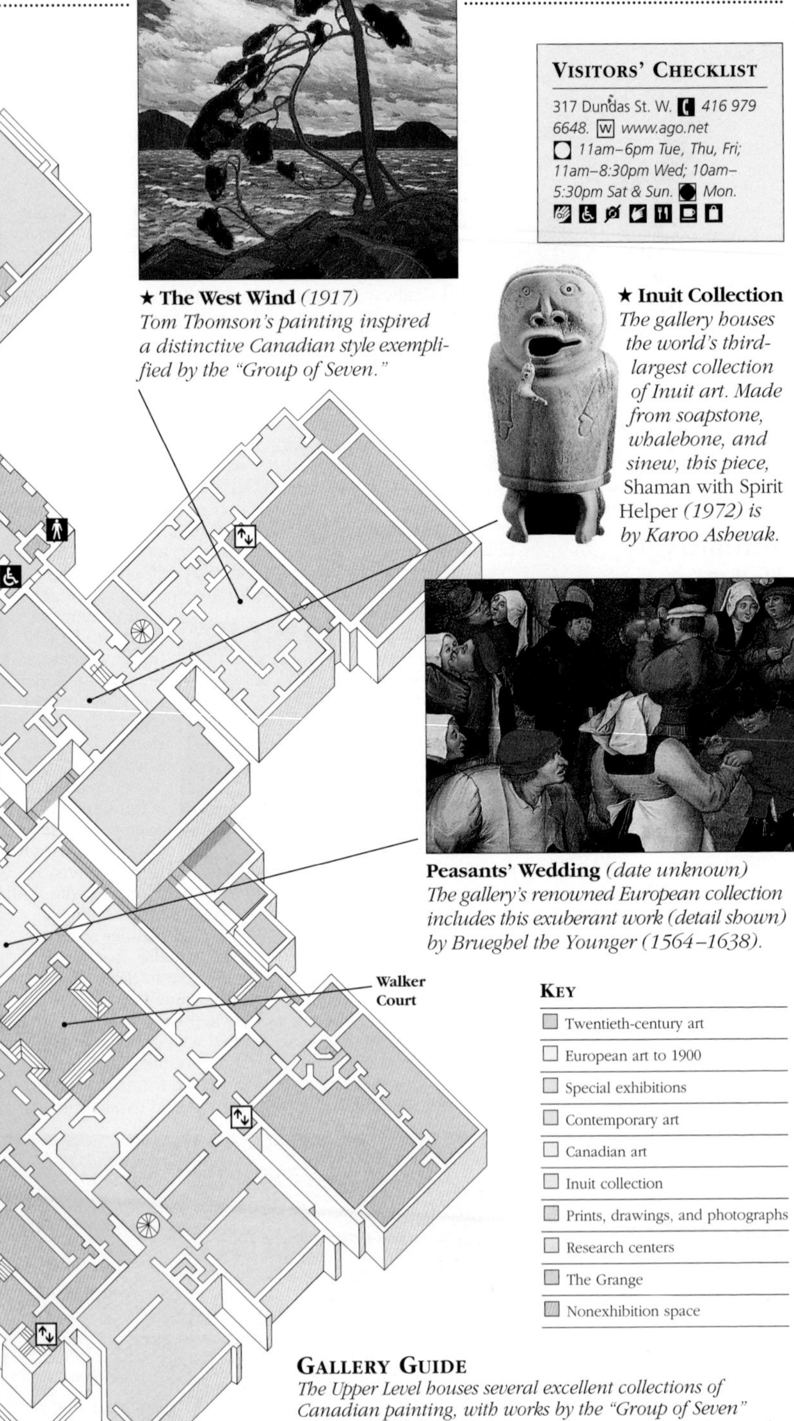

Visitors' Checklist

317 Dundas St. W. 416 979 6648. www.ago.net 11am–6pm Tue, Thu, Fri; 11am–8:30pm Wed; 10am–5:30pm Sat & Sun. Mon.

★ The West Wind *(1917)*
Tom Thomson's painting inspired a distinctive Canadian style exemplified by the "Group of Seven."

★ Inuit Collection
The gallery houses the world's third-largest collection of Inuit art. Made from soapstone, whalebone, and sinew, this piece, Shaman with Spirit Helper *(1972) is by Karoo Ashevak.*

Peasants' Wedding *(date unknown)*
The gallery's renowned European collection includes this exuberant work (detail shown) by Brueghel the Younger (1564–1638).

Key

- Twentieth-century art
- European art to 1900
- Special exhibitions
- Contemporary art
- Canadian art
- Inuit collection
- Prints, drawings, and photographs
- Research centers
- The Grange
- Nonexhibition space

Gallery Guide

The Upper Level houses several excellent collections of Canadian painting, with works by the "Group of Seven" (see pp160–1), and Inuit art. The Upper Level also houses the Henry Moore Centre, which is home to Moore's sculptures, bronzes, and plaster casts, as well as over 700 prints and drawings. European art is found on the ground floor.

Built in the 1960s, the ultra-modern design of Toronto City Hall has proved controversial

Toronto City Hall ⓫

Queen St. W. & Bay St. 416 392 8016. *Union Station.* *Bay Street Terminal.* *Queen St.* *8:30am–4:30pm Mon–Fri.*

COMPLETED IN 1964, Toronto's City Hall was designed by the award-winning Finnish architect Viljo Revell. At the official opening, the Prime Minister Lester Pearson announced, "It is an edifice as modern as tomorrow," but for many cityfolk tomorrow had come too soon and there were howls of protests from several quarters. Even now, after nearly 40 years, the building appears uncompromisingly modern. It is the epitome of 1960s urban planning, with two curved concrete and glass towers framing a central circular building where the Toronto councils meet. Nearby, the Old City Hall is a grand 19th-century neo-Romanesque edifice whose towers and columns are carved with intricate curling patterns.

Chinatown ⓬

Union Station. *Bay Street Terminal.* *505, 77.*

THE CHINESE community in Toronto numbers around 250,000, six percent of the city's total population. There have been several waves of Chinese migration to Canada, the first to British Columbia in the late 1850s during the gold rush. The first Chinese to arrive in Toronto came at the end of the 19th century as workers on the Canadian Pacific Railway, settling in towns along the rail route. The Chinese found work in the Toronto laundries, factories, and on the railways. The last immigration wave saw prosperous Hong Kong Chinese come to live in Toronto in the 1990s. Chinese Canadians inhabit every part of the city but are concentrated in four Chinatowns, the largest and liveliest of which is focused on Spadina Avenue, between Queen and College streets, and along Dundas Street, west of the Art Gallery of Ontario. These few city blocks are immediately different from their surroundings. The sights, sounds, and aromatic smells of the neighborhood are reminiscent not of Toronto but of Hong Kong. Everywhere, stores and stalls spill over the sidewalks, offering a bewildering variety of Chinese delicacies, and at night bright neon signs advertise dozens of delicious restaurants.

Vivid restaurant signs in Chinatown

Kensington Market ⓭

Baldwin St. & Augusta Ave. *Union Station.* *Bay Street Terminal.* *510.*

KENSINGTON MARKET is one of Toronto's most distinctive and ethnically diverse residential areas. It was founded at the turn of the 20th century by East European immigrants, who crowded into the patchwork of modest houses near the junction of Spadina Avenue and Dundas Street, and then spilled out into the narrow streets to sell their wares. The bazaar they established in their small 1930s houses has been the main feature of the area ever since.

Today, Jewish, Polish, and Russian stall owners and shopkeepers rub shoulders with Portuguese, Jamaican, East Indian, Chinese, and Vietnamese traders in a vibrant street scene that always excites the senses. The focal point of this open-air market is Kensington Avenue, whose lower half, just off Dundas Street, is crammed with thrift shops selling all manner of trendy retro bargains, from original punk gear to flares. Kensington Avenue's upper half is packed with fresh food stores filled with produce from every corner of the globe, ranging from iced fish to stacks of cheeses and exotic fruits.

A Torontonian samples exotic nuts in the bazaar of Kensington Market

Façade of the Ontario Parliament Building, home of the provincial legislature since 1893

University of Toronto ⑭

27 King's College Circle. *416 978 2011. Union Station. Bay Street Terminal. St. George.*

THE UNIVERSITY of Toronto, an interdenominational institute, opened in 1850 after opposition from some religious quarters for being seen as challenging church control of education. The new institution weathered accusations of godlessness and proceeded to swallow its rivals, becoming in the process one of Canada's most prestigious universities.

This unusual history explains the rambling layout of the present campus, a leafy area sprinkled with colleges. The best-looking university buildings are near the west end of Wellesley Street. Here, on Hart House Circle, lie the delightful quadrangles and ivy-clad walls of Hart House (1919), built in imitation of some of the colleges of Oxford and Cambridge universities in Britain, and the Soldiers' Tower, a neo-Gothic memorial to those students who died in both world wars. Nearby, King's College Circle contains University College, an imposing neo-Romanesque edifice dating from 1859, Knox College with its rough gray sandstone masonry, and the fine rotunda of the university's Convocation Hall. A visit to the campus can be peacefully rounded off by a short stroll along Philosophers' Walk, where the manicured lawns lead to Bloor Street West.

Reminiscent of old British universities, the University of Toronto

Ontario Parliament Building ⑮

Queen's Park. *416 325 7500. Union Station. Bay Street Terminal. Queen's Park. 97B. May–Sep: 8:30am–6pm Mon–Fri, 9am–5pm Sat & Sun; Sep–May: 8:30am–6pm Mon–Fri.*

THERE IS NOTHING modest about the Ontario Parliament Building, a vast pink sandstone edifice built in 1893 that dominates the end of University Avenue. Ontario's elected representatives had a point to make. The province was a small but exceedingly loyal part of the British Empire and clamored to make its mark and had the money to do so. Consequently, the Members of Provincial Parliament (MPPs) commissioned this immensely expensive structure in the Romanesque Revival style. Finished in 1892, its main façade is a panoply of towers, arches, and rose windows decorated with relief carvings and set beneath a series of high-pitched roofs.

The interior is of matching grandeur. Gilded classical columns frame the main staircase and enormous stained-glass windows illuminate long and richly timbered galleries. The chamber is a lavish affair, with a wealth of fine wooden carving that carries epithets urging good behavior, such as "Boldly and Rightly," and "By Courage, not by Craft."

In 1909, a fire razed the west wing, which was rebuilt in Italian marble. The stone was very expensive, so the MPPs were annoyed to find that a large amount of the marble was blemished by dinosaur fossils, which can still be seen today in the west hallway. Visitors can sometimes watch the parliament in session.

The Parliament Buildings, viewed from inner-city Queen's Park

Queen's Park ⓰

College St. & University Ave. *416 325 7500.* *Union Station.* *Bay St. Terminal.* *506.* *Queen's Park.*

JUST BEYOND the Parliament Buildings lies Queen's Park, a pleasant grassy space for those wishing to stroll and relax in between the closely packed sights in this area. It is fringed to the west by the 19th-century buildings of the University and offers views of the historic campus, from where walking tours regularly depart in the summer.

In June each year a spectacular parade passses by the north of the park on Gay Pride Day. Toronto has a sizable gay and lesbian community, and the gay lifestyle is celebrated in flamboyant fashion in this yearly weekend festival, which started in the 1970s.

George R. Gardiner Museum of Ceramic Art ⓱

111 Queen's Park. *416 586 8080.* *Union Station.* *Bay St. Terminal.* *Museum.* *10am–6pm Mon, Wed, Fri; 10am–8pm Tue & Thu, 10am–5pm Sat & Sun.* *Jan 1, Dec 25, 31.*

OPENED IN 1984, the Gardiner Museum of Ceramic Art is the only showcase of its kind in North America dedicated solely to pottery and porcelain. Skillfully displayed, the collection traces the history of ceramics, with a detailed focus on its principal developmental stages. These start with Pre-Columbian pottery, and the museum has fascinating displays of ancient pieces from Peru and Mexico that incorporate several grimacing fertility gods.

The Greeting Harlequin **Meissen ceramic figure**

Examples of brightly colored *maiolica* (glazed, porous pottery), includes painted pots made first in Mallorca, then Italy, from the 13th to the 16th centuries. Cheerfully decorated everyday wares are complemented by later Renaissance pieces relating classical myths and history. English delftware (tin-glazed earthenware) is also well represented. The Renaissance pieces gathered from Italy, Germany, and England are superb – particularly the collection of *commedia dell'arte* figures. These are derived from the Italian theatrical tradition of comic improvisation with a set of stock characters, notably the joker Harlequin. Intricately decorated in rainbow colors, these figurines were placed on dinner tables by the aristocracy to delight, impress, or even to woo their special guests.

Porcelain here is stunning, with many examples of exquisite Meissen from 1700 to 1780. Packed in its own specially made leather carrying case to accompany a fine lady owner on her travels, a special feature is the embellished tea and chocolate service dating from the early 18th century. Each tiny cup has individual, intricate sailing scenes surrounded in gold. The porcelain collection also contains over 100 carved or molded scent bottles from all over Europe.

The modern façade of the Gardiner Museum of Ceramic Art

Royal Ontario Museum ⓲

See pp182–183.

The Bata Shoe Museum ⓳

327 Bloor St. W. *416 979 7799.* *Union Station.* *Bay St. Terminal.* *St. George.* *10am–5pm Tue–Sat, noon–5pm Sun.* *Jan 1, Good Friday, Jul 1, Dec 25.*

THE BATA SHOE MUSEUM was opened in 1995 to display the extraordinary range of footwear collected by Sonja Bata, the current director of the eponymous shoe manufacturing family, a worldwide concern that sells footwear in 60 countries. To be sure her collection was seen to best effect, Sonja had the prestigious contemporary Canadian architect Raymond Moriyama design the building, an angular modern affair complete with unlikely nooks and

crannies created to look like a chic shoebox. The collection is spread over several small floors and features temporary exhibitions developing a particular theme, for instance "Japanese Footgear and Pādukā: Feet and Footwear in the Indian Tradition," as well as regularly rotated items selected from the museum's substantial permanent collection.

One fixed feature in the museum is the exhibition entitled "All About Shoes," which provides the visitor with an overview of the functions and evolution of footwear. It begins with a plaster cast of the earliest known footprint, discovered 4,000,000 years after it was made in Tanzania, and has an interesting section on medieval pointed shoes. A second permanent feature is the section on celebrity footwear. This displays all kinds of eccentric performance wear, from Elvis Presley's blue-and-white patent-leather loafers and a pair of Elton John's platforms to Michael Johnson's gold lamé sprinting shoes and ex-Canadian Prime Minister Pierre Trudeau's battered sandals.

There is also a display of unusual and improbable footwear including unique French chestnut-crushing boots, Venetian platform shoes dating from the 16th century, and a pair of US army boots made for use in the Vietnam War, whose sole is shaped to imitate the footprint of an enemy Vietcong irregular.

Other fascinating items on display feature the importance of First Nations and Inuit bootmaking skills. The development of snowshoes is generally credited with aiding the Inuit to settle in the very far north of Canada.

The Bata Shoe Museum lobby displays enticing footwear

A lazy Sunday afternoon at Café Nervosa in trendy Yorkville

Yorkville ⑳

Union Station. *Bay St. Terminal.* *Bay.*

In the 1960s tiny Yorkville, in the center of the city, was the favorite haunt of Toronto's hippies. With regular appearances by countercultural figures such as Joni Mitchell, it was similar to London's Chelsea or New York's Greenwich Village. The hippies have now moved on, and Yorkville's modest brick and timber terrace houses have either been colonized by upscale shops and fashionable restaurants, or converted into bijou townhouses. Designer boutiques, specialty bookstores, private art galleries, fine jewelers, wine stores, and quality shoe stores all jam into the neighborhood, attracting shoppers in droves. The area is a lovely place to sit at an outdoor café, nursing a cappuccino and watching the crowds. Yorkville and Cumberland Avenues are the center of all this big spending, as are the elegant and discreet shopping complexes that lead off them, especially the deluxe Hazelton Lanes, at the corner of Yorkville Avenue and The Avenue, with its Ralph Lauren and Versace boutiques. The dropout philosophy has been thoroughly replaced by very chic stores – some of the most exclusive retail outlets in the country are found here. Although the recession in the 1990s affected trade somewhat, the area is still prosperous and thriving. Café society really takes off at night, even so Yorkville can be an expensive place to have fun.

Replica dressing room in BCE Hockey Hall of Fame, Toronto ▷

CLUB DE HOCKEY CANADIEN

Cooper

1962 1963
HON H. de M. MOLSON
F. J. SELKE
T. JOHNSON
H. BLAKE
B. GEOFFRION
R. BACKSTROM
J. PLANTE
B. HICKE
J. BELIVEAU
G. TREMBLAY
J.C. TALBOT
J.C. TREMBLAY
D. MARSHALL
R. ROUSSEAU
D. MOORE
G. BERENSON
C. PROVOST
L. FONTINATO
R. GOYETTE
J. GAUTHIER
H. RICHARD
C. MANIAGO
A. GALLEY
L. AUBUT
1964 1965
HON H. de M. MOLSON
J.D. MOLSON
S. POLLOCK
H. BLAKE
J. BELIVEAU
C. LAROSE
J.G. TALBOT
D. BALON
C. PROVOST
J. LAPERRIER
H. RICHARD
C. HODGE
R. BACKSTROM
L. WORSLEY
G. TREMBLAY
J. ROBERTS
J.C. TREMBLAY
D. DUFF
R. ROUSSEAU
T. HARRIS
G. BERENSON
Y. COURNOYER
T. HARPER
J. FERGUSON
1966 1967
HON H. de M. MOLSON
J.D. MOLSON
S. POLLOCK
H. BLAKE
J. BELIVEAU
D. BALON
J.G. TALBOT
J. LAPERRIERE
C. PROVOST
C. HODGE
H. RICHARD
L. WORSLEY
R. BACKSTROM
J. ROBERTS
G. TREMBLAY
D. DUFF
J.C. TREMBLAY
T. HARRIS
R. ROUSSEAU
Y. COURNOYER
T. HARPER
N. PRICE
J. FERGUSON
R. VACHON
C. LAROSE
L. ROCHEFORT
L. AUBUT
1968 1969
J.D. MOLSON
W. MOLSON
P. MOLSON
S. POLLOCK
C. RUEL
J. BELIVEAU
L. WORSLEY
C. PROVOST
D. DUFF
H. RICHARD
T. HARRIS
R. BACKSTROM
Y. COURNOYER
G. TREMBLAY
J. LEMAIRE
J.C. TREMBLAY
S. SAVARD
R. ROUSSEAU
R. VACHON
T. HARPER
M. REDMOND
J. FERGUSON
C. BORDELEAU
J. LAPERRIERE
L. HILLMAN
L. AUBUT
E. PALCHAK
cooper
JOFA
JDP

Royal Ontario Museum ⓲

Ming headrest in the Chinese Gallery

FOUNDED IN 1912, the Royal Ontario Museum (ROM) holds a vast and extraordinarily wide-ranging collection drawn from the fields of fine and applied art, the natural sciences, and archaeology. The museum is far too large to absorb in one visit, and merits several trips to appreciate its many treasures. Special highlights include a room full of dinosaur skeletons from around the world and the fabulous Far East collection. The latter features the best display outside China of Imperial Chinese artifacts, such as dainty ceramic head cushions, and the Ming Tomb of a grandee, reassembled this century after 300 years and the only complete example in the West.

★ Dinosaur Gallery
The most popular gallery in the ROM, 13 dinosaur skeletons are set in simulations of the Jurassic Age. Animation techniques as used in the 1990s blockbuster Jurassic Park *draw children and adults alike.*

Museum façade
Based in a handsome early 20th-century building, the ROM is the largest museum in Canada. It was finished in 1914 to house 19th-century collections from Toronto University.

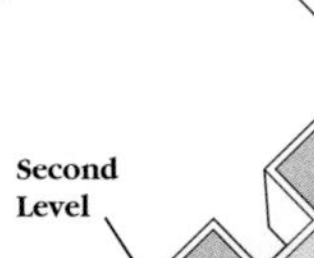

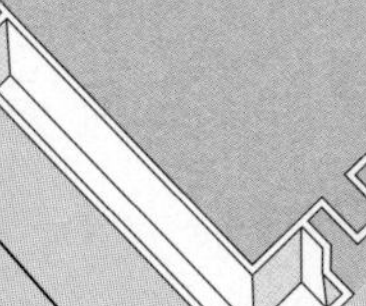

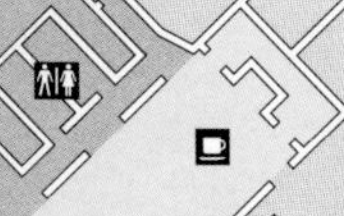

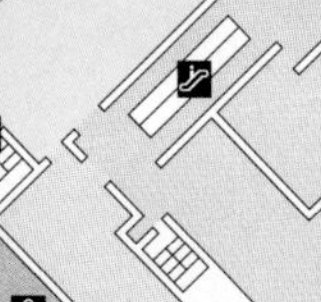

★ Ming Tomb
The ROM's Chinese galleries include this splendid imperial tomb thought to be part of an enormous 17th-century complex that may have been the burial site of a Ming general.

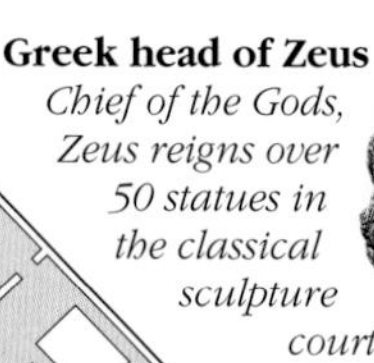

Greek head of Zeus
Chief of the Gods, Zeus reigns over 50 statues in the classical sculpture court.

Visitors' Checklist

100 Queen's Park. 416 586 8000. www.rom.on.ca Museum. 10am–6pm Mon–Sat; 11am–6pm Sun. Dec 25, Jan 1. limited.

Egyptian Mummy
With a large collection of mummies, burial masks, and domestic artifacts, the Egyptian collection in the Mediterranean World galleries contains the remains of a buried court musician, in a painted golden coffin so intricate that scholars dare not open it.

Gallery Guide

The largest museum in Canada with 6 million artifacts and four floors (three shown), the ROM's 40 galleries can each be visited independently or on a guided tour. Canadian culture dominates the lower level (not shown). At entrance level are the Asian Art and Earth Sciences Galleries. The Dinosaur Gallery and Life Sciences are found on the Second Floor. The third level houses the Classical Rooms.

Bat Cave
Painstakingly reconstructed from a 4-km (2-mile) long Jamaican bat cave, some 3,000 wax and vinyl bats fly to greet the visitor in this eerie darkened cavern.

Key

- East Asia galleries
- Samuel Hall Currelly gallery
- Chinese Sculpture Court
- Garfield Weston exhibition hall
- Earth Sciences
- Life Sciences
- Temporary exhibition space
- Mediterranean World
- Europe
- Nonexhibition space

Stuffed Albatross
This huge bird has a wingspan of 3 m (9 ft). It is a main feature of the bird gallery, which offers interactive exhibits.

Star Exhibits

★ **Ming Tomb**

★ **Dinosaur Gallery**

Spadina House ㉑

285 Spadina Rd. *416 392 6910.* *Union Station.* *77+, 127.* *Dupont.* *Jan–Mar: noon–5pm Sat & Sun; Apr–Aug: noon–5pm, Tue–Sun; Sep–Dec: noon–4pm, Tue–Fri; noon–5pm, Sat & Sun.* *Mon; Dec 25, 26, Jan 1.* *obligatory.*

James Austin, first president of the Toronto Dominion Bank in the 1860s, had this elegant Victorian family home, Spadina House, built on the bluff overlooking Spadina Avenue in 1866. The last of the Austins, Anna, moved out in 1982. She left the building, its contents and gardens intact, to the Historical Board of Toronto, and, as a result, Spadina House is an authentic family home illustrating the decorative tastes of four generations of well-to-do Canadians. The general ambience appeals here, but there are several particularly enjoyable features, notably the Art Nouveau frieze in the billiard room and a trap door in the conservatory that allowed gardeners to tend to the plants unseen by the family.

The front door of Spadina House with garlanded Victorian columns

Fort York ㉓

Garrison Rd. *416 392 6907.* *Union Station.* *7.* *Tue–Sun.* *Mon; Good Fri, Dec 18–Jan 2 approx.*

The British built Fort York in 1793 to reinforce their control of Lake Ontario and to protect the city that is now Toronto. Modestly sized, the weaknesses of the fort were exposed when the Americans overran it after a long battle in the War of 1812 *(see p43)*. After the war, the British strengthened the fort, and its garrison gave a boost to the local economy. Fort York's military compound has been painstakingly restored, and its barracks, old powder magazine, and officers' quarters make for a pleasant visit.

Casa Loma ㉒

This unusual fairy-tale building was designed by E.J. Lennox, the man responsible for Toronto's Old City Hall. It has no claim to the history of a stately home and architecturally it is a novelty, but it is a remarkable tribute to the foibles of one man, Sir Henry Pellatt (1859–1939). He made a fortune in hydropower during the early 1900s, harnessing the strength of Niagara Falls for electricity. In 1911, Pellatt decided to build himself a castle in Toronto. Three years and Can$3.5 million later, Casa Loma was built in a mixture of styles – medieval fantasy meets early 20th-century technology.

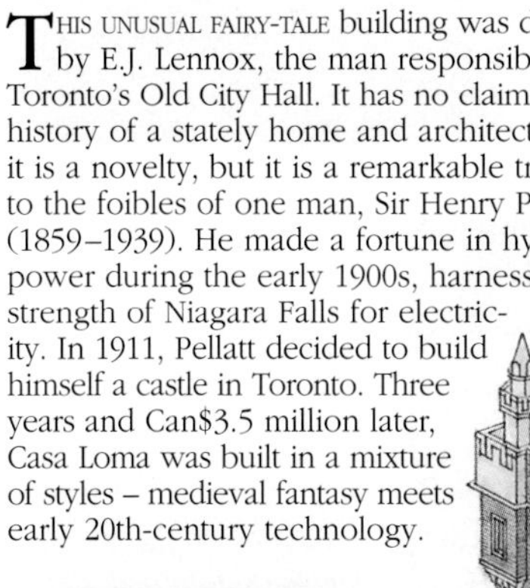

★ The Great Hall
Oak beams support a ceiling 18-m (60-ft) high, with caryatid sculptures and a 12-m (40-ft) tall bay window.

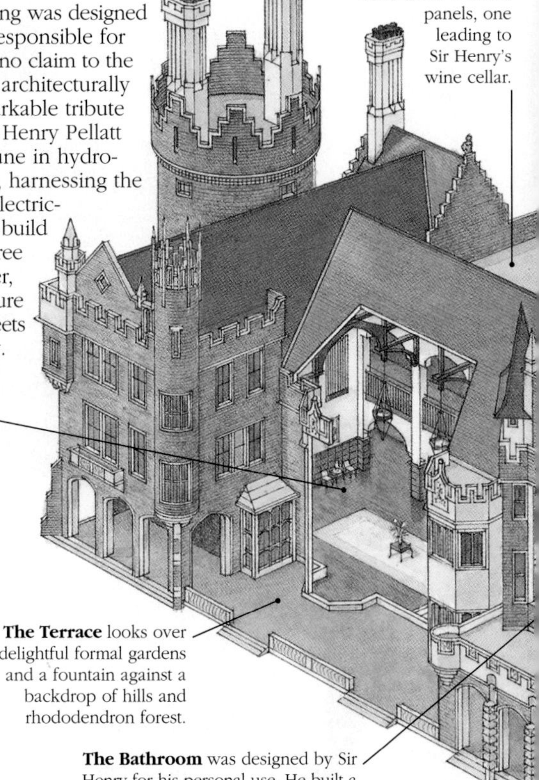

The Study hid secret doors in its wooden panels, one leading to Sir Henry's wine cellar.

The Terrace looks over delightful formal gardens and a fountain against a backdrop of hills and rhododendron forest.

The Bathroom was designed by Sir Henry for his personal use. He built a free-standing shower with six heads and indulged in lavish decoration.

Fresh vegetables on sale in Little Italy

Little Italy ㉔

St. Clair Ave. W. *Union Station.* *Bay St. Terminal.* *512.* *207 Queen's Quay W. 416 203 2500.*

THERE ARE half a million people of Italian descent resident in Toronto. The first major wave of Italian migrants arrived between 1885 and 1924. Italians have been in Toronto since 1830, and their sense of community, together with the instability of Italy after World War II, led to another large influx in the 1940s and 1950s. Italians live and work in every corner of the city, but there is a focus for the community in the lively "Corso Italia," or Little Italy, whose assorted stores, cafés, and restaurants run along St. Clair Avenue West.

Though the architecture is at best unremarkable, many houses are brightly painted in the traditional colors of red, green, and white. More European touches appear in the proliferation of espresso bars, and cinemas showing Italian films. The typically Mediterranean food offered by the many sidewalk cafés is terrific.

Ontario Place ㉕

955 Lakeshore Blvd. W. *416 314 9900.* *Union Station.* *511.* *mid-May–Sep: 10am–midnight.*

AN EXCELLENT theme park, this waterfront complex on Lake Ontario is built on three artificial islets. It provides family entertainment, with rides both tame and terrifying. Inside, the Children's Village is equipped with playgrounds and swimming pools, long water slides, computer games, and bumper boats, while Cinesphere is a huge dome housing a giant IMAX cinema. The HMCS *Haida* is an old World War II destroyer that has been converted into a floating museum to show the layout and naval machinery of a historic ship.

Façade of house and formal gardens
Five acres of garden add to the charm of the estate with perennial borders, roses, lawns, and woodland.

VISITORS' CHECKLIST

1 Austin Terrace. *416 923 11 71.* *Dupont.* *9:30am–4pm.* *Dec 25, Jan 1.* *www.casaloma.org*

★ Conservatory
White walls clad with Ontario marble offset the Victorian stained-glass dome. The marble flowerbeds conceal steam pipes for the rare plants.

STAR SIGHTS

- ★ **The Great Hall**
- ★ **Conservatory**

Visitors on the bicycling paths on the Toronto Islands

The Toronto Islands ㉖

Union Station. Bay St. Terminal. 6, 75. Queen's Quay. 207 Queen's Quay W. 416 203 2500.

IN LAKE ONTARIO, just offshore from the city, the three low-lying Toronto Islands, which are connected by footbridges, shelter Toronto's harbor and provide some easy-going recreation in a car-free environment. Here, amid the cool lake breezes, visitors can escape the extremes of the summer heat, which can reach up to 35°C (95°F). In good weather there are fine views of the top of the CN Tower *(see p168)*.

It takes about half an hour to walk from one end of the islands to the other. In the east is Ward's Island, a sleepy residential area with parkland and wilderness; Centre Island, home to the Centreville Amusement Park for children, is in the middle, and to the west lies the isle of Hanlan's Point with the Islands' best beach.

The Beaches and Scarborough Bluffs ㉗

Union Station. Bay St. Terminal. Queen St. E. routes. 207 Queen's Quay W. 416 203 2500.

THE BEACHES is one of Toronto's most beguiling neighborhoods, its narrow leafy streets running up from the lakeshore and lined by attractive brick houses with verandas. The area lies to the east of downtown between Woodbine Avenue and Victoria Park Avenue. Queen Street East, the main thoroughfare, is liberally sprinkled with excellent cafés and designer clothes shops. Until very recently, the Beaches was a restrained and quiet neighborhood, but its long sandy beach and boardwalk have made it extremely fashionable – and real estate prices have risen dramatically in recent years. Rollerblading and cycling are popular here – a 3-km (2-mile) path travels through the area and is very busy in summer, as is the large public swimming pool. The polluted waters of Lake Ontario are not ideal for swimming, nevertheless many take the risk and surfboards can be rented easily.

At its eastern end, the Beaches borders Scarborough, the large suburb whose principal attraction is also along the rocky lakeshore. Here, the striking Scarborough Bluffs, outcrops of rock made from ancient sands and clay, track along Lake Ontario for 16 km (10 miles). A series of parks provides access: Scarborough Bluffs and the Cathedral Bluffs parks offer great views of jagged cliffs, and Bluffers Park is ideal for picnics and beach trips. Layers of sediment from five different geological periods can be seen in the rocks around the park.

Toronto Zoo ㉘

361A Old Finch Ave., Scarborough. *416 392 5900. Scarborough. Kennedy. 86A. mid-May–Sep: 9am–7:30pm daily; mid-Mar–mid-May & Sep–mid-Oct: 9am–6pm daily; mid-Oct–mid-Mar: 9:30am–4:30pm. Dec 25.*

TORONTO can claim to have one of the world's best zoos. It occupies a large slice of the Rouge River Valley, and is easily accessible by public transportation and car.

The animals are grouped according to their natural habitats, both outside, amid the mixed forest and flatlands of the river valley, and inside within a series of large, climate-controlled pavilions.

Visitors can tour the zoo by choosing one of the carefully-marked trails, or hop aboard the Zoomobile, a 30-minute ride with commentary, which gives an excellent overview. It takes about four hours to see a good selection of animals, including such Canadian species as moose, caribou, and grizzly bear. The Children's Web area has a playground, and child-friendly exhibits.

A mother and baby orangutan at Toronto Zoo

A tinsmith takes a break outside his store in Black Creek Pioneer Village

Ontario Science Centre 29

770 Don Mills Rd. *416 696 3177.* *Oriole.* *Eglinton or Pape.* *Eglinton Ave. E. routes.* *10am–5pm daily.* *Dec 25.*

ONE OF TORONTO'S most popular sights, the Ontario Science Centre attracts children in droves. They come for the center's interactive displays and hands-on exhibits exploring and investigating all manner of phenomena, which are divided into 12 categories. These include the Living Earth, Matter-Energy-Change, the Information Highway, and the Human Body. Visitors can land on the moon, travel to the end of the universe, or have hair-raising fun on a Van de Graaff generator.

Black Creek Pioneer Village 30

cnr Steeles Ave. W. & Jane St. *416 736 1733.* *Jane.* *35b.* *May & Jun: 9:30am–4:30pm Mon–Fri, 10am–5pm Sat & Sun; Jul–Sep: 10am–5pm daily; Oct–Dec: 9:30–4pm Mon–Fri, 10am–4:30pm Sat & Sun.* *Jan–May; Dec 25.*

OVER THE YEARS, some 40 19th-century buildings have been moved to historic Black Creek Pioneer Village in the northwest of the city from other parts of Ontario. Inevitably, the end result is not entirely realistic – no Ontario village ever looked quite like this – but this living history showpiece is still great fun. Staff in period costume demonstrate traditional skills such as candlemaking, baking, and printing. Among the more interesting buildings are the elegant Doctor's House from 1860, and the Lasky Emporium general store, which is open and trading, selling baking products to visitors. The Tinsmith Shop is manned by skilled craftsmen, and there is a Masonic Lodge meeting room too.

Four buildings are credited to Daniel Stong, a 19th-century pioneer; his pig house, smoke house, and two contrasting homes – the first and earlier dwelling is a crude log shack, the second a civilized house with a brick fireplace, outside of which is a herb garden.

McMichael Art Collection 31

10365 Islington Ave., Kleinburg. *(905) 893 1121.* *Yorkdale.* *TTC 37.* *Tue–Sun.* *Dec 25.*

ON THE EDGE OF Kleinburg, about 30 minutes' drive north of downtown Toronto, Robert and Signe McMichael built themselves a fine log-and-stone dwelling overlooking the forests of the Humber River Valley. The McMichaels were also avid collectors of Canadian art, and in 1965 they donated their house and paintings to the government. Since then, the art collection has been greatly increased and is now one of the most extensive in the province, with over 6,000 pieces.

Most of the McMichael is devoted to the work of the Group of Seven *(see pp160–61)*, with a whole string of rooms devoted to an eclectic selection of their works. The keynote paintings are characteristically raw and forceful landscapes illustrating the wonders of the Canadian wilderness. Each of the group has been allocated a separate area, and both Tom Thomson (a famous precursor of the group) and talented Group of Seven member Lawren Harris, are particularly well represented. The McMichael also has fascinating sections devoted to contemporary Inuit and Native American art, including the sculpture *Bases Stolen from the Cleveland Indians and a Captured Yankee* (1989) by the well-known contemporary artist Gerald McMaster (b.1953).

Bill Vazan's "Shibagau Shard" at the McMichael

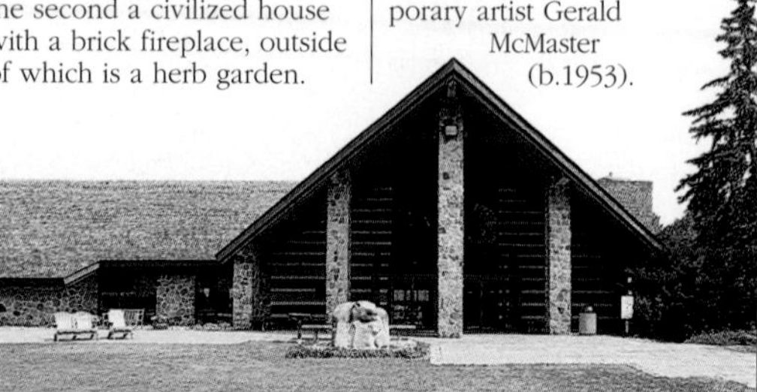

The log and stone façade of the McMichael Art Collection building

Ottawa and Eastern Ontario

One of the most visited regions in Canada, Eastern Ontario is justly famous for its history and natural beauty. The myriad lakes and waterways that dominate the landscape here once served as trade highways through the wilderness for native people and explorers. Today they form a beautiful natural playground, with spectacular opportunities for outdoor activities such as boating, fishing, hiking, and skiing. The St. Lawrence is one of the world's great waterways and has its source in the historic small city of Kingston. North of Lake Ontario lies the Canadian Shield, with the ancient lakes, rocks, and forest that epitomize Canada. A big favorite with many Canadian vacationers, Algonquin Provincial Park is one of the country's most famous wilderness areas. Also popular is the picturesque Kawartha Lakes region. Rising majestically over the Ottawa River, Canada's capital is a storehouse of national history and stately architecture that attracts over five million visitors each year.

Sights at a Glance

Historic Towns and Cities
- Barry's Bay 13
- Combermere 11
- Eganville 12
- Haliburton 10
- Kingston 5
- North Bay 15
- Ottawa 1
- Prescott 3
- Upper Canada Village 2

National and Provincial Parks
- Algonquin Provincial Park 14
- Serpent Mounds Park 8

Islands and Waterways
- Kawartha Lakes 9
- Prince Edward County 7
- Rideau Canal 6
- The Thousand Islands 4

Key
- International airport
- Highway
- Major road
- Major rail routes

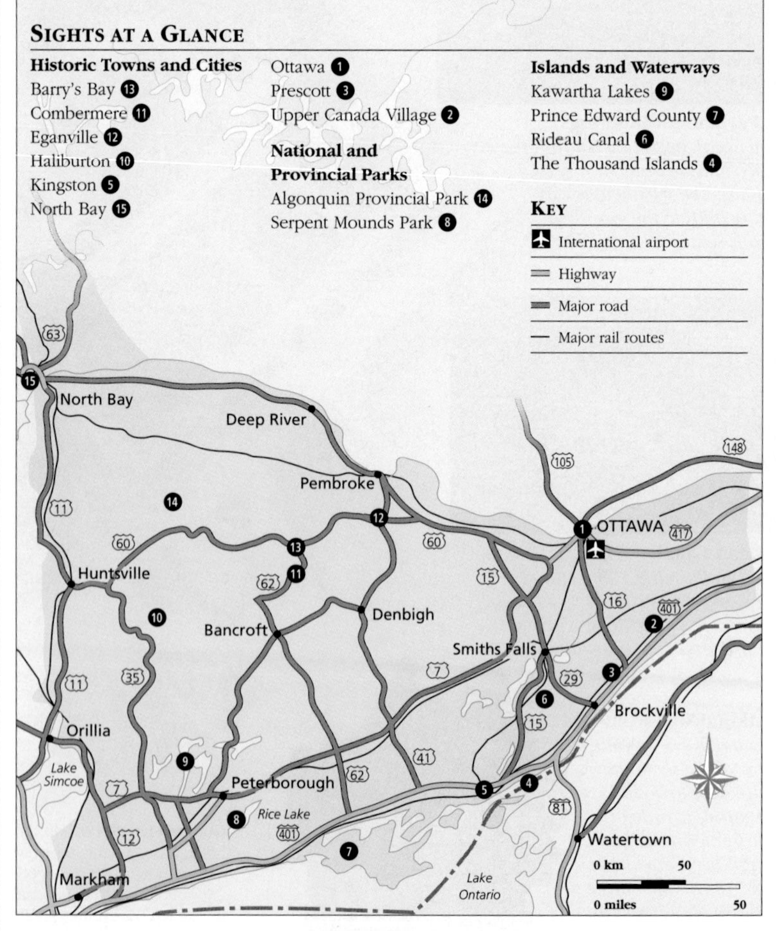

◁ **Pleasure boats on the Rideau Canal at night overlooked by Ottawa's imposing Parliament Buildings**

Street-by-Street: Ottawa ❶

OTTAWA WAS A COMPROMISE choice for Canada's capital, picked in part because of the rivalry between the English and French and the cities that grew into today's urban giants, Toronto and Montreal. This compromise has from its foundation in 1826, grown into a city with an identity all its own. Named capital of the Province of Canada in 1855, Ottawa has a fine setting on the banks of the Ottawa and Rideau rivers. Far more than just the political capital, the city has grown into a mix of English and French residents and historic and modern buildings with plenty of attractions to keep its 4 million annual visitors busy.

A member of the RCMP leading his horse by the Parliament buildings

★ Parliament Buildings
The Changing of the Guard takes place outside daily in July and August. The spectacular ceremony adds to the grandeur of this seat of government.

The Peace Tower has recently been renovated and forms a striking city landmark.

Rideau Canal
Built in the early 19th century, the Canal is now a playground for visitors, its banks lined with grassy cycling and walking paths.

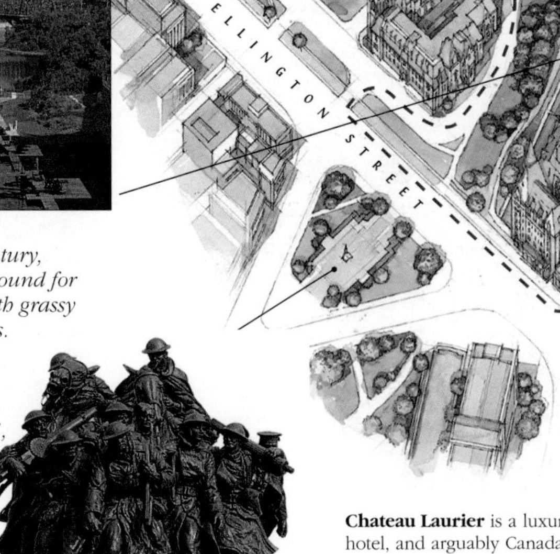

National War Memorial
Annually, on November 11, a memorial service takes place here to honor Canada's war dead. The Centennial Flame is also here. First lit in 1967 to commemorate a century of Confederation, it burns continually.

Chateau Laurier is a luxury hotel, and arguably Canada's most famous. It has been offering sumptuous accommodation to Canada's great and good since it was built in 1901.

Nepean Point
This stunning viewpoint is marked by a statue of a native Canadian at the foot of a monument to Samuel de Champlain (see p41). *From here, the whole of central Ottawa can be seen.*

The Canadian War Museum houses Canada's largest collection of militaria and war art, focusing on World Wars I and II.

Visitors' Checklist

785,000. 18 km (12 miles) south of the city. 265 Catherine St. VIA Rail Station, 200 Tremblay Rd. Canada's Capital Information Centre, 14 Metcalfe St. (613) 239 5000. Winterlude (Feb), Canadian Tulip Festival (May). www.capcan.ca

Key

- - - Suggested route

Royal Canadian Mint
This Can$20 Olympic skiing coin was created by the Mint as a souvenir for the 1986 Winter Olympic Games in Calgary. The mint produces only special edition and investment pieces.

Major's Hill Park is a peaceful open-air space in the heart of the busy capital.

★ National Gallery
Now featuring more than 25,000 artworks, this is the country's premier collection of the fine arts, housed in this outstanding 1988 granite building.

Star Sights

- ★ National Gallery
- ★ Parliament Buildings

Exploring Ottawa

The core of the capital is relatively contained, and many of the top sights can be easily accessed on foot. Traveling south through the city, the Rideau Canal is Ottawa's recreation ground year round, from boating and strolling during summer to skating across its icy surface in the freezing Canadian winter. The National Arts Centre is a focus for theater, opera, and ballet; history and art buffs can spend days visiting museums and galleries, both large and small. Ottawa is a city of festivals too; notably Winterlude, a three-weekend February celebration, while in spring the Canadian Tulip Festival transforms the city into a sea of flowers. Canada Day celebrations, on July 1, also attract thousands of visitors.

Antique doll's dress, Bytown

Away from downtown, it sometimes seems that the suburban National Capital Region is overflowing with museums for every enthusiast. Attractions include the Central Experimental Farm and the National Aviation Museum.

Cash register from a 19th-century shop at the Bytown Museum

Ottawa's Gothic Parliament Buildings rise over the city in majestic style

Parliament Buildings

Parliament Hill. (613) 996 0896. daily. July 1.

Dominating the skyline, the country's government buildings overlook downtown Ottawa in a stately manner. Undaunted by the tall buildings that have crept up around them in the 150 years since they became Ottawa's center of power, the East and West Blocks glow green above the city because of their copper roofing. The gothic sandstone buildings were completed in 1860. Located on a 50-m (165-ft) hill, the Parliament offers a view of the Ottawa River. The Parliament Buildings are distinctly reminiscent of London's Westminster, both in their Victorian gothic style and in their position. Partly destroyed in a fire in 1916, all the buildings are now restored to their former grandeur.

The Parliament Buildings can be toured while the Government, Commons, and Senate are in session. Hand-carved sandstone and limestone characterizes the interior of the government chambers. The Library, with its wood and wrought-iron decorations, is a must. In the summertime Mounties patrol the neat grassy grounds outside the Parliament, where visitors mingle and spot politicians.

Bytown Museum

Ottawa Locks. (613) 234 4570. May–Oct: daily.

Bytown, the capital's original name, changed to Ottawa in 1855. Located east of Parliament Hill and beside the Rideau Canal, in Ottawa's oldest stone building (1827),

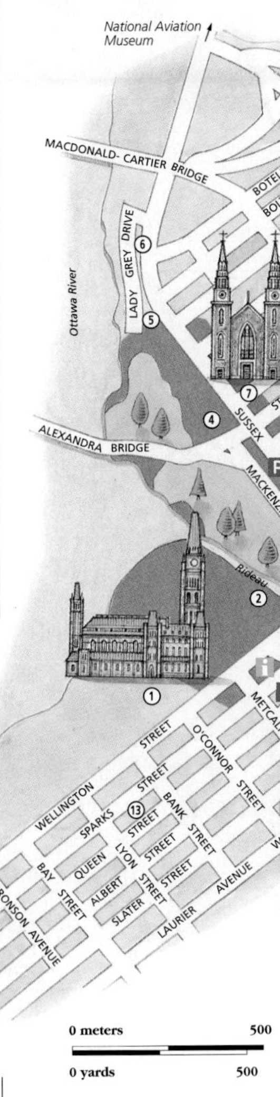

Key

- P Parking
- Visitor information
- Ottawa street-by-street *see pp190–91*

the Bytown Museum is a well-appointed place to learn more about local history. Colonel John By, the officer in charge of building the Rideau Canal, set up his headquarters here in 1826. While work was underway, the building, also known as the Bytown, was used to store military equipment and cash. The ground floor houses an exhibit on the construction of the Rideau Canal. Also very enjoyable is the focus on domestic life of the early 19th century, with a wide variety of homey artifacts on display.

The elegant Zoë's Lounge bar at the Château Laurier Hotel

National Museum of Science & Technology

Sights at a Glance

Bytown Museum ②
Byward Market ⑧
Canadian War Museum ⑤
Cathédrale Notre Dame ⑦
Central Experimentation Farm ⑪
Château Laurier ③
Currency Museum ⑬
Laurier House ⑨
National Arts Centre ⑫
National Gallery *pp196–7* ④
Parliament Buildings ①
Rideau Canal ⑩
Royal Canadian Mint ⑥

Château Laurier Hotel

1 Rideau St. *(613) 241 1414.* FAX *(613) 562 7031.*

This wonderful stone replica of a French château is a fine example of the establishments built by railroad companies in the early 1900s. It has attracted both the great and the good since it opened as a hotel in 1912. Centrally located at the foot of Parliament Hill, its interior features large rooms with high ceilings, decorated with Louis XV-style reproductions. The hotel attracts an upscale clientele, and it is well worth a visit to rub shoulders with celebrities and government mandarins. Within the hotel, Zoë's Lounge, a restaurant with soaring columns, chandeliers and palms, lit by an atrium, is a wonderful place for lunch, as is the larger restaurant, Wilfred's.

Canadian War Museum

330 Sussex Dr. *(819) 776 8600.* *May–mid-Sep: daily; Oct–Apr: Tue–Sun.*

Canadians may have a reputation as a peaceful people but they have seen their share of the world's battlefields. This aspect of their history is well represented in a museum that houses the country's largest military collection. Highlights include a life-size replica of a World War I trench, displays on the American invasion of 1775, the Normandy Landings (1944), and the Canadian Navy's role in the 1942 Battle of the Atlantic, where Allied sailors fought bravely to secure Britain against German U-boats. World War II memorabilia continues, in the form of Goering's personal car, which is riddled with bullet holes; disappointingly, these were added by a past owner trying to increase its value. A gallery is devoted to weapons from clubs to machine-guns. Also worth seeing is the collection of war art, much of it representing both world wars.

Demob sign at the War Museum

Royal Canadian Mint

320 Sussex Dr. (613) 993 8990. daily. obligatory.

Founded in 1908 as a branch of the British Royal Mint, this no longer produces regular Canadian cash currency. Instead, it strikes many special-edition coins and Maple Leaf bullion investment coins. The mint also processes about 70 percent of the country's gold in its refinery, which is among the largest in North America.

The building was refurbished fully in the 1980s and now offers guided tours. These are available daily, but coinage fanatics must make reservations in advance to see the process that turns sheets of metal into bags of shiny gold coins.

The façade of Ottawa's imposing Cathédrale Notre Dame

Cathédrale Notre Dame

Cnr Sussex Dr. & St. Patrick St. (613) 241 7496. daily.

Built in 1839, Notre Dame, with its twin spires, is Ottawa's best-known Catholic church. It is situated in the Byward Market area and features a spectacular Gothic-style ceiling. The windows, carvings, and the huge pipe organ are also well worth seeing (and hearing). Philippe Parizeau (1852–1938) carved the woodwork in mahogany. In niches around the sanctuary, there are wooden etchings of prophets and apostles, crafted by Louis-Philippe Hebert (1850–1917), now painted to look like stone. Joseph Eugene Guiges, the first bishop of Ottawa, oversaw the completion of Notre Dame, and his statue is outside the basilica.

Byward Market is known as a lively area of Ottawa

Byward Market

Ward St. (613) 244 4410. *Jan–Apr & late Oct–Nov: Tue–Sun; May–mid-Oct & Dec: daily.* *Dec 25, 26, Jan 1.* *limited.*

This neighborhood bustles all year round; outdoors in the summer, inside in winter. The area is located just east of Parliament Hill, across the Rideau Canal, and offers a colorful collection of craft shops, cafés, boutiques, bistros, nightclubs, and farmers' market stalls. Special attractions include the artisans' stalls in the Byward Market Building on George Street, and the cobblestoned Sussex Courtyards. The cafés are among Ottawa's most popular places to lunch.

Laurier House

335 Laurier Ave. (613) 992 8142. *9am–5pm Tue–Sat; 2pm–5pm Sun.* *Mon.*

Now a national historic site, Laurier House, a Victorian town house built in 1878, served as the chief residence of two notable Canadian prime ministers, Sir Wilfrid Laurier and Mackenzie King. Beautifully furnished throughout, it houses memorabilia, papers, and personal possessions of both former national leaders.

Rideau Canal

1 (800) 230 0016.

Built in the mid-19th century, the Rideau Canal is a man-made construction that travels through lakes and canals from Ottawa to the city of Kingston *(see p198)*. The canal flows through the capital, providing an attractive pastoral sight with its walking and cycling paths bordering the water. Once used for shipping, the canal is now a recreational area. In summer visitors stroll along its banks, while through Ottawa's freezing winter the canal turns into the city's skating rink, popular with locals during the winter festival.

Central Experimental Farm

Experimental Farm Dr. (613) 991 3044. *9am–5pm daily.* *Dec 25.*

The CEF is a national project researching all aspects of farming and horticulture. It also offers some of the best floral displays in the country, including a spectacular chrysanthemum show every November. There is also an ornamental flower show and an arboretum with over 2,000 varieties of trees and shrubs. The farm's livestock barns and show cattle herds are especially popular with children, and everybody loves the tours of the 500-ha (1,200-acre) site in wagons drawn by huge, magnificent Clydesdale horses.

Children can get close to animals at the Central Experimental Farm

The waterside restaurant at the National Arts Centre, seen from the Rideau Canal

National Arts Centre

53 Elgin St. *(613) 996 5051.* *daily.* *obligatory.*

Completed in 1969, the National Arts Centre has three stages, an elegant canal-side restaurant, and a summer terrace. The building, designed by noted Canadian architect Fred Neubold, comprises three interlocking hexagons opening onto good views of the Ottawa River and the Rideau Canal. Many exponents of Canadian and international dance, theater, and musical forms, including the National Arts Centre Orchestra, perform here regularly. The center's Opera auditorium seats 2,300; the Theatre, with its innovative apron stage, seats 950; the Studio, a marvelous venue for experimental productions, comfortably seats 350. Visitors should note that the center is extremely popular and reserving well in advance is recommended, especially for top international shows.

Currency Museum

245 Sparks St. *(613) 782 8914.* *May–Sep: 10:30am–5pm Mon–Sat; 1–5pm Sun: Oct–Apr: 10:30am–5pm Tue–Sat; 1–5pm Sun.*

Based in the Bank of Canada, displays in the Currency Museum trace the history of money through the ages. This is a fascinating place to learn about the unusual variety of things used as Canadian currency over the years – whales' teeth, glass beads, grain, paper, and metal. The emphasis of the exhibition is on Canadian currency in all its forms. Visitors can also see the workings of the National Bank. Staff are on hand to answer queries.

National Museum of Science and Technology

1867 St. Laurent Blvd. *(613) 991 3044.* *May–Sep: 9am–6pm daily; Oct–Apr: 9am–5pm Tue–Sun.*

Discover a whole new world at this interactive museum whose permanent exhibits include a wide range of fascinating displays exploring Canada's space history, transportation through the ages, and modern and industrial technology. A vintage steam locomotive can be boarded, and the more modern-minded may enter a mini-control room and pull levers to launch a make-believe rocket. Children and adults can also join a mission to save a colony on Mars. More down-to-earth, the biology section includes live chicks incubating.

National Aviation Museum

Aviation & Rockcliffe Parkways. *(613) 993 2010.* *May–Sep: daily; Oct–Apr: Tue–Sun.*

This huge building near Rockcliffe Airport houses more than 100 aircraft, which have flown both in war and peace. The famous 1909 *Silver Dart*, one of the world's earliest flying machines, is here, as is the nose cone from the *Avro Arrow*, the supersonic superfighter that created a political crisis in Canada when the government halted its development in the 1970s. The *Spitfire*, valiant friend of the Allies in World War II, features alongside historic bush planes such as the *Beaver* and early passenger carrier jets. Displays detail the exploits of Canadian war heroes, including World War I ace Billy Bishop, while the audio-visual Walkway of Time traces the history of world aviation.

Model of a rocket at the National Museum of Science and Technology

National Gallery of Canada

OPENED IN 1988, the National Gallery of Canada provides a spectacular home for the country's impressive collections of art. Located near the heart of the capital, architect Moshe Safdie's memorable pink granite and glass edifice is architecture as art in its own right. The National Gallery is one of the three largest museums in the country, and is Canada's top art gallery, with excellent collections of both national and international exhibits. The museum is a short stroll from the Rideau Canal and Major's Hill Park.

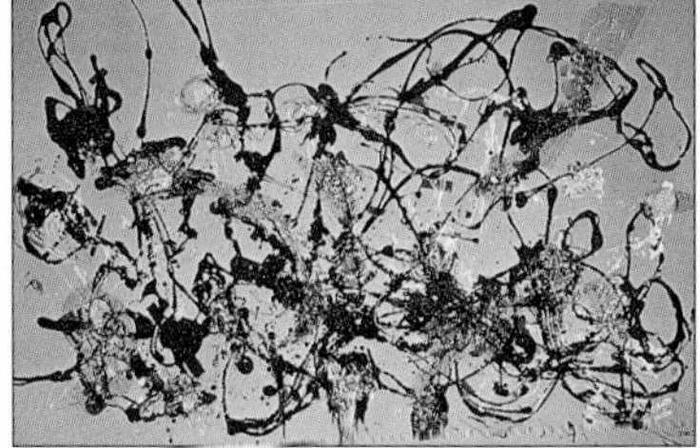

No.29 *(1950)*
A vivid example of Jackson Pollock's idiosyncratic drip technique, this was part of an enormous canvas carefully cut into sections, hence its title, No. 29.

Library

Level 2

★ Rideau Street Chapel
Set in a peaceful inner courtyard, this 1888 chapel was saved from bulldozers nearby and moved here for safety.

Café

GALLERY GUIDE
On its first level the gallery houses the world's largest collection of Canadian art. It also features international displays and major traveling exhibitions. The second level contains the European and American Galleries and the gallery of prints, drawings, and photographs. Visitors can relax in the two courtyards or in the fine café.

KEY

- Special exhibition space
- Canadian gallery
- Contemporary art
- European and American galleries
- Asiatic art
- Prints, drawings, and photographs
- Inuit art
- Nonexhibition space

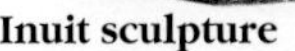

Inuit sculpture
This is represented in ancient and modern forms; Aurora Borealis decapitating a young man *dates from 1965.*

STAR EXHIBITS

- **★ Rideau Street Chapel**
- **★ The Jack Pine by Tom Thomson**

National Gallery façade
In addition to displays of painting, prints, architecture, and photography, the gallery holds regular events for the performing arts, including movies, lectures, and concerts.

VISITORS' CHECKLIST

380 Sussex Dr. *(613) 990 1985.* FAX *(613) 993 4385.* *http://national.gallery.ca* *3.* *May–Oct: 10am–6pm daily, 10am–8pm Thu; Oct–Apr: 10am–5pm Wed, Fri–Sun, 10am–8pm Thu.* *Mon, Tue, Dec 26, Jan 1.* *for special exhibitions.* *in some areas.* *11am & 2pm.*

★ The Jack Pine *(1916)*
In many ways the father of Canada's nationalist art movement of the early 20th century, the Group of Seven, Tom Thomson first attracted notice with his vivid, sketchy, impressionist paintings of Ontario landscape, here shown with a brightly colored oil of a provincial tree framed in wilderness.

Blanche *(c.1912)*
One of the forerunners of the Group of Seven, James Wilson Morrice left Canada for Paris, where he painted his favorite model Blanche Baume in a post-Impressionist style, heavily influenced by Bonnard and Gauguin.

Water Court
This delightful airy space is a sharp contemporary contrast to the treasures of yesteryear that abound in the rest of the gallery. Water Court is used as a contemplative gallery for sculpture.

Upper Canada Village ❷

Cornwall. *Morrisburg 1 (800) 437 2233.*

THIS LITTLE country town was relocated 11 km (7 miles) west of Morrisburg to save it from the rising waters of the St. Lawrence River during construction of the Seaway in the 1950s. Today, it is preserved as a tourist attraction and is a colorful reminder of the province's social history with its collection of 40 authentic pre-Confederation (1867) buildings. Costumed villagers work in the blacksmith's forge and the sawmill while tinsmiths and cabinetmakers employ the tools and skills of the 1860s. A bakery and general store are both in operation. History is also reflected in nearby **Battle of Crysler's Farm Visitor Centre**, a memorial to those who died in the War of 1812.

Battle of Crysler's Farm Visitor Centre
Exit 758 off Hwy 401. *(613) 543 3704.* *mid-May–mid-Oct: 9:30am–5pm daily.*

Prescott ❸

4,000. *360 Dibble St. (613) 925 2812.*

THE MAJOR attractions in this 19th-century town are its architecture and access to the St. Lawrence River. Prescott's recently refurbished waterfront area and its busy marina make for a pleasant waterside stroll.

The 1838 lighthouse overlooks the pleasure boats of Prescott's marina

The town is full of 19th-century homes and is the site for the road bridge to New York State in the US.

Fort Wellington National Historic Site, east from the center of town, attracts many visitors. Originally built during the War of 1812 and rebuilt in 1838, four walls and some buildings remain. These include a stone blockhouse which is now a military museum, incorporating refurbished officers' quarters. Guides in period uniform give tours during the summer, and in July a military pageant includes mock battles.

Fort Wellington
Prescott. *(613) 925 2896.* *late May–mid-Oct: daily.*

The Thousand Islands ❹

2 King St. East, Gananoque (613) 382 3250.

THE St. Lawrence River, one of the world's great waterways, is a gateway for ocean-going vessels traveling through the Great Lakes. Few stretches of the trip compare in charm or beauty to the Thousand Islands, an area that contains a scattering of over a thousand tiny islands, stretching from just below Kingston downriver to the waterside towns and cities of Gananoque, Brockville, Ivy Lea, and Rockport. Cruising opportunities abound from the Kingston boarding site.

River sights include the curious Boldt's Castle, a folly built on one of the islands by millionaire hotelier Boldt and abandoned in grief when his wife died in 1904. It was Oscar, Boldt's head chef at the Waldorf Astoria who, entertaining summer guests at the castle, concocted Thousand Island salad dressing. Landlubbers will enjoy the scenery from the Thousand Islands Parkway, which runs from the pretty town of Gananoque to Mallorytown Landing.

A sailboat travels the Thousand Islands

Kingston ❺

141,000. *209 Ontario St. (613) 548 4415.*

ONCE A center for ship building and the fur trade, Kingston was briefly (1841–44) the capital of the United Province of Canada *(see pp45)*. Constructed by generations of shipbuilders, the city's handsome limestone buildings reflect a dignified lineage.

The host of the 1976 Olympic Games regatta, Kingston is still one of the freshwater sailing capitals of North America and the embarkation point for many local cruises. Kingston is home to more museums than any other town in Ontario. Universally popular, the restored British bastion **Old Fort Henry** is a living military museum brought to life by guards in bright scarlet period uniforms who are trained in drills, artillery exercises, and traditional fife and drum music of the 1860s. Canada's top Army

Guard at Old Fort Henry

Training University is also based in the city and The Royal Military College Museum, housed in a 1846 Martello Tower, tells the story of today's cadets and their forebears.

West of the downtown area lies the **Marine Museum of the Great Lakes**. There are displays on the history of the Great Lakes and the ships that sailed on them, including the first ship built for the Lakes here in 1678. The museum also contains a 3,000-tonne icebreaker which has found a new vocation as a delightfully appointed bed-and-breakfast. Modern-day technology is explored at Kingston Mills, the lock station at the southern end of the Rideau Canal, where boats are lifted 4 m (13 ft).

Old Fort Henry
Kingston. *(613) 542 7388.*
mid-May– late Sep: daily.

Marine Museum of the Great Lakes
55 Ontario St. *(613) 542 2261.*
Apr–Oct: 9am–5pm daily; Nov–May: 10am–4pm Mon–Fri.

Rideau Canal 6

34a Beckwith St. South, Smiths Falls (613) 283 5170.

THE RIDEAU CANAL, originally a defensive barrier protecting Canada against the Americans and finished in 1832, stretches for 200 km (125 miles). The best way to enjoy this sparkling necklace of scenic waterway is by boat. A great feat of 19th-century engineering, which includes 47 locks and 24 dams, the system allows boaters to float through tranquil woods and farmland, scenic lakes, and to stop in quaint villages, as well as visit the **Canal Museum** at Smith's Falls. The canal north of Kingston also contains a number of provincial parks which offer canoe trails. Also popular is the 400-km (250-mile) Rideau Trail, a hiking system linking Kingston and Canada's capital city, Ottawa.

A view of the Rideau Canal as it travels through Westport village

Historic house along the main street of Picton in peaceful Quinte's Isle

Canal Museum
34 Beckwith St. S. *(613) 284 0505.* *mid-Jun–mid-Oct: daily; mid-Oct–mid-Jun: Tue–Sun.*

Prince Edward County 7

116 Main St., Picton.
(613) 476 2421.

CHARMING AND KNOWN for its relaxed pace and old-fashioned hospitality, Prince Edward County is surrounded by Lake Ontario and the Bay of Quinte, and is sometimes referred to as Quinte's Isle. The island is renowned for its two camping and sunbathing beaches in Sandbanks Provincial Park. There, mountains of fine sand reach 25 m (82 ft) and are considered one of the most significant fresh-water dune systems in the world.

United Empire Loyalists *(see p42)* settled in the County following the American Revolution (1775), founding engaging small towns and a strong farming industry. Visitors can absorb the local historic architecture by traveling along the country roads and the Loyalist Parkway, either cycling or by car, pausing to appreciate the island's charming views.

Serpent Mounds Park 8

Rural route 3. (705) 295 6879.
Coburg. Peterborough.
mid-May–mid-Oct: 9am –8pm daily.

SITUATED ON the shore of Rice Lake, Serpent Mounds is a historic native Indian burial ground. A grove of aging oak encloses nine burial mounds of an ancient people who gathered here more than 2,000 years ago. The only one of its kind in Canada, the largest mound has an unusual zigzag appearance, said to represent the shape of a moving snake. The site is still sacred to native people. Rice Lake, which offers shady picnic spots and excellent fishing, provides a pleasant backdrop.

On the tiny Indian River 9 km (5 miles) away, Lang Pioneer Village is a more traditional representation of Canada's past, featuring 20 restored 19th-century buildings, heritage gardens, and farmyard animals. Visitors can watch an ancient restored grist mill in action, and workers in period costumes display ancient skills. Blacksmiths and tinsmiths ply their trade in an authentic smithy and will give lessons.

Lush bullrushes surround a pond in Petroglyphs Provincial Park

Kawartha Lakes 9

Peterborough (705) 742 2201.
Peterborough. Cobourg.

THE KAWARTHA LAKES are part of the 386-km (240-mile) Trent–Severn Waterway that runs from Lake Ontario to Georgian Bay and was originally built in the 19th century. Today the area is a playground for vacationers, with water-based activities including cruises and superb fishing. Renting a houseboat from one of the coastal villages is a popular way of exploring the locality. At the center of the region lies the friendly little city of Peterborough, notable for its university, pleasing waterfront parks, and the world's largest hydraulic liftlock. Thirty-four km (21 miles) north lies the Curve Lake Indian Reserve's famous Whetung Gallery, one of the best places locally for native arts and crafts.

Petroglyphs Provincial Park, 30 km (19 miles) to the north of Peterborough, is better known to locals as the "teaching rocks" for the 900-plus aboriginal rock carvings cut into the park's white limestone outcrops. Rediscovered in 1954, these wonderfully preserved symbols and figures of animals, boats, spirits, and people were made to teach the story of life to aboriginal males. After each lesson, the elders would cover the stones with moss to preserve them. Today, the carvings are under glass to protect them from acid rain. The stones remain respectfully regarded to this day as a sacred site by native peoples.

Petroglyphs Provincial Park
Northey's Bay Rd. off Hwy 28.
(705) 877 2552. May–Oct: 10am–5pm daily.

The Haliburton Highlands 10

Haliburton (705) 457 2871.

THE HALIBURTON Highlands are one of Ontario's year-round outdoor destinations, renowned for their forests, lakes, and spectacular scenery. In the summer, thousands of visitors enjoy boating, fishing, and swimming in this region. In fall, busloads of tourists travel to appreciate the celebrated seasonal colors; other visitors come for the deer hunting. Winter brings skiers, snowboarders, and many snowmobiles.

The Madonna at Pioneer Museum

The village of Haliburton is found along scenic Highway 35, which winds its way through exceptional scenery from Minden north to the considerable charms of Dorset. The fire tower atop a rock cliff overlooking the village gives spectacular views of the Lake of Bays and the surrounding area. This spot is a fantastic viewing point for the myriad colors of Ontario's fall trees with their lovely bright red and orange shades.

Combemere 11

250. Ottawa Valley Tourist Association, 9 International Dr., Pembroke (613) 732 4364.

THE VILLAGE of Combemere is a central point for people heading to a number of provincial parks in Eastern Ontario, including Algonquin *(see pp202–203)*, Carson Lake, and Opeongo River. It is a good tourist center for fuel and refreshments. A few kilometers south of Combermere lies the **Madonna House Pioneer Museum**. Founded by Catherine Doherty, this Catholic lay community has grown to have mission outposts around the world. It is managed by volunteers, who survive from its cooperative farm, and who dedicate themselves to fund-raising. Since 1963, a recycling program has been raising money for the world's poor.

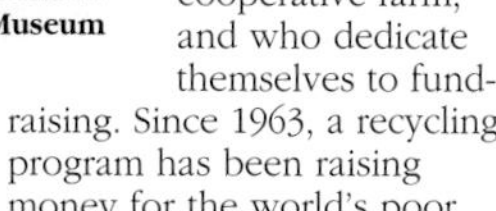

Madonna House Pioneer Museum
Hwy 517. *(613) 756 3713. mid-May–mid-Oct: 10am–5pm Tue–Sat.*

Golfers taking a break between games to enjoy the Haliburton scenery

Farm cottages outside Barry's Bay, home to many Ontarian craftspeople

Eganville ⓬

1,300. Ottawa Valley Tourist Association, 9 International Dr., Pembroke (613) 732 4364.

THIS HIGHWAY 60 village with its little restaurants and gas station provides a handy tourist center for visitors to this picturesque region. Local attractions include the **Bonnechere Caves**, 8 km (5 miles) away. The caves were at the bottom of a tropical sea 500 million years ago. Gradually raised over millennia from the ocean bed, they are covered with fossils of primitive life forms. The privately owned site is open for tours in summer.

Bonnechere Caves
(613) 628 2283. May–early Sep: daily; late Sep–Oct: Sat & Sun.

Barry's Bay ⓭

1,100. Ottawa Valley Tourist Association, 9 International Dr., Pembroke (613) 732 4364.

AN ATTRACTIVE LITTLE town, Barry's Bay has a sizeable Polish population, as does its neighbor Wilno, site of the first Polish settlement in Canada. The area is home to many craftspeople and artisans, who sell their wares in the local villages. Barry's Bay is also popular for stores selling outdoor gear and watersport equipment. Year-round sports facilities can be found at nearby Kamaniskeg Lake and Redcliffe Hills, both of which are popular places for renting cottages. Perched high on a hill, nearby Wilno overlooks scenic river valleys and boasts the fine church and grotto of St. Mary's.

Algonquin Provincial Park ⓮

See pp202-203.

North Bay ⓯

56,000. 1375 Seymour St. (705) 472 8480.

BILLING ITSELF as the Gateway to the Near North, North Bay sits at the eastern end of Lake Nippissing, 350 km (217 miles) north of Toronto. The region's most famous natives are undoubtedly the Dionne quintuplets. Born in 1934, the Quints' original modest family homestead has been relocated and now forms the town's popular **Dionne Homestead Museum**.

Lake Nippissing nearby is famous for its fishing and wilderness scenery. Boat cruises across the lake follow the old French explorers route. North Bay is a good starting-point for trips to the area's many vacation camps.

Dionne Homestead Museum
1375 Seymour St. (705) 472 8480. mid May–mid-Oct: daily.

THE DIONNE QUINTS

The hamlet of Corbeil experienced a natural miracle on May 28, 1934: the birth of the Dionne quintuplets; Annette, Emilie, Yvonne, Cecile, and Marie, the five identical girls born to Oliva and Elzire Dionne. The Quints' combined weight at birth was only 6.1 kg (13 lbs 5 oz), and the babies' lungs were so tiny that small doses of rum were required daily to help them breathe. Experts put the chances of giving birth to identical quintuplets at 1 in 57 million. The girls became international stars, attracting countless visitors to North Bay during the 1930s. A Quint industry sprang up with curiosity-seekers flocking to watch the young girls at play. The Dionne homestead was moved to North Bay in 1985, and visitors can travel back over 60 years to marvel anew at the birth of the Quints in this small farmhouse.

Algonquin Provincial Park ⓮

"Moose Crossing"

To many Canadians, Algonquin, with its lush maple and fir woods, sparkling lakes, and plentiful wildlife, is as familiar a symbol of Canada as is Niagara Falls.

Founded in 1893, Algonquin Provincial Park is the oldest and most famous park in Ontario, stretching across 7,725 square km (3,000 square miles) of wilderness. Wildlife abounds; visitors have a chance to see beavers, moose, and bear in their natural habitats, and the park echoes with the hauntingly beautiful call of the loon, heard often in northern Ontario. Every August, nightly "wolf howls" are organized whereby visitors attempt to elicit answers from these native animals by imitating their cries. Opportunities for outdoor activities are plentiful; most visitors like to try one of the 1,500-km (932-miles) of canoe routes through the forested interior.

Killarney Lodge
One of the park's rental lodges, these rustic buildings are popular places to stay during their summer and fall season.

The Algonquin Gallery exhibits various international art displays, with a focus on nature and wildlife. Painters featured have included Tom Thomson, precursor of the famous Group of Seven *(see pp160–1)*.

Moose near Highway 60
Visitors can usually spot a few moose each day, especially near lakes and salty puddles by roadsides, which these huge animals seem to love.

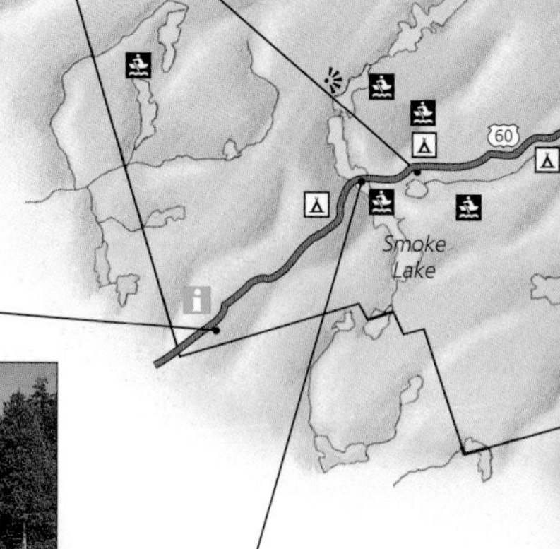

Canoe Lake
Almost a thousand miles of canoe trails lace the park. They range from beginner and family routes, some as short as 6 km (4 miles), to 70-km (50-mile) treks for the experienced. Routes are well planned and marked.

Visitors' Checklist

Hwy 60. (705) 633 5572. daily. from Toronto in summer. for camping. some lodges. www.algonquinpark.on.ca

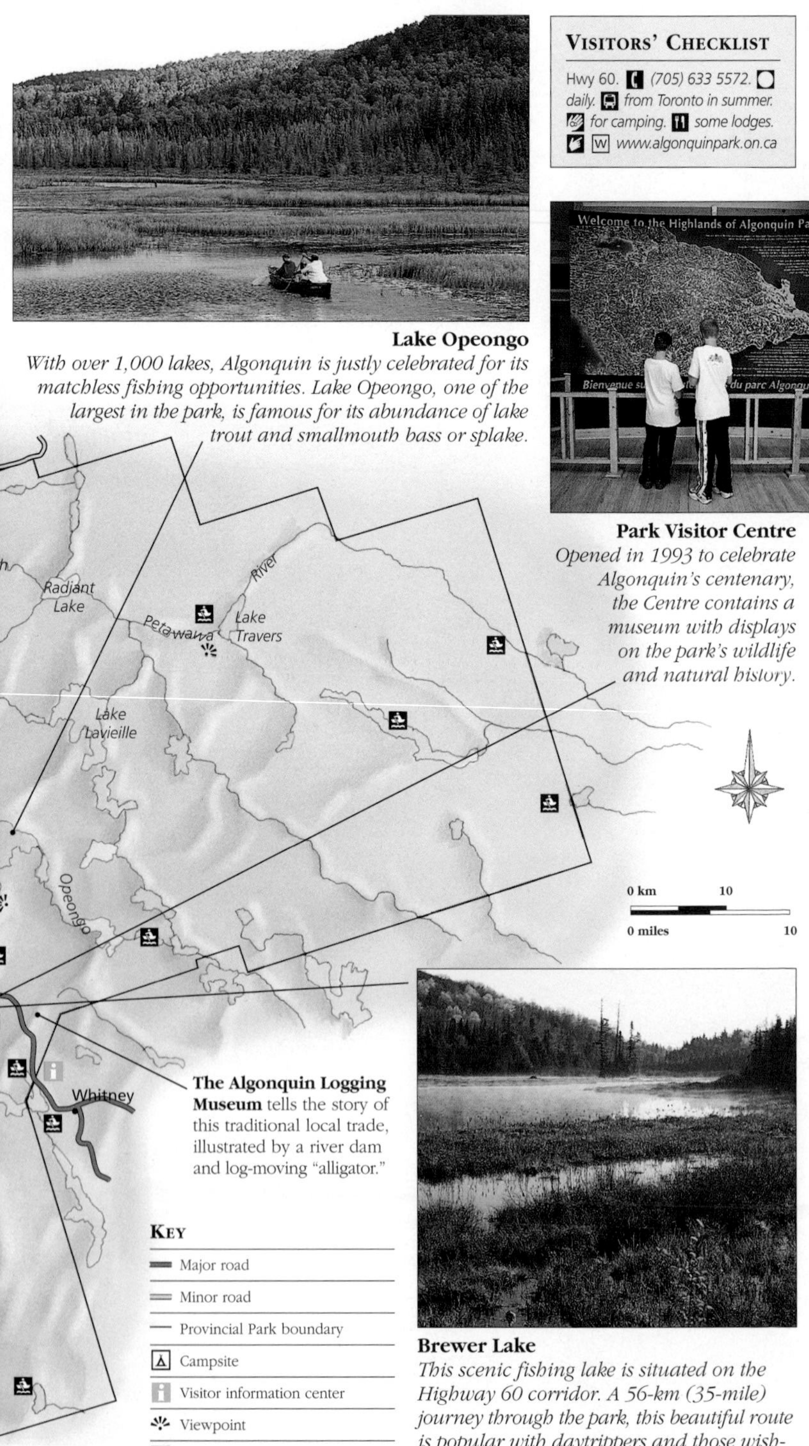

Lake Opeongo
With over 1,000 lakes, Algonquin is justly celebrated for its matchless fishing opportunities. Lake Opeongo, one of the largest in the park, is famous for its abundance of lake trout and smallmouth bass or splake.

Park Visitor Centre
Opened in 1993 to celebrate Algonquin's centenary, the Centre contains a museum with displays on the park's wildlife and natural history.

The Algonquin Logging Museum tells the story of this traditional local trade, illustrated by a river dam and log-moving "alligator."

Key

- Major road
- Minor road
- Provincial Park boundary
- Campsite
- Visitor information center
- Viewpoint
- Canoe route access

Brewer Lake
This scenic fishing lake is situated on the Highway 60 corridor. A 56-km (35-mile) journey through the park, this beautiful route is popular with daytrippers and those wishing to catch the major sights in limited time.

THE GREAT LAKES

The varied charms of the Canadian Great Lakes region, from the sleepy little farming towns bordering Lake Erie to the island-studded bays of Lake Huron and the wilderness encircling Lake Superior, tend to be obscured by the fame of Niagara Falls. One of the world's most famous sights, the falls occur where the Niagara River tumbles 50 meters (164 ft) between Lakes Erie and Ontario. Native tribes once lived on the fertile land around the area's lakes and rivers, but fur traders used the lakes as a vital waterway. The War of 1812 resulted in British Canada securing trade rights to the northern lakeshores. Between 1820 and 1850 settlers established farms, and mining and forestry flourished in Canada's then richest province. Today, the Trans-Canada Highway follows the northern shores of Lakes Huron and Superior for over 1,000 km (620 miles), traveling through the untamed scenery of Killarney Park, past picturesque old towns such as Sault Ste. Marie, and eventually reaching the bustling port of Thunder Bay.

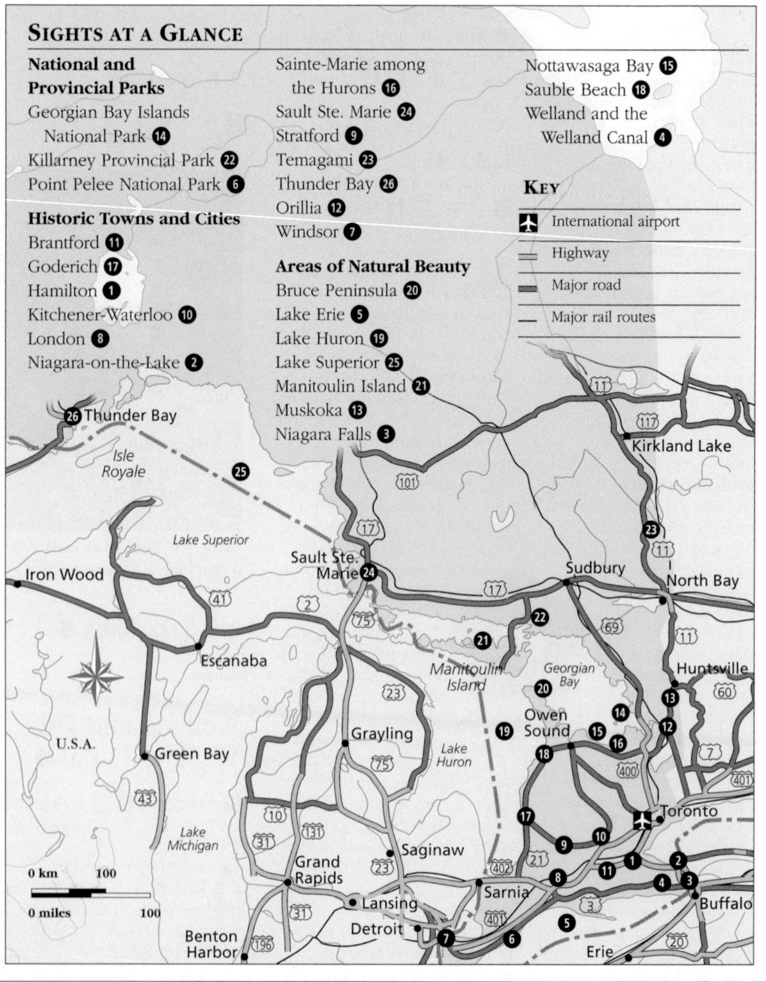

◁ **The warm colors of Killarney Provincial Park reflected in the tranquil waters of Cranberry Lake**

The imposing façade of Dundurn Castle in Hamilton

Hamilton ❶

322,350. 127 King St. East (905) 546 2666.

The city of Hamilton sits at the extreme western end of Lake Ontario, some 70 km (44 miles) from Toronto. Its specialty is steel, and the city's mills churn out around 60 per cent of Canada's total production. Despite the town's industrial bias, it possesses some enjoyable attractions. **Dundurn Castle** is a Regency villa dating from the 1830s, whose interior holds a fine collection of period furnishings. It was built for the McNabs, one of the most influential families in Ontario, who included in their number Sir Allan Napier McNab, Prime Minister of Canada from 1854–6.

Another sight is the **Royal Botanical Gardens**, comprising forests, marshes, and small lakes over some 1,093 ha (2,700 acres) on the north side of Hamilton harbor. Trails crisscrossing the lakeshore conduct visitors to several special gardens, notably a fine Rose Garden, the Laking Garden with its peonies and irises, and the heavily perfumed Lilac Garden. The Mediterranean Garden occupies a large conservatory and contains plants found in this climate zone drawn from every corner of the globe.

Rose in the Royal Botanical Gardens

Also in town, the Canadian Warplane Heritage Museum has a display of more than 30 operational aircraft dating from World War II to the jet age.

Dundurn Castle
610 York Blvd. *(905) 546 2872.* *mid-May–early Sep: 10am–4pm daily; late Sep–mid-May: noon–4pm Tue–Sun.* *partial.*

Royal Botanical Gardens
680 Plains Rd. West. *(905) 527 1158.* *daily.* *partial.*

Niagara-on-the-Lake ❷

13,000. 153 King St. (905) 468 4263.

Niagara-on-the-Lake is a charming little town of elegant clapboard mansions and leafy streets set where the mouth of the Niagara River empties into Lake Ontario. The town was originally known as Newark and under this name it became the capital of Upper Canada (as Ontario was then known) in 1792. It was to be a temporary honor. Just four years later, the British decided to move the capital farther away from the US border, and chose York (now Toronto) instead. It was a wise decision. In 1813, the Americans crossed the Niagara River and destroyed Newark in the War of 1812 *(see pp42–43)*. The British returned after the war to rebuild their homes, and the Georgian town they constructed has survived pretty much intact.

Today, visitors take pleasure in exploring the town's lovely streets, but there is one major attraction, **Fort George**, a carefully restored British stockade built in the 1790s just southeast of town. The earth and timber palisade encircles ten replica buildings including three blockhouses, the barracks, a guard house, and the officers' quarters. There is also a powder magazine store, where all the fittings were wood or brass, and the men donned special shoes without buckles to reduce the chance of an unwanted explosion. Guides in old-style British military uniforms describe life in the fort in the 19th century.

Niagara-on-the-Lake is also home to the annual Shaw Festival, a prestigious theatrical season featuring the plays of George Bernard Shaw and other playwrights, which runs from April to November.

Fort George
Queen's Parade, Niagara Pkwy. *(905) 468 4257.* *9:30am–5:30pm daily.*

Gardens in front of an early 19th-century inn at Niagara-on-the-Lake

Niagara Falls ❸

(See pp210–13)

Welland and The Welland Canal ❹

48,000. Seaway Mall, 800 Niagara St. (905) 735 8696.

An important steel town, Welland is bisected by the famous Welland Canal, which was built to solve the problem of Niagara Falls. The Falls presented an obstacle that made

Aerial view of the small village of Long Point on the shore of Lake Erie

it impossible for boats to pass between lakes Ontario and Erie. Consequently, goods had to be unloaded on one side of the Falls and then carted to the other, a time-consuming and expensive process. To solve the problem, local entrepreneurs dug a canal across the 45-km (28-mile) isthmus separating the lakes early in the 19th century, choosing a route to the west of the Niagara River.

The first **Welland Canal** was a crude affair, but subsequent improvements have created today's version, which has eight giant locks adjusting the water level by no less than 99 m (324 feet). A remarkable feat of engineering, the canal is capable of accommodating the largest of ships. It is possible to drive alongside the northerly half of the canal, on Government Road from Lake Ontario to Thorold, where seven of the eight locks are situated. The viewing platform at Lock No.3 provides a great vantage point and has an information center detailing the canal's history.

Welland boasts another eye-catching attraction: 28 giant murals decorate some of the city's downtown buildings.

A merchant ship on the Welland Canal near the town of Welland

Lake Erie ❺

315 Bertie St., Fort Erie (905) 871 3505.

LAKE ERIE IS named after the native peoples who once lived along its shores. The Erie, or cat people, were renowned for their skills as fishermen. Some 400 km (249 miles) long and an average of 60 km (37 miles) wide, Lake Erie is the shallowest of the Great Lakes and separates Canada from the US. Its northern shore is one of the most peaceful parts of Ontario, with a string of quiet country towns and small ports set in rolling countryside. Three peninsulas reach out from the Canadian shoreline, one of which has been conserved as the Point Pelee National Park, home to a virgin forest and, during spring and summer, thousands of migrating birds.

About 30 km (19 miles) south of Niagara Falls, the small town of Fort Erie lies where the Niagara River meets Lake Erie, facing its sprawling US neighbor, Buffalo. The massive Peace Bridge links the two, and most people cross the border without giving Fort Erie a second look. They miss one of the more impressive of the reconstructed British forts that dot the Canada-US border. Historic **Fort Erie** is a replica of the stronghold, destroyed by the Americans in the War of 1812. Entry is across a drawbridge, and the interior holds barracks, a powder magazine, officers' quarters, and a guard house. The fort became a popular posting among British soldiers. This was because it was fairly easy to desert across the river to join the US army, whose pay and conditions were thought to be better.

Fort Erie
350 Lakeshore Rd. *(905) 371 0254.* *mid-May–Sep: daily.* *partial.*

Point Pelee National Park 6

(519) 322 2365. Windsor. Windsor. daily.

ALONG, FINGERLIKE isthmus, Point Pelee National Park sticks out into Lake Erie for 20 km (12 miles) and forms the southernmost tip of Canada's mainland. The park has a wide variety of habitats including marshlands, open fields, and ancient deciduous forest. These woods are a rarity, as they are one of the few places in Canada where many of the trees have never been logged. There is a profusion of species that creates a junglelike atmosphere, with red cedar, black walnut, white sassafras, hickory, sycamore, and sumac, all struggling to reach the light. Furthermore, this varied vegetation attracts thousands of birds, which visit on their spring and fall migrations. Over 350 species have been sighted in the park, and they can be observed from lookout towers and forest trails. Every fall, hosts of orange-and-black monarch butterflies can also be seen throughout the park. A marshland boardwalk trail winds through Point Pelee and has good observation spots along the way. Bikes and canoes can be rented at the start of the boardwalk, and there is a concession stand here. Farther into the park, the visitor center features displays of local flora and fauna.

Water cascades at the main entrance of Windsor's fashionable Casino

Windsor 7

191,450. 333 Riverside Drive W. (519) 255 6530.

A CAR MANUFACTURING town, just like its American neighbor Detroit, Windsor and its factories produce hundreds of US-badged vehicles every day. Windsor has clean, tree-lined streets and a riverside walkway, but its most noted attraction is a trendy riverside Casino that draws thousands of visitors throughout the day and night. The city has many lively bars and cafés, the best of which are along the first three blocks of the main street, Ouellette. Also of interest, the nearby **Art Gallery of Windsor**, is noted for its excellent visiting exhibitions.

Contemporary painting at Windsor Art Gallery

It is possible to relive the days when the town was a bootleggers' paradise by taking a guided tour of the Hiram Walker Distillery: during Prohibition millions of bottles of alcohol were smuggled from Windsor into the US across the Detroit River.

From Windsor, it is an easy 20-km (12-mile) drive south along the Detroit River to the British-built Fort Malden at Amherstburg. Not much is left of the fort, but there is a neatly restored barracks dating from 1819, and the old laundry now holds an interpretation center. This relates the fort's role in the War of 1812 *(see pp42–43)*, where the English plotted with the Shawnee to invade the US.

Art Gallery of Windsor

401 Riverside Dr. W. (519) 977 0013. daily. donation.

London 8

305,150. 300 Dufferin Ave. (519) 661 5000.

LIKEABLE LONDON sits in the middle of one of the most fertile parts of Ontario and is the area's most important town. It is home to the respected University of Western Ontario, which has a striking modern art gallery and a campus with dozens of Victorian mansions. In addition, the few blocks that make up the town center are notably refined and well tended. The finest buildings in the center are the two 19th-century cathedrals, St. Paul's, a red-brick Gothic Revival edifice built for the Anglicans in 1846, and the more ornate, St. Peter's Catholic Cathedral erected a few years later.

Canoeists alongside the boardwalk at Point Pelee National Park

Located in the northwest of the city, the Museum of Archeology focuses on the 1,100-year history of the settlement of the area. The adjacent Lawson Indian Village is a popular attraction here. This reconstruction of a 500-year-old village, once occupied by the Neutral Indians, has elm longhouses and cedarwood palisades.

Reconstruction of a 500-year-old house at Lawson Indian Village

THE UNDERGROUND RAILROAD

Neither underground nor a railroad, the name "Underground Railroad" (UGRR) was founded by abolitionists in the 1820s. The UGRR helped slaves from the southern United States to escape to both Canada and the free northern states. It was a secretive organization, especially in the South where the penalties for helping a slave to escape were severe. Slaves were moved north from safe house to safe house right up to the end of the American Civil War in 1865. Reverend Josiah Henson was one of those who escaped on the UGRR, and later founded a school for ex-slaves. Harriet Beecher Stowe's 1851 abolitionist novel *Uncle Tom's Cabin* was based on his life story.

Reverend Josiah Henson

Stratford ❾

28,000. 88 Wellington St. (519) 271 5140.

IN 1830, AN innkeeper called William Sargint opened the "Shakespeare Inn" beside one of the rough agricultural tracks that then crisscrossed southern Ontario. Those farmers who settled nearby called the local river the "Avon" and named the town that grew up here "Stratford," after William Shakespeare's home town.

In 1952 Tom Patterson, a local journalist, decided to organize a Shakespeare Festival. This first event was a humble affair held in a tent, but since those early days the festival has grown into one of Canada's most important theatrical seasons, lasting from May to early November and attracting over half a million visitors. The leading plays are still Shakespearean, but other playwrights are showcased too – including modern works.

Stratford is an attractive town with plenty of green lawns, riverside parks, and swans. The town is geared to visitors, offering over 250 guesthouses and several good restaurants. The visitor center produces a book with information and photographs of all the town's bed-and-breakfasts. They also organize heritage walks through the town, which pass its many historic buildings. One of the town's architectural highlights is the Victorian town hall with its towers and turrets. Stratford has a plethora of art galleries, and the central Gallery Indigena features an interesting collection of native works.

The Shakespearean Gardens along Ontario's River Avon are overlooked by Stratford's distinctive courthouse

Niagara Falls ❸

ALTHOUGH THE MAJESTIC RUMBLE of the falls can be heard from miles away, there is no preparation for the sight itself, a great arc of hissing, frothing water crashing over a 52-m (170-ft) cliff amid dense clouds of drifting spray. There are actually two cataracts to gaze at as the speeding river is divided into twin channels by Goat Island, a tiny spray-soaked parcel of land. On one side of Goat Island is the Canadian Horseshoe Falls, and on the far side, across the border, is the smaller American Falls. Stunning close-up views of the falls are available from the vantage point of the Maid of the Mist boat trips. Even better is the walk down through a series of rocky tunnels that lead behind Horseshoe Falls, where the noise from the crashing waters is deafening.

American Falls
The Niagara River tumbles over the 30-m (98-ft) wide American Falls.

Rainbow Bridge
From the elegant span of the Rainbow Bridge there are panoramic views over the falls. The bridge itself crosses the gorge between Canada and the US. Here, on sunny days, rainbows rise through the spray.

Customs

Niagara Falls Museum houses a collection of artifacts and photographs that record the attempts of adventurous individuals to ride the falls – in a kayak, a barrel, and a diving bell.

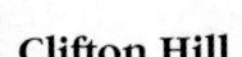

Clifton Hill
This street boasts a range of attractions. Ripley's Believe it or Not Museum features a dog with human teeth as just one of its offerings.

STAR SIGHTS

★ **Horseshoe Falls**

★ **Maid of the Mist boat trip**

VISITORS' CHECKLIST

130 km (80 miles) SW of Toronto. [train] *from Toronto.* [bus] *from Toronto.* [i] *Niagara Falls Canada Visitor and Convention Bureau, 5515 Stanley Ave., Niagara Falls (905) 356 6061 or 1 (800) 563 2557.*

★ Horseshoe Falls
Shaped like a horseshoe, these are the larger set of falls at Niagara and are some 800 m (2,625 ft) wide and 50 m (164 ft) high.

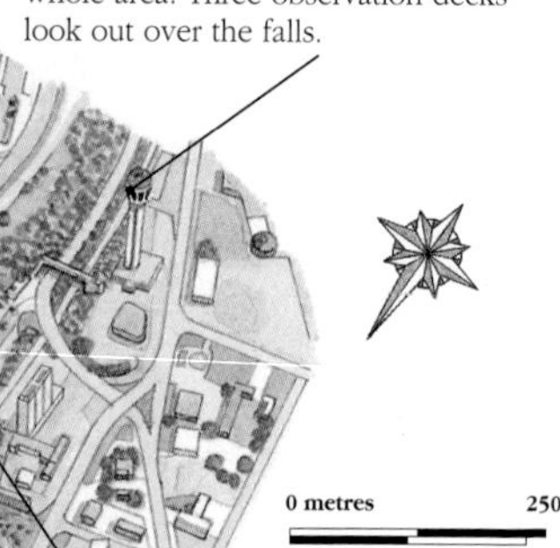

The Minolta Tower, like the Skylon Tower, offers panoramic views of the whole area. Three observation decks look out over the falls.

0 metres 250
0 yards 250

Journey Behind the Falls
An elevator from the Horseshoe Falls leads to the Journey Behind the Falls, where a series of rocky tunnels take visitors behind a wall of water so thick it blocks out daylight.

★ Maid of the Mist boat trip
These intrepid vessels gets very close to the foot of the falls. Raincoats are supplied as passengers can expect to get wet on this thrilling trip.

Skylon Tower
The tower has an observation deck, which gives a bird's-eye view of the falls. It is also open at night so visitors can see the floodlit waters.

Exploring Niagara Falls

NIAGARA FALLS IS A welcoming little town that stretches along the Niagara River for about 3 km (2 miles). Renowned as a honeymoon destination, the town is well equipped to satisfy the needs of the 14 million people who visit the falls each year. It is divided into three main sections: to the south are the falls themselves, and these are flanked by a thin strip of parkland that stretches out along the river bank as far as Clifton Hill, the glitziest street in Ontario, lined with garish amusement park attractions. To the west is the main motel strip, Lundy's Lane. To the north, on Bridge Street, lies the business district and the train and bus stations.

Horseshoe Falls

Named for their shape, the 800-m (2,625-ft) wide and 50-m (164-ft) high Horseshoe Falls are formed by the turbulent waters of the Niagara River roaring over a semicircular cliff to plunge into the bubbling cauldron below. By these means the Niagara River adjusts to the differential between the water levels of lakes Erie and Ontario, which it connects. The falls remain an awe-inspiring sight, despite the fact that the flow of the river is regulated by hydroelectric companies, which siphon off a substantial part of the river to drive their turbines. One result has been a change in the rate of erosion. By the 1900s, the falls were eroding the cliff beneath them at a rate of 1 m (3 ft) a year. Today, the rate is down to 30 cm (1 ft) a year.

The Maid of the Mist pleasure trip

Maid of The Mist

River Rd. *(905) 358 5781.*
mid-May–Oct: daily.

The best way to appreciate the full force of the falls is to experience the Maid of the Mist boat trip. Boats depart from the jetty at the bottom of Clifton Hill and then struggle upriver to the crashing waters under the falls. It is an invigorating (if wet) trip. The boat owners provide raincoats.

A wax museum and an array of other attractions at Clifton Hill

Clifton Hill

No one could say Clifton Hill is refined. This short, steep street runs up from the edge of the Niagara River gorge and is lined with a string of fast food restaurants and gaudy tourist attractions. The flashing lights and giant advertising billboards point the way to such sights as the Guinness Book of World Records, House of Frankenstein, That's Incredible Museum, Houdini's Museum and Ripley's Believe it or Not! Museum, where visitors can speak to a genie in a crystal bottle and see oddities such as a man with a greater-than-usual number of pupils in his eyes.

Great Gorge Adventure

4330 River Road. *(905) 371 0254.*
mid-Apr–mid-Oct: daily.

The great force of the Niagara River's torrent is best admired from down at the bottom of the canyon. The Great Gorge

The dramatic arc of thundering waters at Horseshoe Falls

Wooden boardwalk along the Niagara River at the Great Gorge Adventure

Adventure provides this close-up view by means of an elevator and a tunnel, which lead from the top of the gorge to a riverside boardwalk. The whirlpools and rapids here are some of the most spectacular, yet treacherous, in the world.

The Old Scow

Just above the falls, stranded on the rocks in the middle of the river, is the Old Scow, a flat-bottomed barge that was shipwrecked in August 1918. It was being towed across the Niagara River by a tugboat when the lines snapped. The scow hurtled towards the falls, getting within 750 m (2,460 ft), of the brink, and the two-man crew appeared to be doomed. Luckily the boat grounded itself on this rocky ledge just in time. The crew's ordeal was, however, far from over: they had to wait another 29 hours before being finally winched to safety. The Old Scow has been rusting away on the rocks ever since.

Niagara Glen Nature Reserve

3050 River Road. *(905) 371 0254.* *daily.*

The small Niagara Glen Nature Reserve lies 7 km (4 miles) downriver from the falls. This segment of the gorge has been preserved in pristine condition, with bushes and low trees tumbling down the rocky cliffside. This is how it may have looked before the coming of the Europeans. Seven different hiking trails lead past boulders, caves, and wild flowers. The walks are easy on the way down but a steep climb on the way up.

Whirlpool Rapids

3850 River Road. *(905) 371 0254.* *Apr–Oct: daily; Mar: Sat & Sun.*

The Niagara River makes a dramatically sharp turn about 4.5 km (3 miles) downstream from the falls, generating a vicious raging whirlpool, one of the most lethal stretches of water in the whole of North America. The effect is created when the river pushes against the northwest side of the canyon, only to be forced to turn around in the opposite direction. The most stunning view of the whirlpool rapids is from the Spanish Aero Car, a specially designed, brightly colored cable car that crosses the gorge high above the river. A different perspective of the falls can be seen from here.

Butterfly at the Botanic Gardens and Conservatory

Niagara Parks Botanical Gardens and Butterfly Conservatory

2565 River Road. *(905) 371 0254.* *daily.* *for conservatory.*

The Niagara Parks Botanical Gardens are located 9 km (6 miles) downstream from the falls and comprise over 40 ha (99 acres) of beautifully maintained gardens divided into several different zones. One of the prettiest areas in summer is the rose garden, which displays over 2,000 different varieties. The extensive annual garden, which houses many rare species imported from all parts of the globe, puts on a year-round show. The gardens also include an arboretum that has examples of many different types of trees from beech and mulberry to magnolia and yew.

The butterfly conservatory is even more popular. At the beginning of a visit, a video is shown in the theater. The film explains the life cycle of a butterfly, from egg and larvae through to the emergence of the adult. The butterflies are housed in a huge heated dome that holds several thousand – one of the largest collections in the world. Visitors follow a series of pathways that pass through the dome, leading past the lush tropical flora on which the butterflies make their homes.

The Whirlpool Rapids are best seen from the Spanish Aero Car

Tourists get a close-up view of the magnificent frothing waters of Niagara's Horseshoe Falls ▷

Alexander Graham Bell's study at the Bell Homestead in Brantford

Kitchener-Waterloo ❿

210,300. 80 Queen Street N. (519) 745 3536.

ORIGINALLY CALLED Berlin by the German immigrants who settled here in the 1820s, the town was renamed Kitchener (after the British Empire's leading general) during World War I. Today, the town is a supply center for the surrounding farming communities including religious groups such as the Mennonites *(see box)*. Visitors can see the fascinating sight of traditionally dressed Mennonites in their horse-drawn buggies around town. These descendants of German immigrants provide a key reason to visit Kitchener-Waterloo. Every year they organize the nine-day **Oktoberfest**, a celebration of German culture, with everything from sausages with sauerkraut to lederhosen and lager.

Fruit seller in Brantford

Brantford ⓫

85,000. 1 Sherwood Drive (519) 751 9900.

BRANTFORD IS AN unassuming manufacturing town that takes its name from Joseph Brant (1742–1807), the leader of a confederacy of tribes called the Six Nations. An Iroquois chief himself, Brant settled here in 1784. He soon decided that the interests of his people lay with the British, and his braves fought alongside the Redcoats during the American War of Independence (1775–83). Sadly, he had chosen the losing side and, after the war, his band was forced to move north to Canada, where the British ceded the natives a piece of land at Brantford. The Iroquois still live in this area, and host the Six Nations Pow Wow, featuring traditional dances and crafts, and held here on tribal land every August. Brantford is also known for its association with the telephone. In 1876, the first ever long-distance call was made from Brantford to the neighboring village of Paris by Alexander Graham Bell (1847–1922), who had emigrated from Scotland to Ontario in 1870. Bell's old home has survived and, conserved as the **Bell Homestead National Historic Museum**, is located in the countryside on the outskirts of town. The site has two buildings: Bell's homestead is furnished in period style and houses displays on his inventions as well as telling the story of the telephone; the other, containing the first Bell company office, was moved here from Brantford in 1969.

Bell Homestead National Historic Museum
94 Tutela Heights Rd. (519) 756 6220. 9:30am–4:30pm Tue–Sun. Dec 25, Jan 1.

Orillia ⓬

26,000. 150 Front St. S. (705) 326 4424.

ORILLIA IS A pleasant country town that was the home of the novelist and humorist Stephen Leacock (1869–1944). Leacock's tremendously popular *Sunshine Sketches of a Little Town* poked fun at the vanities of provincial Ontario life in the fictional town of Mariposa. His old lakeshore home has been conserved as the **Stephen Leacock Museum**, containing original furnishings as well as details of his life.

Orillia lies along a narrow strip of water linking Lake Couchiching to Lake Simcoe (once a Huron fishing ground) and is a good base from which to cruise both lakes. On the shore, Orillia's Centennial Park has a marina and a long boardwalk that stretches all the way to Couchiching beach.

Stephen Leacock Museum
50 Museum Drive, Old Brewery Bay. (705) 329 1908. daily.

Bethune Memorial House in the town of Gravenhurst, Muskoka

Muskoka ⓭

50,000. Gravenhurst. Huntsville. 1342 Hwy 11 North RR #2, Kilworthy (705) 689 0660.

MUSKOKA COMPRISES an area north of Orillia between the towns of Huntsville and Gravenhurst. It comes alive in the summer as city folk stream north to their country cottages. The center of this lake country is Gravenhurst, a resort at the south end of Lake Muskoka.

Here, a small museum is devoted to the life and work of Doctor Norman Bethune (1890–1939), who pioneered mobile blood transfusion units during the Spanish Civil War. Bethune Memorial House is the doctor's birthplace, and it has been restored and furnished in late 19th-century style.

Windsurfing off Turgean Bay Island in Georgian Bay

Georgian Bay Islands National Park ⓮

(705) 756 2415. Midland. daily. summer.

THE DEEP-BLUE waters of Georgian Bay are dotted with hundreds of little islands, often no more than a chunk of rock guarded by a windblown pine. The bay is large, beautiful, and flows into Lake Huron. Sixty of its islands have been incorporated into the Georgian Bay Islands National Park. The park's center is Beausoleil Island, the hub of the area's wide range of boating activities, with everything from canoeing to yachting available.

Beausoleil is also crossed by scenic hiking trails, but it is important to come properly equipped since it is a remote spot. The only way to reach the island is by water taxi from the resort of Honey Harbour. The journey takes about forty minutes. Day trips around the islands are also available.

The Mennonite Religious Community

The Mennonite Christian sect was founded in Europe in the early 16th century. The Mennonites were persecuted because they refused to swear any oath of loyalty to the state or take any part in war. In the 17th century, a group split off to form its own, even stricter, sect. These Ammanites (or Amish) emigrated to the US and then to Ontario in 1799. The Amish own property communally and shun modern machinery and clothes, traveling around the back lanes in distinctive horse-drawn buggies and dressed in traditional clothes.

Amish couple driving a buggy

Nottawasaga Bay ⓯

Barrie. Wasaga Beach. 550 River Rd. W., Wasaga Beach (705) 429 2247.

PART OF SCENIC Georgian Bay, Nottawasaga Bay is one of the region's most popular vacation destinations. The Wasaga Beach resort has miles of golden sandy beach and many chalets and cottages. As well as swimming and sunbathing there is the curious Nancy Island Historic Site, behind Beach Area 2. The site has a museum which houses the preserved HMS *Nancy:* one of few British boats to survive the War of 1812 *(see pp42–43)*.

There are more naval relics in Penetanguishene, just to the east of Nottawasaga Bay, where Discovery Harbour is a superb reconstruction of the British naval base that was established here in 1817. Along the inlet are replicas of the barracks, blacksmiths' workshops, houses, and the original 1840 Officers' Quarters. The harbor holds a pair of sailing ships, the *Tecumseh* and the *Bee*, built to 19th-century specifications. In the summer, volunteers organize sailing trips for visitors, who are expected to lend a hand during the voyage.

To the west of Nottawasaga Bay lies Owen Sound. Once a tough Great Lakes port, this is now a quiet place with a Marine-Rail Museum devoted to the town's past. Displays include photographs of Victorian ships and sailors.

Discovery Harbour, Nottawasaga Bay's restored British naval base

Sainte-Marie among the Hurons ⓰

17th-century Iroquoian jug

SAINTE-MARIE AMONG THE HURONS is one of Ontario's most compelling attractions. Located 5 km (3 miles) east of the town of Midland, the site is a reconstruction of the settlement founded here among the Hurons by Jesuit priests in 1639. The village is divided into two main sections, one for Europeans (complete with a chapel and workshops), the other for Hurons, with a pair of bark-covered longhouses. Marking the boundary between the two is the small church of Saint Joseph, a simple wooden building where the Jesuits set about trying to convert the Huron to Christianity. Their efforts met with a variety of reactions, and the complex relationship between the two cultures is explored here in detail.

Exterior of Longhouse
The exterior of the longhouse had bark-covered walls built over a cedar pole frame that was bent to form an arch.

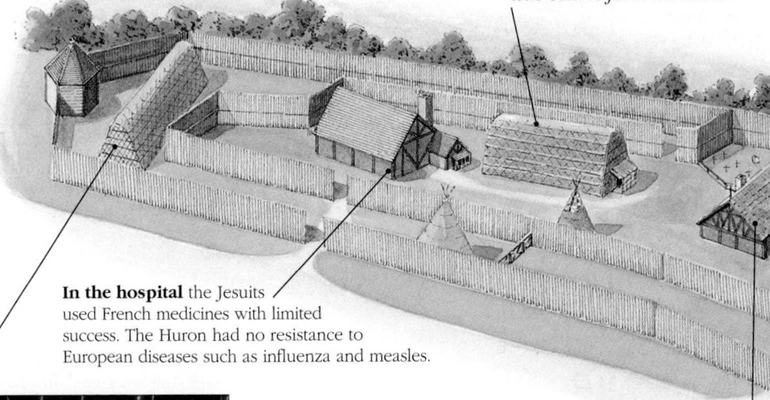

In the hospital the Jesuits used French medicines with limited success. The Huron had no resistance to European diseases such as influenza and measles.

★ Fireside Gathering
Inside the longhouse, fish, skins, and tobacco were hung from the ceiling to dry. An open fire burned through the winter. The smoke caused health problems to the Huron.

St. Joseph's Church
This is the grave site of two Jesuit priests, Jean de Brébeuf and Gabriel Lalement, who were captured, bound to the stake, then tortured to death by the Iroquois.

Ojibway Wigwam by the Palisades
This wigwam is built to Ojibway design and lies next to the wooden palisade which encloses the mission. It is believed that the Jesuits built these to make visiting Ojibway feel at home.

STAR FEATURES

- ★ Fireside Gathering in Longhouse
- ★ Traditional Crafts

★ Traditional Crafts
The costumed guides here have been trained in the types of traditional crafts employed by both the Huron and the French, including canoe-making and blacksmith's work.

Visitors' Checklist

Hwy 12 (5 km, 3 miles east of Midland). *(705) 526 7838.* *May–Oct: 10–5pm daily.* *www.hhp.on.ca*

Interior of Chapel
The old chapel has been carefully re-created and, with the light filtering in through its timbers, it is easy to imagine what it was like for the priests as they gathered to say mass each day before dawn.

The blacksmith's shop was important as Sainte-Marie needed essential items such as hinges and nails, often made by using recycled iron.

The carpenter's shop had an abundant supply of local wood, and craftsmen from France were employed by the priests to build the mission.

Entrance

0 meters 25

0 yards 25

Bastions helped defend the mission from attack. Built of local stone to ward off arrows and musket balls, they also served as observation towers.

The Cookhouse Garden
At Sainte-Marie, care is taken to grow crops the Huron way, with corn, beans, and squash planted in rotation. This system provided a year-round food supply, which was supplemented with meat and fish.

Goderich ⓱

7,450. ✈ ℹ cnr Hamilton St. & Hwy 21. ☎ (519) 524 6600.

Goderich is a charming little town overlooking Lake Huron at the mouth of the River Maitland. It was founded in 1825 by the British-owned Canada Company, which had persuaded the Ontario government to part with 1 million ha (2.5 million acres) of fertile land in their province for just twelve cents an acre, a bargain of such proportions that there was talk of corruption. Eager to attract settlers, the company had the Huron Road built from Cambridge, in the east, to Goderich. The town was laid out in a formal manner, with the main streets radiating out from the striking, octagon-shaped center.

Goderich possesses two excellent museums. The first, the **Huron County Museum**, houses a large collection of antique farm implements, the most interesting of which are the cumbersome machines, such as tractors, pickers, and balers, which dominated the agricultural scene between the 1880s and the 1920s. There is also a huge, steam-driven thresher. The **Huron Historic Jail**, built between 1839 and 1842, is an authentically preserved Victorian prison. Fascinating tours are available of its dank cells, the original jailers' rooms, and the Governor's 19th-century house. The town is also renowned for its sunsets, particularly as viewed from the shore of Lake Huron.

Historic storefront in the charming town of Goderich

The golden sands of Sauble Beach on the shore of Lake Huron

Huron Historic Jail
181 Victoria St. N. ☎ (519) 524 2686. ◯ *May–Sep: 10am–4:30pm Mon–Sat, 1pm–4:30pm Sun.*

Huron County Museum
110 North St. ☎ (519) 524 2686. ◯ *May–Sep: 10am–4:30pm Mon–Sat, 1pm–4:30pm Sun.*

Sauble Beach ⓲

Owen Sound. ℹ *RR1, Sauble Beach (519) 422 1262, open May–Sep.*

One of the finest beaches in the whole of Ontario, the golden sands of Sauble Beach stretch for 11 km (7 miles) along the shores of Lake Huron. Running behind this popular beach is a long, narrow band of campsites, cabins, and cottages. The center of the resort is at the pocket-sized village of Sauble Beach, which has a population of only five hundred. The quiet back streets of the village also offer friendly guesthouses and bed-and-breakfasts. The most attractive and tranquil camping is at Sauble Falls Provincial Park, to the north of the beach.

Lake Huron ⓳

ℹ *Sarnia, Southern shore (519) 344 7403.* ℹ *Barrie, Georgian Bay (705) 725 7280.* ℹ *Sault Ste. Marie, North shore (705) 945 6941.*

Of all the Great Lakes, it is Lake Huron which has the most varied landscapes along its shoreline. To the south, the lake narrows to funnel past the largely industrial towns of Sarnia and Windsor on its way to Lake Erie while its southeast shore is bounded by a gentle bluff, marking the limit of one of Ontario's most productive agricultural regions. Farther north, the long, thin isthmus of Bruce Peninsula stretches out into Lake Huron, signaling a dramatic change in the character of the lakeshore. This is where the southern flatlands are left behind for the more rugged, glacier-scraped country of the Canadian Shield. This transition can be seen clearly in the area of Georgian Bay. This is an impressive shoreline of lakes, forests, beaches, and villages that attract large numbers of visitors every year. The lake's island-sprinkled waters are a popular area for water sports. Outdoor activities here include swimming, hiking, and fishing.

Bruce Penninsula Tour ⑳

THE 100-KM (62-MILE) Bruce Peninsula divides the main body of Lake Huron from Georgian Bay and also contains some of the area's most scenic terrain. Bruce Peninsula National Park lies along the eastern shore and boasts craggy headlands and limestone cliffs with several hiking paths. Beyond the port of Tobermory, at the peninsula's tip, Fathom Five Marine National Park, comprises 19 uninhabited islands. The park is popular with divers because of its clear waters and amazing rock formations.

TIPS FOR DRIVERS

Tour Route: *The route follows Hwy 6 and can be reached from Owen Sound in the south, or Tobermory in the north.*
Length: *100 km (62 miles).*
Stopping-off points: *Diving trips and tours to Flowerpot Island leave fromTobermory, which also has good accommodation.*

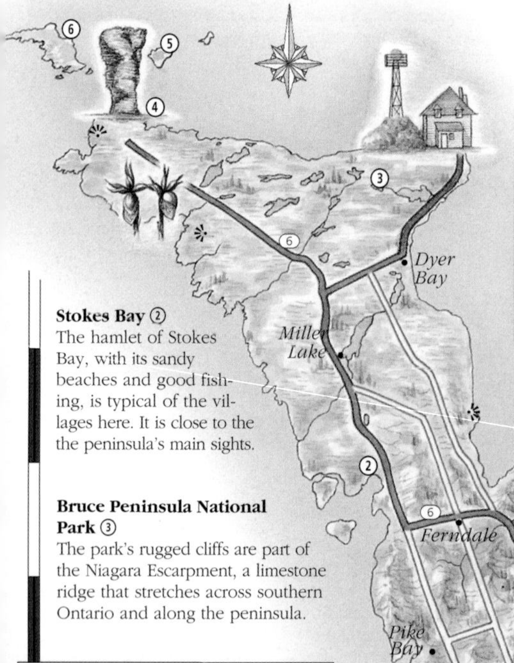

Cape Croker ①
At the tip of Cape Croker, the Cabot Head Lighthouse and keeper's house can be reached via the scenic coast road from the village of Dyer's Bay.

Stokes Bay ②
The hamlet of Stokes Bay, with its sandy beaches and good fishing, is typical of the villages here. It is close to the the peninsula's main sights.

Fathom Five Marine Park ⑥
Off the northern tip of the peninsula, the park's boundaries enclose an area around 19 islands. Divers are drawn here by the clear, calm waters and shipwrecks.

Bruce Peninsula National Park ③
The park's rugged cliffs are part of the Niagara Escarpment, a limestone ridge that stretches across southern Ontario and along the peninsula.

Tobermory ④
At the northern tip of the peninsula, this small fishing village is a hub for tourist acitivities in the area. Ferries to Flowerpot Island leave from here.

Flowerpot Island ⑤
The only island in Fathom Five Marine Park with basic facilities, it is noted for the rock columns that dot the coastline.

0 km 5
0 miles 5

KEY

- Tour route
- Other roads
- Viewpoint

Manitoulin Island ㉑

5,000. Little Current (705) 368 3021.

HUGGING THE northern shores of Lake Huron, Manitoulin Island is, at 2,800 sq km (1,100 square miles), the world's largest freshwater island. A quiet place of small villages and rolling farmland, woodland, and lakes, its edges are fringed by long, deserted beaches. The lake's North Channel separates Manitoulin from the mainland, its scenic waters attracting hundreds of summer sailors, while hikers escape the city to explore the island's numerous trails.

The Ojibway people first occupied the island more than 10,000 years ago, naming it after the Great Spirit – Manitou, (Manitoulin means God's Island). First Nations peoples still constitute over a quarter of the island's population. Every August they celebrate their culture in one of Canada's largest powwows, called the Wikwemikong (Bay of the Beaver).

On the north shore, Gore Bay houses five tiny museums that focus on the island's early settlers. Nearby, the island's largest settlement is Little Current, a quiet town, where there is a handful of motels, bed and breakfasts, and restaurants.

Gore Bay on Manitoulin Island

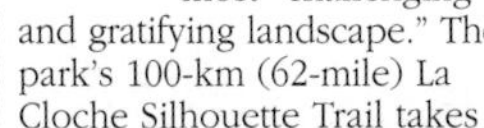

Reflections in George Lake, Killarney Provincial Park

Killarney Provincial Park ㉒

(705) 287 2900. Sudbury. daily. for some facilities.

KILLARNEY PROVINCIAL park is a beautiful tract of wilderness with crystal-blue lakes, pine and hardwood forests, boggy lowlands, and the spectacular La Cloche Mountains, which are known for their striking white quartzite ridges. This magnificent scenery has inspired many artists, particularly members of the Group of Seven *(see pp160–1)*, one of whom, Franklin Carmichael, saw the park as Ontario's most "challenging and gratifying landscape." The park's 100-km (62-mile) La Cloche Silhouette Trail takes between a week and ten days to complete and attracts numbers of serious hikers to its stunning views of the mountains and of Georgian Bay. Canoeists can paddle on the park's many lakes and rivers by following a network of well-marked canoe routes.

Temagami ㉓

1,000. Chamber of Commerce, Lakeshore Rd. (705) 569 3344.

THE TINY RESORT of Temagami and its wild surroundings have long attracted fur traders and trappers, painters, and writers, most famously Grey Owl *(see p248)*, the remarkable Englishman who posed as a Native Canadian and achieved celebrity status as a naturalist and conservationist in the 1930s. The resort sits on the distinctively shaped Lake Temagami, a deep lake with long fjords and bays as

One of Lake Temagami's numerous canoe routes

well as 1,400 islands, which are crisscrossed by numerous scenic canoe routes, hiking and mountain bike trails.

Even more remote is the Lady Evelyn Smoothwater Wilderness Park, farther to the west. The only way in is by canoe or float plane from Temagami, but the reward is some of Ontario's most stunning scenery. Much more accessible is the 30-m (98-ft) high Temagami Fire Tower lookout point, which provides panoramic views of the surrounding pine forests, and the charming Finlayson Provincial Park, a popular place to picnic and camp; both are located on Temagami's outskirts.

Sault Ste. Marie ㉔

81,500. cnr Huron St. & Queen St. W. (705) 945 6941.

WHERE THE RAPIDS of St. Mary's River link Lake Superior to Lake Huron sits the attractive town of Sault Ste. Marie, one of Ontario's oldest European communities. The town was founded as a Jesuit mission and fur trading post by the French in 1688. Called the "Sault" (pronounced "Soo") after the French word for "rapids," the trading station prospered after 1798 when the rapids were bypassed by a canal. Since then, the canal has been upgraded time and again, and today transports the largest of container ships to the interior, thereby maintaining a thriving local economy.

Although there are regular boat trips along the canal, visitors are drawn to Sault Ste. Marie's main tourist attraction, the **Algoma Central Railway**, which offers day-long rail tours from the city into the wilderness. The train weaves north through dense forest, past secluded lakes and over yawning ravines to reach the spectacular scenery of Agawa Canyon where there is a two-hour break for lunch.

In town, the Roberta Bondar Pavilion is a huge tentlike structure decorated with murals depicting Sault's history. Named after Canada's first female astronaut, who was on the *Discovery* mission in 1992, the pavilion is also the venue for concerts, exhibitions, and a summer farmers' market.

Canal locks at Sault Ste. Marie

Algoma Central Railway
129 Bay St. (705) 946 7300. Jun–mid-Oct: once daily.

Lake Superior ㉕

Ontario Travel Information Centre, Sault Ste. Marie (705) 945 6941.

THE LEAST POLLUTED and most westerly of the Great Lakes, Lake Superior is the world's largest body of freshwater, with a surface area of 82,000 sq km (31,700 sq miles). It is known for sudden violent storms, long a source of dread to local sailors. The lake's northern coast is a vast weather-swept stretch of untamed wilderness dominated by dramatic granite outcrops and seemingly limitless forest. This challenging area is best experienced in Pukaskwa National Park and Lake Superior Provincial Park, both reached via the Trans-Canada Highway (Hwy 17) as it cuts a dramatic route along the lake's north shore.

Thunder Bay ㉖

114,000. Terry Fox Information Centre, Hwy 11/17 E. (807) 983 2041.

ON THE NORTHERN shore of Lake Superior, Thunder Bay is Canada's third-largest freshwater port, its massive grain elevators dominating the city's waterfront. Grain is brought to Thunder Bay from the prairies farther west before being shipped to the rest of the world via the Great Lakes.

The town was originally established as a French trading post in 1679. These early days are celebrated at Old Fort William, a replica of the old fur trading post, with costumed traders, French explorers, and natives. Fort William was amalgamated with the adjacent town of Port Arthur to form Thunder Bay in 1970.

Old Fort William
Off Broadway Ave. (807) 473 2344. mid-May–mid-Oct: 9am–6pm daily.

Lake Superior, the world's largest freshwater lake

Central Canada

Exploring Central Canada

Central Canada covers the provinces of Manitoba, Saskatchewan, and eastern Alberta and encompasses the most productive agricultural and energy-rich part of the country. The region is dominated by prairie, (often associated with borderless fields that stretch to the horizon) and covers a vast area of the western interior, which is the size of Mexico. The region is not all prairie, but has a variety of landscapes, from the forested aspen parkland to the west and north of the plains to the tundra of northern Manitoba and the rocky desert of the badlands in the south.

The Broadway Bridge and central Saskatoon overlooking the South Saskatchewan River

Lake Athabasca
58
35
ALBERTA
SASKATC
PEACE RIVER
FORT MCMURRAY
LA LOCHE
63
2
155
2
EDMONTON
PRINC
16
2
RED DEER
NORTH BATTLEFORD
11
SASI
DRUMHELLER
1
MEDICINE HAT
MOC J
1
LETHBRIDGE

Grain elevators and wheat cars punctuate the vast fields of the Canadian prairies

Getting Around

Winnipeg, Edmonton, Regina, and Saskatchewan, the four main cities of the region, are well served by public transportation, with regular air, train, and bus connections from British Columbia and other provinces. All four cities also have international airports. From Winnipeg, the Trans-Canada Highway follows the route established in the 19th century by the Canadian Pacific Railway, going 1,333 km (828 miles) west to Calgary. The more scenic Yellowhead Highway starts at the Forks in Winnipeg and runs through Yorkton and Saskatoon, reaching Edmonton at 1,301 km (808 miles), continuing on through Jasper National Park and British Columbia.

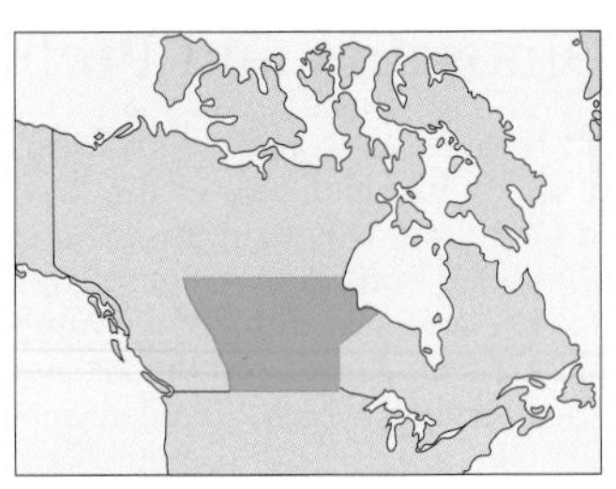

Key

- Highway
- Major road
- River
- Provincial boundaries

CHURCHILL
Hudson Bay
MANITOBA
LYNN LAKE
THOMPSON
106
FLIN FLON
THE PAS
6
60
3
10
Lake Winnipeg
YORKTON
DAUPHIN
16
1
PORTAGE LA PRAIRIE
WINNIPEG
GINA

The prairies of Manitoba, one of Canada's richest agricultural areas

0 km 150
0 miles 150

See Also

- ***Where to Stay*** pp352–3
- ***Where to Eat*** pp372–3

Dinosaurs and Prehistoric Canada

IT IS EASIER TO imagine gunslingers and coyotes in the desert-like badlands of the Red Deer River Valley in Central Canada than it is to envisage the dinosaurs who once lived in this region. Over 75 million years ago the area was a tropical swamp, similar to the Florida Everglades, and the favored habitat of these huge reptiles, which dominated the Earth for some 160 million years. All the dinosaur specimens found here originate from the Cretaceous period (144–65 million years ago). Dramatic changes in the region's weather patterns, from wet and tropical to dry desert, helped to preserve an incredible number of dinosaur remains in the area. Today, the Dinosaur Provincial Park is a UN World Heritage Site.

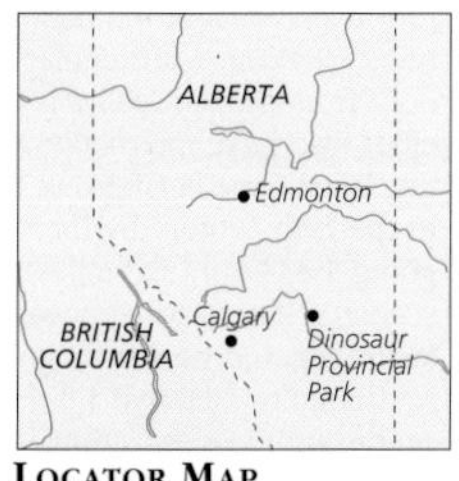

LOCATOR MAP

This Triceratops skull *shows the dinosaur's flaring bony frill, which protected its neck from attack. Its two horns were an awesome 1 m (3 ft) long. More types of horned dinosaurs have been found here in Alberta than anywhere else.*

Trained staff carefully dig out a groove around the bone while it is still in the ground. Once removed it will be carefully matched to its adjoining bone.

The Magnolia *is thought to be one of Earth's first flowering plants, or angiosperms, and became widespread during the Cretaceous period.*

Joseph Burr Tyrrell *found the first important dinosaur skeleton sections in the Red Deer River Valley, Alberta, in 1884. A geologist, Tyrrell stumbled across the skull of a 70 million-year-old Albertosaurus while surveying coal deposits. Subsequently, palaeontologists rushed here to search for fossils. Drumheller's Royal Tyrrell Museum of Palaeontology is named after him* (see p246).

An artist's re-creation *of the Cretaceous landscape depicts the types of flora living at the time. Tree ferns dominated the country, and grew in large forests to heights of 18 m (60 ft). Some species still grow in the tropics.*

Horseshoe Canyon *lies along the Red Deer River, its high, worn hills visibly layered with ancient sediments. Ice Age glaciers eroded the layers of mud and sand that buried the remains of dinosaurs and plants. Erosion continues to form this barren, lunar landscape, exposing more bones, petrified wood, and other fossils.*

This dinosaur nest *on display at the Royal Tyrrell Museum was discovered at Devil's Coulee, Alberta, in 1987, and contains several embryos and eggs of the plant-eating Hadrosaur.*

The Royal Tyrrell *Field Station in the Dinosaur Provincial Park opened in 1987, and offers visitors interpretive displays explaining the history of the area's dinosaurs.*

Dinosaur Dig near Drumheller

The Royal Tyrrell Museum runs a series of different dig programs where visitors can experience the excitement of uncovering a dinosaur skeleton destined for the museum. Several trips are led by Canada's leading palaeontologists, and visitors learn to use the tools of the trade, such as hammers, chisels, and brushes. Gradually uncovering fossils is a skilled business. Technicians have to record the location of every tiny piece of bone before the skeleton can be rebuilt.

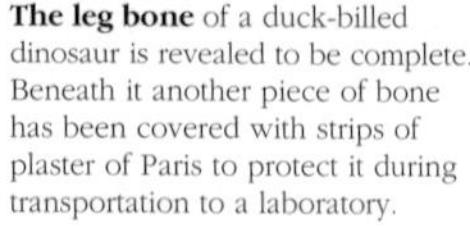

The leg bone of a duck-billed dinosaur is revealed to be complete. Beneath it another piece of bone has been covered with strips of plaster of Paris to protect it during transportation to a laboratory.

The reconstructed skeleton *of an Albertosaurus towers over the Dinosaur Hall at the Royal Tyrrell Museum of Palaeontology. The first dinosaur discovered in the area, Albertosaurus was a fierce meat-eating predator. Despite being eight meters (26 ft) long and weighing some two tons (2,032 kg), this dinosaur was capable of reaching speeds of 40 km/h (25 mph).*

Canadian Mounties

Traditional Mountie

THE ROYAL CANADIAN Mounted Police are a symbol of national pride. Canada's first Prime Minister, Sir John A. Macdonald, founded the North West Mounted Police in 1873 in Ontario after violence in the west of the country (between illicit liquor dealers and local natives) reached a climax with the Cypress Hills Massacre *(see p245)*. Marching west, the Mounties reached the Oldman River, Alberta, 70 km (43 miles) west of the Cypress Hills, where they built Fort Macleod in 1874. The principal aims of the Mounties were to establish good relations with the aboriginal peoples of the Prairies and to maintain order over new settlers in the late 1800s. The Mounties won respect for their diplomacy, policing the Canadian Pacific Railroad workers and the Klondike Gold Rush in the Yukon during the 1890s. In recognition of their service they gained the Royal prefix in 1904.

***The lush Cypress Hills** were the site of a gruesome massacre which led to the founding of the North West Mounted Police.*

***The march west** covered 3,135 km (1,949 miles) from Fort Dufferin, Manitoba to southern Alberta. A force of 275 men, 310 horses, and cattle, was sent to catch the illicit whiskey traders operating in the west. Battling with extreme temperatures, plagues of insects, and lack of supplies, the Mounties arrived at the Oldman River in 1874.*

THE LONG MARCH

Sioux Chief Sitting Bull

Inspector James M. Walsh sealed the Mounties' reputation for bravery when he took only six men on a parley with Sioux Chief Sitting Bull. The Sioux had retreated to the area after their defeat of US General Custer at the Battle of the Little Big Horn in 1876. Although the Sioux were the traditional enemies of the local Blackfoot and Cree Indians, there was no fighting after the arrival of the Mounties. Walsh's force succeeded in enforcing law and order across mid-west Canada, winning respect for their diplomacy. Blackfoot native chief Crowfoot praised their fairness saying, "They have protected us as the feathers of a bird protect it from winter."

James M. Walsh

***The adventures of the** pioneering Mounties have long been a source of inspiration to countless authors and filmmakers. Square-jawed and scarlet clad, the Mountie was the perfect hero. Perhaps the best-known "Mountie" film was the 1936 "Rose Marie" starring crooner Nelson Eddy and Jeanette MacDonald.*

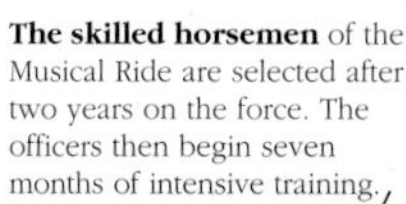

The skilled horsemen of the Musical Ride are selected after two years on the force. The officers then begin seven months of intensive training.

The Musical Ride

The Musical Ride is a thrilling spectacle of 32 riders and horses performing a series of traditional cavalry drills set to music. The drills have not changed since their original use in the British army over a century ago. Staying in tight formation, the horses do the trot, the canter, the rally, and the charge. Every summer the Ride is performed in different venues across Canada and the US.

***As an enduring symbol of Canada** the image of the Mounties has adorned everything from postage stamps and currency to this 1940s promotional tourist poster for Lake Louise in Banff National Park.*

32 specially bred horses take part in the Musical Ride. A mixture of thoroughbred stallion crossed with black Hanoverian mare, the horses train for two years.

***Today's Mounties** are a 20,000 strong police force responsible for the enforcement of federal law across Canada. Their duties range from counting migratory birds to exposing foreign espionage. Jets, helicopters, and cars are all used by modern Mounties.*

CENTRAL CANADA

CENTRAL CANADA covers a vast region of boreal forest and fertile grasslands, often known as the Prairies, which traverses Manitoba, Saskatchewan, and part of Alberta. Originally, First Nations peoples lived here, and depended on the herds of buffalo that provided them with food, shelter, and tools. By the end of the 19th century the buffalo were hunted almost to extinction. European settlers built towns and farms, some taking native wives and forming a new cultural grouping, the Métis. By the 20th century the area's economy came to rely on gas, oil, and grain. Today the Prairies, punctuated by striking, tall grain elevators, are known for the surprising variety of their landscape and the intriguing history of their towns.

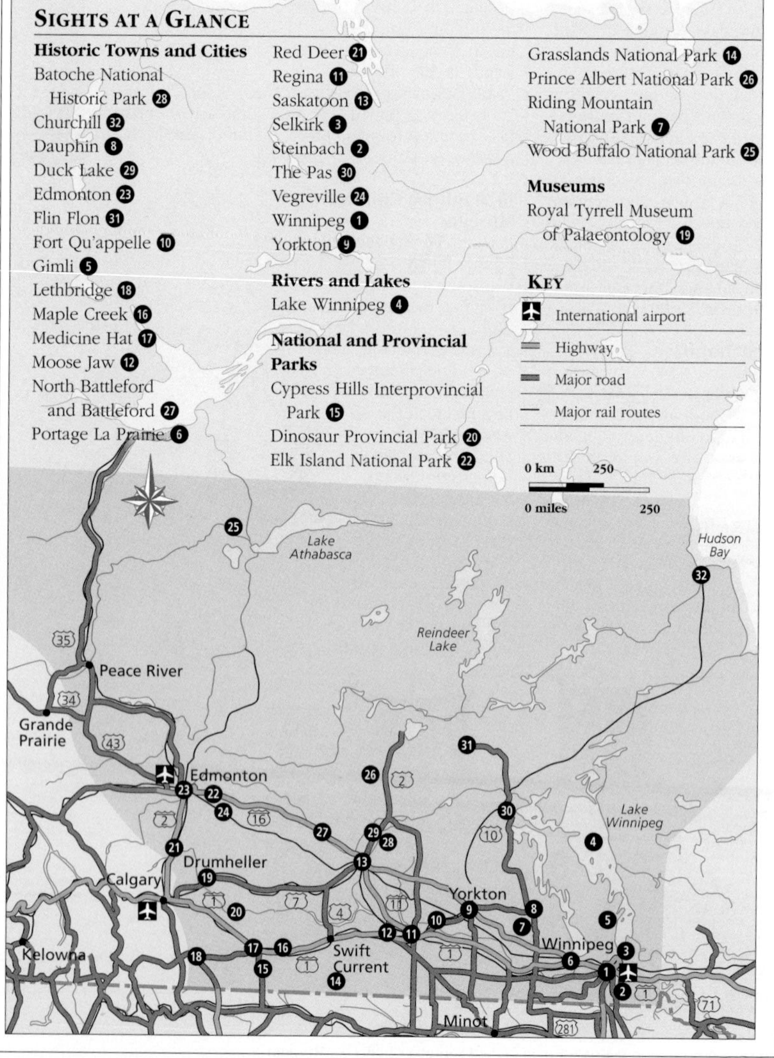

◁ **A young Indian dancer in traditional costume performs a centuries-old dance in Alberta**

Winnipeg ❶

WINNIPEG IS A LARGE, cosmopolitan city located at the geographic heart of Canada. Over half of Manitoba's population live here, mostly in suburbs that reflect the city's broad mix of cultures. Winnipeg's position, at the confluence of the Red and Assiniboine rivers, made it an important trading center for First Nations people going back some 6,000 years. From the 1600s Europeans settled here to trade fur. During the 1880s grain became the principal industry of the west, aided by a railroad network routed through Winnipeg. Today, this attractive city, with its museums, historic buildings, and excellent restaurants, makes for an enjoyable stay.

Exploring Winnipeg
Most of Winnipeg's sights are within easy walking distance of the downtown area. The excellent Manitoba Museum of Man and Nature and the Ukrainian Cultural Centre lie east of the Exchange District.

At the junction of the Red and Assiniboine rivers lies The Forks, a family entertainment center devoted to the city's history. At the junction of Portage and Main streets, lie the city's financial and shopping districts with their banks and malls.

St. Boniface

Cultural Centre, 340 Blvd. Provencher. *(204) 233 8972.* *Mon–Sat.*

The second largest French-speaking community outside of Quebec lives in the historic district of St. Boniface. This quiet suburb faces The Forks across the Red River and was founded by priests in 1818 to care for the Métis *(see p45)* and the French living here. In 1844 the Grey Nuns built a hospital which now houses the St. Boniface Museum. Priests built the Basilica of St. Boniface in 1818. Although the building was destroyed by fire in 1968, its elegant white façade is one of the city's best-loved landmarks. Métis leader Louis Riel was buried here after his execution following the rebellion at Batoche in 1881.

Manitoba Children's Museum

The Forks. *(204) 956 KIDS.* *daily.*

Located within The Forks complex, the Manitoba Children's Museum provides a series of enticing hands-on exhibits aimed at children from the ages of 3 to 11. In the All Aboard gallery children can play at being train drivers for a day on a reconstructed 1952 diesel engine while learning the history of Canada's railroad. They can also browse the internet or produce a TV show in a studio.

The Forks National Historic Site

45 Forks Market Rd. *(204) 983 6757.* *grounds: daily; office: Mon–Fri.* *special events.*

The Forks National Historic Site celebrates the history of the city. The river port, warehouses, and stables of this once bustling railroad terminus have now been restored.

The stable buildings, with their lofty ceilings, skylights, and connecting indoor bridges, house a flourishing market offering a wide range of specialty food, fresh produce, meat, and fish. Crafts, jewelry, and folk art are sold from the converted hayloft.

Set in 23 ha (56 acres) of parkland, The Forks

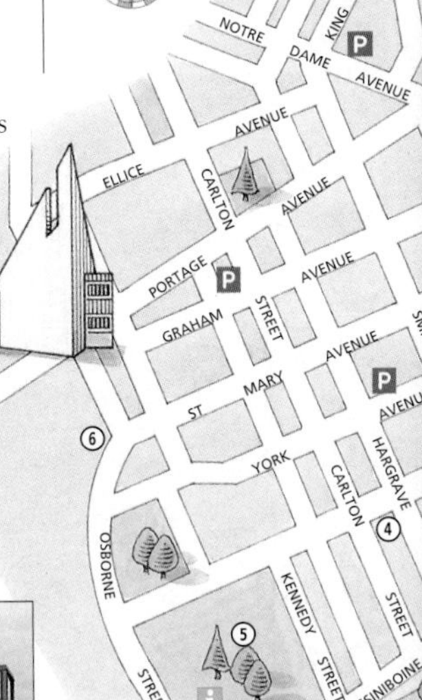

0 meters 500

0 yards 500

KEY

VIA Railroad station

Parking

Visitor information

The brightly colored main entrance to the Manitoba Children's Museum

Cruise boats and canoes can be hired from The Forks harbor

has an open-air amphitheater, and a tower for a spectacular six-story-high view of the Winnipeg skyline. The riverside walkway also offers splendid views of the city center and St. Boniface.

Dalnavert

61 Carlton St. (204) 943 2835. Tue–Thu, Sat, Sun. Mon, Fri.

Built in 1895, this beautifully restored Victorian house is a fine example of Queen Anne Revival architecture. Its elegant red brick exterior is complemented by a long wooden veranda. The house once belonged to Sir Hugh John Macdonald, the former premier of Manitoba, and the only surviving son of Canada's first prime minister, John A. Macdonald. The interior's rich furnishings reflect the lifestyle of an affluent home in the late 19th century.

Winnipeg Town Center

- Dalnavert ④
- Exchange District and Market Square ⑦
- Legislative Building ⑤
- Manitoba Children's Museum ②
- Manitoba Museum of Man and Nature *(see p237)* ⑧
- St. Boniface suburb ①
- The Forks National Historic Site ③
- Ukrainian Cultural Centre ⑨
- Winnipeg Art Gallery ⑥

Visitors' Checklist

670,000. 12 km (8 miles) NW of city. VIA Rail Station, cnr Main St. & Broadway. Greyhound Canada Station, cnr Portage Ave. & Colony St. Tourism Winnipeg, 279 Portage Ave. (204) 943 1970. Red River Exhibition (Jun); Winnipeg Intl Children's Festival (Jun); Folklorama (Aug); Festival Voyageur (Feb).

The Golden Boy statue adorns the dome of the Legislative Building

Legislative Building

Cnr Broadway & Osborne. (204) 945 5813. Mon–Fri for tours.

The Legislative Building is built of a rare and valuable limestone complete with the delicate remains of fossils threaded through its façade. The building is set in 12 ha (30 acres) of beautifully kept gardens dotted with statues of poets such as Robert Burns of Scotland, and Ukrainian Taras Ahevchenko, which celebrate the province's ethnic diversity.

Winnipeg Art Gallery

300 Memorial Blvd. (204) 786 6641. Tue–Sun. but free Wed.

The Winnipeg Art Gallery has the largest collection of Inuit art in the world. Over 10,000 carvings, prints, drawings, and textiles have been acquired since 1957. Especially striking is the large four-panel fabric collage wall-hanging, "Four Seasons of the Tundra" by Inuit artist Ruth Qaulluaryuk. The Gallery also contains Gothic and Renaissance altar paintings and tapestries donated by Irish peer Viscount Gore.

Exchange District and Market Square

Albert St. (204) 942 6716.

When the Canadian Pacific Railway decided to build its transcontinental line through Winnipeg in 1881, the city experienced a boom that led to the setting up of several commodity exchanges. Named after the Winnipeg Grain Exchange, this district was soon populated with a solid array of handsome terracotta and cut stone hotels, banks, warehouses, and theaters. The Exchange District is now a National Historic Site and has been restored to its former glory. It now houses boutiques, craft stores, furniture and antique stores, galleries, artists' studios, and residential lofts.

The center of the district is Old Market Square, a popular site for staging local festivals and outdoor concerts.

Ukrainian Cultural and Educational Centre

184 Alexander Ave. E. (204) 942 0218. *10am–5pm Mon–Fri, 10am–3pm Sat, 2pm–5pm Sun.*

Housed in an attractive 1930s building in the Exchange District, this institute was founded to celebrate the history and culture of Canada's second-largest ethnic grouping.

However, the center's museum, gallery, and research library are gradually being restored following a serious fire in the building in 2000. The museum was known for it's wood carvings, vibrant textiles, and collection of elaborately decorated, often hand-painted, *pysanky* (Easter eggs). It is hoped that new displays will soon open to the public.

Original 19th-century walls enclose the buildings at Lower Fort Garry

Lower Fort Garry

Hwy 9, nr Selkirk. (204) 785 6050. *May–Sep: 10am–6pm daily.*

Located 32 km (20 miles) north of Winnipeg on the banks of the Red River, Lower Fort Garry is the only original stone fur-trading post left standing in Canada. The Fort was established in 1830 by George Simpson, the governor of the Hudson's Bay Company's northern division, whose large house is now one of the fort's major attractions.

Before exploring the fort, visitors can see a film about the fort and its fur at the reception center. Several buildings have been restored, including the clerk's quarters and the store with its stacks of furs.

Sculpture in the Leo Mol garden, Assiniboine park

Royal Canadian Mint

520 Lagimodière Blvd. (204) 257 3359. *May–Aug: 9am–4pm Mon–Fri.*

The Royal Canadian Mint is housed in a striking building of rose-colored glass. The mint produces more than four billion coins annually for Canadian circulation, as well as for 60 other countries including Thailand and India.

Assiniboine Park

2355 Corydon Ave. (204) 986 5537. *daily.*

Stretching for 153 ha (378 acres) along the south side of the Assiniboine River, Assiniboine Park is one of the largest urban parks in central Canada.

One of the park's best-loved attractions is the Leo Mol Sculpture Garden which has some 50 bronze sculptures by the celebrated local artist. The park's Conservatory offers a tropical palm house which has seasonal displays of a wide range of flowers and shrubs. The park also features an English garden, a miniature railroad, and a fine example of a French formal garden. The old refreshment pavilion is now the Pavilion Gallery, which focuses on local artists.

The Assiniboine Park Zoo contains 275 different species, specializing in cold-hardy animals from the northern latitudes and mountain ranges such as polar bears, cougars, elk, and bald eagles. The zoo houses a large statue of Winnie the Bear, which is thought to be modeled on the original Winnie the Pooh of the A.A. Milne books.

The park's numerous cycling and walking trails are popular with both visitors and locals in summer, as is cross-country skiing, skating, and tobogganing in winter.

A pink glass pyramid houses Canada's Royal Mint

Manitoba Museum of Man and Nature

OUTSTANDING DISPLAYS of the region's geography and people are imaginatively presented at this excellent museum, which opened in 1970. The visitor proceeds through chronologically organized galleries with displays that range from pre-history to the present day. Each geographical area also has its own gallery: from the Earth History Gallery, which contains fossils up to 500 million years old, to the re-creation of Winnipeg in the 1920s, including a train station, a cinema, and a dentist's office. One of the museum's biggest draws is a replica of the *Nonsuch*, a 17th-century ketch.

VISITORS' CHECKLIST

190 Rupert Ave. *(204) 956 2830.* *11.* *mid-May–Sep: 10am–6pm daily; Sep–May: 10am–4pm Tue–Fri; 10am–5pm Sat, Sun.* *Mon, Sep–May.*

KEY

- Orientation gallery
- Earth History gallery
- Arctic/Sub-Arctic gallery
- Boreal Forest gallery
- Grasslands gallery
- Discovery room
- Urban gallery
- Nonsuch gallery
- Hudson's Bay Company gallery
- Parkland/Mixed Woods gallery
- Temporary exhibits
- Nonexhibition space

Moose Diorama

A moose and her calf among the conifers of the Boreal Forest are part of a display that includes a group of Cree people rock painting and gathering food before the harsh winter sets in.

Boreal Mezzanine

Earth History Mezzanine

Main entrance

GALLERY GUIDE

The galleries are arranged on two levels with steps connecting to mezzanines in the Earth History and Boreal Forest galleries. Part of a three-story addition built in 1999 houses the museum's Hudson's Bay Company collection.

Nonsuch Gallery

This two-masted ketch, built in England in 1970, is a replica of the Nonsuch *that arrived in Hudson Bay in 1688 in search of furs.*

Buffalo Hunt

A Métis hunter chasing buffalo symbolizes the museum's focus on man's relationship with his environment.

Prairie fields bloom with color across Central Canada during summer ▷

Ploughing with horses at the Mennonite Heritage Village, Steinbach

Steinbach ❷

11,350. *Hwy 12N. (204) 326 9566.*

ABOUT AN hour's drive southeast of Winnipeg, Steinbach is a closely knit community with impressive businesses in trucking, printing, manufacturing, and especially car dealerships. These are run largely by the Mennonites, members of a Protestant religious sect who are noted for their fair dealing.

Steam Engine at the Mennonite Heritage Village

The Mennonites arrived in Steinbach on ox-drawn carts in 1874, having fled from religious persecution in Russia. Despite not having a rail link, the town thrived as the Mennonites were good farmers and, later, car dealers (despite preferring not to use the motor car themselves). The nearby **Mennonite Heritage Village** re-creates a 19th-century Mennonite settlement with some original 100-year-old buildings and a church and school furnished to the period. Its restaurant serves home-made meals such as Mennonite borscht, a soup made with cabbage, and cream according to a traditional recipe. The general store offers locally crafted items, including Victorian candy.

Mennonite Heritage Village

Hwy 12 North. *(204) 326 9661.*
May–Sep: daily.

Selkirk ❸

9,800. *200 Eaton Ave. (204) 482 7176.*

NAMED AFTER the fifth Earl of Selkirk, Thomas Douglas, whose family had an interest in the Hudson's Bay Company, Selkirk was established in 1882 when settlers arrived along the shores of the Red River. Today, on Main Street, a 7.5-m (25-ft) high statue of a catfish proclaims Selkirk as the "Catfish capital of North America." Excellent sport fishing is a year-round activity, attracting enthusiasts from across North America.

The city's main attraction is the Marine Museum of Manitoba, where six historic ships, including the 1897 S.S. *Keenora*, Manitoba's oldest steamship, have been restored.

Lake Winnipeg ❹

Winnipeg. *Winnipeg.*
Winnipeg (204) 945 3777.

LAKE WINNIPEG is a huge stretch of water some 350 km (217 miles) long that dominates the province of Manitoba, connecting the south of the province to the north at Hudson Bay via the Nelson River. Today, the resorts that line the lake are highly popular with both locals and visitors alike.

Numerous beaches line the southeastern coast of the lake, including Winnipeg Beach, renowned for having one of the best windsurfing bays on the lake. An impressive carving of an Indian head by resident native artist Peter "Wolf" Toth stands in the local park. Called *Whispering Giant*, the wood sculpture honors the Ojibwa, Cree, and Assiniboine First Nations people of Manitoba.

Grand Beach in the **Grand Beach Provincial Park** has long powdery-white sand beaches and huge grass-topped dunes over 8 m (26 ft) high. Stretching back from the beach, the marsh, which is also known as the lagoon, is one of the park's treasures, and supports many species of birds, such as the rare and endangered Piping Plover.

Moving west from the lake, **Oak Hammock Marsh** provides an important habitat for some 280 species of birds and animals. The marsh's tall grass prairie, meadows, and aspen-oak bluffs house birds

Historic ships outside the Marine Museum of Manitoba in Selkirk

Carved cedar sculpture in the park at Winnipeg Beach

such as the ruff (a shorebird), the garganey (a duck), and the sharp-tailed sparrow.

Farther north, **Hecla Provincial Park** occupies a number of islands in the lake. A causeway links the mainland to Hecla Island, which was originally inhabited by the Anishinabe (Ojibwa) people. The first European settlers here were Icelanders who arrived in 1875. Today, the seaside village of Hecla is a pretty open-air museum featuring several restored 19th-century buildings. From Hecla there are many hiking and biking trails that lead to viewpoints for sightings of waterfowl such as great blue herons and the rare western grebe.

Grand Beach Provincial Park
Hwy 12, nr Grand Marais. *(204) 754 2728.* *daily.* *partial.*

Hecla Provincial Park
Hwy 8, nr Riverton. *(204) 378 2945.* *daily.*

Gimli 5

2,100. *Centre St. (204) 642 7974.*

LOCATED ON the western shores of Lake Winnipeg, Gimli is the largest Icelandic community outside Iceland. The settlers arrived, having gained the rights to land, at nearby Willow Creek in 1875. They soon proclaimed an independent state, which lasted until 1897 when the government insisted that other immigrants be allowed to settle in Gimli. Today, the **New Iceland Heritage Museum** tells the story of the town's unusual history.

Gimli has a distinctly nautical atmosphere, with cobbled sidewalks leading down to a picturesque harbor and a wooden pier. At the Icelandic Festival of Manitoba, held every August, visitors can play at being Vikings, participate in games, listen to folk music, and eat Icelandic specialties.

Statue of a Viking in the village of Gimli

About 25 km (15 miles) west of Gimli, the Narcisse Wildlife Management Area has been set up to preserve the habitat of thousands of red-sided garter snakes that can be seen here during the summer, on a specially designated short trail.

New Iceland Heritage Museum
Betel Waterfront Centre, 94 First Ave. *(204) 642 4001.* *9am–5pm Wed–Fri, 11am–5pm Sat & Sun.* *Donation.*

Portage la Prairie 6

13,400. *11 Second St. NE (204) 857 7778.*

PORTAGE LA PRAIRIE lies at the center of a rich agricultural area growing wheat, barley, and canola. The town is named after the French term for an overland detour, as Portage la Prairie lies between Lake Manitoba and the Assiniboine River, which formed a popular waterway for early travelers. Today, this thriving farming community contains the Fort La Reine Museum and Pioneer Village, on the site of the original fort built by the French explorer, La Vérendrye, in 1738. The museum offers exhibits of tools and photographs detailing 19th-century prairie life. The popular railroad display features a caboose, a watchman's shack, and the cigar-stained business car of Sir William Van Horne, founder of the Canadian Pacific Railroad. Pioneer Village successfully re-creates a 19th-century settlement with authentic stores and a church.

Pioneer Village, part of the Fort La Reine complex at Portage la Prairie

Riding Mountain National Park ❼

Hwys 10 & 19. 1 800 707 8480. daily. partial.

ONE OF western Manitoba's most popular attractions, Riding Mountain National Park is a vast 3,000 sq km (1,160 sq miles) wilderness. The best hiking trails and some of Manitoba's most beautiful scenery are to be found in the center of the park, where a highland plateau is covered by forests and lakes. To the east, a ridge of evergreen forest including spruce, pine, and fir trees houses moose and elk. A small herd of some 30 bison can also be found in the park near Lake Audy. Bison were reintroduced here in the 1930s after they had been hunted out at the end of the 19th century. The most developed area here is around the small settlement of Wasagaming where information on the park's network of trails for cycling, hiking, and horseback riding is available. Canoes are also available to rent for exploring the park's biggest lake, Clear Lake.

Wasagaming is the park's main settlement, and offers hotels, restaurants, and campgrounds. At nearby Anishinabe village, visitors have the opportunity to camp in traditional tipis.

One of a small herd of bison at Riding Mountain National Park

Dauphin ❽

8,800. 3rd Ave. (204) 638 4838.

A PLEASANT TREE-LINED town, Dauphin was named after the King of France's eldest son by the French explorer La Vérendrye. Located north of Riding Mountain National Park, Dauphin is a distribution-and-supply center for the farms of the fertile Vermilion River valley. The Fort Dauphin Museum in town is a replica of an 18th-century trading post. Exhibits include a trapper's birchbark canoe and several early pioneer buildings, including a school, church, and blacksmith's store.

Today, the town's distinctive onion-shaped dome of the Church of the Resurrection is a tribute to Dauphin's Ukrainian immigrants who began to arrive in 1891. A traditional Ukrainian meal, including savory stuffed dumplings *(piroggi)*, forms part of a tour of the church.

Yorkton ❾

17,000. Jct Hwy 9 & Hwy 16 (306) 783 8707.

YORKTON WAS founded as a farming community in 1882, and is located in central Saskatchewan. The striking architecture of its churches, particularly the Catholic Church of St. Mary's, reflects the town's Ukrainian heritage. The church was built in 1914 and is a city landmark. Its 21-m (68-ft) high dome, icons and paintings are stunning. The Yorkton branch of the **Western Development Museum** (one of four in the province) focuses on the story of immigrants to the region.

Western Development Museum
Yellowhead Hwy. (306) 783 8361. May–mid-Sep: daily.

The magnificent Dome at Saint Mary's Catholic Church, Yorkton

The elegant façade of Motherwell Homestead

Fort Qu'Appelle ❿

2,000. Regina (306) 789 5099.

NAMED AFTER an 1864 Hudson's Bay Company fur trading post, the picturesque town of Fort Qu'Appelle is located between Regina and Yorkton on Highway 10. The **Fort Qu'Appelle Museum** is built on the site of the old fort and incorporates a small outbuilding that was part of the original structure. The museum houses native artifacts such as antique beadwork and a collection of pioneer photographs.

The 430-km (267-mile) long Qu'Appelle River stretches across two-thirds of southern Saskatchewan. At Fort Qu'Appelle the river widens into a string of eight lakes bordered by several provincial parks. Scenic drives through the countryside are just one of the attractions of the valley.

About 30 km (19 miles) east of Fort Qu'Appelle is the **Motherwell Homestead National Historic Site**. Originally built by politician William R. Motherwell, this gracious stone house with extensive ornamental gardens is open to visitors. Motherwell introduced many agricultural improvements to the area and was so successful that, after living in poverty for 14 years, he rose to become agriculture minister of Saskatchewan between 1905 and 1918.

Fort Qu'Appelle Museum
cnr Bay Ave. & Third St. (306) 332 6443. Jul–Sept: daily. limited.

Motherwell Homestead
Off Hwy 22. (306) 333 2166. May–Oct: daily. limited.

Regina ⑪

199,700. Hwy 1 E (306) 789 5099.

REGINA IS A friendly, bustling city and the capital of Saskatchewan. The city was named for Queen Victoria by her daughter, Princess Louise, who was married to the Governor General of Canada. Regina was established in 1882 after starting life as a tent settlement called Pile O'Bones. This is a derivation of "oskana" (a Cree word meaning buffalo bones), from the piles of bones left behind after hunting.

Today, Regina is a thriving modern city whose highrise skyline contrasts with the 350,000 trees of the man-made Wascana Centre, a 930-ha (2,298-acre) urban park which contains a vast man-made lake. The lake's Willow Island is a popular site for picnics and can be reached by ferry. The park is also a haven for some 60 species of waterfowl, including large numbers of Canada geese. The **Royal Saskatchewan Museum** is housed in the park and focuses on the story of the area's First Nations peoples from earliest times to the present day. There are lectures by tribal elders on the land and its precious resources, as well as murals, sculptures, and paintings by contemporary Saskatchewan native and non-native artists.

Canadian goose in Wascana Centre Park

One of several murals on downtown buildings in Moose Jaw

The original headquarters for the North West Mounted Police lies west of the city center. Today, the Royal Canadian Mounted Police Barracks trains all Canada's Mounties and is also the site of the **RCMP Centennial Museum**. Here, the story of the Mounties is told from their beginnings following the Cypress Hills Massacre in 1873 *(see p245)*. Among the highlights of a visit to the museum are the ceremonies and drills that are regularly performed by special trained groups of Mounties, including the Sergeant Major's Parade, the Musical Ride, and Sunset Retreat Ceremonies.

Royal Saskatchewan Museum
Cnr Albert St. & College Ave. *(306) 787 2815.* *daily.* *Dec 25.*

RCMP Centennial Museum
Dewdney Ave. W. *(306) 780 5838.* *daily.*

Moose Jaw ⑫

34,500.
99 Diefenbaker Dr. (306) 693 8097.

THE QUIET TOWN of Moose Jaw was established as a railway terminus by the Canadian Pacific Railroad in 1882. A terminus for the American Soo Line from Minneapolis, Minnesota soon followed. Today, a series of murals celebrates the lives of the early railroad pioneers and homesteaders, decorating 29 buildings around downtown's 1st Avenue. Nearby, River Street has a concentration of 1920s hotels and warehouses that reflect Moose Jaw's time as "sin city" during the 1920s – when Prohibition in the United States meant that illegally produced liquor was smuggled from Canada to Chicago, by gangsters such as the infamous Al Capone.

The Moose Jaw branch of the Western Development Museum focuses on transportation, particularly the railroad.

Cadets of the Royal Canadian Mounted Police Academy in Regina are put through their paces

Traditional powwow dancer in Wanuskewin Park, Saskatoon

Saskatoon ⓭

231,420. *6306 Idylwyld Dr. N. (306) 242 1206.*

FOUNDED IN 1882 by Ontario Methodist John Lake as a temperance colony, Saskatoon is located in the middle of prairie country. Today, the city is an agricultural and commercial hub, and a busy regional center for cattle ranchers and wheat farmers from surrounding communities. The region's history is told in Saskatoon's branch of the Western Development Museum, which focuses on the town's boom years in the 1900s, re-creating the bustling main street of a typical prairie town, including its railroad station and a hotel.

The South Saskatchewan River meanders through the city and is bounded by many lush parks, including the outstanding 120-ha (290-acre) **Wanuskewin Heritage Park**. The park is devoted to First Nations history, with archaeological sites that confirm the existence of hunter-gatherer communities some 6,000 years ago. Some of the digs are open to the public, and the excellent park interpretive center has an archaeological lab explaining current research. The park's wooded hills and marshy creeks are still held to be sacred lands by the Northern Plains peoples who act as interpretive guides. Easy-to-follow trails lead the visitor past tipi rings, buffalo trails, and a buffalo jump *(see p294)*.

Black-tailed prairie dog

The riverbank also houses two fascinating museums, The Ukrainian Museum of Canada with its collection of brightly colored traditional textiles, and the Mendel Art Gallery, which houses a collection including First Nations and Inuit pottery and glassware.

Wanuskewin Heritage Park

Off Hwy 11. (306) 931 6767. daily. Good Fri, Dec 25. limited.

Grasslands National Park ⓮

Jct Hwys 4 & 18. Val Marie (306) 298 2257. Val Marie. daily. partial.

SITUATED IN THE southwest corner of Saskatchewan, Grasslands National Park was set up in 1981 to preserve one of the last original prairie grasslands in North America. The park is an area of climatic extremes where summer temperatures can be as high as 40 °C (104 °F), and winter ones as low as -40 °C (-48 °F). This environment supports a range of rare wildlife, including short-horned lizards and ferruginous hawks. The rugged landscape along the Frenchman River valley is the only remaining habitat of the black-tailed prairie dog in Canada. Visitors may hike and camp in the park, but facilities are basic.

East of the park is the striking, glacially formed landscape of the **Big Muddy Badlands**. In the early 1900s, caves of eroded sandstone and deep ravines provided hideouts for cattle thieves such as Butch Cassidy and Dutch Henry.

Big Muddy Badlands

Off Hwy 34. (306) 267 3312. Tours in summer from Coronach.

Buttes (isolated flat-topped hills) in the Big Muddy Badlands seen from Grasslands National Park

Cypress Hills Interprovincial Park 15

Hwy 41. (306) 662 2645. Maple Creek. daily. partial.

CROSSING THE border between Saskatchewan and Alberta, the Cypress Hills Interprovincial Park offers fine views of the plains from its 1,400-m (4,593-ft) high peaks. The park's landscape is similar to the foothills of the Rocky Mountains, with its lodgepole pine forests and abundant wild flowers. Walking trails through the park offer the visitor the chance to see moose, elk, and white-tailed deer, as well as the 200 or more species of bird that stop here during migration, such as the rare trumpeter swan and mountain chickadee.

In the eastern section of the park, in Saskatchewan, **Fort Walsh National Historic Site** houses a reconstruction of Fort Walsh, which was built in 1875 by the Mounties to keep out the illicit whiskey traders who were causing trouble among the natives. Nearby, the trading posts involved in the illegal liquor trade, Farwells and Solomons, have been reconstructed. Costumed guides tell the story of the Cypress Hills Massacre.

Fort Walsh National Historic Site

Cypress Hills Interprovincial Park. (306) 662 2645. May–Oct: 9am–5pm daily.

Maple Creek 16

2,300. Hwy 1 West (306) 662 2244

LOCATED ON THE edge of the Cypress Hills, Maple Creek is affectionately known as "Old cow town," and was established as a ranching center in 1882. The town still has a look of the Old West with trucks, trailers, and Stetson-wearing ranchers filling the downtown streets. Maple Creek's many original 19th-century storefronts include the elegant Commercial Hotel with its marble-floored lobby. The oldest museum in the province, the Saskatchewan Old Timers' Museum, boasts an excellent collection of pictures and artifacts telling the story of the NWMP, the natives, and the early settlement of the area.

Iron Bridge over the Oldman River, Lethbridge

Medicine Hat 17

50,152. 8 Gehring Rd SE (403) 527 6422.

THE SOUTH Saskatchewan River Valley is the picturesque setting for the town of Medicine Hat, the center of Alberta's gas industry. Founded in 1883, Medicine Hat is noted for Seven Persons Coulee, once a substantial native camp and buffalo jump and now one of the most important archaeological sites of the northern plains. Evidence that aboriginal peoples lived here over 6,000 years ago has been garnered from finds including bones, tools, and arrowheads. Tours of the site are available.

Lethbridge 18

68,712. 2805 Scenic Dr. (403) 320 1222.

COAL, OIL, AND gas are the basis of Lethbridge's success. Alberta's third-largest city was named after mine-owner William Lethbridge in 1885, but First Nations peoples such as the Blackfoot Indians have inhabited the area since prehistoric times.

Lying on the banks of the Oldman River, Lethbridge is home to the notorious Fort Whoop-up, established in 1869 by whiskey traders John Healy and Alfred Hamilton for the sole purpose of profiting from the sale of illicit, and often deadly, whiskey. Many Indians, drawn by the lure of the drink, were poisoned or even killed by the brew, which was made with substances such as tobacco and red ink. Today, a replica of Fort Whoop-up has a visitor's center that describes the history of the trading post.

CYPRESS HILLS MASSACRE

On June 1, 1873 a group of whiskey traders attacked an Assiniboine camp, killing several women, children, and braves in retaliation for the alleged theft of their horses by natives. Many native people had already died from drinking the traders' liquor, which was doctored with substances such as ink and strychnine.

The massacre led to the formation of the North West Mounted Police. Their first post at Fort Macleod in 1874, and another at Fort Walsh in 1875, marked the end of the whiskey trade and earned the Mounties the natives' trust.

Two Assiniboine Indians from an engraving made in 1844

Royal Tyrrell Museum of Palaeontology ⓳

The museum's Albertosaurus logo

THE OUTSTANDING Royal Tyrrell Museum of Palaeontology was opened in 1985 and is the only museum in Canada devoted to 4.5 billion years of the Earth's history. The layout of the exhibits enables visitors to follow the course of evolution through displays of dinosaurs and fossils from different ages. The museum uses interactive computers, videos, and 3-dimensional dioramas to re-create distinct prehistoric landscapes, bringing the age of the dinosaurs to life.

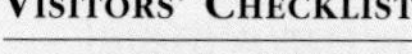

VISITORS' CHECKLIST

Hwy 838, 6 km NW of Drumheller. *(403) 823 7707. Calgary. May–Oct: daily; Nov–Apr: Tue–Sun.* *www.tyrrellmuseum.com*

KEY

- Science hall
- Extreme theropod
- Discoveries
- Burgess Shale
- Dinosaur hall
- Bearpaw sea
- Age of reptiles
- Age of mammals
- Palaeoconservatory
- Terrestrial Palaeozoic
- Nova Discovery room
- Pleistocene gallery
- Nonexhibition space

Dinosaur Hall
In Dinosaur Hall, a T-rex towers over a display of some 35 complete dinosaur skeletons.

The "Introducing Fossils" part of this gallery explains fossils and their formation, from fossilized tree sap (amber) to natural molds and 500-million-year-old casts.

GALLERY GUIDE

The collection is housed on several levels reached by a series of ramps. Each area contains a display on an era of geological time. Introductory exhibits on fossils and dinosaurs are followed by displays on prehistoric mammals and the Ice Ages. The largest and most popular part of the museum is the Dinosaur Hall.

Albertosaurus
A fossilized Albertosaurus was found in 1884, in the Drumheller Valley, by the museum's namesake, Dr. J.B. Tyrrell. A cousin to the meat-eating T-rex, this reptile was a fierce hunter.

MUSEUM ORGANIZED DINOSAUR DIGS

Visitors on a dinosaur dig

Most of the Royal Tyrrell Museum's dinosaur remains have been found in the Alberta Badlands, a barren landscape of fluted gullies and steep bluffs. There is a variety of tours of the area, ranging from 2-hour Dig Watches to camps lasting a week or more. Participants may help the Museum paleontologists to uncover fossils and dinosaur bones.

Elk Island National Park's largest lake, Astotin Lake, is skirted by a popular hiking trail

Dinosaur Provincial Park 20

Rte 544. *(403) 378 4342.*
daily. *partial.*

TWO HOURS' drive southeast of the town of Drumheller, the UNESCO World Heritage Site of Dinosaur Provincial Park, established in 1955, contains one of the world's richest fossil beds. Located along the Red Deer River Valley, the park includes dinosaur skeletons mostly from the Cretaceous period, between about 144 and 66.4 million years ago *(see pp228–9)*. More than 300 significant finds have been made here and more than 30 institutions worldwide have specimens from this valley on display.

From the town of Drumheller it is possible to tour the 48-km (30-mile) loop **Dinosaur Trail**, which takes visitors through the "Valley of the Dinosaurs" and features fossils and displays relating to prehistoric life, as well as stunning views of the strange badlands landscape from highpoints such as Horseshoe Canyon.

Dinosaur Trail
Drumheller (403) 823 1331.

Hoodoos, towers of rock sculpted by glacial erosion, near Drumheller

Red Deer 21

63,100. *Sports Hall of Fame, Hwy 2: (403) 346 0180.*

LOCATED MIDWAY between Calgary and Edmonton, this bustling city was founded in 1882 by Scottish settlers as a stopover point for travelers. A modern city with good cultural and recreational facilities, Red Deer is the hub of central Alberta's rolling parkland district. The city has some interesting buildings, such as the award-winning St. Mary's Church, and the landmark Water Tower, known as the "Green Onion." The city's beautiful reserve of Waskasoo Park is located along the Red River.

Elk Island National Park 22

Hwy 16. *(780) 992 2950.*
daily. *partial.*

ESTABLISHED IN 1906 as Canada's first animal sanctuary, Elk Island became a national park in 1913. It offers a wilderness retreat only half-an-hour's drive from Edmonton. This 194 sq km (75 sq miles) park is exceptional for providing a habitat for large mammals such as elk, the plains bison, and the rarer, threatened wood bison. The park's landscape of transitional aspen parkland (an area of rolling meadows, woodlands, and wetlands) is, according to the World Wildlife Fund for Nature, one of the most threatened habitats in North America.

Aspen trees grow mostly on the hills, while balsam, poplar, and white birch grow near wet areas. Plants such as sedges and willows also thrive in the wetlands alongside a host of birds such as the swamp sparrow and yellow warbler.

Elk Island is a popular day trip from Edmonton as well as being a picturesque weekend picnic spot for locals. There are 13 hiking trails of varying difficulties and lengths. During the summer a wide range of activities is available in the park including swimming, canoeing, and camping. Cross-country skiing is the most popular winter activity.

Ice Palace at West Edmonton Mall

Edmonton 23

890,000. 9797 Jasper Ave. (780) 496 8400.

EDMONTON SPANS the valley of the North Saskatchewan River and sits in the center of Alberta province, of which it is the capital. Established as a series of Hudson's Bay Company trading posts in 1795, this city is now the focus of Canada's thriving oil industry.

Edmonton's downtown area is centered on Jasper Avenue and Sir Winston Churchill Square, where modern glass high-rises sit among shops and restaurants. Without doubt the main attraction in Edmonton is the gigantic **West Edmonton Mall**. Billed as the world's largest shopping center, it contains over 800 stores and services, an amusement park, over 100 restaurants, a water park with its own beach and waves, a golf course, and an ice rink. In contrast, downtown also houses one of Alberta's oldest buildings, the delightful Alberta Legislature, which was opened in 1912. Overlooking the river, on the site of the old Fort Edmonton, the building has beautifully landscaped grounds filled with fountains.

Southwest of downtown, Fort Edmonton Park re-creates the original Hudson's Bay Company fort with reconstructions of street areas in 1885 and 1920. Here visitors can experience past times, wandering around original shops and businesses, as well as taking rides on a horse-drawn wagon, steam train, or street car.

West Edmonton Mall
170th St. & 87th Ave. (780) 444 5200. daily.

Vegreville 24

5,300. at giant Pysanka (780) 632 6800.

ALONG THE Yellowhead Hwy, heading eastward from Edmonton, lies the predominantly Ukrainian town of Vegreville. Its community is famous for producing traditionally Ukrainian, highly decorated Easter eggs (or pysanki). Clearly visible from the road there is a fabulously decorated giant pysanka covered with intricate bronze, gold, and silver designs that tell the story of the region's Ukrainian settlers, and celebrates their religious faith, bountiful harvests, and the protection they received from the RCMP. The egg is 7 m (23 ft) high, and is made of over 3,500 pieces of aluminum.

A giant decorated Easter egg made by Ukrainians at Vegreville

Wood Buffalo National Park 25

main access: Fort Smith, NWT. (867 872 7900). daily.

THE LARGEST national park in Canada, Wood Buffalo National Park is about the size of Denmark, covering an area of 44,807 sq km (17,474 sq miles). The park was made a UNESCO World Heritage Site in 1983 because of the range of habitat it offers for such rare species of animal as the wood bison or buffalo.

There are three different environments here: fire-scarred forest uplands; a large, poorly drained plateau filled with streams and bogs; and the Peace-Athabasca delta, full of sedge meadows, marshes, and shallow lakes. Sightings of such birds as peregrine falcons and bald eagles are common, and the park is the only natural nesting site of the rare whooping crane in the world.

THE GREY OWL STORY

Long before conservation became popular, the renowned naturalist by the name of Grey Owl, took up the cause. Inspired by his Mohawk wife, Anahareo, he wrote the first of several best-selling books, *Men of the Last Frontier*, in 1931, the same year he became the official naturalist of Prince Albert National Park. He built a cabin on the peaceful shores of Lake Ajawaan from where he ran a beaver protection program. When Grey Owl died of pneumonia in 1938, there was uproar when a newspaper discovered that he was really an Englishman. Born in Hastings in 1888, Archibald Stansfield Belaney took on the identity of Grey Owl when he returned to Canada after World War I. He wore buckskins and wore his hair in Apache-style braids. A generation later Grey Owl's legacy remains the protection of Canada's wildlife.

Grey Owl feeding a beaver

Prince Albert National Park ㉖

ESTABLISHED IN 1927, Prince Albert National Park covers 3,875 sq km (1,500 square miles) of wilderness, which changes from the gently rolling terrain of aspen parkland in the south to the spruce and fir trees of the northern boreal forest. These distinct environments house different wildlife populations, with moose, wolf, and caribou in the forests, and elk, bison, and badger in the parkland. The center of the park, and the most accessible areas for visitors, are the hiking and canoeing trails around the Kingsmere and Waskesiu Lakes. The townsite of Waskesiu is the best place from which to begin exploring the park.

VISITORS' CHECKLIST

off Hwy 2. *(306) 663 4522.* *mid-May–Aug: 8am–10pm daily; Sep–May: 8am–4pm. Nature center open Jul–Aug: 10am–5pm daily.*

KEY

- Major road
- Minor road
- Hiking route
- Rivers
- Camping
- Picnic area
- Visitor information
- Viewpoint

Grey Owl's cabin by Ajawaan Lake
A popular hike in the park leads to Grey Owl's log cabin, "Beaver Lodge."

Beach resort at Lake Waskesiu
The village of Waskesiu offers visitors a wide range of facilities, including stores, hotels, and a sandy lakeside beach.

Kingsmere Lake

Crean Lake

EDMONTON

0 km 3

0 miles 3

Waskesiu Lake

Waskesiu

PRINCE ALBERT

The Hanging Heart Lakes form a waterway that leads to Lake Crean – one of the popular canoe trips in the park.

Lakeview Drive Nature Centre explains the park's ecology.

View over Waskesiu Lake
Fall foliage across the boreal forest seen around the lake from Kingsmere Road.

Kingfisher trail is a popular 13-km (8-mile) walk by Waskesiu lake.

Gun with carriage at Fort Battleford National Historic Site

North Battleford and Battleford 27

19,500. *Visitors' center, jct Hwys 16 & 40 (306) 445 2000.*

THE COMMUNITIES of North Battleford and Battleford, together known as The Battlefords, face each other across the North Saskatchewan River Valley. Named after a ford in the Battle River, the area was the site of age-old conflicts between the Blackfoot and Cree. An important early settlement in the West, Battleford was chosen as the seat of the North-West Territories government from 1876 to 1882. Today, the communities are thriving industrial centers, although the North Battleford branch of the Western Development Museum focuses on the rural life of the prairies.

One of the most popular attractions in The Battlefords is the **Allan Sapp Gallery**, housed in the old municipal library. Allan Sapp is one of Canada's best-loved contemporary artists. His work celebrates the traditions of the Northern Plains Cree community in simple, delicately colored paintings and drawings.

Across the river, just south of Battleford, the **Fort Battleford National Historic Site** contains a well-restored North-West Mounted Police post. The stockade has original buildings such as the Sick Horse Stable, where the Mounties' horses were taken to recover from the rugged life of the prairies. Costumed guides tell the story of the time when 500 settlers took refuge in the stockade during the North-West Rebellion.

Allan Sapp Gallery
1091 100th St. *(306) 445 1760.*
1pm–5pm daily. *limited.*

Fort Battleford National Historic Site
Off Hwy 4. *(306) 937 2621.*
mid-May–mid-Oct: daily.

Batoche National Historic Park 28

Rte 225 off Hwy 312. *(306) 423 6227.* *May–Oct: daily.*

THE ORIGINAL village of Batoche was the site of the Métis's last stand against the Canadian Militia, led by Louis Riel and Gabriel Dumont in 1885 *(see p45)*.

From the 17th century, white fur traders in the west had married Indian wives and adopted tribal languages and customs. The resulting mixed raced peoples, known as the Métis, had originally rebeled in 1869 in the Winnipeg area when it seemed the federal government might deprive them of their land rights. When history began to repeat itself in 1885, Métis rebels recalled Riel from exile in Montana to declare a provisional government at Batoche. Violence erupted on May 9, 1885 into what was to become known as the North-West Rebellion. Riel surrendered, was tried for treason, and hanged in Regina.

Today, the Batoche National Historic Park occupies the site of the village and battlefield. The 648-ha (1,600-acre) park houses the bullet-ridden St. Antoine de Padou Church and Rectory as well as the cemetery where the Métis leaders are buried. An interpretive center features an audio-visual presentation telling the history of Batoche and the rebellion through the eyes of the Métis.

St. Antoine de Padou Church and Rectory at Batoche National Historic Park

Polar Bears

Known as the "Lord of the Arctic," the magnificent polar bear can weigh as much as 650 kg (1,433 lb). In the fall the bears begin to congregate along the bay east of Churchill waiting for ice to form in order to hunt seals. Their acute sense of smell can detect a scent up to 32 km (20 miles) away and pick up the presence of seals under 1 m (3 ft) of snow and ice.

Up to 150 bears pass by and through Churchill during the season. The best way to view them is in a tundra buggy, a large buslike vehicle that is warm, safe, and elevated over 2 m (6.5 ft) from the ground.

The majestic polar bear

Duck Lake 29

670. 301 Front St. (306) 467 2277.

A LITTLE TO THE WEST of the small farming village of Duck Lake lies a plaque commemorating the first shots fired in the North-West Rebellion. On March 26, 1885, a police interpreter and a Cree emissary scuffled during a parley, and the officer was killed. During the ensuing battle, 12 NWMP officers and six Métis died. The Battle of Duck Lake is depicted in a series of murals at the town's visitors' center.

The Pas 30

5,900. 324 Ross Ave. (204) 623 7256.

ONCE A KEY fur-trading post dating back some 300 years, The Pas is now a major industrial distribution and transportation center for Manitoba's northwest. Nearby Clearwater Lake Provincial Park is named for the lake itself, which is said to be so clear that it is possible to see the bottom at 11 m (35 ft). The park also offers a walking trail through "the caves," a geological phenomenon where rock masses split away from shoreline cliffs to create huge crevices that provide shelter for a number of animals, including black bears, squirrels, and weasels.

Flin Flon 31

7,200. Hwy 10A (204) 687 4518.

STEEP HILLY STREETS reflect the fact that Flin Flon lies on Precambrian rock (as old as the formation of the Earth's crust itself, roughly 3.8 billion years ago), and the area is famous for its distinctive greenstone. The town bears the name of a fictional character of a popular novel, *The Sunless City* by J.E.P. Murdock. The book was read by a prospector at the time he staked his claim here in 1915. Copper and gold are still mined in Flin Flon, but visitors mostly come to experience the vast wilderness of the nearby Grass River Provincial Park.

The distinctive Grass River, where strings of islands dot the countless lakes of the river system, has been a trade route for centuries, used by both natives and, later, European explorers and fur traders to travel from the northern forests to the prairies. Today, visitors may follow the historic route on guided canoe tours as well as fishing for northern pike, lake trout, turbot, and perch.

Churchill 32

1,100. 211 Kelsey Blvd. (204) 675 2022.

LOCATED AT THE mouth of the Churchill River on Hudson Bay, the town retains the look of a basic pioneer town, with no luxury hotels, no paved roads, and few trees. This vast Arctic landscape is snow-free only from June through to the end of August. Churchill has no road access and can be reached only by plane or train from Winnipeg, Thompson, and The Pas. Despite its remote situation, Churchill was an important point of entry into Canada for early European explorers and fur traders arriving by boat in the 18th century. The Hudson's Bay Company established an outpost for fur-trading here in 1717.

Today, visitors come to see the polar bears, beluga whales, and the splendid array of tundra flora in this region. In the spring and fall the tundra's covering of moss, lichens, and tiny flowers bursts into an array of reds, violets, and yellows. In the summer beluga whales move upriver to the warmer waters and can be seen from boat trips or on scuba dives.

Polar bear warning sign near Churchill

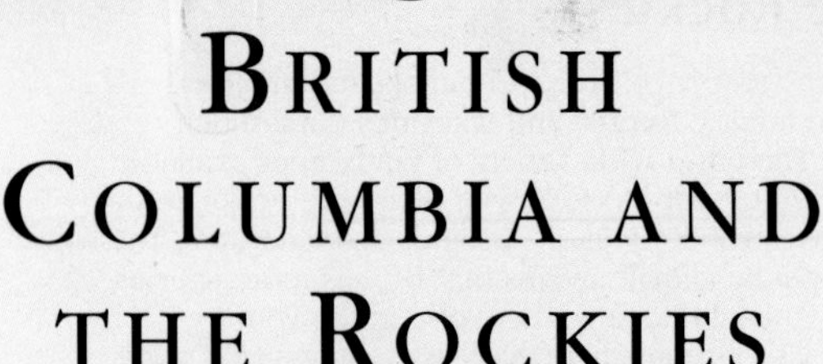

British Columbia and the Rockies

Introducing British Columbia and the Rockies

THE DRAMATIC BEAUTY OF British Columbia and the Rockies' mountain ranges, forests, and lakes make it a much visited area. There is a wide variety of landscapes available here, from the northern Rockies with their bare peaks, to the south's Okanagan Valley with its orchards and vineyards. The region's temperate climate means that BC has more species of plant and animal than anywhere else in the country.

Millions of visitors come here every year, drawn by a wide range of outdoor activities. To the west, Vancouver Island offers ancient rainforest and the impressive coastal scenery of the Pacific Rim National Park. Lying between the Pacific Ocean and the Coast Mountains, Vancouver is a stunningly attractive city, with good transportation links to the rest of the region, including Calgary in the east.

Centuries-old rainforest in the Gwaii Haanas National Park on the Queen Charlotte Islands

Illuminated by 3,000 lights, Victoria's Parliament Buildings are reflected in the waters of Inner Harbour on Vancouver Island

SEE ALSO

- ***Where to Stay*** pp355–59
- ***Where to Eat*** pp375–79

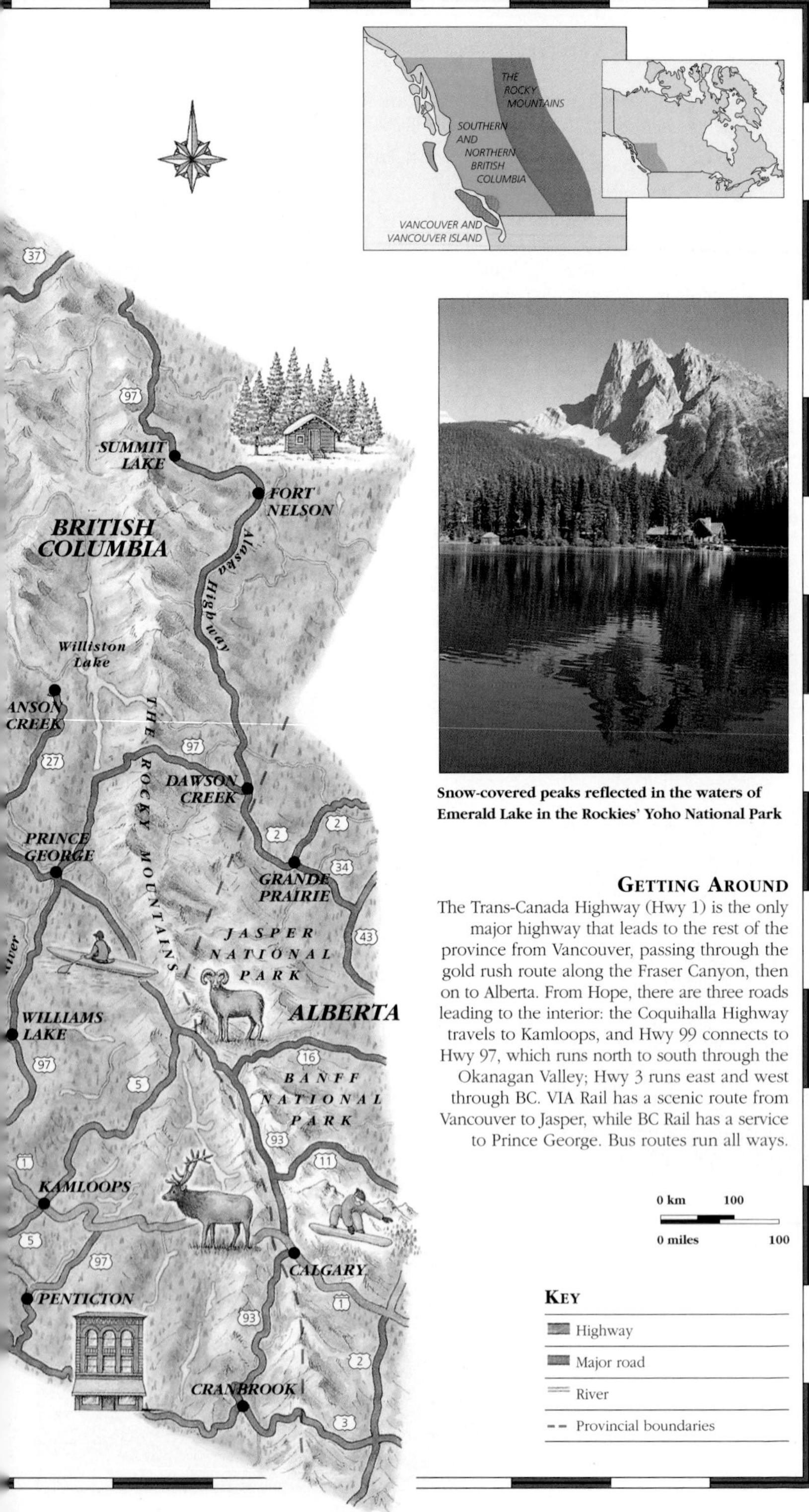

Snow-covered peaks reflected in the waters of Emerald Lake in the Rockies' Yoho National Park

Getting Around

The Trans-Canada Highway (Hwy 1) is the only major highway that leads to the rest of the province from Vancouver, passing through the gold rush route along the Fraser Canyon, then on to Alberta. From Hope, there are three roads leading to the interior: the Coquihalla Highway travels to Kamloops, and Hwy 99 connects to Hwy 97, which runs north to south through the Okanagan Valley; Hwy 3 runs east and west through BC. VIA Rail has a scenic route from Vancouver to Jasper, while BC Rail has a service to Prince George. Bus routes run all ways.

Key

- Highway
- Major road
- River
- Provincial boundaries

The Rocky Mountains

THE CANADIAN ROCKY MOUNTAINS are a younger section of the Western Cordillera, a wide band of mountain ranges that stretch from Mexico to Canada. Formed between 120 and 20 million years ago, they include some of Canada's highest peaks, the 389-sq km (150-sq mile) Columbia Icefield, and glacial lakes. In summer wild flowers carpet the alpine meadows; in winter both visitors and locals take advantage of the snow-covered slopes to indulge in winter sports. The flora and fauna of the Canadian Rockies are protected within several National Parks; the most noted being Banff, Jasper, and Yoho *(see pp298–309)*, which houses the renowned Burgess Shale fossil beds.

Orchid found in the Rockies

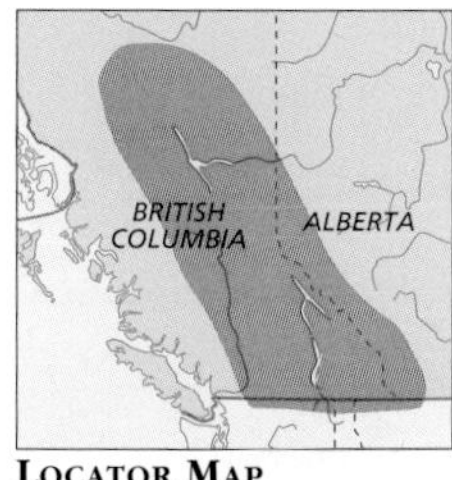

LOCATOR MAP

The Canadian Rockies

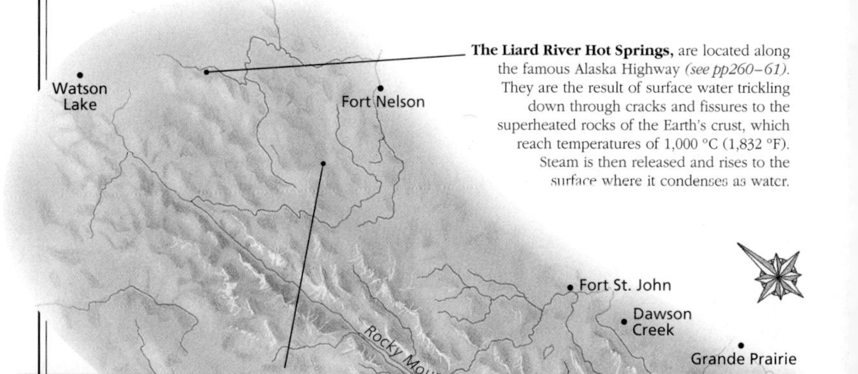

The Liard River Hot Springs, are located along the famous Alaska Highway *(see pp260–61)*. They are the result of surface water trickling down through cracks and fissures to the superheated rocks of the Earth's crust, which reach temperatures of 1,000 °C (1,832 °F). Steam is then released and rises to the surface where it condenses as water.

Hoodoos are *mushroom-shaped pedestals of rock, sculpted by wind and sand. These are found among the bare peaks of Muncho Lake Provincial Park, at the northern end of the Canadian Rockies.*

From the Icefields Parkway *(Hwy 93), a scenic route that runs from Lake Louise in Banff National Park to Jasper, it is possible to view the saw-toothed appearance of the youngest peaks in the range. These were formed during the last episode of uplift, about 20 to 15 million years ago. Older ranges such as the Appalachians* (see p19) *have rounded tops formed by long-term erosion.*

***Maligne Canyon** is a 50-m deep (164-ft), limestone gorge in Jasper National Park. The canyon was formed by the melt-waters of a glacier that once covered the valley. Today, the Maligne River rushes through this narrow channel, which also drains a series of underground caves.*

***The Lewis Overthrust** in Waterton Lakes National Park is a geological phenomenon. When rocks were moving east during the formation of the Rockies, a single mass composed of the lowest sedimentary layer of the Rockies – known as the Lewis Thrust – came to rest on top of the prairies.*

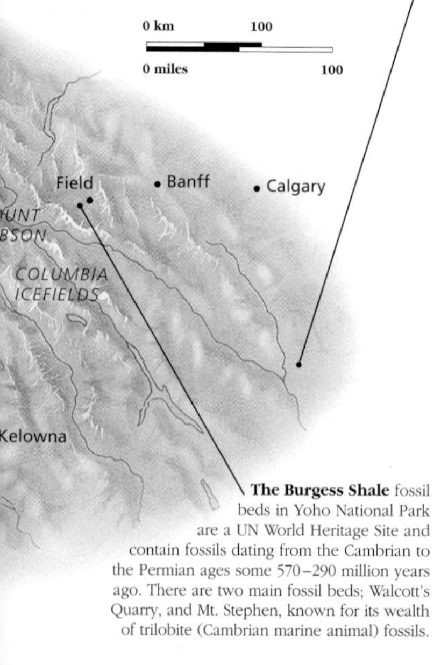

The Burgess Shale fossil beds in Yoho National Park are a UN World Heritage Site and contain fossils dating from the Cambrian to the Permian ages some 570–290 million years ago. There are two main fossil beds; Walcott's Quarry, and Mt. Stephen, known for its wealth of trilobite (Cambrian marine animal) fossils.

The Formation of the Rocky Mountains

There are three main forces responsible for the formation of the Rocky Mountains. First, large areas of the Earth's crust (known as tectonic plates), constantly moving together and apart, created uplift. Second, the North American plate was subducted by the Pacific plate, which caused a chain of volcanoes to form from the molten rock of the oceanic crust. Third, erosion caused by the Ice Ages, as well as rivers and wind, deposited sedimentary rocks on the North American plate, which was then folded by more plate movement between 50 and 25 million years ago. The Rockies' jagged peaks reflect their recent formation.

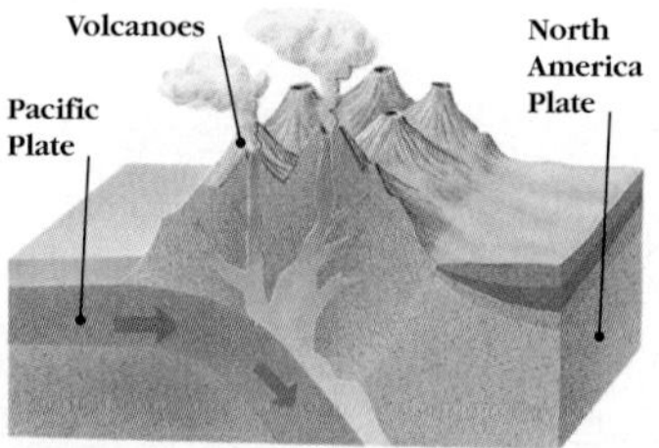

1 Some 150 million years ago, the Pacific plate moved east, adding to the molten rock from great depths of the North American Plate. This then rose up to form the Western Cordillera Mountains.

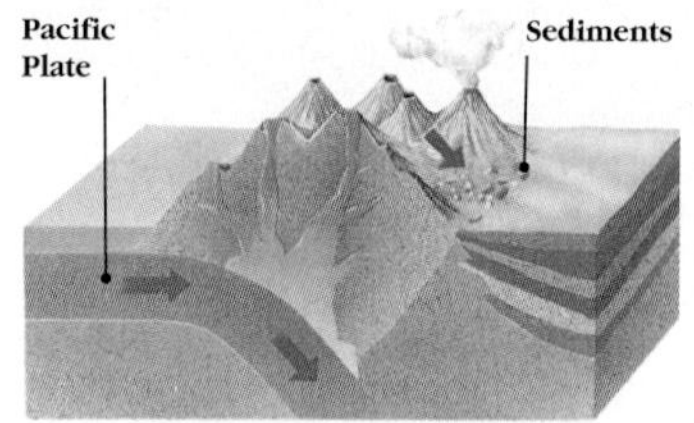

2 The Cordillera was eroded over millions of years and during various Ice Ages. This led to sediments being deposited in the sagging, wedge-shaped crust east of the mountain range.

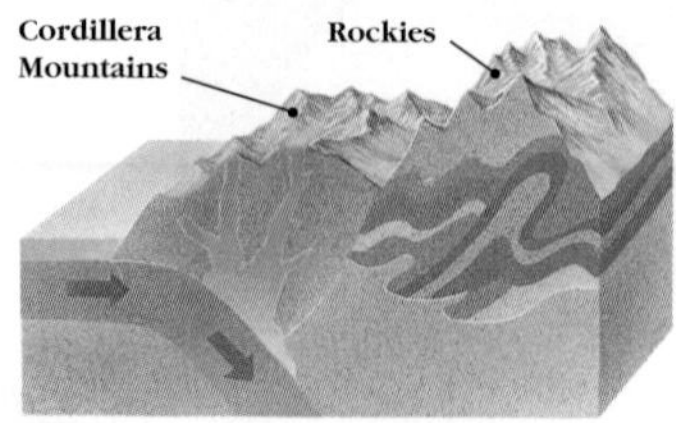

3 Around 50 million years ago, the Pacific plate continued to push east, forcing the Cordillera range eastward, compressing sedimentary rocks, folding and uplifting them to form the Rockies.

Forestry and Wildlife of Coastal British Columbia

FROM ITS SOUTHERN BORDER with the United States to the northern tip of the Queen Charlotte Islands, the coastal region of British Columbia ranks as the richest ecological region in Canada. The warm waters of the north Pacific Ocean moderate the climate, creating a temperate rainforest teeming with life such as the black tail deer, black bear, and cougar. Dense forest still covers many islands, bays, and inlets along the coast, and is home to a large number of plant and animal species, including some of the tallest trees in Canada. Douglas Fir and Sitka Spruce can grow as high as 91 m (300 ft).

***Trumpeter swans** are so-called for their distinctive brassy call. They are found on marshes, lakes, and rivers.*

TEMPERATE RAINFOREST HABITAT

High rainfall and a mild climate have created these lush forests of cedar, spruce, and pine, with their towering Douglas Firs and Sitka Spruces. Housed beneath the dripping forest canopy is a huge variety of ferns, mosses, and wild flowers, including orchids. Today, environmentalists campaign to protect these ancient forests from the threat of logging.

***Bald eagles**, with their distinctive white heads, can be seen in large numbers diving for fish in the ocean near the Queen Charlotte Islands. The area is noted for having the largest bald eagle population in BC.*

***The white black bear** is unique to coastal British Columbia. It is related to the common black bear, and is an agile salmon catcher.*

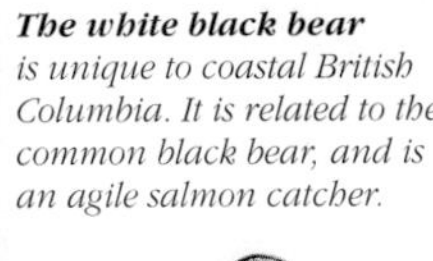

***Harlequin ducks** are small and shy, and the males have striking markings. A good swimmer, the harlequin enjoys fast-flowing rivers and the strong surf of the Pacific.*

***Black tail deer** are found only on the north Pacific coast. They are the smallest member of the mule deer family and are preyed on by cougars in the area.*

Salmon

The coastal waters of BC are home to five species of Pacific salmon: pink, coho, chinook, sockeye, and chum. Together they support one of the most important commercial food fisheries in the world. All Pacific salmon spawn in freshwater streams only once in their adult life, then die. Their offspring migrate downstream and out to sea where they feed and grow to adults ranging in size from 7 kg (15 lb) to over 45 kg (100 lb). At maturity they swim long distances upstream in order to return to the waters of their birth.

***Chinook Salmon** leaping while swimming upstream to spawn.*

***Sockeye Salmon** are highly prized in BC's fishing industry for their firm, tasty flesh.*

Coastline habitat

The warm waters of the north Pacific Ocean provide a habitat for more species of wildlife than any other temperate coastline. This distinctive region is characterized by having thousands of islands and inlets, which provide a home for a range of animals. Mammals such as gray, humpback, and orca whales can be seen here, as can sea otters, seals, and sea lions.

***Northern sea lions** live in colonies along the rocky BC coast. Large, lumbering animals, they have short "forearms" that enable them to move on land.*

***The glaucous gull** is a large, gray-backed sea gull, which nests along coastal cliffs, and on the numerous small islands here.*

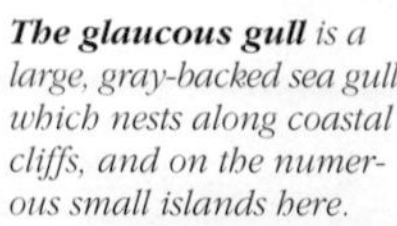

***Sea otters** were hunted, almost to extinction, for their thick fur coats. Today, these playful creatures are numerous off the coast of mainland BC and Vancouver Island.*

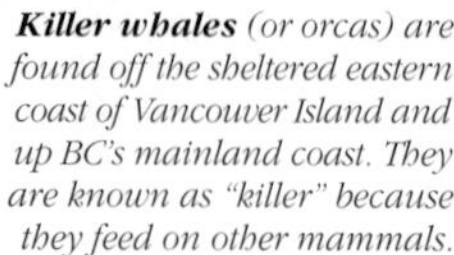

***Killer whales** (or orcas) are found off the sheltered eastern coast of Vancouver Island and up BC's mainland coast. They are known as "killer" because they feed on other mammals.*

The Alaska Highway

THE BUILDING of the Alaska Highway was an extraordinary achievement. Winding through 2,451 km (1,523 miles) of wilderness, mountains, muskeg (moss-covered bog), and forest, the first road was completed in 1942, only eight months and twelve days after construction began. Linking the United States to Alaska through British Columbia, it was built after the Japanese attacked Pearl Harbor in 1941, as a military supply route and to defend the northwest coast of Alaska.

Today, the original gravel road has been replaced by a two-lane, mostly asphalt highway. The highway's many curves are gradually being straightened, shortening its total length, and the present road now covers 2,394 km (1,488 miles).

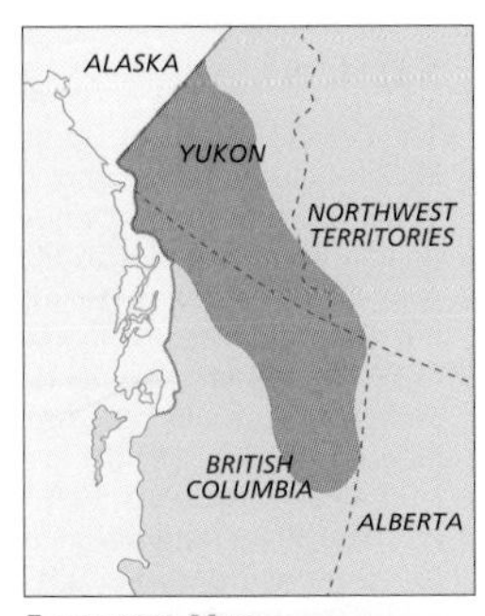

LOCATOR MAP

Map area

Kluane National Park *contains some of the most dramatic scenery to be seen along the highway. The Kluane Mountains are among the highest in Canada, and icefields cover around half of the park's area.*

Whitehorse *is the capital of the Yukon and the center of the province's forestry and mining industries. The town, at mile 910 of the highway, retains a frontier atmosphere, and it is still possible to hear coyotes at night.*

Historical Mile 836 marks the site of the Canol Project. This oil pipeline was built alongside the highway, to aid the military effort. The pipe runs an incredible 965 km (600 miles) to an oil refinery at Whitehorse.

Teslin Lake *derives its name from the Tlingit language, meaning "long and narrow waters." The highway follows the 130-km long (80-mile) stretch of water, lined by snow-capped peaks. Today, the area attracts anglers eager to catch the plentiful trout, grayling, and pike, and hunters looking for game.*

***The Alaska Highway in winter** is often covered in snow and affected by frost heave. Since it was opened to the public in 1949, teams of maintenance workers have ensured that the road is open year round.*

Construction of the Highway

The Alaska Highway was built in under nine months by US army engineers and Canadian construction workers. The recruiting poster for workers warned: "This is no picnic... Men will have to fight swamps, rivers, ice, and cold. Mosquitoes, flies, and gnats will not only be annoying but will cause bodily harm. If you are not prepared to work under these... conditions, DO NOT APPLY."

The workers shared mobile army camps that were moved along the route as construction progressed. If a company got stuck in one of many dismal swamps, they employed such techniques as laying corduroy – where whole trees were laid side by side, then spread with gravel. In some places en route as many as five layers were required.

Bogged-down truck waits for corduroy to be laid

Watson Lake

Fort Nelson

MUNCHO LAKE PROVINCIAL PARK

Kechika River

BRITISH COLUMBIA

KWADACHA WILDERNESS PROVINCIAL PARK

SPATSIZI PLATEAU WILDERNESS PROVINCIAL PARK

T. EDZIZA OVINCIAL PARK

Fort St. John

Dawson Creek

Peace River

4

37

97

The Peace River Valley section of the highway winds through fertile farmland, between Dawson Creek and Fort St. John. Before the Peace River suspension bridge was built in 1943, travelers crossed the river by ferry.

Historic Mile 588 or "Contact Creek" is the point where two teams of builders, from the north and south, met in 1942.

***The Sign Post Forest** at Watson Lake has over 10,000 signs. The first was erected in 1942 by a GI missing his hometown of Danville, Illinois.*

0 km 100

0 miles 100

Key

- Alaska Hwy
- Other roads
- National and Provincial Parks
- Provincial boundaries

VANCOUVER AND VANCOUVER ISLAND

LOOKING OUT TOWARD the waters of the straits of Johnstone and Georgia, Vancouver occupies one of the most beautiful settings of any world city. The coastal mountains form a majestic backdrop for the glass towers and copper-topped skyscrapers of the city. It was Captain James Cook who claimed the area for the British when he stepped ashore at Nootka Sound, Vancouver Island, in 1778. Until then the area had been inhabited for more than 10,000 years by the Coast Salish peoples, whose cultural heritage is celebrated in two of Canada's best museums: the UBC Museum of Anthropology in Vancouver and Victoria's Royal BC Museum. Established as a city after a fire destroyed the fledgling town of Granville in 1886, Vancouver offers historic districts, lush gardens, and wilderness parks within its environs. A short ferry ride away, Vancouver Island's world-famous Pacific Rim National Park is the whale-watching center of Canada.

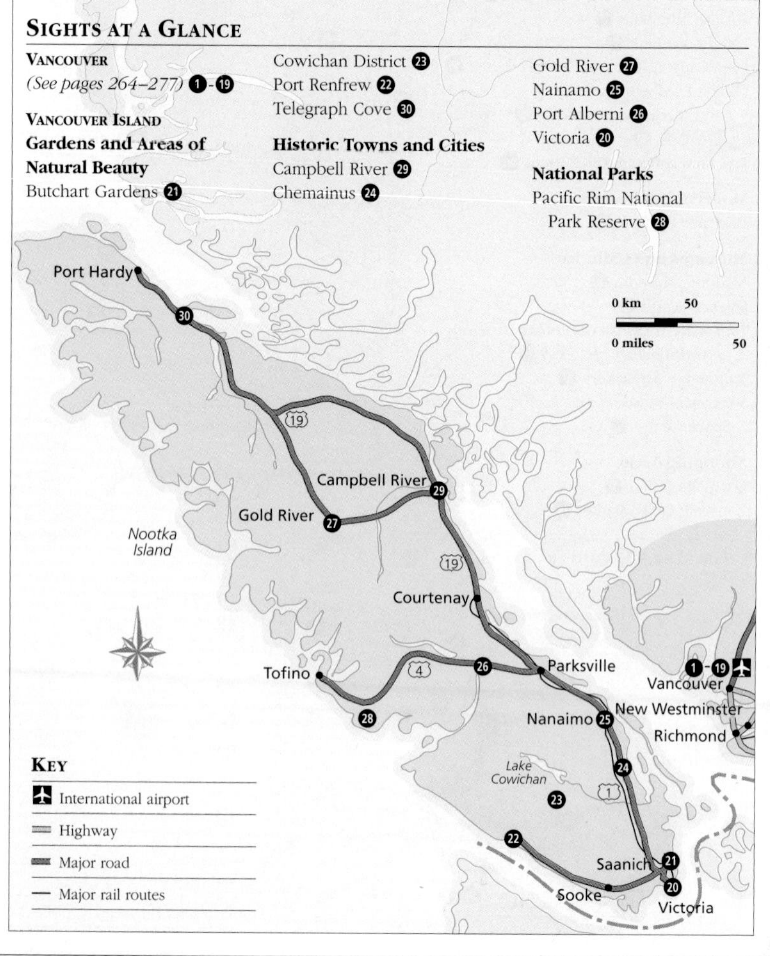

◁ Detail from Haida totem pole carved from cedar wood representing a double-headed snake

Exploring Vancouver

THE HEART OF VANCOUVER is its downtown area, a finger of land bounded by the waters of English Bay. The city center radiates from Robson Square. The 404.7-ha (1,000-acre) Stanley Park occupies the tip of the peninsula, next to the West End. The historic Chinatown and Gastown districts are close to Main Street, the city's south to north axis.

SIGHTS AT A GLANCE

Historic Streets and Buildings

Chinatown 2
Old Hastings Mill Store 12

Historic Sites

Capillano Suspension Bridge 18
Royal Hudson Steam Train 14

Parks and Gardens

Dr. Sun Yat-sen Chinese Garden 1
Grouse Mountain 17
Lighthouse Park 19
Lynn Canyon Park and Ecology Centre 16
Queen Elizabeth Park and Bloedel Conservatory 9
Stanley Park 13
Van Dusen Botanical Gardens 10

Modern Architecture

BC Place Stadium 4

Museums and Galleries

Maritime Museum 6
Science World 3
University of British Columbia Museum of Anthropology pp274–5 11
Vancouver Art Gallery 5
Vancouver Museum and Pacific Space Centre 7

Shopping Areas

Granville Island 8
Lonsdale Quay Market 15

KEY

Waterfront and Gastown: *see pp266–7*
International airport
SkyTrain station
Bus station
SeaBus station
Railroad station
Visitor information
Parking
Highway
Major road
Pedestrian walkway

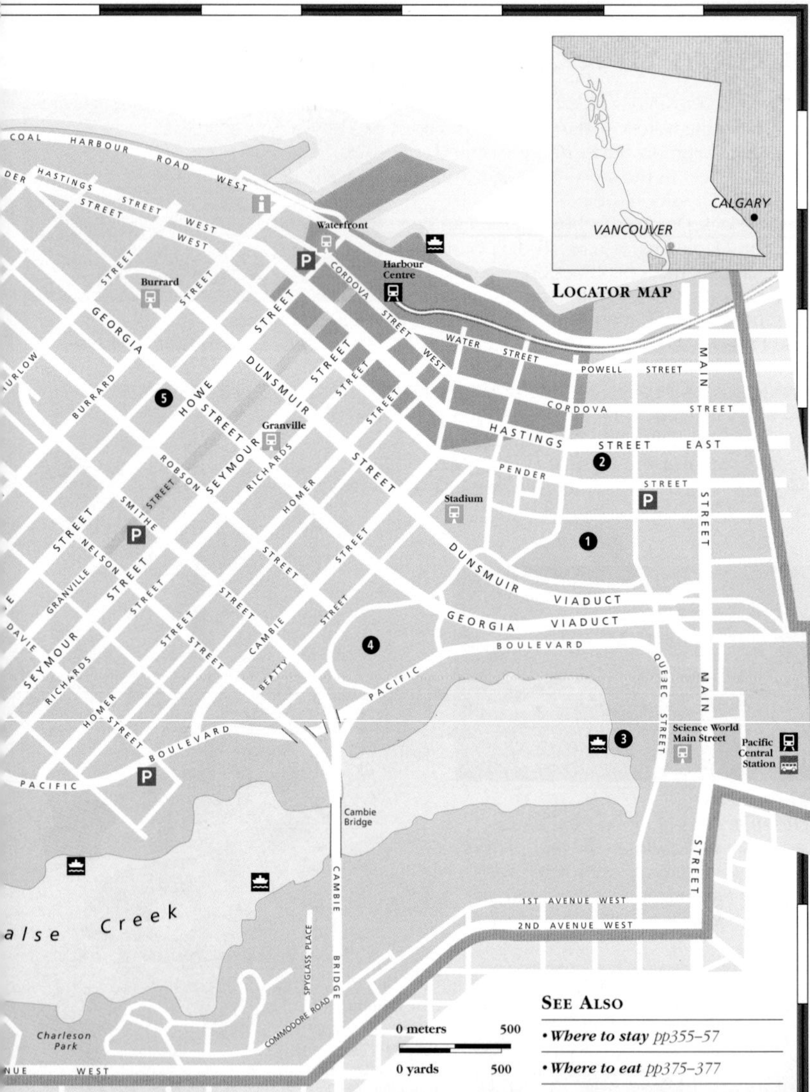

See Also

- ***Where to stay*** *pp355–57*
- ***Where to eat*** *pp375–377*

Getting Around

As most of downtown is surrounded by water, Vancouver's comprehensive transportation system includes the SeaBus, bus, and the light-rail line, the SkyTrain, a driverless system that runs above and below ground. The SeaBus runs between Lonsdale Quay in North Vancouver and Waterfront Station downtown, where it is possible to connect with the bus and SkyTrain system. Many Vancouverites commute by car, and rush hour traffic is to be avoided because access to downtown is limited to a few bridges, including the hectic Lion's Gate Bridge.

Vancouver's stunning harbor with mountains as a backdrop

Street-by-Street: Waterfront and Gastown

One of Vancouver's oldest areas, Gastown faces the waters of Burrard Inlet and lies between Columbia Street in the east and Burrard Street in the west. The district grew up around a saloon, opened in 1867 by "gassy" Jack Deighton whose statue can be seen on Maple Tree Square. Today, Gastown is a charming mix of cobblestone streets, restored 19th-century public buildings, and storefronts. Chic boutiques and galleries line Powell, Carrall, and Cordova streets. Delightful restaurants and cafés fill the mews, courtyards, and passages. One popular café occupies the site of the city's first jail. On the corner of Water and Cambie streets, visitors can hear the musical chimes of the steam clock every 15 minutes, as well as be entertained by local street performers.

★ Canada Place
Canada Place is a waterside architectural marvel of white sails and glass that houses a hotel, two convention centers, and a cruise ship terminal.

The SeaBus
Stunning views of the harbor can be seen from the SeaBus, a catamaran that ferries passengers across Burrard Inlet between the central Waterfront Station and Lonsdale Quay in North Vancouver.

The Waterfront Station occupies the imposing 19th-century Canadian Pacific Railroad building.

HOWE STREET

SEYMOUR STREET

★ Harbour Centre Tower
The Harbour Centre is a modern high-rise building best-known for its tower. Rising 167 m (550 ft) above the city, on a clear day it is possible to see as far as Victoria on Vancouver Island.

Star Sights

★ Canada Place

★ Harbour Centre Tower

Water Street
Much of the quaint charm of Gastown can be seen here. Water Street boasts gas lamps and cobblestones, as well as shops, cafés, and the famous steam clock.

Locator Map
See map pp264–5

Steam Clock
Said to be the world's first steam operated clock, it was made in the 1870s, and toots every 15 minutes on the corner of Water and Cambie streets.

"Gassy" Jack Statue
Gastown is named after "Gassy" Jack Deighton, an English sailor noted both for his endless chatter and for the saloon he opened here for the local sawmill workers in 1867.

The Inuit Gallery on Water Street offers a variety of original Inuit art such as jewelry and paintings.

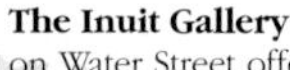

Shopping on Powell Street is a delightful experience with its range of small galleries and trendy boutiques.

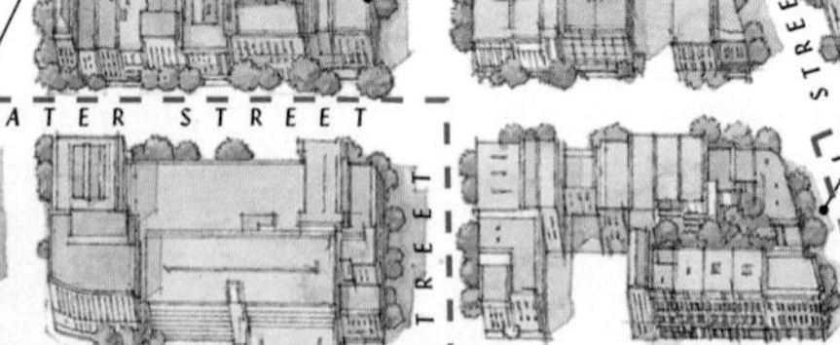

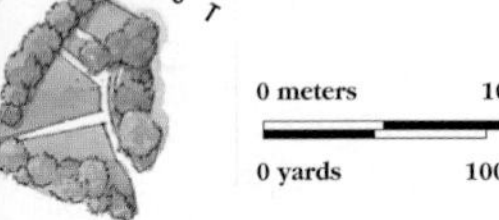

Triangular Building
Reminiscent of New York's Flatiron Building, this striking structure was built in 1908–9 as a hotel and forms the corner of Alexander and Powell streets. It is now an apartment building.

Key

– – – Suggested route

Peaceful pavilion in the Dr. Sun Yat-sen Classical Chinese Garden

Dr. Sun Yat-sen Classical Chinese Garden ❶

578 Carrall St. *(604) 662 3207. Central Station. Central Station. 19, 22. Downtown terminal. Jun–Sep: 9:30am–7pm; Oct–May: 10am–4pm. Dec 25.*

BUILT FOR EXPO '86, this re-creation of an 800-year-old Ming Dynasty garden offers a refuge from Vancouver's bustling city center. The garden owes its tranquillity to ancient Taoist principles, which aimed to create a healthy balance between the contrasting forces of man and nature.

Over 50 skilled craftsmen came from Suzhou, China's Garden City, to construct the garden, using only traditional techniques and tools. Pavilions and covered walkways were all built with materials from China, which included hand-fired roof tiles and the pebbles in the courtyard. Many of the plants and trees symbolize different human virtues. Willow is a symbol of feminine grace, and the plum and bamboo represent masculine strength.

Chinatown ❷

Pender St. *East Hastings & East Pender Sts routes.*

VANCOUVER'S CHINATOWN is older than the city itself. In 1858 the first wave of Chinese immigrants was drawn to Canada by the promise of gold. The Canadian Pacific Railroad attracted even more Chinese workers in the 1880s with jobs to build the new railroad. Today Chinatown stretches from Carrall to Gore Streets and still provides a warm welcome for more recent Asian immigrants.

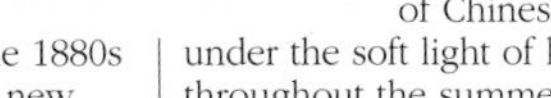

Bilingual sign in Chinatown

Declared an historic area in 1970, Chinatown has restored many of its notable houses with their elaborately decorated roofs and covered balconies. The main drag, Pender Street, is the best place to view the architectural details that decorate the upperstories of the buildings, such as highly painted wooden balconies. Street signs with colorful Chinese characters add to the authentic atmosphere.

Whether buying mouth-watering duck, or watching the spicy dumplings known as won tons being made at top speed, or settling down to taste the myriad dishes available in an array of fine restaurants, the main attraction for the visitor is food. There is also a fascinating range of stores, from bakeries selling a selection of savory and sweet buns to traditional herbalists, and jewelers specializing in jade. In contrast to the bustling markets there are also several relaxing tea-rooms, as well as the nearby Dr. Sun Yat-sen Chinese Garden, which also offers tea and cakes and has weekly evening concerts of Chinese music under the soft light of lanterns throughout the summer.

Science World ❸

1455 Quebec St. *(604) 443 7443. Central Station. Central Station. 10am–5pm Mon–Fri, 10am–6pm Sat & Sun. Dec 25.*

OVERLOOKING the waters of False Creek, near the Main Street Railway Station, stands the 47-m (155-ft) high steel geodesic dome that now houses Vancouver's science

The striking geodesic dome housing Vancouver's interactive Science World

museum, Science World. The dome was designed for Expo '86 by American inventor R. Buckminster Fuller, and is now one of the city's striking landmarks. The highly interactive science museum moved into the structure in 1989.

A range of hands-on exhibits includes activities such as blowing square bubbles, wandering through the insides of a camera, and playing with magnetic liquids, all of which make this a popular day out for children. In the Sara Stern Search Gallery visitors can touch and feel fur, bones, and animal skins while the Shadow Room encourages visitors to chase their own shadows. There is also a wide spectrum of different laser presentations offered.

The museum is renowned for its Omnimax cinema, located at the top of the dome, where a huge screen shows films of flights through such epic landscapes as Mount Everest and the Grand Canyon.

BC Place Stadium ❹

777 Pacific Blvd. S. *(604) 661 7373. Stadium. varies, depending on scheduled events. May–Oct: Tue–Fri.*

STANDING OUT from the Vancouver skyline, the white-domed roof of the BC Place Stadium has often been described as a giant mushroom. When it opened in 1983, it was the first covered stadium in Canada and the largest air-supported dome in the world. Noted for its versatility, the stadium is able to convert in a matter of hours from a football field seating 60,000 people to a more intimate concert bowl seating up to 30,000.

Among the famous guests who have visited the dome are Queen Elizabeth II and Pope John Paul II. Visitors hoping to catch a glimpse of a celebrity or two can take behind-the-scenes tours to the locker rooms, playing fields, and media lounges. The stadium also houses the **BC Sports Hall of Fame and Museum**, which chronicles the history of the region's sporting heroes.

The large white dome of BC Place Stadium

BC Sports Hall of Fame and Museum

BC Place Stadium. *(604) 687 5520. 10am–5pm daily.*

Vancouver Art Gallery ❺

750 Hornby St. *(604) 662 4719. Central Station. Central Station. 3. daily.*

WHAT WAS ONCE British Columbia's imposing provincial courthouse now houses the Vancouver Art Gallery. The building was designed in 1906 by Francis Rattenbury, an architect known for the Gothic style of Victoria's Parliament building and the Empress Hotel *(see p278)*. The interior was modernized in 1983 by Arthur Erikson, another noted architect, who designed the UBC Museum of Anthropology *(see pp274–5)*.

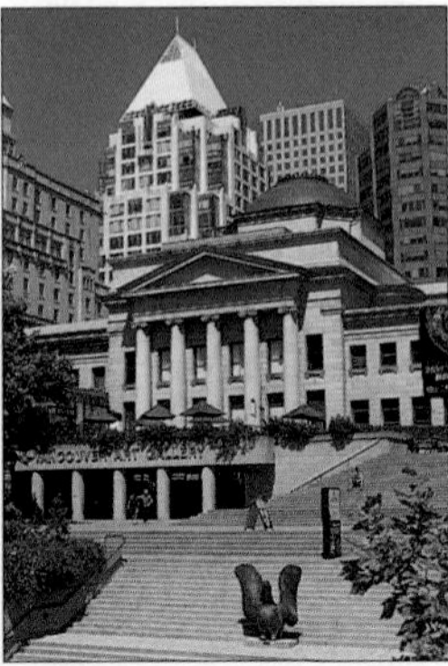

Decorative Victorian features on the Vancouver Art Gallery façade

Among an impressive assortment of historical and modern Canadian art, including works by the Group of Seven *(see pp160–61)*, the gallery also houses the world's largest collection of paintings by one of Canada's best-loved artists, Emily Carr. Carr was born in Victoria in 1871, and studied the local native cultures, capturing their way of life and the scenery of the western coastline in her sketchbook. She often depicted Haida artifacts such as totem poles in her pictures. Her palette is dominated by the blues, greens, and grays of the stormy west coast.

Maritime Museum ❻

1905 Ogden Ave. *(604) 257 8300. Central Station. Central Station. late May–Aug: daily; Sep–mid-May: Tue–Sun. 25 Dec.*

CELEBRATING Vancouver's history as a port and trading center, the Maritime Museum's star feature is the schooner, *St. Roch*, which is on permanent display. Built as a supply ship for the Mounties in 1928, in 1940–42 *St. Roch* was the first ship to navigate the Northwest Passage in both directions.

Other displays include *Man the Oars*, and *Map the Coast*, which tells the story of British Captain George Vancouver and the crews of the *Chatham* and the *Discovery* who charted the inlets of the coast of British Columbia in 1792. The Children's Maritime Discovery Centre has a powerful telescope through which the city's busy port can be viewed.

Vancouver's skyline reflected in the waters of Johnson Strait, backed by the Coastal Mountains ▷

Steel sculpture in front of the Vancouver Museum's distinctive façade

Vancouver Museum and Pacific Space Centre 7

1100 Chestnut St., Vanier Park. *(604) 736 4431. Central Station. Central Station. 22. 10am–5pm daily.*

LOCATED IN Vanier Park near the Maritime Museum *(see p269)*, the Vancouver Museum is a distinctive addition to the city's skyline. Built in 1967, the museum's curved, white, concrete roof has been compared to a flying saucer. Outside, a stunning modern sculpture, which looks like a giant steel crab, sits in a fountain on the museum's south side.

Permanent displays here include the Orientation Gallery which re-creates British Columbia's rocky coastline and mountainous interior. Vancouver's history is explored from the culture of the aboriginal people of the area to the city's pioneering days, celebrated in a series of delightful black-and-white photographs. The museum is particularly noted for its depiction of everyday life, with exhibits such as an 1880s Canadian Pacific Railroad car, 1930s clothes, and classic Vancouver street signs.

Part of the museum, the Pacific Space Centre is particularly popular with children. The Cosmic Courtyard is an interactive gallery that focuses on space exploration, including Canada's involvement in space research and astronomy. Here, visitors can launch a rocket or play at being an astronaut in the Virtual Voyages simulator.

Granville Island 8

1398 Cartwright St. *(604) 666 5784. Central Station. Central Station. 51. Market: 9am–6pm daily; other stores: 10am–6pm daily.*

TODAY, THIS once down trodden industrial district has a glorious array of stores, galleries, and artists' studios in its brightly painted warehouses and tin sheds. The fire of 1886 destroyed almost all of fledgling Vancouver and drove people south across the water to Granville Island and beyond. Many of the early buildings were constructed on land reclaimed in 1915 to cope with the burgeoning lumber and iron industries.

Granville Island Brewing Company sign

There are no chain stores on the island, and the smaller stores are known for their variety, originality, and quality, displaying a range of local arts and crafts such as rugs, jewelry, and textiles.

The island is also a center for the performing arts and boasts several music, dance, and theater companies.

A daily public market offers a cornucopia of foods that reflect Vancouver's ethnic diversity. Waterside cafés and restaurants occupy the False Creek Shore where there was once a string of sawmills.

Queen Elizabeth Park and Bloedel Conservatory 9

Cambie St. *Conservatory: (604) 257 8584. 15. Conservatory: May–Sep: 9am–8pm Mon–Fri; 10am–9pm Sat & Sun; Oct–Apr: 10am–5:30pm daily. for Conservatory.*

QUEEN ELIZABETH PARK is located on Little Mountain, Vancouver's highest hill (152-m/499-ft), and has fine views of the city. Despite being built on the site of two former stone quarries, the park's gardens are continually in bloom, beginning in early spring when multicolor tulips cover the hillsides.

The plastic-domed Bloedel Conservatory is perched on top of the hill, and grows plants from many climactic zones in the world, from rainforest plants and trees to desert cacti. There are also free-flying colorful tropical birds and fishponds filled with Japanese carp.

The plastic dome of the Bloedel Conservatory in Queen Elizabeth Park

A dazzling fall display of reds and oranges, one of many attractions in Stanley Park

Van Dusen Botanical Gardens ⑩

5251 Oak St. *(604) 257 8666.* *Central Station.* *Central Station.* *17.* *year round; call ahead for hours.*

SITUATED IN the center of Vancouver, this 22-ha (55-acre) garden was opened in 1975. In 1960 the land was under threat from its original owners, the Canadian Pacific Railroad, who wanted to build high-rise apartments there. It took a campaign by local people and a donation from Mr W.J. Van Dusen, a wealthy local businessman, to save the site for the gardens.

Today, visitors enjoy a spectacular year-round display of over 7,500 varieties of plants from six continents, set among lakes and marble sculptures. In spring there are narcissi, crocuses, and thousands of flowering rhododendrons. The Perennial Garden is filled with roses in summer, while September heralds the blazing reds and oranges of fall.

Marble statue in Botanical Gardens

University of British Columbia Museum of Anthropology ⑪

See pp274–5.

Old Hastings Mill Store ⑫

1575 Alma Rd. *(604) 734 1212.* *4th Ave. route.* *Jul & Aug: 11am–4pm Tue–Sun; Sep–Jun: 1–4pm Sat & Sun.* **Donation.**

THE OLD HASTINGS Mill Store was Vancouver's first general store and one of the few wooden buildings to survive the Great Fire of 1886. Built in 1865, it was moved by barge from its original site at Gastown in 1930 to the shores of Jericho Beach and then to its present home on Alma Street, at the corner of Point Grey Road. The building was intended to be used as a yacht club, but in the 1940s local people contributed a variety of historic artifacts, and today the house is an interesting small museum. Behind the pretty clapboard exterior, the museum's exhibits include a range of Victorian artifacts such as a horse-drawn cab, several antique sewing machines, and an extensive collection of native artifacts including an impressive range of hand-woven baskets.

The Old Hastings Mill Store, one of Vancouver's oldest buildings

Stanley Park ⑬

2099 Beach Ave. *(604) 257 8400.* *Central Station.* *Central Station.* *135, 123.* *Horseshoe Bay.* *daily.*

THIS IS A magnificent 404-ha (1,000-acre) park of tamed wilderness, just a few blocks from downtown, that was originally home to the Musqueam and Squamish native Canadians. Named after Lord Stanley, Governor General of Canada, the land was made a park by the local council in 1886. It offers visitors the opportunity to experience a range of typical Vancouver attractions. There are beaches, hiking trails, and fir and cedar woods as well as wonderful views of the harbor, English Bay, and the coastal mountains. Bicycles can be rented near the entrance to the park for the popular ride around the 10-km (6.5-mile) perimeter seawall. The park is also home to the **Vancouver Aquarium** where visitors can watch orca and beluga whales through the glass of enormous tanks.

Vancouver Aquarium
Stanley Park. *(604) 659 3474.* *Jun–Sep: 9:30am–8pm daily; Oct–Apr: 10am–5:30pm daily.*

University of British Columbia Museum of Anthropology ⓫

FOUNDED IN 1947, this outstanding museum houses one of the world's finest collections of Northwest coast native peoples' art. Designed by Canadian architect Arthur Erickson in 1976, the museum is housed in a stunning building overlooking mountains and sea. The tall posts and huge windows of the Great Hall were inspired by the post-and-beam architecture of Haida houses and are a fitting home for a display of full-size totem poles, canoes, and feast dishes. Through the windows of the Great Hall, the visitor can see the magnificent outdoor sculpture complex, which includes two houses designed by contemporary Haida artist Bill Reid.

★ The Great Hall
The imposing glass and concrete structure of the Great Hall is the perfect setting for totem poles, canoes, and sculptures.

Outdoor Haida Houses and Totem Poles

Set overlooking the water, these two Haida houses and collection of totem poles are faithful to the artistic tradition of the Haida and other tribes of the Pacific northwest, such as the Salish, Tsimshan, and Kwakiutl. Animals and mythic creatures representing various clans are carved in cedar on these poles and houses, made between 1959 and 1963 by Vancouver's favorite contemporary Haida artist Bill Reid and Namgis artist Doug Cranmer.

Carved red cedar totem poles

Climbing figures
These climbing figures are thought to have decorated the interior of First Nations family houses. Carved from cedar planks, the spare style is typical of Coast Salish sculpture.

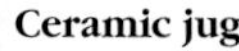

Ceramic jug
This beautifully decorated jug was made in Central Europe in 1674 by members of the Anabaptist religious sect. The foliage motifs are in contrast to the freely sketched animals that run around the base.

Star Exhibits

- ★ The Great Hall
- ★ The Raven and the First Men by Bill Reid

★ The Raven and the First Men *(1980)*
Carved in laminated yellow cedar by Bill Reid, this modern interpretation of a Haida creation myth depicts the raven, a wise and wily trickster, trying to coax mankind out into the world from a giant clamshell.

VISITORS' CHECKLIST

6393 NW Marine Drive. (604) 822 5087. 4 UBC, 10 UBC. Jun–Sep: 10am–5pm Wed–Mon, 10am–9pm Tue; Oct–May: 11am–5pm Wed–Sun, 11am–9pm Tue. Mon, Dec 25–26. www.moa.ubc.ca

GALLERY GUIDE
The Museum's collections are arranged on one level. The Ramp gallery leads to the Great Hall, which features the cultures of Northwest coast First Nations peoples. The Visible Storage gallery contains artifacts from other cultures, and a range of 15th- to 19th-century European ceramics is housed in the Koerner Ceramics gallery.

Wooden Frontlet
Decorated with abalone shell, this wooden frontlet was a ceremonial head-dress worn only on important occasions such as births and marriages.

Red cedar carved front doors
This detail comes from the set of stunning carved red cedar doors that guard the entrance to the museum. Created in 1976 by a group of First Nations artists from the 'Ksan cultural center near Hazelton, the doors show the history of the first people of the Skeena River region in British Columbia.

KEY

- The Ramp gallery
- The Great Hall
- The Rotunda
- Visible storage/Research collection
- Archeological gallery
- Koerner Ceramics gallery
- Temporary exhibition space
- Theatre gallery
- Nonexhibition space

The restored Royal Hudson Steam Train takes visitors to Squamish

Royal Hudson Steam Train ⓮

BC Rail Station, 1311 W. First St. *(604) 984 5246. mid-May–Sep: Wed–Sun. book in advance.*

ONE OF GREATER Vancouver's prime attractions, the Royal Hudson Steam Train was built in 1940 especially for use in British Columbia. A replica of the Royal Hudson that carried King George VI and Queen Elizabeth across Canada in 1939, the train was restored for summer trips to Squamish in 1974. The two-hour ride offers stunning views of the forests and rocky seascapes of British Columbia's coastline from a viewing car. The interior of the Parlor Class dining coach has authentic 1940s wooden and leather furnishings so passengers can dine in style. From Squamish, visitors can tour Shannon Falls or the West Coast Railway Heritage Museum nearby. An alternative to returning on the train is the M.V. *Britannia*, which offers a return cruise through Howe Sound.

Lonsdale Quay Market ⓯

123 Carrie Cates Ct. *(604) 985 6261. Central Station. Central Station. Waterfront. 9:30am–6:30pm Sat–Thu, 9:30–9pm Sun.*

OPENED IN 1986, this striking concrete-and-glass building forms part of the North Shore SeaBus terminal. The Lonsdale Quay Market has a floor devoted to food, with a market selling everything from fresh-baked bread to blueberries, as well as an array of cafés and restaurants serving every type of ethnic food. Specialty shops offering a wide choice of hand-crafted products such as jewelry, pottery, and textiles occupy the second floor. The complex includes a five-star hotel, a pub, and a nightclub.

There are music festivals here in the summer when visitors take advantage of the building's open walkways to take in the view of the port.

Lynn Canyon Park and Ecology Centre ⓰

3663 Lynn Canyon Park Rd. *(604) 981 3103. Central Station. Hastings. 228, 229. Horseshoe Bay. Apr–Sep: 10am–5pm daily; Oct–Mar: 10am–5pm Mon–Fri, noon–4pm Sat & Sun. Dec 25, 26; Jan 1.* ***Donation*** *limited.*

LOCATED BETWEEN Mount Seymour and Grouse Mountain, Lynn Canyon Park is noted for its forests. This is a popular spot for hiking and there are several marked trails, some of which are steep and rugged and take the visitor past waterfalls and cliffs. However, many of the trails are gentle strolls through Douglas fir, western hemlock, and western red cedar. If you venture far enough into the forest it is possible to see black bears, cougars, and blacktail deer, but most visitors keep to the main trails where they are more likely to see squirrels, jays, and woodpeckers. There are wonderful views from the 70-m (230-ft) high suspension bridge that crosses the canyon.

The nearby Ecology Centre offers guided walks, shows natural history films, and features interesting displays on the ecology of the area.

Magnificent forests of Douglas fir and red cedar in Lynn Canyon Park

Grouse Mountain ⓱

6400 Nancy Greene Way. *(604) 984 0661. Lonsdale Quay. 236. 9am–10pm daily.*

FROM THE SUMMIT of Grouse Mountain visitors experience the grandeur of British Columbia's dramatic landscape and stunning views of Vancouver. On a clear day it is possible to see as far as Vancouver Island in the west, the Coastal Mountains to the north and toward the Columbia Mountains in the east.

Although there is a tough 3-km (2-mile) trail that goes to the top of the 1,211-m (3,973-ft) mountain, it is easier to take the Skyride cable-car. At the summit there are all the amenities of a ski resort, including ski schools, a dozen ski runs, equipment rental, and snowboarding as well as restaurants with great views. At night the mountain is brightly illuminated and is popular with locals taking evening skiing lessons.

There are other hiking trails from the mountain top, but they can be demanding. In both summer and winter the resort offers a multitude of activities including mountain bike tours, guided tours for sightings of wildlife, and

Panoramic view of Vancouver's skyline from Grouse Mountain

hang-gliding competitions, not to mention logger sports such as chain-saw sculpture shows. A cinema shows films on the history of Vancouver.

Capilano Suspension Bridge ⑱

3735 Capilano Rd, North Vancouver. *(604) 985 7474.* *Central Station.* *Highlands 246.* *daily (call ahead as hours vary according to season).* *Dec 25.* *May–Oct.* *limited.*

THE CAPILANO Suspension Bridge has been a popular tourist attraction since it was built in 1889. Pioneering Scotsman George Grant Mackay, drawn by the wild beauty of the place, had already built a small cabin overlooking the Capilano Canyon. Access to the river below was almost impossible from the cabin and it is said that Mackay built the bridge so that his son, who loved fishing, could easily reach the Capilano River.

The present bridge, the fourth to be constructed here, is 70 m (230 ft) above the Canyon, and attracts thousands of visitors every year. Nature lovers are drawn by the views and the chance to wander through old-growth woods (old trees that have never been felled) past trout ponds and a 61-m (200-ft) waterfall. Visitors are told the history of the area by guides. The original 1911 tea house is now a gift shop.

Lighthouse Park ⑲

Off Beacon Lane, West Vancouver. *(604) 925 7200.* *Central Station.* *Central Station.* *Horseshoe Bay.* *daily.*

NAMED AFTER the hexagonal lighthouse built at the mouth of Burrard Inlet in 1910 to guide ships through the foggy channel, Lighthouse Park is an unspoiled area with 75 ha (185 acres) of old growth forest and wild, rocky coast. The trees here have never been logged and some of the majestic Douglas firs are over 500 years old.

There is a variety of hiking trails in the park, some leading to the viewpoint near the 18-m (60-ft) Point Atkinson Lighthouse. Here one can see stunning vistas across the Strait of Georgia all the way to Vancouver Island. A typical two-hour hike covers about 5 km (3 miles) of old-growth forests, taking the visitor through the fairly rugged terrain of moss-covered gulleys and steep rocky outcrops where there are good vantage points for watching seabirds wheeling above the sea. Closer to the shoreline, it is possible to sunbathe on smooth rocks.

Lighthouse Park's Point Atkinson Lighthouse

The Capilano Suspension Bridge crossing the dramatic and tree-covered Capilano Canyon

Victoria ⓴

A QUIET, ATTRACTIVE CITY, Victoria's reputation for having an old-fashioned, seaside-town atmosphere is enhanced in the summer by the abundance of flowers in hanging baskets and window boxes that decorate every lampost, balcony, and storefront. Established as a Hudson's Bay Company fur-trading post in 1843 by James Douglas, Victoria had its risqué moments during its gold rush years (1858–63), when thousands of prospectors drank in 60 or more saloons on Market Square. Victoria was established as the provincial capital of British Columbia in 1871 but was soon outgrown by Vancouver, now BC's largest city. Today, Victoria is still the province's political center as well as one of its most popular attractions for visitors.

Fishing boats and pleasure craft moored in Victoria's Inner Harbour

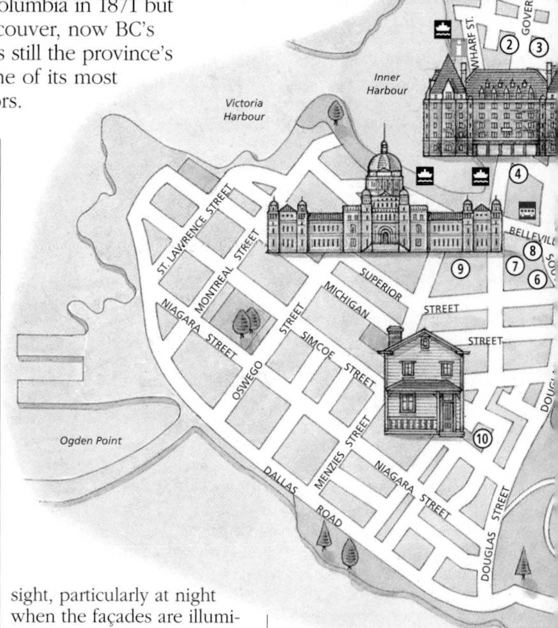

Exploring Victoria

A stroll along Victoria's Inner Harbour takes in many of the city's main attractions, such as the excellent Royal British Columbia Museum with its dramatic depictions of the geology and native cultures of the region. Dominating the area are two late 19th-century buildings: the Empress Hotel and the Parliament Buildings, which were designed by noted architect, and Victoria's adopted son, Francis Rattenbury. Between Fort Street and View Street is the four-story shopping mall, the Eaton Centre. Bastion Square, with its restaurants and boutiques, lies to the west of Market Square and its restored 1850s buildings.

Parliament Buildings

501 Belleville St. *(250) 387 3046.* *8:30am–5pm daily.* *Dec 25, Jan 1.*

Looking out toward the water at Inner Harbour, Victoria's many-domed Parliament Buildings are an impressive sight, particularly at night when the façades are illuminated by thousands of lights. Designed by Francis Rattenbury in 1892, the buildings were completed in 1897. Rattenbury, a 25-year-old British architect who had arrived in British Columbia only the year before, won a

The Parliament Buildings illuminate the waters of Inner Harbour

Sights at a Glance

Art Gallery of Greater Victoria ⑫
Bastion Square ②
Beacon Hill Park ⑪
Carr House ⑩
Craigdarroch Castle ⑬
Empress Hotel ④
Crystal Gardens ⑤
Eaton Centre ③
Government House ⑭
Helmcken House ⑥
Market Square ①
Parliament Building ⑨
Royal BC Museum ⑦
See pp282–3
Thunderbird Park ⑧

national competition to design the new Parliament Buildings. He went on to design several of the province's structures including the nearby Empress Hotel and the Crystal Garden.

British Columbia's history is depicted throughout the buildings. A statue of explorer Captain George Vancouver is perched on top of the main dome. Inside, large murals show scenes from the past.

Empress Hotel

721 Government St. (250) 384 8111. daily.

Completed in 1905 to a Francis Rattenbury design, the Empress is one of Victoria's best-loved sights. Close to the Parliament Buildings, the Empress Hotel overlooks Inner Harbour and dominates the skyline with its ivy-covered Gothic splendor. Visitors are welcome to sample the luxurious decor of the hotel's public bars and lounges, such as the Crystal Dining Room with its antique furniture and lovely Tiffany-glass dome.

Bastion Square

Government St. (250) 995 2440. daily.

This beautifully restored square faces Victoria's picturesque harbor and contains some of the city's oldest 19th-century buildings. What were once luxury hotels and offices, built during the boom era of the late 1800s, now house boutiques and gift shops. Restoration began in 1963 when it was discovered that the Hudson's Bay Company's fur-trading post Fort Victoria, established in 1843, once stood on this site. Today, this pedestrian square includes the MacDonald Block building, built in 1863 in Italianate style, with elegant cast-iron columns and arched windows. The old courthouse, built in 1889, houses the BC Maritime Museum. In summer, both visitors and workers lunch in the courtyard cafés.

Visitors' Checklist

71,500. Victoria Airport. 25 km (15 miles) N of city. Via Station, 450 Pandora Avenue. Pacific Coach Lines, 1150 Terminal Avenue. BC ferries. 812 Wharf Street. (250) 953 2033. Jazz Fest Inter-national, (Jun); Victoria Shakespeare Festival, (Jul & Aug); First People's Festival, Royal BC Museum (Aug).

Bastion Square is a popular lunch spot for locals and visitors

Market Square

560 Johnson St. (250) 386 2441. 10am–5pm daily. Dec 25, Jan 1. limited.

Two blocks north of Bastion Square on the corner of Johnson Street, Market Square has some of the finest Victorian saloon, hotel, and store façades in Victoria. Most of the buildings were built in the 1880s and 1890s, during the boom period of the Klondike Gold Rush. After decades of neglect, the area received a much-needed face-lift in 1975. Today, the square is a shoppers' paradise, with a variety of stores selling everything from books and jewelry to musical instruments and other arts and crafts.

0 meters 500

0 yards 500

Key

- Train station
- Bus station
- Parking
- Ferry
- Visitor Information

One of the giant totem poles on display at Thunderbird Park

Thunderbird Park

cnr Belleville & Douglas Streets.

This compact park lies at the entrance to the Royal British Columbia Museum *(see pp282–3)* and is home to an imposing collection of plain and painted giant totem poles. During the summer months it is possible to watch native artists in the Thunderbird Park Carving Studio producing these handsome carved totems. The poles show and preserve the legends of many different tribes from the aboriginal peoples of the Northwest Coast.

Helmcken House

10 Elliot St. Square. *(250) 361 0021.* *May–Oct: 10am–5pm daily; Nov–Apr: noon–4pm Thu–Mon.*

Located in Elliot Square in the Inner Harbour area, the home of Hudson's Bay Company employee Dr. John Sebastian Helmcken was built in 1852 and is thought to be British Columbia's oldest house. The young doctor built his house with Douglas fir trees felled in the surrounding forest. This simple but elegantly designed clapboard dwelling contains many of the original furnishings including the piano, which visitors are permitted to play. Other exhibits include a collection of antique dolls and the family's personal belongings such as clothes, shoes, and toiletries.

Crystal Garden

713 Douglas St.

(250) 381 1213. *daily.*

Built in 1925 to house Canada's largest salt-water swimming pool, the Crystal Garden was inspired by London's Crystal Palace and was designed by the architect Francis Rattenbury. The swimming pool has now been replaced by lush tropical gardens whose junglelike foliage provides a refuge for some 65 different species of rare monkey and tropical bird. There are also hosts of colorful free-flying butterflies to see while taking tea in the conservatory.

Parrot in the Crystal Gardens

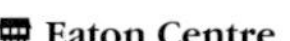

Eaton Centre

Government St. *(250) 389 2228.* *9:30am–6pm Mon, Tue & Sat; 9:30am–9pm Wed–Fri; 11am–5pm Sun.*

The Eaton Centre is a shopping mall within walking distance of the Inner Harbour and was built behind the façades of several historic buildings on Government Street. The Driard Hotel, designed in 1892 by John Wright, was saved from demolition by a public campaign, as were the fronts of the 1910 Times Building and the fine, 19th-century Lettice and Sears Building. Behind these elegant façades, there are three floors of stores selling everything from fashion and gifts to handmade chocolates and gourmet food.

Carr House

207 Government St. *(250) 383 5843.* *mid-May–mid-Oct: 10am–5pm daily.*

Emily Carr, one of Canada's best-known artists *(see pp28–29)*, was born in 1871 in this charming, yellow clapboard house. It was built in 1864 by prominent architects Wright and Saunders, under instruction from Emily's father, Richard Carr. Located just a few minutes walk from Inner Harbour, at 207 Government Street, both the house and its English-style garden are open to visitors. All the rooms are appropriately furnished in late 19th-century period style, with some original family pieces. Visitors can see the dining room where Emily taught her first art classes to local children. Emily's drawing of her father still sits upon the mantel in the sitting room where, as an eight-year-old, she made her first sketches.

The Carr House where renowned painter Emily Carr was born

Beacon Hill Park

Douglas St. (250) 361 0600.
daily.

In the late 19th century this delightful park was used for stabling horses, but in 1888 John Blair, a Scottish landscape gardener, redesigned the park to include two lakes and initiated extensive tree planting. Once a favorite haunt of artist Emily Carr, this peaceful 74.5-ha (184-acre) park is now renowned for its lofty old trees (including the rare Garry oaks, some of which are over 400 years old), picturesque duck ponds, and a 100-year-old cricket pitch.

Art Gallery of Greater Victoria

1040 Moss St. (250) 384 4101.
10am–5pm Mon–Wed, Fri, & Sat, 10am–9pm Thu, 1–5pm Sun.

This popular gallery's eclectic collection is housed in an impressive Victorian mansion on Moss Street, east of the downtown area, and a few blocks west of Craigdorrach Castle. Inside, fine wood moldings, original fireplaces, and tall ceilings provide a home for an array of exhibits, including a wide-ranging collection of Chinese and Japanese painting, ceramics, and pottery. The gallery also has the only authentic Shinto (a Japanese religion worshiping ancestor spirits) shrine in North America. The collection of contemporary Canadian painting includes the work of famous local artist Emily Carr. Executed between the 1900s and 1930s, Carr's paintings are among the most popular exhibits, with their haunting evocation of the stormy northwest and the lives of native peoples.

Shinto shrine detail at the Art Gallery

Craigdarroch Castle

1050 Joan Cres. (250) 592 5323.
Jun–Sep: 9am–7pm daily; Oct–May: 10am–4:30pm daily.
Dec 25, 26, Jan 1.

Completed in 1889, Craigdarroch Castle was the pet project of respected local coal millionaire, Robert Dunsmuir. Although not a real castle, the design of this large house was based on that of his ancestral home in Scotland and mixes several architectural styles such as Roman and French Gothic.

When the castle was threatened with demolition in 1959, a group of local citizens formed a society that successfully battled for its restoration. Today, the restored interior of the house is a museum that offers an insight into the lifestyle of a wealthy Canadian entrepreneur.

The castle is noted for having one of the finest collections of Art Nouveau lead-glass windows in North America, and many of the rooms and hallways retain their patterned wood parquet floors and carved paneling in white oak, cedar, and mahogany. Every room is filled with opulent Victorian furnishings from the late 19th century and decorated in original colors such as deep greens, pinks, and rusts. Several layers of the paint have been painstakingly removed from the drawing room ceiling to reveal the original hand-painted, stencilled decorations beneath, including wonderfully detailed butterflies and lions.

A tower at Craigdarroch Castle in the French Gothic style of a château

Government House

1401 Rockland Ave. (250) 387 2080. *daily (gardens only).*

The present Government House building was completed in 1959 after fire destroyed the 1903 building, which was designed by renowned architect Francis Rattenbury.

As the official residence of the Lieutenant-Governor of British Columbia, the Queen's representative to the province, the house is not open to the public, but visitors can view 5.6 ha (14 acres) of stunning public gardens with beautiful lawns, ponds, an English country garden, and a Victorian rose garden. Marvelous views of the grounds are available from Pearke's Peak, a mount formed from the rocky outcrops that surround the property and which contain rock gardens.

The 1959 Government House, built with blue and pink granite

The Royal British Columbia Museum

THE ROYAL BRITISH COLUMBIA MUSEUM tells the story of this region through its natural history, geology, and peoples. The museum is regarded as one of the best in Canada for the striking way it presents its exhibits. A series of imaginative dioramas re-create the sights, sounds, and even smells of areas such as the Pacific seashore, the ocean, and the rainforest, all of which occupy the second floor Natural History Gallery.

Every aspect of the region's history is presented on the third floor, including a reconstruction of an early 20th-century town. Visitors can experience the street life of the time in a saloon and a cinema showing silent films. The superb collection of native art and culture includes a ceremonial Big House.

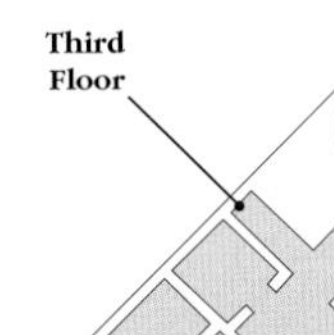

Third Floor

19th-century Chinatown
As part of an 1875 street scene, this Chinese herbalist's store displays a variety of herbs used in traditional Chinese medicine.

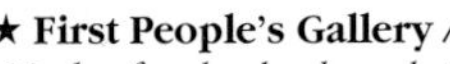

★ First People's Gallery
Made of cedar bark and spruce root in around 1897, this hat bears the mountain goat crest of the raven clan.

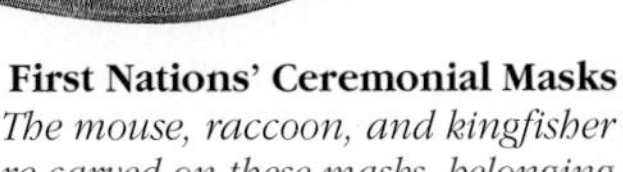

First Nations' Ceremonial Masks
The mouse, raccoon, and kingfisher are carved on these masks, belonging to the Mungo family who wore them to dance on ceremonial occasions.

KEY TO FLOORPLAN

- First People's gallery
- Modern History gallery
- Feature exhibits
- Natural History gallery
- Museum theater
- National Geographic IMAX theater
- Nonexhibition space

Exterior of the museum
The museum's main exhibits building was opened in 1968 after years of having to occupy several sites in and around the Legislative Buildings. The museum also houses an archives building, and a Heritage Court.

Modern History Gallery
A variety of streets, stores and public buildings, from the 1700s to 1990s, are re-created in this gallery. Here, the Grand Hotel occupies an authentic wooden sidewalk.

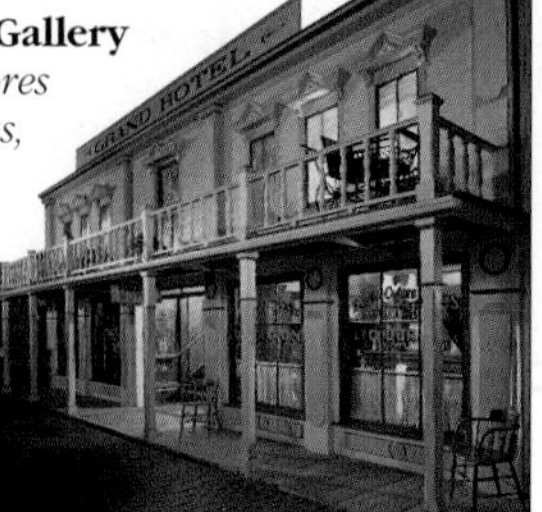

VISITORS' CHECKLIST

675 Belleville St. *(250) 387 3701.* *5, 28, 30.* *9am–5pm daily.* *Dec 25, Jan 1.* *www.royalbcmuseum.bc.ca*

★ Natural History Gallery
A full-size prehistoric tusked mammoth guards the entrance to the Natural History gallery which includes several lifelike dioramas that re-create British Columbia's coastal forests and ocean life since the last Ice Age.

★ Pacific Seashore Diorama
This diorama uses sound, film, lighting, and realistic animals such as this northern sea lion.

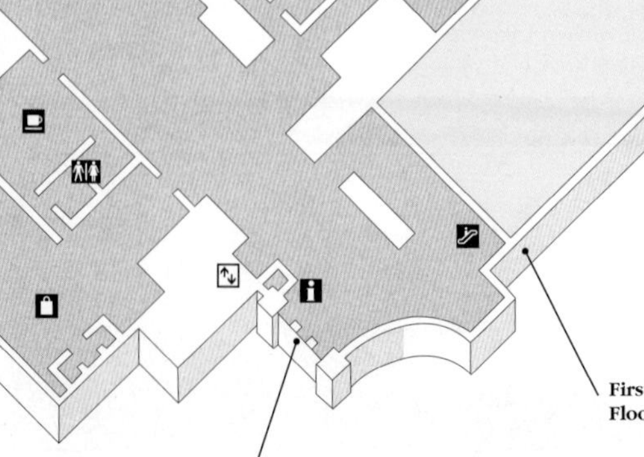

GALLERY GUIDE
The main exhibits of the museum are housed on the second and third floors. The Natural History gallery, on the second floor, reconstructs a range of environments from the Open Ocean to the Boreal Forest displays. The third floor has the First People's and Modern History galleries.

STAR EXHIBITS

- ★ Pacific Seashore Diorama
- ★ Natural History Gallery
- ★ First People's Gallery

The lily pond in the formal Italian garden at Butchart Gardens

Butchart Gardens ㉑

800 Benvenuto Ave., Brentwood Bay. *(250) 652 4422.* *Victoria.* *Victoria.* *9am daily; closing times vary by season.*

THESE BEAUTIFUL gardens were begun in 1904 by Mrs. Jennie Butchart, the wife of a cement manufacturer. When her husband moved west to quarry limestone near Victoria, Mrs. Butchart began to design a new garden, which would stretch down to the water at Tod Inlet. When the limestone deposits ran out, Mrs Butchart decided to add to her burgeoning garden by landscaping the quarry site into a sunken garden which now boasts a lake overhung by willow and other trees laden with blossom in spring. A huge rock left in the quarry was turned into a towering rock garden. Today visitors can climb stone steps to see stunning views from the top. As their popularity grew, so the gardens were filled with thousands of rare plants collected from around the world by Mrs Butchart.

Today, the gardens are arranged into distinct areas. There is a formal Italian garden with a lily pond that features a fountain bought in Italy by the Butcharts in 1924. The rose garden is filled with the scent of hundreds of different blooms in summer. During the summer the gardens are illuminated and play host to evening jazz and classical music concerts.

Port Renfrew ㉒

300. *2070 Phillips Rd., Sooke (250) 642 6351.*

PORT RENFREW IS a small, friendly fishing village and ex-logging town. A popular daytrip from Victoria, the town offers visitors access to Botanical Beach where a unique sandstone shelf leaves rock pools filled with marine life such as starfish at low tide.

Port Renfrew is famed for its hiking along old logging roads: the Sandbar Trail goes through a Douglas fir plantation to a large river sandbar where it is possible to swim at low tide. A more serious hike is the 48-km (30-mile) Juan de Fuca Marine Trail from Port Renfrew to China Beach. This trail offers a range of hikes, from treks lasting several days to short beach walks. The town is one of two starting points for the West Coast Trail in Pacific Rim National Park *(see pp286–7)*.

Cowichan District ㉓

& from Duncan. *381A Trans-Canada Hwy, Duncan (250) 746 4636.*

LOCATED ON the south central coast of Vancouver Island, about 60 km (37 miles) north of Victoria, the Cowichan District incorporates both the Chemainus and Cowichan Valleys. Cowichan means "warm land" in the language of the Cowichan peoples, one of British Columbia's largest First Nations groups; the area's mild climate means the waters of Cowichan Lake are warm enough to swim in during the summer months. The largest freshwater lake on the island, Lake Cowichan offers excellent fishing, canoeing, and hiking.

Between the town of Duncan and the lake lies the Valley Demonstration Forest which has scenic lookouts and signs explaining forest management. Duncan is known as the City of Totems as it displays several poles along the highway. The Cowichan Native Village is a heritage center which shows films on the history of the Cowichan Tribe. The gift shop sells traditional artifacts including Cowichan sweaters. At the large carving shed visitors can see sculptors creating the poles while guides tell the stories behind the images.

Stunning vista over Lake Cowichan in the Cowichan Valley

Chemainus ㉔

4,000. *9796 Willow St. (250) 246 3944.*

WHEN THE LOCAL sawmill closed in 1983, the picturesque town of Chemainus transformed itself into a major attraction with the painting of giant murals around the town that depict the history of the region. Local artists continued the project and today there are more than 32 murals on specially built panels, based on real events in the town's past.

First Nations' faces looking down from a Chemainus town mural

Pleasure craft and fishing boats moored in Nanaimo harbor

Larger-than-life images of Cowichan natives, pioneers, and loggers dominate Chemainus and have revitalized the town. Visitors enjoy browsing in the town's various antique stores and relaxing in the many pleasant sidewalk cafés, espresso bars, and tearooms.

Environs: Some 70 km (45 miles) south of Chemainus, Swartz Bay is the departure point on Vancouver Island for ferries to the Southern Gulf Islands. Visitors are drawn to the 200 mostly uninhabited islands by their tranquillity and natural beauty. It is possible to stroll along empty beaches where sightings of eagles and turkey vultures are common. There are fishing charters for visitors who enjoy catching salmon and cod as well as kayaking tours offering stops on isolated shores to view otters, seals, and marine birds.

Salt Spring is the most populated island, with about 10,000 inhabitants. In the summer, visitors come to wander around the pretty Ganges Village, where a busy marina surrounds the wooden pier. The village offers stores, cafés, and galleries as well as colorful markets.

Nanaimo 25

78,800. 2290 *Bowen Rd. (250) 756 0106.*

Originally the site of five Coast Salish native villages, Nanaimo was established as a coal-mining town in the 1850s. As the second largest city on Vancouver Island, Nanaimo has plenty of malls and businesses along the Island Highway, but it is the Old City Quarter that is most popular with visitors.

The Old City Quarter has many 19th-century buildings, including the Nanaimo Court House, designed by Francis Rattenbury in 1895. The **Nanaimo District Museum** is located at Piker's Park and has a re-creation of Victoria's 19th-century Chinatown, complete with wooden sidewalks, a general store, a barber shop, and a schoolroom. There is also a lifelike replica of a coal mine. Other exhibits include native artifacts displayed in a village diorama.

Nanaimo District Museum
100 Cameron Rd. *(250) 753 1821.* *9am–5pm daily.* *Sep–May; Mon all year.* *book in advance.*

A carved eagle soars over Port Alberni Pier

Port Alberni 26

26,800. *Site 215, C10, RR2 (250) 724 6535.*

Port Alberni sits at the head of Alberni Inlet, which stretches 48 km (30 miles) from the interior of Vancouver Island to the Pacific Ocean in the west. The town depends upon the lumber and fishing industries and is a popular haunt for salmon fishers. Every year the Salmon Derby and Festival offers 5,000 Canadian dollars for the biggest fish caught during the last weekend in August. The town's other attractions include a 1929 locomotive offering train rides along the waterfront during the summer from the restored 1912 Port Alberni Railway Station by the Alberni Harbour Quay. Many visitors come to Port Alberni to cruise on one of two freighters, the 40-year-old M.V. *Lady Rose* and the M.V. *Frances Barkley*. The ships deliver mail all the way down the inlet, as well as offering trips for visitors to Ucluelet near the Pacific Rim National Park. The boats also carry kayaks and canoes for those hoping to sail around the Broken Islands Group *(see p286)*.

Just east of Port Alberni, it is possible to hike among awe-inspiring old growth Douglas firs and red cedars in the outstanding MacMillan Cathedral Grove Provincial Park.

A 1929 locomotive offering rides along Port Alberni's waterfront

Gold River ㉗

1,900. Highway 28 (250) 283 2418.

GOLD RIVER IS a logging village located at the end of the picturesque Hwy 28, near Muchalat Inlet. The village is a popular center for caving, containing over 50 caves in its environs. Just 16 km (10 miles) west of Gold River, the unique crystalline formations of the Upana Caves and the deeper grottos of White Ridge draw hundreds of visitors every summer.

Summer cruises on a converted World War II minesweeper, *M.V. Uchuck III*, take visitors to Friendly Cove where Captain Cook is said to have been the first European to meet local native peoples in 1778.

Gold River is a good base from which to explore **Strathcona Provincial Park** which lies in the center of Vancouver Island. Established in 1911, this rugged wilderness is BC's oldest provincial park and encompasses 250,000 ha (617,750 acres) of impressive mountains, as well as lakes and ancient forests. However, much of the park's outstanding scenery can be explored only by experienced hikers.

Mountain view at Strathcona Provincial Park

Strathcona Provincial Park
Off Hwy 28. (250) 337 2400.
daily. for campsites. limited.
Jul & Aug: call ahead for details.

Campbell River ㉙

30,000. 1235 Shoppers Row (250) 287 4636.

LOCATED ON THE northeast shore of Vancouver Island, Campbell River is renowned as a center for salmon fishing. The waters of Discovery

Pacific Rim National Park Reserve ㉘

THE PACIFIC RIM NATIONAL PARK RESERVE is composed of three distinct areas: Long Beach, the West Coast Trail, and the Broken Group Islands, all of which occupy a 130-km (80-mile) strip of Vancouver Island's west coast. The park is a world famous area for whale-watching, and the Wikaninnish Centre off Hwy 4 has the latest information on their movements. Long Beach offers a range of hiking trails, with parking lots located at all trail heads and beach accesses. The most challenging hike is the 77-km (48-mile) West Coast Trail, between the towns of Port Renfrew and Bamfield. The Broken Group Islands are popular with kayakers.

The Broken Group Islands
This is an archipelago of some 100 islets popular with kayakers and scuba divers.

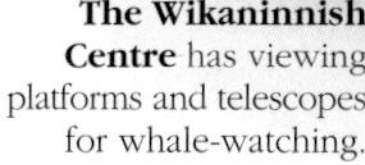

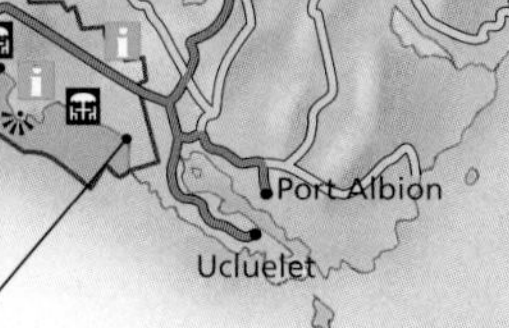

The Schooner Trail is one of nine scenic and easy-to-follow trails along the sands of Long Beach.

The Wikaninnish Centre has viewing platforms and telescopes for whale-watching.

Long Beach
The rugged, windswept sands of Long Beach are renowned for their wild beauty, with crashing Pacific rollers, unbeatable surfing opportunities, rock pools filled with marine life, and scattered driftwood.

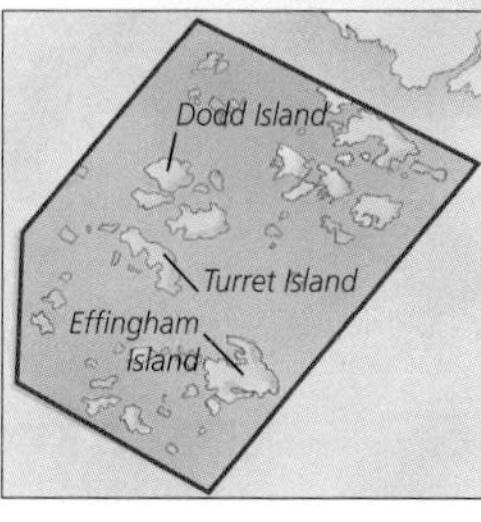

The crashing waters of Elk Falls along the Campbell River

Passage are on the migration route for five major species of salmon, including the giant Chinook. There are boat tours, which follow the fish up river.

As well as renting one of the many available fishing boats, visitors can try their luck catching fish from the 200-m (656-ft) Discovery Pier in the town.

Just 10 km (6 miles) northwest of Campbell River, Elk Falls Provincial Park houses large Douglas Fir forests and several waterfalls, including the impressive Elk Falls.

Telegraph Cove 30

100. Port McNeill. Port Hardy (250) 949 7622.

LOCATED ON THE northern tip of Vancouver Island, Telegraph Cove is a small, picturesque boardwalk village, with distinctive high wooden houses built on stilts that look over the waters of Johnson Strait. In summer, about 300 killer whales, drawn to the area by the migrating salmon, come to cavort and scratch their bellies on the gravel beds in the shallow waters of Robson Bight, an ecological preserve established in 1982. Visitors may view the antics of the whales from tour boats or from the village pier.

Killer whales in the clean waters of Johnson Strait, Vancouver Island

Whale Watching

Migrating gray whales

More than 20 species of whale are found in British Columbia's coastal waters. Around 17,000 gray whales migrate annually from their feeding grounds in the Arctic Ocean to breed off the coast of Mexico. The whales tend to stay near to the coast and often move close enough to Vancouver Island's west shore to be sighted from land. From March to August there are daily whale-watching trips from Tofino and Ucluelet.

Visitors' Checklist

Hwy 4. (250) 726 7721. from Port Alberni. daily. Jun–Sep.

Key

- Major road
- Minor road
- West Coast Trail
- National Park boundary
- Rivers
- Camping
- Picnic areas
- Tourist information
- Viewpoint

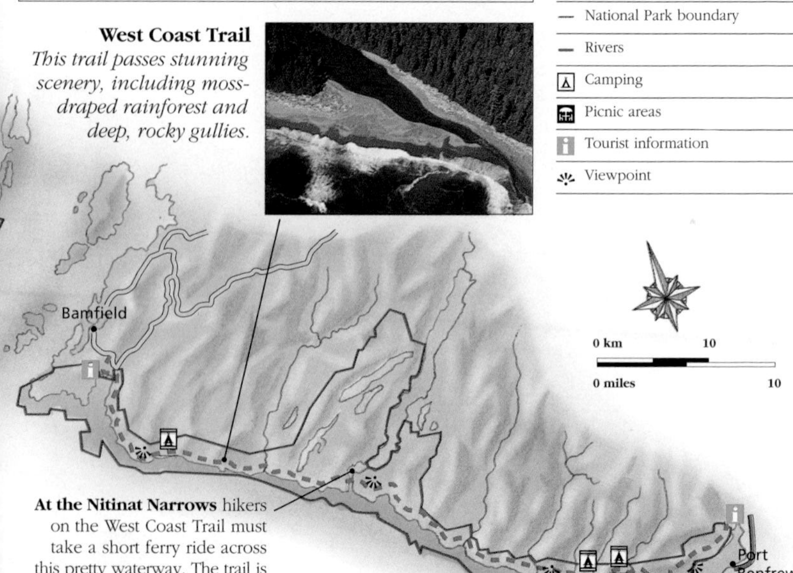

West Coast Trail *This trail passes stunning scenery, including moss-draped rainforest and deep, rocky gullies.*

At the Nitinat Narrows hikers on the West Coast Trail must take a short ferry ride across this pretty waterway. The trail is open from May to September.

C.E.X.&S.

THE ROCKY MOUNTAINS

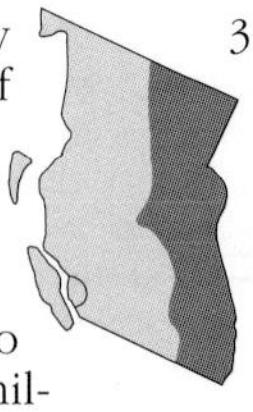

THE CANADIAN ROCKIES occupy a band of the provinces of British Columbia and Alberta nearly 805 km (500 miles) wide, and are part of the range that extends from Mexico through the United States into Canada. Between 65 and 100 million years ago, a slow but massive upheaval of the Earth's crust caused the rise of the Rocky Mountains and the dramatic, jagged appearance of their peaks, 30 of which are over 3,048-m (10,000-ft) high. A region of spectacular beauty, the landscape of the Rockies is dominated by snow-topped peaks, luminous glaciers, and iridescent glacial lakes, now protected in a series of national parks. The discovery of natural hot springs at Banff in 1883 prompted the federal government to create Canada's first national park. Since 1985 Banff, Jasper, Yoho, and Kootenay parks have become UNESCO World Heritage sites.

SIGHTS AT A GLANCE

Historic Towns and Cities
Calgary 1
Cranbrook 7
Fernie 5
Fort Macleod 2
Fort Nelson 19
Fort St. John 18
Grande Prairie 17
Prince George 16
Radium Hot Springs 10

National and Provincial Parks
Banff National Park 13
Glacier National Park 9
Jasper National Park 15
Kootenay National Park 11
Muncho Lake Provincial Park 20
Waterton Lakes National Park 3
Yoho National Park 14

Historical Sites and Places of Natural Beauty
Crowsnest Pass 4
Fort Steele Heritage Town 6
Kananaskis Country 12
The Purcell Mountains 8

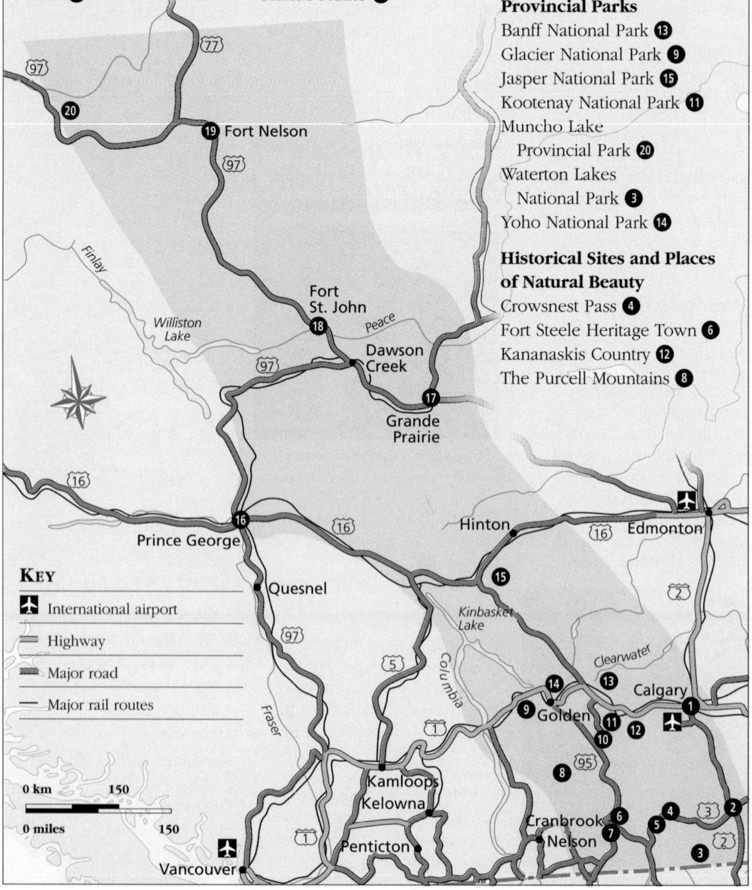

KEY
International airport
Highway
Major road
Major rail routes

0 km 150
0 miles 150

◁ **Skilled horsemanship on display at the Calgary Exhibition and Stampede**

Calgary ❶

Blackfoot shirt in Glenbow Museum

Established in 1875, Calgary is famous for hosting the Winter Olympics of 1988, and for its Stampede. Calgary covers the largest area of any city in Alberta, and lies between the eastern foothills of the Rockies and the Prairies. It is a sophisticated place, with skyscrapers, galleries, and theaters, but it retains the air of a frontier town where pick-up trucks and cowboy boots are not out of place. The city's western atmosphere belies the fact that its modern skyline has grown since the oil boom of the 1960s. Noted for its proximity to Banff National Park, Calgary's center, with its offices and stores, is 120 km (75 miles) east of Banff Townsite *(see p301)*.

Calgary Tower surrounded by the skyscrapers of the city's skyline

Calgary Tower

9th Ave. & Centre St. SW. *(403) 266 7171.* *daily.*

The Calgary Tower is the third-tallest structure in Calgary, with 18 elevators, which hurtle to the top in 62 seconds, and two emergency staircases composed of 762 steps apiece. From street level to the top, the tower measures 191 m (327 ft). At the top there is a restaurant and an observation deck, which offer some half-a-million tourists each year incredible views across to the Rockies and eastward over the vast plains of the Prairies.

Devonian Gardens

317 7th Ave. SW. *(403) 268 3830.* *9am–9pm daily.*

Devonian Gardens is a 1 ha (2.5 acre) indoor garden located downtown on the fourth floor of the Toronto Dominion Square complex. Reached by a glass-walled elevator from 8th Avenue, the gardens are a popular lunchtime haunt for office workers, offering a quiet sanctuary from the bustle of downtown. More than 135 varieties of tropical and native Albertan plants are intersected by winding pathways. There are waterfalls, fountains, and a pool that becomes an ice rink during the winter.

Secluded spot with fountains and fish pond in Devonian Gardens

Shopping at a designer boutique in downtown Eau Claire Market

Eau Claire Market

End 3rd St. SW. *(403) 264 6450.* *daily.*

Housed in a brightly colored warehouse, Eau Claire Market provides a welcome contrast to the surrounding office blocks downtown. Located on the Bow River, opposite Prince's Island Park, the market offers specialty stores selling a fine variety of gourmet foods, contemporary arts, street entertainers, craft markets, cinemas, cafés, and restaurants with outdoor terraces. A network of walkways connects to a footbridge that leads to Prince's Island Park.

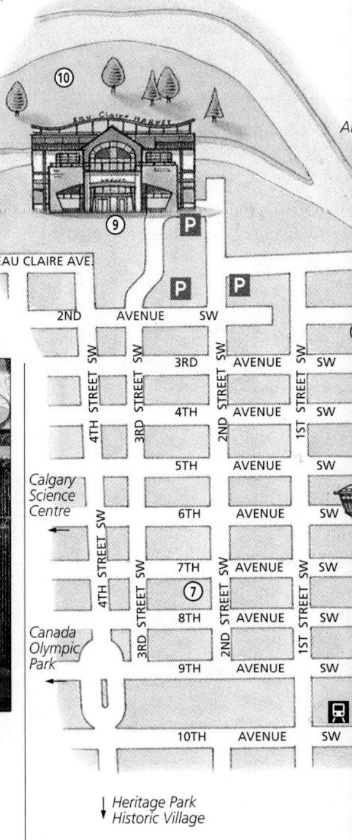

Sights at a Glance

- Calgary Tower ⑥
- Calgary Centre for Performing Arts ④
- Calgary Chinese Cultural Centre ⑧
- Devonian Gardens ⑦
- Eau Claire Market ⑨
- Fort Calgary ②
- Glenbow Museum ⑤
- Hunt House and Deane House ③
- Prince's Island Park ⑩
- Saint George's Island ①

Prince's Island Park

The pretty Prince's Island Park lies close to the city center on the banks of the Bow River. This tiny island is connected to the city via a pedestrian bridge at the end of 4th Street SW. During hot summers, visitors and locals picnic under the cool shade of the park's many trees, as well as using its walking and cycling trails.

Calgary Chinese Cultural Centre

197 1st St. SW. *(403) 262 5071.* *daily.* *for museum.*

Located in downtown Calgary, the Chinese Cultural Centre was completed in 1993. It is modeled on the 1420 Temple of Heaven in Beijing, which was used exclusively by emperors. The center was built by artisans from China using traditional skills. The Dr. Henry Fok Cultural Hall is the highlight of the building with its 21-m-high (70-ft) ceiling and dome adorned with dragons and phoenixes. Each of the dome's four supporting columns is decorated with lavish gold designs, which represent the four seasons.

Blue tiles inside the dome of the Calgary Chinese Cultural Centre

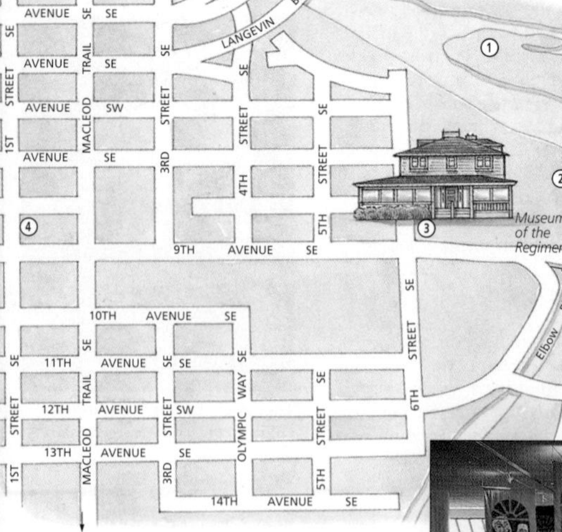

> **VISITORS' CHECKLIST**
>
> *819,700. 16 km (10 miles) NE of city. Greyhound Bus Station, 877 Greyhound Way SW. Calgary Convention and Visitors Bureau, 237 8th Avenue SE (403) 263 8510. Calgary Stampede (Jul); Calgary Folk Festival (Jul); International Native Arts Festival (Aug).*

Glenbow Museum

130 9th Ave. SE. *(403) 268 4100.* *daily.*

Located in the heart of downtown Calgary, the Glenbow Museum is western Canada's largest museum. The vast gallery houses an excellent collection of both European and contemporary Canadian art, as well as a wide range of objects that chronicle the history of the Canadian West. Laid out over four floors, the gallery's permanent displays include both native and pioneer artifacts, ranging from settlers' wagons to a stunning collection of First Nations' dress and jewelry. The fourth floor is devoted to five centuries of military history, with exhibits of medieval armor and Samurai swords.

Calgary Centre for Performing Arts

205 8th Ave. SE. *(403) 294 7455.* FAX *(403) 294 7457.* *daily.*

Opened in 1985, this large complex houses four theaters and a concert hall, as well as having five rental boardrooms. Located in the heart of the city on Olympic Plaza, the center has staged events as diverse as k.d. lang concerts and the High Performance Rodeo.

The lobby of the Calgary Centre for Performing Arts

Mountie's cabin in the Interpretive Centre at Fort Calgary Historic Park

Hunt House and Deane House

750 9th Ave. SE. (403) 290 1875. *Deane House: daily.*

The Hunt House lies across the Elbow River from the Fort Calgary Interpretive Centre. This small log house is one of the few buildings left from the original settlement of Calgary in the early 1880s.

Nearby Deane House was built for the Superintendent of Fort Calgary, Captain Richard Burton Deane, in 1906. Today, the house is a restaurant where visitors can enjoy a meal in a delightful period setting.

Fort Calgary Historic Park

750 9th Ave. SE. (403) 290 1875. *May–Oct: daily.*

Fort Calgary was built by the North West Mounted Police in 1875 along the banks of the Bow River. The Grand Trunk Pacific Railway (later amalgamated with the CPR), arrived in 1883, and the tiny fort town grew to over 400 residents in a year. In 1886, a fire destroyed several of the settlement's key buildings and a new town was built out of the more fire-resistant sandstone. In 1911 the land was bought by the Grand Trunk Pacific Railway and the fort was leveled. Pieces of the fort were discovered during an archeological dig in 1970, and the well-restored site was opened to the public in 1978.

Today, the reconstructed fort offers an interpretive center, which houses a re-created quartermaster's store and carpenter's workshop. There are also delightful walks along the river. Costumed guides participate in dramatic reenactments such as an exciting jailbreak.

Calgary Stampede

An exuberant ten-day festival of all things western, the Calgary Stampede is held every July in Stampede Park. Originally established as an agricultural fair in 1886, the Stampede of 1912 attracted 14,000 people. In the 1920s one of its still-popular highlights, the risky but exciting covered wagon races, became part of the show.

Today's festival has an array of spectacular entertainments that dramatize scenes from western history. They can be seen both on site and in Calgary itself. The fair starts with a dazzling parade through the city, and then features bull riding, calf roping, and cow tackling. The main events are the *Half Million Dollar Rodeo*, and chuck-wagon racing which have combined prize money of over Can$1.2 million.

Saint George's Island

Saint George's Island sits on the edge of the Bow River near downtown Calgary. The island houses the magnificent Calgary Zoo, the Botanical Gardens, and Prehistoric Park.

The zoo prides itself on the exciting presentation of its animals, which can be seen in their appropriate habitats. A series of environments called The Canadian Wilds has been created, highlighting the diversity of both the Canadian landscape and its wildlife. There are aspen woodlands where it is possible to see the endangered woodland caribou, and visitors can wander the pathways of the boreal forest environment, maybe spotting the rare whooping crane feeding in the shallow wetlands area.

The zoo is surrounded by the Botanical Gardens, which has a vast greenhouse displaying plants from different climate zones from around the world.

The Prehistoric Park offers a reconstructed Mesozoic landscape, where visitors can picnic among 22 life-size dinosaurs.

The stately whooping crane at Calgary Zoo, Saint George's Island

Stampede Park

140 Olympic Way SE. (403) 261 0125. *daily.* *some events.*

Famous as the site of the Calgary Stampede, the park offers year-round leisure and conference facilities. There is a permanent horse racetrack, as well as two ice-hockey stadiums, one of which is housed inside the striking Saddledome, named for its saddle-shaped roof. Trade shows, such as antiques and home improvements, are also held here.

Heritage Park Historic Village houses some 70 historic buildings

Fish Creek Provincial Park

Bow Bottom Trail SE. (403) 297 5293. daily. partial.

Established in 1975, Fish Creek Provincial Park is one of the world's largest urban parks, covering 1,189 ha (2,938 acres) of forest and wilderness along the Fish Creek valley. Park guides hold slide shows on both the ecology and history of the region, detailing the park's many archeological sites, such as buffalo jumps dated between 750 BC and 1800 AD.

The park's forest is a mix of white spruce, aspen, and balsam poplar. In winter, many of the hiking trails become cross-country ski trails, popular with locals and visitors alike. The Canada goose, the great blue heron, and the bald eagle are among a variety of birds that visit the park during both summer and winter.

Heritage Park Historic Village

1900 Heritage Drive. (403) 259 1900. May–Sep: daily; Sep–Dec: weekends only. Jan–Apr.

Heritage Park Historic Village sits on the shore of Glenmore Reservoir, and contains over 83 historic buildings, from out-houses to a two-story hotel, which have been brought here from sites all over western Canada. The buildings have been organized into time periods, which range from an 1880s fur trading post to the shops and homes of a small town between 1900 and 1914. Most of the 45,000 artifacts that furnish and decorate the village have been donated by residents of Calgary and the surrounding towns, and vary from teacups to steam trains. Among the most thrilling of the exhibits, a working 19th-century amusement park has several rides, and three original operating steam locomotives. A replica of the SS *Moyie*, a charming sternwheeler paddle boat, takes visitors on 30-minute cruises around the Glenmore Reservoir. One of the most popular experiences is to ride one of two vintage electric streetcars to the park's front gates. The sense of stepping back in time is enhanced by the all-pervasive clip-clopping of horse-drawn carriages, and by the smells and sounds of shops such as the working bakery and the blacksmith's shop, all staffed by costumed guides.

Victorian drink container at Heritage Park

Canada Olympic Park

88 Canada Olympic Rd. SW. (403) 247 5452. 9am–10pm Mon–Fri, 9am–5pm Sat & Sun.

Canada Olympic Park was the site of the 1988 XV Olympic Winter Games. Today, both locals and visitors can enjoy the facilities all year round, including riding on the bobsleds and luge tracks. The views toward the Rockies and over Calgary from the 90-m (295-ft) high Olympic Ski Jump Tower are truly stunning.

Visitors can experience the breath-taking thrills of the downhill ski run and the bobsleds on the simulators housed in the Olympic Hall of Fame and Museum.

Calgary Science Centre

701 11th St. SW. (403) 221 3700. Jun–Sep: daily; Sep–May: Tue–Sun.

The Calgary Science Centre is a popular interactive museum, with over 35 exhibits of scientific wonders such as frozen shadows, laser shows, and holograms. One of the highlights is the Discovery Dome where the latest multimedia technology brings all kinds of images to life on the enormous domed screen. Fascinating shows include detailed explorations of everything from an ordinary backyard to the solar system. On Friday evenings, visitors can observe the stars using the high-powered telescopes in the observatory.

Museum of the Regiments

4520 Crowchild Trail SW. (403) 974 2850. 10am–4pm daily. Wed. **Donation**

Opened in 1990, the Museum of the Regiments is devoted to the history of the Canadian Armed Forces. The largest of its kind in western Canada, it focuses on four regiments and includes realistic displays that depict actual battle situations.

Sherman tank on display outside the Museum of the Regiments

The mountain-ringed Lake Waterton in Waterton Lakes National Park

Fort Macleod ❷

3,100. Fort Macleod Museum, 25th St. (403) 553 4703.

Alberta's oldest settlement, Fort Macleod was established in 1874 as the first North West Mounted Police outpost in the west. Sent to control lawless whiskey traders at the Fort Whoop-up trading post, the Mounties set up Fort Macleod nearby (*see p230*).

Today's town retains over 30 of its historic buildings, and the reconstructed fort palisades (completed in 1957) house the fort's museum, which tells the story of the Mounties' journey.

The world's oldest and best preserved buffalo jump lies just 16 km (10 miles) northwest of Fort Macleod. **Head-Smashed-In-Buffalo Jump** was made a UN World Heritage site in 1987. This way of hunting buffalo, where as many as 500 men wearing buffalo skins stampeded herds of the animals to their deaths over a cliff, was perfected by the Blackfoot tribe. The site takes its name from the brave whose head was smashed in when he decided to watch the kill from below the cliff!

Head-Smashed-In-Buffalo Jump
Rte 785, off Hwy 2. (403) 553 2731. daily.

Waterton Lakes National Park ❸

Calgary. Park Info Centre, open mid-May–Sep (403) 859 5133. daily. partial.

Scenery as amazing as any of that found in the Rockies' other national parks characterizes the less-known Waterton Lakes National Park. Located in the southwest corner of Alberta along the US border, the park is an International Peace Park and manages a shared ecosystem with Glacier National Park in the US.

The park owes its unique beauty to the geological phenomenon of the Lewis Overthurst, which was forged over a billion years ago (before the formation of the Rockies) when ancient rock was pushed over newer deposits. Thus, the peaks of the mountains rise up sharply out of the flat prairies.

Waterton's mix of lowland and alpine habitats means it has the widest variety of wildlife of any of Canada's parks, from bears to bighorn sheep, and from waterfowl to nesting species such as sapsuckers.

Crowsnest Pass ❹

Calgary. Frank Slide Interpretive Centre (403) 562 7388.

Crowsnest Pass is located on Highway 3, in Alberta close to the border with British Columbia. Like most Rocky Mountain passes, it is enclosed by snowcapped mountains.

Visitors on an underground tour of Bellevue Mine at Crowsnest Pass

In the early 1900s this area was dominated by the coal-mining industry and was the site of Canada's worst mine disaster. In 1903, a huge mass of rock slid off Turtle Mountain into the valley below, hitting part of the town of Frank, and scooping up rocks and trees, killing 70 people. The Frank Slide Interpretive Centre offers an award-winning audio/visual presentation called "In The Mountain's Shadow." A trail through the valley is marked with numbered stops and leads hikers to the debris left by the disaster. Visitors can learn more about the history of local mining communities at the Bellevue Mine, which offers underground tours through the same narrow tunnels that working miners took daily between 1903 and 1961. Tours are available of Leitch Collieries, a fascinating early mining complex.

The Rocky Mountains tower over houses in the town of Fernie

Fernie ❺

4,877. Hwy 3 & Dicken Rd. (250) 423 9207.

Fernie is an attractive, tree-lined town beautifully set amid a circle of pointed peaks on the British Columbia side of Crowsnest Pass. The town owes its handsome appearance to a fire that burned it to the ground in 1908, since when all buildings have been constructed from brick and stone. Among several historic buildings, the 1911 courthouse stands out as the only château-style courthouse in BC.

Fernie is known for its winter sports, and boasts the best powder snow in the Rockies. The skiing season runs from November to April. The nearby Fernie Alpine Resort is huge and is capable of taking around 12,300 skiers up the mountain every hour. During the summer, the Mount Fernie Provincial Park offers a broad range of hiking trails through its magnificent mountain scenery. Boat trips on the many nearby lakes and rivers are popular, as is the fishing.

Various companies offer helicopter sightseeing trips that take visitors close to the mountains to see the formations and granite cliffs particular to this region of the Rockies.

Fort Steele Heritage Town ❻

Hwy 95. (250) 426 7352. daily.

A re-creation of a 19th-century pioneering supply town, this settlement was established in 1864, when gold was discovered at Wild Horse Creek. Thousands of prospectors and entrepreneurs arrived by the Dewdney Trail, which linked Hope to the gold fields. The town was named after the North West Mounted Police Superintendent, Samuel Steele, who arrived in 1887 to restore peace between warring groups of Ktunaxa native peoples and European settlers. The town underwent a brief boom with the discovery of lead and silver, but the mainline railroad was routed through Cranbrook instead, and by the early 1900s Fort Steele was a ghost town.

19th-century barber's shop at Fort Steele Heritage Town

Today, there are over 60 reconstructed or restored buildings, staffed by guides in period costume, including the general store, livery stable, and Mountie officers' quarters, where personal items such as family photographs, swords, and uniforms create the illusion of recent occupation. Demonstrations of traditional crafts such as quilt- and ice cream-making are also held here. Tours at the nearby Wild Horse Creek Historic Site include the chance to pan for gold.

The Buffalo

The large, shaggy-headed type of cattle known as buffalo are really North American bison. These apparently cumbersome beasts (a mature bull can weigh as much as 900 kg/1,980 lbs) are agile, fast, and unpredictable.

Before European settlers began moving west to the plains, in the 18th and 19th centuries, the buffalo lived in immense herds of hundreds of thousands. It is estimated that as many as 60,000,000 roamed here. Initially hunted only by the Plains Indians, who respected the beasts as a source of food, shelter, and tools, the buffalo were subsequently hunted almost to extinction by Europeans. By 1900 less than 1,000 animals remained. In 1874 a rancher called Walking Coyote bred a small herd of just 716 plains bison whose descendants now roam several Canadian national parks.

A North American plains bison

The luxurious dining car on a restored train at Cranbrook's rail museum

Cranbrook 7

18,050. 2279 Cranbrook St. N. (250) 426 5914.

CRANBROOK IS the largest town in southeast BC and lies between the Purcell and the Rocky Mountain ranges. A major transportation hub for the Rocky Mountain region, Cranbrook is within easy reach of a variety of scenic delights, including alpine forest and the lush, green valleys of the mountain foothills. A range of wildlife such as elk, wolves, cougar, and the highest density of grizzlies in the Rockies, may be spotted on one of many hikes available here.

The town's main attraction is the **Canadian Museum of Rail Travel**. Housed in the restored 1900 station, the museum possesses an archive of papers and photographs illustrating the history of the railroad. Outside, visitors can explore the lavish interiors of its collection of original trains.

The Canadian Museum of Rail Travel

Hwy 3/95 & Baker St. *(250) 489 3918. Apr–mid-Oct: daily; late Oct–Apr: Tue–Sat.*

The Purcell Mountains 8

Kamloops. Hwy 95, Golden (250) 344 7125.

THE RUGGED and beautiful Purcell Mountains face the Rockies across the broad Columbia River Valley. The region is one of the most remote in the Rockies and attracts hunters and skiers from across the globe. A high range of granite spires, called the Bugaboos, also draws mountain climbers. In the north of the Purcell range, and in one of its few accessible areas, the Purcell Wilderness Conservancy, covers a vast 32,600 ha (80,554 acres). Carefully regulated hunting expeditions for bear, mountain goats, and elk are permitted here.

From the nearby pretty town of Invermere, it is possible to access one of the most difficult trails in Canada; the Earl Grey Pass Trail extends some 56 km (35 miles) over the Purcell Mountains. It is named after Earl Grey, Canada's Governor General from 1904 to 1911, who chose the Purcell range as the place to build a vacation cabin for his family in 1909. The trail he traveled followed an established native route used by the Kinbasket natives of the Shuswap First Nations. Today the trail is notoriously dangerous; bears, avalanches, and fallen trees are often hazards along the way. Hiking along it requires skill and experience and should not be attempted by a novice.

Glacier National Park 9

Revelstoke/Golden. Revelstoke (250) 837 7500. daily.

GLACIER NATIONAL PARK covers 1,350 sq km (520 sq miles) of wilderness in the Selkirk Range of the Columbia Mountains. The park was established in 1886, and its growth was linked to

The Purcell Mountains are noted for remote rivers, forests, and mountains

The Illecillewaet Glacier is one of 420 glaciers in Glacier National Park

the growth of the railroad, which was routed through Roger's Pass in 1885. Today, many of the park's most accessible walking trails follow abandoned railroad lines. Other trails offer visitors stunning views of the park's 420 glaciers, including the Great Glacier, now known as the Illecillewaet Glacier.

The park is known for its very wet weather in summer and almost daily snowfalls in winter, when as much as 23 m (75 ft) of snow may fall in one season. The threat of avalanche is serious here, and skiers and climbers are monitored by the Park's Service.

Taking the waters at Radium Hot Springs

The Roger's Pass line was abandoned by the CPR because of the frequent avalanches, and a tunnel was built underneath it instead. The Trans-Canada Highway (Hwy 1) follows the route of the pass as it bisects the park, en route to the lovely town of Revelstoke. From here, visitors may access the forests and jagged peaks of Mount Revelstoke National Park.

Radium Hot Springs ⑩

1,000. Chamber of Commerce (250) 347 9331.

THE SMALL TOWN of Radium Hot Springs is famous for its mineral springs and is a good base for exploring the nearby Kootenay National Park. During the summer, flower-filled pots decorate the storefronts of the many coffee shops and pubs along the main street, and the town has more motel rooms than residents. Many of the 1.2 million annual visitors come to bathe in the healing waters of the springs. There are two pools, a hot soaking pool for relaxing in, and a cooler swimming pool. Locker rooms, swimsuits, showers, and towels can all be rented, and massages are readily available. Visitors can also explore the nearby Columbia Valley Wetlands. Fed by glacial waters from the Purcell and Rocky mountains, the Columbia River meanders through these extensive marsh lands, which provide an important habitat for over 250 migratory waterfowl such as Canada geese and tundra swans.

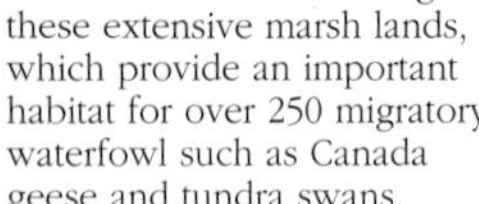

Kootenay National Park ⑪

Banff. Park Info Centre, open May–Sep (250) 347 9505. daily.

KOOTENAY NATIONAL PARK covers 1,406 sq km (543 sq miles) of the most diverse terrain in the Rockies. Much of this scenery can be seen from the Kootenay Parkway (Hwy 93), which cuts through the park from north to south following the Vermilion and Kootenay rivers. Most of the park's attractions can be seen from the many short trails that lead from the highway.

The road winds westward through Sinclair Pass where the high red walls of Sinclair Canyon, a deep limestone gorge, lead to the crashing Sinclair Falls, and the Redwall Fault where rust-colored cliffs form a natural gateway across the highway. Farther north, the magical Paint Pots are reached by a short trail from the road. They are a group of small ochre and red-colored pools that have been formed from iron-rich undergound mineral springs. Farther on lies the high gray granite walls of the stunning Marble Canyon.

The ochre-colored Paint Pot pools in Kootenay National Park

Kananaskis Country ⑫

Canmore. Suite 201, 800 Railway Ave., Canmore. (403) 678 5508.

KANANASKIS COUNTRY is a verdant region of the Rocky Mountain foothills, with mountain peaks, lakes, rivers, and alpine meadows. Located southwest of Calgary on the boundary of Banff National Park, this 5,000 sq km (1,930 sq miles) of wilderness is a popular haunt for both visitors and locals to hike and view wildlife such as eagles, wolves, and bears. The town of Canmore serves as the center of this large recreational area, and has plenty of accommodations, as well as information on outdoor activities such as wildlife tours.

Banff National Park ⓭

THE BEST KNOWN OF the Rockies' national parks, Banff was also Canada's first. The park was established in 1885, after the discovery of natural hot springs by three Canadian Pacific Railroad workers in 1883. Centuries before the arrival of the railroad, Blackfoot, Stoney, and Kootenay native peoples lived in the valleys around Banff. Today, Banff National Park covers an area of 6,641 sq km (2,564 sq miles) of some of the most sublime scenery in the country. The park encompasses impressive mountain peaks, forests, glacial lakes, and mighty rivers. Some five million visitors a year enjoy a range of activities, from hiking and canoeing in summer, to skiing in winter.

Peyto Lake
One of the most rewarding walks in Banff is a short stroll from the Icefields Parkway, near Bow Summit, which leads to a vista over the ice-blue waters of Peyto Lake.

Parker Ridge

View from Icefields Parkway
Renowned for its stunning views of high peaks, forests, lakes, and glaciers, this 230-km (143-mile) road runs between Lake Louise and Jasper.

Saskatchewan River Crossing lies at the junction of three rivers, along the route used by 19th-century explorer David Thompson.

Valley of the Ten Peaks
A scenic road from Lake Louise winds to Moraine Lake, which is ringed by ten peaks each over 3,000 m (10,000 ft) high.

BEAR SAFETY

Both grizzly and black bears are found in the Rockies' national parks. Although sightings are rare, visitors should observe the rules posted at campgrounds by the park wardens. A leaflet, *You are in Bear Country*, is published by the park's service detailing safety tips for encounters with bears. The fundamental rules are: don't approach the animals, never feed them, and don't run. Bears have an excellent sense of smell, so if camping be sure to lock food or trash inside a car or in the bear-proof boxes provided.

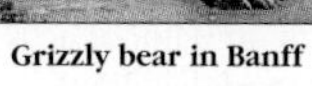

Grizzly bear in Banff

Johnston Canyon
This spectacular gorge boasts two impressive waterfalls, and is one of the most popular trails in the park. The walk can be reached from the Bow Valley Parkway (see p300), *and has a paved trail with wheelchair access, as well as walkways close to the falls. Displays along the way explain the canyon's geology.*

Visitors' Checklist

Hwys 1 & 93. *Banff Visitor Centre, 224 Banff Ave., Banff (403) 762 0270.* *Brewster Bus Depot, 100 Gopher St.* *daily.* *www.banfflakelouise.com*

Key

- Highway
- Major road
- Rivers
- Camping
- Visitor information
- Viewpoint

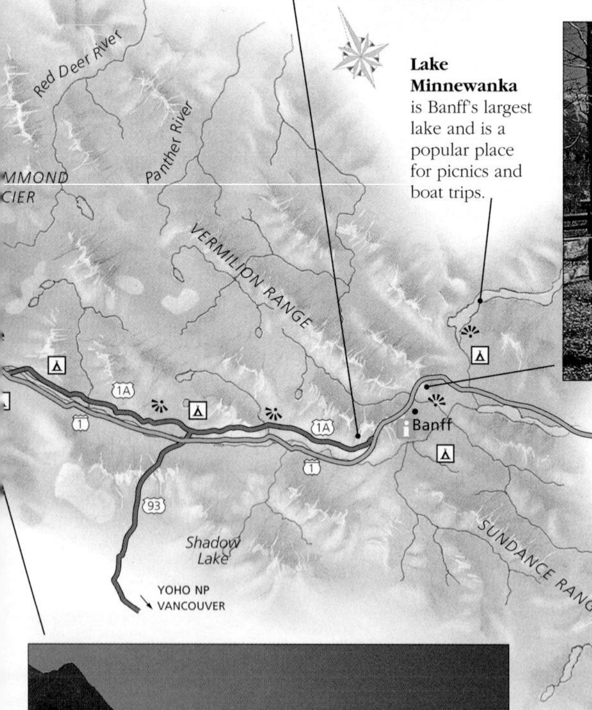

Lake Minnewanka is Banff's largest lake and is a popular place for picnics and boat trips.

Bankhead
An interpretive hiking trail displaying historic photographs leads visitors around this coal mine and ghost town.

Lake Louise
The turquoise waters of Lake Louise are an abiding symbol of the beauty of the Rockies. It was here that one of the first resorts was established in Banff. A giant finger of ice from the Victoria Glacier stretches to the lakeshore.

Exploring Banff National Park

Wild goat by the Icefields Parkway

It is impossible to travel through Banff National Park and not be filled with awe. There are some 25 peaks that rise over 3,000 m (10,000 ft) in Banff, which are magically reflected in the turquoise waters of the park's many lakes. Banff townsite offers visitors a full range of facilities, including the therapeutic hot springs that inspired the founding of the park, and is an excellent base for exploring the surrounding country. Even the highway is counted an attraction here. The Icefields Parkway (Hwy 93) winds through stunning mountain vistas and connects Banff to Jasper National Park, beginning from the renowned Lake Louise.

Icefields Parkway (Highway 93)

The Icefields Parkway is a 230-km (143-mile) scenic mountain highway that twists and turns through the jagged spines of the Rocky Mountains. The road is a wonder in itself, where every turn offers yet another incredible view as it climbs through high passes from Lake Louise to Jasper.

The road was built during the Depression of the 1930s, as a work creation project. Designed for sightseeing, the highway was extended to its present length in 1960, with plenty of pull-offs to allow visitors to take in the views.

Bow Summit is the highest point on the highway, at 2,068 m (6,785 ft), and has a side road that leads to the **Peyto Lake** viewpoint, which looks over snow-topped peaks mirrored in the brilliant blue of the lake. In summer, Bow Summit's mountain meadows are covered with alpine flowers. From here, it is also possible to see the Crowfoot Glacier, a striking chunk of ice in the shape of a crow's foot, hanging over a cliff-face. Farther north a trail leads down from a parking lot to **Mistaya Canyon** with its vertical walls, potholes, and an impressive natural arch. The highway passes close by the Icefields (which cross the park boundaries into Jasper National Park), and the Athabasca Glacier is clearly visible from the road. Mountain goats and bighorn sheep are drawn to the mineral deposits by the roadside.

The Bow Valley Parkway passing scenic country along the river

The Bow Valley Parkway

The Bow Valley Parkway is a 55-km (35-mile) long scenic alternative to the Trans-Canada Highway, running between Banff and Lake Louise. The road follows the Bow River Valley and offers visitors the chance to explore the gentle country of the valley with many interpretive signs and viewpoints along the way. From the road it is possible to see the abundant wildlife such as bears, elk, and coyotes.

About 19 km (12 miles) west of Banff, one of the best short walks leads from the roadside to the **Johnston Canyon** trail. A paved path leads to the canyon and two impressive waterfalls. The path to the lower falls is wheelchair accessible, and the upper falls are a slightly longer 2.7-km (1.5-mile) hike. A boardwalk along the rock wall leads to the floor of the canyon, offering valley views close to the railroad crossing through the mountains. One of the most striking natural phenomena in the canyon is the Ink Pots, a series of pools where vivid blue-green water bubbles up from underground springs. Interpretive signs explain how this fascinating canyon took shape, and how the water created its unique rock formations.

Lake Minnewanka Drive

This narrow, winding 14-km (8.5-mile) loop road begins at the Minnewanka interchange on the Trans-Canada Highway. From here it is a pleasant drive to picnic sites, hiking trails, and three lakes. Lake Minnewanka is Banff's biggest lake, almost 20 km (13 miles) long.

A popular short trail leads to **Bankhead**, the site of an abandoned coal mine that was the first settlement in Banff and whose heyday was in the first half of the 19th century. The footpath displays old photographs and notices which depict the life of the miners.

Lake Minnewanka, the largest lake in Banff National Park

Banff Springs Hotel, styled after the baronial castles of Scotland

Banff

The town of Banff grew up around the hot springs that were discovered here in the 1880s. The Canadian Pacific Railroad's manager, William Cornelius Van Horne, realized the springs would attract visitors, so he built the grand Banff Springs Hotel in 1888. The resort was very popular, and the town expanded to accommodate the influx. Located at the foot of Sulphur Mountain, The **Cave and Basin National Historic Site** is the site of the original spring found by the railroad workers in 1883 and is now a museum telling the story of Banff's development. The **Upper Hot Springs Pool**, also at the base of Sulphur Mountain, is a popular resort where visitors can relieve their aches in the mineral-rich, healing waters.

At 2,282 m (7,486 ft) above sea level, Sulphur Mountain is the highest mountain in the town. Although there is a 5-km (3-mile) trail to the top, a glass-enclosed gondola (cable car) carries visitors to the summit in eight minutes. Here the viewing platforms offer beautiful vistas of the Rockies.

Banff is busy all year round. In winter snow sports from skiing to dog-sledding are available, while summer visitors include hikers, bicyclists, and mountaineers. The **Banff Park Museum** was built in 1903 and houses specimens of animals, birds, and insects.

Banff Park Museum
93 Banff Ave. *(403) 762 1558.*
daily. *Dec 25, Jan 1.*

Gondolas or cable cars taking visitors up Sulphur Mountain

Lake Louise

by Samson Mall (403) 762 0270.
One of Banff National Park's major draws, the beauty of Lake Louise is an enduring image of the Rockies. Famed for the blueness of its water and the snow-capped peaks that surround it, Lake Louise also boasts the Victoria Glacier, which stretches almost to the water's edge. Trails around the lake offer exhibits that explain the lake's formation some 10,000 years ago, at the end of the last Ice Age. The amazing color of the water of this and other lakes in the park comes from deposits of glacial silt, known as rock flour, suspended just beneath the surface. Dominating the landscape at one end of the lake is the imposing hotel Château Lake Louise, built in 1894.

During the summer, a gondola carries visitors up to Mount Whitehorn for stunning views of the glacier and the lake. In winter, the area attracts large numbers of skiers, ice-climbers, and snowboarders.

In Lake Louise village visitors can stock up on supplies, such as food, clothes, and gas.

Moraine Lake

Less well known than Lake Louise, Moraine Lake is every bit as beautiful, with its shimmering turquoise color. The lake has a pretty waterside lodge that offers accommodations, meals, and canoe rentals. There are several trails that all start at the lake: one lakeside path follows the north shore for 1.5 km (1 mile), while the climb, which leads up Larch Valley-Sentinel Pass trail, offers more stunning vistas, ending at one of the park's highest passes.

Yoho National Park ⑭

INSPIRED BY THE BEAUTY of the park's mountains, lakes, waterfalls, and distinctive rock formations, this area was named Yoho, for the Cree word meaning "awe and wonder." Yoho National Park lies on the western side of the Rockies range in BC, next to Banff and Kootenay National Parks.

The Park offers a wide range of activities, from climbing and hiking to boating or skiing. The park also houses the Burgess Shale fossil beds, an extraordinary find of perfectly preserved marine creatures from the prehistoric Cambrian period, over 500 million years ago. Access to the fossil beds is by guided hike and is limited to 15 people each trip.

Shooting star flower

Emerald Lake
The rustic Emerald Lake Lodge provides facilities at this quiet, secluded place in the middle of the park. The lake, which is named for the intense color of its waters, is a popular spot for canoeing, walking, and riding horses.

Natural Bridge
Found in the center of the park, over the waters of the Kicking Horse River, Natural Bridge is a rock bridge formed by centuries of erosion, which have worn a channel through solid rock. The bridge is a short walk from Highway 1.

Hoodoo Creek
These fabulous, mushroom-like towers of rock have been created by erosion and can be accessed from a short off-highway trail.

KEY

- Highway
- Major road
- Rivers
- Campsite
- Picnic
- Visitor information
- Viewpoint

WAPTA ICEFIELD

VANCOUVER, GLACIER NATIONAL PARK

Jasper National Park ⓯

THE LARGEST AND MOST NORTHERLY of the four Rocky Mountain national parks, Jasper is also the most rugged. Covering an area of 10,878 sq km (4,199 sq miles) of high peaks and valleys dotted with glacial lakes, Jasper encompasses the Columbia Icefield *(see p308)*, a vast area of 400-year-old ice that is 900 m (2,953 ft) thick in places. From the icefield, fingers of ice reach down through many of Jasper's valleys.

Some of the most accessible hiking trails in the park start from the Maligne Lake and Canyon, and Jasper town. The town is located roughly in the park's center and is the starting point for many of the most popular walks and sights here, including the Miette Hot Springs.

Pyramid Lake
Ringed by jagged peaks, both Pyramid and nearby Patricia Lake lie close to Jasper town.

Snake Indian River
Jaspe Lake
VICTORIA CROSS RANGE
VANCOUVER
16
93a

The Jasper Tramway
Only a few kilometers out of Jasper town is the popular Jasper Tramway, which takes visitors to a viewing platform near the summit of Whistler's Mountain at 2,285 m (7,497 ft). Panoramic vistas take in the park's mountains, forests, and lakes.

KEY

- Major road
- Minor road
- Rivers
- Camping
- Picnic
- Visitor information
- Viewpoint

Mount Edith Cavell
It is possible to drive up this mountain as far as Cavell Lake from where the trail leads to Angel Glacier and to the flower-strewn Cavell Meadows.

Maligne Canyon
One of the most beautiful canyons in the Rockies, its sheer limestone walls and several impressive waterfalls can be seen from the many footbridges that are built both along and across its walls.

VISITORS' CHECKLIST

Hwys 93 & 16. *Jasper Tourism and Commerce, 409 Patricia St, Jasper (780) 852 3858. VIA Rail, Connaught St. Greyhound Bus Station. daily. www.explorejasper.com*

Miette Hot Springs
Visitors here enjoy relaxing in the warmest spring waters in the Rockies. The springs are said to have healing effects because of their high mineral content.

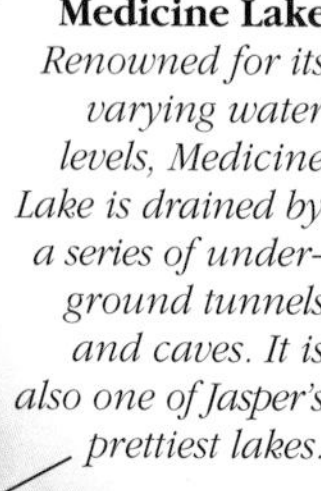

Medicine Lake
Renowned for its varying water levels, Medicine Lake is drained by a series of underground tunnels and caves. It is also one of Jasper's prettiest lakes.

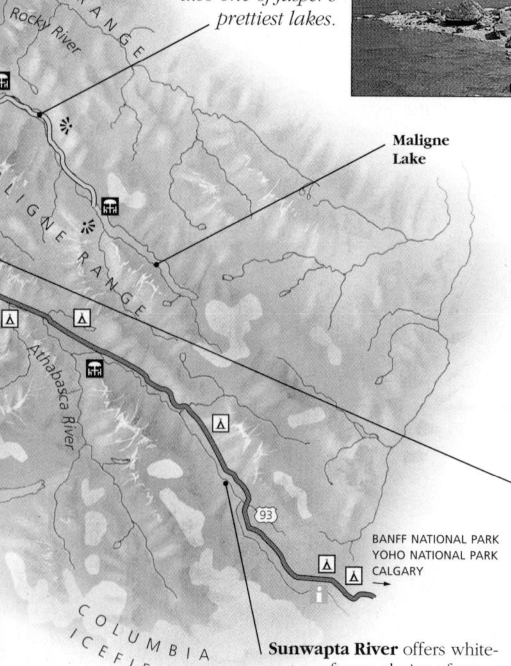

Sunwapta River offers white-water rafters a choice of conditions, from calm to turbulent.

Athabasca Falls
The dramatic, rushing waters of these falls are the result of the Athabasca River being forced through a narrow gorge.

Exploring Jasper

ESTABLISHED IN 1907, Jasper National Park is as staggeringly beautiful as anywhere in the Rockies, but it is distinguished by having more remote wilderness than the other national parks. These areas can be reached only on foot, horseback, or by canoe, and backpackers need passes from the Park Trail Office for hikes that last more than one day. Jasper also has a reputation for more sightings of wildlife such as bear, moose, and elk than any of the other Rockies' parks.

Although most of the park services are closed between October and Easter, visitors who brave the winter season have an opportunity to cross-country ski on breathtaking trails that skirt frozen lakes. In addition, they can go ice fishing, downhill skiing, or on guided walking tours on frozen rivers. In the summertime there are a range of daytrips which are easily accessible from the park's main town of Jasper.

Downhill skiing is just one of the outdoor activities around Jasper

Columbia Icefield and Icefield Centre

Icefields Parkway. (780) 852 6288. May–Oct: daily.

The Columbia Icefield straddles both Banff and Jasper National Parks and forms the largest area of ice in the Rockies. The Icefield covers 325 sq km (125 sq miles) and were created during the last Ice Age.

Around 10,000 years ago, ice filled the region, sculpting out wide valleys, sheer mountain faces, and sharp ridges. Although the glaciers have retreated over the last few hundred years, during the early years of the 20th century ice covered the area where the Icefields Parkway now passes.

The Icefields Centre has an interpretive centre that explains the Ice Age and the impact of the glaciers on the landscape of the Rockies. Tours of the Athabasca Glacier, in specially designed 4-wheel drive Sno-coaches, are available from the Icefield Centre, which also has information on trails in the area.

Athabasca Falls

Located at the junction of highways 93 and 93A, where the Athabasca River plunges 23 m (75 ft) to the river bed below, these are among the most dramatic waterfalls in the park. Despite being a short drop compared with other falls in the Rockies, the force of the waters of the Athabasca River being pushed through a narrow, quartz-rich gorge transforms these waters into a powerful, foaming torrent.

Jasper

The town of Jasper was established in 1911 as a settlement for Grand Trunk Pacific Railroad workers, who were laying track along the Athabasca River Valley. As with Banff, the coming of the railroad and the growth of the parks as resorts went hand-in-hand, and the town expanded to include hotels, restaurants, and a visitor center. Today, many of the park's main attractions are close to the town, which is located at the center of the park, on both Highway 16 and Icefields Parkway (Hwy 93).

Just 7 km (4.5 miles) out of town is the Jasper Tramway station, from where visitors may take a brisk, seven-minute ride up **Whistlers Mountain**. The trip whisks visitors up to the upper terminal at 2,285 m (7,497 ft), where there is a clearly marked trail leading to

The wild waters of Athabasca River make it a popular venue for white-water rafting

the summit at 2,470 m (8,100 ft). On a clear day the view is incomparable. For those who would rather walk than ride the tram, there is a 2.8-km (1.7-mile) trail to the top of the mountain. The trail winds upward, offering panoramic views of both the Miette and Athabasca valleys, and, in July, the lush meadows are blanketed with colorful wild flowers.

Patricia and Pyramid Lakes

North of Jasper townsite, the attractive Patricia and Pyramid lakes nestle beneath the 2,763-m (9,065-ft) high Pyramid Mountain. A popular daytrip from the town, the lakes are noted for windsurfing and sailing. Equipment rental is available from two lakeside lodges.

The deep blue waters of Pyramid Lake beneath Pyramid Mountain

Maligne Lake Drive

Maligne Lake Drive begins 5 km (3 miles) north of Jasper townsite and leads off Hwy 16, following the valley floor between the Maligne and the Queen Elizabeth ranges. This scenic road travels past one magnificent sight after another, with viewpoints along the way, offering visitors panoramas of Maligne Valley. Among the route's most spectacular sights is the Maligne Canyon, reached by a 4-km (2.5-mile) interpretive hiking trail which explains the special geological features behind the gorge's formation. One of the most beautiful in the Rockies, Maligne Canyon has sheer limestone walls as high as 50 m (150 ft) and many waterfalls, which can be seen from several foot bridges. The road ends at the impressive Maligne Lake. The largest natural lake in the Rockies, Maligne is 22 km (14 miles) long and surrounded by snow-capped mountains. There are several scenic trails around the lake, one of which leads to the Opal Hills and amazing views of the area. Guided walks around here can be organized from Jasper, and it is possible to rent fishing tackle and canoes and kayaks to go out on the lake.

A boat cruise on Maligne Lake, the largest natural lake in the Rockies

Medicine Lake

Medicine Lake is also reached from a side road off Maligne Lake Drive. The lake is noted for its widely varying water levels. In autumn the lake is reduced to a trickle, but in springtime the waters rise, fed by the fast-flowing Maligne River. A vast network of underground caves and channels are responsible for this event.

Miette Springs

(780) 866 3939. mid-May–Sep: daily.

Located 61 km (38 miles) north of Jasper along the attractive Miette Springs Road, these springs are the hottest in the Rockies, reaching temperatures as high as 53.9°C (129°F). However, the thermal baths are cooled to a more reasonable 39°C (102°F) for bathers. The waters are held to be both relaxing and healthy – they are rich in minerals, such as calcium, sulfates, and small amounts of hydrogen sulfide (which smells like rotten eggs).

The resort of Miette Springs now houses two new pools, including one suitable for children. The springs are part of a leisure complex that offers both restaurants and hotels.

Mount Edith Cavell

Named after World War I heroine nurse, this mountain is located 30 km (18.5 miles) south of Jasper townsite, and the scenic road that climbs it is well worth the drive. The road ends at Cavell Lake by the north face of the mountain. From here, a guided trail leads to a small lake beneath the Angel Glacier. A three-hour walk across the flower strewn Cavell meadows has views of the glacier's icy tongue.

A peninsula of ice from Angel Glacier seen from Mount Edith Cavell

Typical kitchen of the late 1900s at Grande Prairie Museum

Prince George 16

70,000. 1198 Victoria St. (250) 562 3700.

THE LARGEST town in northeastern British Columbia, Prince George is a bustling supply-and-transportation center for the region. Two major highways pass through here, the Yellowhead (Hwy 16) and Highway 97, which becomes the Alaska Highway at Dawson Creek. Established in 1807 as Fort George, a furtrading post at the confluence of the Nechako and Fraser rivers, the town is well placed for exploring the province.

Today, Prince George has all the facilities of a larger city, including a new university specializing in First Nations' history and culture, as well as its own symphony orchestra and several art galleries. The **Fort George Regional Museum** lies on the site of the original Fort, within the 26-ha (65-acre) Fort George Park, and has a small collection of artifacts from native cultures, European pioneers, and early settlers to the region.

An important center for the lumber industry, the town offers a range of free tours of local pulp mills, which take visitors through the process of wood production, from vast fields of young seedlings to hill-sized piles of planks and raw timber.

Fort George Regional Museum
20th Ave. & Queensway. (250) 562 1612. daily. Dec 25, Jan 1 **donation.**

Grande Prairie 17

28,250. 10632 102nd Ave. (780) 532 5340.

GRANDE PRAIRIE is a large, modern city in the northwest corner of Alberta. Surrounded by fertile farming country, the city is a popular stop for travelers heading north toward Dawson Creek and the Alaska Highway (*see pp260–1*). The city is the hub of the Peace River region; it offers extensive opportunities for shopping in its giant malls and many downtown specialty stores, with the added draw of having no provincial sales tax *(see p380)*.

Running through the city center is the attractive wilderness of Muskoseepi Park. Covering 45 ha (111 acres), the park offers a variety of outdoor activities including walking and biking trails, and cross-country skiing. Boating is very popular with both visitors and locals, and it is possible to rent canoes and rowboats to take out onto the Bear Creek Reservoir. The **Grande Prairie Museum** is also housed in the park and has ten buildings containing over 16,000 historical artifacts. There are several reconstructions, including a 1911 schoolhouse, a rural post office, and a church. A renowned display of dinosaur bones recovered from the Peace River Valley can also be seen here.

Peace River runs through a broad, flat valley over which stand high, ravine-filled canyon walls. The valley is a magnet for bird-watchers, and sightings of eagles are common. The Peace River wetlands, particularly those at Crystal Lake in the northeast corner of the city, contain one of the few breeding grounds for the rare trumpeter swan.

Grande Prairie Museum
cnr 102nd St. & 102nd Ave. (780) 532 5482. May–Sep: daily; Oct–Apr: Sun–Fri. Dec 25, Jan 1.

Fort St. John 18

14,800. 9323, 100th St. (250) 785 6037.

FORT ST. JOHN is located at Mile 47 of the Alaska Highway among the rolling hills of the Peace River Valley. During the construction of the Highway in 1942, the tiny town dramatically expanded from a population of about 800 to 6,000. When completed, the highway turned Fort St. John into a busy supply center that caters to visitors

Lush farmland along the Peace River in northern British Columbia

The Trans-Canada Highway overlooking the Fraser Canyon along the Fraser River

Whistler ❶

4,450. 4010 Whistler Way. (604) 932 2394.

WHISTLER IS THE largest ski resort in Canada. Set among the spectacular Coast Mountains, just 120 km (75 miles) north of Vancouver, the resort is divided into four distinct areas: Whistler Village, Village North, Upper Village, and Creekside. Whistler and Blackcomb mountains have the greatest vertical rises of any ski runs in North America. The skiing here can be among the best in the world with mild Pacific weather, and reliable winter snow. In summer there is skiing on Blackcomb's Hortsman Glacier.

Although the resort is relatively new (the first ski lift was opened in 1961), Whistler Village offers visitors a full range of facilities. There are lots of places to stay, from comfortable bed-and-breakfasts, to luxurious five-star hotels. Café-lined cobbled squares and cozy bars and restaurants cater to a diversity of tastes, while a variety of stores sell everything from ski wear to native arts and crafts in this friendly alpine village.

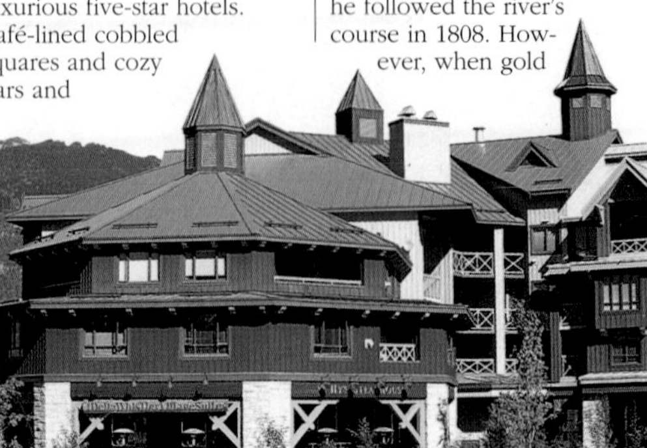

The ski resort at alpine Whistler village in British Columbia

Fraser River ❷

Vancouver (604) 739 0823.

THE MAJESTIC Fraser River travels 1,368 km (850 miles) through some of BC's most stunning scenery. The river flows from its source in the Yellowhead Lake, near Jasper, to the Strait of Georgia, near Vancouver. Along the way, it heads north through the Rocky Mountain trench before turning south near the town of Prince George. It continues by the Coast Mountains, then west to Hope through the steep walls of the Fraser Canyon, and on toward Yale.

It was Fraser Canyon that legendary explorer Simon Fraser found the most daunting when he followed the river's course in 1808. However, when gold was discovered near the town of Yale 50 years later, thousands of prospectors swarmed up the valley. Today, Yale is a small town with a population of 200 and the delightful **Yale Museum**, where exhibits focus on the history of the gold rush, as well as telling the epic story of the building of the Canadian Pacific Railroad through the canyon. This section of river is also a popular whitewater rafting area, and trips can be arranged from the small town of Boston Bar. At Hell's Gate the river thunders through the Canyon's narrow walls, which are only 34 m (112 ft) apart.

Yale Museum
Douglas St. *(604) 863 2324.*
Jun–Sep: 10am–5pm daily.

Hope ❸

3,150. 919 Water Ave. (604) 869 2021.

LOCATED AT THE southern end of the Fraser Canyon, Hope is crossed by several highways, including Hwy 1 (the Trans-Canada) and Hwy 3. Hope is an excellent base for exploring the Fraser Canyon and southern BC, as well as being within easy reach of several provincial parks. The beautiful country of Manning Provincial Park, with its lakes mountains, and rivers, is noted for its outdoor activities. During summer swimming, hiking, fishing, and sailing are popular: in winter there is both downhill and cross-country skiing.

SOUTHERN AND NORTHERN BRITISH COLUMBIA

SOUTHERN BRITISH Columbia covers the region south of Prince George, down to the US border. There is a vast variety of natural beauty here, including the forests and waterfalls of Wells Gray Provincial Park, and the lush valleys, wineries, and lake resorts of the Okanagan Valley. One of the most stunning wildernesses in North America, northern British Columbia spreads north of Prince Rupert, between the Coast Mountains in the west, the Rockies in the east, and the Yukon. Its dramatic landscape, from the volcanic terrain around Mount Edziza with its lava flows and cinder cones to the frozen forests of Atlin Provincial Park, can be reached from the scenic Cassiar Highway. Some of the best sights can be enjoyed on the boat trip to Queen Charlotte Islands. For 10,000 years the archipelago has been home to the Haida people, famous for their totem-carving.

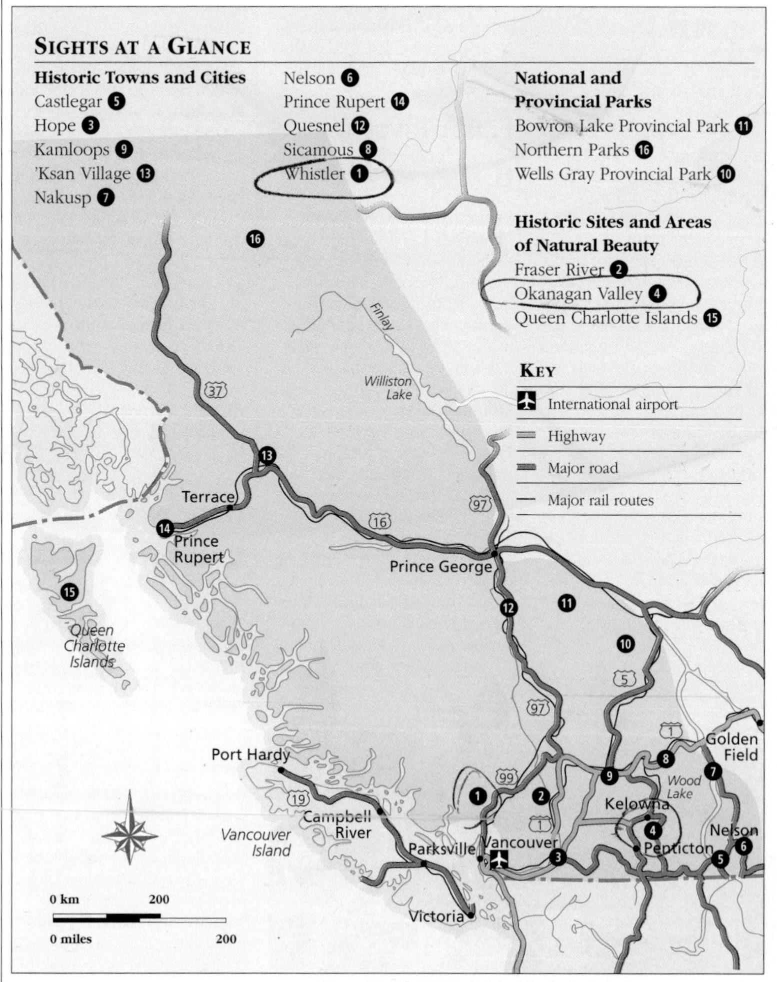

◁ **The Fraser River flowing through Fraser River Canyon in the midst of wooded winter scenery**

SOUTHERN AND NORTHERN BRITISH COLUMBIA

SOUTHERN BRITISH Columbia covers the region south of Prince George, down to the US border. There is a vast variety of natural beauty here, including the forests and waterfalls of Wells Gray Provincial Park, and the lush valleys, wineries, and lake resorts of the Okanagan Valley. One of the most stunning wildernesses in North America, northern British Columbia spreads north of Prince Rupert, between the Coast Mountains in the west, the Rockies in the east, and the Yukon. Its dramatic landscape, from the volcanic terrain around Mount Edziza with its lava flows and cinder cones to the frozen forests of Atlin Provincial Park, can be reached from the scenic Cassiar Highway. Some of the best sights can be enjoyed on the boat trip to Queen Charlotte Islands. For 10,000 years the archipelago has been home to the Haida people, famous for their totem-carving.

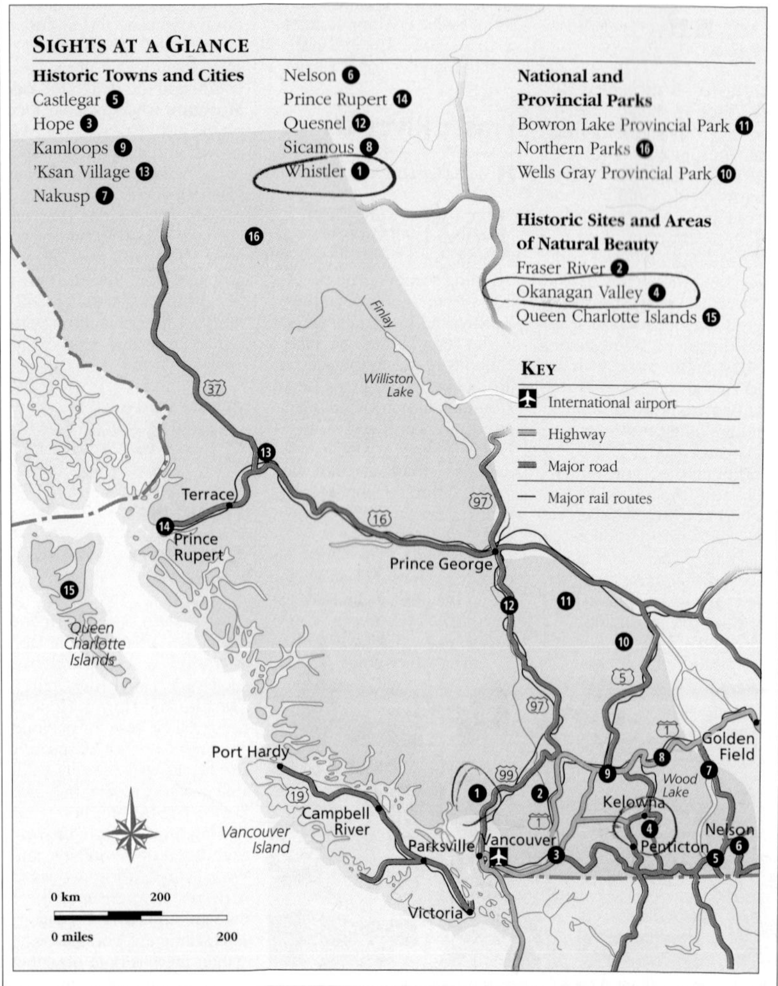

◁ The Fraser River flowing through Fraser River Canyon in the midst of wooded winter scenery

The Trans-Canada Highway overlooking the Fraser Canyon along the Fraser River

Whistler ❶

4,450. 4010 Whistler Way. (604) 932 2394.

WHISTLER IS THE largest ski resort in Canada. Set among the spectacular Coast Mountains, just 120 km (75 miles) north of Vancouver, the resort is divided into four distinct areas: Whistler Village, Village North, Upper Village, and Creekside. Whistler and Blackcomb mountains have the greatest vertical rises of any ski runs in North America. The skiing here can be among the best in the world with mild Pacific weather, and reliable winter snow. In summer there is skiing on Blackcomb's Hortsman Glacier.

Although the resort is relatively new (the first ski lift was opened in 1961), Whistler Village offers visitors a full range of facilities. There are lots of places to stay, from comfortable bed-and-breakfasts, to luxurious five-star hotels. Café-lined cobbled squares and cozy bars and restaurants cater to a diversity of tastes, while a variety of stores sell everything from ski wear to native arts and crafts in this friendly alpine village.

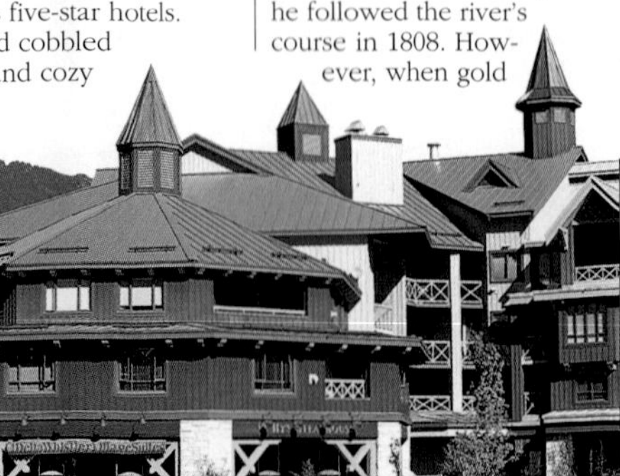

The ski resort at alpine Whistler village in British Columbia

Fraser River ❷

Vancouver (604) 739 0823.

THE MAJESTIC Fraser River travels 1,368 km (850 miles) through some of BC's most stunning scenery. The river flows from its source in the Yellowhead Lake, near Jasper, to the Strait of Georgia, near Vancouver. Along the way, it heads north through the Rocky Mountain trench before turning south near the town of Prince George. It continues by the Coast Mountains, then west to Hope through the steep walls of the Fraser Canyon, and on toward Yale.

It was Fraser Canyon that legendary explorer Simon Fraser found the most daunting when he followed the river's course in 1808. However, when gold was discovered near the town of Yale 50 years later, thousands of prospectors swarmed up the valley. Today, Yale is a small town with a population of 200 and the delightful **Yale Museum**, where exhibits focus on the history of the gold rush, as well as telling the epic story of the building of the Canadian Pacific Railroad through the canyon. This section of river is also a popular whitewater rafting area, and trips can be arranged from the small town of Boston Bar. At Hell's Gate the river thunders through the Canyon's narrow walls, which are only 34 m (112 ft) apart.

Yale Museum
Douglas St. (604) 863 2324.
Jun–Sep: 10am–5pm daily.

Hope ❸

3,150. 919 Water Ave. (604) 869 2021.

LOCATED AT THE southern end of the Fraser Canyon, Hope is crossed by several highways, including Hwy 1 (the Trans-Canada) and Hwy 3. Hope is an excellent base for exploring the Fraser Canyon and southern BC, as well as being within easy reach of several provincial parks. The beautiful country of Manning Provincial Park, with its lakes mountains, and rivers, is noted for its outdoor activities. During summer swimming, hiking, fishing, and sailing are popular: in winter there is both downhill and cross-country skiing.

Okanagan Valley Tour ❹

Okanagan wine

THE OKANAGAN VALLEY is actually a series of valleys, linked by a string of lakes, that stretches for 250 km (155 miles) from Osoyoos in the south, to Vernon in the north. The main towns here are connected by Highway 97, which passes through the desert landscape near Lake Osoyoos, and on to the lush green orchards and vineyards for which the valley is most noted. Mild winters and hot summers have made the Okanagan one of Canada's favorite vacation destinations.

Tips for Drivers

Starting point: *On Highway 97 from Vernon in the north: Osoyoos in the south.*
Length: *230 km (143 miles).*
Highlights: *Blossom and fruit festivals are held in spring and summer, when roadside stalls offer a cornucopia of fruit, and wine tours are available year-round.*

Kelowna ④
The biggest city in the Okanagan, Kelowna lies on the shores of Lake Okanagan between Penticton and Vernon, and is the center of the wine- and fruit-growing industries.

Vernon ⑤
Surrounded by farms and orchards, Vernon owes its lush look to the growth of irrigation in 1908. Several small resorts are set around the nearby lakes.

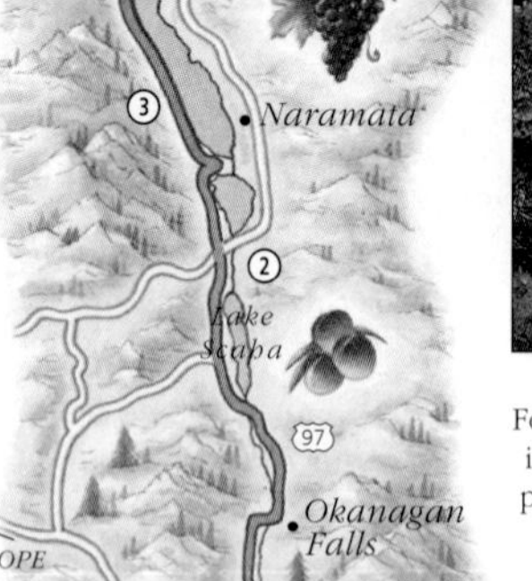

Summerland ③
This small but charming lakeside resort boasts several 19th-century buildings and stunning views from the top of Giant's Head Mountain.

Penticton ②
This sunny lakeside town is known for the long Okanagan Beach, windsurfing, and local winery tours, as well as for its Peach Festival, held every August.

O'Keefe Historic Ranch ⑥
Founded by the O'Keefe family in 1867, this historic ranch displays original artifacts belonging to the family who lived here until 1977. The original log cabin remains, as does the church and store.

0 km 25
0 miles 25

Osoyoos ①
Visitors are drawn here by hot summers, the warm waters and sandy beaches of Lake Osoyoos, and the nearby pocket desert.

Key

- Tour route
- Other roads
- Viewpoint

Impressive and historic stone buildings in the attractive town of Nelson

Castlegar ❺

7,200. 1995 6th Ave. (250) 365 6313.

Located in southeastern BC, Castlegar is a busy transportation hub. The town is crossed by two major highways, the Crowsnest and Hwy 22, and lies at the junction of the important Kootenay and Columbia rivers.

In the early 1900s, a steady influx of Doukhobors (Russian religious dissenters fleeing persecution) began arriving here. The **Doukhobor Village Museum** reflects the group's heritage and houses a variety of traditional clothes and tools, and antique farm machinery.

Traditional Doukhobor tunic

Doukhobor Village Museum
Jct Hwy 3 & 3A. *(250) 365 6622.*
May–Sep: daily.

Nelson ❻

9,000. 225 Hall St. (250) 352 3433.

One of the most attractive towns in southern British Columbia, Nelson overlooks Kootenay Lake. Established in the 1880s as a mining town, with the coming of the railroad in the 1890s, Nelson flourished as a center for transporting ore and timber. The town owes its good looks to its location on the shores of the lake and to the large number of public buildings and houses that were constructed between 1895 and 1920. In 1986 the town was chosen as the location for the Steve Martin comedy film, *Roxanne*. British Columbia's best-known architect, Francis Rattenbury *(see p278)*, played a part in the design of some of the town's most prestigious and beautiful structures, such as the elegant Burns building which was built in 1899 for millionaire cattle rancher and meat packer, Patrick Burns. Rattenbury also designed the Nelson Court House in 1908, a stately stone building with towers and gables.

Today, the town has a thriving cultural scene, with some 16 art galleries, as well as numerous cafés, book, and craft shops. Visitors also enjoy the short ride on Car 23, a 1906 streetcar that operated in the town between 1924 and 1949 (it was restored in 1992), and which today travels along Nelson's delightful waterfront. The infocenter provides visitors with a map and guide for the heritage walking tour of the town's historic buildings.

Nakusp ❼

1,700. 92 W. 6th Ave. (250) 265 4234.

With the snow-topped Selkirk Mountains as a backdrop, and overlooking the waters of Upper Arrow Lake, Nakusp is a charming town. Originally developed as a mining settlement, the town is now known for its mineral hot springs. There are two resorts close to town; the Nakusp and Halcyon Hot Springs, both of which provide therapeutic bathing in hot waters, rich in sulfates, calcium, and hydrogen sulfide, said to be good for everyday aches, as well as arthritis and rheumatism.

The town of Nakusp overlooking picturesque Upper Arrow Lake

Houseboats moored along the waterfront at Sicamous

Roughly 40 km (25 miles) to the south of Nakusp, in the Slocan Valley, are two fascinating abandoned silver mining towns, New Denver and Sandon. Sandon had 5,000 inhabitants at the height of the mining boom in 1892. It also had 29 hotels, 28 saloons, and several brothels and gambling halls. A fire in 1900, poor metal prices, and dwindling ore reserves crippled the mines, and Sandon became a ghost town. Today, the town has been declared an historic site, and its homes and businesses are being carefully restored. The nearby town of New Denver suffered a fate similar to Sandon's, but is also noted as the site of an internment camp for the Japanese during World War II. The Nikkei Internment Centre on Josephine Street is the only center in Canada devoted to telling the story of the internment of over 20,000 Japanese Canadians. The center is surrounded by a formal Japanese garden.

Sicamous 8

3,088. 110 Finlayson St. (250) 836 3313.

Sicamous is an appealing waterfront village known for its 3,000 houseboats, as well as its charming cobblestone streets hung with flower-filled planters. Located between Mara and Shuswap lakes, at the junction of the Trans-Canada Highway and Highway 97A, the town is ideally placed for touring the lakes, and the resort of Salmon Arm, at the northern end of the Okanagan Valley *(see p315)*. Over 250 houseboats are available for renting in the summer, and there are 12 marinas and a houseboat store. From the boats it is possible to view the inlets and forested landscape of Lake Shuswap where wildlife such as black bear, deer, moose, coyote, and bobcat have been spotted along the shore. In summer, visitors and locals enjoy both the good public beach on the lake, as well as the pleasant walk along a marked waterfront trail.

Kamloops 9

80,000. 1290 W. Trans-Canada Hwy. (250) 374 3377.

Kamloops means "where the rivers meet" in the language of the Secwepemc First Nations. The largest town by area in BC's southern interior, it lies at the crossroads of the north and south Thompson Rivers. Three major highways also meet here; the Trans-Canada, Hwy 5, and Hwy 97 to the Okanagan Valley, as do the Canadian Pacific and Canadian National railroad.

European settlement began in 1812, when fur traders started doing business with local natives. The **Museum and Native Heritage Park** in Kamloops focuses on the cultural history of the Secwepemc First Nations and has a variety of artifacts, including a birch-bark canoe, hunting equipment, and cooking utensils. Outside, short trails lead visitors through the archeological remains of a 2,000-year-old Shuswap winter village site, which includes four authentically reconstructed winter pit houses and a summer camp. The village has a hunting shack, a fish-drying rack, and a smoke house. The museum store sells pine-needle and birch-bark baskets, moccasins, and a wide variety of beaded and silver jewelry.

A horse's snow shoe on display at Kamloops

In the town center, the Art Gallery has a small but striking collection that features landscape sketches by A.Y. Jackson, one of the renowned Group of Seven painters *(see pp160–61)*.

Museum and Native Heritage Park

353 Yellowhead Hwy. (250) 828 9801. Jun–Sep: daily; Sep–May: 8:30am–4:30pm Mon–Fri.

Wells Gray Provincial Park 10

(604) 924 2200. Clearwater. Clearwater. daily.

Wells Gray Provincial Park is one of the most beautiful wildernesses in British Columbia, and offers wonders comparable to the Rockies in the east. The park was established in 1939 and is distinguished by alpine meadows, thundering waterfalls, and glacier-topped peaks that rise as high as 2,575-m (8,450 ft). The Canadian National Railroad and Hwy 5 follow the Thompson River along the park's western edge, and both routes offer travelers stunning views.

From the Clearwater Valley Road, off Hwy 5, there are several trails, from easy walks to arduous overnight hikes in remote country. A selection of small trails, just a few minutes from the road, lead to the spectacular sight of Dawson Falls.

Bowron Lake Provincial Park ⓫

(250) 398 4414. Quesnel. Quesnel. daily (weather permitting). partial.

Bowron Lake Provincial Park is located about 113 km (70 miles) east of Quesnel on Highway 26 in the Cariboo Mountains. The park is renowned for having a 112-km (70-mile) rectangular waterway composed of nine lakes, three rivers, streams, small lakes, and many portages (trails linking the waterways). There is a week-long canoe trip here, but it is limited to 50 canoeists at a time, and passes must be obtained from the visitor center. It is a special trip that allows visitors to come quietly upon wildlife such as moose or beaver. In late summer, bears come to feed on the spawning sockeye salmon in the Bowron River.

A grizzly bear standing up

Quesnel ⓬

23,000. 705 Carson Ave. (250) 992 8716.

Quesnel is a busy logging town that started life as a gold rush settlement between 1858 and 1861. The town was the last along the Gold Rush Trail, or Cariboo Road (now Hwy 97), which was lined with mining towns between here and Kamloops. Quesnel occupies an attractive position in a triangle formed by the Fraser and Quesnel rivers. The town's sights include the Riverfront Park Trail System, a tree-lined 5-km (3-mile) path that runs along the banks of both rivers. Just outside the town's limits, Pinnacle Provincial Park features the geological wonder of hoodoos, rocky columns formed 12 million years ago when the volcanic surface was eroded by Ice Age meltwaters.

From Quesnel, 87 km (54 miles) east on Hwy 26, lies the historic mining town of **Barkerville**. The town was born when Englishman Billy Barker dug up a handful of gold nuggets in 1862. Today, it is a good example of a perfectly preserved 19th-century mining town, with more than 120 restored or reconstructed buildings and costumed guides. Visitors can see a blacksmith at work in his forge, see showgirls put on the kind of display the miners would have seen at the theater, or take a ride on a stagecoach.

A 19th-century horse and carriage in the streets of Barkerville

Barkerville
85 km E. of Quesnel, Hwy 26.
(250) 994 3302. daily.

'Ksan Village ⓭

(250) 842 5544. grounds: year round; houses: Apr–Sep: daily.

Some 290 km (180 miles) east of Prince Rupert, 'Ksan Village is a re-creation of an 1870 native settlement, established in the 1950s to preserve the culture of the Gitxsan First Nations. Gitxsan natives have lived in the area for thousands of years, particularly along the beautiful Skeena River valley. Their way of life was threatened by an influx of white settlers who arrived in the 1850s at Prince Rupert to work their way up river to mine or farm.

Noted for their skill in creating carved and painted masks, totems, and canoes, Gitxsan elders are now schooling new generations in these skills at 'Ksan Village. Within the complex there are seven traditional long houses containing a carving school, a museum, and a gift shop.

Gitxsan carved cedarwood totem pole in 'Ksan Indian village

Prince Rupert ⓮

16,000. 100 1st Ave. W. (250) 624 5637.

Prince Rupert is a vibrant port city, and the second-largest on BC's coast. Located on Kaien Island, at the mouth of the Skeena River, the city is circled by forests and mountains, and overlooks the beautiful fjord-studded coastline. The harbor is busy with cruise ships, ferries, and fishing boats and is the main access point for the rugged Queen Charlotte Islands and Alaska.

Like many of BC's major towns, Prince Rupert's development is linked to the growth of the railroad. Housed in the 1914 Grand Trunk Railroad Station, the Kwinitsa Railway Museum tells the story of businessman Charles Hay's big plans for the town, which were largely unfulfilled: he went down with the *Titanic* in 1912.

Tsimshian First Nations were the first occupants of the area, and as recently as 150 years ago the harbor was lined with their large cedar houses and carved totems. The excellent **Museum of Northern British Columbia** focuses on Tsimshian history and culture

and offers archaeological tours, including the Tsimshian village of Metlakatla, describing their culture over 10,000 years.

Museum of Northern British Columbia
100 1st Ave. W. *(250) 624 3207.*
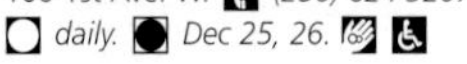
daily. *Dec 25, 26.*

Queen Charlotte Islands ⓯

Prince Rupert. *Prince Rupert.* *3220 Wharf St., Queen Charlotte. (250) 559 8316 (open May–Sep).*

SHAPED LIKE A bent ice-cream cone, the Queen Charlotte Islands, also known as Haida Gwaii, are an archipelago of about 150 islands across from the city of Prince Rupert.

The Queen Charlotte Islands were left untouched by the last Ice Age, and have an ecosystem unique to Canada. The forests house distinctive species of mammal such as the dusky shrew and short-tailed weasel. The islands are also home to a large population of bald eagles, and the spring brings hundreds of migrating gray whales past their shores.

The islands have been the home of the Haida people for thousands of years. Today, the Haida are recognized for their artistic talents, particularly their carvings and sculptures from cedar wood and argillite (a black slatelike stone found only on these islands).

It was the Haida who led environmental campaigns against the logging companies in the 1980s, which led to the founding of the **Gwaii Haanas National Park Reserve** in 1988. The park houses centuries-old rainforest, including 1,000-year-old Sitka spruce, red cedar, and western hemlock.

Atlin Lake in remote Atlin Provincial Park

Gwaii Haanas National Park Reserve
(250) 559 8818. *May–Sep.*

Northern Parks ⓰

Mount Edziza, Spatsizi; Hwy 37. Atlin; Hwy 7. *(250) 624 5637.*

THE PROVINCIAL parks of northern British Columbia comprise Mount Edziza Provincial Park, Spatsizi Plateau Wilderness Provincial Park, and, farther north, Atlin Provincial Park. These offer remote landscapes, with high peaks, icefields, and tundra.

Established in 1972, Mount Edziza Provincial Park is distinguished by its volcanic landscape which includes lava rivers, basalt plateaus, and cinder cones. The park can be reached by a minor road off the Cassiar Highway (Hwy 37). There is no vehicle access within the park, and only long, rugged overland trails or chartered float planes take visitors through open meadows, arctic birch woods, and over creeks.

Across the highway lies the even more rugged country of Spatsizi Plateau Wilderness Provincial Park, which includes the snow-capped peaks of the Skeena Mountains. Gladys Lake, a small lake in the center of the park, is an ecological reserve for the study of sheep and mountain goats. Access to the park is again limited to a small road leading from the village of Tatogga along Hwy 37. The village also offers guides and float plane hire.

The spectacular Atlin Provincial Park is only accessible from the Yukon on Hwy 7, off the Alaska Hwy. About one-third of the park is covered by large icefields and glaciers.

Massett, one of three major towns on Graham Island, the most populous of the Queen Charlotte Islands

Northern Canada

Introducing Northern Canada

Northern Canada covers the Yukon, Northwest Territories, and Nunavut, and stretches up to within 800 km (500 miles) of the North Pole, and from the Atlantic Ocean west to the Pacific, 37 percent of Canada's total area. The landscape is incredibly harsh: barren, treeless, frozen tundra dominates most of the year, with subarctic forest, mountains, glaciers, and icy lakes and rivers. Nonetheless, an abundance of wildlife flourishes, with musk ox, caribou, polar bears, and seals. At the height of the brief summer the "midnight sun" provides 24-hour days, while the Aurora Borealis *(see p335)* illuminates dark winters with ribbons of colored light. Development in the far north has occurred only where conditions are hospitable, often where the land is most scenic and varied. Populated by First Nations people some 25,000 years ago and the Inuit about 3000 BC, this uniquely dramatic land is enjoyed by 500,000 visitors a year.

Glorious flaming fall colors rise above the evergreens in the north of the Yukon

Getting Around

The watchword when traveling in this region is cost; trips, accommodations, and even food are all far more expensive than in the rest of the country. In the Yukon all major towns are connected by bus, but the most flexible way to travel around is by car. Air is the best means of traveling in Nunavut and the Northwest Territories. There are 600 landing strips and small airports here. Visitors should be aware that accommodations are equally restricted. In many settlements only one hotel is available, but the Yukon towns are well-equipped with places to stay.

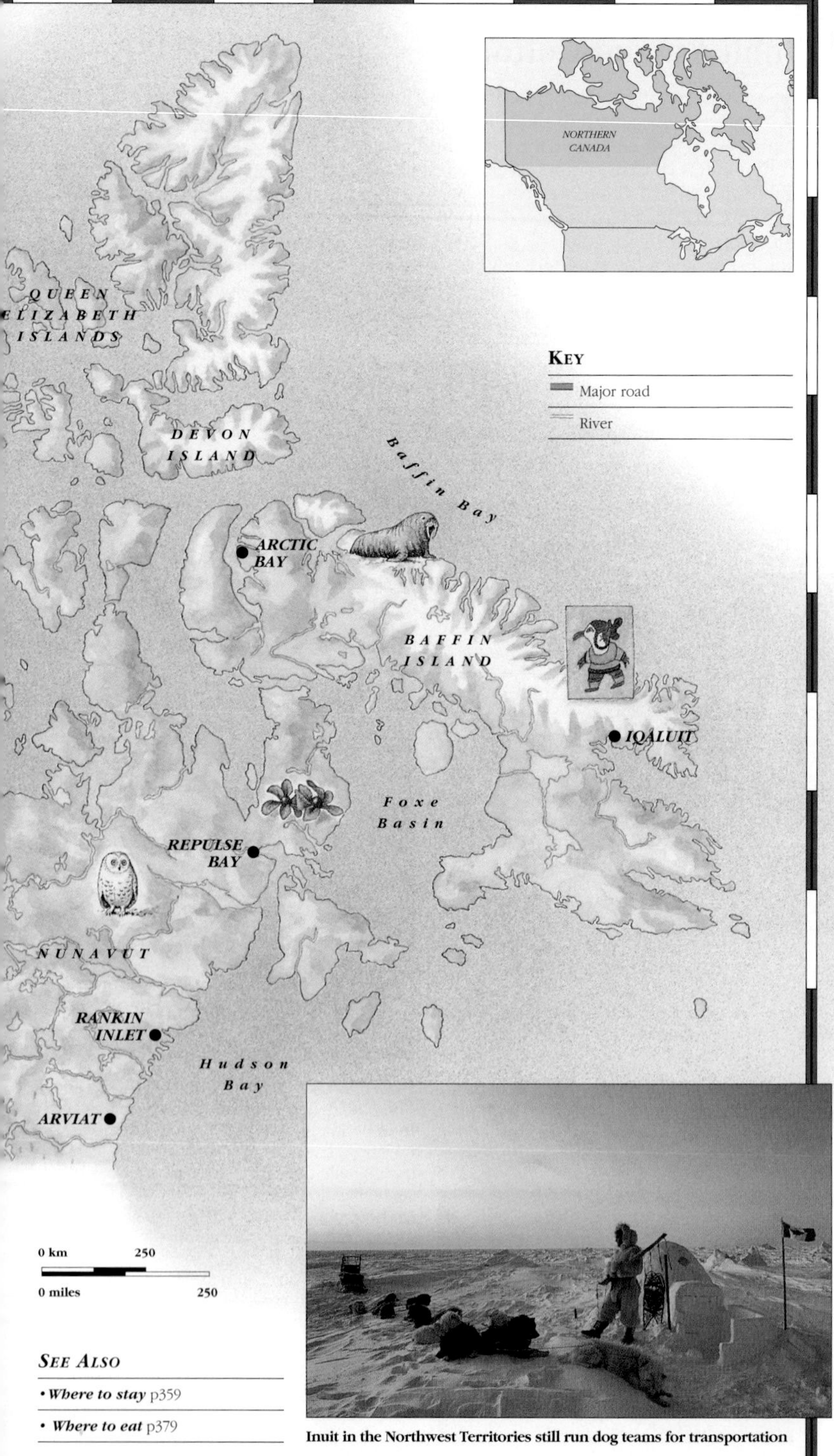

Inuit in the Northwest Territories still run dog teams for transportation

SEE ALSO

- ***Where to stay*** p359
- ***Where to eat*** p379

Inuit Art and Culture

FOR CENTURIES, the hunting and trapping lifestyle has created a distinct culture for the Inuit. Their customs have remained largely the same throughout the communities of eastern and central Northern Canada, although regional differences can be seen in the varied artforms. The Inuit have a limited written tradition, and much of 21st-century culture is still oral. It might seem surprising, given the outstandingly harsh environment and limited natural resources, that their communities offer a flourishing artistic output, but it is the hardship of northern life that has promoted artistic achievement. For example, the Inuit use their tool-making skills for sculpture. Inuit culture is closely tied to their lansdcape and environment, which has inspired many artists and mythmakers.

This woodblock print *of a girl meeting a polar bear represents an artform developed in the 1950s. Stone cuts and stencils are also used to interpret drawings by older artists.*

Warm clothing is both functional and decorative. Often painstakingly handwoven from scraps from the remains of a kill, women dress their families mostly in fur and wool.

Inuit beadwork and jewelry *was made in earlier times from bone and ivory; colored stones and beads are now used. Each piece shows birds, animals, or people, and is unique. Western influences include new designs in silver and gold.*

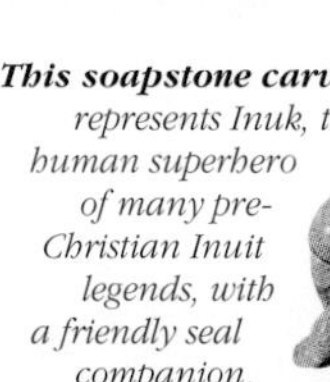

This soapstone carving *represents Inuk, the human superhero of many pre-Christian Inuit legends, with a friendly seal companion.*

INUIT WOMAN PREPARING CHAR

The outdated, if not offensive, name for the Inuit people is "eskimo," a native Cree word meaning "eaters of raw meat." The Inuit traditionally eat their meat uncooked, as the Arctic has no trees for firewood. Much of the caribou, polar bear, and fish was sundried or mixed with sauces made from summer fruits and berries. The arrival of the stone and modern fuels has changed the menu somewhat, although tradition remains at the heart of the community's eating habits.

These dancing costume ornaments *are carved from ivory or whalebone and worn by Inuit dancers to celebrate ceremonial events. As with clothing, Arctic bird feathers are used for decoration.*

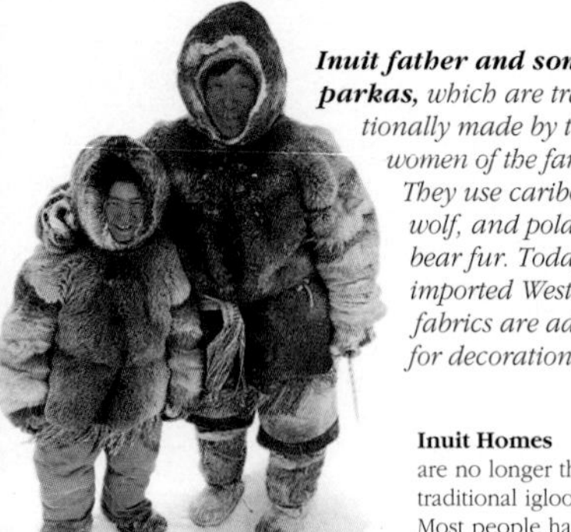

Inuit father and son in parkas, *which are traditionally made by the women of the family. They use caribou, wolf, and polar bear fur. Today, imported Western fabrics are added for decoration.*

Inuit fishermen *have made the best possible use of their often limited natural resources and still rely largely on small-scale fishing for food.*

Inuit Homes are no longer the traditional igloo. Most people have moved to camps or community housing.

Traditional hunting and fishing remains at the core of Inuit culture, although in the 1960s the Ottawa government unsuccessfully tried to stop these ancient practices.

INUIT MYTH

Carving of Inuk fighting his spirit

Set on the very fringes of the habitable world, the Inuit guarded against the threat of starvation with a supernatural belief system based on the respect of the animals they hunted, being careful to guard against divine retribution. Their myths promote the belief that every living creature has a soul, and that the village shaman could travel between the upper and lower worlds to commune with, and appease, the spirits in control of the hunt and the weather. Since earliest times hunting tools and weapons have been carved with the representations of the appropriate guardian spirit, and singers and musicians are well versed in legends of sea spirits and human heroes.

Drum dancing *is one of the varied forms of traditional music, and plays an important part in most of life's great events: births, weddings, a successful hunt, and honoring a person who has died. Another form of music, throat singing, is usually performed by two women facing one another to recount a legend, life event, or myth.*

Northern Canada

Still one of the most remote destinations on Earth, Northern Canada's Arctic beauty is now accessible to adventurous travelers in search of untouched terrain for superlative, challenging hiking and exploring. Many of the settlements at this brink of the world were established only in the 20th century. Some of the first towns grew up around RCMP outposts, established to monitor trappers, explorers, and whalers in Canadian territory; more recently defense outposts have developed new settlements. Local Inuit communities have gradually given up their nomadic life, and many are now settled around these outposts. These small towns are bases for exploring the stunning surroundings. In the winter the north is cold, descending to -50°C (-58°F), yet in summer warm air sweeps over the cold land, and the tundra bursts into bloom. The thaw acts in defiance of eight long months of winter when everything is draped in a blanket of white. This is a startlingly beautiful land with deserted plains, icy trails, rare wildlife, and gentle people, and is ripe for discovery.

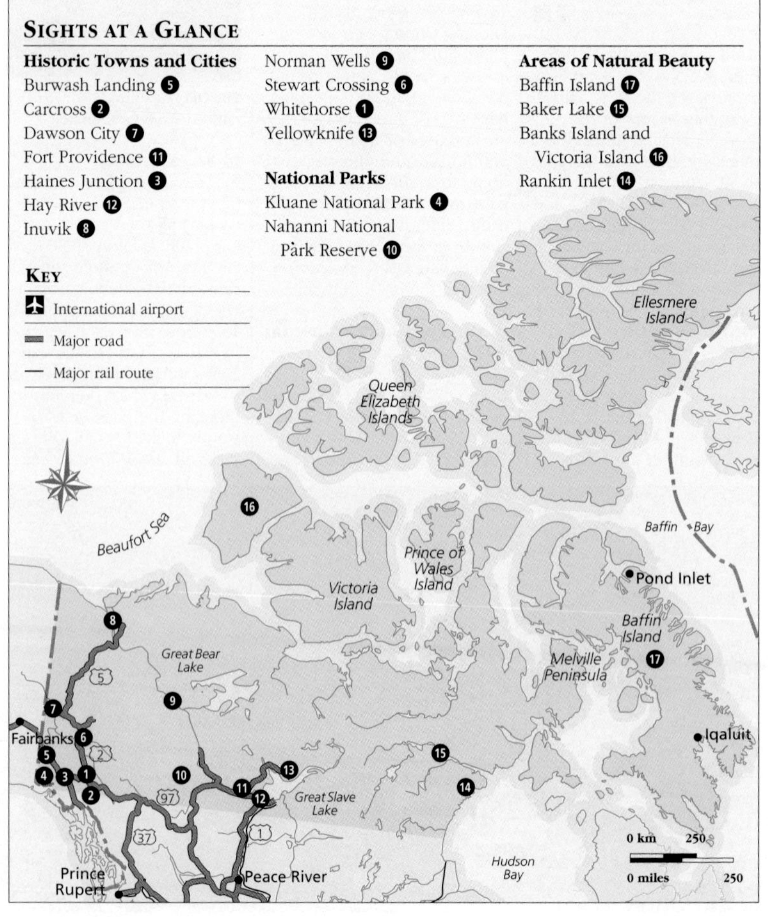

◁ **The frozen seas surrounding the coast of Baffin Island**

Whitehorse ❶

WHITEHORSE TAKES ITS NAME from the local rapids on the Yukon River that reminded miners in the gold rush of "the flowing manes of albino Appaloosas." The town evolved when 2,500 stampeders on the hunt for gold braved the arduous Chilkoot and White Pass trails on foot in the winter of 1897–98 and set up camp here by the banks of Lindeman and Bennett Lakes. Boatmen made over 7,000 trips through the rapids during the spring thaw of 1898 before a tramway was built around them. On the spot where gold miners could catch a boat downstream to the mines of the Klondike and the glittering nightlife of Dawson City in the Yukon, a tent town sprang up and Whitehorse was born. This regional capital is the fastest-growing town in the northern territories, but despite all modern amenities, the wilderness is always only a few moments away.

MacBride Museum

First Avenue & Wood St. *(867) 667 2709.* *late May–Sep: daily; Sep–May: noon–4pm Tue–Thu.*

The MacBride Museum is housed in a log cabin at the corner of Wood Street and First Avenue along the river. Here the exciting history of the Yukon is revealed in its glory, with galleries featuring the gold rush, Whitehorse, natural history, the Mounties (RCMP), and native peoples of the region. Special features include an engine from the White Pass and Yukon Railroad, and a log cabin complete with recorded poetry readings from Yukon poet Robert Service *(see p31)*. Also included is the restored old government telegraph office, originally built in 1899 and used as the focus for the new museum in the 1950s.

Log Skyscrapers

Lambert St. & Third St. *(867) 667 3084.*

Two blocks away from the Old Log Church Museum on Elliott Street are the unique log skyscrapers. Now several decades old, these log cabins have two or three floors. They are still used as apartments and offices, and one was home to a Yukon member of parliament. Worth a detour, the cabins offer a pleasing diversion from the rather functional architecture that characterizes much of the rest of town.

Old Log Church Museum

Elliott St. & Third Ave. *(867) 668 2555.* *Jun–Sep.*

In 1900 Whitehorse's first priest lived and held services in a tent in the town. However, by 1901 the Old Log Church and Rectory had been built. They are now among the few buildings here remaining from the gold rush period. The church was the Roman Catholic cathedral for the diocese and is the only wooden cathedral in the world. Fully restored and now also open as a museum, the church displays exhibits of pre-contact life of the native peoples, as well as early explorers and exploration, the gold rush, long-standing missionary work with the natives in the region, and the church's history.

The Old Log Church, constructed entirely from local timber

S.S. Klondike

End Second Ave. *(867) 667 3910.* *mid-May–mid-Sep: 9am–7pm daily.*

Originally built in 1929, the S.S. *Klondike* paddle-steamer sank in 1936. Rebuilt from its wreckage, the *Klondike* made 15 supply trips each season to Dawson City. In the early 1950s, bridges along the road to Dawson were built too low, blocking the passage of the sternwheelers, so all journeys stopped. The *Klondike* ceased

The city center of Whitehorse, sheltered in the Yukon River valley

S.S. *Klondike* in its permanent home in Whitehorse

operating in 1955 and was beached forever in Whitehorse. It is now restored to its heyday in every detail, right down to the 1937 *Life* magazines on the tables and authentic staff uniforms. Although no longer operational, the boat is a National Historic Site, with regular guided tours of the interior on offer.

Lake Laberge

Klondike Hwy. *(867) 667 5340.* *daily, weather permitting.*

Largest of the lakes in the area, Lake Laberge is 62 km (39 miles) from Whitehorse along the Klondike Hwy. Frozen for most of the year, with temperatures dropping below -30°C (-22°F), this popular summer swimming, fishing, and boating destination comes to life during the annual thaw. The lake is famous among locals as the site of the funeral pyre of Yukon poet Robert Service's Cremation of Sam Mc Gee, which relates the true-life demise of a local hero. Trout fishing is excellent; fish were barged here by the ton during the Klondike gold rush to feed the hordes of hopeful miners.

Local mountain goat

Visitors' Checklist

17,975. *White Pass & Yukon Route.* *Greyhound bus depot, 2191 2nd Ave.* *Whitehorse Visitor Reception Centre, 100 Hanson St. (867) 667 3084.* *Yukon Quest, Yukon Sourdough Rendezvous, Frostbite Music Festival (Feb).* *www.touryukon.com*

Yukon Wildlife Reserve

Takhini Hot Springs Rd.

(867) 668 3225. *daily.*

This sanctuary was set up in 1965 for research and breeding purposes and lies about 25 km (16 miles) from the town off the Klondike Hwy on the Takhini Hot Springs Road. A beautiful reserve of forest, grassland, meadows, and water areas, it has many indigenous animals of the far north roaming free in their natural settings. Moose, bison, elk, caribou, mountain goats, deer, Dall sheep, as well as musk ox can all be seen here protected in the 280-ha (700-acre) parkland of their natural roaming habitat.

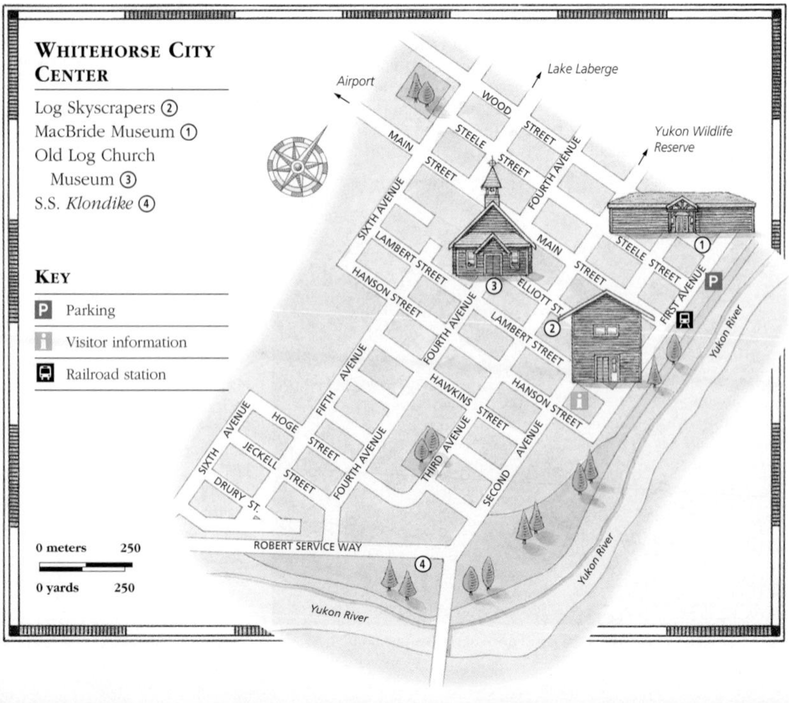

Whitehorse City Center

Log Skyscrapers ②
MacBride Museum ①
Old Log Church Museum ③
S.S. *Klondike* ④

Key

- Parking
- Visitor information
- Railroad station

0 meters 250
0 yards 250

Male caribou resting near Carcross, as herds migrate across the Yukon

Carcross ❷

250. *(867) 821 4431,* *mid-May–Sep daily.*

Carcross is a small village that lies at the picturesque confluence of Bennet and Tagish Lakes, an hour's drive south of Yukon's regional capital, Whitehorse. Early miners crossing the arduous Chilkoot Pass on their journey to the bounty of the gold mines in the north named the site "Caribou Crossing" after herds of caribou stormed their way through the pass between the two lakes on their biannual migration. The town was established in 1898 in the height of the gold rush with the arrival of the White Pass and Yukon railroad. "Caribou Crossing" was abbreviated officially to Carcross to avoid duplication of names in Alaska, British Colombia, and a town in the Klondike.

Carcross has a strong native tradition, and was once an important caribou hunting ground for the Tagish tribe. Tagish guides worked for US Army surveyors during the building of the Alaska Highway in 1942 *(see pp 260–61)*.

Traveling just 2 km (1 mile) north, there is a chance to see the smallest desert in the world, Carcross Desert. Blasted by strong winds, the sandy plain is barren, and the only remnant of a glacial lake that dried up after the last Ice Age. The strength of the winds allows little vegetation to grow, but the spot is memorable.

Haines Junction ❸

862. *Kluane National Park Visitor Information Centre (867) 634 2345.*

A useful service center on the Alaska and Haines highways, Haines Junction is a handy fuel and food stop for visitors on the way to the impressive Kluane National Park. The town has a post office, restaurant, and hotels. Trips into the park for rafting, canoeing, and various hiking excursions can be organized from the town, as the park's administrative headquarters are here. Haines Junction was once a base camp for the US Army engineers who in 1942 built much of the Alcan Highway (now known as the Alaska Highway) that links Fairbanks in Alaska to the south of Canada. The St. Elias Mountains tower above the town, and air trips can be taken from here to admire the views of the frozen scenery, glaciers, and icy peaks of this wilderness.

The St. Elias range dominates the small town of Haines Junction

Kaskawulsh Glacier rising over Kluane National Park

Kluane National Park ❹

(867) 634 2345. *Haines Junction.* *year round.*

This superb wilderness area is a United Nations World Heritage Site. Covering 22,000 square km (8,500 square miles) of the southwest corner of the Yukon, the park shares the St. Elias mountain range, the highest in Canada, with Alaska. The whole park comprises the largest nonpolar icefield in the world.

Two-thirds of the park is glacial, filled with valleys and lakes that are frozen year-round, broken up by alpine forests, meadows, and tundra. The landscape is one of the last surviving examples of an Ice Age environment, which disappeared in the rest of the world around 5–10,000 BC. Mount Logan, at over 5,950 m (18,500 ft), is Canada's tallest peak. Numerous well-marked and established trails make for excellent hiking here, and

Kluane National Park displays radiant foliage in fall, as seen here in the Alsek River area

several conveniently start from the main road. There are some less defined routes, which follow the old mining trails. There are trails to suit both the novice and experienced hiker, ranging from a two-hour stroll to a ten-day guided trek.

Kluane's combination of striking scenery and an abundance of wildlife, including moose, Dall sheep, and grizzly bears, make it the Yukon's most attractive wilderness destination. Trips into the park are organized mostly from nearby Haines Junction. Due to the hazardous weather, untamed wildlife, and isolated conditions, safety measures are mandatory here.

Burwash Landing 5

88. Whitehorse (867) 667 5340.

NORTHWEST OF Haines Junction by 124 km (77 miles), this little village at the western end of Kluane Lake lies just outside Kluane National Park on the Alaska Hwy. A community was established here in 1905, after a gold strike in a local creek, and Burwash Landing is now a service center. Visitors can also enjoy stunning panoramas of Kluane Lake to the south.

The village is noted for its Kluane Museum, with many animal-related exhibits, including a mammoth's tooth and numerous displays on local natural history. Focus is also given to the traditional lifestyle of the region's tribe of Southern Tutchone native people.

Kluane Museum
Burwash Junction. *(867) 841 5561.*
mid-May–mid-Sep: 9am–9pm daily.

Stewart Crossing 6

25. Whitehorse (867) 667 5340.

APPROXIMATELY 180 km (113 miles) east of Dawson City *(see p334)*, Stewart Crossing is a small community at the junction of the Klondike Hwy and the Silver Trail, which leads to the small mining settlements of Mayo, Elsa, and Keno, once famous for their silver trade. During the gold rush in the late 19th century, the area was referred to as the "grubstake," because enough gold could be panned from the river sandbars here during the summer to buy the following year's stake. Stewart Crossing is a modest service center that also operates as the starting-point for canoe trails on the Stewart River. Unusual for this wild terrain, these boat trips are suitable for children and beginners. Trips should be organized in Whitehorse or Dawson City.

Above the community is a scenic viewpoint that overlooks the spectacular Klondike River valley and the **Tintina Trench**. Providing in a glance visible proof of the geological theory of plate tectonics, the trench itself stretches for several hundred kilometers across the Yukon, with layers of millennia-old rock gaping open to the skies. "Tintina" means "chief" in the local native language, and this is one of the largest geological faults in the Yukon system. Stewart Crossing is an ideal place to view the trench, which runs up to here along the route of the Klondike Hwy, from a course parallel with the Yukon River that begins at Fortymile village.

Broad Valley by Stewart Crossing near the Yukon River, Yukon

The stunning beauty of a Yukon river valley in summer ▷

The Gaslight Follies Theatre in Dawson City

Dawson City ❼

2,150. cnr Front & King Sts. (867) 993 5566.

THE TOWN OF Dawson City came into prominence during the Klondike gold rush of 1898 *(see pp46–7)*, when the population boomed and the city grew from a moose pasture into a bustling metropolis of some 30–40,000 people, all seeking their fortune in the new "Paris of the North." Dawson City continues to mine gold, but tourism is now the town's most reliable source of income.

Dawson City Museum has exhibits on the Klondike, with features on the gold rush and artifacts from that period. A popular attraction is **Diamond Tooth Gertie's**, the gambling hall complete with a honky-tonk piano and can-can girls.

Inuvik welcomes its visitors

Dawson City Museum
5th Ave. *(867) 993 5291.*
mid-May–Sep: 10am–6pm daily; late Sep–May: by appointment.

Diamond Tooth Gertie's
cnr 4th Ave. & Queen St. *(867) 993 5575. mid-May–mid-Sep: 7pm–2am daily.*

Inuvik ❽

3,300. W. Arctic Regional Visitors' Centre (867) 777 4727.

ABOUT 770 KM (480 miles) north of Dawson City, Inuvik lies at the tip the Dempster Hwy, the most northerly road in Canada. At the heart of the Mackenzie River delta, Inuvik has only a very recent history. Founded in the 1950s as a supply center for military projects in the NWT, the town prospered in the oil boom of the 1970s. Full of functional contemporary architecture, Inuvik's charm lies more in its location as a very good visitors' center for the region – there are a few hotels and several shops, no mean feat for a town that boasts just a single traffic light. It is, nonetheless, the most visited town in the northern Arctic, popular as a craft center for the Inuit and as a starting point for a tour of the far north.

ENVIRONS: The settlement of Paulatuk lies 400 km (250 miles) east of Inuvik and is one of the smallest communities in the territory. It is well placed for hunting, fishing, and trapping game; these activities remain its staple support after many centuries. Its location is also useful as a stepping-stone to the wilderness. Tourism is becoming popular, and trips leave from here with Inuit guides in search of wildlife. Visitors also come to see the unusual Smoking Hills nearby, which are composed of sulfide-rich slate and coal.

Norman Wells ❾

800. NWT Tourism Office, 52nd St., Yellowknife (867) 873 5007.

IN 1919 CRUDE OIL discoveries were made here near a small Inuit settlement. Oil production surged in World War II when the US estabishd a pipeline to supply oil to the Alaska Highway while it was being built, and the town grew. The wells closed down in 1996 for economic reasons.

Today Norman Wells is the starting point for the Canol Heritage Route, a long-distance path of wilderness trail through to the Canol Road above the Ross River in the Yukon Territory, which links up with the Yukon Highway system. There are few facilities along the trail, making it one of the toughest trekking paths in the world. Despite the difficulties, this is a popular destination with experienced hikers.

Nahanni National Park Reserve ❿

(867) 695 2713. Fort Simpson. year round. Nahanni National Park Reserve, Post Bag 300, Fort Simpson, NWT.

NAHANNI NATIONAL Park Reserve sits astride the South Nahanni River between the border with the Yukon and the small settlement of Fort Simpson. In 1978, it was

Inuvik's town church and hall, shaped like an igloo against the climate

The vast expanses of Nahanni National Park in summer

the first place in the world to be designated a UN World Heritage Site to protect its wildlife. The park is a great wilderness with four vast river canyons, hot springs, and North America's most spectacular undeveloped waterfall, Virginia Falls. The falls, at 90 m (295 ft), are twice the height of Niagara but have less volume, and boast excellent flora and fauna. At least 13 species of fish enjoy the cascades, and more than 120 varieties of bird live overhead. Wolves, grizzly bears, and woodland caribou move freely in the park.

The park's main activities are, surprisingly, not wildlife-watching but whitewater rafting and canoeing. In summer, watersports take precedence over walking tours as the rivers thaw and the landscape bursts into bloom with wild flowers. The park can be reached by boat along the Nahanni River.

Fort Providence ⓫

750. NWT Tourism Office, 52nd St., Yellowknife (867) 873 5007.

THE DENE PEOPLE call this village "zhahti koe," which means mission house in their native tongue. Fort Providence began life as a Catholic mission and was later enlarged by the Hudson's Bay Company *(see pp158–9)*, which set up an outpost here in the late 19th century. Attracted by this and the prospect of employment, the local Dene First Nations people settled here permanently. Today the town is a Dene handicrafts center.

Immediately north of the village lies the Mackenzie Bison Sanctuary. The sanctuary is home to the world's largest herd of 2,000 rare pure wood bison. The park stretches for 100 km (60 miles) north along the banks of Great Slave Lake, and bison can be seen along the road by drivers.

Hay River ⓬

3,600. MacKenzie Hwy (867) 874 3180. Jun–Sep.

SET ON THE BANKS of Great Slave Lake, the small community of Hay River is the major port in the Northwest Territories. A lifeline, the town supplies the High Arctic settlements and the northernmost towns in the country, particularly Inuvik, with essentials. When the river thaws in spring, it supplies freight. The town looks designed for the purpose it serves – the wharves are lined with barges and tugs, as well as the local fishing fleet.

Unusually for this area, Hay River's history stretches back over a millennium. The Dene moved here centuries ago, lured by the town's strategic position at the southern shore of the Great Slave Lake, for its hunting and fishing. Attractions here are based on local industry; as a shipping center, the harbor is a bustling place to spot barges. The original Dene settlement, now a village of 260 people, sits across the river north from the Old Town and welcomes visitors.

THE NORTHERN LIGHTS

The Northern Lights, or *aurora borealis*, are believed to be the result of solar winds entering the Earth's ionosphere some 160 km (100 miles) above the surface of the planet. Emanating from the sun, these winds collide with the gases present in the Earth's upper atmosphere, releasing energy that becomes visible in the night sky. The stunning consequences are visible in the Yukon and the NWT, most often from August to October. Some Inuit groups attach religious significance to the Lights, believing them to be the spirits of dead hunters, while 19th-century gold prospectors mistook them for vapors given off by ore deposits. Whatever one's beliefs, the sparkling ribbons of light are an awesome sight.

Yellowknife ⓭

ORIGINALLY A NATIVE Dene settlement, Yellowknife is named after the yellow-bladed copper hunting knives used by its first residents. The Hudson's Bay Company closed its outpost here in 1823 due to failing profits, but the Old Town thrived again with gold mining in the 1930s and again after 1945. With improved road communications, the city became the regional capital of the Northwest Territories in 1967. Growing bureaucratic needs and the occasional successful goldmine guaranteed that Yellowknife has flourished ever since the 1960s.

Makeshift houseboats built from empty oildrums on the Great Slave Lake

The Old Town

Just 1 km (0.5 mile) north of downtown, the Old Town is situated on an island and a rocky peninsula on the Great Slave Lake. By 1947 Yellowknife had outgrown itself, and the New Town rose from the sandy plain southward. An unusual community thrives here on Yellowknife Bay, many living on makeshift houseboats. Also interesting is the variety of older architecture that can be seen from a stroll around this now residential area. Shops and accomodations are found farther south in the New Town. A good vantage point from which to survey the area is the Bush Pilot's Monument (a blue Bristol airplane) at the north end of Franklin Avenue.

VISITORS' CHECKLIST

15,200. The Northern Frontier Regional Visitors' Centre, 4804 49th St. (867) 873 4262. The Caribou Carnival (Mar); Festival of the Midnight Sun (Jul); Folk on the Rocks (Jul).

The Wildcat Café

Wiley Road. (867) 873 8850.
Jun–Sep: 11am–9pm daily.

The oldest restaurant in Yellowknife, this institution is open only during the summer. A true frontier stop, the sagging log cabin is set under the hill

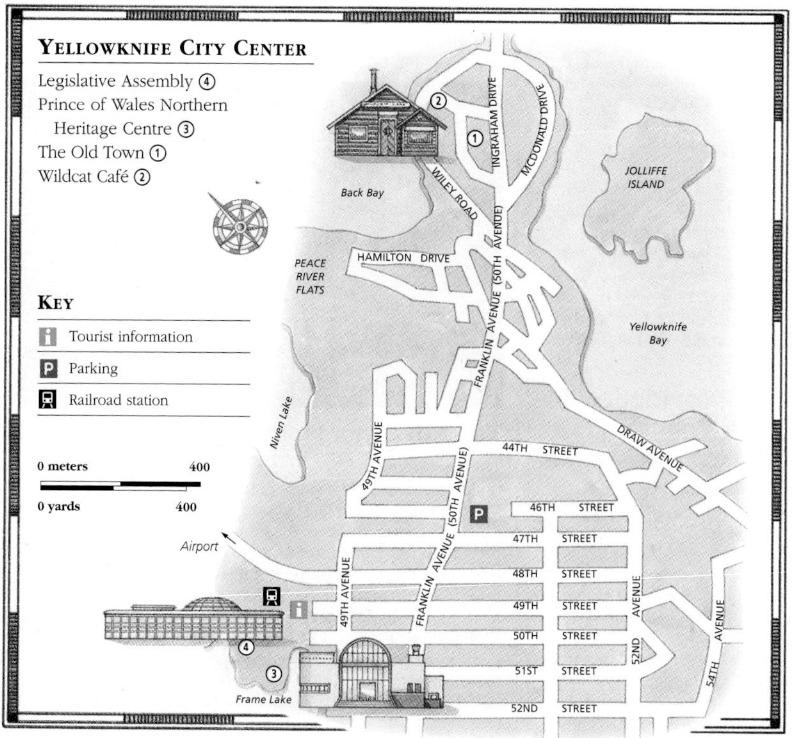

YELLOWKNIFE CITY CENTER

Legislative Assembly ④
Prince of Wales Northern Heritage Centre ③
The Old Town ①
Wildcat Café ②

KEY

Tourist information
Parking
Railroad station

0 meters 400
0 yards 400

Ingraham Drive, McDonald Drive, Jolliffe Island, Back Bay, Wiley Road, Hamilton Drive, Peace River Flats, Franklin Avenue (50th Avenue), Yellowknife Bay, Niven Lake, Draw Avenue, 44th Street, 49th Avenue, 46th Street, 47th Street, 48th Street, 49th Street, 50th Street, 51st Street, 52nd Street, 52nd Avenue, 54th Avenue, Airport, Frame Lake

of the Old Town and has been refurbished in 1930s style. Its atmospheric interior is reminiscent of the pioneer days. Rather showing its age, this establishment is the most photographed building in Yellowknife. It is also the most popular eating place – top dishes include hearty stew and fish.

Sampling the fare at the Wildcat Café is a truly northern experience

The Prince of Wales Heritage Centre
49th Street. (867) 873 7551. daily. public holidays.
This excellent local museum is a good introduction to the history of the Northwest Territories. There is a display on the lifestyles of the Dene and Inuit peoples, followed by one describing European development of the area. Another gallery retells the history of aviation in the Territories, with exhibits on natural sciences.

The Legislative Assembly
Frame Lake. (867) 669 2200. Mon–Fri. *Jul & Aug.*
Built in 1993, this headquarters of local government has a tall domed roof that stands out in the area. Signifying equal rights for all ethnic groups, the government chamber is the only round one of its kind in the country, with a large oval table to give all delegates equal responsibility, in the manner practiced by aboriginals. Decorated with paintings and Inuit art, the chamber is graced with a large polar bear rug. The official public government rooms can be toured when the council is not in session.

Rankin Inlet ⓮

2,058. *(867) 645 3838.*

Founded in 1955 when North Rankin Nickel Mine opened, Rankin Inlet is the largest community in the stony plateau of Keewatin, the mainly Inuit district of Nunavut that stretches east of the Canadian Shield to Hudson Bay. This small town is the government center for the Keewatin region, whose population, now 85 percent aboriginal, has settled mainly on the coast. The Inlet is also the local tourism center.

This region is characterized by its historic rural way of life and stunning Arctic scenery. **Meliadine Park**, 10 km (6 miles) from the town center, contains a traditional Thule (ancestor of the Inuit) restored native site with stone tent rings, meat stores, and semi-subterranean winter houses.

Meliadine Park
10 km (6 miles) northwest of Rankin Inlet. *(867) 645 3838.* *daily, weather permitting.*

Baker Lake ⓯

1,385. *(867) 793 2456.*

Baker lake is geographically at the center of Canada and is the country's only inland Inuit community. Located at the source of the Thelon River, the area has always been a traditional summer gathering place for different Inuit peoples. Today it is an important center for Inuit art, especially textiles.

Heading westward, the **Thelon Game Sanctuary** can also be visited. Visitors can see herds of musk ox in their natural habitat and glimpse other indigenous animals and birds.

Thelon Game Sanctuary
300 km (200 miles) w. of Baker Lake. *(867) 873 4262.* *daily.*

Banks Island and Victoria Island ⓰

(867) 645 3838.

Located in the Arctic Ocean, Banks Island is home to the largest herds of musk ox in the world. They dwell in **Aulavik National Park**, on the remote northern tip of the island. This numbers among the world's most remote wildlife destinations, and is accessible only by plane. In common with large areas of the far north, trips are mostly undertaken by the wealthy and adventurous.

Split between the Northwest Territories and Nunavut, Victoria Island has a town in each – Holman in NWT and the Inuit Cambridge Bay in Nunavut, where local native people traveled each summer for char fishing and caribou and seal hunting. The town today is a service center for locals and visitors along the Arctic coast. Polar bears, musk ox, wolves, and Arctic birds live nearby.

Aulavik National Park
Sachs Harbour. *(867) 690 3904.* *daily, weather permitting.*

An Inuit igloo builder near Baker Lake, practicing this traditional skill

Baffin Island 17

Purple Saxifrage in summer

PART OF NUNAVUT, Baffin Island is one of the most remote places in North America. At 500,000 square km (193,000 square miles), the island is the fifth largest on the planet, with more than 60 percent of its landmass lying above the Arctic Circle. Sparsely populated, the island is inhabited by just 11,000 people, 9,000 of whom are Inuit. Most people live in one of nine settlements scattered throughout the island, the chief of which is Iqaluit, capital of the province of Nunavut.

With its spectacular fjords and knife-edged mountains sparkling with glaciers, Baffin Island offers a chance to experience all the outdoor activities of the Arctic. Canoeing, kayaking, trekking, and thrilling glacial walks are all unbeatable here. Many of the activities often take place in the company of abundant wildlife, including polar bears and whales.

Nanisivik is a mining settlement founded in 1974 to exploit lead and zinc, which can only be shipped when the inlet's sea thaws in summer.

Pond Inlet
Pond Inlet is a jewel in Nunavut's twinkling crown. Blessed with stunning scenery of mountains, glaciers, and icebergs, the town is surrounded by abundant Arctic marine life. Snowmobiling and dogsled rides to the floe's edge are popular.

Auyuittuq National Park

Auyuittuq is the third-largest national park in Canada at 21,470 square km (8,300 square miles). It is a rarity as one of the few national parks above the Arctic Circle on Earth. A spectacular destination, the park displays a pristine wilderness of mountains, valleys, and fjords. In spring the meadows thaw out from under their snowy coverlets, and wildflowers burst into bloom. Within the park borders, wildlife abounds, with animals ranging from snow geese and arctic foxes to polar bears sharing the territory. Even in the brief summer, the weather can be tricky with the risk of heavy snow. Temperatures are low year-round. The nearby town of Pangnirtung is a craft center.

Wildflowers flourish beneath Auyuittuq's frozen peaks

0 km 100
0 miles 100

Cape Dorset is of interest archeologically as predecessors of the modern Inuit, the Thule and Dorset peoples, lived in this area.

Key

- Rivers
- National Park boundary
- Viewpoint
- Domestic airport

Pangnirtung

This little town of 1,100 residents sits at the southern end of the Pangnirtung Pass, the 100-km (62-mile) hiking trail which is the most popular on Baffin. During the summer the Pass is free of snow and can be negotiated quite easily. Views of the fjord below are stupendous.

VISITORS' CHECKLIST

11,400. Nunavut Tourism, Iqaluit (867) 979 6551
www.nunatour.nt.ca
Toonik Tyme (Apr), Iqaluit.

ACCESSING CANADA'S NORTH

While tourism to the Northwest Territories increases every year, visitors should be aware of severely limited travel and communications. The only access to these remote settlements is by air, which is very expensive compared to mainline routes. Despite the cost, the region has over 600 airports and small landing strips covering the region.

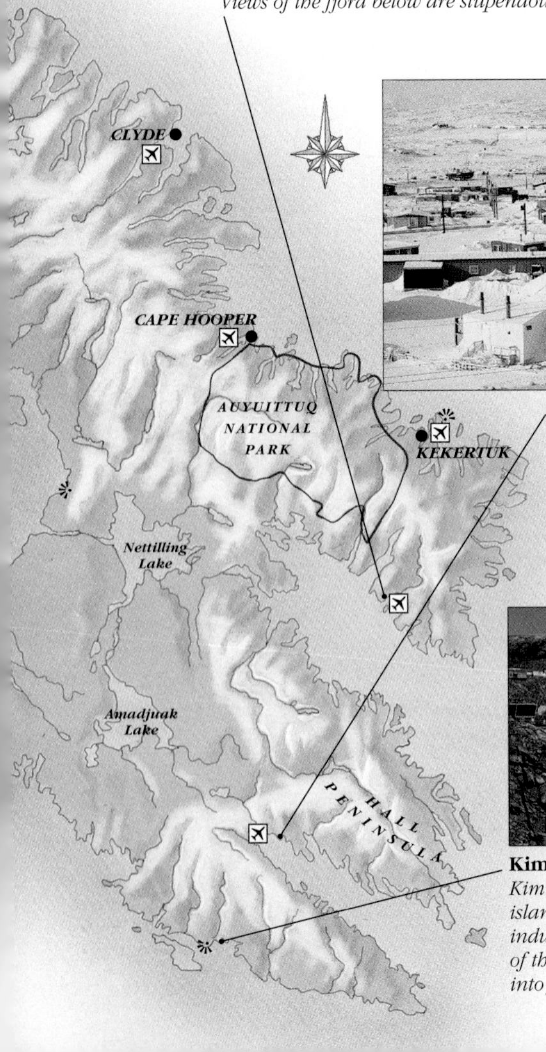

CLYDE

CAPE HOOPER

AUYUITTUQ NATIONAL PARK

KEKERTUK

Nettilling Lake

Amadjuak Lake

HALL PENINSULA

Iqaluit

Iqaluit is the gateway to exploring Baffin Island. Selected as the capital for the new state of Nunavut (see p51)*, the little town has a mainly Inuit population and is a convenient service center.*

Kimmirut

Kimmirut is now the center of the island's famous Inuit stone-carving industry. Slightly warmer than the rest of the island, the meadows here burst into flower during the short summer.

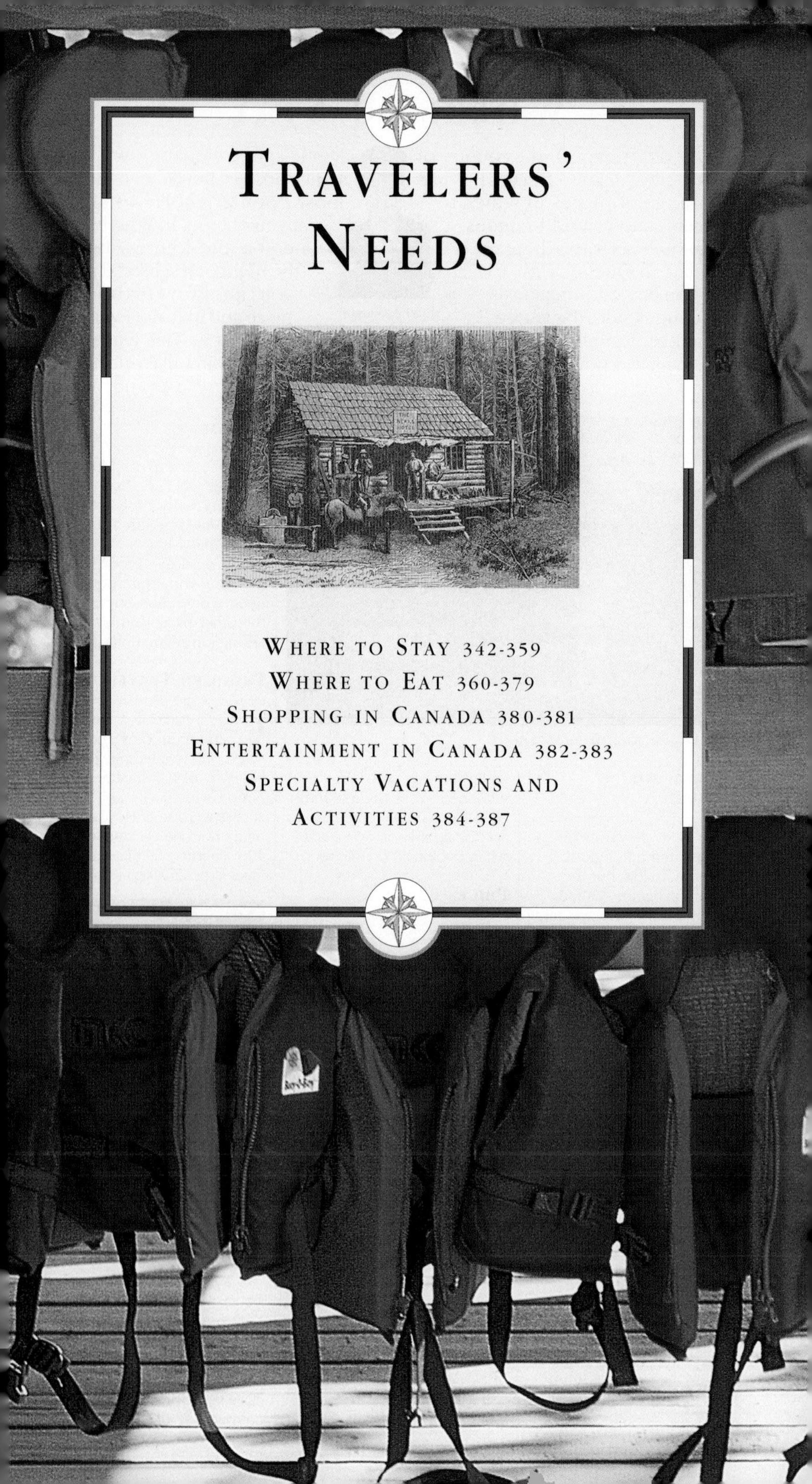

TRAVELERS' NEEDS

Where to Stay

As one might expect in a country of its size, Canada has a wide range of places in which to stay: from stately, world-famous hotels such as the Château Frontenac in Quebec City, to family-run bed-and-breakfasts in the countryside, the variety is immense. Canada offers excellent middle-range accommodations, and you will find rural inns, cottages to rent in scenic spots, elegant town apartments, hostels, houseboats, and the most popular choice of all, the convenient motel. Whether you need a mid-journey bed for the night or a seasonal rental, you can always find the right place and may not even need to book in advance. The listings on *pp344–59* describe in full a selection of destinations for every taste and budget.

Hotel doorman

A rental lodge in Banff National Park

Grading and Facilities

There is no government-sponsored hotel grading system in Canada, but the voluntary program "Canada Select" is usually very accurate. Each establishment is rated by numbers of stars. It is worth bearing in mind, however, that a 4-star hotel in a large city such as Toronto, for example, might not have the same level of facilities as one with the same rating in a small upscale resort with a château hotel.

The Canadian Automobile Association also operates an assessment system, mostly for hotels and motels along main highways, and these, while also non-official, are largely recognized as consistent and accurate. Air-conditioning comes as standard in most of the country during summer, except in national park lodges and cooler coastal and northern regions. Central heating country-wide is efficient. Cable TV, radio, irons and ironing boards, and coffee-making facilities are standard. Private bathrooms are usual, but you will need to specify a bathtub or shower – also remember to ask for double or twin beds when booking a double room.

Prices

With such a wide range of accommodations, prices vary hugely. In a major town, the top hotel's presidential suite may command a daily rate in excess of Can$1,000, while a hiker's hostel will provide a dormitory bed for under Can$25. Budget hotels and B-and-Bs charge Can$50–75 a night per person. Some prices rise in high season, but rates are discounted in low season.

Reservations

Advance reservations are always recommended in the main cities, where festivals, conventions, meetings, and major sports and musical events are held year-round (*see pp34–7*). Provincial tourist offices or airlines (*see p393*) will assist in suggesting and arranging bookings.

Children

Traveling with children is relatively easy. Nearly every property will supply a cot or junior-sized bed in a parents' room. Major hotels offer baby-sitting services. A lone parent traveling with children may need written consent from the other parent under anti-abduction regulations.

Disabled Travelers

Canada's building laws require all new and renovated public buildings to provide wheelchair facilities with ramps, wide doors, and straight access to rooms. However, as many rural hotels date from the 19th century, facilities should always be checked in advance.

The imposing façade of The Royal York Hotel in Toronto *(see p351)*

Luxury Hotels

Although Canada has few five-star hotels, the major cities boast some truly world-class establishments. The railroad age of the late 19th

Bedroom at Elmwood Inn, a B-and-B, Prince Edward Island *(see p345)*

century ushered in château-style hotels, which are unique Canadian architectural features. Nowadays, most of the castle-hotels, including the Château Frontenac, are owned and operated by Fairmont Hotels. Luxury chains are well represented: the Four Seasons, the Hilton, the Radisson, the Sheraton, and Westin chains operate in Toronto, Montreal, Calgary, and Vancouver.

Chain Hotels

Canada offers numerous franchise and chain hotels and motels. Reliable and comfortable, if occasionally a little bland, chains vary in style and price from grand resort areas to the less expensive but equally well-known Best Western, Comfort, and Super 8. Popular with families and business travelers, many of the properties have offices for use, including fax, e-mail, and telegraph equipment. Children's facilities are usually good.

Efficiency Apartments

There is a tremendous variety of these options available in Canada in addition to the traditional cottage rental industry. Motorhomes or RVs (Recreational Vehicles) are gaining in popularity and can be leased in all the major cities. Most nowadays have air-conditioning, refrigerators, ovens, and bathrooms. Campgrounds are found all over the country, from lush fields in the fertile southern national parks to well-insulated zones partly inhabited by the Inuit in the north. The proliferation of this choice guarantees high quality and a well-priced stay: electrical connections, as well as laundry facilities, general store, and sports programs are often available for all ages.

For many, the cottage or cabin option is traditionally Canadian. Ontario is famous for its selection of rural vacation homes, again very well equipped, which are available weekly, monthly, or seasonally, and are always well located for nearby attractions. National parks also rent lodges and offer campgrounds.

Bed-and-Breakfasts

The growing number of bed-and-breakfasts across Canada is testimony to their popularity. From historic inns to rustic quarters on vacation farms, each provides personalized service, a friendly local face, and insight into the region's way of life. Atlantic Canada is renowned for its B-and-Bs, with many located in the elegant Victorian homes of historic towns. Call the provincial tourist office for a detailed list with tariffs. Most establishments have up to four rooms for rent.

Accommodations Taxes

Bear in mind that accommodations of almost every kind are subject to two taxes on top of the basic tariff. The first, provincial sales tax, varies from province to province from about 4–9 percent. It must be paid on accommodations as well as on goods and other services. Rules vary slightly between provinces: Alberta levies only the PST on hotel and motel stays, with campsites, B-and-Bs, and guesthouses tax-free. Manitoba and Quebec offer partial rebates on accommodations tax to foreigners on production of the receipt. Forms are available from **Revenue Canada**, Visitors' Rebate Program, 275 Pope Rd., Summerside, PEI, C1N 6C6. Most provinces charge for every stay and do not offer a rebate of the PST.

The Goods and Services Tax (GST) is a standard national charge of 7 percent throughout the country; this affects most accommodation classes. In some provinces the GST and PST are combined as "general sales tax" of approximately 15 percent. Smaller hotels may not charge the GST, so inquire on arrival. However, the GST is entirely refundable to visitors. Keep receipts and contact Revenue Canada for a refund.

A bed-and-breakfast in the Rocky Mountains

Choosing a Hotel

THE HOTELS in this guide have been selected for their good value, excellent facilities, or location. This chart lists the hotels by region in the same order as the rest of the guide. The color codes of each region are shown on the thumb tabs. Entries are alphabetical within price category. For restaurant listings, see pages 364–79.

Hotel	Price	Number of Rooms	Restaurant	Children's Facilities	Garden/Terrace	Swimming Pool
NEWFOUNDLAND AND LABRADOR						
GRAND FALLS: *Mount Peyton Hotel* www.mountpeyton.com 214 Lincoln Rd., NFD A2A 1P8. *(709) 489 2251.* FAX *(709) 489 6365.* mtpeyton@fortisproperties.com This friendly family and business hotel offers hospitable service and one of the better restaurants in central Newfoundland.	$	150	●			
HAPPY VALLEY-GOOSE BAY: *Labrador Inn* labinn@cancom.net 380 Hamilton River Rd., LAB AOP 1CO. *(709) 896 3351.* FAX *(709) 896 3927.* The staff are big on northern hospitality here.	$	74	●			
L'ANSE AU CLAIR: *Northern Light Inn* www.labradorstraits.nf.ca/nli PO Box 92 L'Anse au Clair, NFD A0K 3K0. *(709) 931 2332.* FAX *(709) 931 2708.* This family-style hotel overlooks the bay. The restaurant serves local favorites, including Caribou.	$$	59	●			
NORRIS POINT: *Sugar Hill Inn* www.sugarhillinn.nf.ca 115–129 Sextons Rd., NFD A0K 3V0. *(709) 458 2147.* FAX *(709) 458 2166.* A quality inn located in the heart of Gros Morne National Park, near Lobster Point Lighthouse. The meals feature local seafood.	$$	7	●			
ST. ANTHONY: *Haven Inn* Goose Cove Rd., NFD A0K 4S0. *(709) 454 9100.* FAX *(709) 454 2270.* This modern hillside motel offers great views of St. Anthony's harbor. There are cozy fireplaces in the lounge and dining room.	$	29	●			
ST. JOHN'S: *Balmoral Inn* www.balmoralhouse.com 38 Queens Rd., NFD A1C 2AS. *(709) 754 5721.* FAX *(709) 722 8111.* This heritage property features elegant Queen Anne architecture, high ceilings, and attractive rooms decorated with antiques.	$	2				
ST. JOHN'S: *Hotel Newfoundland* www.fairmont.com Cavendish Square, NFD A1C 5W8. *(709) 726 4980.* FAX *(709) 726 2025.* Managed by Faimount Hotels. It offers views of Signal Hill and the harbor, as well as two on-site restaurants.	$$$$	301	●	■		■
TRINITY BAY: *Campbell House* www.campbellhouse.nf.ca. High St., Trinity Bay, NFD A0C 2S1. *(1 877) 464 7700.* FAX *(709) 464 3377.* Two of these three waterfront homes are registered heritage properties. The oldest, built in 1842, has period antiques and decor.	$	5			●	
NEW BRUNSWICK, NOVA SCOTIA, AND PRINCE EDWARD ISLAND						
BAY FORTUNE: *The Inn at Bay Fortune* RR4, Souris, PEI COA 2B0. *(902) 687 3745.* FAX *(902) 687 3540.* www.innatbayfortune.com This elegant seaside inn is home to one of Canada's finest restaurants *(see p364).*	$$$$	18	●		●	
BOUCTOUCHE: *Le Vieux Presbytère* 157 Chemin du Couvent, NB E4S 3B8. *(506) 743 5568.* FAX *(506) 743 5566.* This charming Acadian country inn was built in 1880 and has gardens overlooking Bouctouche River.	$	22	●		●	
BRIER ISLAND: *Brier Island Lodge* www.brierisland.com Westport, NS B0V 1H0. *(902) 839 2300.* FAX *(902) 839 2006.* Located on a tiny island in the Bay of Fundy, this small lodge is ideally situated for coastal walks and whale-watching.	$	39	●			
CAPE D'OR: *Cape d'Or Lighthousekeeper's Guesthouse* Cape d'Or Lighthouse, NS B0M 1S0. *(902) 670 0534.* This remote destination is near coastal cliffs and trails on the Minas Basin. The rooms have spectacular views.	$	4	●			

Price categories for a standard double room per night, including breakfast (where served), taxes, and any extra service charges:
($) under Can$100
($)($) Can$100–$150
($)($)($) Can$150–$200
($)($)($)($) Can$200–$250
($)($)($)($)($) over Can$250

RESTAURANT
Hotel restaurant or dining room, usually open to non-residents unless otherwise stated.
CHILDREN'S FACILITIES
Indicates child cribs and/or a baby-sitting service available. A few hotels also provide children's portions and high chairs in the restaurant.
GARDEN/TERRACE
Hotel with a garden, courtyard, or terrace often available for eating outside.
SWIMMING POOL
Hotel with an indoor or outdoor swimming pool.

Hotel	Price	Number of Rooms	Restaurant	Children's Facilities	Garden/Terrace	Swimming Pool
CARAQUET: *Hotel Paulin* 143 Blvd. St-Pierre west, NB E1W 1B6. *(506) 727 9981.* FAX *(506) 727 4808.* Innkeeper Gerard Paulin is the third generation of Paulins to operate this historic seaside hotel built in 1891. P	($)	8	●			
CAVENDISH: *Kindred Spirits Country Inn and Cottages* Route 6, PEI C0A IN0. *(902) 963 2434.* FAX *(902) 963 2434.* W www.kindredspirits.ca This charming inn is located next to Green Gables House *(see p76)*. An oasis of peace amid this busy tourist destination. ● *May–Oct.* TV P	($)($)	39				■
CHARLOTTETOWN: *Elmwood Heritage Inn* 121 North River Road, PEI C1A 3K7. *(902) 368 3310.* FAX *(902) 628 8457.* W www.elmwoodinn.pe.ca @ elmwood@pei.sympatico.ca Based in Charlottetown's historic district, this is one of Canada's famous B-and-Bs. Beautifully furnished, it offers delicious food. TV P	($)($)($)	6			●	
CHARLOTTETOWN: *Delta Prince Edward Hotel* 18 Queen St., PEI C1A 8B9. *(902) 566 2222.* FAX *(902) 566 2282.* W www.deltahotels.com The Prince Edward overlooks Charlottetown Marina. There are three on-site eateries, including a waterfront café. TV P	($)($)($)	213	●	■		■
EDMUNDSTON: *Howard Johnson Hotel and Convention Centre* 100 Rice St., NB E3V 1T4. *(506) 739 7321.* FAX *(506) 735 9101.* W www.hojo.com Clean, friendly, and family-oriented, this hotel is attached to a 22-store mall and well located for Edmundston's attractions. TV P	($)($)	103	●	■		■
GRAND TRACADIE: *Dalvay-by-the-Sea* PEI National Park, Box 8, York PEI C0A 1P0. (902) 672 2048. FAX (902) 672 2741. W www.dalvaybythesea.com This mansion was built by oil tycoon Alexander MacDonald in 1895. The restaurant specializes in island seafood *(see p365)*. P	($)($)($)($)($)	32	●	■		
HALIFAX: *Delta Barrington* W www.deltahotels.com 1875 Barrington St., NS B3J 3L6. *(902) 429 7410.* FAX *(902) 420 6524.* Located in the heart of the city's historic downtown. TV P	($)($)($)	202	●	■		
HALIFAX: *Waverly Inn* W www.waverlyinn.com 1266 Barrington St., NS B3J 1Y5. *(902) 423 9346.* FAX *(902) 425 0167.* This heritage inn opened in 1876. It is just a few minutes' walk from the historic downtown of this maritime city. TV P	($)($)	32				
INGONISH BEACH: *Keltic Lodge* Middle Head Peninsula, NS B0C 1L0. *(902) 285 2880.* FAX *(902) 285 2859.* This grand resort is located on a rocky bluff overlooking Ingonish Harbour. Prices include a four-course dinner and breakfast. TV P	($)($)($)($)($)	104	●	■	●	■
LOUISBOURG: *Cranberry Cove Inn* 12 Wolfe St., NS B0A 1M0. *(902) 733 2171 or 1-800-929-0222.* FAX *(902) 733 2449.* W www.louisbourg.com/cranberrycove This attractive inn offers chic accommodations and European-style cuisine using the best of the local produce. P	($)($)	7	●			
LUNENBURG: *Lunenburg Inn* W www.lunenburginn.com 26 Dufferin St., NS B0J 2C0. *(902) 634 3963.* FAX *(902) 634 9419.* Built in 1893, this beautiful Victorian building is located at the edge of Lunenburg's historic Old Town. P	($)($)	7				
MARGAREE VALLEY: *Normaway Inn* W www.normaway.com 691 Egypt Rd., NS B0E 2C0. *(902) 248 2987.* FAX *(902) 248 2600.* This 1920s resort is set on 100 ha (250 acres) in the Margaree Valley. It offers fishing, barn concerts, tennis, and a fine restaurant. P	($)($)	29	●	■	●	

Price categories for a standard double room per night, including breakfast (where served), taxes, and any extra service charges:
($) under Can$100
($)($) Can$100–$150
($)($)($) Can$150–$200
($)($)($)($) Can$200–$250
($)($)($)($)($) over Can$250

RESTAURANT
Hotel restaurant or dining room, usually open to non-residents unless otherwise stated.
CHILDREN'S FACILITIES
Indicates child cribs and/or a baby-sitting service available. A few hotels also provide children's portions and high chairs in the restaurant.
GARDEN/TERRACE
Hotel with a garden, courtyard, or terrace often available for eating outside.
SWIMMING POOL
Hotel with an indoor or outdoor swimming pool.

Hotel	Price	Number of Rooms	Restaurant	Children's Facilities	Garden/Terrace	Swimming Pool
MONCTON: *Comfort Inn* W www.choicehotels.ca 2495 Mountain Rd., NB E1G 2W4. *(506) 384 3175.* FAX *(506) 853 7307.* A chain motel that offers better-than-average accommodations. Close to Magnetic Hill and the Trans-Canada Highway.	($)	59				
ST. ANDREWS: *Algonquin Resort* 184 Adolphus St., NB E0G 2X0. *(506) 529 8823.* FAX *(506) 529 7162.* This classic resort offers great views of Passamaquoddy Bay. Plenty of amenities, including an 18-hole golf course.	($)($)($)	238	●	■	●	■
ST. ANDREWS: *Kingsbrae Arms, Relais & Châteaux* 219 King St., NB E5B 1Y1. *(506) 529 1897.* FAX *(506) 529 1197.* W www.kingsbrae.com This elegant old-world inn has beautiful rooms with antiques, and superb dining.	($)($)($)($)($)	8	●		●	■
SAINT JOHN: *Parkerhouse Inn and Restaurant* 71 Sydney St., NB E2L 1L5. *(506) 652 5054.* FAX *(506) 636 8076.* W www.parkerhouseinn.net A Victorian mansion in the historic downtown area, with a beautiful stained-glass conservatory.	($)	9	●		●	
SAINT JOHN: *Country Inn and Suites* 1011 Fairville Blvd., NB E2M 5T9. *(506) 635 0400.* FAX *(506) 635 3818.* W www.countryinns.com A homey atmosphere enhanced by country-style decor and a wood fire in the lounge.	($)($)	60				
SUMMERSIDE: *Loyalist Country Inn* 195 Harbour Drive, PEI C1N 5R1. *(902) 436 3333.* FAX *(902) 436 4304.* This is a well-appointed family hotel close to the marina. The hotel is located just 20 minutes from Confederation Bridge.	($)($)($)	103	●			■
WEST POINT: *West Point Lighthouse* O'Leary, RR2, PEI C0B 1V0. *(902) 859 1510.* W www.peisland.com/westpoint/light.html Canada's only inn in a functioning coast guard lighthouse.	($)($)	9	●			
WOLFVILLE: *Blomidon Inn* W www.blomidon.ns.ca 127 Main St., NS B0P 1X0. *(902) 542 2291.* FAX *(902) 542 7461.* This Victorian mansion is set back from the main street amid landscaped lawns. The inn is one of Nova Scotia's finest.	($)($)	26	●		●	
MONTREAL						
CHINATOWN: *Holiday Inn Sélect Montréal Centre-Ville* 99 Ave. Viger, Ouest QUE H2Z 1E9. *(514) 878 9888.* FAX *(514) 878 6341.* W www.hiselect-yul.com Two pagodas on the roof help this modern hotel blend seamlessly into its surroundings. Miniature ponds, Chinese gardens and the *Chez Chine* restaurant dominate the lobby.	($)($)($)	235	●			■
DOWNTOWN: *Hôtel Viger* W www.hotelviger.com 1001 Rue Saint-Hubert, QUE H2L 3Y3. *(514) 845 6058.* FAX *(514) 844 6068.* The rooms are basic, but the rates at this small hotel are low; the location is near Vieux-Montréal, Chinatown, and Mont-Royal.	($)	21				
DOWNTOWN: *Hôtel Château & Tour Versailles* 1808 Ouest Rue Sherbrooke, QUE H3H 1E5. *(514) 933 8111.* FAX *(514) 933 6867.* W www.versailleshotels.com The "château" part of this hotel is housed in two Victorian homes; the "tour" is a modern tower across the street. It has a very good French restaurant.	($)($)	181	●			
DOWNTOWN: *Hôtel de Paris* 901 Est Rue Sherbrooke, QUE H2L 1L3. *(514) 522 6861.* FAX *(514) 522 1387.* The old graystone building with its fanciful turret is a short walk from the nightlife of Rue St. Denis. The rooms are comfortable.	($)($)	39	●		●	

Hotel	Price	Rooms				
Downtown: *Hôtel-Suites Le Riche Bourg* W www.iber.com 2170 Ave. Lincoln, QUE H3H 3N5. *(514) 935 9224.* FAX *(514) 935 5049.* All suites have kitchens and dining areas, which make them ideal for families or for longer stays. TV P	$$	221	●	■		■
Downtown: *Le Nouvel Hôtel* W www.lenouvelhotel.com 1740 Ouest Blvd. René Lévesque, QUE H3H 1R3. *(514) 931 8841.* FAX *(514) 931 3233.* Montreal's amateur comics test their talent at the Comedy Nest, the cabaret of this comfortable, modern hotel near the *Centre Canadien d'Architecture.* TV P	$$	162	●	■	●	■
Downtown: *Delta Montréal* W www.deltamontreal.com 475 Ave. Président Kennedy, QUE H3A 2TA. *(514) 286 1986.* FAX *(514) 284 4342.* This modern hotel has large comfortable rooms. Place des Arts and Montreal's department stores are nearby. 24 TV P	$$$	453	●	■		■
Downtown: *Hôtel du Fort* W www.hoteldufort.com 1390 Rue du Fort, QUE H3H 2R7. *(514) 938 8333.* FAX *(514) 938 3123.* Most of the elegant rooms with kitchen facilities in this modern tower have good views of the harbor or Mont-Royal. TV P	$$$	126				
Downtown: *L'Hôtel de la Montagne* 1430 Rue de la Montagne, QUE H3G 1Z5. *(514) 288 5656.* FAX *(514) 288 9658.* W www.hoteldelamontagne.com A flamboyantly decorated lobby and rooftop pool make this hotel popular. TV P	$$$	134	●		●	■
Downtown: *Marriott Château Champlain* W www.marriott.com 1 Place du Canada, QUE H3B 4C9. *(514) 878 9000.* FAX *(514) 878 6761.* This tall white tower with arch-shaped windows has excellent views of Mont-Royal and the harbor. TV P	$$$	611	●			■
Downtown: *Montréal Bonaventure Hilton* 1 Place Bonaventure, QUE H5A 1B4. *(514) 878 2332.* FAX *(514) 878 3881.* W www.hiltonmontreal.com Built around a garden with an open-air pool that is open winter and summer, this hotel is located over the Place Bonaventure exhibition halls. TV P	$$$	395	●	■	●	■
Downtown: *Residence Inn by Marriott-Montréal* 2045 Rue Peel, QUE H3A 1T6. *(514) 982 6064.* FAX *(514) 844 8361.* W www.residenceinn.com\yulri All suites have fully equipped kitchens. The hotel also has a library with a fireplace. TV P	$$$	190	●		●	■
Downtown: *Hôtel La Reine Elizabeth* W www.fairmont.com 900 Ouest Blvd. René Lévesque, QUE H3B 4A5. *(514) 861 3511.* FAX *(514) 954 2256.* This busy convention hotel is well located with comfortable rooms. The Beaver Club restaurant is on the ground floor. 24 TV P	$$$$	1050	●			■
Downtown: *Hôtel Ritz Carlton* W www.ritzcarlton 1228 Ouest Rue Sherbrooke, QUE H3G 1H6. *(514) 842 4212.* FAX *(514) 842 4907.* Richard Burton and Elizabeth Taylor had one of their two weddings in this Edwardian-style hotel. The Ritz Garden is a good place for tea, and the Café de Paris is a fine French restaurant. 24 TV P	$$$$	229	●		●	
Downtown: *Loews Hôtel Vogue* W www.loewshotel.com 1425 Rue de la Montagne, QUE H3G 1Z3. *(514) 285 5555.* FAX *(514) 849 8903.* The Vogue's elegantly decorated lobby looks out onto one of Montreal's trendiest streets. Its rooms are large and well equipped and each one has a whirlpool bath. 24 TV P	$$$$	142	●	■		
Downtown: *Omni Montreal* W www.omnihotels.com 1050 Ouest Rue Sherbrooke, QUE H3A 2R6. *(514) 284 1110.* FAX *(514) 845 3025.* The marble lobby of this modern hotel has a wonderful restaurant/bar with windows overlooking the street. 24 TV P	$$$$	300	●			■
Downtown: *Renaissance* W www.marriott.com 3625 Ave. du Parc, QUE H2X 3P8. *(514) 288 6666.* Rooms decorated in blond wood and pastels overlook Parc Mont-Royal. A comfortable bar dominates the lobby. TV P	$$$	459	●			
Plateau Mont-Royal: *Hôtel de l'Institut* 3535 Rue Saint-Denis, QUE H2X 3P1. *(514) 282 5120.* FAX *(514) 873 9893.* Students at the *Institut de Tourisme et d'Hôtelerie du Québec* hone their skills by serving guests in the hotel on the upper floors of their college. TV P	$	42	●			

For key to symbols see back flap

Price categories for a standard double room per night, including breakfast (where served), taxes, and any extra service charges:
- $ under Can$100
- $$ Can$100–$150
- $$$ Can$150–$200
- $$$$ Can$200–$250
- $$$$$ over Can$250

RESTAURANT
Hotel restaurant or dining room, usually open to non-residents unless otherwise stated.

CHILDREN'S FACILITIES
Indicates child cribs and/or a baby-sitting service available. A few hotels also provide children's portions and high chairs in the restaurant.

GARDEN/TERRACE
Hotel with a garden, courtyard, or terrace often available for eating outside.

SWIMMING POOL
Hotel with an indoor or outdoor swimming pool.

Hotel	Price	Number of Rooms	Restaurant	Children's Facilities	Garden/Terrace	Swimming Pool
PLATEAU MONT-ROYAL: *Hôtel Le Saint-André* 1285 Rue Saint-André, QUE H2L 3T1. *(514) 849 7070.* FAX *(514) 849 8167.* www.lesaintandre.montrealplus.ca Guests get a surprising amount of style for a modest fee. Near the bistros of Rue Saint-Denis. TV P	$	61				
PLATEAU MONT-ROYAL: *Auberge de la Fontaine* 1301 East Rue St. Rachel, QUE H2J 2K1. *(514) 597 0166.* FAX *(514) 597 0496.* www.aubergedelafontaine.com An adjoining pair of Second-Empire homes has been converted into a small hotel with stylish, eccentrically decorated rooms. TV P	$$	21			●	
PLATEAU MONT-ROYAL: *Le Jardin d'Antoine* 2024 Rue St.-Denis, QUE H2X 3K7. *(514) 843 4506.* FAX *(514) 281 1491.* www.hotel-jardin-antoine.qc.ca The pretty garden that gives this hotel its name offers a peaceful respite from the nearby cafés and nightclubs. The more deluxe rooms at the back overlook the garden. TV P	$$	25			●	
VIEUX MONTRÉAL: *Auberge les Passants du Sans Soucy* 171 Ouest Rue Saint-Paul, QUE H2Y 1Z5. *(514) 842 2634.* FAX *(514) 842 2912.* The lobby of this tiny hotel is a functioning art gallery. TV	$$	9				
VIEUX MONTRÉAL: *Pierre du Calvet AD 1725* 405 Rue Bonsecours, QUE H2Y 3C3. *(514) 282 1725.* FAX *(514) 282 0456.* www.pierreducalvet.ca Fireplaces, marble bathrooms, antique furniture, and Oriental rugs grace this historic hotel's rooms.	$$$	9	●		●	
VIEUX MONTRÉAL: *Auberge du Vieux-Port* 97 E. Rue de la Commune, QUE H2Y 1J1. *(514) 876 0081.* FAX *(514) 876 8923.* www.aubergeduvieuxport.com This romantic hotel overlooks the Vieux Port. The roof terrace is ideal for drinks or tea.	$$$$	27	●		●	
VIEUX MONTRÉAL: *Hôtel Inter-Continental Montréal* 360 Ouest Rue Saint-Antoine, QUE H2Y 3X4. *(514) 987 9900.* FAX *(514) 847 8550.* www.interconti.com Roof turrets on this hotel help it blend into a row of 19th-century buildings. 24 TV P	$$$$	357	●	■		■
QUEBEC CITY AND THE ST. LAWRENCE RIVER						
BAIE SAINT-PAUL: *Auberge La Maison Otis* 23 Rue Saint-Jean-Baptiste, QUE G3Z 1M2. *(418) 435 2255.* FAX *(418) 435 2464.* www.maisonotis.com At the heart of this inn is an old stone house with seven exquisite rooms and one of the finest restaurants in the area. TV P	$$	30	●	■	●	■
CÔTE NORD: *Hôtel Tadoussac* www.famillledufor.com 165 Rue du Bord-de-l'Eau, Tadoussac, QUE G0T 2A0. *(418) 235 4421.* FAX *(418) 235 4607.* Canada Steamships built this hotel in 1942 for its passengers. Rates include breakfast and dinner. *Oct–May.* 24 TV P	$$$	149	●	■	●	■
GASPÉ: *La Gîte du Mont-Albert* Parc de la Gaspésie, QUE G0E 2G0. *(418) 763 2288.* FAX *(418) 763 7803.* This mountain inn looks like a hunting lodge, enhanced by its rustic decor. The hotel also rents cottages. *Oct–Feb.* P	$$	48	●		●	■
ILES-DE-LA-MADELEINE: *Hôtel au Vieux Couvent* Havre-aux-Maisons, QUE G0B 1K0. *(418) 969 2233.* FAX *(418) 969 4693.* A former convent school, the dormitories have been converted into bedrooms, and the chapel is a seafood restaurant. *Sep–Jun.* P	$	7	●		●	
LAC-SAINT-JEAN: *Hôtel du Jardin* 1400 Blvd. du Jardin, Saint-Félicien, QUE G8K 2N8. *(418) 679 8422.* FAX *(418) 679 4459.* This comfortable modern hotel makes a good base for exploring the Lac-Saint-Jean area. TV P	$$	84	●			■

Hotel	Price	Rooms				
PERCÉ: *Hôtel-Motel La Normandie* www.normandieperce.com 221 Route 132 east, Cap de Foi, QUE G0C 2L0. *(418) 782 2112.* FAX *(418) 782 2337.* Most of the rooms of this inn overlook the sea and Rocher Percé. A fine seafood restaurant is on site. *Oct–May.*	$$	45	●	■	●	
POINTE-AU-PIC: *Manoir Richelieu* www.fairmont.com 181 Rue Richelieu, QUE 65A 1X7. *(418) 665 3703.* FAX *(418) 665 7736.* This stone castle sits on a cliff surrounded by gardens overlooking the estuary.	$$$	405	●	■	●	■
QUEBEC CITY: *Hôtel Particulier Belley* 249 Rue Saint-Paul, QUE G1K 3W5. *(418) 692 1694.* FAX *(418) 692 1696.* This old tavern is next to the Marché du Vieux-Port. Some rooms have bare brick walls and others have skylights.	$	8				
QUEBEC CITY: *Le Priori* 15 Rue Sault-au-Matelot, QUE G1K 3Y7. *(418) 692 3992.* FAX *(418) 692 0883.* A whimsical little hotel at the foot of Cap Diamant. Many rooms have stone walls but modern furniture.	$$	26	●	■		
QUEBEC CITY: *Hôtel Clarendon* www.hotelclarendon.com 57 Rue Sainte-Anne, QUE G1R 3X4. *(418) 692 2480.* FAX *(418) 692 4652.* The interior of this 1870 hotel is an Art Deco delight. There is live jazz in the lobby every evening.	$$$	151	●			
QUEBEC CITY: *Hôtel Dominion* www.hoteldominion.com 126 Rue Saint-Pierre, QUE G1K 4A8. *(418) 692 2224.* FAX *(418) 692 4403.* Old photographs decorate the high-ceilinged rooms in this 1912 building. Dozens of attractive restaurants line the picturesque Rue du Petit Champlain nearby.	$$$	40			●	
QUEBEC CITY: *Château Frontenac* www.fairmont.com 1 Rue des Carrières, QUE G1R 4A7. *(418) 692 3861.* FAX *(418) 692 1751.* Probably the most photographed hotel in Canada. Its baronial exterior is reflected inside in the wide hallways, wood paneling, and stonework. The rooms on the river have magnificent views.	$$$$$	611	●	■	●	■
RIVIÈRE-DU-LOUP: *Hôtel Lévesque* 171 Rue Fraser, QUE G5R 1E2. *(418) 862 6927.* FAX *(418) 867 5827.* This waterfront hotel is ideal for families, with its pool, beach, and big rooms. It has two restaurants, one offering simple fare, the other specializing in gourmet menus.	$	91	●	■	●	■
SEPT-ILES: *Hôtel Sept-Iles* 451 Ave. Arnaud, QUE G4R 3B3. *(418) 962 2581.* FAX *(418) 962 6918.* In the 1960s and 70s Sept-Iles' workers were the highest paid in Canada and spent their wages in the restaurant in this bayside hotel.	$	113	●			
SOUTHERN AND NORTHERN QUEBEC						
HULL: *Auberge de la Gare* 205 Blvd. Saint-Joseph, QUE J8Y 3X3. *(819) 778 8085.* FAX *(819) 595 2021.* Serviceable, comfortable hotel in the heart of downtown Hull, close to the bridge and the attractions of Ottawa.	$$	42				
LAURENTIAN MOUNTAINS: *Auberge Le Rouet* 1288 Rue Lavoie, Val-David, QUE J02 2N0. *(819) 322 3221.* Pine trees and cross-country ski trails surround this rustic lodge. The low rates include three meals served in a log-paneled dining room.	$$	30	●		●	■
LAURENTIAN MOUNTAINS: *Hôtel Far Hills Inn* Val-Morin, QUE J0T 2R0. *(819) 322 2014.* FAX *(819) 322 1995.* This mountaintop resort has its own lake, tennis courts, and 130 km (80 miles) of hiking and cross-country ski trails.	$$	70	●		●	■
LAURENTIAN MOUNTAINS: *Château Mont-Tremblant* Station-de-Ski Mont Tremblant, QUE J0T 1Z0. *(819) 681 7000.* FAX *(819) 681 7644.* www.fairmont.com This luxury hotel brings big-city amenities into the Laurentian wilderness.	$$$	316	●	■	●	■
LAURENTIAN MOUNTAINS: *Auberge de la Montagne-Coupée* 1000 Chemin Montagne-Coupée, QUE J0K 2S0. *(450) 886 3891.* FAX *(450) 886 5401.* This modern establishment has a glass wall that looks out onto the mountains. Rates include breakfast and dinner.	$$$$	49	●	■	●	■

For key to symbols see back flap

Price categories for a standard double room per night, including breakfast (where served), taxes, and any extra service charges:
- $ under Can$100
- $$ Can$100–$150
- $$$ Can$150–$200
- $$$$ Can$200–$250
- $$$$$ over Can$250

Restaurant
Hotel restaurant or dining room, usually open to non-residents unless otherwise stated.

Children's Facilities
Indicates child cribs and/or a baby-sitting service available. A few hotels also provide children's portions and high chairs in the restaurant.

Garden/Terrace
Hotel with a garden, courtyard, or terrace often available for eating outside.

Swimming Pool
Hotel with an indoor or outdoor swimming pool.

Hotel	Price	Number of Rooms	Restaurant	Children's Facilities	Garden/Terrace	Swimming Pool
Magog: *Auberge l'Étoile sur le Lac* 1150 Ouest Rue Principale, QUE J1X 2B8. *(819) 843 6521.* FAX *(819) 843 5007.* Many of the rooms have balconies overlooking Lac Memphrémagog. In summer, meals are served on the lakeside terrace. TV P	$$	38	●		●	■
North Hatley: *Auberge Hovey Manor* W www.hoveymanor.com Route 108 E. (Chemin Hovey), QUE J0B 2C0. *(819) 842 2421.* FAX *(819) 842 2248.* Modeled on George Washington's Virginia home, many of the rooms here have fireplaces and four-poster beds. 24 P	$$$$	39	●		●	■
Nunavik: *Auberge Kuujjuaq* Kuujjuaq, QUE J0M 1C0. *(819) 964 2903.* FAX *(819) 964 2031.* Lodging in Quebec's far north tends to be scarce and expensive. Book well ahead for a room in this little hotel. TV P	$$$$	22	●			
Outaouais: *Château Montebello* W www.chateaumontebello.com 392 Rue Notre-Dame, Montebello, QUE J0V 1L0. *(819) 423 6341.* FAX *(819) 423 5283.* Canadian workers built one of the largest log structures in the world during the Depression. It is now part of this charming riverside resort with golf course, riding trails, and tennis courts. TV P	$$$	211	●	■	●	■
Richelieu Valley: *Hostelerie Les Trois Tilleuls* 290 Rue Richelieu, Saint-Marc-sur-Richelieu, QUE J0L 2E0. *(514) 856 7787.* W www.relaischateaux.fr/tilleuls This member of the Château & Relais organization is set in farm country one hour's drive from Montreal. Every room has a balcony overlooking the Richelieu River. TV P	$$$	24	●		●	■
Rouyn-Noranda: *Hôtel Albert* 84 Ave. Principale, QUE J9X 4P2. *(819) 762 3545.* FAX *(819) 762 7157.* This old-fashioned downtown hotel was renovated in 1997 and has large comfortable rooms with some original features. TV P	$	51	●			
Trois-Rivières: *Delta Trois-Rivières* W www.deltahotels.com 1620 Rue Notre-Dame, QUE G9A 6E5. *(819) 376 1991.* FAX *(819) 372 5975.* This modern hotel is just a short walk from the old section of Trois-Rivières and the walkways along the St. Lawrence River. TV P	$$	159	●	■		■
TORONTO						
Airport: *Delta Toronto Airport Hotel* W www.deltahotels.com 801 Dixon Rd, ONT M9W 1J5. *416 675 6100.* FAX *416 675 4022.* A well-maintained modern hotel offering easy access to the airport. It has a lot of pool tables. TV P	$$$	250	●	■	●	■
Airport: *Regal Constellation Hotel* W www.regal-hotels.com 900 Dixon Rd., ONT M9W 1J7. *416 675 1500.* FAX *416 675 1737.* This appealing chain hotel, situated close to the airport, has a splendid seven-story glass lobby. 24 TV P	$$	710	●			■
Downtown: *Bond Place Hotel* W www.bondplacehoteltoronto.com 65 Dundas St. East, ONT M5B 2G8. *416 362 6061.* FAX *416 360 6406.* Right in the center of downtown, a short walk from the Eaton Centre, this simple hotel is popular with package-tour operators. TV	$$	286	●	■		
Downtown: *Days Inn Toronto Downtown* 30 Carlton St., ONT M5B 2E9. *416 977 6655.* FAX *416 977 0502.* A standard hotel, which has competitively priced, plain but functional rooms. It occupies a high-rise near College subway. TV P	$$	537	●			■
Downtown: *Quality Hotel Downtown* 111 Lombard St., ONT M5C 2T9. *416 367 5555.* FAX *416 367 3470.* An unassuming city center hotel with spotless rooms, continental deluxe breakfast included. It is located on a quiet street. TV P	$$$	196				

Hotel	Price	Rooms				
DOWNTOWN: *Toronto Colony Hotel* W www.toronto-colony.com 89 Chestnut St., ONT M5G 1R1. *416 977 0707.* FAX *416 585 3164.* Occupying a central location, close to City Hall, the Colony has pleasant double rooms furnished in a modern style.	$$$$	721	●	■		■
DOWNTOWN: *Victoria Hotel* W www.toronto.com/hotelvictoria 56 Yonge St., ONT M5E 1G5. *416 363 1666.* FAX *416 363 7327.* @ reception@hotelvictoria.on.ca Pocket-sized hotel situated in the heart of the city. It has pleasant, European-style rooms.	$$	48				
DOWNTOWN: *Delta Chelsea Inn* W www.deltahotels.com 33 Gerrard St. W, ONT M5G 1Z4. *416 595 1975.* FAX *416 585 4302.* Located close to the Eaton Centre, this is the biggest hotel in Toronto, with outstanding leisure facilities. The rooms are spacious and attractively furnished.	$$$	1591	●	■	●	■
DOWNTOWN: *Novotel Toronto Centre* W www.novotel.com 45 The Esplanade, ONT M5E 1W2. *416 367 8900.* FAX *416 360 8285.* This stylish establishment occupies a beautiful converted Art Deco building close to Union Station.	$$$	262	●			■
DOWNTOWN: *Ramada Hotel and Suites* W www.ramada.com 300 Jarvis St., ONT M5B 2C5. *416 977 4823.* FAX *416 977 4830.* A convenient, high-rise hotel located on bustling Jarvis Street, five minutes' walk east of Yonge. The hotel is a popular spot with visiting businessfolk.	$$$$	102				■
DOWNTOWN: *Royal York* W www.fairmont.com 100 Front St. W, ONT M5J 1E3. *416 368 2511.* FAX *416 860 5008.* When it was completed in the 1920s, the Royal York was the largest hotel in the British Empire. The public areas have now been refurbished to their original grandeur.	$$$$	1365	●	■	●	■
DOWNTOWN: *Sheraton Centre Toronto Hotel* 123 Queen St. W, ONT M5H 2M9. *416 361 1000.* FAX *416 947 4801.* A massive hotel right in the center of Toronto, boasting a superb indoor-outdoor swimming pool.	$$$	1382	●	■		■
DOWNTOWN: *Sutton Place Hotel* W www.suttonplace.com 955 Bay St., ONT M5S 2A2. *416 924 9221.* FAX *416 324 5654.* This trendy hotel is popular with visiting actors and politicians alike. The rooms are well appointed and just a few steps from the city's business and main shopping areas.	$$$$	230	●	■	●	■
DOWNTOWN: *Radisson Plaza Hotel Admiral* 249 Queens Quay W., ONT M5J 2N5. *416 203 3333.* FAX *416 203 3100.* W www.radisson.com/toronto Prestigious hotel occupying a prime waterfront location. It has stylish, comfortable rooms.	$$$$	157	●		●	■
DOWNTOWN: *Renaissance Toronto Hotel at SkyDome* 1 Blue Jay Way, ONT M5V 1J4. *416 341 7100.* FAX *416 341 5091.* W www.renaissancehotels.com Much loved by baseball fans, this hotel forms part of the SkyDome sports stadium *(see p169)*. Some of the rooms actually overlook the playing area.	$$$$	346	●	■		■
DOWNTOWN: *The Westin Harbour Castle* W www.westin.com 1 Harbour Square, ONT M5J 1A6. *416 869 1600.* FAX *416 361 7448.* A prestige waterfront hotel, many of the rooms offer views of Lake Ontario. It also has a revolving rooftop restaurant.	$$$$	980	●	■	●	■
DOWNTOWN: *Toronto Marriott Eaton Centre* 525 Bay St., ONT M5G 2L2. *416 597 9200.* FAX *416 597 9211.* W www.marriott.com Ardent shoppers need look no further than this elegant hotel adjoining the Eaton Centre.	$$$$	459	●	■	●	■
DOWNTOWN: *King Edward Hotel* 37 King Street E., ONT M5C 1E9. *416 863 3131.* FAX *416 367 5515.* W www.lemeridien-hotels.com Elegant hotel with attractive rooms. The doormen are the most stylish in town.	$$$$$	294	●			
DOWNTOWN: *Hotel Intercontinental Toronto* 220 Bloor Street W., ONT M5S 1T8. *416 960 5200.* FAX *416 960 8269.* W www.toronto.interconti.com This sleek modern hotel offers every amenity, including business floors in some of its suites.	$$$$$	209	●	■		■

For key to symbols see back flap

Price categories for a standard double room per night, including breakfast (where served), taxes, and any extra service charges:
- $ under Can$100
- $$ Can$100–$150
- $$$ Can$150–$200
- $$$$ Can$200–$250
- $$$$$ over Can$250

RESTAURANT
Hotel restaurant or dining room, usually open to non-residents unless otherwise stated.

CHILDREN'S FACILITIES
Indicates child cribs and/or a baby-sitting service available. A few hotels also provide children's portions and high chairs in the restaurant.

GARDEN/TERRACE
Hotel with a garden, courtyard, or terrace often available for eating outside.

SWIMMING POOL
Hotel with an indoor or outdoor swimming pool.

	Number of Rooms	Restaurant	Children's Facilities	Garden/Terrace	Swimming Pool
HIGH PARK: *High Park Bed & Breakfast* $ 4 High Park Blvd., ONT M6R 1M4. *416 531 7963.* www.bbcanada.com/3924.html An attractive old house in the High Park suburb, 5 km (3 miles) west of downtown. P	2			●	
NORTH YORK: *Holiday Inn Toronto, Don Valley* $$$ 1100 Eglinton Ave. E, ONT M3C 1H8. *416 446 3700.* FAX *416 446 3701.* www.holiday-inn.com A pleasant chain hotel located next door to the Ontario Science Centre *(see p187)*. It specializes in free meals and discounted accommodations for children. TV P	298	●	■	●	■
SCARBOROUGH: *Howard Johnson Plaza Hotel* $$ 940 Progress Ave., ONT M1G 3T5. *416 439 6200.* FAX *416 439 0276.* @ reservations@hojotoronto.com Routine but perfectly adequate hotel in Scarborough, a suburb to the east of the downtown area. TV P	191	●			■
YORKVILLE: *Howard Johnson Yorkville* www.hojo.com $$ 89 Avenue Rd., ONT M5R 2G3. *416 964 1220.* FAX *416 964 8692.* This modest hotel has a good location on the edge of Yorkville. The modern rooms are well maintained and spacious. TV	71				
YORKVILLE: *Four Seasons Hotel* www.fourseasons.com $$$$$ 21 Avenue Rd., ONT M5R 2G1. *416 964 0411.* FAX *416 964 2301.* This luxurious hotel is popular with visiting celebrities. Located in chic Yorkville, a short walk north of Bloor Street. 24 TV P	380	●	■	●	■
OTTAWA AND EASTERN ONTARIO					
ALGONQUIN PROVINCIAL PARK: *Arowhon Pines Hotel* $$$$$ off Hwy 60, Algonquin Provincial Park, ONT P1H 2G5. *(705) 633 5661.* *(1 416) 483 4393 (winter).* FAX *(705) 633 5795.* The food inspires rave reviews. Rates include three meals a day. ● *Nov–Apr.* TV P	50	●	■		
BROCKVILLE: *Royal Brock Hotel and Resort* www.hotelbook.com $$ 100 Stewart Blvd., ONT K6V 4W3. *(613) 345 1400.* FAX *(613) 345 5402.* Selected as one of the finest small hotels in Canada, the Brock offers award-winning cuisine prepared by a European chef. TV P	72	●			■
HALIBURTON: *Sir Sam's Inn* www.sirsamsinn.com $$$$$ Eagle Lake, ONT K0M 1N0. *(705) 754 2188.* FAX *(705) 754 4262.* This is an adults-only resort located in the heart of the highlands. Rates include a four-course dinner. ● *mid-Nov–mid-Dec, Easter.* TV P	25	●			■
KAWARTHA LAKES: *Eganridge Inn & Country Club* $$$ RR3 Fenelon Falls, ONT K0M 1N0. *(705) 738 5111.* www.eganridge.com Originally an 18th-century country estate, Eganridge is now an elegant inn located on Sturgeon Lake, on the Trent-Seven Waterway. ● *Nov–Apr.* TV P	13	●		●	
KINGSTON: *Marine Museum of the Great Lakes at Kingston* $ 55 Ontario St., ONT K7L 2Y2. *(613) 542 2261.* FAX *(613) 542 0043.* www.marmus.ca These modest comfortable ship's cabins are a few blocks from the downtown area. ● *Oct–Apr.* P	23				
KINGSTON: *Hochelaga Inn* www.someplacesdifferent.com $$$ 24 Sydenham St., ONT K7L 3G9. *(613) 549 5534.* FAX *(613) 549 5534.* Located in the heart of historic Kingston, this lovely old Victorian manor hotel is the perfect place to pamper yourself. TV P	23				
KINGSTON: *Prince George Hotel* $$$ 200 Ontario St., ONT K7L 2Y9. *(613) 547 9037.* FAX *(613) 547 0056.* Built as a private home in 1809, it has been operating as a hotel for more than 150 years. Within walking distance of all attractions. TV	28	●			

Hotel		Rooms				
North Bay: *Pinewood Park Inn and Conference Centre* 201 Pinewood Park Drive, ONT P1B 8J8. *(705) 472 0810.* FAX *(705) 472 4427.* W www.pinewoodparkinn.com This well kept motel is five minutes from the Dionne Quints Museum *(see p201)*. TV	$$	102	●		●	■
Ottawa: *Gasthaus Switzerland Bed & Breakfast Inn* 89 Daly Ave., ONT K1N 6E6. *(613) 237 0335.* FAX *(613) 594 3327.* W www.gasthausswitzerlandinn.com A charming old stone house just two blocks south of Rideau St. and the Byward Market *(see p194)*.	$	22				
Ottawa: *Lord Elgin Hotel* W www.lordelginhotel.ca 100 Elgin St., ONT K1P 5K8. *(613) 235 3333.* FAX *(613) 235 3223.* This is a 1940s hotel offering a great value in a prime location across from the National Arts Centre. TV P	$$	312				
Ottawa: *Château Laurier Hotel* W www.fairmont.com 1 Rideau St., ONT K1N 8S7. *(613) 241 1414.* FAX *(613) 562 7030.* This famous old hotel looks like a French château and is close to Parliament Hill. TV	$$$$	428	●			■
Ottawa: *Delta Inn* W www.deltahotels.com 361 Queen St., ONT K1R 7S9. *(613) 238 6000.* FAX *(613) 238 2290.* Spacious, modern rooms, and the lobby fireplace is particularly attractive. TV P	$$$	328	●	■		■
THE GREAT LAKES						
Bayfield: *The Little Inn of Bayfield* W www.littleinn.com Main Street, ONT N0M 1G0. *(519) 565 2611.* FAX *(519) 565 5474.* One of the most charming hotels in Ontario occupies a restored 19th-century timber-and-brick building on the shores of Lake Huron. The rooms are decorated in period style. TV P	$$$	29	●	■	●	
Midland: *Park Villa Motel* 751 Yonge St. W., ONT L4R 2E1. *(705) 526 2219.* FAX *(705) 526 1346.* Midland is short on amenities, but this standard motel, 2 km (1 mile) from the waterfront, with air-conditioned rooms is pleasant. TV P	$	41				
Niagara Falls: *Quality Inn Fallsway* W www.fallsresort.com 4946 Clifton Hill, ONT L2E 6S8. *(905) 358 3601 or 1 800 263 7137* FAX *(905) 358 3818.* This Quality Inn is a modern, motel-style place within earshot of the Falls. The rooms are spacious. TV P	$$$	274	●			■
Niagara Falls: *Day's Inn Overlooking the Falls* 6546 Buchanan Ave., ONT L2G 3W2. *(905) 356 4514.* FAX *(905) 356 3651.* W www.daysinn.com A dapper hotel by any standard, the Day's Inn is a sprightly high-rise offering great views of the Falls. TV P	$$$$	167	●			■
Niagara Falls: *Sheraton Fallsview Hotel* 6755 Oakes Drive, ONT L2G 3W7. *(905) 374 1077.* FAX *(905) 374 6224.* W www.fallsview.com @ sheraton@fallsview.com Luxurious hotel providing panoramic views of the Falls. The restaurant is one of the best in town. TV P	$$$$	407	●	■	●	■
Niagara Falls: *Sheraton on the Falls* 5875 Falls Ave., ONT L2E 6W7. *(905) 374 4444.* FAX *(905) 371 0157.* W www.niagarafallshotels.com One of Niagara's older hotels, this pleasant establishment stands at the foot of Clifton Hill. The bedrooms on the upper floors provide spectacular views of the Falls. TV P	$$$$	670	●			■
Niagara-on-the-Lake: *Nana's Iris Manor Bed and Breakfast* 36 The Promenade, ONT L0S 1J0. *(905) 468 1593.* FAX *(905) 468 1592.* W www.nanas.on.ca A charming bed-and-breakfast set in a delightful 19th-century-style villa in the Old Town. All rooms have a fireplace. In summer, take time to enjoy a cool drink on the veranda. P	$$	3			●	
Niagara-on-the-Lake: *Prince of Wales Hotel* 6 Picton St., ONT L0S 1J0. *(905) 468 3246.* FAX *(905) 468 5521.* W www.vintageinns.com This stylish hotel occupies a tastefully refurbished old building right in the center of town. TV P	$$$$$	108	●			■
Sault Ste. Marie: *Quality Inn Bay Front* 180 Bay Street, P6A 6S2. *(705) 945 9264.* FAX *(705) 945 9766.* W www.soonet.ca/bayfront This hotel has a great location in the centre of town, near the prime tourist sights. TV P	$	110		■		■

Price categories for a standard double room per night, including breakfast (where served), taxes, and any extra service charges:
- \$ under Can\$100
- \$\$ Can\$100–\$150
- \$\$\$ Can\$150–\$200
- \$\$\$\$ Can\$200–\$250
- \$\$\$\$\$ over Can\$250

RESTAURANT
Hotel restaurant or dining room, usually open to non-residents unless otherwise stated.

CHILDREN'S FACILITIES
Indicates child cribs and/or a baby-sitting service available. A few hotels also provide children's portions and high chairs in the restaurant.

GARDEN/TERRACE
Hotel with a garden, courtyard, or terrace often available for eating outside.

SWIMMING POOL
Hotel with an indoor or outdoor swimming pool.

Hotel	Number of Rooms	Restaurant	Children's Facilities	Garden/Terrace	Swimming Pool
SAULT STE. MARIE: *Holiday Inn Sault Ste. Marie Waterfront* \$\$\$ 208 St. Mary's River Drive, ONT P6A 5V4. *(705) 949 0611.* FAX *(705) 945 6972.* W www.holiday-inn.com This is a bright, cheerful chain hotel situated within easy distance of all the attractions.	195	●	■	●	■
THUNDER BAY: *Travelodge Airlane Hotel* \$\$ 698 W. Arthur St., ONT P7E 5R8. *(807) 577 1181.* FAX *(807) 475 4852.* W www.travelodge-airlane.com This clean, new hotel has bright modern rooms that are cheerily decorated. The hotel is near the town's prime tourist attraction, Old Fort William *(see p223).*	154	●			■
TOBERMORY: *Blue Bay Motel* \$ Bay St., Little Tub, ONT N0H 2R0. *(519) 596 2392.* FAX *(519) 596 2335.* W www.bluebay-motel.com The small fishing village of Tobermory is an agreeable place to break a long journey.	16				
CENTRAL CANADA					
DRUMHELLER: *Newcastle Country Inn* \$ 1130 Newcastle Trail, AB T0J 0Y2. *(403) 823 8356.* FAX *(403) 823 8356.* W www.virtuallydrumheller.com/nci/ This three-star property is close to downtown. Breakfast is included in the price of the room.	11				
EDMONTON: *Glenora Bed & Breakfast* \$ 12327–102 Ave., AB T5N 0L8. *(780) 488 6766.* FAX *(780) 488 5168.* W www.glenorabnb.com\index.html Each room has a distinct look, furnished with antiques. Close to downtown and Victoria Promenade.	21	●			
EDMONTON: *Fantasyland Hotel* \$\$\$ 17700–87th Ave., West Edmonton Mall AB T5T 4V4. *(780) 444 3000.* FAX *(780) 444 3294.* W www.fantasylandhotel.com Standard rooms have the usual amenities while theme rooms such as African, Hollywood, and Igloo have whirlpools.	355	●			
EDMONTON: *Union Bank Inn* \$\$\$ 10053 Jasper Ave., AB T5J 1S5. *(780) 423 3600.* FAX *(780) 423 4623.* W www.unionbankinn.com Located downtown. Rates include breakfast and evening aperitif. The restaurant is highly recommended.	34	●			
FORT QU'APPELLE: *Company House Bed & Breakfast* \$ Adjacent to Town Office, Company Ave., SASK S0G 1S0. *(306) 332 6333.* FAX *(306) 332 6333.* W www.bbcanada.com\392.html A charming home with guest sitting room, two tiled cherrywood fireplaces, and shared bathrooms.	3				
LETHBRIDGE: *Best Western Heidelberg Inn* \$\$ 1303 Mayor Magrath Drive, AB T1K 2R1. *(403) 329 0555.* FAX *(403) 328 8846.* Heidelberg Inn has tastefully appointed rooms, a laundry service, and sauna. Near Nikka Yuko Japanese Garden.	67	●			
MOOSE JAW: *Temple Gardens Mineral Spa Hotel* \$\$ 24 Fairford St. East, SASK S6H 0C7. *(306) 694 5055.* FAX *(306) 694 8310.* W www.templegardens.sk.ca Located close to "Tunnels of Little Chicago," this hotel is connected to a mineral pool and spa center.	96	●			■
REGINA: *Fieldstone Inn* \$\$ near Craven, PO Box 26038, SASK S4R 8R7. *(306) 731 2377.* FAX *(306) 731 2369.* Located in the lovely Qu'Appelle Valley, this award-winning farm home offers inclusive watersports. Guests are picked up from Regina.	6	●	■	●	■
REGINA: *Radisson Hotel Saskatchewan Plaza* \$\$ 2125 Victoria Ave., SASK S4P 0S3. *(306) 522 7691.* FAX *(306) 522 8988.* W www.hotelsask.com Well appointed rooms and complementary airport pickup. Convenient for downtown stores.	217	●			

Hotel	Price	Rooms				
RIDING MOUNTAIN NATIONAL PARK: *Clear Lake Lodge* Wasagaming, MAN R0J 2H0. *(204) 848 2345.* FAX *(204) 848 2209.* The lodge has a comfortable living room with fireplace and common kitchen where guests have their own refrigerator. *Nov–Apr.*	$	16			●	■
SASKATOON: *Delta Bessborough Hotel* 601 Spadina Crescent East, SASK S7K 3G8. *(306) 244 5521.* FAX *(306) 665 7262.* W www.deltahotels.com Set on the picturesque South Saskatchewan Rive. Popular Japanese restaurant on site.	$$	225	●			■
WINNIPEG: *Fraser's Grove* 110 Mossdale Ave., MAN R2K 0H5. *(204) 661 0971.* W www.bedandbreakfast.mb.ca/frasersgrove Comfortable modern home is near the river, golf courses, downtown, and Lake Winnipeg beaches.	$	3				
WINNIPEG: *Delta Winnipeg Downtown* 350 St. Mary Ave., MAN R3C 3J2. *(204) 942 0551.* FAX *(204) 943 8702.* W www.deltahotels.com Comfortable downtown hotel. Noted for its billiards room and restaurant.	$$$	402	●	■		■
WINNIPEG: *Fairmont Winnipeg* W www.fairmont.com 2 Lombard Place, MAN R3B 0Y3. *(204) 957 1350.* FAX *(204) 956 1791.* Winnipeg's highest-rated hotel, in the heart of the business district. Rooms have data ports, Nintendo, and videos.	$$$	350	●	■		■

VANCOUVER AND VANCOUVER ISLAND

Hotel	Price	Rooms				
MALAHAT: *The Aerie* W www.aerie.bc.ca 600 Ebedora Lane, BC V0R 2L0. *(250) 743 7115.* FAX *(250) 743 4766.* Elegant terraced inn on a hillside, overlooking one of the island's most incredible vistas. Rooms are furnished with hot tubs, and the landscaped grounds contain ponds and fountains.	$$$$	29	●		●	■
NORTH VANCOUVER: *Thistledown House* W www.thistle-down.com 3910 Capilano Rd., BC V7R 4J2. *(604) 986 7173.* FAX *(604) 980 2939.* A heritage property built in 1920. Rooms are furnished with antiques from all over the world.	$$$	5			●	
PORT ALBERNI: *Eagle Nook Resort* W www.eaglenook.com Box 575, Port Alberni, BC V9Y 7M9. *(250) 723 1000.* FAX *(250) 723 6609.* A resort accessible by water taxi or seaplane only. Soak in the hot tub before feasting on a gourmet meal.	$$$$	23	●		●	
SOOKE: *Sooke Harbour House* 1528 Whiffen Spit Rd., BC V0S 1N0. *(250) 642 3421.* FAX *(250) 642 6988.* W www.sookeharbourhouse.com Just 9 m (30 ft) from the sea and 35 km (23 miles) from Victoria, this clapboard inn is a wonderful getaway.	$$$$$	28	●		●	
SURREY: *Astin Pacific Inn* W www.pacificinn.com 1160 King George Hwy, BC V4A 4Z2. *(604) 535 1432.* FAX *(604) 531 6979.* This Mexican-style hotel has rooms facing a covered courtyard with a swimming pool in the center.	$$	150	●		●	■
TOFINO: *Middle Beach Lodge* W www.middlebeach.com 400 Mackenzie Beach Rd., BC V0R 2Z0. *(250) 725 2900.* FAX *(250) 725 2901.* Two rustic lodges set on 16 ha (40 acres) of secluded oceanfront scenery, with a private beach. One resort is for families with young children, one strictly for adults.	$$$	64		■	●	
TOFINO: *Clayoquot Wilderness Resort* W www.wildretreat.com off Osprey Lane, Chesterman's Beach, BC V0R 2Z0. *(250) 726 8235.* FAX *(250) 726 8558.* This floating inn and its surrounding wilderness is a paradise for ecologically minded tourists. Activities include horseback riding, hiking, and whale-watching.	$$$$	16	●			
TOFINO: *Wickaninnish Inn* W www.wickinn.com Off Osprey Lane, Chesterman's Beach. Box 250, BC V0R 2Z0. *(250) 725 3100.* FAX *(250) 725 3110.* This luxury inn lies 10 miles north of Tofino by boat. Rooms boast hot tubs, fireplaces, and ocean views.	$$$$$	46	●		●	
VANCOUVER: *Days Inn Downtown* W www.daysinnvancouver.com 921 W Pender St., BC V6C 1M2. *(604) 681 4335.* FAX *(604) 681 7808.* Off-season rates and passes to the nearby YWCA fitness facility are some of the extras available at this European-style hotel.	$$$	85	●			

Price categories for a standard double room per night, including breakfast (where served), taxes, and any extra service charges:
$ under Can$100
$$ Can$100–$150
$$$ Can$150–$200
$$$$ Can$200–$250
$$$$$ over Can$250

RESTAURANT
Hotel restaurant or dining room, usually open to non-residents unless otherwise stated.
CHILDREN'S FACILITIES
Indicates child cribs and/or a baby-sitting service available. A few hotels also provide children's portions and high chairs in the restaurant.
GARDEN/TERRACE
Hotel with a garden, courtyard, or terrace often available for eating outside.
SWIMMING POOL
Hotel with an indoor or outdoor swimming pool.

Hotel	Number of Rooms	Restaurant	Children's Facilities	Garden/Terrace	Swimming Pool
VANCOUVER: *Best Western Sands Hotel* W www.rpbhotels.com $$$ 1755 Davie St., BC V6G 1W5. *(604) 682 1831.* FAX *(604) 682 3546.* Located close to English Bay and Stanley Park. The shops and bistros on Davie Street make this a pedestrian haven. TV P	119	●			
VANCOUVER: *Georgian Court Hotel* W www.georgiancourt.com $$$$ 773 Beatty St., BC V6B 2M4. *(604) 682 5555.* FAX *(604) 682 8830.* A small, intimate European-style hotel, with one of Vancouver's finest restaurants. It is close to the entertainment district. TV P	180	●			
VANCOUVER: *Quality Hotel Downtown* $$$$ 1335 Howe St., BC V6Z 1R7. *(604) 682 0229.* FAX *(604) 662 7566.* W www.qualityhotelvancouver.com Close to everything, this boutique hotel was recently awarded Hotel of the Year by Choice Hotels. TV P	157	●			■
VANCOUVER: *Delta Vancouver Suite Hotel* $$$$ 550 West Hastings St., BC V6B 1L6. *(604) 689 8188.* FAX *(604) 605 8881.* W www.deltahotels.com This downtown hotel has clean Scandinavian decor with sleek and modern lines, bedrooms off the lounge area, and full business facilities. 24 TV P	225	●			■
VANCOUVER: *Hyatt Regency Vancouver* W www.hyatt.com $$$$$ 655 Burrard St., BC V6C 2R7. *(604) 683 1234.* FAX *(604) 689 3707.* Upscale convention hotel close to shopping and sightseeing attractions, visited by traveling businessmen and other international guests. TV P	644	●		●	■
VANCOUVER: *Four Seasons* W www.fourseasons.com $$$$$ 791 West Georgia St., BC V6C 2T4. *(604) 689 9333.* FAX *(604) 684 4555.* This hotel has achieved five stars for 24 consecutive years. Located in the business center, close to the Pacific Centre shops, the hotel also features the Chartwell restaurant. 24 TV P	385	●	■		■
VANCOUVER: *Hotel Vancouver* $$$$$ 900 West Georgia St., BC V6C 2W6. *(604) 684 3131.* FAX *(604) 662 1929.* W www.fairmont.com This landmark hotel has offered luxurious service under its green copper roof since 1939. 24 TV P	555	●	■		■
VANCOUVER: *Metropolitan Hotel Vancouver* $$$$$ 645 Howe St., BC V6C 2Y9. *(604) 687 1122.* FAX *(604) 602 7846.* W www.metropolitan.com This hotel is one of only 107 members of the "Preferred Hotels & Resorts" worldwide. 24 TV P	197	●	■		■
VANCOUVER: *Pan Pacific Hotel Vancouver* $$$$$ 999 Canada Place, BC V6C 3B5. *(604) 662 8111.* FAX *(604) 685 8690.* W www.panpac.com Located on the waterfront, this hotel draws a corporate and international clientele. 24 TV P	506	●	■	●	■
VANCOUVER: *Sutton Place Hotel* W www.suttonplace.com $$$$$ 845 Burrard St., BC V6Z 2K6. *(604) 682 5511.* FAX *(604) 682 5513.* An impressive property tailored to the needs of both business travelers and tourists. Located in the heart of the city, the hotel offers luxurious rooms and an excellent restaurant. 24 TV P	397	●	■		■
VANCOUVER: *Waterfront Hotel* $$$$$ 900 Canada Place Way, BC V6C 3L5. *(604) 691 1991.* FAX *(604) 691 1828.* W www.thewaterfronthotel.com Modern glass-and-steel hotel across from the World Trade Centre. First-class amenities. 24 TV P	489	●	■	●	■
VICTORIA: *Days Inn* W www.daysinn.com $$ 123 Gorge Rd. East, BC V9A 1L1. *(250) 386 1422.* FAX *(250) 386 1254.* This inn is located five minutes' drive from downtown Victoria. The rooms are comfortable and peaceful. TV P	94	●			■

Hotel	Price	Rooms				
VICTORIA: *Abigail's Hotel* W www.abigailshotel.com 906 McClure St., BC V8V 3E7. *(250) 388 5363.* FAX *(250) 388 7787.* A small Tudor-style inn built in the 1930s. Rooms are furnished with antiques, and there's a cozy library with a wood-burning fire. P	$$$$	22			●	
VICTORIA: *Empress Hotel* W www.fairmont.com 721 Government St., BC V8W 1W5. *(250) 384 8111.* FAX *(250) 381 4334.* This 1908 stately building overlooks the harbor, near the Parliament Buildings. High Tea is served in the grand lobby. TV P	$$$$$	460	●	■	●	■
VICTORIA: *Ocean Point Resort* W www.oprhotel.com 45 Songhees Rd., BC V9A 6T3. *(250) 360 2999.* FAX *(250) 360 5856.* Located on Victoria's famous Inner Harbor with only the boardwalk between the hotel and the water's edge. World-class European spa and business center on premises. 24 TV P	$$$$$	246	●		●	■
VICTORIA: *Humboldt House Bed & Breakfast* 867 Humboldt St., BC V8V 2Z6. *(250) 383 0152.* FAX *(250) 383 6402.* W www.humboldthouse.com A romantic getaway. Gourmet breakfasts delivered to your room, complete with Jacuzzi and fireplace.	$$$$$	6				
THE ROCKY MOUNTAINS						
BANFF: *Rundlestone Lodge* W www.rundlestone.com 537 Banff Ave., AB T0L 0C0. *(403) 762 2201.* FAX *(403) 762 4501.* Renovated in 1997, this lodge includes Jacuzzis and fireplaces in some rooms. The restaurant offers fine cuisine. TV P	$$$$	95	●			■
BANFF: *Banff Springs Hotel* W www.fairmont.com 405 Spray Ave., AB T0L 0C0. *(403) 762 2211.* FAX *(403) 762 5755.* This landmark hotel features fireplaces, tennis courts, a pool, ice rink, golf course, spa, shops, and restaurants. 24 TV P	$$$$$	777	●	■	●	■
CALGARY: *Elbow River Inn* 1919 Macleod Trail, AB T2G 4S1. *(403) 269 6771.* FAX *(403) 237 5181.* The only Hotel Casino in Alberta, this sprawling property offers non-smoking rooms. TV P	$$	75	●		●	
CALGARY: *Quality Inn Motel Village* 2359 Banff Trail, AB T2M 4L2. *(403) 289 1973.* FAX *(403) 282 1241.* W www.qualityinnmotelvillage.com Newly renovated property with a modern lobby and a poolside restaurant. TV P	$$	105	●			■
CANMORE: *Quality Resort Château Canmore* 1720 Bow Valley Trail, AB T1W 2X3. *(403) 678 6699.* FAX *(403) 678 6954.* W www.chateaucanmore.com Château Canmore consists of chalets and suites equipped with fireplace and microwave. TV P	$$$	93	●	■	●	■
CRANBROOK: *Kootenay Country Comfort Inn* 1111 Cranbrook St. North, BC V1C 3S4. *250 426 2296.* FAX *(250) 426 3533.* W http://home.cyberlink.bc.ca/~motel This inn is a firm favorite with anglers fishing for trout in the nearby Premier Lake. TV P	$	36				
FORT NELSON: *The Blue Bell Inn* 4103 50th Ave. South, BC V0C 1R0. *(250) 774 6961.* FAX *(250) 774 6983.* A bright modern motel in a good location, the complex includes a 24-hour convenience store, a laundromat, and a fuel station. TV P	$	46	●			
LAKE LOUISE: *Lake Louise Inn* 210 Village Rd., AB T0L 1E0. *(403) 522 3791.* FAX *(403) 522 2018.* W www.lakelouiseinn.com Just five minutes from the ski hill and Lake Louise, the rooms in this renovated property range from economy to superior. TV P	$$$	232	●			■
LAKE LOUISE: *Simpson's Num-Ti-Jah Lodge* Mile 22, Bow Lake Icefield Parkway, AB T0L 1E0. *(403) 522 2167.* FAX *(403) 522 2425.* W www.num-ti-jah.com Built on the shore of Bow Lake in 1937 by legendary guide Jimmy Simpson. The Elk Horn dining room offers the finest cuisine on the parkway *(see p378)*. P	$$$	25	●			
LAKE LOUISE: *Château Lake Louise* W www.fairmont.com 111 Lake Louise Drive, AB T0L 1E0. *(403) 522 3511.* FAX *(403) 522 3834.* With a bygone elegance, Château Lake Louise has been host to adventurers since 1890. Dining and shopping on site. 24 TV P	$$$$$	489	●	■	●	■

For key to symbols see back flap

Price categories for a standard double room per night, including breakfast (where served), taxes, and any extra service charges:
- $ under Can$100
- $$ Can$100–$150
- $$$ Can$150–$200
- $$$$ Can$200–$250
- $$$$$ over Can$250

RESTAURANT
Hotel restaurant or dining room, usually open to non-residents unless otherwise stated.

CHILDREN'S FACILITIES
Indicates child cribs and/or a baby-sitting service available. A few hotels also provide children's portions and high chairs in the restaurant.

GARDEN/TERRACE
Hotel with a garden, courtyard, or terrace often available for eating outside.

SWIMMING POOL
Hotel with an indoor or outdoor swimming pool.

Hotel	Price	Number of Rooms	Restaurant	Children's Facilities	Garden/Terrace	Swimming Pool
PRINCE GEORGE: *Econo Lodge* 1915 3rd Ave., BC V2L 1G6. *(250) 563 7106.* FAX *(250) 561 7216.* Very quiet downtown location close to all amenities, with a choice of smoking and non-smoking rooms. 24 TV P	$	30		■		■
RADIUM HOT SPRINGS: *The Springs at Radium Golf Resort* 8100 Golf Course Rd., Hwy 93/95, BC V0A 1M0. *(250) 347 9311.* FAX *(250) 347 6299.* This three-story boutique hotel offers views of the mountains, and all rooms face one of two golf courses. TV P	$$	118	●		●	■
WATERTON LAKES: *Prince of Wales Hotel* Waterton Lakes National Park, AB T0K 2M0. *(403) 859 2231.* FAX *(403) 859 2630.* W www.glacierpark.com This historic hotel is at home amid the grandeur of the Rockies. Its alpine style has made it one of Canada's most photographed hotels. P	$$$$	37	●	■	●	

SOUTH AND NORTH BRITISH COLUMBIA

Hotel	Price	Number of Rooms	Restaurant	Children's Facilities	Garden/Terrace	Swimming Pool
BARKERVILLE: *Kelly House* 2nd St., BC V0K 1B0. *(250) 994 3328.* FAX *(250) 994 3312.* Lodging in two heritage buildings. Highlights include delicious breakfasts and the sound of music from the nearby theater. 24	$	6				
HOPE: *Manning Park Resort* W www.manningparkresort.com Manning Provincial Park, BC V0X 1L0. *(250) 840 8822.* FAX *(250) 840 8848.* A year-round family-oriented resort offering cabins, chalets, lodge rooms, and group facilities. TV P	$$	73	●	■		
KAMLOOPS: *Comfort Inn* W www.comfort.kamloops.com 1810 Rogers Place, BC V1S 1T7. *(250) 372 0987.* FAX *(250) 372 0967.* The rooms are spacious in this three-storey stucco property. The water slide on the grounds makes this inn ideal for families. TV P	$$	128		■		■
KELOWNA: *Lake Okanagan Resort* W www.lakeokanagan.com 2751 Westside Rd., BC V1Z 3T1. *(250) 769 3511.* FAX *(250) 769 6665.* This family-orientated destination borders a beach. There is horseback riding, golf, tennis, and a kids' camp in the summer. TV P	$$$	134	●	■	●	■
PENTICTON: *Penticton Lakeside Resort* W www.rpbhotels.com 21 Lakeshore Drive West, BC V2A 7M5. *(250) 493 8221.* FAX *(250) 493 0607.* A modern resort located on Okanagan Lake. A private beach, pier, jet-skiing, and para-sailing make it particularly popular with families. 24 TV P	$$	204	●	■	●	■
PRINCE RUPERT: *Cow Bay Bed & Breakfast* W www.cowbay.bc.ca 20 Cow Bay Rd., BC V8J 1A5. *(250) 627 1804.* FAX *(250) 627 1919.* A tastefully decorated family home within walking distance of museums and the harbor. TV P	$	3				
QUESNEL: *Becker's Lodge* Bowron Lake Provincial Park, 342 Kinchant St., BC V2J 2R4. *(250) 992 8864.* FAX *(250) 992 8893.* Campsites, log cabins, and basic meals. Canoes are for rent for the circuit in the park *(see p318).* *Oct–Dec.* P	$$	9	●	■		
WELLS: *White Cap Motor Inn & RV Park* Ski Hill Rd., BC V0K 2R0. *(250) 994 3489.* FAX *(250) 994 3426.* W www.whitecapinn.bc.ca Suites with kitchenettes, a children's playground, and an adjacent RV park. TV P	$	34		■	●	
WHISTLER: *Delta Whistler Resort* W www.deltahotels.com 4050 Whistler Way, BC V0N 1B4. *(604) 932 1982.* FAX *(604) 932 7332.* Located next to a golf course and the Whistler and Blackcomb gondolas, this resort has luxury amenities. 24 TV P	$$$$	288	●		●	■

Hotel	Rooms				
WHISTLER: *Holiday Inn SunSpree Resort* www.whistlerhi.com $$$$ 4295 Blackcomb Way, BC V0N 1V4. *(604) 938 0878.* FAX *(604) 938 9943.* In the heart of Whistler Village, minutes from Whistler and Blackcomb mountains, shopping, and nightlife, the rooms are equipped with kitchenettes, jetted soaker tubs, and fireplaces.	114				
WHISTLER: *Château Whistler* www.fairmont.com $$$$$ 4599 Château Boulevard, BC V0N 1V4. *(604) 938 8000.* FAX *(604) 938 2099.* Located at the base of Blackcomb Mountain, the hotel features rooms with fireplaces, Jacuzzis, and private check-ins. Golf courses and a health club add to the luxury in this world-class resort.	556	●	■	●	■
WHISTLER: *Pan Pacific Lodge Whistler* www.panpac.com $$$$$ 4320 Sundial Crescent, BC V0N 1B4. *(604) 905 2999.* FAX *(604) 905 2995.* A luxury property with floor-to-ceiling windows. The outdoor pool has spectacular mountain views.	121	●		●	■
NORTHERN CANADA					
DAWSON CITY: *Midnight Sun Hotel* $$ 3rd Avenue and Queen St., YT Y0B 1G0. *(867) 993 5495.* FAX *(867) 993 6425.* An attractive outdoor patio and lounge look over the historic setting of the gold rush, and the hotel's cabins back onto the casino.	44	●			
FORT PROVIDENCE: *Snowshoe Inn* $$ 1 Mackenzie St., NT X0E 0L0. *(867) 699 3511.* FAX *(867) 699 4300.* Kitchenettes, satellite TV, and modern office facilities add to the relaxing charm of this old-style inn.	35	●			
FORT SIMPSON: *Nahani Inn* $ Main St., Fort Simpson, X0E 0N0. *(819) 695 2201.* FAX *(819) 695 3000.* Centrally located, the hotel has suites as well as self-catering facilities in addition to a bar. It is also famous for its delicious meals.	34	●	●		
HAINES JUNCTION: *Kluane Park Inn* $ Mile 1016, Alaska Highway. *(867) 634 2261.* FAX *(867) 634 2273.* The most scenic hotel in the area, an outside deck overlooks dramatic arctic scenery and is host to regular barbecues in summer.	20				
HAY RIVER: *Caribou Motor Inn* $ 912 Mackenzie Highway, NT X0E 0R8. *(867) 874 6706.* FAX *(867) 874 6704.* Conveniently located near this small town, many of the rooms feature luxurious whirlpools, steam baths, and Jacuzzis.	29		■		
INUVIK: *McKenzie Hotel* $$$ 185 MacKenzie Rd., X0E 0T0. *(867) 777 2861.* FAX *(867) 777 3317.* mac@permafrost.com Friendly considerate staff, a jolly atmosphere and comfortable rooms make this a popular choice.	32	●			
VICTORIA ISLAND: *Arctic Islands Lodge* $$$$ 26 Omingnak St., Cambridge Bay, NT X0E 0C0. *(867) 983 2345.* FAX *(867) 983 2480.* This excellent hotel is known for its helpful staff and comfortable rooms. A fascinating range of sporting facilities, including guided hunting trips in the icy wilderness, are offered by the hotel.	25	●			
WHITEHORSE: *Best Western Gold Rush Inn* $$ 411 Main St., YT Y1A 2B6. *(867) 668 4500.* FAX *867 668 7432.* goldrush@yknet.yk.ca This efficient hotel with friendly staff has a lobby packed with antiques from gold rush days.	106	●			
WHITEHORSE: *High Country Inn* www.highcountryinn.yk.ca $$ 4051 4th Ave., YT Y1A 1H1. *(867) 667 4471.* FAX *(867) 667 6457.* One of the province's most stylish and comfortable inns, a grand piano and log fires add to the luxurious atmosphere.	85	●			
YELLOWKNIFE: *Discovery Inn* $$ 4701 Franklin Ave., X1A 2N6. *(867) 873 4151.* FAX *(867) 920 7948.* Rooms offer kitchenettes here, but there is also a very good licensed restaurant in the evenings.	41	●			
YELLOWKNIFE: *Explorer Hotel* www.explorerhotel.nt.ca $$$ 4825 49th Avenue X1A 2R3. *(867) 873 3531.* FAX *(867) 873 2789.* This luxury hotel boasts two restaurants, Berkeley's family dining room, and the Sakura Japanese restaurant.	128	●	■		

For key to symbols see back flap

Where to Eat

WHAT MAKES Canadian cuisine unique is its regional specialties: Alberta beef, goldeye fish in Manitoba, salmon from BC, Nova Scotia lobster, and Quebec French pies and pastries. Game, including rabbit, caribou, and bison, which have been served in aboriginal homes for centuries, are now considered gourmet dishes at cosmopolitan restaurants. A tradition of French haute cuisine is evident in most of the country's major cities, particularly in top hotels. However, as Canada is a nation of immigrants, ethnic restaurants are common everywhere. German, Greek, Chinese, Thai, Indian, Ukrainian, African, and Italian cuisines, along with other international favorites, provide a wide range of choice at a price to suit every budget. Regional specialties can be sampled in their place of origin, but most of the larger towns will also offer a choice of the country's best local produce, and in some areas this includes Canadian wines and beers *(see p363)*. The listings on *pp364–79* describe a selection of restaurants chosen for their variety, service, and good value.

Seafood on offer in Atlantic Canada

The top class Zoë's Restaurant in Château Laurier, Ottawa ***(see p373)***

Types of Restaurants

EATING OUT IN Canada is surprisingly easy on the pocket, particularly compared to European prices. This makes a trip to a top restaurant to sample international cuisine (often made with local produce) very worthwhile. Eating places are extremely varied, with the tearoom, bistro, brasserie, and theater café competing with the more usual café, restaurant, and fast food outlet. Many pubs also serve excellent bar food, at reasonable prices. More unusual, but no less worthwhile, is the uniquely Canadian dining experience of the delicious lobster supper. Held throughout the summer on Prince Edward Island, these lively gatherings usually take place in church grounds on wooden tables surrounded by local fishermen. Equally unique, though by no means public, are Inuit dinners. Traveling through the Arctic north may result in an invitation to join an Inuit family for the evening meal. Traditional dishes might include sun-dried caribou sweetened with berry sauces or smoked and dried local fish. These family dinners are usually alcohol-free and very lively.

Vegetarian

VEGETARIAN options are on the increase throughout the country. Expect to see at least one vegetarian dish on each menu. For those who eat fish, seafood has something of a national reputation. "Health Canada," the government plan for healthy eating, took effect in the 1990s. Restaurants that subscribe to the plan sign menus with a heart symbol denoting low-fat dishes. Anyone on a special or weight-loss diet can feel free to ask the chef to leave out certain high-calorie ingredients. Fresh fruits are easily obtained throughout the south of the country, and are abundant and often day-old in the main growing areas of Ontario and BC's Okanagan Valley. Some of the best berries and peaches in the world can be enjoyed here in the summer. It is worth remembering that most food in the Northwest Territories and Nunavut is imported, and largely canned or frozen; apart from Inuit game kills, fresh food is hard to obtain, and very expensive, in these distant Arctic regions.

Open-air dining in downtown Montreal ***(see pp366–8)***

Arowhon Pines Lodge in Algonquin Provincial Park, Ontario ***(see p372)***

Alcohol

THE MINIMUM age of public purchase and consumption of alcohol is 19 throughout the country, except in Quebec where it is 18. Canada produces some fine wines (*see p363*), which are becoming more widely available. Visitors should know that tipping in bars should be left until the end of the evening rather than at each round.

It is worth noting that many towns in the Northwest Territories and Nunavut, particularly Inuit settlements, are dry – alcohol sale in stores and bars is heavily restricted due to high native alcoholism rates. Some towns, however, have a hotel bar for visitors.

Eating Hours and Reservations

LUNCH TABLES are usually available from noon to 2pm, and dinner reservations from 6pm to 9pm, although later bookings should be accepted in larger cities. Reserving a table in advance is generally a good idea. It is considered polite to call ahead and cancel if you are unable to make your reservation.

Paying and Tipping

IT IS POSSIBLE to eat well in Canada for a bargain price. A snack in a café seldom costs more than Can$5. In a good restaurant, a three-course meal and a shared bottle of wine often costs between Can$30–$60. Even gourmet dinners can start at Can$50. Fixed-priced menus are common. Luncheon items are generally less expensive, and are often similar to the evening menu without the linen and candles. Restaurant tax is the 7 percent GST (Goods and Services Tax), plus a varying provincial sales tax, applicable everywhere except Alberta. Taxes are included on the final check as percentages of the total. Tipping in most restaurants and cafés is expected, and should be about 10–15 percent of the check. Service charges are not usually included. Europeans should note that tipping is expected in bars and nightclubs. In common with most countries, a tip should increase if you are bringing a larger party to a restaurant and for any exceptional service. Penalizing staff for bad service is not common.

Children

CANADA IS A child-friendly society. Most restaurants offer high chairs or booster seats. The more upscale the venue, the more parents are required to keep children seated at table and to take noisy or upset youngsters outside until they calm down. A children's menu or half-portions may well be available for those under eight years old.

Disabled Facilities

ALL NEW restaurants, as well as existing establishments undergoing renovation, have made their sites accessible to wheelchair users. A wide bathroom door and no interior steps from entrance to dining table are now compulsory across the country in new buildings. However, older, rural establishments should be checked out in advance.

Dress Code

VACATIONERS need not worry unduly about bringing formal clothes with them on a trip. Most restaurants operate "smart-casual" policy, especially at lunchtime, but exceptions to this can include sneakers (trainers), cut-off jeans, and dirty or ripped clothes. The rule generally runs as follows: the more expensive and exclusive the restaurant, the more formal the attire required. Evening dress is very rarely required in any venue.

Smoking

OVER 70 PERCENT of Canadians do not smoke, and local by-laws restrict where the dwindling minority of smokers can smoke. Increasingly, restaurants have a no-smoking area, but this does not apply in bars or cafés. Cigars are generally not popular in restaurants, so ask before lighting up. A note of caution: when picnicking in a park, be sure to extinguish your cigarette for fear of starting a forest fire.

Café-bars in cities are always inexpensive and popular options

A Glossary of Typically Canadian Food

WITH A RICH HISTORY of multiculturalism, Canada's culinary heritage is as diverse as it is intriguing. Although there is no national cuisine as such, regional specialties have their own strong identities. The major cities, in particular Montreal and Toronto, are centers of international cuisine, with restaurants ranging from Italian to Caribbean and Asian at prices to suit every budget. French Canada offers haute cuisine at the country's top dining spots in Quebec City and Montreal.

Provincial specialties offer good value and the chance to sample some of Canada's own excellent fish, beef, and homegrown fruit and vegetables. Seafood dominates Atlantic Canada and BC menus, while steaks and burgers should be sampled in the ranching areas of Alberta and Saskatchewan. Old-style Acadian cuisine, reminiscent of French country food, is available in New Brunswick and Nova Scotia. Summer in Ontario brings fresh fruits and vegetables that take less than a day to reach the table. In Northern Canada, age-old Inuit techniques produce a variety of sundried caribou and fish dishes.

SEAFOOD

BORDERED BY oceans on three sides, Canada offers wonderful seafood, particularly on its east and west coasts. Produce from here is freshly caught and can easily make it from the ocean to the dinnerplate within 24 hours. **Oysters**, **clams**, and **scallops** are a main feature of East Coast menus. In New Brunswick, **fiddleheads** (fern shoots) and **dulse** (seaweed) are enjoyed sautéed as a vegetable accompaniment. Prince Edward Island is famous for its **lobster**, which is simply boiled, broiled (grilled), or served whole with corn on the cob at one of the many church socials that run through summer on the little island; those who don't like crustacea can try **Atlantic salmon**.

Pacific salmon, **crab**, **shellfish**, and **shrimp** (prawns) dominate British Columbian fare, along with the typically northern fish the **Arctic char**. More unusual dishes, often incorporating historic pickling and preserving methods, include **Solomon Grundy** (Nova Scotia's fine marinated herring), and **cod tongues**, as well as tasty **seal flipper pie** from Newfoundland. Since it was the fruits of the sea that tempted early explorers to this area, it is no surprise that **cod**, **clams**, and **mussels** are still much enjoyed for their quality, as are the newly-stylish fresh broiled **tuna** and **sardines**. Freshwater fish, both the farmed and wild versions, is caught in the two million lakes dotted across Canada, and offers a delicate contrast to seafood. In the west of the country, the tender **Winnipeg goldeye, trout**, and **pickerel**, which is often cooked over open fires at informal summer outdoor shore lunches throughout the central region, are a uniquely Canadian treat.

Lobster platter from Quebec City

MEAT

BASED IN CALGARY, Alberta's cattle ranches are the source of Canada's finest beef. Huge **burgers** and **steaks** are exceptionally high-grade here. Most beef in rural areas is served simply, with salad and fries, but one much-loved local dish is **Calgary beef hash**, corned beef with baked beans and fried potatoes. Lamb and buffalo are also farmed, albeit in smaller numbers. The Yukon, Northwest Territories, and Nunavut supply much of the country's game; **caribou**, **musk ox**, and **moose** are all sent down south to be cooked in the European style. Local people, particularly the Inuit, smoke meat for the winter months. Their **smoked caribou** is delicious and very popular. Famous for making the most of a kill, native people use every part of the animal for either clothing or food; even **moose fleas** are something of a delicacy. **Goose**, **duck**, and fish are all smoked or sundried too, providing staples for the very long winter. Caribou and birds are preserved by being hung out on lines to dry in the Arctic sun. Sauces made from wild berries moisten the meat, and may be sweetened to taste.

FRUIT AND VEGETABLES

ONTARIO IS the fruitbowl of Canada. In addition to its burgeoning wine industry, the area is known continent-wide for its strawberries and cranberries. Peaches and apples are also cultivated here in large quantities, as are blueberries, which also flourish in Nova Scotia and Quebec.

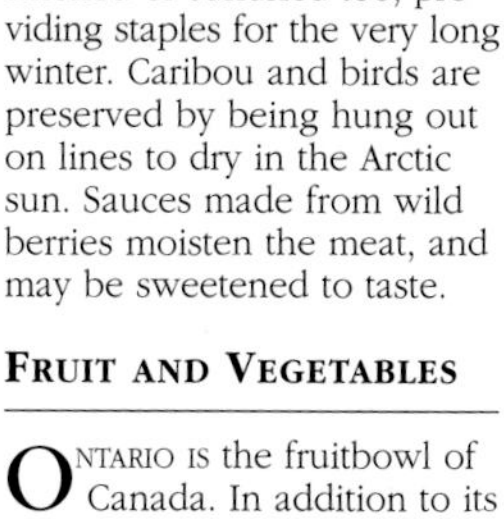

A Chinese vegetable-seller in traditional dress in Toronto

Basket of apples from Ontario in Muskoka market

Many berries grow wild and can be picked while hiking for the evening meal. Corn, black beans, and the gourd vegetable squash (collectively known as the "three sisters") are produced in Ontario alongside zucchini (courgette), huge tomatoes, and fresh herbs, all of which are grown for domestic use and for export.

Desserts and Sweets

Canada has produced a sweet famous the world over: maple syrup. Usually eaten with American (buttermilk) pancakes, the syrup can also be served French-style with ***trempettes***, fried bread soaked in syrup and covered with heavy cream. The syrup is also used in tarts, bread, and pies. It can also round off a meal as maple sugar in coffee or aromatic maple fudge. French-Canadians are known for their rich desserts; ***tarte au sucre*** (sugar pie) is popular, as is ***pudding au chomeur*** (literally "unemployed pudding"), an upside-down cake with a caramel base. Fruit tarts from Quebec are also delicious.

Fast Food

The staple North American fare of hamburgers, hotdogs, French fries, fried chicken, and pizza provides a recognizable selection of snacks for most visitors. For the adventurous, Quebec has managed to break into the world of fast food with ***poutine***, a snack of French fries dripping with melted cheese and a rich beef or onion gravy.

A recent explosion in specialty coffee shops has raised the standard of some outlets; freshly brewed multi-flavored cappuccinos served with a wide choice of muffins and bagels are highly popular. Doughnuts of many varieties are an old favorite: Canadians joke that the easiest way to find a police officer is to visit a doughnut shop, because officers on patrol always seem to be taking a break in one.

French-Canadian Food

The center of French-style gourmet cuisine in Canada is Quebec. Dishes here are reminiscent of the best European food, and Montreal usually boasts at least two well-known French chefs working in its top restaurants at any time. *Canadien* cooks are changing with the times. Many of North America's most innovative chefs work in Montreal and Quebec City, blending elements of centuries-old farmers' traditions with the lighter cuisine of modern Europe and America. For more traditional French-Canadian dishes, both cities and towns in the province usually serve specialties. These include ***creton*** (a spicy pork pâté), ***tourtière***, (a pastry pie filled with ground pork or beef and cloves), and many varieties of ***pâtisserie***. **Smoked beef** is another popular local delicacy.

The Maritime Provinces offer excellent, originally French, Acadian dishes from recipes which are hundreds of years old. As well as meat pies, patés, and stews, rich desserts and cakes feature in their hearty menus.

Maple Syrup

There are several top French restaurants in Canada, based largely in Montreal and Quebec City. Vieux-Montréal boasts a variety of French bistros offering traditional delights such as **snails in garlic**, ***filet mignon*** steak, and delicate **butter tarts** and pâtisserie; in true French tradition, the *prix-fixe* menus are always good value. Quebec City offers more classic country fare such as Quebec **French pea soup**, and **duck**. Breakfast French-style is a treat; local ***brioches*** and ***croissants*** are delicious with ***café au lait***.

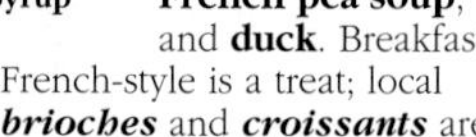

What to Drink

Canada's two favorite beers, the lagers Molson "Canadian" and Labatt "Blue", are known the world over and are drunk, chilled, by Canadians in preference to any other beer. The first Canadian wine was made in 1811 for commercial sale, but it is only in recent years that Canadians have developed a taste for the grape. Canada produces excellent wines from hybrid grapes, thanks largely to European wine makers who emigrated to Canada after rigorous special training. Most wine comes from two areas: a pocket in the southern Okanagan Valley of British Columbia *(see p315)*, and a 55-km (35-mile) strip along the Niagara Peninsula of southern Ontario, where the majority of grapes are grown. Familiar grape varieties such as the Chardonnays, Riesling, and Pinot Noir, are among the better known wines also produced in Ontario, and in the more temperate climate of British Columbia. Rye Whisky is distilled in BC; Canadian Club is the most popular brand, but local distilleries produce specialties.

Molson, the popular Canadian Beer

Choosing a Restaurant

The restaurants in this guide have been selected across a wide range of price categories for their exceptional food, good value, or interesting location. Entries are listed by region, in alphabetical order within price category. The thumb tabs on the pages use the same color-coding as the corresponding regional chapters in the main section of this guide.

Newfoundland and Labrador

Restaurant	Outdoor Eating	Vegetarian Specialties	Bar Area	Fixed-Price Menu	Children's Facilities
Corner Brook: *The Wine Cellar* $$$$ Glyn Mill Inn, Cob Lane. *(709) 634 5181.* This steakhouse has a strong local following. Try the char-grilled Alberta beef and desserts made from wild Newfoundland berries.		●	■		
L'Anse Au Clair: *Northern Light Inn* $$ 58 Main St. *(709) 931 2332.* In an area where there are few restaurants, Northern Light offers dining that is reliable and filling. Seafood and Labrador caribou are specials.		●	■		■
Rocky Harbour: *Ocean View Hotel* $$$ Main St. *(709) 458 2730.* The dining room offers a spectacular view of Rocky Harbour. The menu features fresh seafood and home-made pies.		●	■		■
St. John's: *Bruno's* $$$ 248 Water St. *(709) 579 7662.* Owner Gail Ortichello makes everything in this tiny Italian restaurant by hand, including sausages, breads, and pastas. For dessert, the tiramisu is breathtaking.		●	■	●	■
St. John's: *Bianca's* $$$$$ 171 Water St. *(709) 726 9016.* One of Atlantic Canada's finest restaurants, the extensive menu includes French-cut rack of lamb, baked musk ox, salmon in bittersweet chocolate sauce, and, for dessert, Belgian chocolate torte or apple strudel.	■	●	■		
Saint-Pierre & Miquelon: *Le Caveau* $$$$ 2 Rue Maître Georges Lefevre. *(508) 41 30 30.* Possibly the best restaurant on this very French island, Le Caveau's menu takes full advantage of the local seafood and French bakery goods. A local favorite is the *Brioche d'escargots* in Roquefort dressing.	■	●	■		
Terra Nova National Park: *Clode Sound Dining Room* $$$ Terra Nova Park Lodge. *(709) 543 2525.* This family dining room features a wide variety of pastas, seafood, and steaks, and traditional Newfoundland dishes. *Summer only.*	■	●	■		■
Witless Bay: *The Captain's Table* $ Hwy 10. *(709) 334 2278.* Eat here after a boat tour of the fabulous Witless Bay Bird Sanctuary. The fish and chips are some of the best in Newfoundland, and the rich, creamy chowder is a secret family recipe.					■

New Brunswick, Nova Scotia, and Prince Edward Island

Restaurant	Outdoor Eating	Vegetarian Specialties	Bar Area	Fixed-Price Menu	Children's Facilities
Antigonish: *Sunshine on Main* $$ 332 Main St. *(902) 863 5851.* A favorite here is the Seafood Pot-au-Feu – lobster, shrimp, scallops, mussels, and haddock in a tomato and white wine broth.		●			■
Baddeck: *Telegraph House Inn* $$ Chebucto St. *(902) 295 1100.* Located in a large Victorian mansion, this restaurant prepares traditional Nova Scotia lobster, trout, and salmon. *summer only.*					■
Bay Fortune: *Inn at Bay Fortune* $$$$$ Hwy 310. *(902) 687 3745.* Regularly listed among Canada's finest restaurants, the chef presents a menu of fresh island fish, lamb, and beef. Book the Chef's Table and enjoy seven specially prepared surprise courses.		●		●	■

Price categories for a three-course meal for one, including half a bottle of wine (where available) and service:
$ under Can$25
$$ Can$25–$35
$$$ Can$35–$50
$$$$ Can$50–$70
$$$$$ over Can$70

OUTDOOR EATING
Some tables on a patio or terrace.
VEGETARIAN SPECIALTIES
One menu always includes a selection of vegetarian dishes.
BAR AREA
There is a bar area or cocktail bar within the restaurant, available for drinks and/or bar snacks.
FIXED-PRICE MENU
A fixed-price menu available at a good rate, for lunch, dinner or both, usually with three courses.
CHILDREN'S FACILITIES
Small portions and/or high chairs available on request.

Restaurant	Price	Outdoor Eating	Vegetarian Specialties	Bar Area	Fixed-Price Menu	Children's Facilities
BOUCTOUCHE: *Le Tire-Bouchon* 157 Chemin du Couvent. *(506) 743 5568.* The dining room overlooks the garden. Chowders, scallops, lobster, fresh fish, chicken, and duck are all regular offerings. *Jun–end Sep.*	$$$$			■	●	■
CARAQUET: *Hotel Paulin* 143 Bvld. St. Pierre Ouest. *(506) 727 9981.* The restaurant in this family hotel serves regional fare, including fresh trout and salmon. *summer only.*	$$$			■		■
CHARLOTTETOWN: *Siranella* 83 Water St. *(902) 628 2271.* This Italian eatery is located a short stroll from pretty Peake's Wharf. Try the home-made spinach gnocchi served in cream sauce with gorgonzola and parmesan, or the herb-cured veal grilled in olive oil.	$$$	■	●			■
CHARLOTTETOWN: *Piece A Cake* 119 Grafton St. *(902) 894 4585.* A lively bistro that serves up an eclectic combination of dishes. The open kitchen allows diners to watch as the chef works his magic.	$$$		●			■
DALHOUSIE: *Manoir Adelaide* 385 Adelaide St. *(506) 684 5681.* Part of the Best Western chain, but the dining is far better than the average hotel fare. Fresh fish is grilled, steamed, or poached.	$$$$	■	●	■		■
GRAND TRACADIE: *Dalvay-by-the-Sea* Prince Edward Island National Park. *(902) 672 2048.* This historic inn *(see p345)* serves seafood dishes with an Australian flair including salmon with roasted seaweed and tomato salsa.	$$$$		●	■	●	■
HALIFAX: *Da Maurizio* 1496 Lower Water St. *(902) 423 0859.* An elegant Italian restaurant. Creative offerings include pasta with a range of unusual sauces and luscious creamy desserts.	$$$$		●			
HALIFAX: *Sweet Basil Bistro* 1866 Upper Water St. *(902) 425 2133.* A comfortable but sassy bistro across from the Historic Properties serves innovative dishes such as ravioli stuffed with butternut squash and fresh herbs, covered with a light parmesan and hazelnut sauce.	$$$	■	●			
LUNENBURG: *The Lion Inn* 33 Cornwallis St. *(902) 634 8988.* This small restaurant in Lunenburg's historic Old Town has an excellent menu, including Nova Scotia rack of lamb. Make a reservation.	$$$			■		
MABOU: *Duncregan Country Inn* Hwy 19. *(902) 945 2207.* In this small dining room, Eleanor and Steven Mullendore offer creative takes on regional dishes. The favorite is the fresh salmon grilled over an open flame with a Dijon, lemon, and honey marinade.	$$$		●		●	■
MONTAGUE: *Windows on the Water* 106 Sackville St. *(902) 838 2080.* This delightful spot overlooking Montague Harbour features creative sandwiches and first-class chowders.	$$$	■	●			■
OYSTER BED BRIDGE: *Café St-Jean* Route 6 at Oyster Bed Bridge. *(902) 963 3133.* This restaurant takes full advantage of the local seafood, including fresh lobster from a nearby lobster pound, to present a menu of classic and Cajun dishes. The dessert crêpes are wonderful. *mid-Jun–mid-Oct.*	$$$	■	●		●	■

For key to symbols see back flap

Price categories for a three-course meal for one, including half a bottle of wine (where available) and service:
$ under Can$25
$$ Can$25–$35
$$$ Can$35–$50
$$$$ Can$50–$70
$$$$$ over Can$70

Outdoor Eating
Some tables on a patio or terrace.
Vegetarian Specialties
One menu always includes a selection of vegetarian dishes.
Bar Area
There is a bar area or cocktail bar within the restaurant, available for drinks and/or bar snacks.
Fixed-Price Menu
A fixed-price menu available at a good rate, for lunch, dinner or both, usually with three courses.
Children's Facilities
Small portions and/or high chairs available on request.

Restaurant	Price	Outdoor Eating	Vegetarian Specialties	Bar Area	Fixed-Price Menu	Children's Facilities
Parrsboro: *Harbour View Restaurant* 476 Pier Rd. *(902) 254 3507.* This restaurant is a favorite with locals, serving great chowders, fish and chips, coffee, and home-made pies, all with harbor views.	$	■			●	■
Prince William: *King's Head Inn* Kings Landing Historic Settlement. *(506) 363 4999.* www.kingslanding.nb.ca Set in the Historic Settlement, all the recipes date from 1855, the year the inn was built. *June 3–Thanksgiving.* *dinner.*	$$	■	●	■		■
St. Andrews: *The Europe* 48 King St. *(506) 529 3818.* After a day of beachcombing along the shores of the Passamaquoddy Bay, nothing is better than the hearty French, Swiss, and German dishes on offer here.	$$$			■		
Saint John: *Beatty and the Bistro* 60 Charlotte St. *(506) 652 3888.* www.dineaid.com Lamb is a specialty here, roasted and stuffed with cranberries, pecans, rosemary, and garlic. Another popular dish is chicken florentine, spinach and shrimp.	$$$		●			
Saint John: *Billy's* Old City Market. *(506) 672 3474.* www.billysseafood.com Dinner is chosen from the display of halibut, shrimp, oysters, and other seafood, then drinks are served while it is cooked to order.	$$$	■	●	■		
Shelburne: *Charlotte Lane Café and Crafts* 13 Charlotte Lane. *(902) 875 3314.* Swiss-trained chef Roland Glauser presents delicious menu items such as chicken stuffed with camembert, asparagus, and garlic.	$$$	■	●			■
Sussex: *Broadway Café* 73 Broad St. *(506) 433 5414.* An innovative lunch spot with a tempting assortment of sandwiches and home-made soups. *Sun.*	$$	■	●	■		■
Wolfville: *Acton's Café* 268 Main St. *(902) 542-7525.* Acton's German-trained chef has created an international cuisine featuring ingredients from the farms of the Annapolis Valley.	$$$$	■	●	■	●	
MONTREAL						
Chinatown: *Maison Kam Fung* 1008 Rue Clark. *(514) 878 2888.* This bright, airy restaurant serves the city's most reliable lunchtime dim sum. Dinnertime specialties are standard Cantonese.	$$		●	■	●	■
Downtown: *Schwartz's (Montréal Hebrew) Delicatessen* 3895 Blvd. Saint-Laurent. *(514) 842 4813.* Jewish immigrants from Romania made smoked brisket a staple of the Montreal diet. This place excels in cooking it. No alcohol or credit cards.	$				●	■
Downtown: *Brasserie Magnan* 2602 Rue Saint-Patrick. *(514) 935 9647.* This old-fashioned Montreal tavern serves roast beef, salmon pie, and huge steaks to a mixed clientele. Good selection of draft beers.	$$	■		■	●	■
Downtown: *Biddle's Jazz and Ribs* 2060 Rue Aylmer. *(514) 842 8656.* Jazz musician Charlie Biddle built this restaurant so that his friends would have a place to play a little music and feast on barbecued ribs.	$$	■		■		

DOWNTOWN: *Le Canard* $$
4631 Blvd. St. Laurent. (514) 284 6009.
Brass platters and fish nets decorate this simple restaurant. It is known for its *canard à l'orange*, but the seafood *paella* is equally good.

DOWNTOWN: *Phayathai* $$
1235 Rue Guy. (514) 933 9949.
Classic Thai dishes served in a friendly ambience. Seafood and *galangal* (ginger) soups are excellent, as is the roast duck in curry sauce.

DOWNTOWN: *L'Actuel* $$$
1194 Rue Peel. (514) 866 1537.
This cheerful Belgian-style brasserie serves a few dozen variations on the mussels and French fries theme, as well as other classic Belgian dishes such as smoked herring with potatoes.

DOWNTOWN: *Le Caveau* $$$
2063 Rue Victoria. (514) 844 1624.
Le Caveau's intimate dining rooms are spread over three floors in an old brick house surrounded by glass and steel towers.

DOWNTOWN: *L'Orchidée de Chine* $$$
2017 Peel St. (514) 287 1878.
Diners in romantic little booths can feast on such Chinese delicacies as softshell crab, sautéed lamb with spicy sauce, and crispy duck.

DOWNTOWN: *Moishe's* $$$$
3961 Blvd. Saint-Laurent. (514) 845 3509.
This large noisy dining room is a carnivore's paradise. The Lighter family have been serving their thick steaks for 50 years.

DOWNTOWN: *Restaurant Julien* $$$
1191 Rue Union. (514) 871 1581.
A large canopied terrace makes this French restaurant a charming summer dining spot. The duck-breast tournedos and the chocolate marquise are delicious.

DOWNTOWN: *Café de Paris* $$$$
Ritz-Carlton Hotel, 1228 Ouest Rue Sherbrooke. (514) 842 4212.
During the summer, the formal Edwardian dining room in this upscale hotel spills over into the garden. The kitchen serves classic French cuisine.

DOWNTOWN: *Le Passe Partout* $$$$
3857 Blvd. Décarie. (514) 487 7750.
New York-born chef James MacGuire writes his own menu every day according to his fresh ingredients. Examples include duck terrine, sautéed veal, swordfish, and the best bread in Montreal.

DOWNTOWN: *Toqué!* $$$$
3842 Rue Saint-Denis. (514) 499 2084.
Normand Laprise and Christin LaMarch have reigned as Montreal's most innovative chefs for more than a decade.

DOWNTOWN: *Beaver Club* $$$$$
Hôtel La Reine-Elizabeth, 900 Ouest Blvd. René Lévesque. (514) 861 3511.
An élite ambience with classic roast beef, grilled salmon, and lamb, and the best martinis in town.

DOWNTOWN: *Chez la Mère Michel* $$$$$
1209 Rue Guy. (514) 934 0473.
One of the oldest and most traditional French restaurants in the city. The Dover sole, served *à la meunière* or with lobster, is wonderful.

DOWNTOWN: *Nuances* $$$$$
Casino de Montréal, 1 Ave. du Casino. (514) 392 2708.
The Casino de Montréal's grilled tuna with basil-flavored polenta and lamb with wine and thyme are as spectacular as the views.

DOWNTOWN: *Queue de cheval* $$$$$
1221 Rene Levesque W. (514) 390 0090.
Reservations are recommended at this downtown spot which is highly regarded for both its steaks, service and ambience.

Restaurant	1	2	3	4	5
Le Canard	■			●	
Phayathai		●		●	■
L'Actuel		●	■	●	
Le Caveau		●	■	●	■
L'Orchidée de Chine		●	■	●	■
Moishe's		●	■		■
Restaurant Julien	■	●	■	●	
Café de Paris	■	●	■	●	■
Le Passe Partout				●	
Toqué!			■	●	
Beaver Club		●	■	●	
Chez la Mère Michel		●	■	●	
Nuances	■		■	●	
Queue de cheval	■		■		

For key to symbols see back flap

Price categories for a three-course meal for one, including half a bottle of wine (where available) and service:
- $ under Can$25
- $$ Can$25–$35
- $$$ Can$35–$50
- $$$$ Can$50–$70
- $$$$$ over Can$70

Outdoor Eating
Some tables on a patio or terrace.
Vegetarian Specialties
One menu always includes a selection of vegetarian dishes.
Bar Area
There is a bar area or cocktail bar within the restaurant, available for drinks and/or bar snacks.
Fixed-Price Menu
A fixed-price menu available at a good rate, for lunch, dinner or both, usually with three courses.
Children's Facilities
Small portions and/or high chairs available on request.

Ile Sainte-Helene: *Hélène de Champlain* $$$
200 Tour de l'Isle. *(514) 395 2424.*
It is hard to beat this setting – an old stone house in the heart of the St. Lawrence River region. The food is good too.

Plateau Mont-Royal: *Café Santropol* $
3990 Rue Saint-Urbain. *(514) 842 3110.*
Quiches, thick sandwiches, and great soups in a trendy atmosphere. No alcohol, but the tea selection is wide and exotic.

Plateau Mont-Royal: *L'Anecdote* $
801 East Rue Rachel. *(514) 526 7967.*
Movie posters and chrome fittings give this burger joint a 1950s feel, but concessions to modern tastes include a vegetarian club sandwich.

Plateau Mont-Royal: *Restaurant Salle Gérard-Delage* $$
3535 Rue Saint-Denis. *(514) 282 5121.*
Part of the attraction of eating here is that the waiters and waitresses, like the cooks and bartenders, are students of the Institut de Tourisme et d' Hôtellerie du Québec.

Plateau Mont-Royal: *Faros* $$$
362 Rue Fairmont. *(514) 270 8437.*
Fine fresh seafood prepared in Greek style. The cozy restaurant in blue-and-white decor is full of nooks and crannies.

Plateau Mont-Royal: *L'Express* $$$
3927 Rue Saint-Denis. *(514) 845 5333.*
This almost perfect re-creation of a Paris bistro is very popular. The ambience is lively, and the food good and reasonably priced.

Vieux Montréal: *Stash's Café Bazaar* $$$
200 Ouest Rue Saint-Paul. *(514) 845 6611.*
Stash's Polish kitchen turns out hearty winter sustenance, such as hot *borscht*. Diners sit at pews from a demolished convent.

Vieux Montréal: *Chez Delmo* $$$$
211 Rue Notre-Dame Ouest. *(514) 849 4061.*
Most patrons of this seafood restaurant sit at long bars of polished wood to slurp oysters, crack lobsters, and indulge in Arctic char.

Vieux Montréal: *Les Remparts* $$$$
93 Est Rue de la Commune. *(514) 392 1649.*
Part of the city's original stone walls form the foundations of this cellar restaurant. The chef offers delights such as plum-stuffed rabbit.

Quebec City and the St. Lawrence River

Baie Saint-Paul: *Le Mouton Noir* $$$
43 Rue Sainte-Anne. *(418) 240 3030.*
Overlooking the Gouffre River, this small restaurant marries French techniques with local delicacies in fish and poultry dishes.

Charlevoix: *Auberge Petite Madeleine* $$
Port-au-Persil. *(418) 638 2460.*
This inn serves traditional recipes of Charlevoix, rich in local berries, maple syrup, and wild herbs. Grand views of the St. Lawrence accompany French-style dishes served with flair.

Havre-Saint-Pierre: *Restaurant Chez Julie* $
1023 Rue Dulcinée. *(418) 538 3070.*
This popular local has no pretensions. Huge portions of local seafood – the seafood pizza with béchamel sauce is quite extraordinary.

Restaurant	Outdoor Eating	Vegetarian Specialties	Bar Area	Fixed-Price Menu	Children's Facilities
Hélène de Champlain	■	●	■	●	■
Café Santropol	■	●		●	■
L'Anecdote		●			■
Restaurant Salle Gérard-Delage			■	●	■
Faros	■	●		●	■
L'Express	■	●	■	●	■
Stash's Café Bazaar		●	■	●	
Chez Delmo					
Les Remparts	■	●	■		■
Le Mouton Noir	■		■	●	■
Auberge Petite Madeleine	■	●		●	■
Restaurant Chez Julie		●		●	■

ILES-DE-LA-MADELEINE: *La Saline* $$
1009 Route 199, La Grave, Havre-Aubert. *(418) 937 2230.*
Unpretentious seafood restaurant offers "*pot-en-pot,*" a creamy mix of fish, seafood, and potatoes with a flaky crust. *mid-Sep–mid-May.*

ILES-DE-LA-MADELEINE: *Auberge Marie Blanc* $$$$
1112 Rue Commerciale, Notre-Dame-du-Lac. *(418) 899 6747.*
A Boston industrialist built this romantic lodge on the shores of Lake Témiscouta for his beautiful Creole mistress. The menu focuses on local lamb, venison, rabbit, and partridge. *mid-Oct–May.*

ILE D'ORLÉANS: *Le Vieux-Presbytère* $$$$
1247 Ave. Msgr-d'Esgly, Saint Pierre. *(418) 828 9723.*
This former priests' residence offers lovely views of the St. Lawrence. A game farm next door provides buffalo and elk steaks.

LAC-SAINT-JEAN: *La Volière* $$$
200 4ième Ave. Péribonka. *(418) 374 2360.*
Try local delicacies here such as grilled John Dory, *ouananiche* (land-locked salmon), and blueberry pie. There are also views of the rapids.

MÉTIS-SUR-MER: *Au Coin de la Baie* $$$$
1140 Route 132. *(418) 936 3855.*
The simple decor does not detract from the view of Métis Bay. The scallops and cod fillets are excellent. *mid-Sep–mid-May.*

PERCÉ: *Auberge du Gargantua* $$$
222 Route des Failles. *(418) 782 2852.*
The dining room looks out over the Gaspé interior, so it is appropriate that the menu should list several game specialties from this wilderness hunting area. *Dec–May.*

QUEBEC CITY: *Le Cochon Dingue* $$
46 Blvd. Champlain. *(418) 692 2013.*
This is a fun place, with eccentric decor, brisk service, and a menu of mussels or steak with French fries and sinful desserts.

QUEBEC CITY: *À la Maison de Serge Bruyère* $$$
1200 Rue Saint-Jean. *(418) 694-0618.*
This old house has been converted into three dining rooms, ranging from formal French to a lively Bavarian beer hall.

QUEBEC CITY: *Aux Anciens Canadiens* $$$$
34 Rue Saint-Louis. *(418) 692 1627.*
Venison in blueberry wine and ham in maple syrup are among the Quebec dishes served in this 17th-century home.

SEPT-ILES: *Café du Port* $$
495 Ave. Brochu. *(418) 962 9311.*
Soft colors, fresh seafood, and friendly service make this modest little restaurant worth investigating.

SOUTHERN AND NORTHERN QUEBEC

HULL: *Café Henry Burger* $$$$
69 Rue Laurier. *(819) 777 5646.*
Despite its name, chef Robert Bourassa's specialties are lamb in madeira, or delicately seasoned salmon, rather than hamburgers.

LANIEL: *Pointe-aux-Pins* $$$
1955 Chemin du Ski. *(819) 634 5211.*
A four-course dinner is on offer for those staying in the chalet complex from Thursday to Sunday. The ingredients range from piglet with blue potatoes to lamb with pesto sauce. *Mon–Wed; mid-Oct–mid-May.*

LAURENTIAN MOUNTAINS: *Rôtisserie au Petit Poucet* $$
1030 Route 117, Val-David. *(819) 322 2246.*
A rustic log restaurant serves huge meals of, among other dishes, roasted ham, pork, and caribou. The restaurant also smokes its own meat.

LAURENTIAN MOUNTAINS: *Auberge des Cèdres* $$$$
26 305ième Ave. Saint Hippolyte. *(450) 563 2083.*
A Montreal financier built this rambling lakeside home as a summer retreat. The restaurant is renowned for its duck dishes.

For key to symbols see back flap

Price categories for a three-course meal for one, including half a bottle of wine (where available) and service:
- $ under Can$25
- $$ Can$25–$35
- $$$ Can$35–$50
- $$$$ Can$50–$70
- $$$$$ over Can$70

Outdoor Eating
Some tables on a patio or terrace.
Vegetarian Specialties
One menu always includes a selection of vegetarian dishes.
Bar Area
There is a bar area or cocktail bar within the restaurant, available for drinks and/or bar snacks.
Fixed-Price Menu
A fixed-price menu available at a good rate, for lunch, dinner or both, usually with three courses.
Children's Facilities
Small portions and/or high chairs available on request.

Laurentian Mountains: *L'Eau à la Bouche* $$$$$
3003 Blvd. Sainte-Adèle, Sainte-Adèle. *(450) 229 2991/227 1416.*
Nouvelle cuisine and Quebec cooking are combined here to produce such marvels as roast veal in Cognac and Roquefort sauce.

Montérégie: *L'Auberge des Gallants* $$$$
1171 Chemin Saint-Henri, Sainte-Marthe. *(450) 459 4241.*
The menu of this hilltop inn is rich with rabbit and game dishes, but also offers Atlantic lobster and mussels.

North Hatley: *Auberge Hatley* $$$$$
325 Virgin Hill Rd. *(819) 842 2451.*
Chef Alain Labrie has been voted the best in Quebec four times. He uses his homegrown vegetables and picks his own wild berries to make sherbert. The dining room overlooks Lake Massawippi.

Outaouais: *L'Orée du Bois* $$$$
15 Chemin Kingsmere, Chelsea. *(819) 827 0332.*
Tall trees shade this house at the entrance to Gatineau Park. The seafood *pot-au-feu* and the rillettes of wild boar are menu highlights.

Rigaud: *Sucrerie de la Montagne* $$$
300 Rang Saint-Georges. *(450) 451 0831.*
This rustic barn specializes in such Quebec delicacies as pork and beans, maple-cured ham, and sugar pie, all with maple syrup *(see p146)*.

Rouyn-Noranda: *La Renaissance* $$$
199 Avenue Principale. *(819) 764 4422.*
After dinner in this popular storefront restaurant, diners can retreat to a pleasant lounge for cigars and malt whisky.

Sherbrooke: *La Falaise Saint-Michel* $$$
100 Rue Webster. *(819) 346 6339.*
This welcoming restaurant serves wonderful French specialties – the Barbary duck is particularly good.

Trois-Rivières: *La Becquée* $$$
3600 Blvd. Royale. *(819) 379 3232.*
La Becquée's charming decor offers diners an evening with a light romantic feel.

Toronto

Bloor Street West: *Dang de Lion* $
549 Bloor St. W. *416 538 0190.*
One of the best Vietnamese restaurants in the city, the Dang de Lion is a popular and fashionable spot. The food is inexpensive and delicious.

Bloor Street West: *Kensington Vegetarian Cafe* $
460 Bloor St. W. *416 534 1294.*
This exceptional café serves only organic, sugar-free preparations, with 14 different varieties of home-baked bread and tasty wholefoods on offer throughout the day.

Cabbagetown: *Rashnaa* $
307 Wellesley St. E. *416 929 2099.*
Sri Lankan restaurants are very much in vogue in Toronto, and this little place is one of the most popular. The food is superb.

Cabbagetown: *Real Jerk* $$
709 Queen St. E. *416 463 6055.*
One of the most authentic Jamaican restaurants, offering traditional dishes such as red beans and rice as well as more original fare.

Restaurant	Outdoor Eating	Vegetarian Specialties	Bar Area	Fixed-Price Menu	Children's Facilities
L'Eau à la Bouche	■	●	■	●	■
L'Auberge des Gallants	■	●	■	●	■
Auberge Hatley	■		■	●	
L'Orée du Bois		●	■	●	■
Sucrerie de la Montagne		●		●	■
La Renaissance			■	●	
La Falaise Saint-Michel		●	■	●	■
La Becquée		●	■	●	■
Dang de Lion		●		●	■
Kensington Vegetarian Cafe		●		●	■
Rashnaa	■	●		●	■
Real Jerk		●	■		■

Restaurant	Price					
Cabbagetown: *Margarita's Cantina & Tapas Mexicanas* 229 Carlton St. *416 929 6284.* A lively night out at this authentic Mexican restaurant might include tortillas and *fajitas*, washed down with huge margaritas.	$$$	■	●	■	●	
Downtown: *Il Fornello* 35 Elm St. *416 598 1766.* Atmospheric Italian restaurant highly regarded for its mouth-watering pizzas. A popular spot with chic and attractive furnishings in ultra-modern style.	$$$	■	●	■	●	■
Downtown: *Captain John's* 1 Queen's Quay, West. *416 363 6062.* FAX *416 363 6065.* This family-friendly restaurant offering seafood specialities is located aboard the Jadran ocean liner. Good value lunch buffet.	$$$			■		■
Downtown: *Juice for Life* 336 Queen St. W. *416 599 4442.* Youthful, mostly vegan café. It is not to everyone's taste – the soundtrack is very loud – but the food is tasty and good value.	$	■	●		●	
Downtown: *Ethiopian House* 4 Irwin Ave. *416 923 5438.* Ethiopian restaurants are a rarity, but this appealing establishment serves as an excellent introduction to the cuisine, scooped up by an unleavened piece of bread (*injera*) rather than traditional cutlery.	$$	■	●	■	●	■
Downtown: *Hard Rock Café SkyDome* 1 Blue Jays Way. *416 341 2388.* This burger bar and restaurant is part of the SkyDome sports complex *(see p169)* and is crowded with sports fans during games.	$$		●	■		■
Downtown: *Wayne Gretzky's* 99 Blue Jays Way. *416 979 PUCK.* FAX *416 586 0099.* New York-style diner that celebrates the achievements of ice hockey great Wayne Gretzky. Glass cases display Stanley Cup hockey sticks, magazines and other memorabilia. Large rooftop patio.	$$$	■	●	■	●	■
Downtown: *Shopsy's* 33 Yonge St. *416 365 3333.* Shopsy's was founded as a delicatessen/diner shortly after World War II and has been popular ever since. The meat-loaded sandwiches are still delicious and the diner-style decor appealing.	$$$	■	●	■	●	■
Downtown: *Filet of Sole* 11 Duncan St. *416 598 3256.* Among the many seafood restaurants that dot downtown Toronto, this is one of the most popular, a lively affair situated in a converted warehouse with an emphasis on quantity.	$$$		●	■	●	■
Downtown: *Lai Wah Heen* Metropolitan Hotel, 108 Chestnut St. *416 977 9899.* A chic and well-established restaurant, the Lai Wah Heen serves outstanding Cantonese cuisine from a menu of great originality and flair. Many locals swear by the dim sum.	$$$$		●	■	●	■
Downtown: *Mata Hari Grill* 39 Baldwin St. *416 596 2832.* Malaysian restaurant with jazz as background music and a good choice of wines. Satays and curry are the house specialties.	$$$	■	●			■
Downtown: *Nami* 55 Adelaide St. E. *416 362 7373.* Among Toronto's several Japanese restaurants, this is one of the best. Smoked eel is a particular specialty here.	$$$		●		●	
Downtown: *Picante* 326 Adelaide St. W. *416 408 2958.* Gallant Spanish restaurant in the heart of downtown Toronto. The house specialties are *paella* and an appetizing range of *tapas.*	$$$		●	■		
Downtown: *Ematei Japanese Restaurant* 1st Floor, 30 St. Patrick St. *416 340 0472.* This stylish and attractive Japanese place does a good line in sushi. It is located just to the east of the Art Gallery of Ontario (see pp174–5).	$$$$		●	■		■

For key to symbols see back flap

Price categories for a three-course meal for one, including half a bottle of wine (where available) and service:
- $ under Can$25
- $$ Can$25–$35
- $$$ Can$35–$50
- $$$$ Can$50–$70
- $$$$$ over Can$70

OUTDOOR EATING
Some tables on a patio or terrace.
VEGETARIAN SPECIALTIES
One menu always includes a selection of vegetarian dishes.
BAR AREA
There is a bar area or cocktail bar within the restaurant, available for drinks and/or bar snacks.
FIXED-PRICE MENU
A fixed-price menu available at a good rate, for lunch, dinner or both, usually with three courses.
CHILDREN'S FACILITIES
Small portions and/or high chairs available on request.

DOWNTOWN: *La Fenice* $$$$
319 King St. W. *416 585 2377.*
This classy restaurant, with its chic modern furnishings, offers exquisite Italian cuisine with an imaginative blend of sauces and spices.

DOWNTOWN: *Le Papillon* $$$$
16 Church St. *416 363 0838.*
Quebecois cuisine is hard to find in Toronto, but the French pies and pastries at this first-rate establishment help to fill the gap.

DOWNTOWN: *Rodney's Oyster House* $$$$
209 Adelaide St. E. *416 363 8105.* www.rodneysoysterhouse.com
Oysters galore at this long-established eatery where the bivalve rules supreme. It attracts a mixed crowd of tourists and businessfolk.

DOWNTOWN: *Canoe* www.oliverbonacini.com $$$$$
Toronto Dominion Tower, 66 Wellington St. W. *416 364 0054.*
Canoe prides itself on its use of fresh Canadian ingredients such as Arctic char and caribou. It is situated on the 54th floor of the Toronto Dominion Tower office block. *Mon–Fri.*

DOWNTOWN: *Senator* $$$$$
253 Victoria St. *416 364 7517.* www.thesenator.com
This superb central restaurant makes fair claim to be the best steakhouse in the city. The Art Nouveau decor is striking.

GREEKTOWN: *Avli* $$$$
401 Danforth Ave. *416 461 9577.* www.avlirestaurant.com
This Greek restaurant to the east of the city center is perhaps the best of its type, featuring wonderful casseroles and Greek classics.

YORKVILLE: *Café Nervosa* $$$
75 Yorkville Ave. *416 961 4642.*
This chic café-restaurant is located in Toronto's ritziest neighborhood. The cuisine is a light mix of salads, pastas, pizzas, and seafood.

LITTLE ITALY: *Sweet Spirits* $$$
584 College St. *416 532 3635.*
Celebrated Italian restaurant featuring the best of home-made pastas, seafood, and an excellent range of Italian wines – very popular.

Restaurant	Outdoor Eating	Vegetarian Specialties	Bar Area	Fixed-Price Menu	Children's Facilities
La Fenice		●	■		
Le Papillon		●	■		■
Rodney's Oyster House			■		■
Canoe		●	■		
Senator	■		■		
Avli	■	●			
Café Nervosa	■	●	■		■
Sweet Spirits	■	●	■		■

OTTAWA AND EASTERN ONTARIO

ALGONQUIN PROVINCIAL PARK: *Arowhon Pines* $$$$
off Hwy 60, Algonquin Provincial Park. *(705) 633 5661 or 416 483 4393 winter.*
Even if you're not staying here *(see p352)*, this one is worth the drive off the highway for a meal – the view from the six-sided log dining room is spectacular. Bring your own wine. *Nov–Apr.*

KINGSTON: *Kingston Brewing Company* $
34 Clarence St. *(613) 542 4978.*
A beautifully appointed, 65-seat restaurant, with an outdoor patio. There are no chemicals in the home-brewed ales and lagers.

KINGSTON: *Candlelight Dining* $$$
Fort Henry. *(613) 530 2550.* www.foodandheritage.com
To have dinner right inside Fort Henry *(see p198)* attended by soldier servants in period costume is a unique experience.

KINGSTON: *General Wolfe Hotel* $$$
Wolfe Island. *(613) 385 2611.* www.generalwolfe.com
Getting here is half the fun, with a delightful free ride on the Wolfe Island ferry to Kingston's home of the gourmet dinner.

Restaurant	Outdoor Eating	Vegetarian Specialties	Bar Area	Fixed-Price Menu	Children's Facilities
Arowhon Pines		●		●	■
Kingston Brewing Company	■	●	■		■
Candlelight Dining		●	■	●	■
General Wolfe Hotel			■	●	■

NORTH BAY: *Churchill's Prime Rib* $$$
631 Lakeshore Drive. (705) 476 7777.
This comfortable lakeside spot with fine views draws rave reviews from those who relish a hearty steak meal with local vegetables.

OTTAWA: *Heart & Crown* $
67 Clarence St. (613) 562 0674.
Located in the trendy Byward Market, Heart & Crown specializes in Irish pub fare. There's live Celtic music several nights a week and a selection of Irish whiskies and beers.

OTTAWA: *Mamma Teresa Ristorante* $$
300 Somerset W. (613) 236 3023.
Traditional Italian fare is featured in addition to crispy pizzas, and this is a great place to watch for MPs, cabinet ministers, and media types.

OTTAWA: *Royal Thai* $$
272 Dalhousie St. (613) 562 8818.
The name says it all here – authentic Thai curries at very reasonable prices served in the center of town.

OTTAWA: *The Ritz* $$
89 Clarence St. (613) 789 9797.
Set in the popular Byward Market area with fine 19th-century decor and excellent staff, this is a good spot to watch for local celebrities.

OTTAWA: *Big Daddy's Crab Shack & Oyster Bar* $$$
339 Elgin St. (613) 228 7011.
Very popular with the younger crowd, this place serves lots of Cajun-style cooking, as well as some more exotic fare.

OTTAWA: *Château Laurier Hotel* $$$
1 Rideau St. (613) 241 1414.
This famous hotel *(see p193)* is a must; the twin restaurants of Zoë's and Wilfrid's cater to a wide variety of upmarket diners.

PETERBOROUGH: *Parkhill on Hunter* $$
180 Hunter W. (705) 743 8111.
Parkhill Café is a bistro that is rated by locals and visitors as "the" place to eat in Peterborough.

THE GREAT LAKES

BAYFIELD: *The Little Inn of Bayfield* $$$$$
Main St. (519) 565 2611.
One of Ontario's finest restaurants, located in one of its best hotels. The specialty is fish from Lake Huron – perch or pickerel.

GODERICH: *Robindale's Fine Dining* $$$$
80 Hamilton St. (519) 524 4171.
Set in the pretty country town of Goderich, this first-rate restaurant occupies a tastefully converted Victorian house. The wide-ranging menu features local ingredients – the beef is mouthwatering.

NIAGARA FALLS: *Capri* $$
5438 Ferry St. (905) 354 7519.
Something of a local institution, this family-run restaurant provides excellent Italian fare in generous portions.

NIAGARA FALLS: *The Pinnacle Restaurant* $$$
6732 Oakes Drive. (905) 356 1501.
Perched on top of the Minolta Tower, there are great views of the Falls. The simpler dishes are tasty.

NIAGARA FALLS: *Yukiguni* $$$
5980 Buchanan Ave. (905) 354 4440.
This popular Japanese restaurant offers some of the best food in town. The sizzling dishes are served in style – try the salmon teriyaki.

NIAGARA FALLS: *Skylon Tower* $$$$
5200 Robinson St. (905) 356 2651.
One of the busiest spots in town, the revolving restaurant on top of the Skylon Tower provides unparalleled views of the Falls. Honeymooners and young families alike enjoy favorites such as the Caesar salad.

For key to symbols see back flap

Price categories for a three-course meal for one, including half a bottle of wine (where available) and service:
- $ under Can$25
- $$ Can$25–$35
- $$$ Can$35–$50
- $$$$ Can$50–$70
- $$$$$ over Can$70

OUTDOOR EATING
Some tables on a patio or terrace.
VEGETARIAN SPECIALTIES
One menu always includes a selection of vegetarian dishes.
BAR AREA
There is a bar area or cocktail bar within the restaurant, available for drinks and/or bar snacks.
FIXED-PRICE MENU
A fixed-price menu available at a good rate, for lunch, dinner or both, usually with three courses.
CHILDREN'S FACILITIES
Small portions and/or high chairs available on request.

Restaurant	Price	Outdoor Eating	Vegetarian Specialties	Bar Area	Fixed-Price Menu	Children's Facilities
NIAGARA-ON-THE-LAKE: *Shaw Café and Wine Bar* 92 Queen St. *(905) 468 4772.* Named after playwright George Bernard Shaw, this fashionable café-bar is much favored by theater-goers. The menu is bistro-style.	$$$	■	●	■		■
NIAGARA-ON-THE-LAKE: *The Oban Inn* 160 Front St. *(905) 468 2165.* www.vintageinns.com A classy affair of prettily folded napkins and highly polished cutlery. The food is great too – the poached salmon is recommended.	$$$$		●	■		■
NIAGARA-ON-THE-LAKE: *The Olde Angel Inn* 224 Regent St. *(905) 468 3411.* www.angel-inn.com The Olde Angel occupies a 19th-century roadhouse. Particular favorites include beef cooked in Guinness and roast duckling.	$$$		●	■		■
PENETANGUISHENE: *Blue Sky Family Restaurant* 48 Main St. *(705) 549 8611.* A traditional family-run diner, with bar stools, formica tables, and authentic fare – eggs and bacon, muffins, and the like.	$				●	■
SAULT STE. MARIE: *A Thymely Manner* 531 Albert St. *(705) 759 3262.* This outstanding restaurant, easily the best in town, is noted for its locally raised lamb. The seafood is delicious too – try the lake trout.	$$$$		●			■
THUNDER BAY: *Hoito Restaurant* 314 Bay St. *(807) 345 6323.* Hundreds of Finns emigrated to Thunder Bay in the early 20th century, and Hoito offers traditional Finnish food at reasonable prices.	$			■	●	
WINDSOR: *The Park Terrace* Windsor Hilton Hotel, 277 Riverside Drive W. *(519) 973 5555.* This plush hotel restaurant combines excellent food made from top local produce with fine views of Detroit just across the river.	$$$$$		●	■	●	■
CENTRAL CANADA						
EDMONTON: *Sherlock Holmes* West Edmonton Mall. *(780) 423 0202.* A collection of restaurants in a New Orleans-style street atmosphere, including Sherlock Holmes (noted for its beer), Albert's (Montreal-smoked meat), and Hooters (scantily-clad waitresses).	$	■	●	■	●	■
EDMONTON: *Unheardof Restaurant* 9602 82nd Ave. *(780) 432 0480.* Located in the Old Strathcona district, this popular restaurant's favorites include tenderloins of bison. *Mon.*	$$$$		●		●	■
GULL HARBOUR: *Viking Dining Room* Gull Harbour Resort, Hecla Provincial Park. *(204) 279 2041.* Icelandic fare includes Rulupsa lamb with molasses-based brown bread, fresh fish from Lake Winnipeg, and Vinarterta for dessert.	$$$	■	●	■		■
MEDICINE HAT: *Mario's Ristorante* 439-5th Ave. SE. *(403) 529 2600.* Located in historic downtown, Mario's serves traditional Italian pastas, veal, steak, chicken, and seafood, in a warm, classic atmosphere.	$		●	■	●	■
RED DEER: *Shauney's* 4909 48 St. *(403) 342 2404.* Elegant dining in comfortable surroundings. Ostrich and bison are served, along with other exotic offerings.	$$		●	■	●	■

Restaurant	Price					
REGINA: *The Harvest Eating House* 379 Albert St. (306) 545 3777. Housed in a wooden building decorated with fig trees and rural artifacts, this restaurant features prime rib steak and seafood. The wagon bar is symbolic of Saskatchewan.	$$			■		■
REGINA: *The Diplomat* 2032 Broad St. (306) 359 3366. This elegant restaurant features steak, seafood, and rack of lamb. Paintings of Canada's prime ministers line the walls.	$$$		●	■		■
SASKATOON: *The Granary* 2806-8th St. East. (306) 373 6655. Designed like a country grain elevator, the restaurant features roast prime rib of beef, plus seafood, chicken, and a bountiful salad wagon.	$$	■	●	■	●	■
SASKATOON: *Wanuskewin Restaurant* Wanuskewin Heritage Park. (306) 931 9932. Buffalo burgers, home-made soup, bannock bread, and Saskatoon berry pie are served at this national historic site *(see p242)*.	$	■	●	■	●	■
SASKATOON: *Saskatoon Asian* 136 2nd Ave. South. (306) 665 5959. This restaurant specializes in Vietnamese dishes: rice-paper-wrapped shrimps are a popular delicacy.	$$		●		●	■
STEINBACH: *Livery Barn Restaurant* Mennonite Heritage Village, Hwy 12 North. (204) 326 9661. Tasty Mennonite fare from traditional recipes, served in a pioneer setting. The store sells local stone-ground coffee and old-fashioned candy.	$	■	●		●	■
WINNIPEG: *Wagon Wheel Restaurant* 305 Hargrave St. (204) 942 6695. Lunch stop renowned for its vast clubhouse sandwiches. Traditional thick milkshakes, pickles and homemade soup also on offer.	$					■
WINNIPEG: *Suzy Q's* 1887 Portage Ave. (204) 832 7814. A detailed re-creation of a 1950s-style lunch counter serves delicious hamburgers, French fries, and super-thick milkshakes.	$		●			■
WINNIPEG: *Restaurant Dubrovnik* 390 Assiniboine Ave. (204) 944 0594. The restaurant is one of city's finest. Specialties include pork with mango chutney and lobster with snow pea sauce. Reservations essential.	$$$$	■	●		●	■
VANCOUVER AND VANCOUVER ISLAND						
CAMPBELL RIVER: *Legends Dining Room* 1625 McDonald Rd. (250) 286 1102. www.oakbaymarinagroup.com Overlooking Discovery Passage, patrons indulge on west coast fare while watching ships cruise by. Brandy is served in the fireside lounge.	$$$	■	●	■		
MALAHAT: *The Aerie* 600 Ebedora Lane. (250) 743 7115. www.aerie.bc.ca Sample an excellent menu of local meat and seafood overlooking spectacular views of ocean fjords and mountains.	$$$$$	■	●	■	●	
NANAIMO: *Wesley Street Café* 321 Wesley St. (250) 753 4004. An intimate café for those who appreciate the light, fresh flavors of contemporary west coast food. Live jazz at the weekends adds a touch of sophistication.	$$	■	●	■		■
NANAIMO: *Mahle House Restaurant* 2104 Hemer Rd. (250) 722 3621. www.island.net/~mahle/ This 1904 farmhouse set in an English garden includes "Adventure Wednesday" when the chef cooks a five-course surprise dinner.	$$$$	■	●			
NORTH VANCOUVER: *HiWus Feasthouse* 6400 Nancy Greene Way. (604) 984 0661. www.grousemtn.com A unique dinner-show experience in a Long House, combining traditional native foods and authentic song and dance of the Pacific Northwest Coast First Nations.	$$$$$		●		●	■

Price categories for a three-course meal for one, including half a bottle of wine (where available) and service:
- $ under Can$25
- $$ Can$25–$35
- $$$ Can$35–$50
- $$$$ Can$50–$70
- $$$$$ over Can$70

OUTDOOR EATING
Some tables on a patio or terrace.
VEGETARIAN SPECIALTIES
One menu always includes a selection of vegetarian dishes.
BAR AREA
There is a bar area or cocktail bar within the restaurant, available for drinks and/or bar snacks.
FIXED-PRICE MENU
A fixed-price menu available at a good rate, for lunch, dinner or both, usually with three courses.
CHILDREN'S FACILITIES
Small portions and/or high chairs available on request.

NORTH VANCOUVER: *Pacific Starlight Dinner Train* $$$$$
BC Rail Station, 1311 W. 1st St. *(604) 984 5246.*
Impress your significant other by inviting them for a romantic dinner on a train. The band plays when the train pulls into Porteau Cove.

SALT SPRING ISLAND: *Hastings House* $$$$$
160 Upper Ganges Rd. *(250) 537 2362.*
A historic English manor estate overlooking Ganges' bustling harbor. Homegrown cuisine is served in elegant style in a wood-beamed dining room. Farm buildings have been restored for overnight guests.

SOOKE: *Sooke Harbour House* $$$$
1528 Whiffen Spit Rd. *(250) 642 3421.*
The award-winning menu can include sea asparagus and sea urchins served with vegetables and herbs from the gardens on site.

TOFINO: *Wickaninnish Inn & Pointe Restaurant* $$$$
Osprey Lane at Chesterman's Beach. *(250) 725 3100.*
A beautiful dining room with a circular fireplace and views of the Pacific. The menu includes fresh seafood and Pacific Northwest wines.

VANCOUVER: *The Old Spaghetti Factory* $
53 Water St. *(604) 684 1288.*
Family dining in a lively atmosphere with friendly staff and a varied Italian menu. Dine outside in the heart of Gastown.

VANCOUVER: *Havana* $$
1212 Commercial Drive. *(604) 253 9119.*
This authentic Cuban restaurant, with imported cocktails, is a lively slice of Havana in one of Vancouver's bustling neighborhoods.

VANCOUVER: *Cin Cin Restaurant* $$$
1154 Robson St. *(604) 688 7338.*
Decorated in Italian Mediterranean style, with a clattering open kitchen and a sizzling alderwood grill, this restaurant fills with Vancouver's film types during the week and tourists on the weekend.

VANCOUVER: *Gotham Steak House & Cocktail Bar* $$$$$
615 Seymour St. *(604) 605 8282.*
They serve great steaks and a wide variety of seafood in an elegant, high-ceilinged room. Reservations are recommended.

VANCOUVER: *The Fish House* $$
8901 Stanley Park Drive. *(604) 681 7275.*
Located in Stanley Park, this fine fish restaurant is surrounded by greenery and panoramic views of English Bay. There is an early-bird special between 5 and 6pm.

VANCOUVER: *Villa De Loupa* $$
869 Hamilton St. *(604) 688 7436.*
Mouthwatering Italian food, such as risotto with fresh chives, free-range stuffed chicken, and olive-poached tomatoes.

VANCOUVER: *900 West Hotel Vancouver* $$$
900 West Georgia St. *(604) 669 9378.*
Guests can eat at the kitchen counter, or in the dining room at a table setting. Over 60 wines are on offer in the award-winning bar.

VANCOUVER: *Diva at the Met* $$$
Metropolitan Hotel, 645 Howe St. *(604) 687 1122.*
The terraced floors and open-style kitchen create a casual flair, and the award-winning menu includes pizza topped with barbecued chicken, salmon steaks, and pickled zucchini.

Restaurant	Outdoor Eating	Vegetarian Specialties	Bar Area	Fixed-Price Menu	Children's Facilities
Pacific Starlight Dinner Train		●	■	●	
Hastings House		●		●	
Sooke Harbour House		●			■
Wickaninnish Inn & Pointe Restaurant	■	●	■	●	■
The Old Spaghetti Factory	■	●	■	●	■
Havana	■	●	■	●	■
Cin Cin Restaurant	■	●	■	●	
Gotham Steak House & Cocktail Bar	■		■		■
The Fish House	■	●	■		■
Villa De Loupa		●			
900 West Hotel Vancouver		●	■	●	
Diva at the Met		●	■	●	■

VANCOUVER: *Tojo's Japanese* $$$
777 West Broadway suite, 202. *(604) 872 8050.*
Since opening in 1988, Tojo's has consistently served award-winning Japanese food. Most of the patrons are local media types.

VANCOUVER: *C Restaurant* $$$$
2–1600 Howe St. *(604) 681 1164.*
A contemporary fish restaurant claiming the best seafood in town, with a charming patio bedecked in white linen and white tiles.

VANCOUVER: *Piccolo Mondo Ristorante* $$$$
850 Thurlow St. *(604) 688 1633.*
With 480 Italian wines in the cellar and family recipes to hand, guests can expect delicious northern Italian food in a relaxed atmosphere.

VICTORIA: *Barb's Place* $
Fisherman's Wharf, Erie St. Float. *(250) 384 6515.*
A floating kitchen sitting on the docks of Victoria's harbor. Serves fish and chips and other tasty fare to a happy clientele. *Nov–Apr.*

VICTORIA: *J & J Wonton Noodle House* $
1012 Fort St. *(250) 383 0680.*
Big room with cozy atmosphere serving fresh home-made noodles to the locals and the lucky tourists who go out of their way to find it.

VICTORIA: *Empress Room* $$$$
Empress Hotel, 721 Government St. *(250) 384 8111.*
Fine dining in a 1908 Edwardian dining room. An evening harpist sets an elegant mood, and the menu includes swordfish.

VICTORIA: *Il Terrazzo* $$$$
555 Johnson St. *(250) 361 0028.*
Located in the heart of Old Town, in an original 1890 building, this restaurant boasts the best Italian food in Victoria. A beautiful courtyard is warmed by six fireplaces, ten months of the year.

VICTORIA: *The Victorian* $$$$
Ocean Point Resort, 45 Songhees Rd. *(250) 360 2999.*
Candlelight, fine wine, delicious Pacific Northwest cuisine and views of the harbor can be expected at Victoria's premier resort.

THE ROCKY MOUNTAINS

BANFF: *Giorgio's Trattoria* $$
219 Banff Avenue. *(403) 762 5114.*
An intimate restaurant located in the heart of town, the food is Italian pastas and fresh pizza prepared in a wood-burning oven.

BANFF: *Buffalo Mountain Lodge Dining Room* $$$$
Tunnel Mountain Rd. *(403) 762 2400.*
This wood-beamed dining room slightly off the beaten track serves Canadian Rockies fare: venison, caribou, deer, lamb, and beef.

CALGARY: *Ranchman's* $$
9615 McLeod Trail South. *(403) 253 1100.*
A Calgary tradition, this cowboy café and country music club displays trophy rodeo saddles and a chuck wagon above the stage. The menu features beef and chicken prepared in Texas-style smokers.

CALGARY: *Crosshouse Garden Café* $$$
1240 8th Avenue SE. *(403) 531 2767.*
The 1891 home of Calgary pioneer A.E. Cross offers Arctic char and buffalo as well as many fish and chicken dishes. *Tue–Sat.*

CALGARY: *Mescalero Restaurant* $$$
1315 1st St. SW. *(403) 266 3339.*
With southwestern US influences, the menu here includes enchiladas, black bean soup, and seafood cooked in lime. The building looks like a hacienda, with adobe-style walls and Mexican tile floor.

CRANBROOK: *Sweet Magic* $
20 7th Avenue South. *(250) 426 4565.*
Decorated with BC art and parquet floors, European recipes are prepared in an open kitchen in view of the patrons.

Price categories for a three-course meal for one, including half a bottle of wine (where available) and service:
- $ under Can$25
- $$ Can$25–$35
- $$$ Can$35–$50
- $$$$ Can$50–$70
- $$$$$ over Can$70

Outdoor Eating
Some tables on a patio or terrace.

Vegetarian Specialties
One menu always includes a selection of vegetarian dishes.

Bar Area
There is a bar area or cocktail bar within the restaurant, available for drinks and/or bar snacks.

Fixed-Price Menu
A fixed-price menu available at a good rate, for lunch, dinner or both, usually with three courses.

Children's Facilities
Small portions and/or high chairs available on request.

Restaurant	Price	Outdoor Eating	Vegetarian Specialties	Bar Area	Fixed-Price Menu	Children's Facilities
Faquier: *Mushroom Addition* 129 Oak St. *(250) 269 7467.* Local wild mushrooms are served in nearly every dish. During the summer the place is adorned with fresh-cut flowers.	$	■	●			■
Kimberly: *The Old Bauernhaus* 280 Norton Avenue. *(250) 427 5133.* This 18th-century Bavarian barn was disassembled, shipped to Canada and rebuilt in the 1980s. The first floor is now the restaurant serving hearty German fare. *Tues and Wed.*	$$	■	●			■
Lake Louise: *Poppy Room* Chateau Lake Louise. *(403) 522 3511 ext 1189.* Every table has a view of Lake Louise in this busy dining room. Burgers, salads, pastas, and fish are offered on the menu. Breakfast is buffet-style with a choice of omelettes and waffles.	$$		●			■
Lake Louise: *Elkhorn Dining Room* Mile 22 Bow Lake Icefield Parkway. *(403) 522 2167.* This historic building was built by artist Jimmy Simpson, and his watercolors adorn the walls. The cuisine focuses on local game.	$$$		●	■		■
Nakusp: *Mattie's Family Restaurant* Leland Hotel, 96th 4th Avenue SW. *(250) 265 3316.* Prime rib is the specialty in this restaurant overlooking Arrow Lake. Antique furniture and old photographs create an Edwardian feel.	$	■	●		●	■
Nelson: *The Outer Clove* 536 Stanley St. *(250) 354 1667.* Chefs here use five pounds of garlic a day in a variety of ways, including the desserts, in this brightly painted old brick building. *Sun.*	$	■	●			■
Revelstoke: *The Peak's Lodge Resort* Trans Canada Hwy 1. *(250) 837 2176.* Beneath Boulder Mountain, this old lodge is furnished with antiques. The menu offers Alberta beef and BC salmon smoked on site.	$$$	■	●	■	●	■
SOUTHERN AND NORTHERN BRITISH COLUMBIA						
Fort Langley: *Bedford House* 9272 Glover. *(604) 888 2333.* Located in historic Fort Langley, enjoy good food in a relaxed atmosphere with attentive staff and fine wines.	$$	■	●	■		
Kelowna: *Williams Inn* 526 Lawrence Avenue. *(250) 763 5136.* The menu in this romantic two-storey home is European-style game, steak, lamb, seafood, chicken, and home-made dessert.	$$	■	●		●	
Ladner: *48th Avenue Steak & Seafood House* 5047 48th Avenue. *(604) 946 2244.* Upscale but casual with window seats overlooking the heritage buildings in this seaport village. West coast cuisine of seafood and pasta.	$$	■	●	■		
Naramata: *The Country Squire* 3950 1st St. *(250) 496 5416.* Delicious five-course meals are served over the evening; walk around the garden with a glass of Okanagan wine between courses.	$$$$		●	■	●	
Osoyoos: *The Diamond Steak and Seafood House* 8903 Main St. *(250) 495 6223.* Three dining rooms specialize in Greek and Italian cuisine with a variety of steaks, seafood, pasta, and pizza. Prime rib is a favorite.	$$		●	■	●	■

PRINCE RUPERT: *Smile's Café* $$
1 Cow Bay Rd. *(250) 624 3072.*
A family seafood restaurant in a 1930s wharf building, decorated in netting and with old photographs. A coffee shop is also on site.

WELLS: *Country Encounters* $
4236 Jones Avenue. *(250) 994 2361.*
Home-made breads, pastas, and luscious desserts. Popular with snow-mobilers in the winter; balcony seating in the summer. *Apr and Oct.*

WHISTLER: *Black's Original Restaurant* $$$
4270 Mountain Square. *(604) 932 6408.*
An open-style restaurant located in the Westbrook Hotel at the base of the mountains. Turkey roast is served on Sundays and the British pub upstairs specializes in Guinness.

WHISTLER: *Bear Foot Bistro* $$$$$
4121 Village Green. *(604) 932 3433.*
The acid-washed cement floors, brown leather chairs, live jazz, and North America's largest selection of Cuban cigars create a sophisticated air. The food is innovative French.

NORTHERN CANADA

DAWSON CITY: *Bonanza Dining Room* $$$
Eldorado Hotel, 3rd & Princess Sts. *(867) 993 5451.*
Two rustic restaurants in this hotel serve simple bar food. The specials change daily.

DAWSON CITY: *Klondike Kate's* $$$
3rd Avenue & King St. *(867) 993 6527.*
This popular, friendly café, named after a Dawson City dance hall girl, serves the best breakfast in the Yukon. *winter.*

FORT PROVIDENCE: *Snowshoe Inn* $$
1 Mackenzie St. *(867) 699 3511.*
Home-cooking comes to the fore in the largest restaurant in town; sophisticated seafood is also on offer.

INUVIK: *MacKenzie Hotel* $$$$
185 MacKenzie Rd. *(867) 777 2861.*
Inuit cooking, including char and caribou, can be sampled at this hotel restaurant *(see p359)*.

IQALUIT: *Kamotiq In Restaurant* $$$$
3506 Wiley Rd. *(867) 979 5937.*
Two dining rooms, one shaped like an igloo, serve Arctic cuisine, steaks, seafood, and Mexican dishes.

RANKIN INLET: *Siniktarvik Hotel* $$
(867) 645 2949 FAX *(867) 645 2999.* sinik@arctic.ca
Warming stews and large steaks are available in this newly refurbished restaurant.

WHITEHORSE: *The Cellar Dining Room* $$$$
101 Main St. *(867) 667 2572.*
Part of the Edgewater Hotel, this cellar venue is popular with townspeople and has a great atmosphere and excellent food.

WHITEHORSE: *Yukon Mining Company* $$$
High Country Inn, 4051 4th Avenue. *(867) 667 4471.*
Each evening an outdoor barbecue allows diners to appreciate the stunning scenery surrounding the hotel. Particularly popular are the salmon and halibut, as well as locally brewed beer.

YELLOWKNIFE: *The Prospector* $$$$
3506 Wiley Rd. *(867) 920 7620.*
Seaplane docking is available for fly-in clients looking for a bite to eat in the summer months.

YELLOWKNIFE: *Wildcat Café* $$
3506 Wiley Road. *(867) 873 8850.*
A real slice of wild Canadian life. Local food a speciality, in particular, hearty soups and casseroles *(see p336)*. Dinners only. winter.

For key to symbols see back flap

Shopping in Canada

Shopping in Canada offers more than the usual tourist fare of Mountie dolls and maple leaf T-shirts. Visitors can choose from a wide range of products, and buy everything from electronic equipment to clothes and jewelry. There is also a variety of goods unique to the country – maple syrup from Quebec, smoked salmon from British Columbia, and cowboy boots from Alberta, to name a few. Native art inspired by centuries-old tradition, includes carvings by west-coast peoples and Inuit paintings and tapestries. In each major city there are covered malls, chainstores, specialty shops, and galleries, as well as street markets to explore. In country areas, beautifully-made crafts by local people can be found. Be aware that sales taxes are added to the price of many items.

Doll from Charlottetown

Shopping Hours

Store hours vary, but in larger cities most stores are open by 9am and close between 5pm and 9pm. However, some grocery and variety stores are open 24 hours a day, and in major towns several pharmacies are also open for 24 hours. In most towns, stores have late closing until 9pm on Friday evening. However, in smaller towns and villages you should not expect any store, including the gas station, to be open after 6pm. Sunday openings are increasing: usually hours run from noon to 5pm but vary from province to province. Check first, as many may be closed in rural areas.

How to Pay

Most Canadian stores accept all major credit cards, with VISA and MasterCard being the most popular. Some stores require a minimum purchase in order to use the card. They may limit the use of cards during summer and winter sales. Direct payment, or "Switch" transactions, are also widely used, with point-of-sale terminals for bank cards available in most supermarkets and department stores. Travelers' checks are readily accepted with proper identification; a valid passport or driver's license are the usually accepted forms.

US dollars are the only non-Canadian currency accepted in department stores. Bear in mind that the exchange rate is usually lower, sometimes as much as 15 percent, than a bank will give. Large stores may offer money-changing

Sales Taxes

Canadians love to curse the national Goods and Services Tax (GST), which currently runs at 7 percent. It is added to most retail transactions; the major exception is basic food items. Visitors who are non-resident in Canada can apply for a GST rebate on most goods within 60 days of purchase. This excludes restaurant bills, drinks, tobacco, or transportation expenses. Refund forms are available in airports, duty free stores, hotels, and most Canadian Embassies. Include original receipts when sending the application to Revenue Canada (*see p343*) as photocopies are not accepted.

In addition to the GST, most provinces add a provincial sales tax, varying from 5–12 percent, on meals and store-bought items. Alberta, the Yukon, and the Northwest Territories do not impose this tax, and Quebec, Manitoba, Nova Scotia, and Newfoundland offer rebates to non-residents.

Consumer Rights and Services

Smart shoppers always check a store's refund policy before buying an item. Policies vary, some stores will refund money on unwanted items, others offer store vouchers, and many will not exchange or refund sale merchandise. Reputable stores will take back defective merchandise within 28 days as long as it is accompanied by the original bill. As credit card fraud increases, it is wise to be cautious about buying by telephone using cards.

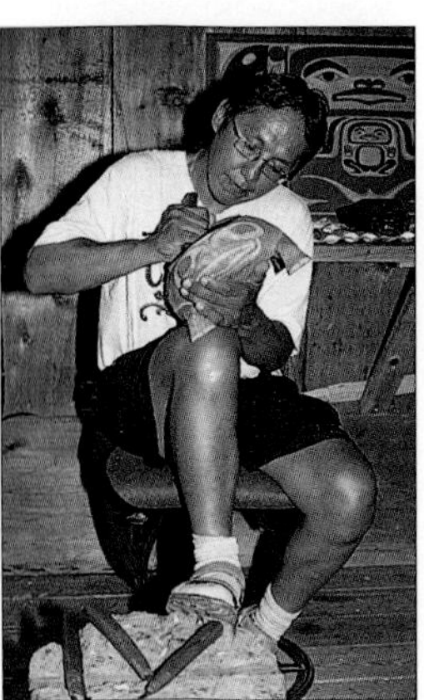

Native Canadian Wayne Carlick, carving soapstone, British Columbia

Completely Canadian

Products made in Canada offer shoppers a wide variety of choice. Although most specialty items are on sale across the country, many goods are less expensive in their province of origin. Hand-knitted sweaters and pottery are particularly good value in Atlantic Canada, as is the much-praised Seagull pewter made in Nova Scotia. The Prairie provinces and Alberta specialize in cowboy attire; tooled belts, vests, cowboy hats, and boots. Farther west, British Columbian artisans produce elaborate carvings,

Shopkeeper at the Lonsdale Quay craft market in Vancouver *(see p276)*

including totem poles. Jade jewelry, from locally mined stone, is also reasonable here. Local specialties from Quebec and Ontario include maple syrup and sugar-related products. Quebec artisans make beautiful wood carvings too. In Ontario, native basketwork is good as a lasting souvenir. For those who need an extra suitcase to carry their finds home, the renowned Tilley travel cases and products are made and sold locally throughout Ontario.

Native carvings can be found across Canada, especially in the far north. Genuine Inuit carvings are inspected and stamped by the federal government. A sticker featuring an igloo marks a true piece; it will also be signed by the artist. Since the 1950s, the Inuit have been producing prints of traditional scenes, which are popular, as is native jewelry. Beautifully handmade parka jackets, embroidered panels, and soft deer hide moccasins make excellent gifts.

Pottery jar, Nova Scotia

Contemporary Canadian art features highly in gift shops and galleries countrywide. Photographs and prints are recommended for the budget-conscious shopper. Recordings of Canadian music are freely available: Europeans will be pleased to find that tapes and CDs are at least 50 percent cheaper in Canada.

Modern sportswear and outerwear is both durable and beautifully designed. Camping, hiking, and boating equipment are fine buys, as is fishing tackle. With such a strong tradition of outdoor life, a wide range of products is usually available at well below European prices.

Department Stores

The Bay is the major middle-range department store chain across the country. Canadian department stores have suffered financially during the last years of the 20th century. They are changing to meet the competition of US chains, such as Wal-Mart and discount stores, and membership stores including Costco and Price Club. Chains such as Sears and Zeller's occupy the middle to lower end of the market place. Canadian Tire sells everything from auto parts to sporting goods and has become a national institution.

Malls and Shopping Centers

Suburbia may not offer the most culture in Canada, but some of the malls are fine destinations in themselves. The renowned modernist Eaton Centre in Toronto is enclosed by a glass and steel arched roof, with a wonderful sculpted flock of geese soaring over shoppers. Over 42 million visitors annually enjoy this showcase of modern architecture, though it has been derided as "brutalism" by conservative Torontonians. Canada has the world's largest mall, the West Edmonton Mall in Edmonton, Alberta. Over 800 stores, more than 100 restaurants, 34 movie theaters, a huge water park, an amusement park, a theme hotel, a mini-golf course, an ice rink, and a zoo with dolphins are just some of the sights that draw Canadians and visitors alike to this retail paradise.

Exclusive stores are largely found in the country's retail capital, Toronto. Bloor Street and Yorkville Avenue are lined with status brands known the world over, such as Tiffany, Holt Renfrew, Ralph Lauren, and Gucci. Both Vancouver and Montreal have their own selection of world-class luxury stores. Montreal is notable as the fur capital of the country; good department stores will stock a selection of winter and summer furs at very reasonable prices. For those unable to travel to the north, Inuit art features highly in craft shops here.

The Underground City, with hundreds of boutiques, in Montreal

Entertainment in Canada

Entertainment in Canada boasts all the sophistication tourists have come to expect from a major North American country, coupled with delightful rural entertainments in relaxing local venues. Covering mainstream world-class productions in Ottawa and the larger cities, Canada also offers the latest in alternative acts and traditional artforms, particularly in its exceptional folk music heritage. Music of the highest quality, both classical and modern, is offered throughout the country, and major cities provide first-rate theater, dance, and film, not to mention many musical shows and film festivals.

Royal Winnipeg Ballerina

Information

Provincial daily newspapers are the most reliable sources of information about forthcoming events; the *Vancouver Sun*, *Montreal Gazette*, *Ottawa Citizen*, and *Toronto Star* are the most popular. Listings are usually published at least once a week. The *Globe & Mail* and *National Post* are produced in Toronto but are sold countrywide and have excellent arts sections containing reviews of the latest attractions. Tourist offices *(see p393)* are helpful; some operators may assist in booking tickets. Visitor centers and hotel lobbies have weekly entertainment guides, such as *Where*, a magazine covering Vancouver. In Quebec, French-language entertainment is chronicled by two papers, *La Presse* and *Le Devoir*. *Macleans* is a national weekly magazine with arts coverage.

Booking

Ticketmaster outlets are found in many shopping malls and represent major halls across the country. Tickets to venues in Quebec are available from Admission Network. Different offices cater to different sports and artistic events in each city. Most venues, however, can be contacted directly for tickets.

Disabled Visitors

Major Canadian venues are well equipped to deal with wheelchair users. All interior halls contain ramps and restroom access. Parking lots will have designated disabled spaces nearby. A hearing loop system is available at Ottawa's National Arts Centre *(see p195)*, and at most other major venues. Call ahead to check their availability. Outside ramps and elevators are provided to reach concerts halls and theaters at most large centers.

Theater

Toronto, Ottawa, Vancouver, and Montreal are the four top theater centers in Canada (most of their productions are in English). Homegrown talent mixes here with shows imported from Europe and the US. Musicals and classical theater are always popular and tend to be fine quality. Shakespeare is popular, but there is a wide spectrum of shows – a stylish revival of the 1980s hit *Fame* was a long-running success in Toronto in the late 1990s. The main theaters listed opposite have a principal season from November to May, but summer attractions are on the increase. Musicals and historical reconstructions are always strong family entertainment; the best-known is the musical *Anne of Green Gables*, performed year-round since the 1950s in Charlottetown.

Film

Imported Hollywood blockbusters have no better chance of success than in Canada, where premieres are often parallel with the US, so visitors may well see films in advance of a showing in their own country. Huge IMAX™ and OMNIMAX™ movie theaters, often with up to 20 screens, are to be found in the center of major cities, particularly in Ottawa and Hull.

Canada has a fine history of filmmaking: the documentary genre was invented here, and more recently its art films have attracted a wider audience. The main centers to see the new trends are Montreal, Vancouver, and Toronto. Robert LePage, Canada's own theater and movie impresario, has an international following among the cognoscenti. The surrealist David Cronenberg, director of *eXistenz* (1999), is also Canadian. Quebec's Denys Arcand directed *Jesus of Montreal* (1986), a film that, despite some controversial scenes, was highly praised. The National Film

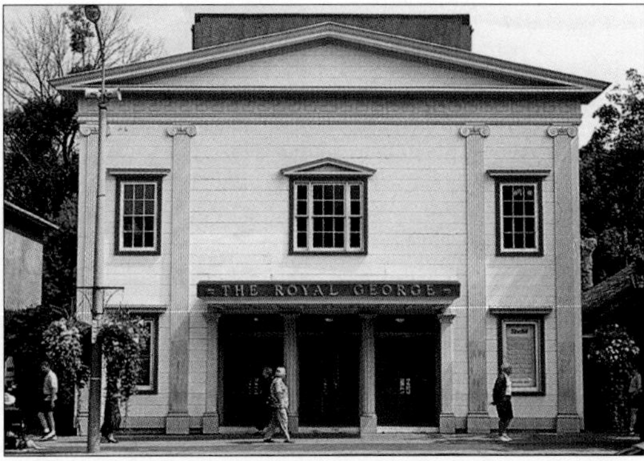

Façade of The Royal George Theatre, Niagara-on-the-Lake

The Ontario Place IMAX™ giant movie theater in Toronto

Board selects and releases a work by native talent each year, comprising feature films, animations, and documentaries. Ideal for spotting new talent in its birthplace, every year the Toronto Film Festival provides a lively magnet to moviegoers, as do parallel festivals held in Montreal and Vancouver.

Classical Music Ballet, and Opera

Classical music and opera draw large audiences in Canada, and this is reflected by the high quality of performers and venues. The Canada Opera Company is based at the Hummingbird Centre for the Performing Arts *(see p176)* in Toronto, with a repertoire ranging from Mozart to cutting-edge pieces sung in English. The National Ballet of Canada is also based here, rival to the Royal Winnipeg Ballet; both companies feature period pieces and experimental work in their seasonal run. Fringe theater takes off in Toronto each summer with 400 shows selected by lottery. Well over 100,000 people annually visit the state-of-the-art Jack Singer Concert Hall in the Calgary Centre for the Performing Arts to hear the celebrated Calgary Philharmonic Orchestra. The Vancouver Symphony Orchestra plays at the Orpheum Theatre in Vancouver.

Rock, Folk, and Pop Music

During the 1990s, Canadian pop music acquired a credibility even its kindest supporters would admit had previously been lacking. Quebec's Celine Dion is a superstar and Shania Twain, Bryan Adams, and k d lang are international stars. Alanis Morissette, a worthy successor to her country's heritage of folk rock, now tours the globe.

Canada is perhaps the best known for its folk music, with such stars as Leonard Cohen, Neil Young, and Joni Mitchell being the best-known faces from a centuries-old tradition. The product of an intensely musical rural people, the nature of Canadian song changes across the country, moving from the lonesome Celtic melodies on the east coast to the yodeling cowboys in the west. Atlantic Canada has numerous tiny, informal venues, where an excellent standard of music can be found. Prince Edward Island often offers a violin accompaniment to its lobster suppers, and New Brunswick's folk festival celebrates both music and dance. Quebec's French folksters include singer Gilles Vigneault *(see p24)* who is also admired in Europe. The Yukon's memories of the gold rush surface in 19th-century vaudeville, reenacted by dancing girls and a honky-tonk piano in Whitehorse.

Celine Dion, one of Canada's best-selling international artists

Directory

Ticket Agencies

Admission Network
(613) 237 3800 Ottawa.
(514) 528 2828 Montreal.
416 861 1017 Toronto.

Ticketmaster
416 870 8000 Toronto.

Major Venues

Hummingbird Centre for the Performing Arts
416 872 2262.

The National Ballet of Canada
416 362 4670 Toronto.

Royal Winnipeg Ballet
(204) 956 0183.

The Newfoundland Symphony Orchestra
(709) 753 6492.

Calgary Centre for the Performing Arts
(403) 294 7455.

Jack Singer Concert Hall and Calgary Philharmonic Orchestra
(403) 294 7455.

Vancouver Symphony Orchestra
(604) 876 3434.

Orpheum Theatre
(604) 665 3050.

Molson Centre
(514) 932 2582.

Specialty Vacations and Activities

The sheer variety of the massive, unspoiled landscape is, in many ways, what attracts visitors to Canada. Taking advantage of the 39 national parks, several of which are UN World Heritage sites, most specialty vacations tend to revolve around Canada's spacious natural playgrounds. The range of activities available in this single country is wide: sledding and snowmobiling with Inuit guides or cruising in the spring through the flower-filled Thousand Islands of Ontario are both possibilities. Other choices include scenic train rides through the Rockies, trout-fishing in pristine secluded lakes, and adventurous world-class hiking.

Hiking sign in National Parks

Hiking

Canada is one of the world's top hiking destinations, with excellent facilities and a wide variety of terrain for beginners and experts alike. Hiking trails range from a leisurely two-hour nature walk to several days' physically demanding trek through starkly beautiful wilderness.

The preferred starting places for hiking trails in each national park are well marked. Accommodations for longer trips are often available in lodges or hostels within a park; alternatively you can bring your own tent or rent one in a nearby town. Large-scale maps of any area, including national and provincial parks, can be obtained from **Canadian Topographical Series** in Ottawa.

Most of the more popular hikes require little preparation and only basic training. The best-known hiking areas are found in Alberta and British Columbia, in particular in and around the "big four parks" of Kootenay, Yoho, Jasper, and Banff, which encircle the Rocky Mountains. The variety of lands here, from the lush, gently rolling country near Calgary to craggy mountain peaks, reinforces the popularity of the area. More centrally, the prairie provinces offer a surprising variety of walking, from the arid badlands of Alberta's dinosaur country to the wilderness hiking in Prince Albert National Park. In the east the mountains resume; the steep scenery of the Quebec park of Gatineau and the untamed wilds of the eastern and central Gaspé Peninsula both have wonderful scenery.

In northern Canada the hiking is more demanding but equally rewarding. Most walking and hiking takes place from April to August, when temperatures do rise slightly, although drops to -30°C (-22°F) are not unusual. At best, the weather remains unpredictable. The Chilkoot Pass is a 53-km (33-mile) trail that follows the path of early gold prospectors in the late 19th century from Bennett in northern British Columbia to Dyea in Alaska. For the area, this is a relatively easy path to follow and gives a good taste of northern scenery. More arduous, not to say dangerous, is the memorable Pangnirtung Trail through the southeast of Baffin Island, which even in the summer has a permanently frozen ice cap. Inuit guides will take hikers through the frozen wastes by arrangement.

Occasionally wildlife-watching hikes are available, and teams of husky dogs carry visitors on sleds across ice paths in the wilderness to reach remote destinations. An unforgettable experience, these tours are expensive due to their remoteness and a lack of other modes of transportation.

Turquoise Lake O'Hara in Yoho National Park

Hikers near Weasel River, Auyuittuq National Park, Baffin Island

Safety Measures

Training and safety procedures must be followed for any hike. Always contact the local park or provincial tourist office for their advice and route maps before setting off. Remember, however unlikely a meeting may seem, wildlife can be aggressive; following instructions on bear safety is a must (*see p298*). While less alarming, insects are a constant irritant: take all possible measures to repel blackflies and mosquitos. However clear and sparkling it may seem, do not drink stream or river water without thoroughly boiling it first as it may contain an intestinal parasite, which can lead to "beaver fever" or giardiasis.

In the far north, freezing weather conditions place a premium on safety measures. Never go on a trip without telling someone your planned route and expected time of arrival. Consult local wardens about wildlife and routes, and take the proper equipment. Even in the summer, freezing weather changes can be sudden, so be prepared. Those venturing into little-known territory must be accompanied by a trained guide or seek local advice on dealing with the unexpected.

Rental lodge by Emerald Lake in Yoho National Park

Equipment

Most hiking areas offer rental outlets for tents and cold-weather clothing. Nonetheless, sturdy walking boots, rain gear, and a change of spare clothing are essentials that hikers have to bring themselves, or buy in a nearby town. Appropriate medication and a first-aid kit should also be taken, in particular bug repellent, and antihistamine. Exposure, resulting in either sunstroke or hypothermia, can be guarded against by using appropriate clothes and medication. On a long trip, carry energy-giving foods such as chocolate or trail mix.

Swimmers at Radium Hot Springs in the Rockies

National Parks

Canada's 39 national parks cover the country's most beautiful mountains, lakes, rivers, forests, and coastline. Areas of unspoiled peace, they are the ideal destination for those seeking an outdoor vacation filled with sports, activities, or even a natural spa. The most celebrated upland areas are the "big four" parks in Alberta and BC, Kluane in the Yukon, and the arctic flower-filled tundra of Auyuittuq National Park in southern Baffin Island.

Most of the parks are administered by the government heritage body, **Parks Canada**, and each has a visitors' center or park office to welcome visitors. Here walking, hiking, canoeing, and fishing information is available, often from guides who know every detail of the terrain. These offices also issue permits for fishing, which are necessary in each park. Hunting of any kind and use of firearms are all strictly forbidden in national parks, as is feeding the wildlife and damaging any trees and plants. Most parks have camping facilities, or rustic lodges and cottages. The parks generally charge for these facilities, and most have a daily, weekly, or yearly entrance fee, but some are free. Season tickets are available from either the individual park or the Parks Canada office in Hull.

Canoeists on Lake Wapizagonke, Parc National de la Mauricie

Canoeing

Native Canadians perfected the canoe to maneuver around the country's vast system of waterways for food and survival; today canoeing is a largely recreational pursuit. In provincial or national parks with many lakes and rivers, canoeists can portage (or trek) to the backwaters, getting away from the most populated areas at a gentle pace.

Over 250,000 lakes and 35,000 km (20,000 miles) of waterways in Ontario make this the most accessible canoeing destination. Rivers and lakes making up more than 25,000 km (16,000 miles) of canoe routes run through the Algonquin, Killarney, and Quetico parks. The Rideau Canal, which travels 190 km (120 miles) from Ottawa to Kingston is a favorite route through the province, taking in the capital, the sprinkling of tiny islands near the historic town of Kingston, and acres of fruit orchards by the fertile waterway. While traveling through the islands, be careful of the other marine traffic. The Canal connects with the St. Lawrence Seaway, the world's largest draft inland waterway, and shipping regulations are tight. Smaller craft may have to make way for tankers.

Most towns near canoeing routes will rent boats by the day, week, or month, and wetsuits, oars, and life jackets are usually available. Because of the popularity of watersports, Canada is an extremely reasonable place to buy fishing and canoeing equipment; many outfitters offer good-quality products at almost half European and US prices.

Whitewater Rafting

Whitewater rafting may be attempted in the national parks of British Columbia. The Mackenzie River system, which runs from BC backwaters through the Northwest Territories, provides occasionally hair-raising rafting and canoeing. Most routes in the far north are for the experienced only. The toughest trek of all is the 300-km (180-mile) run of the South Nahanni River near Fort Simpson in the Northwest Territories. New roads here and in the Yukon have boosted the number of visitors to yet another grueling set of waterways, the Yukon River system.

Inexperienced boaters and rafters can take advantage of two-week basic training courses offered all over the country. Lake canoeing in Wells Gray Provincial Park is popular throughout the province for those seeking a more relaxing alternative.

Windsurfing in Georgian Bay Islands National Park, Lake Ontario

Other Watersports

Although the season may be short, sailing has always been a popular summer pastime. Canada contains a large proportion of the world's fresh

Whitewater rafting on the Athabasca River, Jasper National Park in the Rocky Mountains

Snowmobiling in Ontario across virgin powder snow

water, and there are allegedly more boats per head here than anywhere else in the world. The Great Lakes are the prime sailing and windsurfing areas, as are both east and west coastal regions from May to September. Swimming is also a favorite in warm weather; beaches on Prince Edward Island and Cape Breton off the east coast offer warm waters and sandy beaches, while lakes in Ontario, such as Lake Huron, provide inland swims. Torontonians sometimes swim in Lake Ontario in the summer.

Fishing

Over three million square miles of inland waters go partway to justifying Canada's reputation as a paradise for anglers. There are countless varieties of sports fish *(see p21)*, not to mention the charterboat ocean fishing for salmon off the Pacific coast. Almost all parks offer fishing, often in secluded, pristine lakes and rivers. Be sure to contact the park's main office to obtain a fishing license. While most visitors fish in summer, a tiny wooden structure that sits on the frozen lake makes winter fishing more comfortable. These huts sit over a hole in the ice and are often heated. It may be worth buying rods and reels at your destination; Canadian fishing equipment is very high quality, with a good choice, and is usually very reasonably priced.

Canadian snowboard

Skiing, Snowboarding, and Snowmobiling

Not for nothing is Canada known as the Great White North, providing some of the world's best skiing. In the east, the Laurentian resorts of Mont Tremblant and Mont-Ste-Anne offer excellent skiing. Cross-country skiing is available through the Laurentian mountain range, around Gatineau, and throughout the Eastern Townships of Quebec. Moving west, the international resorts of Whistler, Lake Louise, and Banff provide unforgettable dramatic skiing. High in the Rockies, virgin powder snow awaits the adventurous; heli-skiing (lifting skiiers by helicopter to pristine slopes) takes place on the deserted northern peaks. Many of the runs are higher than those in the European Alps, particularly in Banff and Lake Louise. These sites have held major competitions, in particular the Winter Olympics in 1976. Another advantage to skiing in Canada is the close proximity of the mountains to major cities; each of the main resorts is near a city, and it is perfectly possible to travel out for a day's skiing and to spend the evening dining out in the metropolis.

Snowboarding has become increasingly popular in snowsports centers across the country. In Northern Canada, there are now hotels that cater specifically to snowboarding parties – easily spotted because of the snowboard racks outside. Ontario is noted for its winter weekend deals. The province has almost 50,000 km (35,000 miles) of snowmobile trails. Seasoned riders can cover up to 500 km (300 miles) in two days.

More recently, snowmobiling has also established itself in British Columbia and is available in the principal ski resorts. Traveling in groups is preferable; there are many new and popular pitstops en route. These "snow inns" often offer package deals.

Directory

Maps

Canadian Topographical Series
1(800) 214 8524.

Canada Map Office
Ottawa
(613) 952 7000.

Ulysses Travel Bookshop
Montreal (maps)
(514) 843 9447.

Rand McNally (maps)
1 (800) 333 0136.

Useful Organizations

Parks Canada
(819) 997 0055 Hull.

Cycling Canada
(613) 248 1353.

Canadian Paraplegic Association
416 422 5644.

Travel Operators

Air Canada Vacations
(905) 615 8000 Toronto.
(902) 429 7111 Halifax.
(514) 876 4141 Montreal.

American Express
1 (800) 668 2639.

Cosmos/Globus
1 (800) 556 5454.

Trek America
1 (800) 221 0596.

Questers Worldwide Nature Tours
1 (800) 468 8668.

BC
QUEEN OF SURREY

SURVIVAL GUIDE
PRACTICAL INFORMATION 390-397
TRAVEL INFORMATION 398-411

Practical Information

Canada is a popular holiday destination, and offers visitors a mix of urban sophistication and outdoor pleasures. Visitors' facilities are generally excellent. Accommodations and restaurants are of international standard *(see pp342–79)*, public transportation is efficient *(see pp400–411)*, and tourist information centers are found nearly everywhere.

Whale-watching sign

The following pages contain useful information for all visitors. Personal Security and Health *(see pp394–5)* details a number of recommended precautions, while Banking and Currency *(see p396)* answers the important financial queries, together with taxation details. There is also a section on how to use the Canadian telephone and postal services.

When to Go

Weather and geography dominate any visit to Canada. The vastness of the country means that most trips will be centered on one or the other of the major cities, Vancouver, Toronto, Ottawa, and Montreal, although it is possible to stay in remote areas such as the isolated Inuit settlements dotted west and north of Hudson Bay. Depending on each visitor's individual interests, the best time to go will be dictated by local climate and the time of year.

In general, the climates on both the west and east coasts are temperate, while harsher weather occurs in the center of the country, in Saskatchewan, Manitoba, and Alberta, where the summers are fine but the winters long and hard. Northern Canada is at its most welcoming during July and August when the land thaws, and the temperature is more likely to climb above zero.

In eastern Canada, Nova Scotia, New Brunswick, and Prince Edward Island, there are four distinct seasons, with snowy winters, mild springs, and long, crisp falls; summer is still the best time to visit the provinces' resorts. Quebec and Ontario have hot, humid summers and cold winters, with snow lingering until late March. Spring and fall are brief but can be the most rewarding times to make a visit.

The northeastern province of Newfoundland and coastal Labrador have the most extreme temperatures, ranging on a winter's day from 0°C (32°F) to -50°C (-41°F) in St. John's on Newfoundland's east coast. Winter visitors to British Columbia and the Rockies can enjoy some of the best skiing in the world. This region is also noted for its temperate weather but can be very wet in spring and fall as Pacific depressions roll in over the mountains.

Entry Requirements

All visitors to Canada should have a passport valid for longer than the intended period of stay. Travelers from the UK, US, EU, and all British Commonwealth countries do not require a special visa to visit Canada. Tourists are issued with a visitor's visa on arrival if they satisfy immigration officials that they have a valid return ticket, and that they have sufficient funds for the duration of their stay.

Children play in the Kids' Village at the Waterpark, the Ontario Place leisure complex in Toronto

Visitors can stay up to six months, but to extend their stay they must apply to Citizenship and Immigration Canada in Ottawa before expiration of their authorized visit. As visa regulations are subject to change, it is wise to check with the nearest Canadian Consulate, Embassy, or High Commission before leaving home or buying tickets.

Anyone under the age of 18 who is traveling unaccompanied by an adult needs a letter of consent from a parent or guardian giving them permission to travel alone.

Canadian Time Zones

Canada has six time zones spanning a four-and-a-half hour time difference from coast to coast. Between Vancouver and Halifax there are five zones; Pacific, Mountain, Central, Eastern, and Atlantic Standard Time, with an unusual half-hour difference between Newfoundland and Atlantic time. Every province except Saskatchewan uses Daylight Saving Time to give longer summer days, from the first Sunday in April to the last Sunday in October. Clocks go back an hour in October, forward an hour in April.

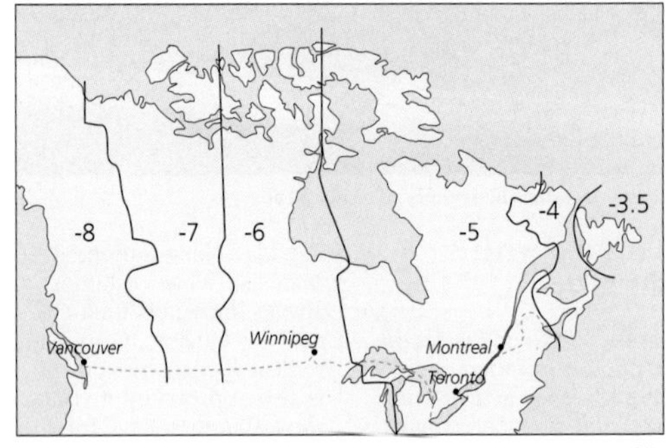

Time Zone	Hours minus GMT	Time Zone	Hours minus GMT
Pacific	*-8*	*Eastern*	*-5*
Mountain	*-7*	*Atlantic*	*-4*
Central	*-6*	*Newfoundland*	*-3.5*

Tourist Information

Canadian tourist offices are famous for the amount and quality of their information, offering everything from local maps to hotel, B-and-B, or campground bookings. Special tours such as wilderness camping, archaeological digs, and wildlife-watching can often be arranged through the tourism service. All the provincial and national parks have visitors' centers, which generally provide maps detailing hiking trails and canoe routes.

The national Canadian Tourism Commission is the central organization, and each province has its own tourism authority. Most smaller towns also have their own seasonal tourist offices, which offer good free maps and detailed information. Each of the large cities has a main office as well as extra booths and kiosks open during busy summer months. Accommodations can usually be booked at the booths found in airports and regional offices.

"The Small Apple" tourist booth in Ontario

Opening Hours and Admission Prices

Most museums, parks, and other attractions throughout Canada charge an admission fee. The amount can vary enormously and many sights offer a range of discount packages for families, children, and seniors. Tourist office leaflets, brochures, and local newspapers often carry discount coupons. Some galleries and museums have free-of-charge days, evenings, or a free hour daily before closing time.

Opening times vary according to the time of the year. As a rule, most of the sights are open for longer through summer but may close completely during the winter months. Many museums and galleries close one day each week, usually on a Monday or Tuesday, but not on weekends. Although many attractions are closed on major holidays, such as Christmas and New Year's Day, a surprising number are open all-year-round. School summer holidays in Canada are from June to Labor Day Weekend, which ends on the first Monday in September. Labor Day generally signifies the end of summer. This is the weekend after which opening hours change over to shorter winter hours of operation. Rural sights generally have shorter hours year-round than those in cities.

Senior Travelers

In Canada people over 60 are refered to as "seniors," and are offered a wide range of discounts. Reduced rates frequently apply to the cost of movie tickets, public transportation, entrance fees, and some restaurant menus. VIA Rail reduce their fares by 10 percent for seniors. When applicable, reductions range from 10 percent to 50 percent for people aged from 55, 60, or 65, depending on the province or attraction. If discounts are not advertised it is always a good idea to inquire.

Educational trips for senior citizens are run by **Elderhostel Canada**, a non-profit organization that offers good, cheap accommodation in university dorms. A typical holiday comprises morning lectures, guided tours in the afternoon, and a communal dinner.

Tourists enjoying the scenery of Niagara Falls

Traveling with Children

Although Canada lacks the numbers of theme parks of the US, its beach resorts, parks, and city centers have much to offer children and families. Most types of accommodations state whether or not they welcome children. Those hotels that do often do not charge for a child sharing a parent's room. They will also normally provide cribs and high chairs, and sometimes have baby-sitting services.

Restaurants now generally welcome children, and many offer kids' menus and high chairs, or will warm up milk and baby food. Some fast food outlets have play areas. It is best to check in advance with more upscale establishments.

Both international and internal airfares are often cheaper for children, and babies under two years old who are not taking up a seat may travel free. On public transportation children under five travel free, and those under 12 have lower fares. If you are renting a car you can reserve one or two car seats for children from your rental firm *(see p411)*.

Etiquette

Canada is very much a multicultural nation *(see pp22–3)*, which welcomes and respects people and customs from the rest of the world. Native Canadians are never referred to as "Indians"; in general they are known as Canada's "First Nations" or "natives," while "eskimos" are always known as Inuit *(see p27)*. In Quebec, be prepared to hear French spoken first. It is also appreciated if visitors show that they have tried to learn a few French words.

Canada's relaxed, informal atmosphere is evident in its dress codes, which tend to be practical and dependent on the climate. Canadians favor jeans and sweatshirts, and dress in layers so they can add or subtract clothing, especially when moving between well-heated malls and winter streets. However, in the cities and larger towns more formal clothing is expected, particularly in more stylish restaurants, theaters, and other formal places. Even the more humble eateries insist on proper attire, and the sign "no shoes, no shirt, no service" is frequently seen in many tourist areas. Topless sunbathing is generally frowned upon in Canada.

Drinking in non-licenced public places is illegal, and it is also illegal to have opened bottles of alcohol in the car when traveling. It is against the law to smoke on buses and trains, in most taxis, in all public buildings, and some restaurants, although some still have smoking areas. Unlike the US, Canada still tolerates smokers, and in some cities, such as Toronto, rules have been drawn up to accommodate them. Ask about smoking policies when booking a restaurant or hotel.

Unless a service charge is included in your check, the standard tip is 15 percent (more if the service is exceptional). Taxi drivers expect a similar tip, while barbers and hairdressers should receive about 10 percent of the total. Porters at airports and train stations, cloakroom attendants, bellhops, doormen, and hotel porters expect Can$1 per bag, and it is customary to leave something for the hotel maids. Tipping bar staff in bars and nightclubs is also expected. Anyone in charge of a large party of visitors should prepare to be generous.

Student Travelers

With an International Student Identity Card (ISIC), full-time students are entitled to substantial discounts on travel as well as admission prices to movies, galleries, museums, and many other tourist attractions. The ISIC card should be purchased in the student's home country at a Student Travel Association (STA) office in the nearest city.

International student I.D. card

There are also a wide range of bus and rail discounts available to students, such as the "Go Canada" Accommodation and Coach Pass, which offers both reduced-cost travel and stays in youth hostels across the country. The pass can be booked through local agents specializing in student travel. VIA Rail also offers students the "Canrail Pass," which allows a period of unlimited travel on all routes. Reasonably priced accommodations are available on university campuses in the larger cities during local student vacations. There are also comfortable hostels throughout the country, most of which are affiliated to the International Youth Hostelling Federation (IYHF). Eating out is inexpensive, so students can easily find great food on a budget.

ELECTRICITY

CANADIAN electrical appliances come with either a two-prong or three-prong plug, and most sockets will accept either. The system is a 110-volt, 60-cycle system. You need a plug adaptor if you are visiting from outside North America. Batteries are universal and are readily available for all appliances. Bear in mind that bargain electrical goods purchased here will probably need modification for use in Europe.

Standard plug

TRAVELERS WITH DISABILITIES

TRAVELERS WITH physical disabilities can expect some of the best facilities in the world in Canada. Increasingly, large towns and cities offer wheelchair access in most public buildings, as well as on public transportation.

Vancouver's buses all have low platforms, and VIA Rail trains can accommodate wheelchairs. Each province has varying requirements for disabled drivers, and information on this is available through the **Canadian Paraplegic Association (CPA)**. This Ottawa-based association also has details on companies that rent specially adapted cars and RV vehicles. Parking permits can be obtained in advance through the CPA but require a doctor's letter and a small processing fee.

There is a wide choice of hotels with disabled facilities in Canada. Most of the big chains such as Best Western and Holiday Inn are easily accessible, as are some luxury hotels and youth hostels. The CPA also has details on the most disabled-friendly attractions. Many of the national and provincial parks have interpretive centers, short nature trails, and boardwalks that are wheelchair accessible.

CONVERSION CHART

Imperial to Metric
1 inch = 2.54 centimeters
1 foot = 30 centimeters
1 mile = 1.6 kilometers
1 ounce = 28 grams
1 pound = 454 grams
1 pint = 0.6 liters
1 gallon = 4.6 liters

Metric to Imperial
1 centimeter = 0.4 inches
1 meter = 3 feet, 3 inches
1 kilometer = 0.6 miles
1 gram = 0.04 ounces
1 kilogram = 2.2 pounds
1 liter = 1.8 pints

DIRECTORY

IMMIGRATION

Canadian High Commission
Macdonald House,
38 Grosvenor Street,
London, W1X 0AA.
(0891) 616644.

Citizenship and Immigration Canada
Jean Edmonds Towers,
365 Laurier Ave. W,
Ottawa, ON K1A 1L1.
(613) 954 9019.

TOURIST INFORMATION

Canadian Tourism Commission
235 Queen St,
Ottawa, ON K1A 0H6.
(613) 954 3943.

Tourism Canada
501 Penn Ave.,
NW Washington DC, USA
(202) 682 1740.

Canadian Tourism Commission
Visit Canada Centre,
62–65 Trafalgar Square,
London, WC2N 5DY.
(0891) 715 000.

PROVINCIAL OFFICES

British Columbia
Tourism British Columbia
865 Hornby St., 8th floor,
Vancouver, BC V6Z 2G3.
(604) 660 2861.

Ontario
Ministry of Tourism
900 Bay St., 9th floor,
Hearst Block, Toronto,
ON M7A 2E1.
416 325 6666.

Travel Manitoba
155 Carlton St.,
7th Floor, Winnipeg,
MB R3C 3HB.
(204) 945 3796.

Tourism Saskatchewan
1922 Park St., SK
F4P 3V7.
1(800) 667 7191.

Newfoundland and Labrador
Department of Tourism,
PO Box 8700,
St. John's, NF A1B 4J6.
(709) 729 2831.

Tourism New Brunswick
PO Box 12345,
Campbellton, NB E3N 3T6.
1 (800) 561 0123.

Travel Alberta
Suite 500,
999–8 St. SW,
Calgary, AB T2R 1J5.
(403) 297 2700.

Tourism Prince Edward Island
PO Box 940,
Charlottetown,
PEI C1A 7M5.
1 (800) 565 0201.

Nunavut Tourism
PO Box 1450,
Iqaluit, NT XOA OHO.
(867) 979 6551.

Northwest Territories
NWT Arctic Tourism
PO Box 1320, Yellowknife,
NWT X1A 2N5.
1(800) 661 0788.

Tourism Nova Scotia
PO Box 519,
1800 Argyle St., Suite 605,
Halifax, NS B3J 2R7.
1(800) 565 0000.

Tourism Yukon
PO Box 2703,
Whitehorse,
Yukon, Y1A 2C6.
(867) 667 5340.

Tourism Quebec
PO Box 979,
Montreal, PQ H3C 2W3.
(514) 873 2015.

SENIOR TRAVELERS

Elderhostel Canada
4 Cataraqui Street,
Kingston,
Ontario, K7K 1Z7.
(613) 530 2222.

STUDENT TRAVELERS

STA Travel
(0207) 361 6262 UK.
(800) 825 3001 Can.

DISABLED TRAVELERS

Canadian Paraplegic Association
National Office
1101 Prince of Wales Dr.,
Suite 230, Ottawa,
Ontario, K2C 3W7.
(613) 723 1033.

Personal Security and Health

WITH ITS COMPARATIVELY low crime rate, Canada is a safe country to visit. In contrast to many US cities, there is little street crime in the city centers, perhaps because so many Canadians live downtown that the cities are never empty at night. However, it is wise to be careful and to find out which parts of town are more dangerous than others. Avoid city parks after dark, and make sure cars are left locked. In the country's more remote areas visitors must observe sensible safety measures. In the remote country, wildlife and climatic dangers can be avoided by heeding local advice. If a serious problem does arise, contact one of the national emergency numbers in the telephone directory.

PERSONAL SAFETY

THERE ARE FEW off-limit areas in Canadian cities. Even the seedier districts tend to have a visible police presence, making them safer than the average suburban area at night. Always ask your hotelier, the local tourist information center, or the police, which areas to avoid. Although theft is rare in hotel rooms, it is a good idea to store any valuables in the hotel safe, as hotels will not guarantee the security of property left in rooms. Make sure you leave your hotel room key at the front desk.

Pickpockets can be a hazard at large public gatherings and popular tourist attractions, so it is a good idea to wear cameras and bags over one shoulder with the strap across your body. Try not to be seen with large amounts of cash, and if necessary use a coin purse and a wallet for larger bills. Keep your passport apart from your cash and traveler's checks. Never hang your purse over the back of your chair in restaurants; put it on the floor beside your feet with one foot over the strap, or pinned down by a chair leg. Male travelers should not carry their wallets in their back pocket, as this makes a very easy target. Safe options for both sexes are zippered purse belts.

LAW ENFORCEMENT

CANADA IS policed by a combination of forces. The Royal Canadian Mounted Police (RCMP) operate throughout most of the country, while Ontario and Quebec are looked after by provincial forces. There are also city police and native police on the reserves. For the most part, the officers are noted for their helpful attitude, but it is illegal to comment on (or joke about) safety, bombs, guns, and terrorism in places such as airports, where it is possible to be arrested for an off-the-cuff remark. Drinking and driving is also taken seriously here, and remember that open alcohol containers in a car are illegal. Narcotics users face criminal charges often followed by moves for deportation.

Canadian policemen on duty

LOST PROPERTY

AS SOON AS something is lost, report it to the police. They will issue a report with a number that you will need in order to make a claim on your insurance policy. If a credit card is missing, call the company's toll-free number and report it immediately. Lost or stolen traveler's checks must also be reported to the issuer. If you have kept a record of the checks' numbers, replacing them should be a painless experience, and new ones may be issued within 24 hours.

If you lose your passport, contact the nearest embassy or consulate. They will be able to issue a temporary replacement as visitors do not generally need a new passport if they will be returning directly to their home country. However, if you are traveling on to another destination, you will need a full passport. It is also useful to hold photocopies of your driver's license and birth certificate, as well as notarized passport photographs if you are contemplating an extended visit or need additional ID.

TRAVEL INSURANCE

TRAVEL INSURANCE is essential in Canada and should be arranged to cover health, trip-cancellation, and interruption, as well as theft and loss of valuable possessions.

Canadian health services are excellent, but if you do not wish to pay you will need insurance. If you already have private health insurance you should check to see if the coverage includes all emergency hospital and medical expenses such as physician's care, prescription drugs, and private duty-nursing. In case of a serious illness, separate coverage is also required to send a relative to your bedside or return a rented vehicle. Emergency dental treatment, and out-of-pocket expenses or loss of vacation costs also need their own policies. Your insurance company or travel agent should recommend the right policy, but beware of exclusions for pre-existing medical conditions.

MEDICAL TREATMENT

A COMPREHENSIVE range of treatment centers are available in Canada. For minor problems pharmacies are often a good source of advice, and walk-in clinics in the cities will treat visitors relatively quickly. In smaller communities, or in more difficult cases, go straight to the emergency room of the closest hospital, but be prepared for a long wait. In a serious medical emergency dial 911 in most areas, or 0 for the operator, to summon an ambulance.

Anyone taking a prescription drug should ask their doctor for extra supplies when they travel, as well as a copy of the prescription in case more medication is needed on the trip. It is a good idea to take a simple first-aid kit, especially for longer trips in the more remote or Arctic areas of the country. Generally this should include aspirin (or paracetamol), antihistamine for bites or allergies, motion sickness pills, antiseptic and bandages or band aids, calamine lotion, and bug repellent. Antibiotic creams are useful for intrepid wilderness hikers.

All the provincial capitals have dental clinics that will provide emergency treatment. The Yellow Pages telephone book lists dentists in each area together with opticians and alternative health practitioners.

NATURAL HAZARDS

THERE ARE times when Canada's mosquitoes and black flies can be so troublesome that moose and deer leave the woods for relief. Insects are a major irritant for tourists in rural areas. They are at their worst during annual breeding periods from late spring to midsummer, and all-year-round in Northern Canada. There are precautions one can take to alleviate the misery. Taking Vitamin B complex tablets for two weeks before traveling is thought to affect the skin's chemistry and reduces the chance of bites considerably. Stick to light-colored clothes as the bugs are drawn to dark ones, and cover as much skin as possible with long sleeves, and pants tucked into boots and socks. It might even be worth investing in a gauze mask for your head and neck if you are planning to venture into deserted areas at peak breeding times.

Canada is notorious for cold winter weather, but tourists are not likely to suffer many serious problems. The media gives daily extensive coverage to the weather, and on days when frostbite is possible they offer detailed reports. Dressing in layers and wearing a hat is necessary. Sunscreen is needed in summer, even on overcast days.

Warning sign for motorists

BEARS

CANADA'S national parks' service, particularly in the Rockies, supplies advice on bear safety *(see p298)*, but unless you are camping or hiking in the woods it is unlikely that you will come across them. Encounters can be avoided by following a few basic rules: never leave food or garbage near your tent, car, or RV, do not wear scent, and make a noise (many hikers blow whistles) as you walk, as bears are more likely to attack if surprised. If you do come across a bear, do not scream or run as bears are very fast, and do not climb trees – they are even better at that. Instead, keep still, speak to them in a low voice, and put your luggage on the ground to try and distract them.

DIRECTORY

EMERGENCY SERVICES

Police, Fire, Ambulance
In most of Canada and in large cities call 911, elsewhere dial 0.

CONSULATES AND EMBASSIES

United States
Vancouver, 1095 West Pender St.
☎ *(604) 685 4311.*

Ottawa, 490 Sussex Drive.
☎ *(613) 238 5335.*

Montreal, Complex Desjardins, South Tower. ☎ *(514) 398 9695.*

Toronto, 360 University Ave.
☎ *(416) 595 1700*

UK
Vancouver, 1111 Melville Street.
☎ *(604) 683 4421.*

Ottawa, 80 Elgin Street.
☎ *(613) 237 1530.*

Montreal, 1000 rue de la Gauchetiére. ☎ *(514) 866 5863.*

Toronto, 777 Bay St
☎ *416 593 1290.*

A polar bear approaching a tourist Tundra Buggy, northern Manitoba

Banking and Currency

ATM or banking machine sign

Canadian currency is based on the decimal system, and has 100 cents to the dollar. Two of the most useful coins are the 25-cent and $1 pieces which operate pay telephones, newspaper boxes, and vending machines. They are also handy for public transportation in the larger cities, where as a matter of policy bus drivers often do not carry any change. It is a good idea to arrive with some Canadian currency, around Can$50–100 including small change for tipping and taxis, but to carry most of your funds in Canadian dollar traveler's checks.

Sandstone façade of the Toronto Stock Exchange

Banks

Canada's main national banks are the Royal Bank of Canada, the Bank of Montréal, the Toronto Dominion, the Canadian Imperial Bank of Commerce, the Bank of Nova Scotia, and the National Bank. These banks generally accept ATM (automatic teller machine) cards, although it is wise to check with your bank first. ATMs can also be found at such places as grocery stores, shopping centers, gas stations, train and bus stations, and airports.

Banks are usually open Monday to Friday, from 9am to 5pm; some stay open later on Fridays, and a few open on Saturday mornings. All banks are closed on Sundays and on statutory holidays.

TD

Toronto Dominion Bank logo

Traveler's Checks

Traveler's checks issued in Canadian dollars are probably the safest and most convenient way to carry money for your vacation. They offer security because they can be easily replaced if they are lost or stolen. They are also accepted as cash in a vast range of gas stations, shops, and restaurants across the country. Buy checks in smaller denominations such as $20 as most retailers prefer not to give out large amounts of change. It is a good idea to find out which Canadian banks charge commission for changing traveler's checks, as many have arrangements with certain issuers of checks and make no charge. The Royal Bank of Canada, for example, charges no commission on American Express checks in Canadian dollars. A passport or other form of ID is needed to cash traveler's checks at a bank or at Bureaux de Changes offices such as American Express or Thomas Cook.

Credit Cards

Credit cards are used extensively in Canada, and American Express, Diner's Club, MasterCard/Access, and VISA are widely accepted. Credit cards are often asked for as a form of ID, and for placing large deposits – most car rental companies in Canada insist on a credit card or require a substantial cash deposit. Some hotels also prefer prepayment by credit card. Credit cards can also be used to secure cash advances, but you will be charged interest from the date of withdrawal.

Wiring Money

If you run out of money or have an emergency it is possible to have cash wired from home in minutes using an electronic money service. Both American Express and Thomas Cook provide this service, as does Western Union which has 22,000 outlets all over North America.

WESTERN UNION | MONEY TRANSFER®
The world's No. 1 money transfer service.

Western Union's familiar logo

Coins and Bank Notes

Canadian coins are issued in denominations of one cent (the penny), five cents (the nickel), ten cents (the dime), 25 cents (the quarter), $1 (dubbed the "loonie" because it has an illustration of the bird, the Canadian loon on one side), and the $2 coin or "twonie," which replaced the old bank note in 1996.

Bank notes are printed in denominations of $5, $10, $20, $50, $100, $500, and $1,000. However, the larger denominations such as $50 or $100 dollar bills are sometimes viewed with suspicion as they are not used very often in small stores, or even in cafés and gas stations.

Directory

Currency Exchange and Wiring Money

Thomas Cook
Check replacement, UK
(0800) 622 101.
Canada and US
1 (800) 223 7373.

American Express
Check replacement, Canada
1 (800) 221 7282.

Western Union
Wiring money, Canada
1 (800) 235 0000.

Media and Communications

Canada has some of the most sophisticated communication systems in the world. There are public payphones everywhere – in cafés, bars, public buildings, gas stations, and post offices. Most operate with coins or cards, and while local calls are a bargain, international calls can be expensive. It is also possible to send telegrams, faxes, and even documents via Intelpost, a satellite communications system.

Canada Post, the country's mail service is certainly reliable, but it is renowned for being slow. It can be quick however, if you are willing to pay an extra fee for priority handling and delivery.

Public Telephones

Public telephones operate on 25 cent coins, although there is an increasing number of phones that accept both credit and phone cards. Rates are generally cheaper between 6pm and 8am, and on weekends. All local calls cost 25 cents (private subscribers have free local calls). For any call outside the local area, including international calls, the operator will tell you how much to pay for the initial period and will then ask for more money as your call progresses. It is usually easier to make long distance calls using card phones than to have the stacks of change required.

Public roadside telephones are found countrywide

Postal Services

All mail from Canada to outside North America is by air and can take between one and five days to arrive. If you are sending mail within the country it can also take days, but it is faster if you include the postal code. To send mail, look for signs that say "Canada Post" since some post offices are located in malls.

Mobile Phones and E-Mail

It is possible to rent a mobile phone while on vacation, or to have your own mobile tuned to local networks.

Visitors can use e-mail in the larger hotels or at one of many city-based Internet cafés.

Fax and Telegram Services

It is possible to send a fax from the commercial outlets found in most towns. Telegrams are dealt with by Canadian National Telecommunications (CNT) or Canadian Pacific (CP). There are two main services, Telepost, which provides first-class delivery, and Intelpost, which sends documents abroad via satellite.

Media

The only papers that see themselves as national publications are *The National Post* and *The Globe and Mail*, both based in Toronto. There is also a national news weekly called *MacLean's*. Most cities have their own daily newspapers and some, such as Toronto, have several. Many areas have weeklies that provide excellent coverage of local events.

Canada has a national 24-hour public broadcasting corporation (CBC), 80 percent of whose programs are produced locally. CBC also provides an excellent radio service, and can be a good source of information on local happenings and weather for visitors. They also have a national service in French.

Directory

Provincial Codes

Alberta - *403 & 780.*
British Columbia - *604 & 250.*
Manitoba - *204.*
New Brunswick - *506.*
Northwest Territories - *867.*
Nova Scotia - *902.*
Newfoundland & Labrador - *709.*
Ontario - *416 & 905 (Toronto).*
705 - (central and northeast).
519 - (southwest peninsula).
613 - (Ottawa region).
807 - (northwest).
Prince Edward Island - *902.*
Quebec - *514 & 540 (Montreal).*
819 - (north).
418 - (east).
Saskatchewan - *306.*
Yukon & Nunavut- *867.*

Useful Information

Canadian Post Customer Services line.
1 (800) 267 1177.

Reaching the Right Number

- For direct-dial calls to another area code: dial 1 followed by the area code and the 7-digit local number.
- For international direct-dial calls: dial **011** then the code of the country (Australia **61**, New Zealand **64**, the UK **44**) followed by the local area/city code (minus the first **0**) and the number. To call the US from Canada dial the state code, then the number.
- For international operator assistance dial **0**.
- For information on numbers within your local area dial **411**.
- For information on long distance numbers call **1** followed by the provincial code then **555 1212**.
- An **800** or **877** or **888** prefix means the call will be toll free.

Travel Information

The majority of visitors to Canada arrive by air, usually at one of the country's three largest international airports – Vancouver, Toronto, or Montreal. It is also possible to fly direct to cities such as Halifax, Winnipeg, Edmonton, Calgary, and St. John's, Newfoundland.

Maple leaf Air Canada logo

The size of the country makes flying between locations popular with visitors who wish to see more than one part of Canada. For example, on a short stay, it could prove difficult to see Toronto and Montreal in the east, as well as the Rocky Mountains in the west without spending some time in the air. There are other transportation choices that allow visitors to see much of Canada. The national rail network, VIA Rail, links most major cities, while long-distance bus routes provide a delightful, and often less expensive, way to see the country. There are short cruises and ferry rides that take in some spectacular scenery. Exploring Canada by car is also a popular choice, enabling visitors to get to locations that can be difficult to reach any other way.

Arriving by Air

Canada is a destination for several international airlines, and the country's major carrier **Air Canada** is linked with national airlines around the world. All Europe's principal airlines fly into Toronto or Montreal, while Vancouver is a gateway for carriers such as Cathay Pacific, Qantas, and national airlines from the Far East.

Visitors who intend to see parts of the US as well as Canada can find plenty of connecting flights to such principal US destinations as New York, Los Angeles, Dallas, Chicago, and Atlanta.

International Flights

Flights between Canada and Europe take from seven to nine hours; from Asia or Australia, across the Pacific, you may be in transit for as long as 25 hours. Older travelers or those with children may wish to consider a stopover for the sake of comfort (Hawaii is a popular choice). It is also a good idea to plan flights so that they account for international time differences.

Canada has 13 international airports, the busiest being at Toronto, Montreal, and Vancouver. It is also possible to fly direct into airports in cities such as Edmonton, Halifax, Ottowa, Winnipeg, and St. Johns, Newfoundland. All the major cities are connected with airports in the US. Several leading airlines offer special deals that allow visitors to fly to one part of North America and leave from another.

In summer 2000 Air Canada bought Canadian Airlines.

Air Fares

Flights to Canada from Europe, Australia, and the US can be expensive, especially during peak holiday periods such as Christmas, New Year, and the summer months between July and mid-September. It is always cheaper to book an Apex

Airport	Information
St. John's	(709) 758 8500
Halifax	(902) 873 1223
Montreal (Dorval)	(514) 394 7377
Montreal (Mirabel)	(514) 394 7377
Ottawa	(613) 248 2100
Toronto	(416) 247 7678
Winnipeg	(204) 987 9402
Calgary	(403) 735 1372
Edmonton	(780) 890 8382
Vancouver	(604) 276 6101

(Advanced Purchase Excursion) fare, which should be bought no less than seven days in advance, (most major airlines, including Air Canada, offer them). These tickets generally impose such restrictions as a minimum (usually seven days) and maximum (of 3–6 months) length of stay. It can also be difficult to alter dates of travel, and it is worth considering insuring yourself against last-minute, unforeseen delays or cancellations.

Charter flights sometimes offer a cheaper alternative, with savings of 20 percent on some tickets. Round-the-world fares are increasingly popular, as are package vacations which provide a variety of choices. The kinds of deals available range from fly/drive vacations with a much reduced car rental as part of the price of the ticket, to a guided tour, including all accommodations, transportation, and meals.

On Arrival

Just before landing in Canada you will be given customs and immigration documents to fill in. On arrival you will be asked to present them, along with your passport, to the appropriate customs and immigration officials.

The larger airports offer a better range of services, but most airports have shops, medical and postal services, foreign exchange bureaus, newsstands, and bookstores. The major car rental companies have outlets at the airport, and buses, limousines, and shuttle buses into town are available. Most terminals offer facilities for disabled travelers.

Visitors hoping to catch a connecting flight to another part of the country will have to claim and clear their baggage through customs before checking in with the connecting airline. Arrangements for transferring to domestic flights are usually made when you book your trip. It is a good idea to ask airline staff if you need more information; as in large airports such as Toronto's Pearson International there are three separate terminals.

Roads to and from airports are well sign-posted

Directory

Airlines in the UK, US, and Canada

Air Canada
UK: (0990) 247 226.
CAN: (1 800) 813 9237.
US: (1 800) 813 9237.

American Airlines
UK: (0345) 789789
(0208) 572 5555 (London only).
CAN: (1 800) 433 7300.
US: (1 800) 433 7300.

British Airways
UK: (0845) 77 99977.
CAN and US: (1 800) 247 9297.

Distance from City	Taxi Fare to City	Bus Transfer to City
8 km (5 miles)	CAN$16	NO SERVICE
42 km (26 miles)	CAN$35	30–45 mins
22 km (14 miles)	CAN$28	25 mins
55 km (34 miles)	CAN$69	40–55 mins
18 km (11 miles)	CAN$20	20–30 mins
24 km (15 miles)	CAN$35	45–55 mins
10 km (6 miles)	CAN$15	20 mins
16 km (10 miles)	CAN$25	30 mins
31 km (19 miles)	CAN$35	45 mins
15 km (9 miles)	CAN$25–30	25–45 mins

Domestic Air Travel

Because of the distances involved, flying around the country has become an accepted part of Canadian life. There is a complex network of domestic flights, with over 75 local airlines, many of which are linked to Air Canada. The smaller operators fly within provinces, and to remote locations where they are often the only means of transportation. In all there are some 125 domestic destinations. It is possible to book domestic flights with a travel agent before departure or, once in Canada, through local agents or the Yellow Pages. Domestic flights are not cheap, but there are often discounts advertised in the local press, or a range of pass deals exclusively for visitors from abroad. Light aircraft can also be chartered for fascinating but costly trips over far-flung landmarks such as Baffin Island.

Dash-7 aircraft during a trip in Canada's far north

Air Routes and Airlines

The impressive array of domestic flights available here means that most of the nation's smaller urban areas are within reach of regular services. However, you will generally have to fly to the major city in the area, principally Vancouver, Toronto, or Montreal, and then take a connecting flight.

Most of the smaller airlines are connected with Canada's major carrier, Air Canada, and it is often possible to book your connection through the national airline. The majority of the country's long-haul domestic routes run east-to-west, connecting the cities: from Halilfax on the east coast, through to Montreal, Toronto, Ottawa, Winnipeg, Calgary, and Edmonton to Vancouver in the west. Longer north-to-south flights to places such as the Yukon and Northwest Territories usually originate from Edmonton and Winnipeg. In the remote north, light aircraft are the best way to reach a destination such as Baffin Island, (which can be reached by boat only in good weather) with the exception of Churchill, Manitoba, which is connected by train.

Apex Fares and Other Discounts

There are several kinds of bargain tickets available within Canada: through charter carriers, Apex (Advance Purchase Excursion) fares, and seat sales. Charter airlines such as Canada 3000, Royal, and Air Transat fly between Canadian cities much like scheduled airlines. However, they are usually up to 20% cheaper than scheduled tickets and can be booked through tour operators. To take advantage of the reductions available through Apex you must book between 7 and 21 days in advance: the earlier the booking, the larger the discount. Each fare will have its own set of rules, which include restrictions on length of stay and time of travel (such as between certain hours or on certain days). Be aware that refunds are seldom given and it might be difficult to change your dates.

Seat sales are another bargain option whereby an airline will advertise exceptionally cheap tickets to boost travel on popular routes during quiet times of the year. There is very little flexibility on these deals, and you have to fly within a specific period of time.

Air Canada offers pass deals for visitors who want to travel all over the country, as well as to the US. The passes are available only outside of North America. Most of the offers involve paying for a number of coupons, each of which represents a single flight within either the continent or a specific region. The passes also usually specify a period of time (7 to 60 days) for which they are valid.

Fly-Drive Deals

A good way to make the most of a visit to Canada is to book a fly-drive vacation. The deal invariably involves a substantial cut in the cost of the car rental. Arrangements can also be made to pick up and drop off your vehicle in different places. It would be possible, for example, to pick

up a car in Toronto, tour Ontario, dropping the car off in Ottawa before flying on to Vancouver on the west coast. Known as one-way car rental, these deals may involve large drop-off fees: from Toronto to Ottawa costs around Can$200. Travel agents offer a wide range of such packages.

Baggage Restrictions

Passengers traveling economy on domestic flights should be aware that there are restrictions on the amount and weight of baggage that can be taken on board. The type of aircraft determines what can be carried, and light aircraft usually accept only hand-baggage. In general, passengers are entitled to have two suitcases, each with an average weight of 32 kg (70 lb) per item. Hand-baggage must fit safely under aircraft seats or in overhead lockers. Garment bags may be carried on board some aircraft but must be soft-sided and comply with size restrictions – length 112 cm (45 ins), depth 11 cm (4.5 ins) – so remember to check with your airline or travel agent when puchasing your ticket.

Canadian Airlines logo

Checking In

Security is a necessity nowadays and can make the boarding procedure take longer. Within Canada you must check in at least 30 minutes prior to departure; for flights to the US, allow 60 minutes; and for international flights, leave at least 90 minutes. Visitors from other countries traveling within Canada should carry a passport to verify that he or she is the traveler named on the ticket.

It is also worth noting that the daily peak periods at the larger Canadian airports are usually from 7am to 9am and from 3pm to 8pm. Passenger volume also increases significantly during the winter holiday season, March break, and the summer, so it is wise to allow extra time for parking, check-in, and security screening during these periods.

Directory

Domestic Airlines

Air BC
(Richmond, BC)
(604) 273 2464.

Air Nova
(Halifax)
(902) 873 5000.

Air Ontario
(London, Ont.)
(519) 453 8440.

Air Transat
(Montreal)
(450) 476 1011.

Bearskin Airline
(Thunder Bay, Ont.)
(807) 577 1141.

First Air
(Ottawa, for far north flights)
(613) 738 0200.

Canada 3000
(Toronto)
(416) 674 0257.

Royal Airlines
(Montreal)
(450) 476 3800.

Skyservice
(Mississauga, Ont.)
(905) 678 3300.

Westjet
(Calgary, AB)
1 800 538 5696.

Principal Domestic Air Routes

Canada's major airline is Air Canada. It acquired Canadian Airlines, which was facing severe financial difficulties, in mid-2000. Air Canada provides links to a number of regional carriers to form a comprehensive domestic air network.

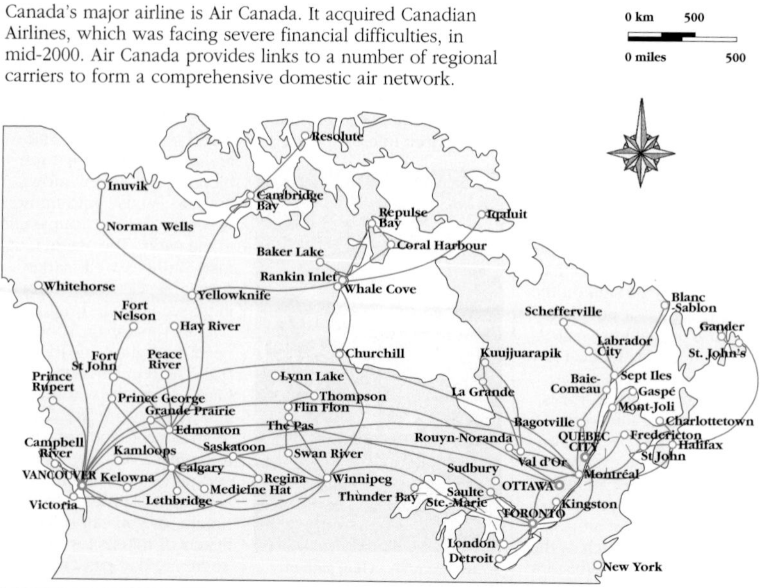

Getting Around Canada's Cities

Although the car is a popular way to travel in Canada, the country is noted for the fast, frequent, and efficient public transit systems of its cities. In general, the best way for visitors to explore Canada's urban centers is primarily on foot, using public transportation as a back up. The streets are clean and safe, and strolling through different neighborhoods is a pleasant way to get to know them. Most municipal transit systems are reasonably priced, with discounted multi-ticket deals and day passes. Driving around downtown areas can be daunting, particularly during the rush hour, and parking tends to be both difficult and expensive.

Tourbus in Toronto

Most transit systems offer free maps, available at stations or tourist information centers. The following pages detail how to get around Canada's three largest cities, Vancouver, Toronto, and Montreal *(see endpaper for detailed transit maps)*, as well as other provincial capitals and the most often visited towns and communities.

Montreal

Montreal's bus and subway network is integrated so that the stations connect with bus routes and tickets can be used on either. Be sure to get a transfer ticket, which should take you anywhere in the city for one fare. Known as the Métro, Montreal's subway is clean, safe, and air-conditioned in summer and heated in the winter. It is by far the fastest and cheapest way to get around town *(see endpaper)*. Free maps are available at any of the ticket booths. Visitors can buy a Tourist Pass for one or three days at major hotels and at the Visitor Information Office downtown.

Driving is not recommended here, as the roads are busy and parking is severely restricted, especially in the old town. It is best to use the city's park-and-ride system. Cabs can be hailed in the street. They have a white or orange sign on the roof; the sign is lit up when the cab is available.

Many streets in Montreal now have bike lanes. The Great Montreal Bike Path-Guide is available free at the tourist office. Bikes can be taken on the Métro anytime except during rush hour, from about 7am to 10am and 5pm to 7pm on weekdays. There are some lovely bike paths, such as the waterfront trail on the historic Canal de Lachine, and those that lead through Cité du Havre and across Pont de la Concorde to the islands. There are a number of bicycle shops offering daily or weekly rental; they generally require a deposit of Can$250 or more in addition to the daily rate.

Toronto

The Toronto Transit Commission (TTC) operates a huge system of connecting subway, bus, and streetcar lines that serves the entire city. It is one of the safest and cleanest systems of its kind anywhere in the world. There are two major subway lines, with 60 stations along the way *(see endpaper)*. Be sure to get a free transfer pass if you intend to continue your trip by bus or streetcar after you leave the subway.

Scenic riverside cyling path in Quebec City

To ride buses and streetcars, you must have exact change, a ticket, or a token. Tickets and tokens are on sale at subway entrances and stores. The "Pick up a Ride Guide" shows every major place of interest and how to reach it by public transit, and is available at most subway ticket offices. A Light Rapid Transit line connects downtown to the lakefront (called Harbourfront). The line starts at Union Station and terminates at Spadina/Bloor subway station.

It is easy to catch a cab in Toronto; they can be hailed in the street, called in advance, or found outside hotels. There are several outlets that rent bicycles, but as downtown Toronto is busy with traffic, it is best to confine your cycling to the parks. The Martin Goodman Trail is a well-marked scenic bicycle route along the long, scenic waterfront.

As in Vancouver, you will need the right coins for the bus. The regular adult fare is Can$2 across the whole system, and transfers are free for up to an hour. If you are going to be in Toronto for an extended period, it is worth considering a MetroPass for one month, or you can buy 10 tickets or tokens for Can$17. There are day passes for use during off-peak hours.

Toronto taxicabs gather at a taxi stand

Ferries to the Toronto Islands run several times an hour at peak times in summer and continue well into the evening. There is also a road bridge.

Vancouver

Vancouver's well-organized network of light rail (called SkyTrain), bus, and ferry services is run by BC Transit. An inexpensive Transit Guide is available from newsstands and information centers. It includes a map of the city showing all routes. Driving is not the best way to see the city as congestion is heavy, and you are unlikely to find a spot to park. There is a park-and-ride system, where commuters can leave their cars at certain points around the city center.

The SkyTrain is a light rail system of driverless trains that connects downtown Vancouver with the suburbs of Burnaby, New Westminster, and Surrey. It travels partially beneath ground and partially overground on a raised track. The main terminal is at Waterfront Station at the bottom of Seymour Street. An alternative to the SkyTrain is to use the city's downtown bus routes. These are worth riding as they offer delightful tours past the city's top attractions, although it is advisable to avoid rush hour traffic. Bus services end around midnight, but there is a scaled down "Night Owl" service.

One of the best ways to get around Vancouver is by water. The SeaBus is a 400-seat Catamaran that shuttles between Lonsdale Quay in North Vancouver and the downtown terminal at Waterfront Station. The trip takes around 15 minutes and includes wonderful views of the mountains and Vancouver skyline. Aquabus Ferries connect stations on False Creek, Granville Island, Stamp's Landing, and the Hornby Street Dock.

If you want to take a cab it is best to call one of the main companies such as Black Top or Yellow Cab, as hailing a taxi in the streets is rarely successful. However, Vancouver is a great city for cyclists, with plenty of bike paths, including the 10 km (6 mile) road around Stanley Park. There is a park-and-ride service for bikes here, similar to the one elsewhere for cars.

Fares are the same for bus, SkyTrain, and SeaBus in the Vancouver area, but the price varies according to time of day and the distance you travel. Adult fares are cheaper after 6:30pm, and all day Saturday, Sunday, and holidays. There are three zones in the city, and the price of the fare depends on how many zones you cross. The off-peak adult fare in zone one is Can$1.75. There are a wide variety of discounts available: a FareSaver book of 10 tickets or a day pass are good value. Children under 4 ride free, and those between the ages of 5 and 13 pay less (as do students with a valid GoCard), and seniors over 65 also get concessions. A transfer ticket is free and lasts for 90 minutes of travel.

SkyTrain traveling over the city bridge in Vancouver on a summer evening

The scenic approach to Château Frontenac in Quebec City, best appreciated on foot

Ottawa

Fortunately for visitors, many of the capital city's major tourist attractions are within walking distance of Parliament Hill. Ottawa's sidewalks are both wide and clean, and you can do most of your sightseeing on foot, using public transportation to cover the longer distances. The region of Ottawa-Carlton operates **OC Transpo**, a 130-route bus network. Fares are among the most expensive in Canada, with a two-tier system that charges more for traveling during rush hour, Can$2.25 per ticket. You need the exact fare unless you buy tickets in advance. These are available at newsstands and corner stores. If you need to change buses, ask for a transfer, which can be used for up to an hour. It is possible to get a transfer for use on the separate Hull bus system across the Ottawa River, although you may have to pay a little more. All routes meet downtown at the Rideau Centre, and the stops are color-coded according to the route.

If you are using a car there are several reasonably priced municipal car lots – look for a green 'P' sign. Taxis can be booked by phone or hailed at stands outside major hotels.

Bicycles are a good way to explore a city that has some 150 km (93 miles) of scenic paths. The Rideau Canal, that crosses the city from north to south, is bordered by delightful walking and bike paths.

Calgary

Calgary transit operates buses and a light-rail transit system known as the C-Train. For a flat fare of Can$1.60 you can transfer to either using the same ticket, although day passes for around Can$5 are good value for visitors hoping to see several sights in one day. The C-Train travels north to the University and airport, and south to Macleod Trail. It is free in the downtown section between 10th Street and City Hall (buses are not). Maps are available from the **Calgary Transit** offices, where you can also buy tickets. C-Train tickets can be bought from machines located on the platforms.

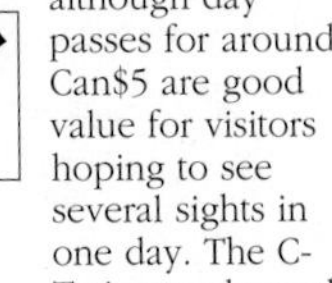

Logo for the C-Train in Calgary

If you wish to travel mostly within the city center, walking and public transportation are your best options. However, the city's blocks are long, (Calgary is Canada's second largest city by area) and any trip to the outskirts and beyond requires a car. There are several rental companies, including all the major outlets, and charges are around Can$50 per day, although weekend rates are much cheaper. Cabs are expensive here and cannot be hailed on the street, but they can be picked up at hotels or ordered by telephone.

Winnipeg

Many of Winnipeg's attractions are within a 20-minute walk of one another in the downtown area, centered on the crossroads of Portage and Main Streets. **Winnipeg City Transit** operates an efficient bus system, which is also ideal for reaching farther-placed sights. There is a flat fare of Can$1.65, or you can purchase a book of 10 tickets for Can$16.00 from the Transit Service Centre based in the underground concourse at Portage and Main. (A transfer, valid for an hour, is available from the driver if you are changing buses.) The center is open weekdays between 8:30 am and 4:30 pm, and offers detailed information

and a free route map of the city. There are also several pleasant bicycle paths that run through the city as well as to outlying districts.

Quebec City

The charming narrow streets of the old city are best seen on foot, especially since most of the historic sights are located within a small area of the walled city. If you need to travel farther to see one of the more distant sights such as the Musée du Québec, the bus system is frequent and reliable. Fares are cheaper if you buy a ticket before boarding and are on sale at several outlets in grocery stores and supermarkets. There are also one-day passes for Can$4.60. The bus station is in the Lower Town on Boulevard Charest Est. Most of the main routes stop centrally on the Place d'Youville in the Old Town.

Taxi stands are located in front of the major hotels or outside city hall. Horse-drawn carriages or *calèches* may be hired for a gentle trot around the Old Town, but expect to pay Can$50 for 40 minutes.

Halifax

The compact city of Halifax is best explored on foot or bicycle, which can be hired for a half or full day. Driving around is difficult: parking is hard to come by and expensive. To reach outlying districts there is the **Halifax Metro Transit** bus system. Fares are cheap, with a flat fare of Can$1.65 charged downtown. It is also possible to purchase budget books of 20 tickets. In the city from Monday to Saturday during the summer season, a free bus service called "Fred" circles the downtown area about every 20 minutes.

Charlottetown

Since the completion of the Confederation Bridge in 1997, Prince Edward Island has become easily accessible by bus and car. Travelers still use the ferry service, which runs from New Glasgow, Nova Scotia between May and November. There is a shuttle bus service from Halifax that travels to the island by ferry. The island's public transportation system is limited to a bus service in Charlottetown run by **Trius Tours**; this operates all year round. However, touring by car is most popular, and it is a good idea to reserve a car during the busiest months of July and August. Several companies offer organized bus, walking, and cycling tours.

Driving over Confederation Bridge to Prince Edward Island

St. John's, Newfoundland

In comparison to most of Canada's cities, parking is easy in St. John's. It is possible to buy a parking permit from one of many well-placed machines. They take quarters (25 cents) or dollar coins. Car rental here is less expensive than in many other Canadian cities and there is a good choice of companies.

The local bus service is run by Metrobus, and tickets cost Can$1.50 every trip. If you are planning on spending some time here it is worth investing in a lo-ride card for Can$13.50. By riding on two routes, such as one downtown and one suburban bus, you get a bargain tour of the city.

Directory

City Transportation Information

Vancouver
British Columbia Transit
(604) 521 0400.

Toronto Transit Commission (TTC)
416 393 4636.

Montreal
STCUM and AMT
(514) 288 6287.

Ottawa
OC Transpo
(613) 741 4390.

Calgary
Calgary Transit
(403) 262 1000.

Winnipeg
Winnipeg City Transit
(204) 986 5700.

Quebec City
STCUQ
(418) 627 2511.

Halifax
Halifax Metro Transit
(902) 490 6600.

Charlottetown
Trius Tours
(902) 566 5664.

St. John's Newfoundland
Metrobus
(709) 570 2020.

Bus traveling over Harbour Bridge in St. John's, Newfoundland

Train Travel in Canada

THE CANADIAN RAIL network is run by the government-owned VIA Rail. The service has been significantly reduced since the late 1980s when many cross-country services, along with other lines, were cut. VIA Rail still provides a service on the famed 1950s *Canadian*, a beautifully restored train that travels across the country between Toronto and Vancouver, passing through stunning Rockies' scenery between Jasper and Kamloops.

Increasingly, Canadians fly long distances or use their cars to cover most of the shorter hauls. For visitors, traveling by train remains a wonderful way to see large parts of Canada (especially in those trains that have glass-domed observation cars). Smaller commuter networks around the major cities are also useful for visitors who wish to explore an area in detail.

Specialty trips on the Rocky Mountaineer travel through the Rockies

The Canadian Rail Network

VIA RAIL CANADA INC. operates Canada's national passenger rail service. Despite the closing of several lines there are still 400 trains every week, which cover some 13,000 km (8,000 miles) on major routes between Vancouver and Toronto, traveling on to Montreal, Quebec, and Halifax. It is possible to cross the country by train – a trip that takes five days – by connecting up with these lines. The longest continuous route remains the Vancouver–Toronto trip on board the stylish and luxurious 1950s *Canadian*, with its observation and dining cars. Places with no road link, such as the town of Churchill in northern Manitoba, rely on the railroad. The line between Winnipeg and Churchill is mostly used by visitors in October, heading north to see the polar bears *(see p251)*.

VIA Rail operates both long-haul trains in eastern and western Canada, as well as inter-city trains in the populous Ontario Corridor, from Quebec City to Windsor, passing through Kingston, Montreal, Niagara Falls, Ottawa, and Toronto. This is a fast service that offers snacks and drinks on board most trains.

It is easy to travel onward to the United States, as VIA connects with the American rail network, Amtrak, at both Montreal and Vancouver. VIA Rail and Amtrak jointly run the Toronto–New York line through Niagara Falls, and Toronto–Chicago trains through Sarnia/Port Huron. The VIA station in Windsor is only a few kilometers from the Amtrak station in Detroit.

Smaller Networks

VISITORS SHOULD also be aware that VIA is not the only passenger rail service in Canada. The larger cities all have useful local commuter lines. Vancouver has **BC Rail** and the West Coast Express to Prince Rupert, while Toronto's Go Transit covers the city's outlying suburbs as far as Milton, Bradford, Richmond Hill, and Stouffville, and Montreal has AMT *(see p405)*.

Specialty Trips

THERE ARE several lines that offer visitors the chance to enjoy Canada's best scenery in comfortable, often luxurious trains. Among the best trips is the **Algoma Central Railway** in Ontario *(see p223)*, which runs from Sault Ste. Marie to Hearst and has an excursion train from Sault Ste. Marie to the Agawa Canyon through spectacular landscapes from early June to October. There is a Snow Train excursion on weekends from late December to early March, also from Sault Ste. Marie.

Ontario Northland Railway operates both freight and passenger services on its main line from North Bay to Moosonee. *The Polar Bear Express* is a summer excursion to Moosonee, which provides a close-up look at the northern wilderness. The passenger service continues south of North Bay to Toronto.

The Cariboo Prospector train, run by BC Rail, travels from North Vancouver to Prince George, through gold rush country in comfortable, air-conditioned cars. An additional summer train, the *Whistler Explorer*, running between Whistler and Kelly Lake, is popular with tour groups from the US and overseas. BC Rail also operates the historic steam train excursion, *The Royal Hudson*, from Vancouver to Squamish between June and September.

The most spectacular train ride in Canada is probably in British Columbia, where, from mid-May until early October, **Rocky Mountaineer Railtours** runs two-day excursions

from Vancouver to Calgary via Banff or Jasper. The *Rocky Mountaineer* follows the original route of the Canadian Pacific Railroad. These trips operate entirely in daylight, and the package includes a night in Kamloops plus meals. There is also a dome car for viewing the stunning scenery that lies around every bend.

Travel Classes

On long-distance routes there are two main classes of travel available, Economy and a variety of Sleeper classes, known as VIA 1. Economy Class offers comfortable, reclining seats in cars with wide aisles and large windows, as well as blankets and pillows for overnight trips. Passengers in Economy class also generally have access to one of the onboard snack bars or restaurants. Sleeper classes offer a range of options from double- and single-berth bunks to double bedrooms, which convert to luxurious sitting rooms by day. VIA services in Western Canada such as the *Canadian,* offer the choice of "Silver & Blue" first-class cars that have access to a private observation car, as well as plush dining cars.

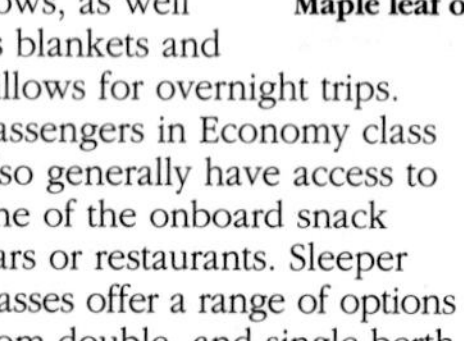

Maple leaf on VIA Rail logo

Tickets and Bookings

Reservations for rail travel can be made through travel agents or direct through VIA Rail. There are a variety of discounts available on both economy and sleeper classes if you book round-trip tickets or in advance. Reductions on Ontario corridor lines are available if you book five days in advance (on most other routes you need to reserve tickets seven days in advance.) There are also discounts for bookings made for travel during the off-peak period between October and December, and from January until the end of May.

The CANRAILPASS gives you 12 days of unlimited travel in economy class during a 30-day period. Just show your CANRAILPASS each time you obtain a ticket. The card is valid on all VIA Rail routes, and you can make as many stops as you like during your trip. Up to three extra days' travel can be added, which can be bought in advance or at any time during the 30-day validity period. It is a good idea to reserve seats in advance during the summer as there are a limited number for pass holders. Throughout the VIA system, travelers over 60 are entitled to an additional ten percent reduction on fares.

Directory

VIA Rail
416 366 8411 Toronto and most other Canadian provinces.

Algoma Central Railway
(705) 946 7300.
Toll-Free 1 800 242 9287.

BC Rail
(604) 631 3500 or (604) 984 5246.

Ontario Northland Railway
(1 800) 461 8558.

Rocky Mountaineer Railtours
(604) 606 7245.

Principal Rail Routes

VIA Rail is the main provider of passenger rail services throughout Canada. It is possible to reach all the major centers of the country, and regional operators link up with most town's outlying districts.

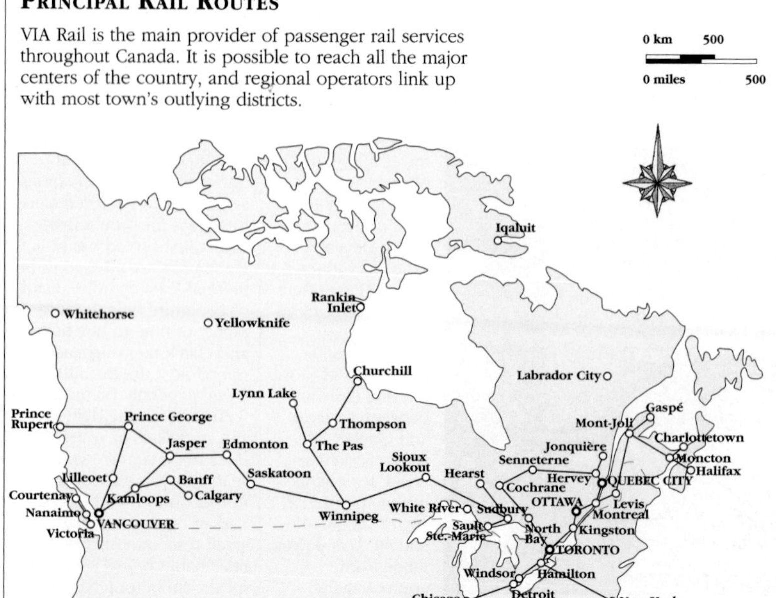

Traveling by Bus

Buses are the least expensive way to get around Canada. The majority of bus routes west of Toronto are run by Greyhound Canada, including the epic trip along the Trans-Canada Highway (Hwy 1) between Toronto and Vancouver. East of Toronto there are several smaller companies that cover most areas. Although a long bus trip can mean one or more nights spent sitting upright, the buses are generally clean and comfortable, and offer plenty of rest stops. The network is also reliable and efficient with buses usually arriving on time. In more remote regions, check timetables in advance as there may be no service or only one bus a week.

Long-Distance Buses

Long-distance buses provide a cheaper and often faster option than the railroad. The main operator, Greyhound Canada, carries more than two million passengers each year to most of the towns and cities across the country. Although Greyhound lines operate in the west and center of the country, many routes are linked to bus lines in the east, and in the United States. West of Vancouver, Greyhound links up with Pacific and Maverick Coach Lines, east of Ottawa, with Voyageur Colonial, Orleans Express, and Acadian SMP. Greyhound's express services offer a faster, highway-based service on buses that have more leg room, movies, music, and snacks.

Although smoking is prohibited, most long-haul buses stop every three to four hours so that travelers can leave the bus for a rest break. Rest breaks or driver changes take place at both bus and service stations, where you will find a variety of facilities ranging from restaurants and cafés to snack vending machines. All the buses are air-conditioned and have washrooms. Buses also offer passengers the advantage of picking up and arriving in convenient downtown areas.

Greyhound bus logo

Discounts and Passes

There is a variety of discounted bus passes available to visitors. Children under five usually travel free, and travelers over 65 are entitled to discounts on both return tickets and pass deals. Fares are also cheaper if you book in advance or travel during the off-peak season, from January to June or from October to December.

The Greyhound Canada Pass offers unlimited travel on both Greyhound and many other lines, such as those running eastward between Ontario and Quebec or across Saskatchewan, for a range of time periods: 7, 10, 15, 21, 30, 45, and 60 days. Prices range from approximately Can$265 for 7 days to Can$640 for 60. The Canada Coach Pass Plus is similar, with the bonus of including travel across the country to Montreal, Quebec City, Halifax, St. John, and Charlottetown, as well as to New York City in the US.

Some pass deals booked overseas and through organizations such as Hostelling International include accommodation in more than 80 hostels from coast to coast; an example is the Go Canada Budget Travel Pass. This pass can also be used to travel on VIA Rail services between Toronto, Ottawa, and Montreal.

Rout-Passes offer access to some 35 intercity bus companies in Ontario and Quebec from mid-April to mid-November. Passengers do not need to decide on their itinerary in advance, and reservations are not necessary. There is a wide range of Rout-Passes to choose from, and some include accommodation vouchers. The 16-day Rout-Pass can be bought only by members of the International Hostelling Association.

Boarding the bus on Ottawa's Parliament Hill

Bus Stations and Reservations

Buses from different carriers all operate from the same stations, making it easy to connect with other bus lines and municipal transit services. Reservations are not usually needed since buses are filled on a first-come, first-served basis. Passengers are advised to be there at least an hour ahead of departure time, leaving plenty of time to buy tickets and check their luggage. Do not panic if the bus fills up; it will generally be replaced with another one right away. Buying tickets in advance does not guarantee you a seat, and you will still have to line up to board the bus.

Most bus stations have a small restaurant or café where reasonably priced snacks and meals can be purchased. On long-distance journeys it is a

Tourists on a bus trip to the Athabasca Glacier in Jasper

good idea to take some food with you, otherwise you will have to rely on the sometimes over-priced, unappealing food available in service stations. At the larger stations it is possible to rent luggage lockers, leaving you free to explore unencumbered by suitcases. In the major cities such as Toronto, you have the choice of boarding in the suburbs or in the city center. Choose the city center since the bus may be full by the time it reaches outlying districts. Always ask if there is an express or direct service to your destination; as some trips involve countless stops en route and can seem very long. A small pillow or traveling cushion, a sweater (to counter the sometimes fierce air-conditioning), and a good book or magazine can often help to make a long trip more comfortable.

Bus Tours

There are several tour companies that offer package deals on a variety of trips. An extensive range of tours is available, from city sightseeing and day trips to particular attractions, to expensive luxury, multi-day tours including guides, meals, and accommodations. There are specialized tours that focus on such activities as glacier hikes, white-water rafting, and horseback riding. A typical ten-day tour of the Rockies may take in everything from a cruise to Victoria, a hike in Banff, and a picnic on Lake Louise, to a trip to the Columbia Icefield, or a look at the history of gold rush country in the Cariboo region. Most companies will send you detailed itineraries in advance, and it is a good idea to make sure that there are no hidden extras such as tips, sales taxes, and entry fees, as these are often included in the price of the package. Some of the most beautiful scenery can also be seen on regular Greyhound routes, such as those in the Rockies.

Directory

Greyhound Canada Inquiries
1 800 661 8747.

Timetable Information
from Canada and US
1 800 661 8747.
from the UK
(44) 0870 888 0223.

Bookings (passes only)
(UK) *0870 888 0223.*

Bus Tour Companies

Brewster Transportation
for tours in the west
(800) 661 1152.

Great Canadian Holidays
for tours in the east
(519) 896 8687.

Bus Routes

This map shows the main bus routes across Canada. It is possible to travel right across the country along the Trans-Canada Highway using Greyhound Canada and the bus companies that operate east of Toronto.

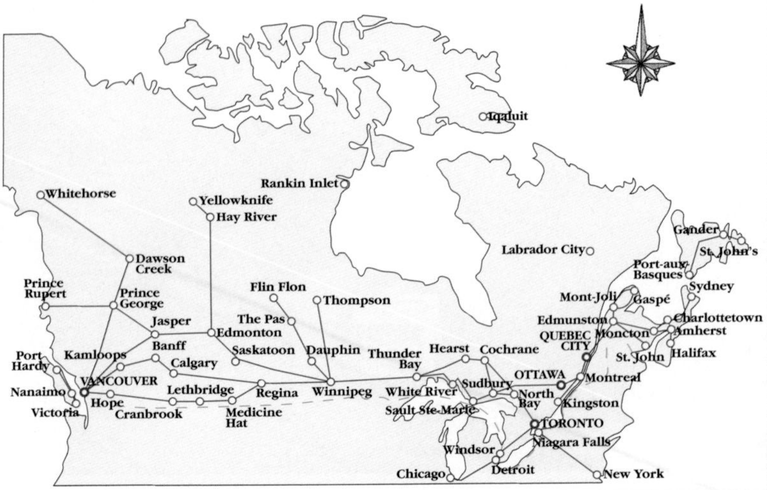

Driving in Canada

Driving Route tour sign

It is a good idea to rent a car when visiting Canada. Other modes of transportation will get you around the cities and from one rural town to another, but once you arrive in a remote country area, a car is the best way of exploring. Tours of regions such as Quebec's wild Gaspé Peninsula *(see pp140–41)*, or British Columbia's Okanagan Valley *(see p315)* are best made by car. Several aspects of Canadian life reflect the fact that this is a driver's country: there is an excellent, well-maintained highway network, and many places have huge out-of-town malls. However, city-center traffic congestion means that visitors to the major cities of Toronto, Vancouver, Montreal, and Ottawa may find that public transportation is quicker and cheaper than driving.

Arriving by Car

Many people drive to Canada from the US. The border here is the longest in the world. There are 13 major crossing points, the two busiest being from Detroit to Windsor and at Niagara Falls. Most of the highways entering Canada connect to the Trans-Canada Highway, which is the longest highway through the country, running for some 5,000 km (8,045 miles) from Victoria, BC, to St. John's in Newfoundland. Customs control ask that visitors declare their citizenship, their place of residence, and proposed length of stay. You may be asked to show your passport and visa *(see pp390–91)*. It is a good idea to fill up with less expensive fuel on the US side. It is also possible to enter the country from the Alaska side by the famed Alaska Highway *(see pp260–61)*, which crosses the Yukon and ends in British Columbia at Dawson City.

Driver's Licenses

An up-to-date driver's license from your own country usually entitles you to drive in Canada for up to three months. There are some provincial variations: in British Columbia, Quebec, and New Brunswick your license will be valid for up to six months, in Prince Edward Island four months, and in the Yukon only one month. It is advisable to carry an International Driving Permit (IDP) with your license in case of problems with traffic officials or the police.

Insurance

Whether driving a rental or your own car you will need proof of insurance coverage, which is compulsory in Canada. If you are using your own car it is advisable to check whether your insurance is valid in Canada, as this may save money. The minimum liability cover is Can$200,000, except in Quebec, where it starts at Can$50,000. Most rental companies offer collision damage waiver and personal accident insurance for an additional charge; it is a good idea to have both. If you are driving a private car that is not registered in your own name, you will need to carry a letter from the owner that authorizes your use of the vehicle. For a rental vehicle you must carry the company's official documentation for the same reason. Arranging summer rentals and insurance in advance is recommended.

A Recreational Vehicle passes mountains and forests on a trip through Banff National Park, Alberta

Car Rental

Rental cars are available just about everywhere in Canada. Most major rental car dealers such as Hertz, Avis, and Tilden, have offices at airports and in towns and cities across the country. Among the less expensive options are booking a fly-drive package from home, or there may be discounts if you rent your car in advance. The cost varies greatly depending on the season, type of vehicle, and length of rental. Ask about hidden costs such as drop-off charges, provincial sales tax, and the Goods and Services Tax (GST). When picking up your car you may be asked to show your passport and return airline ticket. The minimum age for renting a car is usually 25 or, in some cases, 21. You will need a credit card for the deposit as it is all but impossible to rent a car in Canada without one. Children under 18 kg (40 lbs) require a child seat fixed in place with a seat belt. Most companies will arrange for one with a little notice. The biggest rental companies offer a wide choice of vehicles, ranging from two-door economy cars to four-door luxury models. Most cars come with a radio and air-conditioning. Bear in mind that nearly all rental cars in Canada have automatic transmission. Manual models are unusual, although cars with specially adapted hand controls for disabled drivers are available from some of the larger companies. RVs (Recreational Vehicles) or camper vans can also be rented, but they are more expensive. They should be booked well in advance if you intend to travel in summer.

Fuel and Service Stations

Fuel prices are slightly higher than in the US and half the price you pay in the UK, especially in cities and large towns, although rural areas often charge more. Unleaded gas and diesel only are available in Canada. Rental companies generally provide a full tank on departure, and give you the choice of paying for the fuel in advance or on return. Service stations are often self-service, which can be a problem if you need a mechanic. In major cities some stations are open for 24 hours, but in rural areas they often close at 6pm and are few and far between, especially in northerly regions. It is a good idea to fill up before setting off. Credit cards and traveler's checks are widely accepted.

Rules of the Road

Canada's Highway system is well maintained and has mostly two-lane all-weather roads. They are all clearly numbered and signed. Most highway signs are in English, and some bilingual, except for those in Quebec where they are only in French. A good road map is essential and can be obtained from any auto club such as the **Canadian Automobile Association (CAA)**, which is affiliated with other similar clubs in the world. It is worth checking the rules of the road with them as there are numerous small provincial variations.

In Canada you drive on the right. You can turn right on a red light everywhere, except in Quebec. The speed limits are posted in kilometers-per-hour (km/h) and range from 30–40 km/h (18–30 mph) in urban areas to 80–100 km/h (50–60 mph) on highways. On multi-lane highways you pass on the left for safety. Some provinces require cars to keep their headlights on for extended periods after dawn and before sunset, for safety reasons. Seat belts are compulsory for both drivers and passengers.

Driving in the north involves special procedures because most of the roads are extremely hazardous due to ice, and are passable only during the summer months.

Moose warning sign on highway

Directory

Major Rental Agencies

Hertz
800 654 3131.

Avis
800 331 1212.

National
800 387 4747.

Auto Clubs

Canadian Automobile Association
(613) 247 0117.

American Automobile Association
(407) 444 7000.

24-hour emergency road service
1-800-222-help.

Winter Driving and Safety

Canadian winters are harsh, and you should always check road conditions and weather forecasts before setting out on trips. Drifting snow and black ice are frequent hazards in winter or in northern regions. When driving in remote areas, make sure you have a full gas tank, and carry blankets, some sand, a shovel, and emergency food, such as chocolate bars, in case you get stuck. Jumper cables are also useful because extreme cold can drain a car battery quickly. Studded tires are allowed year-round in the Yukon, the Northwest Territories, Alberta, and Saskatchewan and are permitted in winter in most other provinces. Check with local tourist offices.

During the summer months animals such as bears and moose can be a hazard, especially in parts of British Columbia. They can suddenly appear on roads when they rush out of the woods to escape the blackflies during spring and summer. Watch for road signs, and take extra care when you see deer or moose road signs as these indicate an area where animals are most likely to appear suddenly.

General Index

Page numbers in **bold** type refer to main entries

C

I

J

K

S

T

Y

Z

Acknowledgments

DORLING KINDERSLEY would like to thank the following people whose contributions and assistance have made the book possible:

MAIN CONTRIBUTORS

Paul Franklin has recently completed Nova Scotia's provincial travel guide, commissioned by the Government of Nova Scotia. A writer and photographer for both Canadian and world travel guides, he lives in Nova Scotia.
Sam Ion and **Cam Norton** live and work in Burlington, Ontario. A successful travel-writing team, they contribute to newspapers, magazines, and brochures as well as their most recent work, the Ontario Government's millenium website, celebrating the province.
Philip Lee has worked as a travel writer for over a decade, and is the author of numerous articles and travel books about countries throughout the world. He has lived and traveled extensively through the US and Canada and is now based in Nottingham, England.
Lorry Patton lives and works in British Columbia, having recently been travel editor of BC Woman magazine. She currently runs an online travel magazine which includes BC, and lives on the Gulf Islands just outside Vancouver.
Geoffrey Roy is an award-winning freelance travel writer and photographer, based in Surrey, England. He has published numerous articles on Northern Canada.
Donald Telfer is a Saskatchewan-based travel writer with over 20 years' writing experience of Central Canada. He contributes regularly to a variety of Canadian and international newspapers and magazines.
Paul Waters is a Montreal-based journalist who has lived and worked inseveral cities in Quebec and has written extensively on the province. He is currently the travel editor for *The Gazette*, a popular Montreal English-language daily.

ADDITIONAL CONTRIBUTORS

Alan Chan, Michael Snook.

ADDITIONAL PHOTOGRAPHY

James Jackson, Matthew Ward

ADDITIONAL ILLUSTRATIONS

Stephen Conlin, Eugene Fleury, Steve Gyapay, Chris Orr, Mel Pickering, Peter Ross.

CARTOGRAPHY

ERA-Maptec Ltd, Dublin, Ireland.

PROOF READER

Sam Merrell.

INDEXER

Hilary Bird.

DESIGN AND EDITORIAL ASSISTANCE

Gillian Allen, Louise Bolton, Vivien Crump, Joy Fitzsimmons, Emily Green, Marie Ingledew, Steve Knowlden, Lee Redmond, Ellen Root, Anna Streiffert.

SPECIAL ASSISTANCE

Canada Map Office, Ontario; Canadian Tourism Office, London, UK; Claude Guerin and Danielle Legentil, Musée d'art contemporain de Montreal; Jim Kemshead, Tourism Yukon; Wendy Kraushaar, RCMP Museum, Regina, Saskatchewan; 'Ksan Historical Indian Village & Museum, Hazleton, BC; Leila Jamieson, Art Gallery of Ontario, Toronto; Antonio Landry, Village Historique Acadien, New Brunswick; Marty Hickie, Royal Tyrrell Museum, Drumheller, Alberta; Mary Mandley, Information Office, Sainte-Marie among the Hurons; National Air Photo Library, Ottawa, Ontario; Liette Roberts, Manitoba Museum of Man and Nature, Winnipeg; Mark Sayers; Ernest D. Scullion, Aeriel Photography Services, Scarborough, Ontario; Visit Canada office, London, UK; Jennifer Webb, UBC Museum of Anthropology, Vancouver, BC.

PHOTOGRAPHY PERMISSIONS

Dorling Kindersley would like to thank everyone for their assistance and kind permission to photograph at their establishments.

Placement Key - t = top; tl = top left; tlc = top left centre; tc = top centre; trc = top right centre; tr = top right; cla = centre left above; ca = centre above; cra = centre right above; cl = centre left; c = centre; cr = centre right; clb = centre left below; cb = centre below; crb = centre right below; bl = bottom left; b = bottom; bc = bottom centre; bcl = bottom centre left; bottom centre right = bcr; br = bottom right; d = detail.

Works of art have been produced with the permission of the following copyright holders: The work illustrated on page 172c is reproduced by permission of the Henry Moore Foundation; © Bill Vazan *Shibagua Shard*, 1989 sandblasted sheild granite 187c.

The publishers would like to thank the following individuals, companies, and picture libraries for their kind permission to reproduce their photographs:

AIR CANADA: 49b, 398t; AKG, London: 47b; BRYAN AND CHERRY ALEXANDER: 16c, 20t, 21cr, 23c/cr/bl, 26t, 37t, 51c/b, 153t, 321c, 322, 324cb, 324-5, 325c, 332-3, 334t, 338t, 339t/c; ALLSPORT: Scott Halleran 32b; Elsa Hasch 17c; Jed Jacobson 33t; Jamie Squire 35b; Rick Stewart 32c; ANCHORAGE MUSEUM OF HISTORY AND ART, Anchorage, Alaska: B74.1.25 46t; courtesy of THE ANNE OF GREEN GABLES MUSEUM, Silver Bush, Park Corner, Prince Edward Island: 79b; ART GALLERY OF ONTARIO: Karoo Ashevak, Canadian: Inuit 1940–74, *Shaman with Spirit Helper* 1972, whalebone; ivory; dark greystone; sinew 47.7 x 23.6 x 16.6 cm, Gift of Samuel and Esther Sarick, Toronto 1996 © Palaejook Eskimo Co-op Ltd. 175ca; Pieter Brueghel the Younger, Flemish 1564–1638 THE PEASANTS WEDDING n.d., oil on cradled oak panel 36.2 x 44.2 cm 175cb(d); Paul Gaugin French 1848–1903, HINA AND FATU c.1892, tamanu wood, 32.7 cm height, Gift of the Volunteer Committee